THE AMERICAN DREAM

SHADOW & SUBSTANCE

compiled by MARVIN MILLER

A COLLECTOR'S PICTORIAL HISTORY OF AMERICA'S 200 YEARS

Compiled by MARVIN MILLER

RONALD MILLER/Executive Publisher

ROGER LA MANNA/Art Director

CONTRIBUTING EDITORS:

PATRICK ALLAWAY/Journalist, Screenwriter, Teacher, Mt. San Antonio College
MICHAEL ANGEL/Journalist, Screenwriter
MARC DAVIS/Journalist, Novelist, Art Teacher, Book Reviewer for the *Chicago Tribune*
ANDRIA MILLER FLETCHER/Assistant Professor of Political Science, La Verne College
HARRY HEYBOER/Instructor in History, Mount San Antonio College
HERBERT HOGAN, Ph.D./Professor of History, La Verne College, Fullbright Professor, Gottingen, Germany
MARLENE ADLER MARKS/Journalist, Legal Writer
PAUL NEIMARK/Novelist, Author of twelve books on contemporary society

ASSISTANTS: ELEANOR HAZLETT/JOAN B. MARKIEWICZ

First Release Printing Date July 4, 1976

Copyright © 1976
Classic Publications

Library of Congress Cataloguing in Publication Data

Main entry under title: *The American Dream: Shadow and Substance*

Photo Credits: Wide World Photos, White House Historical Association, New York Historical Society, U.S. Army, U.S. Navy, U.S. Marine Corps, U.S. Coast Guard, United Press International, Los Angeles County Public Library, New York Public Library.

The portraits of the Presidents appearing in *The American Dream: Shadow and Substance* are the official White House portraits.

TABLE OF CONTENTS

THE AMERICAN TREE

America. Discovered almost by accident. Named for a man who never saw its shores. Settled by people whose only common denominator was the hope of a new and better life. And through two hundred years of revolution, civil war, world wars, depressions, recessions, and political chicanery the American nation continues, like a new world Tree of Life, to offer that promise of a new beginning to her people.

The seeds of that tree were planted more than two centuries ago by a small group of Englishmen who came to North America searching not for gold as the Spanish and Portuguese had done in South America, but, rather, seeking freedom. Freedom, that elusive abstraction which had flourished under the Greeks, floundered under the Roman Empire, and all but disappeared during the subsequent fifteen hundred years of European civilization. By the time the Renaissance reached England the seed of artistic freedom was well established, but the colonizers of the new world carried across the Atlantic in their hearts and minds the seed of a new kind of freedom—political freedom. Freedom from religious persecution. From taxation without representation. From all the old world archaic strictures which had proscribed their lives in Europe. And they planted their seed of freedom in the fresh earth of the New World.

The seed had barely sprouted before the boot of British oppression attempted to try to stamp it out. But the blood of the American Revolutionaries, determined to rid themselves forever of social and political oppression, nurtured the young tree and it blossomed forth with the richest fruit of political freedom the world has ever known—the American Constitution.

The freedom tree spread its strong roots through the heroic and reasoned thoughts and actions of America's Founding Fathers. Men such as Washington, who took a ragtag group of militiamen and transformed them into an army of freedom fighters, and then went on to lead the new republic through the first stumbling years of democracy; and Jefferson, whose enlightened ideas and majestic pen shaped the basic fibre of American life; and Jackson and Madison and Adams and Franklin and Paine and the whole pantheon of early American leaders. And most particularly the farmers and shopowners and craftsmen and citizens of every rank, whose struggle was the struggle for the common man that he too might be free.

And as the tree grew its roots expanded west across the untamed continent. Across the Adirondacks, across the Appalachians and Smokeys, through the valleys and forests and swamps of the new world the roots spread. Across the Missouri and the Mississippi and out onto the plains the roots spread until they reached the Pacific shore, where the continent stopped but the roots of freedom didn't. And still the roots continued to grow until North, South, East, and West lay within the protective bowers of the American nation.

As the tree continued to grow it was forced to bend to accommodate new ideas and different times, but always it remained strong. But even the most supple young tree can be bent only so far before it breaks, and less than a century after its planting the American tree of freedom faced its most serious bending—the Civil War. The war which pitted American against American threatened to break the tree, but, as it had done during its early years, the nation produced a leader whose dedication and compassion kept the tree intact. Abraham Lincoln, with a father's concern, watched over the tree and nurtured it back to wholeness. And when the Civil War was ended the tree was again upright and stronger than ever.

By the third quarter of the nineteenth century and with its formative years behind it, the tree began to mature and bear fruit. Steel mills and railroads, canals and great dams, public education and new art forms—all of these and more were the tangible proof of the health of the tree. And underlying its growth and feeding its branches was the hard work of the American citizen, who, despite the phenomenal materialistic growth which occurred during the latter part of the nineteenth and early part of the twentieth centuries, never lost sight of the fact that the real wealth of the country was in her political ideals and not in her manufactured objects.

Fed by an almost constant stream of new people from other lands the tree continued to grow and flourish. Spurred on by the hope of a better material life and seeking the same political freedom that the colonists had sought, the immigrants brought their native culture with them to the new world. And the food and dress and customs of a hundred different countries became an integral part of the American lifestyle, adding a richness and a texture to the fruit which bloomed on the tree.

And when, two decades into the twentieth century, the world was thrust into a major war, it was towards America that the other freedom loving countries turned. It was back on the European continent, where the seed had first germinated, that America was able to illustrate for the whole world the material and ideological strength of her people. And when ''the war to end all wars'' had ended, America emerged as a force to be reckoned with in the world.

The Depression which blanketed the world one generation after the end of World War I took its toll on the blooming American tree. Widespread unemployment, bread lines, soup kitchens, and once-proud American workers selling apples on street corners were all signs of the Thirties. But though the disease twisted and withered some of the tree's branches and dried up her leaves, the roots weathered the economic storm, proving as it had so often in the past that the American tree was planted in healthy soil. With the outbreak of World War II the world once again turned toward America for help, and her sons and daughters joined in the fight against Fascism. The economic recovery precipitated by World War II infused new life into the withering tree, and America emerged in 1945 as the leader of the free world.

With the conclusion of the Second World War America was again able to turn her attentions toward peace and regeneration. Through massive outright gifts of money and manufactured goods America, during the next decade, helped rebuild a bombed out world. And as she helped spread democracy in other nations new, fresh buds of personal freedom began to appear on the freedom tree.

As America moved into the Sixties the new buds which appeared were really a mutation, a throwback to an earlier age. The personal freedom of millions of Americans now became the chief trunk in the country's growth, and as the civil liberties of minorities flowered they generated a new bloom of liberty for all Americans. However, these new flowers of personal freedom were not grown without a price. Assassinations, racial unrest, campus disturbances, and street violence marked the generation of the Sixties. But again the American tree, though bent into new and stronger directions, remained solid evidence of the people's compassion for the underdog and their love of liberty for all the country's citizens.

By the time America neared her two hundredth anniversary the tree had shed some of the branches of an earlier age. Gone were the political reactionism and isolationism, the overt racism, the petty sectionalism, and political divisiveness of the immature nation. Replacing them was the new flower of the super state. The tree which, though weakened by economic recession and an unpopular war, subverted by political chicanery at the highest levels, continues to blossom and generate, keeping alive the ideals of freedom inherent in the seed of democracy planted more than two hundred years ago.

But there is much more to the American tree than laws, politics, wars, and social movements. Nearly from the beginning of its history one of the tree's strongest and most fruitful branches has been the multi-layered growth of science, technology, and industry. Nowhere are there better examples to be found of the efficacy of the American way of life than in her scientific and technological breakthroughs and manufactured goods, which have been an almost continual byproduct of the American system of freedom. For it is the same sense of freedom which permeates the political life that makes unfettered scientific investigation possible. A nation which is free in spirit but not in body is only half free, and the material comforts produced during America's two hundred years have made her people the best fed and best housed in the history of the world. America has been called a nation of gadgets, her people referred to simply as consumers of disposable goods. But the same branch of the American tree that produced the gadgets and unnecessary goods also produced a revolution in science and engineering, put the world on wheels, tamed nature to make parts of the globe habitable, and eradicated dozens of diseases. That branch of the tree also produced a technology capable of feeding not only the American people but also countless millions throughout the world. And that branch of the tree has blossomed each generation with inventions and scientific ideas which have made life for the American people the envy of the rest of the world. And that branch has also produced a new language into the lexicon of American life by making space travel a reality. But the tree has other branches intermingled within which have produced goods of a less tangible but no less significant nature.

While the tree flowered and grew politically and scientifically, another equally important branch wound its way through American life. The tree which produced the Constitution, and the automobile and the space ship also produced a culture unique to the world. From the scrimshaw of the whalers to the sculpture in the museums, from brassy notes of the jazzmen to the mellowed tones of the concert halls, and from early shadowy flickerings of the movie camera to the late late show, America has put forth a popular culture to match its political and scientific life. And these manifold expressions of artistry merely mirror the fundamental freedom which underlies all of American life. The tree is bountiful, and the world is filled with the fruits of its bounty.

It has been a productive branch, reflecting a country at thought and play. And sometimes her games have taken on the nature of culture. For more than one hundred years the world has been playing baseball, an American invention just as surely as the atom bomb was. During the two hundred years of American life sports have been an integral branch on the tree and Americans have participated and watched as myriad games came and went, each in its own day capturing the popular imagination. And nowhere is there a better indication of the personal freedom enjoyed by her citizens than in the games America's people play.

There is another branch of the American tree. One which in its own way has been productive, but one which has remained throughout the tree's history a shriveled, dwarfish branch. All nations have had their undersides, their shadows, and America is no exception. It is endemic to the seed of freedom that mixed in with the good fruit should be some of the rotten. The traitors to the American Revolution, the desperadoes of the old West, the robber barons, the war profiteers, the organized mobsters, the political corrupters—all these too grew on the tree, but they never flowered as sweetly or as long, and never once did the American collective mind see them as anything but mutations on a healthy tree.

And the tree stands today. Changed and in some ways slightly disfigured. But it remains. Not because of its technology or science or art or social system. It stands today because of an idea. An idea planted more than two hundred years ago that the individual has the right to be free to live his life to the fullest of his potential. And the tree continues to grow.

Marvin Miller

REVOLUTIONARY WAR CALENDAR

JANUARY 1, 1776

Norfolk, Va., burned by British after defeat of royalist contingent.

JANUARY 10, 1776

First demand for complete independence for American colonies appeared in pamphlet *Common Sense* by **Thomas Paine,** greatly influential in swinging tide in favor of clean break with mother country.

MARCH, 1776

Charleston, S.C., set up an **independent government** under a temporary local constitution which was to be in effect until an agreement with England could be reached. John Rutledge was chosen president. Said to be the first independent government within the recognized borders of the colonies. It was this government which successfully defended Charleston against the British army and fleet on June 28, 1776, thus freeing the South from attack for nearly 3 years.

MARCH 17, 1776

Gen. Howe evacuated Boston Harbor after Washington had seized Dorchester Heights, 2 weeks previously. Howe sailed for Halifax, N.S., to await reinforcements.

APRIL 12, 1776

North Carolina Provincial Congress instructed its delegates to the Continental Congress to vote for independence. She was the **first colony to propose independence formally.**

JUNE 1776

The Declaration of Independence drafted by Thomas Jefferson.

JUNE 27, 1776

Condemned as a traitor, Thomas Hickey was **first American soldier executed by order of military court.** He had conspired to deliver Gen. Washington to British.

JULY 4, 1776

Declaration of Independence adopted.

JULY 5, 1776

President of the Congress, John Hancock, and Secretary of the Congress, Charles Thompson, signed draft copies of the **Declaration of Independence.** These copies were to be sent to the several state assemblies.

JULY 8, 1776

John Nixon gave the first public reading of **Declaration of Independence** to an assembly of Philadelphians. He had been chosen for this distinction by the sheriff of Philadelphia.

AUGUST 2, 1776

Though the **Declaration of Independence** had been adopted July 4, it was not signed by members of Congress until this day. Names of the signers were withheld from public for more than 6 months because, if independence were not achieved, their treasonable act might result in their deaths.

AUGUST 27, 1776

Battle of **Long Island** (N.Y.), in which American forces commanded by Putnam and Sullivan defeated by British under Howe and Clinton. On Aug. 30 Americans evacuated Long Island.

SEPTEMBER, 1776

Benjamin Franklin chosen by Congress to represent the U.S. in negotiations with France for a treaty of commerce.

SEPTEMBER 9, 1776

Continental Congress resolved that the words **"United States"** were to replace the words "United Colonies."

SEPTEMBER 15, 1776

American forces withdrawn from **New York** and city occupied by British under Howe.

SEPTEMBER 22, 1776

Capt. **Nathan Hale** of Connecticut executed by British in New York. Before he was hanged he made his famous statement: "I only regret that I have but one life to lose for my country."

Battle of Bunker Hill, *June 17, 1776. Colonials twice repelled British attackers.*

NOVEMBER 16, 1776

British under Howe captured **Fort Washington,** New York City, taking about 2000 prisoners.

DECEMBER 19, 1776

First number of series of pamphlets, *The Crisis,* by **Thomas Paine,** written to bolster morale of Continental Army:

THE CRISIS

"These are the times that try men's souls: The summer soldier and the sunshine patriot will, in this crisis, shrink from the service of his country; but he that stands it Now, deserves the love and thanks of man and woman. Tyranny, like hell, is not easily conquered; yet we have this consolation with us, that the harder the conflict the more glorious the triumph."

DECEMBER 26, 1776

Washington captured nearly 1000 mercenary Hessian troops in famous early morning raid on **Trenton, N.J.**

JANUARY 3, 1777

Battle of **Princeton, N.J.,** fought and won by Americans. Washington attacked in early morning again as he had at Trenton in previous week.

JUNE 28, 1777

Americans repulsed at battle of **Monmouth, N.J.** Many soldiers overcome by heat.

JULY, 1777

First state to abolish slavery and adopt universal male suffrage without regard to property was Vermont, which drafted its con-

Ethan Allen *and his "Green Mountain Boys" capturing Fort Ticonderoga.*

George Washington, *right, and Lafayette confer among their starved and huddled troops during the terrible winter at Valley Forge.*

Battle of Trenton, *Christmas Day, 1776. In a 40 minute pitched battle Washington's troops captured more than 800 Hessian prisoners.*

stitution this month. It was followed to a lesser degree by other New England states, which with Vermont were destined to become strongholds of abolitionism in the 1850's. Vermont had declared itself an independent state Jan. 16, 1777.

JULY 6, 1777
Fort Ticonderoga, N.Y., abandoned by Americans under St. Clair to superior British force commanded by Burgoyne. St. Clair, with approximately 3000 troops, joined Schuyler at Fort Edward, N.Y.

AUGUST 16, 1777
Americans under Stark defeated British at **Bennington,** Vt., killing about 200 and taking 600 prisoners. British detachment commanded by Col. Baum sent by Burgoyne in search of provisions.

SEPTEMBER 11, 1777
Washington defeated at **Brandywine,** Pa., by Howe. Gen. Lafayette wounded in this battle.

SEPTEMBER 14, 1777
Burgoyne crossed Hudson over **bridge of boats,** and encamped at Saratoga, N.Y.

SEPTEMBER 19, 1777
First engagement of Gates and Burgoyne fought at **Bemis Heights,** N.Y. British gained some ground and lost 500 men. Almost 300 Americans were killed.

SEPTEMBER 27, 1777
British, under Cornwallis, took possession of **Philadelphia.**

OCTOBER 4, 1777
Washington's attack upon **Germantown,** Pa., repulsed by Howe. Americans lost about 600 men in this battle.

OCTOBER 7, 1777
1500 British troops routed in 2nd battle of **Bemis Heights,** N.Y. British Gen. Fraser killed and Arnold wounded while attempting to force an entrance into Hessian camp.

OCTOBER 9, 1777
Burgoyne retreated to **Saratoga.**

OCTOBER 17, 1777
Burgoyne capitulated to Gates at **Saratoga, N.Y.,** surrendering 5642 British and German troops.

NOVEMBER 15, 1777
Articles of Confederation adopted by Continental Congress at York, Pa.

DECEMBER, 1777
David Bushnell, who had invented a man-propelled submarine, launched a **mine attack** against British ships. The mines were kegs of gunpowder which would explode on contact. This was perhaps 1st marine mine field ever laid, and the feat inspired the ballad, "The Battle of the Kegs," written by Francis Hopkinson.

DECEMBER 17, 1777
Washington retired with his troops to **Valley Forge,** Pa., for winter.

FEBRUARY 6, 1778
Treaty with France signed. It was in part a commercial treaty and in part a political and military alliance. France recognized U.S. independence.

MAY 4, 1778
Continental Congress ratified **Treaty of Alliance** with France.

JUNE, 1778
Directed by Aaron Burr, **Secret Service** organized as "Headquarters Secret Service," 1st such in U.S.

JUNE 18, 1778
Fearing blockade by French ships, British evacuated **Philadelphia.**

JULY, 1778
Conrad Alexandre Gerard, appointed Ambassador to U.S. by Louis XVI, arrived in this country; he was **1st foreign diplomatic representative accredited to U.S.**

JULY 3-4, 1778
Inhabitants of Wyoming Valley, Pa., **massacred** by 1600 Indians and Tories led by Cols. Butler and Brant. Some 200 scalped and many others burned alive when fort at Kingston set aflame.

AUGUST 30, 1778
American forces evacuated **Rhode Island.**

DECEMBER 29, 1778
British troops led by Col. Campbell, took **Savannah,** Ga.

1779

MARCH 3, 1779

British victorious at **Brier Creek,** Ga., where 300 Americans under Gen. Ashe were lost.

JULY 15, 1779

Stony Point, N.Y. seized by Gen. Anthony Wayne. More than 600 British killed or taken prisoner.

JULY 26, 1779

Congress awarded **1st decoration to a foreign national** to Lt. Col. François Louis Teisseidre de Fleury. He was presented with silver medallion for his part in attack on fort at Stony Point, N.Y., July 15, 1779, when he commanded part of the American attack forces himself and captured British flag. He was only foreigner so honored during Revolutionary War.

SEPTEMBER 23, 1779

Bonhomme Richard defeated and captured *Serapis,* a British man-of-war. *Bonhomme Richard,* commanded by John Paul Jones, was lashed fast during battle to *Serapis,* which finally struck its colors after 3 hours of brutal fighting.

OCTOBER 9, 1779

Count Pulaski, Polish officer in American service, mortally wounded in unsuccessful attack upon Savannah, Ga.

AUGUST 16, 1780

Gen. Gates defeated at Camden, S.C., by Gen. Cornwallis. Baron **De Kalb,** Prussian officer who joined American forces, mortally wounded during battle.

OCTOBER 2, 1780

Maj. **John André,** British officer, hanged as spy at Tappan, N.Y. He was apprehended by 3 militiamen after he left West Point, which Benedict Arnold, its commander, had agreed to surrender to British.

OCTOBER 7, 1780

British and Tories defeated at **King's mountain,** S.C., by Americans under Cols. Campbell, Shelby, and Cleveland. British commander, Maj. Ferguson, and 150 others killed and nearly 800 prisoners taken.

JANUARY 17, 1781

British under Col. Tarleton suffered heavy losses at **Cowpens, S.C.** American force of about 800 men led by Gen. Morgan.

MARCH 15, 1781

Cornwallis defeated American force led by Gen. Greene at **Guilford Court House** in N.C. Heavy losses suffered by both British and Americans.

SEPTEMBER 5, 1781

French fleet, under command of De Grasse, entered Chesapeake Bay and engaged **British fleet** under command of Admiral Graves. De Grasse drove British back to New York, precluding any possibility of aid to Cornwallis at Yorktown, Va.

SEPTEMBER 8, 1781

New London, Conn., seized and burned by Gen. Benedict Arnold, now with British. He then took Fort Griswold and was responsible for death of many American soldiers after their surrender.

SEPTEMBER 9, 1781

Gen. Greene forced to withdraw at **Eutaw Springs,** S.C., after assault upon British under Col. Stewart.

OCTOBER 9, 1781

Yorktown, Va., surrounded by American and French troops, who began shelling British position.

OCTOBER 19, 1781

Cornwallis surrendered at **Yorktown,** Va., to Washington and Lafayette. Capitulation, which yielded about 8000 British prisoners, brought war virtually to end.

SEPTEMBER 3, 1783

Peace treaty with Britain signed, ending the Revolutionary War. American independence recognized by British and boundaries of Republic agreed upon with Great Lakes and Florida to north and south, and Mississippi R. to west. Franklin, John Jay, and John Adams were American agents during peace negotiations in Paris.

DECEMBER 24, 1783

Gen. Washington resigned his commission as Commander in Chief of American Army.

"I regret *that I have but one life to lose for my country"* –Nathan Hale, *before his execution in New York in 1776.*

Revolutionary War *sea battle between the U.S.S.* Bonhomme Richard *and H.M.S.* Serapis *off Flamborough, England. It was during this battle that the American captain, John Paul Jones, when asked if he had struck his colors, replied, "I have not yet begun to fight."*

THE SEED IS PLANTED

The first English settlers, like the Spanish before them, not only found a vast and wondrous land, but one that was inhabited by a strange breed of men. Columbus, mistaking the New World for Asia, had called them *Indios* and this name has followed them ever since. These native Americans had no name for themselves since they had no knowledge of any other race and simply referred to themselves as "the people".

The Pilgrims, the pioneers of the seventeenth century, were quite unaware of the complexity of the Indian culture. They knew the living habits of a few tribes along the Eastern Seaboard and had learned some important survival techniques from them, but were quite ignorant of the origin of the Indians or of when they first occupied the Americas.

Most historians today, however, no longer debate the issue. They are convinced that the Indians migrated from Siberia across the Bering Sea, probably across a land bridge that at one time connected Alaska and Siberia. The Indians appear to be related to the marginal Mongoloids of Southeast and West Asia, but not from the same stock that produced the modern population of China and Japan. There is less agreement on the dates, but migration probably occurred at intervals with relatively small groups trickling into Alaska, beginning as early as 40,000 years ago. Dr. Lewis Leakey has suggested that the Indians may have occupied the United States as early as 80,000 to 100,000 years ago, but few archeologists agree with him. According to C. W. Cream, Emil W. Haury bet Leakey one hundred dollars in 1965 "that within the next fifteen years he would not be able to actually *prove* that man in North America is between 50,000 and 100,000 years old".[1] Unfortunately death prevented Leakey from any further attempts to prove his theory.

Although the Pilgrims *left behind them in England a society which had strongly discriminated against them on religious principles, once in the New World they established their own faith and in turn discriminated against those who failed to embrace their religious point of view.*

[1] C. W. Cream, *The First Americans*, p. 286.

[2] Wilcomb E. Washburn, *The Indian in America*, p. 28.

[3] Wilcomb E. Washburn, *The Indian in America*, p. 42.

The Indians, pushing ever southward from Alaska, moved in a direction that took them east of the Rocky Mountains into the United States, then traveled south into Mexico and Central America, until they finally reached Tierra del Fuego some 10,000 years ago.

The early settlers, like most Americans since, had difficulty understanding the Indian. The romantics of the eighteenth century glorified him as a "Noble Savage" who represented all that was best in natural man, one who was pure and undefiled, living in peace and harmony with his spiritual and physical world. Much more often, the pioneer viewed him as a barbarian, culturally a child, cunning, savage and merciless. And always there was the White Man's need for more land—the land of the Indians—which ultimately could lead only to misunderstanding, bloodshed and cruelty on both sides.

In some respects the two conflicting views of the Indian—noble and cruel—were correct. Some modern psychologists are suggesting that the Indian understood aspects of the spiritual and psychological world that modern white man is just now discovering. At their best the Indians produced leaders of whom any country would be proud; at the other extreme were tribes that seem to have been habituated to sadism and cruelty. Too often, however, the White Man has emphasized the latter, forgetting the high cultures of the Olmecs, Toltecs, Mayas, and Incas. Too often the White Man has forgotten how skillfully most Indians adapted themselves to their environment. The Cauhilla Indians of Southern California, for instance, discovered "not less than sixty distinct products for nutrition, and at least twenty-eight more utilized for narcotics, stimulants or medicines" from their desert environment![2] Too often the White Man has assumed that the Indian was without laws or regulations, whereas Wilcomb E. Washburn concluded from the facts that:

Indian methods of social control, though based on unwritten law and tribal custom, though ranging from humor and ridicule to whipping and death, provide a form of behavioral regulation as effective as that of any literate white society plentifully stocked with jails, churches, written codes, professional police, and the like. Indeed, white observers frequently remarked upon the greater effectiveness of Indian law than of white law in maintaining harmony within a society.[3]

The indigenous people *of the North American continent, called Indios by Columbus, were often thought of as "noble savages" by some European writers. Here is a highly romanticized drawing of an American Indian by an unknown French artist.*

Many Indians *were taken to Europe as curiosities, friends or to help in promoting future colonization. In 1734 chief Tomo-Chi-Chi, who had led his tribe into friendship with Georgia settlers, had his portrait painted in England. Pictured with him is his nephew.*

Ninigret, *chief of the Niantic Indians who lived in the region of Rhode Island.*

But generalization about the Indians can also be misleading; there were too many tribes, five hundred language groups in North America alone, too many economic, political and cultural problems. The anthropologist may be able to find a few significant similarities between the Digger Indians and the Mayas, but to understand the pre-Columbian American one must attempt to understand the differences between the Blackfoot and the Nez Percé, between the Sioux and the Algonquin, and between the Chinook and the Digger or the Cherokee. Actually more is known about the American Indian than any other aboriginal peoples, but for some reason the old stereotypes and cliches linger on in the public mind.

THE FIRST EUROPEANS: THE SEED GROWS

Neither the Spanish nor the English explorers and settlers were aware that the first Europeans to reach North America had arrived six hundred years earlier. Nor did they know that the first non-native child to be born in America was a Scandinavian, with the endearing name of Snorro, born (even if much further north) some 575 years before that more well-known claimant to the title of "first", Virginia Dare. Yet, since early nineteenth century, Americans have been fascinated by the idea that the Vikings (more properly called Norsemen) had not only reached but lived upon their shores.

A stone tower in Newport, Rhode Island, was discovered and claimed to be a surviving Norse structure. Leif Ericsson's "signature" was uncovered near Martha's Vineyard, Massachusetts, and the famous Kensington stone with "Scandinavian inscriptions" was dug up as far inland as

This portrait of Pocahontas *was painted in London in 1616 when she was about twenty-one years old. She was in England with her husband, John Rolfe, with whom she had fallen in love after being held captive aboard an English ship during an Indian uprising in America. Their marriage lasted only three years, however, because she died of smallpox while waiting to sail back to America.*

A **portrait** *of the Cherokee warrior Cunne Shote, painted by Francis Parsons.*

Minnesota. Each ''find'' created a fierce dispute over its legitimacy, leaving most historians still unconvinced. The stone tower seems to have been a windmill, Leif Ericsson's signature a practical joke, and the Norse statue was an unfinished piece of work from the English Colonial period. The most recent dispute is over the highly publicized Yale Vineland Map, dated at around A.D. 1440, the discovery of which was revealed in 1965.

In 1960, a Norwegian archeologist, Helge Ingstad, located the actual site where Leif Ericsson and others had lived for a short period of time. It took several years of digging at L'Anse aux Meadows in northern Newfoundland before the evidence became conclusive, but there is little doubt that Ingstad had at long last unraveled the mystery and proven the sagas to be history, not myth.

From the sagas and the archeological work in Greenland and L'Anse aux Meadows, we know that Eric the Red, with twelve to fifteen shiploads of Icelanders, colonized Greenland about 985 A.D. Shortly thereafter, Biarni Heriulfson, on his way to Greenland, lost his bearings and skirted lands farther to his west—the first European to see the New World. It was from him that Leif Ericsson, second son of Eric the Red, learned of these lands. In A.D. 1001 Leif and his crew set sail to the westward in search of wood on the shores Biarni had discribed. He sailed along ''Helluland'' (Baffin Island), then to ''Markland'' (Labrador), and south to ''Vineland'' (Newfoundland) where dwellings were constructed for the winter at L'Anse aux Meadows.

And what of the Norsemen in Greenland? The evidence indicates that settlements continued there well into the Fifteenth Century, but during the last century contacts with Iceland ceased, the climate gradually grew colder making farming all but impossible, the people deteriorated physically and eventually disappeared. Did any of the Norsemen migrate to the west and eventually intermarry with the Indians or Eskimos? Or, is Samuel Eliot Morison correct in saying that ''At some time in the second half of the fifteenth century, the last Norse Greenlander died, 'unknell'd, uncoffin'd and unknown'.''[4]

Whatever happened, the mystery of Newfoundland has been solved, leaving us with only the haunting wonder of what may have befallen the once valiant Norsemen of Greenland.

[4] Samuel Eliot Morison, *The European Discovery of America*, p. 61.

In the Fifteenth Century, as the Portuguese began inching down the coast of Africa in search of a route to the spices and wealth of the East Indies, and the Spanish were poised for the exploration of the New World, England was still a third-or fourth-rate power. In spite of the religious discord caused by Henry VIII in steering England away from the Catholicism of Rome and to Protestantism, the England inherited by Queen Elizabeth was relatively stable, united, expanding economically and maturing culturally.

The defeat of the Spanish Armada in 1588 was a significant turning point for a Protestant England fighting against the chief Catholic power of Europe, and an English victory assured the continuance of Protestantism in England, on the Continent, and in America. England had established herself as the supreme sea power. She was now strong enough on the high seas to move into the New World to establish herself there. After several unsuccessful attempts to colonize the Americas, Jamestown was founded in 1607 by the London Company. The men were adventurers seeking gold and not disposed to work even for their own food; the land was swampy and before long the inevitable conflict with the Indians developed. More than half the men died the first year and it was almost four years before survival seemed assured. After 1615 the colony was transformed from what amounted to little more than a trading post, ruled by iron discipline and hated by most of its inhabitants, into a commonwealth that began to open opportunities for a new and wonderful life for large numbers of ambitious and adventurous Englishmen. It was now certain that the seed so precariously planted in 1607 would grow, though only the most gifted prophet could have predicted that this growth would produce the greatest power on earth.

Two significant events occurred in Virginia in 1619 that would have profound effect upon the future of the United States. One was the creation of the first colonial assembly, the House of Burgesses. Its powers were limited, but for the first time in America the inhabitants were represented in the governmental structure. A small step had been taken, but by the middle of the eighteenth century the Virginia House of Burgesses was ready to challenge the Governor, Parliament and, finally, the King of England. The second event was the introduction of slavery to the colony, and the beginning of an institution which, running counter to the development of democracy, would split the Union asunder in 1861. By the end of the colonial period there were close to 400,000 black slaves in the Colonies.

The Pilgrims, landing at Plymouth Rock in 1620, are as much a part of the American legend as of the American reality. They arrived in America, after first migrating from England to Holland, searching for religious freedom. The most ill-fitted in experience or equipment of any of the pioneers, famine stalked them for many years and death took a heavy toll. Eventually they were absorbed by the great influx of Puritans but not before they had bequeathed to the nation an example of tremendous fortitude and perseverance, the democratic ideas set forth in the Mayflower Compact and the tradition of celebrating a season of thanksgiving.

In 1630, with the arrival of the Puritans, the tempo of colonization increased. By 1640 there were 20,000 settlers in Massachusetts. Dissidents from the Puritan ''theocracy'' founded Connecticut (1636) and Rhode Island (1644). In the meantime, the Dutch had settled in New York and Lord Baltimore had established a colony for Catholics in Maryland. Other colonies followed: the Carolinas (1670), New Hampshire (1679), Pennsylvania (1681), New Jersey (1702), and Georgia (1733).

Sir Walter Raleigh, *favorite of Queen Elizabeth, writer, man of affairs, was as influential as any other in establishing England's claims in America. Deeply interested in exploration, he backed a number of expeditions to colonize the New World, among these the famous ill-fated colony that disappeared mysteriously from Roanoke Island.*

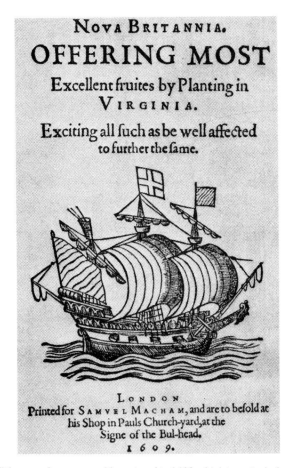

Title page *from a pamphlet printed in 1609 which is typical of many of the promotional tracts offered to entice colonists to various parts of America. This one listed advantages to the Virginia settler.*

Portrait of Thomas Cavendish, *Francis Drake and John Hawkins, three of England's most famous "Sea Dogs." Both Drake and Cavendish circumnavigated the earth.*

Raleigh equipped *an expedition in 1584 to the area that is now North Carolina and these adventurers explored the coast as far as present-day Florida. Raleigh named this entire region Virginia, in honor of "the virgin Queen." The picture represents the explorers offering gifts to the Indians.*

By the eighteenth century distinct economic and social patterns had emerged in three sections of the country: the New England colonies, the southern colonies, and middle colonies. Each was to make its distinct contribution to America.

New England was dominated by small farms, shipbuilding, fishing and commerce. Most early historians were from New England and, not unsurprisingly, for many years American history was conceived as the history of New England written large: New England, the home of the Pilgrims and the Puritans; New England, the home of Yankee ingenuity and the capitalistic work ethic; New England, where sturdy ships were built and manned, and where fishing, and later whaling, inspired the imagination of Americans; New England of the Town Meeting, the Mayflower Compact; New England, with its system of public education and its college, Harvard, which was founded only six years after the British arrived in Massachusetts. Sam Adams, James Otis, John Hancock, John Adams, all from New England, played a crucial role in the Revolutionary movement. But it should be remembered that New England was also parochial, its society relatively homogeneous, primarily of English background, and dedicated to a Protestantism which was mainly of the Puritan persuasion.

Certainly in 1776 Virginia, as the most influential representative of the South, stood equal in importance to Massachusetts. Like the rest of the South, her economy was centered around large plantations which concentrated on a single crop and were operated by slave labor. The plantation economy produced a society which was as dynamic in its own way as the one in New England. Even today, no one can visit the Southern plantations without being impressed with the beauty and comfort of the mansions and the grace, charm, and culture which those mansions represented. The Old Dominion was a jewel in the British crown and its contributions to the new nation perhaps unmatched.

Jamestown was the first colony in English America, the House of Burgesses the first representative assembly, and the first assembly to defy the British. The leadership which Virginians contributed to the new nation has been unexcelled. The contributions of Jefferson in writing the Declaration of Independence won him world-wide acclaim. Washington

was, as Thomas Flexner has called him, the "indispensable man" of the revolution, of the Constitutional Convention, and the adoption of the Constitution. No man could have taken his place as the first President of the United States. James Madison of Virginia made such a significant contribution to the Constitution and the *Federalist Papers* that he has been known, correctly, as the "Father" of the Constitution. Finally there was the Virginia dynasty of Presidents: Washington (1789-1797), Jefferson (1801-1909), Madison (1809-1817), Monroe (1817-1825), occupying the White House for twenty-four years of the first twenty-eight years after the adoption of the Constitution.

Again, however, Virginia was provincial. Its settlers, except for the voiceless slaves, were all British, the religious affiliation largely Anglican, and its way of life the nearest in America to that of the British aristocracy.

The middle colonies produced many leaders during the Revolutionary period and their share of men who fought in the revolution. The names of Benjamin Franklin, Alexander Hamilton, and the Morrises immediately come to mind. But the middle colonies were significant for another reason also. They were more like what America was to become than the other two sections of the country. Their economy was mixed. Philadelphia and New York were becoming important commercial centers along with Boston. Farming was much more varied than in the South.

There were large estates in New York and plantations with slave labor in Maryland, but througout the middle colonies and particularly in Pennsylvania, there were numerous small family farms similar to those of New England. It produced a greater variety of products than did New England or the South. Manufacturing was as significant a part of the economy as it was in the northern states. New York was the center of the fur trade, and farm products, unlike the single crop system of the South, included hogs, horses, corn, wheat, flour, tobacco, cotton and vegetables.

It was, however, the multiplicity of peoples and religions that made the middle colonies what America was to become. Whereas Virginia and New England were essentially English, it was to the middle colonies that the Dutch, Swedes, Finns, Jews and the Germans, along with the English, Scots and Irish, came. New England's religion was essentially

Jamestown, Virginia, as it might have appeared about one year after its founding. Jamestown was the first English-speaking colony in North America, St. Augustine in Florida having been established by the Spanish some forty years earlier.

Puritan, Virginia's, Anglican, but in the middle colonies could be found Quakers, Lutherans, Moravians, the Dutch Reformed, Mennonites, Dunkers and Jews along with Presbyterians, Methodists and other Protestant sects.

EMERGENCE OF THE AMERICAN: THE ROOTS TAKE HOLD

According to John Adams, the Revolution was "already in the hearts and minds of the people" before any overt steps were taken. Something had happened in the one-hundred-and-fifty years following the settlement at Jamestown that made the Americans unique and twentieth century America is still a reflection of that uniqueness. American democracy, American capitalism, the American concept of individualism, liberty, hard work, religious freedom, and social equality all find their roots in Colonial America. Americans in 1776 were different from their English forebears, even though English policy contributed to that difference. Americans in 1776 were also singularly different from the French and Spanish colonists to the north and south of them.

Geography played a significant, though by no means a determining role. Three thousand miles of ocean made it difficult for the British to exert control over the colonies in America; the ocean was a barrier to imperialism and a highway to freedom. Communication was slow and often the ships bearing letters were long delayed because of wars. Not

A page from Captain John Smith's General Historie of Virginia (1624), which is filled with his astonishing feats and near defeats. Never one who lacked for adventure, after settling Jamestown and exploring New England he fought the Spaniards in the Netherlands, then jaunted off to battle the Turks in Hungary where he was taken a slave, only later to escape through Russia and Germany.

until 1755 was there a regular mail service between England and the colonies. Poor communication was accentuated by the inefficiency of the British bureaucracy. It is little wonder that the third, fourth and fifth generation Americans came to have, and would continue to expect, considerable freedom from England.

The frontier gave added impetus to the development of the American character. One does not need to agree with all of the concepts expressed by Frederick Jackson Turner on the importance of the frontier in America to recognize that on the frontier there was more liberty and equality than could possibly exist in the motherland where most of the people were bonded into classes subject to aristocratic rule. There were virtually no man-made restraints on the frontier and any man who could wield an axe or shoulder a gun was the equal of all others. There can be little question that the frontier gave rise to that keen sense of individualism that came to be associated with the American character, which in turn led to a *laissez faire* doctrine of government.

Though seven out of ten white Americans at the time of the Revolution were English, the British colonies were unique in the multiplicity of national groups represented in their population. In Spanish America, whose great expanse of land stretched from the present state of California and New Mexico to the southern tip of South America, could be found only one group of Europeans, the Spanish. The French followed the same restrictive policy in Canada, and only Frenchmen could emigrate to the new world.

In the British colonies of North America, a far different policy was practiced. By the Revolutionary period there were Scots, Irish, Swedes, Finns, Danes, Dutch, Swiss and even a few Jewish people in the colonies. Negro slaves made up about twenty percent of the total population and though American was not yet the "melting pot" it was to become, the process had begun. Americans were developing a greater ease in accepting people of other nationalities (excluding the Blacks) than others in the world. Also, many of these groups made their own contribution to the movement toward independence and to the American character. The Scotch-Irish displayed a fierce sense of their English "liberties", the Germans reinforced the Protestant work ethic, and by 1776 many of these groups could more easily break their ties with England than could the colonists of English extraction.

The dominant economic philosophy of the times was mercantilism, a theory which held that colonies should be the producers of raw materials and the mother country the producer of industrial goods. This created an unfavorable balance of trade for the colonies which became a factor in their growing resistance to English rule. Mercantilism on a broader scale meant control of the economy of the empire for the good of the empire, hence some of the British justification for controlling the currency in the colonies, and for establishing the Trade and Navigation Acts, the Sugar Act and tax on tea.

Colonists at Jamestown, *Virginia, greet their future wives off a Brides' ship in this artist's sketch depicting the year 1619.*

Artist's rendering *of the first Thanksgiving. Despite eventual antagonisms between the colonists and the Indians, the two groups were able to sit down together and enjoy a feast to celebrate, at least in the Pilgrims' minds, the bounty of the Christian God.*

The British system of mercantilism was much less restrictive and less paternalistic than the systems of either the French or Spanish. This provided the settlers in the British colonies with more opportunity to benefit from their own initiative, hard work and frugality. England also was becoming the most important industrial and commercial nation, and the American colonies developed economically much more rapidly as a consequence. The system, as it functioned, was conducive to economic growth, mobility and self-government. By 1776, right or wrong, many in the English colonies were beginning to feel that they could now make their way alone, and thanks to the British mercantile system, they were much better equipped economically to do so than either the French or Spanish colonies.

Other economic factors were important in setting the colonies apart from Britain and leading ultimately to a more democratic society in America. Almost all reports indicate that real wages were considerably higher in America than in England and that working conditions were more humane (particularly in New England and the Middle colonies) thus providing a sizeable number of skilled and unskilled free workers who could move into the middle class. In fact, the craftsman enjoyed a far more reputable position socially and politically in the colonies than he could have in England, or in the Spanish and French colonies.

Even more important was the availability of land. Though practices varied from colony to colony and from Tidewater to back country, land even in the South could be acquired by the man with little means if he desired it. In New England land was widely owned and rather equally distributed, with few large estates. The importance of land in creating much greater equality than existed in Europe is self-evident, but one should also remember that the right to vote was based upon the ownership of land. With ownership widely distributed, voting rights were obtainable by a sizeable proportion of the population. The large plantations of the South, based on the system of slave labor, were less democratic than the New England system, but everywhere in the British colonies land was more readily available than in Europe or in the Spanish and French colonies. In Spanish America the awarding of large land grants to privileged men coupled with differing attitudes toward, and opportunities for, the skilled and unskilled worker divided society between the rich and the poor and precluded the development of a middle class, whereas in America democracy has, to a large extent, been a "middle class" democracy.

Many migrants to the new world were motivated by economic considerations, but large numbers came also for religious reasons. From a practical standpoint the multiplicity of religious sects would lead to tolerance and eventually to the separation of church and state—which is to say, religious freedom. English policy permitted any religious group to settle in the New World. There were as many sects as there were nationalities. The South was largely Anglican, but the Catholics settled in Maryland, Scots-Irish Presbyterians filtered into the back country and some French Huguenots

Having fled *from injustice and determined to establish their own laws of government, 41 Pilgrims sign the Mayflower Compact while still aboard ship in Provincetown harbor in 1620.*

The governor's palace *at Williamsburg. In 1699, the capital of the Virginia Colony was moved from Jamestown to Middle Plantation and named Williamsburg for King William III of England.*

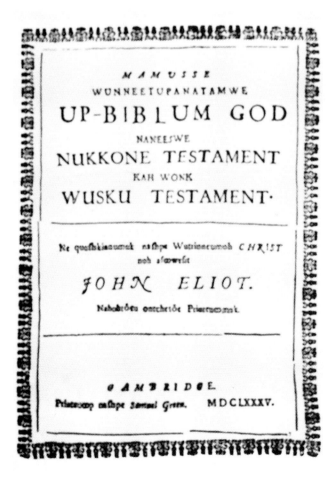

One of the *first books to be printed in America was this Indian-language Bible which appeared in 1663.*

established themselves in the Carolinas. Elsewhere were the Puritans (Congregational and Presbyterian), the Dutch Reformed, German Lutherans, Baptist, Quakers, Mennonites, Dunkers, Moravians, Schwenkfelders and Jews. Constant association frequently brought tolerance and understanding while certain religious groups (most notably the Quakers and Baptists) actively practiced and espoused religious freedom.

Some historians have maintained that Protestantism developed out of capitalism, though others would insist that capitalism developed from Protestantism. Both viewpoints give expression to the close relationship between American economic ideas and practices and the Protestant religion. In the economic sphere Puritanism (and most religious groups in America were influenced by its doctrines) emphasized what has come to be called the Protestant ethic and the work ethic. To the Puritan, hard work was next to (or perhaps the same thing as) Godliness. He was convinced that man should use his talents because an ''idle man's brain is the devil's workshop.'' On the other hand if one worked hard, was frugal, and moral, one would be rewarded by material prosperity. So firmly established was this belief that those who did not prosper were ''obviously'' lacking in moral virtue and those who had succeeded in acquiring wealth were considered virtuous. Benjamin Franklin was to give a classic expression to the Protestant ethic in *Poor Richard's Almanack* and much later John D. Rockefeller was to declare ''God gave me my money.''

Within Protestantism were the seeds, also, of many political ideas associated with democracy. The Protestants were ''protest''ants. They opposed the power and authority of the

An artist's conception *of New York City, circa 1740. Although originally settled by the Dutch, by the time of the American Revolution New York City had become one of the leading centers of mercantilism under the unique British system of trading.*

Cecilius Calvert, *second Lord Baltimore, is portrayed with his grandson. Although a Roman Catholic, he worked to establish freedom of worship and protection of all faiths in Maryland, the area granted to his father in 1632 by Charles I of England.*

Pope and opposed the power and authority of kings. It was not difficult for the eighteenth century Bostonian to move from a belief in the infallibility of the Bible to the belief in the ''higher law'' upon which the Revolution and the Constitution were based. The idea that man needed no priest or Pope to intercede for him, that he could commune directly with God, and the belief that each man could interpret the Bible for himself led to the same intensive individualism as did life on the frontier. It is not surprising that those theological concepts, combined with the American environment, created churches that were self-governing. The Congregational Church of New England best exemplified this. Even Anglican churches in the South reflected greater control by the membership than could have occurred in England.

Some historians have described the Puritans as narrow, bigoted and autocratic, and insist that they attempted to establish a theocracy in Massachusetts in which a theology of

The third largest library in the colonies was housed on the second floor of Stenton, erected near Philadelphia in 1728.

predestination, hellfire and brimstone, and original sin were used to frighten the populace into submission to the state. Their interpretation considers the witch hunt of Salem and the Puritan persecution of the Quakers as the logical outgrowth of that perverted theocracy. The witch hunt finally ended, but not until twenty so-called witches had been executed and two had died in prison. The Puritans found the Quakers hardly less acceptable than the witches and their persecution included whipping (up to fifty lashes), placing them in the stocks and even the hanging of a young woman, Mary Dyer, in 1660.

And yet perhaps American democracy owes more to the Puritans than to any other single group. Covenant theology—the Puritans recognized seven to eight covenants—merged into the social contract theory of the eighteenth century upon which the Declaration of Independence was based. Church government among the Puritans was essentially democratic and the practice of popular government throughout Massachusetts was largely a secularization of Congregationalism. The Massachusetts Town Meeting has frequently been considered the nearest thing to pure democracy ever witnessed in America. Land was divided on a relatively equal basis and the Protestant ethic permeated the economy. Nor could the Puritans be matched for their attention to public education or the founding of Harvard College. Finally, Massachusetts was the only colony in which the owners of the charter all migrated to America and once there extended the right of political participation to all freemen who were members of the church.

Though the seventeenth century colonists accepted an old world class structure, the geographic, economic, and religious factors produced salient social differences between the colonies and the mother country, disparities which were even more pronounced between the English colonies and the Spanish and French colonies. In spite of the development of a native aristocracy, based on wealth and education, and the existence of slavery, the distinctive features of colonial society were the increase in fluidity throughout the social structure and the increasing size of the middle class.

Higher wages for skilled and unskilled labor, the absence of the guild system, the availability of land, the emphasis on individual achievement, and life on the frontier all led to the possibility of upward mobility. Thousands of migrants came to the new world as indentured servants (almost two-thirds of the immigrants to Pennsylvania in the eighteenth century), but later found ample opportunity to move into the middle class. By the time of the Revolution, social fluidity had made middle class values the dominant feature of the American mind and the chief stabilizing influence. Nowhere else in the Western World was the middle class as large, or as socially and politically important; and not surprisingly, nowhere else was social solidarity, liberty, equality and self-government so prevalent.

Popular opinion and stories to the contrary, democratic self government was not practiced in the colonies. But for a hundred and fifty years, slowly, persistently, sometimes two steps backward for one forward, the colonies moved in that direction. They inherited much from England: the Magna Carta, the right of representation, trial by jury, the Bill of Rights, and the English concept of local government. Even during the Revolution the colonists believed they were fighting only for their rights as Englishmen.

The American colonists also took advantage of the complexity of the English colonial administration. On many issues each colony was treated separately—thirteen colonies, thirteen systems of government. Furthermore, in England, responsibility for colonial administration was divided among an amazing array of agencies with overlapping jurisdictions. Even Benjamin Franklin could not have determined where the responsibilities of the Privy Council, the Board of Trade, the Treasury Board, the Admiralty Board, the War Office or the Secretary of State began and ended. The result of the confusion was that a large measure of self-government was left to the colonies. By contrast, both the French and

Tinsmiths *at work, during a period when industry was largely handicraft.*

Cotton Mather, *the son of Increase Mather, became his father's associate in Boston's North Church and almost tripled his father's writing output. He was a student of sorcery and through his writing set off the Salem witch hunt of 1692. His other contributions, however, improved his image, for he published works on biology, physics, medicine and astronomy, helped to found Yale College and was elected to England's Royal Society.*

Mather was the name *of a famous family of clergymen in New England. Increase Mather, although a rigorous Puritan, was of scientific mind and supported the campaign to introduce the inoculation for smallpox and was greatly troubled by the witch trials in Salem. He published 130 books and pamphlets upholding his high religious principles and was president of Harvard College for sixteen of his 84 years.*

Spanish had highly centralized colonial administrations and relatively efficient control over their colonies, leaving little possibility for self-government.

Through a century-long tug-of-war between the colonial assemblies and the appointed governors, the representative assemblies gradually increased their power and influence. Perhaps the most important power they gained was the control of the purse strings, and in all but two colonies, control over the governor's salary. The Revolution was fought in part because the assemblies considered themselves equal, and not subservient, to the English Parliament.

While the colonies were moving toward self-government, a gradual broadening of suffrage was also taking place. The restrictive qualifications for suffrage clearly indicates that democracy as generally defined did not exist, but with all the limitations, by 1770, voting privileges were available to a far larger proportion of the population than anywhere in the Western World. Authorities disagree widely on exact figures, and conditions varied from colony to colony enough to make generalizations precarious. But there can be no doubt about certain groups who were automatically disenfranchised: all women, all slaves, and all indentured servants. In addition, the ownership of property was a general requirement. A number of studies indicate that only one out of four white males was eligible to vote for representatives to the assembly.

The free press, a late colonial development, played the same significant role in the Revolution that it did in Watergate. There was only one newspaper in the colonies in 1715 with a circulation of only 250 and that was "published by authority." By 1763 there were twenty-three reaching tens of thousands of people and printed without censorship. Though these journals in 1763 were devoting eleven out of twelve columns to advertisements an amazing development occurred as tension with England over the Sugar Act and Stamp Tax mounted. By 1765 they were devoting eleven in twelve columns to the political issues of the day.[5]

By the Revolutionary period a number of other important political ideas compatible with democracy were emerging. The "rule of law," not of men, written constitutions as the best guarantee of liberty, faith in local government, and an inchoate conception of federalism. Not all of these ideas were articulated until the revolutionary period, but all of these concepts had been germinating in the American soil.

[5] Clinton Rossiter, *The First American Revolution*, pp. 126-27.

Declaration of Independence

IN CONGRESS, JULY 4, 1776

The unanimous Declaration of the thirteen united States of America.

When in the Course of human events, it becomes necessary for one people to dissolve the political bands which have connected them with another, and to assume among the powers of the earth, the separate and equal station to which the Laws of Nature and of Nature's God entitle them, a decent respect to the opinions of mankind requires that they should declare the causes which impel them to the separation.

We hold these truths to be self-evident, that all men are created equal, that they are endowed by their Creator with certain unalienable Rights, that among these are Life, Liberty and the pursuit of Happiness.—That to secure these rights, Governments are instituted among Men, deriving their just powers from the consent of the governed,—That whenever any Form of Government becomes destructive of these ends, it is the Right of the People to alter or to abolish it, and to institute new Government, laying its foundation on such principles and organizing its powers in such form, as to them shall seem most likely to effect their Safety and Happiness. Prudence, indeed, will dictate that Governments long established should not be changed for light and transient causes; and accordingly all experience hath shewn, that mankind are more disposed to suffer, while evils are sufferable, than to right themselves by abolishing the forms to which they are accustomed. But when a long train of abuses and usurpations, pursuing invariably the same Object evinces a design to reduce them under absolute Despotism, it is their right, it is their duty, to throw off such Government, and to provide new Guards for their future security.—Such has been the patient sufferance of these Colonies; and such is now the necessity which constrains them to alter their former Systems of Government. The history of the present King of Great Britain is a history of repeated injuries and usurpations, all having in direct object the establishment of an absolute Tyranny over these States. To prove this, let Facts be submitted to a candid world.

He has refused his Assent to Laws, the most wholesome and necessary for the public good.

He has forbidden his Governors to pass Laws of immediate and pressing importance, unless suspended in their operation till his Assent should be obtained; and when so suspended, he has utterly neglected to attend to them.

He has refused to pass other Laws for the accommodation of large districts of people, unless those people would relinquish the right of Representation in the Legislature, a right inestimable to them and formidable to tyrants only.

He has called together legislative bodies at places unusual, uncomfortable, and distant from the depository of their public Records, for the sole purpose of fatiguing them into compliance with his measures.

He has dissolved Representative Houses repeatedly, for opposing with manly firmness his invasions on the rights of the people.

He has refused for a long time, after such dissolutions, to cause others to be elected; whereby the Legislative powers, incapable of Annihilation, have returned to the People at large for their exercise; the State remaining in the mean time exposed to all the dangers of invasion from without, and convulsions within.

He has endeavoured to prevent the population of these States; for that purpose obstructing the Laws for Naturalization of Foreigners; refusing to pass others to encourage their migrations hither, and raising the conditions of new Appropriations of Lands.

He has obstructed the Administration of Justice, by refusing his Assent to Laws for establishing Judiciary powers.

He has made Judges dependent on his Will alone, for the tenure of their offices, and the amount and payment of their salaries.

He has erected a multitude of New Offices, and sent hither swarms of Officers to harrass our people, and eat out their substance.

He has kept among us, in times of peace, Standing Armies without the Consent of our legislatures.

He has affected to render the Military independent of and superior to the Civil power.

He has combined with others to subject us to a jurisdiction foreign to our constitution, and unacknowledged by our laws; giving his Assent to their Acts of pretended Legislation:

For Quartering large bodies of armed troops among us:

For protecting them, by a mock Trial, from punishment for any Murders which they should commit on the Inhabitants of these States:

For cutting off our Trade with all parts of the world:

For imposing Taxes on us without our Consent:

For depriving us in many cases, of the benefits of Trial by Jury:

For transporting us beyond Seas to be tried for pretended offences

For abolishing the free System of English Laws in a neighbouring Province, establishing therein an Arbitrary government, and enlarging its Boundaries so as to render it at once an example and fit instrument for introducing the same absolute rule into these Colonies:

For taking away our Charters, abolishing our most valuable Laws, and altering fundamentally the Forms of our Governments:

For suspending our own Legislatures, and declaring themselves invested with power to legislate for us in all cases whatsoever.

He has abdicated Government here, by declaring us out of his Protection and waging War against us.

He has plundered our seas, ravaged our Coasts, burnt our towns, and destroyed the lives of our people.

He is at this time transporting large Armies of foreign Mercenaries to compleat the works of death, desolation and tyranny, already begun with circumstances of Cruelty & perfidy scarcely paralleled in the most barbarous ages, and totally unworthy the Head of a civilized nation.

He has constrained our fellow Citizens taken Captive on the high Seas to bear Arms against their Country, to become the executioners of their friends and Brethren, or to fall themselves by their Hands.

He has excited domestic insurrections amongst us, and has endeavoured to bring on the inhabitants of our frontiers, the merciless Indian Savages, whose known rule of warfare, is an undistinguished destruction of all ages, sexes and conditions.

In every stage of these Oppressions We have Petitioned for Redress in the most humble terms: Our repeated Petitions have been answered only by repeated injury. A Prince whose character is thus marked by every act which may define a Tyrant, is unfit to be the ruler of a free people.

Nor have We been wanting in attentions to our Brittish brethren. We have warned them from time to time of attempts by their legislature to extend an unwarrantable jurisdiction over us. We have reminded them of the circumstances of our emigration and settlement here. We have appealed to their native justice and magnanimity, and we have conjured them by the ties of our common kindred to disavow these usurpations, which, would inevitably interrupt our connections and correspondence. They too have been deaf to the voice of justice and of consanguinity. We must, therefore, acquiesce in the necessity, which denounces our Separation, and hold them, as we hold the rest of mankind, Enemies in War, in Peace Friends.

We, therefore, the Representatives of the united States of America, in General Congress, Assembled, appealing to the Supreme Judge of the world for the rectitude of our intentions, do, in the Name, and by Authority of the good People of these Colonies, solemnly publish and declare, That these United Colonies are, and of Right ought to be Free and Independent States; that they are Absolved from all Allegiance to the British Crown, and that all political connection between them and the State of Great Britain, is and ought to be totally dissolved; and that as Free and Independent States, they have full Power to levy War, conclude Peace, contract Alliances, establish Commerce, and to do all other Acts and Things which Independent States may of right do.—And for the support of this Declaration, with a firm reliance on the protection of divine Providence, we mutually pledge to each other our Lives, our Fortunes and our sacred Honor.

John Hancock

Button Gwinnett
Lyman Hall
Geo Walton.

Wm Hooper
Joseph Hewes
John Penn

Edward Rutledge.

Thos Heyward Junr.
Thomas Lynch Junr.
Arthur Middleton

Samuel Chase
Wm Paca
Thos Stone
Charles Carroll of Carrollton

George Wythe
Richard Henry Lee
Th Jefferson
Benja Harrison
Thos Nelson jr.
Francis Lightfoot Lee
Carter Braxton

Robt Morris
Benjamin Rush
Benja Franklin
John Morton
Geo Clymer
Jas Smith
Geo. Taylor
James Wilson
Geo. Ross
Caesar Rodney
Geo Read
Tho M:Kean

Wm Floyd
Phil Livingston
Frans Lewis
Lewis Morris

Richd Stockton
Jno Witherspoon
Fras Hopkinson
John Hart
Abra Clark

Josiah Bartlett
Wm Whipple
Saml Adams
John Adams
Robt Treat Paine
Elbridge Gerry
Step Hopkins
William Ellery
Roger Sherman
Sam l Huntington
Wm Williams
Oliver Wolcott
Matthew Thornton

THE SEED TAKES ROOT

With an English victory in 1763 in the French and Indian War, France was forced to cede to England all of Canada and all of the Louisiana Territory east of the Mississippi, thus completely excluding France from the North American Continent. This victory was the culmination of the rise of England to the position of the strongest commercial and colonial power in the world. The importance of the victory to the American colonies, however, cannot be overlooked either. A French victory would have bottled up the Americans at the Appalachian Mountains and changed the course of history. The date of 1763 marks a change in British policy toward America which led to the Revolution and in turn to an independent United States in possession of those coveted lands east of the Mississippi.

With the end of the War and the expulsion of France from America, the British were faced with a host of pressing problems which would embroil the mother country and the colonies and result in changing radically the relations of the two. Within thirteen years after the glorious victory in the French and Indian War, the American colonies would declare their independence and a new nation would be born. Britain had two immediate problems which needed attention: one was how to pay for the war and the increased costs of retaining a larger military and civil administration to protect and rule the empire, and second, the need for more systematic organization of the enlarged empire.

During the war the British debt had increased to a staggering £140,000,000 and the budget for her enlarged civil and military needs had jumped five fold, to £350,000. To a considerable degree the war had been fought for the benefit of the American colonies. The men in Parliament thought it

only just that the colonies be taxed to pay their share of the debt. The colonists claimed that they could protect themselves, but the half-hearted support they had given the English during the recent war and in defending the colonies during Pontiac's Conspiracy left the British little recourse but to keep soldiers stationed in America. Nor were the British unmindful that the colonists had enriched themselves in many ways during the war, not the least of which was the treasonable act of trading with the French; nor that the average person in England was paying two to three times more in taxes than the average colonist.

But unsuspected resistance awaited the British at each attempt to implement their new policies, and the colonist's first display of organized opposition was to the Sugar Act of 1764, which actually lowered the tax on foreign molasses imported into the colonies. The English were well aware, however, that under the earlier Molasses Act the colonists had paid little revenue, resorting to smuggling to avoid the British customs agents. The Sugar Act, unlike the Molasses Act, was to be strictly enforced and the colonists were well aware of this difference. New Englanders seemed more alarmed over the Sugar Act than they had been over the French and Indian forays into New England during the recent war.

Opposition to the Sugar Act was based on the manner in which it imperiled the chief commodity of the triangle trade, and the triangle trade was the basis of New England economy. Products were carried by New Englanders in New England-built ships to the West Indies where they were traded for molasses. The molasses was brought back to New England and converted into rum which was then used along the African coast to exchange for slaves, the slaves taken to the West Indies for more molasses to be turned into more rum

George Washington *as represented by Thomas Uully.*

25

Lord George Germain

George Grenville

Charles Townshend

Lord North

Advisors *to King George who advocated taking a strong stand against the colonies.*

Englishmen *who often expressed sympathy toward the colonial cause.*

Charles James Fox

Edmund Burke

John Wilkes

and the pattern continued. The three-sided commerce was not only lucrative, but provided New England with much needed cash to balance its debts with England—debts inevitable under mercantilism. Even more important, most of the molasses was purchased in the French West Indies where the price was twenty-five to forty percent lower than in the English held islands. Trade with the French was illegal, thus all molasses purchased from the French needed to be smuggled into the colonies. If the new tax on sugar, even though only half as much as the original tax in the Molasses Act, was enforced, the New England economy would be seriously crippled. Under these circumstances the Act was looked upon not so much as a tax, but as a virtual prohibition of trade with the foreign West Indies, trade of vital importance to the New England economy.

The Stamp Tax passed by Parliament in 1765 was considered by the British to be one of the most equitable, easy to collect and yet profitable taxes ever devised. It was not designed to raise money to be utilized in England to pay off the British debt, but was meant to raise only a small portion (about one-sixth) of the money needed to maintain the civil and military establishment in America. The cry of "no taxation without representation" echoed throughout the colonies and the severity of the protest forced the repeal of the tax.

Since the colonists had indicated they only objected to "internal" taxing by the mother country, England returned in 1767 with "external" taxes in the form of the Townshend

Acts. Organized opposition, riots, and boycotts developed almost immediately. Resistance this time was based on how the monies received from the duties would be used. The plan included applying the monies to a colonial civil list. This would render the royal judges and governors independent of the colonial assemblies, one of the most coveted powers acquired by the assemblies through lengthy contention with the governors. Finally, the British were forced to repeal in 1770 all the Townshend Acts except the tax on tea.

The resistance to the Stamp Tax was a prelude to the events which would follow the tax on tea. Not only was it an internal tax but also it directly affected those people who were the most vocal in the colonies—the merchants, lawyers, clergymen and journalists. They were quick to recognize that the tax violated a basic right of Englishmen, the right of taxation only with representation, and according to them its enforcement would deprive them of their political liberties. Finally, the colonists were not unaware of the huge British debt and they believed that if the Stamp Tax went unopposed other taxes were sure to follow and the Americans would soon be forced into slavery.

A group called the Sons of Liberty was formed with the express purpose of organizing the opposition to the Stamp Tax. Opposition in New England was especially strong. Several months before the tax was to go into force riots broke out in Boston. There a mob, which had been carefully organized by the Sons of Liberty, hung Andrew Oliver, the tax

Samuel Adams, *although rich in word and deed was a failure in business and lived in "genteel poverty" most of his life. He was a leader in the rebel cause and one of the most outspoken in the drive for independence from England. He organized the Boston Tea Party and recommended that the colonies send delegates to a congress to clarify their position. When such a congress was formed in Philadelphia in 1774, he was selected as one of its members. He was a cousin of John Adams, a signer of the Declaration and one of the great sons of liberty.*

John Hancock, *a wealthy merchant, was regarded by the British—along with Sam Adams—as one of the most dangerous of the revolutionaries. The British plotted to arrest the two in Lexington in 1775 but Paul Revere's warning allowed their escape. Hancock's bold signature on the Declaration of Independence attests to the strength of his character and his open rebellious feelings.*

master, in effigy, marched on the building which was to be the office of the stamp master and completely demolished it, and then, using debris from the wreckage, burned the effigy of Oliver along with one of the Devil. The next target was Oliver's home which suffered considerable damage. Oliver had been out of town and was, therefore, not molested, but he resigned, judiciously, the next day.

Less than two weeks later the Boston mob attacked the house and the first floor office of the register of the Vice Admiralty Court and destroyed all records and papers in a huge bonfire. Not far away was the newly constructed home of the comptroller of customs whose house and belongings suffered the same destructive fury as Oliver's, but this time the mob profited by getting away with his money as well, after obviously enjoying the contents of the wine cellar. The final act of violence was against Lieutenant Governor Hutchinson, but he was forewarned and was able to escape with his family. His mansion, one of the finest examples of colonial architecture, was not fortunate enough to escape the mob's vengeance and was totally gutted with everything in the house cast into the street, pictures slashed, china smashed piece by piece, and a great collection of manuscripts on the history of Massachusetts burned. No one was ever punished for these wanton acts of destruction.

Attempts of the British to reorganize the empire were met with the same lack of success as they experienced in trying to

The Stamp Act *was particularly irksome to the colonists and their resistance to it was not passive. The engraving of the period shows a stamp agent strung up on a liberty pole.*

27

raise taxes in the colonies. A systematic approach to the administration of the colonies was long overdue. After the period of salutory neglect, piecemeal steps had been taken to remedy the situation, but they were still piecemeal and often ineffective. Tightening the entire customs system to prevent smuggling was one of the needed reforms, and a Board of Customs Commissioners was established at Boston and new regulations were imposed. One historian has even suggested that these changes alone were enough to precipitate revolution because of the adverse effect they had on the merchant class in the colonies.

A major attempt at solving the organizational needs of the empire after the French and Indian War was the Proclamation of 1763 involving all lands west of the mountains. During the war the British had made treaties with a number of Indian tribes in the area and they were intent upon keeping their side of the agreements. With these considerations in mind, the British decided that settlers should be excluded from the trans-Allegheny country until the Indians were pacified and a definite land policy worked out. The formal application of this policy in the Proclamation of 1763 wiped out the dreams and hopes of those Americans who were planning, following the war, to settle these rich virgin lands. It also negated every western land claim of the thirteen colonies.

The Proclamation could lead to disaster for many Virginians, including George Washington, who was speculating heavily in western lands. Because the Virginians were forced to send all their tobacco to England and to purchase all their manufactured and luxury goods from the mother country, they experienced an unfavorable balance of trade and an ever increasing debt to her. By the time of the Revolution, the American colonies owed England about £5,000,000 and five-sixths of that amount was owed by the southern colonies. One of the few avenues open to the Virginian to balance his English deficits was to speculate in western lands for resale to the eager pioneers ready to surge across the mountains to new settlements. The Proclamation had now barred that possibility.

The Quebec Act passed in 1774 seemed even more insidi-

Attacks *on Colonials' homes became an increasingly common activity of the British Redcoats, particularly after a mob of colonists attacked and burned in effigy the Boston Tax Collector, Andrew Oliver. Here an artist's view of an American colonial woman defending her home and children from British soldiers.*

This English cartoon *depicts the burial of the Stamp Act which had been repealed soon after its onset. Other taxes, however, were enforced which further entrenched the colonists in their desire to stand alone without British interference.*

ous to the colonists than the Proclamation of 1763. The Act was intended to correct certain mistakes in the Proclamation and to secure for the British the loyalty of the French Canadians who became British subjects as the result of the French defeat in the recent war. To the French Canadians, all of whom were Catholic, England granted complete religious freedom and the restitution of their French legal and political institutions. With considerable justification the Act annexed to the Providence of Quebec all of the lands north of the Ohio River.

Again the western land claims of the colonies, which dated back to their original charters, were being denied, and this time the land was given to the hated French Catholics with whom they had been at war a dozen times in the past hundred years. Enlightened or not, the effect of the Act on the American colonies after all that had transpired between 1763 and 1774, could not have been more devastating.

Finally there was the Boston Massacre which resulted from the British having quartered their troops in Boston. A snow-balling of the troops by the irate Bostonians degenerated, apparently, into a mob attack. A gun was fired, other shots followed, and when the skirmish was over four Bostonians lay dead on the street. It was more a brawl than a massacre, but it added fuel to the propaganda campaign conducted by the Sons of Liberty against the British. The patriots effectively used the event to keep the fires of resentment against the British burning with lurid details of this latest of British ''atrocities''. According to one authority the massacre provided the material for one of the most effective propaganda campaigns in history.

THE SHOT HEARD 'ROUND THE WORLD

The final chain of events which led directly to the Revolution began with the Boston Tea Party. In an effort to assist the near bankrupt British East India Company and thereby buttress the economy of the empire, Parliament granted the East India Company a monopoly of the tea trade in the colonies.

The Boston Massacre on March 5, 1770 was in reality a street fight between a Boston mob and British troops stationed in the town. The mob, hating the presence of the British, had attacked a sentinel whose British compatriots came to his aid, firing upon the crowd, resulting in the death of five citizens. John Adams, to prove there was liberty for all, acted as council for defense of the British soldiers, even in the face of strong adverse public sentiment.

Under the arrangements the company was able to sell tea at one-half the previous price, even undercutting the smugglers. Monopoly, however, was hardly in keeping with the American disposition. Many people were fearful that other monopolies would soon follow, and the middle men and smugglers who were being frozen out of business felt they could look forward only to ruin. To many Americans the conclusion seemed inescapable: the Tea Act threatened the foundation of American liberty.

Like the stamp masters the tea consignees found themselves exposed to the full fury of the Sons of Liberty. In Boston the patriots enforcing the boycott against the sale of the tea were convinced that should the tea be brought ashore, it would ultimately be sold and their boycott would have failed. Thinly disguised as Indians, a group of patriots boarded the three ships in the harbor carrying the tea, which now symbolized all they hated, and hoisted it overboard.

The Boston Tea Party was only the first of a series of tea parties given by the Americans at the expense of the East India Company, but the consequences of that first party were the most drastic. All England was in shock, and the time had come to teach the radicals in Boston a long overdue lesson. Orders were sent to close the port of Boston to all shipping, certain offenders were to be henceforth shipped to England for trial (a denial of the right to be tried by one's peers), and radical changes were made in the government of Massachusetts. These ''Coercive Acts'' were intended not only to punish Boston, but to isolate Massachusetts from the rest of the colonies. Instead of isolating Massachusetts, the ''Intolerable Acts'', as they came to be known in the colonies, rallied the other twelve colonies to her support. All the

Patriots, *disguised as Indians, feeling that the tea represents monopoly, taxes and further British oppression, throw the contents of 342 chests of tea into Boston Harbor.*

This picture *represents the patriots's sentiments against all excisemen. Here they visit reprisal upon Johnny Malcom, a spy for British customs who has been tarred and feathered and forced to drink tea. The Constitution's later stand against cruel and unusual punishment is to be commended in a day when such acts were taken for granted.*

colonies recognized that the Intolerable Acts represented a "tyranny" on the part of England more serious than a Sugar Act or a Stamp Tax, more serious than any distinction between internal and external taxes, or between taxes to control trade or to obtain revenue. A rump assembly meeting in Williamsburg, Virginia, sent out a call for a congress of all American colonies and less than four months later, in September, 1774, the First Continental Congress was in session. After it took official action against the Coercive Acts, adopted a Declaration of Rights and Grievances, and performed other actions which helped solidify the colonies, a date was set for another meeting in 1775. In April of that year before they could convene, however, the "shot heard around the world" had been fired in Lexington and the colonies were locked into a war that would last eight long years.

At the onset, the colonies were not by intention embarking upon a war for independence, they were simply seeking a redress of grievances, particularly those that had grown out of the Coercive Acts. Time, however, seemed to be on the side of the radicals and given the English decision to stand firm, the colonies were inexorably forced into a more militant posture. With Lexington and Concord open warfare was under way. The Continental Congress had adopted a recourse to arms as a defensive measure only, but the patriots were defining what constituted defense as any activity by the British troops in Boston that checked the rebellious activities of the patriots. Citizens of Boston made life as miserable as possible for the English soldiers, constantly heckling them, bludgeoning those out alone, and refusing to provide quarters or supplies. The soldiers increased the tensions by licentious behavior and violence which was easily multiplied and exaggerated by the propaganda of the Committee on Correspondence.

When the second Continental Congress met, military matters were the first order of the day and the members took steps to provide a Continental Army and to select a Commander-in-Chief. John Adams, recognizing the need to unify the

Never has a revolution been conducted with more style and finesse than by many of the young statesmen in America. But it was said by a contemporary that Patrick Henry was one of the most commanding speakers ever heard. His powerful statement concerning liberty or death and his "if this be treason make the most of it" have often been quoted. He was a distinguished leader, the governor of Virginia at Williamsburg and the first politician to address his constituents as "fellow citizens."

"The Shot Heard 'Round the World" *was fired at the Battle of Lexington on April 18, 1775. The skirmish at Lexington occurred before the Continental Congress could meet again later that same year, and thrust the Colonies into an eight year war with England.*

colonies, recommended George Washington of Virginia for the position and he proved to have been an excellent choice. But the organization of the army meant that the Continental Congress now had to take on the activities of a revolutionary government such as printing money for the purchase of supplies and paying its soldiers. Conducting a war also necessitated a more permanent organization, hence the adoption of the Articles of Confederation and Perpetual Union.

On the other side of the Atlantic the British responded by issuing a "Proclamation of Rebellion" and ordering thirty thousand troops to America, supplemented by mercenaries hired from Germany. The patriots now claimed that England had severed her relationship with the colonies, that aid for their defense should be sought from France, and that they should declare their independence. The French government was delighted with an opportunity to thwart England. France, however, waited while Washington retreated from New England to New York, and from there to New Jersey. France waited until America had declared her independence and until the Americans had achieved a major victory in the defeat of Burgoyne at Saratoga. Even after openly declaring war on England, and providing generous financial aid to America, the French navy refrained from taking a significant part in the combat. It was ultimately, however, the combined effort of the French forces, army and navy, along with the American army that assured the defeat of Cornwallis at Yorktown.

The Battle of Yorktown was the final major confrontation of the war and signaled its end even though a treaty of peace was not signed for almost three years. The condition of the American troops was so deplorable that Washington might have found it impossible to continue in battle had England

decided to prolong the struggle, but she had no stomach for protracting the war. None of her generals seemed to be able to match George Washington for sheer character and staying power, and at home a large portion of the English had opposed the war from the beginning. Finally, though not a victor, England did not sue for peace as a defeated nation. She still controlled New York and Charleston, and in the larger sphere of the war had completely defeated the French fleet in the West Indies, put an end to the French threat in India, and raised the siege of Gibraltar.

The day the Declaration of Independence was officially signed has always been celebrated as the day of American independence. An equally appropriate day would be September the third, the day in 1783 when the Treaty of Paris was signed. It was then that the war was officially over, that American independence was fully recognized, and that boundaries were established which provided ample opportunity for expansion. England had agreed to honor the American claim to all the land west to the Mississippi River, south to Florida and roughly the present boundary of the United States in the North, an area larger than England, Germany, France, the Netherlands, Belgium, and Spain put together. One of the earliest and most persistent interpretations of the American Revolution is that the colonists were fighting for their freedom against a tyrannical king and his corrupt bureaucracy. It stressed the political motives for the war and exalted the war into one fought for the highest ideals ever desired by mankind. The Declaration of Independence stands as the key document in these assertions. The principles in the Declaration were the common heritage of English and French thinkers of the eighteenth century, but Jefferson gave them their classic expression:

We hold these truths to be self-evident, that all men are created equal, that they are endowed by their Creator with cer-

In 1765 *Patrick Henry lashed out against British oppression in his famous speech before the Virginia House of Burgesses.*

tain unalienable Rights, that among these are Life, Liberty and the pursuit of Happiness. That to secure these rights, Governments are instituted among Men, deriving their just powers from the consent of the governed. That whenever any Form of Government becomes destructive of these ends, it is the Right of the People to alter or to abolish it, and to institute new Government, laying its foundation on such principles and organizing its powers in such form, as to them shall seem most likely to effect their Safety and Happiness.

Scholars on both sides of the Atlantic have discovered that George III was not the tyrant the colonists considered him to be. Economic determinists have placed the emphasis on the material and economic reasons for the war. They see the need, and at times the greed, of the colonists to expand economically outside the confines of mercantilism as the chief cause of the Revolution. Virginia was being squeezed by an unfavorable balance of trade which under mercantilism could only be remedied by speculation in western lands. That opportunity was closed off by the Proclamation of 1763. New England needed the triangle trade and her trade with the French West Indies; and if the Sugar Act were enforced, which mercantilism dictated, her economy would have been ruined. Certainly one of the results of the American Revolution was the advancement of capitalism at the expense of mercantilism.

During the 1960's it became almost fashionable to stress the role played by the agitators and radicals. Men like Sam Adams and John Hancock, who knew how to stir up trouble, how to organize mobs to destroy property by burning, looting and vandalism, and how also to make the most of it through propaganda, were considered the real heroes of the Revolu-

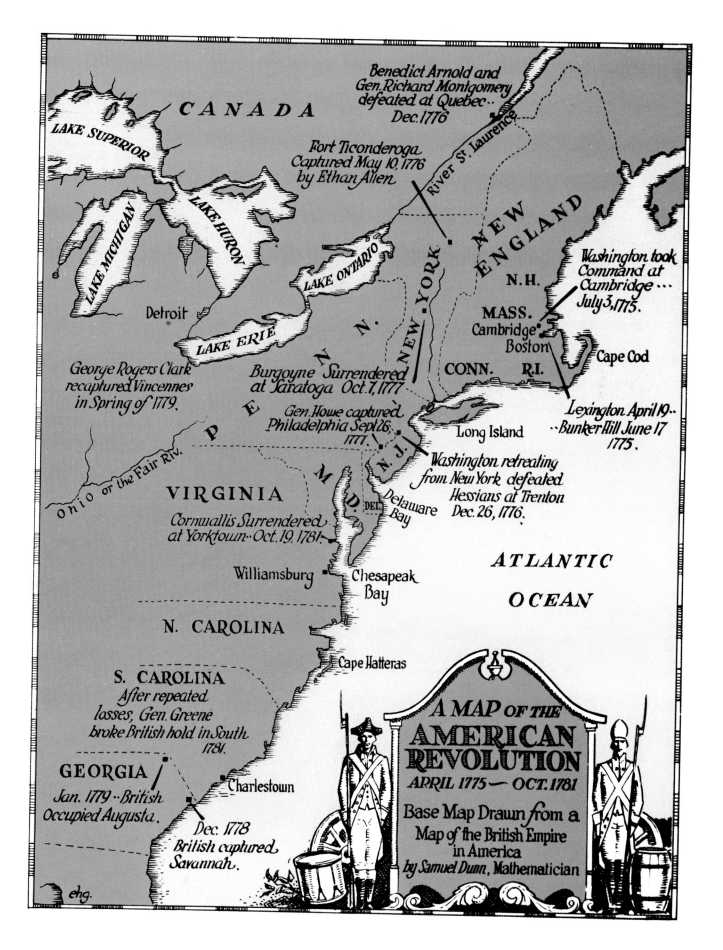

A MAP OF THE
AMERICAN
REVOLUTION
APRIL 1775 — OCT. 1781

Base Map Drawn from a
Map of the British Empire
in America
by Samuel Dunn, Mathematician

CANADA

Benedict Arnold and
Gen. Richard Montgomery
defeated at Quebec.
Dec. 1776

Fort Ticonderoga
Captured May 10, 1776
by Ethan Allen

LAKE SUPERIOR

LAKE MICHIGAN

LAKE HURON

LAKE ONTARIO

Detroit

LAKE ERIE

River St. Laurence

NEW ENGLAND

N.H.

Washington took
Command at
Cambridge...
July 3, 1775.

MASS.
Cambridge
Boston

Cape Cod

NEW YORK

George Rogers Clark
recaptured Vincennes
in Spring of 1779.

Burgoyne Surrendered
at Saratoga Oct. 7, 1777

Gen. Howe captured
Philadelphia Sept. 26,
1777.

CONN.

R.I.

Lexington April 19...
...Bunker Hill June 17
1775.

P E N N

Ohio or the Fair Riv.

VIRGINIA

Cornwallis Surrendered
at Yorktown..Oct. 19, 1781.

Williamsburg

Long Island

Washington retreating
from New York defeated
Hessians at Trenton
Dec. 26, 1776.

N.J.

M D.

DEL.

Delaware
Bay

Chesapeak
Bay

ATLANTIC

OCEAN

N. CAROLINA

Cape Hatteras

S. CAROLINA
After repeated
losses, Gen. Greene
broke British hold in South.
1781.

GEORGIA

Jan. 1779..British
Occupied Augusta.

Charlestown

Dec. 1778
British captured
Savannah.

ehg.

Map of the major battle sites of the American Revolution.

Artist's sketch *shows the Liberty Bell being carted from Philadelphia to Allen, Pennsylvania to prevent its capture by the British Army which was threatening Philadelphia.*

Besides *being known for his famous "midnight ride," Paul Revere was recognized as a master craftsman in silver and a fine engraver. At the start of the war he learned to manufacture gunpowder and the art of casting bullets and cannon. He also designed and printed the first issue of Continental paper money and built the first copper rolling mill in America.*

British General Cornwallis *surrenders to the American forces following the Battle of Yorktown, effectively bringing to an end the American Revolution. At the time of the surrender Washington feared the Colonists might be unable to continue fighting had the British not sued for peace.*

tion. This led to the justification by many radical groups during the sixties for employing similar methods in behalf of their "noble" causes. Though no one has proposed that the continuous barrage of highly effective propaganda issued by the patriots from 1765 on was the real cause of the Revolution, it would not be difficult to deduce from some of the studies that without the propaganda the Revolution might never have occurred. Even in 1776, it would appear that only about one-third of the population was in favor of the Revolution, one-third opposed, and one-third was, in today's terms, *undecided*. The actions and the propaganda of the patriots were significant in swaying part of the population toward a demand for independence from England. Perhaps, the British reaction to them was equally important, which is what agitators depend on. With each defiant action of the patriots, the British became more determined to take strong measures against the colonists, and with each new repressive British action, more colonists were ready to declare in favor of liberty and against "slavery."

Among the more recent interpretations of the War for Independence is an almost opposite concept that views the Revolution as one of the most conservative revolutions that has ever taken place. The colonists, after all, were not fighting for radical or utopian goals, they were fighting only to preserve those things which they already possessed. During the period of a hundred and fifty years since the first settlers appeared, Americans had become different from Englishmen. There was more economic and social equality, more mobility, more self-reliance, more self-government, and more liberty in America than in England, and the Americans were fighting to preserve these achievements. Except for the actual war against England, it was a "law and order" revolution, a period of time when the Americans in an orderly, peaceful, constructive manner drew up constitutions and demonstrated that they could govern themselves. Those who were fighting against the British did not seize power for themselves. Rather the new Constitutions were noteworthy for the manner in which they limited power. And finally, the Revolution did not devour its children as did the French Revolution. None of the leaders of the American Revolution was executed or even jailed. All those who fought for the cause lived to see the revolution fulfilled.

The revolutionary period involved the question of home rule for the colonies, but it also involved the question of *who* would rule at home. One development which encouraged a shift of power was the departure of tens of thousands of Loyalists either during or after the War. Many of the Loyalists were large landholders who had been influential in the colonial governments, and their departure permitted upward mobility for the middle class into the social and governmental structure.

The Articles of Confederation drawn up by the Continental Congress illustrated another "democratic" tendency of the period. To the colonists British government represented centralized and authoritative government. The colonists showed their fear of too much central authority by bestowing a minimum of power on the new central government under the Articles, and a minimum of power on the executive branch within that government.

With the English ties destroyed, state constitutions were drawn up to replace the old charters. By the very act of drawing up their own state constitutions, Americans were demonstrating a principle they had learned during the colonial period: that the best protection of the rights of the people was to be found in constitutional government, in rule of law, not of men. Each of the constitutions was based upon the

Lieutenant General Charles Cornwallis *painted by Gainsborough. He helped capture New York in 1776, then pursued Washington's troops across New Jersey. He invaded North Carolina, but was ultimately defeated at Yorktown. After the war he served with distinction as commander in chief and governor-general of India.*

This picture, *representing the signing of the peace treaty, was never finished by Benjamin West because the British commissioners refused to pose. Those present are (left to right) John Jay, John Adams, Benjamin Franklin, Henry Laurens and their aide, William Temple Franklin, Ben's grandson.*

same authority as the Declaration of Independence, a philosophy of natural rights and the social contract theory. Each of the constitutions began with a bill of rights and each paid tribute to the principle of separation of powers. Most of them limited the governor's term to one year, six states even restricting his re-election following his one year in office. The powers of the governor to pardon, to veto, and to dissolve the legislaure were either limited or abolished altogether.

Perhaps as significant as the constitutions themselves were the methods followed in adopting them. Some states held state constitutional conventions, while other state constitutions were drafted by the legislatures, but were drafted only upon the authority of the people of the state. In only three states were constitutions adopted without the express authority of the people.

In all five of the Southern states, the church was deprived of financial support through state taxes and in most colonies the religious qualifications that had been required for voting were abolished. America had, during the revolutionary period, separated church and state, something new for the Western World.

A new attitude was also demonstrated toward slavery. Within ten years of 1776 all states but Georgia had abolished the slave trade, that is the importation of slaves from outside the United States. Vermont abolished slavery itself in 1777, and all states north of the Mason Dixon Line soon took similar action. Though the feudal systems of Primogeniture and Entail were never rigidly adhered to in the colonies— land was too prevalent, society too fluid—legally, both were in force in a number of colonies. During the revolutionary period they were abolished in many of the states where Primogeniture and Entail were still on the law books.

Henry Knox *was a tremendously capable General in the Revolutionary Army and one of Washington's most trusted officers. It was Knox who suggested establishing a military academy at West Point in 1779 and two years later was present at the surrender of Cornwallis at Yorktown.*

Those who look upon the revolutionary period as one in which all significant political, social, cultural and educational reforms came to America are all too frequently ignoring the roots of some of these reforms in the period before 1763, and are insensitive to the lack of real accomplishments during this period in such areas as prison reforms and education. Political developments of the period were significant, and articulation of constitutionalism, representation by locality rather than class, separation of powers, the need for a bill of rights, expressions of a natural rights philosophy and the social contract theory were to establish extremely important precedents for America. The shift in class structure, the separation of church and state, and the abolition of slavery in the northern states were equally significant in moving America noticeably toward a more democratic society. Movements during the same period such as Shay's Rebellion, which through force closed the law courts of much of western Massachusetts, suggest that in some sections of the new nation the movement toward local control may have gone beyond democracy and was bordering on anarchy.

There was considerable doubt after 1783 that the purpose of the Revolution would be fulfilled.

The situation after the War was not as critical as some historians have implied, and it is a misreading of the period to consider it as one of chaos and utter confusion. The decisions to be made were, however, of utmost importance to the fulfillment of Revolutionary goals and to the future of America. The decisive and creative manner in which the problems facing the new nation were resolved is a tribute to the calibre of leadership which America had produced. No other period in American history would assemble so many statesmen who would possess such a high degree of character, dedication and ability as those men who gathered to write the Constitution and to direct the new nation during its formative years.

Robert Morris, *a wealthy merchant and signer of the Declaration of Independence, called "the financier of the Revolution" by George Washington, was responsible for establishing the Bank of North America to help relieve the shortage of acceptable money. He issued notes based on his own credit that served as money. Unfortunately he lost his fortune later in land speculation and died in poverty and obscurity.*

The drafting committee *presents the Declaration of Independence to Congress.*

King George III *was the handsome erratic ruler of Britain during trying times. He lost the colonies through the revolt of the Americans and later his position was threatened during the French Revolution. Toward the end of his life he became hopelessly insane.*

Thomas Jefferson, *author of the Constitution.*

THE SIGNERS OF THE DECLARATION

CONNECTICUT

Saml Huntington

Roger Sherman

Wm Williams

Oliver Wolcott

DELAWARE

Tho M:Kean

Geo Read

Caesar Rodney

GEORGIA

Button Gwinnett

Lyman Hall

Geo Walton

MARYLAND

Charles Carroll of Carrollton

Samuel Chase

Wm Paca

Thos Stone

MASSACHUSETTS

John Adams

Saml Adams

Elbridge Gerry

John Hancock

Robt Treat Paine

NEW HAMPSHIRE

Josiah Bartlett

Matthew Thornton

Wm Whipple

NEW JERSEY

Abra Clark

John Hart

Fra^s Hopkinson

Richd Stockton

Jno Witherspoon

OF INDEPENDENCE

NEW YORK

Wᵐ Floyd

RHODE ISLAND

William Ellery

Step Hopkins

SOUTH CAROLINA

Thoˢ Heyward Junʳ

Thomas Lynch Junʳ

Arthur Middleton

Edward Rutledge

VIRGINIA

Carter Braxton

Benjᵃ Harrison

Th Jefferson

Francis Lightfoot Lee

Richard Henry Lee

Thoˢ Nelson jr.

George Wythe

Franˢ Lewis

Phil. Livingston

Lewis Morris

NORTH CAROLINA

Joseph Hewes

Wᵐ Hooper

John Penn

PENNSYLVANIA

Geo Clymer

Benjᵃ Franklin

Robᵗ Morris

John Morton

Geo. Ross

Benjamin Rush

Jaˢ Smith

Geo. Taylor

James Wilson

"Votaries of Independence"

First presented to Congress on July 2, 1776, the Declaration of Independence was thereafter signed by 56 patriots. John Trumbull's painting of the document's presentation (above) shows 48 men present—including the drafting committee at center—who may be identified as follows:

Group at far left: George Wythe *(Virginia)*, William Whipple *(New Hampshire)*, Josiah Bartlett *(New Hampshire)*, Thomas Lynch, Jr. *(South Carolina)*, Benjamin Harrison *(Virginia)*; **Standing in back:** William Paca *(Maryland)*, Samuel Chase *(Maryland)*, Richard Stoc *(New Jersey)*, Lewis Morris *(New York)*, William Floyd *(New York)* Arthur Middleton *(South Carolina)*, Stephen Hopkins *(Rhode Islar* William Ellery *(Rhode Island)*, George Clymer *(Pennsylvania)*; **Seated in first row:** Richard Henry Lee *(Virginia)*, Samuel Adams

(Massachusetts), George Clinton (New York), Thomas Heyward, Jr. (South Carolina), Charles Carroll (Maryland), Robert Morris (Pennsylvania), Thomas Willing (Pennsylvania), Benjamin Rush (Pennsylvania), Elbridge Gerry (Massachusetts), Robert Treat Paine (Massachusetts), William Hooper (North Carolina), George Walton (Georgia), James Wilson (Pennsylvania), Abraham Clark (New Jersey), Francis Hopkinson (New Jersey); **At desk:** John Adams (Massachusetts), Roger Sherman (Connecticut), Robert Livingston (New York), Thomas Jefferson (Virginia), Benjamin Franklin (Pennsylvania), Charles Thomson (Pennsylvania), John Hancock (Massachusetts); **Seated and standing beyond desk:** Thomas Nelson, Jr. (Virginia), Francis Lewis (New York), John Witherspoon (New Jersey), Samuel Huntington (Connecticut), William Williams (Connecticut), Oliver Wolcott (Connecticut), George Read (Delaware), John Dickinson (Pennsylvania), Edward Rutledge (South Carolina), Thomas McKean (Delaware), Philip Livingston (New York).

HISTORICAL NOTE

The purpose in this historical note on the formation of the Constitution of the United States, is to portray rapidly that which the Founding Fathers breathed the spirit of life; through every subsequent generation, which spirit has remained vital to this day.

Now, more than 200 years have passed of cataclysmic events, the Constitution has successfully withstood test after test. No crisis-foreign-or-domestic has impaired its vitality. The system of checks and balances which it sets up has enabled our grand nation to adapt itself to every need and at the same time to checkrein every bid for arbitrary power.

America has evolved dynamically and dramatically. The original thirteen colonies, carved out of the wilderness in the eighteenth century, emerges on its 200th anniversary as the leader of the earth-industrial-military-political-economic-psychological, and the broad outline of the Constitution remains today fundamentally intact.

One reading the Constitution's words, its phrases, clauses, sentences, paragraphs, and sections will find that they possess a miraculous quality—a mingled flexibility and strength which permits its adaptation to the needs of the hour without sacrifice of its essential character as the basic framework of freedom.

The test has passed, the Constitution will always remain the blueprint for freedom. It will continue as an inspiration to men and women everywhere, for centuries to come; for our shores are the lighthouse of freedom, in a world where the darkness of injustice hangs so heavily.

HISTORICAL NOTE ON FORMATION OF THE CONSTITUTION

In June 1774, the Virginia and Massachusetts assemblies independently proposed an intercolonial meeting of delegates from the several colonies to restore union and harmony between Great Britain and her American Colonies. Pursuant to these calls there met in Philadelphia in September of that year the first Continental Congress, composed of delegates from 12 colonies. On October 14, 1774, the assembly adopted what has become to be known as the Declaration and Resolves of the First Continental Congress. In that instrument, addressed to His Majesty and to the people of Great Britain, there was embodied a statement of rights and principles, many of which were later to be incorporated in the Declaration of Independence and the Federal Constitution.[1]

This Congress adjourned in October with a recommendation that another Congress be held in Philadelphia the following May. Before its successor met, the battle of Lexington had been fought. In Massachusetts the colonists had organized their own government in defiance of the royal governor and the Crown. Hence, by general necessity and by common consent, the second Continental Congress assumed control of the "Twelve United Colonies", soon to become the "Thirteen United Colonies" by the cooperation of Georgia. It became a *de facto* government; it called upon the other colonies to assist in the defense of Massachusetts; it issued bills of credit; it took steps to organize a military force, and appointed George Washington commander in chief of the Army.

While the declaration of the causes and necessities of taking up arms of July 6, 1775,[2] expressed a "wish" to see the union between Great Britain and the colonies "restored", sentiment for independence was growing. Finally, on May 15, 1776, Virginia instructed her delegates to the Continental Congress

---

[1] The colonists, for example, claimed the right "to life, liberty, and property", "the rights, liberties, and immunities of free and natural-born subjects within the realm of England"; the right to participate in legislative councils; "the great and inestimable privilege of being tried by their peers of the vicinage, according to the course of [the common law of England]"; "the immunities and privileges granted and confirmed to them by royal charters, or secured by their several codes of provincial laws"; "a right peaceably to assemble, consider of their grievances, and petition the king." They further declared that the keeping of a standing army in the colonies in time of peace without the consent of the colony in which the army was kept was "against law"; that it was "indispensably necessary to good government, and rendered essential by the English constitution, that the constituent branches of the legislature be independent of each other"; that certain acts of Parliament in contravention of the foregoing principles were "infringement and violations of the rights of the colonists." Text in C. Tansill (ed.), *Documents Illustrative of the Formation of the Union of the American States*, H. Doc. No. 358, 69th Congress, 1st sess. (1927), 1. *See also* H. Commager (ed.), *Documents of American History* (New York: 8th ed. 1964), 82.

[2] Text in Tansill, *op. cit.*, 10.

to have that body "declare the united colonies free and independent States." [3] Accordingly on June 7 a resolution was introduced in Congress declaring the union with Great Britain dissolved, proposing the formation of foreign alliances, and suggesting the drafting of a plan of confederation to be submitted to the respective colonies. [4] Some delegates argued for confederation first and declaration afterwards. This counsel did not prevail. Independence was declared on July 4, 1776; the preparation of a plan of confederation was postponed. It was not until November 17, 1777, that the Congress was able to agree on a form of government which stood some chance of being approved by the separate States. The Articles of Confederation were then submitted to the several States, and on July 9, 1778, were finally approved by a sufficient number to become operative.

Weaknesses inherent in the Articles of Confederation became apparent before the Revolution out of which that instrument was born had been concluded. Even before the thirteenth State (Maryland) conditionally joined the "firm league of friendship" on March 1, 1781, the need for a revenue amendment was widely conceded. Congress under the Articles lacked authority to levy taxes. She could only request the States to contribute their fair share to the common treasury, but the requested amounts were not forthcoming. To remedy this defect, Congress applied to the States for power to lay duties and secure the public debts. Twelve States agreed to such an amendment, but Rhode Island refused her consent, thereby defeating the proposal.

Thus was emphasized a second weakness in the Articles of Confederation, namely, the *liberum veto* which each State possessed whenever amendments to that instrument were proposed. Not only did all amendments have to be ratified by each of the 13 States, but all important legislation needed the approval of 9 States. With several delegations often absent, one or two States were able to defeat legislative proposals of major importance.

Other imperfections in the Articles of Confederation also proved embarrassing. Congress could, for example, negotiate treaties with foreign powers, but all treaties had to be ratified by the several States. Even when a treaty was approved, Congress lacked authority to secure obedience to its stipulations. Congress could not act directly upon the States or upon individuals. Under such circumstances foreign nations doubted the value of a treaty with the new Republic.

Furthermore, Congress had no authority to regulate foreign or interstate commerce. Legislation in this field, subject to unimportant exceptions, was left to the individual States. Disputes between States with common interests in the navigation of certain rivers and bays were inevitable. Discriminatory regulations were followed by reprisals.

Virginia, recognizing the need for an agreement with Maryland respecting the navigation and jurisdiction of the Potomac River, appointed in June 1784, four commissioners to "frame such liberal and equitable regulations concerning

---

[3] Id., 19.
[4] Id., 21.

the said river as may be mutually advantageous to the two States." Maryland in January 1785 responded to the Virginia resolution by appointing a like number of commissioners [5] "for the purpose of settling the navigation and jurisdiction over that part of the bay of Chesapeake which lies within the limits of Virginia, and over the rivers Potomac and Pocomoke" with full power on behalf of Maryland "to adjudge and settle the jurisdiction to be exercised by the said States, respectively, over the waters and navigations of the same."

At the invitation of Washington the commissioners met at Mount Vernon, in March 1785, and drafted a compact which, in many of its details relative to the navigation and jurisdiction of the Potomac, is still in force.[6] What is more important, the commissioners submitted to their respective States a report in favor of a convention of all the States "to take into consideration the trade and commerce" of the Confederation. Virginia, in January 1786, advocated such a convention, authorizing its commissioners to meet with those of other States, at a time and place to be agreed on, "to take into consideration the trade of the United States; to examine the relative situations and trade of the said States; to consider how far a uniform system in their commercial regulations may be necessary to their common interest and their permanent harmony; and to report to the several States, such an act relative to this great object, as when unanimously ratified by them, will enable the United States in Congress, effectually to provide for the same." [7]

This proposal for a general trade convention seemingly met with general approval; nine States appointed commissioners. Under the leadership of the Virginia delegation, which included Randolph and Madison, Annapolis was accepted as the place and the first Monday in September 1786 as the time for the convention. The attendance at Annapolis proved disappointing. Only five States—Virginia, Pennsylvania, Delaware, New Jersey, and New York—were represented; delegates from Massachusetts, New Hampshire, North Carolina, and Rhode Island failed to attend. Because of the small representation, the Annapolis convention did not deem "it advisable to proceed on the business of their mission." After an exchange of views, the Annapolis delegates unanimously submitted to their respective States a report in which they suggested that a convention of representatives from all the States meet at Philadelphia on the second Monday in May 1787 to examine the defects in the existing system of government and formulate "a plan for supplying such defects as may be discovered." [8]

The Virginia legislature acted promptly upon this recommendation and appointed a delegation to go to Philadelphia. Within a few weeks New Jersey, Pennsylvania, North Carolina, Delaware, and Georgia also made appointments.

---

[5] George Mason, Edmund Randolph, James Madison, and Alexander Henderson were appointed commissioners for Virginia; Thomas Johnson, Thomas Stone, Samuel Chase, and Daniel of St. Thomas Jenifer for Maryland.

[6] Text of the resolution and details of the compact may be found in *Wheaton* v. *Wise*, 153 U.S. 155 (1894).

[7] Transill, *op. cit.*, 38.

[8] Id., 39.

New York and several other States hesitated on the ground that, without the consent of the Continental Congress, the work of the convention would be extra-legal; that Congress alone could propose amendments to the Articles of Confederation. Washington was quite unwilling to attend an irregular convention. Congressional approval of the proposed convention became, therefore, highly important. After some hesitancy Congress approved the suggestion for a convention at Philadelphia "for the sole and express purpose of revising the Articles of Confederation and reporting to Congress and the several legislatures such alterations and provisions therein as shall when agreed to in Congress and confirmed by the States render the Federal Constitution adequate to the exigencies of Government and the preservation of the Union."

Thereupon, the remaining States, Rhode Island alone excepted, appointed in due course delegates to the Convention, and Washington accepted membership on the Virginia delegation.

Although scheduled to convene on May 14, 1787, it was not until May 25 that enough delegates were present to proceed with the organization of the Convention. Washington was elected as presiding officer. It was agreed that the sessions were to be strictly secret.

On May 29 Randolph, on behalf of the Virginia delegation, submitted to the convention 15 propositions as a plan of government. Despite the fact that the delegates were limited by their instructions to a revision of the Articles, Virginia had really recommended a new instrument of government. For example, provision was made in the Virginia plan for the separation of the three branches of government; under the Articles executive, legislative, and judicial powers were vested in the Congress. Furthermore the legislature was to consist of two houses rather than one.

On May 30 the Convention went into a committee of the whole to consider the 15 propositions of the Virginia plan *seriatim*. These discussions continued until June 13, when the Virginia resolutions in amended form were reported out of committee. They provided for proportional representation in both houses. The small States were dissatisfied. Therefore, on June 14 when the Convention was ready to consider the report on the Virginia plan, Paterson of New Jersey requested an adjournment to allow certain delegations more time to prepare a substitute plan. The request was granted, and on the next day Paterson submitted nine resolutions embodying important changes in the Articles of Confederation, but strictly amendatory in nature. Vigorous debate followed. On June 19 the States rejected the New Jersey plan and voted to proceed with a discussion of the Virginia plan. The small States became more and more discontented; there were threats of withdrawal. On July 2 the Convention was deadlocked over giving each State an equal vote in the upper house—five States in the affirmative, five in the negative, one divided.[9]

The problem was referred to a committee of 11, there being 1 delegate from each State, to effect a compromise. On July 5 the committee submitted

---

[9] The New Hampshire delegation did not arrive until July 23, 1787.

its report, which became the basis for the "great compromise" of the Convention. It was recommended that in the upper house each State should have an equal vote, that in the lower branch each State should have one representative for every 40,000 inhabitants, counting three-fifths of the slaves, that money bills should originate in the lower house (not subject to amendment by the upper chamber). When on July 12 the motion of Gouverneur Morris of Pennsylvania that direct taxation should also be in proportion to representation was adopted, a crisis had been successfully surmounted. A compromise spirit began to prevail. The small States were now willing to support a strong national government.

Debates on the Virginia resolutions continued. The 15 original resolutions had been expanded into 23. Since these resolutions were largely declarations of principles, on July 24 a committee of five [10] was elected to draft a detailed constitution embodying the fundamental principles which had thus far been approved. The Convention adjourned from July 26 to August 6 to await the report of its committee of detail. This committee, in preparing its draft of a Constitution, turned for assistance to the State constitutions, to the Articles of Confederation, to the various plans which had been submitted to the Convention and other available material. On the whole the report of the committee conformed to the resolutions adopted by the Convention, though on many clauses the members of the committee left the imprint of their individual and collective judgments. In a few instances the committee avowedly exercised considerable discretion.

From August 6 to September 10 the report of the committee of detail was discussed, section by section, clause by clause. Details were attended to, further compromises were effected. Toward the close of these discussions, on September 8, another committee of five [11] was appointed "to revise the style of and arrange the articles which had been agreed to by the house."

On Wednesday, September 12, the report of the committee of style was ordered printed for the convenience of the delegates. The Convention for 3 days compared this report with the proceedings of the Convention. The Constitution was ordered engrossed on Saturday, September 15.

The Convention met on Monday, September 17, for its final session. Several of the delegates were disappointed in the result. A few deemed the new Constitution a mere makeshift, a series of unfortunate compromises. The advocates of the Constitution, realizing the impending difficulty of obtaining the consent of the States to the new instrument of Government, were anxious to obtain the unanimous support of the delegations from each State. It was feared that many of the delegates would refuse to give their individual assent to the Constitution. Therefore, in order that the action of the Convention would appear to be unanimous, Gouverneur Morris devised the formula "Done

---

[10] Rutledge of South Carolina, Randolph of Virginia, Gorham of Massachusetts, Ellsworth of Connecticut, and Wilson of Pennsylvania.

[11] William Samuel Johnson of Connecticut, Alexander Hamilton of New York, Gouverneur Morris of Pennsylvania, James Madison of Virginia, and Rufus King of Massachusetts.

in Convention, by the unanimous consent of the States present the 17th of September . . . In witness whereof we have hereunto subscribed our names." Thirty-nine of the forty-two delegates present thereupon "subscribed" to the document.[12]

The convention had been called to revise the Articles of Confederation. Instead, it reported to the Continental Congress a new Constitution. Furthermore, while the Articles specified that no amendments should be effective until approved by the legislatures of all the States, the Philadelphia Convention suggested that the new Constitution should supplant the Articles of Confederation when ratified by conventions in nine States. For these reasons, it was feared that the new Constitution might arouse opposition in Congress.

Three members of the Convention—Madison, Gorham, and King—were also Members of Congress. They proceeded at once to New York, where Congress was in session, to placate the expected opposition. Aware of their vanishing authority, Congress on September 28, after some debate, decided to submit the Constitution to the States for action. It made no recommendation for or against adoption.

Two parties soon developed, one in opposition and one in support of the Constitution, and the Constitution was debated, criticized, and expounded clause by clause. Hamilton, Madison, and Jay wrote a series of commentaries, now known as the *Federalist Papers*, in support of the new instrument of government.[13] The closeness and bitterness of the struggle over ratification and the conferring of additional powers on the central government can scarcely be exaggerated. In some States ratification was effected only after a bitter struggle in the State convention itself.

Delaware, on December 7, 1787, became the first State to ratify the new Constitution, the vote being unanimous. Pennsylvania ratified on December 12, 1787, by a vote of 46 to 23, a vote scarcely indicative of the struggle which had taken place in that State. New Jersey ratified on December 19, 1787, and Georgia on January 2, 1788, the vote in both States being unanimous. Connecticut ratified on January 9, 1788; yeas 128, nays 40. On February 6, 1788, Massachusetts, by a narrow margin of 19 votes in a convention with a membership of 355, endorsed the new Constitution, but recommended that a bill of rights be added to protect the States from federal encroachment on individual liberties. Maryland ratified on April 28, 1788; yeas 63, nays 11. South Carolina ratified on May 23, 1788; yeas 149, nays 73. On June 21, 1788, by a vote of 57 to 46, New Hampshire became the ninth State to ratify, but like Massachusetts she suggested a bill of rights.

---

[12] At least 65 persons had received appointments as delegates to the Convention; 55 actually attended at different times during the course of the proceedings; 39 signed the document. It has been estimated that generally fewer than 30 delegates attended the daily sessions.

[13] These commentaries on the Constitution, written during the struggle for ratification, have been frequently cited by the Supreme Court as an authoritative contemporary interpretation of the meaning of its provisions.

HISTORICAL NOTE

By the terms of the Constitution nine States were sufficient for its establishment among the States so ratifying. The advocates of the new Constitution realized, however, that the new Government could not succeed without the addition of New York and Virginia, neither of which had ratified. Madison, Marshall, and Randolph led the struggle for ratification in Virginia. On June 25, 1788, by a narrow margin of 10 votes in a convention of 168 members, that State ratified over the objection of such delegates as George Mason and Patrick Henry. In New York an attempt to attach conditions to ratification almost succeeded. But on July 26, 1788, New York ratified, with a recommendation that a bill of rights be appended. The vote was close—yeas 30, nays 27.

Eleven States having thus ratified the Constitution,[14] the Continental Congress—which still functioned at irregular intervals—passed a resolution on September 13, 1788, to put the new Constitution into operation. The first Wednesday of January 1789 was fixed as the day for choosing presidential electors, the first Wednesday of February for the meeting of electors, and the first Wednesday of March (i.e. March 4, 1789) for the opening session of the new Congress. Owing to various delays, Congress was late in assembling, and it was not until April 30, 1789, that George Washington was inaugurated as the first President of the United States.

---

[14] North Carolina added her ratification on November 21, 1789; yeas 184, nays 77. Rhode Island did not ratify until May 29, 1790; yeas 34, nays 32.

PURPOSE AND EFFECT OF THE PREAMBLE

Although the preamble is not a source of power for any department of the Federal Government,[1] the Supreme Court has often referred to it as evidence of the origin, scope, and purpose of the Constitution. "Its true office" wrote Joseph Story in his Commentaries, "is to expound the nature and extent and application of the powers actually conferred by the Constitution, and not substantively to create them. For example, the preamble declares one object to be, 'to provide for the common defense.' No one can doubt that this does not enlarge the powers of Congress to pass any measures which they deem useful for the common defense. But suppose the terms of a given power admit of two constructions, the one more restrictive, the other more liberal, and each of them is consistent with the words, but is, and ought to be, governed by the intent of the power; if one could promote and the other defeat the common defense, ought not the former, upon the soundest principles of interpretation, to be adopted?"[2] Moreover, the preamble bears witness to the fact that the Constitution emanated from the people, and was not the act of sovereign and independent States,[3] and that it was made for, and is binding only in, the United States of America.[4] In the Dred Scott case,[5] Chief Justice Taney declared that: "The words 'people of the United States' and 'citizens' are synonymous terms, and mean the same thing. They both describe the political body who, according to our republican institutions, form the sovereignty, and who hold the power and conduct the Government through their representatives. They are what we familiarly call the 'sovereign people,' and every citizen is one of this people, and a constituent member of this sovereignty."[6]

[1] *Jacobson* v. *Massachusetts*, 197 U.S. 11, 22 (1905)

[2] 1 Story, Commentaries on the Constitution, 462.

[3] *McCulloch* v. *Maryland*, 4 Wheat, 316, 403 (1819); *Chisholm* v. *Georgia*, 2 Dall. 419, 470 (1793); *Martin* v. *Hunter*, Wheat, 304, 324, (1816)

[4] *Downes* v. *Bidwell*, 182 U.S. 244, 251 (1901); In re Ross, 140 U.S. 453, 464 (1891)

[5] 19 How. (1857)

[6] *Ibid.* 404.

THE CONSTITUTION OF THE UNITED STATES OF AMERICA

We the People of the United States, in Order to form a more perfect Union, establish Justice, insure domestic Tranquillity, provide for the common defence, promote the general Welfare, and secure the Blessings of Liberty to ourselves and our Posterity, do ordain and establish this Constitution for the United States of America.

Article. I.

Section. 1. All legislative Powers herein granted shall be vested in a Congress of the United States, which shall consist of a Senate and House of Representatives.

Section. 2. The House of Representatives shall be composed of Members chosen every second Year by the People of the several States, and the Electors in each State shall have the Qualifications requisite for Electors of the most numerous Branch of the State Legislature.

No Person shall be a Representative who shall not have attained to the age of twenty five Years, and been seven Years a Citizen of the United States, and who shall not, when elected, be an Inhabitant of that State in which he shall be chosen.

Representatives and direct Taxes shall be apportioned among the several States which may be included within this Union, according to their respective Numbers, which shall be determined by adding to the whole Number of free Persons, including those bound to Service for a Term of Years, and excluding Indians not taxed, three fifths of all other Persons. The actual Enumeration shall be made within three Years after the first Meeting of the Congress of the United States, and within every subsequent Term of ten Years, in such Manner as they shall by Law direct. The number of Representatives shall not exceed one for every thirty Thousand, but each State shall have at Least one Representative; and until such enumeration shall be made, the State of New Hampshire shall be entitled to chuse three, Massachusetts eight, Rhode-Island and Providence Plantations one, Connecticut five, New-York six, New Jersey four, Pennsylvania eight, Delaware one, Maryland six, Virginia ten, North Carolina five, South Carolina five, and Georgia three.

When vacancies happen in the Representation from any State, the Executive Authority thereof shall issue Writs of Election to fill such Vacancies.

The House of Representatives shall chuse their Speaker and other Officers; and shall have the sole Power of Impeachment.

Section. 3. The Senate of the United States shall be composed of two Senators from each State, chosen by the Legislature thereof, for six Years; and each Senator shall have one Vote.

Immediately after they shall be assembled in Consequence of the first Election, they shall be divided as equally as may be into three Classes. The Seats of the Senators of the first Class shall be vacated at the Expiration of the second Year, of the second Class at the Expiration of the fourth Year, and of the third Class at the Expiration of the sixth Year, so that one third may be chosen every second Year; and if Vacancies happen by Resignation, or otherwise, during the Recess of the Legislature of any State, the Executive thereof may make temporary Appointments until the next Meeting of the Legislature, which shall then fill such Vacancies.

No Person shall be a Senator who shall not have attained to the Age of thirty Years, and been nine Years a Citizen of the United States, and who shall not, when elected, be an Inhabitant of that State for which he shall be chosen.

The Vice President of the United States shall be President of the Senate but shall have no Vote, unless they be equally divided.

The Senate shall chuse their other Officers, and also a President pro tempore, in the Absence of the Vice President, or when he shall exercise the Office of President of the United States.

The Senate shall have the sole Power to try all Impeachments. When sitting for that Purpose, they shall be on Oath or Affirmation. When the President of the United States is tried the Chief Justice shall preside: And no Person shall be convicted without the Concurrence of two thirds of the Members present.

Judgment in Cases of Impeachment shall not extend further than to removal from Office, and disqualification to hold and enjoy any Office of honor, Trust or Profit under the United States: but the Party convicted shall nevertheless be liable and subject to Indictment, Trial, Judgment and Punishment, according to Law.

Section. 4. The Times, Places and Manner of holding Elections for Senators and Representatives, shall be prescribed in each State by the Legislature thereof; but the Congress may at any time by Law make or alter such Regulations, except as to the Places of chusing Senators.

The Congress shall assemble at least once in every Year, and such Meeting shall be on the first Monday in December, unless they shall by Law appoint a different Day.

Section. 5. Each House shall be the Judge of the Elections, Returns and Qualifications of its own Members, and a Majority of each shall constitute a Quorum to do Business; but a smaller Number may adjourn from day to day, and may be authorized to compel the Attendance of absent Members, in such Manner, and under such Penalties as each House may provide.

Each House may determine the Rules of its Proceedings, punish its Members for disorderly Behaviour, and, with the Concurrence of two thirds, expel a Member.

Each House shall keep a Journal of its Proceedings, and from time to time publish the same, excepting such Parts as may in their Judgment require Secrecy; and the Yeas and Nays of the Members of either House on any question shall, at the Desire of one fifth of those Present, be entered on the Journal.

Neither House, during the Session of Congress, shall, without the Consent of the other adjourn for more than three days, nor to any other Place than that in which the two Houses shall be sitting.

Section. 6. The Senators and Representatives shall receive a Compensation for their Services to be ascertained by Law, and paid out of the Treasury of the United States. They shall in all Cases, except Treason, Felony and Breach of the Peace, be privileged from Arrest during their Attendance at the Session of their respective Houses, and in going to and returning from the same; and for any Speech or Debate in either House, they shall not be questioned in any other Place.

No Senator or Representative shall, during the Time for which he was elected, be appointed to any civil Office under the Authority of the United States, which shall have been created, or the Emoluments whereof shall have been encreased during such time; and no Person holding any Office under the United States, shall be a Member of either House during his Continuance in Office.

Section. 7. All Bills for raising Revenue shall originate in the House of Representatives; but the Senate may propose or concur with amendments as on other Bills.

Every Bill which shall have passed the House of Representatives and the Senate, shall, before it becomes a law, be presented to the President of the United States: If he approve he shall sign it, but if not he shall return it, with his Objections to that House in which it shall have originated, who shall enter the Objections at large on their Journal, and proceed to reconsider it. If after such Reconsideration two thirds of that House shall agree to pass the Bill, it shall be sent, together with the Objections, to the other House, by which it shall likewise be reconsidered, and if approved by two thirds of that House, it shall become a Law. But in all such Cases the Votes of both Houses shall be determined by yeas and Nays, and the Names of the Persons voting for and against the Bill shall be entered on the Journal of each House respectively. If any Bill shall not be returned by the President within ten Days (Sunday excepted) after it shall have been presented to him, the Same shall be a Law, in like Manner as if he had signed it, unless the Congress by their Adjournment prevent its Return, in which Case it shall not be a Law

Every Order, Resolution, or Vote to which the Concurrence of the Senate and House of Representatives may be necessary (except on a question of Adjournment) shall be presented to the President of the United States; and before the Same shall take Effect, shall be approved by him, or being disapproved by him, shall be repassed by two thirds of the Senate and House of Representatives, according to the Rules and Limitations prescribed in the Case of a Bill.

Section. 8. The Congress shall have Power To lay and collect Taxes, Duties, Imposts and Excises, to pay the Debts and provide for the common Defence and general Welfare of the United States; but all Duties, Imposts and Excises shall be uniform throughout the United States;

To borrow Money on the credit of the United States;

To regulate Commerce with foreign Nations, and among the several States, and with the Indian Tribes;

To establish an uniform Rule of Naturalization, and uniform Laws on the subject of Bankruptcies throughout the United States;

To coin Money, regulate the Value thereof, and of foreign Coin, and fix the Standard of Weights and Measures;

To provide for the Punishment of counterfeiting the Securities and current Coin of the United States;

To establish Post Offices and post Roads;

To promote the Progress of Science and useful Arts, by securing for limited Times to Authors and Inventors the exclusive Right to their respective Writings and Discoveries;

To constitute Tribunals inferior to the supreme Court;

To define and punish Piracies and Felonies committed on the high Seas, and Offenses against the Law of Nations;

To declare War, grant Letters of Marque and Reprisal, and make Rules concerning Captures on Land and Water;

To raise and support Armies, but no Appropriation of Money to that Use shall be for a longer Term than two Years;

To provide and maintain a Navy;

To make Rules for the Government and Regulation of the land and naval Forces;

To provide for calling forth the Militia to execute the Laws of the Union, suppress Insurrections and repel Invasions;

To provide for organizing, arming, and disciplining, the Militia, and for governing such Part of them as may be employed in the Service of the United States, reserving to the States respectively, the Appointment of the Officers, and the Authority of training the Militia according to the discipline prescribed by Congress;

To exercise exclusive Legislation in all Cases whatsoever, over such District (not exceeding ten Miles square) as may, by Cession of Particular States, and the Acceptance of Congress, become the Seat of the Government of the United States, and to exercise like Authority over all Places purchased by the Consent of the Legislature of the State in which the Same shall be, for the Erection of Forts, Magazines, Arsenals, dock-Yards and other needful Buildings;—And

To make all Laws which shall be necessary and proper for carrying into Execution the foregoing Powers and all other Powers vested by this Constitution in the Government of the United States, or in any Department or Officer thereof.

Section. 9. The Migration or Importation of such Persons as any of the States now existing shall think proper to admit, shall not be prohibited by the Congress prior to the Year one thousand eight hundred and eight, but a Tax or duty may be imposed on such Importation, not exceeding ten dollars for each Person.

The Privilege of the Writ of Habeas Corpus shall not be suspended, unless when in Cases of Rebellion or Invasion the public Safety may require it.

No Bill of Attainder or ex post facto Law shall be passed.

No Capitation, or other direct, Tax shall be laid, unless in Proportion to the Census of Enumeration herein before directed to be taken.

No Tax or Duty shall be laid on Articles exported from any State.

No Preference shall be given by any Regulation of Commerce or Revenue to the Ports of one State over those of another; nor shall Vessels bound to, or from, one State, be obliged to enter, clear or pay Duties in another.

No Money shall be drawn from the Treasury, but in Consequence of Appropriations made by Law; and a regular Statement and Account of the Receipts and Expenditures of all public Money shall be published from time to time.

No Title of Nobility shall be granted by the United States: And no Person holding any Office of Profit or Trust under them, shall, without the Consent of the Congress, accept of any present, Emolument, Office, or Title, of any kind whatever, from any King, Prince or foreign State.

Section. 10. No State shall enter into any Treaty, Alliance, or Confederation; grant Letters of Marque and Reprisal; coin Money; emit Bills of Credit; make any Thing but gold and silver Coin a Tender in Payment of Debts; pass any Bill of Attainder, ex post facto Law, or Law impairing the Obligation of Contracts, or grant any Title of Nobility.

No State shall, without the Consent of the Congress, lay any Imposts or Duties on Imports or Exports, except what may be absolutely necessary for executing it's inspection Laws: and the net Produce of all Duties and Imposts, laid by any State on Imports or Exports, shall be for the Use of the Treasury of the United States; and all such Laws shall be subject to the Revision and Controul of the Congress.

No State shall, without the Consent of Congress, lay any Duty of Tonnage, keep Troops, or Ships of War in time of Peace, enter into any Agreement or Compact with another State, or with a foreign Power, or engage in War, unless actually invaded, or in such imminent Danger as will not admit of delay.

Article. II.

Section. 1. The executive Power shall be vested in a President of the United States of America. He shall hold his Office during the Term of four Years, and, together with the Vice President, chosen for the same Term, be elected, as follows:

Each State shall appoint, in such Manner as the Legislature thereof may direct, a Number of Electors, equal to the whole Number of Senators and Representatives to which the State may be entitled in the Congress: but no Senator or Representative, or Person holding an Office of Trust or Profit under the United States, shall be appointed an Elector.

The Electors shall meet in their respective States, and vote by Ballot for two Persons, of whom one at least shall not be an Inhabitant of the same State with themselves. And they shall make a List of all the Persons voted for, and of the Number of Votes for each; which List they shall sign and certify, and transmit sealed to the Seat of the Government of the United States, directed to the President of the Senate. The President of the Senate shall, in the Presence of the Senate and House of Representatives, open all the Certificates, and the Votes shall then be counted. The Person having the greatest Number of Votes shall be the President, if such Number be a Majority of the whole Number of Electors appointed; and if there be more than one who have such Majority, and have an equal Number of Votes, then the House of Representatives shall immediately chuse by Ballot one of them for President; and if no Person have a Majority, then from the five highest on the List the said House shall in like Manner chuse the President. But in chusing the President, the Votes shall be taken by States, the Representatives from each State having one Vote; a quorum for this Purpose shall consist of a Member or Members from two thirds of the States, and a Majority of all the States shall be necessary to a Choice. In every Case, after the Choice of the President, the Person having the greatest Number of Votes of the Electors shall be the Vice President. But if there should remain two or more who have equal Votes, the Senate shall chuse from them by Ballot the Vice President.

The Congress may determine the Time of chusing the Electors, and the Day on which they shall give their Votes; which Day shall be the same throughout the United States.

No person except a natural born Citizen, or a Citizen of the United States, at the time of the Adoption of this Constitution, shall be eligible to the Office of President; neither shall any person be eligible to that Office who shall not have attained to the Age of thirty five Years, and been fourteen Years a Resident within the United States.

In Case of the Removal of the President from Office, or of his Death, Resignation, or Inability to discharge the Powers and Duties of the said Office, the Same shall devolve on the Vice President, and the Congress may by Law provide for the Case of Removal, Death, Resignation or Inability, both of the President and Vice President, declaring what Officer shall then act as President, and such Officer shall act accordingly, until the Disability be removed, or a President shall be elected.

The President shall, at stated Times, receive for his Services, a Compensation, which shall neither be increased nor diminished during the Period for which he shall have been elected, and he shall not receive within that Period any other Emolument from the United States, or any of them.

Before he enter on the Execution of his Office, he shall take the following Oath or Affirmation:—"I do solemnly swear (or affirm) that I will faithfully execute the Office of President of the United States, and will to the best of my Ability, preserve, protect and defend the Constitution of the United States."

Section. 2. The President shall be Commander in Chief of the Army and Navy of the United States, and of the Militia of the several States, when called into the actual Service of the United States; he may require the Opinion, in writing, of the principal Officer in each of the executive Departments, upon any Subject relating to the Duties of their respective Offices, and he shall have Power to grant Reprieves and Pardons for Offenses against the United States, except in Cases of Impeachment.

He shall have Power, by and with the Advice and Consent of the Senate, to make Treaties, provided two thirds of the Senators present concur; and he shall nominate, and by and with the Advice and Consent of the Senate, shall appoint Ambassadors, other public Ministers and Consuls, Judges of the supreme Court, and all other Officers of the United States, whose Appointments are not herein otherwise provided for, and which shall be established by Law: but the Congress may by Law vest the Appointment of such inferior

Officers, as they think proper, in the President alone, in the Courts of Law, or in the Heads of Departments.

The President shall have Power to fill up all Vacancies that may happen during the Recess of the Senate, by granting Commissions which shall expire at the End of their next Session.

Section. 3. He shall from time to time give to the Congress Information on the State of the Union, and recommend to their Consideration such Measures as he shall judge necessary and expedient; he may, on extraordinary Occasions, convene both Houses, or either of them, and in Case of Disagreement between them, with Respect to the Time of Adjournment, he may adjourn them to such Time as he shall think proper; he shall receive Ambassadors and other public Ministers; he shall take Care that the Laws be faithfully executed, and shall Commission all the Officers of the United States.

Section. 4. The President, Vice President and all Civil Officers of the United States, shall be removed from Office on Impeachment for, and Conviction of, Treason, Bribery, or other high Crimes and Misdemeanors.

Article. III.

Section. 1. The judicial Power of the United States, shall be vested in one supreme Court, and in such inferior Courts as the Congress may from time to time ordain and establish. The Judges, both of the supreme and inferior Courts, shall hold their Offices during good Behaviour, and shall, at stated Times, receive for their Services, a Compensation, which shall not be diminished during their Continuance in Office.

Section. 2. The judicial Power shall extend to all Cases, in Law and Equity, arising under this Constitution, the Laws of the United States, and Treaties made, or which shall be made, under their Authority;—to all Cases affecting Ambassadors, other public ministers and Consuls;—to all Cases of admiralty and maritime Jurisdiction;—to Controversies to which the United States shall be a Party;—to Controversies between two or more States;—between a State and Citizens of another State;—between Citizens of different States;—between Citizens of the same State claiming Lands under Grants of different States, and between a State, or the Citizens thereof, and foreign States, Citizens or Subjects.

In all Cases affecting Ambassadors, other public Ministers and Consuls, and those in which a State shall be Party, the supreme Court shall have original Jurisdiction. In all the other Cases before mentioned, the supreme Court shall have appellate Jurisdiction, both as to Law and Fact, with such Exceptions, and under such Regulations as the Congress shall make.

The Trial of all Crimes, except in Cases of Impeachment, shall be by Jury; and such Trial shall be held in the State where the said Crimes shall have been committed; but when not committed within any State, the Trial shall be at such Place or Places as the Congress may by Law have directed.

Section. 3. Treason against the United States, shall consist only in levying War against them, or in adhering to their Enemies, giving them Aid and Comfort. No Person shall be convicted of Treason unless on the Testimony of two Witnesses to the same overt Act, or on Confession in open Court.

The Congress shall have Power to declare the Punishment of Treason, but no Attainder of Treason shall work Corruption of Blood, or Forfeiture except during the Life of the Person attainted.

Article. IV.

Section. 1. Full Faith and Credit shall be given in each State to the public Acts, Records, and judicial Proceedings of every other State. And the Congress may by general Laws prescribe the Manner in which such Acts, Records and Proceedings shall be proved, and the Effect thereof.

Section. 2. The Citizens of each State shall be entitled to all Privileges and Immunities of Citizens in the several States.

A Person charged in any State with Treason, Felony, or other Crime, who shall flee from Justice, and be found in another State, shall on Demand of the executive Authority of the State from which he fled, be delivered up, to be removed to the State having Jurisdiction of the Crime.

No Person held to Service or Labour in one State, under the Laws thereof, escaping into another, shall, in Consequence of any Law or Regulation therein, be discharged from such Service or Labour, but shall be delivered up on Claim of the Party to whom such Service or Labour may be due.

Section. 3. New States may be admitted by the Congress into this Union; but no new State shall be formed or erected within the Jurisdiction of any other State; nor any State be formed by the Junction of two or more States, or Parts of States, without the Consent of the Legislatures of the States concerned as well as of the Congress.

The Congress shall have Power to dispose of and make all needful Rules and Regulations respecting the Territory or other Property belonging to the United States; and nothing in this Constitution shall be so construed as to Prejudice any Claims of the United States, or of any particular State.

Section. 4. The United States shall guarantee to every State in this Union a Republican Form of Government, and shall protect each of them against Invasion; and on Application of the Legislature, or of the Executive (when the Legislature cannot be convened) against domestic Violence.

Article. V.

The Congress, whenever two thirds of both Houses shall deem it necessary, shall propose Amendments to this Constitution, or, on the Application of the Legislatures of two thirds of the several States, shall call a Convention for proposing Amendments, which, in either Case, shall be valid to all Intents and Purposes, as Part of this Constitution, when ratified by the Legislatures of three fourths of the several States, or by Conventions in three fourths thereof, as the one or the other Mode of Ratification may be proposed by the Congress; Provided that no Amendment which may be made prior to the Year One thousand eight hundred and eight shall in any Manner affect the first and fourth Clauses in the Ninth Section of the first Article; and that no State, without its Consent, shall be deprived of it's equal Suffrage in the Senate.

Article. VI.

All Debts contracted and Engagements entered into, before the Adoption of this Constitution, shall be as valid against the United States under this Constitution, as under the Confederation.

This Constitution, and the Laws of the United States which shall be made in Pursuance thereof; and all Treaties made, or which shall be made, under the Authority of the United States, shall be the supreme Law of the Land; and the Judges in every State shall be bound thereby, any Thing in the Constitution or Laws of any State to the Contrary notwithstanding.

The Senators and Representatives before mentioned, and the Members of the several State Legislatures, and all executive and judicial Officers, both of the United States and of the several States, shall be bound by Oath or Affirmation, to support this Constitution; but no religious Test shall ever be required as a Qualification to any Office or public Trust under the United States.

Article. VII.

The Ratification of the Conventions of nine States, shall be sufficient for the Establishment of this Constitution between the States so ratifying the Same.

The Word, "the," being interlined between the seventh and eighth Lines of the first Page, The Word "Thirty" being partly written on an Erazure in the fifteenth Line of the first Page, The Words "is tried" being interlined between the thirty second and thirty third Lines of the first Page and the Word "the" being interlined between the forty third and forty fourth Lines of the second Page.

done in Convention by the Unanimous Consent of the States present the Seventeenth Day of September in the Year of our Lord one thousand seven hundred and Eighty seven and of the Independence of the United States of America the Twelfth In witness whereof We have hereunto subscribed our Names,

Gº. WASHINGTON—Presidᵗ and deputy from Virginia

Attest WILLIAM JACKSON
Secretary

New Hampshire { JOHN LANGDON
                NICHOLAS GILMAN

Massachusetts { NATHANIEL GORHAM
                RUFUS KING

Connecticut { W^M.. SAM^L. JOHNSON
              ROGER SHERMAN

New York . . . . ALEXANDER HAMILTON

New Jersey { WIL: LIVINGSTON
             DAVID BREARLEY.
             W^M.. PATERSON.
             JONA: DAYTON

Pennsylvania { B FRANKLIN
               THOMAS MIFFLIN
               ROB^T MORRIS
               GEO. CLYMER
               THO^S. FITZSIMONS
               JARED INGERSOLL
               JAMES WILSON
               GOUV MORRIS

Delaware { GEO: READ
           GUNNING BEDFORD jun
           JOHN DICKINSON
           RICHARD BASSETT
           JACO: BROOM

Maryland { JAMES M^{C}HENRY
           DAN OF S^T THO^S. JENIFER
           DAN^L CARROLL

Virginia { JOHN BLAIR—
           JAMES MADISON Jr.

North Carolina { W^M.. BLOUNT
                 RICH^D. DOBBS SPRAIGHT
                 HU WILLIAMSON
                 J. RUTLEDGE

South Carolina { CHARLES COTESWORTH PINCKNEY
                 CHARLES PINCKNEY
                 PIERCE BUTLER

Georgia { WILLIAM FEW
          ABR BALDWIN

CONSTITUTION OF THE UNITED STATES

In Convention Monday, September 17ᵗʰ 1787.

Present

The States of

New Hampshire, Massachusetts, Connecticut, Mᴿ Hamilton from New York, New Jersey, Pennsylvania, Delaware, Maryland, Virginia, North Carolina, South Carolina and Georgia.

Resolved,

That the preceeding Constitution be laid before the United States in Congress assembled, and that it is the Opinion of this Convention, that it should afterwards be submitted to a Convention of Delegates, chosen in each State by the People thereof, under the Recommendation of its Legislature, for their Assent and Ratification; and that each Convention assenting to, and ratifying the Same, should give Notice thereof to the United States in Congress assembled. Resolved, That it is the Opinion of this Convention, that as soon as the Conventions of nine States shall have ratified this Constitution, the United States in Congress assembled should fix a Day on which Electors should be appointed by the States which shall have ratified the same, and a Day on which the Electors should assemble to vote for the President, and the Time and Place for commencing Proceedings under this Constitution. That after such Publication the Electors should be appointed, and the Senators and Representatives elected: That the Electors should meet on the Day fixed for the Election of the President, and should transmit their Votes certified, signed, sealed and directed, as the Constitution requires, to the Secretary of the United States in Congress assembled, that the Senators and Representatives should convene at the Time and Place assigned;

that the Senators should appoint a President of the Senate, for the sole Purpose of receiving, opening and counting the Votes for President; and, that after he shall be chosen, the Congress, together with the President, should, without Delay, proceed to execute this Constitution.

By the Unanimous Order of the Convention

G^o: WASHINGTON—Presid^t.

W. JACKSON Secretary.

AMENDMENTS

TO THE

CONSTITUTION OF THE UNITED STATES
OF AMERICA

ARTICLES IN ADDITION TO, AND AMENDMENT OF, THE CONSTITUTION OF THE UNITED STATES OF AMERICA, PROPOSED BY CONGRESS, AND RATIFIED BY THE SEVERAL STATES, PURSUANT TO THE FIFTH ARTICLE OF THE ORIGINAL CONSTITUTION [1]

AMENDMENT [I.] [2]

Congress shall make no law respecting an establishment of religion, or prohibiting the free exercise thereof; or abridging the freedom of speech, or of the press; or the right of the people peaceably to assemble, and to petition the Government for a redress of grievances.

[1] In *Dillon* v. *Gloss*, 256 U.S. 368 (1921), the Supreme Court stated that it would take judicial notice of the date on which a State ratified a proposed constitutional amendment. Accordingly the Court consulted the State journals to determine the dates on which each house of the legislature of certain States ratified the Eighteenth Amendment. It, therefore, follows that the date on which the governor approved the ratification, or the date on which the secretary of state of a given State certified the ratification, or the date on which the Secretary of State of the United States received a copy of said certificate, or the date on which he proclaimed that the amendment had been ratified are not controlling. Hence, the ratification date given in the following notes is the date on which the legislature of a given State approved the particular amendment (signature by the speaker or presiding officers of both houses being considered a part of the ratification of the "legislature"). When that date is not available, the date given is that on which it was approved by the governor or certified by the secretary of state of the particular State. In each case such fact has been noted. Except as otherwise indicated information as to ratification is based on data supplied by the Department of State.

[2] Brackets enclosing an amendment number indicate that the number was not specifically assigned in the resolution proposing the amendment. It will be seen, accordingly, that only the Thirteenth, Fourteenth, Fifteenth, and Sixteenth Amendments were thus technically ratified by number. The first ten amendments along with two others which failed of ratification were proposed by Congress on September 25, 1789, when they passed the Senate, having previously passed the House on September 24 (1 *Annals of Congress* 88, 913). They appear officially in 1 Stat. 97. Ratification was completed on December 15, 1791, when the eleventh State (Virginia) approved these amendments, there being then 14 States in the Union.

The several state legislatures ratified the first ten amendments to the Constitution on

CONSTITUTION OF THE UNITED STATES

AMENDMENT [II.]

A well regulated Militia, being necessary to the security of a free State, the right of the people to keep and bear Arms, shall not be infringed.

AMENDMENT [III.]

No Soldier shall, in time of peace be quartered in any house, without the consent of the Owner, nor in time of war, but in a manner to be prescribed by law.

AMENDMENT [IV.]

The right of the people to be secure in their persons, houses, papers, and effects, against unreasonable searches and seizures, shall not be violated, and no Warrants shall issue, but upon probable cause, supported by Oath or affirmation, and particularly describing the place to be searched, and the persons or things to be seized.

AMENDMENT [V.]

No person shall be held to answer for a capital, or otherwise infamous crime, unless on a presentment or indictment of a Grand Jury, except in cases arising in the land or naval forces, or in the Militia, when in actual service in time of War or public danger; nor shall any person be subject for the same offence to be twice put in jeopardy of life or limb; nor shall be compelled in any

---

the following dates: New Jersey, November 20, 1789; Maryland, December 19, 1789; North Carolina, December 22, 1789; South Carolina, January 19, 1790; New Hampshire, January 25, 1790; Delaware, January 28, 1790; New York, February 27, 1790; Pennsylvania, March 10, 1790; Rhode Island, June 7, 1790; Vermont, November 3, 1791; Virginia, December 15, 1791. The two amendments which failed of ratification prescribed the ratio of representation to population in the House, and specified that no law varying the compensation of members of Congress should be effective until after an intervening election of Representatives. The first was ratified by ten States (one short of the requisite number) and the second, by six States. Connecticut, Georgia, and Massachusetts ratified the first ten amendments in 1939.

criminal case to be a witness against himself, nor be deprived of life, liberty, or property, without due process of law; nor shall private property be taken for public use, without just compensation.

AMENDMENT [VI.]

In all criminal prosecutions, the accused shall enjoy the right to a speedy and public trial, by an impartial jury of the State and district wherein the crime shall have been committed, which district shall have been previously ascertained by law, and to be informed of the nature and cause of the accusation; to be confronted with the witnesses against him; to have compulsory process for obtaining witnesses in his favor, and to have the Assistance of Counsel for his defence.

AMENDMENT [VII.]

In Suits at common law, where the value in controversy shall exceed twenty dollars, the right of trial by jury shall be preserved, and no fact tried by a jury, shall be otherwise re-examined in any Court of the United States, than according to the rules of the common law.

AMENDMENT [VIII.]

Excessive bail shall not be required, nor excessive fines imposed, nor cruel and unusual punishments inflicted.

AMENDMENT [IX.]

The enumeration in the Constitution, of certain rights, shall not be construed to deny or disparage others retained by the people.

AMENDMENT [X.]

The powers not delegated to the United States by the Constitution, nor prohibited by it to the States, are reserved to the States respectively, or to the people.

CONSTITUTION OF THE UNITED STATES

AMENDMENT [XI.] [3]

The Judicial power of the United States shall not be construed to extend to any suit in law or equity, commenced or prosecuted against one on the United States by Citizens of another State, or by Citizens or Subjects of any Foreign State.

AMENDMENT [XII.] [4]

The Electors shall meet in their respective states and vote by ballot for President and Vice President, one of whom, at least, shall not be an inhabitant of the same state with themselves; they shall

---

[3] The Eleventh Amendment was proposed by Congress on March 4, 1794, when it passed the House, 4 *Annals of Congress* 477, 478, having previously passed the Senate on January 14. *Id.*, 30, 31. It appears officially in 1 Stat. 402. Ratification was completed on February 7, 1795, when the twelfth State (North Carolina) approved the amendment, there being then 15 States in the Union. Official announcement of ratification was not made until January 8, 1798, when President John Adams in a message to Congress stated that the Eleventh Amendment had been adopted by three-fourths of the States and that it "may now be deemed to be a part of the Constitution." In the interim South Carolina had ratified, and Tennessee had been admitted into the Union as the sixteenth State.

The several state legislatures ratified the Eleventh Amendment on the following dates: New York, March 27, 1794; Rhode Island, March 31, 1794; Connecticut, May 8, 1794; New Hampshire, June 16, 1794; Massachusetts, June 26, 1794; Vermont, between October 9 and November 9, 1794; Virginia, November 18, 1794; Georgia, November 29, 1794; Kentucky, December 7, 1794; Maryland, December 26, 1794; Delaware, January 23, 1795; North Carolina, February 7, 1795; South Carolina, December 4, 1797.

[4] The Twelfth Amendment was proposed by Congress on December 9, 1803, when it passed the House, 13 *Annals of Congress* 775, 776, having previously passed the Senate on December 2. *Id.*, 209. It was not signed by the presiding officers of the House and Senate until December 12. It appears officially in 2 Stat. 306. Ratification was probably completed on June 15, 1804, when the legislature of the thirteenth State (New Hampshire) approved the amendment, there being then 17 States in the Union. The Governor of New Hampshire, however, vetoed this act of the legislature on June 20, and the act failed to pass again by two-thirds vote then required by the state constitution. Inasmuch as Article V of the Federal Constitution specifies that amendments shall become effective "when ratified by legislatures of three-fourths of the several States or by conventions in three-fourths thereof," it has been generally believed that an approval or veto by a governor is without significance. If the ratification by New Hampshire be deemed ineffective, then the amendment became operative by Tennessee's ratification on July 27, 1804. On September 25, 1804, in a circular letter to the Governors of the several States, Secretary of State Madison declared the amendment ratified by three-fourths of the States.

The several state legislatures ratified the Twelfth Amendment on the following dates: North Carolina, December 22, 1803; Maryland, December 24, 1803; Kentucky, December 27, 1803; Ohio, between December 5 and December 30, 1803; Virginia, between December 20, 1803 and February 3, 1804; Pennsylvania, January 5, 1804; Vermont, January 30, 1804; New York, February 10, 1804; New Jersey, February 22, 1804; Rhode Island, between Feb-

name in their ballots the person voted for as President, and in distinct ballots the person voted for as Vice-President, and they shall make distinct lists of all persons voted for as President, and of all persons voted for as Vice-President, and of the number of votes for each, which lists they shall sign and certify, and transmit sealed to the seat of the government of the United States, directed to the President of the Senate;—The President of the Senate shall, in the presence of the Senate and House of Representatives, open all the certificates and the votes shall then be counted;—The person having the greatest number of votes for President, shall be the President, if such member be a majority of the whole number of Electors appointed; and if no person have such majority, then from the persons having the highest numbers not exceeding three on the list of those voted for as President, the House of Representatives shall choose immediately, by ballot, the President. But in choosing the President, the votes shall be taken by states, the representation from each state having one vote; a quorum for this purpose shall consist of a member or members from two-thirds of the states, and a majority of all the states shall be necessary to a choice. And if the House of Representatives shall not choose a President whenever the right of choice shall devolve upon them, before the fourth day of March next following, then the Vice-President shall act as President, as in the case of the death or other constitutional disability of the President—The person having the greatest number of votes as Vice-President, shall be the Vice-President, if such number be a majority of the whole number of Electors appointed, and if no person have a majority, then from

ruary 27 and March 12, 1804; South Carolina, May 15, 1804; Georgia, May 19, 1804; New Hampshire, June 15, 1804; and Tennessee, July 27, 1804. The amendment was rejected by Delaware on January 18, 1804, and by Connecticut at its session begun May 10, 1804. Massachusetts ratified this amendment in 1961.

the two highest numbers on the list, the Senate shall choose the Vice-President; a quorum for the purpose shall consist of two-thirds of the whole number of Senators, and a majority of the whole number shall be necessary to a choice. But no person constitutionally ineligible to the office of President shall be eligible to that of Vice-President of the United States.

AMENDMENT XIII.[5]

SECTION 1. Neither slavery nor involuntary servitude, except as a punishment for crime whereof the party shall have been duly convicted, shall exist within the United States, or any place subject to their jurisdiction.

SECTION 2. Congress shall have power to enforce this article by appropriate legislation.

---

[5] The Thirteenth Amendment was proposed by Congress on January 31, 1865, when it passed the House, *Cong. Globe* (38th Cong., 2d Sess.) 531, having previously passed the Senate on April 8, 1964. *Id.* (38th Cong., 1st Sess.), 1940. It appears officially in 13 Stat. 567 under the date of February 1, 1865. Ratification was completed on December 6, 1865, when the legislature of the twenty-seventh State (Georgia) approved the amendment, there being then 36 States in the Union. On December 18, 1865, Secretary of State Seward certified that the Thirteenth Amendment had become a part of the Constitution, 13 Stat. 774.

The several state legislatures ratified the Thirteenth Amendment on the following dates: Illinois, February 1, 1865; Rhode Island, February 2, 1865; Michigan, February 2, 1865; Maryland, February 3, 1865; New York, February 3, 1865; West Virginia, February 3, 1865; Missouri, February 6, 1865; Maine, February 7, 1865; Kansas, February 7, 1865; Massachusetts, February 7, 1865; Pennsylvania, February 8, 1865; Virginia, February 9, 1865; Ohio, February 10, 1865; Louisiana, February 15 or 16, 1865; Indiana, February 16, 1865; Nevada, February 16, 1865; Minnesota, February 23, 1865; Wisconsin, February 24, 1865; Vermont, March 9, 1865 (date on which it was "approved" by Governor); Tennessee, April 7, 1865; Arkansas, April 14, 1865; Connecticut, May 4, 1865; New Hampshire, June 30, 1865; South Carolina, November 13, 1865; Alabama, December 2, 1865 (date on which it was "approved" by Provisional Governor); North Carolina, December 4, 1865; Georgia, December 6, 1865; Oregon, December 11, 1865; California, December 15, 1865; Florida, December 28, 1865 (Florida again ratified this amendment on June 9, 1868, upon its adoption of a new constitution); Iowa, January 17, 1866; New Jersey, January 23, 1866 (after having rejected the amendment on March 16, 1865); Texas, February 17, 1870; Delaware, February 12, 1901 (after having rejected the amendment on February 8, 1865). The amendment was rejected by Kentucky on February 24, 1865, and by Mississippi on December 2, 1865.

CONSTITUTION OF THE UNITED STATES

AMENDMENT XIV.[6]

SECTION. 1. All persons born or naturalized in the United States and subject to the jurisdiction thereof, are citizens of the United States and of the State wherein they reside. No State shall make or enforce any law which shall abridge the privileges or immunities of citizens of the United States; or shall any State deprive any person of life, liberty, or property, without due process of law; nor deny to any person within its jurisdiction the equal protection of the laws.

---

[6] The Fourteenth Amendment was proposed by Congress on June 13, 1866, when it passed the House, *Cong. Globe* (39th Cong., 1st Sess.) 3148, 3149, having previously passed the Senate on June 8. *Id.*, 3042. It appears officially in 14 Stat. 358 under date of June 16, 1866. Ratification was probably completed on July 9, 1868, when the legislature of the twenty-eighth State (South Carolina or Louisiana) approved the amendment, there being then 37 States in the Union. However, Ohio and New Jersey had prior to that date "withdrawn" their earlier assent to this amendment. Accordingly, Secretary of State Seward on July 20, 1868, certified that the amendment had become a part of the Constitution if the said withdrawals were ineffective. 15 Stat. 706–707. Congress on July 21, 1868, passed a joint resolution declaring the amendment a part of the Constitution and directing the Secretary to promulgate it as such. On July 28, 1868, Secretary Seward certified without reservation that the amendment was a part of the Constitution. In the interim, two other States, Alabama on July 13 and Georgia on July 21, 1868, had added their ratifications.

The several state legislatures ratified the Fourteenth Amendment on the following dates: Connecticut, June 30, 1866; New Hampshire, July 7, 1866; Tennessee, July 19, 1866; New Jersey, September 11, 1866 (the New Jersey Legislature on February 20, 1868 "withdrew" its consent to the ratification; the Governor vetoed that bill on March 5, 1868; and it was repassed over his veto on March 24, 1868); Oregon, September 19, 1866 (Oregon "withdrew" its consent on October 15, 1868); Vermont, October 30, 1866; New York, January 10, 1867; Ohio, January 11, 1867 (Ohio "withdrew" its consent on January 15, 1868); Illinois, January 15, 1867; West Virginia, January 16, 1867; Michigan, January 16, 1867; Kansas, January 17, 1867; Minnesota, January 17, 1867; Maine, January 19, 1867; Nevada, January 22, 1867; Indiana, January 23, 1867; Missouri, January 26, 1867 (date on which it was certified by the Missouri secretary of state); Rhode Island, February 7, 1867; Pennsylvania, February 12, 1867; Wisconsin, February 13, 1867 (actually passed February 7, but not signed by legislative officers until February 13); Massachusetts, March 20, 1867; Nebraska, June 15, 1867; Iowa, March 9, 1868; Arkansas, April 6, 1868; Florida, June 9, 1868; North Carolina, July 2, 1868 (after having rejected the amendment on December 13, 1866); Louisiana, July 9, 1868 (after having rejected the amendment on February 6, 1867); South Carolina, July 8, 1868 (after having rejected the amendment on December 20, 1866); Alabama, July 13, 1868 (date on which it was "approved" by the Governor); Georgia, July 21, 1868 (after having rejected the amendment on November 9, 1866—Georgia ratified again on February 2, 1870); Virginia, October 8, 1869 (after having rejected the amendment on January 9, 1867); Mississippi, January 17, 1870; Texas, February 18, 1870 (after having rejected the amendment on October 27, 1866); Delaware, February 12, 1901 (after having rejected the amendment on February 7, 1867). The amendment was rejected (and not subsequently ratified) by Kentucky on January 8, 1867. Maryland and California ratified this amendment in 1959.

76

SECTION. 2. Representatives shall be apportioned among the several States according to their respective numbers, counting the whole number of persons in each State, excluding Indians not taxed. But when the right to vote at any election for the choice of electors for President and Vice President of the United States, Representatives in Congress, the Executive and Judicial officers of a State, or the members of the Legislature thereof, is denied to any of the male inhabitants of such State, being twenty-one years of age, and citizens of the United States, or in any way abridged, except for participation in rebellion, or other crime, the basis of representation therein shall be reduced in the proportion which the number of such male citizens shall bear to the whole number of male citizens twenty-one years of age in such State.

SECTION 3. No person shall be a Senator or Representative in Congress, or elector of President and Vice President, or hold any office, civil or military, under the United States, or under any State, who, having previously taken an oath, as a member of Congress, or as an officer of the United States, or as a member of any State legislature, or as an executive or judicial officer of any State, to support the Constitution of the United States, shall have engaged in insurrection or rebellion against the same, or given aid or comfort to the enemies thereof. But Congress may by a vote of two-thirds of each House, remove such disability.

SECTION 4. The validity of the public debt of the United States, authorized by law, including debts incurred for payment of pensions and bounties for services in suppressing insurrection or rebellion, shall not be questioned. But neither the United States nor any State shall assume or pay any debt or obligation incurred in aid of insurrection or rebellion against the United States, or any claim for the loss or emancipation of any slave; but all such debts, obligations and claims shall be held illegal and void.

SECTION 5. The Congress shall have power to enforce, by appropriate legislation, the provisions of this article.

AMENDMENT XV.[7]

SECTION. 1. The right of citizens of the United States to vote shall not be denied or abridged by the United States or by any State on account of race, color, or previous condition of servitude.

SECTION 2. The Congress shall have power to enforce this article by appropriate legislation.

---

[7] The Fifteenth Amendment was proposed by Congress on February 26, 1869, when it passed the Senate, *Cong. Globe* (40th Cong., 3rd Sess.) 1641, having previously passed the House on February 25. *Id.*, 1563, 1564. It appears officially in 15 Stat. 346 under the date of February 27, 1869. Ratification was probably completed on February 3, 1870, when the legislature of the twenth-eighth State (Iowa) approved the amendment, there being then 37 States in the Union. However, New York had prior to that date "withdrawn" its earlier assent to this amendment. Even if this withdrawal were effective, Nebraska's ratification on February 17, 1870, authorized Secretary of State Fish's certification of March 30, 1870, that the Fifteenth Amendment had become a part of the Constitution. 16 Stat. 1131.

The several state legislatures ratified the Fifteenth Amendment on the following dates: Nevada, March 1, 1869; West Virginia, March 3, 1869; North Carolina, March 5, 1869; Louisiana, March 5, 1869 (date on which it was "approved" by the Governor); Illinois, March 5, 1869; Michigan, March 5, 1869; Wisconsin, March 5, 1869; Maine, March 11, 1869; Massachusetts, March 12, 1869; South Carolina, March 15, 1869; Arkansas, March 15, 1869; Pennsylvania, March 25, 1869; New York, April 14, 1869 (New York "withdrew" its consent to the ratification on January 5, 1870); Indiana, May 14, 1869; Connecticut, May 19, 1869; Florida, June 14, 1869; New Hampshire, July 1, 1869; Virginia, October 8, 1869; Vermont, October 20, 1869; Alabama, November 16, 1869; Missouri, January 7, 1870 (Missouri had ratified the first section of the 15th Amendment on March 1, 1869; it failed to include in its ratification the second section of the amendment); Minnesota, January 13, 1870; Mississippi, January 17, 1870; Rhode Island, January 18, 1870; Kansas, January 19, 1870 (Kansas had by a defectively worded resolution previously ratified this amendment on February 27, 1869); Ohio, January 27, 1870 (after having rejected the amendment on May 4, 1869); Georgia, February 2, 1870; Iowa, February 3, 1870; Nebraska, February 17, 1870; Texas, February 18, 1870; New Jersey, February 15, 1871 (after having rejected the amendment on February 7, 1870); Delaware, February 12, 1901 (date on which approved by Governor; Delaware had previously rejected the amendment on March 18, 1869). The amendment was rejected (and not subsequently ratified) by Kentucky, Maryland, and Tennessee. California ratified this amendment in 1962 and Oregon in 1959.

CONSTITUTION OF THE UNITED STATES

AMENDMENT XVI.[8]

The Congress shall have power to lay and collect taxes on incomes, from whatever source derived, without apportionment among the several States, and without regard to any census or enumeration.

AMENDMENT [XVII.] [9]

The Senate of the United States shall be composed of two Senators from each State, elected by the people thereof, for six years; and each Senator shall have one vote. The electors in each State shall have the qualifications requisite for electors of the most numerous branch of the State legislatures.

---

[8] The Sixteenth Amendment was proposed by Congress on July 12, 1909, when it passed the House, 44 *Cong. Rec.* (61st Cong., 1st Sess.) 4390, 4440, 4441, having previously passed the Senate on July 5. *Id.*, 4121. It appears officially in 36 Stat. 184. Ratification was completed on February 3, 1913, when the legislature of the thirty-sixth State (Delaware, Wyoming, or New Mexico) approved the amendment, there being then 48 States in the Union. On February 25, 1913, Secretary of State Knox certified that this amendment had become a part of the Constitution. 37 Stat. 1785.

The several state legislatures ratified the Sixteenth Amendment on the following dates: Alabama, August 10, 1909; Kentucky, February 8, 1910; South Carolina, February 19, 1910; Illinois, March 1, 1910; Mississippi, March 7, 1910; Oklahoma, March 10, 1910; Maryland, April 8, 1910; Georgia, August 3, 1910; Texas, August 16, 1910; Ohio, January 19, 1911; Idaho, January 20, 1911; Oregon, January 23, 1911; Washington, January 26, 1911; Montana, January 27, 1911; Indiana, January 30, 1911; California, January 31, 1911; Nevada, January 31, 1911; South Dakota, February 1, 1911; Nebraska, February 9, 1911; North Carolina, February 11, 1911; Colorado, February 15, 1911; North Dakota, February 17, 1911; Michigan, February 23, 1911; Iowa, February 24, 1911; Kansas, March 2, 1911; Missouri, March 16, 1911; Maine, March 31, 1911; Tennessee, April 7, 1911; Arkansas, April 22, 1911 (after having rejected the amendment at the session begun January 9, 1911); Wisconsin, May 16, 1911; New York, July 12, 1911; Arizona, April 3, 1912; Minnesota, June 11, 1912; Louisiana, June 28, 1912; West Virginia, January 31, 1913; Delaware, February 3, 1913; Wyoming, February 3, 1913; New Mexico, February 3, 1913; New Jersey, February 4, 1913; Vermont, February 19, 1913; Massachusetts, March 4, 1913; New Hampshire, March 7, 1913 (after having rejected the amendment on March 2, 1911). The amendment was rejected (and not subsequently ratified) by Connecticut, Rhode Island, and Utah.

[9] The Seventeenth Amendment was proposed by Congress on May 13, 1912, when it passed the House, 48 *Cong. Rec.* (62d Cong., 2d Sess.) 6367, having previously passed the Senate on June 12, 1911. 47 *Cong. Rec.* (62d Cong., 1st Sess.) 1925. It appears officially in 37 Stat. 646. Ratification was completed on April 8, 1913, when the thirty-sixth State (Connecticut) approved the amendment, there being then 48 Sates in the Union. On May 31, 1913, Secretary of State Bryan certified that it had become a part of the Constitution. 38 Stat 2049.

When vacancies happen in the representation of any State in the Senate, the executive authority of such State shall issue writs of election to fill such vacancies: *Provided,* That the legislature of any State may empower the executive thereof to make temporary appointments until the people fill the vacancies by election as the legislature may direct.

This amendment shall not be so construed as to affect the election or term of any Senator chosen before it becomes valid as part of the Constitution.

AMENDMENT [XVIII.] [10]

SECTION. 1. After one year from the ratification of this article the manufacture, sale, or transportation of intoxicating

---

The several state legislatures ratified the Seventeenth Amendment on the following dates: Massachusetts, May 22, 1912; Arizona, June 3, 1912; Minnesota, June 10, 1912; New York, January 15, 1913; Kansas, January 17, 1913; Oregon, January 23, 1913; North Carolina, January 25, 1913; California, January 28, 1913; Michigan, January 28, 1913; Iowa, January 30, 1913; Montana, January 30, 1913; Idaho, January 31, 1913; West Virgina, February 4, 1913; Colorado, February 5, 1913; Nevada, February 6, 1913; Texas, February 7, 1913; Washington, February 7, 1913; Wyoming, February 8, 1913; Arkansas, February 11, 1913; Illinois, February 13, 1913; North Dakota, February 14, 1913; Wisconsin, February 18, 1913; Indiana, February 19, 1913; New Hampshire, February 19, 1913; Vermont, February 19, 1913; South Dakota, February 19, 1913; Maine, February 20, 1913; Oklahoma, February 24, 1913; Ohio, February 25, 1913; Missouri, March 7, 1913; New Mexico, March 13, 1913; Nebraska, March 14, 1913; New Jersey, March 17, 1913; Tennessee, April 1, 1913; Pennsylvania, April 2, 1913; Connecticut, April 8, 1913; Louisiana, June 5, 1914. The amendment was rejected by Utah on February 26, 1913.

[10] The Eighteenth Amendment was proposed by Congress on December 18, 1917, when it passed the Senate, *Cong. Rec.* (65th Cong. 2d Sess.) 478, having previously passed the House on December 17. *Id.,* 470. It appears officially in 40 Stat. 1059. Ratification was completed on January 16, 1919, when the thirty-sixth State approved the amendment, there being then 48 States in the Union. On January 29, 1919, Acting Secretary of State Polk certified that this amendment had been adopted by the requisite number of States. 40 Stat. 1941. By its terms this amendment did not become effective until 1 year after ratification.

The several state legislatures ratified the Eighteenth Amendment on the following dates: Mississippi, January 8, 1918; Virginia, January 11, 1918; Kentucky, January 14, 1918; North Dakota, January 28, 1918 (date on which approved by Governor); South Carolina, January 29, 1918; Maryland, February 13, 1918; Montana, February 19, 1918; Texas, March 4, 1918; Delaware, March 18, 1918; South Dakota, March 20, 1918; Massachusetts, April 2, 1918; Arizona, May 24, 1918; Georgia, June 26, 1918; Louisiana, August 9, 1918 (date on which approved by Governor); Florida, November 27, 1918; Michigan, January 2, 1919; Ohio, January 7, 1919; Oklahoma, January 7, 1919; Idaho, January 8, 1919; Maine, January 8, 1919; West Virginia, January 9, 1919; California, January 13, 1919; Tennessee, Janu-

CONSTITUTION OF THE UNITED STATES

liquors within, the importation thereof into, or the exportation thereof from the United States and all territory subject to the jurisdiction thereof for beverage purposes is hereby prohibited.

SEC. 2. The Congress and the several States shall have concurrent power to enforce this article by appropriate legislation.

SEC. 3. This article shall be inoperative unless it shall have been ratified as an amendment to the Constitution by the legislatures of the several States, as provided in the Constitution, within seven years from the date of the submission hereof to the States by the Congress.

AMENDMENT [XIX.] [11]

The right of citizens of the United States to vote shall not be denied or abridged by the United States or by any State on account of sex.

Congress shall have power to enforce this article by appropriate legislation.

ary 13, 1919; Washington, January 13, 1919; Arkansas, January 14, 1919; Kansas, January 14, 1919; Illinois, January 14, 1919; Indiana, January 14, 1919; Alabama, January 15, 1919; Colorado, January 15, 1919; Iowa, January 15, 1919; New Hampshire, January 15, 1919; Oregon, January 15, 1919; Nebraska, January 16, 1919; North Carolina, January 16, 1919; Utah, January 16, 1919; Missouri, January 16, 1919; Wyoming, January 16, 1919; Minnesota, January 17, 1919; Wisconsin, January 17, 1919; New Mexico, January 20, 1919; Nevada, January 21, 1919; Pennsylvania, February 25, 1919; Connecticut, May 6, 1919; New Jersey, March 9, 1922; New York, January 29, 1919; Vermont, January 29, 1919.

[11] The Nineteenth Amendment was proposed by Congress on June 4, 1919, when it passed the Senate, *Cong. Rec.* (66th Cong., 1st Sess.) 635, having previously passed the House on May 21. *Id.*, 94. It appears officially in 41 Stat. 362. Ratification was completed on August 18, 1920, when the thirty-sixth State (Tennessee) approved the amendment, there being then 48 States in the Union. On August 26, 1920, Secretary of State Colby certified that it had become a part of the Constitution. 41 Stat. 1823.

The several state legislatures ratified the Nineteenth Amendment on the following dates: Illinois, June 10, 1919 (readopted June 17, 1919); Michigan, June 10, 1919; Wisconsin, June 10, 1919; Kansas, June 16, 1919; New York, June 16, 1919; Ohio, June 16, 1919; Pennsylvania, June 24, 1919; Massachusetts, June 25, 1919; Texas, June 28, 1919; Iowa, July 2, 1919 (date on which approved by Governor); Missouri, July 3, 1919; Arkansas, July 28, 1919; Montana, August 2, 1919 (date on which approved by Governor); Nebraska, August 2, 1919; Minnesota, September 8, 1919; New Hampshire, September 10, 1919 (date on which approved by Governor); Utah, October 2, 1919; California, November 1, 1919;

CONSTITUTION OF THE UNITED STATES

AMENDMENT [XX.] [12]

SECTION 1. The terms of the President and Vice President shall end at noon on the 20th day of January, and the terms of Senators and Representatives at noon on the 3d day of January, of the years in which such terms would have ended if this article had not been ratified; and the terms of their successors shall then begin.

SEC. 2. The Congress shall assemble at least once in every year, and such meeting shall begin at noon on the 3d day of January, unless they shall by law appoint a different day.

Maine, November 5, 1919; North Dakota, December 1, 1919; South Dakota, December 4, 1919 (date on which certified); Colorado, December 15, 1919 (date on which approved by Governor); Kentucky, January 6, 1920; Rhode Island, January 6, 1920; Oregon, January 13, 1920; Indiana, January 16, 1920; Wyoming, January 27, 1920; Nevada, February 7, 1920; New Jersey, February 9, 1920; Idaho, February 11, 1920; Arizona, February 12, 1920; New Mexico, February 21, 1920 (date on which approved by Governor); Oklahoma, February 28, 1920; West Virginia, March 10, 1920; Washington, March 22, 1920; Tennessee, August 18, 1920; Connecticut, September 14, 1920 (confirmed September 21, 1920); Vermont, February 8, 1921. The amendment was rejected by Georgia on July 24, 1919; by Alabama on September 22, 1919; by South Carolina on January 29, 1920; by Virginia on February 12, 1920; by Maryland on February 24, 1920; by Mississippi on March 29, 1920; by Louisiana on July 1, 1920. This amendment was subsequently ratified by Virginia in 1952, Alabama in 1953, Florida in 1969, and Georgia and Louisiana in 1970.

[12] The Twentieth Amendment was proposed by Congress on March 2, 1932, when it passed the Senate, *Cong. Rec.* (72d Cong., 1st Sess.) 5086, having previously passed the House on March 1. *Id.*, 5027. It appears officially in 47 Stat. 745. Ratification was completed on January 23, 1933, when the thirty-sixth State approved the amendment, there being then 48 States in the Union. On February 6, 1933, Secretary of State Stimson certified that it had become a part of the Constitution. 47 Stat. 2569.

The several state legislatures ratified the Twentieth Amendment on the following dates: Virginia, March 4, 1932; New York, March 11, 1932; Mississippi, March 16, 1932; Arkansas March 17, 1932; Kentucky, March 17, 1932; New Jersey, March 21, 1932; South Carolina, March 25, 1932; Michigan, March 31, 1932; Maine, April 1, 1932; Rhode Island, April 14, 1932; Illinois, April 21, 1932; Louisiana, June 22, 1932; West Virginia, July 30, 1932; Pennsylvania, August 11, 1932; Indiana, August 15, 1932; Texas, September 7, 1932; Alabama, September 13, 1932; California, January 4, 1933; North Carolina, January 5, 1933; North Dakota, January 9, 1933; Minnesota, January 12, 1933; Arizona, January 13, 1933; Montana, January 13, 1933; Nebraska, January 13, 1933; Oklahoma, January 13, 1933; Kansas, January 16, 1933; Oregon, January 16, 1933; Delaware, January 19, 1933; Washington, January 19, 1933; Wyoming, January 19, 1933; Iowa, January 20, 1933; South Dakota, January 20, 1933; Tennessee, January 20, 1933; Idaho, January 21, 1933; New Mexico, January 21, 1933; Georgia, January 23, 1933; Missouri, January 23, 1933; Ohio, January 23, 1933; Utah, January 23, 1933; Colorado, January 24, 1933; Massachusetts, January 24, 1933; Wisconsin, January 24, 1933; Nevada, January 26, 1933; Connecticut, January 27, 1933; New Hampshire, January 31, 1933; Vermont, February 2, 1933; Maryland, March 24, 1933; Florida, April 26, 1933.

SEC. 3. If, at the time fixed for the beginning of the term of the President, the President elect shall have died, the Vice President elect shall become President. If a President shall not have been chosen before the time fixed for the beginning of his term, or if the President elect shall have failed to qualify, then the Vice President elect shall act as President until a President shall have qualified; and the Congress may by law provide for the case wherein neither a President elect nor a Vice President elect shall have qualified, declaring who shall then act as President, or the manner in which one who is to act shall be selected, and such person shall act accordingly until a President or Vice President shall have qualified.

SEC. 4. The Congress may by law provide for the case of the death of any of the persons from whom the House of Representatives may choose a President whenever the right of choice shall have devolved upon them, and for the case of the death of any of the persons from whom the Senate may choose a Vice President whenever the right of choice shall have devolved upon them.

SEC. 5. Sections 1 and 2 shall take effect on the 15th day of October following the ratification of this article.

SEC. 6. This article shall be inoperative unless it shall have been ratified as an amendment to the Constitution by the legislatures of three-fourths of the several States within seven years from the date of its submission.

AMENDMENT [XXI.] [13]

SECTION. 1. The eighteenth article of amendment to the Constitution of the United States is hereby repealed.

---

[13] The Twenty-first Amendment was proposed by Congress on February 20, 1933, when it passed the House, *Cong. Rec.* (72d Cong., 2d Sess.) 4516, having previously passed the Senate

CONSTITUTION OF THE UNITED STATES

SEC. 2. The transportation or importation into any State, Territory or possession of the United States for delivery or use therein of intoxicating liquors, in violation of the laws thereof, is hereby prohibited.

SEC. 3. This article shall be inoperative unless it shall have been ratified as an amendment to the Constitution by conventions in the several States, as provided in the Constitution, within seven years from the date of the submission hereof to the States by the Congress.

AMENDMENT [XXII.] [14]

SECTION 1. No person shall be elected to the office of the President more than twice, and no person who has held the office

on February 16. *Id.,* 4231. It appears officially in 47 Stat. 1625. Ratification was completed on December 5, 1933, when the thirty-sixth State (Utah) approved the amendment, there being then 48 States in the Union. On December 5, 1933, Acting Secretary of State Phillips certified that it had been adopted by the requisite number of States. 48 Stat. 1749.

The several state conventions ratified the Twenty-first Amendment on the following dates: Michigan, April 10, 1933; Wisconsin, April 25, 1933; Rhode Island, May 8, 1933; Wyoming, May 25, 1933; New Jersey, June 1, 1933; Delaware, June 24, 1933; Indiana, June 26, 1933; Massachusetts, June 26, 1933; New York, June 27, 1933; Illinois, July 10, 1933; Iowa, July 10, 1933; Connecticut, July 11, 1933; New Hampshire, July 11, 1933; California, July 24, 1933; West Virginia, July 25, 1933; Arkansas, August 1, 1933; Oregon, August 7, 1933; Alabama, August 8, 1933; Tennessee, August 11, 1933; Missouri, August 29, 1933; Arizona, September 5, 1933; Nevada, September 5, 1933; Vermont, September 23, 1933; Colorado, September 26, 1933; Washington, October 3, 1933; Minnesota, October 10, 1933; Idaho, October 17, 1933; Maryland, October 18, 1933; Virginia, October 25, 1933; New Mexico, November 2, 1933; Florida, November 14, 1933; Texas, November 24, 1933; Kentucky, November 27, 1933; Ohio, December 5, 1933; Pennsylvania, December 5, 1933; Utah, December 5, 1933; Maine, December 6, 1933; Montana, August 6, 1934. The amendment was rejected by a convention in the State of South Carolina, on December 4, 1933. The electorate of the State of North Carolina voted against holding a convention at a general election held on November 7, 1933.

[14] The Twenty-second Amendment was proposed by Congress on March 24, 1947, having passed the House on March 21, 1947, *Cong. Rec.* (80th Cong., 1st Sess.) 2392, and having previously passed the Senate on March 12, 1947. *Id.,* 1978. It appears officially in 61 Stat. 959. Ratification was completed on February 27, 1951, when the thirty-sixth State (Minnesota) approved the amendment, there being then 48 States in the Union. On March 1, 1951, Jess Larson, Administrator of General Services, certified that it had been adopted by the requisite number of States. 16 *Fed. Reg.* 2019.

A total of 41 state legislatures ratified the Twenty-second Amendment on the following dates: Maine, March 31, 1947; Michigan, March 31, 1947; Iowa, April 1, 1947; Kansas, April 1, 1947; New Hampshire, April 1, 1947; Delaware, April 2, 1947; Illinois, April 3, 1947; Oregon, April 3, 1947; Colorado, April 12, 1947; California, April 15, 1947; New

of President, or acted as President, for more than two years of a term to which some other person was elected President shall be elected to the office of the President more than once. But this Article shall not apply to any person holding the office of President, when this Article was proposed by the Congress, and shall not prevent any person who may be holding the office of President, or acting as President, during the term within which this Article becomes operative from holding the office of President or acting as President during the remainder of such term.

SEC. 2. This Article shall be inoperative unless it shall have been ratified as an amendment to the Constitution by the legislatures of three-fourths of the several States within seven years from the date of its submission to the States by the Congress.

AMENDMENT [XXIII.] [15]

SECTION 1. The District constituting the seat of Government of the United States shall appoint in such manner as the Congress may direct:

A number of electors of President and Vice President equal to the whole number of Senators and Representatives in Congress

---

Jersey, April 15, 1947; Vermont, April 15, 1947; Ohio, April 16, 1947; Wisconsin, April 16, 1947; Pennsylvania, April 29, 1947; Connecticut, May 21, 1947; Missouri, May 22, 1947; Nebraska, May 23, 1947; Virginia, January 28, 1948; Mississippi, February 12, 1948; New York, March 9, 1948; South Dakota, January 21, 1949; North Dakota, February 25, 1949; Louisiana, May 17, 1950; Montana, January 25, 1951; Indiana, January 29, 1951; Idaho, January 30, 1951; New Mexico, February 12, 1951; Wyoming, February 12, 1951; Arkansas, February 15, 1951; Georgia, February 17, 1951; Tennessee, February 20, 1951; Texas, February 22, 1951; Utah, February 26, 1951; Nevada, February 26, 1951; Minnesota, February 27, 1951; North Carolina, February 28, 1951; South Carolina, March 13, 1951; Maryland, March 14, 1951; Florida, April 16, 1951; and Alabama, May 4, 1951.

[15] The Twenty-third Amendment was proposed by Congress on June 16, 1960, when it passed the Senate, *Cong. Rec.* (86th Cong., 2d Sess.) 12858, having previously passed the House on June 14. *Id.*, 12571. It appears officially in 74 Stat. 1057. Ratification was completed on March 29, 1961, when the thirty-eighth State (Ohio) approved the amendment, there being then 50 States in the Union. On April 3, 1961, John L. Moore, Administrator of General Services, certified that it had been adopted by the requisite number of States. 26 *Fed. Reg.* 2808.

to which the District would be entitled if it were a State, but in no event more than the least populous State; they shall be in addition to those appointed by the States, but they shall be considered, for the purposes of the election of President and Vice President, to be electors appointed by a State; and they shall meet in the District and perform such duties as provided by the twelfth article of amendment.

Sec. 2. The Congress shall have power to enforce this article by appropriate legislation.

AMENDMENT [XXIV.] [16]

SECTION 1. The right of citizens of the United States to vote in any primary or other election for President or Vice President,

The several state legislatures ratified the Twenty-third Amendment on the following dates: Hawaii, June 23, 1960; Massachusetts, August 22, 1960; New Jersey, December 19, 1960; New York, January 17, 1961; California, January 19, 1961; Oregon, January 27, 1961; Maryland, January 30, 1961; Idaho, January 31, 1961; Maine, January 31, 1961; Minnesota, January 31, 1961; New Mexico, February 1, 1961; Nevada, February 2, 1961; Montana, February 6, 1961; Colorado, February 8, 1961; Washington, February 9, 1961; West Virginia, February 9, 1961; Alaska, February 10, 1961; Wyoming, February 13, 1961; South Dakota, February 14, 1961; Delaware, February 20, 1961; Utah, February 21, 1961; Wisconsin, February 21, 1961; Pennsylvania, February 28, 1961; Indiana, March 3, 1961; North Dakota, March 3, 1961; Tennessee, March 6, 1961; Michigan, March 8, 1961; Connecticut, March 9, 1961; Arizona, March 10, 1961; Illinois, March 14, 1961; Nebraska, March 15, 1961; Vermont, March 15, 1961; Iowa, March 16, 1961; Missouri, March 20, 1961; Oklahoma, March 21, 1961; Rhode Island, March 22, 1961; Kansas, March 29, 1961; Ohio, March 29, 1961, and New Hampshire, March 30, 1961.

[16] The Twenty-fourth Amendment was proposed by Congress on September 14, 1962, having passed the House on August 27, 1962. *Cong. Rec.* (87th Cong., 2d Sess.) 17670 and having previously passed the Senate on March 27, 1962. *Id.*, 5105. It appears officially in 76 Stat. 1259. Ratification was completed on January 23, 1964, when the thirty-eighth State (South Dakota) approved the Amendment, there being then 50 States in the Union. On February 4, 1964, Bernard L. Boutin, Administrator of General Services, certified that it had been adopted by the requisite number of States. 25 *Fed. Reg.* 1717. President Lyndon B. Johnson signed this certificate.

Thirty-eight state legislatures ratified the Twenty-fourth Amendment on the following dates: Illinois, November 14, 1962; New Jersey, December 3, 1962; Oregon, January 25, 1963; Montana, January 28, 1963; West Virginia, February 1, 1963; New York, February 4, 1963; Maryland, February 6, 1963; California, February 7, 1963; Alaska, February 11, 1963; Rhode Island, February 14, 1963; Indiana, February 19, 1963; Michigan, February 20, 1963; Utah, February 20, 1963; Colorado, February 21, 1963; Minnesota, February 27, 1963; Ohio, February 27, 1963; New Mexico, March 5, 1963; Hawaii, March 6, 1963; North

for electors for President or Vice President, or for Senator or Representative in Congress, shall not be denied or abridged by the United States or any State by reason of failure to pay any poll tax or other tax.

SECTION. 2. The Congress shall have power to enforce this article by appropriate legislation.

AMENDMENT [XXV.] [17]

SECTION 1. In case of the removal of the President from office or of his death or resignation, the Vice President shall become President.

SECTION. 2. Whenever there is a vacancy in the office of the Vice President, the President shall nominate a Vice President who shall take office upon confirmation by a majority vote of both Houses of Congress.

Dakota, March 7, 1963; Idaho, March 8, 1963; Washington, March 14, 1963; Vermont, March 15, 1963; Nevada, March 19, 1963; Connecticut, March 20, 1963; Tennessee, March 21, 1963; Pennsylvania, March 25, 1963; Wisconsin, March 26, 1963; Kansas, March 28, 1963; Massachusetts, March 28, 1963; Nebraska, April 4, 1963; Florida, April 18, 1963; Iowa, April 24, 1963; Delaware, May 1, 1963; Missouri, May 13, 1963; New Hampshire, June 16, 1963; Kentucky, June 27, 1963; Maine, January 16, 1964; South Dakota, January 23, 1964.

[17] This Amendment was proposed by the Eighty-ninth Congress by Senate Joint Resolution No. 1, which was approved by the Senate on February 19, 1965, and by the House of Representatives, in amended form, on April 13, 1965. The House of Representatives agreed to a Conference Report on June 30, 1965, and the Senate agreed to the Conference Report on July 6, 1965. It was declared by the Administrator of General Services, on February 23, 1967, to have been ratified.

This Amendment was ratified by the following States:

Nebraska, July 12, 1965; Wisconsin, July 13, 1965; Oklahoma, July 16, 1965; Massachusetts, August 9, 1965; Pennsylvania, August 18, 1965; Kentucky, September 15, 1965; Arizona, September 22, 1965; Michigan, October 5, 1965; Indiana, October 20, 1965; California, October 21, 1965; Arkansas, November 4, 1965; New Jersey, November 29, 1965; Delaware, December 7, 1965; Utah, January 17, 1966; West Virginia, January 20, 1966; Maine, January 24, 1966; Rhode Island, January 28, 1966; Colorado, February 3, 1966; New Mexico, February 3, 1966; Kansas, February 8, 1966; Vermont, February 10, 1966; Alaska, February 18, 1966; Idaho, March 2, 1966; Hawaii, March 3, 1966; Virginia, March 8, 1966; Mississippi, March 10, 1966; New York, March 14, 1966; Maryland, March 23, 1966; Mis-

SECTION. 3. Whenever the President transmits to the President pro tempore of the Senate and the Speaker of the House of Representatives has written declaration that he is unable to discharge the powers and duties of his office, and until he transmits to them a written declaration to the contrary, such powers and duties shall be discharged by the Vice President as Acting President.

SECTION. 4. Whenever the Vice President and a majority of either the principal officers of the executive departments or of such other body as Congress may by law provide, transmit to the President pro tempore of the Senate and the Speaker of the House of Representatives their written declaration that the President is unable to discharge the powers and duties of his office, the Vice President shall immediately assume the powers and duties of the office as Acting President.

Thereafter, when the President transmits to the President pro tempore of the Senate and the Speaker of the House of Representatives has written declaration that no inability exists, he shall resume the powers and duties of his office unless the Vice President and a majority of either the principal officers of the executive department or of such other body as Congress may by law provide, transmit within four days to the President pro tempore of the Senate and the Speaker of the House of Representatives their written declaration that the President is unable

souri, March 30, 1966; New Hampshire, June 13, 1966; Louisiana, July 5, 1966; Tennessee, January 12, 1967; Wyoming, January 25, 1967; Washington, January 26, 1967; Iowa, January 26, 1967; Oregon, February 2, 1967; Minnesota, February 10, 1967; Nevada, February 10, 1967; Connecticut, February 14, 1967; Montana, February 15, 1967; South Dakota, March 6, 1967; Ohio, March 7, 1967; Alabama, March 14, 1967; North Carolina, March 22, 1967 Illinois, March 22, 1967; Texas, April 25, 1967; Florida, May 25, 1967.

Publication of the certifying statement of the Administrator of General Services that the Amendment had become valid was made on February 25, 1967, F.R. Doc. 67–2208, 32 *Fed. Reg.* 3287.

to discharge the powers and duties of his office. Thereupon Congress shall decide the issue, assembling within forty-eight hours for that purpose if not in session. If the Congress, within twenty-one days after receipt of the latter written declaration, or, if Congress is not in session, within twenty-one days after Congress is required to assemble, determines by two-thirds vote of both Houses that the President is unable to discharge the powers and duties of his office, the Vice President shall continue to discharge the same as Acting President; otherwise, the President shall resume the powers and duties of his office.

AMENDMENT [XXVI] [18]

SECTION 1. The right of citizens of the United States, who are eighteen years of age or older, to vote shall not be denied or abridged by the United States or by any State on account of age.

SECTION 2. The Congress shall have power to enforce this article by appropriate legislation.

---

[18] The Twenty-sixth Amendment was proposed by Congress on March 23, 1971, upon passage by the House of Representatives, the Senate having previously passed an identical resolution on March 10, 1971. It appears officially in 85 Stat. 825. Ratification was completed on July 1, 1971, when action by the legislature of the 38th State, North Carolina, was concluded, and the Administrator of the General Services Administration officially certified it to have been duly ratified on July 5, 1971. 36 *Fed. Reg.* 12725.

As of the publication of this volume, 42 States had ratified this Amendment:

Connecticut, March 23, 1971; Delaware, March 23, 1971; Minnesota, March 23, 1971; Tennessee, March 23, 1971; Washington, March 23, 1971; Hawaii, March 24, 1971; Massachusetts, March 24, 1971; Montana, March 29, 1971; Arkansas, March 30, 1971; Idaho, March 30, 1971; Iowa, March 30, 1971; Nebraska, April 2, 1971; New Jersey, April 3, 1971; Kansas, April 7, 1971; Michigan, April 7, 1971; Alaska, April 8, 1971; Maryland, April 8, 1971; Indiana, April 8, 1971; Maine, April 9, 1971; Vermont, April 16, 1971; Louisiana, April 17, 1971; California, April 19, 1971; Colorado, April 27, 1971; Pennsylvania, April 27, 1971; Texas, April 27, 1971; South Carolina, April 28, 1971; West Virginia, April 28, 1971; New Hampshire, May 13, 1971; Arizona, May 14, 1971; Rhode Island, May 27, 1971; New York, June 2, 1971; Oregon, June 4, 1971; Missouri, June 14, 1971; Wisconsin, June 22, 1971; Illinois, June 29, 1971; Alabama, June 30, 1971; Ohio, June 30, 1971; North Carolina, July 1, 1971; Oklahoma, July 1, 1971; Virginia, July 8, 1971; Wyoming, July 8, 1971; Georgia, October 4, 1971.

THE FEDERALISTS: 1789-1801

CREATING A NATION

The design of the American Constitution was one of the great political achievements of the revolutionary generation—a group comprised of the most remarkable men the country has produced; but the Constitution did not create a government, it only established the framework within which a government could be created, and the framework was recognized even by all concerned as an experiment.

One piece of work the new government found necessary to undertake was the completion of unfinished business left from the Constitutional Convention. The Constitution did not mention a cabinet, it merely provided that the President "may require written opinions of the heads of his departments," but the system proved so cumbersome that Cabinet meetings gradually evolved in the Washington administration. The Constitution provided for a court system, but it was one of the sketchiest parts of the document and it was up to the Washington administration to implement the provision. Congress thus passed the Judiciary Act in 1789 creating a three-level Federal court system with thirteen district courts at the bottom, three circuit courts and the Supreme Court at the top. It was not clear how the Constitution's dictum that the Senate should "advise and consent" should be implemented, and at one point Washington gave the Senate an uncomfortable moment by strolling into the chambers for a consultation. The House spent time in bitter debate on whether the President could remove officials without Senatorial approval and it took the prestige of Vice-President Adams and his tie-breaking vote in the Senate to pass a bill which permitted the President unilateral power of removal.

The most important task which Congress assumed in completing the work of the Constitutional Convention was passing the Bill of Rights, the first ten amendments to the Constitution. Many who believed the Constitution to be basically sound, had opposed it only because it included no such bill. Others had supported the Constitution on the basis that a bill of rights would be added. It was James Madison whose influence at the Convention was so great he has come

George Washington *in his later years.*

to be known as the Father of the Constitution, who undertook the job of organizing the bill and engineering its passage by Congress. At the onset, 210 amendments had been suggested. Madison whittled these down to eighty and then to nineteen, which in the course of debate in the House and Senate were further reduced to twelve. After approval by both Houses, the twelve were sent out to the states for their approval with the result that North Carolina and Rhode Island ratified the Constitution and became a part of the Union. By the end of 1791 a sufficient number of states had ratified ten out of the twelve amendments that they became a part of the Constitution. The Bill of Rights, as finally adopted, protected freedom of religion, of speech, and of the press, and the right to assemble, to petition the government, to bear arms, to be tried by jury, and to enjoy other procedural safeguards and civil rights.

Vital to the new government was a sound financial structure and in this task Washington's brilliant Secretary of the Treasury, Alexander Hamilton, proved to be a financial wizard and one of the most able statesmen in American History.

Hamilton had been one of the least democratic members of the Constitutional Convention, fearing direct rule by the people and desiring a system of government based on the British tradition. He advocated that the President and Senators be elected for life and believed that because the masses were "ever turbulent and changing" their share in the government should be greatly restricted. He worked ceaselessly for the adoption of the Constitution, however, and once it was adopted turned his talents toward serving the new government. He brought to Washington's Cabinet an easy command of the most subtle and intricate matters of finance, an abiding commitment to make his adopted country great, and held the complete confidence of President Washington.

Hamilton's grand design for America's future rested on three interrelated principles: the need for a strong national government, the necessity of a sound financial structure and a viable economy, and the need to tie the rich and well born to the national government in order to give it the strength without which, he was convinced, the experiment in republicanism would fail. To achieve his ends Hamilton made a number of proposals which, again, were all interrelated: The debts incurred during the Revolution and under the Confederation must be assumed; a sound currency system should be established; an adequate revenue system must be developed; and the country should embark upon a long-range plan for economic growth and diversification of its economy to be encouraged and promoted by the national government.

One of the first problems to be confronted was that of the national debt, much of which was owed to foreign powers and some to citizens of the states. There was general agreement in Congress with Hamilton that the debt should be retired, but a storm of protest broke out over his suggestion that the debt should be funded at full value. Many of the notes were no longer in the hands of their original owners, having been bought up by speculators for as low as ten to twenty percent of their value. After heated debate Congress passed the funding proposal, but the decision unfortunately opened the way for skullduggery. Profiteers hurried into the rural areas ahead of the news, buying the depreciated notes from farmers and war veterans for a song. Although Hamilton has been accused of lining his own pockets in this way, he was never a wealthy man and died heavily in debt. It is well known, however, that his Assistant Secretary and other men in government profited personally from their foreknowledge of the funding proposal.

Amid salvos *from cannon and bright flying flags, Washington completes his jubilant inaugural journey from Mt. Vernon to New York, as depicted in this 19th century painting.*

Hamilton was also criticized for not seeking out the original holders of the securities, but such a course would have been impossible. In retrospect it is clear that Hamilton's goal and his methods were those that were needed, because the funding of the entire debt at the original value and to the current holders of securities, helped to establish the credit of the United States more securely than any piecemeal measures possibly could have and at a time when financial creditability was an absolute economic necessity. Funding also helped to achieve Hamilton's other objectives, those of strengthening the national government and of cementing relationships between the national government and the monied interests.

Congress next took under consideration Hamilton's proposal that the national government assume the debts which the states had incurred during the war. The proposal met with immediate and vocal opposition which came from a broader front than had the opposition to the funding of the national debt. It was obvious to many that the financial interests were those who were benefiting most from the funding measure and they would now gain additional advantages. For the national government to assume the debts of all states on an equal basis seemed unfair to those states which had already paid off most of their obligations, such as Virginia, and would now be asked to pay additional taxes to assume

Many people wondered *if the nation would ever achieve unity, when a meeting held in the Maryland capitol, pictured here, to discuss trade problems only drew five delegates from the thirteen states.*

the debts of those states (Massachusetts, for instance) which were still heavily burdened. The struggle over the assumption of state debts took on the semblance of a North-South conflict, and was only ended by some old-fashioned horse-trading. Jefferson agreed to muster enough Southern votes for assumption if Hamilton would return the favor by securing votes to locate the Federal Capitol along the Potomac River. There is little question that the assumption of state debts furthered all three of Hamilton's objectives and his most unique contribution was the manner in which he used both funding and assumption as an asset for revitalizing the failing financial circulatory system of the country.

Most of the revenues to operate the government, according to Hamilton, should come from tariff duties, but he desired these duties to be levied with an eye not only to revenue but to protecting and/or encouraging American industry. The measures passed by Congress, however, were for revenue alone and Hamilton's desire to safeguard native industry by means of protective tariffs was not accepted until after the War of 1812. Since some additional revenue was needed beyond that produced by the tariff, Hamilton recommended, and Congress passed, an excise tax on spiritous liquors.

The Whiskey Tax, as the latter became known, was particularly offensive to the men of the western regions who violated the law in much the same manner as the New Englanders had earlier resisted the Stamp Tax or the Tea Tax imposed by England. Just as sugar and molasses were key ingredients in the economy of the New Englander before the Revolution, so was whiskey in the economy of the farmer of western Pennsylvania. Transportation of corn or wheat over the mountains was almost impossible, and even sending it down the Ohio and Mississippi Rivers was not economical. Thus much of the crash crop went into distilled liquors to reduce the bulky bushels of grain to proportions that could be economically transported or which could be used as a convenient item of barter in an area short of money. Although Hamilton was concerned about furthering the interest of the industrial and commercial sections of America he was not interested in the problems of the western farmer except as they related to the westerner's loyalty to the United States government. The Whiskey tax, he believed would bring an awareness of the central government to the independent states' rights advocates of the west who had not voted for the Constitution and thus further enhance the authority of the new government. It took a minor rebellion, the Whiskey Rebellion, and thousands of troops under Washington and Hamilton, who over-reacted, to enforce the act, but it did strengthen the prestige of the national government, although not that of the Federalist Party.

Hamilton proposed a Bank of the United States as the capstone of his financial system. Hamilton's knowledge of the existing banks in the United States convinced him that they were neither adequate nor trustworthy for national purposes and he chose the Bank of England for his model. The system he envisioned would incorporate a private bank chartered for twenty years with capitalization of ten million dollars, one-fifth of the stock to be subscribed by the national government. The bank, once organized, would issue its notes as loans to private citizens and thus provide the nation with a stable circulation of paper money. As further insurance of stability, the government would accept notes of the United States Bank at par for all taxes and other obligations due it, and the bank would serve as the government's depository and fiscal agent. An integral part of the plan was the manner in which Hamilton was proposing to make the public debt the basis for a sound money system.

The Bank issue was hotly contested and brought that division of political reactions which would develop into the Federalist and the Republic parties.

On April 30, 1789, *Washington was inaugurated as the first President of the United States. He is shown here speaking to the spectators who attended the inaugural.*

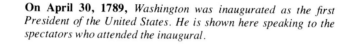

Washington *on his inaugural day.*

Congressmen from the areas south of the Potomac (except those from South Carolina) voted against the bank; most of those from the northeast and a majority from the middle states supported it. Jefferson expressed his opposition on the grounds that the Tenth Amendment to the Constitution prohibited the national government from exercising any power not "expressly" delegated to it, that all such power had been reserved to the states or to the people. Jefferson's position came to be known as the "strict constructionist" interpretation of the Constitution, a position which Hamilton answered by the "loose constructionist" doctrine. Hamilton's position was based on Article 1, Section 8 of the Constitution, "Congress shall have power . . . to enact laws necessary and proper for carrying into effect the foregoing powers . . ." It seemed clear to Hamilton that if the Constitution had granted the Federal Government the power to borrow money, to collect taxes, to coin money, and to regulate the "value thereof" a national bank was not only proper but necessary and Congress would be fully justified in establishing a Bank of the United States. Hamilton's views won out both with Congress and with a troubled President, and Washington reluctantly signed the bill into law.

The final proposal in the Hamiltonian system, contained in his Report on Manufactures, was never adopted. Hamilton was interested in diversifying the

Alexander Hamilton

American economy so that there would be a balance which included manufacture along with agriculture and commerce. He believed that only through such a balance could the United States reduce its foreign debt and its reliance on foreign nations, and attain true independence. To achieve these ends Hamilton proposed a scheme of protective tariffs and bounties which would make investments in industry attractive. America, however, was a nation of farmers and the farmers, and many of the merchants, feared that protective tariffs would prompt retaliatory action by other countries against American exports. Furthermore they preferred free competition to keep down the price of manufactured goods. Others wondered if Americans could afford a tariff system that would reduce imports since the government's principal income came from import duties. Moved by such considerations Congress shelved Hamilton's report.

Forty years after most of the Hamiltonian system had been adopted Daniel Webster paid eloquent tribute to Hamilton declaring, *"He smote the rock of the national resources, and abundant streams of revenue gushed forth. He touched the dead corpse of public credit, and it sprung upon its feet."* But it is not only the financial policy per se for which he is remembered, for the dynamic Secretary, still under forty years of age when he retired in 1795, had also strengthened the government politically during the first crucial years of its existence and did as much to create the American nation as the accomplishments of any other. His goal of building a strong industrial nation was decades ahead of its time, but as America moved in that direction during the second half of the nineteenth century Hamilton was fondly recalled as the founding father who had most clearly foreseen the economic direction of the country and who had been the most responsible for establishing and articulating policies which would further that growth. If Hamilton had understood the development of democratic America as well as the development of fiscal policies, his contributions to his adopted country would have been even greater and, ironically, he helped pave the way for Jefferson's election in 1800 by his impolitic actions during the preceding four years. His earlier contributions, however, cannot be overstressed. He helped create a nation; Jefferson was to help assure that the nation would be a democracy.

DISSENSION WITHIN AND WITHOUT

Hamilton's policies divided the country. It was clear that the financial interests had gained the most from the funding of the national debt and the assumption of state debts. Almost all the stock in the United States Bank was purchased by Northern and European creditors, and Hamilton made it clear that the bank was intended to facilitate the expansion of industry and commerce, not agriculture. He would not even consider a suggestion that the bank lend money to Southern planters on the security of tobacco warehouse receipts. Hamilton's loose construction of the Constitution dismayed others, and by the end of Washington's first term in office the differences between Hamilton on the one hand and Jefferson and Madison on the other was about as wide as government under the Constitution would permit. Washington, however, had stood above the conflict and both sides urged him to accept another term when elections were held in 1792.

The split between the Federalists and the Republicans, as they were now calling themselves, was widened during Washington's second term because of an increasingly bitter debate over foreign policies. For the remainder of the decade, in fact up through the War of 1812, much of American foreign policy was based on the desire to maintain American rights while keeping out of the European wars which had been precipitated by the French Revolution. At times these became total conflicts in which any power attempting to remain neutral found its ships and merchandise confiscated by one side or the other, and at times by both sides. The party division over these problems was accentuated by the open attempt of the French to solicit support for the French Revolution within the United States and by the fact that Revolution was viewed by the Republicans as seeking the same goals as those achieved by the American Revolution but were considered by the Federalists as abhorrent to everything for which they stood.

Neither the Republicans nor Federalists, at the outset, wanted war, and both were committed to the general policy laid down by Washington of neutrality in European affairs in order to preserve peace for the United States, a peace which most men were convinced was essential if the young republic was to survive. But neutrality meant widely different things to the two contending parties. Hamilton had always held the British government in high esteem. Even more important he recognized that the American economy was closely related to British trade, had tied his funding program to duties on that trade, and was reluctant to do anything that might offend England. From a practical viewpoint he was aware that the strength of the British navy made a challenge against England more dangerous than one against France. Hamilton also had strong aversion to the French Revolution, which he felt was overturning the foundations of society—destroying the stability that had been achieved through monarchy and aristocracy by exalting democracy and demagoguery. His horror mounted when the French Revolution launched the "war of all peoples against all kings," with England as one of the chief targets.

Jefferson, on the other hand, had been the American minister to France and had learned to admire French civilization and the French people. At first he was skeptical that their revolution would meet with success since they had lived so long under monarchy, but he became increasingly enthusiastic over their main goal which appeared to be the creation of a democratic society similar to the one he hoped to see in the United States. Furthermore, the United States had made treaties with France in 1778 under which the French had provided the aid so desperately needed to defeat the British, and Jefferson argued that those treaties having been made with the French nation were still binding even though the King had been overthrown. Where Hamilton wanted the United States to declare its neutrality as a means of scrapping the French alliance, Jefferson believed that America would retain greater bargaining power if neutrality were not made official. President Washington issued a proclamation of neutrality, but did not repudiate the French treaties. This compromise did not satisfy Jefferson who believed that all necessary bargaining power had been lost and he angrily resigned from the Office of Secretary of State at the end of that year, 1793.

The first results of the Hamiltonian policy were to be seen in the Jay Treaty, signed by Washington in 1795. Although Hamilton had also resigned from the Cabinet by that time, his influence was as great as when he had served as Secretary of the Treasury, and in the case of the Jay Treaty that influence was to be felt before the treaty was even negotiated. The United States had serious grievances with England and war hysteria was running high. Washington sent John Jay on a special mission to England to avert war if possible. Hamilton first persuaded

An early cartoon *which tells the story of an excise man and the fate that will befall him in the form of tar and feathers and eventual hanging.*

Washington to decline an invitation from other neutral powers that could have helped pressure England into making concessions, and then notified the British minister in America of President Washington's decision and of the general friendly attitude of the United States toward England. Because of this advance information, Jay lost all bargaining power and found it necessary to settle for an agreement in which England won on all major issues. The American public, even many Federalists, were inflamed over the results. A typical toast of the time was "Damn John Jay! Damn everyone who won't Damn John Jay! Damn everyone who won't put out lights in his windows and sit up all night Damning John Jay." After considerable delay Washington reluctantly signed the treaty and, in so doing preserved the peace so necessary to the economic development of the country, but hardly on honorable terms and at the expense of further alienating the Republicans.

Hamilton further weakened the Federalist party by his attempt to manipulate the electoral vote in the 1796 election. It had been understood that if Washington chose not to run, his Vice-President John Adams would be the Federalist candidate because Hamilton, although influential among politicians in the party, did not have enough popular support to assure his own election. Hamilton did not feel he could renounce Adams publicly, but thought that the right political tactics might elevate the Federalist's Vice-Presidential candidate, Thomas Pinckney of South Carolina, to the Presidency. Adams won the election but he was all too aware of how close he had come to defeat, and that Hamilton was responsible. Throughout the first years of his administration, Adams was continually handicapped because three of his cabinet members showed a marked loyalty to Hamilton which affected his presidential policies but he felt he could not remove them since they had been appointed by the country's national hero, George Washington.

During the administration of John Adams, 1797-1801, the Federalists continued to alienate the Republicans by their policies, particularly by passing three oppressive measures, the Alien, Sedition, and Naturalization Acts. The three measures were the result of an increasing fear on the part of the Federalists over French influences in America, and the growing power of the Republicans who were sympathetic to the French cause. There were many refugees from the French Revolution coming to the United States and some of them were radicals who expressed their ideas with a facility that was venomous and persuasive. The Federalists, who were already agitated by the stinging criticism of the Republicans, saw no reason why the United States should have to tolerate these atheistic demagogues who had no loyalty to the Federalist regime. The Naturalization Act prolonged the time of residence required for citizenship from five years to fourteen. The Alien Acts gave the government the right to deport aliens or to license individuals to reside in some particular locality. The Sedition Act provided penalties for seditious activity on the part of aliens or citizens.

The Sedition Act was the most obnoxious to many and was used without much restraint in suppressing the Republican press. Under the Act, twenty-four Republican editors were arrested, including four of the most able journalists in America. Of the dozens of others who fell victim to the law, Matthew Lyons, Congressman from Vermont, was the most prominent. He was sentenced to four months in jail and fined one thousand dollars for asserting that President Adams "had turned men out of office for partisan reasons" and for referring to the President's "continued grasp for power" and his "unbounded thirst for ridiculous pomp, foolish adulation, and selfish avarice." David Brown, an illiterate Revolutionary soldier, helped erect a liberty pole which stated, "No Stamp Act, no Sedition, no Alien Bills . . ." and was sentenced under the Sedition Act to eighteen months in jail and fined four hundred dollars. Since he was unable to pay his fine he remained in jail for two years until pardoned by Jefferson.

Although the excuse for the Sedition Act had been the radicalism of the French, the blatant political purpose of the act was revealed on the date it was to expire: March 3, 1801, when the next President would be inaugurated. The act would be in force long enough to gag Republican criticism of the Administration until the next election was over but would expire soon enough to permit Federalist criticism in case the election brought in a Republican President.

Jefferson and Madison were alarmed, and rightly so. They retaliated by securing the passage of a series of resolutions by the Virginia and Kentucky legislatures declaring the Alien and Sedition Acts unconstitutional. The Kentucky resolution went so far as to declare the acts "void and of no force" and that "nullification" by the states was the proper remedy for unconstitutional actions by the Federal Government. But the Republicans did more than pass resolutions, they began to build a national political organization appointing county committees in the South and township committees in the North to instruct the voters on the vices of the Federalists and the virtues of their own party. Over the local committees were state committees, which in turn took direction from the national level.

The final split within the Federalist ranks came over the matter of foreign policy. The Hamiltonian faction was eager for war with France and was reorganizing and enlarging the army which was to be commanded by George Washington with Alexander Hamilton second in command. There was also evidence that this same clique which was maneuvering for war had in mind the possible use of troops against rebellious Republicans at home, too, if necessary.

At almost the last hour before he had been maneuvered into war with France, Adams took a firm stand. He sent to the Senate the nomination of William Vans Murray as minister to negotiate a new agreement with France. The war faction of the Federalist party was furious, the Republicans delighted. Eventually the negotiating team was increased to three members which upon arriving in France found Napoleon eager for conciliation. On September 30, 1800, a convention was signed that put an end to French spoliation of American Commerce, and Adams almost singlehandedly had saved his country from a needless war. Later in his life Adams wrote that he would defend his mission to France as long as he lived and when he died he desired no other inscription over his gravestone than: "Here lies John Adams, who took upon himself the responsibility of the Peace with France in the year 1800." Adams had put his nation ahead of his party, and although Hamilton could be held more responsible than Adams, the Federalists were never to win another Presidential election.

Thus, while the Republicans were increasing their strength through strong party organization at all levels, the Federalists were hampered by internal dissension within their own party. The rank and file of the party supported Adams' peace mission to France and wholeheartedly backed him for the Presidency in 1800. Hamilton, speaking for the war party, considered Adams a traitor, declared he would never again support Adams, and wrote a pamphlet attacking him. Although Adams was running for his second term and was the Federalist candidate, Hamilton again attempted to manipulate the electoral college in the hopes of obtaining more votes for the Vice-Presidential candidate than would be the case for Adams. The Republican machine, however, had worked smoothly and both Jefferson and Burr received seventy-three electoral votes compared to sixty-five for Adams and sixty-four for his running mate, Charles Cotesworth Pinckney.

It had been understood that Burr was the Vice-Presidential candidate, but since all Republican electors had voted for both Jefferson and Burr they were tied and the election was thrown into the House of Representatives. There the politicking continued through thirty-five ballots without the necessary nine-state majority for one candidate. Hamilton, who had his own score to settle with his New York rival, Burr, finally persuaded some of the latter's supporters to cast blank ballots and Jefferson was elected. Needless to say, a Constitutional amendment, the Twelfth, was immediately forthcoming which required the Electoral College to vote separately for President and Vice-President.

Before leaving office Adams made one last contribution to the nation and to the cause of the Federalist party; he appointed John Marshall as Chief Justice of the Supreme Court. Marshall, a staunch Federalist, was to bring to the Supreme Court the power and prestige which was absolutely necessary to the proper functioning of the American constitutional system, and during the years after 1800 when the Federalist party was disintegrating he continued their work of developing American nationalism.

John Adams, for all his exemplary qualities was not a great President but he was a great American. He was too tactless and immovable to be a party leader and he lacked the enthusiasm to unite his party. He was elected by his home town to the convention that framed the Massachusetts state constitution and wrote almost all of the document including the widely acclaimed bill of rights. He was a member of the mission that negotiated peace with England at the end of the revolution, and acted as the first U.S. minister to Great Britain. Before becoming

President he had held office as the Vice-President during both of George Washington's terms.

Just as he had served his country in England at the end of the American Revolution, so his son, John Quincy Adams, was to mirror his achievements by helping to negotiate the Treaty of Ghent with England after the War of 1812, and his grandson, Charles Francis Adams, was to carry on the tradition as minister to Great Britain during the troubled years of the Civil War. John Quincy is the only son of a President to have occupied that same high office and the only President to have returned to serve in Congress after leaving the White House, his service being continuous down to his death in 1848.

Although Benjamin Franklin was probably close to the truth when he said that John Adams "was always honest, often great and sometimes mad," when judged by his total contributions to the country, not just his Presidency, he must rank with Washington, Jefferson, Hamilton, Franklin, and Madison as one of the founders of the American nation, and few families can equal the contributions of the Adams.

With the election of Jefferson in 1800, the Federalist party with all its talent and virtue—and lack of political common sense—became a minority party and then disappeared altogether. It did not have the sustaining power or the necessary vision to remain nationally viable or to attract new leaders with the character of Washington, the genius of Hamilton, and the dedication of Adams. Their task, to mold an inchoate nation into an enduring union, had been accomplished, and they had built exceptionally well. Many of their principles were revived after the War of 1812 by the National Republicans, later by the Whigs, and finally by the Republican party founded in 1856. Their appeal in 1800, however, was too sectional, too largely based on the commercial and industrial interests in an essentially agrarian nation, and they relied too heavily upon the rich and well born to be effective in the developing democratic milieu—one in which Jefferson and Jackson would be much more at home.

FIRST AMENDMENT

Most cherished among our freedoms and most essential to the life of a free democracy are the liberties guaranteed us by the first amendment to the Constitution. No democracy can endure and thrive without the unabridged right to criticize its own government, in the press or mass media, in peaceable public assemblies, or as private citizens exercising the right of free speech.

Yet freedom of speech and of the press have other implications, and the concept has been repeatedly tested, refined and amplified in the courts over the last two hundred years. In areas ranging from artistic and academic freedom to problems of censorship, political dissent, the distinction between peaceable assembly and incitement to riot, the difference between a public demonstration and an alleged conspiracy to disrupt the government, and in numerous other complex and difficult Constitutional issues, the first amendment has been frequently subjected to judicial interpretation.

In the area of religious freedom, or the separation of church and state, there has been much controversy in recent years. Conscientious objection to military service on religious grounds is regarded as a Constitutional guarantee, providing the objector presents convincing proof of his religious beliefs. Alter-

John Adams *with symbols depicting his life as patriot of the Revolution, Minister to France and England, Vice-President under Washington, and President from 1797 to 1801.*

nate, non-combat service is often required of conscientious objectors in time of war, although complete exemption from military duty has been granted in certain cases. The Viet Nam war inspired both more political dissent and conscientious objections than any other American war in recent times. Among the young men to refuse military service on religious grounds was World Heavyweight boxing champion Muhammed Ali, a Muslim.

In 1963 the Supreme Court ruled unconstitutional all state and local laws requiring the recitation of prayers or readings from the Bible in public schools. The decision reasserted once more the rights of citizens not to have religion imposed upon them by their government. Supreme Court Justice Hugo L. Black wrote in the majority opinion, "It is neither sacrilegious nor antireligious to say that each separate government in this country should stay out of the business of writing or sanctioning official prayers and leave that purely religious function to the people themselves and to those the people choose to look to for religious guidance."

Created to prevent a repetition in the United States of the religious tyrannies of previous English monarchs or colonial theocracies, the first amendment clause prohibiting the establishment of a state religion allows each citizen to serve God as conscience dictates, or to live unmolested as an atheist if he so desires.

The strict abridgments of speech and of the press in England, especially before the enactment of the English Bill of Rights and the earlier Declaration of Right were among the government abuses James Madison and other framers of the Bill of Rights intended to eliminate in the United States by denying Congress the right to make laws restricting such activities. Blackstone, the noted English jurist in his famous *Commentaries* on the law insisted that the only freedom guaranteed the press was the freedom from prior restraint. Speech or writing offensive to the English Crown, government or society was punishable under the common law. Critics of the English government had been punished for centuries by fines, beatings, imprisonment and torture. Constitutional scholars still debate the exact meaning of Madison's first amendment draft, one school of experts claiming it refers to the old concepts of Blackstone, another group claiming it should be construed exactly as written.

The real or debatable ambiguities of the first amendment, however, allow new meanings to be extracted from the law which are appropriate for the times. As the problems of democracy became increasingly complex, the problems of interpreting first amendment guarantees accordingly became more difficult. Freedom of expression took surprising, unforeseen turns—motion pictures, radio, television, mass market publishing, the "underground" press, among so many other recent phenomena, all challenged the flexibility of first amendment freedoms.

Political dissent evolved through the years, finding new forms to affect the new issues. The "sit-in," the mass civil rights and antiwar demonstrations of the 1960's, the burning of draft cards, the boycotts and close-outs and scores of other methods of protest tied new legal knots for the Supreme Court to unravel. Now the national interest and security came in conflict with personal liberty and the imperatives of individual conscience as investigative news reporters revealed classified government documents, or government employees delivered such documents to the press for disclosure.

A variety of judicial opinion and diverse court decisions complicates the issues even further. Inconsistencies remain to be reconciled, and each new first

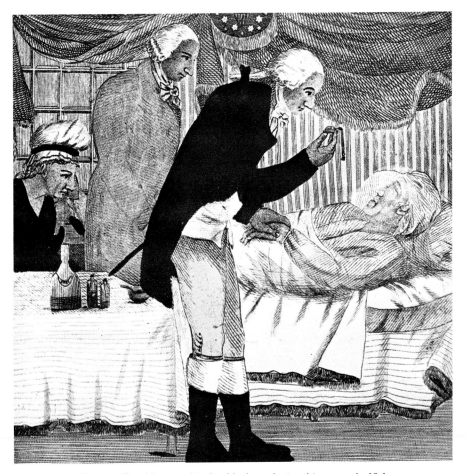

The first President *on his deathbed, as depicted in an early 19th century print. While Martha grieves nearby the two doctors keep watch over the dying Washington.*

amendment case which comes before the Supreme Court poses legal problems of immense complexity which must be resolved in accordance with the ever-changing requirements of the age.

Reduced to its essence, the first amendment guarantees a safeguard against oppression of minorities by a majority. Under dictatorships and totalitarian governments, all such first amendment guarantees are systematically denied. One need only examine the Soviet or Nazi governments with their state-controlled mass media to understand how valuable and necessary are the first amendment guarantees of free speech and freedom of the press. Among the first victims of any totalitarian regime on assuming governmental power are the writers, artists and thinkers of a nation.

First amendment liberties often conflict with public well-being. Public speakers may criticize anyone, pronounce the most unpopular views and attack our most fundamental beliefs. Yet police are obliged to protect the speaker and to maintain peace in the audience no matter how inflammatory the speaker becomes. The free speech guarantee includes the right to pronounce ethnic and racial slurs, reprehensible as such statements may be. This is the price we pay for our freedom.

Limitations, however, do exist. In the case of *Beauharnais* v. *Illinois* (1952) a lower court conviction for group libel on the basis of racist remarks published in a leaflet was upheld by the Supreme Court. Justice Felix Frankfurter in the majority opinion wrote, "… if an utterance directed at an individual may be the object of criminal sanctions, we cannot deny to a State power to punish the same utterance directed at a defined group…". Simply stated, the Supreme Court decided that a group as well as an individual may be protected from criminal libel, and such protection does not constitute an abridgement of free speech. Dissenting opinion on the case argued that "Punishment of printed words … is justifiable only if the prosecution survives the 'clear and present danger' test…".

The "clear and present danger" test refers to an earlier Supreme Court decision first delivered by Justice Oliver Wendell Holmes regarding first amendment rights and later expanded in the case of *Cantwell* v. *Connecticut* (1940). The case involved two religious evangelists convicted of solicitation for religious causes without state certification and inciting a breach of the peace. The Supreme Court decision stated,

> …No one would have the hardihood to suggest that the principle of freedom of speech sanctions incitement to riot or that religious liberty connotes the privilege to exhort others to physical attack upon those belonging to another sect. When clear and present danger of riot, disorder, interference with traffic upon the public streets, or other immediate threat to public safety, peace, or order, appears, the power of the State to prevent or punish is obvious. Equally obvious is that a State may not unduly suppress free communication of views, religious or other, under the guise of conserving desirable conditions.

The Supreme Court overturned the earlier Cantwell convictions, reasserting the "clear and present danger" principle so frequently applied more than twenty years later during the tumultuous 1960's when mass demonstrations and inflammatory rhetoric were so commonplace.

Freedom of speech has other limitations as well. Advocating a revolution is a criminal offense, although the "clear and present danger" test is not necessarily applicable. In the cast of *United States* v. *Dennis* (1950), the secretary general of the American Communist Party and ten Communist officials were convicted under the Smith Act of advocating the forcible overthrow of the government. On appeal to the U.S. Supreme Court, the lower court conviction was upheld.

The Supreme Court decision stated in part, "…We reject any principle of governmental helplessness in the face of preparation for revolution, which principle, carried to its logical conclusion, must lead to anarchy … the Smith Act … is directed at advocacy not discussion."

Here the Supreme Court asserts the individual right to discuss any idea, but denies the right to advocate violent revolution. The "clear and present danger" test is interpreted in this specific case as follows from the majority opinion, "Obviously the words [clear and present danger] cannot mean that before the Government may act, it must wait until the *putsch* is about to be executed, the plans have been laid and the signal is awaited … Certainly an attempt to overthrow the Government by force, even though doomed from the outset … is a sufficient evil for Congress to prevent."

Legal abridgements of freedom of speech may be accomplished through the existing prerogatives of Congress to establish censorship in a state of war or during national emergencies. But this Congressional privilege extends principally to areas concerned with the war effort *per se*.

In matters of local censorship of magazines, books, movies, plays and even nightclub comedians in the case of the late Lenny Bruce, a discrepancy seemed to exist between State government practice and Constitutional principle. On several important occasions in recent years the Supreme Court reversed lower court obscenity convictions, establishing a solid body of precedents which until recently allowed great latitude in the communication of sexual material.

John Marshall *was a staunch Federalist from Virginia. When he was appointed Chief Justice of the Supreme Court in 1801, the Court was so poorly respected that it was difficult to get capable men to serve as Justices. When Marshall's term ended with his death thirty-four years later, the Supreme Court had acquired equal stature with the other branches of government.*

In the landmark *Roth* v. *United States* case, the Supreme Court defined obscenity and held that it was not protected by first amendment guarantees. Sustaining a lower court conviction for mailing obscene circulars and advertising, the majority opinion stated in part,

> ... All ideas having even the slightest redeeming social importance—unorthodox ideas, controversial ideas, even ideas hateful to the prevailing climate of opinion—have the full protection of the guarantees, unless excludable because they encroach upon the limited area of more important interests. But implicit in the history of the First Amendment is the rejection of obscenity as utterly without redeeming social importance...
>
> However, sex and obscenity are not synonymous. Obscene material is material which deals with sex in a manner appealing to prurient interest ... whether to the average person, applying contemporary community standards, the dominant theme of the material taken as a whole appeals to prurient interest...

In the dissenting opinion Justice William O. Douglas wrote,

> When we sustain these convictions, we make the legality of a publication turn on the purity of thought which a book or tract instills in the mind of a reader. I do not think we can approve that standard and be faithful to the command of the First Amendment, which by its terms is a restraint on Congress...
>
> The tests by which these convictions were obtained require only the arousing of sexual thoughts. Yet the arousing of sexual thoughts and desires happens every day in normal life in dozens of ways...
>
> Any test that turns on what is offensive to the community's standards is too loose, too capricious, too destructive of freedom of expression to be squared with the First Amendment. Under that test, juries can censor, suppress and punish what they don't like, provided the matter relates to 'sexual impurity' or has a tendency to 'excite lustful thoughts.' This is community censorship in one of its worst forms...
>
> I reject too the implication that problems of freedom of speech and of the press are to be resolved by weighing against the values of free expression, the judgement of the Court that a particular form of expression has 'no redeeming social importance.'

Although the Roth case decision seemed to signal a return of censorship privileges to local officials, that impression was quickly squelched the same year by a Supreme Court decision declaring a Michigan law unconstitutional which prohibited the dissemination of materials "...tending to the corruption of the morals of youth."

Further Supreme Court decisions since the Roth case tended toward an increasing liberalization of first amendment interpretations, especially in matters of sexual materials. With the Nixon appointments of three conservative justices, however, the Supreme Court in recent years has been somewhat less liberal in first amendment decisions, and certain precedents have been revised by new interpretation.

In the case of *Miller* v. *California* (1973), the Supreme Court voted 5 to 4 to uphold a lower court obscenity conviction, asserting that adult book stores and theaters are not exempt from state regulation. The Court also stated that material may be found obscene if it lacks serious literary, artistic, political or scientific value—a substantial change from the Court's previous position that material is obscene only if utterly without redeeming social value. In the test of allegedly obscene materials offending contemporary community standards, the Court ruled that local rather than national community standards may be applied. Community censorship was thus sanctioned by the decision in a fulfillment of the prophecy made by Justice Douglas in his dissenting opinion in the Roth case.

As a consequence of the Miller case, many State and city governments began drafting new obscenity statutes and ordinances. The motion picture and publishing industries have challenged the ruling, arguing that what one community accepts as legitimate candor in expression, will be rejected by another.

The dissenting opinion in the Miller case held that the decision was an invitation to a state-controlled regimentation of our minds, leaving the determination of obscenity to "average" persons and what they understand of community morality.

Yet the same Court voted 8 to 0 that *The New York Times* and *The Washington Post* could not be prevented from printing the so-called "Pentagon Papers" on American Vietnam war policy. Although the papers were classified, the Court ruled that the government failed to show justification for prior restraint.

In 1975, on the eve of our two-hundredth year as a nation, significant Supreme Court rulings in the area of first amendment freedoms included a decision declaring unconstitutional a Jacksonville, Florida law banning nudity films in drive in theaters that are visible from public places. Such a restrictive law, declared the Court, is an abridgement of free speech. By contrast, however, the Court also decided to uphold a Santa Barbara, California law prohibiting nudity in public parks, beaches and streets.

The Constitution of the United States is extremely flexible and responsive to contemporary requirements, and new interpretations of first amendment principles are bound to occur in the years to come. Yet the Constitution is difficult to amend and its fundamental guarantees are inviolate.

Justice William O. Douglas, recently retired from the Supreme Court after the longest term of service in history, wrote the following regarding first amendment liberties:

"Free speech and free press—not space ships or automobiles—are the important symbols of western civilization. In material things the communist world will in time catch up. But no totalitarian regime can afford free speech and a free press. Ideas are dangerous—the most dangerous things in the world because they are haunting and enduring. Those committed to democracy live dangerously for they stand committed never to still a voice in protest or a pen in rebellion."

As America begins its third century as a nation, advancing into the future with all its uncertainties, among all the coming changes one thing must remain unchanged: our complete commitment to the original principles upon which our freedoms were constructed.

Thomas Jefferson, *third President of the United States.*

DEMOCRACY TAKES ROOT

With independence from England, America continued to broaden and deepen her system of self-government. Although many members of the Constitutional Convention were opposed to democracy, and the Constitution when it was eventually adopted established a republic not a democracy, it was flexible enough to allow for the expansion of the democratic concepts which had been sown in the earlier periods. It was Thomas Jefferson, more than any other, who fashioned and perfected the ideas that resulted in democracy; and it was during the presidency of Andrew Jackson that America, with the serious exception of the institution of slavery, became fully established as a functioning democratic nation.

THOMAS JEFFERSON, FATHER OF DEMOCRACY

Thomas Jefferson, the third child of Peter and Jane Randolph Jefferson, was born into a family that represented all that was best in eighteenth century Virginia. His father was one of those sturdy men who helped break the wilderness, a man of prodigious strength, hard working and God-fearing, who surveyed unbroken land, felled trees, cleared fields, and established himself by the age of thirty-one as a man of property. Jefferson's mother, Jane Randolph, came from one of the more prestigious families of Virginia bringing with her all the social, cultural, and political privileges of the Virginia elite. Although Peter Jefferson died when Thomas was fourteen, he had already inspired his son with a love of learning, a spirit of discipline and hard work, and a zest for vigorous outdoor life.

At William and Mary College, young Jefferson displayed a keen thirst for knowledge and an unrestrained curiosity that was a delight to his professors. It was his good fortune that among their ranks he discovered a small group of men who not only befriended him but challenged his mind, men who were to leave their lasting imprint upon America through their apt pupil. After two years he left college to study law, and at the age of twenty-four was admitted to the bar. He was not by temperament and interest cut out for the legal profession, but in spite of this became a successful attorney and his practice and income grew apace. A happy marriage to Martha Wayles Skelton soon brought added advantage in the form of her inheritance of 40,000 acres of land and one hundred and thirty-five slaves, doubling the Jefferson estate and making Thomas Jefferson at the age of twenty-eight one of the wealthiest planters of Virginia. The outward signs of wealth were misleading, however, for he had to support a family of thirty-four persons as well as several hundred slaves, and the income barely balanced the upkeep and expenses.

The Virginia aristocracy had a keen sense of political responsibility and almost as a matter of course Thomas Jefferson ran for and was elected to the House of Burgesses. As one of the younger and more humble members of that body, his contributions were relatively insignificant until 1773 when he became a member of the party of resistance to England and, before long, one of its most able leaders. He was among the organizers of the Committee of Correspondence, and also a member of the rump assembly which gathered in the Raleigh Tavern to propose that all the colonies should ''meet together in a united congress''; and the author of *A Summary View of the Rights of British America*.

Reproduction *of an oil painting of Thomas Jefferson, whose social philosophy defined and shaped much of the American Constitution.*

He displayed a polished statesmanship as a member of the Second Continental Congress, and his brilliance flared into magnificence as the author of the Declaration of Independence. During the Revolution he was active in the Virginia House of Delegates and, during the two blackest years of the war, was governor. Later he served as Minister to France, Secretary of State, Vice-President under John Adams, and of course, President of the United States for two terms.

No other American has had a more distinguished career in the service of his country, yet it is the political philosophy that was his most lasting contribution. The development of American democracy has been a gradual realization of the implications of Jeffersonian political philosophy. Both the Jacksonians and the Whigs claimed to be his spiritual descendants, Lincoln based his own philosophy on the Declaration of Independence and considered the principles as laid down by Jefferson to be the "definitions and axioms of free society." The Populists re-affirmed Jeffersonian agrarian democracy, and urban progressive thought, particularly as set forth in the classic speeches and essays of Woodrow Wilson, was a twentieth century exemplification of Jefferson's heritage to America.

It was in the crucible of the Revolutionary period that Jefferson began to give expression to the ideas that had been formulating since college in his fertile mind. The motto which he adopted during that time, "Resistance to Tyrants is obedience to God," was a sure clue to the immediate direction this expression would take. In *The Summary View*, written in 1774, he contended that originally in England the ancestors of the British Americans had been free, just as their remote Saxon forefathers had been, and that they had a natural right to emigrate and establish laws of their own in America, just as the Saxons had in England. He claimed that there was a compact between the colonists and the King embodied in the early charters, which had imposed restric-

tions on royal power. He concluded that free trade with all parts of the world was a natural right belonging to the colonists. His position may not have been historically sound, but it was essentially a theory of "imperial partnership"—a commonwealth of nations—a position which Britain would eventually accept, although long after the Revolution. At the time of its first publication, *The Summary View* was too bold to be approved by his fellow Virginians and was sufficiently radical to cause the British Parliament to put Jefferson's name on a bill of attainder for prosecution.

As a member of the Second Continental Congress, Jefferson was appointed to the committee to draw up the Declaration of Independence and was unanimously elected by his colleagues to serve as author of the document. Although it went through several drafts with changes proposed by other members, it was essentially Jefferson's work and the principles it expressed were exemplified throughout his life. That "all men are created equal" was one of those principles and, in a letter to a friend, he underscored his position, stating that he was ready "to say to every human being 'thou are my brother', and to offer him the hand of concord and amity."

Many have contended that Jefferson's "self-evident" truth of man's equality was in reality a self-evident lie, but Jefferson was not referring to a biological or psychological equality, only to political equality, that man was born with the right to enjoy the same political privileges and human opportunities as his neighbor. He explained this stand when he wrote to John Adams, saying that there was "a natural aristocracy among men," adding that the grounds for this aristocracy were not wealth or heredity as in Europe, but "virtue and talents," and *that* aristocracy he considered "as the most precious gift of nature, for the instruction, the trust, and government of society." Yet to uphold equality so staunchly while at the very same time employing slave labor seems quite inconsistent; but the tenor of the times and the complexities of his way of life prevented him from doing more than being one of the first to work earnestly toward the abolition of slavery in Virginia. He never reconciled himself to the institution and in 1814 wrote: "The love of justice and the love of country plead equally the cause of these people, and it is a moral reproach to us that they should have pleaded

Monticello, *Thomas Jefferson's home in Albemarle, Virginia, was designed by him along the classical line of European buildings and was erected in 1768. It was remodeled several times and was not completed until 1809. Many of the mechanical devices invented by Jefferson are at Monticello, including a revolving desk and a calendar clock.*

The formal dining room at Monticello. The room is laid out to catch the afternoon sunlight.

The 18 foot ceiling of the parlor at Monticello and the parquet floors reflect a distinctively French decor. Jefferson, in addition to designing the structure, took a close hand in the decorating of Monticello.

so long in vain.'' At another time he referred to ''the whole commerce between master and slave as a perpetual exercise of the most boisterous passions, the most unremitting despotism on the one part, and degrading submissions on the other.''

One of the inalienable rights listed in the Declaration of Independence is that of liberty. As with his conviction on the equality of man, Jefferson constantly emphasized that ''the God that gave us life gave us liberty at the same time.'' He wrote: ''We acknowledge that our children are born free, that freedom is the gift of nature, and not of him who begot them;'' and later heightened this by saying, ''There are rights which it is useless to surrender to the government. . . . These are rights of thinking, and publishing our thoughts by speaking or writing; the right of free commerce and the right of personal freedom.'' No one was more maligned by the press than was Jefferson, yet none was more consistent in upholding the absolute necessity of ensuring a free press in a democratic society.

Jefferson had written in the Declaration: ''life, liberty and the pursuit of happiness,'' unlike the British political philosopher John Locke, who had written of: ''life, liberty and property.'' Jefferson's use of the inclusive phrase ''the pursuit of happiness'' was deliberate. He took for granted the right to own property; he felt that property, like government, was indispensable, but both were the means to an end. By elevating the end, *happiness*, above the means, *property*, he established a new goal for political institutions.

The entire Declaration was based on the social contract theory, that governments are established for the benefit of man upon a contract drawn up between man and that government. ''. . . whenever any form of government becomes destructive of these ends,'' he wrote, ''it is the right of the people to alter or to abolish it, and to institute a new govern-

Reproduction *of an oil painting of Andrew Jackson, posed as the philosopher/soldier.*

This political cartoon *published during the Presidential campaign of 1828, was captioned, "Jackson is to be President and you will be hanged."*

ment." So firmly did he believe in this principle that he suggested a new constitution should be written every twenty years, so that each generation should have the right to establish its own laws. Along these same lines, although he was by nature too peace-loving to advocate bloodshed, he suggested that a little revolution now and then might be a good thing. As President he insisted upon paying the national debt since ". . . one generation of men cannot foreclose or burden its use to another, which comes to it in its own right and by the same beneficence."

The social contract theory as accepted by Jefferson and exemplified in the Declaration, was based on an optimistic view of human nature, and if there is any one doctrine that is fundamental to Jeffersonian democracy, it is his emphasis on the basic goodness of man. Jefferson was too much the practical politician to overlook the seamy side of man's character, as is attested to by his insistence upon the separation of powers, but he never lost faith in man's ability not only to govern himself, but to govern himself well. This ability, in turn, was centered on what he referred to as the "general existence of a moral instinct . . . the brightest gem with which the human character is studded." On another occasion he wrote: "Strike from man the shackles of despotism and superstition and accord to him a free government, and he will rise to unsuspected felicity." Jefferson was skeptical concerning city dwellers and feared the blindness of uneducated men, but one cannot read his many speeches, essays and letters without sensing his deep and abiding optimism.

Shortly after the adoption of the Declaration of Independence, Jefferson returned to Virginia to resume his responsibilities in the state legislature. From 1776 until 1779, while still in his early thirties, he served as a member of the Virginia House of Delegates, applying his consummate skill toward organizing the social, political, and economic institutions of his native state. He was responsible for a bill which ended the feudal hereditary system of entail, and another that outlawed primogeniture. He drew up a bill for the emancipation of the slaves and recommended that the importation of slaves should cease. The right of expatriation and liberal provisions for naturalization were included in another of his proposals to the House. He favored reducing the property qualifications required for voting, and he coupled this suggestion with a proposal that fifty acres of land be granted to every person of "full age" who did not already have that much acreage, which if adopted would have meant universal white male suffrage.

Two areas of reform considered particularly important to Jefferson were changes in the educational system and a need for religious freedom. He submitted three bills on education:

Reproduction *of an artist's conception of the eventual look of Pennsylvania Avenue in Washington, D.C.*

(1) "for the more general diffusion of knowledge", (2) "for amending the constitution of the College of William and Mary", and (3) "for establishing a public library." The preamble to the first bill set forth principles that were nearly as significant and far-reaching in the evolution of the democratic ideal as those contained in the Declaration of Independence. These principles asserted that democracy cannot long exist without an enlightened citizenry, that the talent and virtue needed in a society should be encouraged through education regardless of "wealth, birth or other accidental condition," and that the children of the poor must be educated at the "common expence."

Of all the achievements in the House of Delegates, the one from which he gained the most personal satisfaction was his bill for establishing religious freedom (The Statute of Virginia for Religious Freedom). In his personal religion he was a rationalist and a deist, believing that every man's soul belonged to himself and that man was answerable for his actions only to God. The bill provided that no man should be compelled to belong to or support any religious body whatsover, that "all men shall be free to profess, and by argument to maintain, their opinions in matters of religion" without prejudice to their political rights. His criticism of religion and religious institutions was political, not theological, deriving from his consuming passion for liberty and from the historical evidence that the partnership of church and state had always led to tyranny and oppression. Although it took six years of debate before the bill was enacted into law, it established for the United States the precedent of the separation of church and state.

Not all the reform measures designed in 1776 by Jefferson and his Virginia colleagues—one of them young James

The first Democratic candidate, *General Andrew Jackson, campaigned from a stagecoach. Jackson is shown here addressing a small gathering during the 1828 campaign. His election was characterized by his political enemies as "triumph of the mob."*

Madison—were enacted into legislation, and it took nine years of struggle before the major reforms were accomplished. By 1785 Jefferson was American Minister to France. When the Constitutional Convention was called, he was still in France and therefore unable to participate, but his letters to friends and later comments reveal that he approved of most of the tenets of the new Constitution, and most certainly approved of the procedures by which it was adopted. "The example of changing a constitution by assembling the wise men of a state, instead of assembling armies," he wrote, "would be worth as much to the world as the former examples we have given them." He was shocked, however, by the absence of a bill of rights, and it was through his efforts and those of James Madison that such a bill was ultimately added to the document as the first ten amendments. Jefferson also expressed concern that no limit had been placed on tenure of office, particularly for the President, and it is revealing that twenty years later Jefferson himself resigned from office after two terms when he could have been re-elected had he chosen to run for the third. Coming after Washington's decision not to seek a third term, Jefferson established a precedent that was not broken until 1940, and when it was, the event aroused sufficient concern that the twenty-second amendment to the Constitution was adopted in 1951 limiting the tenure of the President to two terms. Jefferson also raised the question of how much power the Federal Government should have, but his criticism of what was to become known as the loose construction theory of the Constitution was to come in the following years. Once the Bill of Rights was added, he considered the American constitutional system as "unquestionably the wisest ever yet presented to men."

After the Constitution was adopted and Washington elected President, Jefferson became the first Secretary of State and Alexander Hamilton the first Secretary of the Treasury. Jefferson soon found, however, that he was in conflict with Hamilton, and Hamilton's policies were often the ones that were ultimately supported by Washington. Jefferson did not agree with Hamilton's claim that the mass of the people are "turbulent and changing, they seldom judge or determine right," and, therefore, a "permanent and distinct share in the Government should be given to the rich and the well born." Hamilton took a pessimistic view of human nature, feared anarchy and thought in terms of concentrating power in a governing class in order to preserve order. Jefferson, on the other hand, had an optimistic view of man, feared tyranny and thought that the chief safeguard of liberty was in the diffusion of power among the people, because the people were the most virtuous, although not always the most wise. In his first Inaugural Address, after becoming President in 1801, he defined good government as one "which shall restrain men from injuring one another, which leaves them otherwise free to regulate their own pursuits of industry and improvement, and shall not take from the mouth of labor the bread it has earned." Hamilton wanted to diversify the American economic life through legislation that would encourage shipping and manufacturing, and although he had never been to Europe, wanted America to be a new Europe. Jefferson would have America remain a nation of farmers, and having been in Europe wanted America to be as much unlike it as possible.

But the difference between Hamilton and Jefferson should not be overstated. Although Jefferson was a firm believer in the political equality of man, he believed in an aristocracy of talent and virtue, which in the eighteenth century was essentially the same class that Hamilton accepted as the leaders of the nation. Jefferson was a member of the Virginia aristocracy, whereas Hamilton was only an aspiring aristocrat. Jefferson, the "sage of Monticello," held views that were liberal for his day; he was a practical statesman who was invariably conservative in the means that he used to reach his ends, and as President he was not radically different in his execution of his responsibilities from the Federalists. Jefferson's break with Hamilton, however, led to the formation of the Jeffersonian Republican party and the beginning of the two-party system in the United States. Since it seems inconceivable that democracy can exist in a large nation without at least two major political parties, Jefferson's action provided one more contribution to the practice of self-government.

Jefferson referred to his own election to the Presidency as the Revolution of 1800. Since it constituted the first transfer of power from the Federalists, who had been the ruling party since the adoption of the Constitution, it may well have seemed like a revolution, not only to the Jeffersonians but also to the Federalists as well. In retrospect the election does not appear to have been unlike many another election in the United States in which the voters were presented with an honest choice between candidates with distinct platforms. His inaugural address constituted a re-affirmation of his faith in the democratic principles for which he had been working for a quarter of a century, and once in office he did nothing to disturb the National Bank, showed his willingness to use the powers of the Presidency for the good of the Nation in acquiring the Lousiana Territory, and, in enforcing the Embargo against England, used the power of the Federal Government in a manner that New England found just as offensive as Jefferson had found the Alien and Sedition Acts.

Jefferson did make some reforms in the judicial system, in civil service, in the Treasury Department, and by repealing the Alien and Sedition Acts. In keeping with his promises and his philosophy he reduced the national debt from eighty to fifty-three million dollars, in spite of the expenditure of fifteen million on Louisiana, and the repeal of the obnoxious Whiskey Tax. He abolished the quasi-monarchical forms and ceremonies that had been instituted under the Federalists, and in dress and action provided an example of greater social democracy than the country had witnessed under Washington and Adams. Except for the failure of the Embargo Act, Jefferson's terms in the White House could be considered successful, but in the long view of history it was not the specific accomplishments of his tenure that seem important. It is, rather, that his Presidency had given a practical illustration that the government of the United States could be carried on successfully without tying itself to the monied or any special interest, other than those who consider it a public trust. It provided a practical demonstration that democracy was not dangerous and that restraints upon freedom of speech and of the press were not necessary to make a government strong. Thus Jefferson's administration helped to clinch the ideas which are known as Jeffersonian democracy, which if they had not actually been put into practice might have been deemed inpractical for many years to come.

Jefferson's life-long conviction that without knowledge there could be no liberty inspired him, after his retirement from the Presidency, to design an elaborate educational plan for his native state which would culminate in a publicly

President Jackson's wife, *Rachael, who preferred the peace and tranquility of her home to the hustle and bustle of life in the nation's capital.*

maintained university. His grand design for the University of Virginia became his sole occupation for the last eight years of his life. He developed the curriculum, drew the plans for architecture and landscaping, procured the artisans and even supervised the bricklayers and carpenters.

Jefferson wished to be remembered, according to the instructions he left for his epitaph, as the author of the Declaration of Independence, the author of the Statute of Virginia for Religious Freedom, and as the Father of the University of Virginia. America has remembered him for these, but for much, much more. As the scholars of the twentieth century began to rediscover Jefferson, it became apparent that no other American, except possibly Benjamin Franklin, touched life at more points or left a more lasting contribution in so many fields of endeavor. As America moved toward free education in the last half of the nineteenth century, it was found that Jefferson had been one of its first and most eloquent advocates. About the same time Americans began to realize that Jefferson held a prominent position in American architecture, and that the classic revival in America was traceable to the man who had designed his own home, Monticello, and the University of Virginia, and who was directly responsible for the style of the Capitol buildings in Virginia and the National Capitol in Washington. His *Notes on Virginia* established him as a scientific scholar of high repute in the fields of geography, botany, paleontology, and horticulture. He discovered the proper curvature of the plow, was a pioneer soil conservationist, was at home in French, Italian, Spanish, Latin, and Greek, and an authority on the Anglo-Saxon language; and upon whatever subject he wrote, he did so with a grace, style, and an imperishable rhetoric unequalled in his time. All this was accomplished while he was operating a large plantation, becoming a successful lawyer, devoting over forty years of almost continuous service to political life, and articulating the American concept of democracy.

ANDREW JACKSON AND THE COMMON MAN

Andrew Jackson, the seventh President of the United States, has long been the symbol of the common man and the triumph of western democracy, although he always considered himself an aristocrat, all who knew him testify to the fact that he was the most uncommon of men, and the notion that Jacksonian democracy was born on the American frontier needs considerable qualification. Jackson was, however, the first self-made man to occupy the White House. He was the son of ordinary immigrants arriving in America with little but their personal possessions to seek their fortunes. He was as much a product of the developing American democracy as he was a cause, as much a representative of the age as its leader.

His parents, Andrew and Elizabeth Jackson, migrated to America from Ireland in 1765. The hardships of the Atlantic crossing had not daunted their courage, and shortly after arriving in Pennsylvania they began the five hundred mile journey south to the frontier along the border between the Carolinas where relatives had preceded them. His father died just before Andrew, the third son, was born in 1767, leaving Elizabeth to raise her three boys. Andrew's schooling was sporadic and by 1776 the settlement of Waxhaw, where the Jacksons lived, was in the path of the Revolutionary War. By the time he was fourteen, Jackson was on his own, his entire family having been wiped out either in battle or through the ravages of smallpox. Jackson himself had barely escaped death on both counts, and he was to carry through life the

Margaret ''Peggy'' Eaton, *wife of Jackson's Secretary of War. Her reputation for promiscuity prior to her marriage to Eaton created many problems for Jackson while in the White House.*

marks of smallpox and a livid scar which had resulted from a sabre cut, dealt by a British officer in retaliation for his impudent behavior while imprisoned by the English.

In many respects Andrew was well suited to the rugged life of his frontier environment. He was a born fighter, a reckless horseman, and few could beat him in footracing or jumping. He inherited a legacy of three hundred pounds from his grandfather in Ireland, moved to Charleston, and soon had squandered his money on horse racing and reckless living, while impressing most of the young women in the process. After trying his hand at several enterprises he began the study of law in Salisbury, North Carolina, where he was remembered as ''the most roaring, rollicking, game-cocking, horse-racing, card-playing, mischievous fellow, that ever lived in Salisbury. . .'' After being admitted to the bar, he left Salisbury with two pistols, a beautiful rifle, and a troop of hunting dogs to try his luck farther to the west on the new frontier of Tennessee. Before leaving he had been appointed Attorney General for the new district, but his position was more properly that of solicitor. In the midst of a territory where Indian raids were endemic, lawlessness was commonplace, and quick fortunes were to be made, Jackson was to leave an indelible mark. The twenty-two year old redhead dispensed honest justice with an iron hand, sometimes through the use of personal force or dueling, worked on the side of the larger land speculators, developed a lucrative practice as an attorney, began his own speculation in land and slaves, operated a mercantile business, and before long owned a stable of race horses. At one point, when his luck was down and he was facing foreclosure, a timely five thousand dollar bet on one of his horses kept him solvent.

Jackson served one term in the House representing the new

Reproduction *of an oil painting of Andrew Jackson wearing the uniform of a general.*

This political cartoon, *which appeared in 1833, was titled "Model of a President." Inspiration for the cartoon came from Jackson's public admiration of Napoleon.*

State of Tennessee, was elected to the U.S. Senate, although he was unable to serve out the term, and became a general in the militia. In the latter capacity he fought daringly against the Creek Indians, acquiring the name "Old Hickory," and volunteered for service when the War of 1812 was declared. During the early part of the War, although awarded a commission in the regular army, he saw little action. As the Indian situation became increasingly inflammatory, however, Andrew Jackson was dispatched to resolve the trouble, and before long as Commander of the military district embracing Tennessee, Louisiana, and the Mississippi Territory, he was to rout the British forces under Wellington at New Orleans. Following the war his fortunes continued to fluctuate, but he always managed to recoup his losses. In 1817 he was again commanding his regiment and was sent on a foray to subdue the Seminoles along the Florida border; in the process he invaded Florida to assure its falling into

American hands. The new laurels gained with his success in the Florida campaign assured for the hero of New Orleans an eventual chance at the Presidency. In 1824, what he considered an "unholy coalition" kept him from that high office, but by 1828 there was no stopping his own coalition, and so in that year the voters ushered into office the founder of the Democratic Party, the man of the people, the symbol of the common man.

The men of letters, journalists, and even the politicians of the time who wrote about their Jacksonian persuasions were simply providing an extended commentary on Jeffersonian democracy. Jackson himself had voted for Jefferson and apparently disagreed with him only when he failed to take a militant nationalist stand against England and Spain. Political institutions, however, had changed since the sage of Monticello had been elected. America had moved much closer to the democracy that he had advocated. By the time Jackson was elected in 1828 all of the Western states that had entered the Union had established white manhood suffrage by doing away with all property and religious qualifications for voting. Property qualifications for holding office had also vanished and party management had changed radically. The old caucus system for nominating Presidential candidates, King Caucus as the Jacksonians were wont to call it, gave way to state nominating conventions, and by 1832 the national party convention had become the vehicle for nominating a President. By that time citizens of all states, with the exception of South Carolina, could vote directly for Presidential electors. All these changes had been brought about by popularly elected conventions which in turn submitted their proposals to the people for ratification.

Jackson had had little to do with any of these changes; in fact, he had opposed the Governor of Tennessee who instituted many of the reforms which eventually came to be known as "Jacksonian," but he was directly involved in the death of King Caucus. After 1814 the two-party system on the national level had disappeared, and the executive branch of the government seemed to be self-perpetuating. The Constitution specified that the electors should meet and choose a President, but in addition to this the practice of calling a caucus in the legislature that actually made the nominations. It appeared to many that the government for some time had been controlled by a small clique, not representative of the people at large. Madison had served as Jefferson's Secretary of State and then became President. Monroe had been Madison's Secretary of State, and was virtually unopposed for the Presidency in 1816 and again in 1820. By 1824, opposition groups were stirring up popular sentiment against this "closed" political corporation branding it as a flagrant usurpation of the rights of the people, and insisting that the administration of government must be taken from the hands of the social elite.

The election of 1824, and the involvement of Andrew Jackson in that election, were to provide the wedge needed by the opposition groups. Jackson had agreed to the nomination and one of the chief issues of the campaign centered around the caucus system. Jackson, the national military hero, had considerable edge on his opponents with the new electorate, but fell short of the necessary majority in the electoral college. The election, then, was thrown into the House of Representatives where Clay asked his supporters to vote for Adams, who was accordingly elected. When Adams almost immediately appointed Clay as his Secretary of State, the charge of a corrupt bargain between them was brought by the thwarted Jacksonians, and Jackson's campaign for the election of 1828 was launched.

The Presidential campaign for that year was one of the most bitter in American history, with dirty tricks on both sides. Adams' supporters dug into Jackson's army record and ferreted out his execution of six Tennessee militiamen who had mutinied during the War of 1812, and Jackson's marriage to a divorced woman also became a key issue. Jackson supporters, on the other hand, rigged the tariff to make it appear to industrial sections of the North that Jackson favored the tariff but to the South that he opposed it. The South was assured that Jackson would defend states' rights, but once in office Jackson showed himself to be one of the strongest Nationalists to occupy the White House. Through some peculiar alchemy, however, the people who had voted in such large numbers for Jackson to assure his victory, had voted for the man who most represented them and their needs.

One of Jackson's first contributions to the new democracy was his introduction of the "spoils system," a system politicians had already developed on the local and state levels. The existing Washington bureaucracy at the time he took office was comprised of an honest and efficient but elite corps whose roots stretched back thirty years to the Federalists, so Jackson's actions in cleaning house were prompted by a desire to bring into the government his own supporters, as well as to reward those who had worked so faithfully for the party. Jackson elevated the system to a theory of government, "rotation in office," for he believed that "the duties of all public offices are, or at least admit to being made, so plain and simple that men of intelligence may readily qualify themselves for their performance . . . no one man has any more intrinsic right to official station than another." Rotation in office was thus made a leading principle of the party creed, and one which appealed strongly to the democratic elements in the nation.

By the time he was President, Jackson's manner and dress gave little hint of his frontier background. But in the Peggy Eaton affair, his background emerged in a stubborn unwillingness to bow to the overly genteel Establishment, and in the process he struck a small note for social domocracy. Peggy had been married to a hard-drinking naval paymaster, but resided in his absence at her parents' tavern where her flirtations with the guests, especially with Senator Eaton, caused considerable talk. When her husband died, Peggy delighted the gossip mongers by marrying the Senator. Eaton had been a long-time friend of Jackson's, and, still bitter over the political attacks against his own wife's reputation, Jackson insisted that Mrs. Eaton be accepted into the Washington social life. When Mrs. Calhoun and other wives of government official refused to comply, Jackson went so far as to hold a cabinet meeting at which he pronounced Mrs. Eaton "as chaste as a virgin." The affair resulted in a split in the cabinet and the resignation of Van Buren and Senator Eaton, who hoped by withdrawing from the field to salvage the situation.

Of more direct importance to Jacksonian democracy was Jackson's stand on the National Bank issue. The Bank had ceased to exist in 1811 when President Madison had not renewed its twenty-year charter. Following the War of 1812, however, the Republicans had found fiscal policies in such grave disorder that a second bank had been established, again under a twenty-year charter, and this second charter was due for renewal before the end of Jackson's second term. Jackson had a long-standing prejudice against the National Bank, in fact against most banks. As he told its president, Nicholas Biddle, "I do not dislike your bank more than all banks." But ever since he had read the history of the South Sea Bubble, he had been "afraid of banks." Still, once it had recovered from the Panic of 1819, the National Bank had been operating efficiently and honestly, although exerting considerable political pressure on its own behalf and, despite Jackson's hostility, it appeared that he might be seduced into favoring a renewal of its charter. Henry Clay, however, was overly anxious to make the Bank an issue in the election of 1832 and pursuaded Biddle, against his own judgment, to allow the bill for re-charter to come before Congress four years before its charter expired. The bill passed Congress, but was vetoed by Jackson. When Clay was roundly defeated at the polls in 1832, Jackson regarded his own victory as a mandate against the Bank and immediately proceeded to

undermine its power. In the process his monetary policies, along with the rapid land speculation of the thirties precipitated the panic of 1837.

Although Jackson's antagonism to the Bank may have been motivated largely by personal prejudice and a naive understanding of monetary policy, underneath the bias and naivete ran some good native horsesense, and his outlawing of the Bank was a significant step in opening America for liberal capitalism, for the Bank had been a power, and a highly privileged one. As a fiscal agency it was comparable in magnitude to the government itself, and even Nicholas Biddle had boasted that for years he had been "in daily exercise of more personal authority than any President habitually enjoys."

Jackson's message to Congress concerning his veto of the new charter centered mostly on the unconstitutionality of the Bank, but the social indictment he made against the Bank was perhaps more revealing. He described it as a monopoly, a grant of exclusive privilege which excluded from competition all of the American people. Its stock was held by foreigners or by a few hundred Americans, chiefly of the richest class, and as such it was a menace to the country's liberty and independence. Jackson stated that the role of government should not be to grant exclusive privileges to make "the rich richer and the potent more powerful," but to protect "the humble members of society—the farmers, mechanics, and laborers—who have neither the time nor the means of securing like favors to themselves. . ." If the government "would confine itself to equal protection . . . alike on the high and the low, the rich and the poor, it would be an unqualified blessing."

The struggle against corporate privilege which Jackson had dramatized in the contest with Biddle over the National Bank was also waged on a much wider front. In 1837, Connecticut passed a general incorporation act which opened the process of incorporation to all comers who could meet state requirements, and other states soon followed its example. In 1838, New York passed a banking law that permitted banking associations to operate under general rules, a precedent that has been considered the most important event in

Portrait *of the Executive Committee of the First International Council for Women. Among the members are Susan B. Anthony, second from left in first row, and Elizabeth Cady Stanton, fourth from left in first row.*

American banking history, and while Jacksonian concepts were being written into the law of corporations, a Jacksonian Supreme Court was reading them into the Constitution. The mood of the country was captured by Daniel Webster who observed that "competition comes in place of monopoly; and intelligence and industry ask only for fair play and an open field." Jacksonian democracy had thus wedded free political institutions to freedom of economic opportunity, or democracy to capitalism, more firmly than ever before. In so doing Jackson had become the spokesman for the lower and middle elements of society who were not only the farmers and laborers, but also the rural capitalists, the small businessmen, and the hopeful entrepreneurs.

The Jacksonian period was one of freedom's ferment, not only in the economic and political realm, but in the intellectual and social as well. It was the period of the Transcendentalists with their optimistic views of man and American society, and a period of great religious revival which spoke to both man's loneliness and the intense individualism of the American. It was a period of seething social reform and Utopian ideas.

The social reform movements touched almost every aspect of American life. Women were not content with their status which prevented them from voting, owning property, or obtaining a higher education. Even their wages belonged to their husbands or fathers, as the case dictated, and the professions were closed to them. Frances Wright, Elizabeth Stanton, Lucretia Mott and others were foremost in the revolt. Some states enacted legislation allowing women to own property, and some colleges, led by Oberlin in 1833, opened their doors to women. The inhumane treatment of the insane came under attack without much success. Imprisonment for debt was abolished in all Northern states and Maryland and Kentucky by the time of the Civil War. After a decade of agitation for the ten-hour day, President Van Buren limited working days for government employees to ten hours without reducing their salaries. In 1833 the American Temperance Union was founded, and there were several organizations seeking universal peace, one of which was the League of Universal Brotherhood founded by Elihu Burritt, a blacksmith, who was convinced after his study of thirty languages that all men were descended from a common source and should be brothers.

Utopian ideas were given live expression by the numerous small communities that sprang up throughout the nation. The Transcendentalists established Fruitlands and Brook Farm, the latter remembered especially for its progressive ideas on education. Robert Owen, the British industrialist, founded New Harmony in Indiana, striving to bring to America his concept of an ideal society. Organized along cooperative communal lines, its constitution fluctuated from democratic control by town meetings to guild or occupational socialism, but its membership was unsuited in both temperament and vocational skills for the endeavor and the community was dissolved after two years. There were dozens of Fourierist communities founded in America on the principles of François Fourier, a French Socialist, although none was destined for permanence. The religious communities were by far the most successful. Although one thinks of the Mormons more as a church than as a community, they were a direct product of both the small community movement and the revivalism of the period. The Amana Society, religious in nature, came to America from Germany and settled first in New York, but eventually migrated to Iowa where there are still remnants.

The Oneida Community well illustrates the Utopian ideas behind most of the communal experiences during the Jacksonian period. The community was founded by John Humphrey Noyes, the descendant of generations of sturdy, welto-do New Englanders. He was a graduate of Dartmouth College who had planned to study law until he had a conversion experience under the influence of the great revivalist Charles Finney. Noyes became a minister and began to preach against the "sin system," the "marriage system," the "work system" and the "death system," in the process losing his license because of his radical ideas. He also read all he could about Owen's New Harmony, the Fourier

Ralph Waldo Emerson, *who was one of the leaders in the literary renaissance which flowered in New England in the 19th century.*

phalanxes, Brook Farm, and the Shakers. His first community was organized in Putney, Vermont, but its unusual sexual practices horrified the town and forced the small group to migrate. In 1848 they settled in Oneida, New York, where they retained their communal form of communism until 1879.

The Oneida community made a serious attempt to place women on a more equal basis with men, freeing the women from part of the kitchen drudgery and, when possible, hiring others to do the more monotonous work. Women cut their hair in the fashion of men and wore trousers and short-skirted tunics. Children were placed in the community nursery school as soon as they could walk.

Closely related to the equality granted to women was the complex marriage system instituted by Noyes. He believed that revivals are theocratic and that when the theocratic tendency goes beyond religion it involves socialism. Religious love he considered a very close neighbor to sexual love, hence the practices of the Mormons and the Shakers. Mormonism, which embraced polygamy, he considered a masculine form of revivalism, whereas Shakerism with its polyandry he regarded as the feminine form. The complex marriage system designed for the Oneida community was an attempt to equalize the roles—each woman in the group was the wife of every man and every man was the husband of every woman. But his was not "free love," he maintained, since no sexual intercourse was permitted without the complete willingness of both parties and under close regulation. Male continence was practiced and propagation was regarded as a matter for group discussion. In all, Noyes insisted, sexual matters at Oneida were more strictly regulated than in the outside world.

An unknown artist's *version of what the capitol would eventually look like. The painting, which today hangs in the White House, was completed about 1835.*

This photograph, *taken in the mid-1860's, shows the Mormon Tabernacle nearing completion. The roof is covered with 350,000 wooden shingles which were then covered with aluminum. In the foreground is the foundation for the Mormon Temple.*

The group also practiced a number of the other ideas popular among small communities. Though not strictly vegetarian, they ate little meat, avoided drugs and ate simply. They believed in faith-healing and several seemingly miraculous occasions strengthened their faith in the power of Noyes. Recreation for both old and young was considered important as it was among the Mormons and at Brook Farm. The practice of "mutual critism" was often credited with helping to maintain harmony in the community.

Perhaps one of the reasons for the success of the Oneida community was that it prospered economically almost from the first. The business affairs of the community were controlled by a system of twenty-one standing committees, and a method of frequent rotation of jobs prevented occupational monotony. Initially the community was engaged in farming and logging, but Noyes was interested in obtaining some industrial enterprise that might prove more profitable. This hope materialized when a man who had invented a new type of steel trap joined the community. Before long Oneida traps became the best in the land and were sold as far away as Hudson Bay. The members of the community were not only industrious but were inventive as well, and developed new machines, utilized water power, became skilled laborers and the community was soon reaping large profits. Equally important was the production of silver-plated spoons, and later knives and forks, until eventually Oneida silverware was well-known throughout the United States.

Although the community had been one of the most successful of the social and economic experiments of the period, in 1879 Noyes finally advised that the whole process of complex marriage be given up because of pressure from the outside, and the following year a majority of the group decided to reorganize and became incorporated as a joint stock company—a company that still exists today.

In retrospect it would seem that the Jacksonian period possessed to a greater degree more of the basic ingredients of democracy than any other period of American history. The concept of democracy holds that both equality and liberty are important, yet the only way that any country has been able to achieve complete equality has been to deny liberty to someone, and when a people is granted absolute freedom it is virtually impossible to maintain for any length of time a viable concept of equality. In the Jacksonian period there was a maximum of both. Millions of American moving into an unexploited land had more freedom than Americans were ever to have again, and the availability of land and other opportunities provided a type of equality not know since. With the new democratic institutions of the eighteen-thirties, the destruction of the National Bank, and the adoption of new state corporation and banking laws, there was more political

and economic equality than at any other period. The rugged individualism of an Andrew Jackson, and many of those who supported him, has become known as central to the American character, yet it is difficult to imagine that type of individualism in the twentieth century. The numerous small communities of the period give testimony to the heterogeneous, pluralistic nature of Jacksonian society, an age before national newspapers, radio and television had molded, to some extent, all Americans to a common stereotype.

Though Jacksonian democracy was not the product of Andrew Jackson, he was a symbol of the self-made man, he was the President with whom the new masses could identify, he was a firm believer in Jeffersonian democracy, he brought the common man into the national government, he removed economic restrictions which opened up equality of opportunity for the entrepreneurial, or expectant entrepreneurial class, he was a strong Nationalist in dealing with the South Carolina nullification movement, and he set a pattern of strong Presidential leadership on behalf of the American people that would be followed in the twentieth century.[1] Unlike Jefferson he was intuitive rather than reflective, he had a heightened concept of nationalism, and he believed completely in the need for a strong executive branch in government; he was the rugged individualist in office, not the scholar statesman.

One cannot leave the Jacksonian period, however, without pointing out that there was a section of the country, and one from which Jackson himself had come, which still held to the most undemocratic of institutions, slavery, that women still had few rights, and that Senators were still elected by the state legislatures, not by the people themselves. It would not be until the Civil War and the Reconstruction Period that the thirteenth, fourteenth, and fifteenth amendments to the Constitution would free the slaves and provide, on paper at least, their right to vote and to civil liberties. And the period from 1860 to 1900 would witness the rise of new monopolies and a staggering concentration of wealth that would destroy the Jacksonian balance between liberty and equality and thereby led directly to the Populist and Progressive movements.

Henry David Thoreau, *the man who became a model for non-violent civil disobedience in America.*

CHRONOLOGY   *A timetable of American events:* **1789-1801**

EXPANSION and EXPLORATION	POLITICS	MILITARY and FOREIGN AFFAIRS	ECONOMICS and SCIENCE
1789-90 Friction between Indians and American settlers on Northwest frontier becomes critical	**1789** Organization of federal government at New York; Washington inaugurated		**1789** First tariff legislation
1790 Organization of the Southwest Territory which was to become Tennessee	**1790** House sets site of new national capital on the Potomac		**1790** Hamilton's "Report on the Public Credit"
1791 Vermont statehood	**1791** Creation of city of Washington, D.C.		**1790** Samuel Slater establishes his textile mill at Pawtucket
1792 Kentucky statehood	**1791** Bill of Rights (first 10 constitutional amendments) adopted	**1791** General St. Clair routed near the Wabash	**1790** Philadelphia-Lancaster turnpike begun
1792 Robert Gray discovers the Columbia River	**1792** Presidential Succession Act	**1791** Britain appoints first minister to the U.S.	**1790** First U.S. census reports 3,929,000 inhabitants
	1792 Washington and Adams re-elected for second term	**1793** Citizen Genêt Affair	**1791** First Bank of the United States chartered
	1793 Supreme Court decides *Chisholm vs. Georgia*	**1793** Washington's Neutrality Proclamation	**1791** Hamilton proposes protective tariffs and agricultural bounties
	1793 Impact of French Revolution upon American native political parties becomes clear	**1794** Congress authorizes construction of six warships; foundation of U.S. Navy	**1792** Mint Act establishes decimal system of coinage
	1794 Whiskey Rebellion	**1794** Neutrality Act	**1793** Eli Whitney invents cotton gin
	1795 Naturalization Act	**1794** Battle of Fallen Timbers	**1793** Jefferson devises mold-board plow
	1795 Provisions of Jay Treaty made public. Attack upon treaty by Republicans		**1793** Philadelphia yellow fever epidemic inspires improvements in sanitation and water supply
1796 Land Act provides for survey of public lands and their sale at public auction	**1796** In *Ware vs. Hylton*, Supreme Court declares treaties supreme over state laws	**1795** Treaty of San Lorenzo settles boundary and navigation issues with Spain	**1794** Arrival of Joseph Priestley stimulates interest in study of chemistry
1796 Tennessee statehood	**Sept. 17, 1796** Washington's Farewell Address	**1797** XYZ Affair	**1797** Newbold patents iron plow
1798 Organization of the Missisippi Territory	**Dec. 1796** John Adams elected President	**1798** Commercial intercourse with France suspended	**1797-1809** U.S. ships make voyages to Japanese ports carrying goods for Dutch merchants
	1798 Ratification of 11th Amendment	**1798** Creation of Department of the Navy	**1798** Eli Whitney develops system of interchangeable parts that presages mass production
	1798 Alien and Sedition Acts	**1798-1800** Undeclared war with France on high seas	**1799** Nathaniel Bowditch publishes *Practical Navigator*, pioneering work in navigation
	1798-99 Kentucky and Virginia Resolutions	**1799** *Constellation* defeats *L'Insurgente*	
	1799 General Post Office established		
	1799 Death of Washington		
	1800 National capital transferred to Washington	**1800** By treaty of Morfontaine, U.S. ends defensive alliance with France	**1800** Census shows 5,308,000 inhabitants
	1800 Presidential election; Adams vs. Jefferson	**1801-05** Tripolitan War	**1800** Cowpox vaccination introduced into U.S. by Dr. Benjamin Waterhouse
	1801 Adams defeated for presidency; deadlock between Burr and Jefferson broken by Hamilton	**1802** U.S. Military Academy opened	**1801-14** Albert Gallatin Secretary of the Treasury; carries out Republican policy of financial retrenchment
	1801 "Midnight judges" appointed		

THE LURE OF THE WEST
1789—1853

The Westward movement comprises one of the most dynamic and intriguing periods in American History. In one life-time the United States was transformed from thirteen Brithish colonies along the Atlantic coast into a transcontinental nation, the fourth largest in the world. It is interesting to note that the life-span of John Quincy Adams, President of the United States from 1825 to 1829, covers this exact period. He was born in 1768, the year the Townshend Duties were passed, and died in 1848 just three weeks after the Treaty of Guadalupe Hidalgo, in which Mexico ceded California to the United States. He was with his father, John Adams, in 1783 when the Treaty of Paris was confirmed, received his first political appointment from George Washington, and one member of the committee to make arrangements for his funeral was Abraham Lincoln.

National policy favored western expansion in order to assure adequate protection against foreign powers moving into unoccupied territories and for the commercial advantages which could be obtained from having control over such areas as the outlet to the Mississippi River or the wealth of the Rocky Mountain fur trade. The American people were motivated by similar goals, but more frequently by less articulate reasons for wanting to move West. One of the strongest motives was that they could satisfy, perhaps for the last time in history, one of man's deepest needs: to own land just by walking toward it.

Reproduction of Frederic Remington's famous painting "The Coming and Going of the Pony Express." The Pony Express was the first attempt to link up the western United States with a fast mail service.

An even more subtle reason was the restless individual energies of the people themselves. James Reed, a leader of the Donner Party that came to California in 1846, well illustrates this. Born in North Carolina, he later migrated to Kentucky, then to Indiana; from there he moved to Illinois, to Texas, and finally back to Illinois. All this was accomplished before starting out for California, and not easily, for travel was by foot, horse or covered wagon.

Underlying all else, the American people possessed an aggressive faith in the transcendent destiny of their way of life. It was natural and right, they thought, that America with her superior democratic institutions should eventually occupy lands now being held by the British, French and Spanish. By the 1840's this belief had evolved into the doctrine of Manifest Destiny, which would lead the United States into the Mexican War and later still into the Spanish American War.

The first major impact of the West upon American governmental policy came during the Federalist period. At that time, the British still controlled forts in the Northwest Territory and from them were able to keep some of the Indian tribes as allies to block the Westward expansion of the Americans. The Jay Treaty, signed in 1795 with England, had special significance to future expansion because of its provision for the evacuation of the British forts, thus allowing the United States the opportunity to begin effective control over the Northwest Teritory. In the same year as the signing of the Treaty the Indians were defeated at the Battle of Fallen Timbers, and additional lands were opened for settlement.

During that same year also, President Washington, mindful that the vanguard of pioneers and traders who ventured into the far reaches of the country made up the future strength of the nation, negotiated a treaty with the Spanish which allayed the growing discontent of the settlers over Spanish policies restricting their trade routes. The Spanish controlled all lands west of the Mississippi, the great river itself where it flowed into the Gulf of Mexico, and had closed the port of New Orleans to all but their own people. Because the most economical avenue of trade for the Westerner was down the Mississippi River to New Orleans, the restrictions imposed by the Spanish were particularly irksome to the Americans. With the signing of the treaty of San Lorenzo (Pinckney Treaty), the United States acquired free access to the Mississippi River, the right of deposit at New Orleans, and established an agreement that marked the Florida border (Spain still owned Florida itself) as the thirty-first parallel.

THE LOUISIANA PURCHASE

The first major acquisition of land by America after the establishment of domestic boundaries at the end of the Revolution was the Louisiana Territory. This vast area, which was to double the size of the United States, had belonged to France until her defeat in the French and Indian War, at which time she had ceded all claims west of the Mississippi to Spain. But by 1800 Napoleon was the dominant military figure in Europe and in a position to force Spain to return the Territory to France. Many Americans were alarmed; for although Spain was relatively weak and from her they had little to fear, a France under Napoleon, in possesion of the west bank of the Mississippi and New Orleans, was another matter. Even Jefferson, who had been in sympathy with the French Revolution, was prompted to exclaim that with this threat the United States "must marry herself to the English Fleet." Fortunately, such action was not necessary, for France, in her desire for supremacy, had overextended herself. In a move to take over Santo Domingo, she had sent 35,000 crack troops to the island, only to have them nearly annihilated by a combination of fever and the military tactics of the able Black leader of the Dominican resistance, Toussaint L'Ouberture. With the loss of Santo Domingo Napoleon bowed to the persistent attempts of Jefferson to purchase the Territory. Its cost to the United States was $15,000,000, or approximately 28 cents per acre.

At that price, a twentieth century land broker has to stretch his imagination to understand why the purchase of the

The front view *of the cabin of Dr. Thomas Walker, Nearbourville, Kentucky. Dr. Walker's cabin was the first built in the state of Kentucky.*

Daniel Boone, *legendary explorer and frontiersman. Boone's flamboyant life and adventures paralleled the energy and dynamics of the new American nation. Boone led several expeditions into the unexplored regions west of the Tennessee Valley.*

Louisiana Territory met with the opposition it did. There was, however, a concern over the constitutionality of the act. Jefferson was a strict constructionist and nowhere in the Constitution did he find specific authority granting the President the right to purchase land from a foreign power. Although he sought an amendment to provide the needed Constitutional power, the question was still unresolved when the time came to sign the treaty. He acted decisively, explaining to the nation that his decision was for the good of the country and if there was an opposition from the people he would have to get out of the deal as best he could. One of the concerns over the purchase came from those who argued that France had never really taken control from the Spanish, and because of this, the Spanish forces occupying the territory might not honor an agreement between the United States and France. The constitutionality of the issue was also being questioned on the other side of the Atlantic. Spain, in ceding the territory back to France, had specified that France had no right to transfer the area to a third power and the French Constitution provided Napoleon with no authority to sell her possessions.

Another result of the Purchase was the hatching of the New England Plot which in turn led to the untimely death of Alexander Hamilton. New Englanders, already concerned over the agrarian policies of Jefferson, recognized that he, by acquiring the Louisiana Territory, had in one stroke doubled the farming lands of the northern states. A group of New Englanders, in angry retaliation, plotted to withdraw from the Union and set up their own federation. If they could bring

New York into the scheme, success seemed certain. Aaron Burr, then Vice President, held no love for his superior, Jefferson, feeling that he had been slighted by him. Burr agreed to run for the governorship of New York, apparently promising to swing New York into the New England Federation in exchange for Federalist support in the election. Suspicious and distrustful of Burr, Alexander Hamilton made disparaging remarks about him during the campaign which resulted in Burr's defeat and threatened his political career. When Burr demanded an apology from his detractor, it was not forthcoming and he challenged him to a duel. Hamilton was killed and Burr went on to entangle himself in further intrigue and to become one of the most controversial figures in history.

What motivated Burr to approach the British minister in Washington with an offer to detach the Western states from the Union for a half million dollars? That scheme failing, why did he then proceed down the Ohio River, using his charm to rally the frontiersmen in support of a plan to conquer Mexico and establish himself as emperor? Why did he at a later time accept ten thousand dollars from the Spanish minister in Washington, ostensibly for the purpose of defending the Spanish holdings in America? Was he opportunist, dreamer or fool? In the summer of 1806 he again descended the Ohio River, this time with sixty followers, on his way,

This early daguerrotype shows John Quincy Adams in 1843 at the peak of his powers. This is the earliest photographic likeness of an American President.

perhaps, to take up land claims he had bought in Louisiana; but at this point General Wilkinson, Commander at New Orleans and a former co-conspirator, deciding it was time to betray his partner, sent word to the President of a "deep, dark, wicked. . . conspiracy." Because other Westerners had been sending similar reports also, Burr was arrested for treason; Chief Justice Marshall, no admirer of Jefferson, took care that the constitutional definition of treason was strictly adhered to and Burr was acquitted. By then, however, Burr was a ruined man and sought exile in France.

Another complication that arose from the Louisiana Purchase was over the ownership of West Florida. Without much justification, Jefferson and Madison claimed that West Florida had been a part of the Louisiana Territory and that French exclusion of it from the treaty had cheated the United States. Diplomacy, threats of war, and secret appropriations were all employed but to no avail. Finally in 1810, Madison, now President, encouraged the revolutionary sentiments of the inhabitants of West Florida, with the result that the United States was "obliged" to occupy part of the area to protect them. In 1812 Congress officially incorporated the region into the State of Louisiana and by a second act added to the Territory of Mississippi a further slice of Spanish West Florida. In the meantime, Congress had provided the President with authority to take custody of East Florida if it was in danger of occupation by some foreign power other than Spain. Their concern was over the possibility of English occupation of the area, and although the British did not attempt an occupation during the War of 1812, it seemed clear to many that it was only a matter of time before Spain would have to cede East Florida to the United States.

The life of John Quincy Adams, above, covered the period of the westward movement in American history. He was born in 1768, the year the Townshend Duties were passed, and died in 1848, three weeks after the signing of the Treaty of Guadalupe-Hidalgo which added former Mexican territory to the United States.

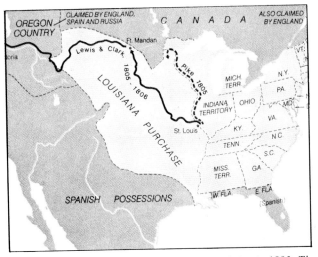

Map *of the route of the Lewis and Clark expedition in 1803. The expedition wintered the first year at Fort Mandan; it was near Fort Mandan that the party met Sacagewa, the Shoshoni girl who led the expedition to the Pacific.*

THE WEST AND THE WAR OF 1812

Before acquiring East Florida, the United States was involved in the inglorious war with a glorious ending, the War of 1812. Ostensibly, the War was over maritime conflicts with England. England and France were once more engaged in a death struggle, and each was attempting to strangle the trade of its opponent. American shipping was caught between the two powers. The British had proclaimed that all vessels trading with France or her allies were liable to capture and declared that in certain instances neutral vessels must first touch at British ports, which meant paying a heavy tribute to a British custom house. If an American ship had paid British customs, had even been stopped by a British ship, or had any British goods on board—it was subject to capture by the French as a violation of the French blockade of England. Since British sea power was superior to that of France, American merchants had more to fear from the English than from the French and resentment of the British grew apace. American sentiments were further enflamed by the British policy of impressing American seamen, forcefully taking Americans—usually claimed by the British to be their subjects—to serve in the British navy.

So, after years of diplomatic protest and the boycotting of British goods, war was declared on England. The reasons given were the impressment of American seamen, British violation of the three mile limit, her "paper" blockades, and the British system of attempting to control trade on the high seas. But were those the real reasons? Ironically, the maritime sections of New England, which should have been the most concerned over British policy and action, voted unanimously for peace, whereas the inland states lacked only one vote of being unanimously in favor of war. It would appear that the real motives behind the declaration of war lay elsewhere, namely in the expansionist spirit of the Westerners.

The Northwest continued to be concerned about the relationship of the British and the Indians. In 1811 the great Indian Chief, Tecumseh, had united a large number of tribes to make a massive stand against American encroachments. The first battle, under William Henry Harrison, ended in disaster for the Americans who suffered over 100 wounded and 61 killed. The desire to avenge the "blood of the murdered" did not stop with the defeat of Tecumseh, for it was generally agreed that he was the agent of London and Quebec with the British, and British guns found in Tecumseh's village confirmed that belief. Many a Westerner thought it was time not only to remove the British influence from the United States but to capture Canada as well. The Southwest had designs on East Florida and Spain was not allied with England in the struggle against Napoleon. Declaration of war

Emperor Napoleon *of France shakes the hand of United States Minister Robert R. Livingston after signing the Louisiana Purchase Treaty at the Louvre in Paris in 1803. The Purchase secured for the United States nearly a million square miles of new and unexplored territory.*

This old painting *depicts the ceremony marking the formal transfer of the lands included in the Louisiana Purchase from France to the United States. The ceremony occurred in New Orleans on December 20, 1803, although the Senate did not ratify the Purchase until October of the following year.*

Treaty

Between the United States of Am.

and the French Republic

Facsimile *of the Louisiana Purchase. The negotiations for the Purchase were completed under the Presidency of Thomas Jefferson.*

with England would open the way for settlement of long-standing grievances against the Seminoles along the Florida border and perhaps result in the conquest of Florida itself.

The Treaty of Ghent which ended the War in 1814 settled nothing officially. Both sides agreed to disagree on everything imporant. Yet the opposing nations had gained a new respect for each other and the United States was never again refused the deference that was due an independent nation. Four boundary commissions were created which ultimately settled the border between Canada and the United States, and America was once more free to continue her march westward. The first new acquisition was East Florida. Although hardly a "Western" territory, the forces which led to its control were typical of those of the Westward movement.

Scrimmages between the Indian and the White Man along the Florida border were part of the frontier tradition; as the Americans had pushed farther into Indian lands, the Seminoles had migrated south establishing themselves either along the border or further south into Florida. With no love for the Americans and a little assistance and prodding from the Spanish, they constituted a continuing menace to the land-hungry pioneer. Trouble had broken out with them in 1816, and again in 1817. On December 16, 1817, General

Andrew Jackson was requested to assume command of the American forces fighting these tribes and if need be to follow the Indians into Florida. In this same month negotiations with Spain over Florida were resumed, but the ultimate outcome of the negotiations was determined as much by Jackson's aggressive acts during the ensuing few months as by any events transpiring in Washington.

Old Hickory was a Westerner, and he shared with his countrymen a keen dislike of the Indians, an intense

The United States warship The Constitution *(right) shown engaging the British warship* Guerriere *in a sea battle during the War of 1812.* The Constitution *and* Guerriere *met and fought a bloody sea battle on August 19, 1812.*

General Andrew Jackson *is shown exhorting his troops during the famous Battle of New Orleans. The Americans, under the leadership of Jackson, defeated the British here in 1815.*

Reproductions *of a painting showing a frontier woman helping to load a cannon during a battle on the Niagara frontier during the War of 1812.*

Reproduction *of a painting of Dolly Madison, wife of James Madison.*

nationalism, and the aggressive temperament of the frontiersman who acts first and questions later. Thinking he had approval from President Monroe for a conquest of Florida, he hastened to begin his campaign, ostensibly against the Indians, and turned what should have been a series of skirmishes into a war against Spain for the possession of Florida and, in the process, once more embroiled the United States with England. The Spanish empire was in an acute state of disintegration—the revolutions in Mexico and South America had taken their toll—and his advance met with little resistance. He occupied and rebuilt Fort Apalachicola, captured Fort Marks, and marched into Pensacola. In the process he captured the Indian Chief Homollimiaco and another known by the name Bowlegs, both of whom were executed.

Engraving *of James Madison, fourth President of the United States.*

He also seized and executed two British subjects whom he accused of conspiring with the Indians against the United States.

As George Dangerfield has written: "The trial of two British subjects before an American court in a fortress legally the property of Spain was a circumstance too complex for anyone ever to make any sense out of it."[1] It took skillful diplomatic maneuvering by John Quincy Adams to persuade the British to accept his rationalization of the event. It also took five cabinet meetings, not to mention the development of life-long enmities, before the Monroe Administration decided not to censor Jackson for his unauthorized invasion of Florida. The enthusiasm that greeted Jackson upon his return home was unbounded; and following upon his impressive victory over the British at New Orleans in 1814, would catapult him into the Presidency.

Although a final settlement was no longer in much doubt, negotiations over Florida with the wiley Spanish minister in Washington dragged on for another year. A treaty was finally signed in 1819 ceding Florida to the United States in return for two million dollars. Before the treaty was approved by both governments, however, additional complications developed over the rights of Spanish land-grants in Florida—in truth Spain had outwitted Adams—and it was not until 1821 that the Treaty was officially signed by the Spanish King and ratified by the U.S. Senate.

THE FINAL SWEEP: THE FAR WEST

Following the acquisition of Florida, no new territories would be incorporated into the United States until the annexation of Texas in 1845 and the signing of the Treaty of Guadalupe Hidalgo in 1848. Contacts with the far West developed from a trickle early in the century to flood-tide by mid-century. The movement consisted of a four-pronged infiltration: exploration of the Rocky Mountains by the fur traders, development of trade with New Mexico along the Santa Fe Trail, migration into Texas, and contact with California and Oregon which led to the migration of the 1840's.

[1] George Dangerfield, *The Era of Good Feelings*, p. 134.

THE ROCKIES AND THE MOUNTAIN MEN

The exploration of the Rocky Mountain region and the Far West began with the Lewis and Clark Expedition (1803-1806), sent by Thomas Jefferson to explore the Louisiana Territory and to discover a transcontinental route to the Columbia River. On May 14, 1804, the 43-man expedition under the leadership of Captain Meriwether Lewis and George Rogers Clark started the long trip up the Missouri River. Their first winter was spent in the last White outpost among the Indians in North Dakota. In the spring of 1805 they pushed off into unexplored country, following a trail of rivers—the Missouri, then across the plains to the Yellowstone, and eventually to the Jefferson which they traveled to what they assumed to be the source of the Missouri. They crossed the mountains after considerable hardship, even eating their horses to keep alive, floated down the Clearwater to the Snake River, then down the Snake to the Columbia (near presentday Pasco, Washington) and on to the Pacific Ocean. After wintering among the coastal Indians they retraced their steps to Montana, divided into several groups to explore additional routes from there, gathered again on the Missouri and on September 23, 1806, reached St. Louis. The United States reaped many benefits from this successful expedition. For the first time Americans had an idea of the tremendous size of the country and the wealth of resources that lay between the Mississippi River and the Pacific Ocean; America had established a claim to the Oregon country; and the expedition had lost only one man and had maintained friendly relationships with the Indians throughout the trip.

The Lewis and Clark Expedition signaled the beginning of the Rocky Mountain fur trade. On their way down the Missouri they met small groups of American fur trappers ascending the river at points farther west than any known White

Reproduction of a painting *of President James Monroe, whose policy toward Latin America became known in American history as the Monroe Doctrine.*

Map *showing the three major trails followed by the Pioneers during their trek into the western United States. The famed Oregon Trail covered a 2000 mile course from Independence, Missouri to the mouth of the Columbia River.*

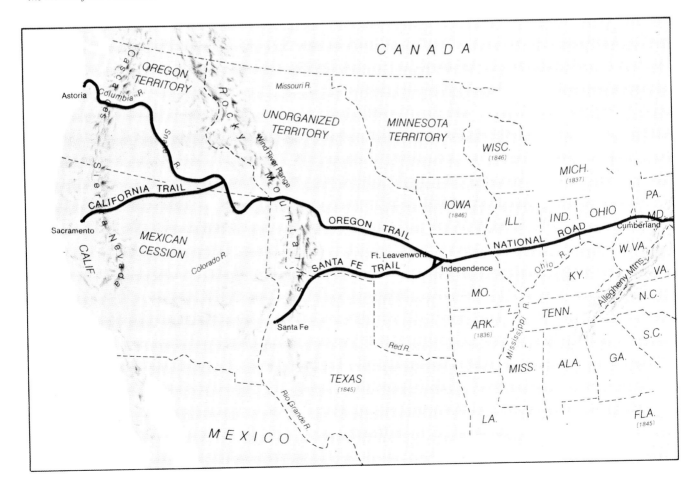

Reproduction of a painting *of George Rogers Clark, who, along with Merriwether Lewis, led an exploration party across the uncharted Rockies and on to the Pacific coast.*

Explorer Merriwether Lewis, *who, under the mandate of President Thomas Jefferson, helped lead an expedition into the Northwest preparatory to the Louisiana Purchase which brought much of the land explored by the Lewis and Clark Expedition under the control of the United States government.*

Men besides themselves had yet ventured. One of their own men caught the fur trading fever and asked to be allowed to turn back with two of the trappers. Each year the trappers moved farther into the interior and in 1810 John Jacob Astor attempted to control both the inland and West Coast fur trade by establishing a trading post at the mouth of the Columbia River. He organized two expeditions, one to go by sea and the other overland. Difficulties plagued the project from the start, and upon arrival his parties discovered that a Canadian explorer, David Thompson, had already established a network of British posts in the interior. With the outbreak of the War of 1812 American trappers, discouraged and threatened by British sea attack, sold out to the Canadians. Although the Pacific Northwest remained exclusively in British hands for a decade, Astor and his men had established another basis for a U.S. claim to the area.

By the 1820's the fur traders had reached the almost legendary beaver country of the Rockies and for a number of years two rivals, the Rocky Mountain Fur Company and the American Fur Company, vied for the wealth found there. The eighteen-twenties-and-thirties were the years of the great mountain men—men who suffered extreme hardships but, possessing amazing courage, fortitude, skill, and determination, explored and trapped the entire mountain area. These intrepid pathfinders included Jim Bridger, Jedediah Smith, William Sublette, Tom Fitzpatrick, Kit Carson, and a host of

Sacagewa, *a Shoshoni girl, helped guide Lewis and Clark up the Missouri River and across the Rockies to the Pacifi coast. The expedition did not return to its starting point, St. Louis, until three years after its departure, and many people felt until their return that the expedition had perished.*

others who outdid the Indians in techniques of survival and warfare, and at times matched them for cruelty. When by 1840 the supply of beaver had been exhausted, and Americans—ever restless and adventurous—were beginning to seek new opportunities in the far West, these were the men who would guide the wagon trains, parley with the Indians, scout for the army, and lead explorers like John Fremont to California. Less praiseworthy was another part they played before the far West was opened to more stable pioneers: they had debauched the Red Men with liquor, infected them with veneral diseases and small pox, and

135

The whaling ship *Platina* which sailed out of New Bedford, Connecticut. It was from this whaler in 1902 that Amos Smalley harpooned a white whale. On deck can be seen the whaleboats which were launched to give chase when the mother ship sighted schools of whales.

Kit Carson *was another legendary character of this period of American history. During his lifetime Carson was an explorer, trapper, Indian fighter, scout for the Cavalry, and a successful rancher.*

Reproduction of the painting *"Halcyon Days" by George Catlin. It shows a scene from a Sioux encampment; the women in the foreground are tanning buffalo skins and drying meat.*

helped to rob them of their self-sufficiency.

It was one of the mountain men, the most remarkable of all, who made the first overland journey to California. In 1826 Jedediah Smith led a group south through Utah across the Colorado River (near present-day Needles, California) and over the Mojave Desert through the San Bernardino Mountains to the Pacific. Returning to California the following year, he and his men headed north through more unexplored wilderness into Oregon, where all but two of his party were killed by Indians.

But most of the early contacts with California were by way of the Pacific Ocean. Trading vessels and whalers had occasionally put in along the California Coast for provisions, although prior to Mexico's independence from Spain, they were not welcomed. Following independence, Mexican civil affairs were in disarray, and the Californians began to pay little regard to policies established by the corrupt and inefficient government of Mexico City. In the 1820's a thriving trade in cattle, hides, and tallow sprang up between California and New England, and eventually the New England firms found it profitable to establish their own agents in California. A few Americans even acquired land-grants and, becoming rancheros, settled down to a leisurely life in a warm climate. Before long Americans in the eastern states were hearing glorious descriptions of the California paradise.

THE SANTA FE TRAIL

New Mexico, like California, had traditionally been closed to Americans, and one of the first to push into the Spanish territory of the Southwest on an exploring expedition, Z. Pike, was arrested and sent to Mexico before being permitted to return to the United States. Yet New Mexico was the center for some 40,000 New Mexicans of Spanish origin who were starved for manufactured goods that their mother country could not provide. A group of merchants hoping to exploit that market reached Santa Fe in 1812 only to be thrown into jail. Six years later another enterprising group was halted before reaching the city, their merchandise confiscated, and the men imprisoned. The situation changed in 1821 when Mexico had finally won its independence from Spain. A Missouri merchant, William Becknell, had been trading on the edge of the Spanish Borderlands when he was informed of the new events in Mexico; he started for Santa Fe at once. For his merchandise he received bags of Mexican silver and returned to Franklin, Missouri, not only unmolested by the New Mexicans but with a handsome profit as well. The exact amount is unknown, but one of his townsmen, who had invested money in the enterprise, realized a return of $900 on his $60 investment. Becknell also brought news from the governor of New Mexico that all American traders would be welcome and that he had pioneered a shorter route to Santa Fe. From 1824 on, wagon trains left Missouri each year to trade with the New Mexicans. By 1831 one caravan alone carried goods worth $200,000. Although the trade diminished after 1837 because of internal problems within New Mexico, and eventually dwindled considerably as war between Mexico and the United States became more imminent, the traders had demonstrated the feasibility of wagon travel across the plains, devised the technique that all migrant trains were to follow in defending themselves against the Indians, had spread word that Mexico's authority in the Southwest was waning, and had established the impression that the northern provinces of Mexico would inevitably fall to America.

Reproduction *of a painting of General Sam Houston who became the first president of the Republic of Texas.*

THE LONE STAR REPUBLIC

The sprawling plains of Texas became a part of the American-Spanish controversy almost as soon as the treaty for the Louisiana Purchase had been signed. At that time, Jefferson claimed that Texas was a part of the Louisiana Territory, and later, during the negotiations with Spain over Florida, John Quincy Adams revived the issue; yet in the final settlement on Florida all claims to Texas were renounced. Within two years of that time, however, Americans were taking up residence there, welcomed by the Spanish—even invited. Spain had decided, after three hundred years of restrictions, that the borderlands might profit from settlers from other countries. Moses Austin, hearing of this new policy, worked out an agreement whereby he would bring three hundred settlers into Texas, all of them willing to become loyal Mexican citizens. Before he could recruit his colony, however, he died and his twenty-seven year old son, Stephen Austin hurried to Texas to determine the status of his father's land claims. The governor assured him that the land grant was his, and authorized him to select a site for the settlement. The first members of his group arrived in December of 1821.

In spite of the normal hardships of pioneering—drought, Indian attacks, sickness—the colony prospered and by 1825 numbered over two thousand persons. More lenient immigration laws passed by Mexico in 1824, the success of Austin, and the availability of land without charge (it was $1.25 per acre in the United States), inspired others to follow Austin's example. By 1836 there were almost thirty thousand Anglo-Americans in Texas, outnumbering the Mexican population by almost ten to one. This could only lead to trouble, for distrust had been brewing on both sides for ten years. As early as 1826 a small group of Texans had been involved in a land dispute and had set up a short-lived republic. Although Austin had raised a small army to quell

Davy Crockett, *famed guide and mountain man who died along with Jim Bowie and the other defenders of the Alamo. The painting shows Crockett as he appeared circa 1830, when he was a member of Congress.*

The Alamo *in San Antonio, Texas, where 180 Texans led by Colonel William Travis were killed in the opening round of Texas' struggle for independence from Mexico.*

the revolt, the Mexicans had viewed the uprising as part of a design by the Americans to wrest the northern provinces from their mother country. To make matters worse, the United States government had chosen this time to open diplomatic negotiations for the purchase of Texas. It was almost inevitable that the distrust would mount as the American population grew. The Americans were mostly Protestants, living in a country where Catholicism was dominant. Most of the Americans had come from the South and expected to employ slaves as conditions warranted, but the Mexican government under which they lived was not in favor of slavery and abolished it in 1829. The Mexican tradition stressed the authority of rulers; the American, the authority of individuals and the right of self-government. Americans considered their civilization to be the highest in the Western world and looked down upon the Mexicans as slovenly, inefficient and cowardly.

Disputes between Texas and Mexico erupted periodically. After an armed rebellion broke out in 1831, a convention was held in 1932 to demand reforms from the Mexican government, and a second convention was convened a year later. Some reforms were made by General Santa Anna, then President of Mexico, but in 1834 he repudiated these reforms, dissolved Congress, wiped out the entire federal system, and proclaimed himself dictator of a centralized state. Dissension flared again among the Texans, armed resistance broke out, and finally on November 3, 1835, a convention of

Painting of the Battle of the Alamo. *Davy Crockett, out of ammunition, uses his rifle as a club to fend off the attacking Mexican soldiers under the generalship of Santa Anna. The Alamo was defended by 180 Americans, who fought valiantly against the 2,500 Mexican attackers.*

delegates from the Texas communities issued a "Declaration of Causes" which explained why they were impelled to take up arms and named Sam Houston as commander of the army. A more formal declaration of independence was issued in March.

In that same month the famous and tragic Battle of the Alamo was fought. Some 4,000 Mexican soldiers were on hand to put down the rebellion, and their first objective was the defeat of the garrison at San Antonio. The defenders, who numbered less than 200, were resolved to make victory for the enemy worse than defeat:

> For ten days the Mexicans made thrust after thrust, only to be beaten back with frightful losses. Then, in the grey dawn of March 6, the whole enemy force surged forward, shouting as they came. Twice they were beaten back, but on the third assault they came swarming over the walls like sheep. Gradually the Texans fell back, fighting with rifle butts and knives, until by noon, the last survivor was dead.[2]

The defenders of the Alamo, who included such frontier heroes as Davy Crockett and Jim Bowie, had been true to their convictions. Although all 187 Texans were killed, Mexican losses reached a total of 1,544, and "Remember the Alamo" became the rallying cry that stirred the Texans to an eventual victory.

Sam Houston, not yet ready to sacrifice his unorganized and untrained men to Santa Anna, retreated to the east. In April, however, with his own army strengthened by recruits and discipline and Santa Anna's army dwindling in size, Houston attacked the enemy forces near the San Jacinto River. Catching the Mexicans at their noon siesta, the Texans

[2] Ray Allen Billington, *The Far Western Frontier*, p. 128.

revenged the Alamo in the short span of fifteen minutes. Santa Anna, along with 730 of his troops, was captured and 630 Mexicans were killed. Some 2,000 Mexican troops still in the country hurried home, leaving the Texans in charge of the field. Santa Anna was released after promising his support for an Independent Texas, support which he almost immediately revoked.

Texas was not long in seeking admission to the Union, but sectional rivalries precluded the government in Washington from taking favorable action. It was clear to all that debate over bringing the Lone Star Republic into the Union would center on the slave issue and split the nation in two. It was not until 1844, when James K. Polk elevated the Texas question above sectionalism, that action by Congress was taken. Polk had campaigned for the Presidency on the slogan, "Reoccupation of Oregon and reannexation of Texas," and "Fifty-four forty or fight." His victory assured Texas a place in the Union, and even before he was inagurated Congress voted by joint resolution (February, 1845) to admit Texas to Statehood.

OREGON

The Oregon territory had been claimed by four countries on the basis of discovery and exploration: England, Russia, Spain, and the United States. Spain had withdrawn from the controversy in 1821, ceding to the United States its claims north of the forty-second parallel. Russia followed in 1824, surrendering to England and the United States its rights south

Reproduction of a painting *showing the landing of General Scott's 12,000 man army in Vera Cruz, Mexico in 1847. The American forces occupied the Mexican city for several months.*

of the fifty-four-forty line. The United States and England, not ready for a show-down, agreed to a treaty of joint occupation that allowed the nationals of both countries to trade and settle there. American enthusiasts immediately began to advertise the advantages of Oregon, but it was not until the Methodist and Presbyterian Churches sent missionaries into the area that the Oregon fever spread.

The Methodists were the first to arrive there with the Reverend Jason Lee, and two years later Marcus Whitman was appointed to carry the Gospel to the Indians of the Oregon country. Their records, judged by the number of souls saved, was not impressive, but both made significant contributions to history as promoters of Oregon, and more than any others they were responsible for the surge of pioneers into the Willamette Valley. As the number of settlers increased so did the propaganda reaching the East. The Willamette Valley was painted as a modern Garden of Eden with rich lands, healthy climate, and readily available markets for produce. The propagandists were confident that only a few American settlers were needed to drive out foreign interlopers and make this West Coast paradise a part of the United States. They did not have long to wait. A small party reached Oregon in 1839, larger parties in '41 and '42; and only a year later nearly one thousand emigrants assembled at Elm Grove, thirty miles from Independence, Missouri, the rendezvous point for the wagon trains that would soon be heading for Oregon and California. In July, 1843, the American settlers so out-numbered the English, who were there with the Hudson Bay Company, that they established their own government which was to function in the Territory until "such time as the United States of America extended their jurisdiction over us."

At times Polk seemed ready for war with England over Oregon, even though war with Mexico was becoming daily more imminent. When war actually broke out with Mexico, he was more willing to compromise on the Oregon question, and by then the British were ready for a peaceful settlement as well. They were aware that there were 5,000 Americans in the southern portion of the Oregon territory as compared to 750 British subjects, and that the Hudson Bay Company had already moved its fort to Victoria from Vancouver, where it was vulnerable to American attack. In June, 1846, the U.S. Government received the formal British offer to settle on the forty-ninth parallel, which left England the Oregon territory from there to the southern boundary of Alaska and the United States the territory from the forty-second to the forty-ninth parallel. The treaty was formally ratified by the Senate on June 15, 1846.

THE MEXICAN WAR

After 1820 Americans had penetrated the Far West, some as settlers in Texas, some as fur traders in the Rockies, others as merchants along the Santa Fe Trail and on the California Coast, and by the eighteen-forties an increasing number were risking the arduous overland trek to settle in Oregon or California. Except for the settlement of Texas the number of people involved was relatively small, but the spirit of expansion was permeating the entire nation, and the four years from 1844 to 1848 would see the culmination of these movements in an unequalled burst of enthusiasm for new territories. Bernard DeVoto has captured the significance of the period in the title of his volume, *The Year of Decision, 1846*. It was in that year that the Donner Party headed to California, symbolizing its importance as a new frontier, that the Mormons migrated to the great salt basin to colonize the desert; that Polk gave notice to England that in twelve months' time the joint occupation of Oregon would expire, and it was in that year also that the United States declared war on Mexico, ostensibly over a dispute concerning the Texas boundary.

The Mexican War has had its share of critics, both at the time it was waged and since. Henry Thoreau went to jail rather than pay taxes which might be used to support the War, and no less a person than Abraham Lincoln denounced the War in Congress. Some modern historians describe it as a war of aggression against a helpless neighbor, while others consider James K. Polk one of the great American Presidents because of his role in acquiring California and the Southwest territory while at the same time forcing England to settle the Oregon controversy on a basis favorable to the United States.

The abolitionists considered the war as part of an expansionist conspiracy of slaveowners to acquire more and bigger pens into which to cram more slaves, an interpretation which cannot be substantiated since many Southern slaveowners were opposed to the War. Other historians justify the War on the basis of disrespectful treatment given to American diplomats sent to Mexico City to negotiate the purchase of California and other lands from Mexico. The Mexican government during this time was in near chaos. Between 1823 and 1858 there were forty-eight different executives with an average tenure of under nine months each. Even before Mexico had gained independence, Spain had lost most of her

control over the distant states of Texas, New Mexico, Arizona and California. After independence, conditions continued to deteriorate: Californians were warring among themselves and ready to break with Mexico, New Mexicans in Santa Fe talked of similar action, all attempts to control the Indians in Arizona had been abondoned, and Texas, through a Mexican policy of encouraging immigration, had ten American settlers for every Mexican. Refusal of the Mexican government to pay "legitimate" claims of Texans against that government is another justification for the War. Fear of British or French control of California—both France and England were active in the Pacific—gave added impetus to the desire for the possession of California.

The underlying cause for the Mexican War, however, was probably "manifest destiny", a term coined during the 1840's, but one which simply picked up the exaggerated feeling of the period of a concept which has run throughout American history. Americans were convinced that their democratic government and the American way of life were superior to all others, and that it was their destiny to spread across the continent into the scarcely occupied lands of the west which were claimed, but very inadequately governed and developed, by less civilized people. As one popularizer of this theme wrote: "What do I consider the boundaries of my country? On the East we are bounded by the rising sun, on the west by the procession of the equinoxes, on the north by the aurora borealis and on the south by the day of Judgment."

One of the reasons given by Polk for declaring war was stated in his war message to Congress wherein he said that "American blood" had been shed "upon American soil." In the light of the evidence, however, that statement must be considered the pretext for war, not the reason. The reason for the war, however it is justified, was that Polk and many other Americans wanted California, and Polk was using the dispute over the Texas boundary in his bargaining with Mexico. He wanted California without war, but ultimately accepted war as the only remaining alternative.

Congress had agreed to the annexation of Texas even though her independence had never been recognized by Mexico. Since Texas had been unofficially independent for nine years, this came as no surprise to Mexico, but the boundary between Texas and Mexico was a more serious problem. Texas claimed all territory to the Rio Grande River, and Mexico insisted, with considerable justification, that the boundary stopped at the Nueces River. Polk sent General Zachary Taylor to the Nueces River, and then ordered him to invade the disputed territory and position his troops on the left bank of the Rio Grande. The Mexican general, stationed on the other side of the river, commanded Taylor to return to the Nueces, but he responded by blockading the Rio Grande in order to cut off food supplies for the enemy troops. Following this, a Mexican force crossed the Rio Grande and engaged in a skirmish with the U.S. troops, killing a few and capturing the rest. Polk interpreted this as the spilling of American blood on American soil. The Mexican government had made no military disposition that threatened Texas, had not occupied the disputed territory (Taylor had), and made no moves against Taylor until his blockade had threatened the Mexican troops.

In the meantime, Polk and his Cabinet had been busy meddling in the affairs of California. In 1845 the State Department had sent word to a representative in Monterey that the United States would send help in case of difficulty, and in the same year Captain John C. Fremont was sent on a

The Siege of Monterey *in 1846 was effected by the skillful leadership of General Zachary Taylor. In the action pictured above, he succeeded in defeating the Mexicans, and thus paved the way for the war with Mexico to settle disputed boundaries.*

mission to explore California, even though it was still a foreign territory. In June of that year the Secretary of the Navy sent word to Commodore Sloat, who was then commanding the Pacific station, to seize San Francisco in the event that Mexico should declare war. In October the Secretary of War wrote to the American Consul at Monterey that if the people of California wished to become part of the United States they would be welcomed as brethren, and in the same month a second army officer, Lieutenant Gillespie, was sent on a secret mission through Mexico to California to seek out Fremont. Whatever their official reasons for being in California, both Gillespie and Fremont took part in fomenting the rebellion that established the Bear Flag Republic.

It is true that Polk's war message was sent to Congress only after American blood had been spilled, but Polk had not learned of the incident until the night of May 9th. On April 25th he had already begun to prepare a message to Congress urging war, on the grounds that the Mexican Government would not receive the American minister and that there were unpaid damages and claims owed by Mexico to the Texans which amounted to just over $3,000,000. On Saturday the 9th, before receiving word of the fighting along the Rio Grande, he had told his Cabinet that he felt it his duty to send the war message to Congress on the following Tuesday. That night the dispatch from General Taylor reached the White House, and Polk rewrote the message. On May 13, 1846, Congress declared war on Mexico.

The conquest of New Mexico and California were achieved in a relatively short time, but the invasion of Mexico dragged on for fifteen months. The Americans were not as well prepared for war as they had optimistically thought, political considerations too often took precedence over military, and the Mexicans fought more valiantly than expected. Once Mexico City was occupied, Santa Anna promptly abdi-

cated for the third time, and two months elapsed before General Scott and Nicholas Trist, the peace commissioner, could find any formal Mexican government with which to negotiate peace. The Treaty of Guadalupe Hidalgo was signed in February, 1848. Mexico ceded Texas with the Rio Grande boundary, New Mexico, and Upper California to the United States. The New Mexican territory included what later became the states of New Mexico, Arizona, Nevada and Utah. The United States assumed the unpaid claims and paid fifteen million dollars to Mexico. With the exception of a narrow strip of land purchased from Mexico in 1853 (the Gadsden Purchase), the United States had rounded out her continental area to its present limits.

The war had other consequences as well. The United States gained new respect from Britain for its military prowess, and new hostility from Mexico for depriving it of half its territory. The battles fought in Mexico were the blood-spattered school rooms for future officers on both sides of the Civil War, and inadvertently, Polk's acquisition of so much new territory made the Civil War almost inevitable. Even before the Mexican War was over, the snarling dog of slavery had been aroused. Would the new lands be added to Freedom's airy domain, or provide "bigger pens to cram with slaves"? With considerable foreboding, the elder statesman, John C. Calhoun said in the Senate:

> I said to many of my friends that a deed had been done from which the country would not be able to recover for a long time, if ever . . . it has dropped a curtain between the present and the future, which to me is impenetrable. . . it has closed the first volume of our political history under the Constitution and opened the second and. . . no mortal could tell what would be written.[3]

[3]John C. Calhoun in Bernard DeVoto, *The Year of Decision: 1846*, p. 214.

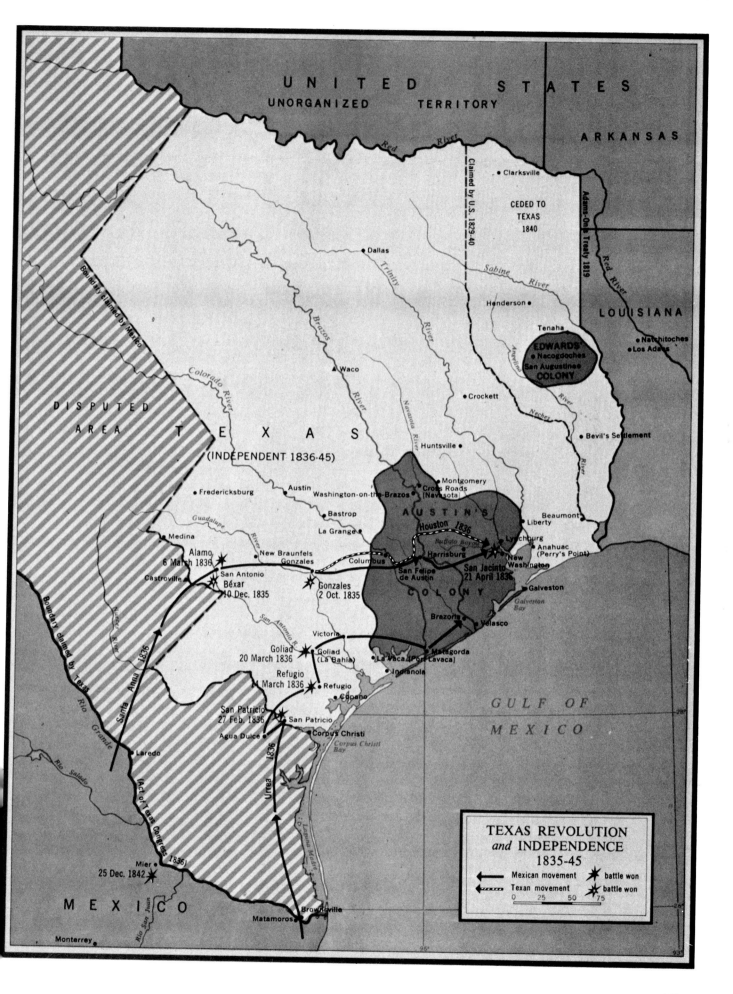

UNITED STATES

UNORGANIZED TERRITORY

ARKANSAS

• Clarksville

CEDED TO
TEXAS
1840

Claimed by U.S. 1829-40

Adams-Onís Treaty 1819

Red River

Sabine River

LOUISIANA

• Henderson

Tenaha

EDWARDS'
• Nacogdoches
San Augustine
COLONY

• Natchitoches
• Los Adaes

Boundary claimed by Mexico

Colorado River

• Dallas

Trinity River

Brazos River

Navasota River

• Crockett

• Bevil's Settlement

DISPUTED
AREA

T E X A S

(INDEPENDENT 1836-45)

• Huntsville

Neches River

• Fredericksburg

• Austin

Washington-on-the-Brazos

• Montgomery
Cross Roads
[Navasota]

AUSTIN'S

Beaumont
• Liberty

• Bastrop

Guadalupe River

• La Grange

Houston 1836

• Medina

New Braunfels
Gonzales

Columbus

Buffalo Bayou

Harrisburg

Lynchburg

• Anahuac
(Perry's Point)

Alamo
6 March 1836

San Felipe
de Austin

New
Washington

Castroville

San Antonio
Béxar
10 Dec. 1835

Gonzales
2 Oct. 1835

San Jacinto
21 April 1836

COLONY

• Galveston

Santa Anna 1836

Nueces River

San Antonio R.

Victoria

Brazoria

Velasco

Galveston
Bay

Boundary claimed by Texas

Goliad
20 March 1836

Goliad
(La Bahia)

• La Vaca [Port Lavaca]

Matagorda

Refugio
14 March 1836

• Refugio

• Indianola

Rio Grande

San Patricio
27 Feb. 1836

Agua Dulce

Urrea 1836

• San Patricio

• Copano

• Corpus Christi

Corpus Christi
Bay

GULF OF

MEXICO

(Act of Texas Congress 1836)

Rio Salado

• Laredo

Laguna Madre

Mier •
25 Dec. 1842

M E X I C O

Rio San Juan

Matamoros

• Brownsville

• Monterrey

TEXAS REVOLUTION
and **INDEPENDENCE**
1835-45

⟵ Mexican movement   ✸ battle won
⟵╍ Texan movement   ✸ battle won

0   25   50   75

143

THE WAR BETWEEN THE STATES: THE TREE IS BENT

The "second volume" of political history referred to by Calhoun hinged upon the acquisition of the new Western Territories. Most of man's destiny has centered around his relationship to land and the utilization of it to his own purposes, but although he may shape the land to his needs, often the very nature of the land itself can dictate his fortunes.

From the very beginning, the geographic differences between the New England Colonies and the Southern settlements pushed hem into separate patterns of growth. Over the years the agrarian interests of the South and the commercial interests of the North led to a widening division of their political views and the coming of the Industrial Revolution greatly broadened that division. With the opening of the new territories in the West, another issue had been raised to spark more trouble between the two sectors. The questions involved in this issue were not only whether the agrarian or commercial interests would control the national government, but whether or not slavery would be extended into the territories, for by then slavery had become a moral issue.

In 1619 the first representative assembly in the New World, the Virginia House of Burgesses, was formed and paradoxically that was also the same year the first Negro slaves were sold in Jamestown, and slavery soon spread throughout the South. Geography was a cardinal factor in determining where slavery would take root and where free labor would predominate. New England, with its barren coast and rocky soil, did not lend itself to the plantation system and the small family farm became the dominant way of life for the early settler. Fishing opportunities along the New England and Newfoundland coasts soon led to a thriving ship building industry and the beginning of an economy based on trade and manufacturing. Although the shrewd Yankee traders made a fortune from bringing African slaves to the South, slavery proved to be unprofitable on the New

England farm or in the North's commercial and industrial enterprises. The warm climate and fertile soil of the South lent itself to the growing of tobacco, rice, indigo, sugar and cotton, and these were crops most economically raised on large plantations employing slave labor.

By the American revolution the incompatibility of slavery and democracy was becoming apparent and the northern states, which had not found slavery profitable and therefore had few slaves, abolished the institution. Many a Southerner agreed that slavery was evil and looked forward to the time when it might be outlawed, but the large number of slaves in the South and the dependence of the economy upon forced labor, had produced complications that they did not know how to solve. At this point the industrial revolution came to America, heightening the differences between both sections of the country and making it increasingly difficult for the two to maintain a harmonious relationship.

The year 1793 is significant for both the North and South. It was in that year that Eli Whitney invented the cotton gin, its use greatly enhanced the profits to be made from cotton and thus further entrenched slavery into the Southern economy. The development of the textile industry in England and America, one of the first fruits of the industrial revolution, assured the South of ready markets for her steadily increasing production of cotton. It was in the same year Whitney invented the cotton gin that an immigrant from England, Samuel Slater, incorporated into one factory in Rhode Island all three processes required in the manufacture of cloth, and the North was on its way to becoming the chief industrial section of the country—and dependent on free labor.

The diverging Northern and Southern economies led to conflicting views by the two factors as to the nature of the Federal government and what each should expect from it. During the 1790's these views were expressed in the philosophies of Hamilton and Jefferson, with Hamilton contending that the National government should serve the commercial and industrial interests, and Jefferson holding that the strength of the country lay with the agrarian interests. During the Era of Good Feelings which followed the War of 1812, many of the noticeable differences between Northern

Reproduction of a painting showing slaves being transported from the Gold Coast of Africa to the United States. Painting depicts the forced exercise slaves had to do while on board ship during the journey to keep them healthy for the slave markets of the South.

and Southern expectations from the National government were temporarily submerged—even that Southern advocate of states' rights, John C. Calhoun, supported a national bank, new protective tariffs, and internal improvements subsidized by the Federal government.

By the 1820's, however, Southerners were recognizing the error of their ways and were ready to return to a Jeffersonian agrarian philosophy. Thus, the North favored a national bank to provide sound currency and economic stability, while the South opposed the bank, believing that it furthered Northern commercial interests while increasing Southern indebtedness to Northern capitalists. The North favored protective tariffs to encourage infant industry, whereas the South opposed them since no benefit accrued to the agrarian interests and the prices she paid for manufactured goods were correspondingly higher. The North advocated Federal subsidies to provide internal improvements—roads, canals, eventually railroads—which were so essential to commerce; the South opposed these subsidies because most of the improvements benefited the North, yet were paid for in part by tax dollars from the South. The North, seeking governmental action in each of these areas, thought in terms of a stronger national government; the South, opposing governmental interference, developed a states' rights doctrine that would lead directly to the secession of the South in 1861. Underlying all of the issues that divided North and South was the "peculiar institution," slavery, which by 1830 had been accepted as an absolute necessity by the South.

SECTIONALISM AND SLAVERY

Sectionalism had plagued the new nation from the begin-

Scene of a slave auction *conducted in Virginia in 1861. Little consideration was made for family unity during the selling of the slaves, and families were often broken up with the children being separated from the parents.*

ning. Centrifugal forces almost destroyed the government under the Articles of Confederation and so a new Constitution was adopted. With Washington as the first President, the success of the government may have been assured, but none was more aware than he that the country was experimenting with a new type of government, a federal republic, and there were many who doubted its ultimate success. Yet, with each sectional threat, the National government appeared to grow more secure. The Whiskey Rebellion in western Pennsylvania threatened the new government and was forcefully subdued by troops under Washington and Hamilton. When the Federalists passed the Alien and Sedition Acts, the Jeffersonians responded with the Kentucky and Virginia resolutions that declared a State possessed the right to declare Federal laws unconstitutional. When Jefferson became President, the Alien and Sedition Acts were repealed and no serious harm had come to the prestige of the National government. During Jefferson's term of office the country witnessed the New England plot of 1804, the Burr conspiracies, and the strong opposition of New England to Jefferson's Embargo Act. During the War of 1812 it was again New England that talked of secession to redress her grievances against the Jeffersonian Republican policies that seemed destined to ruin her commercial and industrial economy. The successful conclusion of the war brought the dissolution of New England opposition and ushered in the Era of Good Feelings.

The issue that destroyed the harmony of the era of Good Feelings was the question of the admission of Missouri to the Union. The problem was two-fold: (1) would the admission of Missouri, which was pro-slavery, upset the existing balance of eleven free and eleven slave states, and (2) did Congress have the power to place qualifications upon the admission of new states? The debate, and the animosity it engendered, continued for almost two years until the famous Missouri Compromise of 1821 was reached. The power struggle was solved by allowing Missouri to enter the Union as a slave-holding state, but balanced its entrance by admitting Maine, which had just detached herself from Massachusetts, as a free state and thus maintaining an equal number of free and slave states in the Union. Under the Compromise slavery was prohibited in the territory north of latitude 36°30'. Under this provision the land south of the 36°30' line remaining for settlement by the Southern slave-holder was considerably less than that open to the free men of the North, but more important, the North had maintained the principle established in the Northwest Ordinance that Congress could legislate on slavery in the territories if it so ordained. Although passions did subside and the Compromise was to keep the peace for a quarter of a century, John Quincy Adams wrote in his diary: "I take it for granted that the present question is a mere preamble—a title-page to a great, tragic volume." After the Missouri Compromise, sectionalism next threatened national unity over the tariff issue, although the entire Southern system based on slave labor was at stake.

By 1830 planters in South Carolina were suffering economically from their land-destroying system of cotton culture, and much of their trade with Europe was being funneled through New York, thus further reducing their profits. Many of her enterprising planters had emigrated to the black belts of Alabama and Mississippi where virgin soils provided them with bumper crops, but those who remained were becoming increasingly convinced that their economic plight was caused by the rising interest rates. As their plight deepened they began to claim that protective tariffs were unconstitutional.

When Congress passed a new tariff in 1828, many in South Carolina were ready to contest the position of the Federal government. The State legislature approved a document written by Calhoun, the South Carolina Exposition, which asserted that the Federal Constitution was a compact between

The interior *of a slave holding pen at Alexandria, Virginia. The slaves were held in pens like these until their numbers were called and they were taken to the auction area. Pens similar to these were constructed throughout the South.*

the states established by the thirteen original sovereign states and not by the American people. Since each state possessed indivisible, indestructible sovereignty, each had the right to judge when its agent, the Federal government, exceeded its powers. If a state convention determined an act of Congress to be unconstitutional, it could take measures to prevent its enforcement within the states' borders. The South Carolina Exposition was a clear statement of the theory of Nullification and the strongest states' rights position yet taken by any state.

For two years the unionists and the states righters jockeyed for position in the Senate and in President Jackson's Cabinet, and during that time Calhoun and the South Carolina nullifiers were held in check by the unionists within South Carolina. Then in 1832 Congress passed a new tariff bill which seemed to challenge South Carolina directly. The state-rights party carried the Fall elections in South Carolina, and the new legislature promptly called a state convention which declared the Tariff Act as "unauthorized by the Constitution of the United States . . . null, void, and no law, nor binding upon this State, its officers or citizens." The ordinance also forbade Federal officials the right to collect customs duties within the state, and threatened secession from the Union if the Federal government attempted to use force against their State.

President Andrew Jackson prepared to take strong measure, measures which almost anyone would have expected from such a strong nationalist, but no one wanted actions that would lead to bloodshed. Fortunately, within a few weeks Henry Clay was able to push through Congress a compromise tariff which provided for a gradual scaling down of all sched-

Photograph of field slaves *bringing their cotton loads to the cart at the end of the working day in the fields.*

Eli Whitney, *whose invention of the cotton gin made cotton the mainstay of Southern economy. Because of the gin it became necessary to have more slaves in the fields to supply the machine, and consequently, the value of the slave increased as a source of free labor.*

John C. Calhoun, *Vice-President under President John Qunicy Adams, resigned from the Vice-Presidency following a disagreement with Adams. Calhoun was a strong defender of states' rights.*

Frederick Douglass, *who escaped from slavery in Maryland and traveled to the North in 1838, became one of the most famous and outspoken leaders of the Northern abolitionist movement.*

Photograph of Henry Clay, *who led the fight in Congress for the Compromise of 1850, which was intended to cool the antagonisms growing between North and South over the question of slavery.*

ules over a ten-year period. Jackson signed the new tariff and on the same day the Force Act, which authorized him to use the army and navy whenever necessary to collect duties if judicial process was obstructed. A re-assembled South Carolina Convention then repealed the nullification ordinance, but saved face by declaring the Force Act null and void. The Union was preserved without resorting to open conflict, but many observers recognized that slavery itself would be the next pretext for the threat of secession.

From 1833 to 1846 the outward harmony of the union was maintained by a gentlemanly and informal agreement in Congress to ignore the question of slavery. When Texas petitioned to join the Union, Congress hesitated to take action, knowing that the issue was too explosive for either party to handle. James K. Polk succeeded in 1844 in lifting the Texas question out of its slavery setting only when he combined it with the re-occupation of Oregon, and thus put the annexation of Texas into a context of national expansion and prestige. Polk did not enjoy his victory for long. During his negotiations with Mexico over the purchase of the Spanish borderlands, he had asked Congress for two million dollars for the enterprise, and a Congressman named David Wilmot tacked onto the bill authorizing the money, a proviso that "neither slavery nor involuntary servitude shall ever exist in the territory so acquired." The Wilmot proviso did not pass, but the debate over it in Congress was heated and left little question that when the territories acquired from Mexico were organized, the country would most certainly divide over the question of whether the area would be free or slave.

MOUNTING TENSIONS

In the decade of the 1850's tensions between the North and South mounted as the political power struggle over the territories continued. The Mexican War had brought vast new lands into the Nation, and almost immediately Southerners and Northerners began vying with each other over whether or not slavery would be extended into these new holdings. The South grew more aggressive in her demands and increasingly anxious over the stand which had been intensifying among the Abolitionists in the North. The situation was aggravated because the issue was no longer purely economic; the North had come to consider slavery as morally wrong, and the South thought it morally right.

The decade opened with bitter conflict over the admission of California as a free state. Until this issue came before Congress, Southerners had accepted the right of states to prohibit slavery, but if a free California were brought into the Union, the South would have lost its chance to spread its "peculiar institution" into over half the land gained from the recent Mexican War. A number of related issues were in need of resolution, and Henry Clay once more came forth with a complicated compromise package in an effort to satisfy the demands of each section. The package included: (1) immediate admission of California as a free state; (2) the organization of territorial governments in New Mexico and Utah, without mention of slavery; (3) a new and stringent fugitive slave law; (4) abolition of the domestic slave trade in the District of Columbia; and (5) adjustment of the boundary dispute between Texas and New Mexico with the assumption of the Texas national debt by the Federal government.

Debate over the Clay proposals lasted for almost eight months with impassioned appeals by the Senate greats—Webster, Clay, Calhoun, Douglas, Seward, Chase and Davis. Calhoun demanded that the North do justice to the slave interests by allowing slavery in the territories, admitting slavery into California, and by ceasing agitation on the slave question. For a time the secession of South Carolina and possibly other Southern states seemed imminent, but as the debate progressed a sufficient number were won over to ensure passage of the essential bills, known collectively as the Compromise of 1850. Another year elapsed before it was certain that the secession movement would crumble, and

Reproduction *of a painting showing the infamous Marais des Cygnes massacre of 1858. A band of border desperadoes, led by Charles Hamilton, marched into the town, rounded up a group of prisoners, marched them to a ravine, and there shot them down. Five prisoners were killed in the attack.*

then for a time it appeared that the Compromise of 1850 had preserved the Union just as the early Missouri Compromise had in 1821. The divisive forces in the Nation, however, were already too far advanced to warrant such optimism.

A revival of the conflict flared up in 1854. North and South were in competition over the area which would be selected for the route carrying the first transcontinental railroad, and the North was at a disadvantage since the Kansas-Nebraska Territory (the most direct route) had been left by treaty in the hands of the Indians "as long as grass shall grow and water shall run." Stephen A. Douglas, a Democrat from Illinois, highly favored establishing the route through the Indian lands, but had to devise a method of assuring Southern support for the legislation needed to secure that area. To accomplish this purpose he proposed a bill to organize the Kansas-Nebraska Territory on the basis of "popular sovereignty." The passage of the bill would mean that settlers moving into this newly opened territory could of themselves decide the issue of slavery, thus negating the tenets set down by the Missouri Compromise. Although bitterly contested by no less a person than Abraham Lincoln, the bill received the support of many Southern Democrats and was enacted into law. Immediately Southerners from Missouri poured across the border into Kansas only to be met by an influx of Northerners, many of them imbued with Abolitionist ideals. A frontier war broke out between the contending factions, with considerable loss of property and lives. John Brown and his sons, in retaliation for violent acts performed by slaveowners in the area, murdered five Southerners in the dead of night with old fashioned Navy cutlasses. After some political maneuvering, the slave interests in Kansas adopted a constitution permitting slavery while their more numerous opposition submitted to Washington a constitution banning slavery. It eventually became obvious that the slave interests were a minority and the anti-slave constitution was accepted. In 1856 a new party, the Republican, emerged with the slogan, "Free soil, free speech, and Fremont." The Republican candidate, John C. Fremont, swept all the Northern states except

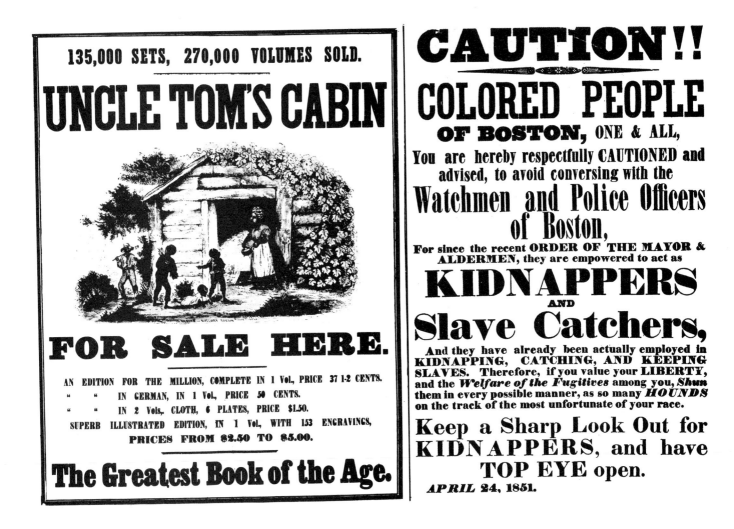

Dred Scott, *whose legal fight for freedom went all the way to the Supreme Court, which ruled in 1857 that, in the words of Chief Justice Taney, "(the Negroes) had no rights which the white man was bound to respect." Shortly after this appalling decision Scott's owner freed him, but the freed slave died in St. Louis less than a year after his freedom was granted.*

Signs *of the times in the 1850's.*

Pennsylvania, Illinois and Indiana, and even during the campaign Southerners made it clear that they would not remain in the Union if a party made up solely of Northerners elected a President. The Democratic nominee, James Buchanan, won the election and the Union held. But just two days after Buchanan's inauguration the North was to receive its most severe shock, the Dred Scott decision (Dredd Scott v. Sandford).

Dred Scott was a slave who sued in the Missouri courts for his freedom on the grounds that he had resided for periods of time in Illinois, and in unorganized territory north of 36°30′ where slavery had been forbidden by the Missouri Compromise. The decision of the Supreme Court delivered by a Southerner, Chief Justice Taney, was devastating to the Northern cause. It declared that because he was a Negro, Scott could not be a citizen of the United States and therefore had no right to sue in Federal court; and that as a resident of Missouri, the laws of Illinois had no longer any effect on his status. The most sweeping statement of all proclaimed that as a resident of the territory north of 36°30′, he had not been emancipated because Congress had no right to deprive citizens of their property (slaves) without "due process of law." It followed from this that the Missouri Compromise was unconstitutional and void. The Southern victory over slavery was now complete: Southerners could take their slaves into any corner of the Nation and be protected by the Supreme Court, and Northerners could not outlaw slavery anywhere.

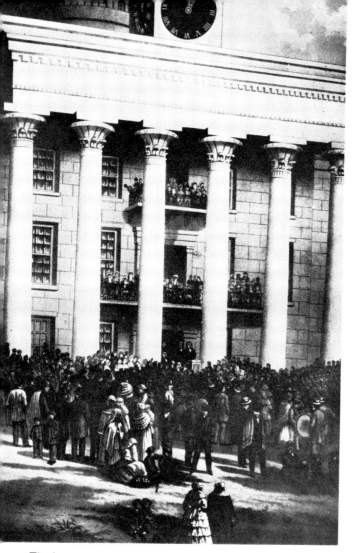

The inauguration *of Jefferson Davis as President of the Confederacy on February 18, 1861, in Montgomery, Alabama.*

Charles Sumner *was caned in the United States Senate chambers by a vengeful "Bully" Brooks during the heated debates prior to the Civil War.*

SECESSION

One might argue that as late as 1861 there were still possible solutions to the North-South conflict that could have prevented war, but it would have taken the most dispassionate, perceptive and self-denying statesmanship any country has ever witnessed. The times were not suited to these qualities, though both Abraham Lincoln and Jefferson Davis possessed them in a unique degree. They were tense and angry times. On the floor of the Senate, Charles Sumner had condemned the pro-slavery men as "hirelings picked from the drunken spew and vomit of an uneasy civilization," and for his ill-advised remark was beaten almost to death in the Senate chamber. Senator Hammond reported that every man in both houses was armed with "a revolver—some with two—and a bowie knife." John Brown gathered a group about him in 1859 and raided Harper's Ferry with the intent of providing Negroes with guns with which to begin an insurrection. Though he was hanged by the Federal government for treason, he became a symbol to the Southerners of the true intentions of the North, and a symbol to some Northerners of the need for exactly the type of action the South so feared. Henry David Thoreau wrote that John Brown "had the courage to face his country herself when she was wrong," and the perception to point out that "when you bury a hero a crop of heroes is sure to spring up." Thoreau rejoiced that he was a contemporary of Brown's and concluded: "Eighteen hundred years ago Christ was crucified; this morning perchance John Brown was hung. These are the two ends of a chain." Ralph Waldo Emerson referred to Brown as "that new saint, than whom nothing . . . more brave was ever led by love of men into conflict and death" and believed Brown would "make the gallows glorious like a cross."

In the elections of 1856 Southerners had threatened secession if a purely Northern party elected a President. Their threat was not allowed to die in the off-year elections and was employed even more vigorously in the Presidential elections of 1860. In that election the North had found its spokesman in the person of a gangly, homely, shrewd lawyer from Illinois, Abraham Lincoln, and the South was about to find its leader in a gentlemen planter, a hero of the Mexican War, and a brilliant statesman of national reputation, Jefferson Davis. Both men had been born in Kentucky, a microcosm of the

The transition of Southern thought on slavery constitutes one of the more fascinating aspects of the Civil War. At the time of the Northwest Ordinance (1787) Southerners had accepted the right of Congress to limit slavery in the territories. In 1808 there had been little opposition to the abolition of the slave trade. In 1821, although with more opposition, the South had accepted the right of Congress to bar slavery in the territories north of the 36°30' line. By 1850, however, many Southerners were demanding the right to migrate with slaves into any of the western areas. In 1854 that right was allowed by the Kansas-Nebraska Bill when it officially adopted "popular sovereignty" for the lands involved, and with the Dred Scott decision all previous legislation became null and void and the Southerners had acquired the right to import slaves even into the original Northern states where slavery had been outlawed for more than fifty years.

Accompanying this change in their demands for the political protection of slavery was a change in their philosophical position. During the Revolutionary period many Southerners believed that slavery was an evil and should ultimately be abolished. By the time of the Missouri Compromise, the Southern position seemed to be that slavery was an evil, but a necessary evil. By the 1850's slavery was being advocated as a positive good. Jefferson Davis and other Southern leaders began to compare Southern society to that of the Greeks and insisted that only through the institution of slavery could a high civilization develop.

President *of the Confederacy Jefferson Davis.*

The Republican *nominating convention in Chicago, 1860. It was at this convention that the name of Abraham Lincoln was brought up as a candidate for the Presidency. Many easterners, who had at first not supported Lincoln, finally joined forces with the westerners who supported Lincoln, and the two groups were able to have Lincoln nominated on the third ballot.*

Abraham Lincoln *as he appeared at the time he took office.*

This picture shows *the death scene of Abraham Lincoln. Mrs. Lincoln kneels beside the bed as members of his cabinet stand grouped around it. The picture was reportedly given to a friend by Mrs. Lincoln and passed on within the family from generation to generation.*

Nation, but one had gone South and developed a Southern view of government and slavery, and the other had migrated West, never losing contact with middle America.

Abraham Lincoln had served in the Illinois legislature, had represented Illinois for a term in Congress, but had before 1850 little to recommend him for the herculean tasks which he would be called upon to face in 1861. But during those eleven years of apprenticeship he had matured politically and spiritually, and with each new issue that faced the Nation, had demonstrated greater clarity of perception and a deeper dedication to the principles upon which the Nation was founded. In his arguments against the Kansas-Nebraska Act, his speeches during the election of 1856, his stand on the Dred Scott Decision, and his stellar performance in his famous debate with Douglas, he was honing his thought and perfecting his style. When he received the Presidential nomination of the Republican party, he was a seasoned politician with a profound understanding of the American tradition and a discerning political wisdom.

In discussing the Kansas-Nebraska Act he stated flatly that ''The spirit of seventy-six and the spirit of Nebraska, are utter antagonisms.'' He went on to add that although the Fathers of the Republic had seen slavery as an evil to be contained, the spirit of Nebraska had proclaimed slavery a sacred right to be extended. Although Lincoln was frankly admitting what the South tried to avoid facing—that the Negro was a man—he was not advocating that slavery be abolished in the South. Like the Founding Fathers he saw

General Robert E. Lee *on his famous war horse Traveler.*

MULLIGAN'S BRIGADE!

LAST CHANCE TO AVOID THE DRAFT!

$402 BOUNTY!

TO VETERANS!

$302 to all other VOLUNTEERS!

All Able-bodied Men, between the ages of 18 and 45 Years, who have heretofore served not less than nine months, who shall re-enlist for Regiments in the field, will be deemed Veterans, and will receive one month's pay in advance, and a bounty and premium of $402. To all other recruits, one month's pay in advance, and a bounty and premium of $302 will be paid.

All who wish to join Mulligan's Irish Brigade, now in the field, and to receive the munificent bounties offered by the Government, can have the opportunity by calling at the headquarters of

CAPT. J. J. FITZGERALD

Of the Irish Brigade, 23d Regiment Illinois Volunteers. Recruiting Officer. Chicago. Illinois.

Each Recruit, Veteran or otherwise, will receive

Seventy-five Dollars Before Leaving General Rendezvous,

and the remainder of the bounty in regular instalments till all is paid. The pay, bounty and premium for three years will average **$24** per month, for Veterans; and **$21.30** per month for all others.

If the Government shall not require these troops for the full period of Three Years, and they shall be mustered hono[...] out of the service before the expiration of their term of enlistment, they shall receive, UPON BEING MUSTERED O[...] the whole amount of BOUNTY remaining unpaid, the same as if the full term [...] been served.

J. J. FITZGERALD.

Chicago, December, 1863.

Recruiting Officer, corner North Clark & Kenzie Stre[...]

HENRY W. HALLECK   AMBROSE E. BURNSIDE   JOSEPH HOOKER   GEORGE G. MEADE

Four generals *Lincoln called upon to lead the Union forces during the Civil War.*

slavery as a problem too well entrenched and complex to be eradicated at one stroke. Lincoln, like most men of that time, repudiated any thought of racial equality between the Blacks and the Whites, but unlike many of his time he held fast to the idea that the Negro shared with the rest of humanity the right to life, liberty and the pursuit of happiness. For Lincoln freedom was indivisible; once admit that enslaving the Negro was right, and the same arguments could later justify enslaving the factory worker, or the immigrant.

In speaking on John Brown, Lincoln revealed the position he would later take as President. He denied any connection between the Republican party and John Brown, and firmly denounced the lawlessness of Brown's act. Violence and bloodshed and treason are wrong, he said, but went on to warn the South that they are wrong in whatever guise they appeared, and if the Southern states should ever attempt to break up the Union, "it will be our duty to deal with you as old John Brown has been dealt with."

After his election Lincoln had not only to face the complications stemming from slavery, but the issue of secession, and once in office he had to abide by his oath to uphold the Constitution. In his inaugural address he indicated that he would work with the South to enforce the fugitive slave law, uphold the domestic slave trade, and even support a Constitutional amendment guaranteeing no Federal interference with slavery in the states where it then existed; but he flatly rejected any extension of slavery into the territories, insisted that no state upon its own motion could lawfully get out of the Union, warned that if force and violence were used from another quarter, it would be met by force, and that whatever happened, the power confided to him would "be used to hold, occupy, and possess the property and places belonging to the government."

A badly divided Democratic party, and a new feeling of

A Black soldier *serving in the Union Army during the Civil War.*

Recruitment poster *from 1863.*

A Rebel soldier *killed during the Battle of Gettysburg.*

Photograph *of Private Edwin Jennison, a member of the Georgia forces serving in the Confederate Army. Jennison was killed at Malvern Hill.*

General William Tecumseh *Sherman, whose infamous march to the sea laid waste to virtually all in the path of his conquering army.*

unity in the North had assured Lincoln's election in November even though he received only forty percent of the total votes cast. South Carolina seceded in December, followed by other Southern states and the Confederate government was formed in February 1861, almost a month before Lincoln was inaugurated. By that time all the hitherto nationally owned forts and navy yards in the seceded states had fallen without resistance to the Confederate authorities except Fort Sumter at Charleston and Fort Pickens at Pensacola, and the Confederacy made it clear that any attempt to reinforce Sumter would be considered a hostile act. Lincoln delayed sending supplies and reinforcements, hoping that Virginia, Kentucky, Tennessee, Missouri and Arkansas could be saved for the Union if precipitous action was held in check. Toward the end of March, Lincoln decided to face the issue squarely and ordered that a relief expedition be sent to Fort Sumter. In response, Jefferson Davis ordered General Beauregard to fire on Sumter only if necessary to prevent its reinforcement; the situation got out of hand and on April 12th, firing on the fort began, an act considered by all in the North, Democrats and Republicans alike, to be one of treason.

THE DELUSION OF SECESSION

The reasons given by Southerners for secession from the Union seem in retrospect to be ill-conceived and raise tantalizing questions about the actual motives behind their decision. They claimed to have withdrawn because the Northern states had enticed their slaves from them and hindered their return. But the very act of withdrawing from the Union cut off any possibility of exerting an influence upon the North to desist from its efforts to help the slaves escape, to enforce the fugitive slave law, or to prevent the Abolitionists from spreading their propaganda.

The Southerners stated that they had left the Union because the North claimed the right to prohibit slavery in the territories and from the states henceforth to be admitted to the Union. But, certainly they would have had no control over the territories or any other privileges there once they were out of the Federation. The Federal government could have freed the slaves only through a Constitutional amendment, but an amendment would not have been possible for many years to come had the slave states remained in the Union to vote it down.

Soldiers *from the 24th Michigan, part of the Army of the Potomac, killed during the battle of Gettysburg. The 24th Michigan lost more than eighty percent of its men during the bloody battle.*

Armed hostilities *between North and South which opened the Civil War occurred on April 12-13 with the bombardment of Fort Sumter in the harbor at Charleston, South Carolina.*

Reproduction *of a painting showing the battle between the* Monitor *(foreground) and the* Merrimack. *The battle between the two ironclad ships occurred on March 9, 1862.*

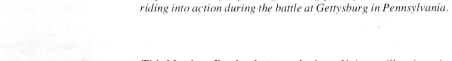

Reproduction *of a painting showing part of the Union artillery riding into action during the battle at Gettysburg in Pennsylvania.*

This Matthew Brady photograph *shows Union artillery in action during the Battle of Fredericksburg in December, 1862. The Confederate forces were victorious in this battle.*

Reproduction *of an ink sketch showing the celebration of Emancipation Day in Charleston, South Carolina, on January 8, 1877.*

Photograph *of U.S. Army troopers fighting somewhere in the west during the Civil War.*

Photograph *of John Wilkes Booth, Lincoln's assassin.*

They also seceded, they said, because a purely Northern party had elected a President, but the South dominated the Supreme Court and Southerners and Democrats would have possessed a majority of both houses of Congress for several more years. The South seemed to believe she could have seceded without war, yet America had been ready on several previous occasions to go to war over control of the outlet to the Mississippi River which was now in her hands. The vision which the Southerners had entertained of a cultured feudal aristocracy based on great landed estates hardly seemed consistent with the exploitative modern capitalism that had created the cotton kingdom of the South after 1800. As William and Bruce Catton have pointed out:

> They were counterrevolutionaries consciously embarked upon revolution. . . . defenders of the status quo who had to keep altering it in order to protect it. . . . and would soon try to wage something approaching total war on the basis of a devout belief in state sovereignty, local autonomy, and individual liberty. . . . And at bottom, they were fighting for their freedom in order to preserve slavery.''

To explain the Southern mind, it is not enough to recognize the dissimilar geographic conditions which led one section to have an economy based upon the single crop plantation system and slavery, and the other to have free labor, commerce and industry. Nor is it sufficient, although it is closer to the heart of the matter, to point out that the North favored a protective tariff, a national bank and government appropriations for internal improvements, whereas the South, convinced that such legislation aided the North at her expense, opposed them; or that the North advocated a stronger national government and the South, as protection against the legislation she opposed, resorted to a states' rights doctrine.

Slavery was an integral part of the Southern culture and for both North and South it had become a moral issue which was

Scene showing *the capture of Harrold and the shooting of John Booth in the barn of Garath's farm by a detachment of the 16th New York Cavalry under the leadership of Colonel Baker.*

inextricably bound to the causes of the war; but taken by itself slavery does not explain the irrational position of the South in 1861, even if it was interwoven into the fabric of the economic differences and the consequent political demands of the two sections. Some historians have even suggested that if there had been no West—no additional territories to be fought over, the war would never have occurred, and the Cattons hint that the simplest explanation of the war was the fact that neither side had the haziest notion that when an actual showdown came it would result as it did.

The ingredient which was the catalyst for all other considerations may have been a growing fear throughout the South: fear of the Negro, who in many sections of the South outnumbered the White, and the fear—a combination of apprehension and pride—caused by the relative decline of the South in relationship to the North. The fear of the Negro was precipitated by the Abolitionists at home and abroad who were encouraging the slaves to escape and demanding the abolition of slavery itself; and each year their tactics grew more militant and their demands more absolute. The fear was accentuated by occasional insurrections in the South of which Nat Turner's was a chief example, and climaxed during John Brown's raid on Harper's Ferry. Able to control the Black only through harsh measures on the plantations and a host of restrictive laws, it seemed obvious that the push for the immediate freedom of the illiterate Black population by the Abolitionists could only result in chaos for society and a

bloody death for many of the Southern Whites.

The decline of the South in relationship to the North was very real indeed. By 1860 the population of the North was double that of the South, and the Northern states possessed ninety-two percent of the Nation's industry, sixty-seven percent of the Nation's railroads, almost all the iron, coal and copper deposits, and sold goods each year that were worth three times the goods produced in the South. Although the South had experienced a booming economy based on cotton, the old Tidewater states had clearly lost their prestigious position in the Union. Virginia had twice the population of New York in 1790, but by 1850 had dropped to half that of New York. In 1790 the exports and imports from Virginia and New York were virtually equal; in 1852 New York was exporting products worth more than twenty-five times those being exported by Virginia, and in 1855 was importing 165 million dollars worth of goods compared to Virginia's imports of one million dollars. In spite of all the Southerner's boasts that only a slave economy could create a great civilization, it was the free society of the North that was producing such eminent figures as Emerson, Thoreau, Parker, Alcott, Cooper, Stowe, Hawthorn, and Melville. Even the period of Southern leadership in national politics, which had made such a significant contribution to American life, seemed to have come to an end.

Fear, pride, resentment and poverty, when combined with the moral issue of slavery, basic economic differences with the North and her losing struggle for control and direction of national policy, brought the South into embracing the delusion that secession would solve her problems—and secession could lead only to war.

HISTORICAL HEADLINES
ON
THE CIVIL WAR

CHARLESTON

MERCURY

EXTRA:

Passed unanimously at 1.15 o'clock, P. M., December 20th, 1860.

AN ORDINANCE

To dissolve the Union between the State of South Carolina and other States united with her under the compact entitled "The Constitution of the United States of America."

We, the People of the State of South Carolina, in Convention assembled, do declare and ordain, and it is hereby declared and ordained,

That the Ordinance adopted by us in Convention, on the twenty-third day of May, in the year of our Lord one thousand seven hundred and eighty-eight, whereby the Constitution of the United States of America was ratified, and also, all Acts and parts of Acts of the General Assembly of this State, ratifying amendments of the said Constitution, are hereby repealed; and that the union now subsisting between South Carolina and other States, under the name of "The United States of America," is hereby dissolved.

THE

UNION

IS

DISSOLVED!

The Charleston Mercury Extra.

Saturday Evening, April 13, 1861.

THE BATTLE OF FORT SUMTER!

END OF THE FIGHT!

MAJOR ANDERSON SURRENDERS!

All last night the mortar batteries were throwing shells into the Fort. At an early hour this morning the gun batteries re-opened their fire, which had been suspended during the night. Major ANDERSON replied about seven o'clock with a vigorous fire. It appeared that he had become convinced that his fire against the Cummings' Point Batteries was ineffectual, for he now devoted his attention almost entirely to Fort Moultrie, the Dahlgren Battery and the Floating Battery. At ten minutes after eight, A. M., a thick smoke was seen issuing from the parapet, and the roof of the southern portion of Fort Sumter barracks was soon in flames. The fire was produced either by a hot shot or a shell. During the progress of the fire, three explosions were produced by the fall of shells into the combustibles of the Fort.

At a quarter to one o'clock the flag and flag-staff of the United States was shot away. For some twenty minutes no flag appeared above the fort. Col. L. T. WIGFALL, in a small boat, approached it from Morris Island, with a white flag upon his sword. Having entered, he called for Major ANDERSON, stated that he was an Aid-de-Camp of Gen. BEAUREGARD; that seeing his distress and the impossibility of his holding the post, he claimed, in the name of his Chief, its surrender. In reply to the inquiry "what terms will be granted," he stated that Gen. BEAUREGARD was a soldier and a gentleman, and knew how to treat a gallant enemy, but that Major ANDERSON could not make his own terms, and must leave the details to Gen. BEAUREGARD.

Major ANDERSON then agreed to surrender to General BEAUREGARD, in the name of the Confederate States, and hauled down his flag, which he had again lifted, accompanied by a white flag.

The batteries then ceased firing, and Colonel WIGFALL reported to General BEAUREGARD, in Charleston.

The following are substantially the terms of the capitulation :

All proper facilities will be afforded for the removal of Major ANDERSON and command, together with company arms and property, and all private property.

The flag which he has upheld so long, and with so much fortitude, under the most trying circumstances, may be saluted by him on taking it down.

Major ANDERSON is allowed to fix the time of surrender, which is some time to-morrow (Sunday). He prefers going from Fort Sumter to the fleet off our bar.

A detachment of the regular army from Sullivan's island will be transferred to Fort Sumter; and one detachment from Morris Island.

No one has been killed or wounded upon our side. A few of the garrison of Fort Sumter were slightly wounded.

The Catawba will take Major ANDERSON to the fleet.

LATEST FROM MORRIS ISLAND.

HOSTILITIES SUSPENDED FOR THE NIGHT.

MORRIS ISLAND, Saturday, April 13, 6 P. M.

A boat sent in by the fleet of war vessels off the Bar, has just been brought to by a shot from one of our batteries. It contained, besides the oarsmen, Lieut. MARCY, of the Powhatan, bearing a flag of truce. He reports the vessels in the offing to be the Baltic, Illinois, Powhatan, Harriet Lane, and Pawnee.

Lieut. Marcy, in the name of his superior officers, has announced a suspension of hostilities until to-morrow morning.

It is rumored that he demands that Major ANDERSON and his men be allowed to join the fleet.

SOUTH CAROLINA IS INDEPENDENT!

Lincoln AND HIS Contemporaries

By WILLIAM DAY SIMONDS.

IF THIS article is to be of value to any one its nature and purpose must be clearly understood. It is not an essay upon the life of Abraham Lincoln, nor an attempt to pass judgment upon him. We seek merely to see him through the eyes of his contemporaries, of those who knew him and have left on record their impressions. We would know the man as his neighbors thought they knew him, as strangers thought they saw him, even as his enemies misread him.

It would be false to suppose that these first-hand conclusions are correct. Many are grotesquely incorrect, some evidently malicious, and more are simply mistaken. But all are important, for they answer the question, "What did the men who knew Abraham Lincoln in private and public life think of him while he was still a living man among them? How was he held in public opinion before the assassin's bullet gave him an immortality of fame?" Surely our study of Lincoln lacks completeness unless these questions are honestly answered, and this the writer attempts in what he believes to be the scientific method and spirit.

Perhaps the first surprise awaiting the impartial student is the discovery of Lincoln's obscurity prior to 1858, when his debate with Stephen A. Douglas made him a national figure. Two years later, when a candidate for the Presidency, he deprecated an attempt to prepare a campaign biography, saying: "It is all folly to try to make anything out of me or my early life. It can all be condensed into a single line of Gray's Elegy: 'The short and simple annals of the poor.'"

In those days, and of this the evidence is conclusive, Lincoln was believed to be of very humble ancestry. "Poor white trash spawned by Kentucky upon Southern Illinois," said Wendell Phillips, voicing the general opinion. It was darkly whispered that some mystery clouded his origin, and touching all such matters Lincoln was known to be extremely reticent. A man of little schooling, less than twelve months altogether, in the indifferent frontier schools of the period, this fact gave currency to the idea that he was ignorant, boorish and vulgar. Fond of anecdotes, according to the fashion of his time, he never outgrew the reputation early fastened upon him as a retailer of doubtful stories. Lincoln was a poor man whose exceeding simplicity of life masked his greatness. Up to the hour of his election to the Presidency he "did his chores," taking care of his old horse Tom, and looking after the family cow, just like the humblest of his neighbors.

A German traveler, seeing Lincoln when a Presidential candidate, enter a meat shop at Springfield, make his purchase and walk home, was heard to remark: "You can not convince me that a man who buys a pound of steak, has it wrapped in brown paper, and carries it home himself, is fit for the high office of President of the United States."

He Did Not Know Himself.

That he was a good lawyer, an able politician, that given a good cause, he could speak with convincing power—of all that he had given good proof. But that he was really a great man—one of those rare men who change the course of history—no one so much as suspected, unless it might have been his unhappy wife, who seems to have dreamed of coming greatness and impending tragedy. The people did not know this man. He did not know himself.

In 1858, only two years before the famous debate with Douglas, Lincoln said in a public address: "With me the race of ambition has been a failure—a flat failure." So he honestly thought, and so he had a right to think. A frontier lawyer, a member, many years before, of the Illinois Legislature, one term in Congress, several political campaigns in which he and his party had suffered defeat, this was the record at the age of 45. Quite true, the race of ambition had been a flat failure, embittered by the renown of his rival, Douglas.

In 1860 the New York Herald pronounced Lincoln a fourth rate country lawyer wholly unfit for the Presidency. About the same time a large audience in Boston was found to contain but three men who could give their inquiring fellow citizens even a meager account of the new leader of Republicanism. Perhaps no man ever entered upon the duties of President so little known to the people at large. It should be remembered that Lincoln was not the first choice of the strong men of his party as a Presidential candidate, nor was he the choice of the majority of voters in the election which carried him to power. He was what is known as a minority candidate and a minority President. That is, a majority of Republicans preferred some other candidate, and the majority of voters divided their ballots among Lincoln's three opponents in the campaign of 1860.

Coarse Epithets Applied to Him.

So much for his popularity as he entered the White House. But this is only the beginning of the story. For reasons it is now difficult to understand, many public men conceived for the new President a violent dislike. Coarse epithets were habitually applied to him by men high in official position. Southern statesmen and Southern papers did not scruple to call Mr. Lincoln "the Illinois ape." Congressmen—some of them of his own party—were in the habit of speaking of "the babboon at the other end of the avenue." Richard H. Dana, writing of affairs in Washington in February, 1863, says: "The most striking thing here is the absence of personal loyalty to the President. He has no admirers. He likes rather to talk and tell stories with all sorts of people who come to him for all sorts of purposes than to give his mind to the main duties of his great post."

"I know Mr. Lincoln," said Wendell Phillips. "I have been to Washington and I have taken his measure. He is a first-rate second-rate man, and that is all there is of him. He is a mere convenience, and is waiting, like any other broomstick to be used." The New York Independent, then a power in the land, thought Lincoln's official papers "cold, lifeless, dead."

Edwin M. Stanton, afterward Secretary of War, was accustomed during the earlier months of Mr. Lincoln's administration, to refer to "the painful imbecility of the President," and Nicolay and Hay affirm that the attitude of Secretary Chase varied between the limits of active brutality and benevolent contempt."

Just how long this prevailing sentiment of distrust and dislike continued it is hard to determine, but it is safe to say that for full three years Mr. Lincoln was the most bitterly reviled of American Presidents. Standing the central figure of the fiercest civil war of history, upon his head rained calumny and curse, until the vocabulary of rage and hate was exhausted. For battles and elections lost; for Generals defeated and disgraced; for the people's poverty and the soldiers' suffering; for the dire distress of those terrible days, he was held responsible. Nor did the tide begin to turn until his life was almost at an end.

The people, the plain people, had learned to love him for the very qualities that aroused the hatred of politicians. Generals in the Army despised his weakness in granting pardon to military offenders, but the people loved him for the mercy he granted their own sons. His honest devotion to Union and liberty at last conquered the head and heart of the Nation and he was elected to the Presidency for a second term, this time by a larger majority than had been given to any candidate. At length his Generals gave him victories, and the people gave him applause until all the glory of successful war crowned his Administration. And then, as though it were the will of heaven that hate should make his glory secure, a madman's murderous deed gave him the crown of martyrdom.

His Warmest Admirers Cautious.

But not at once did the stricken President enter into his just renown. His warmest admirers spoke cautious words beside his coffin, if measured by the lofty praise that to-day the world willingly bestows. Contemporary opinion was accurately expressed in an eulogy by Dr. J. G. Holland: "Strong without greatness, acute without brilliancy, penetrating but not profound, he was in intellect an average American in the walk of life in which nature found him."

At a memorial meeting in Tremont Temple, Boston, Wendell Phillips atoned for years of merciless criticism in a manly tribute, not yet without implied qualification of distrust: "Fortunate man! God has graciously withheld him from any fatal misstep in the great advance, and withdrawn him at the moment when his star touched its zenith, and the Nation needed a sterner hand for the work God gives it to do.

"With the least possible personal hatred; with too little sectional bitterness, often forgetting justice in mercy; tender-hearted to any misery his own eyes saw; and in any deed which needed his actual sanction, if his sympathy had limits—recollect he was human, and that he welcomed light more than most men, was more honest than his fellows, and with a truth to his own convictions such as few politicians achieve. With all his shortcomings, we point proudly to him as the natural growth of democratic institutions. Coming time will put him in that galaxy of Americans which makes our history the day star of nations."

That prophecy has come to earlier fulfillment than the orator dreamed, for though but a single generation has passed, the fame of Lincoln as the foremost man of his age and country is secure.

A NEW LINCOLN ANECDOTE

"An incident illustrating the kindness of heart of Abraham Lincoln and his consideration of the feelings of others, was told by the late Noah Brooks," said J. H. Morse recently.

"At a time when the camp fires of the Confederate Army were in sight of Washington, and, of course, when the whole time and thought of the President were strained to the limit, a man appeared at the door of the White House insisting on seeing the President personally, but for several days he was denied admission. The matter finally coming to Mr. Lincoln's ears, he gave instructions that the man on his next appearance should be admitted. He proved to be a common laboring man living on the outskirts of the city, his habitation commanding a view of the Smithsonian Institute and Arlington Heights as well.

"After looking about very carefully and satisfying himself that the doors were all closed and no one within earshot, he gravely informed the President that every night at midnight for the several weeks past a signal had been flashed from the tower of the Smithsonian Institute to the Confederates encamped across the river, and he thought it should be brought to the attention of the President, the only official in whom he had absolute confidence.

"Mr. Lincoln, placing his hand on the man's shoulder, very kindly informed him that that was the lantern of the man whose duty it was to take the reading of the weather instruments located there, and assured the man that his loyalty was appreciated by the Government, and urged him always to come and inform the President of anything suspicious that he might observe. Most men would have sent the man away with a reminder that the time of the Chief Magistrate of the Nation should not be taken up by trifles, but not so Abraham Lincoln."

IF HE HAD A TAIL.

Dressed in the latest and most approved motocycling costume, with goggles all complete, the motocyclist gayly toot-tooted his way toward the Zoo. Suddenly he slackened, dismounted, and said to a small, grubby urchin:

"I say, boy, am I right for the Zoo?"

The boy gasped at so strange a sight, and thought it must be some new animal for the gardens.

"You may be all right if they have a spare cage," he said, when he could find his tongue, "but you'd ha' stood a far better chance if yo [illegible] a tail."—Tit-Bits.

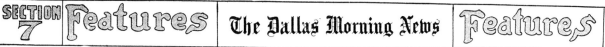
Supreme in Texas   Copyright, 1925 A. H. Belo & Company   DALLAS, TEXAS, SUNDAY, MAY 17, 1925   Copyright, 1925 A. H. Belo & Company   Supreme in Texas

Jeff Davis Visited Dallas in Year 1875

Idol of Followers of the Gray Spent Few Colorful Hours Here Ten Years After War Ended

By Remarkable Coincidence Coming Confederate Reunion Is Exactly Fifty Years Later

BY STUART McGREGOR.

Come Tuesday, the nineteenth, and we will be at the fiftieth anniversary of one of the great days of the early history of Dallas—the memorable visit of Jefferson Davis, ex-President of the Confederacy, on May 19, 1875.

Now-a-days, great men are as thick as grasshoppers and whiz about over the country by airplane, rail and auto. To make an occasion of every visit would turn the calendar into a succession of red letter days and work the village band overtime. The President can still draw a house, and a Babe Ruth, or a Baron Renfrew or a Valentino can make a splash in certain circles, but as for the average man, he just drops into the hotel like John Doe and registers, and may count himself lucky if a luncheon club invites him to make a ten-minute address or a newspaper reporter calls for an interview. Thus great men come and go, and great occasions pass like ships in the night.

Not so in 1875. In those days a great man was great and it was a privilege to travel fifty miles by horseback or prairie schooner to look at him. And if there ever was a great man in the eyes of his admirers it was Jefferson Davis or Robert E. Lee in those dark days following the close of the Civil War. So the visit of the former President of the Southern Confederacy to Dallas on May 19, 1875, was most distinctly a great occasion.

Indeed, as the times quieted down they were ideally suited to making a tremendously great occasion of such a visit. The South had just emerged from the sorrowful days of reconstruction. Less than two years prior to the visit of Davis to Dallas, the election of Richard Coke as Governor had ended "carpetbag" rule in Texas. The memory of negro Judges, "scalawag" public treasurers, and voting places guarded by Union troops was still fresh in the minds of Dallas residents.

Then, too, Dallas' growth had been stimulated greatly by the recent acquisition of her two first railroads (in 1872 and 1873) and she had jumped from the status of a little frontier village to that of a thriving city of 5,000 or more population. It was, indeed, a day of renewed confidence and high hopes, following a period of disaster and gloom.

Why He Came a Mystery.

Just why Jefferson Davis came to Dallas is not plain, except that he was very cordially invited by Dallas citizens when they heard that he was in Houston. Just why he was in Texas at that time is not made plain by the old Dallas Herald clippings announced by The News, although it carries several preliminary announcements in addition to the five-column story of the great day.

In those days when salesmen took town from doors and climb up five escapes when candidates for public office inquire into the conduct of their opponents during the boyhood, when more stars in angle in divorce suits for the public it grieves—in such bold days as now, newspaper reporters are not paid to ask the questions of the mighty what his business is. But back in 1875—well, that was a day bowing and scraping—there was more polish and less push. So the editor of the Dallas Herald didn't question the train that the mission of Mr. Davis about his mission to Texas, probably he thought it a Mr. Davis' private business, however, history records that the President of the Confederacy as at that time interested in certain railroad extensions and other commercial development in the lower Mississippi Valley and it is probable that it was his duties in that connection therewith that brought him to Texas.

Invited by Dallas Delegation.

At any rate, it became known in Has that Jeff. Davis was in Huston and a delegation of Dallas—most prominent citizens, including Gen. W. L. Cabell, Barry Brown, John Brokaw, Bart Gibbs and others was sent to the South Texas city to lay before him and urge upon other invitation of the city. Accordingly, Jeff Davis became the distinguished guest of Dallas—it became at once the mecca every ex-Confederate and Confederate sympathizer within hundreds of miles.

A Gala Occasion.

All was hurry and bustle of preparation until the day of arrival—and such a day! Five closely-printed columns in the Dallas Herald tell of the glories of the occasion. "The team deliberately spent Jeff Davis." Jeff Davis picture on the street corners, Jeff the banners bedecked the city's roughfares. Jeff Davis drinks were served and here, and it is recorded in Herald that the Scotch bakery made a "Jeff Davis" bun in honor of the occasion.

Great Crowds Arrive.

The day preceding the 18th the roading little Dallas were eded. Came the slow moving wagon and from nearer locations in the country about came carry-alls and the buckboards every train brought a load of varsity. Streets were given over to ing and wagon yards were overing. Husky country boys rode from far and near, tying their the reins over the hitching posts Main street, dismounted and astrwalkway with glad steps the "Five Brothers" to relievegorged thereots and heighthalr mentil firmaments tie a see befitting such a great occasion. The gas lights along Dallas—downtown streets (only recently installed) burned late that night.

The Expected Moment.

The train bringing Mr. Davis from Houston was scheduled to arrive at 3:30 o'clock in the morning, the thousands of spectators half an hour or more in the station around the little frame house before a shrill blast from the directions of the "cee" announced the arrival of the station train. No doubt then an aroused the throttle gave a longer than usual caper to ring in the station yard with a loader clang of couplings and the little, big-funneled lo...

A STRANGE COINCIDENCE OF EVENTS

Jefferson Davis, President of the Confederate States of America during the Civil War, came to Dallas for a short visit on Tuesday, May 19, 1875. And on Tuesday, May 19, 1925, the few remaining men who comprise the rapidly thinning ranks of the Confederate Army will meet here for their latest reunion.

It is most unusual that the Confederate veterans should have chosen a time to meet in Dallas that coincides exactly with the fiftieth anniversary of the visit of Jeff Davis to this city. The coincidence is the more noteworthy when the completeness of it is realized.

First, the two occasions are just fifty years apart—1875 and 1925.

Second, the date is the same—May 19 of both years.

Third, it just happens that May 19 of 1875 was a Tuesday while May 19 of this year also is a Tuesday.

If someone had consciously and purposefully chosen an auspicious time for the coming reunion to get under way, they could not have done better than this. The weird angle to the whole business is that no one thought of the coincidence at all. It just happened!

federacy as he stepped from the station platform into a carriage for a few remarks after which he was chicked away to the San Jacinto Hotel for a brief rest. Then came the "big push." The program called for a march to the old fair grounds where a general picnic and speechmaking was to be indulged in.

Military Escort.

First in that great procession came the Lancaster Band, then the Sterewall Greys and the Lamar Rifles. In carriage bearing the city's guest, Major Cabell and Gen. Lubbock, the fire boys in their red shirts and blue caps (the Hook and Ladder Co.), members of the city lodges mounted on horses bearing the Dallas Commercial Club and then more carriages with city and county officials. Over Elm street near Lamar was a great banner bearing the words "God Bless Jeff Davis."

A Grand Parade.

The procession formed near the courthouse square and marched on Austin street and thence up Elm, up past Adam's hardware store. Wheat's dry goods store and Bell's hardware store with their numerous signboards consisting respectively of a bundle of wheat and a boll on past Sanger's and then on out Elm street, to the old fair grounds with thousands crowded the sidewalks, jammed upper story windows and thronged the flat-topped roofs of the buildings which lined the street. "God Bless Jeff Davis."

How Dallas Looked Then.

Truly it was a great day for Dallas, and it must have been a great day for Jefferson Davis. As he rode up Elm street he saw no towering skyscrapers, but instead a line of one and two-story buildings of frame and rough stone structure with plank and flagstone sidewalks and small dingy display windows. A random corner was crammed with a newly installed gas light, but the pavement consisted of good black ways soil, and no doubt the procession had to detour slightly to avoid a deep hole at Elm and Poydras with a warning fence rail stuck in the midst of it. But Davis was a man of vision; no doubt he read the future as he beheld that day the raw but rampant Western city with its vibrant, whooping citizenship.

The Big Picnic.

The old fair grounds was located in the vicinity of the present Baptist Hospital and Baylor Medical College. Remnants of that stately grove of oaks remain today on the campus of that institution and on the spacious lawns of some of the homes in that vicinity. It is almost downtown today, but then it was on the outer fringe of the downtown section.

Here white tablecloths were spread upon the grass and fried chicken, layer cake and all that sort of thing was spread in turn on the tablecloths. The distinguished guest joined informally in the merrymaking and Thomas F. and S. Beverley Scott, who reside in Dallas today, recall eating at the same table with Davis. Indeed, there are many Dallas residents today who remember that famous occasion. One of them, June Peak, took an important part in the formalities in his double capacity as City Marshall and First Lieutenant of the Stonewall Greys.

Davis Speaks.

Then came the speechmaking. Judge John J. Good delivered the address of welcome. In replying Davis stated that he had been deeply touched by "such outpouring of hearts, for surely the interests of none can be promoted by paying honor to me." But he spent little time reflecting upon the sorrows of the past; his was a hopeful, courageous message looking solely toward the future. He talked about the agricultural and industrial development of Texas, indeed, his speech sounded, more like the address of a present day Chamber of Commerce official than anything else.

"Diversity of soil and climate," he said, "will make yours a great State." He predicted that Texas would become a great exporter of raw products and pleaded for "free trade and protection of farmers' rights." He concluded his speech with the remark: "And whereever I go, give me a Texas welcome."

Gov. Lubbock Responds.

Ex-Governor Lubbock followed at the conclusion of his speech Goslin and Cox, color sergeants for the Lamar Rifles and the Stonewall Greys, advanced with the Lone Star flag. The Lamar Rifles were composed largely of former Union soldiers, while the Stonewall Greys were ex-Confederates, thus the two companies represented the "Blue" and the "Gray" for this great occasion. As the color sergeants came forward the band played "Bonnie Blue Flag" and Davis, called by the throng to his feet again, said: "Brave men can always meet on common ground."

Governor Throckmorton Speaks.

Ex-Governor Throckmorton then spoke, welcoming "not a conqueror but one who embodies the great cardinal principles of honor, truth and bravery." There was a ringing speech also by John Henry Brown and Captain Ed A. Bower of the Stonewall Greys called for three cheers for Captain O'Dell of the Lamar Rifles, who was absent from the city and whose company was then under command of Lieutenant Rivers.

"Among Those Present."

Among the ladies present, as mentioned by the Herald, was Mrs. Peak Mrs. Harwood, Mrs. J. M. Stemmons, Mrs. Juliette Fowler and Mrs. Tom Fields. Among the distinguished out of town visitors were General Walter P. Lane of Marshall, Col. George W. Clinton of Tyler, Col. Ed Burleson of San Marcos, Major Tom Dugan of San Antonio, Miss J. M. Hurt of Sherman and Mrs. Tibithia Rhinc of McKinney.

At the conclusion of the speechmaking program the crowd surged about the veteran Southern leader eager to grasp his hand and hear a word of greeting from his lips. Finally General Cabell arose and asked the remainder of the great crowd to refrain from shaking hands with the earnest remarking that the strength of his right arm is not equal to the warmth of his heart."

Davis' Departure.

But now the sun was sinking low and time for the departure of the train was drawing near. The great man was whisked away to his hotel for a brief rest before taking final leave of the city.

A great ball was given at the courthouse that evening by the elite of the city, but Jefferson Davis had gone and there wasn't much kick in a ball without his presence—not so far as most of the populace was concerned, at least. So the farmer and his family wandered back to the wagon yard and hitched up Pete and Beck, the prominent attorney from Greenville mounted his buckboard and the husky country boy took another drink and crawled into his saddle, and presently the roads were thronged again—outward bound.

Jeff Davis as he appeared during the war.

Jeff Davis at the age of 32 years.

Jeff Davis at the age of 73 years.

The capitol of the Confederate States at Richmond.

The Oldest Twins of the Gray

The Haw Brothers of Virginia, 87 Years Old, Think They Have Distinction of Being Further Along in Years Than Any Other Set of Twins That Fought Under Lee's Banners.

BY VERA PALMER.

To the Old Dominion goes the honor of having what are believed to be the oldest surviving twins who fought throughout the War between the States, and possibly the oldest in the entire country. They are George P. Haw, who until three years ago was a prominent attorney of Richmond, and for forty years Commonwealth's Attorney for Hanover County, Virginia, and John H. Haw of King William County. They are the sons of the late John and Mary Watt Haw and were born July 29, 1838, at "Oak Grove," near Studley, in Hanover county. That home of their childhood is still in the family, and is within a mile distance of the spot where Patrick Henry gave forth his first infant utterances.

These "boys" volunteered in the Hanover Grays before Virginia seceded, and on April 23, 1861, they were mustered into service as members of Company I, Fifteenth Virginia Infantry, to be trained at Camp Lee, just west of the city of Richmond.

The pair saw their first fighting on the Peninsula against McClellan, and took part in the battle of Malvern Hill, together with a number of small actions and skirmishes. Their company is said to have been known as the best fighting unit of the regiment.

During their fighting on the Peninsula the Haws formed a part of the line held by Gen. Lee from Mulberry Island, on the James River, to Yorktown, on the York River, a distance of eleven miles, in which they were only 500 men to the mile.

Saw Much Action.

When falling back on Richmond their company participated in a heavy battle near West Point. The Haws also took part in the defense of the lines of Company B, Fifteenth regiment, to help later, when the force moved to Drewry's Bluff on the James River, and became desperately ill with typhoid fever and was on sick leave for a year.

Meantime his brother now promoted to the rank of First Lieutenant, remained with the company encamped at Richmond when Gen. Lee left for Maryland in 1862. Later Lieut. Haw went to train to Doswell as the only commissioned officer with his company, and from three marched to Harper's Ferry, arriving the morning it was captured by Jackson's corps.

Then came the forced march to the battle of Antietam, more familiarly known as Sharpsburg, in which the regiment was a part of Sim's Brigade in McClaus' Division, reaching the field just as Jackson's exhausted troops were retiring. They forced the enemy back and as they constituted the last man fate had to put in the field, turned defeat into victory.

Of the original Company I there were only sixteen enlisted men and Lieut. Haw, and in that engagement there were killed and eleven wounded, the sole officer losing his left arm. He was wounded just in front of the Dunkard Church but walked to the hospital, where his arm was amputated.

Made Prisoner.

Several days later he fell into the hands of the Federals, and was held prisoner for thirty days, until exchanged at Varina Landing, just below Richmond. On his recovery Lieut. Haw was assigned to light duty as enrolling officer for Hanover, King and Queen and King William Counties, all in Virginia. He served in this capacity until the close of the war.

John H. Haw returned to the army as First Sergeant of his old company, then a part of Pickett's Division. He participated in a campaign in Tennessee and fought in other skirmishes around Johnston, then later taking part in the second battle of Cold Harbor. Sergt. Haw was transferred then to Selma, Ark. and assigned to a gun foundry until the cessation of hostilities.

Diploma Signed by Lee.

Almost immediately following the war George P. Haw entered Washington College Law School, now Washington and Lee University, and was graduated June 20, 1867. His diploma, signed by Gen. Robert E. Lee, then president of that institution, is one of his most cherished possessions. He married Elizabeth Winston Fontaine, formerly Miss Price, elder daughter of the late Dr. Thomas Price of "Dundee," near Hanover Courthouse, where he has lived ever since. Mr. Haw has always been interested in politics and a consistent Democrat. Many years in Congress, owing to the ill health of that time of Mrs. Haw.

"Brother John" has eschewed both politics and matrimony, but he is a mighty fox hunter. In this respect he has more than a State wide reputation, and the "hounddawgs" bred at his kennels have ace high in sporting circles. He is the owner of the famous old "Piping Tree Ferry" plantation in King William County, Virginia, where until a few years ago he used to give house parties for his young relatives and their friends. Invitations to these gatherings at which the proverbial milk and honey could not be compared with the chicken feed and hot biscuits which used to flow ceaselessly from the kitchen, were eagerly sought and highly valued. Immediately after the war John Haw opened a foundry at Garlick's Ferry, Va., but very soon he turned his attention to farming, at which he has been very successful in one does not hunt foxes in the summertime. Both his and his two brothers are devout members of the Presbyterian church, in which George P. Haw has been an elder for a great many years, an office also held by his son.

Tarnish-Resisting Silver.

A new kind of tarnish-resisting silver has been developed by a British silver manufacturing company. The material which is 92.5 per cent silver alloy, has been put to practical test by the manufacture of articles from it and the results have been reported to the Silver Trade Technical Society. The new alloy is said to stand up to the heat necessary for soldering, and to keep shape while being heated. It will bear more heat than standard silver and will allow of a considerable amount of manipulation without developing any defects. British housewives are following the experiences with interest as in the hope that gold and silver dinnerware will soon solve problems of the past.

John Haw (left) and George Haw (right) of Virginia. These two Confederate veterans believe that they are the oldest living twins that served under the Stars and Bars.

THE TREE IS REASSEMBLED

The real issue resolved by the termination of the Civil War was the supremacy of the Federal Government, if it chose to accept that position through the adoption of Constitutional Amendments. The manner through which decisions were made to expand the dominance of the national government relate directly to the development of the Civil Rights movement and to the constitutional question of equality under the law. In a series of acts passed by a Congress which was led by abolitionists who had become Republicans, the origins of Civil Rights as a basic concept in American history began to emerge.

The most fundamental action was the passage of the Thirteenth Amendment which abolished slavery as a legal institution. Two controversies arose simultaneously: the outcry against the change in the status of Blacks and the allegation that the Act was a violation of the Constitution. The second charge was predicated on the belief that it produced a centralization of power and a consolidation of government that was in direct conflict with the intent of the Constitution. The concept of state's rights versus national jurisdiction became the central focus of the controversy.

The direction which the issue would take was in part determined by three situations: the death of President Lincoln, the intransigence of his successor, Andrew Johnson, and the operation of the Black Codes protecting a semi-slavery status in the South. All of these combined to provide the Republicans with a new base of power in Congress. The efforts of three men in particular contributed to the introduction and passage of legislation which was designed to grant Blacks the same rights which were inherently and constitutionally guaranteed to Whites. Thaddeus Stevens, John Bingham, and Charles Sumner aimed their energies and their talents at creating a bill which would, in effect, overturn the Dred Scott decision.

Reproduction *of an ink sketch showing the Republican convention of 1868.*

The success of the passage of the Civil Rights Act of 1866 was superficially an accomplishment of this objective. This comprehensive piece of legislation did establish for Blacks the same rights enjoyed by the White population in almost every aspect of citizenship. However, the fact that they were the same rights did not mean that they were equal or even substantially equal rights.

This potential problem did not escape the attention of the Republicans in Congress. In an effort to prevent a possible repeal of the Act or a reinterpretation of its intent by some future Democratically controlled Congress, they proceeded to construct the Fourteenth Amendment as a means of constitutionally codifying the Civil Rights Act. In 1868 they secured the ratification of the amendment and within two years were able to draft and force the passage of the Fifteenth Amendment, providing Blacks with access to the ballot box.

Taken collectively, the Civil Rights Amendments encouraged Republicans to believe that, because each contained the phrase ''Congress shall have the power to enforce this article by appropriate legislation'', they had successfully placed the Dred Scott decision in a position which was beyond the possibility of legislative appeal or judicial interference.

The accomplishments of the amendments appeared monumental. Blacks had gained six new and vital areas of status within the American community. They were free and not slaves. They were protected as citizens of the United States and as citizens of the states within which they resided. They were presumably insured against an abridgement of their rights, privileges and immunities through the Fourteenth Amendment and granted equal protection under the law and due process within the law. Not only were Blacks' rights to be protected by the Federal Government, but also the power to enforce this protection was placed in the hands of the currently favorable Congress and not the Supreme Court or the States which had been and continued to be, in many cases, hostile to the implementation of civil rights. The work of Congress culminated, at this point in time, with the

Civil War Act of 1875 which protected the right to vote, forbade discrimination in jury selection, established punishment for denial of Constitutionally guaranteed rights of Blacks, and proscribed racial discrimination in inns, theaters, trains, and all other places of public accommodation.

The atmosphere in which this legislation was passed is worth examining in light of the difficulty of actual implementation and in the context of events occurring outside of Washington. Two factors are especially critical. First, although the Civil rights legislation was extremely comprehensive, there were notable exceptions and omissions. For example, as originally proposed the bill would have included articles requiring an end to racial segregation in schools, cemeteries, and churches. The Senate was victorious in striking out the prospect of church integration—arguing basically that it would be asking too much of Christians. Similarly, the House of Representatives abandoned sections securing integration in schools and cemeteries. Consequently, resistance to Civil Rights within the lawmaking bodies at the Federal level had a significant impact in three vital areas. That equality would not mean integration was apparent from the onset of the Civil Rights movement.

The Supreme Court had been in a period of partial eclipse since it had ruled on the Dred Scott case. During the Civil War years, the Court had been characterized by vacillation and its stature had been temporarily weakened by charges that it had precipitated the war and acted unconscientiously during its continuation. Even in the wake of bitter disagreements over Lincoln's reconstruction plan, however, the Court was unable to reassert itself very fully and it was not for another decade that it would be able to gather the force and the will to take an active role in reconstruction.

Lincoln's proposal for reconstruction was predicated on two primary points: the desire to restore the Southern states to the Union with all possible speed, and the objective of allowing loyal Southern governments to proceed with a minimum of Federal intervention in their own internal affairs. For radical Republicans in Congress, this plan was both

The period *of Reconstruction in the South, despite the social turmoil it created between southerners and Carpetbaggers and Scalawags, did bring a significant measure of industrial expansion to the South. Note the juxtaposing of the railroad and the horse drawn wagons.*

too conservative and too generous. Programs for widespread guarantee of amnesty, for special pardons to Confederate leaders, for minimal equality of Blacks following emancipation, and for full power to Southern states to re-establish their own governments were met with serious and whole-hearted resistance by dominant individuals in both Houses of Congress. Against this resistance, Lincoln was able to hold to his plan by vetoing Congressional bills which presented alternatives and by standing his own ground with opponents elsewhere. With his assassination on April 14, 1865, came the first real opportunity to change the course of reconstruction.

With the succession of Andrew Johnson, the radical Republicans were convinced that a new climate of opinion would prevail in the White House. Within a few months, Johnson offered rewards for the arrest of Confederate leaders as well as for the accomplices of John Wilkes Booth. He spoke in a determined way about bringing prominent Confederates to trial for treason and showed an interest in resurrecting the Confiscation Act of 1862 as a means of breaking up large Southern states. In addition, he went a step further than his predecessor had in making a clear commitment to the total abolition of slavery.

The new President also assured Congress that the governments Lincoln had organized in four Southern states would be disbanded, that the Cabinet would be reorganized and that either Congress would be called into special session or political reconstruction would be delayed until Congress reconvened in regular session the following December. It became clear within a matter of a year or so that the grounds of agreement between Congress and the President were, in fact, very small however. It was only in three areas that there was concrete correspondence in viewpoints. First, they shared the objective of restoring the Union and suppressing the rebellion in the South once and for all. Second, they mutually supported the Thirteenth Amendment. And, third, they both held on to a hatred for White Southern planters and aristocracy. Apart from these areas, the divergence between the radicals and the President was extremely wide.

His approach to reconstruction began moderately, by revising Lincoln's plan and adding his own segments. On May 9, 1865, he formally recognized the Pierpont government as the legal government of Virginia. Two weeks later he announced his reconstruction program in a two-edged proclamation, outlining prescriptions for an oath of allegiance that the mass of Southerners would be able to take, providing them with political and civil rights, immunity from trials for treason or conspiracy and exemption from the Confiscation Act. He also outlined the necessary steps to be take for the formation of provisional governments at the state level. In each of the Southern states, the President would appoint a provisional governor whose duty it was to call a state convention and supervise the election of delegates to it. The purpose of the convention was to establish requirements for permanent voting rights and office-holding, after which a general election would be held for a regular governor, other state office positions and members of Congress. With the accomplishment of these minimal requirements, Johnson believed he had completed reconstruction and announced to Congress in December that the process had been both swift and successful. Congress felt otherwise however. Within months, the President's plan had been repudiated and Congress began to assert itself in taking control of reconstruction. Within three years after he became President, Johnson's program for reconstruction was in shambles and he was standing trial for impeachment—a measure which was defeated by a single vote.

For a period of several years, the radicals were able to

This Matthew Brady photograph *shows the members of Congress who were involved in managing the impeachment proceedings against President Andrew Johnson. From left to right they are Senators: Butler, Wilson, Stevens, Boutwell, Williams, Logan, and Bingham.*

successfully channel reconstruction along their chosen lines. The heart of the radicals' program centered on their ability to gather the support of the four million Blacks who lived in the South and constituted a key base of support for any political action. The radicals also focused their attentions on providing aid to the freedmen, and controversies within their own ranks began to emerge over issues of civil, political and economic rights and responsibilities. Meanwhile, opposition was mounting among their opponents in Washington and their rivals in the South.

Increasingly, the roles of three groups within the South became instrumental to the outcome of the radical reconstruction program. These were the Blacks, the Scalawags and the Carpetbaggers.

Of the more important statements which can be made about the role of Blacks in Reconstruction, one stands out: although many were elected to public office in Southern radical governments, none were in a position of control. Even collectively, they were never able to dominate state governments or extend their influence to Washington. Typically, Blacks were elected to lieutenant governorships, or to offices such as the secretary of state, the superintendent of education, or the treasury. In national congressional patterns the same thing held. Fourteen Blacks were elected to the United States House of Representatives and two secured a position as United States Senator. Although this represents a high point in American history in terms of the numbers of Blacks holding high office, in all cases Whites dominated the key positions and were able to control policies which ensued from all levels of government.

Blacks however turned their attention to another area—the development of their own leadership. They began to counsel with Black preachers for their political activities and attitudes. As expressed in a letter to Thaddeus Stevens in 1868, ''The Colored preachers are the great power in controlling and uniting the colored vote, and they are looked to, as political leaders, with more confidence . . . than any other

source of instruction and control.'' Importantly, most of the Black Southern preachers were conservative on almost all issues except civil and political rights.

Compared with the radical Republicans, however, the degree of activity and the pressure for change was mildly expressed by Black leaders throughout the South. In no Southern state did any responsible Black leader or any sizeable Black organization attempt to gain full or complete political control. In each case the demands were the same: equal political rights and equality under the law. There was no expression of a desire for a separate political party or for the division of existing political parties on the basis of race. Rather, they expressed an anxiousness to work with Whites within the operational party framework. Many Blacks were even willing to delay action of social integration, and on the issue of school desegragation, in an attempt to avoid further conflict in these areas while they pursued the solidification of fundamental civil rights.

Even at State conventions, establishing new constitutions under the directives of the United States government, the tenor was moderate. The documents expressed what appeared to be an acceptable, theoretical compromise; the Arkansas constitution was typical in its inclusion of this phrase: ''(It) is recognized and shall ever remain inviolate that equality of all persons exists before the law; no citizen shall be deprived of any right, privilege or immunity, nor exempted from any burden or duty, on account of race, color or previous condition.'' Apart from Louisiana and South Carolina, which made provisions for some degree of social integration in schools and elsewhere, the new constitutions made no recognition of social integration at any level of interaction. The ambiguity of the equality statements left room for considerable discretion within the states and this set up a situation which would provide for the denial of such integration for decades to come— despite legislation made by the United States Congress or rulings handed down by the United States Supreme Court.

A second group of some considerable importance came to be called the Carpetbaggers, a term applied to all northern settlers in the South who actively supported the radical Republicans. Contrary to many popular opinions, the carpetbaggers were not a homogeneous, lower class group of people who uniformly benefitted from corruption practiced in the South during Reconstruction. Within their ranks were many people who had no political careers available to them when they migrated to the South because of existing laws prior to 1867; others were veterans of the Union Army who had enjoyed the Southern climate and believed there were better opportunities available to them in the South than in the North; still others came as teachers, clergymen, officers of the Freedmen's Bureau or representatives from a number of Northern societies established to assist Blacks after the termination of the Civil War. What they all had in common was simply one thing: they became supporters of the radical Republicans and their programs after they settled in the South. Their primary offense, and hence, the negative connotation which has surrounded the term Carpetbagger was not so much corruption as it was the organizing of Blacks for political action.

There were a number of carpetbaggers who reached positions of particular importance in the South whose records were especially distinguished. The second governor of Mississippi during Reconstruction was Adelbert Ames, a man well recognized for his integrity, ability and sincerity in protecting the rights of Blacks and securing a better post-War

Photograph *of the Republican convention of 1880. The Republican Party during this period was one of the strongest forces in the nation for trying to re-establish the South along the lines of the industrialized North.*

Reproduction *of a painting showing a debate in the United States Senate during the period of Reconstruction. Southern Senators opposed any attempt of the Northern and Western Senators to impose laws upon them which took power away from the individual states and gave it to the Federal government.*

set of conditions for all citizens of his state. Ames was successful in developing a system of education which was far superior to any previous system in the South, in reorganizing the judiciary and adopting a new code of laws which was substantially more equitable and just than had existed before, in renovating and rebuilding new public facilities (including state hospitals serving all residents), and in building better facilities for the deaf, blind and handicapped. No major

political corruption was exposed during his tenure in office and Mississippi was generally recognized as the best governed state in the South during Reconstruction.

A third notable group of individuals who joined in tentative alliance with the Blacks, carpetbaggers and radical Republicans was called the Scalawags. In general usage, the term Scalawag referred to anyone who was a White southerner who collaborated with the radicals. The term took on its pejorative connotation because of the number of people who betrayed the South for the spoils of office presented to them through the establishment of new governments. Some Scalawags supported the radicals for legitimate reasons: that prominent people in the South had an obligation to join with the radicals in order to control and monitor their actions; that for humanitarian reasons the position of Blacks needed to be improved; and that the course of action pursued by the radicals was the appropriate one for the best interests of the country as a whole.

Throughout Reconstruction, the Scalawags remained a minority in the South, but their impact was felt in a number of ways, especially when it coincided with actions taken by radical politicians in government besides themselves and by Blacks or Carpetbaggers acting in concert regardless of the motive. This unusual coalition offered the Radical Republicans a base of support which enabled them to move forth with their plans for a considerable period of time despite tensions and conflicts in the national Capitol.

These activities and attitudes existed against a background which was corrupt in one sense or another, either deliberately or unintentionally, due to lack of political or economic experience. Issuing fraudulent bonds, giving and accepting

Reproduction *of an ink sketch showing a session of the South Carolina Assembly during the period of Reconstruction. For a few years following the end of the Civil War the Black majority was able to elect a Black Assembly.*

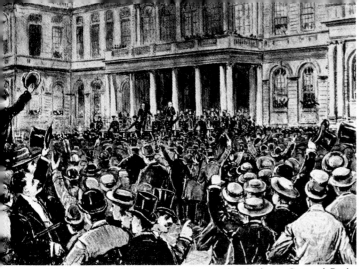

This reproduction *of a newspaper sketch shows General Butler making a campaign speech for Horace Greeley during the election of 1866 in New York City.*

bribes, using graft in land sales or purchases and in contracts for public works, and excessive extravagance and waste were fairly typical. By their own admission, several governors of Southern states testified to having engaged in corrupt practices on a regular basis.

Each of the eleven states of the former Confederacy during all or part of the decade between 1867 and 1877 fell under the control of the radical Republicans. In many states elected officials had extremely little experience in handling governmental matters; on many occasions the temptation toward corruption, whether on a small or large scale, was overbearing. In the halls of state, county, and city legislatures, opportunities for private financial benefit emerged easily and readily. Issues of conflict of interest were rarely considered and attention to mutual private and public interests were emphasized.

While public debts throughout the South increased the tax burden to residents skyrocketed. Throughout the South the tax assessment during Reconstruction varied, but it was never less than four times as great as it had been prior to the Civil War. A great deal of it can be explained in terms of the largely unqualified and sometimes incompetent individuals who were elected to office in the new governments. And, it was by no means a phenomenon isolated in the South.

The moral and ethical tenor for the nation was set in Washington, under the auspices of the Grant administration which was notable for its numerous scandals. Both the Credit Mobilier and the Whiskey Ring, two of the most remarkable scandals, involved members of Congress as well as individuals high in administrative circles. In addition, there were blatantly corrupt Republican machines operating in and controlling the politics of a number of Northern states including New York, Massachusetts and Pennsylvania. Consequently, Reconstruction as an era was characterized not simply by corruption and scandal in the South, but by an enigma.

By 1876 the Democrats fought their last great battle of Reconstruction with the radical Republicans. Eight of the Southern states had already fallen to the Democrats, but three of them were still under the control of a coalition of Carpetbaggers, Scalawags and Blacks. In the elections of 1876, the Democrats claimed victory in South Carolina, Florida and Louisiana and the new President, Rutherford B. Hayes, was not inclined to argue the point even though he was a Republican. Within months, he ordered the removal of the remaining Federal troops in the South and sanctioned political control by the Democrats in the three disputed states.

Internal fragmentation, corrupt leadership in President Grant and his Cabinet, opposing attitudes on the part of Southern and Northern Whites over civil and political rights for Blacks and an overly radical approach to Reconstruction had contributed to the demise of the radical Republicans over the course of a decade.

Moreover, the Supreme Court had begun to reassert itself and was gradually able to substitute its own judgments for those which had been rendered by Congress. The dominance of the radicals, regardless of the Presidential administration in office, had meant that the jurisdiction for civil rights law-making had been within the purview of the Congress. However, changes in the composition of state legislatures in the South was accompanied by changes in the party membership of representatives sent to Washington and the make-up of Congress had begun to be altered. This signalled a time when conditions began to favor a stronger Supreme Court say in the affairs of government, both nationally and with regard to states.

Within a brief period the Supreme Court directly overturned the intent of the amendments and Congressional bills which provided the basis for civil rights. It was successful in incorporating a racial caste system into the Constitution despite the termination of slavery as a legal institution. The consequence, as John Marshall Harlan argued in his dissenting opinion of 1883, made Blacks "a class of human beings in practical subjection to another class, with power in the latter to dole out to the former just such privileges as they may choose to grant."

Despite Harlan's observations, the practice of civil rights implementations was based on the Court's majority opinion. States merely stood back silently while individuals joined together in voluntary organized form and exercised rampant discrimination which subjected the Black population to harassment, terror, poverty, and second class citizenship. Insofar as the Black citizen could claim protection through the Fourteenth Amendment only when it could be proven that a state had participated in the violation or lent specific assistance to the actual offense, he or she was rendered helpless in the South where the protection was most desperately and urgently needed.

The "separate but equal doctrine" established by the Court in the Plessey versus Ferguson decision of 1896 merely codified behavior which had been sanctioned by earlier decisions. Carrying the 1875 Act to a broader and somewhat different conclusion, the Court maintained that all that was required was "substantial equality", and substantial was interpreted as satisfactory if the most minimal conditions were met. Whatever claims to potential integration through civil rights legislation which had been made by earlier Congressional Republican leaders had vanished into the shadows. The substance of laws now revealed the effective, practical meaning of civil rights—separate, but minimally equal.

Recourse was largely precluded. If Blacks had had an opportunity to influence the political process through their enfranchisement through the Fifteenth Amendment, this prospect was largely lost by the turn of the century. State control of voting rights had resulted in virtually the total exclusion of Black citizens from the polls. By the last decade of the nineteenth century the voting turnout of Blacks had dropped by 99 percent.

To the extent that the Civil War had marked a high point for the predominance of the federal government over the union, the Supreme Court decisions of the ensuing years demonstrated a victory for States in the arena of civil rights.

CIVIL RIGHTS BILL NOW THE LAW OF THE LAND

Ike Backing Scranton Or Isn't He?

LOS ANGELES EVENING AND SUNDAY

Herald Examiner

EXPRESS

CLASSIFIED ADVERTISING Richmond 8-4111   All Other Calls Richmond 8-1212 or Richmond 8-4141

LARGEST EVENING CIRCULATION IN AMERICA

VOL. XCIV   Four Sections Section A   10 CENTS   THURSDAY, JULY 2, 1964   S   NO. 98

SUNSET Race Results
Complete N. Y. Stocks

House Votes 289 to 126; LBJ Signs

From Herald-Examiner Wire Services

WASHINGTON, July 2—Conflicting reports on whether former President Dwight D. Eisenhower had agreed to put Gov. William W. Scranton's name in nomination for President threw confusion today into the Republican presidential race.

Two major television-radio networks aired the conflicting reports last night. There was no direct comment from Eisenhower. Scranton, campaigning in Eugene, Ore., said he knew nothing about the report.

Aides close to Eisenhower, who was at his Gettysburg, Pa., home, also said they knew nothing about it. The former President's son, John, also denied the report.

"It's not true," said John Eisenhower last night at his home in Gettysburg. He said that with him were his father and mother, celebrating thier 48th wedding anniversary.

NBC's first report quoted "sources close to Gen. Eisenhower." Later, on a scheduled newscast, NBC said.

"NBC News has learned that in his 45-minute conversation with Gen. Eisenhower in Walter Reed Hospital yesterday (Tuesday) Henry Cabot Lodge suggested that Mr. Eisenhower put the name of Gov. Scranton in nomination. . . Sources close to Gov. Scranton have told NBC that the general had agreed."

John Eisenhower said the report may have come out of conversations with Lodge, who quit as ambassador to South Viet Nam to aid Scranton's candidacy. "But I assure you," said Eisenhower, "it is not true."

Later the American Broadcasting Co quoted Gen. Eisenhower as saying in a phone inquiry that Lodge sought to get him to nominate Scranton but he had received no

(Continued on Page 8, Col. 3)

Pilot Saved

Navy Jet Explodes: 1 Killed

SAN DIEGO, July 2 (AP)— A Navy jet fighter exploded 'n flight about 25 miles off he coast today, killing one man and injuring the other of the two-man crew.

The pilot, identified as 'ndr. William R. O'Connel, as picked up by a Navy 'e'icopter shortly after he 'jected from his F4B Phanom jet.

He was taken to a dispensary for treatment of superficial burns.

BODY DISCOVERED

The duty officer at the Los Angeles office of the Federal Aviation Agency said the body of the other crewman was recovered by a Navy patrol plane.

His identity was not immediately available.

The military originally reported a mid-air collision and the sighting of four parachutes. A military spokesman said the multiparachute report probably

(Continued on Page 4, Col. 3)

AN OLD-FASHIONED GOWN

LONDON, July 2 (AP)—Princess Margaret danced in a "near topless" dress last night.

Her gown was in the style of the Georgian era of 200 years ago when the low cut gown was all the rage.

Her husband, Lord Snowdon, sported a wig with a bow in it.

Along with the wig, the princess' ex-photographer husband wore an eggplant-colored velvet jacket with huge lace cuffs and a flyaway panel at the back. Knee breeches, white stockings and a gold waistcoat completed Snowdon's ensemble.

The princess wore a wig, too, a smoky blue creation to match a jeweled gown of pale blue silk. The neckline plunged down to a corselet embroidered in gold and pearls.

A huge butterfly clasp holding a fichu ensured it stopped somewhat short of toplessness.

Neither the princess nor Lord Snowdon was setting a new fashion. They were guests of London's Lord Mayor Clement Harman at a Georgian ball and all the guests wore the styles of two centuries ago.

In those days the very low neckline was customary and raised no eyebrows.

Another 'Zoom Day' For Stocks

NEW YORK, July 2 (AP)—The stock market rally rolled on today, carrying the averages again to new all-time highs.

However, its strength failed to match yesterday's surge as caution and profit-taking set in ahead of the long Fourth of July holiday weekend. The market will be closed tomorrow.

The Dow Jones averages of 30 industrials rose 3.41 to 841.47. This was a little more than half the size of its gain yesterday.

Volume again was heavy, exceeding 5 million shares for the second consecutive session. The total of 5.24 million compared with 5.35 million yesterday.

American Telephone, still reacting to a report of record earnings in the three months ended May 31, was most active, up ¼ to 74⅛.

PRINCESS MARGARET WEARS NEAR-TOPLESS COSTUME AT BALL
She came dressed in the fashion of two centuries ago, even to the wig

—United Press International Telephoto

New L.A. Ontario Airport?

Acquisition of Ontario International Airport by the Los Angeles Department of Airports loomed as a possibility today with disclosure of informal discussions toward taking set in motion that end are underway between the two cities.

Francis T. Fox, general manager of the Los Angeles airport, was instructed by the airport commissioners and Mayor Yorty to negotiate

with the city's revenue bond consultants for a financial and economic analysis of the Ontario facility.

The proposed study would include the effect of the acquisition of the airport by Los Angeles upon the sale and interest of the revenue bonds which the Department of Airports proposes to issue this year.

"Ontario is a vital airport

for Southern California," said Melvin J. Erickson, commission president, "and we feel it has a fine future as evidenced by the recent United Research survey of the airport's passenger traffic potential."

Air traffic into Los Angeles International is diverted to Ontario when bad weather interrupts takeoff and landings here, Erickson added.

WASHINGTON, July 2 (UPI) — The civil rights bill, born in the violence of the Negro protest movement against discrimination, completed its congressional journey today and was signed by President Johnson into the law of the land.

The President acted only hours after the House, by a 289 to 126 vote, stamped final approval on the compromise version worked out by the Senate and passed there June 19.

STRICT RULES

The House, operating within strict procedural rules that limited debate on the milestone measure today to one hour, acted one year and two weeks after President Kennedy sent the rights bill to Congress.

289 TO 126

The vote was 289 to 126. When the House originally passed the measure l a s t February, it did so by a 290 to 130 vote.

President Johnson originally had considered signing the bill into law on the 4th of July.

Voting for the bill today were 153 Democrats and 136 Republicans. Voting against were 91 Democrats and 35 Republicans.

SWITCH VOTES

Six members switched from their original House vote, but they consisted of three from each side, thus balancing out.

Reps. Edward Hutchinson, R-Mich.; John J. Rhodes, R-Ariz., and Charles L. Weltner, D-Ga., changed from an original "no" vote to "aye."

Reps. Charlotte Reid, R-Ill.; Bob Wilson, R-Calif., and Earl Wilson, R-Ind., who voted for the bill last

(Continued on Pg. 4, Cols. 3-7)

City Council

Demand Taxi Refunds

The City of Los Angeles should institute a $1 million-plus suit against Yellow Cab Co. for asserted over charges, City Councilwoman Rosalind Wyman urged in a resolution introduced in council today.

Mrs. Wyman said that the city attorney should act as a trustee for patrons of Yellow Cab in bringing the suit.

"If recovery is made," she said, the money should be transferred to the general fund to benefit all the people."

Councilman Harold Henry said that he believed that Mrs. Wyman's resolution for a law suit was of "doubtful legality" based on conversations with attorneys.

"I believe the court to follow would be to force the cab company to reduce its rates until the over charges are made up. This would be giving a break to the cab using public and would in a large part compensate them for what they have lost to taxi meter errors."

The idea stems from revelations by Mayor Samuel W. Yorty and the City Board of

(Continued on Pg. 4, Cols. 1-2)

TODAY'S BASEBALL

AMERICAN LEAGUE

	R.	H.	E.
At Boston—			
Minnesota	500 106 030—15	17	0
Boston	200 000 304— 9	13	0

NATIONAL LEAGUE

	R.	H.	E.
At Milwaukee—			
St. Louis	001 100 200— 4	7	0
Milwaukee	020 001 000— 3	7	2

HOLLYPARK RACES

1 MoolahBob 7.20,4.40,2.80; AutumnRoyal 7.20,5.00;Silk Star 4.20
2 PerformingArts 9.60,6.20,5.20;Dakine 4.20,3.80;SealBeach 6.80
Daily double (10 and 4) paid $79.00.
3 Amer.Fancy 8.20,5.00,3.80;FairLegend 15.00,9.80;BabyDoll 5.00

FOURTH: 4 fur., f. and m., 4-yr. up. clmg., purse $6000:

4-EL CIELITO	7:20	3:80	3:20
ITS SMART		6:80	4:80
CURRA FLIGHT			5:20

No scratches.

Copy-Cat

(U.S. Weather B-4, Tides D-8)

With the approach of July 4th—traditionally the start of summer in Southern California, no matter what astronomers mumble about equinoxes — temperature highs have leveled off at 85 and probably will stay there.

At least for a few days.

Tomorrow, the Weather Bureau predicted, will be a copy-cat, again hitting today's and yesterday's 85.

The smog picture for tomorrow: moderate to heavy across the basin.

The low will be the same s this morning's: 56.

THE PROGRESSIVE MOVEMENT: A FURTHER GRAFTING 1900-1917

The Progressive Movement for which Theodore Roosevelt became a spokesman, had its roots in a number of late nineteenth century developments. It adopted many of the Populist ideas, but reflected equally the growing concerns of the social worker movement which had spread through the cities, the social gospel movement which was influencing much of Protestantism, the new scholarship that emphasized the economic factors in the development of American government, and it drew strength and widespread support from the Muckraking movement which developed during the first decade of the twentieth century.

It was Roosevelt who applied the term "Muckrakers" to those engaged in uncovering corruption in American life. Borrowing the name from Bunyan's *Pilgrim's Progress,* he used it as one of scorn, but like many another epithet its meaning evolved into one of approval, and Roosevelt himself was to be influenced by the movement. The term simply refers to the literature of exposure, the bringing to light of graft and corruption in business, government and other areas of American life during the period 1900-1917. What distinquished the first decade of the twentieth century was the concerted effort on the part of a large number of writers, not just a few isolated individuals, and on the part of many of the popular magazines, to delve deeply into the evils of society. The movement was unique in that the attack was more than a general indictment, the articles named names and dates, the amount of money that exchanged hands, or the exact methods used in the control of a city by the bosses.

Considering the type of material they were using, it is amazing how few successful law suits were brought against them. A single article might blast a political reputation or ruin a business, and the nation was exposed not to a few articles but hundreds. Week after week, month after month,

McClure's, Everybody's, Hampton's, The Arena, Ladies Home Journal, Cosmopolitan and a host of other magazines hit the newsstand. These magazines devoted a considerable proportion of their space to articles of exposure, sometimes as much as twenty percent. It was estimated that the combined circulation of the ten leading muckraking magazines ran over three million, and this did not include the newspapers which participated in the movement, or the books that were published. Lincoln Steffens in his articles in *McClure's* magazine, uncovered the corruption in city governments across the land and later the state governments. Ida Tarbell wrote on the Standard Oil trust, others exposed the railroads, the patent medicine racket, the meat packing industry, the influence of big business on the Senate, the White Slave traffic, or the relationship between the liquor industry and crime. No area of American life escaped their pens and the public was aroused to support the legislation sponsored by the Progressive Movement.

As with Muckraking, it can be misleading to refer to "a" Progressive Movement. The term is one given by historians to a group of movements that came together during the first two decades of the twentieth century and which collectively accomplished major reforms in the United States. On the local level were many concerned mayors who wrested the government from boss rule and corruption—Tom Johnson of Cleveland, 'Golden Rule' Jones of Toledo, and Seth Low and J. P. Mitchell of New York. Reforms at the state level soon followed with Robert La Follette of Wisconsin taking the lead. La Follette challenged the political power of the railroads and utilities by creating a regulative commission which had the power to determine rates based on an evaluation of their physical assets. He sought to regulate industrial monopolies, secured passage of a state inheritance tax and workmen's compensation laws, set aside state forest reserves for the benefit of the people, and introduced the direct primary, initiative, referendum and recall. Somewhat later Woodrow Wilson was to achieve a similar program in New Jersey, and Hiram Johnson in California.

A **campaign poster** *from the election of 1900, Bryan's second attempt to win the Presidency. Notice on either side of his name the analogy between the crown of thorns and the cross of gold, Bryan's most enduring campaign slogan.*

William McKinley, *twenty-fifth President of the United States. He was assassinated while in office.*

A number of the accomplishments of the Progressive Movement had little relationship to either major political party, and in fact on the national level, the two major parties, Republican and Democrat, shared somewhat equally—with Roosevelt, a Republican, in office for two terms and Wilson, a Democrat, for two. By World War I, over twenty states had adopted the initiative and referendum, and a number of states had adopted the recall. Following the example of Wisconsin, more than two-thirds of the states had adopted direct primary legislation and the Australian, or secret, ballot was universally adopted. By 1912 thirty states already had provided for the expression of popular opinion in the choice of Senators, and the Seventeenth Amendment, ratified in 1913, established direct election of Senators throughout the nation. In the meantime the Sixteenth Amendment had passed making the income tax Constitutional, and two amendments were ratified after the War, both of which owed their impetus to the Progressive Movement, the prohibition amendment (Eighteenth) and women's suffrage (Nineteenth).

THEODORE ROOSEVELT AND THE SQUARE DEAL

McKinley's running mate in the elections of 1900 was a young, able, and bellicose man with national ambitions, Teddy Roosevelt. The Republicans recognized that Roosevelt would strengthen the ticket, but they were also playing shrewd politics by nominating him to the Vice Presidency, a method by which they shunted his ambitions into an innocuous office. The ticket was eminently successful but as President McKinley was shot by an anarchist in September 1901, six months after his inauguration, rather than exiling Roosevelt to the Vice Presidency, the Republicans had placed him in the most prominent position in the nation.

Teddy Roosevelt was not unprepared for his new role. He had served in the New York State Assembly, as Civil Service Commissioner under Harrison and Cleveland, Police Commissioner of New York City, Assistant Secretary of the Navy, as the organizer and commanding officer of the famous Rough Riders in the Spanish American War, and was Governor of New York at the time of his elevation to the position of Vice President of the United States.

Throughout his career, although a strong critic of many reform groups, Roosevelt had been identified with the reform element in his party, and he appeared on the national scene just as the reform spirit of the Progressive Movement was emerging. The growth of the nation had been astonishing, yet the system under which Americans lived was strangely out of kilter. Agriculture had grown beyond even the fondest dreams of Jefferson, yet the farmers of the nation were on the verge of ruin. The nation was fabulously rich, yet the masses of people were poor. American industrial production was outstripping the countries of Western Europe, yet those who worked in the factories put in a twelve to fourteen hour day, earned rock bottom wages, suffered an excessive accident rate, and lived under deplorable conditions. Everyone seemed to believe in democracy, yet corruption corroded the system from top to bottom. Many at both ends of the economic scale feared for the future of the country. Would the United States develop into a benevolent feudalism, or would the socialists and anarchists, breeding upon the cancer of discontent, foment a revolution, or would democracy prove its ability to right the ship of state?

During the Pullman strike Roosevelt had written to a friend: "I know the Populist and the laboring men well and their faults. . . . I like to see a mob handled by the regulars, or by good State-Guards, not over-scrupulous about bloodshed." Yet it was Roosevelt who first gave labor a "square deal." In 1902 the anthracite coal miners, working long hours for small pay and living in squalid company-owned towns, decided to strike. They demanded a twenty percent raise in wages, a nine-hour day and union recognition. The strike lasted five months while coal prices soared, schools closed and disaster faced Roosevelt's administration. On every other occasion when the government had stepped in, it had been to use troops to break the strike; but this time Roosevelt believed that labor had conducted itself in a more commendable fashion than management and threatened to order in troops, not to break the strike, but to keep the mines open. At the same time he used the office of the President to mold public opinion in favor of arbitration, and his own political prowess to bring management to the arbitration conference. The significance of the President's action was not that he ended the strike or that a service had been rendered to the American labor movement, although he took satisfaction in both; it was, instead, that he had fostered a series of innovations that would have far-reaching effects. For the first time the threatened use of troops was not on behalf of big business, but was used as a third force to bring an equitable solution. Never before had the representatives of both capital and labor been called to the White House where the influence of the Federal government was employed to negotiate a settlement, and, for the first time, the President of

Teddy Roosevelt, *center, resigned his position as Assistant Secretary of the Navy in 1898 to lead a cavalry regiment he had recruited for the Spanish-American War. The group, which was known as the Rough Riders, became famous for their victory at San Juan Hill.*

the United States had appointed an arbitral board whose decision both sides promised to accept.

One of the most publicized aspects of Roosevelt's tenure was his trust-busting policy. In his first message he had called for a greater measure of regulation for the trusts, and his administration almost immediately found a case, a monopoly of the transcontinental railroads, which would dramatize the need for government action. Edward H. Harriman, with outside financial backing, had succeeded in merging the already extensive Southern Pacific and Union Pacific roads. His rival James J. Hill, with Morgan's support, had combined the Northern Pacific and Great Northern lines.

General Philander Knox announced the intention of the Roosevelt Administration to file suit against the Northern Securities Company under the Sherman Anti-Trust Act. The defeat of the Northern Securities Company, even though by a narrow margin in the Supreme Court decision, gave new life to the Sherman Act, brought Roosevelt considerable popularity, and indicated to a wide cross-section of Americans that Roosevelt intended to give the country a square deal. This success was followed by suits against Swift and Company, Armour and Company, the American Tobacco Company and a suit in 1907 against Standard Oil carrying a fine of twenty-nine million dollars. Most of the fine against Standard Oil was rescinded at a later date, but by then trust-busting had become the hallmark of Teddy Roosevelt.

Actually, Roosevelt was never convinced that trust-busting was the answer to the problem which he had recognized as crucial to America. He early made a distinction between ''good'' and ''bad'' trusts, and advocated other types of legislation which may have been more significant in the long run. During his administration the Department of Commerce and Labor was created, and a Bureau of Corporations with provisions for inspection and partial publicity of corporative mis-deeds. A Meat Inspection Act and a Pure Food and Drug Act were passed and became operative. Under Roosevelt additional steps were taken to strengthen the

This scene of *poverty and squalor was typical of the kind of living conditions the recently arrived immigrants were forced to live in. The low wages generally meant that all the members of the family, except the very young, had to work to make ends meet.*

Interstate Commerce Act—the Elkins Act and the Hepburn Railroad Act—which gave the government most of the regulatory powers needed. The two acts were supplemented by the Mann-Elkins Act druing the Presidency of William Howard Taft.

Taken collectively Roosevelt's corporation program was a creative and effective undertaking, but perhaps his greatest contribution was the manner in which he dramatized the issues. His approach was essentially a moral one, and he continually used the Presidency as a ''bloody pulpit'' from which he could preach to the American people, publicize corporate mis-deeds, insist that the interests of the entire nation must be served, and in the process made the Federal government and the American President a third force with which to be reckoned. Those critical of Roosevelt conclude that it was all a sham battle since there were more than five times as many trusts at the end of his term as there were when he became President, but the solution to the problem created by giant trusts is one that the best minds in the White House, Congress and the Supreme Court have not been able to agree upon even today.

In retrospect, one of the most creative and far-reaching of Roosevelt's programs was in the field of conservation. The

The immigrants' *living conditions changed very little during the decade of the 1890's. Despite huge profits by the industrialists, the laborers and the families continued to live in grossly overcrowded tenements and company towns. The basic amenities, which later generations of Americans have taken as their birthrights, were totally lacking in the squalid homes of the working class during this era.*

The sympathies *of the American people were stirred by the writing of Jacob Riis, who wrote about the inhuman conditons of life in the city slums near the turn of the century.*

program was marked by sustained intellectual and administrative force in which the President effectively blanded a knowledge of science and a strong feeling of morality. He pressed for his program for seven years, frequently against the most powerful leaders of his own party, and at the end of his term even against the combined opposition of both parties. The man most directly influential, along with the President, and the one who saw most of the enterprise through to a successful conclusion, was Gifford Pinchot, Chief of the Forest Service. In 1902 Roosevelt signed into law the Newlands Bill, a Democratically sponsored bill which the leaders in his own party had blocked, but which he had thrown his weight behind to secure passage in Congress. The bill established a creative, heavily-subsidized program for the reclamation of arid western lands. Under the act thirty irrigation projects, including the Roosevelt Dam in Arizona, were in progress or completed when Roosevelt left office, and ultimately a total of more than 1,500,000 acres of land were brought under cultivation. In 1903 Roosevelt vetoed a bill that would have turned Muscle Shoals over to piecemeal private development because he believed that the exploitation of such a valuable natural resource should be considered in a comprehensive way and in terms of general policy based

Child labor *was an economic fact of life during the 1890's. Pictured here is a group of young boys who worked as coal miners. Although the legal minimum age was 14, most parents had their children lie about their ages so that they could go to work at an earlier age. None of the boys pictured here is more than 12 years old.*

upon public interests. He withdrew 50 million acres believed to contain coal and other minerals from public entry to protect the interests of the American public and just before he left office he withdrew another 18 million acres in Alaska. During Roosevelt's Presidency, Pinchot withdrew more than 2,500 power sites from entry.

Roosevelt and Pinchot were so active in setting aside forest reserves that Congress actually passed a bill which specified that no more forest reserves could be created in the Western states. The two men, however, out-maneuvered Congress by creating new reserves in those states (totaling 16 million acres) during the ten days Roosevelt had in which to sign the bill. In all, the forest reserves of the nation tripled during Roosevelt's term. In 1903 he set aside the Yellowstone area as a national park and proceeded to create four additional national parks, sixteen national monuments, four game preserves and fifty-one wild bird refuges before leaving office. In 1907 he appointed the Inland Waterways Commission which made the first thorough study of all American waterways and established the principles upon which the Tennessee Valley Authority would be based thirty years later. To dramatize the entire program and to secure additional support for it, he called a Governor's Conference on conservation (1908) which made a declaration on the subject which has often been called the Magna Charta of the conservation movement.

Upon leaving office in 1909, Roosevelt could afford to be proud of his record. He had made the Federal government a decisive force in the American system, had enlarged the powers of the President, had in many ways provided the American people with a square deal, and had been instrumental in developing a conservation program unequalled in that age and not to be matched again until the time of the New Deal. On the foreign scene he had acquired the Panama Canal Zone and begun the construction of the Canal, had taken an active part in the affairs of the Far East, set forth an aggressive—though later to be recognized as a mistaken— policy in the Caribbean and South America, and in general advanced the prestige of the United States among

The ebullient Teddy Roosevelt, *whose exploits during the Spanish-American War, as well as his outspoken criticism of the Trusts had earned him a favorable national reputation, was the Republican Presidential nominee in 1904. Here he is shown campaigning during that election year.*

The disparity *between the rich and the poor during the era of the 1890's was visible everywhere. This ink sketch shows the two groups: the rich returning from a pleasure cruise, the poor being shipped off to one of New York City's institutions.*

the world powers.

Roosevelt left his hand-picked successor, William Howard Taft, in the Presidency and departed for an extended big game hunt in Africa. When he returned, he was sorely disappointed with what he found. Taft had not kept Roosevelt's cabinet, was on bad terms with Roosevelt's family, had dismissed his able Chief of the Forest Service, Pinchot, and, in spite of a valiant trust-busting drive, had tied himself so closely to the conservative wing of the Republican Party that the Republicans had lost the elections in 1910 and appeared to be headed for defeat in the Presidential elections of 1912. Roosevelt, never humble about his prowess, decided to challenge Taft for the Republican nomination. As one wit remarked, Roosevelt needed to be the center of the stage, "The bride at every wedding, the corpse at every funeral." Or, as another added, he wanted to be "the preacher, the bride and the bridegroom."

Although Roosevelt had considerable popular support, Taft had the Republican machine behind him, and the protégé won out over his patron. Not receiving the Republican nomination Roosevelt bolted and accepted the nomination of the Progressive Party. His actions, by splitting the Republicans, virtually assured victory to the Democratic nominee Woodrow Wilson. In the elections Wilson received only forty-two precent of the vote, but won an overwhelming 435 electoral votes compared to the eighty-eight cast for Roosevelt and the eight for Taft. The real significance of the election, however, was that it constituted a mandate for progressivism. Almost seventy percent of the popular vote was cast in favor of Wilson and Roosevelt, both of whom ran on progressive, although not identical, platforms.

PROGRESSIVISM: THE HYBRID FRUIT

Progressivism had won at the polls in 1912, but at least in theory there was considerable difference between Wilsonian progressivism, a concept which Wilson thought of as the "New Freedom," and Roosevelt's brand of progressivism, which came to be known during the campaign as the "New

While the leading industrialists *were very rich, the poor of America were very poor. Here two children of the poor rummage through a trash basket looking for something they might be able to sell.*

Reproduction *of an ink sketch showing the Bradley Martin Ball held at the Waldorf in 1897. So extravagant was the setting and costuming that Martin's tax assessment was doubled, and criticism of his family's lavish expenditures, coming as they did near the end of the Depression, was so widespread that the family moved to Europe to avoid the unfavorable opinion.*

This is a SENATE
of the MONOPOLISTS
BY the MONOPOLISTS AND
FOR the MONOPOLISTS!

Nationalism.'' The Wilsonian variety was close to that described by George E. Mowry.[2] His study of Progressives in California revealed that they were young, born in the Middle-West, of Northern-European stock, strongly religious (Protestant), considerably above average in education, and although coming largely from the professional and business class, were not representative of the industrial or financial corporations. On the basis of his study he concluded that the origins of progressivism were quite dissimilar from Populism, the former being urban, not rural, drawing its leaders from a different class, and when it did involve agrarian groups they were not the ones from the Populist wheat, cotton and mining regions, but from states with much more diversified economy. In many respects this brand of progressivism was representative of the middle class American who was revolting against the manner in which the new industrialism on the one hand and the growing labor movement on

the other, was squeezing him out of his traditional role of leadership in the nation.

Woodrow Wilson represented this type of progressivism. He was a WASP with little understanding of the new immigrant, a man of Southern birth whose attitude toward the Negro was paternalistic. He thought in idealistic Jeffersonian terms and held an abiding faith in the Anglo-American democratic heritage. Along with Thomas Jefferson and Andrew Jackson, he considered that the duty of the government was not to control and regulate big business, but to emancipate men from its domination. Where Jefferson had thought in terms of freedom from political tyranny, Wilson was working for freedom from economic tyranny, the tyranny of concentrated wealth. He did not want a ''benevolent'' government, but a ''free and a just government.'' He considered Hamilton a great man, but not a great American, and viewed the business combinations as the artificial product of the unrestrained activities of ambitious men not as the natural outgrowth of new economic conditions. He felt, too, that regulation of business was not the answer, for once attained, who would control the regulating agencies? Even uncontrolled competition he considered to be superior to regulated monopoly, but better than either of these, he believed was regulated competition.

In contrast Roosevelt's New Nationalism was based on Hamiltonianism. Where Wilson thought in terms of freedom, Roosevelt thought in terms of order and stability. The

Teddy Roosevelt, *left, and famed naturalist John Muir in Yosemite, California. Roosevelt was a strong believer in the outdoor life, and during his administration steps were taken to set aside areas of natural beauty as national parks. The first national park was Yellowstone. Yosemite became a national park in 1906.*

A view of Roosevelt Dam, *one of the many conservation measures pushed to completion by Teddy Roosevelt while he was President.*

New Nationalism was concerned with the morale of the nation, the New Freedom with the morality of the individual. Wilson's dream was to prevent a benevolent state, Roosevelt's was decidedly paternalistic. Wilson hoped to keep the power of the Federal government at a minimum, Roosevelt to enlarge it. The New Nationalists considered competition as causing exploitation, evil working conditions, unemployment and low wages, and regarded the great corporations as not only inevitable, but a positive good in that they produced greater efficiency. It thus became the responsibility of government, according to the New Nationalists, not to regulate competition but to regulate monopoly for the good of all, and this should be done through the establishment of government commissions with appropriate jurisdiction and power. Underlying the philosophy of the New Nationalism was the conviction that the United States was not predestined to achieve success and that American life was not automatically self-fulfilling. The hope to transform the nation rested in the possibility of developing a conscious sense of national purpose and national destiny. The New Nationalists considered Wilson's program a revival of Jeffersonian individualism, a policy of drift compared to Roosevelt's policy of mastery, not a new freedom, but an old bondage.

The theories underlying the New Nationalism had a strong appeal for the new immigrants. They had not suffered the downward mobility of the middle class at the hands of the new industrialists, and shared few of the aspirations of the small businessmen. Indeed, they recognized that the latter were all too frequently identified with the sweatshop, and they looked with favor upon governmental regulation as a better guarantee of economic security and stabilization than could be provided by government anti-trust drives. Perhaps their political experiences with the paternalistic ward boss conditioned them to transfer the same function to the city, state or national governments. In any case, in places like New York and Massachusetts, large numbers from among the immigrant population voted for progressive legislation of the type that most directly affected them and of the type that was more typical of the New Nationalism than of the New Freedom, and they frequently supplied the necessary votes to ensure passage. They voted for workmen's compensation, widows' pensions, wages and hours legislation, factory safety regulation and tenement laws. They also produced a number of outstanding leaders who, though not of the old Anglo-Saxon, Protestant strain, were effective in working for progressive legislation, men such as Robert Wagner, James Foley, James Michael Curley, and David I. Walsh.

WOODROW WILSON AND THE NEW FREEDOM

Woodrow Wilson was one of the least prepared of men to become President of the United States, if by preparation one means the rise from ward politics through the rough and tumble of electoral offices. Yet in many ways he was one of the best prepared Presidents to reach the White House. He had been born into a family which, in addition to making the Presbyterian Church central in their lives, had a keen interest in politics and a passion for edcuation. Young Woodrow had early developed similar traits and had visions of someday entering the field of public leadership. One of Wilson's pet phrases during his college years had been "when we meet on the floor of the Senate," and even earlier he had written a number of cards in his own hand:

Thomas Woodrow Wilson
Senator from Virginia

Teddy Roosevelt *as he appeared as President. This photograph was taken in 1908.*

While at Princeton he formed a "solemn covenant with his friend Charles Talcott:

> ... that we would school all our powers and passions for the work of establishing the principles we held in common; that we would acquire knowledge that we might have power; and that we would drill ourselves in all the arts of persuasion, but especially oratory ... that we might have facility in leading others into our ways of thinking and enlisting them in our purposes.

Wilson set about this task of "schooling" all his powers and passions with admirable persistence. His study of politics led to the publication of a classic volume on American government, *Congressional Government*, and later two other volumes, *The State and Constitutional Government*. His immersion in the study of history resulted in the publication of a five-volume history, *A History of the American People*, a biography of George Washington, and again a classic little volume, *Division and Reunion*, on the Civil War and Reconstruction periods. His written and oral expression was attested to by all who read his numerous essays or heard him speak. Before becoming President of the United States he had served a distinguished term as President of Princeton University and then a term as Governor of New Jersey, where he received attention for the Progressive legislation enacted during his two years. No one can review the masterly fashion with which he conducted the Presidency, and served virtually as Prime Minister of his Party, without having a keen appreciation for his consummate political acumen and skill, an appreciation which must, however, be qualified by his dismal performance after World War I.

The legislation passed during the Wilson administration was the culmination of the Progressive movement, and although World War I and its aftermath nullified many of Wilson's achievements, his record was a brilliant one. In line with the philosophy of the New Freedom, the Underwood Tariff was pushed through Congress. Tariff rates were reduced on the average by one-third, to the lowest rate since the Civil War, and the free list greatly extended. It was an honest tariff since duties were based on the easily understood valorem duties instead of a host of specific rates with all kinds of hidden devices and jokers. An anti-dumping provision, the re-creation of a tariff board, and provisions for reciprocity agreements all helped to make it one of the most rational tariffs ever enacted. To compensate for loss of revenue the tariff bill included an income tax, considered the first in American history, since a similar attempt in 1894 had been declared unconstitutional. Rates, by today's standards were amazingly low. A married man with an income of $4,000 or more (equal to at least $20,000 today) paid one percent. Those with incomes of $20,000 ($100,000 in today's currency) paid two percent. The highest tax reached six percent. The eventual use of the progressive income tax (particularly during World War II), to equalize the personal incomes of the rich and the poor, made the income tax provision of the Underwood Tariff one of the most far-reaching legislative acts of the twentieth century.

High on the Democratic party list of priorities was the need to reform the American banking system. Though Wilson had been opposed to governmental control of banking, he was well satisfied with the ultimate compromise which was embodied in the Federal Reserve System. The National Banks established under the act of 1863 lacked centralized control, but in function were too centralized. Their relationship to the Federal Treasury was defective, the system encouraged speculation on the New York Stock Exchange, and above all

Sometimes called "Battling Bob," *Robert M. LaFollette of Wisconsin was the most important man in the Progressive Party of 1912 until Theodore Roosevelt broke with the Republican Party and ran as the Progressive candidate for the Presidency. LaFollette was a reform governor of Wisconsin, a senator from Wisconsin from 1905 to 1925, and received nearly five million votes in the Presidential elections of 1924 as the Progressive Party candidate.*

it could not provide an elastic currency. The Federal Reserve system corrected all these weaknesses. By creating a Federal Reserve Board, whose members were appointed by the President, it provided for centralized control and planning. By establishing twelve separate districts, with a Federal Reserve Bank in each, and each with its own board of directors, it decentralized the banking functions uniformly throughout the nation. It also brought stability to the entire banking system by the provision that Federal Reserve banks were bankers' banks, and could not by law make profits. The Federal Reserve system provided for an elastic currency (the demand of the Greenback Party, followed by the silver interests and the Populists) by decreasing the amount of reserves in gold that needed to be on deposit in the Federal Reserve banks, by the open market operation, by providing for the re-discounting of commercial paper, and by allowing the Federal Reserve system to adjust interest rates as needed by the economy.

Since the system was no better than the men who controlled it, it was unable to prevent the depression of the thirties, but proper use of its prerogatives could have mitigated that depression, and the system was a much needed and important reform in the field of banking and monetary regulation. The fact that the Bryan group at first thought it too favorable to the bankers, while the bankers opposed it as too restrictive of their activities, is some evidence of its balance.

Two significant legislative acts passed during the Wilson administration dealt with the problem of monopolies. The Pujo Committee of the House of Representatives had reported that the three New York financial concerns of Morgan, First National Bank and National City Bank together held 341 directorships in 112 corporations of various types which had total resources of over twenty-two billion dollars. This financial pyramiding made it possible for the banking institutions to shape policies of numerous concerns in their own interests, not in the interests of the corporations involved. Wilson asked for legislation that would not only solve the problem of financial pyramiding, but would correct the weaknesses of the Sherman Anti-Trust Act. One result was the Federal Trade Commission Act. The intention of the Act was to be preventive rather than punitive. It established a non-partisan commission of five members that was authorized to investigate corporations engaged in interstate commerce and if found guilty of unfair methods to issue "cease and desist" orders.

The second piece of legislation was the Clayton Anti-Trust Act. The Act prohibited discrimination in prices which might tend to prohibit competition, prohibited "tying" agreements, forbade interlocking directorates in companies that had reached a certain size, and forbade the practice of buying stock in competing firms. If officers of the corporations were involved in these violations they were made personally responsible under the law. Labor organizations, which had complained bitterly over the fact that the Sherman Anti-Trust Act was passed to control business monopolies but seemed to be used only against labor, were rewarded by being specifically exempt from the Clayton Act.

In the course of his administration, Wilson had made a significant transition away from the New Freedom and toward the New Nationalism of Teddy Roosevelt. The transition was most notable in his acceptance of the Federal Trade Commission Act which was exactly what Roosevelt advocated and Wilson had rejected, but was reflected in later Wilsonian legislation as well: the Seamen's Act, Rural Credits, Child Labor and Workmen's Compensation for industries involved in interstate commerce, and the Adamson Act

Woodrow Wilson *on the campaign trail as the Democratic candidate for President in 1912.*

establishing an eight-hour day for employees of interstate railroads. One of Wilson's most trusted advisors, Edward M. House, had published a utopian novel, *Philip Dru, Administrator* (1921) which had described a nationalism so comprehensive that it might have been questioned even by Teddy Roosevelt. Yet in 1918 another member of Wilson's Cabinet could remark that "All that book has said should be, comes about slowly. The President comes to Philip Dru in the end." By the time the United States entered World War I, Wilson had fused Jeffersonian ideals with Hamiltonian methods to create one of the most constructive and consistent legislative programs in the history of the country.

In retrospect, then, Roosevelt and Wilson were not as far apart as the 1912 campaign implied. They were both from the middle class which was being squeezed by big business and big labor, and both had a bit more fear of labor than of business. Both were strongly moralistic in their approach, both fervent believers in democracy, though Wilson's con-

A great humanitarian, *founder of Hull House in Chicago, leader of the social workers movement, and Nobel Peace Prize winner, Jane Addams was active in the Progressive Party.*

victions ran deeper than Roosevelt's. Both believed firmly in private property and the profit system. Although they outwardly disagreed on whether to regulate monopoly or regulate competition, neither was really opposed to competition, and Wilson moved toward Roosevelt's position of the need to regulate monopoly. Both were strongly opposed to the development of classes in the American society, and both had an abiding faith in the individual, although again, Wilson's faith was more profound.

By the time war clouds began gathering for World War I, the Progressive movement on the city, state and Federal level, had achieved a high percentage of its goals, and in fact had written into law most of the Populist program in the process. As the country moved toward war, Wilson's idealism, and in a sense that of the Progressive movement, was projected onto the international scene. Wilson felt, and led the country to believe along with him, that it was a war to end all wars, a war to make the world safe for democracy, a war for peace and justice and freedom for everyone, including the Germans. The war was to end, according to Wilson, without revenge and he set down fourteen points that he thought would assure this. The last of the fourteen points called for the formation of a "general association of nations," which would ensure the peace of the future, but events precluded the United States from joining that League of Nations for which Wilsonian idealism labored so long and hard at Versailles and at home.

This cartoon *shows President Woodrow Wilson as a stern parent admonishing a recalcitrant Congress.*

Woodrow Wilson *as he appeared on his departure to Europe for negotiations over the peace treaty which ended World War I.*

Teddy Roosevelt *is shown here campaigning in the 1912 election as the candidate of the Bull Moose Party. By this election Roosevelt had broken his ties with the Republican Party. The Republican candidate in 1912 was William Howard Taft.*

THE GILDED AGE

Between the Civil War and 1900 the United States became the foremost industrial nation in the world. America produced more steel, iron, coal, oil, timber, gold, silver and meat than any other country. She led the world in miles of railroad and telegraph lines, and had more telephones and electric lights than any other country. The era is commonly called "The Gilded Age," which was the title of a novel that Mark Twain wrote about a shady politician and a crooked businessman. Like the dime-store trophy, the exterior glistened brightly golden, but if one scratched through the paint, it was only a cheap pot metal. Twain pointed out that under the surface of sensational economic development, American society had a scabby center of corruption and greed. Others have termed it the "Era of Good Stealing" and called the business leaders "Robber Barons," but Twain's phrase has prevailed.

Certainly the heroes of the age were not its elected leaders. Politicians expressed little understanding of the enormous changes in American life brought by industrialization. Between Lincoln and Theodore Roosevelt, a succession of presidents—Johnson, Grant, Hayes, Garfield, Arthur, Cleveland, Harrison, McKinley—provided little leadership to the nation. One journalist, noting the prevalence of beards and moustaches among them, implied they were ashamed to show their faces. The young Woodrow Wilson, later to help end the political blight, complained that America had "no leaders, no principles, no parties."

Republicans and Democrats differed little on what might have been basic issues. Both parties supported protective tariffs and "sound" currency. Both were pro-business and used governmental power to break strikes. After the end of Reconstruction, civil rights for Blacks were seldom mentioned. Republicans waved the "Bloody Shirt," urging voters to remember which party preserved the Union and "vote as you shot." The Democrats less successfully asked voters to forget the tragic war and vote for the party that wanted to heal the old wounds.

Corruption in government was rampant at all levels. The Spoils System frustrated the efforts of well-meaning presidents to bring honesty or efficiency to the Federal Government. Corporations bought and sold state legislatures. It was claimed that Standard Oil did everything with the Pennsylvania legislature except refine it into oil. Californians called the Southern Pacific Railroad "The Octopus" because its tentacles reached out into all areas of commerce with benign approval of the state government. Many cities were run by the likes of New York's Boss Tweed, with his ingenious ways to spend a budget. Some politicians sold valuable public assets; others gave it away. After losing a battle in the New York legislature, one frustrated businessman defined an honest legislator as "one who stays bought."

America looked to its John D. Rockefellers, Andrew Carnegies and J.P. Morgans for leadership; the businessman seemed the truly creative force in the land. In a few short years, they transformed the society, linked the nation with railroads, built a marvelously efficient steel industry, opened oil fields, poured out a flood of new gadgets, and introduced a ruthless efficiency into production. These men preferred that government not interfere with their efforts, and America discovered they had concentrated wealth and power beyond

anything the nation had experienced before.

BIG INDUSTRY

The United States industrialized under highly advantageous conditions. The land was rich in raw materials, and they were generally conveniently located. Millions of immigrants came to America during these years, forming a cheap and mobile labor force. Because America lacked a rigid social structure that might have resisted major changes, the Industrial Revolution received a generally enthusiastic response.

Railroad construction created the first post-Civil War economic boom. By 1900, the United States had approximately 200,000 miles of railway, by World War I, about 250,000. Railroads opened the West to farming, ranching, and trade. Other industries, such as iron, bridge building, and manufacturing of rolling stock, flourished by supplying the railroads. Generous government grants of land and loans financed many railroads; some were built more with an eye to speculative profits than the creation of a sound operating company. In areas of high competition, rate wars broke out; where one railroad provided the only outlet to market, its customers complained of excessively high rates.

During the 1870's, business entered a new phase based on efficient, large scale operations. "Captains of Industry" saw that ruthless cost-cutting and control or stabilization of the industry against excessive competition would generate production miracles. It was said of the meat packers that they used everthing from the hog except its squeal. Often the process was led by someone within the industry, such as Duke in tobacco or Armour in meat packing. But a knowledge of the specific industry was not required, since Carnegie in steel and Rockefeller in oil came from other occupations.

When John D. Rockefeller first considered investing in the oil industry, he was shocked at the chaos of competing companies drilling and refining oil. Only when an oil technician convinced him that they could enter the field as the leading refiners did this department store executive become an oil-man. Armed with rebates from railroads as a weapon against competitors, he rapidly built Standard Oil into a dominating position.

Andrew Carnegie worked for the Pennsylvania Railroad as a telegraph operator. A shrewd investor in growth stocks, he anticipated retiring in his early thirties with a nice yearly income of $50,000. On a European trip he saw the new methods of mass-producing steel and decided to introduce this revolutionary change to America. Joining with Henry Clay Frick, they acquired iron ore from the Mesabi Range, brought it to Pittsburgh where plentiful supplies of coal lay nearby, and soon they were producing steel for about a penny a pound. Carnegie's role with the company was primarily that of selling the steel and goading the plants to higher production. In 1901, Carnegie sold out to J.P. Morgan for almost half a billion dollars and retired to devote his life to philanthropic activities.

J.P. Morgan illustrates another evolution of American business, the rise of the financier. Huge industries required vast amounts of capital, and bankers expected a protective role in the use of their money. Morgan combined Carnegie Steel with a number of smaller competitors into United States Steel, capitalized at $1,400,000,000. This one corporation was worth more than the entire estimated wealth of the United States in 1800. A congressional investigation in 1911 discovered that the Morgan bank controlled 112 corporations worth twenty-two billion dollars, about one tenth of the national wealth. One reform magazine quoted Morgan as saying: "America is good enough for me" and added: "Whenever he doesn't like it, he can give it back to us."

Mass production introduced an almost inhuman efficiency into factory work. Frederick W. Taylor, whose time and motion studies increased production by leaps and bounds, admit-

Jane Addams *as she appeared about 1892, shortly after she had started Hull House in Chicago.*

ted that the most desirable workers were stupid, unemotional, and resembled an ox. Henry Ford added the final touch to the assembly line, with the complete standardization of the work and the product. As Ford liked to say of his cars: "You can have any color you like, as long as it's black."

By the 1890's, it became clear that monopolization was an increasing tendency in business. By using trusts, pools, mergers, holding companies, and interlocking directorates, a few hundred corporations controlled most of the national production. Even conservative politicians became concerned that there was a trust for everything from sugar and nails to oil and steel. The men who controlled these monopolies also dominated government; an American plutocracy had been created.

THE GOSPEL OF WEALTH

What were the values of these business tycoons; what motivated their tremendous achievements? Carnegie, a man of somewhat philosophical mind, called their views "The Gospel of Wealth." Obviously the gospel not only motivated them, but also justified their actions. One basic faith was in *laissez faire* economics. Government should keep its hands off business, allowing the free market to regulate the economy. The customers would buy the best product at the best price; wages of labor and profits would be determined by supply and demand. The free enterprise dogmas did not seem to prevent assistance from government such as land grants for railroads and protective tariffs to limit foreign imports.

The influence of their religious training also conditioned the businessmen's thinking. Many were reared in the Protestant Ethic with its Calvinist emphasis on hard work and thrift as a service to God. The just Calvinist God rewarded his followers with wealth and punished the lazy with poverty. Many of America's most popular preachers taught that "to make money honestly is to preach the gospel." Rockefeller confidently believed that: "God gave me my gold." A railroad

president claimed a new version of divine right, referring to "the Christian men to whom God in His infinite wisdom, has given control of the property interests of the country."

Rugged Individualism offered a secular version of the same doctrine, stressing that through thrift and hard work a poor boy could go from rags to riches. Here the reward was not from God, but from the open and equal opportunity in a free enterprise economy. Horatio Alger was one of the most popular writers of the era, with 135 novels which sold 200 million copies, telling of poor boys succeeding through "pluck and luck." In real life, Andy Carnegie was the embodiment of the ideal. He came to America as a poor immigrant lad and became one of the richest and most powerful men in the world. Carnegie firmly believed that the millionaires had been trained in the stern, but efficient, school of poverty.

Carnegie also believed that Herbert Spencer's use of the evolutionary theories of Charles Darwin explained much of his success. The world of business resembled the jungle, where only the fittest survived. On first reading Spencer's *Social Darwinism*, he exclaimed: "Light came in as a flood and all was clear." Rockefeller taught his Sunday School class that the Standard Oil Company was, like the American Beauty Rose, an example of survival of the fittest. Like the botanist, he had presumably clipped off the inferior little oil companies to allow his own masterpiece to flower.

Businessmen defended their actions by the American devotion to "Progress." Did critics carp about little children in factories or low pay for workers? Such malcontents should hold their tongues and return in twenty years to see what miracles had been wrought to improve the living standard of everyone. The final results would surely justify some hardshhips en route to success.

The Gospel of Wealth was not just a rationalization of business tactics, but a set of ideas that spurred businessmen on to great achievements which the public generally accepted. The modest life style of many millionaires indicated their love of imperial creations rather than mere pursuit of money. Yet the philosophy did eliminate grounds for criticism of their behavior. If they were morally or physically superior to their fellow men, and those who failed could only blame their own weakness, then nothing could be done about the results. Nor was there any obligation, as Spencer pointed out, to create "a forcible burdening of the superior for the support of the inferior." The Gospel of Wealth rendered reform impossible; if a worker made $450 a year and Carnegie made forty million, there was nothing either of them could do to alter it. The corporate leaders seemed to have an air-tight defense.

For those non-believers in the dogma, the argument contained some weak elements. While singing the praises of free enterprise, businessmen ruthlessly eliminated competition. Some of them hardly reflected Christian virtues in the conduct of their business. Social Darwinism was fatally flawed in that these men were changing the environment, rather than merely adapting to it. A study of the background of business leaders by the Harvard Business School demolished the rags to riches thesis. Most executives came from middle and upper class families, and they began with the advantage of a substantial education for that era. Probably Morgan, who inherited his family's bank, is more representative of the wealthy than Carnegie.

As part of his Gospel of Wealth, Carnegie argued that the rich acquired certain obligations with their wealth. Although seeming to contradict Social Darwinism, he felt obligated to care for his less fortunate countrymen by providing them with libraries, schools, music, and even world peace. The Rockefellers also contributed large sums to schools, churches, the cause of world peace, and other worthy charities. Although not universal, many of the new millionaires assumed the duties of an American aristocracy, providing culture for the masses. Certainly their generosity is admirable, but critics questioned whether a larger paycheck might not be more advantageous to workers who could then take their children out of the factories for the benefits of education. Critics also questioned whether the American concept of economic opportunity and political freedom could survive this paternalistic attitude.

THE FARM REVOLT

The farmers were the first to rebel against the power of big business and the *laissez faire* philosophy. After several decades of rapid expansion following the Civil War, over-production brought falling prices and an economic squeeze. The farmer angrily blamed the railroads, bankers, and moguls of Wall Street for his plight, and demanded governmental action.

The number of farms and agricultural production approximately tripled in the fifty years following the Civil War. The rapid growth was made possible by the opening of the West by railroads, generous government land grants to individuals and to railroads, and by increased mechanization of farming. The Department of Agriculture taught the farmer advanced scientific farming techniques. Farming became more and

A soldier wounded *during a battle of the Spanish-American War receives first aid on the battlefield from a member of the American Red Cross.*

more a business, dependent on profits for survival, but the farmer's place in the economy was a precarious one. The railroad, which made it possible to send products to market, charged rates that prevented profits. Bank loans carried exhorbitant interest rates, and bankers would not loan against crops in storage. The tariff that protected manufacturers added heavily to the cost of the farmer's purchases. The "middlemen" who marketed the products seemed to earn a higher profit than he did. Added to the economic frustrations, the farmer felt increasingly isolated from American society. He seldom enjoyed the new inventions—electrical lighting or indoor plumbing—even worse, people sneered at his backwardness. Once honored as the virtuous heart of the American republic, now he was a "hick" or "hayseed."

The cure to the problem was plainly not to "work harder." The more he produced, the more prices fell, sometimes as much as sixty percent. So the farmer turned to the state for help. Since an active governmental policy got him into this mess, it must now protect him against his enemies and help him make more money.

The Patrons of Husbandry, commonly called the Grange, had originally been formed primarily as a social organization. Soon it turned to economic problems and political solutions. Through cooperative marketing and purchasing, Grangers hoped to break monopolistic pricing. The major target was railroad rates. Centering in the Middle West, notably Illinois, the Grangers joined with small businessmen to lobby through the state legislatures regulation of railroad rates, the end of tax evasion and dubious financing. The "Granger Laws" were soon struck down by the Supreme

Court on the grounds that only Congress has the power to regulate interstate commerce. In 1887, Congress passed the Interstate Commerce Act which outlawed discriminatory rates and rebates, and which was the first Federal regulatory agency. Although initially too weak to end railroad abuses, later legislation toughened the controls. The Grangers at least established the principle that business must submit to control by the public for the common good.

A decade later the farm revolt shifted to the Western Great Plains and the South. The Farmers Alliances joined corn, wheat, and cattle farmers of the West with the cotton share-croppers of the South. This farm protest emerged from a much harsher background than the Granger movement. Tenant farmers of the South, both white and black, suffered under a cruel burden of debt peonage which they could hardly hope to escape with low prices for cotton. Western farmers lived the collapse of the American Dream.

Political action posed a problem as the Western farmer was traditionally a Republican and the Southerners were Democrats. After the flush of early victories, the Alliances decided to create a new political party, the Peoples Party. The Populists, as they were commonly called, hoped to attract other dissident groups, especially factory workers, so the new reform party would replace one of the old parties wedded to the status quo.

The populists elected some of the more colorful politicians America has seen. Jerry Simpson, the "Sockless Socrates of the Prairees," became Governor of Kansas. (His opponent stood accused of the effete practice of wearing silk socks; and the new governor complained about the bathtub in the governor's mansion!) The Governor of Colorado was nicknamed "Bloody Bridles" Waite after vowing that when the revolution came he would be immersed in gore up to the bridles of

IT TAKES TWO TO MAKE A CONTRACT.

HOW TO WRITE A CONTRACT.

Rule :—1. The parties to a Contract are taken in the order in which they are written and referred to as "the party of the first part," "the party of the second part," without repeating their names. It matters not which name is written first.

2. After writing the date, names of the parties and their places of residence, state fully all that the first party agrees to do, and then state all that the second party agrees to do.

3. Next state the penalties or forfeitures in case either party does not faithfully and fully perform, or offer to perform, his part of the agreement.

4. Finally, the closing clause, the signatures and seals, the signatures of witnesses are written. (A seal is simply the mark of a pen around the word "seal," written after the signature.)

The period of business *development gave rise to such advertisements as this one, showing the average citizen how he could make a contract.*

his horse. Tom Watson of Georgia and "Pitchfork Ben" Tillman of South Carolina were elected to the United States Senate. Tillman promised he would prod conservative Senators into action with his sharp pitchfork in their ribs. Probably the leading orator of the movement was Mary Ellen Lease who advised Kansas farmers to "Raise less corn and more Hell," shocking advice from a woman in those days. She proclaimed: "Wall Street owns the country," and she denounced politicians for speaking of overproduction of food while American children starved. In revolutionary terms she warned: "The people are at bay, let the bloodhounds of money who have dogged us thus far beware." The Populist assault on Wall Street took on all the fervor of a religious crusade against the devil.

The Populists were widely regarded as dangerous radicals, perhaps even Communist revolutionaries, in conservative Eastern circles. One journal in New York editorialized: "We do not want any more states until we can civilize Kansas." By minimizing farm problems, the farmer looked like a malcontent. After all, he did not have to borrow the banker's money, so why complain now of the interest rate. Businessmen had not forced farmers to open more land and produce more goods than the market could support. With considerable justification, critics pointed out that these agricultural areas needed to diversify their economies, move into other crops and bring industry into their states.

What did these rural radicals propose that frightened Easterners? In politics they advocated the secret ballot, the direct election of Senators, the initiative and referendum. In economics they proposed government action against monopolies, Federal control of currency with at least fifty dollars per capita in circulation, and adoption of the graduated income tax. Probably the only proposal that might sound radical today was for government ownership and operation of railroads and telegraph. Most of these reforms were passed in subse-

Andrew Carnegie, *one of the leading industrialists during the Gilded Age.*

A new railroad *financed by Andrew Carnegie, center, was built in Pennsylvania in 1886.*

quent years under the leadership of respectable Republicans and Democrats.

The Populists failed to build a permanent political force and Federal legislative results were almost nonexistent. Since farmers formed a majority of the population, the lack of success of Populism requires some speculation. Not all farmers suffered the same economic problems, nor was there a kinship among farmers. In the East, agriculture benefitted from the favorable railroad rates of business, and farmers saw their Western counterparts as competitors forcing them into dairy farming and truck gardening for the burgeoning cities. As the Populists turned to an over-simplified approach of inflation through free coinage of silver, factory workers feared the effect of inflation on their already inadequate paychecks. Many of the workers were recent immigrants, and they sensed that farmers had an underlying hostility to new Americans of non-white-Anglo-Saxon-Protestant background. The Populist hero, William Jennings Bryan, running as a Democratic candidate for President, showed clearly the lack of understanding or sympathy for the plight of urban workers. The Populists erred in thinking there was a natural alliance with factory workers; the farmer was a small businessman with dissimilar problems. Finally, many people potentially sympathetic to reform were frightened by the rhetoric of Populism. No matter how moderate and reasonable the program really was, the speeches frightened an essentially conservative America. It would require a Teddy Roosevelt to make the reforms sound necessary and imminently practical.

The greatest failure of all in the Populist program was that the reforms ignored the heart of the problem. All could be passed without curing the overproduction of farm commodities. After 1900, farmers turned to more practical and promising methods. Ignoring broad reforms and third parties, groups such as the Farm Bureau turned to lobbying in Congress for favorable governmental action. By the 1920's, the farm bloc, based on the same alliance of Southern Democrats and Western Republicans, could pass legislation bringing government subsidies through the purchase of surplus commodities. However, not until the 1930's would a President endorse such an approach and grant the farmer his claim on government protection of farm income.

LABOR ORGANIZES

Factory workers were also trying to organize and deal with the power of big business during these years. Industrialization did little to improve the condition of workers, but much to jeopardize it. Mass production methods erased the priority of skilled workers; women and children could do many of the jobs as well as a man and for less wages. In case of a strike, a new labor force could be trained to operate the plant in short order. Arbitrary wage cuts, fines for lateness or imperfections in the work, even charging workers for the use of the machines were common practices. Company stores and towns controlled employees' spending and even their private lives.

Wages were theoretically determined by supply and demand. With millions of new immigrants, the supply was always large and the pay low. As corporations became national in scope, labor costs tended to fall to the lowest available wage level in the nation. The enormous size of the modern corporation created an impersonal relationship between the employer and his workers. Employees were simply part of the cost of production, and as one hard-hearted textile manufacturer put it, when they "get starved down to it, then they will go to work at just what you can afford to pay."

In 1870, a survey of industrial workers' wages in manufacturing states indicated a yearly average salary of $405.64. Three decades later it had increased by less than fifty dollars. A printer said of his fellow workers that the inadequacy of

Immigrants from eastern Europe *as they have lunch soon after completing their processing for entry into America. Immigration was encouraged during the Gilded Age, because the large cartels needed a cheap source of labor to maintain the economic and industrial growth which had begun with the decades of the 1890's.*

their income and the squalor of their living conditions was creating a revolutionary mood. Ten to twelve-hour working days were common; seasonal lay-offs without any income prevailed in many industries.

When workers organized unions to change conditions, leaders were fired and blacklisted. During strikes, private detective agencies like Pinkertons could provide rental guards for the plants. If private power could not break the strike, government could be called on. The mayor would use the police force to maintain "order," the governor would use the National Guard in major strikes. If these forces were inadequate, the president would send in the regular army. Until the administration of Theodore Roosevelt, such interventions were almost universally on the side of management.

American attitudes did not provide a favorable environment for labor's efforts to organize. The ideas that assisted businessmen handicapped workers. Collective bargaining violated the concept of Rugged Individualism. Each man should bargain with his boss on a personal basis, no matter how impractical it might be for one employee to negotiate alone with Standard Oil. Collective bargaining implied a class system, that the economic interests of the workers differed from their employers. Since Americans conceived of their society as classless, with each man succeeding or failing on his own merits, such an appeal smacked of Socialism. With strikes often came violence as men resisted being replaced by "scabs," Americans denounced the violation of "law and order."

The public and the authorities generally blamed the strikers and not management for violence. The moderate New York *Times* probably accurately reflected public opinion when it denounced the methods of strikers as "un-American." It recommended imprisoning strike leaders, and rather ominously proposed to "pick out the leaders and make such an example of them as to scare others into submission." Less moderate newspapers called on the government to use guns and grenades on strikers. A Protestant religious journal even proposed Gatling guns as the most effective remedy for

strikes.

If workers could overcome the obstacle of hostile public opinion, they still faced internal disagreements on how to organize and what methods to use. Union leaders disagreed on whether to form along craft lines or industry-wide. Should they use the strike, the boycott, or seek governmental legislative help? Should they work within Capitalism for a larger share of the pie or turn to Socialism?

Early attempts at unionization often reflected the same mixture of idealism and impracticality with solid reforms as the farm movement. Labor leaders also believed in Rugged Individualism and were reluctant to accept their followers as life-time factory workers. William Sylvis led the National Labor Union to a membership of 600,000 with a dream of making workers the owners of business through cooperatives. Uriah Stephens, a Baptist minister and humanitarian, led the Knights of Labor principally by speeches urging employers to respect the humanity of their workers. His successor, Terence Powderly, favored the boycott over the strike as a tactic. Ironically, its membership soared by 600,000 within a year after they won a railroad strike. The Knights of Labor may have been the most liberal of all unions in accepting workers without discrimination, including women and blacks. Membership was closed only to bartenders, professional gamblers, lawyers and bankers. Although the union had little direct involvement in the strike that led to the violence, the Haymarket bombing in Chicago in 1886 led to its collapse. The public assumed a "Red" threw the bomb, and a wave of hostility to all unions as radical destroyed the moderate Knights of Labor.

The rise of tough, practical unionism came with the American Federation of Labor under the leadership of Samuel Gompers. Rejecting political action or radicalism, the AF of L worked for better wages and hours within the capitalist system. Gompers was probably more conservative than Andrew Carnegie. Amid the reforms of the Progressive Era he argued: "Doing for people what they can and ought to do for themselves is a dangerous experiment. In the last analysis the welfare of the workers depends upon their own initiative." He felt if the government would stop helping business, labor could win its share of the battles. Besides providing little support for possible reforms for workers, this passive approach left large new industries—steel, automobiles, rubber workers—unorganized until the creation of the Congress of Industrial Organizations in the 1930's.

Bloody strikes, especially during economic panics in the 1870's and 1890's, frightened Americans with images of class warfare reminiscent of Europe. In 1877, a railroad strike resulted in twenty-six deaths and millions in property damage before federal troops crushed it. In the coal fields of Pennsylvania, ten members of the "Molly Maguires" were executed for union acts of terrorism. In 1886, after repeated clashes with police by strikers at the McCormick Harvester plant in Chicago, a mass meeting called by radicals at Haymarket Square led to a violent ending. As police arrived to break up the meeting, a bomb thrown into their midst killed seven and wounded seventy more officers.

The 1890's brought even more labor disturbances. At the Homestead, Pennsylvania, plant of Carnegie Steel, 8,000 National Guardsmen broke the small union in that firm. Two years later the federal government sent troops into Illinois, against the wishes of the Governor, to break the peaceful strike of the American Railway Union against the Pullman Coach Company. Eugene Debs, head of the union, was jailed for violation of an injunction against the strike; he came out converted to Socialism.

Like the farmer, workers had failed miserably in their at-tempt to deal with business on an equal footing. In 1900, seventy percent of the industrial workers still labored ten or more hours per day for a salary well beneath the estimated minimum living costs compiled by the federal government. The only hopeful sign for workers was in the stirrings of reform within the new Progressive Movement; perhaps others could give them what they had failed to achieve for themselves.

AN URBAN SOCIETY

The cities underwent a spectacular growth during the last part of the nineteenth century. Between 1880 and 1900, New York almost doubled in size and Chicago more than tripled. Industrialization opened job opportunities, and new inventions made city life attractive. Technological changes were making larger populations possible. Electrical commuter trains enabled masses of people to travel to work, and the telephone brought speedy communication. Electric power provided a new source of clean, portable energy to run factories, light streets, and run elevators.

The American city was not generally a healthy place to live in 1900. Few cities had an adequate water supply, and sewage disposal was rudimentary. Regular garbage collection was rare; uncollected wastes around apartments provided breeding ground for rats and vermin. Building codes gave little protection against overcrowding or lack of sanitary facilities. Tenement houses often featured two-room apartments, one room nine by fourteen feet, the other about nine by six feet. Many families could not even afford this space; they were forced to take in boarders or share with another family. The tenement might contain one toilet per floor, or even one in the yard for the whole building. Space between the tenements was inadequate to let in sufficient sunshine or clean air.

In these conditions disease spread rapidly, and families often disintegrated under the pressures of inadequate privacy, squalor, and poverty. Fathers not infrequently quit the struggle for survival, turning to liquor or gambling for release, or even abandoning their families.

Many city dwellers were poorly prepared for the urban experience. They had no job skills, only their brute strength to offer on the labor market. Country people had trouble adjusting to the new life style of the city. Without relatives or friends, the impersonality of life in the city could swamp the individual.

The situation was worse for the immigrants from abroad. For them, it was a double migration, from farm to city, and to a strange new land. At the turn of the century, there were about thirteen million foreign born, and they tended to concentrate in the worst city ghettos. After 1880, another significant change was a shift in migration to people from Southern and Eastern Europe. They would face a special hostility in that they were not Anglo-Saxon Protestants like the majority of Americans.

The same forces at work in European agriculture as in American drove them from their homes. The industrial and commercial revolution brought consolidation of farm lands and replacement of peasant workers by machines. The population explosion in crowded Europe meant no land for children to inherit. Government oppression, and often ethnic hostilities, created an intolerable situation. Most migrants went from a feudal village to urban, industrial America. Illiterate and unskilled, they had to take the work available at whatever wages they could get. When native Americans

Child labor *was a fact of economic life during this era. These boys are pictured at the end of their 16 hour work day in a coal mine in West Virginia.*

earned to little too live decently, the immigrant made only half or two-thirds of that wage.

The immigrants found the American doctrine of Rugged Individualism foreign to their family and communal background and ineffective in solving problems. They formed mutual aid societies to provide insurance against death or illness and to bring companionship among one's countrymen. They developed their own cultural activities—newspapers and the theatre—to help interpret and learn the American culture. Within several decades, some immigrants began to achieve power and wealth through organization, notably in political machines, in the church, in entertainment, and in crime.

Politics offered a new form of expression for immigrants. In Europe they had little or no voice in government, but in America their votes were eagerly sought by urban bosses. They were assured that America was a democracy, and they had an obligation to "vote early and vote often." The boss had his own interest of course; the votes kept him in office. The rapidly growing city needed many services—gas, electricity, trains—chartering them gave him many opportunities for kickbacks from business. The urban boss has had an odious reputation for graft, but too little has been said in his defense. The immigrants needed jobs, assistance in brushes with authorities, groceries and coal during hard times. The urban political machines gave personal assistance, providing an essential service when no formal welfare facilities existed. And they governed their cities. As some political scientists warned the reformers, bad government was better than none. Today as so many big cities seem unable to manage themselves, the one notable exception is the last major American city controlled by a boss.

The immigrants discovered that middle class Americans were eager to reform them, to bring honest (and impersonal) government by destroying the power of the political boss. The reformers seemed a strange breed, full of absurd ideas about drinking being evil, of the desirability of Sunday blue laws, and even of giving women equal rights. They claimed the bosses stole money, but the immigrants knew they did not have anything worth stealing. Uprooted from his native land, feeling alienated in America, the immigrant generally clung to traditional values in the face of the reform fervor.

WAR WITH SPAIN

At first glance, the American involvement in the Cuban rebellion against Spain seems an unlikely disturbance of internal economic development. For decades Americans had isolated themselves from foreign affairs while the West was settled and the industrial base created. But to a large degree the domestic problems we have been considering and the popular ideas of the time led naturally to a bellicose foreign policy.

By the 1890's, the Western frontier, in terms of available open land for settlement, was gone. Americans believed the roots of their democracy lay in the westward movement. As explained by Frederick Jackson Turner, one of America's most inflential historians, the availability of free land produced an individualistic, classless society. With the end of the frontier, the source of American democracy was en-

Market Street *in San Francisco, California, late in the morning of April 18, 1906, minutes after the great San Francisco earthquake.*

dangered. Recent trends in business concentration and strife between workers and employers indicated that already America was becoming more authoritarian and torn by class hostilities.

Perhaps America could open a new frontier across the Pacific. The old theory of Manifest Destiny, that Americans are God's chosen people to spread democracy, was dusted off and trotted out to justify expansion. After all, did Americans not have an obligation to "civilize our little brown brothers" in the Orient? Social Darwinism reinforced this duty; the Anglo-Saxon skill at government would be exported to the natives. Senator Henry Cabot Lodge argued that America must not "fall out of the line of march;" apparently if England and Germany colonized, then the United States should also share in the "white man's burden."

Economic considerations seemed to compel expansion. America needed new markets for her products and new sources of raw materials. This argument was not put forth primarily by businessmen, who began with little enthusiasm for the war, but by politicians such as Theodore Roosevelt. Captain Alfred T. Mahan of the Naval Academy argued that great trading nations need strong navies and large merchant fleets. A powerful navy would require bases throughout the world. Roosevelt felt that a "bit of a spar" with Germany would do wonders to teach Americans the need for a strong military, but if Spain was a convenient target, she would have to do.

Although difficult to prove, expansion may also have been useful to divert the nation's mind from internal problems. At least, one Texas Congressman followed this view in urging President Cleveland to be belligerent with England. He promised that a little shooting would lance the boil of Populism and crush Socialism.

Teddy Roosevelt received a letter from his friend John Hay describing the war with Spain as "a splendid little war." In less than three months and with minimal casualities, the United States forced Spain to leave Cuba. It acquired a base in Cuba, the island of Puerto Rico, and the Philippine Islands. During the war, Hawaii was annexed. The United States had enlarged its military power in the Caribbean and become involved in the Far Eastern power struggle. America demonstrated to the world its arrival as a major power by thoroughly thrashing a third rate power. The vast trade expansion anticipated never developed and the burden of empire led even Roosevelt a few years later to question whether expansion had been wise.

PROGRESSIVE REFORM

Criticism of business and political practices had been slowly building in the intellectual community for some years. Henry George, a journalist in California, was one of the first to attack the Gospel of Wealth. He wondered why, after a life of hard work, he was not prospering as Carnegie promised. Was it really possible that the American Dream of rags to riches was a fraud; that a man could struggle all his life and remain poor? George spent several years trying to answer this question and produced his conclusions in a very influential book. In *Progress and Poverty*, George argued that child labor, hoboes, and grinding poverty were as much characteristic of industrialism as the mansions of the millionaires. No longer did man struggle with the problem of producing sufficient goods, but now the distribution of the fruits of technology had become the central issue. In the midst of plenty, many went to bed hungry every night. He claimed business

defined democracy as the "liberty to compete for employment at starvation wages."

Several economists, notably Richard T. Ely, broke with dogmas of laissez faire. He claimed it did not operate along scientific principles beyond the reach of human improvement. While retaining a belief in private property, Ely stressed the need for social responsibility in an economic system. Only the government could, and should, protect the public interest from the abuses of business leaders.

In religion, the rise of the Social Gospel repudiated the use of the Protestant Ethic to defend the rich and prevent the church from assisting the poor. They rediscovered that Jesus was a carpenter and not a corporate executive. Although some ministers turned to a humanist Socialism, most sought a middle ground ethic between the ruthless competitiveness of Capitalism and the collectivist emphasis of Socialism. As many of their parishioners moved to the suburbs, they needed to reach out to the newer migrants to the city. Through recreational facilities and social clubs, they hoped to restore the church to a vital community role amid the impersonality of the modern city.

Probably William James and John Dewey in their philosophy of Pragmatism best expressed the optimism that man could govern himself that underlay Progressivism. They argued that truth is relative and man is his own creator; every idea should be tested in the laboratory of experience. If a concept works and improves society, it is valid. If behavior does not improve, the idea should be junked. A harmful environment would probably produce bad people, but man has an infinite capacity to improve conditions. As some critics warned, the approach was shallow-minded, ignoring the dark side of human nature, and more of a method of doing without a philosophy. They had simply stated very well the American tradition of doing what is practical without regard to inherited dogmas. As we have seen, such ideas as laissez faire and the Protestant Ethic were used more to explain actions than to limit behavior. Americans would have no trouble now turning to new economic practices such as publically owned utilities without worrying if it was Socialism.

Few Americans read John Dewey or Richard T. Ely, but they did read their magazines, and here they were bombarded with detailed accounts of hanky panky in the world of business and government. From 1900 to the first world war, almost every issue contained a new exposé about some prominent American or about the methods of a major corporation, written by people Teddy Roosevelt named the Muckrakers. Henry Demarest Lloyd and Ida Tarbell attacked the practices of Standard Oil with moralistic fervor. Lincoln Steffens described municipal corruption in a series called the *"Shame of the Cities."* The eager public read about dirty dealings in the stock market and the United States Senate.

American society was questioned from top to bottom. Jacob Riis wrote the first exposé of life in American ghettos. He argued, in words that still ring true, that America cannot rob a child of its childhood, or let men live like pigs, when we need their participation in our society as free men. Typical of the muckraking style was Upton Sinclair's description of immigrant workers packing meat in Chicago's stockyard. The novel, *The Jungle*, pictured men with tuberculosis working without safety precautions in unsanitary conditions. Spoiled meat, trash, even rats and rat poison, all went into the public's food supply. Workers fell into vats and went out of the plants as "Durham's Pure Leaf Lard."

Like all the Muckrakers, Sinclair's basic question was how such conditions could be tolerated. His answer was the

The gild *in the Gilded Age is illustrated here in this picture of a private barber chair and salon aboard a private railroad car.*

same found by the other writers, that the government of Chicago was literally a branch office of the packers, thanks to bribery. Only by collusion between elected officials and businessmen could the public be treated so contemptuously.

The Muckrakers succeeded in tearing away the halo of the businessman and the claims to respectability of politicians. They did so, not out of a spirit of despair about Capitalism or democracy, but rather out of a conviction that government and business could be reformed by an aroused public opinion. They performed an indispensable task in preparing the nation for the Progressive reformers. When Teddy Roosevelt denounced ''Malefactors of Great Wealth,'' most people did not have to ask who or what he was referring to.

Progressivism began within the Republican Party, under the leadership of men such as Robert La Follette of Wisconsin, Hiram Johnson of California, and Theodore Roosevelt of New York. The Democrats carried the movement forward under Woodrow Wilson until World War I ended domestic reform. Progressivism drew its membership largely from urban, middle-class backgrounds. Many of the activists came from business and the professions, but notably more from the independent, self-employed than from the ranks of big corporations. Social workers and others close to the problems of workers also contributed to the reform spirit.

After the failure of the farmers and workers to effectively challenge the power of business, it may seem puzzling that those who suffered much less from industrialism should revolt. The middle class feared that traditional American values—political democracy and free economic opportunity —were being crushed by political machines and business monopolies. Watching the labor strife of the 1890's and the Populist farm revolt, they also worried that the swing towards a right-wing plutocracy might be reversed by a counter revolution of the oppressed leading to Socialism. By destroying the political bosses' power and disciplining big business, the Progressives hoped to restore the democratic tradition to America. And, as Roosevelt argued, social justice was necessary to prevent Socialism.

The political solution was to replace the political party with direct democracy, involving the people in the decisions affecting their lives. Essentially it was the same program as Populism: the initiative, referendum and recall, direct election of Senators, the secret ballot, the direct primary, and women suffrage. In the cities, public ownership of utilities and equitable taxation would break one of the boss's source of power. City managers and commissions would replace the mayor's relatives and professionalize administration.

Dealing with corporate power produced a split within the Progressive Movement. Theodore Roosevelt represented one line of thought with his New Nationalism. Roosevelt did not believe that big business could be successfully ''trust-busted,'' in fact bigness often brought efficiency. Therefore strong government should strictly regulate corporations in the public interest. Workers would be protected by safety legislation, accident compensation, even public medical insurance.

Woodrow Wilson, with substantial agreement from Republicans like La Follette, believed that business could be broken up into competitive units. Wilson was very reluctant to see the creation of a welfare state, although he saw the political advantage in not opposing some of the reforms. Wilson may even have acknowledged Roosevelt's approach as more effective by the creation of the Federal Trade Commission rather than emphasize new anti-trust legislation.

A strong vein of social reform ran through Progressivism, dominated by a concern for the consumer, and especially for urban victims of poverty. Settlement workers like Jane Addams sought to teach needed skills and to encourage city dwellers to rebel against bossism. Pure food and drug acts, slum clearance, public parks and playground, aimed at making urban life more tolerable. While much of the concern was paternalistic, especially the desire to make recent immigrants conform to Anglo society, it also reflected a sympathy for the oppressed seldom seen in the American middle class.

The strong moralistic strain of the middle class led the Progressive to vigorous efforts against social evils. Not only did they wish to improve the behavior of politicians and businessmen, but they set out to eliminate sin through legislation. Prohibition of alcoholic beverages was finally imposed on the nation after a century of effort. A combination of state and Federal laws banned prostitution, gambling and prize fighting.

From the perspective of the passage of half a century, the Progressive program failed in many aspects. Most people today would agree that the moral legislation, especially prohibition, was disastrous. Certainly it is clear that business continues to wield enormous power in American politics, and that the concentration into fewer and larger corporations continues. Political corruption was not ended by direct democracy; soon the Harding Administration would prove how easy the rules could be evaded. Perhaps instead of weakening political parties, the Progressives should have tried to make them more responsible. In these days of calls for "participatory democracy," it might be wise to examine the results of Progressivism and ask what burdens of decision-making the average citizen is able or willing to assume.

Progressivism illustrates that it is not governmental techniques that ensure honest, responsive government, but the election of public spirited, concerned leaders. Here the Progressive record was outstanding. Theodore Roosevelt was a volcano of energy; he had to be "the bride at every wedding,

and the corpse at every funeral." Equally at home with cowboys and intellectuals, boxers and artists, he restored the White House as the center of national power. Although he managed to push little of his program through a reluctant Congress, he preached reform until the American people accepted it and later legislatures passed it. This gifted politician was a "combination of St. George and St. Vitus" as he led Americans on an emotional and moral crusade for social justice. He did not always win, but he took on business tycoons like J.P. Morgan, and ended the crushing of labor by the Federal Government. Probably his greatest achievement was the beginning of a Federal program of conservation; Roosevelt was the first president to realize we could not waste our resources so carelessly.

One reporter noted that government under Roosevelt was a three-ring circus, but under Woodrow Wilson it was an Easter sunrise service. Wilson's idealism inspired millions of Americans; during World War I much of the world thrilled to his vision of democracy. His first six years as president showed his ability to lead as well as inspire, and Progressives enacted the rest of their program. His last two years in office, when he became crippled with illness and failed to bring the nation to accept his peace treaty, illustrate both his inability to work with opponents and the lack of unity in Progressive ranks about America's role in the world.

Throughout all levels of government, in numbers too numerous to begin a listing of them, Progressives illustrated the ability of good people to work actively on social problems. They brought a new spirit to politics and business, and the beginnings of national commitment to promote the public over the private interest. They demonstrated that government can be a positive force to protect citizens from unbridled personal power. In this era of cynicism about government, Progressivism is an example that all politicians are not crooks, that people of integrity, ability, and concern for the conditions of American life can be found to lead us.

The opulence *of the age was manifest in* The Breakers, *the seaside mansion built for Cornelius Vanderbilt between 1893 and 1895.*

George Washington
FIRST PRESIDENT   1789-1797

John Adams
SECOND PRESIDENT   1797-1801

Thomas Jefferson
THIRD PRESIDENT   1801-1809

James Madison
FOURTH PRESIDENT   **1809-1817**

James Monroe
FIFTH PRESIDENT   1817-1825

John Quincy Adams
SIXTH PRESIDENT   1825-1829

Andrew Jackson
SEVENTH PRESIDENT   1829-1837

Martin Van Buren
EIGHTH PRESIDENT   1837-1841

William Henry Harrison
NINTH PRESIDENT   1841

John Tyler
TENTH PRESIDENT   1841-1845

James K. Polk
ELEVENTH PRESIDENT   1845-1849

Zachary Taylor
TWELFTH PRESIDENT   1849-1850

Millard Fillmore
THIRTEENTH PRESIDENT   **1850-1853**

Franklin Pierce
FOURTEENTH PRESIDENT   1853-1857

James Buchanan
FIFTEENTH PRESIDENT   1857-1861

Abraham Lincoln
SIXTEENTH PRESIDENT **1861-1865**

Andrew Johnson
SEVENTEENTH PRESIDENT   **1865-1869**

Ulysses S. Grant
EIGHTEENTH PRESIDENT   1869-1877

Rutherford B. Hayes
NINETEENTH PRESIDENT   1877-1881

James A. Garfield
TWENTIETH PRESIDENT   1881

Chester A. Arthur
TWENTY-FIRST PRESIDENT   1881-1885

Grover Cleveland
TWENTY-SECOND PRESIDENT   1885-1889
TWENTY-FOURTH PRESIDENT   1893-1897

Benjamin Harrison
TWENTY-THIRD PRESIDENT   1889-1893

William McKinley
TWENTY-FIFTH PRESIDENT   **1897-1901**

THE ERA OF REFORM

As Henry Steele Commager has pointed out, the eighteen nineties constituted a great watershed in American history.[1] America before that time was predominantly agricultural; after that predominantly urban and industrial. The America of the nineteenth century was primarily concerned with domestic problems, but in the eighteen nineties she became involved in world affairs and from then on was inextricably tied to the economy and politics of the entire globe. By 1890 the constant struggle with the Indians was over and the battle of Wounded Knee, fought in that year, symbolized the disintegration of the Red Man's world. By 1890 the Civil War was no longer a cardinal issue in the political battle between the Democrats and the Republicans. In that year, too, an official report indicated that the Frontier no longer existed in America, and the Frontier had been an integral part of the American scene for almost three hundred years. By the 1890's it was obvious to all that it was not just business that was important, but "Big" business, which included the Standard Oil Trust, Carnegie Steel, J. Pierpont Morgan's banking interest, and the railroad magnates. Toward the end of the century the value of industrial production was greater than that of agriculture. By the 1890's the city had become a dominant feature of American life, and the "new" immigrants coming to the country in increasingly large numbers (up to a million a year) were from Southern and Catholic Europe rather than from the Western Protestant countries.

The Depression of 1893 is a poignant illustration of the fact that by the nineties the nation was being confronted by

[1] Henry Steele Commager, *The American Mind: An Interpretation of American Thought and Character Since the 1880's*, Ch. I.

Labor-Management strife *of the 1890's was climaxed with the riots at Homestead, Pennsylvania, in 1892. The riots began following the lockout of steel workers at the Edgar Thompson Works. Ten men were killed in the battles which occurred between the strikers and the Pinkertons, shown here in the foreground.*

the same political and economic problems that have plagued the United States since, and which were to have such devastating consequences in the Depression of the 1930's. That earlier depression was the darkest period since the Civil War and the first industrial depression the nation had experienced. Millions of people were unemployed (15,000 commercial houses failed in 1893 alone, 158 national banks closed, along with countless state banks). Within two years sixty percent of the railroads were not paying dividends, and almost a fifth of the nation's railroad mileage was in receivership. Jacob S. Coxey, a successful businessman who desired government reform of the currency system, led an "army" of the unemployed to Washington as a "petition . . . with boots on." Other armies formed throughout the country. Although few of them reached Washington, they symbolized the hunger, poverty, and discontent of the poor and unemployed. It was in 1894 that the Pullman Strike tied up all railroads going in or out of Chicago, virtually bringing the nation's transportation system to a halt and throwing fear into the souls of American businessmen.

THE POPULIST MOVEMENT

The Populist Movement was the culmination of a number of unsuccessful attempts by various groups to reform the American political system as it had developed after the Civil War. It provided a focus for all the frustrations of an agrarian population which was not benefitting economically from the industrial revolution and the rise of big business, but was witnessing the disintegration of the American way of life which had been characteristic of the eighteenth and nineteenth centuries.

The rise of big business was based not only on the development of new technology, but also upon new business methods that were only dimly understood by most of the population. Many of the new techniques greatly increased

227

New arrivals *from eastern Europe near America's shores. During the decade of the 1890's thousands of immigrants came to America seeking a better life. They were welcomed with open arms by American industry as a source of cheap labor.*

efficiency and production, but others, like the formation of the "trust" by Standard Oil, were to provide business with powerful new means of exploiting the nation. Even as the strength of business developed it raised doubts in the minds of those who thought bigness was in and of itself un-American, and many more were convinced that monopoly was completely opposed to the competitive American system. The seemingly unlimited opportunities of the post-Civil War period probably accentuated the tendency of that generation to grab what it could at the expense of the less fortunate or the less skilled. The Sherman Anti-Trust Act was passed by Congress in 1890, but it was singularly ineffective in controlling monopolies or preventing others from being created.

Westerners were even more directly affected by the corrupt, and at times, vicious practices of the railroads. Homesteaders in the West were completely dependent on railroads to transport their crops to the East and excessive rates charged to them by the railroads could ruin their economy. The railroads had long abused their power through the system of rebates, pooling agreements, different charges for long and short hauls, granting favors and bribes to Congressmen, and watering their stock. During President Grant's term of office, the exposure of the Credit Mobilier scandal brought ruin to several Congressmen and to the Vice President, Schuyler Colfax. The company was used by a group of corrupt executives in the Union Pacific to enable them to pocket exorbitant profits (384%) in the construction of the line, even while the Union Pacific was going bankrupt.

It is estimated that in 1885 one-third of all railroad stock was "water", this in spite of the fact that railroads received large land grants from the Federal, State and even local governments. The Northern Pacific cost some seventy million dollars to build, but it had received land grants that sold for 136 million, with much of the most valuable land still remaining to be sold. Total cost of the five transcontinental railroads has been estimated at 634 million dollars, but without graft and dishonest practices, the same roads could have been built for 286 million. The Interstate Commerce Act of 1887 was the first legislation of its kind in America, and it was probably expecting too much to assume it would correct

the grave abuses that had been coming to light; but whatever the expectations, it, like the Sherman Anti-Trust Act, was ineffective.

With big business had come big labor, but the labor movement could make little headway against the former. Pinkerton detectives were used to spy on labor organizers and were often employed as a private army to put down strikes. State and Federal troops were called in on many occasions, not to keep peace, but to break strikes. Civil Service reform had taken a significant step with the passing of the Pendleton Civil Service Act, but there was still corruption at the ballot box, and at all levels of government with city government, perhaps, being the most corrupt. Tariff rates continued to rise throughout the period with big business reaping the benefits of a protected market whereas the farmer was forced to pay more for manufactured goods.

By 1890 the situation of the farmer in the South and the Middle Border states (the Dakotas, Kansas, Nebraska, Iowa) was becoming desperate. In the years after the Civil War the production of wheat had doubled and then doubled again, the production of corn and cotton tripled. But the benefits did not accrue to the farmer. With the advent of farm machinery, the average farm ceased to be a self-sufficient unit which produced most of the family's food, clothing and other necessities. Instead it became a cog in an industrial system, devoted to raising a staple crop. No longer independent, the farmer was tied to the banking and industrial sections of the country, and with the tremendous increase in production of wheat, corn and cotton, was dependent upon overseas markets and prices set by the world market. Wheat prices dropped from a dollar a bushel in the seventies to fifty cents a bushel in the nineties, corn from seventy-five cents to twenty-eight cents, cotton from thirty-one cents a pound to six cents. And, while prices of farm products were falling, the cost of farming was rising. Transportation costs were high, the price of farm machinery, protected by tariffs, con-

George Pullman, *who perfected the sleeper coach which revolutionized the railroad in this country. Strikes at the Pullman factory were some of the worst in a decade of labor violence.*

John Pierpont Morgan, *whose financial manipulations created one of the most powerful and prestigious banking cartels in the world. Morgan's banking interests reached down into several interrelated industries, and were a foreshadowing of the huge conglomerates which developed sixty years later.*

tinued to increase as did the cost of other manufactured goods which the farmer was no longer able to provide for himself.

The plight of the farmer was accentuated by other factors. Like most Americans he had erroneously assumed that the soil of the nation was inexhaustible, but soil depletion and erosion, drought and flood, took a heavy toll on millions of acres of Western land. Earlier, many of those who had farmed out an area simply moved on to virgin lands farther West, but in 1890 the Frontier had come to an end. To purchase necessary equipment farmers had borrowed heavily from banks which charged almost prohibitive rates. Throughout the farm belts of the South and the West, interest rates were frequently above twenty percent and seldom below ten. And, as if to underscore all their other difficulties, farmers who had borrowed money suffered additional losses through the operation of the currency system. In 1865 thirty-one dollars per capita was in circulation, but this shrank before long to nineteen dollars per person. Money had thus become more valuable, or on the farmer's terms, he had to exchange more wheat, corn, or cotton to receive a dollar in currency. If he had borrowed money on the basis of one bushel of wheat as equal to one dollar, he now found that he had to pay off his debt on the basis of a bushel-and-a-half for each dollar.

The first organized attempts of the farming community to obtain relief from economic difficulties came shortly after the Civil War. In the eighteen seventies the Greenback Party was organized for the express purpose of gaining a more elastic currency by seeking legislation requiring the printing of more paper money, but its Presidential candidate in 1876 polled less than one percent of the popular vote. The Grange movement (founded as the Patrons of Husbandry in 1867) attempted to organize the farmer for both political and economic action. In the latter sphere it was successful in establishing

Adlai E. Stevenson, *the grandfather of the 1956 Presidential Democratic candidate, served as vice-president under Grover Cleveland. Stevenson was one of the few voices within the Cleveland administration to speak out against the political spoils system which had infected the goverment.*

229

hundreds of cooperative stores which benefited the farmer for a period of time. In 1880 the Farmers' Alliances assumed the political rôle originally filled by the Grange, and entered the economic field through cooperative buying and selling, cooperative insurance and the establishing of farmers "exchanges." In the eighteen nineties the Alliance groups merged into the Populist Party. The final impetus to the organization of the People's Party can be directly attributed to the weather. In 1887 the drought in the Middle Border was so severe that crops withered, farm animals died, and the folks who had been part of the over-settlement of the more arid regions (often their fortunes based on inflated land prices and inflated interest rates) faced ruin. Thousands of farm

mortgages were foreclosed and many people now returned eastward, often bearing signs on their wagons, "In God we Trusted, in Kansas we busted."

In the elections of eighteen ninety the new party, even without national organization, was successful in electing four Senators, over fifty Congressmen, and in gaining control over a dozen state legislatures. Flushed with success, the party leaders prepared to organize in a formal fashion and to present a full ticket in the 1892 elections. In Omaha, on Independence Day of that election year, there gathered a colorful and passionate group of men drawn from the ranks of the Greenbackers, the Knights of Labor, free-silverites, members of "Bellamy" clubs who had been inspired by Edward Bellamy's *Looking Backward*, followers of Henry George the "single taxer", and above all, from the powerful Farmers' Alliances, North and South. The platform, drawn up by Ignatius Donnelly, painted a melancholy scene of American life. It pictured the nation as teetering on "the verge of moral, political, and material ruin." The urban workmen and the farmer alike had been denied the fruits of their labor and the nation was breeding "two great classes—tramps and millionaires." To the tune of "Save a Poor Sinner Like Me" the delegates shouted that "the railroads and old party bosses together did sweetly agree" to deceive and exploit "a hayseed like me." And over and over again they sang the "People's Hymn" to the music of the "Battle Hymn of the Republic":

This political cartoon, *from* Harper's Weekly, *shows Congressmen scuttling needed Civil Service and Tariff reform, while President Cleveland, at the stern of the ship of state, cuts the lines on those Democrats who were advocating a silver-purchase bill in Congress.*

Benjamin Tillman, known as "Pitchfork Ben," gained a reputation while serving as a senator from South Carolina for being a hot tempered and flamboyant legislator.

Besides a falling market for their farm products, American farmers during the 1890's were also hit by one of the worst droughts in the country's history.

They have stolen our money, have ravished our homes;
With the plunder, erected to Mammon a throne;
They have fashioned a god, like the Hebrews of old,
Then bid us bow down to their image of gold.

The planks of the platform were specific and far-reaching in intent. Although regarded by many throughout the East as an attack on the American system that could be regarded as little short of communism, within the next fifty years every one of the planks had been incorporated into law in whole or in part. In an attempt to unite the farmer and the industrial laborer in the movement, the platform advocated an eight-hour day, denounced "the maintenance of a large standing army of mercenaries known as the Pinkerton system," favored the right of labor to organize, and advocated the limitation of injunctions in labor disputes. To correct political abuses and clean up corruption the Party urged the adoption of the secret ballot, endorsed the popular election of U.S. Senators, advocated the initiative, referendum, recall and direct primaries, and with less zeal, women's suffrage.

In the economic field one of the most important platforms set forth was for the free coinage of silver to provide an elastic currency system, but other planks also were far reaching: no further government aid to corporations directly or indirectly; the strengthening of the Interstate Commerce Act and the Sherman Anti-Trust Act; the ownership of the railroads, telegraph and telephone systems by the Federal government; a graduated Federal income tax; a subtreasury system that could loan money to farmers at no more than two percent interest; government loans on crops enabling the farmer to hold his crop for higher prices; and government operated postal savings banks.

There is little question that the strength and the heart of the movement were agrarian. The attempt to rally the labor movement around the platform was not successful, and at the polls it was the Middle Border and the South that provided support. The Populists were comprised mainly of the poor and middle classes, but it was a sectional not a class movement. Its philosophy had its roots deep in the American past. It reflected Jeffersonian agrarianism in its distrust of urbanization and industrialism and in its conviction that the abiding virtues of morality and self-reliance were the peculiar product of a good life on the farm. It subscribed wholeheartedly to the ideas in the Declaration of Independence: the goodness of man, the social contract theory, the belief that man can govern himself, that all men are born equal and possess the inalienable rights of life, liberty and the pursuit of happiness. Along with the Jeffersonian philosophy, Populist ideals combined the strong individualism of frontier Jacksonian democracy with its emphasis on a rugged equality, equal rights for all and special privileges for none, and the need for a stronger federal government to ensure this goal. *A Call to Action* written by James B. Weaver, the Presidential candidate for the Party in 1892, drew up an indictment against business corporations which reads like the Jacksonian polemic which was aimed at the National Bank sixty years earlier.

It was natural that the Populists should turn to the government for help since the government had very materially aided the development of the West. Large tracts of land had been given away to encourage immigration, the railroads had received both money and lands, states had been given thousands of acres of land from the public domain for educational purposes, the national government had built roads and aided in the construction of canals, and the Homestead and Pre-emption laws passed by Congress had provided the acre-

Grover Cleveland, *Democratic President of the United States during the Depression of the 1890's. In addition to serving as President from 1893-1897, he had also served a first term from 1885-1889.*

While farmers were suffering *untold hardships and laborers were working for as little as eight cents an hours, the Vanderbilts (and other industrialists) were spending millions on mansions such as this.*

Reproduction *of an ink sketch showing Mary Lease, who was one of the earliest and the only influential woman to speak out in favor of the Populist Movement.*

age for most of the settlers of the Middle Border.

The Populists also included in their philosophy an ingredient which made them suspect by some later historians. Though strongly pro-American and imbued with their share of the belief in the transcendent destiny of the United States, nevertheless they embraced conspiratorial theory to explain the country's "deplorable" situation. Since man was considered basically good and capable of governing himself, they felt the problems of the country must have been caused by a small parasitic minority which was to be found in the highest places of power. "On one side," said William Jennings Bryan, "stand the corporate interests of the United States, the moneyed interests, aggregated wealth and capital, imperious, arrogant, compassionless. On the other side stand an unnumbered throng, those who gave to the Democratic party a name for whom it assumed to speak." In its most simple form, the theory suggested that all American history since the Civil War could be understood as a sustained conspiracy of the international money power (sometimes referred to as the Anglo-American Gold Trust). Thus to some extent the international Jewish bankers became the symbol of all evil. Although the Populist movement was characterized by neither a strong anti-foreign nor an anti-Semitic position, the seeds of these ideas were present and were later expanded by other "populist" groups in America into fascist or near fascist philosophies.

An amazing development, for the times, was the close working relationship between the Negroes and the Whites in the Populist Party. In 1890 the two Farmers' Alliances in the South, one Black and one White, agreed to work together and throughout the country Blacks were an integral part of the movement. In 1890 the Party in Kansas ran a Negro minister as their candidate for State Auditor, and although he lost, he ran well ahead of the ticket. In Louisiana twenty-four Negroes were elected as state delegates to the first state convention; in Georgia Tom Watson openly mustered White and Black audiences to fight for the rights of man regardless of color. "My friends," he cried when speaking to one group, "this campaign will decide whether or not your people and ours can daily meet in harmony, and work for law, and order, and morality, and wipe out the color line and put every man on his citizenship irrespective of color." In North Carolina hundreds of Negroes were appointed or elected to local offices and in the election of 1896 a Negro, George C. White, was elected from the state to serve in Congress. The collapse of the Populist movement after 1896 put an end to this most promising possibility for an emancipated South.

The election of 1896 was the crucial test for the Populist movement. Two years before, with the country in the depths of depression and people looking for a way out of their problems, the Party had increased its votes, largely at the expense of the Democrats in the South and the West, and therefore by 1896 the Democratic Party was on the verge of disintegration. The key issue centered around the free coinage of silver, and it appeared that either the "silver wing" of the Democratic Party would capture control of the organization or the silverites would secede to the Populists, making the latter one of the major parties.

The silver issue was more than a matter of politics, for both sides attached a moral significance to it which turned the campaign into something of a religious crusade. The classic theory of money, widely accepted prior to the Civil War, had held that the value of money was determined by the bullion which was kept as security for its redemption and any interference by the government with the bases was economically unsound. As long as the relation between gold and silver remained relatively stable, those in favor of the bullion theory of money accepted a bi-metallic standard, but a decline in the value of silver had disrupted the ratio and so, after the Civil War, orthodox economists reversed to a single metallic standard, gold. But a new theory had also emerged at that time partly as a result of the government method of financing the War, and its adherents considered money a token of credit rather than a token of bullion, and advocated that it was the proper business of government to regulate the supply of money in the interest of society. They saw the post Civil War period as one of rapid expansion, and thus believed it was the responsibility of the government to expand the currency to facilitate the business of a growing economy. To fail to do so, they felt, forced the value of money up, made continual expansion difficult, and worked to the disadvantage of those who had borrowed cheaper money and must now repay their debts in dear money.

The situation was further complicated by the fact that the government, in 1873, had de-monetized silver just as immense deposits of this metal were being discovered in the mountains of the West and the price of silver was plummeting. The Greenback Party had made an unsuccessful attempt to solve the currency issue by advocating legislation that would put more paper money into circulation. The silver interests became convinced that a more adequate supply of money would be in circulation *and* the price of silver would be restored if the government would return to a bi-metallic system and coin silver as well as gold. Although the silverites had pushed through the Bland-Allison Act in 1878, the amount of silver purchased under the Act had not been sufficient enough to be of any appreciable help. In 1890 the Sherman Silver Purchase Act had attempted to remedy the situation by sizeably increasing the amounts of silver which must be purchased each month by the Treasury Department. Again the legislation had failed to remedy either the price of silver or to increase the amount of money in circulation. By 1893, President Cleveland, faced with a country in the midst of a depression, considered the Sherman Act as one of the reasons for the economic failure and with an obliging Congress had the Act repealed. This was the situation as the political forces began to organize for the election of 1896, and Cleveland's insistance upon the repeal of the Sherman

Act had already driven a sizeable wedge into the Democratic Party.

In many sections of the country silver Democrats had already effected a fusion with the Populists, and in many states it was difficult to distinguish between the two parties. By the time of the Democratic convention in July of 1896, the silver interests had captured the Democratic Party, and their nomination of William Jennings Bryan as their standard-bearer for the election, assured the support of the Populists. Only thirty-six years old, William Jennings Bryan was known as the Boy Orator of the Platte, and for the previous two years had been organizing the silver interests of the party in order to achieve the triumph which had resulted at the convention. He represented all the passion, conviction and courage that were needed to articulate the quarter of century of frustration felt by the distraught West and South. "I come to speak to you," he told the convention, "in defense of a cause as holy as the cause of liberty—the cause of humanity." And he concluded his famous Cross of Gold Speech with: "You shall not press down upon the brow of labor this crown of thorns, you shall not crucify mankind upon a cross of gold."

Not only on the silver issue, but on most other issues, the Democrats had stolen the Populists' thunder, but it was the money issue that brought the election to fever pitch. Bryan's opponent in the Republic Party was William McKinley from Ohio who was well known for his support of high tariffs and other legislation favorable to the interests of big business. So worried were those members of the business community over the monetary policies of Bryan that they rallied behind McKinley with lavish financial support and flooded the country with their propaganda. In reality, the election was over more than money—it was a clear-cut issue of who would control the government, the business interests of the East or the agrarian interests of the West. The election turned out to be the last major protest of the agrarian interests against the encroaching industrialism and urbanization.

At the polls McKinley garnered over fifty percent of the popular vote and in the electoral college he received 271 votes to Bryan's 176. Almost a hundred years after the death of Alexander Hamilton, Hamiltonian ideas, apparently, had won out over Jeffersonian. Big business would immediately have its reward in the Dingley Tariff (1897), the highest in the history of the country, the Gold Standard Act (1900), and in the refusal of the government under William McKinley to put teeth into the Interstate Commerce Act or the Sherman Anti-Trust Act. The Populist Party was not able to survive the capture of its issues by the Democratic Party and soon faded from the political scene. It had, however, in its short duration proposed solutions to a host of very real problems, solutions which would prove themselves in the future, and that the future was much closer than anyone in 1896 imagined. It was only five years later that Theodore Roosevelt was installed in the White House and the Progressive Movement was launched.

William Jennings Bryan, *known for his oratory, was a three time loser as the Democratic nominee for President. His first attempt at the Presidency was made in 1896—it was during the Democratic convention that year that he made his famous "cross of gold" speech—but he was beaten rather easily by William McKinley in the election.*

HISTORICAL HEADLINES
ON
THE ERA OF REFORM

The Daily Inter Ocean.

VOL. XXVII., NO. 29. CHICAGO, FRIDAY MORNING, APRIL 22, 1898.—TWELVE PAGES. PRICE—IN CITY CARRIER DISTRICTS, ONE CENT. OUT OF CITY CARRIER DISTRICTS, TWO CENTS.

WAR

From This Time On Spain and This Nation Are Enemies Ashore and Afloat.

M'KINLEY SO DECIDES

Proclamation Is Already Written Declaring That War Exists with Spain.

CORDON ABOUT CUBA

News That the Island Is Surrounded by Our Ships Is Now Awaited.

DONS MAKE REPLY

Their Action in Dealing with Our Minister Considered an Answer by This Government.

CHALLENGE IS ACCEPTED

Presenting Mr. Woodford with Passports Regarded as an Act to Provoke Hostilities.

Arrangements Have Been Made to Call for 100,000 Volunteers as Soon as Authority Is Given by Congress.

Special Dispatch to The Inter Ocean.

WASHINGTON, D. C., April 21.—A proclamation has been prepared at the State Department announcing the blockade of Cuban ports and is withheld from promulgation only awaiting news from Captain Sampson of the arrival of the fleet off Havana harbor. This proclamation will contain the assertion that a state of war exists.

The precedent for this action can be found in the action of President Madison, in the war of 1812, when he issued a proclamation declaring the existence of war in the absence of legislative declaration to that effect. All diplomatic representatives of the United tSates abroad have been notified of the intention to issue this proclamation, and will inform the governments to which they are accredited of the fact.

The call for 100,000 volunteers, which is also ready, and only waits for conclusive action by Congress authorizing its publication to issue, will also contain the declaration that a state of war exists. These declarations, it is held by competent authorities, sufficiently cover the legal formalities of the case, and render unnecessary any formal declaration of war by Congress.

Special Dispatch to The Inter Ocean.

WASHINGTON, D. C., April 21.—There need be no longer any doubt that a state of war exists between the United States and Spain. Whatever technical quibbles there may be over the question whether or not war has actually come, the government has decided that with the dismissal of Minister Woodford the conflict has been inaugurated, and that from now on until a treaty of peace is made Spain and this Nation are enemies ashore and afloat.

The President today accepted the responsibility of whatever may follow when he directed the Secretary of the Navy to order the vessels of the North Atlantic squadron to proceed without delay to Cuban waters to blockade Havana and the other ports of the island. Just as soon as a report is received from Captain Sampson, the commander-in-chief of the United States naval forces in Cuban waters, that he has established the blockade, a proclamation stating that fact will be issued by the President.

The proclamation was drawn up at the State Department this evening and is ready for the signatures of the President and the Secretary of State. It is the belief of official quarters that a dispatch vessel bringing the news that Captain Sampson's vessels have been distributed around the island, thus forming a cordon through which no vessel will be allowed to pass without fighting its way, will reach Key West early tomorrow morning. The issuance of the proclamation will follow the receipt in Washington of Captain Sampson's report.

In the proclamation will be the explicit statement that war exists between the United States and Spain.

Stirring scenes marked the day in Washington. The members of the naval strategy board, headed by Assistant Secretary Roosevelt, appeared before Secretary Long to urge him to secure permission from the President for Captain Sampson's ships to sail for Cuba immediately. They based their request on a dispatch from Lieutenant Dyer, the United States naval attache at Madrid, that the Spanish squadron at St. Vincent had "apparently" sailed from that port. Secretary Long laid the advice of the board before the President, but decision on the matter was deferred until the Cabinet meeting.

While the meeting was in progress news came from official sources that the fleet had not left St. Vincent, but this information had no effect on the determination of the President and his advisers. It was decided that Spain had given her answer in dismissing Minister Woodford and there should be no further delay in carrying out the directions of Congress.

At 3 o'clock orders had been sent by Secretary Long to Captain Sampson directing him to proceed to blockade Cuban ports. The meeting was given up almost entirely to considering the naval and military situation and in arranging plans for bringing victory to the American arms. Major General Miles and Captain Crowninshield, chief of the naval bureau of navigation, were present part of the time. They explained the condition of the army and navy to cope with the enemy, and gave their views as to the best means of securing strategical advantage.

When the Cabinet adjourned at 2:30 o'clock, after a session lasting an hour and a half, the immediate offensive programme of the United States had been mapped out. In substance this provided for the blockade of Cuban ports, without any attack on the defenses of Havana, the blockade of Manila and other places in the Philippine islands by the Asiatic squadron, now mobilized at Hong Kong under Admiral Dewey, the establishment of a base of supplies in Cuba by Captain Sampson's squadron, and the organization of a military expedition to occupy this base within one week and protect it from attack from Spanish troops.

It was also arranged that a call for 100,000 volunteers should be issued as soon as the House bill granting the President authority to that effect had passed the Senate.

M'KINLEY WAITS FOR CONGRESS

President Cannot Call for Volunteers Until Bill Is Passed.

Special Dispatch to The Inter Ocean.

WASHINGTON, D. C., April 21.—The Senate having amended the volunteer army bill so that it will have to go to a conference committee and cannot become a law before tomorrow, has necessarily delayed the President's call for volunteers. This call will be issued as soon as the bill becomes a law to give him the power to call out the militia.

It is still the purpose of the President and Secretary of War to make the call upon the states so as to bring the National guard into service first. The states will be called upon for their quotas, based on the proportion of military service population, and the National guard will be preferred. Secretary Alger has had offers of more than 60,000 men from Governors of states up to the present time, and has no doubt that he can secure 100,000 men from the National guard, who will be drilled and equipped for almost immediate service. Illinois' quota would call for four regiments and three batteries. Indiana, two regiments and two batteries. Iowa, [illegible] Michigan, two; Wisconsin, two regiments and one battery, Minnesota, one regiment and one battery.

While the call for volunteers will be issued at once and the volunteer army placed in the field, the President and Secretary of War are considering plans that will not necessitate sending this army to Cuba at once, especially if the rainy season sets in to make it dangerous to send troops. The insurgents in Cuba are anxious to show that they can drive Blanco out of Cuba, and two of their Generals, Nunez and Castillo, are here to present to General Miles plans for placing a Cuban army in the field to co-operate with the United States troops in driving Spain out of the island. The insurgent Generals claim to have an army of 35,000 men in the field and say that they can enlarge it to 60,000 men if they can be armed and supplied with ammunition. They know the ground and are natives not to be affected by the climate as would either an American army or the Spanish army.

If this plan suggests itself to General Miles and Secretary Alger they can keep their volunteer army on the Southern coast or in camp during the rainy season in Cuba and allow the insurgent army to do the fighting while this government furnishes the supplies and munitions of war. Then in the fall when the weather is good and the climate healthy, the American army can be rushed over and clear up the whole business in short order.

This is the plan of one of the high military authorities in the War Department. It will depend upon the climatic conditions in Cuba, for the President does not desire to sacrifice thousands of the young men of America to the ravages of yellow fever. And, while the general idea is that this shall be a thirty or sixty days' war, military authorities do not depend on that short time to free Cuba of the Spaniards, and establish a free and independent government on the island. They look at war as war until peace is re-established, and whatever the result in Cuba the war cannot end until Spain is ready to sign a treaty of peace.

EQUIPMENTS FOR 75,000 MEN.

War Department Sends Order to the Rock Island Arsenal.

Special Dispatch to The Inter Ocean.

ROCK ISLAND, Ill., April 21.—Orders came late this afternoon from the War Department to Rock Island arsenal to provide at once equipments complete for 75,000 men for field service.

WAR

Flying Squadron Starts South Between Midnight and Daybreak.

SCHLEY IS ORDERED

He May Go to Protect the Battle-Ship Oregon in South American Waters.

CONCERN IS FELT

Massachusetts Ready to Sail at Any Moment for Key West or Havana.

SUPPLIES TAKEN ABOARD

Captain Higginson, It Is Reported, Will Report to Captain Sampson.

This Great Fighting Ship Is Wanted in His Fleet to Make the Bombardment of the Cuban City More Effective.

Special Dispatch to The Inter Ocean.

NEWPORT NEWS, Va., April 21.—The flying squadron today received "thirty-minute sailing orders," and these were supplemented tonight. It is officially stated, by an order which will start the warships under Commodore Schley to sea between midnight and daybreak, probably for South American waters, until countermanding orders are received.

An officer from the Brooklyn said tonight that it is not unlikely that the flying squadron will sail under a high rate of speed to join the battle-ship Oregon, for the safety of which considerable apprehension is felt.

Report has it that Captain Higginson, commanding the Massachusetts, has been ordered to hold his ship in readiness to sail at any moment for Key West or Havana, where he is to report to Captain Sampson.

The united fighting strength of the queen of the American navy, as officers regard her, is wanted in the North Atlantic squadron, to make the bombardment of Havana more effective, should that course be adopted.

Unusual activity aboard the Massachusetts has been apparent all the afternoon. At 6 o'clock a quantity of medical supplies, which ordinarily would have waited over till tomorrow, were hastened aboard the ship. A coal barge is alongside tonight, filling the coal bunkers.

Two six-inch rapid-fire rifles arrived at Fort Monroe today from New York. They will be followed by another shipment of four this week.

The War Department has decided to construct a rapid-fire battery at Point Breeze, one mile below this city, for the protection of the ship yard and the battle-ships Kentucky and Kearsarge, recently launched.

The armored ram Katahdin sailed from Hampton roads today for Provincetown, Mass., where she will be stationed.

The torpedo-boat Rodgers passed out for Key West to join the flotilla, and was loudly cheered by crowds as she steamed by the warships at twenty knots.

NEW YORK MILITIAMEN READY.

Imminence of War Causes a Rush of Young Men to Enlist.

Special Dispatch to The Inter Ocean.

NEW YORK, April 21.—National guard officers, who were in such a stew on Wednesday because they thought the Hull bill was designed to rob them of their commissions, were feeling easier today. The amendment to the Hull bill, giving the power of appointment, from colonels down to lieutenants, to the Governors of the states from which militia are called, was practically assurance that they would remain undisturbed in their places. David Humphries of Brooklyn called on General Roe today and offered him the services of 1,000 Italians, who, he said, had been in service in Africa.

Everything about the armory of the Seventy-First regiment, the Second battery, and the First Signal corps tonight indicates war. In the basement there was an artillery drill, on the floor above was a battalion drill of the Seventy-First, on the next floor the signal corps men were wig-wagging, and on the mezzo floor above that two squads of recent recruits to the Seventy-First were learning the manual of arms.

The busiest place in the building was the rooms of the medical examining board of the Seventy-First. The imminence of war has caused a rush of young men to join the regiment, and the three surgeons on the board have been unable to examine all that present themselves. They work up to midnight, and if any are left unexamined they are told to come back.

The surgeons of the Sixty-Ninth regiment were kept busy up to a late hour examining a crowd of applicants who wanted to join.

At the armory of the First battery Captain Louis Wendel and his officers remained until midnight, in expectation of an official notice of the calling out of the National guard. The officers then departed, but a plan of action had previously been mapped out which would be effectual in getting the battery together at short notice in case word was received later.

SPAIN LACKS COAL FOR FLEET.

Run on Barcelona Branch of the Bank of Spain.

Special Cable Dispatch to The Inter Ocean.

LONDON, April 22.—The Barcelona correspondent of the Daily Telegraph claims to have learned from an excellent source that Spain is incomparably worse off for coal than has hitherto been imagined.

He attributes the government's neglect to obtain a proper supply to its reliance upon the success of the intercession of the Pope and the powers.

The result, the correspondent adds, is likely to be the premature collapse of hostilities, followed in the end by the downfall of the government and the monarchy.

There is extreme depression among the few who have been intrusted with the painful secret.

Run on the Bank of Spain.

A news agency dispatch from Barcelona says that the Bank of Barcelona this afternoon withdrew 7,000,000 pesetas ($1,900,000) from its account at the local branch of the Bank of Spain.

When this fact became known the people became excited and large numbers of them presented notes issued by the Bank of Spain, demanding cash for them.

All notes so far presented have been cashed, but the bank must fail if the news spreads to other cities.

Special Cable Dispatch to The Inter Ocean.

CHARLOTTE AMALIE, St. Thomas, April 21.—Spanish agents from Porto Rico are trying to purchase coal here and in the Windward islands (British). So far they have not been able to obtain any supplies.

There are 7,000 tons of coal afloat, consigned to the island of St. Thomas. Mr. Van Horne, the United States consul here, is reported to be negotiating for a part of the coal afloat.

Mr. Shand, an agent of the United States State Department, has arrived here with special instructions for the United States consuls in the West Indies.

CLARA BARTON BOUND FOR CUBA

Red Cross President Will Return with Twenty-Five Nurses.

Special Dispatch to The Inter Ocean.

NEW YORK, April 21.—Miss Clara Barton, president of the National Red Cross, left for Washington today. After a brief stay at the capital she will proceed to Key West with twenty-five nurses, and Dr. and Mrs. A. Monal Lesser. Miss Barton expects to reach Key West with her party in time to join the Cuban relief ship, State of Texas, upon its arrival there. The State of Texas took about 100 tons of supplies, and was then towed over to Atlantic basin, where the loading of 1,000 tons more was begun. It was expected that the steamer will sail for Key West, under the Red Cross flag, at [illegible] Saturday afternoon. This should bring her into Key West next Wednesday afternoon. Orders will be awaiting for her there from the State Department. As the situation is now, the steamer will probably go under convoy of a United States warship to Cuba.

TAMPERING WITH MINE CABLES.

Suspected That Wires in New York Harbor Were Maliciously Cut.

Special Dispatch to The Inter Ocean.

NEW YORK, April 21.—The submarine cables which connect the mines laid in the upper portion of the bay and the Narrows with Fort Wadsworth were tampered with a few nights ago, and the wires severed. The fact became public today, and members of the garrison at the fort admitted that such was the case, while refusing to discuss the matter further. The wires were cut or broken. There is well-grounded suspicion, however, that some person cut the wires maliciously, inasmuch as it is almost impossible for the wires to have broken without assistance. The break has been repaired and caused no permanent injury.

LONG AND SHERMAN MAY QUIT.

President Contemplates Reorganization of His Cabinet.

Special Dispatch to The Inter Ocean.

NEW YORK, April 22.—The Journal's Washington correspondent says:

A reorganization of the Cabinet is contemplated. The resignation of Postmaster General Gary today, ostensibly on account of his health, but in reality, many persons allege, because he is opposed to war in any form, is the first of a series of resignations expected.

Secretary Long, it may be stated on good authority, wrote his resignation today and signed it. The President is understood to have decided to withhold it for several days. Admiral Walker is slated for the naval portfolio.

Secretary of State Sherman will also resign shortly. The place was offered to Senator Cushman Davis three weeks ago and he declined it.

TO PROTECT PACIFIC COAST.

Rear Admiral Miller to Be Recalled from Honolulu.

Special Dispatch to The Inter Ocean.

WASHINGTON, D. C., April 21.—Rear Admiral Joseph S. Miller, in command of the Pacific naval squadron, is to be recalled to San Francisco to assume charge of the naval defense of the Pacific coast. He is now on the Bennington, at Honolulu, whence orders were sent him by the steamer Alameda, sailing from San Francisco today. Admiral Miller will have quite a formidable squadron under his command. The cruiser Charleston will probably be his flagship.

Special Dispatch to The Inter Ocean.

WASHINGTON, D. C., April 21.—Lieutenant Commander W. S. Cowles will be assigned to the command of the cruiser Topeka, formerly the Portuguese ship Diogenes.

STEAMER PARIS CALLED HOME.

Will Leave Southampton for New York This Morning.

Special Cable Dispatch to The Inter Ocean.

SOUTHAMPTON, April 21.—An urgent telegram was received here today, ordering the immediate dispatch of the American line steamship Paris for New York, and she will sail tomorrow morning.

WAR

Seizure of Mules for the Spanish Army the First Hostile Act.

TAKEN FROM VESSEL

Collector of Port Seizes Animals and Treats Them as Contraband.

APPEAL BY CONSUL

Protest to United States Officials by Spanish Agents Avails Them Nothing.

SCENE IN NEW ORLEANS

This Government's Vigorous Rebuke to Dons Cheered by Big Crowds.

If Naval Operations Are Under Way When Ship Reaches Cuban Waters She Will Steer Clear of the Island and Go to Cadiz.

Special Dispatch to The Inter Ocean.

NEW ORLEANS, La., April 21.—The mules destined for the Spanish army in Cuba were taken from the Spanish steamship Catalina just before she left here today and held by the authorities as contraband of war.

These were part of a batch of 1,200 mules and horses purchased here by a Spanish agent for the use of the army in Cuba. They would have been shipped some time ago but for the Morgan line discontinuing its steamers to Havana.

The Catalina loaded the mules today and was to have left with them. There was quite a crowd of people at the wharf when she was loading and loud protests went up against allowing the vessel to leave here with coal for the enemy's fleet and mules for the enemy's army. The ship's officers were notified by the customs officers that the mules and horses could not be shipped.

The Spanish consul and Spanish agent went before Collector Wilkinson and a long and heated controversy ensued, they claiming that the vessel had cleared before noon, and she had the right to carry the mules. This was denied, however, and the mules were finally taken from the vessel and driven to their stables amid the cheers of the crowd present.

The Catalina then set sail for Havana, her cargo consisting mainly of provisions. Her ultimate destination is Cadiz, and she may not stop at Havana if she finds naval operations under way there.

The Spanish steamer Miguel Jover will sail tomorrow. She also was to have carried a cargo of mules and horses to Havana.

SAMPSON NOW REAR ADMIRAL.

Made Senior Flag Officer of Force in North Atlantic.

Special Dispatch to The Inter Ocean.

WASHINGTON, D. C., April 21.—President McKinley today authorized Captain W. T. Sampson, commander-in-chief of the North Atlantic squadron, to hoist the flag of a Rear Admiral.

By this act the President has made Captain Sampson the senior flag officer of the entire force of war vessels on the North Atlantic coast.

Should Commodore W. S. Schley, commanding the flying squadron, or Commodore Howell, commanding the Northern patrol squadron, fall in with Rear Admiral Sampson's vessels, it will be their duty to report to Rear Admiral Sampson and to carry out any orders that that officer may consider it necessary to give.

SAYS CHINA HAS SOLD SHIPS.

Hamburger Correspondent Insists America Has Bought Them.

Special Cable Dispatch to The Inter Ocean.

BERLIN, April 21.—The Hamburger Correspondent emphatically reasserts, despite denials, that the United States has bought three warships that were built by the Vulcan company at Stettin for China.

Special Cable Dispatch to The Inter Ocean.

LONDON, April 21.—The Liverpool correspondent of the Central News says the United States has bought the British steamer Lake Ontario.

ARMIES ARE NOW FACE TO FACE.

War Between Nicaragua and Costa Rica Almost Certain.

Special Cable Dispatch to The Inter Ocean.

MANAGUA, Nicaragua, April 21.—The armies of Nicaragua and Costa Rica are face to face on the frontier, the peace negotiations having failed, and war is almost certain. The Nicaraguan officers and troops are anxious that President Zelaya should leave them and keep out of danger. Business is at a complete standstill.

EXTRA

4:00 A. M.

ON THE WAY TO HAVANA

Flagship New York Starts to Begin the Blockade.

Rest of the Fleet of Warships and Monitors Follow in Quick Order.

Special Dispatch to The Inter Ocean.

KEY WEST, Fla., April 22.—The flagship New York sailed shortly after midnight to begin the blockade of Havana. The other warships will get under way about 4 o'clock.

Several of the slower vessels of the fleet got under way a little earlier.

The torpedo fleet will leave at 7 o'clock.

The three monitors, the Puritan, Terror, and Amphitrite have just been ordered to get up steam and start for Havana. They will not make more than six knots an hour, so that they will be overtaken by the rest of the fleet before sighting Morro.

Special Dispatch to The Inter Ocean.

NEW YORK, April 21.—The Herald's Washington correspondent says:

Resistance attempted by the Spanish vessels now in Cuban and Porto Rican waters to the blockade instituted by the North Atlantic squadron will be followed by their destruction.

Under the instructions given him it will be the duty of Rear Admiral Sampson, as he has been officially designated, to capture or destroy every ship Spain has in those waters, and when this has been accomplished, to impose the blockade contemplated by the government's plan of campaign.

The department officials are not at all certain of the number of ships Spain has in Cuban waters, and of the number she has in Porto Rican waters, but it is known that, distributed among the islands, there are fifty-eight ships.

It is believed that at least twelve or fifteen of these are in the harbor of San Juan awaiting the arrival of the flying squadron.

HONG KONG FLEET TO MOVE.

Will Leave Station for the Philippines Saturday.

Special Dispatch to The Inter Ocean.

WASHINGTON, D. C., April 21.—The strategy board has been not a little concerned regarding the squadron gathered at Hong Kong under Admiral Dewey. The administration had practically decided that it would hold that formation at Hong Kong and not carry out immediately the previous understanding that Admiral Dewey should menace Manila and other Philippine ports. The strategy board urged Secretary Long to dispatch the Asiatic squadron to the Philippines at once. After some discussion the views of the board were adopted, and it was decided that policy dictated that Admiral Dewey should be instructed to blockade Spain's possessions in the far East. For some reason he will not move on the Philippines for a day or two, perhaps not until Saturday. Orders directing him to leave Hong Kong for Manila were cabled to Admiral Dewey tonight.

BOMB SENT TO THE PRESIDENT.

Infernal Machine Intercepted and Rendered Harmless.

Special Dispatch to The Inter Ocean.

WASHINGTON, D. C., April 21.—An infernal machine was sent to the President today. Fortunately its character was suspected and measures taken to prevent its explosion, and no harm was done. The incident was carefully concealed, and all efforts are being made to capture the sender. There was nothing to suggest from whom it came, and no clew was afforded as to the villain who sent it.

The machine was inclosed in a harmless looking cigar box. An ingenious contrivance had been arranged so that when the lid of the box was opened there would be a flash of powder, which would explode a stick of giant powder, sufficient to blow a man to atoms.

Lieutenant Cross, in charge of the White House police, to whom the machine was handed, discovered its nature, and took precautions to render it harmless. He soaked it in a tub of water until the contents were thoroughly saturated, and then opened it. As a result of this incident additional measures were taken to guard the executive mansion. The police force was doubled, and tomorrow it is expected that a detail from the District militia will form an additional outside guard to the approaches to the White House grounds.

REVOLUTION IN PORTO RICO.

Rioting Is Reported in All Parts of the Island.

Special Dispatch to The Inter Ocean.

NEW YORK, April 21.—Advices from San Juan, Porto Rico, state that a revolution has broken out there, and that there is rioting all over the island. Residents of other countries now in Porto Rico are panic-stricken. They feel that there is no safety in ports of the island, as they are momentarily expecting a bombardment by American warships. This feeling is particularly strong in San Juan.

CUBANS REFUSE TO TALK PEACE

Reject the Overtures Made by the Spanish Government.

Special Cable Dispatch to The Inter Ocean.

HAVANA, April 21.—It is admitted that the insurgents have refused to treat for peace with the commissioners of the Spanish government upon any terms except absolute independence.

The committee that went early in the week to Santa Cruz del Sur, as agents of the autonomists to try to persuade the insurgents to accept the armistice offered by Spain, are expected to return here Sunday. Its mission was an utter failure. It did not even get a chance to speak to the insurgent leaders.

WAR

North Atlantic Squadron Ordered to Start for the West Indies.

HAVANA TO BE TAKEN

Sampson Will Blockade the Cuban City and Bombard It if Necessary.

NO MORE DIPLOMACY

Mr. Woodford Notified by Spain That Friendly Relations Are Severed.

QUICK MOVE IS MADE

President Confers with Cabinet and Decides to Act Without Any Delay.

NO TIME WAS WASTED

After Blanco Has Had a Chance to Notify Madrid the Havana Cables Will Be Cut.

Government Has Moved Into Position and Is Now in Line of Battle Prepared to Enforce the Ultimatum—Spaniards Must Fight or Surrender.

Special Dispatch to The Inter Ocean.

KEY WEST, Fla., April 21.—General Graham was aboard the flagship New York this afternoon in conference with Captain Sampson.

After a long council Captain Sampson said the fleet would not sail before tomorrow at 9 o'clock.

It is said that this delay is due to an order to await the arrival here of transports with troops.

Special Dispatch to The Inter Ocean.

WASHINGTON, D. C., April 21.—Without a formal declaration of war, the North Atlantic squadron is ordered to proceed to Havana without delay to blockade that port, and to bombard it in case of resistance.

There has been much talk and discussion of a formal declaration of war, but it has not been considered necessary at this time, nor until there has been an actual exchange of shots. The ultimatum of this government was served on the Spanish Minister yesterday morning, but Minister Woodford was notified that all diplomatic relations were severed this morning before he could present the ultimatum to the Spanish Minister of Foreign Affairs at Madrid. The State Department knew of this diplomatic trick contemplated by Spain, and for that reason served its ultimatum on Minister Polo before the President had signed the resolutions of Congress. The President knew that if he signed the resolutions before he sent the ultimatum that fact would at once be cabled to Madrid, and Woodford would be dismissed before he could present the ultimatum. For some reason Minister Woodford was again caught napping, probably through no fault of his own, as it is suspected that the Spanish censor held his telegram from Secretary Sherman until Minister Polo's telegram was received to the effect that the resolutions had been signed, the ultimatum sent, and the Spanish Minister here had asked for his passports. But for the suspicion that this was the plan of Spain, and the sending of the ultimatum to Minister Polo before he asked for his passports, the President would have been unable to present his demand to Spain, except, perhaps, by

NEW YORK JOURNAL

POSTSCRIPT. | NO. 5,676—P. M.   NEW YORK, WEDNESDAY, JUNE 1, 1898.   PRICE ONE CENT. | **POSTSCRIPT**

SANTIAGO FORTS

IN RUINS!

Washington Does Not Believe the Rival Fleets Have Met at Santiago.

Bombardment Follows a Vain Attempt of Spanish Torpedo Boats to Destroy the Battleship Texas---Sampson There?

Washington, June 1.—The Navy Department is anxiously awaiting news from Commodore Schley before Santiago. Unless Cervera's fleet attempted to leave the harbor, the Navy Department believes, there has been no engagement between the rival fleets.

There is good reason to believe that Schley did not enter Santioga harbor to give battle to the Spaniards. It is not necessary, Secretary Long believes, for us to risk our ships to get what is surely ours. If Cervera sees fit to take the chances of battle (which are all against him) to being slowly starved to death, then Schley will give him all the fight he wants.

Until official details are received noth-

Continued on Second Page.

SCHLEY BATTERS SANTIAGO.

Defences of Cervera's Refuge Showered with Shot and Shell by Our Warships.

Cape Haytien, June 1.—Partial reports have been received of the battle of Santiago. They show that Commodore Schley has bombarded the three forts at and near the mouth of the harbor, and there can be no doubt that the cannonading was extremely destructive and that the enemy's loss of life must have been very great. Even the Spaniards, from whom comes the story of the engagement, acknowledge that the Americans had the advantage.

Particulars of the fight, as sent by the Spaniards, which will be open

Continued on Second Page.

NO OFFICIAL DETAILS OF THE BATTLE

Washington a Little Sceptical About a General Engagement Off Santiago.

Washington, June 1.—No official report has yet been received by the Government of the battle which is said to have taken place at Santiago between Sampson's and Schley's combined fleets and the Santiago forts and Cervera's ships.

So many wild stories have been sent out from Cape Haytien by the Associated Press that the authorities here would have been chary about crediting the latest had it not been preceded by the Evening Journal's special cable from Kingston, Jamaica, yesterday, which gave practically the same story that is published this morning.

Even the Kingston dispatch was probably based upon rumor and the skirmish that took place between the Texas and Brooklyn and the two Spanish torpedo boats which tried to steal upon and sink the Texas.

It is highly improbable that firing at Santiago, 200 miles away, could be heard on any part of the Haytien coast, as is alleged.

The story that Sampson's fleet was with Schley is also an improbability. Sampson was off Key West Monday at a. m. He could hardly have reached Santiago, even at top speed, in time to have taken part in a battle there yesterday.

If a battle has taken place at Santiago the Navy Department should officially have at least an intimation of it by

NO. 2

2D NEW JERSEY REGIMENT STARTS FOR CHICKAMAUGA

SEA GIRT, N. J., June 1.—The Second Regiment has left for Chickamauga. The men were early astir this morning, and in a few minutes their tents had been struck. After burning their straw beds and having breakfast the men marched to the railroad station, where they boarded the cars. They were off amid the cheers of their friends.

The regiment is fully equipped.

1898-----DEFEAT OF SPAIN BRINGS U.S. TO FRONT AS WORLD POWER

San Jose DAILY Mercury.

VOL. LIII. SAN JOSE, CALIFORNIA: MONDAY MORNING, JULY 4, 1898.—EIGHT-PAGE EDITION. NO. 185.

GLORIOUS NEWS FOR DAY WE CELEBRATE

Bold Sampson Utterly Destroys the Spanish Fleet Under Cervera in the Harbor of Santiago.

STARS AND STRIPES WILL CERTAINLY WAVE OVER THE CITY TO-DAY.

WASHINGTON, July 3.---The following dispatch was received at the War Department: ment that all the Spanish fleet ex hat the ships are burning on the Captain Smith, who told the opera ALLEN, Signal Officer."

WASHINGTON, July 3.---The fol t the White House: "Playa del Cervera's fleet is confirmed.

"Playa del Este, July 3.---Siboney office confirms the state- cept one warship was destroyed and beach. The sight was witnessed by tor. No doubt of its correctness.

lowing cable dispatch was given out Este, July 3.---The destruction of "ALLEN, Lieutenant-Colonel."

SURRENDER OF THE CITY DEMANDED.

WASHINGTON, July 3.---The following statement was to-night given at the White House. General Shafter telegraphs: "Playa del-Este, July 3.-Early this morning I sent a demand for the immediate surrender of Santiago, threatening to bombard the city. I believe the place will be surren- dered." This contradicts the report that General Shafter has fallen back.

WASHINGTON, July 4.---Glorious news from Cuba affords the American people just cause for the celebration of this, the Nation's holiday. Ad- miral Sampson has accomplished the work which he was directed to perform when he left Key West for the coast of Cuba. He was ordered to find and destroy Cervera's fleet. Several weeks ago Commodore Schley located the fleet in the Bay of Santiago. Yesterday, after being bottled helplessly in the arbor for weeks, the fleet was destroyed. Nothing now remains of the Spanish squadron but shattered and burning hulks. In addition to this splendid work accomplished by Admiral Sampson, General Shafter, in command of the land forces before Santiago, had so far progressed in the carrying out of his plans for the reduction of the city that at 10:30 yesterday morning he demanded the immediate surrender of the Spanish forces. At 3:30 yesterday after- noon General Shafter's demands had not been complied with so far as was officially known. That the demand will be complied with, however, General Shafter fully believes, and that the Stars and Stripes will on this Fourth of July be raised over the former capital of Cuba is regarded as practically certain.

FIRST EXPEDITION ARRIVES AT MANILA.

Was Delayed Because It Captured the Ladrone Islands on the Way===Governor and Other Officials Brought to Cavite.

Hongkong, July 4.—The United States dispatch boat Zafire which left Cavite, Manila harbor on July 1st, has arrived here. She reports that the American troops on the transports City of Sydney, City of Peking and Australia, convoyed by the Charleston arrived at Cavite June 30th, having taken Ladrone Islands on the way and having left men there. The Spanish Governor and other officials captured were brought to Cavite. The United States troops commenced to disembark at Cavite on July 1st.

"THE WAR TO END ALL WARS"

Prior to the first week of August, 1914, the international system had operated to the advantage of the United States by providing almost guaranteed assurances of the integrity of the Monroe Doctrine through the balance of power in Europe. With the outbreak of war, however, the balance was shattered and the situation changed dramatically. Although public opinion reflected a continuing belief that the United States was far enough removed from the theatre of conflict to remain essentially unaffected by it, the Administration was receiving daily reports of the closing of European trade markets which were vital to American economic prosperity. Within a month after the President had announced that the official position of the government was neutrality, proclaiming that impartiality should be accomplished in fact as well as in name, it was evident that the events on the Continent were directly precipitating an economic crisis in the United States.

To prevent European stockholders from unloading shares of securities on the American market and creating a panic on Wall Street, the Stock Exchange had been closed on July 31st. To enable American products to be transported to Europe, Congress had agreed to allow foreign ships to sail under the United States flag; and, to protect the nation's gold supply, the Administration had adopted a policy of discouraging loans by American banking institutions to participants in the war. Nonetheless, by the early part of 1915, it became clear that the international economic system was on the verge of collapse and that adherence to the policy of prohibiting loans was both contributing to that crisis and destroying the only major foreign trade in which the United States could engage.

On March 15th, Secretary of State Bryan publicly announced that the Department would not oppose a fifty million dollar loan by J.P. Morgan and Company to the French government, thereby initiating a series of relationships with the Allied governments which would begin to transform official neutrality into informal support for those nations during the war. In conjunction with this measure, the Administration entered into agreements with France and Great Britain to engage in the sale of munitions—an action which did not violate neutrality under international law, but which augmented American ties with these countries. The immediate effects of these decisions were dramatic. Within a brief period of time, the export figure had reached 467 million dollars and economic depression had been elevated to prosperity.[1] The situation improved steadily with the floating of bond issues amounting to half a billion dollars and, indirectly, because of the increase in German submarine warfare in Europe.

By September, 1916, the Administration's concern was focused on the German policy and the effects which it was having on international trade. The President launched a series of statements which established a new policy. On the 2nd of the month, Wilson summed up the basis of the policy by announcing that "This is our guiding principle: that property rights can be vindicated by claims for damages when the war is over . . . but the fundamental rights of humanity cannot be. The loss of life is irreparable."[2] In order to prevent such actions as had previously occurred with the sinking of the Lusitania and the Sussex and the attendant loss

[1] The export of explosives alone constituted a turn about for the economy and later supplements in the form of sales and credits for foodstuffs added to American economic prosperity.

[2] The President's approach following this speech was to focus on attempts at mediation with the German Imperial Government—an effort which was marginally successful during the 1915-1916 period.

Another scene *of the Armistice Day celebration in New York City on November 11, 1918.*

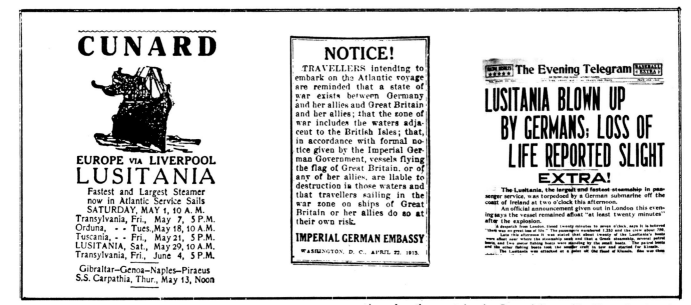

An advertisement *by the Cunard Steamship Lines showing the announced sailing date for the* Lusitania, *followed by a notice from the German government, and finally the newspaper headline telling of the sinking of the* Lusitania. *Although the headline reports slight loss of life, in fact 1,198 of the 1,924 passengers were killed in the attack on the luxury liner.*

of American lives and material goods, the government was prepared to take all necessary steps and to hold the German government strictly accountable.

In the Capitol, advocates of military preparations were gaining in strength and several interpreted the President's message as a signal of the initiation of such actions as were necessary to accomplish this task. Recognizing that continued opposition to military preparedness would provide the Republicans with a central political issue in the 1916 campaign, the President and his key partisan advisors requested the Secretaries of War and of the Navy to recommend programs to Congress which would satisfy existing national security requirements. Proposals were drafted and made available to the appropriate committees in Congress for examination. The issue was considerably more controversial than the President had anticipated, however, and several months passed before approval was finally granted in the form of the Army Reorganization bill, a Naval Expansion act and a Merchant Marine act.[3]

In order to finance the military preparedness program, the legislature was forced to find new and substantial sources of revenue. After several amendments and extensive compromise, the Congress produced the Revenue Act of 1916—a measure which was designed to meet the present demands on the budget minimally without placing an undue tax burden on the American public. With the passage of the Act, the President was able to campaign on the slogan of peace, prosperity, and progressivism. The Act had been a clear attempt at spreading the tax burden across the socio-economic spectrum of society, with the high income

[3] The Army Reorganization Bill was passed on May 20, 1916, increasing the regular army to 11,327 officers and 208,338 soldiers, integrating the National Guard into the National Defense Structure and authorizing the War Department to establish volunteer training camps. The Naval Act called for a five-year building program and the Merchant Marine Act authorized the appointment of a United States Shipping Board, empowered to own and operate all vessels engaged in foreign commerce.

[4] The Act doubled the normal income tax, without lowering exemptions, to approximately two percent of total individual income; raised the minimum surtax to 13 percent; repealed the consumption tax of the Emergency Tax Act of 1914; levied a new corporate tax on excess profits and raised the estate tax to twelve-and-a-half percent. In addition, an existing tax on munitions manufacturers was increased to twelve and a half percent.

categories financing a major proportion of the revenue, and it contributed in major part to the re-election of the President in November, 1916.[4]

Two of the three campaign promises were kept. Prosperity continued to characterize the American economic situation, and progressive policies began to dominate the management of the military preparedness programs. The third, however, was seriously threatened with the resumption of unrestricted German submarine warfare—a policy announced on February 1, 1917, after a temporary cessation of such activities. Wilson responded immediately, asking Congress for authority to arm merchant vessels against German attack and to use any method necessary for the protection of American lives.

In the Senate, opponents of the measure were able to conduct a successful filibuster which settled the request by default when the sixty-fourth Congress adjourned its session. In an attempt to circumvent the legislature, the new Secretary of State, Robert Lansing, advised the President that the necessary authority existed without explicit Congressional approval. On the 21st of March, Wilson accepted the advisor's interpretation and announced the policy of armed neutrality. Within three weeks, it became obvious that the new status was operationally impotent, and that submarine attacks were being levelled equally against American and belligerent ships. On April 2, the Chief Executive called a special session of Congress to request a formal declaration of war.

In the final sentences of his speech, Wilson's words captured a tone which would become symbolic of his philosophy: "We shall fight for the things which we have always carried closest to our hearts—for democracy, for the right of those who submit to authority to have a voice in their own government, for the rights and liberties of small nations, for a universal dominion of right by such a concert of free peoples as shall bring peace and safety to all nations and make the world itself at last free." In addition to being an official request for Congressional authorization of war, the President's speech also embodied the basis of what would become his guiding principle throughout the period of

President Woodrow Wilson, *center, is shown marching with military unit to try to create sympathy for the British already fighting in Europe in 1914. America was reluctant to enter the war, believing it to be a strictly "European" affair, and Wilson did many such activities to convince the American people of the need to come to the aid of the forces fighting Germany and Austria.*

American military involvement and participation in the post-war agreements—the concept of an international community of nations, a league of nations.

Four days later, on April 6, Congress resolved that a state of war between the United States and the Imperial German Government existed. The vote in both houses had been overwhelming.[5] By 5:00 p.m. the President completed the process by signing the declaration, and the nation which had attempted in a variety of ways to remain outside of the actual hostilities found itself directly engaged in war.

Despite the fact that a military preparedness program had been launched several months earlier, it became immediately apparent that the provisions available for actual combat were gravely insufficient. Within two weeks after the declaration became effective, Congress was submerged with demands for new sources of revenue and new means of administrative organization. The latter issue was resolved through the establishment of numerous national boards, designed to regulate and direct the nation's resources toward the war effort. Between April 10 and August 23, the government created a War Industries Board which served as a clearing house for purchases, a central vehicle for the allocation of raw materials and control production, and a supervising agency over labor relations; established a Fuel Administration which was given broad powers over the production, manufacture, and distribution of natural resources; and, extended the authority of the Food Administration. In order to achieve unified policies and direction of the administration of labor programs and activities, the Chief Executive, through his sweeping powers under the Lever Act, created a National War Labor Board as the Supreme Court for labor controversies. Lacking separate judicial authority, the Board enforced its rulings through the President's war powers and produced policies which represented a clear break with the past.[6]

[5] The vote in the Senate was eighty-two to six and in the House of Representatives, three-hundred-and-seventy-three to fifty.

[6] In addition to giving the President extensive powers over the production, manufacture, and distribution of goods, the Lever Act also gave him authority to institute price controls and to enforce regulations.

In attempting to provide the necessary revenue, Congress became engaged in a prolonged debate over the relative merits of bond issuances versus taxation—a controversy which continued until October 3 when a new Revenue Act was finally passed and signed into law. Income tax was increased from two to four percent; graduated excess profit taxes were raised to a range from twenty to sixty percent; income tax exemptions were reduced by a half to two-thirds; the maximum surtax was increased to twenty-five percent; and new taxes were imposed on luxuries, services and facilities. The Act placed seventy-five percent of the tax burden on large individual and corporate incomes alone, signifying the President's efforts at expanding democracy at home as well as abroad. Additionally, Congress passed the first War Loan Act, allowing the Treasury to issue two billion dollars in short-term notes and another five billion dollars in bonds, stipulating that the bonds would be sold through popular subscription. It would subsequently become obvious that the revenue generated by this combination of policies would remain inadequate to the task of financing the war and additional sources of money would be required, but the basic formula was established at this juncture.

As public opinion became increasingly supportive of the war effort, concerns arose over the statements and actions of those individuals and organizations which expressed dissent-

The first group of draftees *to be called up for service in World War I. The first group of military conscripts are lined up in front of their barracks, at Camp Upton, Yaphank, Long Island. Note that they are still in their civilian clothing.*

243

General Pershing, *second from left in first row, leader of the American forces, with his staff. Picture was taken while the American force was enroute to France.*

ing viewpoints or attempted to obstruct the war effort without specifically violating the law of treason. The White House produced a means of dealing with the situation in the form of the Espionage Act of 1917, which allowed for imprisonment of up to twenty years and/or a fine of up to ten thousand dollars for individuals who willfully made false reports to help the enemy, incited rebellion among the military forces, or attempted in any way to obstruct recruiting operations of the draft.[7] As the war progressed, interpretations of the Act were expanded, including approval for the censoring of all international communications, the mailing of all Socialist publications in the United States, and the suppression of the International Workers of the World—a left-wing organization which had unionized thousands of laborers in the western part of the country. Congress also broadened the ability of the government to control words and actions which appeared to be injurious to the war effort through the passage of the Sedition Act on May 16th. The Espionage Act had empowered the government to impose sanctions on individuals only when it could be proven that statements made resulted directly in injurious consequences; the Sedition Act

[7] The Espionage Act was passed by Congress on June 15, 1917, and also provided authority to the Postmaster General to deny the use of the mails for any purpose which, in his opinion, advocated treason, insurrection or forcible resistance to American laws. This was the first time in United States' history that such broad powers had been given to that office.

went a step farther in extending control over speech and printed matter, regardless of consequence. In total, 1,532 persons were arrested under these two Acts for reasons less than that required by the original piece of legislation. Only ten of the arrests were made for actual sabotage.

With the development of the war and the increasing use of governmental control over civil liberties, the public assumed a similar psychology. Outside of the scope of governmental procedures and due process of law, instances of private harassment and violence against dissenters became prevalent. As the President had predicted in conversations prior to the announcement of the declaration of war, the American people in general had replaced tolerance, justice, and compassion with hostility, repression, and vindictiveness. Federal Courts provided no effective defense against accusations which were made under the existing conditions; none of the sedition cases reached the Supreme Court until the war was over; and, hundreds of individuals were deprived of their rights as American citizens.

On November 7, 1918, reports of an armistice agreement swept across the country. A hundred and fifty tons of ticker-tape and torn paper were thrown out of windows overlooking

Fifth Avenue; parades formed on main streets across the nation; businesses closed for the day; and, millions of people joined in triumphant celebration which lasted until an official report was released late in the afternoon, announcing that the earlier statement had been only rumor and no agreement to end the war had been reached. Ecstasy was shattered and disappointment increased as the hours, and then the days, passed with no further word from the White House.

First American troops *to land on French soil parade in St. Nazaire on June 26, 1917. This contingent was part of the 1st Division, which had debarked a week after General Pershing and his staff had arrived for consultations with French military leaders.*

A "Liberty Loan" parade *showing marchers parading through New York City to try to encourage Americans to support the war effort by purchasing Liberty Loans to finance the war. Such parades were common in many major cities as the American forces were fighting in Europe.*

Then, shortly after midnight on the 11th, the President wrote a brief message on an ordinary piece of stationery. The statement was precise: it captured the essence of Wilson's idealism and validated the official news which he had received minutes earlier. By 3:00 a.m. the document was transmitted to the Department of State for public release. It read simply: "My Fellow Countrymen: the Armistice was signed this morning. Everything for which America fought has been accomplished. It will now be our fortunate duty to assist by example, by sober, friendly counsel, and by material aid in the establishment of just democracy throughout the world."[8] Within an hour and a half, the word was being dispatched to every newsroom in the country. Immediate skepticism was transformed into exhuberant enthusiasm as the public realized that the announcement was, indeed, official. The events four days earlier were surpassed in their magnitude and in city after city seemingly paradoxical incidents occurred—citizens joined to sing the Doxology and proclaim their relief and gratitude that the War was over, while others burned the Kaiser in effigy, signifying their bitterness and hostility. These responses would persist as it became increasingly apparent that the transition to a peacetime environment would be long and difficult.

The formal armistice signalled the end to the most dramatic war in history. Yet, three and a half million remained in the armed forces and almost two-thirds were still in Europe. The Expeditionary Forces waited in the trenches for orders to begin the long and arduous march into Germany, while civilians at home persisted in subscribing to war time rationing practices. The Government maintained its operation of the railroads and the press its daily listing of American war casualties. The impact of the preceeding nineteen months had been emphatic. Even after the processes of demobilization were well under way, a war time psychology prevailed.

A week after the President's announcement, this attitude found expression. In New York City, Mayor Hylan banned the display of Russian flags in the streets and ordered the police force to disperse unlawful crowds. A few nights later, five hundred soldiers and sailors stormed Madison Square Garden, protesting the Socialist meeting taking place inside. Police officers were able to control the mob and restore order, but the incident triggered another similar activity the next evening. This time protest was levelled against the Interna-

[8] *The New York Times*, November 11, 1918.

The Supreme Court *in 1917, with Oliver Wendell Holmes, seated in the center, serving as head. Because of the war and the scare it caused in America, many civil liberties were abridged in the name of national security. The Holmes Court failed to stop such abridgement of rights on the part of the government against individual citizens.*

Scene *of a victory demonstration in New York city following the announcement of the signing of the Armistice ending the war. Here a group of ship-workers, filling their trucks, parade up Lower Broadway on November 11, 1918.*

tional Women's League which was holding a meeting to register sympathy for the Russian Revolution. Again, the agitators were military men, and again police were required to restore order. Six people were seriously injured, including a Wall Street conservative who had been mistakenly identified as a Bolshevik.

These two incidents were the first overt manifestations of a shift in public opinion. During the war, attention had properly been focused on the events in Europe; with the Armistice signed, the target became the danger of subversion by Bolshevism. Intolerance was coupled with feelings of moral righteousness and the combination produced an explosive situation. In the weeks to come, this would be the catalyst for urban riots, labor strikes, isolated instances of violence and major changes in civil liberties protections, and in expanding the Sedition Acts.

In the White House, however, there was only one exclusive concern—the impending peace settlement. The President devoted his full attention to preparations for the forthcoming conferences, designing in detail a proposal which he believed would guarantee international peace. Popular support for the Chief Executive had reached its highest point and disagreement with his conduct of foreign policy was virtually nonexistent. Senator Lodge had announced as early as December 21, 1918, that the Senate had co-equal Constitutional authority with the President in matters related to treaty-making and that that role would be fulfilled. Yet, even this did not suggest an indication of the resistance which was to come.

Leaving the Capitol to sail for Europe to participate personally in the talks, Wilson typified supreme self-confidence. If there had been any reluctance in his speech announcing America's entry into the war, it had been dispelled by the events which followed. The United States had emerged as a clear victor, and Wilson's mission seemed defined by historical and moral forces. His self-assurance seemed equal to the task. In the first few weeks of his six month tour, the President's speeches were eloquent and promising. Gradually, however, the environment on the Continent began to change. While Wilson spoke Utopian idealism, European allies emphasized pragmatic na-

General Pershing, *left, stands on the balcony of the old Waldorf-Astoria Hotel in New York City reviewing returning American troops. This parade of returning American soldiers occurred on March 26, 1919.*

An effigy *of the German leader Kaiser Wilhelm is carried aloft by happy Americans in a celebration which lasted for days.*

tionalism. The gap widened in governmental chambers as Clemenceau, Lloyd George, and Italian Premier Orlando prepared to muster unanimous support for radical annexations of territory as their primary concern. Wilson persisted in listing the development of the League of Nations as his chief objective. The confrontation of perspectives occurred in Paris in the summer of 1919.

In the Council of Four, the key mechanism for reaching a peace agreement, the political skills of the European leaders proved a formidable match for the President of the country which held the dominant international position. To a creditable extent, Wilson achieved a compromise in moderating the terms of the agreement by restraining demands for massive annexations of territory and by gaining acceptance of the mandate principle. But, by the time the Treaty of Versailles was signed, it was evident that it was not the document that the President had expected. In many ways, it paralleled the ubiquitous secret treaties which had been devised during the War, while at the same time it included the League Covenant in a form which was inherently rigid in its provisions for American military obligations in the future. Despite Wilson's valiant efforts, the issue of nationalism had prevailed over the concept of unity; the bitterness of the war triumphed over idealism; and, fear transcended optimism.

In the final week of June, Wilson returned to the United States, prepared to announce to Congress and the public that the conference had been successful and that the Treaty contained all of the essential points of his proposal. This was not a completely accurate interpretation of either the events or the document itself, but in order for the League of Nations to be actualized, the Treaty had to be ratified. This was the President's sole intent as he lobbied for approval.

The atmosphere in the United States had changed during his absence, however, and international affairs were becoming less and less important to the public. Making the world safe for democracy increasingly sounded like idyllic rhetoric in the midst of the events which were taking place on the domestic scene. Shortly after Wilson had departed for Europe, workers had united in a nationwide strike against low wages and long hours. Strikes had occurred almost simul-

President Woodrow Wilson *passes through a phalanx of French soldiers on his way to a meeting with other world leaders in Paris in 1918.*

taneously in the building trades, the shipping industry, the telephone business and elsewhere, affecting several vital areas of American life. On April 29, Senator Hardwick, the Chairman of the Immigration Committee, received a brown paper package in the mail, containing a bomb which exploded in the hands of his housekeeper. At 2:00 p.m. the next afternoon, sixteen similar packages were discovered in a New York City post office, addressed to prominent officials in the government and business.[9] The packages had not been sent because of insufficient postage, but news of their existence created widespread hostility toward aliens, and especially Russian aliens, who were alleged to have been behind the scheme. A month later, there was another series of bomb explosions, the most successful of which damaged the Attorny General's house and killed a passerby.

Before extensive governmental operations could be implemented to deal with these acts of violence, several other incidents had occurred. On May Day, two major confrontations between military personnel and Socialists resulted in hundreds of injuries and one death. The offices of the New York *Call*, a Socialist newspaper, were vandalized and all of the equipment was destroyed. In Cleveland, the Socialist Headquarters were destroyed. Similar, more minor, incidents occurred across the country.

On July 10, Wilson formally presented the Treaty to the Senate for ratification. The document was referred to the Senate Foreign Relations Committee for investigation and deliberation. The Chairman of the Committee, whose position was critical to the development of the course of events leading up to a full vote on the Senate floor, was Henry Cabot Lodge. His viewpoint emerged clearly and quickly—he believed that American foreign policy should be aimed at keeping the United States out of foreign entanglements unless involvement was absolutely required by a direct threat to national security. After a series of debates, and by a narrow margin, the committee reached its verdict favoring Lodge's position by offering an amended version of the document which altered Articles X and XI of the League Covenant.[10] It began to appear as if the process of deliberation would be interminable before an actual, final vote could be taken on the Senate floor.

[9] These included: the Secretary of Labor, the Attorney General, the Commissioner of Immigration (who had recently proposed restrictions on immigration to keep Bolsheviks out of the country), a Supreme Court Justice, the Postmaster General and other governmental officials and business entrepreneurs.

The "Big Four" leaders *of the Allies who met in Paris following the end of World War I to set up a peace treaty. Seated from left to right are, Vittorio Orlando, from Italy; Lloyd George of England, Georges Clemenceau of France, and Woodrow Wilson from the United States.*

Steel workers *massed to listen to speaker on organizing a strong union. The steel workers were among many groups of industrial workers who struck for better working conditions following the war.*

Wilson announced a decision to take the issue to the American public in anticipation of stimulating the public to petition their representatives for ratification. His physicians warned against a prolonged speaking tour, but Wilson remained convinced that this was the best approach. His vision of the public was as it had been prior to his departure for negotiations in Europe; he failed to gauge accurately the interests and the support of public opinion and was bitterly disillusioned when the response he had expected when he left the White House on September 3 was not forthcoming. International issues were of utmost importance to the President; to the public, they were becoming secondary and somewhat tiring.

While he continued to give two or three speeches a day across the nation, the Senate agreed to take a test vote on the Treaty. The results were approval of ratification, by the slim margin of forty-three to forty. The Senate appeared to be a reasonable reflection of public opinion and as the days progressed, prospects for ultimate passage dwindled. The Presi-

One view *of the Boston Police Riots which broke out in 1919 following days of unrest in the city.*

The American Federation of Labor *organized a strike among steelworkers in September, 1919. Here a group of strikers hold up their strike bulletins. By the following January, however, the strike had been broken and the workers were back at the foundries.*

In Lawrence, Massachusetts, *striking workers carrying American flags paraded to protest working conditions in nearby factories. At the urging of their leaders the strikers did not engage in any violent acts during this demonstration, and thereby won support from a public which was becoming more and more hostile to violence on the part of striking workers.*

dent was beginning to express disillusionment. His health worsened, and a day after the test vote he was taken seriously ill. Speaking commitments were cancelled and he was rushed back to the Capitol, where, three days later, he suffered a cerebral thrombosis which left him partially paralyzed.

During the following seventeen months he remained in precarious health. Experts testified that he was mentally competent to carry out the duties of the office, but he avoided all matters except those of utmost importance. The White House was sealed off by security guards and the Chief Executive counselled with a minimum number of advisors. The business of government was left to the Cabinet and Congress, and a number of issues required immediate attention.

On September 9, a few days after the President's speaking tour had begun, a police strike had been launched in Boston. In response to low salaries and other complaints, officers formed a union and affected an affiliation with the American Federation of Labor—despite the fact that the police commissioner had explicitly forbidden identification with any outside organization. Charges were brought against nineteen officers and union members for having violated orders and guilty verdicts were rendered. The defendants were suspended from the force. The remaining officers threatened a full-scale strike as a means of protest, and a committee was constituted to arbitrate the dispute. The Commissioner staunchly refused to compromise and a walk-out resulted, leaving the city without police protection.

Taking advantage of the situation, vandals smashed store windows and looted merchandise. Tensions throughout the city increased and the mayor called for assistance from the Governor of Massachusetts in the form of sending State Guard soldiers to the scene to restore order. On the morning of September 10, the Guard arrived and was joined with a volunteer police force consisting primarily of college students and ex-soldiers. Violent confrontations between the law enforcement officers and the vandals continued for four days. Samuel Gompers arrived from Washington, trying to intervene on the basis that the action of the police Commissioner had been unwarranted and autocratic. The Governor of the state, Calvin Coolidge, replied that there was "no right to strike against the public safety by anybody, anywhere at any time."[11] Overnight, Coolidge became a national hero. The strike collapsed, vandalism receded, a new police force was recruited, and, order was reconstituted in the city.

The impact was felt across the nation, however. A few days after the police strike, several hundred thousand steel workers protested low pay and long hours in a national strike which continued for several months. It was accompanied by threats of an impending coal strike of similar proportions. The coal miners had made their position somewhat clear in earlier statements which had enthusiastically supported the nationalization of the industry. Despite the fact that economic conditions were worsening—the cost of living was increasing, business prosperity was slowing down, unemployment figures were up, and there was a general malaise among labor leaders—most of the American public continued to believe that the coal miners' stance was tantamount to support for Bolshevism. Demands for governmental intervention strenghthened, but the President remained isolated in

---

[10] Article X was changed to read that the United States assumed no obligations to preserve the territorial integrity or political independence of any country without the passage of a joint Congressional resolution.

[11] This became one of the initial positions of those who would later openly and insistently resist the rights of public employees in general to engage in strikes for whatever reasons.

This unusual photograph *shows the Ku Klux Klan in their regalia parading through the streets of Tulsa, Oklahoma, in 1923. At the left is Tulsa sheriff Bill McCullough who tried to prevent the Klan from making this particular parade. Note the uniformed police marching alongside the Klansmen.*

Attorney General A. Mitchell Palmer *who conducted a series of "raids" in 1919 and 1920 to ferret out suspected members of the communist party. The Red hunt led by Palmer resulted in the deportation of many people suspected of being communists.*

the White House. The task of responding to the situation was assumed by the Attorney General—a man whose house had been bombed in the activities of the week of May 29th.

Mitchell Palmer initiated a series of activities in late 1919 which began with the securing of a Federal Court injunction against the leaders of the coal strike to desist from any further demonstrations against employers. He did this under the provisions of the Food and Fuel Control Act which forbade restriction of coal production during the war. The peculiar set of circumstances which made this action legal related directly to the fact that although the war was officially over, the peace treaty was still being subjected to debate in the Senate. In a strict sense, then, the legislation remained applicable. However, the provisions of the Act and their interpretation by the White House at the time it was signed into law were clearly outside of the domain within which the Attorney General was operating. The Administration had been explicit in stating that the Act did not prohibit peaceful strikes or peaceful picketing. Palmer disregarded this fact and proceeded to enforce the injunction.[12] Nonetheless, the next day four hundred thousand coal workers, without the benefit of their leaders because of the decree of the Federal Government, walked out of the mines. The press and the public applauded the inunction just as they had praised Coolidge for his actions in Massachusetts.

The Attorney General took this as a signal to begin a second phase of activities, this time in the form of multiple raids in which alleged Communist leaders were arrested and deported, without regard to due process of law or respect for their civil rights. Again, public opinion supported the actions

[12] With the confinement of the President to the White House and his accompanying unwillingness to take part actively in the making decisions which were not regarded as being of primary importance, Palmer was relatively free to exercise a unilateral role in the judicial interpretation of administrative policies.

despite the fact that no crimes had been committed. A new record was set in American history for administrative violations of constitutional rights.

The justification which was used in support of the deportations was found in the drastic Sedition Act of 1918, under which the Secretary of Labor had the authority to deport aliens who were anarchists, or who advocated the overthrow of the government, or who were affiliated with any organization which believed in or advocated the overthrow of the government.[13] This authorization clearly did not apply to the office of the Attorney General; nonetheless, Palmer proceeded to conduct raids as if it did.

On November 19, 1919, the Senate settled the issue of ratification of the Versailles Treaty and participation in the League of Nations by defeating the amended document. This action raised issues as to the status of the laws which had been passed during the war and their applicability in view of the fact that an official recognition of the termination of the War had not been rendered. As an alternative, the Senate began to draw up plans for a separate treaty with Germany—a measure which would clarify the issue. In the interim, the public continued to side with the exercise of such laws in cases where they worked against the rights of aliens suspected of engaging in pro-Russian activities.

On New Year's Day, 1920, Communist sympathizers and Communist Party members were meeting at their various headquarters in scores of cities throughout the United States. On this and succeeding nights, Palmer ordered massive raids. Over six thousand individuals were arrested. In Detroit, five hundred were interned in a bull pen measuring twenty-four by thirty feet and forced to remain there for a week under conditions which the mayor of the city described as intolerable. In Hartford, suspects were jailed along with visitors who were arrested and incarcerated on the grounds that their acquaintance provided evidence of affiliation with the Communist Party.

The national environment within which these activities were occurring sheds some light on their acceptance by the general public, even though it is obvious in retrospect that they were largely illegal and unwarranted. By late 1919, approximately two million workers had engaged in strikes. In addition to the traditional grievances of long hours and low pay, other wider questions had been raised by the strikes and further demands had been articulated. In September, for example, the United Mine Workers had made the first major demand in peace-time history for the nationalization of an industry. Shortly thereafter, the I.W.W. was proclaiming the need for One Big Union. In North Dakota and contiguous grain states, two hundred thousand farmers had joined Townley's Non-Partisan League—an organization which derived its structure from Socialist concepts. By the final day of the year reliable estimates of the number of people who were members of the Socialist Party reached 39,000. The figure for the Communist Labor Party was set as somehere between ten and thirty thousand and the statistic for the Communist Party ranged between thirty and sixty thousand members.[14] In total, this meant that Socialist and Communist organizational membership represented less than two tenths of one percent of the entire adult population in the United States. Nonetheless, most of the general public and a number of governmental officials believed that the activities of labor were directly or indirectly instigated by these organizations,

[13] The Act was signed on May 16, 1918, and broadened the powers of the Postmaster General to deny the right of individuals to use the mails if it could be shown that the content of materials violated in any way the provisions of the Act. In addition, any abusive remarks about the President, the flag or the country constituted violations of the Act. Under this last provision, sixty-five persons were arrested for what were interpreted as threats against the President.

[14] These figures do not include the estimated number of people who could be called supporters of the organizations; only actual members are estimated.

The Ku Klux Klan *rose to new strength during the period of the Red Scare following World War I. Here they are shown parading past the Treasury Building in Washington, D.C.*

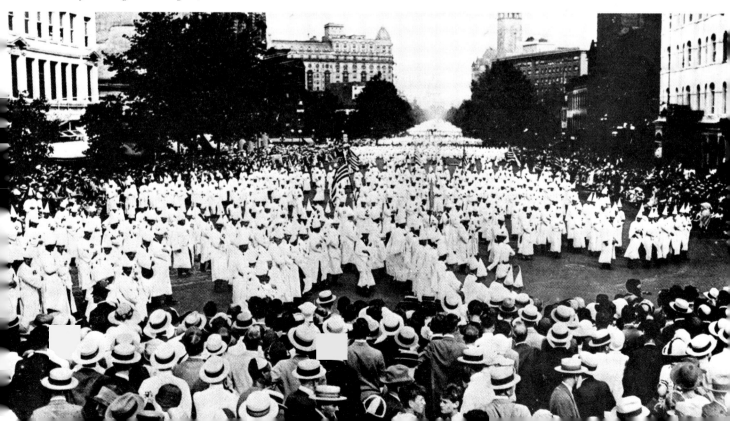

The United Klans *of Mississippi hold an open air torch light ceremony around a burning cross. Although the popularity of the Klan rose during the period following the war, their violent excesses and government crackdowns on meeting combined to reduce the Klan's membership in the late Twenties.*

with the ultimate goal of overthrowing or radically transforming the American government. If the President disagreed, there was no indication from the White House where he remained confined to bed, seriously ill and gravely disillusioned by the Senate's failure to support his foreign policy plan.

Almost simultaneously, intolerance found expression in hostile acts against Black Americans who had migrated to Northern cities in large numbers during the War because of higher wages and more numerous jobs. One sultry afternoon in the summer of 1919 a seventeen-year-old black youth was swimming in Lake Michigan in a section reserved by Chicago authorities for non-Whites. The young man drifted across the invisible boundary as he held on to a railroad tie. Whites on the adjacent beach began to throw stones at him, causing him to let go of the tie. He swam a few yards and sank, drowning moments later. Whether he had been hit by a rock was uncertain, but Blacks on the beach accused Whites of killing him a fight began. Disorder spread throughout the city and the ensuing race riot was the most massive and violent occurrence since Reconstruction. When order was finally restored, fifteen Whites and twenty-three Blacks had

been killed; five hundred and thirty-seven people had been injured and a thousand had been left homeless and destitute.

Anti-Semitism and anti-Catholicism were growing at an almost equal pace. Charges of an international Jewish conspiracy coincided with accusations that Catholics took their orders from the Pope and not the President. Prejudice prevailed and found its manifestation in the organizational resurrection of the Ku Klux Klan. Taking its conceptual premises from the Klan of the Reconstruction era, the newly formed organization incorporated principles of salesmanship, artifacts of ritualism, and bigotry against all three groups — the Blacks, Jews, and Catholics—into its format. Early in 1920, Colonel William Simmons, who had headed the revitalization of the organization since 1915, put the task of consolidating the KKK into the hands of Edward Clark, a staff member of the Southern Publicity Association. Members were recruited and memberships sold for the modest sum of ten dollars. Salesmen were given the title of Kleagles and the country was divided into Realms which were organized by King Kleagles. Each Realm was further divided into Domains, headed by Grand Goblins. Clark, the primary organizer, assumed the title of Imperial Kleagle and Colonel Simmons was bestowed the title of Imperial Wizard. As ludicrous as this nomenclature may have seemed, the strategies employed were extremely successful in soliciting significant numbers of Americans for active membership. Gradually, as the new decade got under way, the Klan was able to capture major political offices in several states and exert major political influence in others.

When five Socialist Party members were expelled from the New York State Assembly in April, 1920, on the grounds that they were members of a "disloyal organization composed exclusively of perpetual traitors,"[15] the Klan applauded the Judiciary Committee which had initiated the proceedings on the basis that several of the delegates were Jews, and, therefore, threats to American integrity. When a Republican member of the Union League Club in New York City protested the action, accusations were made that he might be a Communist sympathizer. Nothing could have been farther from the truth, but the expression of support for civil liberties and political rights was becoming an extremely unpopular stand.

On May Day, Attorney General Palmer announced that fully mobilized police forces were on alert to crush the activities of thousands of communists and socialists who, according to Palmer, had selected that date to engage in massive strikes, assassinations and revolution. Nothing happened. The interest of the American public had shifted again, this time to the forthcoming Presidential elections. Strikes and riots continued, accompanied by legislative enactments and judicial rulings, but with the coming of the summer of 1920 there were a significant number of other things to compete with them for public attention. The impact of the war and the period immediately following its conclusion had had a substantial effect on the American people as well as the government—an effect which would see its culmination in the New Deal policies of the 1930s and the entrance of the United States into the Second World War in the 1940's. In the interim of the 1920's, the direction of American public policy began to change as the priorities which had been established because of American participation in the War ultimately gave way to new concerns.

[15] This decision clearly violated both State and national constitutional laws insofar as the delegates had been elected through democratic procedures and no violations of law had been committed.

HISTORICAL HEADLINES
ON
WORLD WAR ONE

CALIFORNIA FORECAST
Los Angeles and vicinity: Increasing cloudiness Thursday; light west wind, becoming southerly.
San Francisco and vicinity: Rain Thursday; moderate southerly wind.
COAST TEMPERATURES
Los Angeles..... 48 | Portland 16
San Diego....... 48 | Spokane 4
San Francisco... 44 | Tacoma 24
Sacramento 38

Los Angeles Examiner

AN AMERICAN PAPER FOR THE AMERICAN PEOPLE

The Great Newspaper of The Great Southwest

A House or a Lot—
Buy a home now or a lot to build on. The best bargains in residence property can be found by glancing at the "Want Ads"
IN TODAY'S EXAMINER

VOL. XIII—NO. 33, Registered in S. Patent Office. Official Forecast—Increased Cloudiness. LOS ANGELES, JANUARY 13, 1916 THURSDAY PRICE 2½ CENTS Delivered to Subscribers 5 CENTS On News Stands and Trains

CONGRESSMEN DEMAND U. S. ACTION IN MEXICO

Capture Murderers and Punish Them, Secretary Lansing Wires Carranza

SEVEN OF THE AMERICANS KILLED BY MEXICAN BANDITS

Top (Left to Right), Thomas Evans, Charles R. Watson, C. A. Pringle, John Pope Coy, W. J. Wallace; (Below), Richard P. McHatton and Maurice Anderson. These Photographs Are From Snapshots Furnished by A. L. Lathrop, Now of Los Angeles, Who Until Recently Was General Manager of the Madera Company, Limited of Madera, Chihuahua, and Who Knew Well Most of the Victims of the Mexican Bandits.

SCHMIDT GETS LIFE SENTENCE AS PLEA FAILS

Convicted Dynamiter, With New Trial Denied, Refuses to 'Squeal' in 'Last Words'

CAPLAN SOON ON TRIAL

Stay of Execution Granted Until Companion Faces Judge on Same Charge

"It is the judgment of this court that you be confined for the remainder of your life in the State prison at San Quentin."

M. A. Schmidt, convicted dynamiter, heard Superior Judge Willis pronounce those words yesterday. For a moment he said nothing, but swayed slightly. Then, bowing to the judge, he asked permission to express himself for the last time in public. The request was granted.

Schmidt had prepared. He had what he wanted to say written and before him. Ever since the jury found him guilty he has carefully written line by line that last address. He charged that an avenue of freedom had once been opened to him, but if he had trodden that road, he would have been branded a "squealer." Then he spoke on history and politics and ended with poetry.

Sees Fight on Labor

Schmidt prefaced his remarks by a few words relative to capital being arrayed against labor, saying:

> "And it is these forces which insist that they must deal with the workers individually and collectively. They demand that the workers enter the industrial arena unprotected and disarmed and there meet the trained forces of greed and gold.

Court Warns

Several times during his remarks the court halted Schmidt and instructed him to tone down his speech, and once was about to stop him altogether, but for the insistence of Attorney Nathan C. Coghlan.

When Schmidt was brought into court Attorney Coghlan launched a lengthy argument for a new trial, in which he charged that the grand jury which returned the indictment and the trial jury were biased. Among other things, he claimed that during the trial several of the jurors were allowed to go to their homes. The motion for a new trial was denied.

When sentence was passed Schmidt was granted a stay of judgment until January 24. On that date David Caplan will be brought to court to have his trial set. It is probable that his trial will be placed for the early part of February.

'Too Much Money' Seen in East by Philadelphian

Rudolph Blankenburg, famous reform Mayor of Philadelphia, who went out of office with the close of 1915, predicted last night that "a day of reckoning will come" as a result of the tremendous accumulation of money in the East.

Mr. Blankenburg arrived on the Sunset Limited from New Orleans with his wife and adopted daughter, Miss Louise Adolphson, and left on the midnight train for San Diego to visit his son, Frederick Rudolph Blankenburg, who is in business there.

"There is too much money in the East," exclaimed the rugged septuagenarian.

"A time will come when this will be an embarrassment and then must be solved difficult problems.

The distinguished Philadelphian and his family will spend several weeks in San Diego and then will come to Los Angeles for a visit.

Huerta Dying and End Is Not Far Off

(By Associated Press)

EL PASO, Texas, Jan. 13.—The death of General Victoriano Huerta, once provisional President of Mexico, was momentarily expected early this (Thursday) morning. At 3:50 p. m. yesterday Huerta's family was called to his bedside. At 4 o'clock the final sacraments were administered. Gen. Huerta suffered two hemorrhages during the night, greatly weakening his already weakened condition.

Son of H. H. Boyeson Weds Miss Stovell

(By International News Service)

SAN FRANCISCO, Jan. 12.—Miss Marion Stovell became the bride of Hjalmar Hjorth Boyeson this evening, the Rev. Mr. Clampett performing the ceremony. The bride is the daughter of Mr. and Mrs. Charles J. Stovell and a granddaughter of Mrs. Jane Martel, one of the prominent matrons of early days in San Francisco society. The groom is the son of the late Hjalmar Hjorth Boyeson, the author and professor of literature.

Count Okuma Target for Bomb Thrower

(By Associated Press)

TOKIO, Jan. 12.—An attempt to assassinate Count Shigenobu Okuma, the Japanese premier, was made today by a man who threw two bombs into the premier's automobile. Count Okuma was not injured.

HERE IS AUTHENTIC LIST OF VICTIMS ON DEATH TRAIN

(BY INTERNATIONAL NEWS SERVICE)

EL PASO, Texas, Jan. 13, 2:30 a. m.—Following authentic list dead Americans whose bodies reached border at 2 a. m. today:

C. R. WATSON.	J. F. COY.
WILLIAM J. WALLACE.	ALEXANDER HALL.
E. L. ROBINSON.	J. W. WOON.
GEORGE W. NEWMAN.	CHARLES A. PRINGLE.
M. B. ROMERO.	W. D. PEARCE.
THOMAS W. EVANS.	R. H. SIMMONS.
R. P. M'HATTON.	MAURICE ANDERSON.
H. C. HASE.	A. H. COUCH.
CHARLES WADLEIGH.	THOMAS JOHNSON.

Automobiles Mean "Class"

During the year of 1915, the Los Angeles Examiner published a total of

697,998 Agate Lines

of Automobile, Accessory and Tire display advertising (not including the advertising of Department Stores).

This was 1330 agate lines more than the next Los Angeles newspaper published—*and 154,070 agate lines more than the other three Los Angeles newspapers combined* published of this class of advertising.

Quality readers buy automobiles—and the *"Examiner"* is read by many thousands more *Quality* readers than any other Los Angeles newspaper. Hence its lead in Automobile and other high-class advertising. Shrewd Los Angeles advertisers demand *Quality-Quantity* circulation—and get it in

The LOS ANGELES EXAMINER

The Great Newspaper of the Great Southwest
Los Angeles' Greatest Home Paper.

HOLMES RELATES STORY OF MERCILESS MASSACRE

THE following interview given by Tom D. Holmes to John W. Roberts, special correspondent of the International News Service, was pronounced correct and signed by Holmes before he left El Paso for Los Angeles:

By John W. Roberts

(BY INTERNATIONAL NEWS SERVICE)

EL PASO, Tex., Jan. 12.—Tom D. Holmes, the only American survivor of the band of fifteen foreigners who early Monday morning fell victims to General Villa's wrath against the Washington Government, reached the border late this afternoon.

Half crazed by the sight of seeing his eighteen companions clubbed, bayonetted and shot down like dogs by savage Villistas, his clothes and flesh torn by mesquite and cactus and other prickly brush while making his escape to the border, Holmes was a pitiful-looking object when he reached American territory.

He told a horrible story of fiendish cruelty by the Villistas, practiced on his unfortunate companions, and an unequaled tale of suffering while he was making his escape to the American border. His speech was broken by sobs when he told of his companions' misery and suffering, and several times Holmes broke down and cried like a child when he related details of the horrible assassinations of other members of the party.

"Monday afternoon our special was stopped near Lavisa by the derailment of some of the cars of the train ahead of us," he said. "I was sitting in a passenger coach wth Tom Evans when our special came to a sudden stop. Tom invited me to go out to see what the trouble was.

"Our intention was to get a bit of fresh air and stretch ourselves while we waited. Mr. Watson and one of the others of the party joined us.

Mexicans Open Fire, Yelling "Viva Villa!"

"No sooner did we alight from the rear platform than a group of about twenty Mexicans appeared from the thick brush nearby and immediately opened fire, yelling 'Viva Villa, down with the Gringoes.'

"Tom Evans, who was the first to alight, fell a victim of the first bullet fired. I jumped back into the car and hid in the lavatory, but saw Watson start to run in the opposite direction from the bandits.

"By this time the firing grew into a regular fusillade, and bullets crashed through the windows and sides of the coach. I heard one of my companions in the car yell, 'There comes Villa himself; run for your lives,' and a moment later I heard some Mexicans board the train and order every American out.

"I saw Watson trying to climb the embankment, and while doing so fall back with a bullet through his throat. My other companions were suffering similar fates. I could hear the Mexicans order them to remove their clothes and shoes, and saw two of the Americans stabbed in the back with bayonets until blood flowed when they refused. Hall, who was trying to follow Watson, fell dead beside him.

"What became of the other members of the party I don't know, because they were taken off the other side of the train and marched away. Occasionally I could hear a shriek as one of my companions was either clubbed over the head or struck with a bayonet by the savages.

Trips on Grass and Escapes Bullets

"When I heard the Mexicans approach the train again I left my hiding place, dismounted from the train and began to run. Five or six shots were fired at me without effect, but at the same moment I tripped on the prairie grass and fell down. This is what saved my life for the Mexicans believed I had been shot and gave up their chase. I did not arise. Instead I lay there without daring to breathe, even though I was lying on a clump of cactus.

"I could hear the Mexicans then assault the passenger coaches ahead. Two other Americans who were in there tried to escape, but were shot down and their assassins immediately began to remove their clothing and shoes. When these men walked away, I crawled on my stomach in a direction away from the train. When I reached the taller mesquite brush I broke into a run and did not stop until I reached a Mexican farm house near Santa Izabel; I gave the ranchman some money to permit me to hide there until I recovered from my exhaustion, and he nursed the bruises and scratches I had received in trying to escape. That night he drove me into Chihuahua and I arrived there early Tuesday morning.

"When I reached there I became unconscious for some time and cannot remember all I told the Americans, but they un-

(Continued on Page 3, Columns 6-8.)

INDIGNATION VOICED IN SENATE OVER AMERICAN MASSACRE BY MEXICANS

Resolution by Senator Sherman Urges Protection of Citizens; Time for 'Watchful Waiting' Has Passed, Says Gallinger in Speech

Death Train Bringing American Victims to U. S. Arrives in Juarez

EL PASO, Jan. 13, 2:30 a. m.—The train containing the bodies of the Americans massacred by Mexicans arrived at Juarez at 2:05 o'clock this morning.

Eighteen bodies were brought by the train and their transfer to El Paso is expected to be made at once.

Military guards at the bridge to Juarez have been trebled by order of General Pershing and extra policemen have been sworn in to help the regular force handle the situation. Fears of an anti-Mexican demonstration are freely expressed, as the race feeling is running high.

(BY ASSOCIATED PRESS)

WASHINGTON, Jan. 12.—Congress was swept by a wave of indignation today over the killing of American citizens by Mexican bandits near Chihuahua City. Demands for action came from minority members and while the administration's leaders counseled peace, even Senator Stone, chairman of the Senate foreign relations committee, admitted that if Carranza, after a fair trial, failed to protect foreigners in Mexico intervention was inevitable.

The atmosphere was surcharged with excitement when the Senate and House met and the storm broke quickly. Senator Sherman, Republican of Illinois, introduced a resolution to express the sense of Congress that there should be intervention by the United States and Pan-American nations unless General Carranza could comply at once with a demand that he protect the lives and property of foreigners. In the House, Representative Dyer of Missouri, offered a resolution asking President Wilson whether he did not think the time had arrived to abandon "watchful waiting" and invade Mexico.

The resolutions were not acted upon, both being referred to the foreign affairs committee. But there was aroused by the latest Mexican atrocity a general spirit of resentment that most conservative leaders found it difficult to restrain. Senators Gallinger and Borah, on the Republican side of the chamber, echoed the terms of the Sherman resolution, which declared that the Carranza government appeared powerless to cope with the lawlessness in Mexico, and declared intervention the only alternative unless reparation for the Chihuahua outrages were speedily made and the de facto government in future showed itself capable of controlling the situation.

Senator Stone urged patriotic support of the President and patient forbearance until the experiment of trying out the Carranza government should prove a failure. He said:

> If Carranza proves himself inefficient, however, if he is unable to punish criminals and to insure safety to foreigners in Mexico, I think with the Senator from Idaho, Mr. Borah, that there is only one thing to do and that it to go down there armed and intervene."

Senator Thom as of Colorado, also advised against intervention except as an unavoidable resort, declaring that the United States never would get out of Mexico if its armies once crossed the Rio Grande. He made a vigorous speech assailing the Standard Oil Company and the Pearson Oil Syndicate, charging that these interests, through rival efforts to monopolize the oil properties in Mexico, had been responsible for the revolutions of that country and for strife along the border.

Senator Sherman's resolution prompted Senator Gallinger to read a telegram from Judge L. W. Holmes of New Hampshire, asking that every pos-

CALIFORNIA FORECAST

Los Angeles and Vicinity—Fair Saturday, with frost in early morning; light west wind.

San Francisco and Vicinity—Generally cloudy weather Saturday; light southwest wind.

COAST TEMPERATURES

Los Angeles	54	Portland	38
San Diego	52	Spokane	35
San Francisco	51	Tacoma	38
Sacramento	50		

Los Angeles Examiner

An American Paper for the American People

The Great Newspaper of The Great Southwest

VOL. XIII—NO. 105 Registered in U. S. Patent Office Official Forecast—Fair LOS ANGELES, MARCH 25, 1916 SATURDAY PRICE 2½ CENTS Delivered to Subscribers 5 CENTS On News Stands and Trains

A House or a Lot

Buy a home now or a lot to build on. The best bargains in residence property can be found by glancing at the "Want Ads."

IN TODAY'S EXAMINER

VILLA REPORTED CAUGHT ON RANCH

R. WAITE AYS HE OUGHT RSENIC

der Suspect Claims His ather-in-Law, John E. Peck, ow Dead, Once Asked Him to uy Poison for Use in Suicide

red Bribe of $1000 to Maid Corroborate Story, Detective leges; Druggist's Record of ales Confronts the Prisoner

(By Associated Press)

EW YORK, March 24.—Confession was made to- by Dr. Arthur Warren ite, according to District orney Swann, that he ght the poison believed the authorities to have ,ed the death of his er-in-law, John E. Peck, Grand Rapids, Mich, but asserted that he made the chase at the request of the ionaire, who was despon- , and wished to commit ide.

other remarkable development in the day was the statement to Mr. Swann by Raymond ndler, a private detective, that Vaite had asked him to attempt ribe Waite's negro maid, Dora r, to corroborate the dentist's

she will say in court that she Mr. Peck ask me to buy the ic," Schindler told the district ney Waite said, "and that she me give him the package un- d, I will give her a check for ."

ck for $1000 by Prosecutor

Waite, according to the detec- hereupon signed what purported a check for $1000 to the order e girl, written by Schindler on eet from his notebook. This k" now is in the possession of wann. Schindler said Waite did now he was a detective.

Waite was taken to the prison at Bellevue Hospital tonight. wann said he wanted the den- ept under the closest possible llance, because Waite had ex- ed regret that the drugs he took esday had not killed him and e wishes he were dead.

en first questioned by Mr. n on Tuesday, Waite is said to laughed heartily, and declared, , this is rich. I never purchased c in my life and have never had

$40,000 Fund ally, Is Claimed

making his statement to the t attorney today, Waite was ossessed and spoke with evi- deliberation. But when he was oned about the alleged misuse),000 entrusted to him for in- ent by Miss Catherine Peck, of John E. Peck, and in re- to a woman he had previously ted having lived with, he ap- ly became indignant, saying, has nothing to do with the t in hand."

," he said, according to Mr. , "I bought the arsenic, but I you won't believe what I am to tell you, so I'll probably go electric chair. Mr. Peck was d man and he was very de- ent over the death of his wife. ay he asked me to buy some for him. I do not remember er he said he wanted arsenic . I went to see a physician ac-

nued on Page 3, Columns 5-6)

Ship Once Sunk, Arrives in Port Worth $1,200,000

Republic, Seized by French, Wrecked by German Shells, Recovered From Harbor

(By Associated Press)

SAN FRANCISCO, March 24.—The American steamer Republic, formerly the German steamer Walkuere, which was seized by the French in 1914 and later sunk in Papeete (Tahiti) harbor by shells from an attacking German squadron and which was granted American register while still a sunken derelict, arrived here tonight from Papeete under its own steam.

The vessel was sunk September 21, 1914, and for more than a year lay in eleven fathoms of water. Then the French Government sold the vessel to a San Francisco syndicate for $29,000.

Under the direction of Captain Lebbeus Curtis of San Francisco, surveyor for the Marine Underwriters' Association, the vessel was raised. This work, which began November 9, 1915, and was completed January 11, involved the construction, under water, of huge cofferdams, and was said by experts here to have been a notable performance.

The cargo recovered from the Walkuere was said to have reimbursed the purchasers for the cost of the ship and the expense of of the salvage operations, and it was reported today that they were considering an offer of $1,200,000 for the vessel.

Eastern Lobsters at 75 Cents a Pound

(By Associated Press)

BOSTON, March 24.—Lobsters reached the highest price ever known in New England today when they were quoted in the local market at 75 cents a pound.

Boisterous weather, an unusually late Spring and small imports from the Canadian provinces are given as the cause of the advance.

E. O. Holland Now College President

(By Associated Press)

PULLMAN, Wash., March 24.—Surrounded by the heads of twenty colleges and universities of the East and West, all wearing the robes and insignia of their academic honors, Ernest O. Holland was formally inducted into office here today as president of Washington State college.

Judge J. J. Carrillo in Same Condition

Judge Juan J. Carrillo, pioneer resident of Southern California, who is seriously ill here at the residence of his daughter, Mrs. A. H. Calkins, was reported last night to be in the same condition as during the past few days.

PACKET SHIP TORPEDOED OFF DIEPPE

Twenty U. S. Citizens, Including Embassy Couriers, Reported on Board; Towed Into Unnamed French Port, Says Dispatch

Sudden Renewal of Submarine Activity Brings Disaster to Allied and Neutral Shipping; Danish and Norwegian Vessels Victims

German War Fleet Seen Steaming East

(BY INTERNATIONAL NEWS SERVICE SPECIAL CABLE)

LONDON, March 24.—A Central News dispatch from Amsterdam states that fifteen German warships and one airship had passed the Dutch island of Ameland last night. Their course lay eastward.

COPENHAGEN, March 24.—Politiken says it is reported that a large number of submarines are in the North Sea near the British coast.

Yesterday was a disastrous day on the sea for neutral and allied shipping. Two British vessels, the Channel packet Sussex, and the Dominion liner Englishman, as well as the Norwegian steamer Blanklokken and the Danish steamer Christianssund were reported sunk, all presumably by torpedoes.

(BY INTERNATIONAL NEWS SERVICE SPECIAL CABLE)

LONDON, March 24.—Probably with Americans among her 380 passengers, the Channel packet Sussex, bound from Folkestone to Dieppe, was torpedoed this evening near the French coast.

The Sussex has been towed into a French port, the name of which was not announced, according to a dispatch to the Central News from Polkstone received here at midnight.

She had steamed away from Folkestone at 1:20 this afternoon and at 7 o'clock when she came to grief, was not far from Dieppe. She sent out alarm signals, and a number of vessels hurried to her assistance.

She was near enough to her destination when struck for vessels to reach the spot from Dieppe harbor and this gives rise to the expectation that all on board may be saved. Reports received by the continental traffic office of the Brighton railroad encourage the belief that all are already safe.

The Sussex is managed by the Brighton railroad, although she belongs to the French State railroads.

(Continued on Page 4, Column 4.)

Irvin Cobb and His "Active Adjectives"

TURN to the Sporting Section of today's Examiner and read **Irvin Cobb's** advance story on tonight's Willard-Moran heavyweight championship fight in New York. Tomorrow's Examiner will contain another **great exclusive feature,** as this famous humorist's impression of the contest will be printed therein.

Every day the Examiner has a great exclusive news feature. Yesterday it was Damon Runyon's account of the Mexico campaign. Today it is Irvin Cobb's story. You should read the Examiner EVERY DAY, and then PRESERVE it, for a newspaper file of today's happenings will be valuable in future years. Phone your subscription to the Examiner—Main 8300 or 10195—or fill out the coupon below and mail it in.

Name ....

Address ....

Make the Examiner Your Breakfast Companion

Roosevelt Back, Describes Bird Which Eats Nuts

'Big as Barn Owl, Nocturnal and Lives in Caves;' Mum on Politics

NEW YORK, March 24.—Colonel Roosevelt returned tonight on the steamship Matura from the West Indies, silent on politics, by announcing the discovery in Trinidad of what was to him a new variety of bird in which he was much interested. He and his wife had been absent six weeks on what he termed a vacation.

The bird, he said, was about as big as a barn owl. It lives in caves, is nocturnal in its habits, and eats nuts. Its native name, he added, was the "guacharo."

Colonel Roosevelt laid full responsibility for the Mexican complication at the door of President Wilson. He declared that the events of the past month in Mexico are the exact working out of the policy of "furnishing arms and munitions to one set of bandits in order to help them against another set of bandits, instead of helping Uncle Sam against all of them."

C. A. Towne to Seek N. Y. Seat in Senate

(By Associated Press)

NEW YORK, March 24.—Charles A. Towne, former United States Senator from Minnesota, announced today that he would enter the primaries in New York for the Democratic nomination to succeed Senator James A. O'Gorman.

Mr. Towne in 1904 was elected to Congress from this city. Recently he has been supporting President Wilson's preparedness program.

Foot of Snow Falls in Salt Lake City

(By Associated Press)

SALT LAKE CITY, Utah, March 24.—The season's heaviest snowfall and the record snowfall for the month of March in Salt Lake began last night and continued today, following a heavy rain. The storm ended late today, after more than a foot of snow had fallen. Street traffic was retarded early in the day. It is believed no damage to crops was done.

Bryan Starts Fight to Go as Delegate

(By International News Service)

FALLS CITY, Neb., March 24.—William Jennings Bryan tonight opened his campaign as a candidate for delegate-at-large to the Democratic National convention.

During the evening Mr. Bryan announced himself as a friend to President Wilson and said he wished to go to the convention to act a friend's part towards the President.

Ship and Crew of 20 Believed Lost

(By International News Service)

GULFPORT, Miss., March 24.—The Norwegian bark Dova Lisboa, which left Rio Janeiro January 8, for Gulfport, carrying a crew of twenty, is missing. Her owners here today said they feared she had been lost.

Bishop Ortynsky of Ruthenian Rite Dies

(By Associated Press)

PHILADELPHIA, March 24.—Bishop Stephen Soter Ortynsky, head of the Ruthenian Rite of the Roman Catholic Church in the United States, died today at his home in this city after a three days' illness from pneumonia. He was 50 years old.

General Otis Said to Remain Unchanged

Physicians attending General Harrison Gray Otis, who is threatened with pneumonia at the California Hospital, reported last night that their patient's condition was unchanged.

SOUTH POLE EXPEDITION IN TROUBLE

Shackleton's Ship Aurora Damaged and Failing to Get Help Is on Her Way to New Zealand Short of Fuel for Repairs

No Word of Leader of Party Who Landed for Cross-Country Dash; Wireless Appeal Long Delayed, Says Message Received

(By Associated Press)

LONDON, March 25, 1:46 a. m.—A wireless message from the auxiliary ship Aurora of the Shackleton Antarctic expedition was received in London yesterday. The Aurora at the time the message was sent was in the Far South Pacific. The wireless said the steamer had been damaged and was proceeding to New Zealand for repairs.

The fate of Lieutenant Sir Ernest Shackleton and the party with him, which set out to cross the South Pole, is not known.

Apparently an attempt had been made to send the wireless for several months, but it had just been received at the New Zealand station, which forwarded it to England. The message was sent by a member of the staff of the Aurora, which went from Australia to Ross Sea at the end of 1914 for the purpose of bringing back Shackleton's party, when they had crossed the South Polar continent. It was not known that the Aurora had wireless on board and the dispatch was delivered to an officer of the expedition which had been closed for some time.

The news as received in London leaves the world completely in the dark as to the doings or whereabouts of Lieutenant Shackleton and his immediate party. If they have carried out their program they now are presumably at the Ross Sea base, but without the expected ship to take them off.

Even if Shackleton has been unsuccessful in the attempt to cross the Pole and has had to retrace his steps to the Widdel Sea base, thence to return to Buenos Aaires, the relief expedition will have to be reorganized to effect the rescue of Lieutenant Aeneas MacIntosh, R. N. R., in command of the Aurora, and a number of his companions who were left on shore at Ross Sea when the Aurora broke from her moorings. The great question is, will the stores which the men possessed be sufficient to sustain the lives of the party for a year.

King George Hears News of Accident to Vessel

The information contained in the message received at London was at once communicated to King George, who presented Lieutenant Shackleton with a flag to carry during his march and who had taken great interest in Shackleton's task. The news caused grave consternation among the relatives and friends of the explorers.

Until the Aurora arrives at some port and a full story of her adventures is available, the extent of the loss sustained by the party cannot be definitely known.

The full text of the wireless message received in London contained about 400 words. It said that the Aurora had reached her destination late in January, 1915, and landed two parties under Lieutenant MacIntosh and also a considerable quantity of stores. Meanwhile the Aurora lay at her moorings off Cape Evans. Several attempts were made to find a safe harbor, but these all failed owing to the extremely bad season.

A blizzard on May 6 drove the Aurora from her moorings. The vessel became lodged in pack ice, which carried her northward around Cape Adare. She lost her rudder and suffered a severe strain to her hull in the ice about July 21 when ninety miles south of Coulman Island.

The message gives the following names to those ashore: Gase, commissariat officer; Richards, physicist; Hayward, secretary, and Jack, biologist; Lieutenant MacIntosh, H. Wild and Messrs. Joyce, Cope, Stevens and Smith.

The breaking away of the Aurora and her consequent inability to pick up the members of the Shackleton expedition on their arrival at the Ross Sea side of the Antarctic was almost the only contingency that had not been foreseen.

Villa Band Fires Mexican Town as U.S. Troops Pass

Janos, With 500 Population, Laid Waste by Marauders Who Escape Soldiers

(By International News Service)

COLUMBUS, N. M., March 24.—Marauding Villistas have fired the town of Janos, midway between Ascencion and Corralitos, according to a report brought into Columbus tonight by Americans returning to the border.

Janos is a small place with a population of about 500, and at one time was the military base of General Bertani of the Carranzista forces.

The Americans passed within two miles of the town and witnessed the fire, but saw nothing of the pillagers.

It is not known that any Americans were in the town.

Poison Lays Aside 200 Factory Hands

(By International News Service)

DAYTON, Ohio, March 24.—Two score or more girls and women employed by the Recording and Computing Machines Company of this city, manufacturers of war munitions, are in local hospitals, sufferers from poisoning, while at least 200 men and girls are at their home, more or less ill from the same deadly agent.

The statement was made that the poison probably developed in food at the company's restaurant, and was not due to the intentional act of any one.

Guatemalan Rebels Win Four Battles

(By Associated Press)

MEXICO CITY, March 24.—A special dispatch to El Democrata from Tapachula, State of Chiapas, and near the Guatemalan frontier, says that fighting between the rebels and the forces under President Manuel Estrada Cabrera was proceeding vigorously on the 18th.

The rebels under General Jose Prado entered the Peten district, capturing the towns of San Pedro, Providencia, Naranjo and El Progreso. Cabrera's forces are said to have been defeated in four separate engagements.

U.S. Ownership of Oil Lands Up Tuesday

(By International News Service)

WASHINGTON, March 24.—Representative Charles H. Randall of Los Angeles, author of a resolution looking toward Government ownership of all the oil lands in the United States, today arranged with Chairman Foster of the House mines and mining committee for a hearing on the resolution next Tuesday.

It is understood that a majority of the committee are in favor of reporting the resolution favorably.

Married Men Ask Derby Resignation

(By Associated Press)

MANCHESTER England, March 25, 3:07 a. m.—The Earl of Derby's resignation as director general of recruiting is demanded in a resolution passed at a meeting of married men who have attested under the Derby scheme.

The meeting was held for the purpose of protesting against married men being called to the colors before all available single men had joined the army.

Similar meetings of protest were held simultaneously in other cities.

Bay City Mail Chief Removed From Office

(By Associated Press)

SAN FRANCISCO, March 24.—Orders were received from Washington today removing from the postal service here Edward McGrath, superintendent of the railway mail service, and James O'Connell, city inspector. The telegram containing the orders assigned no reason for action. McGrath has been in the service for twenty-eight years and O'Connell for twenty.

BANDIT LEADER SURROUNDED AND VIRTUAL CAPTIVE

Official Dispatches From Chihuahua Declare Carranza Troops Have Outlaw Cut Off From Retreat South, Americans Are Closing in From the North and Escape Is Impossible

(BY INTERNATIONAL NEWS SERVICE)

QUERETARO, Mexico, March 25.—Official dispatches from Chihuahua today reported that Francisco Villa is captured on the Hearst ranch, which he has raided several times. The Constitutionalist troops have him cut off from farther retreat to the south, and the American forces are reported to be advancing rapidly toward him from the north.

In any case, official circles in Queretaro today regarded his capture as a probability within a few days. Villa's forces are said to have disintegrated to a few score followers.

(BY INTERNATIONAL NEWS SERVICE)

QUERETARO, Mexico, March 24.—Latest reports from the north indicate that Francisco Villa is in a tight place following a three-day battle with Government forces commanded by Generals Benjamin Garza and Cabazos.

The battle is still raging at a point in the vicinity of Namiquipa, a mountain town in Western Chihuahua. Government reinforcements are being rushed to the scene.

General Obregon, minister of war, stated that the Government has sufficient troops in the region to surround Villa.

(BY ASSOCIATED PRESS)

MEXICO CITY, March 24.—Villa is surrounded and cannot possibly escape, according to a message received tonight by the minister of war from General Luis Gutierrez.

The message adds that General Gutierrez's troops are spread out fan-shaped in front of Namiquipa and that the general has divided his forces into four commands, under General Benjamin Garza, General F. Cabazos, Colonel Hernandez and Colonel Cano, for the purpose of hemming in Villa and his followers from four points of the compass.

The forces of General Gutierrez have been for several hours in contact with the outposts of the Villa party.

MEXICANS MURDER THREE AMERICANS ON BORDER

(By Associated Press)

DOUGLAS, Ariz., March 24.—Three Americans, two women and one man, were killed near Gibson's Line Ranch on the New Mexico-Mexican boundary, eight miles west of Columbus, N. M., between 4 and 5 o'clock Wednesday afternoon, presumably by Mexicans, according to the story brought here by a party of five Douglas people, who said they arrived on the scene shortly after the bodies had been removed by soldiers.

A command of United States soldiers stationed at the Gibson ranch was said to have crossed the line in pursuit of the slayers.

Samuel Collins, automobile dealer; Mr. and Mrs. Russell T. Childers, Miss Lottie Milinowski and Edward Freeman, all of Douglas, were the automobilists who told of the alleged killing.

The names of the persons said to have been killed were not learned.

According to the story told tonight by Mr. and Mrs. Childers and Miss Milinowski, the party had been to El Paso on a pleasure trip. They decided that they would visit Columbus to view the ruins left by the raid of Villa's men instead of returning here through Deming and Lordsburg, N. M.

After leaving Columbus Wednesday afternoon they were stopped at Hermanas by the railroad section foreman, they said, who warned them that something was wrong at the Gibson Ranch a few miles further on. **He said that he had been watching through a pair of binoculars and had seen a mounted band of 100 or more men, supposedly Mexican bandits, cross the border near the ranch and ride to a waterhole a mile and a half north.**

After watering their horses, they rode back across the line. He added that within a short time a number of troopers of the Twelfth Cavalry had come to the ranch house and moved about in an excited manner.

The automobilists proceeded toward the ranch, but before they had arrived there they were stopped by a Twelfth Cavalryman who advised them to come to the ranch house immediately so that the detachment there could afford them protection. They were guarded at the house all

Mr. Fone-Ad Says—

SPEAKING OF PREPAREDNESS, EXAMINER PHONE ADS ARE THE BEST PREPARATIONS FOR GOOD BUSINESS
PREPARE FOR THE TROUT AND BASEBALL SEASONS NOW

Many people are preparing for the opening of the trout season and others for the opening of the baseball season. Congress is doing a lot of talking about preparedness for the army and navy. Are you prepared to make sales or rent your property tomorrow? You can easily gain preparedness. Just phone a small Want Ad to the "Examiner." The "Examiner" gets the customer, you close the sale.

Phone Sunset Main 8300 or Home 10195.

Los Angeles Examiner

The Great Newspaper of The Great Southwest

AN AMERICAN PAPER FOR THE AMERICAN PEOPLE

VOL. XIII—NO. 110 — Registered in U. S. Patent Office — Official Forecast—Fair. — LOS ANGELES, MARCH 30, 1916 — THURSDAY — PRICE 2½ CENTS Delivered to Subscribers — 5 CENTS On News Stands and Trains

CALIFORNIA FORECAST
Los Angeles and vicinity: Fair Thursday; light westerly wind.
San Francisco and vicinity: Fair Thursday; continued warm; light northerly wind.

COAST TEMPERATURES
Los Angeles .. 80 Santa Barbara .. 67
San Diego .... 82 Portland 65
San Francisco.. 60 Spokane 44
Sacramento ... 60 Tacoma 44

A GOOD TURN
Today's exchange columns offer many fine opportunities for making a profitable exchange. Read the "Want Ads" today in **THE EXAMINER**

ROOSEVELT SAYS WILSON INVITES DISASTER IN MEXICO

U.S. ANGRY OVER NEW UNDERSEAS CAMPAIGN

Washington Probing Circumstantial Evidence That Germany is Engaged in a War That Has No Regard for American Rights

Unless Berlin's Reply Changes Situation All Recent Incidents Will Be Combined in One Formidable Indictment of Acts

(BY INTERNATIONAL NEWS SERVICE SPECIAL CABLE)

LONDON, March 29.—The Daily News publishes a report from Paris that the Tubantia and Sussex were torpedoed by Austrian submarines.

(By Associated Press)

WASHINGTON, March 29.—The accumulation of circumstantial evidence indicating that Germany is engaged upon a campaign of submarine warfare which has no regard for the rights of American citizens traveling on merchant ships of belligerent nationality, the Administration considers, has created one of the most serious situations which has confronted the United States since the beginning of the war in Europe.

Every agency open to the State Department tonight was being employed in an effort to gather an impeachable array of facts regarding the explosion which damaged the British Channel steamer Sussex, the sinking of the British ships Manchester Engineer, Englishman, Eagle Point and the Dutch steamer Tubantia, and the alleged firing of a torpedo at the French passenger ship Patris. All of these ships carried American citizens, and all apparently were attacked in violation of Germany's recently renewed assurances to the United States.

Indictment to Cover Aggravating Incidents

The next step of the United States is said authoritatively to have been determined upon. Unless Germany, in reply to the inquiries made by the United States through Ambassador Gerard makes some statement to cause the State Department to change its present intentions, it is understood that all the recent aggravating incidents will be combined in one general formidable indictment which will bring the entire subject to a clear-cut issue.

Should Germany admit responsibility for any of the attacks and attempt to satisfy the United States by saying that a mistake had been made, offer to make reparation and to punish the submarine commander, the issue would not by any means be disposed of.

It is regarded as certain that the United States will not accept such an explanation as satisfactory, at least until time has shown what punishment actually was meted out to the offending submarine commander, and whether any value longer could be attached to Germany's promises.

Number of Attacks Held Significant

In the event of Germany disclaiming responsibility for the disasters, the United States will proceed with its investigations to determine to its own satisfaction whether the evidence which now strongly indicates that the Sussex and other ships were torpedoed without warning can be regarded as conclusive. If the Government probably would act promptly. Officials refrain from discussing the accumulating array of evidence.

(Continued on Page 4, Column 1.)

War Secretary and Gregory in Conference

New Developments in Mexican Border Situation May Be Forthcoming

(By International News Service)

WASHINGTON, March 29.—Following a half hour's conference between Secretary of War Baker and Attorney General Gregory late this afternoon it was reported that some new developments in the situation along the Mexican border may be expected shortly. The Department of Justice has maintained a small army of secret service men along the border and it is believed that information which they have collected was turned over to the War Department by Mr. Gregory.

It was recently announced at the Department of Justice that its agents had discovered that a plot was being hatched in Texas to revive the "plan of San Diego." This plan called for an invasion of Arizona, New Mexico and Texas by an army of Mexicans.

Both Secretary Baker and Mr. Gregory declined to discuss their conference.

Villista Band Is Reported Near Army

HEADQUARTERS PUNITIVE EXPEDITION, NEAR CASAS GRANDES, March 29.—(By wireless to Columbus, N. M.)—An aerogram received here tonight reported that a small band of armed Mexicans, declared to be followers of Villa, had been seen fifty-five miles south of here. If that report is true, that is farther north than Villistas have been reported for more than a week.

One Term Bill for President in House

(By International News Service)

WASHINGTON, March 29.—President Wilson is again confronted with the "one term" plank of the Democratic platform adopted at Baltimore. Representative Bailey of Pennsylvania, an enthusiastic Bryan supporter, today introduced in the House a resolution providing for a constitutional amendment prescribing a single term for the Presidency. Representative Bailey invited the Administration to support his resolution as a means of "disarming criticism" and of helping the party in the coming election. The Bailey amendment would provide that the President be elected for a term of six years and be ineligible for re-election.

Georgia to Regain Innes Case Couple

(By Associated Press)

ATLANTA, Ga., March 29.—Governor Harris received assurances today from Governor Ferguson of Texas that Victor E. Innes and his wife would be extradited to Georgia and officers left for San Antonio tonight to bring them here.

Innes and his wife were acquitted on murder charges at San Antonio and told Governor Ferguson that they feared mob violence if they were returned to Georgia to answer indictments for larceny after trust.

Death Penalty for Sonora Opium Sales

(By International News Service)

DOUGLAS, Arizona, Marc 29.—Governor Calles of Sonora is having prepared a decree making the importation of opium into that State punishable. The possession of opium or paraphernalia for its smoking will be punished by a heavy prison sentence.

Chinese in Sonora for months have been supplying opium to agents in the United States.

Wilsons Guests at Ball for Red Cross

(By Associated Press)

WASHINGTON, March 29.—President and Mrs. Wilson were the guests of honor tonight at a ball given here tonight for the benefit of the American Red Cross.

ENGINEER, TOWERMAN, BLAMED FOR 30 DEATHS

Federal and State Probers Are Started in Effort to Place Blame for Crash of Three Limited Trains at Amherst, O.

List of Dead in Disastrous Collision May Be Increased as Force of Rescuers Clear Away Pile of Wreckage 35 Feet High

(By International News Service)

CLEVELAND, March 29.—State, Federal and railroad investigation of the double wreck on the Lake Shore Railroad at Amherst, O., near here, early this morning, which cost the lives of fully thirty persons and injured forty, was begun here today.

Railroad officials declare the blame for the crash which piled up the Twentieth Century Rar and two other crack Lake Shore passenger trains into a tangled heap of junk probably will be shared by two railroad employes.

While relief parties were still digging dead bodies from the debris, and doctors and nurses were rescuing trapped human beings and caring for maimed victims, three separate investigations were begun. Three men stood out tonight as swiftly become the objects of cross-fire investigation, luckless enough to have been actors in the melodramatic spectacle that sprang out of the fog of early morning hours, when the second section of the Chicago-Buffalo flier rammed into the rear of the first section and both in turn were struck by the west-bound limited.

Towerman and Engineer Are Blamed for Wreck

One is a towerman, Ernst, dozing in his lonely cupola as speeding trains slid by him—a man trying to perform his duties of watching over thousands of lives in the railroad's care and under the handicap of sleepless hours caring for his wife, who Sunday had given birth to a baby. The other is Harman Hass, engineer of the second section of the east-bound flier, who escaped from the cab of his engine after it had plowed into the first section—a man who saw no red warning signal through the fog and relied upon the mysteriously halted first train.

These are the men who became the center of an investigation by New York Central officials, led by General Superintendent A. S. Ingalls. A coincident inquiry was begun by Coroner Garver of Lorain county, while State Railroad Inspectors Packard and Heffernan rushed to the scene to conduct the State Public Utilities probe, and Safety Experts Belknap, Ellis and McAdam started for Amherst to begin a Federal investigation for the Interstate Commerce Commission.

Recover Twenty-six Bodies From Mass of Wreckage

Survivors of the disaster streamed into Cleveland as a port of refuge all day today, bringing with them tales of horror and of magic escapes. Grisly scenes they had witnessed, that shocked and stunned men among them and stunned men.

Out of the chaos at the spot, a mile out of Amherst, rescue parties spent a struggling day taking bodies out of the debris. Twenty-six were recovered, but others were believed to have remained hidden under the tons of wreckage that was strewn over four tracks and reared thirty feet in the air.

Twenty-two bodies are packed in a morgue at Amherst, two are dead at Elyria Memorial Hospital and two are dead at Lorain. Eighteen have been identified. Of the other eight, all in the Amherst morgue, six are men and two are women.

Scattered over many miles are men, women and children, suffering with cuts, bruises and broken bones. Bodies are still thought to be in the wreckage.

(Continued on Page 10, Cols. 2-3)

EXPORT BAN ON GASOLINE PROPOSED IN HOUSE BILL

Authority to Fix Maximum Price of Oil Products is Also Sought for Federal Trade Commission by New Measure

Department of Commerce, Seeking Fuel Contract Renewal, Faces Demand for 40 Cents a Gallon, Compared With 11 Now

(By International News Service)

WASHINGTON, March 29.—Drastic steps to reduce the continued advance price of gasoline throughout the United States were proposed in two bills introduced in the House today. The measures were:

A bill by Representative Howard of Georgia, authorizing the President to impose an embargo on the exports of gasoline and other petroleum products.

A bill by Representative Steenerson of Minnesota, giving the Federal Trade Commission authority to fix maximum prices of petroleum, gasoline, kerosene and fuel oil.

Both of these measures were referred to the House Interstate and Foreign Commerce Committee. An effort will be made to force early action on them. Representative Howard, in a sensational statement accompanying his resolution, asserted the continual rise in gasoline prices has "not only reached the limit of endurance, but is becoming a national scandal."

U. S. Office Faces 40-Cent Demand

The Howard bill was introduced after its author had held a consultation with Secretary of Commerce Redfield. Representative Howard said he had been informed the Department of Commerce, in its efforts to renew annual contracts for gasoline for the next fiscal year, had been confronted with a demand for 40 cents a gallon for the product which is bought under this year's contract for 11 cents. Representative Howard said:

Secretary Redfield told me that the producers of gasoline now seeking contracts will not listen to any suggestion that the prices shall be less than 40 cents. The present price under Government contract is 11 cents.

What we ought to have is action to be taken similar to that taken by former President Roosevelt when the coal strike threatened to cut off the nation's supply of fuel. The people were in dire distress because of increased coal prices due to the strike and President Roosevelt sent for President Baer of the coal roads. He told him that unless the strike was settled within forty-eight hours, Federal troops would be sent to the mining district and the operation of the mines would be taken over by the Federal Government. The strike ended right there.

Has Become Scandal, Howard Declares

In his statement accompanying his resolution, Representative Howard said:

No one in Congress desires to interfere with or impede the great prosperity with which this nation is blessed, so long as that prosperity is derived from legitimate profits, but the continual rise in the price of gasoline, arbitrarily fixed by the refiners, has not only reached the limit of endurance but is becoming a national scandal.

If the people do not demand the immediate passage of this bill you may look for forty-cent gasoline by June the first.

The Steenerson bill would give the Federal trade commission authority to fix maximum prices for petroleum and its products and would force wholesale dealers to publish authoritative prices lists for review by the commission.

Noted Canadians Named in Shell Contract Scandal

Charges Involving Gen. Sam Hughes and Sir Alexander Bertram Hurled in Parliament

(By International News Service)

OTTAWA, Ont., March 29.—Allegations that high Canadian officials crushed with Americans to mulct the Canadian government of thousands of dollars in shell contracts were made in Parliament today by George W. Kayte, M. P., for Richmond.

He charged that the American Ammunition Company, while incorporated for $1,000,000, had actual capital of only $10,000; and the $1,000,000 International Arms and Fuse Company actually only a $3000 concern.

Gen. Sam Hughes, minister of militia, and Sir Alexander Bertram, chairman of the shell committee, are mentioned in connection with the scandal. It is alleged that E. R. Cadwell and R. F. Yoakum of New York and E. W. Bassick of Bridgeport, Conn., all connected with companies mentioned, signed a formal agreement for which they apportioned among themselves as commission $1,000,000 out of which money they were to receive from the shell committee for a contract of 2,500,000 fuses promised by Sir Alexander Bertram.

Nine days later they were awarded contracts for $22,000,000 worth of fuses.

'Waite Tried Gas, Too'

Wife Makes Statement

Mrs. Peck Nearly Victim

JOHN E. PECK, Aged Michigan Millionaire, and His Wife, Who Were Killed by Deadly Germs and Poison Administered by Dr. Arthur W. Waite, Their Son-in-Law.

Unsuccessful Attempt at Asphyxiation Told by Spouse of Confessed Slayer

—International Film Service Photo.

(By International News Service)

GRAND RAPIDS, Mich., March 29.—Dr. Arthur Warren Waite, a week before he killed Mr. John E. Peck, made an unsuccessful attempt to asphyxiate her with illuminating gas, according to a statement made today by Dr. Waite's wife. She said:

Shortly before mother died, I think perhaps a week, I was awakened by the smell of gas in the apartment and getting up to investigate, I found a gas jet in mother's room turned full on. Luckily a window had been left open and she suffered little from the gas.

"He Placed Something in Crack of Door"

At that time we thought nothing of it; we believed that when mother retired, had failed to turn off the gas, and the wind blew out the flame. At least, that was the explanation Warren gave, but I know different now.

I remember he had placed something above the crack under the door, as if to keep

(Continued on Page 9, Cols. 2-4)

Amazing Plot Confession

Poison Experiments Told

HERE are amazing statements made yesterday by Dr. Arthur Waite to Detective Ray C. Schindler, in amplification of his confession to murdering by poison the parents of his wife:

★ ★ ★ ★

I began experimenting upon Mr. and Mrs. Peck as soon as they arrived in the city to visit us. I put morphine and all sorts of germs in the food of Mrs. Peck. I thought I would try my schemes out on her first.

★ ★ ★ ★

I kept the culture tubes in my library. I would get the germ cultures and put them in Mrs. Peck's food. These did not seem to harm the old lady much and finally I gave her cocaine.

★ ★ ★ ★

Mrs. Peck was going to die anyway. She was an old woman. She was sick. "He" (the alter ego) gave her germs, but she would have died anyway. "He" did not murder her.

★ ★ ★ ★

Mr. Peck was old and ill also. The bad man (the alter ego) tried to kill him. But he, too, would have died anyway.

GIVES AID TO ONE BANDIT IN HIS FIGHT ON ANOTHER

In Statement Regarded as Opening Gun of Stirring Campaign ex-President Takes White House Occupant to Task

Cites Three Years of Murder Anarchy in Mexico and Declares Wilson Has Actively Interfered for Representatives of Outlaws

'Now Waging War Against With Whom Little More Than Year Ago He Concluded Treaty of Peace and Friendship'

(By International News Service)

OYSTER BAY, L. I., March 29.—Colonel Roosevelt tonight made a smashing attack on President Wilson's Mexican policy. It is at once an answer to the President's statement of last Sunday and a careful summing up of the situation below the border. Tonight's attack is direct and personal and may be fairly regarded as the opening gun of a vigorous campaign which will be waged without cessation from now until the assembling of the Chicago convention. The statement follows:

I have received many requests from good American citizens in Mexico, asking there is not some way by which the American people may be made to understand the utter baseless character of President Wilson's recent charge that American property owners in Mexico were responsible for stirring up the trouble there. All that is necessary is to put President Wilson to answer these perfectly simple questions:

Who Secured Killing of 276 Americans?

What American or cattle property owners in Mexico cured the killing of the Americans who have killed by Mexicans?

Does Mr. Wilson mean it was American property owners who inspired him to be the shipping to the Villistas the thousands of rifles and munitions of war which have now used to kill our people?

Does Mr. Wilson mean American property owners who inspired his then friends, Villistas and Carranzistas Shooting across our border on different occasions, to kill our own soil nine American soldiers and wound many others?

Does Mr. Wilson mean it was the owners of property in Mexico, native or foreign, who inspired the Villistas or Carranzistas in repeated

(Continued on Page 9, Cols. 2-4)

Los Angeles Examiner
The Great Newspaper of The Great Southwest

VOL. XIII—NO. 111 Registered in U. S. Patent Office   Official Forecast—Fair   LOS ANGELES, MARCH 31, 1916   FRIDAY   PRICE 2½ CENTS Delivered to Subscribers   5 CENTS On News Stands and Trains

CALIFORNIA FORECAST
Los Angeles and Vicinity—Fair and warmer Friday; light northerly wind. San Francisco and Vicinity—Fair Friday; continued warm; light northerly wind.
COAST TEMPERATURES
Los Angeles ...... 63 Portland 56
San Diego ...... 60 Fresno 44
San Francisco .. 67 Tacoma 48
Sacramento 63

VILLA CAPTURES CARRANZA GARRISON, KILLS 172

ONE TEUTON HOLDS UP BRITISH SHIP AND 57 MEN

Captain of Matoppo Bound Hand and Foot and Locked Up in His Cabin While Stowaway Rifles Safe and Destroys Documents

In Lining Up Crew on Bomb Threat, Daring German Orders Boat to Take Him Ashore; Is Intercepted by U. S. Vessel

(By Associated Press)

LEWES, Dela., March 30.—How one German stowaway held up the captain fifty-six members of the crew of the British steamer Matoppo, compelling them at the point of a pistol to change the course of the vessel and put him at the Delaware breakwater after he had rifled the ship's safes and taken all valuables, was told here tonight by Captain Bergner, master of the Matoppo.

The stowaway, who said his name was Ernest Schiller and that he had in Hoboken, for the last eight days, is in jail here awaiting the arrival of the United States district attorney from Wilmington, Del., and British consul general from Philadelphia.

The holdup took place outside the three-mile limit and Federal authorities here say that this government, these circumstances, probably have nothing to do with the matter. Schiller, they say, will be remanded to the Matoppo and turned over to British officials at Sta. Lucia, the vessel will stop for coal.

"Hands Up" Command Gets Captain

Matoppo sailed from New York yesterday for Vladivostok with its cargo consisting chiefly of barbed wire and farm implements. She [...] I Sandy Hook at 6 o'clock in the evening and two hours later, upon taking his cabin, Captain Bergner said he was confronted by a young man with a revolver in each hand.

"Hands up and not a sound if you your life," was the command directed him.

The captain was bound hand and locked in his cabin, promising under penalty of death, not to give an alarm. Then cautiously he his way to the wireless where the stowaway, who is about 26 old, put the instruments out commission, and threw the ship's consisting of six rifles, overboard.

He then returned to the captain cabin, rifled the safe and destroyed many important papers. He had expected, he told Captain Bergner, to find at least £2000 in the safe aboard the Matoppo, this his hopes were shattered, was not a penny in the safe, however, Schiller compelled the captain and the first officer to use their pocketbooks, containing a total of about £30.

Captain Bergner said a pistol his own cabin, Schiller proceeded to round up the crew of 56, but a few of whom were in their bunks. He lined all hands up the end of the ship and threatened everybody to pieces with he said he had placed in different parts of the vessel if anyone a move.

A Steamer Headed for Shore

o'clock this morning Schiller Captain Bergner and, still a revolver in each hand, the steamer headed 'toward Other officers and members crew were likewise ordered places and told to put on all coats. The Delaware Capes. When Matoppo came within sight of about noon, Schiller ordered a

(Continued on Page 8, Columns 1-2.)

Bones on Beach Denied Those of F. Lewis Clark

Skull and Arm Near Santa Barbara First Thought Millionaire's

(By Associated Press)

SANTA BARBARA, March 30.—Coroner A. M. Ruiz declared tonight there was no foundation for a story that has gone out from here to the effect that an arm and skull found near Naples might be that of F. Lewis Clark, the missing Spokane millionaire. Mr. Clark is believed to have committed suicide by leaping into the bay more than two years ago.

The bodies of persons drowned near here have been found to the south, that being the direction of the ocean current off this coast. The two bodies were found twelve miles from here, but these were mistaken.

The original rumor has been traced to the undertaker in whose charge the bones were placed, and he stated tonight he is now satisfied he was mistaken.

The skull and bones of a man were found today on the beach about twenty-five miles from Santa Barbara. Shortly after the find the rumor was spread that the bones were part of the skeleton of Clark.

Col. Harding Believes Canal Open April 15

(By Associated Press)

PANAMA, March 30.—Notwithstanding the official prediction by the War Department at Washington that the Panama Canal would be open for traffic on April 15, many shipping concerns are importing Lieutenant Colonel Harding, engineer of maintenance, with cablegrams asking for a positive statement whether the canal will be ready for reopening on that date. Colonel Harding invariably informs these inquirers that conditions in the Gaillard cut justify the prediction.

Eight $10,000 Air Craft Ordered by U.S.

WASHINGTON, March 30.—Eight new aeroplanes, higher powered and with greater plane surface than any heretofore used by the United States army, have been ordered by the War Department as a result of imperative demands by General Funston and General Pershing. Secretary of War Baker instructed General Scriven, chief signal officer, to purchase four Curtiss biplanes and four Sturtevant biplanes, each to cost about $10,000.

Bishop Glass Names New Salt Lake Vicar

(By International News Service)

SALT LAKE CITY, Utah, March 30.—The Right Rev. Joseph S. Glass, C. M. D., today announced the appointment of the Very Rev. F. M. Cushnahan of Ogden as vicar general of the Catholic diocese of Salt Lake. This is the first appointment which Bishop Glass has made since his installation last September.

Mr. Phone-Ad Says—

[ILLUSTRATION: "I'M ALWAYS IN STYLE"]

This is Dress-Up Week. The dress-up habit is a sign of prosperity. People that have it look prosperous, which is a sign that they use Examiner Want Ads. No matter what you have to advertise, the Examiner Want Ads will get you prosperity-bringing results. You can phone in your ads and have them charged.

Sunset, Main 5300, or Home 10195.

WED AGAIN HER NAME AND ROLE UNCHANGED

Mrs. Sarah Bixby Smith, Divorced Wife of Former Berkeley Pastor, Takes Second Husband Bearing Same Cognomen

Year From Day She Was Freed of First Marriage Bonds, Daughter of Long Beach Millionaire Is Led to Altar by New Spouse

Couple, in Book They Produced Together, Exalt 'Lie for Love' as 'Highest Truth;' Helpmeet of Other Days Indifferent

Just a year from the day she was granted a decree of divorce from her husband, a Unitarian minister, Mrs. Sarah Bixby Smith, daughter of the late Llewellyn Bixby, Long Beach millionaire, last night married a second husband, who is a Unitarian minister named Smith.

She married the second Dr. Smith last night at the home of her brother, Llewellyn Bixby, 1465 Ocean avenue, Long Beach. He is now pastor of the First Unitarian Church of Berkeley. The Rev. Mr. McReynolds of Berkeley performed the ceremony, and members of several branches of the Bixby family were present. The marriage license shows that Dr. Smith is 40 and Mrs. Smith, 42.

The repetition characterizing the matrimonial selection of Mrs. Smith ends with the name and the profession. The first husband was Dr. Arthur Maxon Smith. The second is Dr. Paul Jordan Smith. Mrs. Smith charged the first with infidelity, naming Miss Alice Giffin of this city. He was then pastor of the First Unitarian Church of Berkeley.

She married the second Dr. Smith last night at the home of her brother, Llewellyn Bixby, 1465 Ocean avenue, Long Beach. He is now pastor of the First Unitarian Church of Berkeley. The Rev. Mr. McReynolds of Berkeley performed the ceremony, and members of several branches of the Bixby family were present. The marriage license shows that Dr. Smith is 40 and Mrs. Smith, 42.

Dr. Smith will continue to the Mr. Smith and wife of the pastor of the Berkeley Unitarian Church. Her role as assistant to the minister will not be a new one, however; long before Mrs. Smith had become pastor of divorce the two had collaborated in the writing of "The Soul of Woman," a book containing much exalted philosophy. In it occurs this line:

"To lie for love is the highest truth." Dr. Smith proved that he could put this unconventional theory into practice by denying, about the time Mrs. Smith sued for divorce, that they were going to be married. Later, he calmly admitted that they were in love, and confirmed the announcement of Mrs. Smith that there would be a marriage. He explained that he had deceived in order to spare Mrs. Smith unnecessary grief.

Dr. Arthur Smith, who is living at the Bronx Apartments in this city, has declared his indifference to the fact that his former wife was to marry his successor in the Berkeley pulpit. Even before their separation he had informed Mrs. Smith she was "unresponsive," that their married life had been a disappointment and that he loved another. Thus although he was considered very "unreasonable" at the time of the divorce trial, and also the alleged relations of Smith and Miss Giffin.

Improper Relations With Girl Student Are Charged

Mrs. Smith's story, as related during the trial was that her husband, while professor of philosophy in Pomona College, had led Alice Giffin, a student, astray, and had continued relations with her after both had left the college.

Detectives testified that the two had registered at the Hayward Hotel, Los Angeles, and the Glenwood Inn, Riverside, also that they had taken an Eastern trip together.

Rev. Thomas Giffin of Fowler, Cal., and Leslie Giffin of Fresno, preferred charges against Smith with the church trustees in Berkeley, but the minister won over the board by declaring that a man named Benedetti had impersonated him. Miss Giffin, at her home on Irolo street, this city, denied the charge of improper relations. The court awarded Mrs. Smith custody of the five children. After a short honeymoon journey in Southern California, Dr. and Mrs. Paul Jordan Smith will return to Berkeley.

Mrs. Northam and Auto Racer Toft Tell of Wedding

Couple's Interest in Speed Contests Built Romance; to Enter Corona Event

Mutual interest in automobile racing led Mrs. Leotia K. Northam, widow of the late Colonel "Bob" Northam, and Omar Toft, mechanician and racing driver, to the altar yesterday afternoon. They were married by Rev. J. L. Myers at the Alhambra Apartments, and within fifteen minutes after the ceremony was performed they were arranging to enter an automobile in the Corona races. They will leave Los Angeles this morning and go to the racing camp, where the machines are being tried out.

The wedding yesterday did not come as a surprise to their close friends. Several weeks ago when Toft was injured in a tryout at Ascot Park, Mrs. Northam announced their engagement from his sick bed.

Mrs. Northam, since the death of her husband, who left her a fortune, figured in the sensational disappearance of a large amount of diamonds which were the property of Mrs. Clara Baldwin Stocker. After it had been published that Mrs. Northam had taken the jewels, she made a sensational statement in which she protested her innocence and accused a man who was known to both Mr. and Mrs. Stocker.

Formal Turk Peace Plea Is Reported

(L. A. EXAMINER AND LONDON DAILY TELEGRAPH EXCLUSIVE WAR SERVICE)

PETROGRAD, March 30.—During the last few days the Turkish government, through the Vali of Smyrna and the Sultan's representatives in neutral States, has tried to induce Great Britain to enter into informal negotiation with a view to arranging terms of peace.

The answer was immediate and decisive. The British government refused to have anything to do with such a proposal.

Britain's view is that of her allies. With the Russians mastering the Turkish armies and with disaffection widespread throughout the Sultan's empire, a collapse of Turkish resistance is thought to be inevitable.

Yuan Shi Kai Will Resign, Says Report

(BY INTERNATIONAL NEWS SERVICE SPECIAL CABLE)

LONDON, March 30.—A Reuter dispatch from Tokio says that the resignation of Yuan Shi Kai is regarded as imminent.

"Li Yuan Hung, it is said, is regarded as the most probable successor to the presidency.

Gen. Li Yuan Hung was one of the leaders of the 1912 revolution, which established the republic. He was elected Vice President of the new Yuan Shi Kai government. On September 5, 1915, he resigned.

While Vice President he was known as a "prisoner." He was never allowed to leave the Forbidden City without a guard, to prevent his flight.

Bopp and Aides Must Face Trial

(By Associated Press)

SAN FRANCISCO, March 30.—Judge Maurice T. Dooling overruled today demurrers to the bomb plot indictments against Franz Bopp, German consul general; Baron E. H. von Schack, vice consul; Baron George Wilhelm von Brincken, of the German army, identified with the consulate, and four others. The ruling means that all will have to go to trial.

Posses Search Hills for Trace of Robber

There are but two roads leading out of Nordhoff, one to Santa Paula and one to Ventura, and one line of single track railway, with one train a day. All these routes the belief that the thief was alone, on foot, and has escaped to the hills, where he probably has a cache of food and water. Posses are beating the bush and searching the hills.

The thief was evidently familiar with the customs of the bank and of the town, which is very quiet during the noon hour, and came prepared. It is remembered by some who were at the station when the only train of the day came in at 11:40 that two strangers alighted. One of these was arrested and gave a satisfactory account of himself. The other in some respects answered the description of the thief, but had no beard. There are many tourists in the Nordhoff valley, so strangers cause less comment than in many small towns.

POSSES HUNT FOR DARING BANK BANDIT AT NORDHOFF

Hills Are Searched for Man Who Held Up Miss Mabel R. Eisenberg in Ojai State Institution and Escaped With About $3000

Assistant Cashier Is Driven Into Vault and Her Face Covered by Armed Robber; Woman Believes Beard He Wore Was False

VENTURA, March 30.—Posses are searching the hills in an effort to capture the bandit who held up and robbed the Ojai State Bank of Nordhoff of nearly $3000, shortly after noon today. Miss Mabel R. Eisenberg, the bank's assistant cashier, was alone in the bank when the bandit appeared; E. L. Weist, the cashier, being at lunch.

About 12:15, while serving a customer at the window, Miss Eisenberg noted a bearded man peering in through a window for a moment, but thought nothing of it, believing he wanted to see the cashier. Ten minutes later, while working with her back to the door, she was confronted by the man, who at the point of a revolver forced her to go into the vault, where with a piece of cloth, tied at each end with string, he covered her head and face and ordered her to remain for five minutes.

"After counting five hundred 'very slowly,'" said Miss Eisenberg, "because he had the money anyway and there was not any use of my taking chances." Miss Eisenberg called Cashier Weist on the phone and an alarm was immediately turned in to the sheriff's office here. The thief told Miss Eisenberg that he had a machine and two confederates, who would "fix her" if she made any fuss.

Girl Counts Five Hundred and Then Summons Help

He was about five feet eleven inches tall, rather spare, had large blue eyes and a heavy beard and mustache, according to the assistant cashier, "looked as if they would come off if I gave them a pull, they didn't belong on his face." He was tanned, but not as dark as a Mexican or Spaniard, and wore a long tan or gray ulster, and an inconspicuous hat of some soft material.

The bank is set back from the street about 40 feet, with dense live oak trees on each side, and an outcry, had Miss Eisenberg made one, ordinarily would not have been heard on the street. The location of the bank also explains why citizens did not see the man. He could easily have slipped in through a side entrance.

Intimate Views of Mexico

Negro Troops Amaze Natives

Runyon Depicts Camp Life

'More Rivers, Less Water; Longer Vistas, Less to See Than Anywhere Else'

By Damon Runyon

Staff Correspondent of the International News Service

WITH U. S. ARMY HEADQUARTERS IN THE FIELD, IN MEXICO, March 25.—(Via Motor to Columbus, N. M., March 30.)—Ambition is where you find it. Let us tell you the story of "Dutch," the teamster with the headquarters wagon train of the punitive expedition.

He has another name, no doubt, but no one ever hears it. To all who know him he is "Dutch"—a short, bandy-legged fellow, with an engaging smile, which is just at present somewhat concealed by a black, brigandish stubble of beard.

This beard looks like a section of the State of Chihuahua after the American soldiers have burned off some of the sacaton grass to make room for their camp.

"Dutch" has his head closely cropped, which is the tonsorial fashion of both officers and enlisted men with the expedition. There is a good reason for the convict hair-cut. It is to prevent the acquisition of the typhus-toting bugs. Typhus is said to be prevalent in some parts of Mexico, and while it has not been encountered by the soldiers, they are taking no chances.

Mules That Have Personality

"Dutch" swings a blacksnake over the backs of four as sorrowful looking mules as you could find in the United States army, or in the State of Missouri. To the casual eye they look very much like any other mules, but to "Dutch" they are wholly different. It seems that each of "Dutch's" mules has an individual personality. Each mule is "Dutch's" friend and pal.

As "Dutch's" mules look like any other mules, so, too, does "Dutch" look like any other army teamster when he is mounted at the forefront of his wagon, speaking in the singular language of the man who knows mules. This language can be expressed in print only in blank spaces, and interrogation points.

Yet within the bosom of "Dutch" burns a great ambition. He wants to bring Rip, Nell, Paddy and Mack, which are his mules, through this trip safe and sound. It is a larger task than may appear. Mules are but flesh and blood. Heat and dust and the exertion of dragging a load of 4500 pounds over the dry stretches of Mexico is mighty wearying work. But "Dutch" is determined to return his longeared four-in-hand to the United States just as he took them out.

American Flag Unfurled

He has succeeded so far. He has nursed three over a hundred miles of Mexican territory, and tonight they are as hale and hearty as ever, and can bite into a bale of hay, or a man's leg, with amazing vigor. On the last jump, however, one of them—maybe it was Nell, and maybe it was Mack, they all look alike—seemed to be failing somewhat. Big tears were in "Dutch's" eyes as he nursed her along slowly over the bumps, gently over the rough ruts, and so safe into camp.

"Look at them now!" he said, proudly. "I'll give you $10 if you find a pimple on their backs. I'll get 'em through all right, you can bet on that."

Sellers Minus Change

He denies now that he felt bad about the ailing mule; he scoffs the idea of a man's having any sympathy for a mule, but those who watched him coming down the long, white road saw the tears, and saw, too, when he swabbed the black muzzles of the mournful-looking creatures with water from his own canteen.

During the morning the Germans attempted counter attacks against the positions won by the French, with the especial object of recapturing the strong redoubt near the southeastern edge of the forest. All these attacks failed, Paris states, especially heavy losses being inflicted by French fire from the redoubt.

The American flag is flying over the camp where this is written, probably for the first time since the columns entered Mexico. Nearly all the regiments brought their colors and regimental standards, but they were carried cased on the march. Some of the cavalry outfits had their guidons fluttering as they marched, but the Stars and Stripes were not displayed until they were unfurled to the winds from the mountains of Mexico in this camp. They are flying over the camps of several organizations, and over the hospital tent, side by side with the crimson barred flag of the Red Cross. It is a gracious bit of coloring against the dusty skyline.

Today parties of Mexicans came into camp on commercial bent. Some of them carried...

GERMANS FAIL IN DUAL DASH AT DOUAUMONT

Attempts With Liquid Fire to Debouch From Fort Repulsed; Seven Aeros Felled

(BY INTERNATIONAL NEWS SERVICE SPECIAL CABLE)

LONDON, March 30.—Fighting north of Verdun today switched to the east bank of the Meuse where despite strong artillery preparation and the use of flaming liquids the Germans were twice repulsed in efforts to debouch from Fort Douaumont.

During the day seven German aeroplanes were shot down, five in the Verdun region, one in Champagne and one in the Somme district.

According to the Paris midnight statement the Crown Prince during the day made no effort to follow up his successes on the Malancourt sector. Instead the Germans were kept busy meeting French attacks in the Avocourt woods. Berlin reports that in these attacks, made with the object of extending the gains of the previous night, were repulsed.

During the morning the Germans attempted counter attacks against the positions won by the French, with the especial object of recapturing the strong redoubt near the southeastern edge of the forest. All these attacks failed, Paris states, especially heavy losses being inflicted by French fire from the redoubt.

"Piles of dead bodies," according to the Paris report, were left in front of the field fort.

An intense artillery fire is being directed against the French positions in the village of Malancourt and along contiguous lines, apparently in preparation for renewed infantry attacks.

The attempts of the Germans to advance south of Fort Douaumont were made in great strength, advices from Paris say. The first attack was launched during the morning hours, only to be broken up by the infantry and barrier fire of the French. On the same front in the afternoon the Germans again tried to break forward only to meet a similar fate.

OUTLAW IS REPORTED WOUNDED, IN FLIGHT

Declared to Have Executed All Mexican Soldiers at Guerrero, in Advices Reaching General Funston's Headquarters

Message to Gavira from Madera Asserts Bandit Chief Shot in the Leg in Skirmish With De Facto Government Troops

Villa Battles Carranzistas

Bandit Said to Be in Trap

BY DAMON RUNYON

Staff Correspondent of the International News Service

U. S. ARMY HEADQUARTERS IN MEXICO, March 29, by army radio to Columbus, N. M., March 30.—Sounds from advanced points bring the report of another engagement between Villa and Carranza forces.

Villa is now said to be in a trap.

The fight indicates that the Carranzistas are fully co-operating with the American army.

Two miles of motor trucks with the "empties" arrived here from the front today.

(By International News Service)

EL PASO, March 30.—(Bulletin.)—Francisco Villa captured and executed the Carranza garrison at Guerrero, consisting of 172 men, some time during the last seventy-two hours.

This report was received at General Funston's headquarters in San Antonio tonight and is partly confirmed by State Department representatives here. The information received officially in El Paso merely tells that the Guerrero garrison was captured. Nothing is known of the fate of the Carranzistas.

Tonight Villa is reported to be at Rancho Geronimo. This is about thirty miles northeast of Guerrero, near the head waters of the Santa Maria River.

Several detachments of United States troops, believed to be under Colonel Dodd's command, are within thirty miles of the place where Villa is located.

Further evidences of Villa's activities in the Guerrero district were received late tonight in a telegram via Chihuahua City. It said Herman Blankenberg, a German subject, and two other foreigners were murdered at Minaca yesterday.

Blankenberg left El Paso only a few weeks ago to look after the mining interests of his employers.

Villa Reported Wounded; Barely Able to Ride

By H. H. Stansbury

(By International News Service)

EL PASO, March 30.—In the news from Mexico and along the border today these facts stand out:

Gen. Gabriel Gavira, the Carranza commander, received a telegram from General Bertani, at Madera, that Francisco Villa was wounded in the leg near Guerrero in a skirmish with Carranzistas Wednesday afternoon.

Mexican Consul Andres Garcia and...

LOS ANGELES IS THE LARGEST CITY ON THE PACIFIC COAST

THE WEATHER
For Los Angeles and vicinity: Cloudy Monday. Yesterday's temperature: High, 66.

MORNING TRIBUNE

INDEPENDENT PROGRESSIVE LOS ANGELES PIONEER PENNY MORNING DAILY

TO SUBSCRIBERS
Daily and Sunday Tribune, including Rural World, 45 cents per month by carrier. By mail, $5.50 per year.

VOLUME VI NO. 287 FOURTEEN PAGES ** MONDAY MORNING APRIL 16 1917 ONE CENT In Los Angeles and Suburbs 5 Cents Elsewhere Hotels, Trains 5 Cents By Carrier 45 Cts. Per M

WILSON CALLS WHOLE NATION TO WAR SERVIC

PLAN CAMP IN SOUTH FOR 'SPY' SUSPECTS

overnment Agents Seize Three Germans Aboard Ship Outward Bound; 'Cleanup' of 250 in L. A. Is Hinted

Developments followed fast yester-ay in the alien enemy situation in os Angeles. Three suspects were rrested by immigration inspectors San Pedro as they were trying to scape from the United States. Fed-al agents in Los Angeles admitted 0 suspects were under investigation them. The government, it became own, has completed plans for an ien interning camp near San Diego. Acute as the situation evidently is, deral officers in Los Angeles are waiting word to launch a wholesale mpaign to jail all men suspected of ing enemies of the United States. is thought the order will be gen-al for all Southern California, and e men arrested will be detained in e proposed interning camp at La laya, Point Loma.

Need of Camp Told

Several men under suspicion for al-ged efforts against the nation have en placed under arrest in Los An-eles. Twenty are held in San Diego. ther cities in the Southland also old suspects. Hence the necessity r the camp for interned foreigners. is pointed out by Los Angeles of-cers that it is impractical as well as pensive to send all men arrested to e Presidio at San Francisco.

The three men arrested at Los An-eles harbor all are Germans who ave been in the United States only short time. They said they are: einrick Mooler, twenty, a sailor; Joe lein, twenty-one, a seafaring en-neer, and E. Geisendorser, a sailor. They were taken from the steam-ip Sinaloa as it was clearing from e harbor bound for Chilean ports. mmigration inspectors, acting upon formation the source or nature of hich they did not make public, oarded the boat from a launch and rrested the three Germans.

They were booked at the San Pedro olice station on suspicion. They will transferred today to the county il at Los Angeles.

Twenty Held in South

The twenty men held at San Diego e charged with conspiring to dam-e defense works and manufacturing ants. Most of them are reported prisoned at Fort Rosecrans. Of-cials at the fort refused to discuss nditions attendant upon the intern-g of military prisoners.

It is understood, if the expected eanup in Los Angeles materializes, e prisoners will be hurried to Fort osecrans for trial and later confined the interning camp on Point Loma.

Lifting the government veil of crecy, investigation at San Diego s revealed plots to destroy the orth island aviation plant, the Her-les powder plant, the dye factory

[CONTINUED ON PAGE 4, COLUMN 2]

¶ It matters not what may be your needs, an Express and Tribune Want-ad is equal to the task of getting them quickly for you. Somebody somewhere in Los Angeles wants what you have to offer or else has to offer what you want. Express and Tribune Want-ad pages are a medium for business introductions.

BROTHER OF JOHN D. DIES IN OHIO

Frank Rockefeller, Estranged With Oil Magnate Since 1898, Expires; Bitter Feeling Long Marked His Life

[By Tribune Leased Wire]

CLEVLAND, O., April 15.—Frank Rockefeller, brother of John D., died at his apartment in the Hollenden hotel here this morning. Death followed an operation performed several months ago.

Mrs. Rockefeller and daughters, Mrs. W. F. Nash, Mrs. Walter S. Bowler and Miss Alice Rockefeller, were at the bedside when the end came.

Frank Rockefeller's life was marked by bitter feeling for his multi-millionaire brother. From the beginning of an estrangement in 1898 over money matters until the end he refused to entertain a charitable attitude toward John D.

"There's not the slightest possibility of a reconciliation," he said no later than last September. "I said I'm through in 1898 and I mean it. I'm through."

Frank Rockefeller was a younger brother of John D. and William A., and was for many years associated with them in the oil business.

Helped Start Company

He was born in Richford, N. Y., in 1845, and when his brothers organized the Standard Oil company he beacme identified with them, serving for a time as one of the vice presidents. He acquired considerable wealth, but his relations with his brothers became strained and he severed business connections with them.

In 1900 he turned his attention to stock raising, purchasing 12,000 acres at Belvedere, Kan., for a stock farm.

Attired as a farm hand he was the active "boss"of his ranch, and when fences were to be repaired, ditches dug or other heavy work done he did his part. Some of the purest bred cattle in the world were to be found on his Kansas farm, and he also directed range interests in Texas and Arizona.

Frank Rockefeller always manifested aversion to being referred to as "John D. Rockefeller's brother" or "the other Rockefeller."

"I am Frank Rockefeller, stockman," he would say, "not Frank Rockefeller, a brother of John D."

He studiously avoided newspaper publicity.

Fond of Horses

Although fond of horse trotting as a sport he confined his indulgence in it to his own track, on his own place, with his own horses.

"Next to my family," he remarked, "I love animals more than anything else in the world, and by simply having fun with them I have found out a good many things and learned a good many lessons that I could never have learned otherwise."

One of his desires was to prevent the disappearance of the buffalo. He presented many wild beasts and birds to the zoological gardens in Cleveland and to other cities.

During five months in the year Mr. Rockefeller lived in Cleveland, as did his brother, John D., but they were never seen together.

Chicago Priest Urges Young Men to Enlist

[By Tribune Leased Wire]

CHICAGO, April 15.—The Rev. John L. O'Donnell, pastor of St. Patrick's Catholic church, became an enlisting officer today. Before services he circulated among the young men of his congregation and urged them to enlist. His sermon was a patriotic appeal for every man able to carry arms to join the colors. He declared it to be the duty of every Catholic to serve the country.

Here Is Text of the President's Appeal to All in America to Do Their Part

MY Fellow Countrymen: The entrance of our own beloved country into the grim and terrible war for democracy and human rights which has shaken the world creates so many problems of national life and action which call for immediate consideration and settlement that I hope it will permit me to address to you a few words of earnest counsel and appeal with regard to them.

We are rapidly putting our navy upon an effective war footing and are about to create and equip a great army, but these are the simplest parts of the great task to which we have addressed ourselves. There is not a single selfish element, so far as I can see, in the cause we are fighting for.

Fighting for Rights of Mankind

We are fighting for what we believe and wish to be the rights of mankind and for the future peace and security of the world. To do this great thing worthily and successfully we must devote ourselves to the service without regard to profit or material advantage, and with an energy and intelligence that will rise to the level of the enterprise itself. We must realize to the fullest how great the task is, and how many things, how many kinds and elements of capacity and service and self-sacrifice it involves.

These, then, are the things we must do, and do well, besides fighting, do the things without which mere fighting would be fruitless:

We Must Supply Abundant Food

We must supply abundant food for our armies and our seamen not only, but also for a large part of the nations with whom we have now made common cause, in whose support and beside whose sides we shall be fighting.

We must supply ships by the hundreds out of our shipyards to carry to the other side of the sea, submarines or no submarines, what will every day be needed there, and abundant materials out of our fields and our mines and our factories, with which not only to clothe and equip our own forces on land and sea, but also to clothe and support our people for whom the gallant fellows under arms can no longer work, to help clothe and equip the armies with which we are co-operating in Europe, and to keep the looms and manufactories there in raw material.

Materials of All Kinds Needed for Allies

Coal to keep the fires going in ships at sea and in the furnaces of hundreds of factories across the sea; steel out of which to make arms and ammunition, both here and there; rails for worn-out railways back of the fighting fronts; locomotives and rolling stock to take the places of those every day going to pieces; mules, horses, cattle for labor and for military service; everything with which the people of England, France, Italy and Russia have usually supplied themselves, but cannot now afford the men, the materials or machinery to make.

Industries Must Be More Efficient

It is evident to every thinking man that our industries, on the farms, in the shipyards, in the mines, in the factories, must be made more prolific and more efficient than ever, and that they must be more economically managed and better adapted to the particular requirements of our task than they have been; and what I want to say is that the men and the women who devote their thought and their energy to these things will be serving the country and conducting the fight for peace and freedom just as truly and just as effectively as the men on the battlefields or in the trenches.

Industrial Forces to Be Great Army

The industrial forces of the country, men and women alike, will be a great national, a great international, service army—a notable and honored host engaged in the service of the nation and the world and the efficient friends and saviours of free men everywhere. Thousands, nay, hundreds of thousands of men, otherwise liable to military service, will of right and of necessity be excused from that service and assigned to the fundamental sustaining work of the fields and factories and mines, and they will be as much part of the great patriotic forces of the nation as the men under fire.

Supreme Need Now Is Foodstuffs

I take the liberty, therefore, of addressing this word to the farmers of the country, and to all who work on the farms: The supreme need of our own nation and of the nations with which we are cooperating is an abundance of supplies, and especialy of foodstuffs. The importance of an adequate food supply, especially for the present year, is superlative. Without abundant food, alike for the armies and the peoples now at war, the whole great enterprise upon which we have embarked will break down and fail.

The world's food reserves are low. Not only during the present emergency, but for some time after peace shall have come both our own people and a large proportion of the people of Europe must rely upon the harvests in America.

Fate of Nations Up to Farmers

Upon the farmers of this country, therefore, in large measure rests the fate of the war and the fate of the nations. May the nation not count upon them to omit no step that will increase the production of their land or that will bring about the most effectual cooperation in the sale and distribution of their products? The time is short. It is of the utmost importance that everything possible be done and done immediately to make sure of large harvests. I call upon young men and old alike and upon the able-bodied boys of the land to accept and act upon this duty—to turn in hosts to the farms and make certain that no pains and no labor is lacking in this great matter.

Appeals to South to Plant Foodstuffs

I particularly appeal to the farmers of the south to plant abundant foodstuffs as well as cotton. They can show their patriotism in no better or more convincing way than by resisting the great temptation of the present price of cotton and helping, helping upon a great scale, to feed the nation and the peoples everywhere who are fighting for their liberties and for our own. The variety of their crops will be the visible measure of their comprehension of their national duty.

The government of the United States and the governments of the several states stand ready to cooperate.

Government Ready to Expedite Work

They will do everything possible to assist farmers in securing an adequate supply of seed, an adequate force of laborers when they are most needed, at harvest time, and the means of expediting shipments of fertilizers and farm machinery, as well as of the crops themselves when harvested. The course of trade shall be as unhampered as it is possible to make it, and there shall be no unwarranted manipulation of the nation's food supply by those who handle it on its way to the consumer. This is our opportunity to demonstrate the efficiency of a great democracy, and we shall not fall short of it!

Service Expected of All Middlemen

This, let me say to the middlemen of every sort, whether they are handling our foodstuffs or our raw materials of manufacture or the products of our mills and factories: The eyes of the country will be especially upon you. This is your opportunity for signal service, efficient and disinterested. The country expects you, as it expects all others, to forego unusual profits; to organize and expedite shipments, supplies of every kind, but especially of food, with an eye to the service you are rendering and in the spirit of those who enlist in the ranks, for their people, not for themselves. I shall confidently expect you to deserve and win the confidence of people of every sort and station.

Speed Activities in Transportation

To the men who run the railways of the country, whether they be managers or operative employes, let me say that the railways are the arteries of the nation's life, and that upon them rests the immense responsibility of seeing to it that these arteries suffer no obstruction of any kind, no inefficiency or slackened power.

To the merchant let me suggest the motto, "Small profits and quick service"; and to the shipbuilder the thought that the life of the war depends upon him. The food and the war supplies must be carried across the seas, no matter how many ships are sent to the bottom. The places of those that go down must be supplied and supplied at once.

Work of World Also Waits on Miners

To the miner let me say that he stands where the farmer does: The work of the world waits on him. If he slacks or fails, armies and statesmen are helpless. He also is enlisted in the great service army. The manufacturer does not need to be told, I hope, that the nation looks to him to speed and perfect every process; and I want only to remind his employes that their service is absolutely indispensable and is counted on by every man who loves the country and its liberties.

Let me suggest, also, that everyone who creates or cultivates a garden helps, and helps greatly, to solve the problem of the feeding of the nations; and that every housewife who practices strict economy puts herself in the ranks of those who serve the nation.

Time to Correct Extravagance

This is the time for America to correct her unpardonable fault of wastefulness and extravagance. Let every man and every woman assume the duty of careful, provident use and expenditure as a public duty, as a dictate of patriotism, which no one can now expect ever to be excused or forgiven for ignoring.

In the hope that this statement of the needs of the nation and of the world in this hour of supreme crisis may stimulate those to whom it comes, and remind all who need such a reminder of the solemn duties of a time such as the world has never seen before, I beg that all editors and publishers everywhere will give as prominent publication and as wide circulation as possible to this appeal.

Supreme Test Here, Act Together

I venture to suggest, also, to all advertising agencies that they would perhaps render a very substantial and timely service to the country if they would give it widespread repetition. And I hope that clergymen will not think the theme of it an unworthy or inappropriate subject of comment and homily from their pulpits.

The supreme test of the nation has come. We must all speak, act and serve together!

WOODROW WILSON.

BRITISH ARE STORMING DEFENSES OF LENS

Battle Declared to Be Costliest of War in Number of Lives Believed Ended as Great Allied 'Jaws' Close In

BULLETIN

[By Cable to The Tribune]

BRITISH HEADQUARTERS IN FRANCE (via London), April 15.—The civil population of Lens evacuated Friday. The Germans then seized three months' rations gathered in Lens by the American relief commission.

[By Cable to the Tribune]

LONDON, April 15.—So irresistible seemed the onrush of the Canadians as early this morning they resumed their great "nutcracker" drive against Lens, that early this afternoon word was flashed broadcast that the great French coal mining center had fallen.

In the initial sweep of the new assaults, launched shortly after dawn amidst a heavy downpour of rain, the Canadians captured the Teuton defenses east of Lievin from Riaumont wood to the eastern corner of Cite de Pierre, both of which are close to the outskirts of the city.

News Is Flashed

When a column of patrols was seen shooting across the blood-soaked approaches of Lens, actually reaching the city lines, correspondents at the front telegraphed the "news" of its "capture."

But in the eleventh hour, it developed later in the day, Hindenburg had managed to hurl sufficient reserves into the gaps on the Lens front to stem the British advance, for the time being at least.

Actual capture is believed to be only delayed, for in the course of the afternoon the British pushed steadily forward east of Lievin, and tonight they were "approaching the outskirts of Lens," the bulletin from headquarters announced.

Third Time Prize

Thus for the third time in the war Lens is the prize of a battle transcending in fury and in cost of life anything previously seen. Each time the entente attackers were halted as they were within the very shadow of the city's walls. In 1915, when General Foch led the French in the battle of Artois, his army lost 100,000 in killed and wounded. Later the British, in trying to take it from the north, lost 66,000 during the battle of Loos. But in both those battles Vimy ridge stood a firm bulwark to the allies' onslaughts. Today Vimy ridge is in British hands and wide gaps have been cut into the Teuton defense lines.

Slaughter for Teutons

Moreover in the battle now raging, all dispatches from the front, official and unofficial, agree that where there previously was blood in rivers on the entente side, it is now floating in torrents on the Teuton side.

The same is true, according to the British night report, of the gigantic battle under way to the south, on the front astride the Bapaume-Cambrai road.

Here on a six-mile front the Germans early this morning opened up a terrific counter drive. It was stifled in the British barrage and machine gun fire.

"In addition to 300 prisoners captured," says the British night statement, "1500 dead Germans were left in front of our positions."

Further Gains Made

The earlier statement said that only at one point, Lagnicourt, had the Germans succeeded in gaining a temporary grip upon British trench sectors. They were thrown back by a vigorous counter attack.

To the northwest of St. Quentin the British captured today further

[CONTINUED ON PAGE 8, COLUMN 1]

U. S. FACE SUPREM TEST; ACT IS PLEA

Speed Up All Industries crease Food, Small P and Quick Results, to Bring Victory and F

[By Tribune Leased Wire]

WASHINGTON, April The whole nation was upon for war servic formal proclamation tonight by President Wilson.

Declaring that "mere fightin be fruitless," the president de ed the active support and co tion of men and women in walk of life—"a great intern service army."

From the farmer to the hou each individual was called u do his or her share in com and making available for w the vast resources of the nat

"The supreme test of the has come," said the president must all speak, act and se gether."

The president declared tha the navy is rapidly being pla an effective war footing and army is about to be create equipped, "these are the s parts of the great task to wh have addressed ourselves."

Must Supply Food

He declared that the first thing to be done was to abundant food, and not only United States and its fighting but for a large part of "the with whom we have now mad mon cause."

The imperative need for Ar ships was emphasized by the dent, who declared that the be built by the hundreds to vast quantities of supplies acr sea, "submarines or no subm They must, he declared, carry people of England and Fran Italy and Russia the thing which "they have usually s themselves, but cannot now the men, the materials or t chinery to make."

Greater Production

"It is evident to every man," said the proclamation our industries, on the farms shipyards, in the factories, made more prolific and more than ever, and that they economically managed and adapted to the particular ments of our task than th been; and what I want to say the men and women who dev thought and their energy t things will be serving the and conducting the fight fo and freedom just as truly as effectively as the men on tlefield or in the trenches. dustrial forces of the count and women alike, will be a g tional, a great international army—notable and honored gaged in the service of the and the world."

Call Made to Farmers

The president called on th ers of the nation for an in increase in the production stuffs, asserting that "upon th ers of this country in large rests the fate of the war, and of the nation." He urged yo old alike to turn to the far appealed particularly to the of the south to plant abund crops as well as cotton.

The proclamation pledged operation of the governmen United States and the seve governments in the campa service. It declared that the assist the farmer to get adeq plies and fertilizers. The declared that the governme see to it that there was no m tion of the nation's food su that trade would continue hampered as possible."

The middlemen of the nat

SINK LINER ON WAY TO U. S.

ONE CENT
CITY AND COUNTY

LOS ANGELES
EVENING HERALD
AN INDEPENDENT NEWSPAPER
Reg. U. S. Pat. Off. The Evening Herald Grows Just Like Los Angeles.

BASEBALL EDITION

VOL. XLII. ONE CENT In Los Angeles City and County Elsewhere Two Cents Hotels and Trains Five Cents FRIDAY, JUNE 8, 1917 ONE CENT In Los Angeles City and County Elsewhere Two Cents Hotels and Trains Five Cents NO. 188

ROLL HINDENBURG BACK

Persining in England on Way to Front

EDSKINS ON MOUND IN THIRD OF SERIES

on Leader Sends Chief nson to Firing Line; Smith Opposes Tiger Team

.S—	TIGERS—
vo, rf.	Daley, lf.
k, 3b.	Snodgrass, cf.
sel, cf.	Hunter, ss.
aller, lf.	Griggs, 1b.
rner, 1b.	Galloway, 3b.
lywood, 2b.	Doane, rf.
han, ss.	Callahan, 2b.
Kee, c.	Simon, c.
th, p.	Johnson, p.

ef George Johnson and "Indian" Smith, members of the Vernon an Francisco tribes respectively, ed in a baseball battle on the ngton park diamond this after-

verton claims that Johnson has d time finishing a game against eals, while Stovall said that was forced to leave the box st time he tried to tame the

air-sized crowd was out to the n the hope of seeing the veneer ilization rubbed off the "red- and an old-fashioned tommy- ng result.

y Downs is troubled with the . in addition to an attack of y.

rge Stovall says that his infield nation, with Callahan at second Hunter on short, will be better ager they play together.

Guthrie and Ed Finney umpired.

vall to Stick, Declares His Boss

aring that George Stovall has wonders with the team, Tom dy, president of the Vernon today denied the report that rebrand" was to be deposed. ory emanated from San Fran-

vall has done wonderful work is team," said Darmody. "He onscientious worker, the kind anager we need in the Coast

Snodgrass, who was men- as Stovall's successor, said was the first he had heard he matter and that he consid- a joke.

all deserves great credit for e has done," said Snodgrass. is nothing to the report."

verton Has Eye on New Twirler

pitchers were offered to Har- verton in the past two days nagers of ball clubs in the ut not one has come up to uirements of the Seals' leader. e my eye on one pitcher who ke us a good man and I will n unless the directors decide down to a 16-player limit," olverton.

Big Golf Tourney At San Gabriel to Aid Red Cross

A big Red Cross golf tournament will be held June 30 on the links of the San Gabriel Country club, according to an announcement made today by George Cline, Captain Wharton and J. M. Kerr of the Greens committee.

It will be an open invitation tourney. All other tourneys have been closed to professional players.

The professionals are to play from scratch and the amateurs will be given handicaps.

A tennis tourney and a two-ball mixed foursome golf tourney will be played at the San Gabriel club, July 7.

Entries for the golf tourney will be received by Mrs. C. A. Perley and the tennis entries by Mrs. Shoemaker.

Catalina Fishing Better Than Ever

Yellowtail and barracuda are being caught in large numbers in the waters around Catalina island, according to a report received here today from George E. Daul.

One day's catch consisted of fourteen yellowtail, nine white sea bass, 250 barracuda, one black sea bass, sixty mackerel and many rock bass.

Practically every fisherman landed a big mess of fish.

COUNTRY CLUB GOLFERS TO PLAY FOR TITLE JUNE 17

Golfers of the Los Angeles Country club will gather June 17 to play for the championship of that club, according to the announcement made today by Edward B. Tufts, president of the Southern California Golf association. Norman McBeth, president of the Southern California Golf association. Norman McBeth, Armstrong, Frederickson and Cash are looked upon as the favorites for the club title.

Italy Denies Loss of 27,000 Soldiers

By International News Service

WASHINGTON, June 8.—Official denial was received at the Italian embassy of the claims of the Austrian war office that 27,000 Italians have been captured since May 12.

LAPAN ON SHORT VISIT

Pete Lapan, the catcher for the Angels who was left at home by the Angels when the club went north, has been granted leave of absence for a few days to visit friends at Patton.

DARMODY BACK FROM MAGNATES' MEETING

Tom Darmody, owner of the Vernon Tigers, returned home today from the meeting of the Pacific Coast league directors at San Francisco, bringing with him the report that nothing had been officially decided at the meeting in regard to changes.

"The belief in major league baseball circles is that baseball will not be taxed," said Darmody. "If our gate receipts are assessed 10 per cent we might as well close the gates of the park.

"The directors agreed that the proposition of cutting down players should be left to the various managers."

It is understood that there will be no penalty for the violation of the "Four Busher Rule," although that rule was not abolished.

UNCLE SAM'S AVIATORS ON FIRING LINE

Yankee Flyers to Join Allies in Drive on Hindenburg

WASHINGTON, June 8.—The first regular American fighting force was today on French soil. It comprised 100 expert and prospective naval aviators who are to co-operate with the French navy in meeting the submarine peril of the French coast and also to aid the badly pressed American aviation section on the western battle front.

These experts are all officers in the United States navy. They landed at a French port today and will proceed to get into active service immediately.

The expert aviators include among others Lieut. Grattan of Richmond and Lieut. Kenneth Whiting and Lieutenants, junior grade, Godfrey De Chavellere and Virgil C. Griffin as well as others who already have made their mark in the United States aviation service.

NEW MAJOR GENERALS

The names of the officers who will command the three grand divisions of General Pershing's expeditionary forces on the western battle line in France were made known by President Wilson today when he sent the nominations of the three brigadier generals of the army to be major generals to the senate committee. They are General Morrison, General William L. Sibert, General Charles G. Morton.

Morrison has seen service in Cuba and the Philippines and was military attache with the Japanese army during the Russo-Japanese war in 1914. He was later senior instructor in the army war college. Morrison was born in Charlottesville, N. Y., Christmas day, 1857. He entered the service of the army at 21 years of age.

The nominations were accompanied by the nomination of Captain Hugh Rodman of the navy to be a rear admiral.

Those who will hold other commands in the expeditionary force were nominated to be brigadier generals of the army by the President. They are:

Col. Edward F. Glenn, Col. John Biddle, Col. Henry C. Hodges, Jr., Col. Adelbert Crenkhite, Col. William Sage, Col. Omar Bundy, Col. Richard M. Blatchford, Col. David G. Shanks, Col. Robert L. Bullard, Col. Augustus C. Blocks, Col. George T. Brittlet, Col. Joseph T. Dickinson, Col. Henry T. Allen, Col. Charles W. Kennedy, Col. Harry Hale, Col. Samuel D. Sturgis, Col. William M. Wright, Col. Peyton C. March.

NAVAL PROMOTIONS

The following commanders of the navy were nominated to be captains: Harley C. Christy, Waldo Evans, Charles S. Preston, Noble Irwin, Thomas J. Senn, Richard H. Leigh.

Immediate confirmation of the nominations by the senate is expected

(CONTINUED ON PAGE FIVE)

YANKEE ARMY HEAD READY TO BATTLE

British War and Civic Officials Join in Ovation to American Leader

WASHINGTON, June 8.—"Black Jack" Pershing, commander-in-chief of the American army in the field, is "on the job" in Europe.

He landed at a British port today, accompanied by his entire staff.

With his arrival in England actual participation by America in the land fighting of the war against Germany began.

From this time forward American units will be sent to the battle lines as soon as they can be perfected in the deadly art of war.

The trip overseas of Gen. Pershing and his staff was uneventful. No German submarines were sighted.

Dispatches received by the war department, which officially confirms news of the arrival, give full details of the ceremonies.

ESCORTED BY DESTROYERS

General Pershing's ship was escorted through the danger zone by three United States destroyers.

The American commander was officially welcomed to battle-torn Europe by Rear Admiral Stilman, Lieut. General Sir William Pitcairn Campbell and the Lord Mayor of Liverpool.

As the party stood upon the deck of the ship the band played the "Star Spangled Banner" and afterward "God Save the King." All present stood at salute until the band ceased.

Included in the Pershing party were detachments of internes and nurses. They said that a squadron of British destroyers joined the American convoy about 100 miles off the Irish coast.

"We are glad to be the standard bearers of our government in this war of civilization," Genral Pershing said. "To land on English soil and receive such a welcome is significant. We appreciate it very deeply.

CONCERT ON SHIP

"We expect to be playing our part soon.

"We hope it will be a large part on the western front."

During the voyage a concert was given on shipboard at which General Pershing made an address.

There was great enthusiasm on board when United States destroyers were sighted.

It was an inspiring sight to see the Stars and Stripes flying above the gray war ships and the members of the Pershing party lined the rail and cheered.

General Pershing was active all the way over, conferring with his staff on plans for the work in hand.

The ship docked at 9 o'clock and a

(CONTINUED ON PAGE FIVE)

Uncle Sam's Steps Today in World War

General Pershing arrives in England with staff.

One hundred American aviators are on French soil.

Paris Le Matin declares another American destroyer flotilla expected in European waters soon.

Col. Fabry, "blue devil of France," declares U. S. army not mere expeditionary force, but will be distributed to the western front.

U. S. announces officers to command army in Europe.

Country wide reports on the Liberty Bond campaign show many districts exceeding their allotment.

Vernon Will Get Along Without New Hurlers, Says Chief

No more pitchers are to be added to the staff of the Vernon club.

George Stovall stated today that Art Fromme will be ready to take up part of the burden next week and that Frank Decanniere will be out only ten days because of his broken rib.

Because of the injuries of two of his pitchers Stovall is handicapped. Mitchell is slated to pitch tomorrow's game, while Quinn, who worked yesterday, will pitch Sunday morning, and Chief Johnson, today's selection, will work in the afternoon. Valencia and Walter Doane will finish up games if necessary.

Police Search for Missing Patient

The police and life guards of Venice today began a search for Mrs. T. E. Golf, an inmate of a Hollywood sanitarium, who escaped yesterday. The woman is 60 years old, was lightly clad and had no money. Once before, when she escaped the institution, she attempted to hurl herself into the ocean, and only the prompt action of the life guards saved her life. The mountains are being searched, as it is thought Mrs. Golf may have wandered into the hills and become exhausted.

Breakdown to Auto Halts College Girls

The failure of nine Pomona college girls to return to the college after they had given a glee club entertainment at Redlands, alarmed their friends there today. The girls, chaperoned by Prof. Hartley, music supervisor of the college, reached their homes at daylight. It was explained one of their automobiles had broken down on the trip home from Redlands and the delay in repairing the machine held them on the road half the night.

VICTORIOUS ALLIED FORCES CLOSING IN ON LENS AND LILLE

LONDON, June 8.—The whole great Hindenburg front, stretching like a snake across the edge of Belgium with its head in the vitals of France, is endangered by the great allied advance on the north flank.

Field Marshal Haig, British commander in chief, in his official dispatches to the war office today said that the position captured yesterday south of Ypres was "one of the most important strongholds on the western front."

By the capture of Wytschaete ridge, the single promontory south of Ypres, the British from a height were able today to pour cannon fire on the Germans below them.

The Germans made three tremendous efforts today to storm the great crater caused by the 1,000,000 ton explosion on Wytschaete ridge, but were thrown back in disorder.

Then the British advanced and swept the Teutons back two miles in one of the greatest bayonet charges of the war.

Tonight the British are within four miles of Lille, the great French industrial city. Lille is flanked by Haig's men and its fall is imminent.

The same crushing flanking movement spells the doom of Lens, the great coal city that General Haig has been pressing upon for weeks.

More than 6000 German prisoners have arrived at the stockades back of the British front and reports tonight indicate that fully 10,000 Germans have been taken.

BIG BRITISH GAINS

More than 200 machine guns have been captued in the new drive. Scores of other guns were destroyed by artillery fire.

The British along a front of nine miles have advanced between four and five miles. At Messines they advanced eight miles.

The Germans have delivered powerful counter thrusts with troops massed along the Warneton road, but all these attacks were defeated with tremendous losses.

Correspondents at the front declare that the explosion of 1,000,000 tons of explosives on the Wytschaete ridge yesterday literally buried hundreds of Germans. The earth opened and whole lines of German trench disappeared.

HILL DISAPPEARS

It was worse than an earthquake and the hill shook like jelly as explosion followed explosion. Hill No. 60 disappeared completely in a cloud of dust. A whole regiment of Germans held this hill.

Hindenburg's reserves arrived today and the flower of the German army has been thrown into action to save some of the heights that control all southwest Flanders.

In a gigantic effort to save the kaiser from a stupendous defeat, costing Germany the cities of Lille and Lens and imperiling the whole Teuton

(CONTINUED ON PAGE TWO.)

LATEST NEWS

BIG ATLANTIC LINER LOST AT SEA

NEW YORK, June 8.—The Red Star liner Southland has been lost at sea, according to word received from London at the local offices of the International Mercantile Marine this afternoon. The Southland was bound from Liverpool to Philadelphia when she met with disaster. There were about 125 men in the liner's crew, a number of them Americans. So far as known the Southland carried no passengrs. Further details have not been received here. The Southland was formerly the Vaderland and was engaged in transatlantic service until March, 1915, when she was taken over by the British government.

SHOTS ROUT AUTO STAGE ROBBER

Search was made today in the mountains near Saugus for a masked and armed bandit who attempted to hold up an outbound Santa Barbara stage one mile northwest of Burbank. His plan was thwarted by a fusilade of shots and he was pursued for several miles.

TITLE DECLARED FAULTY IN TAX SUIT

That titles to millions of dollars worth of property sold by the city for taxes may be invalidated under a decision issued by the state supreme court today was the announcement of Attorney George W. Crouch this afternoon. Crouch brought suit for I. W. Leonard against J. R. Jaffray to recover title to a piece of land sold to the city by Jaffray. The supreme court declared Jaffray's title faulty.

LAVA AND QUAKE WRECK SAN SALVADORE

WASHINGTON, June 8.—San Salvador, capital of Salvador, a city of 60,000 persons, has been visited by a devastating earthquake and volcano eruptions.

While no loss of life is reported yet, Consul Long cabled the state department this afternoon that most of the buildings in the city, including the American legation were rendered uninhabitable.

The quake was recorded in the seismograph of the Georgetown university here last night.

It was announced today it was 2000 miles from Washington, but it was not until this afternoon the exact location was learned through Long's cablegram from the Central American city.

He wired the tremors lasted more than two hours and in the midst of

(CONTINUED ON PAGE EIGHT)

GEN. GOETHALS DISMISSES HIS CRITICS

WASHINGTON, June 8.—F. Huntington Clarke and F. A. Eustich, who conceived the plan to span the Atlantic with a bridge of wooden ships, were discharged from their positions with the emergency fleet corporation by General Goethals today.

They had been acting as engineers for the corporation and in public statements had attacked Goethals' plan to substitute steel for wooden ships in the government's plan to defeat the submarine by making gigantic strides in shipbuilding.

Before General Goethals dismissed Clark and Eustis both engineers declared they had nothing to retract from their statements that the wooden program had been abandoned in favor of steel and that the result would be a great delay in getting ships into the service.

The action of General Goethals is

(CONTINUED ON PAGE EIGHT)

LOS ANGELES IS THE LARGEST CITY ON THE PACIFIC COAST

THE WEATHER
For Los Angeles and vicinity: Fair Sunday. Yesterday's temperatures: High 70, low 57.
5☆CENTS

MORNING TRIBUNE
INDEPENDENT ☆ LOS ANGELES ☆ PROGRESSIVE

BEST WAR NEWS ALWAYS
5☆CENTS

VOLUME VII, NUMBER 117. ✦✦ SUNDAY MORNING, OCTOBER 28, 1917. SUNDAY FIVE CENTS

Evening Express, Morning Tribune and Sunday Tribune, 13 papers a week, for 13 cents, or 50 cents a month by carrier in Los Angeles and immediate vicinity. Elsewhere, when by carrier, 60 cents a month.

YANKEES SURGE TO BATTLE

ACTUAL PHOTO OF AMERICAN TROOPS IN TRENCHES BACK OF FIRING LINE IN FRANCE

LOAN SUCCESS; FIVE BILLION GOAL PASSED —M'ADOO

'Defiance of Kaiser Answered in Unmistakable Terms by Free Americans,' Exultant Shout of Treasury Chief

[By Tribune Leased Wire]

WASHINGTON, Oct. 27.—At 9:30 o'clock tonight Secretary McAdoo authorized the following statement:

"It is a great honor to be able to announce to the American people that the second Liberty loan is an overwhelming success. It has been greatly oversubscribed.

The extent of the splendid oversubscriptions of the $3,000,000,000 issue cannot be definitely stated now because full reports have not yet been received and banks all over the country are holding open into the night to accommodate subscribers. **It will be several days before final figures can be given.**

The patriotic people of America, men and women alike, have responded generously and nobly to the call of their government to support and supply the gallant soldiers and sailors of the republic. **The challenge of the German kaiser has been answered by the free people of America in unmistakable terms."**

Enthusiasm Marks Campaign

Three million workers today roused the country to unparalleled fervor. Hundreds of cities and several entire federal reserv. districts exceeded their maximum quotas.

[CONTINUED ON PAGE 4, COLUMN 2]

17TH WEEK

Express Tribune Want-Ads are making a remarkable record of successive weekly gains — BIG GAINS, too — the week just ended makes the 17th consecutive week with a gain of OVER 1000 separate ads.

The Latest Figures·

6236 Want-Ads in Express Tribune Last week.

4564 Want-Ads in Express Tribune same week last year.

1672 GAIN

Fort Rosecrans Plans Stolen; Suspect Held

[Special to the Tribune]

PORTLAND, Ore., Oct. 27.—William Dolfen, chief cook of the Third Oregon regiment, alleged German spy, is charged with having stolen and sold the plans of Fort Rosecrans, San Diego, to a German official in Portland for $1000, in a statement today by United States Attorney Rankin to the United Press.

Dolfen was arrested at Pendleton early today as the troop train, carrying several companies of the Third Oregon regiment to an unnamed eastern point, passed through that town.

Dolfen refused to make a statement of any kind. He did not even ask of federal authorities who examined him on what charge he was arrested.

This afternoon he arrived at Portland in the custody of a United States deputy marshal.

Acting upon instructions from the United States marshal's office at Portland, deputy sheriffs arrested Dolfen on a presidential warrant.

Instructions received here stated Dolfen is charged with being an alien enemy.

German Republicans Circulating Pamphlet to Overthrow Kaiser

Wilson Gives Approval of Teutons' Propaganda Article Against Autocracy

[By United Press]

WASHINGTON, Oct. 27.—German republicans are sowing the seeds of democracy to overthrow the kaiser's autocracy. They have informed the German people how the Prussian war lords are striving for a "humbug peace" while still holding to their mania for world rule.

President Wilson's approval was given to the efforts of the republicans tonight, when the Creel committee made public a propaganda article German republicans in Switzerland are using to unseat Hohenzollernism and establish a republic. The article, in effect, is also another note from President Wilson to the German people, amplifying his ideas on peace.

The pamphlet is headed Peace? A New Humbug?

It is a bitter attack on the German ruling class, an expose of their insincere peace overtures and a clear statement of the allies' case against a "rotten" peace dictated by the German militarists.

Almost paraphrasing the president's own words in previous statements, the article declares that a peace on the kaiser's terms now would signify "nothing but an endless period of everlasting wars, a period of renewed competition in armaments, that will destroy the last rem-

[CONTINUED ON PAGE 4, COLUMN 3]

RAISE IN WAGE AVERTS COAL FAMINE

45-Cent Increase for Fuel at Mines Means 50 to 78 Per Cent More Pay

[By Tribune Leased Wire]

WASHINGTON, Oct. 27.—Wage increases, approximating 50 to 78 per cent, are in store for coal miners of the United States.

To enable operators to meet the higher scale President Wilson tonight authorized a general increase of 45 cents a ton for bituminous coal at the mines.

The president's order becomes effective at 7 o'clock Monday morning, October 29.

The higher prices will not apply to coal sold under existing contracts or in districts in which the operators and miners do not adopt the so-called penalty provision.

This applies to the collection of fines for violation of agreements entered into by the opeators and miners at Washington, October 6.

Order Follows Letter From Garfield

The order tonight followed receipt of a letter by the president from Fuel Administrator H. A. Garfield summarizing present coal conditions.

The president's executive order follows:

"The scale of prices prescribed August 21, 1917, by the president of the United States for bituminous coal at the mine, as adjusted and modified, by order of the United States fuel administrator, to meet exceptional conditions in certain localities, is hereby amended by adding the sum of 45 cents to each of the prices so prescribed or so adjusted and modified, subject, however, to the following express exceptions:

"1. This increase in prices shall not apply to any coal sold at the mine under an existing contract, containing a provision for an increase in the price of coal thereunder, in case of an increase in wages paid to miners.

"2. This increase in prices shall not apply in any district in which the operators and miners fail to agree on a penalty provision, satisfactory to the fuel administrator, for the automatic colection of fines in the spirit of the agreement entered into between the operators and miners at Washington, October 6, 1917.

Order Effective Monday

"This order shall become effective at 7 a. m. on October 29, 1917.

"WOODROW WILSON."

Dr. Garfield had written President Wilson as follows:

"Dear Mr. President:

"It is my understanding that in fixing provisional prices for the sale of coal it was intended to allow a fair profit to the operators. The public does not desire, nor is it necessary to meet the present emergency, that the coal industry should be asked to make

[CONTINUED ON PAGE 6, COLUMN 5]

Evacuation of Russian Capital Is Postponed

[By United Press]

PETROGRAD, Oct. 27.—Evacuation of Petrograd and transfer of the Russian capital to Moscow is not an "urgent matter," Premier Kerensky told the preliminary parliament conference today.

A resolution was adopted noting the government's purpose "to defend the capital with every energy and to remain there as long as possible." It was declared that the constituent assembly would be convened at Petrograd.

The first meeting of the constituent assembly has been set for December 5. This of itself is indication that the Russian government does not propose an immediate shift of the capital from Petrograd to Moscow.

Miss Helen Cudahy En Route War Zone Drowns in Atlantic

Milwaukee Packer's Daughter Believed to Be Unnerved by U-Boat Joking

[By Tribune Leased Wire]

CHICAGO, Oct. 27.—Miss Helen Cudahy, daughter of Patrick Cudahy, the Milwaukee packer, and a niece of the Chicago Cudahys, ended her life by drowning in mid-ocean October 19, according to cables from Paris today.

It is believed that Miss Cudahy's act was the result of brooding over the danger of submarine attack. **There had been joking about the imminent danger of being sunk in mid-ocean, and this conversation is thought to have preyed on the young woman's mind.**

Miss Cudahy sailed as a member of the Red Cross unit organized in Milwaukee. The party was on its way to France and was to proceed immediately to the front. Each member of the unit was to pay her own expenses. Miss Cudahy is said to have been in the best of spirits until the night of October 19.

A friend called at her stateroom to ask her to participate in some festivities. An open porthole aroused suspicion. Miss Cudahy was gone. This note was found:

"It is all for the best. Keep as much as possible from father and mother. Please notify my brother, Michael."

There was no other word. Inasmuch as the vessel was traveling at a good rate of speed, it was impossible to make a search for the body and the boat proceeded on its course.

Friends of Miss Cudahy arriving in Paris told the story of her death.

Miss Cudahy was twenty-six years old. She attended Dana Hall, near Boston, and was abroad two years. One of her instructors there interested her in the mission on which she left the United States.

ITALIAN FRONT FOR 25 MILES CRUMBLING

Austro-German Sweep Led by Kaiser Charles and Mackensen Making Gains

[By Cable to the Tribune]

LONDON, Oct. 27.—Italy's battlefront between Tolmino and the Wippah (Vipacchio) river—twenty-five miles—threatens to cave in completely before the Austro-German sweep.

"The situation is certainly grave," was Rome's official admission today. General Cadorna is admittedly preparing for further withdrawals on a wide front.

From Berlin came a war office statement describing the Teuton successes in glowing terms. It disclosed that Emperor Charles personally is directing the big smash. The immediate high command is in the hands of Germany's most successful army leader, Field Marshal von Mackensen. This bears out the theory exclusively advanced in these dispatches yesterday that "in its large outline the offensive has all the earmarks of a Mackensen drive."

Teutons Menace Rear

Goritz and the entire positions to the east and southeast are menaced in the rear by the Teuton sweep in the direction of Cividale.

On the Carso front, alone, the Italians stand firm. Berlin officially admits this.

Sixty thousand prisoners have been taken by the Teutons so far.

The number of captured guns has reached 450. Inestimable booty is claimed besides.

The attackers have captured the steep mountain ridge of Stol and the strongly fortified summit of Monte Matajur, 1641 meters high. The latter was taken Thursday morning, twenty-four hours after the beginning of the drive.

"The achievements in battle and

[CONTINUED ON PAGE 4, COLUMN 4]

Notice to Subscribers

THE management will consider it a favor if subscribers will phone immediately any failure on the part of carriers to render prompt and satisfactory service.

Use phones: Home 60266 or Main 8100.

Ask for circulation department, day or night.

Subscribers in outside towns see list of agents on first classified page.

Auto Making May Stop

[By Tribune Leased Wire]

WASHINGTON, Oct. 27.—Possible suspension of the manufacture of pleasure automobiles and the certain suspension of much highway and theater construction work is forecast in an order of Robert S. Lovett, administrative officer under the priority shipments act, made public today.

The railroads after the first of the month, are forbidden to furnish open top freight cars for the transportation of luxuries and to confine their use to the shipment of coal, sugar and sugar cane, ore and other commodities necessary to actual war industries.

It has been ascertained, Judge Lovett reported to the president, that the shortage of gondola cars, largely responsible for the shortage of coal in many localities, was due to the diversion of these cars to other purposes.

Seven Survivors of Wrecked Fruit Ship Taken to Vera Cruz

Vessel Founders Off Fronteras, Mex.; 14 Other Crew Members Missing

[By Tribune Leased Wire]

VERA CRUZ, Mex., Oct. 27.—The fishing vessel Dolores Llarena has arrived here with seven survivors of the American fruit vessel Olympia. The Olympia was bound from New Orleans and was wrecked near Fronteras. The survivors were in two small boats when rescued.

Fourteen other members of the lost vessel's crew are missing.

[By United Press]

NEW ORLEANS, Oct. 27.—With the loss of eight lives, including John B. Cefalu Jr., purser, and one of the stockholders in the Mexican-American Steamship company, owners, the steamship Olympia foundered in the Gulf of Mexico, sixty miles off Fronteras, Mexico, Thursday. A severe storm battered many other boats.

The Olympia, according to the advices reaching here today, was caught in the vortex of the storm. Apparently she was trying to reach land, being so close to the Mexican coast.

J. Beninato, president of the Mexican-American Steamship company, received a cablegram today announcing the disaster to the Olympia and the loss of eight, including Cefalu. Thirty-two men were on the ship.

The Tegucigalpa of the Vaccaro Brothers' Fruit company, upon arriving here, reported a tremendous gale in the gulf.

PRESSMEN THREATEN STRIKE

[By Tribune Leased Wire]

NEW YORK, Oct. 27.—Asking a flat increase of $4 a week in wages, press feeders and printers' pressmen of New York will walk out next Monday if the demand is not met.

AMERICAN FORCES MARCH JOYOUSLY INTO BAPTISM OF FIRE TO FREE WORL

Eager Army Follows First U. S. Shell, Sen Hurtling Across No Man's Land Again German Artillery Positions, to Secto Few Hundred Yards From Teuton Trench

By Newton C. Parke

AMERICAN FIELD HEADQUARTERS IN FRANC Oct. 27.—America is on the firing line in Fran

At the stroke of 6 of a recent morning a re haired Irish-American sent America's first sh sizzling across No Man's Land at a German ba tery position, heralding to the world the grim, triumphant me sage that "the Yankees are coming!"

That afternon they came. They marched to battle throu slush and rain. But on their faces was a sacred sunshine, a in their hearts a song.

That night American infantry joined American artillery first line trenches on a quiet sector of the western front. Cri cross firing has been going on ever since. Only a few hund yards away is the nearest German trench. Pershing's boys on the watch.

Cheering News Is Withheld

Not until today—for excellent military reasons—were c respondents permitted to send the cheering news to Ameri The following official statement—America's first "communiqu in the great war—was issued from American headquarters:

"In continuation of their training as a nucleus for the struction of later contingents, some battalions of our first c tingent, in association with veteran French battalions, are in first line trenches of a quiet sector of the French front.

"They are supported by some batteries of our artillery, in sociation with veteran French batteries.

"The sector remains normal. Our men have adapted the selves to actual trench conditions in a most satisfactory m ner."

There it is, the plain, matter-of-fact, typically militaŕy, ty cally American bulletin that ushers in an epoch in the history mankind. For a mere war correspondent to try to elucidate add to all that its simple words imply would be foolish and fu

Details for Future Bulletins

"Have they gone over the top yet? Will they go so Have the Germans tried to 'strafe' them yet and what sor punishment did the Sammies deal out?" These and all thousand and one questions undoubtedly in the minds of folks at home must be left to future bulletins to answer.

All that can be told in this dispatch is the story of t going, from the moment that the first mysterious whisper m the rounds of the correspondents to that picturesque and ne to-be-forgotten scene when our Sammies, sloshing through mud, **turned frontward at the crossroads, their dark, ponch**

THE EXAMINER
DELIVERED TO THE HOME
85c PER MONTH
Daily & Sunday

CHARACTER QUALITY ENTERPRISE ACCURACY
Los Angeles Examiner
AN AMERICAN PAPER FOR THE AMERICAN PEOPLE — THE GREAT NEWSPAPER OF THE GREAT SOUTHWEST
Reg. U. S. Pat. Off.

CALIFORNIA FORECAST

Los Angeles and Vicinity—Tuesday, fair; heavy to light frost in morning; light northerly winds.

San Francisco and Vicinity—Tuesday, fair; light northwesterly winds.

COAST TEMPERATURES

Los Angeles	68	Portland	52
San Diego	63	Spokane	44
San Francisco	59	Tacoma	51
Sacramento	56		

VOL. XV—NO. 336 Official Forecast—Fair; frost. LOS ANGELES, NOVEMBER 12, 1918 TUESDAY TELEPHONES—MAIN 8300, HOME 10195

EX-KAISER IS INTERNED

ILSON MADLY HEERED

nt's Announcement of s End Turns Capital Victorious Pandemonium

ors Who Authorized Call rms Hear That Autocra- Rule Has Been Crushed

James R. Nourse
orrespondent Universal Service)

SHINGTON, Nov. 11. —"The war thus comes nd."

xactly 1:21 o'clock this on President Wilson these words in the the House of Repre- es to the joint session Senate and House.

his official announcement of g of the war. It was his n to the Congress which orized the call to arms that and hopes and aspirations of ce of militarism and autoc be a fully and definitely

onium broke loose with the nent. Senators and Repre- leaped to their feet with a hout of enthusiasm. They heir hands and cheered the as they never cheered him of the previous occasions addressed them, when the ongress, Republicans and s alike, was united in that of applause and approval. eath the rostrum, directly stand whereon the Presi- ed, sat the venerable jus- the Supreme Court, with stice White in the center. arose and applauded with

ts Applaud Address

eft of the President, in the the great hall, sat the corps and the members of ent's cabinet. As the sen- ull of portent, though con- y of seven words, fell from ent's lips, they were up rest of them, cheering and heir hands.

galleries, where applause forbidden, while the House on, forgot the rules utterly them to the winds as the pplause sweeping upward floor of the chamber was in a tremendous echo. son was seated in the ex-

ed on Page 4, Column 1)

Full Victory, Says Wilson Proclamation

WASHINGTON, Nov. 11.—President Wilson issued a formal proclamation at 10 o'clock this morning announcing that the armistice with Germany had been signed.

The proclamation follows:

"My Fellow Countrymen:

"The armistice was signed this morning. Everything for which America fought has been accomplished. It will now be our fortunate duty to assist by example, by sober friendly counsel and by material aid in the establishment of just democracy throughout the world.—WOODROW WILSON."

FORMER CROWN PRINCE SAID TO HAVE BEEN SHOT

Another Rumor Current in Paris States Prince Eitel, Kaiser's Second Son, Tried Suicide

(By Universal Service)

AMSTERDAM, Nov. 11.—Friedrich Wilhelm, ex-Crown Prince of Prussia, eldest son of the former Kaiser, has been shot by a would-be assassin, according to a strong Berlin report just received here. Details are lacking.

PARIS, Nov. 11.—(Havas)—Many sensational rumors became current here as a result of the news of the signing of the armistice between the Allies and Germany. These reports were to the effect that Prince Eitel Friedrich, the second son of William II, was prevented from committing suicide and that the empress was dying.

Three German generals are said to have committed suicide.

(By The Associated Press)

LONDON, Nov. 11, 2:35 p. m.—Field Marshal von Hindenburg has placed himself and the German army at the disposition of the new people's government at Berlin, says a dispatch from the German capital by way of Copenhagen.

The field marshal asked the Cologne soldiers' and workers' council to send delegates to German main headquarters at once. A delegation left Cologne Monday morning. Field Marshal von Hindenburg said he had taken this action "in order to avoid chaos."

(By Universal Service)

WASHINGTON, Nov. 11.—Marshal von Hindenburg, contrary to former reports, is not with his former Kaiser in Holland, but at grand headquarters in Germany, having aligned himself with the new government. A dispatch giving this information over the wireless from Nauen was received at the State Department tonight.

WORLD IN RIOT OF JOY OVER PEACE

Demonstrations Cause Practical Cessation of All Business While Millions Celebrate

Paris and London Throngs Cheer American Soldiers; New York Festivities Are Just Begun

(Staff Correspondent Universal Service)

PARIS, Nov. 11.—Paris has been throughout the day, and is all night, a pandemonium of joy.

American doughboys, followed by a huge throng, marched to the statues of Strassbourg and Metz in the forenoon and placed golden leaved crowns upon the monuments to take the place of the crepe that have hung on them for 47 years.

There was a monster celebration in front of the American Red Cross headquarters at the Hotel Regina.

An American major climbed the statue of Joan of 'Arc and placed a huge American flag in her hand. She now rides on her steed waving the Stars and Stripes.

As the cry "Fini la guerre" sounded through Paris all shops and factories closed and signs of "the war is finished" appeared in the windows. Out poured thousands of Midinettes to join the parades forming spontaneously in every part of every street, boulevard and alley. As the day wore on the cheering grew more frequent and more thunderous. The American habit proved infectious, and the Parisiens liked it.

It was announced that all cafes and restaurants may remain open until eleven tonight, instead of the wartime closing hour of 9:30.

Brokers and clerks crowded the bourse steps early in the afternoon. The "Wall Street district" of Paris did its hearty share in the celebration. The Place de l'Opera swarmed all day with thousands of men, women and children. All approach was impossible.

In the afternoon important conferences took place at Colonel House's residence, General Bliss and Admiral Benson attending. Colonel House declined to comment on the armistice news.

It is understood that General Pershing first learned the news from Paris by telephone and immediately communicated it to army headquarters, where it was flashed to every corps and divisional headquarters.

A thousand helmeted poilus paraded through Paris carrying French and American flags. In the midst of the marching soldiers four husky men carried a big Australian on their shoulders, who waved the Union Jack. An American darky entrenched on a mule waved all Allied flags in one hand.

Barrels of champagne flowed all afternoon and evening in the restaurants and cafes.

The aged Premier of France,

(Continued on Page 2, Columns 3-4)

Day of Glory Has Come, Says Paris Council

(By The Associated Press)

PARIS, Nov. 11.—The Municipal Council of Paris has had the following posted on walls in all parts of the city:

"Citizens! Victory is here—triumphant victory. The vanquished enemy lays down his arms. Blood ceases to flow. Let Paris emerge from her ordered reserve. Let us give free course to our joy and enthusiasm and hold back our tears.

"Let us testify to our infinite gratitude to our grand soldiers and their incomparable chiefs by festooning our houses in the colors of France and our allies. Our dead can sleep in peace. The sublime sacrifice they have made for the future of their race and the salvation of their country will not be in vain.

"The day of glory has come. Long live the republic! Long live immortal France!"

'SOFTEN TERMS,' PLEA TO WILSON

Hun Minister Begs That 'Fearful Conditions' of Armistice Be Modified

(By Universal Service)

AMSTERDAM, via London, Nov. 11.—Dr. W. S. Solf, who was German foreign minister under Prince Max's chancellorship, and who appears to have retained that office—though this is not certain at this moment—today issued a signed appeal to President Wilson in the name of the German people, "to use his influence with the Allies to mitigate these fearful conditions," meaning the armistice terms.

Dr. Solf says:

"After a blockade of Germany lasting fifty months, and still in force, the armistice conditions, especially the surrender of the transport and sustenance of the army of occupation, make it an impossibility to provide Germany with food and would cause the starvation of millions of German women, children and men.

"The enforcement of those terms would produce a feeling among the German people contrary to the reconstruction of the community of nations.

"The German people appeal to President Wilson to influence the Allies to mitigate these fearful conditions."

Dr. Solf's appeal says:

"Convinced of the common aims of democracy, the German government requests President Wilson to re-establish the peace principles which President Wilson has always maintained."

ARMISTICE STIRS IRE OF HUN FLEET

Revolutionary Council, Commanding, Declares Pact Unjust and Calls on Submarines to Act

Directs All Sea Divers of Baltic to Assemble at Once Off Prussian Island of Ruegen

(By Universal Service)

LONDON, Nov. 11—(8:39 p. m.—The German revolutionary council in command of the German fleet, denouncing the armistice terms as "unjust," particularly the continuation of the blockade, has summoned all sailors "to defend the country."

It has ordered all submarines in the Baltic to assemble immediately in the harbor of Sassnitz, on the east coast of the Island of Ruegen, Prussia.

It announces that a strong British naval force is off the Skaw (Skagen), a Danish seaport at the northern extremity of Jutland, off which island the great sea battle was fought in 1916.

The German order was intercepted by the British Admiralty wireless and was given out here tonight. It was sent by the "command and sailors' council," which appears to have headquarters on the German battleship Strassburg. The order reads as follows:

"To all ships, destroyers and submarines in the North Sea and Baltic:

"The enemy terms are unjust. The blockade of the German people, in defiance of international law, continues.

"The Allies' armistice terms are drastic. They entail our destruction.

"German comrades! Defend your country against such unheard of presumption. A strong British force is off Skaw.

"All submarines in the Baltic are to assemble immediately in the harbor of Sassnitz."

More German Rulers Toppled Off Thrones

(By Universal Service)

LONDON, Nov. 11.—The German garrison at the Belgian fortress of Liege is reported in full revolt.

Crown Prince Rupprecht of Bavaria, commander of Germany's northern front in the west, has fled.

(By Universal Service)

BASEL, via Paris, Nov. 11.—The king of Saxony has been deposed, according to a Berlin dispatch late today.

The king of Saxony is Friederich August III. He succeeded to the throne on the death of his father October 15, 1904.

(By The Associated Press)

COPENHAGEN, Nov. 11.—The grand duke of Oldenburg has been

(Continued on Page 2, Column 6)

Ousted Monarch's Train Fired Upon

Holland Places Wm. Hohenzollern in Custody and May Intern Prince Joachim With Entire Imperial Party.

BULLETIN

(BY UNIVERSAL SERVICE)

LONDON, Nov. 12 (Tuesday).—The Kaiser has been interned by Holland in [illegible] chateau [illegible] learns from its correspondent at Amsterdam.

Prince Joachim, the Kaiser's youngest son, and fifty other persons accompanied the ex-Emperor on his flight into Holland, the correspondent adds.

It is presumed the entire party will be interned along with the ex-monarch.

(BY ASSOCIATED PRESS)

LONDON, Nov. 11.—A special dispatch from Eysden, Holland, says that when William Hohenzollern's train arrived here he was not aboard. Later he arrived by motor car, having abandoned the train because of shots fired at the window of his car.

He joined his officers on the platform of the station of Eysden. He was looking haggard, but walked up and down the platform slowly until the train was ready to leave.

A dispatch to the Daily Mail from The Hague dated Sunday says the former Empress of Germany was not on board the train and that no women were among the party.

This dispatch asserts it was the intention of the former Emperor to remain on board the train at Eysden throughout the night and leave Monday morning for internment in a chateau between Utrecht and Arnhem. It was added his suite would be interned at Arnhem.

A dispatch attributed to the Maastricht, Holland, Handelsblad says the presence of the former German Crown Prince with the Hohenzollern party has not been confirmed, but that it is known former Prince Joachim and General von Falkenhayn were with the former Emperor.

On the other hand, the Daily Mail describes the ex-Emperor and the former Crown Prince walking on opposite ends of the Eysden platform without exchanging words.

(BY UNIVERSAL SERVICE)

AMSTERDAM, Nov. 11.—It is reported here that the Kaiser attempted to enter the British lines to surrender, but was prevented by revolutionary troops. It was only after this unsuccessful attempt to hand himself over to the enemy that he went to Holland, the report says.

The report persists that Field Marshal von Hindenburg and twelve German staff officers fled to Holland.

AMSTERDAM, Nov. 11.—The Handelsblad says it learns the Dutch government will object to the former German Emperor residing in Holland.

BIG U. S. GUNS IN FINAL SALVO TO BEATEN FOE

The following is one of the last "spot news" fighting dispatches from the American front. It was filed by the Universal Service man at noon Monday. The great war was in its dying hours, but America's boys swept on relentlessly until Foch gave the signal to stop.

(Staff Correspondent Universal Service)

WITH THE AMERICAN FIRST ARMY, Nov. 11, noon.—On the dot of 11 o'clock this morning the great war passed into history.

All American batteries along a 75-mile front with blazing salvos christened "the Kaiser's knockout."

The army was notified that the armistice was signed at 5:45 o'clock a. m. and headquarters sent out orders by wireless and telephone that hostilities were to cease at 10:55 a. m., on the German side and at 11 a. m., on the American side, there being five minutes difference between German and French time on the front. This resulted in the cessation of fighting at the same instant by both sides.

One division of our troops on the front north of Verdun was making a sharp advance just before the armistice orders were received.

Mud-smeared foot couriers were forced to run through the mire over the hills, to spread the glad tidings.

The lion's share of the homage to heroes in this war belongs to the gallant lads that bled and died in the last hours of the great conflict, performing their final duties with the

(Continued on Page 2, Column 1)

ENVOYS OF PEACE PLANNED

Lansing Mentioned as Probable Head of American Delegation to Decide Fate of Nations

Armistice Finally Signed Aboard Foch's Train; Ally Leader and Germans Affix Names

(By Universal Service)

WASHINGTON, Nov. 11.—"The when and wherefore" of the peace conference is tonight the subject of much speculation in official quarters here.

It is generally believed Secretary Lansing will head the American delegation which, with its attaches, secretaries, clerks, stenographers, typists and the like, is expected to make up a party of 100 persons.

Col. E. M. House, the President's personal adviser and the representative of this Government in the momentous conference of the Supreme War Council at Versailles, also is mentioned as a peace envoy.

Another prospective envoy is Senator Gilbert M. Hitchcock of Nebraska, chairman of the Senate foreign relations committee and therefore the outstanding figure in Congress as far as peace negotiations are concerned.

In order to give our delegation a non-partisan aspect, the President, it has been said, may select former President Taft, who has rendered yeoman service to his country during the war by serving as head of the National War Labor Board, and former Justice Charles Evans Hughes.

Justice Brandeis of the Supreme Court also has been mentioned as a prospective envoy. He is known to have the President's confidence and it is entirely possible that he will be chosen as one of the delegation.

It is not known when or where the peace conference will be held. If Germany carries out the terms of the armistice, however, negotiations are expected to begin very shortly thereafter. The scene of the peace conference may be in any one of the four places—The Hague, Brussels, Paris or London.

Armistice Signed Aboard General Foch's Train

(Staff Correspondent Universal Service)

PARIS, Nov. 11.—Details of the signing of the armistice are yet outstanding but it occurred aboard Foch's headquarters train.

It is reported here the German courier failed to arrive from Spa, but a wireless message sent to the German delegates from German head-

THE NINETEEN-TWENTIES

The center of international government and corporate finance converged on the corner of Broad and Wall Streets as the decade of the 1920s began. Shortly before noon, secretaries began to clear their desks to leave for lunch in a cafe down the street from the J. P. Morgan and Company building. Across the way, junior executives in the Assay office closed their books. Two hundred feet down Wall Street, the Stock Exchange was filled with a record number of spectators, anxiously watching the board as prices continued to rise. Then, at 11:56, a massive bomb exploded. Thirty people were killed instantly—five inside the House of Morgan and twenty-five others on the street outside. Hundreds were injured as fragments of glass and stone were hurled through the air. The demeanor of the intersection turned to panic everywhere except at the Stock Exchange, where the heavy velvet curtains had prevented shattered glass from causing injuries. The director mounted the rostrum, sounded the gong announcing the closing of trading for the day, and methodically emptied the room.

The next day, as police were searching for any clue which might help solve the mysterious bombing, the market opened again and prices continued to rise as if nothing had happened. The press followed the investigation with absorbed interest for the next few weeks and the evidence progressively pointed to the involvement of anarchists. Yet, there were no similar bombings in other cities and none of the great financial entrepreneurs of the country had been injured. The attention of the public subsided within a brief period of time. Had the event occurred six months earlier, national repercus-

sions would have been harsh and comprehensive. But, conditions had changed, and with them attitudes had begun to shift as well. The Red Scare was essentially over in America, if not on the Continent.

Another incident attests to the differences of opinion which were being expressed internationally. On April 20th of the same year, a paymaster and a guard were transporting two cases containing the payroll of the company for which they worked. They were accosted by two men and shot with handguns. The money was stolen and the men escaped. Two weeks later, the Massachusetts police apprehended two suspects—Italian radicals named Sacco and Vanzetti. The story was not covered by news reporters on the grounds that it was commonplace enough not to be considered newsworthy. The *New York Times* was anxiously covering the Dempsey-Carpentier fight and photographers were absorbed with the Washington bathing beauty contest, both of which had more public appeal than the arrest of two more radicals. The trial itself attracted little attention and the men were found guilty of premeditated murder and sentenced to death.

A few months later, however, national and local papers were filling their front pages with information on the case, largely because of the intense efforts of three young men who had been working in a bleak Boston office sending releases to European radical papers and magazines about the case. The information they transmitted was of keen interest to Europeans. Their political sympathies explained their interest in part, but there was an additional factor. Sacco and Vanzetti were clearly remarkable men whose interest in anarchism

The manufacturing of automobiles *for a relatively affluent public begin in earnest in the 1920's. Mass production brought the price of the automobile within the reach of many Americans, and the expanded use of the auto for leisure became a part of the American way of life. This crowded parking lot at the beach near New York City illustrates the proliferation of the auto during the decade of the 1920's.*

was primarily philosophical; both were intellectuals and neither had any record of past involvement in violent activities—political or otherwise. It was extremely difficult to believe that they had participated in such a mundane act as murdering a payroll officer and guard for a reasonably small amount of money. As European papers began to report major demonstrations against the jury's decision in Massachusetts, the American press was forced to carry the stories. A bomb had exploded in the United States ambassador's house in Paris as a signal of protest; twenty people were killed in another bomb explosion in France. Crowds mobbed the American embassy in Rome and an attempt was made to bomb the consul-general's house in Lisbon. In Montevideo, Uruguay, a general strike was launched and efforts were made to boycott all American goods. The case was appealed for a duration of seven years, during which time it received

lessening attention until the final decision was made on August 22, 1927, and the men were executed.

In general, the American public had recognized that the threat of communists and socialists and anarchists in the United States was never as dangerous as they had believed. Conservatism prevailed, but interests were channeled into economic activities and the forthcoming national elections.

On the morning of March 4, 1921, Woodrow Wilson, broken from the defeat of his League of Nations dream in the Senate and gravely ill from the effects of the cerebral thrombosis he endured earlier, left the White House and was driven down Pennsylvania Avenue to the seclusion of his private house on S Street. President-elect Warren Harding had been precisely what the American public wanted in a chief executive from what the election returns indicated, although he had emerged as a compromise candidate at the Republican Convention several months earlier. His earliest actions were well-received. He once again opened the White House to the public and to his advisors, whom he modestly stated that he would rely on for counsel and advice. He emphasized that businesses would be given as free a hand as possible to resume "their normal onward way." Shortly after he assumed office, reporters were writing that the atmosphere in Washington was like that of old home week or a college class reunion. The change was astonishing—an era of good feelings appeared to have been ushered in. The President was genuinely well-liked, friendly and open. Most importantly, he seemed extremely willing to allow the country to move in the direction it chose, a direction in which business interests would dominate other governmental controls.

To the public, the Harding Administration appeared dignified and statesmanlike. On the surface this was true. In foreign affairs, the President had made admirable choices for cabinet positions, particularly in appointing Charles Evans Hughes as Secretary of State. The addition of Herbert Hoover as Secretary of Commerce and Andrew Mellon as Secretary of the Treasury was made out of the vague sense that they would provide the administration with a favorable appearance to the public and a strong degree of good judgment on financial affairs. In both instances, this premonition was verified as the months passed.

In other areas, however, the President made a number of strategic mistakes in appointing key leaders and in adhering to their advice over the counsel of his more knowledgeable and respected cabinet members. In three particularly dramatic cases, the consequences of his judgment would contribute to his downfall. Harry Daugherty, a long-time friend of Harding's, was given the position of Attorney General, Albert Fall was hired as the Secretary of the Interior and Charles Forbes was given the role of directing the Veterans' Bureau. Each of these men, acting in a different but equally disastrous capacity, took advantage of the President's lack of political expertise and participated in activities which culminated in widespread corruption in the highest circles of government—activities which the public at large knew very little about and about which they cared even less during the first three years of the decade.

The focus of attention, when it could be diverted away from social interests, advertising, fashion and sports, was on the accomplishments of the Administration and there were a few very notable ones. Peace with Germany, which had so long been deferred because of the unwillingness of Wilson to compromise with the Senate, was formalized by a resolution signed by the President on July 2, 1921. Domestically, the budget was put on a unified basis for the first time in history

A wave of xenophobia *spread across America in the 1920's and hundreds of recent immigrants were quickly sent back to their native countries because of their professed beliefs in "un-American" political ideologies. Here Alexander Beckman, a self-proclaimed anarchist, addresses an outdoor meeting of the Industrial Workers of the World. Beckman, who had been jailed previously for attempted murder, was ultimately deported.*

and Charles Dawes was appointed as Director of the Budget. Immigration was restricted through a quota system to the satisfaction of labor and the high surtaxes on large incomes were lowered, to the pleasure of big business. Congress raised the tariff, pleasing the Republican party. All in all, the record of the first months of the Harding Administration appeared to conform almost perfectly with the interests of the public. Even when the Attorney General confronted striking railway workers with an injunction, the majority of Americans applauded the action. The emphasis on business interests was increasing exponentially.

The most outstanding achievement of the Administration was attributable almost exclusively to Secretary of State Hughes, however, in the accomplishment of a reduction of world armaments at the Washington Conference—a feat which had widespread implications both domestically and internationally. President Harding opened the first session of the Conference with a profuse welcome speech and then disappeared, true to his earlier statement that he would leave the details of government to his advisors. In this case, the decision paid off. Hughes began, as chairman of the Conference, with a few introductory remarks and then hastened to produce a long and detailed plan for a ten-year naval holiday, during which no capital ships would be built, no plans for ship-building would be projected, and three nations—the United States, Great Britain and Japan—would scrap almost two million tons of ships. In addition, the Secretary called for a new formula, limiting the replacement of obsolete ships according to a 5-5-3 ratio. The American and British navies

The rise of the Klan *in the South was intense but short lived. Although the Klan's appeal was to white Christian ideals, the truth of its bigoted ideology was often demonstrated through atrocities such as this one.*

would be kept at parity and the Japanese navy would be maintained at a level of three-fifths of the size of each.

"With acceptance of this plan, the burden of meeting the demands of competition in naval armament will be lifted. Enormous sums will be released to aid the progress of civilization. At the same time the proper demands of national defense will be adequately met and the nations will have ample opportunity . . . to consider their future course. Preparations for offensive naval war will stop now." The Secretary's words were spoken amidst breathless silence. To the amazement of delegates seated along rows of mahogany tables, the plan announced settled the need for the Conference. Delegates broke into prolonged applause and the success of the conference became almost inevitable as the applause resounded throughout the world via the press.

After three months of negotiations a treaty was agreed upon, incorporating the general lines of the Hughes plan and adding provisions to cover some other matters which were still outstanding following the termination agreements after World War I.[1] The armaments which were built by a particular nation were now recognized as having direct and immediate importance to international affairs and were, therefore, subject to international agreement. This was a monumental breakthrough in history and the credit was given to the Harding Administration. Ironically, the League of Nations, which had been Wilson's dream for international peace, was being accepted by European councils at the same time, though it received almost no attention in the American press.

In the midst of this triumph, however, several other activities were occurring which were hidden from the public and from the government itself. The most dramatic of these was the Teapot Dome Scandal, a widespread misuse of governmental authority resulting in fraud, graft and general corruption. Although the scandal did not become public until a few weeks after Harding's death, the events had been initiated shortly after Fall was appointed Secretary of the Interior. The Secretary had come to office as the ally of big oil interests and as a politician without illusions of idealism, he saw an opportunity to do his friends a favor as concerns about fuel supplies for the armed forces increased.

Less than three months after Harding had been elected to the Presidency, he signed an Executive Order transferring oil reserves at Elk Hills, California, Teapot Dome, Montana, and Buena Vista, California, from the custody of the Secretary of the Navy to the Secretary of the Interior. The decision was made in deference to Fall's insistence that the property was properly under the Department's jurisdiction—a questionable argument at best. On November 17, 1921, Fall secretly entered into negotiations with a small group of oil officials in a room at the Vanderbilt Hotel in New York. Those present included Colonel E. A. Humphreys, the owner of the rich Mexia oil field; James O'Neil, President of Prairie Oil Company; Robert Stewart, Chairman of the Board of Standard Oil of Indiana; Harry Blackmer of the Midwest Oil Company; and Harry Sinclair, the presiding officer of the Sinclair Consolidated Oil Company. In the course of the meeting, Humphreys agreed to sell a third of a billion barrels of oil from his field at $1.50 a barrel, under the imposed condition that he sell through a business which had recently been incorporated—the Continental Trading Company, Limited. The contract was guaranteed by Sinclair and O'Neil.

[1] Additional sections included an agreement to settle all disagreements by conciliatory negotiations, preparations for the withdrawal of Japan from Shantung and Siberia, and an agreement to respect the principle of the open door in China.

Warren G. Harding, *twenty-ninth President of the United States, as he appeared when he took office.*

In the meantime, arguments persisted about whether the Oil Reserves should be leased to private operators who would meet the needs of the armed forces through the use of royalty oil which would be paid to the government for use of the property or whether they should continue to be operated exclusively by the Navy Department. With the transfer of authority to the Secretary of the Interior, and the increasing demand for free enterprise with minimum governmental interference, Fall was able to persuade Congress and the President that private ownership on a lease agreement was preferable.

On April 7, 1922, less than five months after the secret deal had been made at the Vanderbilt, Fall announced that, without competitive bidding, the Teapot Dome Reserve had been leased to Harry Sinclair's mammoth oil company. On December 11th, a similar announcement was made with regard to the Elk Hills Reserve, which was turned over to Doheny's Pan-American Company. The justification given for the absence of competitive bidding was that these leases were fair to the government and that no undue profits would accrue, and that secrecy was essential because military installations were involved. From Fall's perspective, this provided the necessary means for operationalizing the Continental Trading Company and almost immediately the oil was resold to Sinclair's and O'Neil's companies for $1.75 a barrel—thereby diverting a profit of twenty-five cents per barrel which might otherwise have gone to the other companies whose representatives had gathered together months earlier. In turn, the money was kept in secret accounts and the Secretary of the Interior received $260,000 in Liberty Bonds from Sinclair and another $100,000 in cash from Doheny—both without interest or security.

At the time of Harding's death, on August 23, 1923, there

was no direct evidence of the scandal. There were rumors of corruption in some segments of the federal government and a few isolated incidents of actual graft were revealed, including the illegal mismanagement of the Veterans' Bureau by Charles Forbes, who was fired from his post but not convicted of actual crimes. When the President died, allegedly of a heart attack, in San Francisco, the headlines of newspapers across the nation reflected profound grief. As a train carrying his body proceeded along its route to Washington, hundreds of thousands of mourners gathered to pay their respects. A reporter for the *New York Times* captured the sense of loss by stating briefly, but accurately, that "this is the most remarkable demonstration in American history of affection, respect and reverence for the dead." It was only afterwards that the truth would emerge about the Administration, primarily in the form of a prolonged Senate investigation of the Teapot Dome situation, which resulted in several criminal convictions and the knowledge that much of the money provided to Sinclair and Doheny had been used to fill the coffers of the Republican Party.

In the same year that this disclosure was made public, another major case involving the Attorney General under the Harding Administration was being uncovered. During the War, the Alien Property Act had been passed by Congress, authorizing the Director to take over companies whose ownership was primarily foreign. This had happened in the case of the American Metal Company, on the grounds that forty-nine percent of the stock should be held in custody since the operation was conducted by German stockholders. In 1921, Richard Merton appeared at the Custodian's office, claiming that this percentage had not been German, but rather Swiss, and that the office should rightfully return the shares as a form of reimbursement. The claim was allowed after Merton gave $441,000 in Liberty Bonds to John King, a member of the Republican National Committee, for "services" rendered. The services amounted to an introduction to the Custodian and to Jess Smith, an assistant to the Attorney General. In the ensuing trial, a number of interesting facts were brought to light. At least two hundred thousand dollars worth of bonds

The last photograph *of President Harding ever taken. While in office Harding became ill, and the illness is evident on his face in this picture, taken in 1923 when he arrived for a visit to San Francisco. Harding was taken seriously ill while in San Francisco and died shortly after this picture was taken.*

had been paid to Smith for expediting the claim through Washington acquaintances; $49,165 dollars were deposited in the Attorney General's personal account; and, the Attorney General's brother received at least $40,000 dollars for his connections and influence in convincing the Custodian that the claim was valid. At the trial itself, Daugherty refused to testify on his own behalf, indicating that the extent of criminal activities had involved the White House as well as the Department of Justice.

Coupled with other similar cases, the existing evidence which emerged over a two and a half year period made it clear that the Harding Administration had been responsible for more concentrated corruption than had existed in the history of Federal Government. Yet, even though Daugherty and others were forced out of office, and the new President, Calvin Coolidge, appointed a special counsel to oversee oil cases, the general public refused to treat the scandals as if they were of major importance or particularly harmful. The harshest condemnation by the press and the public was reserved not for those individuals who had defrauded the government, but for those who insisted on bringing the facts out into the open. The Senate Investigating Committee was accused of acting irresponsibly and when, a few months later, John Davis was campaigning for the Presidency on the basis of the corruption of the previous administration, his speeches were viewed as being in bad taste. The extent of this attitude was clearly reflected in the landslide victory of Coolidge at the polls in November, 1923.

Prosperity was what the public wanted, and under the

Samuel Gompers, *first president of the American Federation of Labor, at his office in Washington, D.C. The cotton rabbit on the desk was Gompers' mascot, and accompanied him on all of his travels around the country.*

Banker J.P. Morgan, *whose genius for financing was the primary thrust behind America's rise in productivity during the 1920's.*

Socialist Eugene V. Debs, *who was a tireless worker for the rights of the American working class during the decade of the 20's.*

leadership of Coolidge business boomed in an unprecedented degree. For nearly seven years, as Stuart Chase expressed it, American industry and salesmanship combined to become "the dictator of our destinies, the statesman, the priest, the philosopher . . . the creator of standards of ethics and behavior . . . the final authority on the conduct of American society." The automobile was one of the chief contributors to the remarkable changes in society. In 1919 there had been a little over six million passenger cars owned by private citizens; by 1929, there were no less than twenty-three million. During the ten year period, the impact on the economy was monumental-—gas stations flourished, highways were constructed everywhere, road-side stands were erected, tourism increased, and the railroad gave way to passenger buslines. Simultaneously, the manufacture of the radio and its sale on a massive scale transformed the society. Despite fluctuations in the economy in 1924 and 1927 during a brief downward trend, the sale of radios soared from sixty million dollars in 1922 to $842,548,000 in 1929. Emphasis changed from philosophical idealism on the part of intellectuals and pragmatic thrift on the part of farmers to this vast and increasing affluence of the middle class in general and the wealthy in particular.

The spirit of capitalism and the Protestant ethic, so long embedded in American history, were replaced by an ethic of materialism. Coupled with the radio, newspapers and magazines produced thousands of pages of advertising and the public hastened to respond to new trends. The tobacco industry quadrupled its campaign to sell cigarettes and within a brief period of time sales reached heights well beyond manufacturers' expectations. With the passage of the Nineteenth Amendment, women had acquired a new status politically, economically and socially and much of the consumption was directed towards the clothing and cosmetics industries. The United States became the banker and the financial arbitrator for the world and American governmental officials were called in time and again to organize the economies of foreign nations. The limestone buildings on the corner of Broad and Wall Streets, which still bore the scars of the bombing in 1920, were internationally and undisputedly the financial center of the world. Military intervention was used only rarely—in restoring order in Nicaragua and Haiti; elsewhere, financial penetration characterized America's foreign involvement.

The influence of business, and the immediate gratifications which could be offered, became pervasive. Free from external entanglements and experiencing unprecedented prosperity, Americans replaced the symbols of democracy with the slogans of advertising. Even the Ku Klux Klan became a champion of advertising and salesmanship in the mid-1920's, converting tens of thousands of people to its ranks through the sale of memberships costing the modest sum of ten dollars. Other, less political organizations flourished. In every city, service clubs gathered together for weekly luncheons, proclaiming the paramount value of free enterprise. Religious groups associated themselves with business in one of the most significant phenomena of the decade; frequently, quotations from the Bible were enjoined to support business activities and in return, business enterprises contributed substantially to the coffers of organized religion. Church attendance remained constant—no longer was spiritualism the overriding concern; it had been replaced by business, psychology and a general disillusionment with traditional values. Church attendance was, primarily, important from a perspective of business and social association.

Science emerged as the doctrine of the decade and the

Henry Ford, *right, and his son, Edsel, pose with the ten millionth car to come off the Ford production line. The ten millionth car was completed in 1924. The smaller car on the right is the first automobile Ford built, which was completed in 1896.*

The use of the automobile *for advertising purposes in the 1920's.*

prestige of the discipline was colossal. Even the least scientific branch of the field was receiving vast interest. Psychology, transmitted to the United States through the works of Freud and Jung and others captivated the minds of the public and appeared to be overshadowing religion. As Americans lined up on the respective sides of the debate, Fundamentalists found themselves in a position which seemed hopeless. More liberal churches attempted to incorporate science into their dogma and support for their cause was gaining significantly. Then, in the summer of 1925, the controversy reached a climax.

An oil gusher *in Oklahoma in 1923.*

Prohibition agents *hold part of the $300,000 worth of illegal liquor they uncovered in a coal pile aboard a coal steamer in New York Harbor. Federal agents were constantly on the lookout for caches of illegal liquor during the period of prohibition during the 1920's.*

Improvements in industrial technology *did not always find their way to the farm. Here is a scene typical of the farming centers of the decade, with farmers still bringing their crops to market in horse drawn vehicles.*

The issue began with the passage of a bill in the Tennessee State legislature prohibiting any teacher in any school which was supported in whole or in part by public funds from teaching any theory which denied the story of the divine creation of man as taught in the Bible and taught instead a theory of evolution. Within a matter of days after the bill was signed by the governor, a small group in Dayton, Tennessee, became determined to put the law to a test. George Rappelyea, a mining engineer and prominent citizen in the community, approached John Scopes, a twenty-four year old biology teacher at Central High School, proposing that he should allow himself to be caught teaching the theory of evolution in order to challenge the legislature's dictum. Scopes agreed and was soon thereafter arrested. William Jennings Bryan, who had been extremely prominent in national affairs for several years, volunteered his services to the prosecution. Rappelyea wired the American Civil Liberties Union, requesting that it provide the defense. The New York offices complied, securing the counsel of Clarence Darrow.

For the general public, which followed the course of the trial with particular interest, the issue at stake was not that of the rights of taxpayers versus academic freedom; rather, it represented a battle between Fundamentalism and Modernism. The attorneys were well-recognized nationally and the formerly insignificant town of Dayton was pictured on the front pages of newspapers throughout the nation. It was a bitter trial, climaxing on July 20th, when Bryan himself took the stand, testifying as an expert on the Bible. The crowd that filled the courtroom reached such proportions that the judge was forced to reconvene on a platform outside. The shirt-sleeved attorney for the defense, with a Bible on his knee, put the Fundamentalist champion through one of the most astonishing tests in the history of the American judicial system. Darrow, quoting from the Bible, inquired repeatedly as to Bryan's understanding of the events of the creation, the flood, the Tower of Babel, Jonah and the Whale, Cain and Abel, and on and on until the judge mercifully refused to let the ordeal continue. At one point, Darrow had declared that his purpose was "to show up Fundamentalism . . . to prevent bigots and ignoramuses from controlling the educational system of the United States." Bryan had jumped up from the witness chair, screaming that his purpose was "to protect the word of God against the greatest athiest and agnostic in the United States!" The confrontation was clear-cut; it reflected the general atmosphere of the country. The jury in Dayton found Scopes guilty as charged and fined him one hundred dollars. The defense promptly appealed the case to the State Supreme Court, which later upheld the anti-evolutionary law but freed Scopes on a technicality, thereby precluding further appeal.

Theoretically, Fundamentalism was the victor in the Scopes case, but among the population as a whole, the ideas and concepts espoused by the prosecutor were beginning to wane rapidly.

Public attention shifted to a presumably more interesting and critical turn of events—the violation of the Prohibition

The Harding administration was characterized by corruption. Harding, right, was never implicated in any of the shady deals, but his Secretary of the Interior Albert B. Fall, left, became deeply entangled in the Teapot Dome scandals.

Amendment and the violence which was thwarting the enforcement of the Volstead Act. The Eighteenth Amendment, denying the manufacture and sale of alcoholic beverages, had been passed by the Senate and the House of Representatives in 1917 after an extremely brief debate, lasting less than two days. The grounds for the Amendment appeared justifiable considering the need for efficiency and sobriety during the war. Yet, in January, 1919, two months after the Armistice had been signed, the necessary three-quarters of the state legislatures had ratified the measure, incorporating it into the Constitution. Public opinion overwhelmingly had favored the new law and it continued to do so for the ensuing year or so. The Volstead Act was passed with little commotion, providing means of enforcement and even the American Federation of Labor, which opposed the strict terms of the Act, could rally only a moderate number of demonstrators in protest.

As the years progressed, however, it became evident that widespread enforcement was virtually impossible. Between illegal distilling and smuggling, liquor continued to be available and was used in large quantities. Speak-easies flourished and were quickly taken over by gangs which controlled the flow of alcohol through connections with police, bribes and assassinations. As the profits from illegal sales increased, the organization of crime became more sophisticated. By 1923, Al Capone had several hundred men at his disposal, many of

Albert Fall *as a Senator from New Mexico before he became Secretary of the Interior. Fall and Attorney General Daugherty were the two central figures in the Teapot Dome scandals which rocked the country during the 20's.*

whom were adept in the use of sawed-off shotguns and Thompson machine guns. Gradually, he gained complete control over the Chicago suburb of Cicero by installing the mayor of the city, posting his agents in gambling resorts and running 161 bars which openly served liquor to their patrons. Rival gangs, whose interests were being threatened by Capone's success, took matters into their own hands. In the mid-point of the decade, the O'Banions, the Gennas and the Aiellos brought their grievances to the streets in open warfare and with the new technique of wholesale murder. This persisted until the end of the decade and the revenue acquired by Capone and others amounted to what is estimated at sixty million dollars a year.

Other enterprises developed in the wake of these activities. In some instances, labor unions engaged in criminal activities such as extortion; in other cases, rackets spread throughout almost every major city. By 1929, according to the State Attorney's office in Illinois, there were ninety-one rackets in Chicago, costing the average citizen one-hundred-and-thirty-six million dollars a year. Bootleggers and racketeers chose their favorite weapons, for use when persuasion failed. Between October, 1927, and January, 1929, 157 bombs exploded in the Chicago district alone; none of the people who had set them off was ever brought to trial. The network of corruption and violence had pervaded the city government and the police department so thoroughly that enforcement of laws was impossible. Similar systems existed in New York in particular, but almost every major urban center in the country was affected by the adoption of the Eighteenth Amendment.

Harry M. Daugherty, *Attorney General during the Harding administration. Daugherty amassed more than $100,000 in two years illegally by selling bootleg permits for oil drilling, pardons, and immunity from anti-trust prosecution. He was one of the central figures in the Teapot Dome oil scandals.*

Coupled with these illegitimate enterprises, much of the prosperity of the latter half of the decade was concentrated in

273

The crusading Senator *from Wisconsin Robert M. La Follette, speaking to a radio audience in 1928. La Follette was a reformer who spoke out against government corruption and unfair business practices by the large corporations.*

a growing but still reasonably limited, proportion of the society. In a real sense, increases in expendable income were attributable to factors other than actual income gains, per se. The real strength of prosperity resided in the attitudes which supported it.

As the 1928 election approached, it had become apparent that a widespread and profound change had occurred in the values and behavior of the American public. Materialism had made it possible to argue, as many did, that liberal democracy and laissez-faire capitalism were synonomous. Growth became coterminous with progress; liberty was defined through prosperity; and freedom was equated with wealth. Yet, the interplay between illusion and reality was often difficult to discern.

Although prosperity generally characterized the country, there was a certain fragility to it. Advancing technology had been responsible for the extraordinary increase in production during the 1920's. But, technology had its drawbacks. Income inequality was one of these. Clearly, those who most benefitted from rising levels of production were the same individuals who had already achieved a reasonably high standard of living prior to the business boom. And, although the middle class was expanded significantly, due to an increase in the number of white-collar positions available, the average unskilled or semi-skilled worker continued to experience a reasonably low standard of living.

A broadening base of consumption, accompanied by a sharp improvement of free services and the growth of installment buying tended to obscure this fact and to prevent social protest from emerging as a dominant form of behavior. Material possessions were possible because of the extension of credit on a very free basis; but the actual foundation upon which the credit rested was weak. In addition, as production increased and profits became an over-riding interest of the business community, mechanization replaced unskilled labor, affecting every segment of the economy. Between 1919 and 1929, output per man-hour rose seventy-two percent in manufacturing, thirty-three percent in railroads and forty-one percent in mining. Unemployment figures matched the changes, though not completely. While substantial ad-

vances were made in the employment ranks of white-collar workers—trade, finance, real estate, education, government employment, and professional services increased by forty-five percent—the industries hit the hardest by technological advances suffered a net loss of three and a half percent in employment.[2] Similarly, transformations in unionization worked against the extension of the benefits of national prosperity into the lower-class segments of the society.

Although the population residing in cities rose to 92.3 million shortly after the First World War, the growth of labor unions declined. Membership dropped from five million in 1920 to three-and-a-half million in 1923, where it stabilized for the duration of the decade. Effective unionization was concentrated in very few industries—coal, railroads, construction and clothing. In many of the newer and most productive industries, labor organizations were either absent or ineffectual. The strikebreaking tactics of the last few months of 1919 contributed to this decline, along with the pervasive public sentiment against collectivism of any form, the crusades against the union shop and welfare unionism.

The results were not always highly visible because of the practice of conspicuous consumption on a credit basis even among the lower income stratum, but they profoundly affected the income distribution across the nation. Typically, union employees received as much as twice the income of nonunion members performing roughly equivalent tasks. Business prospered through marked increases in manufacturing and production and sales; the national income grew steadily; and, superficially, at least, the era was one of unprecedented wealth. Yet, it was not the labor force itself which benefitted equally, even though the prosperity would have been impossible without it. If anything testifies to the impact of the change in values during the decade, it is the relative absence of movements for social and economic reform which were so comprehensively overshadowed by the ethics of laissez-faire capitalism, and materialism which had supplanted traditional norms. The emphasis on the glorification of free enterprise had become so essential to the American way of life that even those who failed to reap the fruits of prosperity were unwilling to challenge its supremacy.

[2] Figures for unemployment during the decade vary, but the most generally accepted ones indicate that severe unemployment existed, reaching as high as 13 percent in 1924 and 1925, 11 percent in 1926, 12 percent in 1927 and 13 percent in 1928.

Upstate Forest Fires Rage Anew As More Incendiary Blazes Are Reported

SHOPPING'S GOOD IN HOLLYWOOD

HOLLYWOOD DAILY CITIZEN

HOLLYWOOD'S LEADING NEWSPAPER

VOL. 25. NO. 112 HOLLYWOOD, CALIFORNIA, FRIDAY, AUGUST 9, 1929 Price 2 Cents Per Copy

STOCKS IN WORLD WIDE COLLAPSE

Graf Zeppelin Rapidly Nearing Homeland

HELPFUL WIND SPEEDS SHIP OVER SEA

Dirigible Expected To Reach Home Port Tomorrow Afternoon

NEW YORK, Aug. 9. United Press) — The Graf eppelin was approaching the orst of Europe today, havig encountered splendid eather and favorable winds the first day of its roundie-world commercial flight rom Lakehurst, N. J. Friedichshafen, Germany, is the raf's immediate objective.

It was calcuated that the dirigic should reach its home station about 2:30 P. M., E. S. T. tomorw. A continuation of fresh winds hich expected to add 20 to 25 iles per hour to the Graf's speed ould hasten its arrival.

All Well Aboard

All was well aboard the great ey airship as it sped eastward ross the Atlantic with its 22 pasngers and 40 crew members. Prite messages from the group of voyagers indicated that the pasngers were having the "time of eir lives."

The Graf [illegible] due [illegible] New York [illegible] Dr. Eckener having abandoned his idea following the Great Circle course an effort to take advantage of rthwest and west winds.

Tail Wind Aids

The government weather report m Washington said that during first half of today the Graf uld be favored by brisk tail nds and that it would be flying ough "mostly fair weather."

The course the Graf was following would take her north of the ores this morning. Dr. Eckener s expected then to veer northrd, pointing almost directly for iedrichshafen.

The speed with which the Graf s clicking off the miles gave omise of a record for a dirigible ss. During the first 19 hours of flight the airship maintained average of close to 70 knots and speed at times went nearly to miles per hour.

SENATE TARIFF SESSION DELAYED

Pictured above is the Senate finance committee which, despite the hot weather in Washington and the beguilements of seashore and country, is deep in hearings on the tariff bill, under the chairmanship of Senator Reed Smoot of Utah.

Postponement Caused By Long Time Needed To Consider Bill

WASHINGTON, Aug. 9. (U.P.)—Republican members of the Senate finance committee today [illegible] considered decreases made in the tariff duty on figs and, reversing themselves, voted to retain the House rate of 5 cents and 40 percent advalorem.

WASHINGTON, Aug. 9. (U.P.)—A gentleman's agreement has been worked out between Republicans and Democrats to delay the opening of the Senate tariff session from August 19 until September 3, because the Senate finance committee Republicans now rewriting the House tariff bill will not have it ready for Senate consideration until two weeks after the date set originally.

Republicans have arranged to finish all rates in the bill by August 19 when they will be made public officially and turned over to the Democrats for inspection. This courtesy was granted in order that the Democrats might be ready to debate the bill September 3, the two weeks being allowed in order that they may familiarize themselves with its new duties.

The arrangement had to be effected by a gentleman's agreement because under the constitution the Senate can recess no more than three days at a time without consent of the House and the House will not return until September. The Senate therefore will meet every third day after August 19 and adjourn without doing any business until September 3.

Nun Burned To Death Trying To Save Host

PORTSMOUTH, Eng., Aug. 9 (U.P.)—Sister Celestine, acting mother superior of St. Patrick's Convent on Hayling Island, gave her life attempting to save the blessed sacrament, prime object of her devotion, when fire broke out in the convent today.

First Sister Celestine directed the rescue of 54 convalescent children and seven other nuns from the burning wing, which was destrowed. Then she dashed back to save the host, but was overcome by smoke.

Lightning Kills 15 In Terrific Rain Storm

BERLIN, Aug. 9. (U.P.)—Fifteen persons were killed by lightning in a terrific storm in eastern Galicia, it was reported here today. The town of Stanislas was completely under water, the dispatches said.

Snook Leaves Stand After Long Grilling

COURTROOM, Columbus, O., Aug. 9. (U.P.)—The battle of wits between Dr. James Howard Snook, [illegible] alleged murder of Theora Hix, and Prosecutor John J. Chester, Jr., who was cross examining Snook, came to a sudden end at 2:25 p. m. today when Chester broke off in what seemed to be the midst of his questioning, came to the defense table and said "he is your witness."

Dr. Snook had just completed repudiation of his entire alleged confession. His redirect and surrebuttal examinations were completed at 3:25 p. m., and he left the witness stand with evident relief after having testified for more than 16 hours.

UPSTATE FIRES RAGE ON NEW FRONTS

Timber, Brush Lands Aflame In Northern California, Northwest States

By FRANK H. BARTHOLOMEW
(United Press Staff Correspondent)

SAN FRANCISCO, Aug. 9.—While investigation was still under way into 20 fires of incendiary origin in the forests and grazing lands of San Joaquin Valley counties, almost the same number of new blazes broke out during the night in the northern part of the state.

The Klamath National Forest in Trinity County was fired in a dozen places, according to forest service headquarters here.

State authorities were advised that additional blazes of incendiary origin had broken out in Butte and Tuolumne Counties.

Flames Are Fought

Meantime the original San Joaquin fires, set by firepots and burning-glasses so arranged that the rays of the sun would ignite matches, were for the most part still being fought over miles of front.

Belief grew that a state-wide campaign of incendiarism was [illegible] opposed to the [illegible] service or the timber and [illegible]ing interests.

Danger increased as the humidity continued below the fire-hazard point in the "Great Valleys"—the San Joaquin and the Sacramento.

Many other new fires were reported throughout the state, due to sparks from logging locomotives, cigarettes thrown from automobiles and carelessly handled camp fires.

The great Badger Creek fire was brought under control late this morning, and the town of Hawkinsville saved. The fire left a wide

(Continued On Page Three)

DRY AGENTS TO BE REFUSED RIFLES

Pistols To Be Only Weapon Except In Isolated Territories

By JOSEPH S. WASNEY
(United Press Staff Correspondent)

WASHINGTON, Aug. 9.—Prohibition Commissioner J. M. Doran today drafted an order to dry administrators forbidding the carrying of rifles by prohibition agents except when they work in isolated sections. The new regulation was adopted after a Texan had been killed accidentally by dry agents.

Hereafter agents will be armed only with revolvers, as a previous order of Doran banned the carrying of sawed off shot guns and similar weapons.

Sees No Necessity

"There appears to be no necessity for prohibition agents to carry rifles when working in settled communities," Doran said. "The rifle is essentially an offensive weapon and the prohibition service does not bear arms for offensive purposes. In communities pistols must be used exclusively.

"However, in mountain country [illegible] long range defe[illegible] an agent's life may be ne[illegible], rifles will be permitted."

No Machine Guns

The new order was promulgated after the killing of Tom Chandler, Poteet, Tex., by Agent Charles Stevens. Doran said reports in this case showed Sevens fell and the rifle he carried was accidentally discharged, causing the death of the farmer.

Doran said no prohibition agents were armed with machine guns nor automatic rifles but added that some bootleggers and rum runners, especially in the vicinity of Detroit have adopted a highly aggressive attitude toward federal enforcement officers.

PRICES CRASH AFTER REDISCOUNT RATE IS RAISED BY U.S. BANK

Traders In Rush To Unload Send Values Of American Securities To Low Levels; Billions Lost in Paper Profits As Selling Orders Pour In

By ELMER C. WALZER
(United Press Staff Correspondent)

NEW YORK, Aug. 9.—Practically every stock market in the United States, Canada and Europe witnessed a hammering down of American share prices today because the New York Federal Reserve Bank raised its rediscount rate overnight from 5 per cent to 6 per cent.

Traders felt the rise was a forerunner of similar action throughout this country and in England. Fearing a tightening of speculative credit which would make their stockholdings expensive to carry, they preferred to unload while prices still were high.

The result was an unprecedented accumulation of "sell" orders, which forced down every issue on the New York stock exchange and caused one of the worst breaks in Wall Street history. Prices crumpled and repeated attempts to rally the market failed.

At the opening values were down one to more than 20 points. Orders were bunched in blocks of 5000 to 25,000 shares and execution of these huge amounts set a new record for the first half hour with business at the rate of more than 13,000,000 shares for a full day.

Rush Slows Down

Later dealings quieted down from the opening rush. At 1:30 the volume amounted to 3897,100 shares. Tickers were 17 minutes behind before the end of the first hour, but they gradually caught up.

Prices came back in the second hour, but around noon further selling [illegible] very. The list then seesawed back and forth with the trend lower.

Late in the session prices of the majority of issues were off 5 to 10 points, representing a reduction in market value of several billion dollars.

This terrific decline resulted primarily from the unexpected raising of the New York rediscount rate from 5 to 6 per cent.

Call Money The Same

The increased rediscount rate had no effect on call money today and the rate held at 8 per cent all day with supplies fairly comfortable. Incidentally the heavy selling was swinging stocks from weak to strong hands able to finance larger ventures and therefore the money

(Continued On Page Three)

Soviet Aviators Continue Hop To U. S.

NOVOSIBIRSK, Russia, Aug. 9. (U.P.)—The airplane Land of the Soviets, en route from Moscow to New York via Siberia and Alaska, landed here from Omsk at 11:20 a. m. today. The plane left Omsk at 8 a. m., flying the distance of approximately 360 miles in 3 hours and 20 minutes.

The plane, which is manned by four of Russia's crack aviators, will make the 12,500 mile voyage in easy stages. The fliers expect to fly across to Alaska [illegible] Pacific ocean [illegible] they reach Seattle.

From Seattle the fliers probably will proceed to New York, via California and Chicago.

Many Persons Drown In Manchurian Flood

LONDON, Aug. 9. (U.P.)—Daily Express dispatches from Peiping today reported that many persons were drowned in South Manchuria as a result of torrential rains which crippled the railways of the district and destroyed many homes and buildings in the city of Mukden. The Yellow River was reported on the verge of flowing over, threatening to inundate a vast area.

Death, Insanity Caused By Heat Wave In Japan

TOKIO, Aug. 9. (U.P.)—Death, insanity and the prostration of hundreds of persons followed in the wake of an unprecedented heat wave which struck this portion of Japan.

The police reported today that six persons were drowned while seeking relief in surrounding lakes, that several others were driven insane by the depressing heat and that 64 persons were missing. Hundreds of people were reported incapacitated.

Some of the thermometers in the streets here registered as high as 120, although officially the temperature was given out as 97.4. Vegetation and trees were dying in several localities. The heat wave followed a drought of five weeks.

The Weather

Hollywood and Vicinity: Fair tonight and Saturday with moderate temperature. Probably fog or clouds in the morning.

Southern California: Fair but with fog on coast tonight and Saturday; no change in temperature; moderate north to west winds on coast.

TEMPERATURES

Hollywood today at 12 m., 81; minimum today, 65; maximum yesterday, 86.

(Figures by E. G. Cheesman)

What Kind of a Pet ?

Does YOUR Family want? Dog? Cat? Canary?

There's unlimited variety in pets offered daily in the CITIZEN Classified Section—under the "Pet Stock" classification.

Buy or sell pets and supplies through the Classified Ads; get acquainted with this service today.

READ and USE
CITIZEN "Classified Ads"
Phone HO-6111.

Latest News Bulletins

UNSPOKEN BY LINER

HORTA, Azores, Aug. 9. (U.P.)—The radio station here at 4:45 p. m., G.M.T. (11:45 a. m., E.S.T.), heard the French liner Degrasse asking the Graf Zeppelin for her position. The question was unanswered. The radio station was trying to get in touch with the Zeppelin.

WIN BOTH MATCHES

WEST SIDE TENNIS CLUB, Forest Hills, N. Y., Aug. 9. (U.P.)—The United States started brilliantly in the Wightman Cup tennis matches today, winning both of today's singles matches. Miss Helen Wills, the national champion, defeated Miss Phoebe Watson, 6-1, 6-4, while in the second match, Miss Helen Jacobs, the No. 2 United States player, defeated clever Betty Nuthall of Great Britain, 7-5, 8-6.

THERMOMETER GOES UP AS ICE CREAM MEN WALK OUT

CHICAGO, Aug. 9. (U.P.)—With the thermometer around the 90 degree mark, a strike of the ice cream workers union was on here today. About 450 men and 35 factories were affected due to the fact that union demands for a $60 week wage scale have not been met.

DECREASED GRAIN YIELD PREDICTED

WASHINGTON, Aug. 9. (U.P.)—The condition of the corn crop on Aug. 1 was 78.8 per cent of normal, indicating a production of 2,740,514,000 bushels as compared with 2,836,000,000 bushels harvested in 1928, the Agriculture Department announced today.

Production of winter wheat for 1929 was estimated at 568,233,000 bushels, compared with 578,000,000 bushels last year. The average yield of winter wheat per acre was placed at 14.2 bushels and the quality of the crop at 86.7 per cent.

The department announced the condition of other spring wheat at 56.2 per cent of normal, which was indicative of a production of 156,389,000 bushels, compared with 231,000,000 bushels last year.

The indicated production of all wheat was estimated at 773,885,000 bushels for 1929, compared with 902,000,000 bushels in 1928.

The condition of the oats crop Aug. 1 was 75.6 per cent of normal.

'Eruption' Of Mt. Lassen Leaves Historic Peak Strewn All Over

SACRAMENTO, Aug. 9. (U.P.)—Mt. Lassen, pride of Tehama County, burst out in an eruption today that could be heard for blocks.

The volcano emitted smoke, water pipes, trees, mud and dust in a way that was nobody's business, except, perhaps George Collins, state forest ranger.

For months, Collins has been shaping the plaster of Paris replica of the volcano for Tehama County's exhibit at the Diamond jubilee state fair and western exposition.

The miniature, weighing two tons, faithfully represented every characteristic of the big mountain. It was built at the entrance to the Mt. Lassen park and brought from Tehama County to Sacramento by truck.

The volcano, fastened to a big crane, was being shifted from the main floor of the pavilion to the second floor, when the crash came. Down went Mt. Lassen. Its sides split to pieces, plaster of Paris was scattered all over the place, the mountain was a mess.

P. H. Ramsay, Red Bluff member of the fair board, immediately ordered the volcano to be reconstructed.

One Killed, Seven Hurt As Standard Oil Tanker Is Shaken By Explosions

BAYONNE, N. J., Aug. 9. (U.P.)—One man was killed and seven were known to have been injured in a series of explosions aboard the tanker William E. Rockefeller at Pier 6 of the Standard Oil Company today.

The blasts shook Essex County, New Jersey, broke windows along the New Brighton, Staten Island, waterfront, and sent hundreds of persons to their telephones in a panic.

The tanker caught fire and poured blazing oil into the Kill Van Kull. The flames spread across the Kill toward Staten Island, and tugs immediately scouted through the inferno picking up the tanker's crew members from the missing waters.

The body of the dead man found floating near the tanker was taken to the Bayonne morgue. The seven injured men, some with broken bones and all of them burned, were picked from the water and hurried to Staten Island hospital.

All seven had jumped from the decks when the first explosion was followed by several other blasts and by belching fire in the forward hold. Fifteen minutes after the first concussion, there was a final puff and roar.

Black smoke rolled in palls from the huge tanker as tugs and the New York City fireboat Zophar Mills sped to the scene.

The dead man was identified as John Ward, watchman.

Today's Scores

NATIONAL LEAGUE

At Philadelphia—		R.	H.	E.
Chicago	304 000 005—	12	13	0
Philadelphia	050 000 001—	6	10	0

Batteries: Bush and Taylor; Benge, Collins, Elliott, Koupal and Lerain.

At New York—		R.	H.	E.
Cincinnati	010 000 000—	1	4	3
New York	010 132 00x—	7	15	0

Batteries: May, Kolp and Sukeforth; Fitzsimmons and Hogan.

At Pittsburgh—		R.	H.	E.
St. Louis	040 000 200—	6	10	0
Pittsburgh	003 120 01x—	7	14	1

Batteries: Mitchell, Frankhouse, Johnson and Wilson; French, Swetonic and Hemsley.
(Only games today).

AMERICAN LEAGUE

At Chicago—	R. H. E.
St. Louis	301 300 1
Chicago	001 003 3

(Only game today).

INJURIES FATAL

LONG BEACH, Aug. 9.—Mrs. Rhoda A. Speer, 82, of this city, died last night from injuries sustained when she was knocked down by an automobile.

Doeg Tennis Winner In Thrilling Match

SOUTHAMPTON, N. Y., Aug. 9. (U.P.) — John Doeg, California's blonde giant of the tennis court, gained the finals of the Meadow Club invitation tournament here today in a thrilling five set battle with Gregory Mangin, of Newark, N. J.

The match was one of the greatest ever played at Southampton. Doeg coming from behind after losing the first two sets, to win by a score of 8-10, 4-6, 6-3, 6-3, 6-5.

SAN ANTONIO THEATER IS BADLY DAMAGED BY BOMB

SAN ANTONIO, Tex., Aug 9. (U.P.)—A bomb hurled through the door of the Victors Uptown Theater today caused several thousand dollars worth of damage, blowing three sets of double doors from their hinges, ruining valuable draperies and cracking the walls, ceiling and floor of the theater lobby.

PENSION FUND FOR PASTORS DESIRED

SEATTLE, Wash., Aug. 9. (U.P.)—Plans for an $8,000,000 pension fund for ministers occupied today's session of the seventy-eighth annual international convention of Christion churches.

W. R. Warren, Indianapolis, executive vice president of the church pension fund, presided. F. E. Smith, Indianapolis, presented a report.

Talks were made by Dr. George A. Campbell, St. Louis, J. G. Warren, Los Angeles, and J. I. Muffley, Tacoma.

Muffley served as chairman of the Washington state committee for the Presbyterian church when that organization established a pension fund for its ministry two years ago.

"In the two years during which the Presbyterian pension plan has been in operation the benefits have greatly exceeded the fondest hopes of the sponsors," Muffley said.

Helen Wills Victor In Wightman Cup Match

FOREST HILLS, L. I., Aug. 9. (U.P.)—The United States took an early lead in the Wightman cup tennis matches today when Miss Helen Wills, the American champion, defeated Mrs. Phoebe Watson, England's No. 2 singles player. The score was 6-1, 6-4.

After disposing of Mrs. Watson easily in the first set, the California star was forced to the limit to win the second set.

A crowd of more than 6000 saw the British star twice pull up even in the second set after Miss Wills had assumed leads of 2-0 and 4-2.

Mrs. Watson was on the verge of deucing the second set when she led 40-15 in the tenth game, but Miss Wills won four straight points in a row to clinch the match.

Helen Jacobs, whose only reverse this season was at the hands of Miss Wills, met Betty Nuthall, the pink cheeked 18 year old English beauty, in the second singles matches.

Three Youths, Girl In Bank Holdup, Caught

ELK RIVER, Minn., Aug. 9. (U.P.)—Two hours after they held up and robbed the Elk River First National Bank of approximately $7200 three youthful bandits and a girl companion were captured at Zimmerman, a village near here today.

One of the robbers was seriously wounded in a gun battle with two state highway patrolmen, who apprehended them. All of the loot was recovered.

Crust—

"WHAT is more important than a good pie?" responded a department editor, when we asked her if she had anything worth mentioning in this space today. "There's not more than one woman in a hundred who knows how to make a good meringue," she continued. That's sad news. In plain American, what she said was that if your cook, or your wife who is the cook, knows how to make good pie crust, you are lucky. Henceforth, no Citizen reader needs to eat a poor pie crust or the kind of a tart that prompts you to eat the fruit and leave the wear-ever casing. In today's Home Economics Section you will find a story telling you how to make "a meringue that really classifies as a crowning glory!" And if that dosen't interest every American-born man in Hollywood, we make another poor guess. Look to the Home Economics Section every Friday for helpful and interesting items.

DEPRESSION AND THE NEW DEAL

Herbert Hoover was elected President in 1928 as the "candidate of prosperity." His supporters promised that his victory would bring to Americans "a chicken in every pot, a car in every garage." Hoover assured the Republican Party in his acceptance speech that America was "nearer to the final triumph over poverty than ever before ... the poor house is vanishing from among us" and given the chance to go forward with the Republican policies of the last eight years, America would soon, "with the help of God, be in sight of the day when poverty will be banished." In October, 1929, within eight months of his inauguration, the magnificent financial structure of America and the much lauded prosperity of the Twenties came tumbling down around him, and like the fall of Humpty Dumpty, no one could put the pieces together again.

The crash of the stock market in the Fall of '29 was even more spectacular than the bull market which had preceded it. The bull market had gotten underway in 1927, picked up momentum in '28, and reached its grand crescendo in September of 1929. If there was a break now and then and stock prices fell, speculators shrugged off the warning, for each time a new rally carried the market to a higher point than before. John Jacob Raskob, Chairman of the Democratic National Committee, stated that "anyone not only can be rich but ought to be rich," and pointed out that a savings of fifteen dollars a week invested in good common stock would make a man rich in twenty years. From 1926 to 1929 the daily average top price for twenty-five industrials rose from $186.03 to $469.49, providing a possible profit, not counting dividends, of 250%. Individual stocks had shown even more

The little girl, *daughter of an Oklahoma farmer driven from his farm by foreclosure, holds up a scrap of bread. She was one of six children in the family, which lived in a tent near Camp Blanding, Florida. Thousands of families abandoned their homes in Oklahoma and migrated to Florida in search of work.*

spectacular records. Insull Utility Investment jumped from $12.00 to $159.00 a share in nine months. In an eighteen-month period, peaking on September 3, 1929, Montgomery Ward leaped from 132 to 466, Radio Corporation of America from 94 to 505 and General Electric from 128 to 396. Buying stock in those days was like betting on a horse race where most of the horses won.

On October 24, 1929, the stock market cracked and panic began to spread on the floor, but prices held the following day and it appeared that the worst was over. Never was optimism more ill-advised; five days later the dam burst, dwarfing the events of the 24th. Huge blocks of stock were thrown on the market, five thousand, ten thousand, even twenty thousand lots, offered for whatever they could bring. The tape was a half-day behind and the entire accounting system hopelessly snarled. A clerk collapsed and had to postpone his wedding, people fainted, and brokers, fearful of losing collateral, fought each other to get to buyers, and in the melee lost shoes, glasses, and false teeth. Some newspapers described the sound emanating from the floor as "an eerie roar" but others found it more like the howling of hyenas. A young man put in a bid of a dollar a share for White Sewing Machine stock which had been selling for forty-eight, and in the confusion made the transaction. By the end of the day more than 16,000,000 shares of stock had changed hands at bottom prices and 14 billion dollars had been lost; within two months a total of 40 billion dollars disappeared in the transaction, leaving the entire financial community stunned and severely tarnishing the image of the American businessman.

The sudden collapse of the stock market was not the cause of the depression, although the "get rich" psychology which had led to the great bull market was a significant element in precipitating it, and the effects of the crash were to leave an indelible pessimism on the mood of the thirties. Nor did the depression develop spontaneously with the crash. There had been many indications of economic disequilibrium as early

Herbert Hoover, *the thirty-first President of the United States, is shown campaigning during a ''whistle stop'' speech in the mid-west.*

as 1926, and there were many who continued to feel that the failure of the stock market had no direct relationship to American prosperity. Hoover, although apparently less optimistic in private, pointed out that the ''fundamental business of the country, that is, production and distribution of commodities, is on a sound and prosperous basis,'' and some of the indices of 1930 appear to back him up; but by the winter of 1931 it became apparent that prosperity was not just around the corner, and by 1933 America was in the throes of the most serious depression it had ever faced, and one from which it would not recover until it became enmeshed in the war economy of 1939 and 1940.

What then had caused the depression? The problem is complex and stems from the cyclical nature of capitalism and the financial imbalance which followed World War I. Within the United States one of the more significant problems which developed during the twenties was that of overproduction and underconsumption. Although there were errors in judgment that might have mitigated its results, one must also remember that the depression was worldwide, and that ultimately both the height of the optimism of the twenties and the depths of the despair of the thirties were in part psychological.

Business cycles seem to be endemic to capitalism. In the free enterprise system which affords no over-all plan or authority to regulate business and production, a farmer is free to produce the maximum in order to gain a maximum profit. Trouble can arise, however, when too many farmers produce too much and cause prices on the free market to drop; then the farmer may discover that his extra work is rewarded only by prices which are insufficient to cover his costs. When this happens an agrarian depression sets in.

In the industrial society, because of the unusual acceleration which takes place in durable goods, the results of individual freedom are more complicated and far-reaching. Assume that each year twenty million men's coats are sold, produced by 210,000 machines, each of which can make only 1,000 coats in a year. If the average life of each machine is ten years, then 2,000 machines must be produced each year for replacement. If the demand for coats increases by ten

percent it will take 22,000 machines to make the coats and in addition to the 2,000 machines normally required for replacement, another 2,000 machines must be purchased. In other words, with a ten percent increase in the sale of coats, there is a one hundred percent increase that year in the machines needed. This means that the producer of the machines must be able to double the number of his employees and purchase twice the amount of material. If his existing facilities will not allow for expansion, he is forced to invest in new buildings and equipment which will amount to an expenditure many times more than that required for doubling the number of machines to be sold. In an industry which is more than once removed from the consumer, this pyramiding effect is even greater, and when a sizeable number of busi-

This photograph, *taken on October 24, 1929, shows crowds milling about the Wall Street financial district of New York City. The large crowds were a result of the heavy trading on the stock market that day.*

Another view *of October 24, 1929, showing huge crowd amassed in front of the Sub-Treasury Building across the street from the New York Stock Exchange. The crowd soon heard the news they had feared: Wall Street had suffered the worst crash in its history.*

White collar workers *protesting the lack of jobs in 1930.*

nesses are involved in expansion, then a boom period is underway.

When the demand for a product drops, however, the snowballing effect begins; the maker of coats decides to order no new machines and the producer of machines who has recently doubled his capacity for making them, finds he has no business whatsoever. He lays off his workers, whose own buying power is now greatly reduced, thus affecting other businesses. In the meantime, he cannot pay back the loan he needed to expand his plant and the bank is forced to foreclose. If the bank has already foreclosed on other mortgages it may discover it is holding a great deal of property which no one wants and that it must call in other delinquent loans in order to keep up its reserves, which results in more foreclosures, and the downward cycle is accelerated.

The cyclical nature of capitalism was severely strained by World War I. Following the war, Britain was left weakened and was unable to take industrial leadership or impose European peace as she had after the Napoleonic struggle, and industrial competition and economic nationalism were taking the place of the world division of labor. America had become the chief creditor nation of the world, but European countries were finding it increasingly difficult to make their payments to her because of an unfavorable balance of trade, which had resulted in a flow of gold from Europe to America and, therefore, to a further weakening of the financial structure of European countries. During the war the United States had

produced huge quantities of wheat to supply the market normally filled by Russia, but when Russia began to recapture its European markets, the United States was caught with overproduction. The 1918 Peace found not only America but also the world as a whole still producing to over-capacity those things the war had demanded—cereals, steel, copper, nitrates, oil, rubber, and textiles. In "Balkanizing" Europe the Treaty of Versailles had encouraged nationalism and the resultant protective tariffs with which the new countries surrounded themselves greatly diminished international trade. The passage of the Hawley-Smoot Tariff by the Hoover administration in June 30 had the same diminishing effect.

The final chain of events leading to world-wide depression began when Russia dumped huge quantities of wheat on an already glutted European market in the fall of 1930. When world wheat prices broke, the two leading banks of Austria broke with them. Both banks held sizeable short-term credits, deposits, and loans in the banking centers of Europe and America, and when they attempted to fend off disaster by withdrawing the funds deposited in other countries they brought Germany to the verge of collapse. England tried to save the Austrian economy and then tried to save the German and shortly stood in need of help herself. When England went off the gold standard in September 1931, most of the British Empire followed suit, and the ensuing chain reaction in the United States dwarfed even the severity of the stock market crash. During the twelve days following the British action American banks with assets totaling $500 million dollars collapsed. A run on U.S. banks then began in earnest and by the end of the year, more than 2,000 banks had failed and of the 18,000 that remained open, no more than half were solvent.

While world events were emerging which drastically affected the United States, disequilibrium had been developing in America herself. During the Twenties hourly output of goods had increased almost forty percent, whereas hourly

The long line *pictured here is of unemployed men waiting to apply for a few jobs that became available in a New York City store.*

earnings had increased only about eight percent with the result that the purchasing power of most of the nation was inadequate to absorb the goods flooding into the market. Installment buying, an innovation of the Twenties, fed by a new and persuasive advertising business, diverted the recognition of the reduced purchasing power, and compounded the problem when it became obvious that credit had been overextended. Even before the stock market crash there had been a drop in automobile production, construction contracts, pig iron production, and electric power consumption which signaled serious employment problems.

Disequilibrium at home and abroad was accentuated by the speculative attitude of Americans who were caught up in schemes for quick riches. The land booms in Florida and California which created many overnight fortunes and an equal number of bankruptcies were indicative of the speculative mood of the Twenties. On the industrial level financial pyramids were being built, particularly in the field of utilities, in which holding companies were sometimes three and four deep, and able to drain off the profit into the pockets of a fortunate few at the top. On the international level there were pools in copper, cotton, wheat, coffee, sugar, and wool which kept commodity prices disproportionately high, profits for a time excessive, and ultimately an overproduction in these goods which became more dangerous the longer the situation remained unnoticed.

The final step to disaster was directly related to the stock market into which a large percentage of United States capital was being funneled to purchase stock or to finance brokers' loans. As was characteristic of the optimistic Twenties, a large portion of the trading was done on margin. This meant that a broker required only a ten or twenty percent downpayment from his customer and in a real sense loaned him the remainder. If the price of the stock went up as it habitually did between 1926 and 1929, the purchaser could realize a handsome profit on very little investment. If the price dropped, however, and the broker called in the loan, the purchaser was then required to pay off his obligation based on a higher rate than the stock was now worth and in addition had assumed an interest payment to the broker of between ten and twenty percent. At the time of the crash it is estimated that three-hundred million shares of stock were owned on margin with

loans totaling nine billion dollars, and the rapid decline in stock value spelled ruin for most of those who had invested on margin—both the broker and his customer—and put a serious strain on the entire banking institution as well.

In the same boat as those who had "bought on margin" and lost, were those who had put money into the investment trusts. In 1926 there had been fewer than a hundred of these trusts, but by the summer of 1929 more than five hundred had spawned, with more than three billion dollars in shares held principally by small investors. The shareholders were unaware of the shaky foundations underlying the trusts, and that they may have paid three times the total value of the stock and other assets they represented. Furthermore, the trusts were often "inbred," a practice that almost guaranteed their eventual collapse. Goldman, Sachs and Company, for example, floated the Shenandoah Corporation, a third of whose assets was stock in another investment trust, the Blue Ridge Corporation, eighty percent of whose capital consisted of stock in the Shenandoah Corporation. Under such circumstances the small investor who had selected the investment trust as his avenue to "a piece of the rock," was destined to receive the same disillusionment as those dealing directly with Wall Street. In practice the trusts were little more than gambling establishments in which the innocent placed their bets with a croupier whose main goal was to represent the "house." In October, 1929, the investment trust virtually disappeared, and the stock of those still listed on the exchange was worth only a fraction of their September value.

DEPTHS OF DESPAIR

Whatever ingredients went into the alchemy that produced the economic collapse, the results were disastrous. Herbert Hoover, in attempting to avoid the alarming term "panic" and to provide a more optimistic attitude toward the economic situation, suggested that the United States was in a "depression"; but that word backfired and came to represent one of the most abhorrent terms in the economic vocabulary. The physical volume of production fell by 1933 to one-half of

A familiar sight *during the Depression was the Soup Kitchen. Here a Salvation Army officer hands out cups of soup to out of work men in Detroit.*

With the lack of jobs *during the Thirties many men took to the road in search of part time work. Here a "bindlestiff", the term applied to those who had no transportation and carried their belongings on their backs, moves down the highway to the next farm. Note the pair of transient farmworkers also carrying their belongings further ahead.*

The shacks of the unemployed *dot the Seattle, Washington, waterfront during the Thirties. This site had been a busy shipyard just two years earlier. Shanty towns such as this one sprang up all over America during the Depression, and were generally referred to as "Hoovervilles" after President Herbert Hoover, whom many believed was personally responsible for the Depression.*

This crude shack, *built of loose boards and parts of boxes, was situated on a vacant lot in New York City in 1932. Fifteen out of work men called this hovel home; hundreds of such shacks were erected around the country.*

the 1929 level. Unemployment grew from one-and-a-half million in 1929 to somewhere between 12 to 14 million in 1933 (not counting those who were underemployed), which was one out of every four in the labor market. Farm prices, already depressed, dropped another thirty-three percent. Commercial failures from 1929 to 1933 amounted to 129,678 with a total value of three-and-a-half billion dollars. By the end of 1932 more than five thousand banks had failed and in the first two months of 1933 bank failures accelerated at such an alarming rate that bank holidays had been declared in many states even before Roosevelt was inaugurated. The Dow-Jones averages dropped from 364.9 to 62.7. Exports and imports fell off by 67%. Some industries were hit harder than others. Jewelry sales reached a bottom of 15% of their 1929 volume, and the lumber and building materials industries had a similar slump. By 1933 architects were doing less than one-seventh of the business they had enjoyed in 1928.

Bread lines grew in length daily, soup kitchens multiplied, the jobless walked the streets seeking opportunities to work when no opportunities existed, literally millions took to the road riding the freight cars or tramping the highways and byways, and others huddled on the outskirts of the cities in shanty-towns which soon came to be known as Hoovervilles. Local and state relief agencies were unable to cope with the problem, for much of their tax base had been stripped away and they were facing their own deficits and possible bankruptcies. Various barter schemes were devised whereby the unemployed might cut wood or shovel snow in exchange for food. Chicago even resorted to paying its police and other employees in scrip based upon the hope of future tax collections. A city official in Oklahoma proposed a nationwide program whereby restaurants would put their food scraps into covered metal buckets for distribution to the "deserving poor." And, as if things weren't already bleak enough, in the midst of the depression the "black blizzards" hit the plains. Dust could be seen as far away as the Atlantic Coast as soil from a one hundred fifty thousand square mile section of America was blown away and tens of thousands of additional Americans became destitute and left their homes, most of them heading for California where they were immortalized in John Steinbeck's *The Grapes of Wrath.*

The human toll was staggering. The broker or purchaser of stocks who committed suicide was only the spectacular sym-

A cloud of thin black top soil *blowing across the Oklahoma panhandle in 1935. Drought and wind storms created the "Dust Bowl", and farm families by the thousands were forced to leave the region in search of a better life somewhere else.*

The dust storms in the Oklahoma panhandle continued for several years. Here is a farm near Guymon, Oklahoma, with its expensive farm machinery all but buried by the shifting top soil.

bol of the time and by no means typical, although statistics indicate that the percentage of suicides increased as unemployment grew. The President of the Studebaker Company, after repeatedly announcing that the depression was over, and paying out five times the net profit of the company in dividends to prove he was right, went bankrupt and shot himself to death in his bathroom. The decline in birth rates was dramatic during the depression years. By the end of the period there were nearly three million fewer babies than would have been born at the 1929 rates. When the decade ended one study showed that almost half the workers were in jobs for which they had not been trained, or for which they were vastly overtrained, emphasizing the tragic waste of human skills. Unemployed miners were boot-legging coal obtained by the most primitive and dangerous hand methods and selling it cut-rate in cities. A family in Connecticut worked at stringing safety pins on wires late into the night for less than five dollars a week.

Typical roadway scene *during the Thirties showing a family from the Dust Bowl region, their belongings packed in trailers, heading for California. Thousands of families like this one simply packed up what they owned and headed for greener pastures during the Depression.*

Even more difficult to calculate was the effect on the human spirit. A well known inventor, who had assisted in laying the first transpacific cable, had invented sound movies and was working in 1929 for the movie industry with earnings of about four thousand dollars a week. He had invested everything in the stock market and with the crash lost so heavily that it was all he could do to save his home. The effect was so catastrophic that he was a ''dropout'' throughout the depression. What the unemployed person really wanted was work, but how many months could a man pound the streets applying for job after job, when there were a hundred applicants for every opening, before his morale was depleted? Or how many nights could a man stand outside an automobile plant with his feet wrapped in gunny-sacks to keep them from freezing so that he would be at the head of the line when the office opened in the morning? By 1934 there were nineteen million people on some kind of relief, and for many Americans that was the final humiliation. Even if it was an honest job with the WPA, or PWA, or some other government agency, a man often tried to hide his place of employment

Robert Stevens, *one of millions of out of work white collar workers, appeared in the business district of Baltimore, Maryland, on August 26, 1938, wearing this sign.*

An offer *of 2000 jobs in Cleveland, Ohio, brought this response from out of work Ohioans. More than 5000 men lined up in front of the Cleveland City Hall waiting for a chance to apply for the 2000 jobs.*

from friends, and frequently was unable to look the members of his own family in the eye. Many of the unemployed took on piecework at ruinous rates. People seemed to be superfluous, and nothing is more damaging to the human spirit than not to be needed. When a man had lost his job and was unable to find work, he shunned his former friends and refused invitations since often there was not money enough to offer a visitor a cup of coffee.

HOOVER'S RESPONSE

Herbert Hoover was a living example of the American success-story. Orphaned at the age of eight, and brought up by relatives, he worked to earn money whenever he could. One summer during his high school years he weeded onions at fifty cents a day. Later he worked in his uncle's real estate office as an office boy. During his years studying engineering at Stanford he managed a laundry agency, delivered newspapers, worked part-time as a secretary for the head of the university's geology department, and spent his summer vacations doing geological work in Arkansas, California, and Nevada. In 1896, at the age of twenty-three, he was employed by a London company to manage its gold mines in Australia and, two years later, accepted the post of chief engineer for the Chinese Imperial Bureau of Mines. After several other positions he established his own engineering firm in London which reorganized mines in many parts of the world and made him a millionaire by 1914.

Still in London at the outbreak of World War I he was asked by U.S. officials to aid the 120,000 Americans who had been stranded in Europe and needed to get home, and later undertook the organization of food relief for Belgium, at which time he was asked by President Wilson to head the U.S. Food Administration. Following the war he returned to Europe to direct the feeding of millions of people, with such success that he became internationally famous. In 1921 he was called back to the United States to serve as Secretary of Commerce, a position he held with distinction for eight years under both the Harding and Coolidge administrations and

until he was elected President in 1928. As the President during the first three years of the depression, Hoover was torn by two conflicting sides of his character, the practical and the philanthropic. Convinced that the individualist system of free enterprise with its virtues of industry, thrift and self-reliance was what had made America great, he could not bring himself to condone government handouts; yet as a humanitarian he was deeply distressed by the heartbreaking plight of the unemployed. His abiding faith in the basic soundness of the American industrial system increased his determination not to provide direct help to the needy, and led him to deprecate the seriousness of the depression.

Hoover's first efforts, therefore, were directed at the restoration of confidence in the country and toward soliciting and coordinating support to this end. He called together industrial leaders and urged them to maintain existing employment rates and wages. He pleaded with farmers to voluntarily

A common sight *during the Depression was the corner apple stand. The two pictured here were in New York City, but they were typical of such street corner vendors in every major city in America.*

283

reduce planting those crops which were the most affected by
world markets and asked labor to cooperate by avoiding
strikes. He exhorted the state and local governments and
private charities to shoulder the burden of direct relief. He
called the depression ''a temporary halt in the prosperity of a
great people,'' and in essence indicated that if business,
industry, agriculture and labor would cooperate voluntarily,
prosperity, which was just around the corner, would return.

But the depression continued to deepen and Hoover reluctantly agreed to help those at the top—the hard-pressed
railroads, banks, and rural credit corporations—which he
hoped would then be stabilized and be able to employ those at
the bottom. In 1932 he signed into law the Reconstruction
Finance Corporation (RFC) to lend money to banks, railroads, agricultural agencies, and industry. The bill also provided for 300 million dollars to lend to the states for relief
since it was becoming increasingly clear that the states could
no longer carry this burden alone. The RFC set an important
precedent and provided some stabilization in the financial
structure, but the ''trickle-down'' philosophy did not solve
the problem of unemployment nor feed the needy; nor did it
save the banking institutions of the country.

Hoover also recommended that immense sums be appropriated for public works and secured from Congress two-
and-one-quarter billion dollars for such projects. Boulder
Dam (now Hoover Dam) was started on the Colorado river,
and work was begun to develop inland waterways for navigation and flood control. Under the Federal Farm Marketing
Board several millions in government funds were used to
market the 1929-30 and 1930-31 crops. The Glass-Steagall
Act was designed to counteract the contraction of money and
credit by broadening the kinds of commercial loans that were
acceptable for re-discount, and the Federal Home Loan Bank
was formed to prevent home mortgage foreclosures and to
stimulate residential construction. No one worked harder
than Hoover at trying to save the economy, and many of his

One of the *''Bonus Armies'' meeting on the steps of the Capitol.
These members of the American Legion arrived in Washington,
D.C., carrying thousands of petitions seeking cash payments of
adjusted Service Compensation certificates.*

A group *of Bonus marchers shown clashing with police in Washington, D.C., in 1932. Police and Army veterans clashed repeatedly in 1932, and such rock throwing incidents often ended in many
injuries to both groups.*

Another form *of American financial ingenuity during the Depression was the scrapman. This Chicago scrapman hauls his load several miles each day collecting scrap paper, averaging around fifty cents a day for his labors. Despite the low pay and hard work, 5000 men in the Chicago area alone preferred to become scrapmen rather than go on the public assistance programs.*

The Army *was called in to disperse veterans who had set up a camp outside of Washington, D.C., in 1932.*

proposals were creative and constructive, but it was all to no avail. In retrospect it seems that everything that was done was too little and too late.

The similarities between some of the later Hoover proposals and those of the New Deal led Walter Lippmann to view the New Deal as scarcely more than the extension of Hoover's innovations. One needs, however, to look no further than Hoover's own words to refute such a contention. In *The Challenge to Liberty* he made a scathing indictment of the New Deal, and did so in 1934 before Roosevelt had shifted to the left. Hoover was appalled at the centralization of power in the executive branch of the government, the regimentation of Industry and Commerce, the regimentation of agriculture, the entry of government into business in competition with private enterprise—in fact, looked upon it as Socialism, and the manner in which the New Deal had assumed the management of currency, credit, and foreign trade. He considered the underlying intent of the monetary measures to be "the transfer of income and property from one individual to another, or from one group to another, upon enormous scale without judicial processes." Roosevelt's monetary policies, he pointed out, had wiped out ten billions of endowments in educational, hospitalization, and welfare activities.

Just as prosperity had been the chief factor in bringing Hoover into the Presidency in 1928, so the seriousness of the depression virtually predetermined that he would be ushered

out of office in 1932. It appeared to many Americans that the great humanitarian who had fed Belgians would not use Federal funds to feed Americans, that he would lend money to the big bankers who had gotten the country into the mess in the first place, but not to the man on the streets, that he would lend money to agricultural organizations to feed pigs, but did nothing about feeding people. Although the Hawley-Smoot tariff had been opposed by over a thousand economists, the American Bankers Association, and by a host of businessmen engaged in the export business, Hoover signed the bill anyway.

More damaging was his stand against the Bonus Expeditionary Force. In 1932, World War I veterans, who had been hard-hit by the depression, requested that the government prematurely pay the bonuses that would come due in 1945; and some seventeen to twenty thousand men, forming the "Bonus Army," marched on Washington that summer. The House passed a bonus bill but the Senate rejected it. Authorities in the capitol were edgy over the outcome. Some of the demonstrators' camps were unsanitary, there were reports that Communist organizers were within the ranks, and riots broke out resulting in the loss of two lives. Although Hoover asked the members of the Bonus Army to disperse and made money available for their return home, many refused to leave. The army, under General Douglas MacArthur, was ordered to evacuate the uninvited guests and employed bayonets, tear gas and more severity than Hoover had planned. Injuries resulted, with more following, when the troops put the torch to the ex-soldiers' shanties. Many people added this dark episode to the other infamies they connected with the President, the engineer who had "ditched, drained, and damned the country." Hoover lost the 1932 election by an even wider margin than he had won in 1928 and for years suffered the humiliation, undeservedly, as the man who caused the depression, the "Hoover Depression" as it was dubbed by the Democrats.

ROOSEVELT AND THE NEW DEAL

Given the mood of the country, the Democrats would probably have won the 1932 election with any candidate. The vote was more a vote for *a* new deal, not *the* New Deal. Roosevelt was not a national figure prior to his nomination

The infantry, *with fixed bayonets, moves in against the encamped Bonus marchers on July 28, 1932. The infantry was called in when Washington, D.C., police were unable to evict the veterans from government property along Pennsylvania Avenue.*

With machine guns *lining the route, outgoing President Herbert Hoover and President-elect Franklin Roosevelt ride to Roosevelt's inauguration in January, 1933.*

and he did little during the campaign to clarify the issues. He was critical of Hoover for deficit financing, yet he advocated programs that would necessitate even larger expenditures of money. He was a man without any particular economic theories or specialized knowledge and seemingly without specific plans for ending the depression. But he electrified the nation by his vigor, his self-confidence, his ability to communicate, and his personal charm. He was a striking contrast to Hoover who seemed stiff, formal, gloomy, and tired, with feet that appeared to be perpetually stuck in the mud. Granted that any of a number of Democrats could have won in 1932, it seems inconceivable that any other could have met the challenge as Roosevelt did.

Roosevelt was from the old New York aristocracy, a distant cousin of Teddy Roosevelt, a graduate of Groton, Harvard, and Columbia Law School. He had served a term in the New York legislature, then for seven years as Assistant Secretary of the Navy under Wilson, and had been an unsuccessful candidate for Vice-President. In 1921 he contracted polio, from which he never fully recovered, and was out of politics until his friend Al Smith encouraged him to run for the Governorship of New York in 1928, in which capacity he served two terms.

As President, Roosevelt was a man of unbounded energy and buoyancy, ready to tackle the entire range of problems that beset the country. Immediately he called Congress into special session and with unprecedented dispatch fired proposal after proposal to a cooperative Congress until the New Deal seemed to many to constitute a revolution. Broadly speaking, there were two New Deals: the first during 1933 and 1934 concerned mainly with recovery, the second beginning in 1935 more concerned with reform. That there was a shift in 1935 is clear, but both reform and recovery were in evidence in the two periods. By 1937 what might properly be called the New Deal had run its course but a final shift in direction late in that year presaged what might be referred to as a third New Deal.

Faced with the collapse of the banking system during the weeks just prior to his inauguration, Roosevelt immediately declared a national banking holiday and placed an embargo on the export of gold. During the next four days, when business was almost totally suspended—there are all sorts of stories like that of the businessman who found himself with-

out money for subway fare to reach his office—the national and state banks belonging to the Federal Reserve System were quickly inspected, and those shown to be solvent were re-opened. A degree of order was restored, as well as a degree of confidence. Within weeks the United States officially went off the gold standard, and this was followed by an inflationary policy, in the hope of raising commodity prices and providing a stabilized currency value, of printing millions of dollars in paper money and reducing the gold value of the dollar to 59.06. In spite of the fears of many, the inflationary measures were carried through with caution and the dangers of valueless printing-press money were avoided. In line with his inflationary policy, more generous credit facilities were provided through the Reconstruction Finance Corporation—for business, industry, and agriculture; through a new Federal Farm Credit Administration—for loans at drastically reduced interest rates to the farmer; and the Home Owners' Loan Corporation—to refinance small mortgages on privately owned homes.

Reform of the banking system itself came through the Glass-Steagall Banking Act passed in the summer of 1933. It provided for the separation of commercial and investment banking in order to check the use of bank credit for speculative purposes, expanded the Federal Reserve system to include banks previously excluded, gave permission to national banks to establish statewide branch banking, and established the Federal Deposit Insurance Corporation to insure bank deposits up to a fixed sum.

The Truth in Securities Act and a later act which created the Securities and Exchange Commission, brought the same type of reform to Wall Street. The Truth in Securities Act provided that all new securities for interstate sale be registered before the Federal Trade Commission (subsequently the SEC), that every offering should contain full information to enable the purchaser to judge the value of the offering, and that officers of the corporation were to be criminally liable for withholding significant information. The Security and Exchange Commission (SEC) was authorized to license stock exchanges and require the registration of all securities in which they dealt. The act also prohibited pools, options, and

President Roosevelt, *center, with Vice-President Henry Wallace, left, and Secretary of Agriculture Claude Wickard, prior to Roosevelt's broadcast to the nation announcing his national program for farm relief.*

The NRA Blue Eagle banner *was a common sight in store windows in the late Thirties. Here a furniture dealer in Harriman, Tennessee, puts up the banner indicating his acceptance of Roosevelt's economic policies designed to pull America out of the Depression.*

other devices for manipulating the market, and empowered the Federal Reserve Board to determine the extension of credit for marginal and speculative loans.

Two of the most important innovations of the New Deal, both considered by Roosevelt as vital to recovery, were The Agricultural Adjustment Act (AAA) and the National Recovery Act (NRA). Both acts were eventually declared unconstitutional by the Supreme Court, thus leading to Roosevelt's attempt to "pack" the court.

The AAA attacked the long-standing problem of overproduction of basic farm products through a system of subsidies and other agreements with farmers to reduce their acreage. To many it seemed incongruous that the United States had more wheat, more corn, more food, more cotton than any other nation yet people were starving in the streets

and the New Deal was paying farmers to plow under crops and kill hogs. Yet the objectives of the plan were not different from those desired by Hoover when he sought voluntary cooperation from the farmer to reduce crops, and particularly if viewed as a method of bringing relief to the farmer at the same time as solving the problem of overproduction, the plan had considerable success. Nearly three-fourths of the cotton growers agreed to reduce their acreage by one-third in return for cash payments of from seven to twenty dollars an acre or an option on the purchase of some of the cotton held by the government. In 1933 cotton production dropped by four million bales and cotton prices rose from five-and-one-half to nine-and-one-half cents a pound. In addition, the planters who participated received 200 million dollars in benefit payments.

Half a million wheat farmers participated in the AAA program, removing eight million acres from production, and doubled their incomes for 1933 from the increase in price and the government subsidies. Corn acreage was reduced by twenty-five percent and the government slaughtered for relief or other purposes some six million pigs which led to substantially higher prices for corn and pork. One of the most

The NRA Blue Eagle flag *was raised above the Wisconsin state capital building on August 2, 1933. The NRA was one of Roosevelt's first moves to get the country back on its feet following the crash of the stock market.*

spectacular successes of the program—from the farmers' point of view—was in tobacco. Ninety-five percent of the growers participated, raising their incomes from fifty-six million in 1930 to 120 million in 1934.

In 1936 the Supreme Court declared the AAA unconstitutional on the grounds that it was an improper exercise of the taxing power of the Federal government, one which "obliterated" the individual states and "converted" the United States "into a central government exercising uncontrolled police power in every state of the Union, superseding all local control or regulation of the affairs or concerns of the states."

Other attempts were made to improve the status of the farmer, some with more success than others. A Resettlement Administration was set up to remove from cultivation or to improve ten million acres of marginal land; an attempt was made to abolish tenant farming; credit to farmers was broadened, and eventually a new trade policy with foreign countries was adopted in the hope of re-establishing the foreign market for American products.

The New Deal's attempt to rehabilitate industry was embodied in the National Recovery Act (NRA). It was designed to speed up production, spread employment, provide funds for a system of public works and emergency relief, and through a widespread system of codes cooperatively adopted to reduce hours and raise wages. The codes were to be enforced through a complex system of national, regional, state, and local compliance boards. Each industry or business that participated displayed an emblem with a blue eagle. Citizens were encouraged to boycott stores that did not participate and the government announced that it would conduct its business only with cooperating industries and businesses. Many of the relief activities prescribed under the NRA were soon transferred to other agencies, but the entire program still remained too ambitious and cumbersome. Industry refused to hold down profits, codes were habitually violated, and the system led to the growth of monopoly. By May of 1935, when the Supreme Court declared it unconstitutional, the NRA was breaking down under its own weight. The Court found that the Act had made an unconstitutional delegation of legislative power to the executive and an unconstitutional invasion by the Federal Government into the realm reserved to the states.

As it turned out, one of the most significant parts of the NRA was Section 7(a) which provided that workers "shall have the right to organize and bargain collectively." To implement this policy, a National Labor Board was created to settle all controversies between labor and management by using mediation, conciliation, or arbitration. The act gave a tremendous impetus to labor to organize itself and it set about recruiting members on the basis that the President wants "you" to join a union. General Hugh Johnson, national administrator of NRA, however, was not sympathetic to labor; the authority of the National Labor Board (NLB) was ill-defined; and many employers questioned the constitutionality of Section 7(a). The situation precipitated a number of strikes and a counter-offensive by corporations which threatened many of the gains labor had secured. With the invalidation of the NRA by the Supreme Court it was obvious that new legislation was needed and Congress promptly passed the Wagner-Connelly Act which set up a permanent, independent National Labor Relations Board (NLRB) with authority to investigate unfair practices and issue cease and desist orders. This act was also challenged in the Supreme Court but the Court, by a five to four decision, validated the

Wagner Act. Under the more sympathetic attitude of government and with the spectacular rise of the Committee for Industrial Organization (CIO) which organized the unskilled as well as the skilled on an industry-wide rather than a craft basis, labor became for the first time a third force in the American system.

The New Deal instituted a far-reaching program in the realm of conservation and power regulation. The initial step was the creation of the Civilian Conservation Corps (CCC) designed to provide work for young men and to develop a sweeping conservation program. By World War II three million men had served in the program, seventeen million acres of new forest land had been added to the nation's resources, a billion fish had been stocked in hatcheries, soil erosion had been controlled by the construction of six million check dams, and the members of the Corps had fought forest fires, made trails in national parks, built bridges and carried out projects of pest and mosquito control.

In 1931 Hoover had vetoed the Muscle Shoals Bill, but in 1933, Roosevelt, motivated by a radically different philosophy, desired to see the entire area viewed as an

Steel workers *and police engaged in a struggle during the steelworkers strike near Chicago in 1937. Note the patrol wagon on the right.*

Walter Reuther, *right, president of the United Automobile Workers, distributes leaflets to women volunteers during the auto strike at the Ford plant in 1937. On May 27, 1937, fighting between striking auto workers and company guards broke out, which closed the plant.*

Female employees *of Woolworth's Department Store in New York City shown during their sit-down strike in March, 1937. The girls were striking for the 40 hour week, and a minimum $20 weekly wage.*

Longshoremen *in San Pedro, California, crowd around the hiring hall waiting for work. The Pacific Coast maritime strike threw hundreds of longshoremen out of work in 1937.*

Violence *between striking steel workers and company "scabs" flared again in Cleveland, Ohio in 1937. Here a non-union strike breaker at Republic Steel near Cleveland beats a fallen striker while another strike breaker chases after more strikers.*

experiment in regional reconstruction. The Tennessee Valley Authority (TVA) did exactly that by candidly accepting a socialistic approach to public utilities and economic planning on the regional level. TVA was provided with authority to acquire, construct, and operate dams in the Tennessee Valley, to manufacture and distribute nitrate and fertilizer, and to generate and sell electric power particularly with a view to rural electrification. All this was to be accomplished in keeping with long-term needs in conservation. The TVA was to inaugurate flood control through reforestation, withdraw marginal lands from cultivation, develop the Tennessee River for navigation, and advance "the economic and social well-being" of the people living in the river basin. The program for the Columbia River basin, though on a smaller scale, was of similar import. The Grand Coulee Dam was built some seventy miles west of Spokane and the Bonneville Dam on the lower Columbia. The constitutionality of the TVA reached the Supreme Court where, with only one dissenting vote, the Court sustained everything the TVA was doing.

One of the most pressing problems facing the administration was relief for the twelve to fifteen million unemployed. The creation of the Civilian Conservation Corps had been the first step in putting the unemployed to work. The Federal Emergency Relief Administration appropriated money for direct emergency relief to states and local communities and eventually dispersed over three billion dollars, and the NRA had included a provision for a comprehensive system of public works which were administered by the Public Works Administration (PWA). Under a slight shift of philosophy the Works Progress Administration (WPA) was created in 1935. There were probably more jokes about the WPA and PWA than any other of the New Deal programs, and it is difficult to balance the accounts on New Deal relief. In a three-year period relief and public works had been appropriated eight-and-a-half billion dollars and the end was not in sight. There was considerable waste and some projects were ridiculous, but millions of people were put to work and there was hardly a city in the country that did not have a city hall, a school, a hospital or roads that were built under one of the programs, or

had not been aided in the construction of water works, sewage plants, bridges, and power plants. The Federal deficit also soared and there was considerable question whether the country could afford an indefinite continuation of such expenditure.

Although some of the programs advanced by the New Deal after 1934 had long been in the hopper, Roosevelt clearly shifted to the left in 1935. Huey P. Long of Louisiana had organized the Share Our Wealth Society and advocated that every family be given a homestead worth five thousand dollars and an annual income of two thousand five hundred dollars. As the 1936 elections approached it appeared that Long was a chief contender for the Presidency and New Deal circles were afraid he might be able to split the Democratic Party wide open just as Teddy Roosevelt had stolen much of the Republican vote from Taft in 1912. It was at this juncture

The Civilian Conservation Corps *was set up to provide jobs for young men during the Depression of the 1930's. Young men from all over the country, including thousands of city boys, were put to work in the national forests fighting fires, building fire lanes, and clearing brush. This picture was taken less than a year before America entered World War II, when many of the CCC volunteers would change uniforms and serve in the armed forces.*

One of the first *of the work programs instituted by President Roosevelt during his first 100 days in office was the Civilian Conservation Corps. Here a contingent of young volunteers lines up for equipment at Camp Dix, New Jersey in 1933.*

that labor was becoming disillusioned over the provisions of Section 7(a) of the NRA, referring to the Roosevelt policy as the "National Run Around." William Green, head of the American Federation of Labor, threatened that the entire labor movement would oppose Roosevelt. Father Charles Coughlin, the radio priest who had the heaviest mail of any person in the United States and who spoke to the largest radio audience in the world, was advocating a system suspiciously close to that adopted in Italy under Mussolini. And while these groups were becoming more vocal, the Supreme Court had torn up Roosevelt's programs for both labor and industry by declaring the NRA unconstitutional.

Perhaps Roosevelt was also baited into a leftward turn by die-hard conservatives. The conservative press and the hate-Roosevelters unleashed a vicious attack on him which he received with hurt and surprise, and before long his struggle with the economic royalists became an intensely personal one. Raymond Moley, a conservative member of the Roosevelt "Brain Trust" during the first years of the New Deal, reported later that Roosevelt was "amazed at his own moderation," yet the press was against him; big business as symbolized in the Liberty League deserted him; smaller businessmen as represented by the Chamber of Commerce were critical; and to add the final touch, a conservative Supreme Court declared both the NRA and AAA unconstitutional.

So in 1935 two striking measures were added to the President's list of "must" legislation. One was the Wagner-Labor Relations Act which he had earlier resisted, the other was a new "wealth tax," apparently designed to steal Long's thunder. He soon included a strong holding-company act and one of the most far-reaching pieces of legislation enacted during the New Deal, The Social Security Act. The latter provided for pensions to the needy aged, old-age insurance, unemployment insurance, benefit payments to the blind, dependent mothers and children, and appropriations for public health work. Much of the Act was based upon participation by the states, and in the course of the following two years all the states set up old-age pensions and unemployment insurance systems that met the standards set by the Social Security Board.

In 1936 Roosevelt won an overwhelming victory against the Republican candidate, Governor Alfred Landon of Kansas. In the first two years of his second term he sponsored a new Housing Act, the Fair Labor Standards Act, the Farm Security Act, an unsuccessful attempt to set up a national

Sunday afternoon *at the CCC camp in the George Washington National Forest in May, 1933.*

A view of the Norris Dam *which was part of the Tennessee Valley Authority project. The dam was completed in November, 1938.*

string of seven TVA's, and an unsuccessful attempt to reform the Supreme Court. In the latter he over-reached his support and suffered the worst defeat of his Presidency.

Assuming he had a mandate for his programs from the people, and still chafing under the setbacks he had received at the hands of the Court of "old men" which seemed out of touch with the times, he proposed legislation that would permit him to appoint one new judge, up to a maximum of six, for every justice of the Supreme Court who, having passed the age of seventy and having served for ten years, failed to retire. Much could be said in favor of the proposal, but it was immediately denounced, even by some of his own party, as a plan to "pack" the Court and as an example of the President's lust for power. Many, with some justification, believed that if the plan were adopted it would be the end of an independent judiciary in the United States. Although public opinion as well as that in Congress was rising against the bill, it may have been the retreat of the Court from its earlier stand that brought ultimate defeat to the bill and a pyrrhic victory to Roosevelt. While debate still raged, the Supreme Court found reasons for sustaining no less than eight New Deal programs including the National Labor Relations Act. A month later it gave its blessing to the Social Security Act in a decision so broad that had it been adopted earlier it might well have sustained the AAA. Before debate was over, Justice Van Devanter announced his retirement

Workers *in the Public Works Administration prepare the highway behind the White House for new pavement. More than $400,000,000 was spent resurfacing roads in every state in the country under the Public Works Administration direction.*

and other Justices soon followed suit, so that within a few years the Court had been entirely remade with eight new appointees by Roosevelt.

By 1937 the industrial production of the country had risen from its March, 1933, low of 55 on the index to 120 which was higher than the 1929 figure of 110. The New Deal seemed to be running out of steam, and Roosevelt, believing that recovery had been complete, cut back drastically on expenditures for relief. Almost immediately the index of physical production took a sharp decline, hitting a low by April, 1938, of 80—a drop of one-third. The Roosevelt answer was twofold: trustbusting and deficit financing—the latter, not only in practice but for the first time, in principle. By 1939 when the index again rose to about 120 the United States was profiting from European war contracts, and in 1940 the U.S. moved into a wartime economy which boosted the index to 140 by the end of that year. Unemployment, however, was still high, with almost fourteen percent of the labor force out of work (seven-and-a-half million persons) as compared to just over three percent in 1929, and just under nine percent in 1930. There were just over half as many people still unemployed in 1940 as there had been in the worst year of the depression, 1933.

The unemployment statistics would indicate that it was World War II and not the New Deal which brought the country out of the depression, but only the most conservative still felt that the New Deal had lengthened the depression rather than providing constructive answers to it. In 1940 Wendell Willkie ran against Roosevelt on a Republican platform which endorsed much of the New Deal. In spite of the one-hundred-and-fifty-year-old two-term tradition which lost Roosevelt some votes, he won an unprecedented third term with a comfortable margin. In the midst of World War II the ailing President was nominated for a fourth term and again won over his Republican opponent by capturing 432 electoral votes to 99 for Thomas E. Dewey. Roosevelt died at Warm Springs, Georgia, on April 12, 1945, of cerebral hemorrhage, just three months after his fourth inauguration.

Men with wheelbarrows *were a common sight on WPA projects throughout the country during the Depression. This is a picture from construction on the Arkansas River Flood Control project in May, 1939.*

Huey Long *of Louisiana, whose state-wide solutions to the Depression gained him a national reputation, shown here as a Senator in Washington, D.C. Long became an outspoken critic of Roosevelt's programs for solving the country's economic ills. Long was assassinated in 1935.*

THE ROOSEVELT LEGACY

Roosevelt's strengths were many. He came into office at a time when action was needed and he personified action. In his first inaugural he said, "This nation asks for action and action now," and the rapidity with which he proposed legislation brought assurance to the public that something was being done. The first one-hundred days of his administration were the most feverish in the history of the country and it was Roosevelt who set the pace.

Roosevelt's leadership rested to a major degree in his personality. He exuded confidence at a time when the nation had lost it. "There is nothing to fear but fear itself," he told the American people, and even among his closest associates he rarely displayed moods of dejection or pessimism. The pictures flooding the press of his smiling face, jutting jaw, and impertinently tilted cigarette holder, caught the mood of

Sign announcing *the White Fringed Beetle Project which was administered by the WPA in 1939 in Louisiana.*

President Franklin Roosevelt *signing the Social Security Bill on August 14, 1935. The bill was the first in the nation's history to give government guaranteed pensions to workers who reached the age of 65 who had contributed to the program.*

the President and inspired a new confidence among millions of Americans. He was able to articulate great ideas in simple language and he possessed an uncanny ability to know and understand what the majority of people wanted. He also was able to inspire the love and devotion of those closest to him and most of the masses out beyond. Crusty Harold Ickes, his Secretary of the Interior, melted under Roosevelt's charm, and the polls of 1938 showed that of those who responded, eight out of ten Americans liked Roosevelt's personality.

Roosevelt was a master politician—an artist in government. Whether in working with Congress or campaigning for office, his timing has, perhaps, never been equaled. His extensive and effective use of radio, his skillfully written speeches, his handling of patronage, his adroit but constant application of pressure to achieve his ends, his face-to-face persuasiveness, and above all, the sheer joy he exhibited in his work, when taken together can only be considered as superb. Critics believed that Roosevelt was thirsty for power and built a dynasty in the White House to enhance his own selfish ambitions. There is little doubt that he enjoyed power and knew how to use it, but the charge viewed in the light of his earlier political performance seems unjust, and during the first few years in the White House Congress frequently gave him more power than he asked for.

The New Deal has frequently been characterized as "pragmatic" and if one does not define the term too scientifically, it can be a help in understanding the Roosevelt approach. When confronted with two distinct economic theories over how to deal with the tariff, he told his amazed subordinates to combine the two into a single bill and bring it back. At one of his earliest press conferences he compared himself to the quarterback in a football game, saying that the quarterback knows what the next play will be, but beyond that he cannot plan too rigidly because "future plays will depend on how the next one works." In a period when it seemed that everyone—the Fascists, the Communists, the Socialists, the Townsendites, the ultra-conservatives, Huey Long, Father Coughlin—held doctrinaire solutions, many of them Utopian in nature, Roosevelt displayed skepticism about final solutions and Utopias, and contented himself with a series of improvisations, many adopted very suddenly, many seemingly contradictory. Progressive government, he once said, "must be a living growing thing. . . ."

Beneath the pragmatic Roosevelt, however, lay a philosophy that stretched back to Jefferson and Jackson, Theodore Roosevelt and Woodrow Wilson. It was a broadly based democratic humanism and a belief that life could be made better for the masses. In the platform for the 1936 election, largely written by Roosevelt, is the statement:

> We *hold* this *truth* to be *self-evident*—that government in a modern civilization has certain inescapable obligations to its citizens, among which are: (1) Protection of the family and home; (2) Establishment of a democracy of opportunity for all people; (3) Aid to those overtaken by a disaster.

He wanted to help the underdog, although not necessarily at the expense of the top dog, he made it perfectly clear that private and special interests must be subordinated to the general interest.

Roosevelt viewed his role as President as a challenge to find "among many discordant elements that unity of purpose that is best for the nation as a whole," to work toward the "unity and leadership of all groups," to help cement American society, "rich and poor, manual worker and brain worker, into a voluntary brotherhood of free men, standing together, striving together, for the benefit of all." As a leader of all the people, he adopted a program for all the people—something for business (NRA), something for labor (Section 7[a], and NLRB), something for the farmer (AAA), something for the unemployed (WPA, PWA, CCC), the Home Owners' Loan and Federal Depositors Insurance for the middle class, and the list could go on and on.

One may search the speeches and writings of Roosevelt in vain for anything that was revolutionary, yet some liberal historians and a host of conservatives view the New Deal in that light. James Burnham, author of *The Managerial Revolution* and later contributor to conservative journals, considered the New Deal as the major phase in developing in America a new managerial class to replace the traditional democratic capitalistic leadership of the country and a new value structure to replace that of nineteenth century America. Whittaker Chambers, a Communist turned convervative, believed that the New Deal was a "genuine revolution, whose deepest purpose was not simply reform within existing traditions, but a basic change . . . in the power relationships within the nation . . . In so far as it was successful the power of politics had replaced the power of business. . . This shift *was* the revolution," and the revolution was being achieved, he felt, by the Communists and near-Communists in the New Deal who had both greater commitment and clearer direction than the liberals with whom they worked.

The historian Lewis Hacker referred to the New Deal as the Third American Revolution, a revolution in which the concept of the state underwent a metamorphosis, to become an interventionist state rather than a passive or impartial force which had been its traditional role. It now imposed all sorts of controls and regulations on free business enterprises, openly entered business itself often in competition with the private sector, used its great fiscal and financial powers to redistribute wealth and income, and established social security which promised protection from the cradle to the grave. Previously, political power had been in the hands of industrialists and bankers, the larger agrarian interests and the middle class, but Roosevelt brought a shift of power to the lower middle class, to the small farmers, the urban dwellers, the workers, those on relief rolls, and the small distributors and manufacturers. Hacker might have buttressed his case for revolution by pointing out the speed with which the New Deal set up the unparalleled host of government agencies through which it attempted to achieve its ends.

If, however, the New Deal was a revolution—and much depends on how that term is defined—it was one that began in the 1890's, not 1933, and only culminated in the New Deal legislation. There is a direct line from the New Deal leading back to the Progressives and the Populists, to Woodrow Wilson, Theodore Roosevelt and William Jennings Bryan, a line interrupted only the 1920's. Many of the ideas that influenced the Roosevelt Brain Trust can be traced back to Thorstein Veblen, the Muckrakers, Herbert Croly, John Dewey, and others who were writing at the turn of the century. The legislation of the New Deal for the regulation of business stretches back to the Interstate Commerce Act of 1887, the Sherman Anti-Trust Act of 1890, to the Bureau of Corporations and the railroad legislation under Theodore Roosevelt, and to the Clayton Anti-Trust Act and the Federal Reserve Act passed during Wilson's Presidency. FDR's con-

AVERAGE MONTHLY WAGE OF DECEASED WORKER.	MONTHLY BENEFIT FOR ONE CHILD	MONTHLY BENEFIT FOR TWO CHILDREN
$ 50	$10.30	$20.60
100	12.87	25.74
150	15.45	30.90
200	18.02	36.04
250	20.60	41.20

MORE SECURITY FOR AMERICAN FAMILIES

MONTHLY BENEFITS ARE PAYABLE TO THE ORPHANS OF DECEASED WORKERS QUALIFIED UNDER OLD-AGE AND SURVIVORS INSURANCE.

THESE EXAMPLES ASSUME THAT THE WORKER WAS COVERED BY THE SYSTEM FOR THREE YEARS. WITH EACH ADDITIONAL YEAR OF COVERAGE THE BENEFIT INCREASES.

FOR INFORMATION WRITE OR CALL AT YOUR NEAREST SOCIAL SECURITY BOARD FIELD OFFICE.

FEDERAL SECURITY AGENCY

SOCIAL SECURITY BOARD

A poster *outlining the benefits of the newly enacted Social Security Bill.*

Old lady *in Denver, Colorado, puzzled over the bureaucratic maze that quickly grew up with the administration of Social Security benefits.*

servation policies were clearly preceded by those of Theodore Roosevelt, the Water Power Act of 1920 and the Boulder Dam project initiated under Herbert Hoover. His agrarian policy was preceded by legislation during the twenties and policies advocated by the Populists. In this light the New Deal can be seen as a part of a continuous effort on the part of the United States to cope with the problems of industrialization in the factory and on the farm, the rise of big business, urbanization and the radical shift of populations from the farm to the city, the rise of big business, and the lack of new land for exploitation as signaled by the end of the frontier in 1890.

Something of the balance achieved by Roosevelt can be appreciated by viewing the New Deal in broader terms. The world-wide depression and economic conditions gave rise to

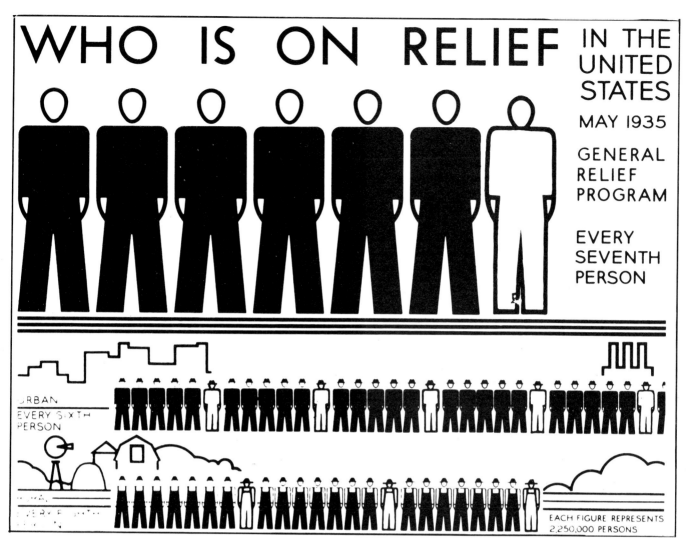

WHO IS ON RELIEF

IN THE UNITED STATES

MAY 1935

GENERAL RELIEF PROGRAM

EVERY SEVENTH PERSON

URBAN EVERY SIXTH PERSON

EACH FIGURE REPRESENTS 2,250,000 PERSONS

This chart, *taken from a 1935 government pamphlet on the relief situation, shows that one in every seven Americans was on relief by May, 1935.*

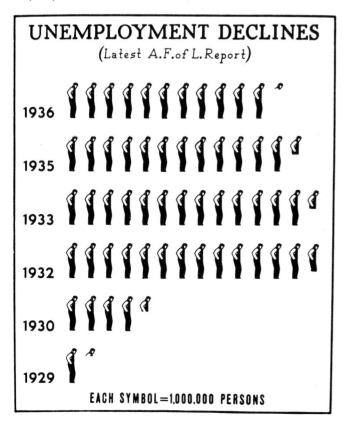

UNEMPLOYMENT DECLINES

(Latest A.F. of L. Report)

1936

1935

1933

1932

1930

1929

EACH SYMBOL=1,000,000 PERSONS

Mussolini and Fascism in Italy, in Germany to Hitler, in England to Fabian Socialism, and gave a tremendous impetus to Communism throughout the world; yet the United States became neither Fascist nor Communist, nor by any classical definition, Socialist. In this sense Roosevelt saved both American Democracy and American Capitalism. When Norman Thomas, the senior statesman of the American Socialist Party, was asked if the New Deal hadn't adopted the socialist platform, he answered "Emphatically no." What had the New Deal done about the banks? Roosevelt had put them on their feet and then turned them back to the bankers. Socialists would have nationalized holding companies, not tried to break them up. The NRA Thomas considered to be an elaborate scheme for stabilizing capitalism and maintaining profits. The CCC he looked upon as forced labor, the AAA was a capitalist scheme to subsidize scarcity. At the opposite end of the scale, J.P. Morgan publicly announced his approval of the bill signed by Roosevelt to take the country off the gold standard, and Russell Leffiingwell, a partner of Morgan's, wrote the President, "Your action in going off the gold standard saved the country from complete collapse. It was vitally necessary and the most important of all the helpful things you have done."

The balance sheet indicates that the New Deal—if judged by the entire period of the depression and World War II—brought significant changes to America. The most ob-

This chart, *with each figure representing 1,000,000 workers, shows the sudden increase in unemployment following the Stock Market crash in 1929, and the gradual lessening of unemployment as the decade progressed.*

Louis D. Brandeis

Willis Van Devanter

Pierce Butler

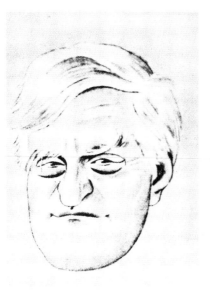

Benjamin N. Cardozo

Charles Evans Hughes

James C. McReynolds

Harlan Fiske Stone

Owen J. Roberts

George Sutherland

Roosevelt's *"nine old men" of the Supreme Court.*

Franklin Roosevelt, *who never fully recovered from polio, is shown relaxing in Warm Springs, Georgia in 1937. Warm Springs became know during the Thirties as the ''Little White House.''*

vious was enlarging the role of the Federal Government and of the executive branch within that Government. A striking aspect of this is the conviction of almost all Americans that it is the job of their government to see that there is never another great Depression, which means that most Americans have accepted the need for, within limits, a managed economy. It seems obvious, also, that never again will the Federal Government delay as it did during the early period of the depression in meeting the needs of the unemployed. The New Deal made a lasting contribution to the stability of the economy through unemployment insurance, social security and other legislation which helped to establish a floor to the business cycle.

Roosevelt's administration also brought a basic shift in the power structure of America. The rise of labor during the New Deal and the War provided labor with an influence of a magnitude that would have appalled the post-Civil War Presidents and industrialists and surprised the labor leaders. When Roosevelt took office the government still represented to a very large degree the White Anglo-Saxon Protestant property-holding class. By 1945, Catholic as well as Protestant and a host of ethnic groups had been brought into the mainstream. Although the Black was hardly in the mainstream, unlike Theodore Roosevelt who had founded a lily-white progressive party in the South, or Woodrow Wilson who had actually furthered segregation in the Federal Government, Roosevelt quietly brought the Negro into the New Deal Coalition. On the other side of the coin, the enormous lead of the well-to-do in the economic race had been considerably reduced. In 1918 the top five percent had received twenty-eight percent of the national income, but by 1945 they were receiving only seventeen percent. The share of the national income for the top one percent had been reduced during that

Eleanor Roosevelt, *wife of the President, shown speaking to the annual convention of the American Red Cross in Washington, D.C.*

period from thirteen percent to seven percent. Nor was this simply "robbing Peter to pay Paul" since the total disposable income for all Americans rose by seventy-four percent between 1929 and 1950. And amazingly, all this had been achieved without violence or bloodshed, but on the American basis of a continuous, experimental, cooperative, and democratic approach.

Whether or not one accepts all the New Deal legislation, or even the main thrust of the New Deal, it is obvious that Franklin Delano Roosevelt was an exceptional President. He restored confidence to millions of Americans, he made outstanding contributions to the human and physical rehabilitation of the country, he guided the United States through the

troubled waters of the darkest period in American History, and, as Commander and Chief during most of World War II, assured American victory in a global war of unprecedented magnitude, he maintained popular support through four Presidential elections, and he shifted—some would call it a revolution—the direction of American political and economic institutions. Since 1945 the political struggle has, to a considerable extent, been over whether the course set by the New Deal should be sustained and broadened, or contained and perhaps curtailed.

I. PHYSICAL VOLUME OF INDUSTRIAL PRODUCTION, 1929-1941
(Index numbers 1925-1935 average equals 100)

Source: Broadus Mitchell, *Depression Decade from New Eras through New Deal, 1929-1941*, p. 439

II. ESTIMATE OF UNEMPLOYMENT 1929-1940.

	numbers	% of total labor force
1929	1,497,000	3.1
1930	4,284,000	8.8
1931	7,911,000	16.1
1932	11,901,000	24.0
1933	12,634,000	25.2
1934	10,968,000	21.6
1935	10,208,000	19.9
1936	8,598,000	16.5
1937	7,273,000	13.8
1938	9,910,000	18.7
1939	8,842,000	16.5
1940	7,746,000	13.9

III. COMMERCIAL AND INDUSTRIAL FAILURES
(Mitchell—Appendix, p. 439)

	No.	Value
1929	22,909	$483,252,000
1930	26,355	668,282,000
1931	28,285	736,310,000
1932	31,822	928,313,000
1933	20,307	502,830,000
1934	19,000	457,000,000
1935	12,000	333,000,000
1936	12,000	310,000,000
1937	9,000	203,000,000
1938	9,000	183,000,000
1939	12,000	246,000,000

IV. EXPORTS AND IMPORTS 1929-1941
(Mitchell—Appendix, p. 444)

	Exports*	Imports	Excess of Ex.
1929	$5,240,995	$4,399,361	$ 841,634
1930	3,843,181	3,060,908	782,273
1931	2,424,289	2,090,635	333,654
1932	1,611,016	1,322,774	288,242
1933	1,674,974	1,449,559	225,435
1934	2,132,800	1,655,055	477,745
1935	2,282,874	2,047,485	235,389
1936	2,455,978	2,422,592	33,386
1937	3,349,000	3,084,000	265,499
1938	3,094,000	1,960,000	1,134,012
1939	3,177,176	2,318,031	859,000
1940	4,021,146	2,625,000	1,395,800
1941	5,147,154	3,345,000	1,802,149

* in thousands of Dollars

HISTORICAL HEADLINES
ON
THE DEPRESSION & THE NEW DEAL

QUAKE JURY HEARS SAFE SCHOOL PLANS

Maria Caselotti, Beautiful Opera Singer and Radio Star, Today Filed Suit for Divorce Here Against Guido Hocke-Caselotti, on Charges He Became Indifferent, Refused to Take Her Out Socially and Once Wrecked Furniture During a Quarrel. Their Romance Began When She Was a Choir Singer and He an Organist Who Coached Her for Opera, It Was Stated. Attorney William Dellamore Represents Her

Only Los Angeles Newspaper With All Leading News Services—Associated Press, International News, United Press, Dow-Jones

LOS ANGELES EVENING
HERALD AND Express

AN INDEPENDENT NEWSPAPER

Reg. U. S. Pat. Office. Copyright, 1933, by Evening Herald Publishing Company

The Evening Herald and Express Grows Just Like Los Angeles

NIGHT EDITION

VOL. LXII   THREE CENTS   Hotels and Trains Five Cents   WEDNESDAY, MARCH 22, 1933   Two Sections Section A   THREE CENTS   NO. 309

BILL LEGALIZING BEER SIGNED BY ROOSEVELT

Wife Tells Dr. Wilson Shooting by Friend

NAZIS FREED IN AMERICAN ATTACKS

Von Hindenburg Balks U. S. Attempts to Have Assailants Punished

By International News Service

BERLIN, March 22—Colonel von Bredow, an intimate friend of former Chancellor Kurt von Schleicher, was detained in the course of the Hitler government's drive against opposition.

By United Press

STRASBOURG, Alsace, March 22—Advices from Nuremburg, Germany, reported today that Otto Lenz, a Jewish storekeeper, had been tortured to death by a squad of Nazis. Lenz, who fought in the German Imperial army in the World war, was said to have brothers in America.

By International News Service

BERLIN, March 22—Attempts of the United States government to obtain punishment of the alleged Nazi storm troopers who assaulted 10 American citizens were thwarted by President von Hindenburg today.

The chief executive signed a sweeping amnesty canceling all charges against Nazis and Nationalists who prior to yesterday committed crimes "in furtherance of the national revolution."

Eight of the 10 Americans who complained of being attacked by Nazis were Jews.

The American embassy, which is following all phases of the German political upheaval carefully and reporting upon it to the state department, is making a detailed investigation of the question of anti-semitism.

American consulates throughout Germany have been asked for reports.

U. S. PROBES REPORTS OF MISTREATMENT OF JEWS IN GERMANY

WASHINGTON, March 22.—Ready to make a formal diplomatic protest if necessary, the American government today sought to learn officially if Jews in Germany are being mistreated by the new Hitler regime.

On the heels of a protest from prominent American Jews headed by Rabbi Stephen S. Wise, the state department immediately informed Ambassador Sackett at Berlin of its concern felt here on the basis of press reports and asked

(CONTINUED ON PAGE FOURTEEN)

Tomorrow Last Day to Register For Primary Vote

Tomorrow will be the last day on which voters may register for the municipal primary election of May 2, Registrar of Voters William R. Kerr warned today.

Registration books will be closed at midnight tomorrow night, and those who have not been duly registered will not be permitted to cast their ballots in May.

The municipal election was looked upon by city officials as one of the most important to Los Angeles in several decades and citizens were urged to register today or tomorrow. Persons who voted at the last primary or general election need not re-register unless they have changed their residence or desire to change party affiliation.

Autopsy May Solve Mystery of Girl's High Temperature

Doctors who were mystified by the ability of Alice Tolan, 20-year-old Mexican girl to live despite the fact she had at times a temperature of 112 degrees, five degrees higher than the mark considered fatal, planned today to perform an autopsy on the girl, who died at the General hospital yesterday. They hope to solve her unusual case.

Last January Miss Tolan's high temperature dropped to below normal and her condition, believed due to tuberculosis, became worse.

But just before she died yesterday Dr. Edna Winters, her physician, said Miss Tolan's temperature rose again to 107 degrees—the fatal point.

2 French Officers Backed by Guns Cross German Line

By International News Service

BERLIN, March 22—Intense excitement was caused here tonight by news that two French mounted officers had crossed the German frontier at Hilst, in the Palatinate, and advanced 200 yards.

They stopped several villagers and inquired about the concentration of Nazi storm troops in the vicinity.

After a few minutes they rode back to French soil. Their movements were covered by a platoon of French infantry and two machine guns stationed on the French side of the border.

YACHT BLAST FATAL

TACOMA, Wash., March 22.—(A.P.)—Dr. E. A. Rich, prominent Tacoma surgeon and yachtsman, died in a hospital here early today of burns and shock suffered in a gasoline explosion on his yacht, the Argosy, last Sunday. He was killed.

VIVID DRAMA AT DR. ZORB HEARING

Another Witness Tells of Four Women Playing Dice in Kitchen

In a hearing fraught with intense drama, pretty Mrs. Louise Wilson, wife of Dr. Clair Wilson, fashionable Hollywood physician, today related in municipal court the tragic details of a scuffle, following a gay yacht party, that resulted in the serious shooting of Dr. Wilson by his best friend, Dr. George Anthony Zorb.

The wife testified at Dr. Zorb's preliminary hearing on a charge of assault with a deadly weapon before Municipal Judge Joseph L. Call.

DICE GAME TOLD

Just before the shooting, four women guests were in the kitchen of the Wilson home shooting dice, according to the testimony of another witness, Mrs. Roy L. Groom, who said she was one of those in the kitchen. Mrs. Groom testified her companions in the dice game were Mrs. Vera Price, Mrs. Dolores Bonnett and Mrs. Vernon Morse.

All four of the women testified they had seen nothing of the scuffle or shooting.

According to Mrs. Groom's testimony, H. A. "Kewpie" Morgan, one of the men guests, had rushed into the kitchen exclaiming: "Get your coats—beat it!" Mrs. Groom said they immediately departed from the house.

As Mrs. Wilson related details of the shooting, she waved the revolver that fired the shot. It was a .32 caliber weapon, described by another witness as "a bad man's gun with a hair trigger."

MRS. WILSON'S STORY

"We were in the kitchen of my home, after returning from the yacht party," Mrs. Wilson commenced in a low voice. "My husband and I. There was a party at the house that afternoon—and Tony came in.

'He was muttering something about 'get my blonde wife.' We told him Mrs. Zorb had gone home.

"Then Tony pulled out the gun and began waving it around. My husband said: 'You had better put that down, for you might hurt someone.'

"I went into the bedroom about that time. In a few minutes I heard a shot.

"When I ran out to the living room there were so many people bending over Dr. Wilson I did not get a chance to see him, but they told me he was desperately

Mrs. Wilson, attired in a dark gray suit and a fox fur, entered the courtroom with an arm in arm with Mrs. Zorb.

Body of Man Shot To Death Is Found In Topanga Canyon

A man's body, believed to be that of Lewis L. Clark, 54, of 1328 North Oxford boulevard, Los Angeles, was found with a bullet wound in his head three miles up Topanga canyon road from the ocean, police reported today.

He was slumped down in the seat of a touring car with a rifle by his side, the officers said.

Police and sheriff's officers who investigated declared the man was a suicide.

FARM AID BILL WINS, 315-98, IN HOUSE

By Associated Press

WASHINGTON, March 22—The farm relief bill, integral part of President Roosevelt's emergency program, was passed by the house today by a strong bi-partisan majority.

The vote was 315 to 98.

California congressmen voted as follows: For—Buck, Burke, Church, Colden, Collins, Dockweiler, Kramer, Lee McGrath, Stubbs, Traeger and Welch.

Against—Englebright, Evans, Hoeppel and Kahn.

Eltse was paired against the bill.

Passage was voted after two days of committee consideration and two days of debate by the house, during which amendments were barred. It was the fourth major recommendation of President Roosevelt to receive house approval in less than three weeks.

Slower action is expected in the senate where opposition is formidable and there is no restriction on debate, or rule to the invoked against the proposal of amendments. Yet, today a number of senators were predicting it would pass very much in its present form.

POINTS IN MEASURE

The bill places enormous powers over American agriculture in the hands of the secretary of agriculture. Its policy was termed by Mr. Roosevelt a "new and untried path." Its purpose is to increase farm buying power.

The chief provisions:

Names wheat, cotton, tobacco, corn, rice, hogs, cattle, sheep, milk and its products as major agricultural commodities.

Authorizes the secretary of agriculture to enter into voluntary agreements with producers of these commodities to secure acreage on crop reductions. In return for curtailments, the producer would receive rent or benefit payments.

CAN LEVY TAX

Empowers the secretary to levy processing taxes on the commodities to raise the funds for paying the rent or benefits. The tax would be limited to the amount necessary to bring the aggregate farm return to its pre-war purchasing power.

Also gives him full powers to regulate, through a licensing system, the handling in interstate and foreign commerce of the nine commodities, and it permits him to make marketing agreements.

Creates a government cotton pool as proposed in last session's Smith bill. Growers would receive options in return for production slashes and benefit by any price increase.

EXPERT GIVES ADVICE AT INQUEST

Modern Education Structures at Beach Unharmed, Quiz Is Told

A series of recommendations for future earthquake-proof construction of school buildings in Southern California was presented this afternoon at the coroner's inquest into the March 10 earthquake by Allen E. Sedgwick, former head of the geology department of University of Southern California.

Declaring that Class A buildings should stand up under an earthquake shock of maximum intensity, Sedgwick recommended:

1. That use of brick in schools and public buildings be prohibited for supporting columns, fire walls, facing and decorations.

ONE-STORY STUCCO

2. That one-story stucco buildings with no "architectural gim-cracks" be used for public school buildings wherever practicable.

3. That structures should be built in square shapes and that L-shaped structures be prohibited because of the counter pull of one wing against the other under earthquake stress.

Sedgwick declared brick walls not properly sealed with the strongest possible mortar are "exceedingly dangerous and invite disaster."

He said all Class A type buildings should stand up under the worst earthquakes, unless they should happen to be built right across an earthquake fault.

'SAFETY VALVES'

Sedgwick declared he did not believe there was cause for alarm over earthquakes in the Los Angeles county section if buildings are properly constructed. He said there is less possibility of disastrous earthquakes in Southern California, because the minor shocks that have been occurring act as safety valves, providing minor slips that relieve the pressure which creates danger of disastrous shocks.

Sedgwick also declared that he conducted a survey for the state corporation commissioner in 1928 in connection with the earthquake situation and that as a result of that survey the commission decided it would not be necessary to require earthquake insurance on Class A buildings represented in securities issues.

MODERN BUILDINGS SAFE

At the close of the second day of the inquest being conducted by Coroner Nance before a jury of nine technical experts, the salient testimony of experts on earthquakes and construction was that

(CONTINUED ON PAGE TEN)

Do Something, Buy Something, Edison Orders

By Associated Press

WEST ORANGE, N. J., March 22.—The following bulletin was posted in all plants of Thomas A. Edison, Inc., today by Charles Edison, son of the inventor and president of the company:

"President Roosevelt has done his part; now you do something.

"Buy something—buy anything, anywhere; paint your kitchen, send a telegram, give a party, get a car, pay a bill, rent a flat, fix your roof, get a haircut, see a show, build a house, take a trip, sing a song, get married.

"It does not matter what you do—but get going and keep going. This old world is starting to move."

Stocks in Slight Rally at Close After Weakness

By International News Service

NEW YORK, March 22—Stocks reacted further today within the adverse influences of weakness in the bond and commodity markets.

The utility shares continued to be the target for the shorts.

However, the list rallied slightly from the lows in the final minutes of trading under the impetus of scattered short covering.

Final prices were: United States Steel 28⅝, up ¼; American Can 58¼, off ¼; American Telephone 95½, off 2¼; General Electric 13¾, off ¼; General Motors 12¼, up ⅜; Standard Oil of New Jersey 25⅛, unchanged; New York Central 18¾, off ⅞; Atchison 42¼, off 1¼.

Indianapolis Blast Kills 1 and Hurts 3

By International News Service

INDIANAPOLIS, Ind., March 22.—One man was killed, and three injured, one critically, when a terrific explosion wrecked the Plaza motor inn in the downtown district here this afternoon. The dead man was Robert Kennedy. The blast was believed to have been caused by the ignition of a large gasoline storage tank.

Spring Weather to Continue in L. A.

Fair spring weather prevailed in Los Angeles today, and the weather bureau forecast that tonight and tomorrow would continue fair, with moderate temperatures and gentle northwest winds. A high pressure area over the Pacific ocean was said to preclude possibility of rain for the time being.

BIG PROJECT TO BEGIN

NEW ORLEANS, March 22.—(U. P.)—A project which will provide several thousand men with steady work for two years will be begin next month when the McClintic-Marshall Co., a Bethlehem steel subsidiary, starts work on a $13,000,000 bridge across the Mississippi river here.

ACTION PUTS O. K. ON BREW SALES AFTER MIDNIGHT, APRIL 6

By Associated Press

WASHINGTON, March 22.—President Roosevelt today signed into law the bill allowing sale of 3.2 per cent beer and wines from midnight April 6 onward.

The President signed the bill at 2 p. m., eastern time.

From congressional halls it had been taken to him, done up neatly in red ribbon, by Representatives Cullen and O'Connor of New York, McCormack of Massachusetts, and Parsons and Sabath of Illinois, all Democrats.

Cullen sponsored the law on the legislative course.

In his seat at the head of the cabinet table and in the presence of newspaper men and photographers, the President glanced over the five and one-half pages of the enrolled measure.

USES FOUR PENS

Upon completing the reading he folded over the last page and picked up the first of the four pens he used in signing.

The delegation of house members which carried the bill to the White House stood just outside the cabinet room during the signing and later were received by Mr. Roosevelt.

Looking up after he had signed, the President smiled.

Later he remarked to photographers that he hoped they "got the smile" at the end.

The President directed that the four pens be given to the American Federation of Labor, the American Legion, Representative Cullen and Senator Harrison of Mississippi, who as chairman of the finance committee, was in charge of the legislation in the senate.

INSTRUCTIONS GIVEN

Joint instructions for carrying out the law were issued at once by Commissioner Doran of the industrial alcohol bureau and Commissioner Burnett of the internal revenue bureau.

Doran said licensing of breweries will begin late today or tomorrow. Beer and wine of 3.2 content may be removed from warehouses and breweries prior to April 6 for the purpose of bottling and storage on the premises of wholesale and retail dealers.

EXPECT LEGAL FIGHT

Once sale of beer gets under way, a long legal controversy is expected to follow as to constitutionality of the law, reaching the supreme court eventually.

President Roosevelt today asked the attorney general to report the status of federal prisoners convicted under the dry laws but who would not have been guilty of vio-

(CONTINUED ON PAGE EIGHT)

DRYS' STRATEGY IN FIGHT ON BEER BARED

By Associated Press

WASHINGTON, March 22.—Edward B. Dunford, attorney for Anti-Saloon League of America, said today "an attack on the (beer) law will certainly be made when the requisite circumstances arise."

He indicated that the Anti-Saloon League would sponsor no attempt to obtain an injunction to restrain issuance of licenses for sale of beer, but would await the actual beginning of distribution about April 7.

Meanwhile, however, Dr. Clarence True Wilson of the Methodist Episcopal board of temperance and public morals has said court proceedings would be filed to obtain an injunction.

Attorneys said an injunction might be sought by a taxpayer to restrain the commissioner of internal alcohol from issuing licenses. Dunford listed six points under which he said the law could be attacked. Briefly the points are:

A dry state could ask an injunction against transportation of beer through the state.

A brewer arrested for not having a permit could plead the beer requiring the permit is illegal in violation of the eighteenth amendment.

Any state prohibiting beer could contest in the courts the constitutionality of the 3.2 beer content.

A soft drink manufacturer could sue to block granting of beer permits on the ground that grants violate the eighteenth amendment and he is constitutionally denied protection of the law.

If intoxication results, injunction could be sought as a nuisance abatement.

A person purchasing beer might be prosecuted for the status of his 3.2 beer content that it violates public policy rendered by the eighteenth amendment.

Night-Club Hostess Shoots Suitor

9 A·M EDITION

Los Angeles Times

LIBERTY UNDER THE LAW — TRUE INDUSTRIAL FREEDOM

9 A·M EDITION

VOL. LII   WEDNESDAY MORNING, JUNE 28, 1933.   DAILY, 5 CENTS

CALIFORNIA 3 TO 1 FOR REPEAL

Race-Track Betting Measure Wins

MOLEY FINDS TRADE PARLEY IN MIDST OF BITTER CRISIS

LONDON, June 28. (Exclusive)—Breathing the utmost optimism, Prof. Raymond Moley, assistant Secretary of State and "special messenger" of President Roosevelt, arrived in London early today in the midst of another crisis threatening early dissolution of the World Economic Conference.

Whether Prof. Moley, wielding the power behind the White House throne, will make the concessions demanded of the United States by the European nations as the price of continuing the conference as the paramount question as the Roosevelt adviser stepped from the boat train at Paddington Station and was hurried to the American Embassy where he will be housed during his London visit.

Prof. Moley declined to comment on the critical situation in the conference that arose yesterday, details of which members of the American delegation who met him were awaiting opportunity to lay before him. He confined himself to guarded generalities of an optimistic tenor.

"PREARRANGED PLAN"

Prof. Moley said he had not come to supersede the present American delegation to the conference.

"I expect to return to New York next week aboard the Manhattan, he said, "and I will then be able to give the President full information of the conference up to the time of my leaving.

"I come to London in pursuance of a plan made before the conference began. I am bringing to my present chief, Mr. Hull, and other members of the delegation a report of the latest economic and legislative developments in America.

"My associate in this mission, by direction of the President and at my own request is Herbert Bayard Swop."

GOLD BLOC ENDANGERED

The new crisis in the life of the conference developed concurrently with a further decline in value of the dollar and the flight of capital from Holland and Switzerland, two of the remaining gold standard countries.

The utmost excitement prevailed among delegations as rumors flew that abandonment of the gold standard by both Holland and Switzerland is imminent and that France and Belgium will be forced off the gold basis soon thereafter. Heads of the French, Belgian, Dutch and Swiss delegations held a meeting to consider the crisis. They were a unit in saying immediately

(Continued on page 7, Column 1)

JOBS AND WAGES FOR MAY SHOW SHARP INCREASE

NEW YORK, June 27. (P)—The amount of pay in the weekly envelope of the average worker in the manufacturing industry increased 8.6 per cent in May over April, the National Industrial Conference Board reported today in its monthly summary of wages.

The number of workers increased 4.1 per cent and their hours of work a week 10.7 per cent.

Combining the increased number of hours with the increased number of workers the board found that the total number of man hours worked in the reporting establishments gained 15.1 per cent.

"As average hourly wages decreased only slightly," the board said, "probably because of the addition of new workers, these changes indicate a substantial increase in the purchasing power of these workers dependent on these establishments.

Weekly earnings of men wage earners averaged $17.65 for all industries in May, against $16.37 in April. Weekly earnings of women wage earners averaged $11.03 in May, against $10.09 in April.

The average work week for all wage earners in the twenty-five industries combined, increased from 33.8 hours in April to 37.4 hours in May.

(Continued on page 7, Column 1)

STILL PEGGING AWAY!

STABILIZATION

DEPRECIATION

WHEE-HEE-HEE-HEE!

UNITED STATES

THE DOLLAR

THE CRASH

—GALE

GREEN ATTACKS TEXTILE GROUP'S PAY-HOURS' CODE

WASHINGTON, June 27. (P)—From union labor and minority groups sudden opposition sprang today as the nation's textile operators formally placed before the National Recovery Administration their proposal to stabilize industry and establish minimum wages and maximum working hours.

Hardly had the broad outlines of their agreement been sketched before the crowd of spectators present, when William Green, president of the American Federation of Labor, objected to the wage and labor provisions of the code and several manufacturers came forward with requests that their plants be exempted.

Presented by more than two-thirds of the domestic spindle and loom operators, the proposed code of fair competition must be approved by the Roosevelt administration before it takes the effect of

(Continued on Page 4, Column 2)

Doug, Jr., Unable to See Visitors

NEW YORK, June 27. (P)—Douglas Fairbanks, Jr., suffering from lobar pneumonia, was reported "about the same" tonight.

Although he passed a fairly comfortable day, he was said by his stepfather, Jack Whiting, to be too ill to receive visitors except his mother.

Two Injured in Trawler Crash

BOSTON, June 28. (P)—The Boston trawler Flow was reported disabled shortly after midnight with her lifeboat stove in and two men badly injured after a collision with the British freighter Cornerbrook four miles off Highland Light.

WHEAT SWEEPS UP TO NEW HIGH IN WILD TRADING

(BY THE ASSOCIATED PRESS)

It was hot in the grain pits today as well as in the grain fields where withered crops set off one of the wildest speculative orgies of trading seen on the Chicago Board of Trade since the World War.

Prices soared in spectacular fashion in all grains for the second successive day as news continued to pour in that crops were "burning up" in the heat that once more was threatening the excessive heat and prolonged drought.

With grains sweeping up from 3 to 8 cents a bushel on a huge volume of business, prices of wheat for future delivery crossed the dollar mark, reaching a peak of $1.06 3-8 a bushel on the May (1934) delivery, with December touching $1.01 7-8.

It was a record-smashing day with the boards behind the market.

The New York Stock Exchange was strong in spots and hesitant in others, the average net change being a gain of 46 cents. This rise, however, was sufficient to put the Associated Press-Standard Statistics closing composite at a new high since November 1931, of $87.20. A number of shares closed $1 to $3 higher; a few leaders were off slightly.

Cotton blossomed hopefully during the first quarter-hour, dabbing higher than Norman H. Davis, American but $1 a bale to Monday's advance. Heavy profit-taking nipped the rally and the market thereafter was

(Continued on Page 7, Column 5)

VIMY RIDGE GENERAL DIES

TORONTO, June 27. (P)—Maj.-Gen. W. B. Lindsay, who commanded the Royal Canadian Engineers at the battle of Vimy Ridge in the World War, was found dead today, apparently a victim of heart disease.

KAHN TELLS HOW HE ESCAPED TAX TODAY

WASHINGTON, June 27. (Exclusive)—For the last three years Otto H. Kahn, New York banker and lavish patron of the arts, has paid no income tax. Tomorrow he will be asked by Ferdinand Pecora, counsel of the Senate investigating committee, to explain his nonpayment, and the minutes of the investigation of Kahn, 66-year-old financier of German nativity, on hitherto undisclosed facts and figures, and operating practices of the private banking house.

According to information now in the hands of the investigators, other associates of Kahn in the banking house of Kuhn, Loeb & Co. also failed to pay income taxes for 1930, 1931 and last year.

WASHINGTON, June 27. (P)—Senate banking investigators decided late today to question Otto H. Kahn, senior partner of Kuhn, Loeb & Co. on his income-tax returns, but deferred this line of inquiry until tomorrow after hearing from Kahn that Norman H. Davis, American ambassador-at-large, had received $35,000 in 1925 for promoting Chilean loans.

Ferdinand Pecora, committee counsel, announced he would take up the income-tax phase, after an all-day examination of Kahn, 66-year-old financier of German nativity, on hitherto undisclosed facts and figures and operating practices of the private banking house.

Kahn discussed the Chilean loans, underwritten by his house and the Guaranty Company of New York, reluctantly, because, he said, it was a "sore point" and the only foreign loans his concern floated that is in default.

He said Davis, whose name recently figured among clients of J.

(Continued on Page 5, Column 3)

WEST VIRGINIA VOTES REPEAL AFTER YEARS AS DRY STATE

CHARLESTON (W. Va.) June 28. (P)—In 1716 precincts reporting complete counts, out of 2238 in the State, West Virginia's vote on prohibition early today was: For repeal, 185,341; against repeal, 106,976.

CHARLESTON (W. Va.) June 27. (P)—Bone dry for twenty years, West Virginia voted tonight to cast off prohibition.

The wet tide added the Panhandle State to the fourteen others which have voted to ratify the Twenty-first Amendment.

With 1718 of the 2338 precincts tabulated, the vote was 186,742 to 110,508, a lead for repeal of 76,234. The repealists were gaining steadily as ballots from the industrial centers rolled in, offsetting the staunch prohibition stand of the hill dwellers and farmer folk in the less populous areas.

Repeal started strongly in early returns with a 2-to-1 trend. That ratio sagged somewhat as returns came in from the hill counties and the farming regions. At no time, however, was the wet lead threatened.

Commenting on the repeal vote, Patrick D. Koontz, chairman of the repeal council, said the returns "show conclusively" the State will lead the way to repeal in the South.

No statements were immediately forthcoming from dry leaders. Throughout the campaign they had expressed themselves as merely hopeful that West Virginia would be the first to throw an obstacle in front of the repeal parade.

Without exception the large counties in the coal and industrial centers, poured thousands of votes into the wet bins.

NEW YORK STATE RATIFIES REPEAL

ALBANY (N. Y.) June 27. (P)—New York, home State of President Roosevelt, today ratified the Congressional repeal of the Eighteenth Amendment at a convention of 150 wet delegates, including twenty-six women.

The gathering in the huge Assembly chamber at the Capitol was marked by a vigorous attack on government by "organized minorities," delivered by former Gov. Smith, and a declaration by former United States Senator Root that "there will be no thirteen States" to block repeal.

WETS AND DRYS MEET IN TEXAS

AUSTIN (Tex.) June 27. (P)—Texas' campaign on repeal of the national prohibition amendment and legalization of 3.2 per cent beer was started here today when proponents and opponents held conventions simultaneously.

Both sides picked separate tickets of candidates for delegates to the November 24 repeal convention when Texas will decide whether it wants national prohibition repealed. The electorate will choose between the repeal and the anti-repeal tickets at a special election on August 26.

BEER SPONSORS DEFY GOVERNOR OF VIRGINIA

RICHMOND (Va.) June 27. (P)—A definite movement to convene the Virginia General Assembly in special session, without call from the Governor, to legalize beer and provide for a repeal referendum, is under way tonight.

With Gov. Pollard remaining firm in his decision not to issue the

(Continued on Page 5, Column 6)

Will Rogers Remarks:

BEVERLY HILLS, June 27.—[To the Editor of The Times:] Had lunch today at the studio with Udet, the greatest living German ace, with sixty-three planes to his credit, a marvelous stunt flyer, and Lieut. Falconi, Mussolini's crack acrobatic ace flyer. A young fellow just 25. Both speak English. A couple of fine young fellows. Saturday we see these babies do their stuff, along with all our crack boys.

During the war we wouldn't let our boys have parachutes for somebody "decided they wasn't safe." The latter part of the war Germany had chutes, and Udet had had his only eleven days when his plane was shot down. Had there been no chute there would have been no Udet today.

It makes you sick when you think of the boys we might have saved. But they was afraid maybe some of the chutes wouldn't open.

Yours

WILL ROGERS.

NIGHT-CLUB GIRL SHOOTS MAN ON BUSY BROADWAY

NEW YORK, June 28. (P)—An attractive young woman fired a bullet into the head of Albert Pearson, 29, near one of the busiest corners in the Broadway theatrical district about dawn today.

Leaving Pearson prone on the sidewalk, she stepped into a taxicab and sped away.

A moment or two later, a young woman entered a police station near by.

"I am Marquita Lopez, a night-club hostess," she said. "I've just shot a man."

She refused to say anything else. Police, after taking a pistol with one exploded cartridge from her handbag, took her to a hospital where Pearson lay near death.

He refused to identify her as the woman who shot him.

"I like her. I like her," he moaned again and again.

HEAT SEARS MIDWEST CROPS, FELLS SCORES

(BY THE ASSOCIATED PRESS)

Most of the nation baked under a sizzling sun yesterday. Scattered showers in a few farm sections brought only scant relief to seared crops.

Scores of persons were prostrated and a few died as the mercury climbed to record highs.

The temperature registered on semi-official thermometers in Chicago was as high as 102 deg. and an official thermometer showed 100.1, the hottest June 27 since 1872.

Two persons died in Illinois.

Two persons died in Indiana and the mercury veered from the mid-nineties to the century mark. Detroit reported one death and a reading of 96 deg. Ohio temperatures were in the 90's.

The Southwest boiled—it was 105 for the second day at Alva, Okla. Some farmers in the State were

forced to haul water for miles to relieve suffering live stock. Texas temperatures stood near 100 and there was no rain in sight.

Salina, Kan., reported a reading of 103. Scattered showers in Missouri brought the thermometer somewhat.

St. Paul, Minn., sweltered as the reading climbed to 100. There was scattered rain in Minneapolis.

Milwaukee reported a reading of 101; Omaha, 84; Lincoln, Neb., 91 and Iowa around 90.

New York was uncomfortable with excessive humidity while the mercury stood at 75. Fog delayed ships. It was 87 in Pittsburgh, 84 in Baltimore. West Virginia saw rising temperatures. It was slightly cooler in Washington with frequent thunderstorms breaking a two-day heat wave.

RILEY-STEWART PLAN, RELIEF BONDS LEADING; PRIVATE SCHOOLS LOSE

California yesterday joined the so-far-unbroken procession of States to vote for repeal of the Eighteenth Amendment, making sixteen in the list to date.

The twenty-two delegates pledged to vote for repeal of the national dry law at the California State convention were elected over a similar slate of anti-repeal delegates by a margin of about three to one throughout the State, though this ratio was far exceeded in many of the northern communities. Returns early this morning showed only Riverside county in the dry column and that by a very narrow margin.

GASOLINE TAX DIVERSION DEFEATED

Of the ten propositions on the general State ballot, victory was indicated for the Riley-Stewart tax plan, the $20,000,000 unemployment relief bonds, the proposal to permit pari-mutuel betting at race tracks, a new assessment of property damaged in the earthquake of March 10, technical dating of 1933 legislative acts and the county home-rule amendment.

Apparently defeated were the proposals to issue $55,000,000 in bonds, backed by State credit, to take up the securities of financially embarrassed irrigation districts, to exempt non-profit private schools from taxation, and to divert some $17,000,000 from the State gasoline tax to pay interest and sinking fund charges on highway bonds.

The local proposition to incorporate territory in and around Belvedere Gardens to form a new sixth-class city to be known as Garden City was overwhelmingly defeated.

All-State returns, mostly from populous centers, compiled up to 5:30 o'clock this morning, showed the following:

For repeal of the Eighteenth Amendment (6312 precincts out of 9347,) 718,723; against, 228,083.

STATE VOTE ON TEN PROPOSITIONS

Proposition No. 1, Riley-Stewart Plan (5005 precincts,) Yes, 316,993; No, 240,898.

No. 2, $20,000,000 Unemployment Bonds (5114 precincts,) Yes, 403,772; No, 168,536.

No. 3, Race-Track Betting (4946 precincts,) Yes, 394,434; No, 217,800.

No. 4, Tax-Exemption of Private Schools (4493 precincts,) Yes, 232,770; No, 354,801.

No. 5, Assessing Quake-Damaged Property (3012 precincts,) Yes, 227,010; No, 115,617.

No. 6, $55,000,000 Irrigation District Bonds (4338 precincts,) Yes, 189,880; No, 293,400.

No. 7, Dating Acts of Legislature (2996 precincts,) Yes, 203,767; No, 117,200.

No. 8, County Home Rule (2998 precincts,) Yes, 143,090; No, 410,887.

No. 9, Gas-Tax Diversion, 1933 (4601 precincts,) Yes, 130,119; No, 402,286.

No. 10, Gas-Tax Diversion, 1935 (4480 precincts,) Yes, 130,119; No, 402,286.

+Will cast their votes for the ratification of the Twenty-first Amendment, which repeals the Eighteenth Amendment.

Los Angeles city and county voted more than two to one for the slate of prohibition repeal delegates. The heaviest wet vote was tallied up in San Francisco, where the majority was about fourteen to one with a capable vote of: For repeal, 127,665; against repeal, 8975. Riverside county gave a small majority for the anti-repeal delegates, but the rest of Southern California voted for the wet ticket headed by H. H. Cotton of San Clemente. Northern California, both valley and mountain, gave heavy majorities for the repeal ticket.

When the returns have been canvassed and certified by Secretary of State Jordan, he will call a session of the delegates to meet at Sacramento, at which time they will

This plan provides that the properties of public utilities, now subject to State taxation alone, be returned to the local assessment roll, that the State assume the counties' share of school costs, that governmental expenditures be limited to a 5 per cent per annum increase. It is designed to ease the tax burden on real estate. It is expected that the Legislature, when it convenes July 17, next, will enact a sales tax of at least 2 per cent to meet the added expense of the school contribution. Adoption of the Riley-Stewart plan will have a distinctive influence on the county budget, now in preparation, as it will relieve taxpayers of the school costs to a very large extent. The plan was sponsored by State Controller Riley and Fred Stewart of the State Board of Equalization, although amended many times by the Legislature.

Los Angeles gave the $20,000,000 unemployment relief bonds a majority of about 2 to 1, which was equaled by San Francisco. In the county, apparently, did the bonds meet defeat and their favorable margin was large throughout the State.

State officials, under the act of the

(Continued on Page 2, Column 1)

Los Angeles Examiner

CHARACTER QUALITY · AMERICA FIRST! · ENTERPRISE ACCURACY

AN AMERICAN PAPER FOR THE AMERICAN PEOPLE · THE GREAT NEWSPAPER OF THE GREAT SOUTHWEST

Reg. U.S. Pat. Off.

VOL. XXXIV—NO. 216   P   LOS ANGELES, THURSDAY, JULY 15, 1937   Two Sections—Part I—FIVE CENTS

HUGE WELCOME PLANNED HERE FOR POLAR FLYERS

CHINA, JAPAN WAGE BATTLE FOR RAILWAY

Machine Guns, Bayonets and Swords Spit and Clash During Night at Lofe Terminal

LINE VITAL WAR FACTOR

Possession by Nanking Troops Would Halt Tokyo's Troop Shift; Long Struggle Seen

By John Goette

(Copyright 1937, Universal Service)

PEIPING, July 15.—(Thursday)—Violent hostilities for possession of vital Peiping - Tientsin railway raged early today as both Japan and China rushed huge reinforcements toward this war zone in preparation for a prolonged conflict.

The new battle between Japanese and Chinese troops broke out at the Lofe Railroad terminal and bridge, midway between Peiping and Tientsin on the north China coast.

NIGHT-LONG FIGHT

Fighting with machine guns, mortars, bayonets and swords lasted throughout the night as contingents of China's Twenty-ninth Route Army struggled to prevent the Japanese from seizing the railroad and a highway running parallel to it.

A Chinese victory at Lofe, situated 30 miles southeast of Peiping, would hamper, if not halt, the surge of Japanese troops to reinforce the 20,000 Japanese soldiers already massed in this battle-torn vicinity.

Chinese railway authorities said the fighting was precipitated when 700 Japanese troops, proceeding from Tientsin to their Fengtai base south of Peiping, encountered a large Chinese force that sought to intercept them by surprise. Both sides hurried fresh troops to the scene as the battle, which began at 1 p. m. last night, mounted in ferocity.

CHINESE RUSH AID

The clash came after the Japanese, defeated by Chinese swordsmen and machine gunners in an initial attempt to pierce Peiping's guarded gates, succeeded in getting 2000 additional troops to Fengtai from Tientsin, which is 60 miles southeast of here.

At the same time a huge force of at least 30,000 Chinese troops with full war equipment neared the Peiping area from the south after crossing the southern borders of Hopei Province, traveling along the Peiping-Hankow railroad.

Smiles of Triumph After Epochal Hop

LEFT TO RIGHT: PILOT MIKHAIL GROMOFF, COPILOT ANDREI YUMOSHEFF AND NAVIGATOR SERGEI DANILIN

First Man to Greet Flyers Describes Tense Scene

By Walter E. Harvey

(Mr. Harvey furnishes the following and first-hand report of the three Russian aviators when they landed on American soil.)

There I stood, right in the middle of a vast cow pasture, anxious to tell them where they were.

But I couldn't—I can't talk Russian and they couldn't talk English.

I was in the San Jacinto Cemetery taking care of some graves when I first sighted the giant red-winged plane.

It seemed to be gliding smoothly down the airlanes headed toward San Diego. I knew immediately it was the Russian plane I had been reading about.

In about five minutes the

(Continued on Page 4, Col. 3)

Aces Complete Longest Aerial Trip in History

Here is the program for the three Russian flyers:

Last night they were scheduled to speak in San Diego.

Today they will be in Los Angeles. They will be guests of the Russian Consulate here.

They will probably be here at least two days and their public appearances will be announced later.

Their plane was to be dismantled last night and taken to March Field, Riverside.

By Marjorie Driscoll

Farther than any man has ever flown an airplane in nonstop flight.

Over the top of the world they came, from Moscow to Southern California, the three Soviet aces who landed their plane at 6:27 a. m. yesterday in a pasture near San Jacinto.

And when the wheels touched the earth the wheels that had left the ground at Moscow—Mikhail Gronoff, Andrei Yumosheff and Sergei Danilin had flown for approximately 6700 miles.

They had been in the air for 62 hours, five minutes.

Los Angeles will welcome the three daring Russians when they arrive from San Diego, probably this morning.

Adolph Hoch, Public Works commissioner, acting as the personal representative of Mayor, hastened to March Field yesterday to extend the city's invitation.

Joining in plans for a celebration to greet the Soviet airmen are representatives of the city, Chamber of Commerce, the motion picture industry and others. Details awaited news of definite plans for the expected visit.

First Desire Granted---a Bath

Taken to March Field by automobile, the flyers had their first desire granted—a bath.

Then they breakfasted.

And then, after the first statements and greetings, slept—their first sleep since they left Moscow.

Grigori Gokhman, Russian consul at San Francisco, flew to March Field to welcome his countrymen.

The landing in the San Jacinto pasture ended hours of anxiety for the hundreds who watched and waited along the line in California.

Nobody Knew Where They Were

Nobody knew where the Russians were, except they were somewhere south of Oakland. Nobody knew where they planned to land.

Only three persons were not worried. They were the three men who, for three nights and two days had seen the miles speed beneath them, as they flew on and on.

They knew where they were; knew so well that they did not bother about asking for information.

About 1 o'clock yesterday morning, they passed over Oakland.

The long distance record was already theirs, but there was fuel in the tanks, the single 1000-horsepower motor was running sweetly. So they kept going.

Down over central California they came through the

HUGHES LANDS IN NEW YORK!

THE WEATHER: Generally fair; continued warm; gentle to moderate northerly winds. (See Report, Page 29.)

The Seattle Daily Times

8 NIGHT SPECIAL CLOSING MARKETS

Published Daily and Sunday and Entered as Second Class Matter at Seattle, Washington. Vol. LXI, No. 195.

SEATTLE, WASHINGTON, THURSDAY, JULY 14, 1938.

PRICE FIVE CENTS

IN NEW YORK THIS AFTERNOON! . . . A. P. Wirephotos . . . HOME AGAIN

TODAY AT FLOYD BENNETT FIELD It's over! Howard Hughes' around-the-top-of-the-world plane stands in the center of an admiring welcoming crowd after its historic, record-shattering flight from New York to New Yorok by way of Paris, Moscow, Omsk, Fairbanks and Minneapolis. Police battled the crowd at this field to clear a way for the flyers to land. The Hughes plane's time for the jaunt was 3 days 19 hours 17 minutes.—A. P. wirephoto. (For other wirephotos of the Hughes flight, see Page 10.)

TODAY AFTER HAPPY LANDINGS Tired and unshaven, the crew of Howard Hughes' 'round-the-world plane received heroes' welcomes from Mayor Fiorello LaGuardia when they landed at Floyd Bennett Field. From left to right are Hughes, Richard Stoddart, Harry P. Connor, Mayor LaGuardia and Thomas Thurlow.—A. P. wirephoto.

New July Heat Mark Looms; 94-Maximum Is Forecast

TODAY'S TEMPERATURES

6 a. m.	72	10 a. m.	82
7 a. m.	73	11 a. m.	82
8 a. m.	77	Noon	85
9 a. m.	79	1 p. m.	86

July's maximum temperature record of thirty-six years' standing was threatened in Seattle today when the mercury climbed steadily upward and the Weather Bureau announced it expects a high of 94 degrees late this afternoon.

At 6 o'clock this morning, the temperature stood at the 72-degree mark. By noon the mercury had surged upward into the 80's.

The all-time July maximum temperature mark was established in 1902, when it reached 95 degrees. Warmest day Seattle ever has had was 98 degrees in June, 1925.

Although continued warm weather is forecast for the next twenty-four hours, forecasters said tomorrow's temperatures will be slightly lower, fixing the maximum at 88 degrees, which was yesterday's high and also the warmest day of the year.

U. S. Files On 'Black Sheep's' Prize Money

Shukichi Atarashi, the Seattle "Black Sheep," who recently won $150,000 in the Irish Hospital Sweepstakes, found out today that his lucky star apparently had taken a tumble when the United States Internal Revenue Bureau filed a $64,548.84 tax lien against him with County Auditor Earl Milliken.

Atarashi used the name "Black Sheep," when he bought the sweepstakes ticket.

The lien, according to Internal Revenue Bureau officials, represents taxes due the government from the prize money which Atarashi declares he hasn't even seen.

King Better; Visit To France Assured

LONDON, Thursday, July 14.—(AP) King George VI had recovered enough today from an attack of gastric influenza to leave his bed and it was believed assured he would be able to make his scheduled visit of state to France with Queen Elizabeth next week.

The King and Queen are scheduled to leave for Pa is Tuesday.

DEMOS SPLIT BY ROW AT CONVENTION

Right Wing Asserts All Action Taken Followed Adjournment; Meyers Repudiates Commonwealth

By J. W. GILBERT

The Democratic Party of Washington today faced a widened rift between right and left wings as a result of yesterday's tumultuous state convention in Tacoma.

Right wingers declared the speeches of Senator Lewis B. Schwellenbach and congressmen, and the passing of various left-wing resolutions came after State Chairman D. Elwood Caples had adjourned the convention in the midst of the disorder.

Left-wingers insisted Caples had merely abdicated and that the convention still was in session—a session incidentally which was so nearly riotous that police were called.

Another effect of the convention

(Continued on Page 8, Column 4.)

Woman Slain At Wimbledon, Tennis Center

By Associated Press.

WIMBLEDON, England, Thursday, July 14.—The body of a pretty, smartly dressed young woman was found barely a hundred yards from the famed center court of the All-England Tennis Club today.

Scotland Yard's noted pathologist, Sir Bernard Spilsbury, and high police officers hurried to the scene, where two weeks ago crowds watched the Wimbledon finals between the two Helens—Moody and Jacobs.

Preliminary investigation showed the black-clad victim was stabbed about the head and then run over with a motor car, from which she apparently had been thrown.

Scotland Yard ordered intensive search for a blood-stained motor car, tire marks of which were found on the girl's clothing.

The dead woman was about 36 years old, slim, brunette, with scarlet fingernails and stenciled eyebrows. She wore a black dress trimmed with fur and black gloves. On her finger was a wedding ring.

Asylum Failed To Tell Police Of Mead Escape

Cole Says State Patrol Would Have Spotted 'Mattson Suspect' as Fugitive

No "pickup order" was broadcast to police last week for the detention of Lester Mead, inmate of the Eastern Washington Hospital for the Insane, after Mead walked off the hospital vegetable garden—later to confess falsely the Mattson kidnaping—Dr. M. W. Conway, superintnedent, said today.

State Patrol Chief William Cole said such an order might have saved his officers most of the time they spent on Mead, but Dr. Conway said the State Patrol should have "sized up" the runaway quickly and could have inquired about him at the state's hospitals for mental cases.

Returned to Hospital

Cole said officers never believed Mead sane but were struck at first by the plausibility of some parts of his varying confessions. Capt. F. H. Morgan of the State Patrol's Spokane office returned Mead to the hospital at Medical Lake last night, the Associated Press reported, authorities having written off his confession Tuesday evening as another one of a long series of fruitless leads.

Dr. Conway said no alarm was broadcast when Mead escaped a week ago, because the patient is harmless.

"Sure, we issue pickup orders lots of times in the case of dangerous people," Dr. Conway said. "But if we did it whenever one of these harmless fellows wanders away—they get hot feet this time of year—we'd have all the sheriffs' offices and the State Patrol and everybody busy.

"Mead's type always locate themselves. Of course, we scout around for them whenever one walks away. But Mead left in the middle of the day and wasn't missed until evening.

Officers Are Criticized

"Whenever we have anyone escape who's been a convict, we realy get out and find him and ask the help of all the officers. But we've had no escape from the criminal building since I've been here—five years."

Dr. Conway said that although no general "pickup order" was broadcast after Mead's escape, state patrolmen "could have told in two or three minutes" that the man was insane.

"If they'd checked on the hospitals they'd have found out about him right away, as we're only fifty miles away from where they found him."

"He (Mead) will be given detail work to do and will be placed under constant supervision," said Dr. Conway.

Mead has been a hospital patient since 1925 and was an inmate at the time of the kidnaping, the superintendent said.

POLITICOS ARE BANNED BY HOPKINS

Administrator Orders W.P.A. Payrolls Purged of Candidates, Managers and Others; Demands Day's Work

WASHINGTON, Thursday, July 14.—(AP)—Harry L. Hopkins, Works Progress administrator, barred W. P. A. employes today from certain federal as well as state political activities.

In a letter to all state administrators, Hopkins explained that the law prohibited the use of relief funds "to pay the salary, or expenses, of any person in a supervisory, or administrative position who is a candidate for any state, district, county or municipal office" which would pay compensation and require his full time.

It also is against the law, he said, to act as campaign manager or assistant manager for a candidate seeking such an office.

"It is the policy of the Works Progress Administration that this regulation also shall be applicable to candiates for federal offices, and to campaign managers, or assistants thereto, for any such candidates," Hopkins said.

"Furthermore," he wrote, "it is the policy of the Works Progress Administration that no such person while holding an elective office, the duties of which would necessitate being absent from a W. P. A. position during regular W. P. A. working hours, or to which a salary in excess of $200 per year is attached, shall be employed."

Solons to Probe Charge Official Was Gouged

WASHINGTON, Thursday, July 14.—(AP)—Chairman Sheppard, Democrat, Texas, said today the special Senate elections committee would look into charges made by a former California postmaster that he was asked to contribute part of his salary to the Democratic Party.

James B. Ogden, 45 years old, former postmaster at Avalon, Santa Catalina Island, made the charges.

Ogden, Sheppard said, was placed on probation after admitting embezzling postal funds.

The postmaster said he was forced to take the money to meet demands for contributions of 10 per cent of his salary to Democratic campaign funds.

WOMAN SHOT BY ACCIDENT, SAYS YOUTH

Victim to Recover From Flesh Wound, Received After Swimming in Sound; Daschunds Ride Stretcher

(See Page 9 for photographs)

William Scoppettone, 21 years old, confessed to deputy sheriffs today that he fired the rifle shot which yesterday injured Miss Meredyth Danks, also 21, as she was walking with a friend near her home, 13020 Seventh Ave. N. W.

Scoppetton said th shot was accidntal and that he had aimed at a bird and not the girl.

The young man was held without charge.

Miss Danks was in Harborview County Mospital today recovering from a flesh wound in her back.

"I didn't even know a bullet hit the woman," Scoppettone told O. K. Bodia, chief criminal deputy sheriff.

Miss Danks and Miss Edna Dawson, 7805 Fremont Way, went swimming in the Sound before the shooting occurred and told officers they had seen a youth with black hair shooting at birds along the beach while they were there.

"I had a feeling that someone was following us as we walked up the path going home," Miss Danks said. "I told Edna that someone was behind us. The next thing I knew I was hit. I turned as I fell and I saw the fellow with the black hair and the blue sweatshirt, who had been shooting on the beach. As I saw him he ducked behind a log."

James Hyllengren, former Roosevelt High School athletic star, was walking up the path with his wife, ahead of the two girls. When Miss Danks screamed, the Hyllengrens retraced their steps and found the girl lying on the ground with her frightened friends attempting to aid her and with her two Dachshunds, Fritz and Zipper, whining beside her.

When Deputy Sheriffs Earl Allen and Roy Hoam, with Hyllengren's aid, carried Miss Danks up the steep trail 400 yards in getting her to an ambulance, the two Dachshunds jumped on the stretcher and had to be lifted off before the ambulance started.

Pulitzer's Daughter Succumbs to Illness

NEW YORK, Thursday, July 14.—(AP)—Mrs. William G. Elmslie, daughter of the late Joseph Pulitzer—founder of The New York World and The St. Louis Post-Dispatch—died today after a long illness.

Tour Line Protests Trips in City Busses

The Board of Public Works today referred to the Municipal Railway Department a protest of the Gray Line Tours, Inc., against the city's practice of chartering busses for private picnics and other trips.

Sand Point, Navy Yard get $225,000 more. Page 5.

150 killed in new Canton air raid. Page 7.

Ross Kidnaper Dies Saying 'I've Got It Coming'

'My Business Was Crime; Money Was My Assets; Electric Chair My Liability'

By Associated Press.

CHICAGO, Thursday, July 14.—John Henry Seadlund, who said "I've got it coming to me," paid with his life today for the crime of kidnaping.

The 27-year-old lumberjack, confessed abductor of Charles S. Ross and confessed killer of the man who helped him commit the crime, was electrocuted at 12:08 a. m. in the Cook County jail.

Seadlund shared his last dinner with his undertaker.

Shaved and masked, Seadlund walked tensely into the execution chamber almost unaided. "You don't have to hold my arms," he told the guards on each side of him. "I can get there alone." After seating himself he made a visible effort to relax and held his arms out for the clamps.

25 See Him Die

Twenty-five witnesses saw Seadlund die. Among them was Severin E. Koop, a Crosby, Minn., undertaker selected by Seadlund to carry his body back to his home in Irontown, Minn. Three newspapermen, three doctors, five business men and state and federal officers were other witnesses.

Seadlund in his last hours expressed no regret, voiced no bitterness. He fitfully read the Bible and talked with the jail chaplain. In his death cell, an hour and a half before the execution, he partook of a light lunch.

Seadlund and James Atwood Gray, his 19-year-old accomplice, kidnaped Ross in Northern Illinois last September 25. They took the 72-year-old retired manufacturer of greeting cards to a hideout in Wisconsin's north woods, near Spooner.

He Killed His Aide

There, Seadlund confessed to agents of the Federal Bureau of Investigation, he killed Gray during a quarrel. Ross was fatally injured in the struggle, Seadlund said, so he shot him, too.

Mrs. Mae C. Ross of Chicago, the kidnap victim's widow, paid a $50,000 ransom. Most of this money, traced across the country, was recovered after federal agents arrested Seadlund at the Santa Anita race track in California.

Seadlund's trial was almost a formality. He pleaded guilty to a charge of kidnaping and was sentenced to die. An appeal was taken to the United States Circuit Court of Appeals. When that court affirmed the sentence, Seadlund told his lawyers to close the case.

"I'm all square and ready," he declared.

Koop, the undertaker, was the only person that Seadlund asked be permitted to witness his execution.

Slayer Eats Chicken

The undertaker paid a visit to Seadlund in his death cell last night. The prisoner, he said, was standing, pecking at a tray of food. "I asked for chicken," Seadlund said. "But I don't think this is chicken. It tastes more like veal cutlets."

Koop, a tall, thin, be-spectacled Minnesotan, asked him if he had any regrets.

"No. I think I've got it coming to me," he quoted Seadlund as saying. "But I'm sorry that my family will have to suffer after I am gone."

"My business was crime," the condemned man said. "Money was my assets." He paused, put a piece of chicken in his mouth and nodded toward the execution chamber. "That's my liability."

25,000 JAM AIR FIELD, CHEER FIVE

Big Monoplane Circles Top of World in 3 Days and 19 Hours; Flyers Make Surprise Stop at Minneapolis

By Associated Press.

FLOYD BENNETT AIRPORT, N. Y., Thursday, July 14.—Howard Hughes and his four unshaven, dog-tired companions completed their 14,824-mile round-the-world flight at 1:37 p. m. (E. S. T.), today, in the amazing, record-smashing time of 3 days, 19 hours, 17 minutes.

Aided by a strong tail wind which shoved their big Lockheed plane at top-speed on the final 1,054-mile leg of the flight from Minneapolis, they lopped off nearly four days from the old record of 7 days, 18 hours and 49 minutes, made by the late Wiley Post, flying alone in July, 1933.

Weary by their long vigil in the air, and wearing the same clothes they wore when they left here Sunday night at 6:20, the five men came down to earth to be greeted by the biggest and most tumultuous crowd ever assembled at this airport.

Officials said 25,000 were there.

Hughes' speed for the elapsed time was approximately 161 miles per hour, as compared to 88 for Post.

A fire whistle let go with a screeching blast as the aerial argonauts set their plane down on the concrete runway and taxiied toward the administration building.

Hundreds of automobile horns joined in a tumultous welcoming.

Despite elaborate precautions to protect the plane, a surging crowd drove through to get a close-up glimpse of the unshaven, dishevelled heroes.

Hughes apparently did not notice a path which had been cleared for him and he taxiied toward a commercial transport plane, which was immediately moved.

Hughes and his companions' last stop before New York was at Minneapolis, Minn., at 7:38 a. m. (E. S. T.) after a 2,441-miles flight from Fairbanks, Alaska, over the Canadian Rockies, down the great wastes of the Yukon and the barrens of Northwest Canada.

After a thirty-three-minute halt at the airport there they roared off at top speed for New York. A strong tail wind shoved the ship along at high speed over this 1,054-mile last lap.

They were reported at various points along the route, their progress cheered by the crowd which had gathered at Flyod Bennet Field. It was estimated by officials at about 25,000.

Grover Whalen, president of the World's Fair, 1939, for which the flight was designed as a good-will venture, was the first to greet the flyers.

Whalen Impeccable

In striking contrast to the tired flyers, he entered the plane immediately after it came to a stop. Following him came Mayor F. H. La Guardia, himself a flyer of World War days.

The impeccably dressed Whalen presented two large baskets of flowers.

Hughes took his time about emerging from the plane, stepping partly out once and then return-

(Continued on Page 3, Column 1.)

WORLD WAR II

While Americans turned their attention almost exclusively to the policies and ramifications of the New Deal during the 1930's, Europeans anxiously watched the activities of the Nazi regime in Germany. In a relatively brief period of time, the devastating effects of the depression had been transformed into a significant amount of support for Adolf Hitler. Cautiously at first, and then with increasing disregard for international law and national integrity, the Fuhrer was launching a well-planned program of rapid military mobilization and territorial conquest.

Although State and War Department officials were receiving cables on a regular basis monitoring the activities of the German government, the general public had little knowledge and even less interest in the events which were transpiring. Roosevelt expressed growing concern about a potential role for the United States as early as 1937, but few of his advisors shared his concern. Domestic considerations prevailed, obscuring international activities.

During a brief tour of the nation, however, the President was encouraged by a close confidant to take a more forceful stance against the tactics of the German regime. Cardinal Mundelein discussed his position with Roosevelt and the Chief Executive was impressed by his sincerity and approach.

The next day, Roosevelt announced his response. The tenor of the speech was low-keyed; he was well aware of public opinion and of the tenuous position which he held. In colorful homilies, now typical of his style, the President stated: "The epidemic of world lawlessness is spreading. When an epidemic of physical disease starts to spread, the community approves and joins in a quarantine of the patients in order to protect the health of the community against the spread of the disease." Peace-loving nations, he continued,

must act in concert with other nations of the international community. His words were met with a response similar to Wilson's after his return from Paris—the public was not interested in becoming engaged in relationships which involved Europe.

In part, public opinion could be explained by the fact that on almost every occasion in which a major event had transpired in the build-up of Nazi activities, something in the United States had diverted attention away from those events. In March, 1933, when Hitler had consolidated his political position in Germany, Roosevelt had just become President; when Germany rearmed in 1935, the Roosevelt administration was in the midst of the famous Second Hundred Days; when Italy invaded Ethiopia, Huey Long had been assassinated; when the Rhineland was reoccupied by the Germans, the Supreme Court challenge to the New Deal reached its apex; when the Rome-Berlin Axis was being formed, the re-election campaign of the President was underway; when the war between China and Japan was initiated, labor battles in the United States captured the headlines; and, in March, 1938, when the Austrian Anschluss events occurred, the country was confronted with a recession. Any Presidential move towards greater involvement in the European conflicts was met with popular charges against interventionalism. The concept of a Fortress America had allies throughout the nation and within both parties in Congress. Even *Time* magazine, which had a wide circulation of readers, was staunchly isolationist and replied to the President's speech in its editorials section that Roosevelt was "warmongering."

Almost simultaneously, the Dies Committee claimed that the New Deal was a Communist conspiracy, while ignoring the right-wing extremist activities and propaganda which were becoming increasingly prevalent. The House of Rep-

resentatives denied the President's request for aid to Guam, on the grounds that it might provoke a negative response from Japan, even though most of the public—with the exception of those residing on the West Coast—had little interest in events occuring in the Orient. In the Spring of 1937, Congress extended the Neutrality Act, but the decision was not strong enough for constituents who continued to write their congressmen, pressing for a stronger position against American involvement. The memory of the transition from neutrality, to armed neutrality to a declaration of war twenty years earlier still lingered in the minds of tens of thousands of citizens.

By January of the following year, sentiment had become persuasive enough to prompt Louis Ludlow to introduce a resolution to the House, stating that the authority of Congress to declare war could not become effective until it was confirmed by a majority vote in a national referendum. In the process of carrying the resolution from committee to the floor, opinion polls indicated that almost three-fourths of the public favored the idea. The President, recognizing that the enactment of such a law would make it impossible to conduct foreign affairs in a reasonable and expeditious way, lobbied strongly against its passage. After Roosevelt's stance was made clear to Congress, the House returned the bill to committee for reconsideration. In the intervening months, public support dropped to sixty-eight percent—still a strong indication of favor, but not adequate to the test as the bill re-emerged once again. When the floor vote was finally taken, the resolution was narrowly defeated, by a margin of 209 to 188. Requiring a two-thirds majority, the bill had failed by fifty-three votes and the President was able to resume his drive for control over the direction of international relations.

The situation continued, despite the fact that events in Europe and the Orient worsened. Opposition to American involvement fluctuated, but the nature of the composition of the resistance expanded. At the forefront was Charles Lindbergh, who for years had been America's greatest national hero. Alongside him were a variety of people, respresenting

an exceptionally diverse number of philosophies and interests.

As the election year approached, Roosevelt's convictions became stronger. Although there was no Constitutional injunction against a President serving more than two terms, precedent had dictated this period of time and the tradition was powerful. Prior to the capitulation of France on June 22, 1940, and the establishment of the Vichy government, the President had expected to retire at the conclusion of his second term; but, the events in Europe and the increasing magnitude of the crisis in Great Britain encouraged Roosevelt to change his mind. On August 14, Lewis Hershey was appointed director of the Selective Service System, in accordance with a measure passed by Congress providing for peacetime conscription. This bill had been ardently and persuasively promoted by the President and enactment was accompanied by anticipated protest. In fact, however, the fall of France, coupled with the Italian declaration of war against France and the development of the Axis alliance between Germany and Italy, had altered public opinion in a perceptible way. On October 16, over sixteen million men registered for the armed forces without incident. The Secretary of War drew the first numbers for induction on October 29, and the President rested in the Oval Office, assured that his decision to run for a third term was both appropriate and potentially successful.

The Democrats concurred, announcing their decision that the President would be their candidate. Among the pledges made in the party platform was the simple promise that American troops would not be sent overseas except in case of attack. The Republicans were divided. Thomas Dewey ran in several primaries and emerged as the victor all the way to the convention. Robert Taft, however, was a favorite among party regulars and the battle increased as the first hours of the Convention wore on. The verdict on the first ballot for nomination was indecisive. On the second ballot, no victor emerged. And, on and on, until the sixth, when the delegates

compromised with the announcement that Wendell Wilkie would be the Party's choice. Wilkie's campaign was subjected to a series of mistakes and minor disasters. The fact that he had, until recently, been a registered Democrat worked against him among solid party supporters; the Republican National Committee became excessive in its anti-war propaganda, eliciting support among party members for the Democratic candidate. Even though his campaign strategists urged him to take a strong stand against Roosevelt's decision to send arms to England, to support the draft and to deal with Allied belligerents by providing matériel, Wilkie found himself increasingly in support of the same measures. The campaign dragged on, until on election day Roosevelt emerged as the first President to serve a third term—by the closest margin in his career, twenty-seven million votes to twenty-two million.[1]

On the morning of December 16, the President called a news conference, announcing inconspicuously what was to become one of the most monumental actions taken prior to direct American military participation in the Second World War. In a period of forty-five minutes, Roosevelt provided the substance of the lend-lease program, formally entitled the House of Representatives Bill 1776.[2] Less than two weeks later, he elaborated on the proposal to the public in a fireside chat. The bill was designed to provide the Chief Executive with the power to decide what to lend, when to lend it and to whom. The source of the leases was a combination of tanks, airplanes and ships and the obvious recipient was Great Britain—the target of massive strikes by the Germans—although the legislation included a section allowing the President to direct assistance to "any country whose defense [is] deemed vital to the defense of the United States." The speech was an exceptionally effective one and it was broad-

[1]On the issue of foreign affairs, public opinion fluctuated dramatically during the campaign months. For example, in late 1940, only 7.7 percent believed that America would be drawn into the war, although 40 percent had thought so eight months earlier when there was less real chance of that happening.

[2]The formal title of the bill was "A Bill to Further Promote the Defense of the United States, and For Other Purposes."

Franklin Roosevelt, *right, meets with his Secretary of State Cordell Hull, center, and Attorny General Homer Cummings during a speaking tour of the country in 1938.*

cast on the night of one of London's worst firebombings. Taken together, these factors resulted in substantial support for the policy. Polls taken in the following days indicated that well over two-thirds of the public approved of lend-lease, with fifty-four percent believing that the program should be started at once. The bill, however, had not yet been sanctioned by Congress. And, this was to prove the most decisive battle of the internal struggle against intervention in the war.

Roosevelt's floor managers worked conscientiously day and night to assure the victory of the proposal. Moderate Republicans were aligned with liberal Democrats; congressmen who had opposed activities which might induce American involvement on greater scales were shown pictures of the devastation of Great Britain; and, finally, Wilkie testified on behalf of the bill, in a brief, but pointed, statement: "It is the history of democracy that under such dire circumstances, extraordinary powers must be granted to the elective executive."[3] The Congress, which had argued for the requirement of a national referendum prior to a declaration of war, had been convinced through the events of the preceding year that expediency was essential. In March, 1941, the bill became law.

Within a matter of hours, the President made a formal request for the authorization of nine billion dollars as an initial expenditure for the development of the lend-lease and for the improvement of the military capacity at home. The monies appropriated for domestic uses were gravely needed. At best, America was unprepared for the eventuality of war.

[3]February 11, 1941, speech to the Joint Session of Congress.

A press conference *called by Roosevelt in 1939 while he was visiting Warm Springs, Georgia, produced this famous photograph. Roosevelt, a victim of polio, was a regular visitor to the Georgian therapeutic resort.*

The Presidential campaign *of 1940 matched Roosevelt against Republican candidate Wendell Wilkie. Wilkie is shown here addressing a crowd gathered on the Iowa capital grounds in Des Moines.*

Troops which had been drafted had been using obsolete equipment and cardboard replicas of tanks during maneuvers at training bases. Heavy industry was operating at a marginal rate of production. Military installations were severely under-staffed and under-equipped. And, most importantly, the economy was far from prepared for a massive assistance program, much less engagement in war. Almost immediately, production began; many of the seven million people who were unemployed during the first quarter of 1941 were hired by the government, and public enthusiasm for the effort mounted. As rapid as the changes were, however, they were not sufficient to meet the impending disaster which precipitated the timing of America's entrance into the War.

PEARL HARBOR

On Saturday, December 6, 1941, Richard Nixon had been married almost five months. The young attorney was applying for jobs—one of which was with the F.B.I. Justice Brandeis was buried in Washington, ending an era in which he had been extremely influential in Supreme Court decisions. Edward R. Murrow was preparing for a dinner engagement with the President and his wife. John Kennedy had tickets for a baseball game in the evening. Intelligence agencies were receiving reports indicating that an aggressive move by the Japanese was expected within the next few days. General Walter Short, the commanding officer in Hawaii, was handed a brief message from Army intelligence stating that "Japanese negotiations have come to a practical stalemate. Hostilities may ensue. Subversive activities may be expected." The officers and enlisted men were given their customary Saturday evening liberty, on the grounds that they would become exhausted if placed on constant alert. No special guards were called to protect the United States Pacific Fleet, which included ninety-four ships—the only American force which could prevent Japanese invasions.

At 7:02 a.m., a radar operator on Oahu reported sightings of a large squadron of aircraft approaching the Hawaiian Islands. His commanding officer reviewed the message and replied that the incoming planes were probably American, arriving from the mainland, telling him to disregard the information. Fifty-two minutes later, the Japanese attack began in full force. The Navy's traffic chief sent an urgent wire to the White House, relaying the events with precise clarity: "Air raid on Pearl Harbor. This is not a drill." Within an hour, the United States no longer had a Pacific Fleet. All eight Navy battleships were destroyed, along with three cruisers and several other vessels. The American aircraft were still on the ground when Japanese planes had completed their assignment.

In Washington, the news was transmitted to the Secretary of State, Cordell Hull. He conferred briefly with the President and then admitted two Japanese envoys to his office. The delegates were almost an hour and a half late for their scheduled appointment. On orders from their superiors in Tokyo, they were supposed to have turned over a fourteen-point proclamation to the Secretary at 1:00 p.m., Eastern Standard Time—approximately a half an hour before the air attack was launched. Complications with decoding the message had thwarted the deadline and the message, culminating with a declaration of war against the United States, arrived too late. This fact, coupled with the intensity of the surprise raid and the destruction of the Pacific Fleet, contributed substantially to the events of the next few days. Hull met with the representatives briefly, accepting the document, and ordered them out of his office.

The President was stunned. In a meeting with Walter Lippmann late in the evening he repeatedly shook his head, muttering, "Our planes were destroyed on the ground! On the ground!" Intelligence reports which he had received indicated that the main thrust of Japanese activities were in Southeast Asia and Indonesia; there was little indication that their forces were strong enough to attack in the Pacific simultaneously. This, of course, proved to be a gross underestimation of their capabilities. What evidence there was to suggest an attack on Pearl Harbor had been bypassed in deferrence to the hostilities occurring in Europe and those officials who had access to such information were generally passed by. Nonetheless, in retrospect at least, there had been considerable forewarning of the attack.

On November 27, the Signal Corps had transcribed a conversation between Tokyo headquarters and the Japanese embassy in Washington, indicating that military preparations were underway for an attack against the United States Navy.

lthough Europe *had been in the throes of war since 1939, many mericans in 1940 felt that the United States should stay out of hat they considered to be a strictly European war. Among the famous Americans who adopted an isolationist position was Charles indbergh, center.*

A Japanese bomber *making a run over Pearl Harbor, Hawaii, on December 7, 1941. The rising black smoke is from the battleships which had been caught in port by the sneak attack.*

In response, the commanding officer in Hawaii had notified his staff that a declaration of war against America might be preceded by a surprise attack on Pearl Harbor. Still, no immediate preparations for defense against such a contingency were made. On the 29th, intelligence officers decoded a message which placed the time and location of the attack in the hands of the American military; again, there was no serious response. On December 5, two days before the attack, FBI agents in Honolulu reported that the Japanese High Command on the island was burning its confidential papers, and leading members of the Navy War Plans Division in Washington expressed their urgent concern that Pearl Harbor was a highly probable target within the next few days. Despite all of these indications, including the interception of the message containing the exact place and time of the attack, the Navy was caught by what appeared to be complete surprise.

There are only two reasonable explanations for this, one of which is the fact that events in the European theater were allowed to significantly overshadow activities in the Pacific.[4] The second, and more realistic explanation in many ways, is the fact that the United States had been engaged in lengthy negotiations with the Japanese government for several months and had been lulled into a false sense of dominance over the leaders of that government. After the Japanese officials entered into a Tripartite Pact with Germany and Italy in October, 1940, the American position began to harden. Under the direction of Hull, demands increased for a reduction of Japanese activities throughout the Orient and the Pacific. In the interim between the time Japan entered into the Axis alliance and the attack on Pearl Harbor, Japanese oil supplies had been reduced monumentally. Estimates of the impact of this turn of events indicated that the military activities being directed by Prince Konoye, dramatic as they were, could not be sustained much beyond Christmas of 1941. Within the Japanese governmental chambers, debates raged about the conduct of relations with the United States and, on October 16—almost precisely a year after the

[4]A third, though not documented, possible explanation is that the President knew that public opinion would not tolerate a direct American military involvement in the war and thus allowed the attack on Pearl Harbor as a means of providing an excuse for United States' entrance.

trialist had had extensive experience in construction prior to the war and had acquired shipyards in Oakland, California, shortly after the attack on Pearl Harbor. Within his factories, engineers discovered a prefabrication and assembly process which allowed for mass production without a loss of quality. The process represented a decisive breakthrough in the mobilization effort, and within a year the quantity of matériel available for war use prompted Stalin to observe, at the Teheran Conference, that without American production, the war would have been lost.

The impact of such production on the economy was equally startling. By 1943, corporate profits surpassed the figures set in 1929, prior to the crash. The Treasury Department estimated that Americans, who were readily accepting an austerity program, had saved as much as seventy billion dollars in cash, checking accounts, and redeemable war bonds. Randolph Paul, the Department's General Counsel, referred to the situation as "liquid dynamite," but his words were lost in the intensity of the mobilization effort. In the same month, the total number of armed forces volunteers and

The USS Casin, *right, and the USS* Downes *as they appeared after the bombing attack on Pearl Harbor. Aircraft carriers from the American fleet were out to sea with military maneuvers at the time of the attack, or they might have been destroyed also.*

draftees reached a figure of sixteen million, twelve million of whom were assigned a combat-ready status. Domestic preparedness was so strong a commitment on the part of the public that one of the most serious violations of Constitutional rights ever experienced in American history was largely obscurred and, when observed, was generally applauded in the name of military expediency and security.

JAPANESE-AMERICAN INTERNMENT

Following the attack on Pearl Harbor, the question of Japanese-American citizens emerged as a major controversial issue. In Hawaii, authorities had moved quickly and rationally to augment security measures. FBI and other government officials worked closely with Japanese community leaders and few incidents occurred which reflected either subversive activity or discrimination.

On the West Coast, the response was entirely different. Although the Japanese-American population constituted less than one percent of the total number of residents of the state of California, Governor Olsen and Attorney General Earl Warren initiated a concerted effort at removing them from all civil service posts and revoking state-issued licenses to prac-

EXTRA

AMERICA FIRST

San Francisco Examiner
Monarch of the Dailies

REG. U.S. PAT. OFF.

THE WEATHER
Fair and Mild
in San Francisco Bay Region
Monday

VOL. CLXXV, NO. 161   CC   SAN FRANCISCO, MONDAY, DECEMBER 8, 1941—28 PAGES   DAILY 5 CENTS, SUNDAY 10 CENTS   DAILY AND SUNDAY PER MONTH $1.50

U. S.-JAP WAR!

HAWAII, MANILA BOMBED; TWO U. S. WARSHIPS SUNK

President Announces Attacks

WASHINGTON, Dec. 7.—(INS)—President Roosevelt issued the following statement at 2:25 p. m. through Secretary Stephen T Early:

"The Japanese have attacked Pearl Harbor from the air and all naval and military activities on the island of Oahu, the principal American base in the Hawaiian Islands.

Twenty minutes after announcing officially that the Japanese air force had attacked American naval bases in Hawaii, the White House announced the Japanese also attacked Manila.

The announcement of the attack on Manila read:,

"A second attack is reported. This one has been made on the American and naval station in Manila."

S. F. Defenses on War Basis; Leaves Cancelled

San Francisco's defenses swung Full crews manned every one into action within minutes of the of the eight to sixteen inch rifles Japanese attack on Manila and that from seaward from both Honolulu yesterday. sides of the Golden Gate.

The Navy, Army and Coast Brig. Gen. E. A. Stockton, commander of the Pacific Guard cancelled all leaves, rounded manding harbor defenses, published at once an order cancelling up every man and sent them to all leaves and furloughs. battle stations.

Agents began streaming into San Francisco police responded offices of the Federal Bureau of at once to requests from the Investigation, apparently to re-Army and Navy and began stopceive final orders preparatory to ping all soldiers and sailors on a roundup of all suspected spies downtown streets to order them and dangerous aliens. to report to their stations.

All San Francisco police of all There still was no police guard details were ordered to report, ap-at the Japanese consulate late in parently to participate in the the afternoon. roundup. Yoshio Muto, the Japanese con-

There was intense activity at sul, appeared stunned. Fourth Army headquarters, "I don't understand! I don't where Lieut. Gen. John L. DeWitt, understand!" he kept repeating. top Army officer of the Pacific San Francisco outwardly maincoast as Fourth Army com-tained its customary Sunday mander, was closeted throughout quiet. the afternoon with his staff.

Busier still was the office of Rear Admiral John W. Green-slade, who as commandant of the Twelfth Naval District is in charge of San Francisco's defense at sea.

$700,000 Granted Monterey Airport

MONTEREY, Dec. 6.—(AP)—Word was received today that President Roosevelt has author-

Great Navy patrol bombers ized a $700,000 improvement proj-swept up and down the Califor-ect for the Monterey airport. nia co ast off the Golden Gate Runways will be extended and on a ceaseless patrol. Vessels of paved, the field will be lighted, the Navy Patrol Force operating and extensive grading and re-from Treasure Island were sent alignment will be done. The WPA to stations at sea in vastly in-will do the work. A $250,000 bond creased numbers. issue will be authorized by the

ALL SHIPS HALTED. district board to cover the spon-

All marine operations in San sor's share of the cost. Francisco Bay except those of the Navy were brought to a halt,

WASHINGTON, Dec. 7.—(INS) — President Roosevelt has ordered the Army and Navy to use their full power for the defense of the United States.

"As soon as word of the attack was taken to the President," Early said, "The President directed the Army and Navy to execute all previously prepared plans for defense of the United States."

War Secretary Stimson and Navy Secretary Knox immediately conferred with the President at the White House.

The White House revealed that the attacks by Japan were made "wholly without warning."

Steps immediately were taken by the White House to notify congressional leaders of the g rave situation.

WASHINGTON, Dec. 7. — (AP) — The President decided today after Japan's attack on Pearl Harbor and Manila to call an extra-ordinarily meeting of the Cabinet for 8:30 p. m. tonight and to have congressional lead-ers of both parties join the conference at 9 p. m.

NEW YORK, Dec. 7.—(AP)—Untold damage has been done to the United States Naval Base at Pearl Harbor and to the city of Honolulu itself by unidentified bombing planes, an NBC observer reported today in a broadcast direct from Honolulu.

The observer, standing on the roof of the Advertiser Building in Honolulu, said the planes, undoubtedly Japanese, made the raid unexpectedly. His report was suddenly broken off.

BULLETINS

MANILA, Dec. 7.—(INS)—The American naval base at Cavite, Island of Luzon, was sub-jected to enemy attack this morning.

Army and Navy authorities commanded all forces to their stations to resist the attack.

There were no immediate reports on dam-age.

HONOLULU, Dec. 7.—(INS)—The United States Army issued an official state-ment this morning declaring enemy aircraft have been shot down.

WASHINGTON, Dec. 7.—(INS)—Senate leaders were preparing today for an emergency session tomorrow in an-ticipation of a message from President Roosevelt asking for a declaration of war against Japan.

SAN PEDRO, Dec. 7.—(INS)—Every naval officer and mechanician attached to the San Pedro air base was ordered by broadcast today to report immediately to his station.

WASHINGTON, Dec. 7.—(INS)—The White House said at 3:30 p. m., that the Japanese attacks upon Hawaii and the Philippines apparently were still in progress at that time.

First news of the attacks was received by the War and Navy Departments, and it was instantly transmitted to President Roosevelt.

There was deep amazement as well as resentment in officialdom over the attacks while the United States and Japan were still holding conferences in an effort to maintain peace.

Even as Japan's envoys were professing that they were trying to find a peaceful solution of the Far East situation the attacks were launched.

WASHINGTON, Dec. 7.—(INS)—The War Department announced that an American transport has been torpedoed 1,300 miles west of San Francisco.

WASHINGTON, Dec. 7.—(INS)—Presiden-tial Secretary Stephen T. Early announced at 3:35 p. m. that the Army has received distress signals from a vessel believed to be one of its cargo ships 700 miles off San Francisco. It was not immediately known if this ship might have been the same one referred to shortly before in an announcement by the War Department, or whether it constituted a second attack.

Severe Explosion Rock Pearl Harbor In Surprise Attac

HONOLULU, Dec. 7.—(AP)—Japan bombs killed at least five persons and inju many others, three seriously, in a surpr morning aerial attack on Honolulu today

HONOLULU, Dec. 7.—(INS)—Americ outpost of the Pacific, mighty Pearl Har naval base was under enemy attack today.

A number of attacking planes, with insignia were sighted shortly after 8 a. m.

(In Washington Presidential Secret Early identified the attacking planes as Ja nese.)

Antiaircraft guns opened fire when planes dived low over the base and relea repeated sticks of bombs.

Two Warships Sunk

Two warships lying in the harbor w sunk.

The planes later returned to the attack. The attack was a complete surprise w minimum forces of the Army and Navy on S day morning duty.

A pall of heavy black smoke hung o Pearl Harbor.

Sporadic Air Raids

Army intelligence said:

"Peal Harbor was subjected to a spora air raid. We have no further details."

Antiaircraft guns are still firing from p tions near the center of Honolulu.

United States Army fighter planes ha taken to the air.

A round of explosions of great magni were heard at 9:30 a. m., more than an he after the first raid.

Los Angeles Examiner

CHARACTER · QUALITY · AMERICA FIRST! · ENTERPRISE · ACCURACY

AN AMERICAN PAPER FOR THE AMERICAN PEOPLE · THE GREAT NEWSPAPER OF THE GREAT SOUTHWEST

Giant of Journalism

Remember PEARL HARBOR

VOL. XXXIX—NO. 10   LOS ANGELES, SUNDAY, DECEMBER 21, 1941   CCC   Six Sections—Part I—TEN CENTS

U-BOATS RAID CALIFORNIA WATERS, ATTACK 2 TANKERS

Greatest Philippine Battle On at Davao; Japs Land Big Army

Hong Kong Holds Out; U. S., Dutch Blast 5 More Enemy Ships

Outstanding developments in the war in the Pacific yesterday were:

HONG KONG—British still waging an epic battle against overwhelming odds in strategic city, with Japanese claiming fall of city only a matter of hours.

MALAYA—British effect orderly withdrawal to new line of defense, and prepare to block all roads to Singapore, despite serious loss of Penang; American submarine sinks another Japanese transport.

BATAVIA—Dutch air force makes direct bomb hits on two Japanese cruisers and two Japanese transports off Miri, seacoast of Sarawak in Borneo; destroys two enemy seaplanes.

CHUNGKING—Chinese claim army has relieved pressure on Hong Kong by fierce attack on Japanese north of Kowloon; American flyers with Chinese army shoot down four Japanese planes at Kunming.

By Robert Robb
Staff Correspondent International News Service

MANILA, Dec. 21 (Sunday).—American and Filipino troops were reported fighting heroically today to hold Davao, seaport capital of Mindanao Island in the Southern Philippines, against a powerful new Japanese invasion, but it was officially acknowledged this morning that the situation in that sector is "obscure."

General Douglas MacArthur's Manila headquarters in a terse communique, issued at 8:30 a. m. today (6:30 p. m. E. S. T., Saturday), announced:

"Due to difficulties of communication, the situation at Davao is obscure."

The communique further stated that the situation on the main Philippine Island of Luzon, where the Japanese hold two beach-heads in the north and

(Continued on Page A, Cols. 4-5)

U.S. War Zone Map Tomorrow

To help you follow the war moves intelligently and with complete clearness, the Examiner tomorrow publishes a full-page map of the entire Pacific theater of the war.

Printed in full color, the map shows the West Coast of the United States, Mexico and Panama Canal. It also displays Alaska, the Pacific side of Soviet Russia, China, Japan, Manila, Singapore, the East Indies, Australia, New Zealand and the Hawaiian Islands.

Naval bases, air bases and fortified areas are indicated, including the distances, measured in miles, between the most important American Pacific Coast city to the countries named.

Here is a map well worth saving for reference as developments occur in the Far Eastern situation. It is the most complete map of the path of war in the Pacific the Examiner has published.

Egypt Cuts Wheat Content of Bread

CAIRO, Dec. 20.—The Egyptian government today decreed that all bread must have only 50 per cent wheat flour and took steps for the rapid importation of additional wheat from Australia and Canada.

HITLER ADMITS RUSS SUPERIOR TO HIS ARMY

Appeals to People for Warm Clothing for Soldiers; Admits Nation Faces Long, Hard War

Setbacks to the Nazi cause, preceding Propaganda Minister Goebbels broadcast yesterday, can be summarized as follows:

1. Red army advancing westward with desperate German rear guards attempting to delay it.
2. Russians take Volokolamsk.
3. Reds report advances against Finns in Lake Ladoga region.
4. Germans in pell-mell retreat in Libya, with British capturing key cities of Derna and Mekili.

By Associated Press

LONDON, Dec. 20, —An appeal from Adolf Hitler read in every radio station of the Reich tonight acknowledged his army faced an enemy superior in numbers and material and begged the straitened German people to contribute their warm clothing to enable the soldiers to endure the rigors of the bitter eastern front.

The appeal, sounded on Hitler's behalf by Propaganda Minister Paul Joseph Goebbels, said the German people must show their gratitude by making a Christmas gift of every article of warm clothing that possibly can be spared to the men in the army.

While Goebbels was thus reading his own appeal and the proclamation of Hitler, the high command admitted its African army was withdrawing westward "according to plan" and that on

(Continued on Page B, Cols. 3-4)

Japs May Pay Taxes, Thank You!

WASHINGTON, Dec. 20. —The Treasury relaxed today restrictions on impounded funds of Japanese nationals — but not enough to make any Japanese happy.

Funds will be released, it said, to permit them to pay taxes and fees to Federal and state Governments.

Subs Shell U. S. Ships 90 and 225 Miles From S.F.

King Commands All U. S. Fleets

ADMIRAL ERNEST KING
New Commander-in-Chief of United States Fleet
Wide World photo.

Ingersoll Is Named Head of Atlantic Flotilla

WASHINGTON, Dec. 20. — (INS) — Stressing the vital role of aircraft in America's war against Japan and the Axis, President Roosevelt tonight named Admiral Ernest J. King, one of the Navy's outstanding fleet airmen, as commander-in-chief of the United States Fleet.

The President's action completed the drastic shakeup of the High Command at Hawaii resulting from the Pearl Harbor debacle of Sunday, December 7.

In naming Admiral King to be Supreme Chief of all U. S. Naval Forces, President Roosevelt followed the same precedent set in placing an Army Air Force Commander, General Delos C. Emmons, in charge of all Army forces in Hawaii.

Admiral King, who has been Commander-in-Chief of the Atlantic Fleet during the counter thrusts of U. S. Sea forces at German U-boat, bomber and surface raider attacks on U. S. Lend-Lease shipping during the past seven months, succeeds Admiral Husband E. Kimmel, who was relieved of duty both as Commander of the U. S. Fleet and the Pacific Fleet earlier this week. Admiral Chester W. Nimitz was named Commander of the Pacific Fleet.

The President's action in selecting Admiral King as Supreme Commander of all U. S. Sea forces also clothed him with the broad authority to take personal command and of U. S. Naval Forces at Sea or to direct all naval operations from Washington.

Admiral King, 63 years old and a native of Loraine, Ohio, will be in supreme command of the Pacific, Atlantic and Asiatic Fleets.

Rear Admiral Royal E. Ingersoll, Assistant Chief of Naval operations, succeeds Admiral King as Commander of the Atlantic Fleet.

U.S. Freezes Sugar at Present Prices

WASHINGTON, Dec. 20.—Sugar prices were "frozen" by the Government today at current levels.

The Office of Price Administration placed temporary emergency ceilings on primary and wholesale prices of all forms of refined and other "direct consumption" sugar which it said would "remove any reason for higher retail sugar prices."

Announcing the order, Price Administrator Leon Henderson declared:

"The OPA has removed all possibility that retail outlets will be forced to pay more for their supplies of sugar.

"Hence there is no reason for American housewives to pay any higher prices for this fundamental foodstuff than they did before the attack on Pearl Harbor December 7."

Douglas C. Mackeachie, OPM purchases director, said that within 24 hours after Japan attacked the United States a consumer run on sugar developed.

One Vessel Sends SOS; Allies Plan Unified War Command

At the naval district headquarters, an aide to Admiral Greenslade said it had been reported without confirmation that the Blunt's Reef Lighthouse had picked up an S. O. S. from the Emidio.

SAN FRANCISCO, Dec. 20—(INS)—Confirming receipt of reports that two American merchantmen had been attacked by enemy submarines in the Pacific less than 300 miles from San Francisco, officials of the 12th Naval District refused to either confirm or deny the reports.

The reports, which naval aides said did not come from official sources, were that the 6750-ton tanker Agwiworld was shelled an undivided distance off Cypress Point, which is some 90 miles south of San Francisco, and that the 6900-ton tanker Emidio was attacked somewhere off Eureka, about 225 miles north of San Francisco.

The reports were that the submarines had surfaced, fired their deck guns at the ship, and then disappeared hastily below the surface. The Emidio dispatched an S O S because of the advices, but this could not be confirmed from any commercial wireless agency because of naval restrictions upon information.

Twelfth Naval District headquarters confined its discussion of the rumored attacks to saying, none of which had been received.

French Legion Cut Off by Red Attacks

VICHY, Unoccupied France, Dec. 20—(P)—Reports from Paris said today that Jacques Doriot, former Communist who was a leader of the French legion fighting with the Axis against Soviet Russia, had been posted as missing for several days and that the legion had been cut off by Russian counterattacks.

EIGHT SHOTS FIRED

Waterfront reports at Santa Cruz said that the Agwiworld, plying off the coast, was attacked at 2 p. m. by a submarine that suddenly surfaced a half-mile away.

Eight shots were fired by the submersible, crew members said, none of which hit the ship. The captain of the vessel immediately turned to port for a coastal haven, showing only the craft's stern as a

Assembly Raps Ship Slayers' Parole

EXAMINER BUREAU, Sacramento, Dec. 20.—A resolution calling upon Governor Olson to revoke the King-Ramsey-Coner paroles was adopted by the State Assembly tonight by a 43-10 vote.

Introduced by Assemblyman Gardiner Johnson of Berkeley, resolution, which now goes to the Senate for concurrence, denounced the "goon squad brutality and lawlessness" of the shipboard-slaying of Chief Engineer George Alberts of the S. S. Point Lobos at Oakland in 1935.

Johnson, in pleading for adoption of the resolution, charged the "parole system of this state was very badly shaken by these paroles."

"There has been a great feeling this case was not heard in

considerate fashion by the parole board," Johnson declared.

"Unequivocally, the sentiment has always been against granting these paroles."

Speaking in opposition to the resolution were Assemblymen Paul Richie of San Diego, Edward O'Day, San Francisco, Cecil King, Los Angeles, and George Gaffney, San Francisco.

O'Day declared that in his opinion "it was a terrible thing to ask the members of the Legislature to pass upon this resolution."

"If we start a precedent like this, we are breaking down the democratic form of government," O'Day said. "We are asked to sit as a jury and without giving these three men the benefit of trial, which is nothing better than passing judgment in a star chamber session."

O'Day suggested that the resolution should be directed against the parole board.

"Why not investigate the activities of the parole board, then determine if these paroles were the result of political pressure as charged here tonight?" O'Day asked.

Assemblyman Jack Tenney, Inglewood, chairman of the legislative committee investigating subversive activities, charged that "the reason these three men are now out of the penitentiary

(Continued on Page 15, Cols. 5-6)

Ban on Tire Sales Extended to January 5

WASHINGTON, Dec. 20.—(INS)—The ban on sale of new automobile tires, which was to expire December 22, was extended today to January 5 in an order issued by Donald M. Nelson, director of priorities of the Office of Production Management.

The extension, Nelson said, was made necessary to complete the rationing plan which is being worked out jointly by the OPM and the Office of Price Administration.

tice medicine and law. The press hastily followed suit, campaigning bitterly against their presence and their position within society. Insurance companies began to cancel policies; markets adopted an informal policy of refusing to sell groceries to Japanese shoppers; restaurants denied them service; and, progressively, within a matter of weeks, eight thousand people were forced to flee the state in hopes of finding more congenial surroundings in the interior of the country.[5]

California officials demanded that the Federal government intervene with a policy to remove Japanese-Americans from the public. Roosevelt was absorbed in the events occurring in Europe and referred the matter to Stimson, the Secretary of War. In turn, he passed the request on to his assistant, McCloy, who became the Administration's prime proponent of resettlement. Taking the President's general instructions as carte blanche for whatever approach he designed, McCloy alerted the Under-secretary of the Interior Department and the chief of the War Department's Aliens Division to prepare for supportive roles. In addition, he drew up extensive plans and submitted them to the President, arguing that relocation was essential to the war effort and to American security. His request was supported by high-ranking and distinguished members of the Administration and Congress, including Milton Eisenhower, Abe Fortas, Henry Stimson and Hugo Black. The response was immediate and favorable; the chief executive issued a declaration on February 19, 1942, authorizing the War Department to establish "military areas" for the relocation of Japanese-Americans on the West Coast. Under Executive Order 9066, all people of Japanese descent were given forty-eight hours to dispose of their property, businesses and personal possessions; investments and bank accounts were forfeited.[6]

At 7:00 on the morning of March 30, 1942, copies of the Civilian Exclusion Order, the War Department's version of the Executive Order, were nailed to front doors, designating the residences of Japanese-Americans to be picked up by truck convoys and transported to temporary assembly areas at

Once America had entered the war against the Axis Powers, she turned the vast resources of her factories to the production of war material. Here a "liberty" ship slides off the dry dock after being launched. American war production was the most valuable asset the United States brought to the war effort.

The drawing *of the first name in the first lottery ever to be held in America for peacetime conscription.*

fifteen different locations in California. Simultaneously, seventy million dollars worth of farm acreage was confiscated by governmental authorities and nearly a half billion dollars worth of assets were frozen, pending a decision regarding their future disbursement. Under the supervision of General De Witt, the army moved expeditiously, relocating tens of thousands of people in race tracks, community centers and arenas, where they would remain until eleven permanent centers could be constructed on desolate Federal lands farther from the coast.

On January 28, 1943, almost a year after the internment process had been initiated, the first indications of a change in Federal policy were announced. Secretary Stimson revealed a proposal to the press, outlining prospects for the Army's acceptance of Japanese-American volunteers for active duty. More than thirteen thousand young men responded to the opportunity and signed loyalty oaths required of recruits while they were still behind barbed wire fences in the camps. Their motive was made clear—those who joined the armed forces believed that if they served well the government would relax its policy and improve camp conditions or release prisoners and terminate the system altogether. In spite of the outstanding contributions which they made in the war effort in Europe, however, there was no commensurate change in policy for almost two years.

Less than a week before Christmas of 1944, the Supreme Court ruled on the issue of the constitutionality of the relocation centers and the internment of the 110,000 Japanese-American people—70,000 of whom had been citizens of the United States at the time of their incarceration. In a divided decision, the Court upheld the War Department's actions, on the grounds that the West Coast had been threatened by invasion and that the military authority exercised was reasonable under such circumstances. In a related decision, however, the Court ruled that there was no longer any reason to detain people whose loyalty was unquestioned. On December 19, the army again began transporting Japanese-Americans—this time in convoys headed away from the centers and back to the coast. The epic was over, but it had taken its toll in civil liberties and constitutional abuses and in individual and collective injustices during the three year period of its existence.

In part, the duration of time can be attributed to, though not justified by, the preoccupation of the President with the conduct of the war in general and the development of plans for the construction of the atomic bomb in particular. Although the White House was petitioned to modify the War Department's policies on the West Coast during the latter part of 1942 and on several occasions thereafter, Roosevelt was focusing most of his energies on the Manhattan Project and continued to defer the issue to the judgment of subordinates.

THE MANHATTAN PROJECT

On the night of December 1, Westinghouse had delivered three tons of uranium to an obscure building on the University of Chicago campus. The shipment was requested by the White House, with no indication of its use, several months earlier. Inside the building, several of the nation's leading

[5]Declarations were soon issued in contiguous states against the entrance of Japanese-Americans into their territory and hostilities were especially prevalent in Nevada and Utah.

[6]Japanese-Americans were entitled to take with them only one bag, containing their personal possessions; everything else was to remain where they were taken away by convoys.

scientists were working on the task of producing a viable chain reaction which could produce an atomic explosion. By 3:30 the following afternoon, they had accomplished their objective—for the first time in history, the chain was self-perpetuating and the prospects for transforming massive amounts of energy into a deliverable bomb seemed possible. Three blocks away, in Room 209 of the University's Eckhert Hall, another group was working on a method of providing the technology to do this. Neither group of scientists knew of the other's presence in the city; secrecy was paramount. On direct orders from the White House, the scientists had been effectively isolated from society and from those among them who were working on different aspects of the problem. They were not informed as the the purpose of their efforts except to the extent that they were assured that the project was vital to the war effort and that the government would pay the bills—which ultimately totalled an amount exceeding two billion dollars.

As scientists attempted to devise a way of combining the reactor process with weapons technology in New Mexico, the President began his annual State of the Union Message to a joint session of Congress. His words reflected his pleasure in the accomplishment of the mobilization efforts and the effects which they were having in the Allied prosecution of the war. A single sentence captured his optimism: "The Axis powers knew that they must win the War in 1942 or eventually lose everything; I do not need to tell you that our enemies did not win the war in 1942." The role of the President had greatly increased internationally as the American contribution increased. After completing his speech, Roosevelt left Capitol Hill in a small cavalcade of cars destined for the President's train, where his leading military advisors awaited his arrival. Together, they traveled to Miami, where a Pan American Clipper was preparing to fly the entourage to Casablanca for a summit meeting with Winston Churchill. At that meeting, amidst Roosevelt's controversial demand for unconditional surrender by the Axis governments, the President ascended to the position of commander-in-chief of all Allied Forces—a post he would hold until his death and a position which was readily accepted by Allied officials at

First Lady Eleanor Roosevelt *addressing a Joint Distribution Committee meeting on March 6, 1941. The committee was organized to bring relief to European refugees made homeless by the war. Mrs. Roosevelt was instrumental in raising millions of dollars during the war for refugee relief.*

several ensuing conferences in the next few weeks.

Domestically and internationally, the President had reached an unprecedented degree of stature. Although there were critics of his policies both at home and abroad, the vast majority of people willingly gave him their full support. The American economy was flourishing and despite the continuation of austerity programs, the standard of living for the average citizen had improved substantially. The Gross National Product, which had been ninety-one billion dollars in 1939, was approaching two-hundred billion in 1944. The total number of goods and services produced had reached an unprecedented high in an extremely brief period of time.[7]

Still, few people, including the President himself, believed that a fourth term in office was probable. It was clear that Roosevelt's health was failing, even though he continued to meet the demands of a rigorous schedule. As the campaign approached, his feelings became ambivalent. He simultaneously believed that he should retire on the one hand, and that he had a moral obligation to continue, if elected, on the other. A week before the Democratic Convention he wrote a letter to the National Committee Chairman, revealing his position. The core of the message read: "If the people command me to continue in this office and in this War I have as little right to withdraw as a soldier has to leave his post in the line. For myself I do not want to run. By next Spring I shall have been President and Commander-in-Chief of the Armed Forces for twelve years. . . . Reluctantly, but as a good soldier, I repeat that I will accept and serve in this office if I am so ordered by the Commander-in-Chief of us all—the sovereign people of the United States."[8]

[7]Production figures are instructive on this point. Between 1940 and 1945, Americans turned out almost 300,000 warplanes, 102,000 tanks, 372,000 artillery pieces, 2,455,964 trucks, 87,620 warships, 5,425 cargo ships, 5,822,000 tons of aircraft bombs, 20,086,061 small arms and 44 billion rounds of ammunition.

[8]Letter published by Robert Hannegan, Chairman of the Democratic National Committee, July 12, 1943. The events which seem to have been instrumental in Roosevelt's decision to make himself available for the nomination focused on growing isolationism in the Capitol and in the press which he feared might sabotage American foreign policy.

For the delegates at the Chicago convention, this was enough. They were united on Roosevelt's candidacy for a fourth term; what they were divided on was the issue of who would be the vice-presidential selection. Henry Wallace had been charged with neglecting his responsibilities and his record had been undistinguished. Although the President refused to take a stand against him publicly, it was rumored that he would accept an alternative running mate. Among the likely prospects were William O. Douglas, Alben Barkley, James Byrnes and Harry S. Truman. Of the four, Truman seemed the least probable choice as the first ballot was taken. No victor emerged, however, and party leaders caucused to re-evaluate the situation. Their decision, and the selection confirmed on the second ballot, was Truman—a man whom they believed would be a reasonable, if not outstanding, contribution to the ticket.

Roosevelt concurred, after discussions with the National Committee, although he indicated that he had never met Truman and could not remember anything about the Senator's career. On a radio address from San Diego, the President accepted the delegates' vote and announced the Democratic team. The New York *Times* responded immediately, charging that Truman's nomination was "the second Missouri compromise," calling it a "triumph of the bosses."

Nonetheless, the campaign resulted in an overwhelming triumph for the Democrats and Roosevelt was returned to office by a margin in the Electoral College of 432 to 99. Over the course of the next few months, the President's schedule intensified and he was confronted with major demands on the home front which actively competed for his time and efforts as Commander-in-Chief of the Allied Forces. Including Truman only marginally in decision-making processes, Roosevelt was forced to participate in a series of activities which included drafting the GI Bill of Rights, convincing Barkley to withdraw his resignation as Senate Floor Leader,

American troops *and their native carriers take a break from the march through the jungle in Burma. Americans joined British forces in the Burma Theatre to help push back the Japanese in that part of the world.*

General George C. Marshall, *Secretary of Defense, as he appeared in 1941.*

Lieutenant General George Patton, *who led the American forces in North Africa for a while. Following his North African campaigns, Patton led a mechanized cavalry unit on the European continent.*

Aerial view *of American landing craft streaming ashore at Iwo Jima. The American forces in the Pacific had to fight an island hopping war as they drove the Japanese out of their Pacific strongholds and moved toward the Japanese homeland islands.*

submitting the largest budget in the history of the world, carrying out secret negotiations with both labor and management in the atomic fission plants, deciding whether Eisenhower or Marshall should lead the invasion of Europe, and studying a proposed moratorium on insurance company premiums. The schedule was taking its toll; on several occasions, Roosevelt complained of chest pains and difficulty in breathing.

By the time the Yalta Conference began, the President was weak and gaunt. His American staff at the meeting believed he was representing the United States effectively and skillfully; but his European counterparts had a different impression. Anthony Eden expressed concern that the President was confused and uncertain on the evening of the first session; Churchill's personal physician told the statesman that he believed Roosevelt was a dying man. In any case, the record of the conference testifies to the fact that the American delegation was able to convince Stalin to enter into an alliance against Japan in exchange for several concessions in other areas. Notably, these included the redrawing of Poland's borders, adding territory which had been German; guaranteeing the Soviet Union an occupation zone in Korea; providing a United Nations Security Council position accompanied with veto power; and, allowing the Russians certain privileges in Manchuria, the Kurile Islands and part of Sakhalin Island. Stalin, in response, solemnly promised to guarantee all Eastern European countries, including Poland, the right to elect their own leaders and determine their own forms of government at the conclusion of the war. To delegates, the greatest beneficiary seemed to be Chiaing Kai-shek, who was recognized as the ruler of China by Stalin and other representatives of the Allied nations, along with the promise that efforts would be made to persuade Mao tse-tung's forces to cooperate with him. The American and British press praised the outcome of the conference, although Soviet experts in the United States were skeptical and Churchill urged Eisenhower to "shake hands with the Russians as far east of the Elbe as possible."

Within two months, Roosevelt was taken seriously ill, complaining of an intense headache at his home in Warm Springs. At 1:15 p.m., he slumped in his chair, suffering a massive cerebral hemorrage. With doctors in attendance, everything possible was done to revive the unconscious President, but the efforts were in vain. At exactly 3:35 p.m., he

died. Eleanor Roosevelt was in Washington at the time, preparing to deliver a speech to the Sulgrave Club on the proposed United Nations. She was notified that something serious had happened and she suspected the worst; nonetheless, she gave the address before returning to the Executive Mansion where she was informed of her husband's death. Her first action was to call for the Vice President, to convey the news to him personally.

HARRY S. TRUMAN

Truman was stunned. On April 12, 1945, he had become President of the United States, yet his knowledge of the events which were transpiring internationally was almost nil. He had never been in the White House War Room; he had no information about the Manhattan Project; and he was unaware of troop movements in either the Orient or Europe. By the end of his first week in office, however, Truman had gained the respect and admiration of many people who had formerly regarded him as a compromise Vice President. He was efficient, quick to learn, and concise in his evaluations of situations; he had a keen understanding of problems and an

unusual ability to grasp their meaning. Most importantly, he was not reluctant to make decisions, whether they related to American or international issues.

In late April, events began to occur in rapid succession. On May 1, Hitler's death was publicly announced. The next day, Berlin fell to Allied forces and by 5:00 p.m., German soldiers in Italy had surrendered. Two days later, German commanders in Holland, Denmark, and northwest Germany capitulated and on the 7th, General Jodl and his staff signed unconditional surrender documents at Reims while Field Marshall Keitel went through the same procedure in Berlin. At 11:30 p.m., for the first time in modern history, the entire armed forces of a nation had become prisoners of war. The next morning marked both V-E Day and Harry Truman's sixty-first birthday. The President announced over the radio at 9:00 a.m. that the war in Europe was over. Jubilantly, thousands of people rejoiced by throwing tons of ticker tape out of Wall Street windows, dancing in the streets and proclaiming victory throughout the nation. Yet, Tokyo retained its resolution never to surrender, and the war in the Pacific

General Eisenhower, *the Allied Commander in Chief, talks with members of a paratroop unit just before they boarded their planes to participate in the assault of Normandy.*

raged on. The victory was only half complete.

On April 24th, Truman had received his first briefing on the Manhattan Project and now, with the surrender of Germany and Italy, the issue came to the forefront as a controversy. Stimson had informed the President that a test was scheduled for July in an uninhabited desert near Los Alamos. If the test proved successful, it would yield five hundred tons of TNT, while the actual bomb would release double the explosive energy. The President's first choice was to seek out other alternatives and two groups, working independently, were assigned the task. On May 31 and June 1, the two teams met together for the first time, and shared the same conclusions—there were no other viable alternatives. In the afternoon of the same day, Truman's advisors recommended that the "bomb should be used as soon as possible against Japan" and that it be directed at a dual target, a military installation near other buildings more susceptible to damage, and that it should be dropped without prior warning.

THE ATOMIC BOMB

On Friday, July 13, exactly three months after Roosevelt had died, preparations for the test were completed. While the scientific community involved in the project waited, two B-29's flying overhead radioed weather conditions, indicating that the scheduled 4:00 a.m. detonation would have to be delayed. At 5:30, the weather had cleared and the countdown began. Thirty seconds after the explosion, the local command headquarters were jarred with winds up to hurricane force. A deafening roar swept across the desert and a giant column shot into the sky, spreading out like a mushroom and

American paratroopers *landing in France on D-Day, June 6, 1944. The Allied invasion force was the largest military armada ever assembled.*

319

Allied and German representatives *sign peace treaty ending the war in Europe in May 1945. General Walter Bedell Smith, fourth from left seated facing camera, was the American representative at the signing.*

Although the war *in Europe had ended, fighting again[st] Japanese in the Pacific continued. Here is a scene typical type of warfare that was waged throughout the Pacific as the moved toward the Japanese mainland.*

The mushroom-shaped cloud *from the atomic bomb which was dropped on Nagasaki, Japan, on September 9, 1945.*

Survivors *moving through the devastated city of Nagasaki following the dropping of the atomic bomb on the city.*

finally disappearing into the darkness at an altitude of 41,000 feet. When the immediate effects of the explosion subsided and the area was declared safe, scientists cautiously entered the target zone and discovered that all life had been destroyed, that the sand within a four-hundred yard radius of the center of the explosion had been transformed into an unidentifiable substance, and that the scaffolding used to support the bomb had completely disappeared. Everything had combined together at the correct time; the test was a complete success and the possibility of releasing an even greater amount of energy in an actual bomb over Japan became a reality. General Groves, who had been a witness to the explosion, captured the impact in a single sentence: "The War's over."

At the time of the test, Truman had been on route to Potsdam to engage in a conference. On the morning of July 16, the President received word of the success of the project and conveyed the information to Churchill directly, adding in general terms to Stalin that the United States had developed a new weapon of unusual destructive force. Eight days later, Truman tentatively adopted a proposal for atomic strikes at Japan, but he remained unconvinced that a warning should not be given. On his initiation, a Potsdam Declaration was issued, providing means by which the Japanese could avoid what was termed "prompt and utter destruction."[9] By August 2, no positive reply from the Tojo government had been received and the point of no return had been passed.

Four days later, Colonel Paul Tibbetts, Jr., and his crew boarded the B-29 *Enola Gay*. No one on the plane knew precisely what would occur in the next several hours except Captain William Parsons, who had been given the responsibility of assembling the bomb en route to the target destination. The Colonel had told his fellow officers that the mission

[9]Demands included the unconditional surrender of the Japanese armed forces, to be accompanied by an occupation which would end as soon as conditions stabilized.

A miniature reproduction *of the Statue of Liberty dominates the crowds which thronged Times Square following the announcement of the end of World War II.*

WAR OVER!

H SPORT .:. NIGHT FINAL   HIGH FOG Details on Page 11

THE CALL-BULLETIN

San Francisco Independent Newspaper

VOL. NO. 10 TUESDAY, AUGUST 14, 1945   5c DAILY

M'Arthur Named To Accept Surrender

WASHINGTON, Aug. 14 (AP).--President Truman announced at 7 p. m. E. W. T. (4 p. m. P. W. T.) today Japanese acceptance of surrender terms. They will be accepted by General Douglas MacArthur when arrangements can be completed. Mr. Truman read the formal message relayed from Emperor Hirohito through the Swiss government in which the Japanese ruler pledged the surrender on the terms laid down by the Big Three conference at Potsdam.

President Truman made this statement:

"I have received this afternoon a message from the Japanese government in reply to the message forwarded to that government by the secretary of state on August 11.

"I deem this reply a full acceptance of the Potsdam Declaration, which specifies the unconditional surrender of Japan. In this reply there is no qualification.

"Arrangements are now being made for the formal signing of surrender terms at the earliest possible moment.

"General Douglas MacArthur has been appointed the supreme Allied commander to receive the Japanese surrender."

V-J Proclamation Waits Signing

"Great Britain, Russia and China will be represented by high ranking officers.

"Meantime, the Allied armed forces have been ordered to suspend offensive action.

"The proclamation of V-J Day must wait upon the formal signing of the surrender terms by Japan."

Simultaneously Mr. Truman disclosed that selective service is taking immediate steps to slash inductions from 80,000 to 50,000 a month.

Henceforth, Mr. Truman said, only those men under 26 will be drafted for the reduced quotas.

Jap Text to Big Four

The White House made public the Japanese government's message accepting that ended the war which started December 7, 1941.

The text of their message, which was delivered by the Swiss charge d'affaires, follows:

"Communication of the Japanese government of August 14, 1945, addressed to the governments of the United States, Great Britain, the Soviet Union and China:

"With reference to the Japanese government's note of August 10 regarding their acceptance of the provisions of the Potsdam declaration and the reply of the governments of the United States, Great Britain, the Soviet Union and China sent by American Secretary of State Byrnes under the date of August 11, the Japanese government have the honor to communicate to the governments of the four powers as follows:

"1. His majesty the emperor has issued an imperial rescript regarding Japan's acceptance of the provisions of the Potsdam declaration.

"2. His majesty the emperor is prepared to authorize and insure the signature by his government and the imperial general headquarters of necessary terms for carrying out the provisions of the Potsdam declaration.

Vm. Knowland Named Senator by Warren

TRUMAN FORECASTS BIG CUT IN ARMY

WASHINGTON, Aug. 14 (AP).—President Truman today forecast that 5,000,000 to 5,500,000 men now in the may be returned to civilian life within the next twelve eighteen months.

HIROHITO WILL GO ON AIR

AN FRANCISCO, Aug. 14 (AP)—Tokio radio announced for Hirohito in a special broadcast will read the imperial pt of Japan's capitulation at 8 o'clock tonight (P. W. T.).

MOSCOW ANNOUNCES JAP SURRENDER

LONDON, Wednesday, Aug. 15 (AP).—The Moscow radio ced at midnight the unconditional surrender of Japan.

ATTLEE TELLS BRITAIN OF WAR END

LONDON, Wednesday, Aug. 15 (AP). — Prime Minister announced Japan had surrendered.

EL MAR—4TH: Joey B., 133.10, 35.80, 10.00; Hand 3.30, 2.60; Gisimo, 4.10. Time, 1:11 3-5.

rrender Sends Japs to Tears of Shame

By International News Service

el news agency said today he "imperial decision was d" on August 14, 1945, Japan's, at 10 p. m. Monday, T., and that weeping people hered outside the imperial bowing in shame, "hetheir efforts were not

Domei transmission, sent by the FCC.

d not give details of the al decision, but another transmission said an instant transmission will be at noon August 15. Japan

monitors, who intercepted gan summarizing the disas it was being wirelessed, ated that the Japanese

agency would go on to disclose the nature of the "imperial decision," but Domei transmitted only about 130 words and then broke off to say to editors: "Hold this item."

The portion of the Domei dispatch on the "emperor's decision" claimed that Hirohito had felt "extreme concern" ever since his rescript of December 8, 1941 (December 7, 1941, in the United

mp Beale Executes wo Army Privates

P BEALE, Marysville, Aug soldiers who had been con today by Brigadier General car B. Abbott, post com-

Those hanged were Private Clinton Stevenson, 30, found guilty of stabbing a fellow soldier at Isleton last fall, and Private Herbert W. Reid, 21, convicted of raping a Marysville white girl.

Johnson Toga For Oakland GOP Leader

By JAMES ADAM
Call-Bulletin Political Writer

Major William F. Knowland of Oakland was appointed today by Governor Warren as United States senator to succeed the late Hiram W. Johnson.

He is a former state senator and Republican national committeeman and is now stationed at Army headquarters in Paris.

YOUNGEST SENATOR

Only 37, he becomes the youngest United States senator and the

MAJOR WM. F. KNOWLAND
Senator From California

first Army officer to be named to an upper House seat.

In announcing the appointment at his Los Angeles office, Warren said he felt "the new senator should be a veteran of this war, because there is no time like the present to give our fighting men an opportunity in Congress to help shape the post-war program of the country they have saved."

Knowland's selection, however, splits the Republican ranks wide open for Lieutenant Governor Fred Houser, an aspirant for the

DAMAGE BIG IN WILD S.F. FETE

Police, and Army and Navy officials, took emergency steps today to curb victory demonstrations here after frenzied throngs, in one of the wildest downtown celebrations in San Francisco history, caused damage running into uncounted thousands of dollars.

The outburst was touched off late last night by a surrender announcement broadcast from Tokio.

Bannered in newspaper headlines, the word that the Japs had quit snapped the tension of days of eager waiting.

It wasn't V-J Day—officially.

But churning thousands of civilians and service men, mostly sailors, filled Market street, roaring their jubilance, smashing store windows, overturning autos, and swarming over street cars, taxicabs and fire engines which

Report Hunt For Hitler Intensified By Allies

LONDON, Aug. 14 (INS)—The London Daily Herald, quoting a dispatch from Hamburg, said today that an intensive search is being waged in belief that Adolf Hitler may be in hiding.

Despite Nazi reports that the Reichsfuehrer died in the last days of the war, the search is being made among 1,500,000 troops in Schleswig-Holstein.

Job Control Out; New Plan Set Up

Government manpower controls are revoked effective immediately and the government has set forth a new plan aimed at speedy re-employment of veterans and jobless war workers.

In an action timed to coincide with Japan's surrender, the War Manpower Commission announced a seven-point program to stimulate "reconversion activities and the speedy re-employment of displaced workers, being waged in belief that Adolf at the same time restoring a free labor market."

Among the controls lifted are those providing for hiring through the U. S. Employment Service, employment ceilings to channel workers to essential

industries and the requirements or certificates of availability in changing jobs.

Acting WMC Chairman Frank L. McNamee said regional directors had been instructed to put the new program into effect at once in the 1,500 local USES offices throughout the country. Specifically it provides that:

1. All manpower controls are to be lifted immediately, in their place voluntary community action to speed reconversion will be substituted.

2. The number of displaced workers and returning veterans in each community will be determined in co-operation with local management-labor.

groups. Action will be taken by the WMC and local USES offices in co-operation with the communities to speed reconversion and re-employment.

3. Labor will be channeled by voluntary methods into civilian industries "especially into industries which may become reconversion bottlenecks and thus delay mass re-employment throughout the country as a whole."

4. Full facilities of the USES again will be made available to all employers, including those for whom services were restricted because of war requirements.

5. Extended services will be

rendered to veterans in their readjustment to civilian employment.

6. Increased emphasis will be given to job counseling and other personalized services to assist job seekers to adapt their wartime experience to peacetime job opportunities.

7. Displaced war workers, many of whom have migrated during the war, will be assisted in finding employment in other communities where civilian production has expanded.

USES offices will continue to give preferential treatment to all reconversion activities, McNamee said.

Continued on Page A, Column 7

Continued on Page C, Column 3

Continued on Page 4, Col. 1

Call-Bulletin Today

"G" indicates Green Flash Section

Bridge	3G	Lawrence, David	A
Casualties	11	Movies	2G, 3G
Comics	8G	Patterns	8G
Crossword	8G	Peeler	A
Deaths	11	Radio Log	8G
Drama	2G, 3G	Ration Data	A
Editorial	8	Society	12
Finance	11	Sadofsky, George	3
Hatlo	10	Sports	9-10
Health	A	Weather	11
Horoscope	8G	Women's Page	12

As General Douglas MacArthur *looks on, a Japanese minister signs the unconditional surrender treaty aboard the USS* Missouri *on October 4, 1945.*

was to drop a bomb which was different from any other in history, but even he was unable to gauge the monumental impact of what was to come. At 9:15, the single missile was released over Hiroshima. It descended in less than a minute, operating perfectly. Through their goggles, the crew watched as a small fire became visible, followed immediately by a fireball half a mile wide, which produced a smoke column rising 10,000 feet into the air. As the base of the column approached three miles, a mushroom-shaped cloud appeared and at fifty thousand feet, a second mushroom cloud was formed. Even after the B-29 reached a point 270 miles from the target, the clouds were still visible. At 9:20, Tibbetts radioed his report to command headquarters: "Mission successful."

At 9:14 a.m., Hiroshima had been a thriving city. Thousands of the 344,000 residents were working in factories and shops, beginning a Monday morning in what seemed a usual way. By 9:16, over sixty thousand had been killed instantly and thousands of others were mortally wounded or missing. In the ensuing months and years, the devastation would be complete as previously unknown diseases and effects appeared. For the moment, however, the American government turned its attention to a second target—Nagasaki. On August 9, the city was devasted and 35,000 lives were lost in a matter of minutes. Simultaneously, squadrons of United States' planes flew over Japan, dropping leaflets which proclaimed that *"America asks that*

you take immediate heed of what we say in this leaflet. We are in possession of the most destructive force ever devised by man . . . we have just begun to use this weapon against your homeland."

On the same day, notice of Stalin's declaration of war against Japan reached Hirohito's command post. The Japanese leaders were in unanimous agreement—the terms of the Potsdam Declaration would have to be accepted. Yet, this did not result in capitulation immediately. After prolonged debate among military officials and politicians, the decision was finally made at 3:30 a.m. on August 10. Cables were sent half an hour later to Washington, London, Moscow, and Chungking, announcing Japan's acceptance of the demands in the document. Four days later, Hirohito formally taped a broadcast to the Japanese people, telling them of the surrender to the Allied forces. The surrender ceremonies aboard the *Missouri* on September 2, 1945, marked the end of the Second World War.

Troops were given orders to return home, on a schedule similar to the one devised following V-E Day, but the country they had left had changed during their absence. By 1945, mobilization had been transformed into prosperity, though it was not yet openly visible. The cost of the war had been 245 billion dollars—more than the combined annual budgets from 1789 to 1940. The total Gross National Product had reached 215 billion, taking the greatest jump in the short period from 1939 that had ever been imagined in history. Life-styles had changed commensurately and the American of 1945 was vastly different from the America of 1940. In the five-year interim, the character of the country had been altered in a dramatic way and its consequences would be felt as the post-War era began.

HISTORICAL HEADLINES
ON
WORLD WAR TWO

'Shootin' Talk' on the Firing Line

By United Press

WASHINGTON, May 7.—Secretary of War Henry L. Stimson's summons for direct naval action to aid Great Britain—the most important of a number of belligerent official statements—aroused the capital today.

Direct comment by officials and congressmen was meager. Noninterventionists denounced the Stimson speech made last night on two nation-wide radio networks as a proposal to go to war, recalling President Roosevelt's recent statement that "convoys mean shooting, and shooting means war."

Stimson's sensational address startled the capital because it was by far the most direct summons to action yet heard from any official in a position of comparable responsibility.

A dozen officials of various rank have spoken in the past four weeks with increasingly emphatic demands for more American action. Some notable examples include:

APRIL 9—CHAIRMAN EMORY S. LAND of the Maritime Commission: In the field of shipping aid to Britain there is a huge bonfire burning, the submarine menace. We might as well ask ourselves in our all-out aid if we could not give greater help by aiding the British to put out the fire rather than concentrating most of our efforts on feeding it with fuel.

APRIL 24—SECRETARY OF STATE CORDELL HULL: It is high time that the remaining free countries should arm to the fullest extent and in the briefest time humanly possible and act for their self-preservation.

APRIL 24—SECRETARY OF NAVY KNOX: We have declared that the fight that England is making is our fight. We cannot allow our goods to be sunk in the Atlantic. We shall be beaten if they are.

APRIL 29—ADMIRAL HAROLD R. STARK, chief of naval operations: Our patrol (extends) 2000 miles out from the high latitudes to the equator in both oceans.

APRIL 30—PRESIDENT ROOSEVELT: We must fight this threat (of aggression) wherever it appears, and it can be found at the threshold of every home in America.

MAY 1—SENATOR JOSEPH F. GUFFEY, Republican of Pennsylvania: Whatever risks are involved (in convoying) they are justified in the face of the peril that confronts us.

MAY 4—PRESIDENT ROOSEVELT: Freedom of democracy....is the kind of faith for which we have fought before, for the existence of which we are ever ready to fight again.

MAY 6—SENATOR PEPPER, DEMOCRAT OF FLORIDA: The American people are ready to spill their blood to prevent dictators from ruling the earth. A few bombers flown by American pilots wouldn't leave enough of Tokio to build a bonfire.

MAY 6—SECRETARY OF WAR STIMSON: Use the American Navy right now in the Battle of the Atlantic to protect the lifeline of Britain.

'Trial Balloon for Battle'

U. S. AT VERGE OF WAR

7 STAR COMPLETE SPORTS ★★★★★★★
Only Los Angeles Newspaper With All Leading News Services—Associated Press, International News, United Press, Dow-Jones
LOS ANGELES EVENING HERALD AND Express
The Evening Herald and Express Grows Just Like Los Angeles
HERALD-EXPRESS PHONE Richmond 4111
RACE RESULTS NIGHT FINAL
VOL. LXXI FIVE CENTS WEDNESDAY, MAY 7, 1941 Two Sections Section A NO. 36

Mayor Bowron And Mrs. Allen Are Re-Elected

Mayor Bowron defeated Stephen W. Cunningham by approximately 32,000 in yesterday's mayoralty election, according to figures in the semi-official count nearing its end today.

At the same time councilmanic elections showed that the Mayor would have five out and out supporters in the new council, in contrast with nine members whom he has opposed or who have opposed him, and one member noncommittal.

Adoption of the $3,500,000 bond issue for completion of the Municipal Airport by well over the necessary two-thirds majority was assured.

And in a close contest for fourth place on the Board of Education, Mrs. Fay E. Allen, Negro incumbent, pulled through by a narrow margin over Mrs. Ethel G. Brown and was reelected for a two-year term.

Other highlights of the voting were:

Defeat of two incumbent councilmen and re-election of four.

Re-election of all four incumbent members of the Board of Education — Dr. E. Vincent Askey, John F. Dalton, Dr. Clarence W. Pierce and Mrs. Allen.

AIRPORT BONDS CARRY

Apparent approval of 12 proposed charter amendments, including strengthening of police and firemen's pensions, financing of airport bonds, changing the recall election system, reorganizing the City Planning Department and restricting the use of the initiative.

Defeat of 14 amendments, among those being the strengthening of the mayor's powers, abolition of the Board of Public Works, provision of additional safeguards for civil service employes, establishment of a board of administrative appeal and abolition of the municipal primary election.

In 2653 out of 2749 precincts Mayor Bowron's vote was 174,237 to Cummingham's 142,546, a majority of 31,691.

The vote fell far short of expectations, having been but little above the primary election figure of 37½ per cent of the registration.

BRIGGS DEFEATED

Biggest upset of the election was the defeat of Councilman Arthur E Briggs in the Fifth district by Ira J. McDonald, West Adams attorney and World War veteran, by approximately 2000 majority.

Briggs was backed by Mayor Bowron, who made a special appeal for him just before the election.

Almost as surprising was the defeat of Councilman Jim Wilson in the First district, composed chiefly of the San Fernando Valley, which he had represented for eight years. The new councilman from the First district is Delamere Francis Mc-

(CONTINUED ON PAGE FOURTEEN)

(For today's eastern baseball, see Page A-22.)

Election Returns

Following are latest returns on election of mayor, councilmen and Board of Education:

MAYOR

2653 Precincts Out of 2749

Bowron (Incumbent)	174,237
Cunningham	142,546

CITY COUNCIL

DISTRICT NO. 1	
186 Precincts Out of 186	
McCloskey	12,826
Wilson (Inc.)	12,148
District NO. 3	
178 Precincts Out of 178	
Austin	10,446
Parker	8,649
DISTRICT NO. 5	
183 Precincts Out of 183	
Briggs (Inc.)	9,492
McDonald	12,420
DISTRICT NO. 7	
171 Precincts Out of 171	
Davis	8,340
Rasmussen (Inc.)	11,726
DISTRICT NO. 8	
193 Precincts Out of 193	
Allen	12,031
Massion	8,408
DISTRICT NO. 9	
177 Precincts Out of 177	
Christensen (Inc.)	12,838
Waxman	7,644
DISTRICT NO. 14	
184 Precincts Out of 184	
Roth	11,386
Thrasher (Inc.)	12,623
DISTRICT NO. 15	
186 Precincts Out of 186	
Buyer	7,917
Hartley (Inc.)	11,877

BOARD OF EDUCATION

2850 Precincts Out of 2946

Askey (Inc.)	181,085
Dalton (Inc.)	164,350
Pierce (Inc.)	163,482
Allen (Inc.)	126,393
Brown	124,242
McManus	119,486
Bradford	82,032
Carlyle	78,100

Vote on Measures

Following are latest returns on the vote on the airport bonds and 26 charter amendments:

PROPOSITION A

AIRPORT BONDS

2653 Precincts Out of 2749

Yes	188,196
No	73,681

CHARTER AMENDMENTS

Following are latest returns on the vote on 26 charter amendments:

No. 1—Fire-Police Pension	
2653 Precincts Out of 2749	
Yes	128,046
No	93,060
No. 2—Civil Service Rules	
2653 Precincts Out of 2749	
Yes	81,712
No.	116,873

(CONTINUED ON PAGE TWELVE)

(For Bay Meadows results see Page A-22, and for tomorrow's Bay Meadows entries and for eastern races, see Page A-23.)

Seize Nazi Seamen

CONFIDENCE VOTE GIVEN CHURCHILL

By United Press

LONDON, May 7.—David Lloyd George, former prime minister, warned today in the House of Commons that Japan is ready to seize the first opportunity to wrest control of the Pacific ocean from the United States.

By Associated Press

LONDON, May 7.—Winston Churchill won today from the House of Commons a tremendous 447-to-3 vote of confidence despite a strident charge from David Lloyd George, World War premier, that "America has got to do more" if she is to enable Britain to beat Germany.

The white-maned elder statesman, in his most outspoken utterance in many months, warned the government against exaggerating the speed or amount of United States aid and declared American war organization traditionally is "full of disappointments" for the British.

He demanded a "real war cabinet" and "an end to the kind of blunders which have discredited and weakened us."

However, Lloyd George cried: "I thank God" for Secretary of War Stimson's speech of last night, and said it was clear that President Roosevelt, by his "changed" attitude, and Stimson both realized the gravity of Britain's position.

Nevertheless, Lloyd-George was not among the trio who voted "No" on the confidence test. They were Communist William Gallagher, Socialist Denis Pritt and Dr. Arthur Salter, a Laborite.

Lloyd George, in his speech, said:

"There never has been a war in which diplomacy has counted so much as in this war. Our worst defeats have been diplomatic defeats; our greatest triumph has been a diplomatic triumph. That is the work of Lord Lothian in the U. S. A....

"I have had the experience of American war organizations. It is full of disappointments.

You must remember the U. S. A. never has had Europe's experience of preparing for wars with millions. They have very efficient arsenals, but their me-

(CONTINUED ON PAGE SEVENTEEN)

U. S. Ships in Combat Zone to Be Sunk, Say Nazis of Stimson Talk

By Associated Press

TOKIO, May 7.—The Japanese gave evidence today of increasing uneasiness over their relations with the United States. Marked declines on the Tokio Stock Exchange were attributed to reaction to Secretary of War Stimson's call for protection of shipments to Britain by United States naval forces.

For details see Page A-15).

By International News Service

BERLIN, May 7.—Fulfilment of Secretary Stimson's demand that the United States Navy be used to insure delivery of war materials to England will have "gravest consequences," the German government warned today.

One thing is certain, an official Wilhelmstrasse spokesman said any American ship entering the combat zones will be torpedoed.

"For the moment," the spokesman continued, "the speech may be regarded as an unofficial declaration.

"It appears to have been an address by a notorious war-monger rather than one by a secretary of war.

"Nevertheless, the United States should be aware what fulfilment of this demand will lead to.

Stimson again has proved himself a poor expert in international law. German submarine warfare is a perfectly legitimate countermeasure to the illegal British hunger blockade of German civilians.

"It is a pity that Stimson did not see fit to protest against the latter."

Stimson's declaration that Germany is seeking bases in Africa for a drive against Brazil and the Western Hemisphere was termed an "untrue, unheard of insinuation."

With regard to the shift in Moscow by which Josef Stalin took over the post of Soviet premier, the spokesman termed it purely a "domestic problem."

"It is no secret that Molotov (former Premier V. M. Molotov) wanted to be relieved of his duties as premier."

The spokesman added there was no change in the status of German-Iraqi relations.

ON RECLAMATION BOARD

SACRAMENTO, May 7.—(I.N.S.) —Governor Culbert L. Olson today appointed J. O. Stemmler, attorney of Stockton, as a member of the State Reclamation Board, replacing J. C. Marshall of Clarksburg, resigned. Stemmler serves at the pleasure of the governor.

GOVT. NABS SCORES IN U. S. PORTS

By Associated Press

NEW YORK, May 7.—More than 100 German seamen were taken into custody today in a secret before-dawn roundup by squads of city detectives and immigration agents—a move which one high immigration official "guessed" was a precautionary measure against "Fifth Column activities."

The roundup in New York and suburban areas was part of a nation-wide action ordered by Attorney General Jackson to bring into official custody 160 German sailors on formal charges of having overstayed their leaves in this country. Nazi seamen were being rounded up in San Francisco, Miami, Philadelphia, Baltimore and Kansas City.

Commenting on the swift, unannounced maneuver, Byron Uhl, district director of immigration, said that "as far as we know these men have been behaving themselves and have not been engaging in propaganda or anything like that."

When he was asked if he thought the action had anything to do with "precautions against Fifth Column activities by the seamen," he replied:

"Well, I'd be just guessing the same as you, but I'd say yes."

Herald-Express Special Features

AUTOMOBILE NEWS	B-12, 13, 14, 15
BEATRICE FAIRFAX	A-8
CLUBS	B-6, 7
COMICS	A-19
COOK'S CORNER	B-4
CROSSWORD PUZZLE	A-19
DALE CARNEGIE	B-3
DRAMA and SCREEN	B-10, 11
FASHIONS, by MARIE MODE	B-4
FINANCIAL NEWS	B-16, 17, 18
GARRISON, ADELE	B-4
HATLO'S "They'll Do It Every Time"	A-21
HENRY, by CARL ANDERSON	B-1
HILL, EDWIN C.	B-2
HOROSCOPE	B-4
LOS ANGELES QUIZ	B-8
"MODEST MAIDENS"	A-8
"PRIVATE BUCK"	A-18
RADIO	B-3
"RANDOM HARVEST," by JAMES HILTON	B-1
ROOM AND BOARD, by GENE AHERN	A-19
SHIPPING NEWS	B-18
SOCIETY	B-6, 7
SPORTS	A-20, 21, 22, 23
"STRICTLY PRIVATE," by QUIN HALL	A-6
"THE NEIGHBORS," by GEORGE CLARK	A-2
VITAL STATISTICS	B-18
WANT ADS—Classified	B-18, 19
WEATHER AT OLD HOME	B-8

Knox Says U. S. Navy Ready For Action

By Associated Press

WASHINGTON, May 7.—Secretary Knox said today that Navy is "readier now than ever" to undertake the job of assur delivery of war supplies to Britain—if and when it is assigned such duty.

(For text of Secretary Stimson's speech see Page A-16)

By GRIFFING BANCROFT

International News Service Staff Correspondent

WASHINGTON, May 7.—Secretary of War Stim assertion that the American Navy alone can insure deli of munitions to Britain today drew the fire of the cong sional noninterventionist bloc, with Senator Nye, Repub of North Dakota, acting leader of the group, terming speech a "trial balloon for war."

Although administration supporters in congress regarded Stimson's address as a declaration of inevitable policy if the aid program is to be carried out, anti-war members called for the American people "to make their voices heard as never before."

Stimson's speech was the third momentous address by members of President Roosevelt's cabinet within the last 10 days, previous ones by Secretary of State Hull and Secretary of Navy Knox having contained the theme that this country must take more belligerent steps if the Axis powers are to be defeated. As in the case of the Knox and Hull speeches, Stimson submitted his utterances to President Roosevelt before delivering them.

KNOX SPEAKS TONIGHT

Secretary Knox, who is to deliver tonight an address generally expected to go at least as far as Stimson's and, perhaps, further, said his colleague's address was "a forthright, courageous and high-spirited utterance."

"Secretary Stimson's word, when reduced to their lowest terms, mean war," said Senator Charles W. Tobey, Republican of New Hampshire, one of the most active of the noninterventionist group.

Senator Rufus C. Holman, Republican of Oregon, said he was not in sympathy with Stimson's ideas and suggested that "those who advocate war see to it that at least one member of their immediate family is in the combat forces."

In what was admittedly the most outspoken statement to date from the cabinet inner circle, Stimson declared that Britain's life-line is being threatened, that this country has done so fa not sufficient," and asked wha we going to do about it?

"While we are strugglin build up an uncompleted A and an uncompleted Air F we have at our hands a instrument prepared and r for just such an emergency, said.

"Right now, at this cross-r of history, it is within power, if we chose to use instrument, to turn the tid darkness back from the Atl world, and, while it is hel check, to gain the means w will preclude it forever fron taining its fell purpose.

"If today that Navy sh make secure the seas for deli of our munitions to Great ain, it will render as great a s ice to our own country an the preservation of Ame freedom as it has ever renc in all its glorious history."

Presidential Secretary Steph Early, asked whether Stin speech had the approval o President, said: "You may a that Secretary Stimson talk the President about the speec

The speech had immediate cussions on Capitol Hill, where ator Nye, a non-intervent leader, termed it "a trial balloo war."

"The organized forces for i vention will now flood of Washington with propaga he declared. "It is time for unorganized forces opposing to be heard from and punc these trial balloons."

Senator Hill, Democrat of

(CONTINUED ON PAGE SEVENT

L. A. Mercury Hits 97 to Set Recor

Ninety-seven degrees.

To that scorching mark sunshine and warm wind sent the mercury today, giving Los Angeles its hottest May 7 on record and causing at least one heat prostration.

It was 5 degrees hotter than yesterday—which was the hottest May 6 on record — and 25 degrees above the normal May peak of 72. And last night, with a minimum of 67, was the warmest night of May 6-7 on the Weather Bureau's 63-year-old records here.

A little cooler weather, with a maximum of "only" 87, was forecast by the weather man for tomorrow.

The heat-prostration victim was Mrs. Jessie White, 65, of 1157 South Normandie avenue. Waiting for a street car on the curb at Pico street and Mariposa avenue, she collapsed to the sidewalk and fractured her right wrist. She was taken to Georgia Street Receiving Hospital.

Comparative temperatures today and yesterday were:

	Today	Yesterday
2 a. m.	73	60
3 a. m.	68	60
4 a. m.	68	60
5 a. m.	68	60
6 a. m.	70	62
7 a. m.	72	65
8 a. m.	77	70
9 a. m.	83	75
10 a. m.	85	79
11 a. m.	88	85
12 noon	92	89
12:30 p. m.	93	90
1 p. m.	94	91
2 p. m.	96	92
3 p. m.	97	91
4 p. m.	95	90
5 p. m.	93	88

The 97-degree temperature was recorded atop the 17-story Federal Building. The Weather Bureau said temperatures on the street probably were over 100.

Last night the mercury dropped no lower than 67, which made it the warmest night in the 63-year-old records here for the night of May 6-7. The previous warmest night on that date was in 1936, when the minimum was 62.

Last night was 7 degrees hotter than night before last, and it was the warmest night, in fact, since last Oct. 19, when the low temperature was 74.

N. R. Williams of the Weather Bureau staff predicted:

"Variable high clouds today, tonight and Thursday. Continued warm today; cooler Thur with maximum near 87. G to moderate, variable winds

Williams blamed the heat flow of warm air from inlan said cooler air from the ocean cause somewhat cooler tem tures over the coastal area T day, with night and early mo fog."

Before today the hottest M on record here was in 1895, the maximum was 88.

Like yesterday, today was hottest day in Los Angeles last Oct. 19, when the me reached 99.

Humidity at noon was 29 cent, which Weather Bureau taches said was "a little h than usual with such warm we but not extreme."

'Random Harvest' By James Hilton, Author of 'Good-By Mr. Chips' and 'Lost Horizon' Begins Today on Page 1, Part

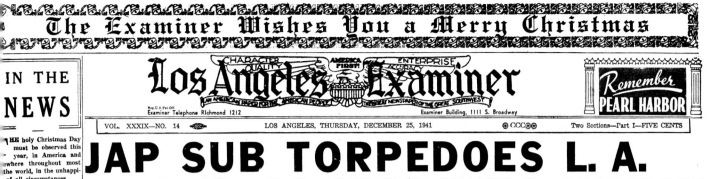

IN THE NEWS

Los Angeles Examiner
AN AMERICAN PAPER FOR THE AMERICAN PEOPLE — THE GREAT NEWSPAPER OF THE GREAT SOUTHWEST

Reg. U.S. Pat. Off.
Examiner Telephone RIchmond 1212

Examiner Building, 1111 S. Broadway

Remember PEARL HARBOR

VOL. XXXIX—NO. 14   LOS ANGELES, THURSDAY, DECEMBER 25, 1941   CCC   Two Sections—Part I—FIVE CENTS

JAP SUB TORPEDOES L. A. SHIP AS HUNDREDS WATCH

THE holy Christmas Day must be observed this year, in America and everywhere throughout most the world, in the unhappiest of all circumstances.

It is the greatest possible proof of human faith in Biblical precepts that this is true.

"On earth peace," sang the angels when Christ was born, "good will toward men."

And of course there is very little peace on earth, and very little more good will.

But let us remember that the angels did not sing of a thing accomplished, or even GOING to be accomplished.

It is not accomplished YET, after nearly two thousand years.

Nor are we to despair, and to become skeptical of our faith, because permanent peace and universal good will are STILL unachieved?

People are too quick to say, when wrongs oppress them, wars engulf them, that things in which they have believed have failed them.

They wonder how such visible events can occur in the world—events like the provoked assault on Pearl Harbor and the consequent involvement of America in an unsought war—if God is just and merciful, and indeed if there IS a God at all.

They should remember that when Christ foretold his own persecution and death his disciples protested that surely such things could not be done with the consent of God, and the Savior answered that evil events were "not things that be of God, those that be of men."

Faith is not sustained in only by blessings received.

"Faith," the Bible tells us, "is the substance of things HOPED for, the evidence of things not seen."

Now let us apply this definition of faith to our present situation.

We face the fact that evil forces, capable of implacable cruelty, have violated our faith and have obviously had power to compel us to undertake a war when peace our desire.

Therefore, we wonder if it has availed us to believe in the ultimate triumph of good over evil.

Those with the least faith among us even wonder what avails us now to repeat the observance of Christmas, after two thousand years the aspirations for peace and the professions of will have borne so little fruit.

And the answer is that it is not the apparent or temporary frustration of hope which is capable of accomplishing our defeat and destruction, but only the ABANDONMENT of hope and faith that dire capacity.

Christ did not come into this mortal world to make BARGAIN with mankind, promising that those who believed in and followed him should thereafter have immunity against all remaining evil in the world.

Christ was not even a law maker, but simply a good and wise and good TEACHER.

Did not St. John write:

"the law was given by Moses, but grace and TRUTH came by Jesus Christ."

Christmas is not less beautiful and real because of the present war.

Wars have prevailed almost continuously throughout the whole Christian era, but there has never been a Christian in all that time when men and women and children have not had justification and renewal of hope and strength.

Christian people have observed Christmas ESPECIALLY in circumstances of trial and ordeal.

(Continued on Page 2, Column 7)

Manila Attack Stemmed as MacArthur Takes Field

Japs Pour More Troops Ashore in Big Pincer Assault on Capital

MANILA, Dec. 25.—(AP)—An unofficial indication that belligerents consider Manila already an open city was seen today when three waves of Japanese bombers circled over the capital for an hour and neither dropped bombs nor drew anti-aircraft fire.

MANILA, Thursday, Dec. 25.—(AP)—U. S. Army forces with General Douglas MacArthur personally in the field staved off Japanese advances toward Manila from both the north and south this Christmas Day, but the invaders continued to land in such numbers that they left no doubt that the battle for this Philippine capital itself now is on.

Bitter fighting occurred throughout yesterday in both the Lingayen sector, about 125 miles north and west of Manila, and in the Atimonan area, 75 miles to the southwest.

Only minor skirmishes occurred during the night, however, the Army command announced in a communique issued shortly before 8 a. m. today (3 p. m. Wednesday, P.S.T.), and a spokesman added that there were no important changes in the front line position overnight.

The command left no doubt, however, that the Japanese pressure continued. The statement said:

"It was a very quiet night, but there still was Japanese pressure both north and south. Practically the only activity overnight was small skirmishes by patrols."

Earlier it was disclosed that Japanese reinforcements continued landing in the Lingayen and Antimonan sectors as their advance forces battled their way toward Manila.

Yesterday General MacArthur and his aides disclosed they were considering declaring Manila an open city, in which case it would not be defended and

(Continued on Page A, Cols. 7-8)

Mexico to Give U. S. Troops Way

MEXICO CITY, Dec. 24—(AP) —The senate, in a secret session, approved today a bill permitting United States troops and airplanes to pass over Mexican territory and allowing United States ships to anchor, repair and refuel in Mexican waters.

Typhus Epidemic Reported in Spain

NEW YORK, Dec. 24.—(AP)—A British radio commentator said in a broadcast heard here tonight by C. B. S. that "there is reason to believe that Spain is in the grip of a typhus epidemic," and that it was therefore unlikely that Adolf Hitler was planning a drive through that country now.

British, Dutch Blast Japs in the Far East

The Hong Kong garrison was still holding; in Malaya, the British had halted the Japanese drive, and the Dutch naval flyers and submarines were again in action. These were the highlights of the Far Eastern war outside of the Philippines.

The British, Canadian and Indian troops defending Hong Kong were reported giving ground slowly, while in some sectors of the island they had regained lost positions. Chungking (China) dispatches reported that the Japs had withdrawn troops from the Hong Kong front in an effort to strike at the flanks of the Chinese who were driving on Jap attackers near Hong Kong.

But it was the Netherlands East Indies forces that were striking telling blows at the Nipponese. Batavia claimed that the Dutch air force and navy had sunk a Japanese ship a day since the war began, December 7.

Heavy Japanese troop losses were reported after the Dutch sank one transport in one action, and a tanker and other transports in another action near Borneo. The Dutch claimed that the entire Japanese supply fleet which aided in the invasion of the Miri old fields at Sarawak had been destroyed.

In Malaya, the British were raiding the Japanese bases in force and the Japanese drive down the Malayan Peninsula appeared to have bogged down for the moment.

(Detailed dispatches from these sectors on Page 2.)

Christmas - 1941

By Alfred Noyes
World-Famous Poet
(Copyright, 1941, by International News Service)

WHO dreamed that earth's one light was now in danger,
The eternal drama but an idle tale,
While Herod dreads the memory of that manger
Which challenges his might, and shall prevail?

THROUGH endless time shall Rachel not remember
Her children drowned beneath the midnight seas;
Or Freedom's land forget, this bleak December,
Christ and His mother, once, were refugees?

MAY we, who in our own wide frontiers gather
All races to one freedom, kneel this night,
Praying one prayer, repeating one "our Father . . .",
Hoping one hope, and cherishing one light,
Till all men cry "good news!"—there is no way,
No truth, no light, but leads thro' Christmas Day.

The above Christmas poem, written by Alfred Noyes, one of the world's greatest living poets, and dedicated by him to America and the other powers fighting the Axis, is published herewith for the first time, having just been composed by the famous poet especially for the 1941 Yuletide.

F.D.R., Churchill Give World Victory Message

(Text of addresses by President Roosevelt and Prime Minister Churchill on page 6.)

By Robert G. Nixon
Staff Correspondent International News Service

WASHINGTON, Dec. 24.—President Roosevelt and Prime Minister Churchill, in joint Christmas messages broadcast throughout the world, tonight dedicated the English-speaking democracies to the stern task of winning victory over the forces of Hitlerism, and to the perpetuation of freedom and decency in the world.

Solemn, but be-speaking grim determination that ultimate victory shall be won from the Axis powers, the Yuletide messages of the two leaders were shadowed by the black tidings from the far Pacific that Wake Island has fallen to Japanese hordes, and that the Philippines are threatened by a three-point Nipponese invasion of the island of Luzon in overwhelming force.

CALL TO PEOPLE

Both spoke briefly. Neither referred directly to the present tides of battle in the world-wide arena of conflict.

President Roosevelt called upon the American people to "make ready our hearts for the

Paul Revere Rides Again! Today It's 'Japsh (Hic) Coming

SEATTLE, Wash., Dec. 24.—(INS) — Police tonight were seeking a tipsy "Paul Revere" who startled residents of a Seattle north end district by riding full tilt on horseback from house to house shouting:

"The Japsh are coming!"

Police were at a loss to explain where the intoxicated equestrian got the false information that an invasion was imminent. They were at a loss even to explain where he got his horse.

POPE OUTLINES '5 PRINCIPLES' IN PEACE PLEA

Message Filled With Distress for World Suffering and Calls for 'Just' Settlement

(Complete text of Pope's important address on Page 8)

VATICAN CITY, Dec. 24.—(Official broadcast recorded by Associated Press.)—In a Christmas Eve message filled with distress for the world's suffering and foreboding for the future, Pope Pius XII enunciated today five principles he said all mankind must observe to "guarantee for all peoples a just and lasting peace."

His message and blessing were delivered before the College of Cardinals, a breach in their customary Christmas greeting to the Pontiff, and broadcast by radio throughout the world.

The Pope's five points for a "new order founded on moral principles" essentially made a demand for a post-war halt to offensive arming and a bill of rights for the little man, the little nation and the little minority.

But even before they can be realized, he said, there must be a return to the true ideals of Christianity, a breach with the prophets of "a new religion without a soul or a soul without religion, a mask of dead Christianity without the spirit of Christ."

"Within the limits of a new order founded on moral principles," Pope Pius said, "there is no room for the violation of the freedom, integrity and security of other states. . . .

"There is no place for open or occult oppression of the cultural and linguistic characteristics of national minorities, for the hindrance or restriction of

(Continued on Page 9, Column 2)

Governor Miles Fights for Life

ALBUQUERQUE, N. M., Dec. 24.—(AP)—Governor John E. Miles was waging a grim, and apparently successful, fight for life at a hospital today.

Undergoing an emergency operation late last night for an intestinal obstruction and peritonitis, he rallied and although his condition was described as critical, his physician said he was not in immediate danger.

Rommel Flees British Trap, Races to Tripoli

Russian forces piled added woes on the Axis last night, but in Libya it was disclosed that General Erwin Rommel, crack Nazi tank leader, had apparently fled an Allied trap. These were the highlights of the European and African fronts:

RUSSIA—Soviet forces met the Germans in fierce engagements along the whole line extending north and south through Russia. The Red army high command reported Soviet forces were still advancing. The Berlin high command countered with claims that

---

Sinking Freighter Saved 6 Miles Off California Coast

Two Others Attacked in Vicinity Escape; Area Bombed by Planes

Killing one crew member, a Japanese submarine torpedoed the Los Angeles-bound 5686-ton McCormick Line freighter Absaroka six miles off the California coast yesterday, in full view of hundreds of persons ashore.

The lumber-laden ship, commanded by Captain Louis Prendle, did not sink.

Her hold filling with water, the Absaroka was towed to port after Coast Guard vessels rescued the 31 survivors, many of whom were hurled into the sea by the torpedo blast.

Seaman Dies Hero's Death

Joseph Ryan, 63-year-old able seaman of San Francisco, died a hero's death.

Ryan was crushed when the freighter's after deck load of lumber was loosened by the torpedo impact.

He died a few seconds after he had saved the life of Herbert Stephens, 20, seaman, of Portland, Ore.

"I tripped over a lashing and was trapped in the path of the sliding lumber when Joe grabbed me," Stephens said.

"He yanked me out of danger and grinned, 'Head for the lifeboats, fellow.'

"That was the last I saw of him. The lumber was roaring all around us and it got him."

Planes Drop Depth Bombs

Within a few minutes after the Absaroka was torpedoed Army and Navy airplanes dropped depth bombs in an attempt to destroy the submarine, which submerged almost immediately after firing the second torpedo at the cargo ship, the first projectile having missed its mark.

The attack on the Absaroka was the ninth enemy submarine onslaught against shipping in California waters. Two of the victims, the Union Oil tanker Montebello and the General Petroleum tanker Emidio, were sunk.

With astounding boldness, the 300-foot submarine lay close inshore waiting to trap the merchantman.

The raider, on the surface, was in the sun path of the Absaroka and thus was invisible to the crew of the Absaroka until the first torpedo was fired.

"I saw the first one coming," said Able Sea-

Free Postage for Service Men Out of U.S. Asked

WASHINGTON, Dec. 24.—(AP)—Postmaster General Frank C. Walker recommended to Congress today that letters written and mailed by soldiers, sailors and Marines assigned to duty outside of the continental United States be mailed free of postage.

At the same time, Walker announced that preferential reduced postage rates on air mail and parcel post carried to and from American forces stationed outside of the United States would be placed in effect immediately.

The ordinary air mail rate of 6 cents a half ounce will apply to all matter carried by airplane to and from the armed forces stationed outside this country.

Merry Christmas
★

EXTRA!

9 A.M. FINAL

Los Angeles Times

LIBERTY UNDER THE LAW — EQUAL RIGHTS — TRUE INDUSTRIAL FREEDOM

9 A.M. FINAL

VOL. LXI   WEDNESDAY MORNING, FEBRUARY 25, 1942.   DAILY, FIVE CENTS

L.A. AREA RAIDED!

Enemy Girds for Knockout Burma Blow

Reinforcements Moved Up as Defenders Fear Fall of Vital City Ne.

BY THE ASSOCIATED PRESS

Japan moved up reinforcements for the Battle of Burma and dispatched a strong naval force toward Dili, capital of Portuguese Timor, in widely separated theaters of the Pacific war today.

Australians announced a Japanese war fleet had been sighted off Dili and that invasion parachute troops had landed near Koepang, capital of the Dutch half of the island.

SHIPS REPORTED FIRED

Japanese transports in Dili Harbor, however, were reported afire and presumably this was a result of blows struck by the Dutch-Australian garrison of the Portuguese area or United Nations warplanes based on Australia or Java. The Japanese gained a foothold in both the Dutch and Portuguese sections of Timor last week.

Japanese raiders who flew at 20,000 feet killed one person and injured five yesterday in dropping 70 bombs on Port Moresby, Southern New Guinea island outpost less than 400 miles off the north tip of Australia, but were said to have caused no important damage to service buildings. The port was attacked again this afternoon.

Domei, Japanese news agency, said warships operating against Koepang had captured a Dutch freighter and a tanker.

The battle crisis heightened in

Turn to Page 2, Column 3

Today's Latest War Bulletins

BANDOENG, Feb. 25. (AP) — Allied aircraft sank two large Japanese transport ships in a raid on a concentration near Macassar, in the Southern Celebes, and a third elsewhere, a Netherlands Indies communique said today. Allied planes also raided an airdrome near Palembang, Japanese-occupied city in Southern Sumatra, and set three enemy planes afire, it was announced.

LONDON, Feb. 25. (AP)—An official spokesman said today the Consul General at Batavia, capital of the Netherlands East Indies, had been arranging since last December for evacuation to Australia of British subjects in the East Indies, "particularly women and children."

TOKYO, Feb. 25. (From Japanese Broadcasts) (AP)—Japa-

Turn to Page A, Column 6

In Colorado— 56 Below Zero

KREMMLING (Colo.) Feb. 25. (AP)—The temperature in this Central Colorado mountain town —not today but a week ago— was 56 degrees below zero.

The report is unofficial, from a railroad station agent's thermometer, but the weather bureau permits its publication now —for whatever aid and comfort it may give the enemy to know that Colorado can match Russian temperatures.

Fifth-Column Acts Reported During Raids

Three Japanese Seized; Mystery Movements and Lights Stir Residents

Mysterious lights, suspicious Japanese, robbery attempts marked the city's first air raid.

In the Tarzana Hills Burbank police saw a string of lights in V-form pointing toward the Lockheed aircraft plant.

Other lights were seen off Point Fermin.

Still others were reported at Redondo and in the hills back of Hermosa Beach.

Air Raid Warden Leo Schukin of Beverly Hills saw winking green and white flashes in the Windsor Hills.

Three suspicious Japanese, two men and a woman, were taken into custody on the Venice pier.

Police were called to stop prowlers who were trying to break in a bank at Laurel Canyon Drive and Ventura Blvd.

A garbage can was thrown through a jewelry store window at First and Broadway.

Home Damaged by Metal From Sky During Raid

Fragments of metal early today hailed from the sky to damage the home of Mrs. H. G. Landis, 1738 W. 43rd St., as Army searchlights and antiaircraft fire probed the heavens for foreign planes menacing Los Angeles.

Mrs. Landis reported to author-

Turn to Page A, Column 2

Jap Planes Peril Santa Monica, Seal Beach, El Segundo, Redondo Long Beach, Hermosa, Signal Hill

Roaring out of a brilliant moonlit western sky, foreign aircraft flying both in large formation and singly, flew over Southern California early today and drew heavy barrages of anti-aircraft fire—the first ever to sound over United States continental soil against an enemy invader.

No bombs were reported dropped.

At 5 a.m. the police reported that an airplane had been shot down near 185th St. and Vermont Ave. Details were not available. Earlier, the Fourth Air Force in San Francisco said that at least one plane had been downed in the raid.

Sirens shrieked throughout the Southland at 2:23 a.m., and an immediate blackout was enforced.

Almost instantly the great fingers of light from the giant Army searchlights shot into the sky, clustering first in an area appearing above the vast El Segundo oil refineries.

Simultaneously the anti-aircraft defenses of the city roared into action and soon the entire southwestern skies of the city were ablaze with orange bursts.

The planes, flying in number variously estimated at from 8 to 20, flew at an altitude of

Turn to Page A, Column 1

BUY WAR BONDS!
Buy them for your country!
Buy them for your future!
Buy them for your children!
BUY STAMPS!

BUFFALO
Courier-Express
Buffalo's Best Newspaper

WEATHER FORECAST
Much colder today with some light rain or snow. Tomorrow cloudy and continued cold. Strong winds. Warnings displayed on Lake Erie and Lake Ontario.

VOL. CX—No. 259 **** Registered U. S. Patent Office BUFFALO 5, N. Y., THURSDAY MORNING, APRIL 5, 1945 22 PAGES — THREE CENTS

Yanks Racing Over Reich Plain; British Hurdle Two River Barriers

Treasury to Launch Seventh Loan Here

City Will Be Setting For Ceremonies

Government, Military And Entertainment Celebrities to Come To Buffalo for Show

The U. S. Treasury has selected Buffalo as the site for the official national opening of the Seventh War Loan on May 14th, it was learned yesterday. Despite strong bids by Boston, Chicago, New York and Hollywood to have the drive begin there, Buffalo was selected because the Treasury decided it is "a typical war production area," and most suitable for launching the campaign.

Scores of notables, including high federal officials, representatives of the military, and theater and motion picture celebrities are scheduled to arrive May 13th to take part in the function, which promises to be the most spectacular Buffalo has witnessed in many years. Opening of the national campaign here will give Buffalo international publicity.

Among those planning to come to Buffalo for the War Loan drive launching, according to the press section of the Treasury, are Secretary Henry J. Morgenthau and Gen. Joseph W. Stilwell of Burma Road fame and his entire staff.

corps of motion picture stars will be here, as will prominent actors and actresses from Broadway.

As part of the drive opening, a large contingent of veterans will present an exhibit of war equipment, captured ordnance, a pageant entitled This Is Your Infantry and will take part in a realistic sham battle simulating actual conditions on the European Front.

To Require Large Space

For this display the arrangements committee in Washington has asked for a space at least 100 feet wide and 300 feet long. It has not been decided whether Civic Stadium will be suitable for the exhibit and sham battle, or whether it may have to be presented on the Delaware Park Meadow or Centennial Park.

There will be a national radio hookup from 10 to 11 o'clock on

SEVENTH LOAN
Continued on Page Seven

365,437 Axis War Prisoners in U. S.

Washington, April 4 (AP)—The War Department reported today that 365,437 Axis prisoners of war were held in this country as of April 1st.

Included were 311,630 Germans, 50,549 Italians and 3,258 Japanese. They were held at 141 base camps and approximately 319 branch camps located near work projects.

Approximately 35,000 of the Italians are members of service units engaged in war work.

Of the remainder, more than 43,000 are working under contract and more than 150,000 at military installations.

Poll Tax Bill Backed

Columbia, S. C., April 4 (AP)—The House judiciary committee reported favorably today a Senate bill to remove South Carolina's poll tax by constitutional amendment. If the House passes the legislation, voters would decide the issue in the 1946 general election.

N. Y.'s Women 'Bulls' Stalking Enemy Aliens

"Lady cops" of metropolis prove successful in new role, turning many suspects over to FBI. Alice Hughes, Page 14.

Also on inside pages:

	Page		Page
Theaters	8	My Day	14
Comics	20	A. Hughes	14
Editorial	16	Crossword	20
Radio	10	Rationing	14
Sports	18-19	Bugs Baer	2
Society	12-13	Your Baby	14
Pictures	14	Horse Sense	14
Your Health	16	Ed Sullivan	20
E. K. Lindley	16	Markets	17

Deaths

Agate, Alfred	Marquardt, William
Bosworth, Ruth	MacLeod, Mary
Cartonia, Maria A.	Mohring, Mary H.
Catalano, Felix L.	O'Brian, Lillian H.
Caulfield, Daniel	Patt, Josephine
Curtin, William J.	Rajkowski, Frank
De Bray, Wilhelmine	Rich, Winfield F.
Gardner, Richard A.	Salamone, Dominic
Guy, Clarendon	Snoor, S/Sgt. J. R.
Hartman, Mary E.	Stadlmeier, Paul
Hofmayr, Mary A.	Stinson, Sarah D.
Johnson, Fred	Tourtellot, Jerry
Kirker, George A.	Walsh, Ellen P.
Lowke, George F.	Warner, Julia

Death Notices on Page 7

Briton in Nazi Helmet Keeps Watch on Rhine

Wearing a Prussian helmet of World War I and sporting a cigar, this British soldier looks across the Rhine River. This is an official British picture.
(AP) Wirephoto

72,000 Miners Of Hard Coal Ask 25% Raise

Royalty of 10 Cents A Ton Also Is Sought

New York, April 4 (AP)—The United Mine Workers today asked a 25 per cent salary increase for 72,000 workers in the hard coal field.

The miners also demanded a royalty of ten cents a ton, as they did in the bituminous negotiations, and asked severance pay for suspensions, dismissals and layoffs.

30 Demands Presented

A set of 30 demands was presented by President John L. Lewis to the representatives of 190 hard coal producers in Eastern Pennsylvania as negotiations opened for a new contract to replace the one expiring April 30th.

Lewis said before the negotiations began that the miners had received "only a 15 per cent increase since 1928" and that they now deserved "a considerable increase" because "we know industry is prosperous."

At a press conference following the first negotiations session, Thomas Kennedy, UMW secretary-treasurer, said "we believe there is enough leeway in our demands to keep within the Little Steel formula."

Requests To Be Studied

Kennedy also said there was no way at present to estimate the over-all cost of the demanded increases to the operators.

Ralph E. Taggart, president of the Philadelphia and Reading Coal & Iron Co., said the operators would give "full consideration" to the demands.

The negotiations were recessed until next Tuesday (2 p. m. EWT) at which time the operators are expected to make a detailed statement.

Baruch Sees Great Wave Of Prosperity

Says Vets Won't Need To Worry About Jobs; Asserts He's Holding Big Stick Over Peace

London, Thursday, April 5 (AP)—Looking confidently into the future, Bernard Baruch, adviser to President Roosevelt, asserted in an interview published today that American service men would not have anything to worry about when they get home, that "there will be more work in the United States than there will be hands with which to do it."

This wave of prosperity, he told a reporter for the Army newspaper Stars & Stripes, would carry over for five to seven years after the war "no matter what is done or not done."

Confers With Churchill

The 75-year-old financier, who has held several conferences with Prime Minister Churchill, was reluctant to talk about the exact nature of his mission to London. But he spoke freely in expressing confidence in the immediate future, and added:

"What happens after those five or seven years depends on the peace the big boys are preparing for us now."

Baruch's interview was given to A. Victor Lasky, Stars & Stripes staff writer. As originally prepared for publication it quoted Baruch as saying at this point:

"And one reason I am over here is to hold the big stick over the big boys to make damn sure they're not going to foul up the peace.

After Lasky's version of the story had been put into type and an abstract had been transmitted by the Associated Press to the United States, where it was widely published, Baruch's secretary asked that it be withheld from publication. However, after deletion of the foregoing paragraph, it was published by Stars & Stripes.

Lasky said that during the interview, in Baruch's suite in the Claridge, the telephone rang and Baruch's secretary told him the prime minister was calling. Baruch, he said, gave Churchill a mild brushoff to continue his talk with the soldier-reporter.

"Hello, Winston, this is Bernie," Baruch said into the phone, according to Lasky. "Look, Winston, I'm busy this afternoon. I'll drop over later." Lasky's account of this incident also was deleted from the final version carried by Stars & Stripes.

In the published interview, Baruch said that one thing that should be more effective than at present was the "GI Bill of Rights."

"When a veteran is discharged he should be told his rights—rights which are not charity dispensed by a beneficent community but rights which he earned," Baruch said. "He should be protected from supersalesmanship designed to sell him everything from a piece of useless property to a used car.

"He should be advised authoritatively what he can do with the money he borrows."

Allied Armies Driving Forward on Two Fronts

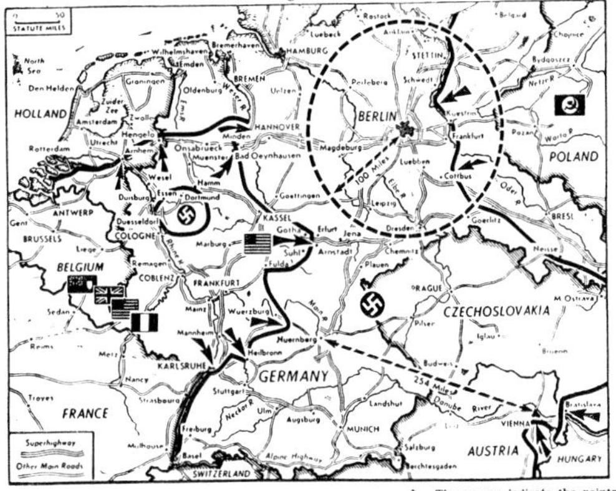

The arrows indicate the points where the Allies are moving in strength against the Germans. British troops crossed the Weser River north of Minden as Canadian-British drives to cut off Holland continued. Americans fought to clear out the Ruhr trap and other units drove across Germany toward Plauen. Karlsruhe fell to the French. The Russians took Bratislava and entered Vienna's Outskirts.

Slovakian Capital Falls; Hungary Cleared of Foe

Reds Take Bratislava, Fight Into Vienna's Suburbs in Day of Sensational Successes

Map on Page Four

London, Thursday, April 5 (AP)—The Russians captured Bratislava, cleared the last Germans out of Hungary and fought into Vienna's southern suburbs yesterday in a day of sensational successes all along the Southeastern Front.

The combined blows of the Second, Third and Fourth Ukrainian Army groups also hurled the Nazis back in Northeast Yugoslavia in the Mura River Valley and overcame the enemy foothold in the Little Carpathian Mountains north of Bratislava, presaging the early clearance of all Slovakia.

Premier Stalin announced the storming of Bratislava, capital of the Nazi puppet state of Slovakia and a key Danubian stronghold of 160,000 population, less than 24 hours after Marshal Rodion Y. Malinovsky's Second Ukrainian group had laid siege to the city.

The subsequent Moscow broadcast communique announced that Marshal Feodor I. Tolbukhin's Third Ukrainian forces seized more than 30 communities south and southwest of Vienna, one of them — Zwoelfazing — only 1½ miles from the southern city limits and 7½ from the very center of the Austrian capital.

Almost due south of Vienna the Russians announced they had hurled the last of the Germans off Hungarian territory and were pressing their liberating invasion of Yugoslavia.

This drive, which took ten Yugoslav towns during the day, was aided by Bulgarian troops.

Similarly, Czechoslovaki Army forces aided in the southwestward thrust of the Fourth Ukrainian Army in Northwest Slovakia, which captured more than 60 populated places.

This resumed offensive by Col. Gen. Ivan Petrov's Fourth Ukrainians was apparently the long-expected push to team up with Malinovky's northern units and put the squeeze on the German-held remainder of Slovakia.

Link of Forces Looms

Another more significant linkup was indicated in Malinovsky's capture of Bratislava. This laid open the traditional invasion gate to Austria and promised early union with the Tolbukhin forces that already were in Vienna's southern suburbs.

Berlin, taking cognizance of the imminent consolidation of Red forces, said that advances by the Soviets made it necessary to move back the German front in Slovakia to a shortened line.

Meanwhile, to the north new offenses seemed impending along the Neisse and Oder rivers. The Germans said Marshal Gregory K. Zhukov, peer of Red Field commanders, was ready to roll his First White Russian Army against Berlin and toward a junction with the Americans in the West. Official silence in Moscow shrouded developments in this area, but dispatches said the Russian offensive—perhaps the last of the war—was near.

U.S. Invades 36th Island In Philippines

Japanese Lifeline To East Indies Severed

Manila, Thursday, April 5 (AP)—Masbate Island in the Central Philippines was invaded by Maj. Gen. Rapp Brush's veteran 40th Infantry Division Tuesday, Gen. Douglas MacArthur announced today in a communique which proclaimed the American blockade of Japanese shipping "in complete operation."

MacArthur also reported that escorted heavy bombers scored their first concerted strike on the great shipping base at Hongkong, hitting the Kowloon and Taikoo dock areas with 126 tons of bombs. Innumerable fires and explosions dotted the target. Not a plane was lost.

Twenty-eight Japanese vessels, including a destroyer-escort, were sunk or damaged in the China Sea and waters to the south.

MacArthur said the Eighth Army Yanks invading Masbate, fairly large sugar island just west of Samar, on the main shipping lane through the Central Philippines, were aided by guerrilla forces, and added: "We are rapidly securing the entire island."

Masbate is the 36th Philippine island invaded.

MacArthur, in a lengthy summary of operations in his theater, said that Monday's seizure of Tawitawi Harbor at the southern end of the Sulu Archipelago "severs the so-called empire lifeline to the East Indies," cutting off Japan's shipping from her conquered holdings.

He said the blockade already had sunk many hundreds of thousands of tons of enemy shipping "and now with the acquisition of the Tawitawi base, is in complete operation."

American forces now control more than 1,000 miles from the northern end of Luzon to the southern tip of the Sulu Archipelago with seizure of Tawitawi and establishment of blockading airfields.

Chief of Coast Guard Becomes Full Admiral

Washington, April 4 (AP) — The Senate today confirmed the promotion of Vice Admiral Russell R. Waesche, commandant of the Coast Guard, to the rank of full admiral.

The appointment — raising a Coast Guard officer to four-star rank for the first time was made possible under legislation recently approved by Congress.

Chevrolet Will Expand For Jet-Engine Output

By LEONARD G. FELDMANN
Courier-Express Financial-Industrial Editor

Assured of large contracts in the Army's plans for mass produced jet engines for the Lockheed P-80 jet-propelled plane known as the Shooting Star—the Chevrolet Aviation Engine plant in Tonawanda yesterday had up for contractors' bids a $1,000,000 to $2,000,000 building expansion program. The project includes 24 engine testing cells.

Although refusing to disclose expansion costs until final bids are received on April 12th, Alfred G. Gulliver, Chevrolet district plant manager, confirmed the expansion.

To Face Kenmore Ave.

He said the new structure will be built on the company's properties facing Kenmore Ave., and that it will be 315 feet long and 240 feet deep. It will be a one-story brick, steel and concrete structure. Albert Kahn Associates of Detroit are the architects.

Contractors' estimates on the expansion deal solely with the building. Machinery and equipment will cost considerably more.

The Defense Plant Corp. office here said is it expecting funds to come through for the Chevrolet expansion "almost any day."

That the local plant will be an important cog in the Army's production plans was confirmed by an AAF representative here yesterday with the announcement that "Chevrolet is scheduled to be included in the production of the new P-80 jet engine."

Program Huge One

Robert E. Cross, Lockheed president, reported Army orders for jet-propelled P-80 fighter planes called for what was believed to be the largest production program in number of planes a month and the most rapid acceleration in output ever assigned to a single air-frame manufacturer.

JET ENGINES
Continued on Page Seven

Arthur Lee Simpkins in Person! Glen Casino! 1st floor show at 7.30. —Adv.

All week in person, Pinkey Tomlin, composer, movie star, song stylist, McVan's Nite Club. Two shows, 9 and 11 P. M. —Adv.

Brace-McGuire invites new laundry customers. Buffalo's Finest Laundry Service. GA. 0078.—Adv.

KEN'S SPECIAL! Genuine "Wind King" Foxhole Lighter—the light that never fails—only $2.00. Ken's Jewelers, 640 Main near Shea's Buffalo, 93 Grant near Breckenridge. —Adv.

Yanks Advance On Okinawa In First Big Fight

Attack Defense Line; Rule Sixth of Isle

Guam, Thursday, April 5 (UP)—The U. S. Tenth Army brought more than 80 square miles of Okinawa — one sixth of the island — under control Wednesday as American infantry smashed southward in the first big clash with Japanese forces since the landings Sunday.

The 24th Army Corps advanced steadily toward the estimated 60,000 Japanese troops compressed in the southern sector. They gained 3¾ miles on the east coast and were less than two miles from the Yonabaru Airfield. On the west they gained two miles and were 1¾ miles from Machinato Airfield, just above Naha City.

Flame-throwing tanks spearheaded the assault against the enemy's defense line above the capital and the big guns of Pacific Fleet warships and bombs of carrier aircraft raked the Japanese' positions in support of the ground troops.

Fleet Admiral Chester W. Nimitz announced that Marines of the Third Amphibious Corps in the north advanced from 3,000 to 4,000 yards above Ishikawa, pushing north and east.

By nightfall Wednesday the Americans held an area that measured some 15 airline miles from north to south along the center of the island. On the east coast, the Yanks control a stretch of 11¾ air miles from Yaka in the north to Kuba Town in the south. On the west coast the distance controlled is approximately 17 miles.

Patton's Men Take Three Cities; French Capture Karlsruhe

Montgomery's Forces Plunge On Toward Bremen and Emden Ports; American 9th Reaches Weser River

Paris, Thursday, April 5 (AP)—U. S. Third Army tank forces, breaking into the open Thuringian Plain, captured Kassel, Gotha and Suhl yesterday and closed in on Erfurt, 130 miles southwest of Berlin, in their swift race to split the dying Reich.

In the north, British armored forces hurdled two major river barriers, the lower Weser and Ems rivers, and plunged on toward the great German North Sea ports of Bremen and Emden.

One force pushing into Lingen, 55 miles south of Emden, and sweeping onward, was only 45 miles from cutting the last Nazi escape route out of all Holland, and Canadian troops on the western flank were overrunning V-bomb sites.

Karlsruhe, capital of Baden on the upper Rhine, fell to the French First Army at the extreme southern end of the front, a French communique announced. The adjoining U. S. Seventh Army pushed to Uffenheim, 34 miles northwest of Nuernberg, Nazi convention city and key road city controlling the Berlin-Brenner Pass routes into Italy. The Americans and French also were threatening Stuttgart, big South German city.

All Allied armies were pounding ahead in a swelling tide that overran underground Nazi factories, vital airfields, and other war plants. The Nazis were losing more than two divisions daily in prisoners alone.

British Aim at Hannover

Field Marshal Montgomery's British 11th Armored Division swept around Osnabrueck, where the last bitter German resisters were being slain, and crossed the Weser River, one of the last two water barriers before Berlin, in an apparent double strike aimed at Hannover and Bremen.

Although the exact point of the crossing was not divulged in a late front dispatch, it apparently occurred above Minden which is 53 miles south of Bremen and 32 miles west of Hannover.

The British "plunged beyond against light opposition," said a dispatch from William Frye, Associated Press correspondent.

The American Third Army, pacing the Allied drive in the center, ran through surrendered Gotha and moved on toward Erfurt, 11 miles beyond, astride the Frankfurt-Dresden military superhighway. The Germans said 40 Allied gliders set down troops, fuel, and munitions to aid in the capture of ancient Gotha.

The American Ninth Army charged up the 240-foot Weser River, next to the last barrier on the high road to Berlin, 170 miles away. Reaching the river at Bad Ceynhausen, the Americans menaced the large Prussian communications center of Hannover, 38 miles from Ninth Army tanks. The naval base of Bremen lay 57 miles to the north.

The Ninth pressed down from the north on the shrinking Ruhr trap where up to 150,000 Germans faced surrender or annihilation. Field Marshal Albert Kesselring, supreme Nazi commander in the West, was in the doomed pocket, a dispatch from the Ninth Army front said. Advancing infantry moved within five miles of Dortmund on two sides.

Street fighting erupted through the rubbled streets of Wuerzburg, Heilbronn, Hamm and Zutphen, all of which were falling on a curving 400-mile front as the Allies ripped

WESTERN FRONT
Continued on Page Two

Allies Near Deadlock On Polish Regime

U. S. May Try to Seek Solution at Moscow

Washington, April 4 (AP)—Signs appeared tonight that the Russian-British-American negotiations at Moscow on the subject of revamping the Polish government are approaching a deadlock which the United States may move to break.

This situation developed even as Secretary of State Stettinius expressed confidence that "a fair solution will be reached."

The three-power talks started almost immediately after the Crimea Conference in February. No accomplishment has been reported.

Representatives of the three countries cannot agree on which Poles should come to Moscow to discuss formulation of a new, unified government for Poland.

Diplomats Impatient

Diplomats involved are getting impatient, and the hush-hush talks may break open in a few days.

Stettinius made his statement in a letter to Sen. Taft, Rep., O. Taft had written the secretary urging that the U. S. "refuse approval to any provisional government which is predominantly under the influence of the Russian government or is not proportionately representative of the Polish people."

He suggested the treatment accorded underground fighters in Poland and Polish troops fighting with the Western Allies as a test of a new government.

"It would be a tragic error for the United States to recognize any government," Taft said, "under whose rule the existing Polish armies would be unable or afraid to return to Poland."

Stettinius said in his reply that "progress (in the Moscow talks) has not been as rapid as we had hoped for but I am still confident that a fair solution will be reached."

The U. S. representative, Ambassador W. Averell Harriman, he continued, "is consistently and steadfastly working for the reestablishment of a Polish government that will be broadly representative of the Polish people and the creation of conditions in Poland that will permit the holding of a free and fair election."

Kesselring Is Injured As Yanks Bomb Quarters

By PIERRE HUSS

Hitler's Former Headquarters Near Bad Nauheim, April 4 (INS)—Here in a sprawling pine forest, where Adolf Hitler formerly had his headquarters, we learned today that Field Marshal Albert Kesselring was injured and nearly killed by a surprise American air attack shortly after he assumed German command on the Western Front.

At least two high-ranking Nazis were gravely wounded or severely shocked as U. S. fighter-bombers swept out of the sky in midafternoon two weeks ago and scored direct hits on the living section used by heavily braided German officers.

Kesselring, who had taken over command from Field Marshal Karl von Rundstedt only a few days earlier, was eating lunch with a dozen officers when the first explosions cracked the stonewalls of the dinning room.

The chandelier crashed into the table in front of Kesselring. Pieces of the ceiling inflicted a deep gash in the left side of his face.

Gravely wounded at the side of the Nazi commander was the German high command's quartermaster, Col. Von Kulhmann. Armaments Minister Albert Speer suffered severe shock.

The combined bombing and strafing attack left only smoking walls, but Kesselring and his staff members managed to reach an underground shelter.

TO HELP in the nationwide transit crisis, ODT asks you to have your exact fare ready when using buses or streetcars. It saves time and fuss. IRC.—Adv.

ODT REQUESTS your co-operation in the nationwide transit crisis, not to ride in rush hours except to and from your job. International Railway Co.—Adv.

Hitler Promises Attack in East

By the Associated Press

Adolf Hitler was quoted by a West German radio station last night as promising an army unit on the Eastern Front that a Nazi "counteroffensive" was "no longer far off."

The domestic broadcast, reported by the FCC, said Hitler told his troops it was necessary to hold the attackers only until "our offensive army is ready for a counter-offensive."

The remark was made, the broadcast said, during a visit by Hitler to the Eastern Front where he decorated a unit commander.

Joins Pacific War

Sydney, Australia, April 4 (AP)—HMCS Uganda, the Royal Canadian Navy's first cruiser, has joined the British Pacific fleet. It is the first unit of the Canadian fighting services to enter the war in the Pacific.

DeSoto and Plymouth motor repairs by experts. Montana Motors, Inc., 369 Niagara St., phone MAdison 3188. —Adv.

Rise and Fall of Adolf Hitler in an Era of Hatred and Fear

Wide World photo

THE PUTSCH — The Fuehrer and his aides on the anniversary of the 1923 beer hall putsch, which marked Hitler's first grab for power in Germany. Hitler's attempt to realize dream of conquest created a war such as the world had never seen.

THE CORPORAL — Adolf Hitler shown at right in picture taken in the field during World War I. The budding Fuehrer already was dreaming of his world conquest.

EARLY PORTRAIT — This photo of Hitler, rising fast amid wobbling German politics, was furnished in 1934.

PRISONER — Above, Hitler in prison in 1923 during his five-year sentence resulting from the ill-fated beer hall putsch. Above, at right, Hitler returned to the cell, after it was made flower-decorated shrine by Nazis.

CONTRAST — The ride with President Von Hindenburg after call to the Chancellorship was Hitler's big moment. Impetuous Hitler offers contrast with "grand old man."

Wide World photo

FUTILE — Late Neville Chamberlain, British Prime Minister, and Hitler at one of their conferences as war clouds gathered in 1938. Chamberlain's pleas were futile.

LOW AND HIGH — At left Hitler leads some followers over bomb rubble of German town in 1944. At right, he dances jig of joy at Compiegne in 1940 at fall of France.

BEGINNING OF END — Hitler, second from left, inspects damage caused by bomb aimed at him on July 20, 1944.

Germany's Scourge of Nazidom Ends

HITLER SUCCESSOR—Admiral Karl Doenitz, who was named successor April 30, 1945, to Fuehrer Adolf Hitler whose death was reported in Berlin on May 1. Doenitz had been in command of U-boat forces.
—Associated Press wirephoto.

ANTI-SEMITIC CHIEF—Julius Streicher, right, who instigated the first onslaughts against the Jews—ordering horsewhippings and beatings. Here he greets Roberto Farinacci, his counterpart in Italy.
—International News photo.

NEVER GIVE IN'—German Foreign Minister Joachim von Ribbentrop, Hitler's personal negotiator on arms problems, boasted that the Axis would never quit, even if it cost *"the blood of our best and bravest."*
—International News photo.

FALLEN LEADERS—Adolf Hitler, who ruled Germany with a dictatorial hand since 1933 and since 1938 conquered most of Europe, is dead, his Reich beaten down by the power of Allied military might. And with it has tumbled Hermann Goering, right, who developed Germany's once great air fleet.
—International News photo.

Military Machine Breaks Up

NO MORE FIGHT—As the Allied and Russian forces kept pressing against the west and east lines, the once mighty Wehrmacht buckled—then broke into a desperate, unorganized flight. Unable to gain time for counterattacks, thousands upon thousands of Nazis like these were taken captive. Just before the end, officers of all ranks offered to surrender. British captured more than 100,000 in one day.
—International News photo.

GOEBBELS—Throughout the years of Hitler's power, Paul Joseph Goebbels served as propaganda minister. His suicide was reported by the Russians.
—Associated Press wirephoto.

TROUBLE SHOOTER—Franz von Papen, Hitler's ace trouble shooter, was captured April 10 by American glider borne troops at a small hunting lodge in the Ruhr pocket. He had been ambassador to Turkey.

HESS— Rudolf Hess was the No. 3 Nazi. On May 10, 1941, he flew to Britain, landed by parachute and was captured. Hess, it was reported, made the flight in hopes of reaching an understanding with Great Britain.

HIMMLER—Head of the ruthless Gestapo and the SS Elite Guards was Heinrich Himmler. He terrorized the Reich as well as all of Europe and was credited with the slaughter of thousands of hostages and Jews.
—Wide World photo.

U. S. Sub in Surface Battle, Sinks 5 Jap Convoy Ships in 46 Minutes

By Associated Press

WASHINGTON, June 5.—Sneaking into the middle of a Japanese convoy, the U. S. Submarine Parche blasted five enemy vessels in 46 minutes of furious fighting.

The story of the exploit was released by the navy today under its new policy of disclosing as much as it deems feasible of its hitherto hush-hush submarine operations. Time and place, however, were not disclosed.

Under the command of Commander L. P. Ramage of Lowville, N. Y., the Parche had stalked the big convoy for several hours on a stormy night. Once, it had closed in for the kill only to be blocked off by escorting war vessels.

On the second run, the Parche maneuvered inside the escort screen. The submarine was running on the surface when it came smack up against the first target.

The submarine swerved off a short distance and loosed torpedoes. There was a loud explosion and the ship was not seen again.

A tanker was the next victim. A torpedo knocked off her bow and she sank almost immediately.

Another tanker came into the Parche sights and again torpedoes found their mark. The ship slowed but stayed afloat.

While the convoy's escort frantically sent up flares and opened up with machine guns, the Parche found a new target—a vessel "with a sizeable superstructure."

A bullseye shot amidships broke the vessel in two.

The Parche, under a hail of machine gun fire, turned on her course and again spotted the tanker it had hit earlier. The tanker's small guns laid down a hot barrage. Ramage, who got the Congressional Medal for his work that night, ordered the lookouts below but himself remained on the bridge with the quartermaster.

Soon the submarine fired another torpedo into the tanker, sending her to the bottom.

The Parche then started for the biggest ship of the group. Suddenly, however, a small enemy ship loomed up on the submarine's starboard bow and raced forward, apparently intending to ram. The Parche swung around almost alongside the Japanese ship but on an opposite course.

"The Japs," Ramage said later, "were screaming like a bunch of wild pigs as we cleared all around by less than 50 feet. Mutual cheers and jeers were exchanged by all hands."

Dead ahead again was the biggest ship of the convoy. The ship's bow presented a narrow target and left, as Ramage put it, only the alternative of firing "down his throat."

The Parche opened fire, however, and hit the huge ship end on, stopping it. Then the Parche swung out and scored a torpedo bullseye from the side. A few minutes later the big ship sank with a rumbling gurgle.

The Japanese escorts, meanwhile, were firing wildly at the Parche and even at each other. With dawn at hand and a job well done, the Parche sped to safety.

DIVIDE UP GERMANY

NIGHT FINAL

Only Los Angeles Newspaper With All Leading News Services—Associated Press, International News, United Press, Dow-Jones

LOS ANGELES EVENING HERALD AND EXPRESS
AN INDEPENDENT NEWSPAPER

HERALD-EXPRESS BUILDING 1243 TRENTON ST ZONE 15 — Registered United States Patent Office — HERALD-EXPRESS PHONE RICHMOND 4141

The Evening Herald and Express Grows Just Like Los Angeles

VOL. LXXV — Two Sections Section A — FIVE CENTS — TUESDAY, JUNE 5, 1945 — H★ — NO. 61

Allies Bare Occupation Zones, Reduce Reich to Pre-War Size

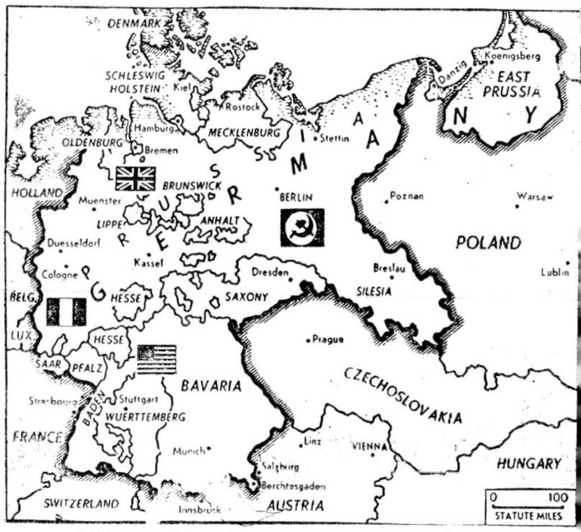

OCCUPATION ZONES IN GERMANY REVEALED

Germany's boundaries of Dec. 31, 1937 (white area), today were fixed as the frontiers of the Reich in a joint occupation statement by the Allies. Occupation zones were not defined in detail but it was announced British would have a northwestern zone, the French a western zone, the United States a southwestern zone and the Russians an eastern zone, as shown by flags on map. An area of "Greater Berlin" is to be administered jointly.

—Associated Press Wirephoto Map

By Associated Press

WASHINGTON, June 5.—Germany was stripped down to pre-Anschluss size today for the purposes of an indefinite Allied occupation.

Zones of supreme authority were allotted to Russia, Great Britain, France and the United States, and a "greater Berlin" area was set aside for occupation by forces of each of the four powers.

Gen. Dwight D. Eisenhower, U. S. representative on the Allied Control Commission, flew to the bomb-shattered Reich capital to sign the joint declaration. Great Britain was represented by Field Marshal Sir Bernard L. Montgomery, Russia by Marshal Gregory Zhukhov, and France by Gen. Jean de Lattre de Tassigny.

Duration of the occupation arrangements was specified in a joint Allied statement as being for "the period when Germany is carrying out the basic requirements of unconditional surrender."

"Arrangements for the subsequent period will be the subject of a separate agreement," the statement said without further elaboration.

The statement, setting up occupation zones for the United States, Great Britain, France and Russia, recreates the German nation as it was before Hitler's annexation of Austria and Czechoslovakia. The declaration was made simultaneously in Washington, Moscow, London and Paris.

With Germany's unconditional surrender, the statement said, there no longer is any central government or authority there "capable of accepting responsibility for the maintenance of order, the administration of the country and compliance with the requirements of the victorious powers."

"It is in these circumstances necessary, without prejudice to any subsequent decision that may be taken respecting Germany," the pronouncement went on, "to make provision for the cessation of any further hostilities on the part of the German armed forces, for the maintenance of order in Germany and for the administration of the country, and to announce the immediate requirements with which Germany must comply."

Four occupational zones were set up and allotted to the

(Continued on Page 6, Column 2)

(For Santa Anita Wednesday selections and today's results see Page A-11.)

Kobe Aflame in Giant B-29 Attack

By ROBBIN COONS

Associated Press War Correspondent

GUAM (Wednesday), June 6.—Great fires raged in Kobe yesterday hours after approximately 450 Superfortresses struck their heaviest blow at this sixth city and largest port of Japan at a cost of eight bombers.

The bomber losses—less than half the record total of 19 shot down over Tokio in the big fire raid of May 29—were announced in Washington by the Twentieth Air Force, which said results of the raid were excellent.

The Japanese agency Domei, which had claimed 56 of the B-29s were shot down, was heard admitting six hours after the last bomber turned for home that the fires were only then "gradually being extinguished."

DROP 3000 TONS

Three thousand tons of fire bombs plummeted into a square mile area of eastern Kobe, embracing the vast Kobe steel works, near a nine-square-mile area laid in ashes by two other raids in February and March.

The big bombers resolutely pressed home their attacks against the worst that the Japanese and the weather could offer.

Heavy and accurate anti-aircraft fire greeted the bombers as they sailed out of the banks of thunderheads and fog into the fair skies over Kobe, 250 miles southwest of Tokio.

At least 40 aggressive Japanese fighter planes came barreling up to meet them, and by enemy account some crashed into the Superforts in suicidal attacks.

ATTACK FOR HOUR

But for all the opposition, the heavyweights cruised the skies over Kobe for an hour, dumping their incendiary loads on the steel works, two main railway stations, shipyards and docks.

The weather was too bad for fighter escort to make the trip, and one returning navigator said the storms knocked out all his instruments, forcing him to reach the target by dead reckoning.

BOMBED OFF 2 SHIPS, MITSCHER DISCOUNTS NIP SUICIDE PLANES

By International News Service

WASHINGTON, June 5.—Vice Admiral Marc A. Mitscher disclosed today that he was bombed off two flagships by Japanese suicide planes during battles near Okinawa.

The commander of the famed carrier task force 58 revealed at a news conference that after an enemy suicide plane crashed onto his first flagship he made his headquarters on another, which later was bombed in the same manner, forcing him to leave that warship.

Despite his near experience with death, Mitscher does not consider the Jap suicide planes a "serious" threat to American success in the Pacific.

Admiral Mitscher revealed that no combat ship in his command had been sunk by the suicide planes. He also announced that 1660 suicide fliers had been shot down at the outer fringes of his force while it operated off Okinawa.

Only one plane out of 100 gets through to make a direct hit, he declared, although admitting that they could be more accurate than a dive bombing operation.

In a statement, which was underscored by Secretary of the Navy Forrestal, Mitscher made an urgent plea for men and materials in the Pacific war and minimized reports of disagreement between the army and the navy in the Okinawa operation.

"There have been some remarks I have seen in the papers, that the navy has had to stand off shore too long," he said. "Airfields don't spring up overnight."

Proudly displaying a button from a Jap suicide pilot's uniform, he said that the flier had crashed on the first of his ships struck and added, "He's dead."

On another ship he said he had lost most of his uniforms. In one attack, he added, four planes got through, two of which were shot down. One went over into the water and one struck.

"They all burned up," he added.

More Tires

June Quota Upped to 2,500,000

By Associated Press

WASHINGTON, June 5.—The War Production Board today made available an additional 500,000 passenger car tires for June, increasing the month's total to 2,500,000.

This brought to 10,000,000 the number of passenger car tires made available for replacement use during the first half of the year.

Distribution of the additional 500,000 tires will follow the same pattern as the original allocation for June. Each of the eight O. P. A. regions will receive a 25 per cent addition to its June quota.

Only B and C ration holders are eligible for new tires.

The W. P. B. also released an additional 25,000 medium truck tires for distribution in June.

Weather

Light Showers Fall in Southland

Drizzles and light showers over the Southern California area today brought only a trace of precipitation to Los Angeles, but varied amounts to other sections, the Weather Bureau said today in issuing its forecast:

"Partly cloudy tonight and Wednesday with intermittent sunshine in the afternoon. Little change in temperature."

Recorded rain included .02 at the Los Angeles Airport; .05 at Mt. Wilson; .07 in Topanga Canyon; .04 at Venice; .15 at San Diego; .03 at Long Beach; .04 at Santa Monica and .03 at Redlands.

Minimum temperature today was 57 degrees, rising to 71.

Eastern Baseball

AMERICAN LEAGUE

New York at Washington, Detroit at Cleveland, St. Louis at Chicago, night games. Philadelphia at Boston, postponed, rain.

NATIONAL LEAGUE

At Pittsburgh (1st game)—		R.	H.	E.
Cincinnati	0 0 0 1 1 0 0 0 2—	4	10	1
Pittsburgh	0 0 0 0 0 0 0 0 0—	0	7	0

Batteries—Heusser and J. Riddle; Strincevich and Lopez.

Chicago at St. Louis, Boston at Philadelphia, Brooklyn at New York, night games.

Russ Got 8 U.S. Ships —Churchill

By Associated Press

LONDON, June 5.—Prime Minister Churchill disclosed today that Britain met Russian demands for part of the Italian fleet by turning over eight former American destroyers among other ships.

The United States also turned over some ships, mostly merchantmen, but also including the U. S. cruiser Milwaukee, Churchill told Commons.

The Russians, he said, raised the question of the disposition of the Italian navy immediately after Italy's surrender. They asked for one battleship, one cruiser, eight destroyers, four submarines, and 40,000 tons of merchant shipping.

The agreement to turn ships over to Russia was reached at Teheran, he said.

Since Italian ships were built mostly for temperate waters of the Mediterranean, Churchill continued, it was decided that they would continue in service in the Allied cause, and an equivalent number of British warships and merchantmen would be delivered to the Red navy on temporary loan. Churchill said this was the action taken:

"Half of the merchant ships and all the warships with the exception of the United States cruiser Milwaukee were provided by the British government.

"The British warships handed over were the battleship Royal Sovereign, eight former American destroyers, and four modern submarines.

"Further, a destroyer was made available to provide spare parts."

Churchill said he assumed "full personal responsibility" for the transaction.

He did not make clear just what the United States contribution was outside of the cruiser Milwaukee, but it was presumed the Americans supplied half of the 40,000 tons of merchant shipping the Russians sought.

The disposition of the Italian fleet will be left to the peace conference, Churchill said.

Laborite Ivor Thomas suggested that, with the war against Germany over, the time had come for Russia to return the ships so that they could be used in the Pacific.

Winchell's Daughter Elopes

By WALTER WINCHELL

Walda Winchell, 18, daughter of the well-known Herald and Express and King Features Syndicate, writer, and Mrs. Walter Winchell, eloped today and was married to William Lawless, 29, in New Jersey.

The newlyweds then reported the fact to the stunned wife of the columnist who after giving her blessing to the newlyweds, telephoned her husband in Hollywood. The bride became 18 only a few weeks ago. The groom will return to art school in Boston. His family live in Cambridge, Mass., and up until January, he was staff sergeant in the Signal Corps.

The couple met last winter at a party in the Waldorf Astoria in the apartment of Wayne Morris. The groom is studying to be a scenic designer. The young lady appears in the play called "Dark of the Moon."

Offering my congratulations to the couple over the long distance telephone, the bridegroom said, "How do you do?"

I said, "I'm all right, considering."

He said, "What do you mean."

I said, "Well, you're the first person to scoop me in a long time. Good luck to you."

Mrs. F. D. R.

$5000 Annual Pension Proposed in Bill

By Associated Press

WASHINGTON, June 5.—A $5000 annual pension for Mrs. Eleanor Roosevelt, widow of the late President, was proposed today in a bill offered by Representative Lesinski, Democrat of Michigan.

Lesinski, chairman of the House Committee on Invalid Pensions, said such a pension—like the free mail privilege recently given Mrs. Roosevelt—is customarily allowed widows of Presidents.

Special Features

Ike Greets Ally Chiefs In Berlin

By Associated Press

PARIS, June 5.—A proclamation issued at supreme headquarters tonight said the Allied Control Council assumed all governmental functions in Germany effective at 6 p. m. The declaration of assumption of authority was signed at Berlin by General Eisenhower for the United States, Marshal Zhukov for Russia, Field Marshal Montgomery for Britain and Gen. De Lattre De Tassigny for France.

By International News Service

LONDON, June 5.—The Moscow radio today announced that the United States, Britain, France and Russia had signed an agreement "assuming supreme power in Germany."

By DREW MIDDLETON

New York Times Correspondent Representing the Combined American Press

BERLIN, June 5.—General Eisenhower landed here at Tempelhof Air Field at 11 a. m. today to attend the first meeting of the Allied Control Council for Germany and to sign a joint declaration by the United States, Great Britain, Soviet Russia and France proclaiming assumption of government of Germany by the four victorious powers.

General Eisenhower flew from his headquarters at Frankfurt to foregather with three other Allied commanders, Marshal Gregory Zhukov of Russia, Field Marshal Montgomery of Great Britain and

(Continued on Page 6, Column 5)

Okinawa Battle Near End

By United Press

GUAM, June 5.—Fleet Admiral Chester W. Nimitz announced today the principal enemy forces on Okinawa have been destroyed, while the remnants were given the familiar choice of annihilation, surrender or suicide.

Front reports disclosed that the U. S. Marines who landed on Oroku peninsula south of Naha harbor were advancing swiftly against scattered resistance while army troops cut other enemy forces into pockets in the southernmost hills of the island.

The fall of Naha and its excellent air field appeared imminent, and any Japanese last-ditch stand south of the city was being forestalled by quick exploitation of the Oroku peninsula landings.

Admiral Nimitz, in a statement of congratulation to Lieut. Gen. Simon Bolivar Buckner, said:

"The manner in which the Tenth Army is exploiting results of the destruction of the principal enemy forces and the main enemy defensive position on Okinawa is most gratifying. To you and to your fine corps and division commanders, 'Well done.'"

United Press War Correspondent Edward Thomas reported from Okinawa that the Oroku peninsula was being gained at ridiculously low cost. He saw only five dead Japanese on the beach. After silencing a few enemy guns and machine gun nests, Fourth Regiment Marines moved quickly down a ridge on the southern bank of Naha harbor.

Japanese reports said American warships were standing off southern Okinawa, directing gunfire at Japanese defense positions on the tip of the island. The enemy acknowledged his Naha-Yonabaru line was broken.

U. S. Marines

Work Out Points for Discharges

By United Press

WASHINGTON, June 5.—Gen. A. A. Vandegrift, marine corps commandant, revealed today that the marine corps was working on a point-system for marine discharges "when partial demobilization of the marine corps is directed by higher authority." He said no point discharge of marines was planned "at present."

Postmaster Briggs Dies

CHARACTER QUALITY — AMERICA FIRST — ENTERPRISE ACCURACY

Los Angeles Examiner

AN AMERICAN PAPER FOR THE AMERICAN PEOPLE — THE GREAT NEWSPAPER OF THE GREAT SOUTHWEST

Examiner Telephone RIchmond 1212   Examiner Building, 1111 S. Broadway

VOL. XLII—NO. 203   LOS ANGELES, MONDAY, JULY 2, 1945   ⓟ PCC   Two Sections—Part I—FIVE CENTS

WAR EXTRA

MACARTHUR LEADS NEW INVASION OF BORNEO

B-29s in Record Fire Raids on Japs

Postmaster Briggs Dies

FLIGHT DECK CRASH—Crewmen (arrows) aboard an U. S. aircraft carrier in the Pacific are knocked down like ten pins as a runaway plane skids around on one wheel and rips into other craft. As the pilot attempted a landing, the arresting gear on the fighter failed to catch.

I. N. P. Soundphoto from U. S. Navy.

OPA CONTROLS STAY IN PEACE, SAYS TRUMAN

President to Ask Senate Today For O. K. of World Charter

WASHINGTON, July 1.—President Truman returned today from an eight-day, 5500-mile air trip to the Pacific Coast during which he addressed the final session of the United Nations Conference at San Francisco.

Tomorrow he will carry personally to the Senate the fruit of the conference—the United Nations Peace Charter—and legislation calling for United States participation in a world court.

The document, flown back to President this afternoon by Alger Hiss, State Department official and Secretary of the Conference.

In compliance with his request ratification of the charter is a foregone conclusion. More than the necessary two-thirds of the Senate membership already has committed itself for approval.

NO OPA BILL

Shortly after Mr. Truman stepped down from his big luxury transport plane, definite plans for everyone at the White House for his appearance before the Senate at 1 p. m. Eastern Time, (10 a. m. P. W. T.) tomorrow.

At the same time it was disclosed that he had signed shortly before midnight the bill extending stabilization and price control for another year. An accompanying statement said that the controls will be carried into the postwar period as a safeguard against inflation.

The President asserted:

"Everyone of us must refrain from making unnecessary purchase of scarce goods ... everyone of us must put many of his dollars as possible into war bonds. In this way we can speed the day of victory and make sure that we will bring a sound and lasting prosperity."

He declared that the renewal of the legislation without weakening amendments "gives our country reassurance that the fight against inflation will be carried on during the difficult year that lies ahead," and added:

"We shall have need for stabilization not only in fighting the war but in solving the

(Continued on Page 6, Column 6)

Postmaster Briggs Dies

Mary Dennis Briggs, postmaster of Los Angeles since 1936, died in Good Samaritan Hospital shortly after 8 a. m. yesterday of a heart attack. She was 67.

Mrs. Briggs apparently was in excellent health until last Monday, when she suffered the first of what developed into a series of heart attacks. She entered the hospital that day, and was reported improving until a second major stroke Friday. She continued to sink after the Friday attack until the end.

Three of her four sons were at the hospital with their mother when she died, and the other was en route here.

The sons are Lieutenant Reid R. Briggs, U. S. Navy, stationed in Washington, D. C.; Lieutenant Colver R. Briggs, U. S. Army, stationed at Fort Monmouth, N. J.; Captain Deane A. Briggs, U. S. Army, stationed at Camp Fannin, Texas, and Alan C.

(Continued on Page 3, Column 6)

Thousands at Youth Jubilees

New Youth for Christ jubilees in Redondo Beach and Bellflower Saturday night attracted more thousands of Southern California teen-agers while thousands of regular attendants flocked to the rally in the Church of the Open Door here.

While the new rallies in Redondo Beach and Bellflower drew crowds to high school auditoriums more than a score of boys and girls attended the first rehearsal of the Los Angeles Youth for Christ band, which the Examiner is furnishing instruments.

Under the direction of Harry Stillwell, leader of the Congress Hall Salvation Army band, the teen-agers practiced simple melodies for more than an hour before the opening of the Saturday Night Jubilee in the Church of the Open Door here.

NEED MEMBERS

Another rehearsal was called for next Saturday at 5:30 p. m. and a plea for additional band members was made by Hubert C. Mitchell, leader of the movement here, during the jubilee program.

Preliminary plans for a gigantic rally in Hollywood Bowl on October 6 were revealed by the Rev. Porter L. Barrington, pastor.

(Continued on Page 4, Cols. 4-5)

Australian Troops Land at Balikpapan

Four New Enemy Cities Blasted

By John R. Henry
Staff Correspondent International News Service

GUAM, July 2 (Monday).—The largest fleet of Superforts yet to take the skies, between 550 and 600, today turned four Japanese cities into blazing kindling.

More than 4,000 tons of the new, deadly fire bombs were scattered unto Shimonoseki, Kure, Ube and Kumamoto in an attack that was described by 21st Bomber Command headquarters as "the largest ever airborne against Japan and many planes bigger than we've ever launched before."

Striking out of the pre-dawn skies in a medium altitude assault, the huge armada blitzed the four industrial targets into flaming infernos, and brought the total of Jap cities subjected to incendiary attacks to 22.

Three of the target cities, Kure, site of the huge naval arsenal with a population of 238,000; Shimonoseki, 100,000, and Ube, 100,000, are located in the Yamaguchi sector of southwestern Honshu.

FIRST ATTACK

Kumamoto, on western Kyushu and fourth largest city on that island, has a population of 210,000. It was the first attack on Kumamoto.

Shimonoseki's compact cement, lime and fertilizer plants and 50,000 square mile population make it one of the most inflammable targets in all Nippon. In addition, the city controls the western entrance to the inland sea and is one of the most vital communication points in the enemy empire.

One of the main targets was the Natabu railway shops in the

(Continued on Page 2, Column 2)

Beachhead Secured, Move Inland

MANILA, July 2 (Monday). —(AP)—Rugged Australian Seventh Division infantrymen landed in force Sunday on the sandy beaches before the great Borneo oil port of Balikpapan and quickly pushed inland after the most intensive preinvasion bombardment yet made in the Southwest Pacific. Losses were light.

General Douglas MacArthur, who personally commanded the invasion forces, announced the landing today.

In a triumphant communique, he declared that this third landing on Borneo, following those May 1 at Tarakan and June 10 at Brunei Bay, had "secured domination of Borneo and driven a wedge south, splitting the East Indies and virtually completing our tactical control of the entire Southwest Pacific."

An Allied invasion fleet of more than 300 ships, including the U. S. Seventh Fleet and Royal Australian and Royal Netherlands units, put the first wave of troops ashore at Balikpapan's burning foreign district at 8:55 a. m. Sunday.

MEET BULLETS

The troops were met by a spattering of small-arms fire from the Japanese who somehow had survived more than two weeks of daily heavy air assault and a devastating rocket barrage that preceded the landing.

Succeeding waves of troops landed on schedule, and by 11:30 a. m. the Australians possessed a mile-long stretch of beach fronting on Macassar Strait and pushed up to a half-mile inland. As the morning progressed, the invaders met accurate Japa-

(Continued on Page 2, Column 1)

419,035 Jap Casualties

By Lee Van Atta
Staff Correspondent International News Service

MANILA, July 2 (Monday).—General Douglas MacArthur disclosed today that enemy casualties in the Philippines campaign have risen to the staggering total of 419,035, including 9774 prisoners.

These include 5240 killed during the past week and 711 captured. Our losses during the same period were 126 killed and 765 wounded.

On Luzon, American patrols carried out extensive operations without "major" contacts, the communique said, and pressure was being continued against Jap centers of resistance in Kiangan and Mankayan in the mountains surrounding the Cagayan Valley.

Meanwhile, Eighth Army forces on Mindanao, engaged in cleaning out last resistance pockets of disorganized Jap troops, found many abandoned vehicles as the fleeing

(Continued on Page 2, Cols. 1-2)

Enemy Suicide Plane Bases Battered in Day-Long Raids

SAN FRANCISCO, July 1.—(AP)— American bombers and fighters, in formations up to 90 planes, today constantly raided Kyushu island in southern Japan, Tokyo radio reported.

Kyushu, where many Nipponese suicide plane bases are located, was attacked in various parts from 3 a. m. to midafternoon, said the broadcasts heard by the Federal Communications Commission.

Domei News Agency reported that the Satsuma and Osumi Peninsulas at the southern end of Kyushu were hit for two and one-half hours in the morning by about 70 Mitchell medium bombers and Lightning fighters.

Another force of around 90 planes, including three Superforts and Corsair and Lightning

(Continued on Page 2, Column 3)

FREE Today
THE EXAMINER
4 Page Color

FULL PAGE OF PICTURES ON PAGE 1, PART 2

Los Angeles Times

LIBERTY UNDER THE LAW — EQUAL RIGHTS — TRUE INDUSTRIAL FREEDOM

IN TWO PARTS

PART I — GENERAL NEWS

Times Office: 202 West First Street
Los Angeles 53, Cal.
Times Telephone Number MAdison 2345

VOL. LXIV   C M   WEDNESDAY MORNING, JULY 18, 1945   DAILY, FIVE CENTS

U.S. PREPARES TERMS FOR JAPAN

Big Three Meet With Truman as Chairman

End Pacific War Soon, Build Peace Foundation, Called President's Aims

POTSDAM, July 17. (U.P.)—President Truman, Prime Minister Churchill and Marshal Stalin opened their momentous Big Three conference today and, dispensing with formalities at the President's request, got to work at once on the sweeping program of world problems they are to discuss.

It was reported that as soon as the meeting got under way the President stated American aims: to end the Pacific war as soon as possible and form a foundation for a peace that would last for generations.

It was reported also that the President took an immediate liking to both Stalin, whom he met for the first time today, and Churchill, with whom he conferred yesterday.

Meet for 90 Minutes

Meeting one day late due to Stalin's delay in arriving, the Big Three got together at 5 p.m. and met for 90 minutes.

Churchill and Stalin paid the President the honor of naming him presiding officer for all meetings.

The three Allied leaders discussed their program and delegated their foreign ministers to meet regularly and prepare information on problems for them to consider.

First Communique

The first communique said: "The Berlin conference of heads of governments of the United Kingdom, United States of America and Soviet Union met this afternoon at 5 o'clock.

"By invitation of his two colleagues, the President of the United States of America will preside at meetings of the conference.

"A preliminary exchange of views took place on matters requiring decision by the heads of the three governments.

"It was decided that the three foreign secretaries should hold regular meetings with a view to preparing the work of the conference."

Before the plenary meeting the President and Secretary of

Turn to Page 6, Column 1

Wacs From California in Switchboard Crew

WASHINGTON, July 17. (AP)—When President Truman wants to phone Prime Minister Churchill or Generalissimo Stalin at the Big Three conference maybe a California Wac will handle the call.

The War Department said today that 27 Wacs, members of the 3341st Signal Service battalion stationed in Paris, have been chosen to operate the Big Three switchboard.

Those selected include the following from California: Pvt. Cecile M. Van Houten, 3873 Eagle St., Los Angeles; Pvt. Margaret E. Kelly, Sonoma, and Pvt. Myrtle C. Harmon, Stockton.

cussed their program and delegated their foreign ministers to meet regularly and prepare information on problems for them to consider.

23 Marines Ill in Train Ordeal From El Centro

MIAMI (Fla.) July 17. (AP)—Twenty-four marines — 23 of them sick with dysentery apparently caused by bad food—arrived in Miami today to tell another chapter in the controversial issue of railroad transportation furnished to America's fighting men.

The marines, all air crewmen with an average of 50 missions in seven Pacific campaigns, were sent here by troop sleeper from El Centro, Cal., to attend operational training school at Opalocka Naval Air Base.

Nazis Well Treated

Pfc. Ed Linebarger of Batesville, Ark., wearer of four battle stars and a Presidential unit citation, cited the following instances of hardship on the journey:

1—Meals of "moldy green stuff they told us was chicken liver."

2—Having to pass through air-conditioned coaches occupied by German prisoners of war en route to the dining car.

3—Traveling in an unventilated car.

4—A water supply that sometimes worked but generally didn't.

Their 3000-mile trek started five days ago in El Centro, Linebarger said, and the marines "sweated, cussed and carried on" through the discomforts of the regulation troop sleeper with their ordeal made more difficult by the dubious quality of the food.

Food Moldy

"The chow they served us for the first two days they wouldn't dare offer a civilian," Linebarger declared. "We noticed the chow improved considerably when the car was thrown open to civilians."

"It was rugged," said Cpl. G. F. Answell of Pittsburgh, who was wounded at Bougainville, "especially when we passed through P.O.W.'s riding air-conditioned coaches in Arizona."

CLOSING OF 222 CAFES LAID TO FOOD SHORTAGE

Comes now the "cafe shortage" to further upset Southern California's eating habits.

In the last 60 days at least 222 restaurants in the metropolitan area have been forced to close, ostensibly because of food shortages and red-point reductions, according to William W. Bradford, executive vice-president of the Southern California Restaurant Association.

Most of the restaurants that locked their doors are small operations, Bradford declared yesterday.

Discovery of the unprecedented number of shutdowns came after the War Labor Board had asked the association to notify some 4479 licensed restaurants in Los Angeles, Culver City, Beverly Hills and Huntington Park of new wage rates.

"We sent out 4479 notifications by mail and we've already had 222 of them returned by the postoffice with the notation, 'Closed,' 'Moved' or 'No Forwarding Address,'" he said.

"We have to assume that these establishments closed because they couldn't get supplies. There couldn't be no other reason for closing when the restaurant business is booming."

FIRST PICTURE OF BIG THREE TOGETHER

WORLD LEADERS MEET—Marshal Stalin, left; President Truman, center, and Prime Minister Churchill stand together before opening session of their Victory conference at Kaiser Wilhelm Palace in Potsdam, Germany. (AP) Wirephoto from Signal Corps Radiophoto from Paris.

Campers Flee Big Forest Fire

Nearly 300 Los Angeles Girl Scouts and more than 300 members of the Crusaders, Angelus Temple youth organization, last night had been evacuated from camps in the San Bernardino Mountains northeast of Redlands after a forest fire started by the crash of a Navy plane had developed into the area's worst conflagration since 1938.

The Girl Scouts, due to end a two-week encampment tomorrow at Camp Osito, on Converse Flat, had been removed from the camp yesterday to Camp Osito Cove on Big Bear Lake after it was feared that flames might sweep the former camp site.

Wind Change Eases Peril

Camp Radford, city of Los Angeles playground, yesterday was threatened as a wind from the west carried the flames up the north side of the Upper Santa Ana River Valley.

Last night a down-canyon wind was reported to have eased the danger, but hundreds of men, equipped with bulldozers, were throwing a line around Radford to guard against another change in wind direction at dawn today.

The Crusaders were moved to the U.S. Forest Service public camp grounds at Barton Flats.

Turn to Page 2, Column 6

Howling Dog Reveals Body

A dog's howl that told of death ended a frantic two-hour search by police, neighbors and the mother yesterday of a 20-month-old San Fernando girl.

The child, Donna June Del Signore, of 11039 Sharp St., San Fernando, was found in a sedan facing the sun, all its doors and windows closed. She was dead, apparently from heat prostration.

Mrs. Vera Del Signore, the mother, told police she left Donna in the backyard of their home, playing with the dog. A short time later the child was missing and two hours later the dog's howl was heard. It was under the automobile and the child's body was found on the front seat of the car. An autopsy will be performed today.

National A.F.L. Unions Sanction Studio Strike

Possibilities that further studio walkouts of a nature decidedly more crippling to the employers may take place in the five-month-old motion - picture strike appeared yesterday in a striker announcement.

It declared that the strike has been proclaimed and authorized by one by the national headquarters of the six principal unions in the A.F.L. faction that has been either directly on strike or has been participating by observing the strikers' picket lines.

Support Pledged

Word to that effect was sent to Pat Casey who handles labor relations matters for the major studios, by William Hutcheson, national president of the Carpenters' Union.

Hutcheson's telegram to Casey concluded with the statement that the presidents of the six unions "recognize the strike and stoppage of work as being legal and will support it to the limit."

The official sanction for the strike, which ordinarily means that all of the various unions' local must recognize the strike, came from the national head-

quarters of the Painters', Carpenters', Plumbers' and Building Service unions and from the International Association of Machinists and International Brotherhood of Electrical Workers, it was declared by striker representatives.

Some of the national headquarters, especially that of the Painters', originally had denounced the strike as unauthorized.

Principally, the A.F.L. non-striking faction includes the International Alliance of Theatrical Employees, Screen Actors' Guild and Teamsters' Union.

Face New Problem

A number of locals of the Painters' Union, notably Screen Office Employees' Guild, Story Analysts and Screen Publicists (press agents) some time ago voted not to join the strike. The new attitude of their national headquarters confronts them with a problem.

Meetings among many locals' officials already have begun and the whole strike situation, as

Turn to Page 2, Column 3

COMPANY FILES ACTION IN VETERAN JOB DISPUTE

The right of an employer to give a returned soldier a job under better conditions than those enjoyed by union employees who did not go to war figures in a union-employer dispute that the Superior Court has been called on to adjudicate.

The complaint against the C.I.O. Western Mechanics Local 700 of the International Mine, Mill and Smelter Workers, Union Stewards and Aaron Weiselman and others. It asks the court to interpret the contract between the two and to settle the dispute, which concerns seniority.

At the company's office it was stated that Frank Stolo worked for it for about two years and left to go into the Army in 1942; he served in the Attu campaign and was wounded; he served also in the Kiska campaign and was wounded; he was given a Bronze Star, is to get the Purple Heart

decoration and was medically discharged.

Last May the company reemployed the veteran of two years and ranked him in seniority according to the length of his service with the company before he went to war, plus a regular accumulation of seniority for such time as he served his country before being discharged.

According to management, the C.I.O. union's officials raised seniority objections about a month after Stolo's re-employment and took the position, company officials said, that the returned soldier was entitled to seniority in his re-employment job only from the time of his re-employment. The union officers were declared to have interpreted the union-employer contract to provide only for such seniority.

The company took a contrary position and, after the union had made a regular grievance of the dispute, now comes to court for declaratory relief.

Argentina Looks Into Hitler Report

BUENOS AIRES, July 17. (U.P.)—Argentine Foreign Minister Cesar Ameghino said tonight that the government is alert to the possibility that Adolf Hitler and Eva Braun had landed on the Argentine coast by submarine and had "taken measures, although there is no evidence to support the belief that such landings were made."

"All reports on the matter are suppositions and conjectures

without any basis of fact," he said.

The government announced that it will deliver German U-Boat 530 to the United States and Great Britain, as recommended by the Foreign Ministry following an investigation.

French Radio Reports Hitler in Antarctic

NEW YORK, July 17. (AP)—The French Brazzaville radio, tonight quoted "the South American newspaper, La Critica," as saying Adolf Hitler and Eva Braun have taken refuge on Queen Maude Island in the Antarctic.

State Department Will Check Report

WASHINGTON, July 17. (AP)—The State Department is going to check up on a report that Adolf Hitler and Eva Braun are hiding out in Argentina.

It directed the U.S. Embassy in Buenos Aires to follow up a Chicago Times story from Montevideo which said Hitler and his alleged wife have found haven in Patagonia.

Argentina has assured other Allied governments that it would not harbor Axis war criminals.

Four German U-boats Still Unaccounted For

LONDON, July 17. (AP)—Four German submarines on the Admiralty's list of U-boats known to have been commissioned before VE-Day still are not definitely accounted for, an Admiralty spokesman said today, but he expressed belief they probably are at the bottom of the sea.

Enemy Must Yield All Conquered Territory as Part of Price of Peace

WASHINGTON, July 17. (U.P.)—The United States has almost completed the terms which Japan will be required to meet after unconditional surrender, it was disclosed tonight. They are much the same as those imposed on Germany. They would give the Allies immediate control of the Japanese military machine and war industry and would force the enemy to yield all conquered territory, including Manchuria, Korea and Formosa.

The terms cover the initial phases of occupation. Permanent controls would be worked out by the United Nations later.

A high quarter reiterated that Japan will be occupied—that under no circumstances will the United Nations send only a token force into the islands. This source emphasized that occupation is the only weapon which will convince the Japanese that they have been beaten.

Sen. Homer E. Capehart (R.) Ind., recently asserted that the Japs had put out peace feelers and he demanded that the government define the terms which Japan must meet. But Acting Secretary of State Grew denied there had been peace offers, either official or unofficial. He reiterated that U.S. policy "is and will continue to be unconditional surrender."

The terms will require constitution and agrarian reforms, the major Pacific Allies who have had few conferences on what will be exacted from Japan.

To Destroy Fleet

The basic objective, however, is to strip the island empire of her military strength and to eliminate her capacity for future war. The following objectives were mapped by U.S. policy makers:

1—Destruction of the Japanese fleet and air force.

2—Elimination of heavy industries capable of turning out aircraft and munitions.

3—The surrender by Japan of her conquests, including Manchuria, Korea and Formosa.

4—Dismantling of her ship-building facilities.

5—Strict control over Jap imports.

6—Provisions for an Allied occupation force in Japan.

It is assumed that President Truman and Prime Minister Churchill will discuss the conditions while attending the Big Three meeting.

Hint Surrender Offer

There are unconfirmed reports, meanwhile, that important developments are imminent in the Jap war. One rumor is that Premier Stalin may have carried a Japanese surrender offer to the conference.

Persistent reports circulated in the London Stock Exchange that Stalin had received a Jap peace offer for submission to the Big Three meeting. Most observers in London now are debating how, rather than when, Japan will surrender. Their talk centers around what Japan will surrender and whether Japan's leaders will be able to command a general surrender if they should decide on it.

Speculation that something big impends already had been prompted by President Truman's decision to hurry back to

Turn to Page 5, Column

U.S. and British Shell Nip Plants at Tokyo Gates

GUAM, July 18. (U.P.)—Guns of the U.S. and British Pacific fleets blasted and seared a sprawling industrial area 25 miles north of Tokyo today while more than 2000 Allied planes struck devastating new blows at the Jap homeland in a continuing series of air raids.

Adm. Nimitz Sends His Congratulations

GUAM, July 17. (AP)—Fleet-Adm. Chester W. Nimitz today sent a message to the 3rd Fleet and Task Force 38 saying:

"Hearty congratulations on the damage inflicted in North Honshu and Hokkaido."

British and American fleet — the greatest striking force ever assembled in the Pacific—hurled tons of explosives into a cluster of war factories on Honshu Island's shore line. The bombardment lasted two hours.

The Allied warships paraded in battle formation within six miles of Japan.

British in Action

Britain's 35,000-ton battleship King George V and lighter units of the British Pacific fleet joined the 3rd Fleet in the bombardment which brought the British into action against Japan for the first time since their one-man-of-war struck Satsuma 82 years ago.

Scores of land-based aircraft teamed with British and American carrier planes to deal new blows to Japan's quaking mainland. Fleet-Adm. Chester W. Nimitz disclosed that at least 30 more enemy vessels had been sunk or damaged in sweeps ranging over Southern Japan, its surrounding waters and off Korea and China. Gen. Douglas MacArthur reported that the U.S. 5th and 7th Army air forces on Okinawa also sent 200 fighters and bombers against Kyushu during Tuesday's swirling action.

Blast Formosa

Other planes of the MacArthur command again swept Formosa as heavy bombers roared across the China Sea to bomb an arsenal, an airfield and shipping. More than 100 river boats were wrecked when the Jap flyers

Turn to Page 4, Column 3

Austin Indorsed for Roberts Post

WASHINGTON, July 17. (AP)—Sen. Warren R. Austin, Vermont Republican, received an indorsement for the Supreme Court duty from Sen. Hatch (D.) N.M. as one of President Truman's closest friends and supporters in the Senate.

Hatch's action cut off virtually all speculation as to other possible appointees to fill the vacancy caused by the retirement of Justice Owen J. Roberts.

Hatch entered a formal survey of sentiment among labor leaders, political figures and others as to whether they thought the President should appoint a Republican.

Atom Moon Trip Visioned

WAR EXTRA

Los Angeles Examiner

CHARACTER QUALITY — AMERICA FIRST! — ENTERPRISE ACCURACY

AN AMERICAN PAPER FOR THE AMERICAN PEOPLE
THE GREAT NEWSPAPER OF THE GREAT SOUTHWEST

Reg. U.S. Pat. Off.
Examiner Telephone RIchmond 1212

Examiner Building, 1111 S. Broadway

VOL. XLII—NO. 240   LOS ANGELES, WEDNESDAY, AUGUST 8, 1945   PCC   Two Sections—Part I—FIVE CENTS

U. S. Official Report:

ATOM BOMB BELIEVED TO HAVE LEVELED CITY

UNRRA NEEDS 2 BILLION MORE SAYS LEHMAN

Declares 'Refinancing Vital if Program Is Carried On

LONDON, Aug. 7.—(AP)—A highly responsible American source said today that U. N. R. R. A.'s program through 946 would require new contributions from participating nations of between $1,500,-000,000 and $2,300,000,000.

Details of the financial program will be presented to the U. N. R. R. A. Conference here by Director General Herbert Lehman, he said. The larger figure was reported to depend upon whether the council grants Russia's request for $700,000,000 worth of supplies.

It was learned that financial questions would be discussed in executive session until the program has been whipped into shape. The United States' contribution to the organization's and to date has amounted to about 72 per cent of the total.

'FOOD NEEDED—

Ernest Bevin, Britain's new Foreign Secretary, told the opening session of the third U. N. R. R. A. International Council that liberated Europe must be succored during the next 12 months to prevent "disease, anarchy and bloodshed."

Listing food as the major need in helping the liberated countries, Bevin asserted that there are members of U. N. R. R. A. who were "in a position to make a much bigger contribution" to the work than they have in the past. He told the delegates from 44 nations that "some of the great tions have already been impoverished" by the demands of war.

The Foreign Minister spoke shortly after Herbert Lehman, N. R. R. A.'s general director,

Continued on Page 4, Column 5)

Truman Speeds to Capital; Docks at Newport News

NEWPORT NEWS, Va., Aug. 7.—(AP)—The U. S. S. Augusta, bearing President Truman and his party returning from the Big Three Conference at Potsdam, docked at Hampton Roads port of embarkation here today 5:15 p. m.

The President and his party left immediately by special train for Washington.

Hitler Refugees Play Vital Part in Great Discovery

REFUGEE IN BOMB RESEARCH—Dr. Lize Meitner, German-Jewish physicist driven from Germany by Hitler's racial laws, who, through her mathematical calculations, contributed important aid to the development of the atomic bomb. She has been at the Stockholm Academy of Science since 1938.
—Associated Press wirephoto.

LEFT DENMARK—Another scientist who fled from his homeland during Nazi occupation is Dr. Niels Bohr, refugee from Denmark. The Nobel Prize winner, whose work on the uranium atom was of great importance in the research on the atomic bomb, was the head of an institute of scientific study in Copenhagen.
—International News soundphoto.

Trip to Moon Possible

By Prof. Archibald M. Low
Written Expressly for International News Special Service

LONDON, Aug. 7.—The use of atomic explosives for ordinary travel purposes may not come for at least a half century, but to think of traveling from England to New York in five hours will one day be commonplace.

And, what's more, within the next century man will have the power to reach the moon if he wants to do so.

It's not so mad as one might think. In fact, 18 years ago some of the best scientists in

(Continued on Page 4, Cols. 3-4)

Bomb Fear Grips Tokyo Warlords

By Kenneth McCaleb

GUAM, Aug. 8 (Wednesday).—Japan's war lords admitted today that "considerable devastation had been wrought by America's new atomic bomb dropped on Hiroshima, and warned the Jap people to expect further attacks with the super-missile.

With Tokyo itself facing the threat of seeing its remaining war plants obliterated by the fantastically powerful bomb, Jap propagandists worked themselves into a frenzy of professed indignation.

They screamed over the radio that the "new type weapon," with its "considerable destructive power," was "barbaric," "cold-blooded" and an indication of American "desperation" to bring the war to an early end.

They claimed American "impatience" over the alleged "slow progress" of plans to invade Japan lay behind the decision to introduce this new instrument of warfare. Fear of

(Continued on Page 4, Cols. 5-6)

U. S. AWAITS PEACE APPEAL FROM TOKYO

Japan Cabinet Is Called Into Special Session After Blast

NEW YORK, Aug. 7.—(INS)—The B. B. C. said tonight that the Japanese cabinet had been called into special session to discuss "internal and foreign matters," and interpreted this action as precipitated by the atomic bombing of Hiroshima.

The broadcast was recorded by N. B. C.

By Frederic Tuttle
Staff Correspondent International News Service

WASHINGTON, Aug. 7.—The Allied high command waited tonight to see whether doomed Japan would choose unconditional surrender or death—whether she would quit the war or be annihilated by atomic energy, deadliest force unleashed by man.

It was pointed out that President Truman, in announcing that the cosmic bomb had blasted the Japanese city of Hiroshima, had warned the enemy that more and more atomic bombs are to come. The American Government was awaiting complete reports on the havoc wrought in Hiroshima, where the first of the bombs fell like a wrathful messenger from another planet.

JAPS CONFUSED—

Japanese reports still were confused and described the damage as very great.

Smoke clouds billowed from the smashed Japanese garrison city and it was suggested that the damage had been so unprecedented that Hiroshima was cut off from the outside world, her communications mute, if any remained alive to report her fate.

State Department quarters described the atomic bomb as the final ultimatum to the Japanese.

They expressed doubt that the President would issue another "give up or perish" warning upon his return from the Big Three Potsdam conference.

ULTIMATUM—

It was recalled that Mr. Truman and former Prime Minister Churchill told the Japs that they must surrender or die in an ultimatum issued from Potsdam. This ultimatum, they recalled, was approved by Generalissimo Chiang Kai-Shek. The leaders of the Allied

(Continued on Page 2, Column 3)

Jewish Scientist Race Law Victim

PROVES POINT

NEW YORK, Aug. 7.—Dr. Lize Meitner, woman physicist whose calculations played an important part in developing the atomic bomb, was driven from Germany because she is Jewish and now is in Stockholm, her sister, Dr. Fride Meitner, said last night.

She has been in Stockholm since 1938, connected with the Swedish Academy of Sciences the sister said.

A brilliant scientist, she was connected with the Kaiser Wilhelm Academy of Science in Berlin before she became a victim of Hitler's racial laws.

Then she fled to Denmark, where she conferred with Dr.

(Continued on Page 4, Column 4)

Plane 10 Mi. Away Rocked by Blast

Explosion 'Tremendous, Awe-Inspiring,' Says Pilot

GUAM, Aug. 7.—(AP)—America's new weapon, the atomic bomb, struck squarely in the center of the industrial city of Hiroshima August 6 (Pacific time) with a flash and concussion that brought an exclamation of "My God" from a battle-hardened Superfortress crew 10 miles away.

Crewmen who carried the awful new bomb which is declared to have an explosive power the equivalent of bombs that 2000 Superfortresses would have had to carry previously, although they were far away, felt the concussion like a close explosion of antiaircraft fire.

Colonel Paul W. Tibbets Jr. of Miami, Fla., who piloted the Superfortress, and Navy Captain William S. Parsons of Santa Fe, N. M., Navy ordnance expert, described the explosions as "tremendous and awe-inspiring."

Neither man could give an estimate of what damage the bomb had wrought, but they declared it "must have been extensive."

There is reason to believe, however, that this southern Honshu city of 343,000 no longer continues to exist.

Turned Plane to Get View

"It was 0915 (9:15 a. m.) when we dropped our bomb and we turned the plane broadside to get the best view," said Captain Parson. "Then we made as much distance from the ball of fire as we could.

"We were at least 10 miles away and there was a visual impact, even though every man wore colored glasses for protection. We had braced ourselves when the bomb was gone for the shock, and Tibbets said 'close flak' and it was just like that—a close burst of anti-aircraft fire.

"The crew said 'My God' and couldn't believe what had happened.

"A mountain of smoke was going up in a mushroom with the stem coming down. At the top was white smoke, but up to 1000 feet from the ground there was swirling, boiling dust. Soon afterward small fires sprang up on the edge of town, but the town was entirely obscured. We stayed around two or three minutes and by that time the smoke had risen to 40,000 feet. As we watched the top of the white cloud broke off and another soon formed."

Obscured 4 Hours Later

Details of the bombing were disclosed at a press conference attended by General Carl Spaatz, who termed the new bomb the "most revolutionary development in the history of the world."

Spaatz was obviously highly elated at the new bombing weapon. He said if he had had it in Europe "it would have shortened the war six to eight months." Major General Curtis Lemay said that if this bomb had been available there would have been "no need to have had D-Day in Europe."

Just what damage was done to Hiroshima was not known. Photographs taken at the time of bombing showed only smoke. Photographs taken four hours later showed smoke still obscuring the city and rising to 40,000 feet. The Superfortress which carried the bomb took off

---

Tokio Radio Report

JAPS OFFER PEACE IF MIKADO STAYS!

EXTRA
BLUE STREAK EDITION R   **HIGH FOG** Details on Page 11

THE CALL BULLETIN
AN INDEPENDENT NEWSPAPER

CALL AND POST, VOL. 158, NO. 7
THE CALL-BULLETIN, VOL. 178, NO. 7   FRIDAY, AUGUST 10, 1945   5c DAILY

HIROHITO, THE 124TH EMPEROR OF JAPAN
—Associated Press Wirephoto.

Truman Text, Page 2

NO DIRECT WORD TO U.S., SAYS TRUMAN

WASHINGTON, Aug. 10 (AP).—The White House said at 10:40 a. m., Eastern War Time (7:40 a. m. Pacific Time), today that the United States is continuing to fight Japan in the absence of any official surrender offer.

WASHINGTON, Aug. 10 (AP).—The White House announced today that President Truman has not received any official word of a Japanese surrender offer. The announcement was made by Press Secretary Charles G. Ross at 10:35 a.m. (7:35 a. m. P.W.T.).

Ross told reporters:

"The President has received no official word of a surrender offer by Japan. Like all of us he has just been waiting."

(Shortly before this announcement the Moscow radio reported that the Japanese premier had informed the Soviet ambassador that Japan was ready to accept the Potsdam terms.)

The Developments

There were these immediate developments as Tokio broadcast a Domei News Agency report that Nippon would quit if she could keep her emperor:

1. President Truman called in Secretary of State Byrnes, Secretary of War Stimson and Secretary of Navy Forrestal. Departing, Byrnes said there still had been no official surrender offer and that even when it came it would be a matter for Allied consideration—not U. S. consideration alone. Forrestal said he expected a development "soon."

2. At the Swiss and Swedish legations, it was explained that the reported Japanese offer—which Domei said would come through those neutral governments—would not be

Continued on Page A, Column 8

Russ Invade Korea, Karafuto, Japs Say

By the Associated Press

Soviet forces have invaded Korea on a wide front and have speared into the southern half of strategic Sakhalin (Karafuto) Island, Tokio radio announced today (Friday) as other Red Army troops plunged deeper into Japanese-held Manchuria in a multi-pronged invasion.

On the second day of Russia's war with Japan, Tokio quoted an imperial headquarters communique as saying Russian troops had penetrated Korea in the vicinity of Keiko in the extreme northeastern part of that country.

The invasion of Karafuto — Japanese name for the southern half of Sakhalin Island — evidently was made at several points. Tokio said that at the same time a Soviet force "carried out a light bombardment of areas southwest of Buika," in the vicinity of the invasion, and west of Handa. The broadcasts were recorded by the F. C. C.

YANKS AID RUSS

American airforces in China, meanwhile, were being deployed for close co-ordination with the Russians in the north.

Lieutenant General George E. Stratemeyer, quoted in a Chungking dispatch, said his U. S. 10th and 14th Air Forces already were being deployed to meet the tactical situations created by the new Russian front, and would "reach out deep into enemy territory everywhere."

As waves of Russian infantry, tanks and cavalry, backed by massed artillery, battered into Manchuria from the east, west and north in a huge pincers operation against the Japanese Kwantung army, Moscow reported swift initial gains.

The Russians plunged fourteen miles into the stolen province from the east and thirty-three miles from the west. Moscow reported the capture of Jin-Jin Sume, which maps show to be an airport town thirty-three miles from the border of outer Mongolia.

OWNERSHIP DIVIDED

Tokio said the invasion of Sakhalin took place at 2 p. m. yesterday (Thursday) Japanese time. The northern half of Sakhalin island, directly north of the Japanese main islands, is owned by Russia and the southern half by Japan.

From the Russian border on the island to the southern tip of Karafuto is a distance of about 275 miles. Then across a forty mile wide strait is Hokkaido, one of the four main Japanese home islands.

Tokio said Russian troops at—

Continued on Page C, Column 2

Surrender Bid Not Official

By Associated Press

Japan told the world today through her official news agency that she is willing to surrender under the terms of the Potsdam declaration so long as Emperor Hirohito is permitted to remain in power.

Russ Invade Korea, Karafuto, Japs Say

Soviet Gets Official Bid From Tokio

LONDON, Aug. 10 (AP).—A Tass broadcast from Moscow said today the Japanese minister of foreign affairs, Shigenori Togo, had informed the Soviet ambassador to Tokio, Jacob A. Malik, that Japan was ready to accept the Potsdam terms, subject to maintenance of Emperor Hirohito as sovereign.

The text of the Soviet news agency broadcast:

"Today (August 10) a meeting of the Soviet ambassador in Japan, Malik, with the Japanese minister for foreign affairs, Togo, took place. Minister Togo made the following declaration to the Soviet ambassador:

"'The Japanese government is ready to accept the terms of the declaration of July 26 this year, to which the Soviet government has also adhered.

"'The Japanese government understands that this declaration does not comprise any demand which prejudices the prerogative of the Japanese emperor as sovereign of Japan. The Japanese government asks for definite information with regard to this matter.'

"Minister Togo also announced that similar statements have been handed to the governments of the United States, Great Britain and China through Sweden."

Under ordinary diplomatic procedure, upon a declaration of war, Malik and his Tokio embassy staff would be interned, just as the Russians yesterday confined Japanese Ambassador Naotake Sato and his staff to the Japanese embassy in Moscow.

Apparently, the Japanese allowed Malik continued access to some kind of communications with Moscow, however, and still treat him as the representative of his country instead of as an internee.

The Domei Agency broadcast that this offer had been communicated to the Allies through neutral intermediaries and expressed hope that an answer will be "speedily forthcoming," thus ending the Allied wrath which has unloosed upon Japan the atomic bomb and the combined forces of the United States, Britain, China and Russia.

President Truman conferred hurriedly with part of his cabinet less than two hours after the original Domei broadcast at 4:30 a. m. (Pacific War Time). Secretary Byrnes said nothing official had been received from Japan. Secretary Forrestal expressed hope that the offer was genuine and said he expected a development soon.

Big Four Confer on Report

An official announcement from the residence of Prime Minister Attlee said the British government is in communication with the United States, Russia and China on the Tokio broadcast offer to usrrender.

A Tass broadcast from Moscow reported that the Japanese minister of foreign affairs, Shigenori Togo, had informed the Soviet ambassador to Tokio, Jacob A. Malik, that Japan was ready to accept the Potsdam terms subject to maintenance of the emperor as sovereign.

(Federal Communications Commission monitors reported here that up to 8 a. m. (P.W.T.) the Japanese surrender offer had not been broadcast to the people of Japan. Domei transmissions of the surrender offer, the FCC said, were made only to the United States and Europe, International News Service reported.)

Would Give Up Conquests

Japanese acceptance of the Potsdam ultimatum would mean that the nation would surrender unconditionally, disarm and give up her conquests, returning Manchuria and Formosa to China and paving the way to an independent Korea. She would withdraw from Malaya. The Netherlands East Indies and China

Following is the text of the Japanese Domei Agency broadcast, as recorded by the Associated Press:

The Japanese government today addressed the following communications to the Swiss and Swedish governments respectively for transmission to the United States, Great Britain, China and the Soviet Union:

In obedience to the gracious command of His Majesty the Emperor, who, ever anxious to enhance the

BIG FOUR CONFER ON PEACE BID

LONDON, Aug. 10.—An official announcement from the residence of Prime Minister Attlee said today the British government is in communication with the United States, Russia and China about the Tokio broadcast offer to surrender.

WHITE HOUSE TO FLASH OFFER

WASHINGTON, Aug. 10 (INS).—The radio networks today made preparations at the White House for flashing the news of a Japanese surrender whenever an official offer is made and in event the offer is acceptable to the Allies.

N. Y. Stocks Up on 'Peace' News

NEW YORK, Aug. 10 (INS).— The stock market greeted Japanese surrender overtures with a strong and active opening today. Gains ran to three points in leading issues and trading was at near-boom proportions.

Dupont, Douglas, Montgomery Ward, and U. S. Rubber soared sharply. Rails advanced fractionally in a heavy trade. U. S. Steel jumped nearly a point in the first few trades. Auto stocks were a bit higher.

HARRISBURG TELEGRAPH EXTRA

Founded 1831

VOL. CXV No. 191 14 PAGES Daily Except Sunday. Entered as Second Class Matter at the Post Office at Harrisburg HARRISBURG, PA., TUESDAY EVENING, AUGUST 14, 1945 Only Evening Associated Press Newspaper in Harrisburg. News Around the Clock SINGLE COPIES THREE CENTS

WAR IS OVER; ALLIES ACCEPT JAP SURRENDER

Washington, Aug. 14, (AP). President Truman announced at 7 p. m. EWT tonight acceptance of surrender terms.

They will be accepted by General Douglas MacArthur when arrangements can be completed.

Mr. Truman read the formal message relayed from Emperor Hirohito through the Swiss government in which the Japanese ruler pledged the surrender on the terms laid down by the Big Three Conference at Potsdam.

President Truman made this statement:

"I have received this afternoon a message from the Japanese Government in reply to the message forwarded to that government by the Secretary of State on August 11.

"I deem this reply a full acceptance of the Potsdam declaration which specifies the unconditional surrender of Japan. In this reply there is no qualification.

"Arrangements are now being made for the formal signing of surrender terms at the earliest possible moment.

"General Douglas MacArthur has been appointed the Supreme Allied Commander to receive the Japanese surrender.

V-J will be proclaimed only after the surrender has been formally accepted by MacArthur.

"Great Britain, Russia and China will be represented by high ranking officers.

"Meantime, the Allied Armed Forces have been ordered to suspend offensive action.

"The proclamation of V-J Day must wait upon the formal signing of the surrender terms by Japan."

Simultaneously Mr. Truman disclosed that selective service is taking immediate steps to slash inductions from 80,000 to 50,000 a month.

Henceforth, Mr. Truman said, only those men under 26 will be drafted for the reduced quotas.

The White House made public the Japanese government's message accepting that ended the war which started December 7, 1941.

The text of their message which was delivered by the Swiss Charge d'Affaires follows:

"Communication of the Japanese government of August 14, 1945, addressed to the governments of the United States, Great Britain, the Soviet Union, and China:

"With reference to the Japanese government's note of August 10 regarding their acceptance of the provisions of the Potsdam declaration and the reply of the governments of the United States, Great Britain, the Soviet Union and China sent by American Secretary of State Byrnes under the date of August 11, the Japanese government have the honor to communicate to the governments of the four powers as follows:

"1. His Majesty the Emperor has issued an Imperial rescript regarding Japan's acceptance of the provisions of the Potsdam declaration.

Fighting Ends

"2. His Majesty the Emperor is prepared to authorize and insure the signature by his government and the Imperial General Headquarters of necessary terms for carrying out the provisions of the Potsdam declaration. His Majesty is also prepared to issue his commands to all the military, naval and air authorities of Japan and all the forces under their control wherever located to cease active operations, to surrender arms, and to issue such other orders as may be required by the Supreme Commander of the Allied Forces for the execution of the above mentioned terms."

Tokio radio said this morning that an imperial message accepting the surrender conditions set forth by the Allies in a proclamation from Potsdam "will be forthcoming soon."

Through neutral Switzerland, acting as go-between in surrender negotiations, came a note from the Japanese government.

Max Grassli, Swiss charge d'affaires, hustled to the State Department and into Byrnes office. He left five minutes later, grinning and nodding confirmation when reporters inquired: "was it the note you took in."

Stuffing a bundle of papers into an inside pocket of his coat, Byrnes walked through a side door of the White House at 6.16 p. m. (EWT).

For the moment there was no indication that once arrogant Japan had decided to surrender

(Continued on Page 8. Col. 4)

725 B-29s Drop About 6000 Tons Of Fire Bombs On Set Targets

Guam, Wednesday, Aug. 15, (AP) — Between 950 and 1000 Superforts and fighter planes smashed heavily in dreaded fire, demolition and strafing attacks against Japanese war industries yesterday and early today while the world awaited the Emperor's answer to Allied surrender demands.

About 6000 tons of bombs were dropped on six military targets in the last 24 hours, Strategic Air Forces headquarters announced. This made that period one of the busiest days in the history of the 20th Air Force.

Guam, Aug. 14, (AP)—American Naval forces won't accept any Japanese broadcasts as authentic and will recognize only an official dispatch from Washington as proclaiming the end of the war, Pacific Fleet Headquarters announced today.

The B-29s hurled their might against the enemy hard on the heels of devastating attacks by carrier aircraft of Admiral Halsey's Third Fleet and attached British warships, still hovering off the Japanese coast.

More than 725 B-29s from the Marianas and 180 fighters based on Iwo Jima participated in the Superforts smash.

Targets for the assault included war industries at Isezaki and Kumagaya, only an hour's automobile ride from the Emperor's Palace, and the Nippon oil refinery at Akita.

Kumagaya was one of the cities on the Superforts' "death list."

Other targets were the Marifu

(Continued on Page 8, Col. 2)

WLB Allows Pay For Time Spent In Celebrations

Washington, Aug. 14, (AP).—The War Labor Board today formally lifted the lid on pay for time not worked—if the boss wants to allow a holiday for V-J celebrations.

The board said that following an official announcement of Japanese surrender employers may:

Excuse employes from work without loss in pay for V-J Day or such holiday period as may be specified by Presidential proclamation and, in addition, for a period not exceeding eight working hours which may intervene between the official announcement and the period so specified by Presidential proclamation.

Consider the regularly scheduled hours not worked by employes so excused during such periods as hours worked for the purpose of computing overtime or premium pay.

Compensate employes who are required to work during such period at rates equivalent to the rates paid by the employer for work performed on any other holiday recognized by the employer, or grant compensatory time off.

TRUMAN DECORATES BYRNES—President Truman (left) pins the Distinguished Service Medal on Secretary of State James F. Byrnes on the White House lawn. The medal was awarded yesterday for outstanding service to nation.

Pavements Covered Ankle Deep By Paper Blizzard in New York

New York, Aug. 14, (AP)—A noisy, turbulent celebration gathered momentum in the streets of New York today in anticipation of a V-J announcement.

Jostling, cheering crowds increased by the minute—passing the 100,000 mark in Times Square by mid-morning—and a breeze-whipped blizzard of torn paper covered pavements ankle deep.

Fireworks exploded over the heads of Chinatown's joyful residents, who were joined by neighbors from Little Italy in the quarter's jam-packed, narrow streets.

Church bells pealed and worshippers in unusually large numbers knelt in gratitude. The Rev. D. G. Warfield Hobbs, at St. Thomas Episcopal Church on Fifth Avenue, asked his congregation to "accept in this mood the obligations of peace."

The din of the celebration could be heard in Grand Central Induction Center, where the induction process went on uninterrupted.

"It's tough, going in when it seems all over," some selectees

(Continued on Page 8, Col. 1)

Martin Expected To Fix Holiday Here on V-J Day

Plans were advancing in the Dauphin county courthouse for observance of V-J Day.

A message from Goveror Martin's office indicated that if President Truman declared a national holiday, all groups would participate, but if he did not, the Governor was expected to declare a holiday for State, county, city and municipal offices.

Chief clerk to the county commissioners, Charles A. Madden, said the commissioners did not have the power to authorize clos-

(Continued on Page 8, Col. 5)

7,000,000 Expected to Lose Jobs During Shift to Peacetime Output

Washington, Aug. 14, (AP) — Government officials helping supervise the return of American industry to a peacetime basis today saw prospects of 7,000,000 unemployed by Christmas.

These leading Federal economists say temporary mass unemployment is sure to come regardless of anything industry can do.

They add, however, that if this mass unemployment is only temporary "it will not be alarming."

Alike in their views although representing separate agencies, these economists—anonymous at their own request—said unemployment might rise to eight or nine million next year unless the Government moves to prevent such an increase.

(The number hunting jobs now has been estimated at 1,400,000; it stood at 13,000,000 in 1932, low point of the depression.)

The economists added that unemployment should begin shrinking late in 1946 or early 1947.

(Continued on Page 14, Col. 4)

AMG Is Ready To Take Over Jap Homeland

Washington, Aug. 15, (AP)—The Army's Military Government Forces are ready to go into Japan with the first troops landing after the Nipponese surrender, it was learned today.

Officers now on Okinawa and in the Philippines are only awaiting the signal to move, and others will be speeded from the Monterey Staging Base for civil affairs officers. Within a few weeks some 2000 or more are expected to be on the job.

The Navy also will send in military government officers for a joint administration similar to the setup on Okinawa where the task is shared by the two services.

Details of the military government plan for Japan had not been disclosed but informed forces say it calls for a stern rule similar to the administration effective in Germany.

The Military Government is expected to establish headquarters only in key areas, largely on the large Japanese island of Honshu.

26 Die in Crash

Goch, Germany, Aug. 14, (AP)—Twenty-first Army Group authorities said today 26 British and Canadian soldiers were killed and 50 injured, some seriously, in a head-on collision of two leave trains near Goch, early yesterday.

Treaty Signed

London, Aug. 14, (AP).—The Moscow radio said tonight the Soviet Union and the Chinese Republic had signed a treaty of friendship today.

Victory Parade

Chief of Police Oscar Blough announced the victory parade moves at 9 p. m.

Congress Called Back to Capitol On September 5, Barkley Asserts

Washington, Aug. 14, (AP).—Congress will reconvene Wednesday, September 5.

Senate Majority Leader Barkley (Ky.) made the announcement today. He said he and Rep. McCormack (Mass.) House majority leader, will file a joint call for return of the lawmakers, under terms of the resolution which recessed both houses until the tentative date of October 8.

"We are going back into session regardless of Japanese surrender developments," Barkley told newsmen. "The war is bound to be over soon, and we have a great deal of important work to do."

The House quit July 21, the Senate August 1.

Barkley has announced a five-point program from the Senate topped by measures designed to provide jobs and to expand the unemloyment compensation law. Other items on his agenda are creation of a one-man surplus property disposal system, consideration of what wartime agencies should be retained, and power for the President to reorganize the executive department of government.

The Senate Banking Committee will resume hearings August 21 on the so-called full employment bill, while the Unemployment Compensation measure will come before the Senate Finance Committee August 29.

Chairman Doughton (D-NC) of the House Ways and Means Com-

(Continued on Page 8, Col. 5)

Russians Invade Jehol Province In North China

London, Aug. 14, (AP).—Russian troops made a sensational spurt of 93 miles from outer Mongolia, invading Jehol Province, and capturing Linsi and Tapansburg, 260 miles north of Peiping in North China, the Soviet communique announced tonight.

London, Aug. 14, (AP).—Russia's tank-tipped armies continued their whirlwind thrusts into Manchuria today after capturing the three-way rail junction of Linkow and cutting the last rail communication line for Japanese troops fighting in the Sungari-Ussuri River valley.

The capture of Linkow by Marshal Kirill A. Meretskov's First

(Continued on Page 8, Col. 8)

U.S. Revokes Manpower Controls In Plan to Speed Up Re-employment

Washington, Aug. 14, (AP)—The government today revoked all war-time manpower controls, effective immediately, and set forth a plan aimed at speedy re-employment of veterans and released war workers.

In an action timed to coincide with Japan's surrender, the War Manpower Commission announced a seven-point program which it said would stimulate "reconversion activities and the speedy re-employment of displaced workers, at the same time restoring a free labor market."

Among the controls lifted are those providing for hiring through the United States Employment Service, employment ceilings to channel workers to essential industries, and the requirement for certificates of availability in changing jobs.

Acting WMC Chairman Frank L. McNamee said regional directors have been instructed to put

(Continued on Page 8, Col. 3)

THE WEATHER
Increasing cloudiness today.
Mostly cloudy Saturday. Little
change in temperature.
(U. S. Weather Bureau Forecast)
Buy MORE War Bonds and Stamps

The Detroit News

THE HOME NEWSPAPER FOR MORE THAN 71 YEARS

Largest A. B. C.-Recognized Home Delivered Circulation in America

FRIDAY, AUGUST 10, 1945, 72nd Year, No. 353

Night-Home Edition
MARKETS ON PAGE 24

32 PAGES   C   FIVE CENTS

JAPS ASK PEACE

Accept Potsdam Terms If Hirohito Can Stay

WASHINGTON, Aug. 10.—(UP)—President Truman summoned the cabinet today to consider Japan's surrender offer.

(BY THE ASSOCIATED PRESS)

A Japanese Domei broadcast announced today that "the Japanese government are ready to accept the terms of the Potsdam Conference with the understanding that the said declaration does not compromise any demand which prejudices the prerogatives of His Majesty (Emperor Hirohito) as a sovereign ruler."

The Domei broadcast was recorded by the Associated Press.

The text of the transmission:

"The Japanese government today addressed the following communications to the Swiss and Swedish governments respectively for transmission to the United States, Great Britain, China and the Soviet Union:

"In obedience to the gracious command of His Majesty the Emperor, who ever anxious to enhance the cause of world peace, desires earnestly to bring about an early termination of hostilities with a view to saving mankind from the calamities to be imposed upon them by further continuation of the war, the Japanese government asked several weeks ago the Soviet government, with which neutral relations then prevailed, to render good office in restoring peace vis-a-vis the enemy powers.

"Unfortunately these efforts in the interest of peace having failed the Japanese government in conformity with the august wish of his majesty to restore the general peace and desiring to put an end to the untold sufferings entailed by war as quickly as possible, have decided upon the following:

"The Japanese government are ready to accept the terms enumerated in the joint declaration which was issued at Potsdam on July 26, 1945, by the heads of the governments of the United States, Great Britain and China and later subscribed to by the Soviet government, with the understanding that the said declaration does not comprise any demand which prejudices the prerogatives of his majesty as a sovereign ruler.

"The Japanese government . . .

(The Tokyo station went off the air at this point and was still silent 10 minutes later.)

★ ★ ★

'Sensational News' Promised on Monday

(BY THE ASSOCIATED PRESS)

Tottering Japan will broadcast next Monday a "sensational message people of the war-torn world have been longing to hear," Radio Tokyo reported today.

The startling announcement said the broadcast would be made at 1:30 p. m., Aug. 13 (12:30 a. m. Detroit time), but gave no indication of its nature other than it would be "direct from the people of Japan."

The Tokyo radio interrupted a regular program to warn its listeners that "they will not want to miss the urgent news of vital importance to everyone."

The announcement aroused intense speculation among officers and newsmen attached to Gen. MacArthur's headquarters, Spencer Davis, Associated Press correspondent, reported from Manila. Davis said the Tokyo statement was generally interpreted by observers as the "beginning of the end."

Areas of Hiroshima Devastated by Atomic Bomb as Reported by Army Observers

This photo-diagram, based on a diagram issued by Army Air Forces, locates areas damaged in the Japanese homeland city of Hiroshima by the first atomic bomb dropped by U. S. Army Air Forces. The large circle is drawn on a diameter of 19,000 feet. Shaded areas indicate devastated sectors, according to information based on intelligence reports. Key to numbers, with percentage of total destruction when available:

1. Army transport base .... 25 per cent	11. Oil storage .... On fire
2. Army ordnance depot	12. Electric RR power station ....100 per cent
3. Army food depot .... 35 " "	13. Electric power generator ....100 " "
4. Army clothing depot .... 85 " "	14. Telephone company ....100 " "
5. E. Hiroshima RR Station .... 30 " "	15. Gas works ....100 " "
6. Unidentified industry .... 90 " "	16. Hiroshima RR station ....100 " "
7. Sumitomo rayon plant .... 25 " "	17. Unidentified RR station ....100 " "
8. Kinkwa rayon mill .... 10 " "	18. Bridge, debris intact.
9. Feikkoku textile mill ....100 " "	19. Bridge, one-fourth missing.
10. Power plant	20. Large bridge, shattered, intact.
21. Bridge, large hole, west side.	
22. Bridge, intact, banks caved in.	
23. Bridge, intact, debris covered.	
24. Both bridges intact.	
25. Bridge destroyed.	
26. Bridge, severely damaged.	
27. Bridge, destroyed.	
28. Bridge, shattered, inoperative.	
29. Bridge, intact, slight damage.	
30. Bridge, intact, severely damaged.	

Daughter of Lehman Gains Divorce in Reno

RENO, Nev., Aug. 10.—(U.P.)—Hilda Jane Lehman de Vadetzky, daughter of Herbert H. Lehman, former governor of New York, was divorced in district court here Thursday from Boris de Vadetzky, of Saranac, N. Y. The complaint charged cruelty. Miss Lehman asked for and was granted restoration of her maiden name.

JERRY McCARTHY WILL BUY YOUR CAR, 5111 Cass, Madison 9610.—Adv.

111,000 Idle in Strikes

COMPLETE RACES

CHARACTER · QUALITY · AMERICA FIRST! · ENTERPRISE · ACCURACY

Los Angeles Examiner

AN AMERICAN PAPER FOR THE AMERICAN PEOPLE · THE GREAT NEWSPAPER OF THE GREAT SOUTHWEST

Reg. U.S. Pat. Off. Examiner Telephone Richmond 1212 — Examiner Building, 1111 S. Broadway

VOL. XLII—NO. 271 — LOS ANGELES, SATURDAY, SEPTEMBER 8, 1945 — PCC — Two Sections—Part I—FIVE CENTS

M'ARTHUR RAISES FLAG ABOVE TOKYO!

'I'm Born Again'

JOYFUL REUNION—As MMM 3/C Clayton O. Decker stepped from the plane at Oakland and clasped his wife, Lucille, and son, Harry, 4, he cried in exultation: "Oh, God, I'm born again." Decker, a survivor of the submarine Tang, related how the Japanese thrust burning cigaret butts into the ears and noses of their captives. Here he plants a hearty kiss on the cheek of his overjoyed wife.

—Associated Press wirephoto.

Freed Yanks Bare New Bestialities

Sub Crew Tortured by Nips on Ship's Hot Steel Deck

OAKLAND, Sept. 7.—(INS)—More blood-curdling tales of Jap bestiality were recounted today by more than 80 liberated American prisoners of war who arrived home today aboard Navy transport planes.

Motor Machinists Mate Third Class Clayton O. Decker, 25, of Oakland, a survivor of the submarine Tang, told how the Japs tied him and other survivors of the Tang on the hot steel deck of a Jap vessel in the burning sun while Jap sailors thrust burning cigaret butts into their ears and nose.

Decker's wife, Lucille, collapsed as he told the story to reporters. She was revived by Red Cross nurses.

'BORN AGAIN'—

Mrs. Decker, a Richmond shipyard secretary, had come to the airport with Decker's 4-year-old son, Harry, for a joyous reunion.

As he stepped from the plane and clasped his wife and son in his arms, Decker cried in exultation:

"Oh, God, I'm born again."

Commander Richard H. O'Kane, famed skipper of the Tang, was imprisoned in the same camp with Decker.

"I saw the Japs beat Commander O'Kane on the kidneys with their rifle butts," Decker said. "I saw several men beaten to death in Ofuna prison camp, which was a torture farm."

HIT CONVOY—

"It was 2 a. m. last October 25 and we were on surface throwing torpedoes into a Jap convoy in the Formosa Straits 10 miles off the Chinese port of Foochow," Decker began his story.

"We had knocked off seven of them and we fired a torpedo at a big troop transport. Something went wrong with it. It circled back and before officers on the bridge could get us out of the way it struck us on the port side aft. Down we went.

"The four officers on the bridge—one of them was Lieutenant (j. g.) Henry Flanagan, 36, of Alameda—were swept into the sea. Flanagan is now on the hospital ship Benevolence, being treated for beri beri.

"Myself and 35 other men were in a large room forward. We locked water tight doors and waited as she settled to the bottom. We went down 180

(Continued on Page 2, Cols. 7-8)

Airliner Crash Fatal to 22

Wreckage Found in S. C. Swamp

FLORENCE, S. C., Sept. 7.—(AP)—An Eastern Air Lines transport crashed into a swamp near here early today, killing and burning all its occupants. The line said there were 22 soldiers and civilians aboard.

The passengers and members of the crew of the Miami to New York plane were burned almost beyond recognition. Most of the bodies were piled up in a heap beside the wreckage and a few were scattered near by.

The plane tore a 50-feet-wide, 200-foot-long path through the swamp before coming to a stop and burning.

LOUD EXPLOSION—

Mrs. W. L. Rankin, who lives on a plantation about two miles from the scene of the crash, said she was awakened about 2 a. m. by a thunderous explosion, then heard several other loud blasts.

Twelve hours after the crash the bodies had not been removed. It was planned to bring them here. Rescuers had to cut a road through the almost impenetrable swamp to reach the wreckage. Previously other searchers waded

(Continued on Page 4, Cols. 4-5)

JAP GENERAL SLAIN IN PLOT TO BALK PEACE

Chief of Hirohito Guards Dies; Young Officers Forge Name

TOKYO, Sept. 7.—(AP)—Japanese sources said today the murder of a general near the Emperor's palace grounds, the forging of a military order and a wild chase to the radio station climaxed attempts of a group of fanatical Japanese Army officers to prevent the imperial surrender announcement from reaching the people.

The dramatic battle in the closing days of the fight between two factions in Japan—one for peace, the other to continue the war—was revealed by well-informed Japanese sources.

These sources said that young Japanese officers on August 14 killed the commanding general of Emperor Hirohito's personal guards division, Lieutenant General Mori, and by forging his name to an order sent troops to surround the palace. They hoped to prevent a recording of the Emperor's historic surrender rescript from leaving the grounds.

FORGERY—

The plan to capture the surrender announcement failed, however, when the forgery was detected.

When other members of the "fight on" faction learned of the failure of the original scheme they raced through the streets of Tokyo to the radio station and began a search of the building for the document.

Their efforts failed when a radio station employee eluded the conspirators and telephoned a near-by army garrison for help.

All the time, the recording was still at the palace and was delivered to the radio station shortly before it went on the air at noon, August 15.

Organized resistance to the Emperor's decision to surrender

(Continued on Page 2, Cols. 2-3)

Famed 1st Cavalry First in Foe Capital

Seventh Regiment Leads Way for U. S. Invasion Troops

NEW YORK, Sept. 7.—(INS)—The Tokyo radio reported tonight that the United States Flag is flying over the Japanese capital.

A Jap broadcast, monitored by the FCC, declared that General Douglas MacArthur's headquarters had been established in Tokyo.

The broadcast said:

"With the transfer of MacArthur's headquarters to Tokyo, the American Flag is now floating over the American embassy there."

TOKYO, Sept. 8 (Saturday).—(AP)—The first troops of the famed First Cavalry Division entered Tokyo this morning (Friday U. S. date)—the first tread of a conqueror's feet in that war-ravaged capital city—and arrival of General MacArthur is expected shortly.

The Seventh Regiment, modern counterpart of that which fought under General Custer at the Little Big Horn, led the way in covering the last triumphant mile of the road back from Australia which General MacArthur began in the grim early days of 1942.

By Kenneth McCaleb

Staff Correspondent International News Service

YOKOHAMA, Sept. 8 (Saturday).—Conquering American legions led by General Douglas MacArthur were due to march triumphantly into war-shattered Tokyo this morning.

The tense Japanese capital will see the Stars and Stripes unfurled over the United States Embassy building, where MacArthur will make his headquarters, at 11 a. m. (7 p. m. Friday, P. W. T.).

The American Flag selected for the historic ceremony flew over the White House the day Japan plunged the United States into the war by attacking Pearl Harbor.

Official Flag Raising Rites

MacArthur himself, surrounded by members of his small official party and a color guard of honor, will officiate at the flag-raising ceremony in the heart of beaten Nippon's capital city.

All elements of the 11th Airborne Division, veterans of the Philippines campaign, were disclosed to have landed at Atsugi airdrome, just outside Tokyo, and first units of the 27th Infantry Division, self-styled the "Tokyo Express Division," were beginning to arrive.

First troops to enter Tokyo, however, will be battle seasoned veterans of the First Cavalry Division, fully armed and clad in white leggings and helmets.

With MacArthur on the brink of reaching his long-sought goal after achieving one of the greatest victories in military annals, disarming of Japanese forces progressed smoothly and the vanguard of 100,000 American troops who will occupy southern

2 Semesters U. S. History Study Vital

Recently tests showed many college freshmen—just out of high school—didn't know Abraham Lincoln was President during the Civil War—or that Woodrow Wilson was at the helm during World War I.

They didn't know because the United States history course, such as that given in the Los Angeles high schools, has been shriveled to a one-semester "quickie" affair.

A full year of United States history—two semesters—obviously should be required in the 11th grade. And, it must be in addition to civics or government. The Examiner today presents another article summarizing the findings on the basic necessity for prompt change in the curriculum.

By Carl Greenberg

"Carryalls."

"Vans."

These two biting definitions have been applied to the currently taught courses in United States history and civics.

They sharply define the ailment that has afflicted the method and content of teaching United States history.

They bring into bright focus the gradual sabotage that is being accomplished under the guise of "vision" and "progress"—to use the bogus dialectic of some of the educational theoreticians and experimentalists.

With sledgehammer effect they make indisputable the necessity for swift action to institute a full one-year, two-semester course in United States history in the Los Angeles high schools, as a separate and distinct course from that given in civics or government.

Yesterday's article highlighted the observations of the Institute of American History of Stanford University. Let us today examine further into the background of the institute's observations.

For several years conferences of California teachers of American history have been held at Stanford. Obviously

(Continued on Page 4, Cols. 4-5)

111,000 Idle in Strikes

By Associated Press

The national total of strike idle mounted yesterday to 111,000, highest in months, as A. F. L. President William Green declared labor's no-strike pledge ended with Japan's surrender.

A labor-management conference will meet in Washington October 29 or November 5 to work out means to minimize labor disputes. The conference was called by Secretary of Labor Schwellenbach and Secretary of Commerce Wallace.

Records showed yesterday's high total of idle over the country compared with a previous high of 92,815 on June 27, reached during the wave of optimism growing out of victory in Europe.

HARDEST HIT—

The Detroit automobile industry, racing to supply the peacetime market with new cars, was hardest hit by the new wave of stoppages. Approximately 45,000 were idle in the motor capital.

A continuing strike at the Kelsey-Hayes Wheel Company prompted the Ford Motor Company to halt all its passenger car and truck production in eight cities and lay off more than 30,000 workers.

Ford officials said, however, 22,000 of those laid off would be

(Continued on Page 4, Col. 3)

300 Naval Ships Will Return Yanks

WASHINGTON, Sept. 7.—(INS)—Fleet Admiral Ernest J. King today announced plans to assign more than 300 U. S. naval vessels, including the 33,000-ton aircraft carrier Saratoga, to return American soldiers and sailors from the Pacific following the occupation of Japan.

The Saratoga, one of the world's largest naval vessels, and 18 escort carriers have already been put on troop transport duty in the Pacific.

Admiral King said that 40 additional escort carriers—they range from 5000 to 10,000 tons—and 197 attack transports will be added to the troop transport fleet as soon as they are relieved of their present assignment of moving soldiers and airplanes from the Philippines, Marianas and Okinawa to the Japanese homeland.

These 256 ships, Admiral King said, will be in addition to the Navy's 48 large transports, already engaged in moving high-point troops from the Pacific to the United States.

Navy officials said the transfer of combatant ships to a transport role will speed the redeployment of troops from this country as replacements in the Far East and thus make possible the earlier demobilization of men not needed for occupation duty.

AMERICA, THE SUPER POWER

One of the major strengths of the Constitution lies in its flexibility and ambiguity. Central issues are not always clearly resolved and tensions between conflicting ideas tend to emerge in periods of crisis, whether internal or foreign. When a particular crisis combines both domestic and international relationships, the magnitude of the Constitutional interpretation becomes strikingly apparent. In the immediate post-World War II years, a central question emerged: how are the rights and liberties guaranteed to individuals protected against the claims of the government acting in the name and interests of national security? Although this issue was not altogether new in American history, the development of its partial resolution had wider and more profound repercussions than had occurred previously.

In part, the dramatic events of the Cold War had their origin in activities and attitudes which existed prior to World War II. Concern had been mounting for several years over communism and its presumed threat to American security, both at home and abroad. Congressional committees had been established for dealing with investigations of anti-American propaganda, subversion, espionage and the like. Although much of the work carried on by these committees resulted in little substantive practice, there are a few cases which became fundamental to the events of the immediate post-War period.

In 1940, amidst concern over the war in Europe and the apparent alliance between Germany and Russia, Congress adopted the first explicit Alien and Sedition Act since 1789. The Smith Act, in addition to providing for the registration of aliens and the deportation of the seditious among them, also made it a criminal offense to teach or advocate, or to conspire to teach or advocate, or to have membership in a party which taught or advocated the "violent overthrow of the government." The Act was written in such a way as to be impartially directed against all political heresies, but clearly the communists were the real target.

Few believed that the communists were in a position to organize a violent overthrow of the American government. The protection was aimed not at the preservation of the Constitution, per se, but rather against any hostile acts, beliefs, or allegiances which might inspire lesser actions inimical to the government. Jefferson had thought the Sedition Act of 1789 completely unconstitutional; there were many governmental officials in 1940 who felt the same way about the Smith Act. However, the issue was obscured by the attack on Pearl Harbor and the entry of the United States into the Second World War. The Act itself went largely unused during the war years and the matter of its constitutionality was not dealt with until 1951.

Questions of civil liberties raised during the war were generally muted. The most flagrant violation of civil liberties prompted almost no objection—110,000 people of Japanese heritage (70,000 of whom were native-born American citizens) were interned or deported. Secrecy seemed vital and few people argued against the concept of "security risk" which was becoming progressively paramount in intelligence and security circles. Similarly, there was no public outcry against the system which required the testing of personnel for loyalty on the basis of their personal beliefs, speech and associations.

The termination of the War and the immediate concerns over the position of the Soviet Union in the international arena altered the domestic environment however. A chain of events was initiated by governmental officials and translated to the public through the press, signalling the onset of the Cold War and the dual policies of containment at home and containment abroad.

Secretary of State Dean Acheson *addressing the opening meeting of the Atlantic Security Treaty signing ceremony in Washington, D.C. on April 4, 1949. Seated behind him in a semi-circle are the ambassadors and foreign ministers of the signing countries.*

Special Army Counsel Joseph Welch, *left, and Senator Joseph McCarthy talk in the hearing room June 4, 1954 during the Army-McCarthy hearings into communist influence in the military.*

Although the key elements of containment did not really emerge until the beginning of 1947, it is evident that the groundwork was laid immediately following the conclusion of the War. The fundamental position which would later emerge in a variety of forms, including the Truman Doctrine, the Marshall Plan, and the military intervention in Korea in the early 1950's, was openly articulated by Navy Secretary James Forrestal in late 1945. In a public speech, Forrestal outlined the need for a unification of the armed services, a move designed to enable the nation "to act as a unit in terms of its diplomacy, its military policy, its use of scientific knowledge, and, finally, of course, in its moral and political leadership of the world." It was the last phrase that captured the flavor of what was to come, of the philosophical substance of the containment policy.

The National Security Act, passed in 1947, initiated the process of administrative and military reorganization. The three branches of the Armed Forces were brought together under a national military establishment which was converted soon thereafter into the Department of Defense. The same Act brought into being the Central Intelligence Agency, the National Security Council, and the National Security Agency, each of which was designed to bridge both military and diplomatic services and activities and create a force which was altogether new in American history. In the words of the Act, the National Security Council was "to advise the President with respect to the integration of domestic, foreign and military policies related to the national security." Consequently, the military branch of government was given, via this channel and others, a new source of influence and status in the creation and implementation of diplomatic policy.

Concurrently, the machinery established to fulfill security requirements proliferated in intelligence operations throughout the government. Within a matter of months, intelligence agents were hard at work collecting and reporting and evaluating data throughout the world. Intelligence gathering abroad and investigations of alleged communist activities at home heightened American concern over the deteriorating situation in Europe. It was becoming apparent that the United States could not take the isolationist stance that popular opinion stressed. Within a brief period of time, the political and geographic boundaries of central Europe had been reconstituted, establishing Soviet-dominated governments in virtually all of the Eastern European nations. By the early weeks of 1947 another chain of actions became apparent. Rarely singular in style, Communist-directed pressure had begun to penetrate the territorial boundaries of Greece, Turkey, Italy, Germany and France, complicating the already devastating task of reconstruction following the War.

Of particular concern in America was the fact that despite the variety of activities, each was becoming more difficult to counteract. The more subtle the enterprises, the greater the concern that was aroused about the possibility of domestic espionage, subversion and the like in America. In Greece, the Communist threat took the form of guerilla warfare; in Turkey it was characterized by diplomatic pressure backed by the threat of military force. In France and Italy it was manifested in powerful domestic communist parties working to destroy the already fragile framework of economic growth and disrupt the delicate democratic processes which were beginning to emerge. In Germany, Soviet pressure was more covert, but similarly aimed at preventing economic recovery and delaying the unification of the three Western zones linked to Berlin.

Significantly, these events provided a concrete measure of the strength of Soviet ideology and military ingenuity, while at the same time demonstrating the fact that the possession of an American atomic weapons capability was not sufficient to deter such maneuvers.

Increasing frustration was witnessed in governmental circles although the public remained content to proceed with economic recovery and to hold to the expectation of peace and prosperity. Most Americans believed, after the founding of the United Nations in particular, that an era of international peace and goodwill was being ushered in; most anticipated an increasingly relaxed atmosphere at home and abroad. But, their expectations were short-lived.

By March, 1946, the origins of the Cold War were being revealed. On the fifth of the month Truman and Churchill flew to Fulton, Missouri, where the Prime Minister delivered what became the primary document explaining the onset of the Cold War. In short, Churchill portrayed a picture of Red Russia bent on conquering the world. Backed by his immense authority through his war record and the great charm of his personality, Churchill was able to convey to millions of listeners the necessity for a giant cordon sanitaire around Russia, accompanied by a world crusade aimed at destroying international communism in the name of Anglo-Saxon democracy. The reality of the existing threat in Europe was coupled with the words of Secretary of State Forrestal to produce a moral fervor which far surpassed Wilson's desire to "make the world safe for democracy."

The famous Iron Curtain Speech had its impact on the American public as well as on the leadership circles. On the day following Churchill's speech only 18 percent of the American people approved of his ideas. A month later a survey demonstrated that a full 85 percent supported them and were willing to proceed with positive actions. A crisis atmosphere had been created in Washington: realities in Western Europe and allegations of conspiracies at home provided the means for making a viable policy of containment credible. In 1945 only thirty-two percent of the public believed that there would be a new world war within the

ensuing twenty-five years; a year later the percentage jumped to forty-one; by the time Truman announced the first concrete containment policy the figure had reached sixty-three percent. In the Gallup poll taken in 1948, almost three-fourths of the American people believed that world war was inevitable.

In part this can also be explained by the visibility of European events reported by the press. In an article published on March 17, 1948, in the New York *Herald Tribune*, Joseph and Stewart Alsop summed up the situation: "The atmosphere in Washington today is no longer a post-war atmosphere. It is, to put it bluntly, a pre-war atmosphere." There was considerable evidence to substantiate this assessment. American foreign policy could by then be described in terms of the Truman Doctrine, which put specifically, was a policy that had as its key objective the absolute containment of communism to its existing borders. In practice, this policy was being implemented primarily through massive military and economic assistance as provided through the Marshall Plan first and later through military aid to Greece and Turkey.

The primary consideration of the assistance programs was to strengthen the capacity of individual countries to meet external and internal threats to economic and political viability, while at the same time allowing the United States to remain uncommitted militarily, at least in terms of direct intervention. There were, of course, no guarantees that this particular formula would be successful, and the uncertainty of the future of Europe raised considerable doubts in the minds of Americans at the same time that they were being subjected to continual news barrages proclaiming the evils of communism. In the midst of this, attention was gradually being internalized and investigations of possible domestic subversion were stepped up.

The extent of reinterpretation of previously established guidelines for investigations was evident in authorizations produced by Congressman J. Parnell Thomas, the chairman of the House Un-American Activities Committee in 1947. The committee announced an eight point program designed to accomplish the following tasks: to expose and ferret out the Communists and Communist sympathizers in the Federal Government, to spotlight the spectacle of having outright communists controlling and dominating some of the most vital unions in American labor, to institute a counter-educational program against the subversive propaganda hurled at the American public, to investigate those groups and movements which were trying to dissipate atomic knowledge for the benefit of a foreign power, to investigate Communist influences in Hollywood and in educational institutions, to organize a research staff so as to furnish reference services to members of Congress, and to continue to accumulate files and records to be placed at the disposal of investigative units of the Government and armed services.

A series of events in 1947 and 1948 magnified the growing beliefs about the potential Communist influence in and danger to the United States. The testimonies of Elizabeth Bentley and Whittaker Chambers provided the House Un-American Activities Committee with its first tangible evidence that there had been Communist cells operating in the Federal Government. Further testimonies indicated the existence of extensive Communist espionage networks in both Canada and the United States and when British scientist Alan Nunn May was imprisoned for revealing atomic information, it was demonstrated that the espionage had penetrated at least the periphery of the most carefully guarded of all national security secrets. By the end of 1948 the government had initiated its case against Alger Hiss, the high-

nator Joseph McCarthy *of Wisconsin in 1954 as he replies to a estion during the dispute which arose at the Senate hearing over esidential handling of secret papers.*

Senator Joseph McCarthy, *center, listens to testimony during the Army-McCarthy hearings. Senator McCarthy had charged that the Army was riddled with enemy agents operating under the control of the Russian secret police.*

ranking governmental official who had participated in the Yalta Conference and in negotiations with the United Nations, as a Communist espionage agent. Mounting governmental concern and public fear added to the fervor of the Committee and investigations under its newly acquired guidelines gathered force.

Instances of violations of civil liberties became more frequent and more noticeable. Denials of due process, suspensions of freedom of speech, resorts to self-incrimination under oath, and invasions of privacy accompanied public and official fear, hatred and partisan politics. By the end of 1948, President Truman was pressured into demonstrating a stand in favor of the measures being used and agreed to resurrect the Smith Act in order to secure the indictment of the principal leaders of the American Communist Party for the crime of conspiring to teach and advocate the overthrow of the American government. The extraordinary trial continued for several months and exacerbated the issue of whether Communists were entitled to exploit civil liberties protected under the American system as a means of attempting to overthrow that very system.

The Smith Act convictions were essential to the domestic history of the Cold War. They encouraged and strengthened the development of a formal anti-Communist crusade, created an environment conducive to the rise of Senator Joseph McCarthy, and signaled the passage of the Internal Security Act of 1950. The latter, often referred to as the McCarran Act, represented a departure from the Smith Act in that it was directly aimed at Communism. It was both explicit and drastic in its formulation and intent.

In February of 1950, Senator Joseph McCarthy entered into the political arena in an ambitious and forthright way. The conviction of Alger Hiss provided the touchstone of the Senator's career. In the political maneuvering of the midterm election year the Truman Democrats, the Dixiecrats, and the Republicans vied with each other to demonstrate that each could claim the most accomplished record of anticommunism. McCarthy became publicly recognized when he stepped into the spotlight carrying a list of two-

344

hundred-and-five names which he claimed were made known to the Secretary of State as being members of the Communist Party and who were working and shaping American foreign policy. He made this statement in Wheeling, West Virginia, on the ninth of the month. A day later, in Denver, Colorado, the list of individuals had been converted from card-carrying communists to "bad security risks." On the third day, in Salt Lake City, Utah, he had reconverted the list to actual members of the Party, but had reduced the number to fifty-seven. By the second week of February, McCarthy had made the headlines of all major and most minor newspapers throughout the country. He would remain on the front page for more than four years. When the Senator returned to Washington, he was both exuberant and confident, anxious to provide evidence to the doubtful Senate committee which was convening.

Late in the afternoon of February 20 a three-bell quorum call sounded in the Senate. McCarthy entered the chamber, carrying with him his tan briefcase which he claimed contained all of the documented evidence needed in support of the charges he had made during his trip around the country. The Democrats demanded evidence and twice since his return to the Capitol he had told newsmen that if he could not provide it he would resign from office. In his briefcase, McCarthy had 108 photostated copies of two year old information which had been presented by the Department of State to an investigating committee in the Senate. Only forty of the individuals listed in the dossier still worked for the State Department, and all of them had undergone extensive FBI field investigations and been cleared. In spite of this, McCarthy stacked eighty-one of the files on his desk and announced that he had "penetrated Truman's iron curtain of secrecy."

Shuffling the first folders, he told the Committee that he would identify each case by number and not by name—ostensibly in the interests of privacy. But the information provided in Senate chambers had always been governed by privilege and Senators in the room began to express

Senator Joseph McCarthy *shown after he accused President Truman of endangering the nation's security by what McCarthy called the President's "arrogant refusal" to release loyalty files of State Department employees accused by McCarthy of having pro-Communist sympathies. In actuality, Truman had not refused to release the files at the time McCarthy made his charge.*

General Douglas MacArthur *waves his arm to acknowledge the applause after his introduction to a joint meeting of Congress on April 19, 1951. It was during this farewell appearance that MacArthur made his famous "Old Soldiers Never Die" speech.*

suspicions that the information was invalid. Within minutes, the Senator from Wisconsin began reading the information in front of him. It was obvious from the start that he had not seen the files before. For six hours he refused to yield the floor, struggling from one file to the next and uncovering nothing to substantiate his charges against State Department employees. Of the cases he read, many had nothing to do with the State Department—five of the files related to members of the Voice of America and one to a staff worker at the Department of Commerce. Several of the numbers cited were duplications of documents which had been filed more than once. At least four of the files were empty and one, perhaps the most dramatic, contained information on a person who was singled out as an example because he clearly was not a communist.

The fiasco in the Senate chamber left members of the Committee with the belief that McCarthy had once again led them astray. They had convened for most of the evening and nothing of substance had emerged. The press revealed the same story to the public the next morning, but the headlines, focusing on McCarthy without providing the basis of the ensuing articles, obscurred the issue. Most Americans, who were already enamoured with the Senator, assumed that he had, once again, uncovered another Communist agent who posed a serious threat to United States security. In a Gallup poll taken shortly after the news of McCarthy's experience with the committee, more than fifty percent of the American public expressed a favorable attitude towards the Senator and believed that he was helping the country.

Buffeted by popular support and undaunted by the fact that the files had provided him with no basis for his charges, McCarthy announced on March 21 that he was about to name the "top Russian espionage agent in the United States." The Tydings Committee convened in a special emergency session to hear the Senator. Without hesitation, he announced that Owen Lattimore, a professor at Johns Hopkins University and a specialist in Asian affairs who was well-known throughout the country for his skill, expertise, and integrity in shaping American foreign policy in the Orient, was "definitely an espionage agent" and that his file would prove it. The file, of course, merely reiterated Lattimore's splendid accomplishments and cleared him of any doubt as to his loyalty to the American government. The next morning, McCarthy called a press conference, explaining that he would shortly make public the name of a man who had been "Alger Hiss's boss in the espionage ring in the State Department." On Sunday, Drew Pearson broke the story, including Lattimore's name.

The professor returned on his own from Afghanistan to defend himself and his record as advisor in East Asian matters. On the floor of the Senate the following day, McCarthy charged him with being the chief architect of America's Far Eastern policy—a fact that was indisputable and irrelevant. Lattimore's response was precise and well-documented. He produced letters from Chiang Kai-shek and Madame Chiang testifying to his remarkable work and expressing profound gratitude for his services. Tydings announced shortly thereafter that the committee had investigated Lattimore's record thoroughly and could find absolutely no evidence to support an allegation of subversion. Lattimore received a standing ovation from the crowded Senate gallery and departed from the chamber, confident that the matter was over.

Four days later it was clear that his optimism had been premature. McCarthy returned to the Senate chamber, this time producing a new witness, Louis Budenz. Budenz had worked as a managing editor of the *Daily Worker* and McCarthy enticed him to swear that he had been instructed by American Communist Party leaders to consider Lattimore a communist. The right-wing supporters of McCarthy in the Senate were ecstatic, believing that at last there was tangible evidence to support the Senator's charges. Under incisive cross-examination by Lattimore's attorneys, Abe Fortas and Paul Porter, however, the witness's testimony dissolved and the committee was again left with a refuted allegation.

In the midst of the inquiries in Washington and the moves to discredit the charges being leveled by McCarthy, elections for Congress were looming. Candidates running on McCarthy-styled platforms and with similar tactics were gaining support in a number of states. Ultimately, they were often victorious. The American public, by the tens of millions, had come to regard the Senator as the symbol of anticommunism and as long as communism was an issue he would remain a hero to them—regardless of the lack of integrity he demonstrated.

While the government continued its search for possible examples of subversion and attempted to trace rumors about in-house espionage agents, the government of North Korea was deploying nine fully-equipped divisions to invade the almost defenseless Republic of South Korea. Spearheaded by twenty thousand Korean communists who had served in World War II, the 120,000-man North Korean Peoples' Army was an elite military force by any standard. Against it was an army of 65,000 troops which had been deliberately weakened by the American government in an attempt to reduce the possibility of major conflict between the two Koreas. Moreover, the American military establishment found itself far from prepared for this contingency. Attention had been myopically focused on European affairs and the retention of the post-World War II status quo, and only minor attention had been paid to events in the Far East. Defense budgets in the immediate postWar era had been slashed and armed forces budgets had been cut from thirty billion dollars

to 14.2 billion during those few years. By 1950, immediately preceeding the deployment of North Korean troops to the south, the Soviet Union had as many combat planes as the United States, four times as many troops and thirty times as many tank divisions. Only one infantry division approached combat-readiness and the four divisions of American occupation forces in Japan had deteriorated rapidly as their presence seemed less and less warranted. The problem of the American Containment policy became clear as the first blasts of North Korean artillery were fired—the United States was neither ready nor able to prevent communist attacks everywhere in the world. The fact that the American government possessed atomic weapons seemed to make very little, if any, difference. That possession did not directly imply use and the clear component of deterrence was absent.

On the morning of the fifth anniversary of the establishment of the United Nations, reports of conditions in Korea poured into New York and Washington. North Korean troops had ignored a United Nations' appeal for a cease-fire and were enveloping Seoul in a six-pronged drive. President Truman called his advisors together to discuss the rôle of the United States. The "War Cabinet", as this group was called, strongly recommended a resolution to the United Nations, calling for direct and expedient action in the form of military intervention led by American troops. Additionally, the President agreed to direct naval and air force units in MacArthur's command to provide tactical support to the Republic of Korea's troops south of the 38th Parallel and, at Secretary of State Acheson's request, he agreed to sanction additional military assistance in the form of materiél to the French forces in Indochina.

Seoul fell to North Korean troops. At noon, three diplomats met for a regular luncheon meeting at the Stockhold

Scene from one *of the sessions of the Senate hearings into communist infiltration in the Army. The hearings were broadcast live on national television.*

President Harry Truman, *who served as President during the first years of the Cold War, was the thirty-third president of the United States.*

Restaurant on Long Island. Trygve Lie, the Secretary General of the United Nations, Jacob Malik, the ambassador from the Soviet Union, and Ernest Gross discussed the military conflict and the Security Council meeting scheduled for later in the afternoon. Lie urged Malik to attend the meeting, primarily because of the United States' recommendation which would be read, but he refused. The refusal provided a rare opportunity—the United States could secure the support of the United Nations in committing troops to Korea and at the same time lead those troops and its own in a manifestation of the Containment policy it had espoused.

The intervention in Korea spotlighted the danger of communism abroad and signalled a restoration of major fears of communist subversion at home. The military campaigns met with little success in the beginning and frustrations began to mount. Public attention was captured by daily headlines depicting McCarthy's allegations on the domestic scene and MacArthur's military maneuvers in Korea. The two policies were supported either by silence or by active praise from Congress and the President. Their coincidence resulted in a central focus on communism which sustained the investigations of the House and Senate committees and the press. The issue of civil liberties faced a serious dilemma: so long as

direct charges against specific individuals of violations of the law were not leveled, Grand Juries could not intervene even though accusations often resulted in the destruction of a person's career as well as his or her personal and public life. The press realized this and in the name and behind the code of objective reporting were careful to state time and again "McCarthy says . . ." as a preface to claims of anti-American activities.

The issue of the constitutionality of the Smith Act, upon which many of the indictments and convictions were rendered, was not resurrected as a major question for civil liberties until 1951 in the Dennis Case. In a six to two decision, the Vinson Court maintained that the basic tenets of the Smith Act were indeed constitutional and reaffirmed the convictions accomplished under it. The Supreme Court argued that since the Smith Act was constitutional by reason of present or probable dangers that it was designed to avert, then it was only reasonable to maintain that other, often more extensive measures were also constitutional insofar as they were simply the logical consequence of that Act.

The impact of the Dennis decision was far-reaching. It settled, for the moment, the issue of national security versus civil liberties in favor of the former. It formally and legally sanctioned and made legitimate the activities of public and private organizations whose sole aim it was to ferret out communists or alleged communists from all segments of American life. And, perhaps most importantly, it codified the concept of guilt by association or by intent—a principle which was and had been throughout the American experience inimical to fundamental theories of justice.

On the wake of the Dennis decision came a new surge of investigations and blacklists. Congressional committees became massive organizations aided by private pressure groups who were zealous in exposing "communists" and "security risks" in all dimensions of American life. Not only were the government in general and the defense industry in particular subject to scrutiny, so also were the motion picture industry, schools and colleges, private industry and, of course, individual citizens. In the name of national security, hundreds of people lost their jobs and were confronted with the improbability of finding another one. These people were often never tried for the crime of which they were accused. Rather, they were informally and extra-legally convicted for what they were thought to be or for what it was assumed they might become.

In part the excesses at home must be attributed to the frustrations stemming from American military intervention in Korea. The early successes of the containment policy in Europe—the reconstruction of economies, the development of the NATO Alliance, the exit of the Soviet Union from Iran, the reduction of pressure by the Soviets in Turkey, the failure of Stalin's promise to honor recognition to the would-be government in Greece, and the terminated blockade of Berlin in particular—lulled a number of government officials into a sense of overconfidence prior to the outbreak of the Korean crisis. The occupation of North Korea by the communists offered the first real test of the containment policy in areas which were not more or less contiguous to the Soviet Union and, initially at least, the prospects for a hasty and successful victory seemed bright.

The problems inherent in the conduct of the war and its relatively lengthy duration raised issues fundamental to containment. It became clear that military intervention was an element which had not previously been anticipated but which was now essential to the restriction of communism, at least in

347

Roy Cohn, *center, shown testifying during the Army McCarthy hearings in April, 1954. To the right, directly behind Cohn, is Army defense counsel Joseph Welch, whose humane defense of those accused by McCarthy of having communist sympathies did much to turn the tide of public opinion against the Wisconsin Senator.*

Asia. Secondly, under the pressure of General MacArthur and his slogan "There is no substitute for victory" the matter of whether containment meant holding the line or actually pushing communism back to the frontiers of the Soviet Union became problematical. Thirdly, the prospects of a stalemate prompted increasing frustration, particularly since it was evident that the United States was clearly the most dominant and militarily strong nation in the world. And, finally, the fact that the United States' government held the exclusive possession of atomic weapons but was unwilling, if not unable, to use them effectively as a deterrent or as an actual weapon caused further frustration. Taken together, these factors help to explain an environment domestically which allowed McCarthy and those with similar attitudes and methods to flourish.

The 1952 Presidential campaign raised several issues pertinent to containment in both theaters. On the domestic scene, Eisenhower privately supported McCarthy and was present in the Senator's home state when he was campaigning for re-election. In statements related to McCarthyism, Eisenhower was cautious but forthright in making the point that it was necessary "to clean up the mess in Washington" and to protect the American citizens from internal subversion, infiltration and espionage. At the same time, however, he was quick to establish his position as differing from the Senator's in terms of methods and tactics. In terms of foreign policy, the General made his strongest bid for the Presidency in criticizing Truman for his conduct of the War and in proclaiming shortly before the election that he would go to Korea to help end the conflict. The Republican ticket of Eisenhower and Nixon won the election by a margin of almost seven million votes.

In keeping with his campaign speeches, Eisenhower was successful in bringing a conclusion to the Korean War, even though negotiations had been in process for two years before the armistice was reached on July 27, 1953. Many people expected that the end of an immediate threat of communism overseas would herald a similar end to internal security probes at home; this was not to be the case. The process which had been initiated years earlier had gained its own

peculiar dynamic.

The election of Eisenhower did not mark an end to the process. In some ways, the activities were, at least for a short time, heightened. Under the President's 1953 revision of the Truman Security Order the procedures involving testimony and appeal were improved, but the real problems were more substantive than procedural. In most instances, the testimony upon which a defendant was convicted was factually correct but the question of what he or she had been convicted of remained elusive. For example, when Ensign Landy was denied a commission in the Naval Reserve because he had continued to have close associations with a former communist the facts were not to be denied. The associate was, in fact, his own mother. However, the conclusion that he was therefore unfit to be commissioned bordered on the absurd. The absurdity of the witch hunts culminated in McCarthy's own undoing and in the ultimate reversal of major decisions which had allowed internal containment to flourish.

Shortly after Attorney General Brownell was proudly listing the accomplishments of the Eisenhower Administration, McCarthy began a national tour sponsored by the Republican Party. The Senator's confidence reached an all-time high during these weeks and he returned to Washington anxious to undertake an investigation of the Army loyalty-security programs, a quest which was seen to conflict with the President's values and interests. McCarthy's initial move was to denounce a respected Army officer, Brigadier General Ralph Zwicker, as "unfit to wear the Uniform." Investigations made into Army bases proved to be fruitless and no evidence of subversion or security risk turned up. The antagonism of the President and the Congress mounted and in a new tactic from the White House, Eisenhower responded to the challenge and defended the Army. Shortly thereafter, the Senate ordered an investigation of its own member and the press began to shift its attention away from McCarthy's allegations and toward his demise.

The Army-McCarthy hearings were televised in a manner which made it clear that the pursuit of the communist heresy in the United States had become the pursuit against the basic principles of American democracy. The stormy proceedings and the testimonies in particular of both McCarthy and Secretary of the Army Robert Stevens laid the issues open to the American public and the ensuing censure of the Senator terminated a major chapter in American history.

The Cold War had begun to lose its intensity and the perils of communism for American internal security were beginning to be put in more appropriate perspective. It became clear that the actual dangers had in fact been grossly exaggerated. The damage done by infiltration, sedition and espionage had really been very slight even though the anti-communist crusade had been massive. The Warren Court, beginning with the Parker versus Lester case in 1955, began to re-establish narrower limits on the denials of due process, the invasion of individual rights and the disregard of the government for simple fairness and constitutional justice which had been laid aside during the immediate post World War II years.

In June, 1957, the Court exercised one of its most telling decisions in setting aside a Smith Act conviction and came very close to reversing its earlier Dennis decision. Although this move outraged individuals and organizations who still clung to anti-communist beliefs and zeal, the general public, with the decline of the Cold War and the exposure of the excesses of containment at home, paid less and less attention. In decisions to follow the trend of the Court continued to be hallmarked by a quest for civil liberties.

HISTORICAL HEADLINES
ON
AMERICA THE SUPER POWER

EXTRA

LATE NEWS

Los Angeles Times
EQUAL RIGHTS
LIBERTY UNDER THE LAW • TRUE INDUSTRIAL FREEDOM

9 A.M. FINAL

VOL. LXX   IN FOUR PARTS   WEDNESDAY MORNING, APRIL 11, 1951   68 PAGES   DAILY, SEVEN CENTS

TRUMAN FORCES MACARTHUR OUT!

Hayden Names Reds in Hollywood

Film Star, Marine Veteran, Was in Party Seven Months, He Says

WASHINGTON, April 10 (U.P)—Movie Actor Sterling Hayden, World War II marine veteran, testified today he joined the Communist Party in a burst of misguided emotion in June, 1946, but quit in disgust seven months later.

The actor, who ticked off the names of several members of his Hollywood cell including former Actress Karen Morley, said he returned from highly dangerous war service with Marshal Tito's Yugoslav partisans imbued with the idea of righting the world's wrongs.

Hayden, ex-husband of Screen Actress Madeleine Carroll, told ings. Kearney said he could go the House Un-American Activities Committee it was in this mood he was recruited into the party by a woman named Bea Winter, then secretary to his agent, Berg Allenberg. He said she now is employed by Sam Spiegel, independent producer.

Names Given

The actor, second Hollywood figure to confess former Red affiliations, also revealed he had handed investigators a list of film colony persons he believes "in conjecture" to be Communists. He refused to tell reporters how many he had listed.

Rep. Moulder (D) Mo., told Hayden he was satisfied "you gave honest testimony. I have concluded that you are an intensely loyal American citizen." Hayden thanked him.

But Rep. Kearney (R) N.Y., said he was not satisfied with Hayden's testimony that he could not remember more persons at Communist cell meet-ings. Kearney said he could go to an Elks lodge meeting and "tell you at least 15 people who had been there."

The first witness in the committee's revived Communism-in-Hollywood hearings was Larry Parks, leading actor in "The Jolson Story." Parks who likewise admitted he was a onetime Communist Party member who later repented. Two other previous witnesses, Actor Howard de Silva and Actress Gale Sondergaard, refused to answer questions and were threatened with contempt prosecution.

When Hayden concluded the committee recessed until tomorrow when it will question Actor Will Geer, one of some 40 other figures of screen, radio, stage and television subpoenaed by the group.

Back Lot Workers

Hayden said he attended a series of party meetings at which a principal subject was the 1946 studio workers strike. He was

Turn to Page 9, Column 1

Recording of Truman Phone Talks Revealed

Investigators Disclose Sen. Tobey Has Transcriptions of Two Calls on RFC

WASHINGTON, April 10 (U.P)—Sen. Charles W. Tobey (R) N.H., has told Senate investigators he has recordings of two telephone conversations with President Truman about the RFC investigation, it was learned tonight.

In the first conversation, Mr. Truman reportedly told Tobey that RFC records show some Congressman had gotten fees for getting loans from the Reconstruction Finance Corp.

In the second conversation which one informed source said Tobey originated, the President told the Senator he had

THE WEATHER

U.S. Weather Bureau forecast: Cloudy nights and mornings today and tomorrow, with partly cloudy skies and hazy sunshine in the afternoons. Warmer today, with a high today near 68. Highest temperature yesterday, 64; lowest, 56.

been mistaken about the fees to Congressmen.

Tobey made the disclosures at a secret meeting of the RFC investigating subcommittee headed by Sen. J. William Fulbright (D) Ark., it was learned.

According to informed sources, Tobey caught only part of the first conversation with Mr. Truman on an office recording device. One source said Tobey told the subcommittee he recorded all of the second one.

Members of the subcommittee declined to comment on the reports. Tobey, a former member, was not immediately available.

Exact dates of the two conversations with the White House were not established. However, the first phone call from Mr. Truman was believed to have been made shortly after the President demanded from the RFC copies of all correspondence regarding RFC loans written by Senators and House members.

The second conversation was

Turn to Page 6, Column 5

EIGHT AIRMEN DIE AS GLIDER PICKUP FAILS

FAIRBANKS, Alaska, April 10 (P)—Eight airmen perished today in the crash of an Air Force C-54 in a glider pickup attempt.

Witnesses said the four-engine transport 'exploded and burst into flames after striking the south runway of Ladd Air Force Base. There was no chance for any of the men aboard to escape.

Tonight the names of three of the eight victims were released by the Air Force. They were Capt. George H. Wood, pilot, Battle Creek, Mich.; Capt. Bernard W. Mark, navigator, East Orange, N.J., and Staff Sgt. George W. Hollister, crew chief, Herington, Kan.

Jury Indicts Walker for Cook Slayings

An indictment charging Lawrence J. Walker, 20, with the murders of Richard and Doris Cook and five other felonies was returned by the Riverside County grand jury in a special session yesterday.

The Cook couple, both 18, were murdered in desert wastelands near Lake Mathews, Riverside County, last March 26. Cook's body was found beside his automobile on Cajalco Road at 11:23 a.m. that day. Mrs. Cook's body was not found until two days later, being located near an abandoned quarry 11.4 miles east of the spot where her husband was slain.

Heard 14 Witnesses

Yesterday's indictment was returned by the grand jury after two-and-a-half hours' deliberation that followed testimony by 14 witnesses.

The true bill was returned before Presiding Judge John G. Gabbert, who remanded Walker to Riverside County Jail without bail. Judge Gabbert ordered Walker arraigned at 9:30 a.m. today.

At a press conference immediately prior to the grand jury meeting yesterday, Dist. Atty. William O. Mackey announced that full information regarding evidence gathered by investigators from his office, the Riverside County Sheriff and the Riverside Police Department, will

Turn to Page 12, Column 1

Visibility Cut by Drizzles, Fog and Smog

Drizzles, fog and smog yesterday held Los Angeles visibility to three-fourths of a mile at 8 a.m. and two miles at 4 p.m.

The haze was somewhat lifted slightly in the afternoon, with the maximum visibility measuring 2½ miles at 2 and 3 p.m. Temperatures ranged from a low of 56 deg. at 6:51 a.m. to a high of 64 at 3:14 p.m.

The Weather Bureau forecast cloudy skies during the nights and mornings and hazy afternoons for today and tomorrow.

FEATURES INDEX

Red Rallying Base Blasted by U.N. Guns

TOKYO, April 11 (Wednesday) (P)—U.N. forces had the Reds cleared out of all South Korea except for one small northwest fragment today—their last day under Gen. MacArthur's command.

As reports of new allied successes arrived from Lt. Gen. Matthew B. Ridgway's 8th Army headquarters, announcement came from Washington that President Truman had removed MacArthur from all his commands in favor of Ridgway.

The announcement, first heard here over Army radio, struck headquarters like a thunderclap.

Out on the battlefield in Korea, allied planes and artillery were reported to have wiped out Chorwon, the rallying center of three Chinese Red armies in West-Central Korea.

Reds Abandon Town

East of the Hwachon power site the Reds were reported to have abandoned the town of Inje. Inje, four miles north of the 38th parallel and 25 miles east of the town of Hwachon, is in a sector where the Reds have been putting up a stiff fight.

Allied ruining of Chorwon deprived the Reds of one of their most important supply and assembly centers. Artillery began pounding Chorwon three days ago.

Gen. MacArthur's intelligence officers estimated last week that the Reds were massing up to 500,000 men in the Chorwon-Kumhwa-Hwachon triangle for an expected counteroffensive.

But MacArthur's midmorning communique said his U.N. forces held the initiative all across Korea yesterday and scored gains.

Turks Cross River

Just north of the 38th parallel on a highway leading up to Chorwon Turkish infantry crossed the Hantan River yesterday. Brushing aside light Red resistance, the Turks seized a hill southeast of Yonchon, 13 miles southwest of Chorwon.

Chinese and North Korean Reds now have been driven back

Turn to Page 2, Column 4

General to Lose All Commands at Once; Ridgway Is Successor

WASHINGTON, April 11 (P)—President Truman fired Gen. Douglas MacArthur today on grounds he failed to support—and publicly sought to change—the grand strategy of the United Nations war against Red aggression in Korea.

In a sensational statement released at the White House at 1 a.m. (EST) after days of soul-searching and indecision, the President announced:

"With deep regret I have concluded that General of the Army Douglas MacArthur is unable to give his wholehearted support to the policies of the United States government and of the United Nations in matters pertaining to his official duties."

Relieved of Fourfold Duties

Acting on that conclusion, once he had reached it, the President:

1—Relieved the 71-year-old MacArthur of his fourfold duties as supreme allied occupation commander in Japan;

For full page of pictures showing Gen. MacArthur in various phases of his military career, turn to Page 3, Part 1.

U.N. commander in chief for Korea; U.S. commander in chief for the Far East; and commanding general of the U.S. Army in the Far East.

2—Named Lt. Gen. Matthew B. Ridgway, field commander in Korea, to succeed MacArthur in all these commands. That means Ridgway not only will direct the U.N. campaign in Korea but also wind up the Japanese occupation, assuming peace treaty plans go through.

3—Named Lt. Gen. James A. Van Fleet, commander of the 2nd Army at Ft. George G. Meade, Md., to take over the 8th Army command in Korea from Ridgway.

4—Issued a set of secret messages exchanged between MacArthur and the Joint Chiefs of Staff here. The evident aim was to show that MacArthur had scorned successive Washington directives to clear anything he said on major political or military policy with either the State or Defense Departments.

Free to Travel; May Come Home

The order relieving MacArthur of command was Mr. Truman's answer to the general's persistent campaign of public statements to get the United States to follow a different policy in the Far East and especially, with its U.N. allies, in the Korean war.

Essentially he has advocated expanding the war to include direct attacks on Red China. He has presented Asia rather than Europe as the critical theater of conflict with aggressive Communism.

His dramatic amounts to reaffirmation by Mr. Truman of United States policies for a strictly limited war in Korea, if possible, and for treating Europe as the ultimately decisive area of contest with Soviet Communist power.

The bombshell announcement was made by Press Secretary Joseph H. Short as a hastily summoned White House news conference.

The President told MacArthur he is free to "travel to such places as you select"—thus freeing the general to return to this county, after an absence of nearly 14 years. There were immediate demands in Congress that he come at once to Washington to give his views.

Order Made Effective at Once

The President's order, telegraphed to MacArthur over the Army network, was brief and pointed:

"I deeply regret that it becomes my duty as President and Commander in Chief of the United States military forces to replace you as supreme commander, allied

Turn to Page 2, Column 2

OUSTED—Gen. Douglas MacArthur, forced out as allied commander in Far East by President Truman, who said the general was unable to support U.S. policies in Asia.

MacArthur Takes News of Ouster 'Magnificently'

'This Has Been His Finest Hour,' Military Secretary Says as Tokyo Crowds Gather

TOKYO, April 11 (U.P)—Gen. Douglas MacArthur received news of his dismissal "magnificently," his military secretary said tonight.

The 71-year-old five-star general "never turned a hair" on learning that he had been relieved by President Truman as U.S. and United Nations Far Eastern commander, Maj. Gen. Courtney Whitney said.

"His soldierly qualities were never more pronounced," Whitney said. "I think this has been his finest hour."

Whitney said MacArthur had no comment on his dismissal "for the time being."

"Not now, not now!" MacArthur said when asked about his discharge.

Crowd Gathers in Rain

The general was at his official residence in the U.S. Embassy for lunch when news of his recall reached Tokyo. With him were Mrs. MacArthur and their 13-year-old son, Arthur.

One guard said the Embassy had been "a madhouse for the past hour."

A crowd began to gather in the rain outside the Embassy gate waiting for MacArthur to emerge. There was an air of bewilderment among them.

"It's a ——— low blow," a GI said.

"I can't figure out why they did it. Do you know?"

News Stuns Staff

The President's announcement took MacArthur's headquarters completely by surprise and stunned staff officers. Most were home at lunch when the news broke shortly before 3:30 p.m. (10:30 p.m. PST).

Maj. Gen. Doyle Hickey, MacArthur's chief of staff, said: "I just heard about it when I came home for lunch and I cannot say anything about it at this time."

There was no immediate indication whether MacArthur learned of his impending dismissal in advance of the President's announcement.

U.S. Army Secretary Frank Pace Jr. conferred at length with MacArthur Monday night

Turn to Page 2, Column 7

ELECTION EXTRA

Los Angeles Examiner

CHARACTER QUALITY · AMERICA FIRST! · ENTERPRISE ACCURACY

AN AMERICAN PAPER FOR THE AMERICAN PEOPLE — THE GREAT NEWSPAPER OF THE GREAT SOUTHWEST

Examiner Building, 1111 S. Broadway, Zone 54   Examiner Telephone RIchmond 1212

In This Section:
Looking Around PAGE 9
Editorials PAGE 14
Fulton Lewis Jr. PAGE 15

OFFICIAL WEATHER

VOL. XLIX—NO. 330   LOS ANGELES, WEDNESDAY, NOVEMBER 5, 1952   CCC   Four Sections—Section 1—TEN CENTS

IKE LANDSLIDE

Cal., 35 Other States Back Eisenhower

GOP Wins State First Time Since '28

Nixon Swept Into Vice Presidency

By Carl Greenberg

California gave Dwight D. Eisenhower a landslide victory yesterday.

With a 3-2 Democratic lead in registration, the state swung into the Republican column for the first time in 24 years.

There never was any doubt from the start.

From the time the first flash began to roll in from Los Angeles County with nearly the state's votes—the GOP mounted inexorably over Ike and engulfed Adlai E. Stevenson, Ike's Democratic rival, for California's 32 electoral votes.

NIXON SEAT—

The sweep carried to the Vice President's office California's favorite son, U.S. Sen. Richard Nixon whose seat will be vacant and whose unexpired term of four more years filled by appointment of Earl Warren, the GOP vice presidential nominee in 1948.

In counties and cities, it was the same.

Nationally, there was a majority for Stevenson, but it was and as the hours ticked the tallies grew larger, the Republican nominee gained on the Illinois Governor.

LAST TIME—

It was since 1928, when Herbert Hoover defeated Al Smith, had California given its electoral votes to a Republican presidential candidate.

Yesterday's record-smashing 4,000,000 vote statewide election the Democrats had a better 200,000 lead in registration, but the figures plainly showed that Democrats by the thousands joined in helping sweep the Truman Administration and its adherents for Ike's "all to all."

In such isolated instances as Humboldt and Ventura counties did Stevenson gain a lead.

In Los Angeles County, most of the 45 cities went for Ike, for such areas as Venice

(Continued on Page 2, Cols. 7-8)

GOP Picks Up 2 Senate Seats, Leads in Other Races

WASHINGTON, Nov. 4.—(AP)—Republicans picked up two Senators tonight in a hot fight for control of Congress and leading in several other races represented by Democrats, many of the races were ugly close.

The first GOP triumph was in Connecticut where Sen. William Benton who won his seat by only 1,000 votes two years ago, was beaten by William A. Purtell, a

manufacturer, for a full six-year term.

The second Republican seat was gained in Maryland where Rep. J. Glenn Beall defeated Democrat George Mahoney in a close fight. Sen. Herbert O'Conor, Democrat, did not seek reelection.

The present Senate lineup is 49 Democrats, 46 Republicans, and one Independent-Republican. The

(Continued on Page 2, Column 3)

Propositions Backed Here

In 101 Los Angeles County precincts, State Proposition 1, authorizing $150,000,000 bond issue for veterans' farm and home purchase loans, was being favored six to one in early returns.

Proposition 2, increasing state aid for schools, was leading more than nearly two to one.

No. 3, tax exempting non-profit private elementary and high schools, was ahead by a closer margin.

No. 6, requiring loyalty oaths from public employees and officers, had a near two to one lead.

No. 7, under which primary election candidates would designate party affiliations on the ballot, also had a more than two to one lead. This measure was proposed as an alternate to No. 13, which would abolish cross-filing.

No. 10, sponsored by Pension Promoter George McLain, prohibiting public fund appropriation to Chambers of Commerce and other private organizations influencing legislation, was running behind.

No. 11, also a McLain measure, to place state aged pension aid under state instead of county controls, was behind, about to five.

No. 13, to ban California's 40-year practice of cross-filing of political candidates, was leading four to three.

No. 24, authorizing issuing of $189,000,000 in state school bonds, was approved three to one.

General Election Without Complaint

WASHINGTON, Nov. 4.—(AP)—The Justice Department said shortly after 4 p. m. (EST), today that it had not received a single complaint concerning the nation-wide voting for the presidency— a rarity for a general election.

Statewide Returns

PRESIDENT
5159 Precincts Out of 8148
Eisenhower (R.) 364,995
Stevenson (D.) 304,928

PROPOSITIONS
1. VETERANS' LOANS
Yes 946
No 213
2. SCHOOL FUNDS
149 Precincts
Yes 649
No 335
3. TAX EXEMPT SCHOOLS
179 Precincts
Yes 682
No 699
5. SUBVERSIVES
137 Precincts
Yes 218
No 90
6. LOYALTY OATHS
23 Precincts
Yes 582
No 284
7. PARTY AFFILIATIONS
148 Precincts
Yes 497
No 503
11. AGED PENSIONS
225 Precincts
Yes 1,045
No 1,536
13. CROSS-FILING
218 Precincts
Yes 1,344
No 1,255
24 SCHOOL BONDS
79 Precincts
No 1,150
Yes 451

L. A. County Results

PRESIDENT
4329 Precincts out of 8148
Eisenhower (Republican) 466,803
Stevenson (Democrat) 362,524

STATE PROPOSITIONS
101 Precincts out of 8148
1. VETERANS' LOANS
Yes 4,103
No 690
2. SCHOOL FUNDS
Yes 3,040
No 1,818
3. TAX EXEMPT SCHOOLS
Yes 2,864
No 2,501
6. LOYALTY OATHS
Yes 2,927
No 1,639

(Continued on Page 2, Column 4)

IN THE LEAD—Gen. Dwight Eisenhower could wear this confident grin last night as returns in a record election put him ahead of Adlai Stevenson.

Associated Press wirephoto

Series of Tidal Waves Lash Hawaii

HONOLULU, Nov. 4.—(AP)—A thundering 13-foot wall of water, powered by one of recorded history's mightiest earthquakes 3500 miles away, struck the evacuated northwest shore of Oahu in the Hawaiian Islands today.

It was the fourth and largest tidal wave to hit Hawaii in little more than an hour.

The waves were built up by a seismic shock that raced through the Pacific at more than 400 miles an hour from a point in the sea of Okhotsk between Siberia and Japan.

The shock also threw nine-foot waves at Adak in the Aleutians and Midway in the Central Pacific.

The 13-foot wave on Oahu knocked down telephone lines and bowled over a United States Navy photographer but he was reported uninjured.

In Honolulu harbor, on the lee of the seismic shock, rising water tore a cement barge from its moorings. The barge struck the Matson freighter Hawaiian Packer a glancing blow amidships and caved in 25 feet of the freighter's rail and stanchions.

At Hilo oh Hawaii Island a recently-completed $13,000 territorial boathouse was demolished by a wave, the Coast Guard reported.

Coast Guard buoys, weighing 10 to 12 tons, were torn from their moorings.

Hilo police ordered the evacuation of Keauhaha Beach, badly hit by a tidal wave in 1946.

(Maps, other stories on Page 16)

GOP Claims 375 Electoral Votes

General Breaks Into Solid South, Wins Virginia, Maryland

SPRINGFIELD, Ill., Nov. 4.—(AP)—One of Governor Stevenson's top aids said at 12:25 (EST) tonight:

"It's all over but the concession to Ike."

CHICAGO, Nov. 4.—(INS)—Col. Jake Arvey, Democratic national committeeman, tonight conceded Illinois to General Eisenhower.

The nation's election picture on latest returns:

Eisenhower led Stevenson in popular vote by 9,229,091 to 8,451,400 in 37,944 of 14,338 precincts.

The Republican candidate had majorities in 36 states with 375 electoral votes; the Democratic nominee led in 11 with 147. Needed to win 266.

SENATE: (35 races) elected: Democrats 5, Republicans 6. GOP gained one seat in Connecticut, defeating Benton (D).

HOUSE: (435 races) elected: Democrats 97, Republicans 27.

GOVERNORS: (30 races) elected: Democrats 3, Republicans 1.

WASHINGTON, Nov. 4.—Dwight D. Eisenhower took vital New York state and split the solid South tonight in a tidal wave of votes that swept a Republican toward the White House for the first time in 20 years.

With reports from 37,944 precincts of the nation's 146,338, here were the figures:

Eisenhower, 9,229,091.
Stevenson, 8,451,400.

The hero of World War II built himself such a lead in yesterday's presidential election that it seemed nothing could stop his landslide.

The South had crumbled. Virginia went definitely into the Republican column for the first time since 1928. So did the border state of Maryland, which has voted for the winner every time save once in the last four decades. He also captured Florida's ten votes.

Ohio Conceded to Republicans

Ohio was conceded to Eisenhower shortly before midnight.

With 3416 of the state's 10,877 polling places counted Ike had a 171,500 vote lead. The count stood Eisenhower 623,346; Stevenson 451,834.

A spokesman for the Volunteers for Stevenson in Cleveland conceded at 10:35 p.m. CST.

The vote-counting was still far from complete, and the possibility remained that Gov. Adlai Stevenson would gain strength in later returns.

But at 11:20 p.m., eastern standard time, Eisenhower and his running mate, Richard M. Nixon, were leading in 34 states with 352 electoral votes—86 more than they needed to win.

Eisenhower was ahead in 20 states carried by Harry S Truman four years ago.

Stevenson held a slight lead over General Eisenhower in Illinois with one-third of the state's precincts reporting. Latest returns gave the Governor 1,052,295, while Ike had 905,337, and 2951 of the state's 9680 precincts reporting.

Eisenhower's power continued in the traditionally downstate Republican rural areas where he polled more

CIVIL RIGHTS MOVEMENT

The record of the Civil Rights Movement during the past three and a half decades testifies to the complexity of what is generally taken to be nationally accepted beliefs. Liberty versus equality, majority rule versus minority rights, and social order versus distributive justice came to the forefront during the 1950's and 1960's as major social issues. And, even though theoretically such beliefs are compatible, in the day to day life of the nation they often have proved to be diametrically opposed

Madison, during the debates preceding the ratification of the Constitution, observed that under a democratic form of government, the majority can manipulate government in such a way as to deny the very objectives of democracy to the to the minority. The so-called silent majority, a term coined by Richard Nixon but applicable to the dominant white population throughout most of this century, has directly fulfilled much of what Madison prophesised: "When a majority is included in a faction, the form of popular government . . . enables it to sacrifice to its ruling passion or interest both the public good and the rights of other citizens."[1]

The original argument for a republican form of government was predicated on the assumption that it would best prevent the majority from carrying out programs detrimental to minority populations. Institutionalizing behavior through republican structures and processes was based on the belief that neither moral nor religious motives could be relied upon as adequate controls over impassioned interests. Interestingly, the thrust of Dr. Martin Luther King's philosophy was predicated on just the opposite assumption—that an innate sense of human justice would, in the end, triumph over racism and prejudice. The history of the civil rights movement provided greater justification for Madison's concerns than for King's faith.

Much of the conflict inherent in the tensions between liberty and equality in particular is attributable to the fact that although the Supreme Court was given the power to render decisions favorable to a greater expression of both concepts, it was denied the ability to enforce those decisions. Throughout American history the judiciary has been by and large dependent upon the willingness or consent of the governed to abide by established laws and to concur with them both in letter and intent. To the extent that Supreme Court decisions have been acceptable to the majority and compatible with its values, they have been upheld and incorporated into the fabric of society; to the degree that they have run counter to the majority's perceptions of its interests, they have been thwarted.

The dilemma of enforcement was easily witnessed in the number of rulings which the Supreme Court had seen virtually ignored because of their widespread unpopularity, the persistence of governmental officials at the state and county levels in maintaining the status quo, and the complicated legislative provisions used in their circumvention. Between 1935 and 1950 eight major civil rights judgments had been rendered. Taken collectively, these decisions resulted in legal guarantees of the rights of Blacks in almost all major areas with the exception of public school desegregation. In transportation, two decisions provided for an end to dis-

The Warren Court *as it appeared in 1958. Seated from left to right, William O. Douglas, Hugo L. Black, Chief Justice Warren, Felix Frankfurter, and Tom C. Clark. Standing, from left to right, Charles Evans Whittaker, John Marshall Harlan, William J. Brennan, Jr., and Potter Stewart. It was the Warren Court's decision in the Brown versus Board of Education suit that said that "separate but equal" education facilities for Blacks and Whites were discriminatory.*

The Federalist Papers, Number Ten.

crimination and segregation in interstate travel; with respect to the judicial system, two judgments guaranteed Blacks the right to serve in jury trials and to vote in primary elections; in the area of housing, restrictive covenants proscribing residential sections of cities were prohibited; in the field of education, unequal advantages in higher education were outlawed on the basis of race, and White law schools were required to open their doors to Blacks; and, in similar decisions in two different cases, labor unions were ordered by the Supreme Court to discontinue the practice of barring Blacks from membership.[2]

Operationally, these rulings had little impact. The conditions which the Court's mandates had been designed to change were in fact maintained through the inability or the unwillingness of political and social systems to relinquish their firm hold on the status quo. When federal and state law conflicted, the latter usually prevailed. Recourse through the judicial process was cumbersome and expensive and frequently unsuccessful. When lower courts upheld rights guaranteed by the High Court's decisions, individuals profited, but the majority of people subject to violations continued to experience them.

Progressively, it became evident that theoretical and legal foundations for civil rights were inadequate as a means for transforming existing patterns of behavior. In the months preceding the Court's decision to hear a major case on public school segregation in 1954, the status of Blacks as second class citizens was abundantly evident. That their position had seriously deteriorated since the demographic changes following World War I was everywhere observable. Although federal law had made restrictive covenants illegal in housing matters, residential segregation prevailed in almost all major cities. In the educational system, segregated schools continued to be required by law in seventeen states, and the number of segregated public schools outside of the South had

[2] Respectively, these decisions were: *Mitchell v. U.S.* and *Morgan vs. Virginia, Norris vs. Alabama* and *Smith vs. Allright, Shelly vs. Kraemer, Gaines vs. Canada* and *Hurd vs. Hodge,* and, finally, *Sweatt vs. Painter* and *The Brotherhood of Trainmen vs. Howard.*

Three reactions from President Eisenhower upon hearing the decision of the Supreme Court in the Brown versus Board of Education case. These pictures were taken during news conference Eisenhower held in Washington, D.C.

skyrocketed in correspondence to residential separation of the races. In employment, jobs were becoming less frequently available to Blacks; when they were hired, their tenure was shortlived and their tasks were more often than not menial. Dependency on relief and welfare systems, massive incidences of crime and thwarted expectations produced an environment which was becoming increasingly volatile. In the summer of 1954, the hopes of many Blacks, including the leaders of the National Association for the Advancement of Colored People, resided with changes in the educational system which might offer Black students a realistic prospect for equality of opportunity, if not for equality itself.

Against this background, it is not surprising that the halls of the Supreme Court building were filled with reporters and spectators on the morning of May 17, 1954. Shortly after noon, all nine Justices entered the formal chamber, prepared to present their judgment in the *Brown versus the Board of Education* case. In order to assure that a full Court was in attendance, Justice Jackson had left his hospital room, where he was recuperating from a heart attack. In a departure from usual practice, and signalling the critical nature of the issue, reporters had not been provided with an advance copy of the ruling. The text of the decision was read by Chief Justice Earl Warren, indicating his agreement with the majority opinion. Instead of delivering a short, concise statement, Warren proceeded slowly and deliberately for over an hour, detailing justifications for the decision which relied on sociological and psychological evidence not previously introduced into Supreme Court rulings.

The basis for the judgment resided in the Court's interpretation of the Fourteenth Amendment in general and specifically in the phrase ''nor shall any state deny to any person the equal protection of the laws . . .'' This dictum had been at the center of civil rights controversies since Reconstruction and to date there has been no clear-cut interpretation of its actual application. Importantly, as it was originally involved, the clause prohibited state action, but not private action urelated to or without the direct support of governmental officials within the state. Consequently, a necessary predicate to the issuance of a federal court order to apply the protection within state borders was the finding of some evidence of *de jure* violations. Also the precedent for termination of public school segregation was unavailable. The Supreme Court had conscientiously avoided the topic on a number of occasions and the only clear historical basis for the current case, from a Constitutional perspective, resided with the 1896 *Plessy versus Ferguson* case which had ordained the doctrine of ''separate but equal.''[3] In short, the implications of the *Brown versus the Board of Education* decision involved for the first time the fundamental issue of States' rights to enforce racial separation.

The approach of the Warren Court in dealing with the Brown case went beyond the scope of the legally entangling controversies of the Fourteenth Amendment and directly to the center of the issue at stake: the compatibility of separation and equality as operational concepts and practices in Amercian society. Weighing a variety of evidence not generally introduced in judicial decision-making processes, the Supreme Court unanimously concurred in overturning the 1896 decision and applying it to public school segregation.[4] The Chief Justic announced to the crowded chamber and to the American public that: ''To separate Negro children from others of similar age and qualifications solely because of their race generates feelings of inferiority as to their status in the community which may affect their hearts and minds in a way never to be undone . . . We conclude that in the field of public education the doctrine of 'separate but equal' has no place. Separate educational facilities are inherently unequal.''[5]

The ruling applied to all states and to the District of Columbia, requiring an end to public school segregation. The Court proceeded to instruct all participants to begin to prepare arguments as to the timing and implementation of the decision which it would hear during the ensuing Fall session.

To characterize the decision as a landmark ruling is not out of line. In the year it was handed down, a total of seventeen states, plus Washington, D.C., required public school segregation by law. In four other states, segregation was permitted though not forced. Altogether, the decision directly and immediately affected twelve million students. The initial reactions of state and school district authorities varied according to geographical location and historical background and were not particularly surprising. In border states and in Kansas and Oklahoma, governors and superintendents of schools stated with relative calm that the required changes could be made and that committees would be constituted to study plans for desegregation. In the North and West, public officials expressed relief that attention had been directed exclusively at *de jure* segregation, since the conditions of racial separation in schools in those regions were a product of *de facto* segregation and they were thus exempt from the

ruling. In Southern states, the reactions ranged from extremely reluctant indications of a willingness to comply to forthright charges that the Court had acted unconstitutionally and that its mandate would be refused. After studying the full opinion of the Court, Governor Stanley of Virginia agreed to call representatives from state and local agencies together to explore methods of compliance which were acceptable to residents of the state. In Texas, Governor Shivers told the press that he would comply but that he was convinced that it would take years. South Carolina's Governor Byrnes threatened to carry out plans to close all public schools within the state in order to continue segregation, and Georgia's Senator Richard Russell argued that the decision was a flagrant abuse of judicial power. Governor Talmadge concurred, issuing a press release charging that Georgia was prepared to map out a program which would ensure the continued and permanent segregation of the races.

The Supreme Court, in view of these reactions and in light of the difficulty of implementing previous major decisions in civil rights, set a flexible schedule for compliance in its Fall session. Warren instructed District and lower courts and school districts to evaluate their own situations and study administrative problems inherent in the transformation process. Additionally, the Court ordered them to take whatever steps were necessary toward a ''prompt and reasonable start'' in carrying out the Brown decision ''with all deliberate speed''as soon as was ''practicable.''[6]

Reluctantly supported by President Eisenhower, who was inclined to believe that integration was already moving at an appropriate pace, the demands of the Court began to be carried out. At his direction, all segregated schools in the nation's Capitol were desegregated immediately. Over the next several months, Kentucky, Oklahoma, West Virginia, Maryland, Arkansas, Tennessee and Delaware reported partial integration in 350 school districts. Elsewhere, however, the picture was less than encouraging. School districts in Virginia and the Deep South echoed their governors' earlier words and hastened to devise long and complicated measures which were designed to produce entrenching Court battles and delay, if not preclude, the implementation of the decision. Method upon method was drawn up and passed by state legislatures for the purpose of circumventing compliance with the Court's order to desegregate.

Simultaneously, a number of activities within Southern White society began to re-emerge. The Ku Klux Klan, which had been largely inoperative for some time, experienced an almost overnight resurrection. White Citizens Councils began to organize to resist desegregation, and the FBI reported a dramatic increase in handgun sales, particularly Southern state sales which in some communities were up as much as 400 percent. Volatile rhetoric, random violence, and massive threats spread rapidly and extensively. White militants vowed to maintain the status quo regardless of the cost—a price which was to prove in the months ahead to be extremely high.

On the other side, Blacks were once again encouraged by the judgment of the High Court, and the National Association for the Advancement of Colored People expressed openly its enthusiams for the victory achieved in the decision. In fact, the 1954 ruling marked the high point in the organization's long and tedious career with the judicial system for equality of Blacks through litigation. Voicing confidence that school

---

[3] It is important to note that this decision related to separate facilities on public means of transportation and not in educational facilities, although it set the precedent for separation by law in a substantial number of areas of life.

[4] Among the evidence introduced were a number of studies by sociologists and psychologists, including Gunnar Myrdal and Kenneth Clark who had written extensively and authoritatively on the mental development of Black children.

Brown v. Topeka Board of Education

[6] *Brown v. Topeka Board of Education II*, 349 U.S. 294 (1955). The decision made occurred almost exactly one year after the original judgment had been rendered.

desegregation would soon become a reality, the NAACP anticipated prematurely that all aspects of society would, in the foreseeable future, be witness to integration. With considerably less optimism and with convictions equal to those of the Southern Whites, another group was expanding rapidly, however. During the winter of 1954-1955 the Black Muslims, with their gospel of Black separatism and retaliatory violence, were attracting members and sympathizers in Northern ghettos in numbers previously unanticipated. The contrast between and within Black and White organizations in both the North and the South left little doubt that the accomplishment of desegregation would be expensive in terms of violence, manpower, and values.

The first major event to signal the incidents to come occured in Tuscaloosa, Alabama. Represented by Thurgood Marshall, who had received extraordinary prominence as a leading attorney in civil rights, a young Black woman announced her intention of enrolling in the State University. After three days of demonstrations, the Board of Trustees presented Autherine Lucy and her legal counsel with a telegram at the Registrar's Office stating simply that ''For your own safety and the safety of the students and faculty members of the University, you are hereby suspended from classes until further notice.'' Marshall quickly petitioned the Federal District Court and the suspension was lifted. In response, and supported by scores of angry protesters, the Trustees reconvened and ordered her permanent explusion. Again, the Federal court system was available and the prospects for a second favorable action were assured. However, it was equally obvious that the prospect for violence in general, and for Ms. Lucy in particular, had heightened to the point where such a judgment would, in all probability, lead to her murder. Taking this into direct consideration and weighing the anticipated gains to be made by her admission under the circumstances, Marshall and his client withdrew the petition.

The first murder following the Brown decision occurred in Greenwood, Mississippi, in August, 1955. Emmett Till, a fourteen year old Black from Chicago had traveled South to visit relatives. Rumors soon spread that he had insulted a White woman. In response, three men, two of whom were later identified, dragged the boy from his relatives' home and drowned him in a nearby river. Federal agents brought the two men to trial, but they were acquitted by an all-White jury. Later, they were charged with kidnappping by a United States attorney, but an all-White Grand Jury failed to bring in an indictment and the case was permanently closed. The pattern was to be repeated on numerous occasions over the decade.

On December 1, 1955, new course of action was initiated. As a result of the treatment of a Black woman who refused to give up her seat on a Montgomery bus, a city-wide Black boycott of public transportation was initiated. The strength of the boycott, consisting of seventy-five percent of the passengers, forced major changes in the company's policies, but not without serious disagreements and antagonisms. The segregationists, led by W. A. Gayle, the mayor of the city, confronted the leader of the Blacks, a young, twenty-six year old clergyman named Martin Luther King who had recently come to Alabama from Harvard University where he had received a Doctoral degree. The philosophy of the boycott, through King's interpretations, became as signifiicant as the action itself. Speaking from the pulpit of his church he declared that: ''This is not a tension between the Negroes and Whites. This is only a conflict between justice and injustice. We are not trying to improve Negro Montgomery. We are trying to improve the whole of Montgomery. If we are arrested every day; if we are exploited every day; if we are triumphed over every day; let nobody pull you so low as to hate them.''[7] This was the formal beginning of the movement of passive resistance—a movement which would

[7]*The New York Times*, December 20, 1955. This speech reflected the attitude of a number of leaders in the National Association for the Advancement of Colored People and the specific philosophy of Dr. King's, which was based on the teachings of Ghandi in particular and other subscribers to passive resistance in general.

The push *for complete civil rights equality for all Americans in the late 1950's generated a new interest in the Klu Klux Klan in certain sections of the country. Here the Klan conducts a meeting with the ominous burning cross in the background.*

Kentucky National Guardsmen *escort a Black youth to school in Sturgis, Kentucky in 1956. Hundreds of scenes such as this were repeated throughout the South following the Brown versus Board of Education decision, as southern politicians at first refused to acquiesce to the Federal government's attempts to end segregation in public schools.*

characterize Civil Rights for the decade. King was arrested and convicted, but later freed, and the movement had gained substantial momentum. After a year of boycotts, King had become a national celebrity and Alabama had been dealt a severe blow. Public transportation within the city was integrated and the first viable step towards desegregation in the Deep South had been taken.

The fact that the boycott had been successful and that it represented a legitimate political activity is important to an understanding of the Civil Rights Movement as it progressed into the late 1950's and early 1960's. Even though the move to direct action in the streets brought protests out of the courtrooms and into the general society, substituting what was called "creative disorder" for litigation, the tactics remained legitimate within the American political order. Inherently, the strategies of the NAACP, The Urban League and other established organizations represented an on-going faith in the ability of the Federal government to deal effectively with civil rights issues. Moreover, both the leadership and the rank and file promoters of passive resistance shared Dr. King's belief in an innate, human sense of justice and morality which they believed would ultimately prevail over racism and prejudice. Nonviolence was cast as a philosophical issue rather than a tactical or strategic question, and King's famous words "We shall overcome!" were exemplary of the prevailing attitudes held by the majority of Black civil rights activists in the immediate post 1954 decision years.

Increasingly, the activities of formal Black organizations took on a moderate tone. The NAACP, the Urban League and the Southern Christian Leadership Conference progressively focused their attentions on explicit and customary forms of racism in the South, and their tactics on legal reform and their aspirations on full integration and assimilation into American society. Against a background in which discrimination continued to prevail and change, the strategies of nonviolent resistance began to lose their appeal among a growing segment of the Black community. The more middle-class and interracial the formal organizations became, the more popular counter-organizations seemed to be. In the Northern ghettos, Elijah Muhammad and the Nation of Islam gained widespread support among a segment of the Black community which reacted unfavorably to the moderate activities of the established organizations. Focusing on Black nationalism and separatism, the Black Muslims, under the leadership of Malcolm X, offered a direct challenge to the integrationist, pacifist approach of other Black groups. Ideologically positioned between these extremes were two other emerging organizations—the Student Nonviolent Coordinating Committee and the Congress on Racial Equality. Activists in both SNCC and CORE were by and large both younger and more militant than their counterparts in the NAACP and the SCLC, but more tempered in their objectives than Black supporters of Islam. The events of the late 1950's and early 1960's further fragmented the civil rights movement because it was becoming abundantly evident that the strong protective action expected of the Federal government was not forthcoming.

White Southern terrorism, as exemplified by the murder of Medgar Evers, of four Black childern in a dynamited church in Birmingham, of three civil rights workers in Mississippi, and of many others in the early 1960's was not accompanied by a willingness on the part of the Federal government to take an active stance in guaranteeing the protections it claimed were due all citizens of the United States regardless of color. Throughout the South, civil rights workers met with greater and more violent resistance. Freedom riders were beaten by mobs in Montgomery, demonstrators were clubbed in Birmingham and Selma, and voting-rights organizers throughout the South were victimized by local officials as well as by angry crowds. It is not surprising, then, that activists in the South were becoming increasingly disillusioned. In the North and West, conditions worsened, and by the mid-1960's it was easier to manipulate the processes of government to maintain the status quo than it was to enforce the laws which required change.

Still, the federal government moved in the direction of constructing further laws—this time in the form of Congressional legislation—to alter the existing situation. During the summer of 1963, President Kennedy proposed a comprehensive measure, including a section outlawing discrimination in public accommodations. Five days after his assassination, President Johnson, in his first address to Congress, urged the passage of the bill as the best memorial to his predecessor. The House of Representatives passed the Act late in February, after nine days of debate. This was a record for the House in acting expeditiously. On June 10, after almost three months of a Senate filibuster which was terminated, again historically, by involving cloture to cut off debate, the President was given the Civil Rights Act of 1964 for signature. The most comprehensive piece of Civil Rights legislation to date was signed into law on July 2.

The principal provisions of the Act fell into six categories: racial discrimination in public accommodations which affected interstate commerce was prohibited,[8] discrimination

---

[8] This provision included hotels, motels, restaurants, cafeterias, lunch counters, gas stations, motion picture houses, theaters and sports arenas.

on the basis of race, color, sex, religion or national origin by employers or labor unions was banned, voting registrars were barred from adopting different standards for White and Black applicants, the Attorney General was permitted to bring suit to enforce desegregation of public accommodations and individuals were allowed to sue for their rights under the Act, the Executive branch of the Federal Government was given the right to halt the flow of public funds to public or private programs engaging in discrimination, and the life of the Civil Rights Commission was extended—along with the creation of a Community Relations Service to conciliate racial disputes and an Equal Employment Opportunity Commission to enforce the fair employment section of the Act.

Despite the passage of this bill, conditions in 1964 had deteriorated substantially. The results of the Brown decision were minimal, even though the Court had ruled on it a decade earlier. Eighty percent of all Black students in the first grade were attending schools which were between ninety and one hundred percent Black. In the South, Black students continued to attend exclusively Black schools in almost every instance. The Court began to reconsider its early phrase designed to enforce its decision, but it was not until 1968 that the words "with all deliberate speed" were replaced with the single dictum, "immediately." In states which were generally regarded as somewhat liberal, residential segregation persisted and efforts to codify separation of Blacks from Whites through democratic procedures were attempted. In California, a few months after the passage of the 1964 Civil Rights Act, voters turned out two-to-one in favor of a State constitutional amendment which would provide them as property owners with complete freedom to sell or rent to anyone they chose.[9] The amendment was sponsored by the California Real Estate Association and was in direct conflict with the provisions of the Supreme Court and the intent of the legislation which had been passed in the Civil Rights Act passed by Congress. Proposition 14, designating the amendment, was generally referred to as the anti-forced housing proposal. It clearly reflected the concerns of Californians in protecting what they considered individual liberty—the right to refuse to sell property to Blacks. The Supreme Court overturned their decision in 1967 on the basis that it was in direct conflict with the Fourteenth Amendment.[10]

Employment practices reflected similar denials of equality of opportunity, much less equality per se. Title VII of the 1964 Civil Rights Act prohibited racial discrimination by employees and thus covered an estimated seventy-five percent of the national labor force. To enforce this statute, a five-member Equal Employment Opportunity Commission (EEOC) was created. In the first three years of its existence, the Commission received a total of 28,537 complaints. Of these, only 882 were dealt with in conciliation and a mere 112 were successfully resolved. According to the chairman of the EEOC, approximately eighty percent of the complaints were valid—they simply were never processed, completed, or referred for conciliation.[11] In short, the law designed to terminate discrimination in employment practices was, during the 1960's, obscured by a lack of reasonable enforcement.

In virtually all dimensions of life, the Black population in the first half of the 1960's was experiencing increasing deprivation. In 1966, the median income of Black families was only fifty-eight percent of the White median income. The purchasing power of Blacks was declining even faster, and the gap between the two groups has widened substantially in the preceding twenty years. Annually since 1954, the unemployment rate was continuously above six percent—a cut-off point which is used as a signal of serious economic difficulties when it is prevalent for the entire work force. Progressively, the number of Blacks dependent upon welfare assistance had increased to a point where one in every seven received aid.

Malcolm X, *a leader in the Black Muslim organization, holds up a copy of* Muhammad Speaks, *newspaper of the all-Black sect. The Black Muslims were one of the most extreme Black groups to rise to prominence during the Sixties.*

The most liberally enshrined features of democracy had served to block aspirations to equality. Local rule, referendums, trade unionism, the jury system, and neighborhood school systems had proven to be the means through which democratic procedures resulted in anti-democratic ends. To complete the irony, the most elitist institution of the government, the Supreme Court, was for a time at the forefront of the quest for egalitarian principles and practices—for which it came under considerable populist attack. The recognition that civil rights laws would not suffice to bring Blacks into full equality in American society furthered the search for more intractable causes of disadvantage in political and economic institutions. Liberals, bureaucrats, and academics came under fire and their motives became increasingly suspect. Faith in the political process and especially in the traditional alliance between Blacks and the liberal elements of the Democratic Party suffered a severe blow in the failure of the Party to seat the Mississippi Freedom Democratic Party delegation at the 1964 convention. The MFDP represented a rejection of White exclusionary practices in Southern politics and a fundamental belief that the Democratic Party subscribed to the ideal of equality. The Party's offer to seat two of the delegates along with the regular Mississippi delegation climaxed the growing disillusionment of Blacks with White liberals, with democratic processes, and with existing political institutions.

Shortly after the election of Lyndon Johnson to the Presidency, Black militancy was catalyzed by the assassination of Malcolm X. Murdered in upper Manhattan's Audubon Ballroom on February 21, 1965, by fellow Blacks, he had just reached the apex of his career. His assassination reflected the

[9] Proposition 14 was designed to overturn the Rumford Act which had been passed by the State legislature and signed into law on October 20.

[10] *Reitman v. Mulkev*

[11] *EEOC, Third Annual Report* (Washington, D.C., 1969)

depth to which divisions among Black militants had plunged and the extent to which violence was becoming an accepted means to achieve political ends. Shortly thereafter, the first of a series of major race riots exploded in Harlem, followed by multiple demonstrations and murders in the South. Almost simultaneously, Martin Luther King called for a freedom march from Selma to Montgomery to dramatize the voting rights issue—a matter which had clearly not been settled by the Civil Rights Act of 1957, which had been specifically designed to provide for the practical enfranchisement of Blacks throughout the country. The contrast in activities paralleled the differences between factions of the Civil Rights movement. King persisted in emphasizing nonviolent means of working within the system, condemning Blacks who engaged in violent actions. His efforts often led to results which were positive within the scope of his objectives. In March, he spearheaded a fifty mile trek from Selma to Montgomery that culminated in the passage of the Voting Rights Act later in the year, which strengthened the earlier provisions of the 1957 Act.[12] Frustrated with his moderate tactics and anticipating the eventuality that the Act would have minimal ramifications, however, the more militant groups in Northern and Western ghettos expressed increasingly volatile concerns. In the midst of summer heat and violent police confrontations, the decade's most massive riots exploded.

The first major riot occurred in Harlem and the second and most dramatic in the Watts district of Los Angeles. On August 11, during a brutal heat wave in Southern California, a Highway Patrol officer stopped a young Black man on suspicion of drunk driving. It seemed low-key and typical of the activities which occurred in Watts—an area which was ninety-eight percent Black and had a population density of 27.3 people per acre. Of the 205 men on the police force which regularly patrolled the district, only five were Black and tensions had increased as animosities toward White officers grew. Shortly after the Black youth was stopped, a crowd began to form. By 10:00 p.m., the spectators had been transformed into a mob and other officers arrived. The famil-

Dr. Martin Luther King *as he preached from the pulpit, exhorting his followers to urge the American government to abandon what he once termed the "reckless adventure in Vietnam." Although King rose to prominence as a leader in the civil rights struggles in the early Sixties, within three years he had expanded the scope of his peaceful resistance campaign to include demonstrating for an end to the Vietnam war.*

iar stages of riot began to escalate and the police sealed off eight blocks by 11:00 p.m. In the midst of violent assaults on property within the area, police tightened security but were unable to constrain the rioters. Two hours later, rioters broke free of the cordon and, two thousand strong, spread through the streets vandalizing property, waylaying strangers and looting stores. For a day, the violence subsided and then on Thursday evening the riot erupted again. This time the violence approached the level of insurrection. Dick Gregory drove through Watts with a bullhorn, trying, unsuccessfully, to convince the rioters to cease their activities and restore order. He was shot in the leg and taken to the hospital. Later, a wedge of police officers cleared the darkened streets and announced that the riot was over and the situation was under control. The announcement was premature by four days.

On Friday morning, two White salesmen were attacked in the first incident of daytime violence. By midmorning, a policeman had wounded a Black looter. Governor Brown's office was called, but he was in Greece; the Lieutenant Governor granted a request from the Los Angeles police chief for National Guard troops and the first contingent

Scenes such as this *were a common sight in certain cities in the South as racial confrontations flared in the Sixties. Here a bus carrying "Freedom Riders" outside Anniston, Alabama, burns. The riders, who were testing bus station segregation in the South, escaped injury in this incident.*

[12] The 1957 Voting Rights Act had been a compromise which, although it was the first major piece of such legislation since 1875, had minimal results. The 1965 Act suspended literacy tests and gave the Civil Service Commission power to appoint federal examiners to enroll voters.

reached Watts that afternoon. More than 5,000 rioters were roaming the 150-block area, firing buildings with Molotov cocktails and ambushing firemen who answered the calls. Watts had its first fatality that evening when a policeman was shot in the stomach. Three other deaths quickly followed and National Guard troops entered the district in increasing numbers, with bayonets attached. Their way was illuminated by hundreds of fires; their path was blocked by looters.

The next morning, snipers began firing at and killing National Guard soldiers and police officers. The number of soldiers increased to 14,000 and a curfew was imposed on a forty square mile area. Early Wednesday morning, thirty-five Blacks were arrested after a shoot-out in a Black Muslim mosque. The violence ended a few hours later and order was restored.

The devastation of the Watts riot was historically unprecedented. Thirty-four people were killed, 898 were injured and four thousand were arrested. The damage to property was estimated at forty-five million dollars. Moreover, riots were triggered elsewhere at the same time. In the West Side of Chicago, a firetruck was overturned and riots exploded for two nights. In Springfield, Massachusetts, the National Guard was called to bring order to a rioting city. By the end of the summer, urban violence had quieted but the pattern was not to end. A year later, riots occurred in a dozen major cities in the United States. By the end of 1966, the death toll was seven, with over forty-three injuries and 3,000 arrests. The total damage to property was over five million dollars. Clearly, the extent and degree of violence in 1966 was substantially less than it had been a year before, or even in the Watts riot alone. Nonetheless, the decrease in the magnitude of riots did not signal their termination as a political tactic.

View from the top *of the Lincoln Memorial of the half million demonstrators who converged on Washington, D.C. in December, 1963, to protest the government's failure to pass new legislation giving full civil liberties to every American. Many famous Americans from different backgrounds joined with the demonstrators for one of the largest and most effective public protests in America's history.*

Nor did it appease Black militants who continued to raise the call for Black Power—a term which was becoming increasingly prevalent, even though it was rigidly opposed by the NAACP and the Southern Christian Leadership Conference.[13]

In 1967, riots in Newark and Detroit were even more destructive than the 1966 riots had been. During the Detroit riot, President Johnson appeared on national television to make a plea for the restoration of order and to announce that he had appointed a National Advisory Commission on Civil Disorders. In recognizing that in a very real sense urban riots were bound up in the civil rights protest and were not random acts of violence triggered spontaneously, the President stated that "the only genuine, long-range solution for what has happened lies in an attack—mounted at every level—upon the conditions that breed despair and violence." Conditions did not change, however, and the attempts of both the moderate Black leadership and the Federal government to reduce violence and to alleviate the conditions which produced it were in vain.

Martin Luther King, Jr., was assassinated on April 4, 1968, following a rising incidence of civil disorders during the first three months of the year. In the aftermath, violence

[13] The term was originally coined by Stokely Carmichael and opposed by King, Roy Wilkins and other moderates.

President Johnson *addressing a joint session of Congress, told the legislators in 1965 that the time had come for effective action in implementing the recently passed and signed Civil Rights Law.*

President Lyndon Johnson, *with Senate Minority Leader Everett Dirksen, left, and Vice-President Hubert Humphrey, behind Johnson, looking on, signs the 1964 Civil Rights Bill. The bill was the first significant civil rights legislation to be passed by Congress in more than one hundred years.*

accelerated at an unprecedented rate. In the ensuing three weeks after King's death, there were nearly as many disorders as had occurred in all of 1967. There were more arrests and more injuries, more National Guard and Federal troop commitments to cities and almost as much property damage. Major riots erupted in Washington, D.C., Chicago, Baltimore, Kansas City (Missouri) and Wilmington (Delaware). In these cities there were 32 deaths and 2,913 reported injuries. Elsewhere, racial violence of some degree of seriousness occurred in 36 states and at least 138 cities. In Wilmington, Federal troops, enforcing a series of harsh anti-riot and curfew provisions, occupied the city and re-there until January, 1969.

In the middle of summer, racial violence flared up again in a number of cities. Although there was not a massive ghetto riot as such, violence in 1968 began earlier in the year than it had in the past and continued for a longer period of time. Importantly, however, there was an emerging trend which differed from the past in one especially significant way—in several militant Black organizations, leaders made direct and markedly successful efforts to restrain ghetto communities from violent actions. Blacks did not participate, except peripherally, in the Chicago Democratic Party Convention demonstrations and there were no accompanying riots in the Black neighborhoods of Chicago. Similarly, where opportunities for massive violence such as occurred in the Watts, Newark, and Detroit riots earlier, were available, they were bypassed. At least in part, this can be explained by the new level of massive official response which occurred in 1968. Further, there is evidence to suggest that the decline in the scale of riots coincided with an increase in more strategic acts of violence and a shift from general population protests to sporadic guerilla warfare in urban areas.

In July, for example, Cleveland police battled with armed Black militants and the resulting violence led to the death of three policeman. There were a number of attacks on policemen in Brooklyn in the later summer and in August two policemen were wounded by shotgunfire; in mid-September, a police communications truck was firebombed and two police officers were hit by sniper fire while they waited for a

Firemen *(in the background) stand amid debris and litter while trying to save burning structures during the infamous Newark, New Jersey, riots in July, 1967. The destruction from the Newark riot covered a mile long area.*

A California Highway Patrolman *stands guard over a group of Blacks outside a looted store in the Watts area of Los Angeles. The rioting in Watts in the summer of 1965 was the first major racial disturbance to grow out of the civil rights movement of the Sixties.*

Police *try to seal off both ends of a city block in Detroit where racial violence also broke out in 1967.*

Two Black rioters *are marched at gunpoint to a police bus after their arrest near a Black Muslim Mosque in the Watts section of Los Angeles. Armed confrontations between police and Blacks intensified during the mid-Sixties.*

Aerial view *of the firebombed businesses and homes during the height of the racial unrest in Detroit in 1967. As was the case in most other riots in major American cities during this period, the National Guard was called in to restore order.*

Dr. Martin Luther King, *center, with Jesse Jackson, left, and Ralph Abernathy, on the balcony of the motel where he was staying. It was when King stepped out onto this balcony on April 4, 1968, that an assassin's bullet killed him.*

The Reverend Jesse Jackson *speaks from the floor of the National Black Political Convention in Gary, Indiana in 1972.*

traffic light to change. In Harlem, two policemen were shot and wounded by Blacks as they sat in their patrol car. Scattered attacks on police simultaneously occurred in several other cities throughout the United States.

In March, 1968, a Task Force of the National Commission on the Causes and Prevention of Violence had reported that some Black Americans had turned to violence because peaceful efforts had failed to bring social change; that official violence was too frequently overlooked; and, that America had had a history of violence or militant action used to bring about political goals. The National Advisory Commission on Civil Disorders (The Kerner Commission), concurred, adding in the most comprehensive study of the urban riots of the 1960's, that ''White racism is essentially responsible for the explosive mixture which has been accumulating in our cities since the end of World War II.'' The commission validated its finding by pointing out the existing pattern of racial discrimination, segregation and inequality in occupation, housing and education, making a distinction between individual racism and institutional racism. Importantly, the Report emphasized the latter.

Institutional racism was, and continues to be, described as subtle, often subconscious, patterns of behavior which originate in the operation of established and respected forces in society. In essence, such behavior had become so well institutionalized that the individual did not generally have to exercise a deliberate choice to operate in a racist manner. The rules and procedures of society and of the political and economic structures had already preconditioned the choice. Consequently, Supreme Court decisions and Congressional acts had only a minimal effect in changing existing attitudes and insuring equality. *De facto* segregation replaced *de jure* segregation, but the conditions of separation remained basically the same; Fair Employment regulations were established, but the extent of Black unemployment and underemployment were not altered to much of a degree; school integration was reinforced in Court decisions subsequent to

The funeral procession *for Dr. Martin Luther King on April 9, 1968. In the front rank are, left to right, King's daughter Yolanda, the Reverend A.D. King, King's second daughter Bernice, his widow Mrs. Coretta King, and his sons Dexter and Martin Luther King III.*

the 1968 reaffirmation of the Brown decision, but schools continued to reflect little change. In almost all instances, the web of institutional racism was so subtle and yet so firmly entrenched in the American way of life that democratic procedures could be effectively used to maintain inequality. Conformity to basic norms resulted in the perpetuation of Black political, economic and societal inferiority; majority rule produced a deprivation of minority rights; and, claims of individual liberty sanctioned group inequality. Additionally, during the Nixon Administration, Presidential speeches and statements by the Attorney General which were notably fallacious added to the insistence of the White majority that they were morally and historically right in adhering to existing patterns of behavior. One example stands out: the busing issue.

In 1971, the Supreme Court ruled in the *Charlotte versus Mecklenburg* case that busing was *one* reasonable means of integrating public schools. It did not, as was charged by the administration and by a large segment of the public, insist on busing as a major means, or, in fact, as a means at all. Nonetheless, the President appeared on national television in 1972 condemning busing for having reached "massive and unreasonable" proportions, urging a moratorium on all busing until the passage of the Equal Opportunity Education Act—a bill which was replete with means of evading public school integration. The "massive" busing to which President Nixon referred amounted to less than three percent of all school busing since 1954. Regular school busing, not used

for the purpose of integration, had increased forty-five percent during the same period and was applauded as being highly beneficial. Nixon was using the Office of the Presidency to sanction resistance to the implementation of national law—a device he had used before and would use again and again until his resignation was forced.

In the years subsequent to 1964, Congress had produced a series of Civil Rights laws which covered virtually all areas of political, social and economic life. By any reasonable standard this should have resulted in the attainment of equality under the law and a progressive move toward equality of opportunity. The federal government, or at least the Congress and the Supreme Court, had taken a firm stand on distributive justice, on the expansion of equality as a fundamental right of groups within the United States, and on the protection of minority rights against the tyranny of majority rule. Implementation and enforcement of these laws, however, fell under the jurisdiction of a reluctant Administration. Clearly the values of Congress and the judiciary were not those of the Executive office, or of the central cabinet member involved in civil rights—the Attorney General.

The replacement of Nixon with Ford as President of the United States did not have much impact for the development of the movement. In fact, civil rights as an issue was so monumentally overshadowed by the Watergate events that little attention was given to it. The problems remain, however. Conditions in central cities have deteriorated since 1974. Black concentrations in ghetto areas and inner cities have increased, along with unemployment, underemployment and welfare dependency. The causes of urban riots have not been ameliorated; rather, the means of official control have been strengthened. Despite the massive amounts of money provided to urban areas following the riots of the 1960's, there are few indications of significant change.

Martin Luther King:
I Have a Dream

One of the greatest orators of modern times, the Reverend Martin Luther King, Jr., used his verbal power as a crusader in the civil rights movement. The Baptist preacher from Atlanta, who headed the Southern Christian Leadership Conference, provided an example of nonviolence for his followers during the 1957 Montgomery bus boycott, the 1960 sit-ins, the 1961 "freedom rides," and the 1963 confrontation with Birmingham police. King was arrested and jailed in the U.S. on such charges as "loitering" in Montgomery (left), but he was regarded as a hero in other lands and in 1964 he received the Nobel Peace Prize. Despite threats on his life and the bombing of his home, he was still advocating nonviolence in 1968 when he was shot dead at age 39. On his tomb are words from a slave song: "Free at last, free at last, thank God Almighty I'm free at last."

THE ANTI-WAR MOVEMENT: A NEW LEAF

While the Civil Rights Movement represented a continuation of struggles which had started during Reconstruction, the anit-war movement was clearly a break with the past. The core of the movement originated in student protest—a phenomenon which had never before reached widespread proportions in the United States. With few exceptions, student activism had been isolated to localized events. Even the Civil Rights Movement had not inspired large-scale participation by students, although several worked during the summer months to recruit voters for registration and marched in demonstrations against governmental policies.

When student protest existed, it was confined in almost all instances to domestic issues. In 1863, for example, anti-draft riots preceeding the Civil War had more to do with ethnic rivalries than with principled objections to the war itself. During the Mexican-American War, Thoreau attempted to enlist the support of students by encouraging civil disobedience to what he considered an illegal war, but his efforts were largely in vain. In the First and Second World Wars, magnified patriotism generally obscured protests against military policies, including the bombing of Hiroshima and Nagasaki.

Students during the 1950's did not actively protest American intervention in Korea, even though the basis for the entry was somewhat questionable and the pursuit of the war was unprecedented in its limitation. When Marines were sent to Lebanon in 1957, hardly anyone noticed, much less protested. This was understandable in view of the impact of McCarthyism and the magnitude of repressive sanctions which were placed on individuals and groups who were charged with opposing the American government in any

conceivable way; in a more profound sense, however, it simply represented a continuation of what had been and what continued to be the norm.

Most of the antagonism against the Bay of Pigs invasion was aimed at the fact that it failed, not at the questionable legitimacy of the American government in perpetrating the action. The deployment of 55,000 United States troops to Thailand and the attempted overthrow of the neutralist Laotian government elicited almost no response from the student population or from the public at large. When 16,000 alleged military advisors were stationed in South Vietnam in 1963, very few people took notice at all. Even the first major indication of what was to come—the rise of the Free Speech Movement at the University of California, Berkeley,—did not raise the issue of American involvement in Southeast Asia.

In the late summer of 1964, a variety of Berkeley undergraduate and graduate students and junior members of the faculty met together to discuss means of expressing their grievance against a new university policy which prohibited on-campus solicitations for off-campus political and civil rights demonstrations. Despite considerable ideological diversity, the students and faculty participants were able to reach an agreement on one central principle:—the protection of freedom of speech. Pro-Goldwater students viewed the issue as the preservation of individual liberty; self-identified leftists saw it as a threat to support for the activities and movement they actively encouraged; others hoped it would provide an opportunity to bring the university into the mainstream of society and out of the ivory tower.

Regardless of motive, the students were able to consolidate their position under the leadership of Mario Savio, a twenty-two year old philosophy student from the East Coast. The week before classes began, speeches were made at Sather Gate, denouncing the administration's policy. Interest in the issue increased as the Fall term began and demands escalated. Negotiations were attempted, but agreements

This photograph illustrates the broadening base of support that the students were receiving for the protests against the Vietnam War. With the Capitol in the background the protestors move down Pennsylvania Avenue, their banners a clear sign of the growing support for the anti war movement in 1969.

could not be met. By the first week of December the first full-blown demonstration was in progress in front of Sproul Hall, the main administration building.

Hundreds of students entered the building, demanding an immediate revocation of the policy on free speech as well as a number of other campus policies. The police were called to restore order. By late afternoon, six hundred uniformed policemen arrived on campus, dragged students out of the building and placed several hundred of them under arrest. A total of eight hundred students had been active participants in the demonstration. In full view of the public, through widespread coverage by the media, the first massive protest against institutional authority had occurred. The magnitude of the event and the attention which it was given signalled a change in the direction of the decade. In an era which had been dominated by the activities of Martin Luther King, Malcolm X and other Black leaders and had been typified by

Mario Savio, *facing the camera in the foreground, was the leader of the Free Speech Movement at the University of California at Berkeley in the early 1960's. The Free Speech Movement was the beginning of the student protests which characterized the turbulent Sixties.*

sit-ins, boycotts and civil rights legislation, the Berkeley demonstration was fundamentally new—its focus was civil liberties, not civil rights; its target was "the establishment."

The Students for a Democratic Society moved into prominence and turned their attentions toward the increasing American military commitment in Southeast Asia. Shortly after the Berkeley events, the SDS called for a march on Washington to protest the escalating war effort. The march was scheduled for April, 1965. Six weeks after the announcement was made by SDS leaders, Johnson publicly announced the bombing of North Vietnam.

American public opinion continued to favor the Administration's policies, approving the bombing by 83 percent. Nonetheless, it was becoming increasingly clear that the public as a whole saw very little, if any, prospect for an outright victory. The pattern of Korea lingered in the subconsiousness of the country—seventy-five percent said that they would favor a negotiated settlement of the sort agreed upon in that conflict.

In the White House, opinions on the utility of the bombing were divided. Although the Joint Chiefs of Staff generally favored it, the CIA indicated strongly that they believed it would not improve the American-South Vietnamese situation. Body counts were the most frequent indicator of the course of the war, but it was abundantly clear that very little was changing. Frustrations occurred at two extremes: those who wanted an immediate escalation of ground force commitments argued that this was the only means of crushing the enemy, while those who favored a decrease in activities stressed the possibilities for a negotiation without increasing the United States' military presence. The President openly sided with the first group, and progressively eliminated the second from the ranks of his counsel.[1]

While Johnson and his advisors met in the White House to

University of California *at Berkeley students watch deputy sheriffs march off campus following the arrest of student protestors. In this particular demonstration 76 protestors were arrested after they refused to vacate Moses Hall on the campus. Police and students clashed often during the first half of the Sixties.*

discuss the deteriorating situation in Saigon, on April 15, twenty thousand anti-war demonstrators gathered in the streets outside. The protest was the first nationally visible attack on the Administration's policies. The SDS was catapulted into prominence as the central expression of the anti-war movement and the President's position hardened. The protestors openly indicated a willingness to be reconciled with the government if certain basic questions could be satisfactorily answered. The questions focused directly on the explanation for American military presence in South Vietnam. The President continued to refer to the Geneva Accords of 1954, which, he claimed, "guaranteed the independence of South Vietnam." In fact, the Accords made no mention of South Vietnam and instead provided a timetable for the reunification of the northern and southern sections, of the country. The students knew it; progressively, they were becoming experts on the history of the area and on the legal dimensions of military involvement by the United States. When the Administration argued that American military presence was essential to provide the South Vietnamese self-determination, the statement did not seem credible. Premier Diem had explicitly refused to follow the election procedures established by the Accords; following his assassination, the new leadership followed the same pattern in refusing to comply with election regulations. The 1965 State Department White Paper omitted any reference to elections that year and applauded the former governments for not having taken part in elections which might have been a sham.

Claims by the Administration of massive North Vietnamese infiltration into the South also failed to ring true. In supporting its statement, the Defense Department could only produce biographical sketches of twenty-three "North Vietnamese prisoners"—seventeen of whom were, in fact, born in South Vietnam.[2] The most important revelation came with the President's announcement that American military escalation was justified because of a clear case of aggression by Hanoi. This charge lost its impressiveness when it was shown that the 16,000 military advisors who had been committed during the Kennedy Administration in late 1963 had been opposing a revolutionary movement which was at least ninety-eight percent indigenous to South Vietnam. In short, the credibility gap had been exposed.

On August 7, 1964, a decision had been made which was, a year later, becoming essential to the attractiveness of the anti-war movement. On that day, the Gulf of Tonkin Resolution was passed by Congress, authorizing the President to "take all necessary measures to repel any armed attack against forces of the United States and to prevent further aggression." Whether Congress had intended the President to be given free hand in the conduct of the war or not by passing the act, Johnson responded by claiming that he had been given the legitimate authority for his subsequent actions. Under-secretary of State Nicholas Katzenbach agreed, stating to the Senate Foreign Relations Committee that the Constitutional clause granting the Congress the right to declare war was "outmoded in the international arena."[3] In

Flags *of the First Brigade of the 101st Airborne Division are dipped in salute after arrival of the American paratroopers at Cam Ranh Bay in South Vietnam in 1965.*

Students on the streets *in front of the White House protesting the government's policies in Vietnam. Student protest against the Vietnam War grew out of the Free Speech and Civil Rights movements.*

fact, there was considerable precedent in foreign affairs for this claim. On 197 occasions, the President of the United States had, over the course of American history, committed troops to foreign lands without the express consent of Congress. By the middle and latter part of 1965, however, a number of Senators were beginning to express their deep concern over the President's interpretation of the resolution and their previous support for it. The ranks of the anti-war movement were beginning to be enlarged by it as well, as pacifists joined student activists in claiming that the conduct of the war was illegal—that it violated the Constitution, the United Nations Charter and the Geneva Accords.

Most of the activities in 1965 were characterized by moderation on the part of protestors. In the final month of the year, sit-ins, teach-ins, and a variety of peaceful demonstrations occurred across the nation. Typically, debate and discussion were encouraged. When acts of civil disobedience were committed, such as refusal to be inducted into the armed services, the consequences were paid by going to jail. And, such activities were not especially widespread. The SDS continued to be active, but nonviolent. In some instances, the organization was charged with being too moderate, as in the case of the refusal of the group as a whole to endorse a national program of opposition to the draft which was designed, above all, to broaden the status of conscientious objection. In the spring of 1966, their decision had its repercussions.

In the midst of a rapid escalation of military activities in Vietnam, and in the face of growing frustrations within the

[1] Among those who were transferred or eased out of the Government service were Roger Hilsman, Averell Harriman, Michael Forrestal, William Truehart and Paul Kattenburg. Others who protested, but remained, included George Ball and John Kenneth Galbraith.

[2] United States' State Department Publications, Far East Series, December 1, 1965.

[3] *Senate Congressional Record*, September 18, 1967 (S25834-35).

Stop the Draft demonstrators *fill the street in front of the Oakland City Hall protesting the conscription of American males for service in Vietnam. This scene, which occurred in 1968, is typical of the demonstrations which occurred in several major American cities in 1968.*

Demonstrators *line the balcony of Hamilton Hall on the campus of Columbia University during student riots on that campus in 1968. Students, often frustrated with the government's failure to end the war in Vietnam, often turned their anger and protests onto the college campus.*

Administration, General Hershey, the Director of the Selective Service System, announced that students would no longer be automatically exempt from military service. Student deferments would be terminated for those individuals whose class standings were poor or who had failed to reach a satisfactory level of performance as determined by the newly-devised Selective Service Qualification Test. Student protest increased proportionately. Students who had stood by the sidelines now found themselves actively demonstrating alongside militants in order to prevent their potentially required participation in the war.

SDS chapters demanded that information be withheld by authorities concerning the status of students' academic positions. At the University of Chicago, five-hundred students staged a sit-in which led to a three-day siege of the administration building. Similar activities occurred at the City Col-

lege of New York, Oberlin University, and the University of Wisconsin. The Chicago siege produced a result which was typical—it did not lead to punitive actions against students, nor did it have any immediate effect on the position of the administrators in complying with the Selective Service order. The major consequence of the campus demonstrations was to produce a nation-wide debate on the draft itself—a debate which for many students provided the impetus to refusing to cooperate with the draft as a means of resisting governmental policies in the war. For the SDS, these events provided a new strategic orientation and a turning point in its development. Attacks against the government ranged from specific cases of the conduct of the war to wholesale charges that the existing system, in total, was abhorrent.

In the Spring of 1967, scores of demonstrators throughout the nation protested the presence of the military, CIA, and Dow Chemical Company recruiters on campuses. Evidence that the South Vietnamese government was becoming increasingly repressive in its assaults on its own population were becoming more widely available. Of the ten regimes which had existed since 1963, none were opposed to imprisoning thousands of their own people for alleged political differences. Religious persecution, corruption, reluctance by the armed forces to take part in dangerous missions, press censorship, rigged elections, summary executions and an officially expressed eagerness on the part of the government to extend the commitment of American troops and financial assistance were becoming obvious characteristics of South Vietnam regimes.[4] Still, Congress continued to appropriate monies for the conduct of the war and the President and his staff continued to assure the American public that with another increase in the troop level the war would be closer to an end. Congressional participation reduced the impact of the charge that the administration was single-handedly waging the war, and the target of the protesters broadened to all branches of government despite growing dissent by a few members of the House and Senate. Arguments for approving appropriations ranged from genuine commitments to the Administration's stance to beliefs that such spending would avert a recession—which it apparently did prior to producing conditions of extreme inflation. It was becoming clear that Congress was not to be the institution to force the end of the war, even though it had that capability in its power of the purse.

By late 1967, support for the anti-war movement had broadened well beyond the confines of the campuses, although it was still students who received the greatest amount

[4] For further descriptions of the record of the Saigon regimes, see Jerome Skolnick, *The Politics of Protest*, pp. 44-45.

Columbia University students *use a bucket to haul up food and supplies to a window ledge of one of the campus buildings during the riots which occurred at Columbia in April, 1968.*

was held and actively supported by CORE and SNCC; the Black Panthers stated as a key element in their Ten-Point Program the importance of refusing to participate in military service.

The alliance between Blacks and Whites on the war issue was to prove fragile, however. The assassination of Martin Luther King, Jr., in April, 1968, signalled the split between the two segments of the population. Urban riots broke out in an unprecedented degree! Within three weeks more cities experienced riots than had occurred in all of the preceeding years, more injuries were sustained, more property damage was done, more Federal troops were called and more militant proclamations were issued. In that short period of time it became obvious to Blacks that their real interest centered in the Civil Rights Movement and not in the anti-war movement. Whites, and particularly White Students, continued to emphasize the importance of the war as the central issue.

Between January 1 and June 15, 1968, there were 221 major anti-war demonstrations on 101 college campuses. Nearly 40,000 students participated actively and according to polls taken during those six months, approximately fifty percent of the remaining students were sympathetic to the activists' demands. Buildings were firebombed, college administrators were jeered, obscenities were shouted at police officers stationed on campuses and in college communities, and demands for the complete withdrawal of American troops from Southeast Asia were intensified. In April, the month which had witnessed the most violent and extensive urban riots, students at Columbia University participated in the most massive demonstration since the Berkeley protest four years earlier. After occupying five buildings on campus for almost a week, students led by SDS leader Mark Rudd were demanding that the administration abandon its plan for the construction of a gymnasium—the original issue,—terminate all university contracts with defense-related agencies, and end the school's association with the Institute for Defense Analysis. The demands were not met and the hostilities continued. A thousand policemen were

of press coverage. A new activist group was formed—the Clergy and Laymen Concerned About Vietnam. In contrast to their relative silence during previous wars, clergymen became a prominent force in what was progressively being called "the peace movement." Partly because of the decline of abstract theology and partly because of the visible effects of the war on innocent people, the clergy became more and more involved in the protest against the Vietnamese war. Several well-known ministers, including Martin Luther King, Jr., William Sloan Coffin, Robert McAfee Brown and Phillip and Daniel Berrigan associated themselves with draft resistance. Sermons from the pulpit devoted increasing time to the issue of the war and as the movement progressed, the clergy would find itself increasingly alienated from the government.

Although Black student support for the anti-war movement had been divided because of the continuing emphasis on civil rights issues, there was a strenuous attempt made on the part of Black community organizations to encourage Blacks to resist induction into the armed forces on the grounds that there was no justification for the government to demand that they participate in a war when that same government refused to grant them equality at home. In Oakland, California, between October 16 and 20, *Stop the Draft Week*

Two protestors *raise their arms in a mock Fascist salute to Illinois National Guardsmen called in during the riots surrounding the Democratic Convention in Chicago in 1968. The rioting in Chicago marked a turning point in America's attitudes towards the Vietnam War.*

directed to the campus and given instructions to clear the buildings, using whatever means necessary. 698 students, almost exclusively White although there had been several Black participants, were arrested; 300 were injured by the police in what Archibald Cox was later to call "brutal and unprofessional conduct, which was not remotely commensurate with the activities of students involved in the occupation of the buildings,"[5] and, seventy-two students, including Rudd, were suspended from the college for a year. President Johnson's announcement, on the 31st of March, that he did not intend to run for re-election to the Presidency had not been sufficient to change students' minds—the central issue was no longer the role of the Chief Executive and the military, it had spread to all institutions of authority which represented "the establishment."

The President had made his announcement in the face of very telling evidence about the divisions of opinion in the country on the war issue. In the New Hampshire primary, a month earlier, Eugene McCarthy had surprised almost everyone by polling forty-two percent of the vote to Johnson's forty-eight percent. On the following Sunday, Robert Kennedy announced his candidacy. In the Wisconsin primary it became obvious that the President's campaign organization was disintegrating while the McCarthy campaign was becoming increasingly strong. Aimed almost exclusively at the war issue in the beginning, the McCarthy campaign was operating as a national poll on dissatisfaction of the war; the base of the anti-war movement had spread into the general public and was expanding. Americans who had been unwilling to participate in demonstrations or openly protest the Administration's policies were willing to express their concern at the ballot box.

Kennedy's campaign stressed the war issue, along with support of civil rights and concern for poverty in America. His ranks were filled with anti-war activists and sympathizers and civil rights promoters as well as a number of people who simply admired the Kennedy family in general and the role of Robert Kennedy in the Cuban Missile Crisis of 1962 in particular. Both Kennedy and McCarthy were running ahead of the President; their combined support indicated a shift of major proportions among the American public—no longer was protest against the war limited to a minority of students on college campuses.

Hubert Humphrey announced his candidacy for the Democratic nomination on April 27, but declined to run in most of the primaries which were taking place across the nation. Kennedy won in Indiana, defeating McCarthy by forty-two percent to twenty-seven percent. In Nebraska, he collected fifty-one percent of the vote to McCarthy's thirty-one percent. On Tuesday, June 4, Kennedy won the biggest of all of the primaries, California, by defeating both McCarthy and Humphrey. That same evening he was killed by an assassin's bullet as he left his campaign headquarters at the Ambassador Hotel in Los Angeles. Just three months after the murder of the major figure in the Civil Rights Movement, Martin Luther King, Jr., the major symbol of the anti-war movement was struck down.

While Richard Nixon calmly accepted the Republican Party's nomination in Florida, preparations of an unprecedented sort were being made in Chicago for the Democratic Convention. The tightest security ever used in the history of Mayor Daley's administration was assembled. A chain link fence, seven feet high, was set up around the International Amphitheater—the site of the convention. Manholes in the streets outside were sealed with tar. Eleven thousand policemen were put on twelve-hour shifts. Five thousand National Guardsmen were alerted and seventy-five hundred United States Army troops were airlifted from Fort Hood, Texas, with orders to standby. The city took on the tone of an armed camp.

Anti-war demonstrators *in San Francisco throb down Van Ness Avenue on their way to the Presidio to protest America's continued involvement in Vietnam. This demonstration occurred in 1969.*

On August 3, a week before the Convention activities formally began, members of the Youth International Party (the Yippies) arrived in the city and settled in Chicago's 1,185-acre Lincoln Park. Jerry Rubin acted as their leader and cautioned them against any acts of violence. On August 5, after two days of peaceful activities and orderliness in the Park, the Chicago police moved in and arrested twelve students for violation of the 11:00 p.m. curfew law. No one resisted arrest. The following day, two thousand young people were situated in the Park. Rubin again counselled strongly against any acts of violence. That same day he was arrested for disturbing the peace. The tensions of the authorities in the city mounted as more students and anti-war activists poured in. Officials expressed their belief that at least 100,000 "radicals" would arrive before the Convention got under way. At most, the actual figure reached twenty-five thousand, many of whom were far from what could be legitimately considered radical.

On August 7, the police launched a full-scale assault against the people in the Park, using tear gas and clubs to drive the demonstrators out. Twenty-one newspapermen were injured, along with numerous by-standers and demonstrators. There was minimal resistance on the part of the demonstrators. The following day, seventy priests and clergymen erected a ten-foot cross in a nearby park. Demonstrators sang "We Shall Overcome" and "The Battle Hymn of the Republic" as delegates in the convention hall listened

[5]Crisis at Columbia: Report of the Fact-finding Commission Appointed to Investigate the Disturbances at Columbia University. (Generally called the Cox Commission), 1968.

to the National Anthem. The conflict was clear.

On August 9, the situation reached a climax. Ron Dellinger, who was the official coordinator of eighty peace groups who were represented in Chicago, told eight-thousand demonstrators that they would begin a march in the city to more visibly express their sentiments against the war. He had received a permit from the city for the march, but immediately prior to its proposed starting time, the officials withdrew the permit and massive numbers of police officers moved in to disperse the crowd. In what was later called a "police riot", the most violent events of the period occurred—in the full view of millions of Americans who were watching the nominating process at the Convention on national television.

Inside the International Amphitheater, several hotel guests were arrested and injured by police who had mistaken them for demonstrators. Outside in the streets, tear gas was being used extensively and violent confrontations between the police and the protesters were rampant. While he watched his nomination being secured on the first ballot from the television in his hotel room, Humphrey began to experience the effects of tear gas being funneled in through the air-conditioning system by accident. Down the hall, in McCarthy headquarters, police stormed in, without a writ or a warrant, and attacked the occupants of the suite on the unsubstantiated assumption that rocks and other debris were being thrown out of the window and down onto the street below. The activities of the week and a half had resulted in a full-scale riot, in which it became clear that the Democratic Party was unmercifully split. Mayor Daley praised the work of the police and other law enforcement agents and was supported by millions of people who believed that law and order were substantially more important than the right to dissent; McCarthy and millions of other Americans expressed their horror at what had happened. The events would mark a critical point in American history.

In November, in the general election, Nixon became President of the United States by one of the slimmest margins in history. With 43.4 percent of the vote to Humphrey's 42.7 and Wallace's 13.5 percent, the difference between the two major candidates had been less than a seventh of a percentage point. Democrates retained control of Congress, but the key

Some of the reasons *for the anti-war movement in America during the Sixties. Here an American soldier, using mostly sign language, tries to communicate with his South Vietnamese guide during the early days of America's military presence in southeast Asia.*

office in terms of the war effort went to a man who had campaigned vigorously on the label of "law and order." Those anti-war demonstrators who had believed that the ballot box was an ineffective means of levelling dissent were soon to be proved tremendously wrong.

After Nixon's inauguration, a new wave of demonstrations flared up. This time, national moratoriums against the war were held. On May 15 ninety thousand protesters convened in Boston, twenty thousand in New York City, and twenty-two thousand in the Capitol. To date, 33,639 Americans had been killed in Vietnam—exceeding the total figure for the Korean War. The cost was running at over $25 billion a year. The injuries were monumental and the prospects for a settlement continued to be minimal. In the midst of all of these frustrations, Nixon announced the first phase of what

A peace demonstrator *is led away to jail by Chicago police during a disturbance in Lincoln Park in 1968. Police fought Hippies, Yippies, and other anti-war demonstrators throughout the summer of 1968.*

Members *of the Ohio National Guard line the campus center of Kent State University during campus disturbances there in 1970. In foreground is the burned out ROTC building. Behind building in upper left is the area where four students were killed by the National Guard.*

he had called his "secret plan for the termination of the war"—Vietnamization of the forces. In essence, Nixon intended to gradually withdraw American forces while at the same time strengthening the ARVN troops in an effort to encourage them to take on a greater role in the fighting. On June 8, the first American forces were withdrawn. Of the 550,000 stationed in South Vietnam and the surrounding areas, twenty-five thousand were given orders to return to the United States.

To anti-war demonstrators, this figure was not an indication of a major change in the direction of the Administration. On November 15, the second national moratorium was held in Washington. This time, 250,000 people attended and the protests continued for three days—quietly and peacefully. In groups of 40,000, demonstrators marched from Arlington to Washington, carrying cards with the names of American soldiers who had been killed and villages which had been destroyed. The marches were orderly; the cards were placed in a coffin draped in an American flag within view of the White House. Reserves of nine thousand army troops which had been alerted for the event were not called. The President remained inside, watching a football game and insisting that the demonstrators would have no influence whatsoever on him.

In Saigon, the response to Vietnamization was to be expected. The Thieu regime insisted that the United States increase its financial aid, provide more, not fewer, American troops and give the government more time to train its own forces. Unless its demands were satisfactorily met, the regime announced that it "could not take responsibility for the consequences."[6] Nixon insisted on continuing the process of Vietnamization, but announced that a minimum of two hundred thousand American soldiers would remain in South Vietnam indefinitely.

In an important way, the resignation of Earl Warren as Chief Justice of the Supreme Court during the same year marked a turning point in the history of the anti-war movement. The major accomplishments of the Court had resided in the restoration of civil liberties which had been severely damaged by the era of McCarthyism in the early 1950's. The appointment of Abe Fortas by President Johnson was blocked in the Senate and the way was cleared for the new President, Richard Nixon, to appoint the replacement. The President-elect had been highly instrumental in the anti-communist crusade and his concern with internal subversion had not subsided. Nixon was convinced that the anti-war movement was communist-inspired and controlled. Supported by FBI Director J. Edgar Hoover and his immediate colleagues in the White House, Nixon began a search for a Chief Justice who would share his concerns and translate them into judicial decision-making. The appointment of Warren Burger was accepted quickly by the Senate and soon thereafter the course of events began to change.

In April of 1968 a distinguished commission had been appointed by Johnson to investigate the basis for and effects of the anti-war demonstrations. The commission reported that "the First Amendment is meaningless unless dissenting individuals attempt to take advantage of the rights it affords. If such individuals do not make the attempt, it is true that there is no violence, no conflict, no overt repression of speech; there is also no freedom. . . In a democracy it should not require courage to defy authorities in order to express dissenting views."[7] By the same month a year later, it was clear that the new Administration differed in its interpretation of civil liberties. Nixon consistently urged the passage of legislation which was aimed at inhibiting the ability of individuals and groups to express dissent, even in a peaceful way. Lower courts were instructed to enforce new and often harsh anti-riot control measures; police officers were given greater latitude in dealing with protesters; and severe sentences were imposed on anti-war demonstrators.

Unknown to the American public, the Administration had been engaged in another war in Southeast Asia for over a year. The Air Force, under a veil of extreme secrecy, had been hammering away at communist bases in Cambodia. On orders from the White House, and without knowledge of Congress, B-52s had conducted 3,630 raids on jungle sanctuaries. The Joint Chiefs of Staff urged the President to commit infantry forces, but he refused, recognizing that Cambodia was a neutral country and that Prince Sihanouk would protest immediately. On March 18, while the Prince was out of the country, a coup occurred and Lon Nol was installed as the new leader. A well-known Rightist, the new premier was favorable to the entrance of American forces to defeat communists who were allegedly taking over villages in the eastern section of the country. Nixon made the announcement that a new phase of the war had begun and that this time an end to the war was in sight. His credibility, however, had reached an unprecedented low.

So great was the public outcry against this new involvement that the Congress resurrected the issue of its right to declare war and passed a resolution demanding the evacuation of all American troops in Cambodia and an end to air support there by July, 1970. On campuses, the reactions were so widespread as to eclipse all previous protests. By the end of May, 415 colleges had been disrupted. The first general student strike in the United States had occurred, and it was altogether spontaneous. At the end of the semester, 286 schools were closed; 129 others in forty-three states were reopened, but most of the classrooms were empty.

On the weekend of May 9-10, more than one hundred thousand students stormed the Capitol to protest the Cambodian excursion. In Wisconsin, a bomb exploded at the University's Army Mathematics Research Center, killing a physicist, wounding four others and doing six million dollars'

[6] *New York Times*, March 18, 1970.

[7] The April 27 Investigating Commission, "Dissent and Disorder," Chicago, August 1, 1968.

worth of damage. At predominantly Black Jackson State, in Mississippi, a confrontation between students and policemen resulted in tragedy when officers opened fire with buck-shot, machine guns and rifles, killing two students and wounding nine more. Manhattan construction workers marched into a crowd of anti-war demonstrators and were commended by the White House for their actions. And, then, in Kent, Ohio, the most telling event of the anti-war movement occurred.

Kent State University was the kind of school the President most admired. While other campuses experienced uphèaval over the Administration's war policies, Kent State students had no tradition of activism. Their major concerns focused on the President's favorite sport, football, and there were beer busts and other activities which had been reminiscent of campus activities in the late 1950's and early 1960's. Ironically, the trouble at Kent State began on a Friday night with a beer bust at a local bar. Several students decided to have a dance in the street and when an angry motorist headed for them, they climbed on the car, broke the windows and began to set fires in trash cans and smash store windows. The police were called and they drove the students back toward campus, using tear gas when a few refused. The events did not seem exceptional.

The next day, however, a few of the militants on campus petitioned the administration for a permit for a rally that evening. The approval was granted and about eight hundred students attended. The crowd chanted against the war and

Ohio National Guardsmen *move into rioting students on the Kent State campus in May, 1970. Smoke is tear gas which the National Guard had used earlier to try to disburse the students.*

shouted obscentities at student marshalls who had been enlisted to maintain peace; within a short period of time, the rally had been transformed into a full-scale demonstration. Lighted railroad flares were thrown through the windows of a one-story ROTC building and when firemen appeared they were pelted with rocks. A few students slashed the fire hoses and the building burned to the ground.

Without notifying the university administration, the mayor of the city appealed for help from the National Guard. Governor Rhodes responded by sending five-hundred soldiers, equipped with M-1 rifles, Colt revolvers, and tear gas. Calling a press conference, the Governor declared a state of emergency and announced that ''We're going to use every weapon of law enforcement to drive them out of Kent. . . They're worse than the Brownshirts, and the Communist element and also the night riders and the vigilantes. They're the worst type of people that we harbor in America.''[8] Rhodes was running in the Republican Senatorial primary which was scheduled for the next day. He had been trailing badly and the situation at Kent State seemed politically exploitable. As of late 1969, public opinion polls revealed that over ninety-percent of all Americans believed that college administrations should take a stronger stand on student disorders. Ninety-six percent of the Repubicans believed this, and this was the audience to which the Governor was appealing.

In Kent, the mayor was making inflammatory statements and Brigadier General Robert Canterbury of the National Guard was virtually inciting to riot. For several hours, the situation seemed under control, however, and classes re-

[8]*New York Times*, May 4, 1970.

sumed on Monday morning. The Guard remained on campus and at noon a thousand students gathered for a peaceful demonstration while another two thousand watched. Guardsmen shouted at them to disperse, claiming that they had no right to assemble. Students replied with jeers and gestures. Canterbury told reporters that the students were going to find out what law and order was all about. Major General Del Corso of the Guard, in full view of the troops, picked up a rock and hurled it at the demonstrators. At 12:15, two rows of Guardsmen fired tear gas cans at the crowd. A few students intercepted them and tossed them back, but they fell short of their target. Other students began to run from the area, pursued by troops. The students escaped but the tempers of the Guardsmen flared. What happened next is uncertain; there is evidence to suggest that a single bullet was fired and that a group of troopers decided after a conference to go ahead and fire on the students, but it was not conclusive.[9] What is certain is that troops reached the top of a slope overlooking the students, knelt down on their knees and aimed their rifles at the students who were over a hundred yards away—too far away to harm the soldiers. At 12:24 p.m., the National Guardsmen opened fire in a thirteen second salvo. Thirteen students were shot, four of them fatally. None of the students were militants; one was an ROTC cadet. None of the troops attempted to aid the students in the aftermath.

In the ensuing investigation of the tragedy, by three hundred FBI agents, the conclusion was clear. The Guardsmen had been in no physical danger and they had

[9]*The Scranton Commission*, Report on the Violence at Kent State University. There is also evidence to suggest that if a single person fired the initial bullet, it was not a member of the guard. One film of the incident indicated it may have been a member of the FBI.

[10]*New York Times*, May 18, 1970.

Demonstrators at Kent *cover their eyes to try to escape the effects of tear gas discharged at them by the Ohio National Guard during the campus riots in May, 1970. The National Guard fired into the unarmed students and killed four of them.*

conspired later to blame the incident on a threatening mob which had never existed. The Justice Department, under Attorney General Mitchell, declined to convene a federal grand jury and it was not until March, 1974, that eight indictments were handed down against the National Guard. Locally, the Ohio Grand Jury exonerated the Guard and indicted instead twenty-five students. Although none of the students was convicted, the local sentiment reflected Nixon's attitude on the subject—"the incident," he said, "should remind us once again that when dissent turns to violence it invites tragedy."[10]

The campus disorders in 1970 formed the key link in a chain of events which culminated in the decision to burglarize the Democratic National Committee's offices in the Watergate complex two years later. The President's insistence on external direction of the campus activities escalated; charges that the student demonstrations were clear-cut cases of communist influence pervaded the Oval Office and Nixon began to distrust even his most ardent supporters—CIA Director Richard Helms and FBI chief J. Edgar Hoover—who could not find evidence of such influence. Dissatisfied with their efforts, the President turned to illegal forms of behavior to locate evidence to substantiate his beliefs. The following spring, the New York *Times* began publishing Pentagon leaks about the military activities in Southeast Asia and the White House took on an increasingly tight lipped tenor.

On February 8, 1971, a new phase of the war was initiated. The White House authorized the commitment of American troops to the borders of Laos to protect ARVN regulars who were directed to cross the demilitarized zone, penetrate Laos along Route 9 and cut the Ho Chi Minh Trail—a path which was as wide as fifty miles in some places. The first reports claimed success, then disaster struck. The North Vietnamese attacked with tanks, heavy artillery, and rockets, destroying four of the best divisions of the South Vietnamese army. Infantrymen panicked and abandoned their positions and only the intervention of American air power prevented a complete disaster. At the end of a forty-five day campaign the South Vietnamese army had experienced thousands of casualties and roughly fifty percent of the forces were destroyed. Nixon appeared on national television, in early April, immediately after these events had occurred and been publicized, and stated that at last Vietnamization had succeeded.

The response from the anti-war movement was inevitable. On April 18, the Vietnam Veterans Against the War demonstrated on Capitol Hill and picketed the Supreme Court. On the 24th, a peaceful march was held in the same city by 200,000 protesters. A week later, the Peoples' Lobby filled the streets and demonstrated against the Selective Service System. By the end of the month the Mayday Tribe, as the new demonstrations were called, arrived in Washington to participate in the most massive protest ever—this time designed to bring the government to a standstill. On the evening of May 1st, 12,000 young people invaded the Capitol. Seven hundred police officers swinging riot sticks drove them into the streets. They dispersed, but two days later the largest confrontation in the history of the capitol began. The overriding instruction of the police, National Guard, and Army troops was to keep the traffic moving. To accomplish this goal, they broke up large concentrations of demonstrators with tear gas. Assault units hovered overhead in military helicopters. Seventy-two hundred arrests were made and in many cases those arrested were peaceful picketers and spectators. Altogether, over a four day period, 12,614 people were taken into custody where their civil rights were repeatedly violated. The Administration responded with high praise for the Washington Chief of Police.

Six weeks after the Mayday demonstrations, the New York *Times* carried the first installment of the *Pentagon*

Daniel Ellsberg, *center, former Pentagon researcher, who gave top secret papers concerning the conduct of the Vietnam War to the Press. Charges against Ellsberg were ultimately dropped when it was discovered that the Plumber's Unit, which had been involved in the Watergate break-in, had tried to get damaging information on Ellsberg by breaking into his psychiatrist's office.*

Papers, revealing the history of American involvement in Southeast Asia. Mitchell and Nixon agreed to go to Court to get an injunction against the printing of further installments on the ground that the material was violating governmental secrets. The *Times* was temporarily restrained, but the Washington *Post* picked up the story and carried it itself. The Supreme Court was enjoined, and it decided in a six to three vote that the press could continue to print the *Papers*. The nine judges handed down six opinions. Along with John Harlan, Nixon appointees Burger and Blackman were in the minority.

On June 28, Daniel Ellsberg surrendered to authorities in Boston and was released on $50,000 bail. The same day, in Los Angeles, he was charged with stealing government property and violating the Espionage Act. Six months later, twelve additional charges were leveled at him, including conspiracy. The indictments did not result in any convictions, but the trial was protracted and widely publicized.

During the same year, there were a number of other notable trials. Conspiracy continued to be a major means of attempting to apply legal sanctions to political dissidents. In 1968, William Sloan Coffin, Dr. Benjamin Spock and three others had been charged with conspiracy to resist the draft; they were acquitted after the U. S. Court of Appeals overturned a lower Court decision. In 1971, along with the Ellsberg trial, the Chicago Seven trial was underway. Demonstrators at the Chicago Convention had been charged by the District Court in Illinois with "crossing state lines in order to incite riot", a new provision included in the anticonspiracy laws passed in the wake of student demonstrations. After a long trial, the defendants were found guilty. But, with the Spock trial, the decision was overturned by a higher court. The pattern had been set, and within months there were several similar trials throughout the United States, including the nationally publicized Harrisburg Seven trial, the Evanston Four, the Seattle Seven and the Camden Seventeen.

At the same time, the most famous court martial of the era was underway. In March, 1968, Lieutenant William Calley led a platoon of American soldiers into the village of My Lai. They were under orders to "clear" the village, which was a suspected Viet Cong stronghold. At daybreak, they found 567 people who appeared to be defenseless villagers The Lieutenant ordered his men to round up the men, women, and children in the center of the hamlet. The first round of ammunition was fired. Then villagers were herded into a hut and a hand grenade was thrown in after them. By midday, the

Members of the Third Battalion, *60th Infantry, march up the rain soaked Fourth Avenue in Seattle following their return from Vietnam. This group of 800 men was the first of 25,000 ordered returned from Vietnam by President Nixon in 1969.*

third phase of events occurred. Hundreds of people were ordered into a large drainage ditch where they were murdered. Twelve days after the event, Colonel Barker, the commanding officer in the area, filed an official report stating that the attack had been "well planned, well-executed and successful." Two and a half years later, Calley was convicted after a four month trial of killing 109 civilians. He was sentenced to life imprisonment.

Ironically, although the convictions of American dissenters were being overturned in the courts because of the lack of evidence that any actual crimes had been committed, the President continued to condemn dissidents as being the worst elements of society. The Vice President took an even stronger stand, stating that he would trade all the student activists in America for one platoon of soldiers in Vietnam. In an interesting way, he got his wish—President Nixon intervened in the Calley case to place him under house arrest instead of confining him to the army stockade. It was not long afterwards that the Lieutenant was discharged from the Armed Services and granted parole.

On October 8, 1972, a month before the Presidential election, the North Vietnamese government dropped its insistence that the Thieu government be ejected before a peace settlement could be reached. The decision amounted to a major breakthrough in the Paris Peace talks and Secretary of State Kissinger announced that peace was at hand. The announcement proved to be premature, however. On October 23, the White House announced that the signing of the cease-fire agreement was being postponed pending new sessions needed to clarify some matters. Apparently, these matters concerned the resistance of the Thieu regime to comply with American demands. The North responded by charging that the offer had been a farce. The President was reported to be equally angry with both governments, but maintained that troop withdrawals would continue and that the war would end before Christmas.

Nixon was re-elected by an overwhelming majority in November. Taking the vote as a mandate, he proceeded to

harden his position with the Vietnamese governments. On December 14, 1971, Kissinger left Paris in despair and Nixon cabled North Vietnam's Premier Pham Van Dong, warning him that unless serious discussion resumed within seventy-two hours, he would initiate massive bombing attacks. The Premier failed to respond, and the President kept his word. The result was the most savage chapter in the history of the war. Over fourteen hundred sorties were conducted in the first week alone. Americans were stunned. Only a few days earlier they had expected an end to the war and a complete disengagement of American troops from Southeast Asia. Nixon offered no public justification for the activities. However, the President had misjudged the public's capacity for moral indignation. The anti-war movement was no longer confined to a minority of the population. Pressures increased from every sector of society, demanding a termination of the American military presence in Vietnam.

In late January, the Paris Peace talks entered their twenty-fourth round of negotiations in forty-two months. The formal end of the war came in the conference room of the Majestic Hotel and simultaneous announcements were broadcast from Washington and Hanoi. Nixon declared that he had achieved "peace with honor." The war concluded with an awesome record. 46,000 Americans had died in battle, 300,000 had been wounded, and the cost had exceeded 100 billion dollars. The nation was left with a spiritual malaise, a rapidly increasing rate of inflation and a rift between the government and the people which was only to be broadened by the events to come in the Watergate experience. Yet, among the shadows, something vital emerged.

The events of a decade had made it abundantly clear that dissent was a fundamental part of the American political process. Despite repeated attempts by two Presidents to repress opinions which were antagonistic to their policies, these opinions ultimately prevailed, testifying to the importance of dissent as a vital component of liberty and a key dimension of freedom. Dissent had on occasion trespassed the boundaries which make it meaningful and useful, by levelling charges and violence against random corridors of government, but for the most part the protests were well-defined, specific, and understandable. The right of the people to participate in the determination of policies which affect their daily lives had, once again, been reaffirmed.

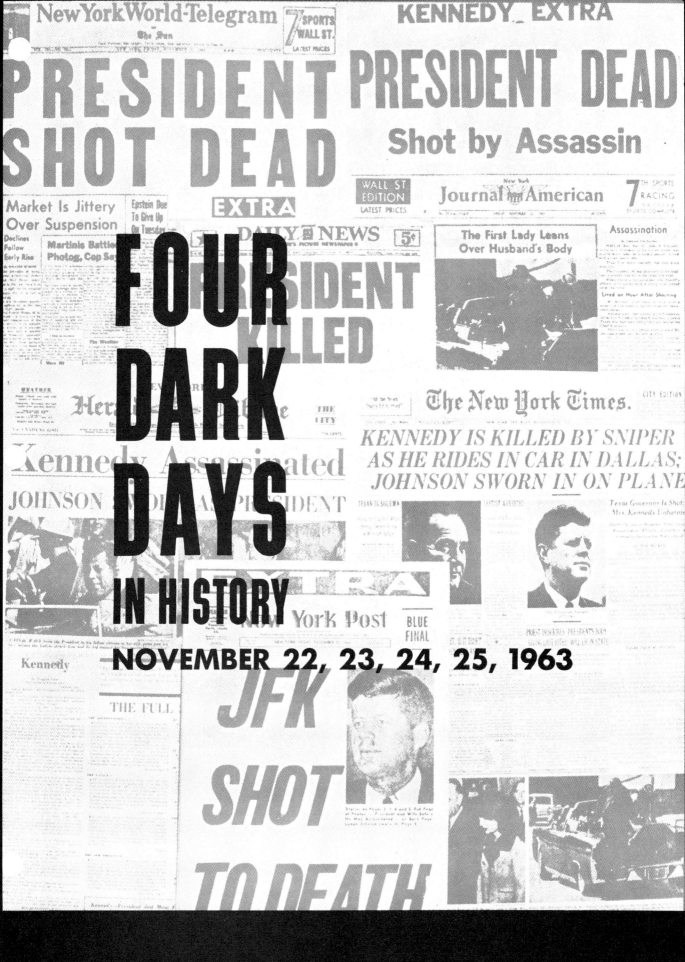

NOVEMBER 22, 1963, THE START OF A HAPPY TEXAS

TOUR: BREAKFAST -THE SPEECH THAT WAS HIS LAST

The President's party appears in good spirits at Fort Worth breakfast (above) with Jackie Kennedy chatting with Vice-President Johnson. Mrs. Johnson and Mr. Kennedy are at each side. President Kennedy makes what was his last speech (at right)   flanked by Gov. Connally left and the Vice- President at right.

START OF THE MOTORCADE

The motorcade, with Governor Connally, Mrs. Connally, President Kennedy and Mrs. Kennedy gets underway with the foursome waving and smiling.

ARRIVAL IN DALLAS

President Kennedy and his wife Jacqueline are a smiling couple as they arrive in Dallas. The sun was brilliant and large crowds were on hand to "see" their President.

MOTORCADE PASSES DALLAS SCHOOL BOOK DEPOSITORY AND THEN...

...THE ASSASSIN'S BULLETS STRIKE

President Kennedy suddenly slumps against his wife as one of three bullets from an assassin's rifle strikes him in the head. Another of the bullets struck down Texas Governor John Connally.

Action moves swiftly. Secret Service Agent Clinton Hill leaps from car behind to the rear deck of the President's car (above) aided by Mrs. Kennedy. The motorcade picks up speed (below). Destination is now Parkland Hospital. White arrow is the President's foot. Black arrow is the Governor's wife. Both men are seriously wounded. Agent Hill protects Mrs. Kennedy who is not visible as she tries to aid the President. Note how some of the watching crowd are still not aware of what has happened.

per had this view
e fired from the
floor of the
las book storage
ding. Rifle, with
ower scope
unted on it, was
nd near open
dow.

Detectives and newsmen are
shown checking sixth floor
open corner window (upper
left). Sniper fired bullets
from his advantage point.

Dallas police (above) start
downtown search for killer
as word is received that
President Kennedy died, the
victim of a sniper's bullet.

Dallas School book building
(left), the sixth floor window
marked, is spot sniper
fired from, President's car
was approximately at point
of white truck, lower left.
Bullets traveled 100 yards.

Refer to SecNav

Lee H. Oswald
U.S.M.C.R. 1653230
Kalinina St. 4-24
Minsk, U.S.S.R.
January 30, 1961

Secretary of the Navy
John B. Connally Jr.
Fort Worth, Texas

Dear Sir.

    I wish to call your attention to a case about which you may have personal knowlege since you are a resident of Ft. Worth as I am.

    In November 1959 an event was well publicised in the Ft. Worth newspapers concerning a person who had gone to the Soviet Union to reside for a short time, (much in the same way E. Hemingway resided in Paris.)

    This person in answers to questions put to him by reporters in Moscow criticized certain facets of american life. The story was blown up into another "turncoat" sensation, with the result that the navy department gave this person a belated dishonourable discharge, although he had received an honourable discharge after three years service on Sept. 11, 1959 at El Toro, marine corps base in California.

    These are the basic facts of my case.

    I have and allways had the full sanction of the U.S. Embassy, Moscow U.S.S.R. and hence the U.S. goverment. In as much as I am returning to the U.S.A. in this year with the aid of the U.S. Embassy. bring with me my family (since I married in the U.S.S.R.) I shall employ all means to right this gross mistake or injustice to a boni-fied U.S. citizen and ex-service man. The U.S. goverment has no charges or complaints against me. I ask you to look into this case and take the neccessary steps to repair the damage done to me and my family. For information I would direct you to consult the american Embassy, Chikovski St. 19/21, Moscow, U.S.S.R.

Thank You

Lee H. Oswald 2 Y75

Lee H. Oswald
W. KALININA 4-24
MINSK.
U.S.S.R.

tor John G Tower
shington, D.C.

Dear Senator Tower,

My name is Lee Harvey Oswald, 22. Fort Worth up till October 1959, when I came to the Soviet Union for a residential stay. I took a residential document for a non-Soviet person living for a time in the U.S.S.R. The American embassy in Moscow is familiar with my case.

Since July 20th 1960, I have unsuccessfully applied for a Soviet Exit visa to leave this country, the Soviets refuse to permit me and my Soviet wife, (who applied at the U.S. Embassy Moscow, July 8, 1960 for immigration status to the U.S.A.) to leave the Soviet Union. I am a citizen of the United States of America (passport No. 1733242, 1959). And I beseech you, Senator Tower, to rise the question of holding by the Soviet Union of a citizen of the U.S., against his will and expressed desires.

Yours Very Truly,
Lee H. Oswald

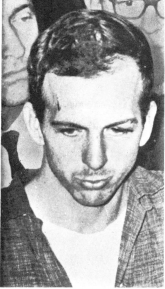

Was this the motive behind **Lee** Oswald's assassination of President Kennedy and the shooting of Texas Gov. John Connally? While living in Russia in 1961, Oswald petulantly demanded that Connally, then Secretary of the Navy, reverse the dishonorable discharge he received after leaving the Marines and traveling to the Soviet Union. Was Governor Connally the true target for killing by Oswald?

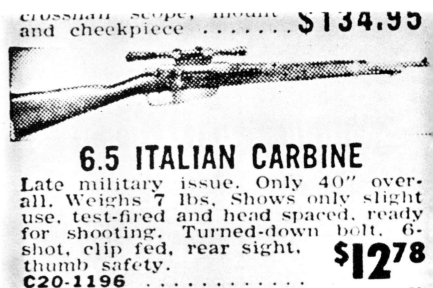

Dallas detective J. C. Day holds aloft the bolt-action rifle with telescopic sigh
used by assassin who killed President Kennedy. Gun was purchased through
magazine ad from out of state. Death of the President was starkly told in
brief Homicide Report.

HOMICIDE REPORT

FORM OP HR-405

POLICE DEPARTMENT   CITY OF DALLA

Last Name of Person Killed	First Name	Middle Name	Race	Sex	Age	Residence of Person Killed	Offense Serial No.
KENNEDY, John F (PRESIDENT OF U. S.)			W	M	47	Washington, D. C. (White House)	F-8595

Reported By		Title or Relationship	Race	Sex	Age	Address of Person Reporting	Phone of Person Reporting

Offense as Reported (Crime)	After Investigation Changed to
MURDER	

Place of Occurrence — Street and Number or Intersection	Division	Platoon	Beat	Officers Making Report	I.D. No.	Name	I.D. No.
Elm St. (approx. 150' W of Houston)	H&R)	2	101	CN Dhority 476	HH Blessing 698		

Day of Week	Date of Occurrence	Time of Day	Date Reported	Time Reported	Report Received By	Received—Time—Typed
Fri	11/22/63	12:30PM	11/23/63	5:10PM	Mayo	5:10PM

DESCRIPTION OF DEAD PERSON

Age	Height	Weight	Eyes	Hair	Beard	Complexion	Identifying Marks, Scars, Etc.	Clothing

Coroner Notified	Name of Coroner Attending—Time of Arrival	A.M. P.M.	Name of Prosecutor Attending—Time of Arrival
Joe B. Brown			

Pronounced Dead by Physician	Address	Person With Whom Accused Lived or Associated
Dr. Kemp Clark, 1PM, Parkland Hospital		

DETAILS OF OFFENSE (Give Circumstances of Occurrence of Offense and its Investigation) Use Both Sides of This Sheet.

The expired was riding in motorcade with wife and Governor John Connally, and his wife. Witnes
heard gun shot and saw the expired slump forward. More shots were heard and the expired fell i
his wife's lap. Governor Connally was also shot at this time. Car in which they were riding
was escorted to Parkland Hospital by Dallas Police Officers.

Witness Taken Into Custody	Address	Witness Taken Into Custody	Address
All witnesses affidavits are in Homicide Office.			

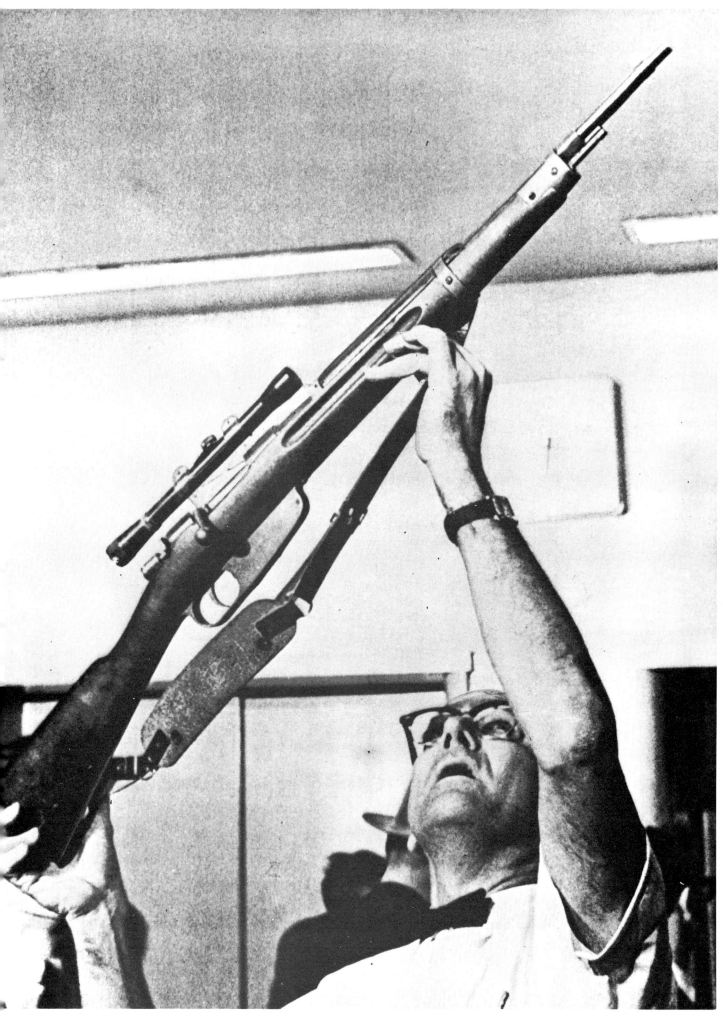

PRESIDENTIAL FIRST

Lyndon B. Johnson solemnly takes
oath as the 36th President. The ceremony
historically took place in the cabin
of the Presidential plane which
brought President Kennedy to Dallas
and carried his body back
to Washington. Federal Judge
Sarah T. Hughes, a Kennedy
appointee delivered
the oath as Mrs. Johnson (left),
and the still stunned Mrs. John
F. Kennedy stood by
his side. Moments later, the
new President and his wife offered the
grief-stricken Mrs. Kennedy
somber words of solace as she looked
blankly into space.

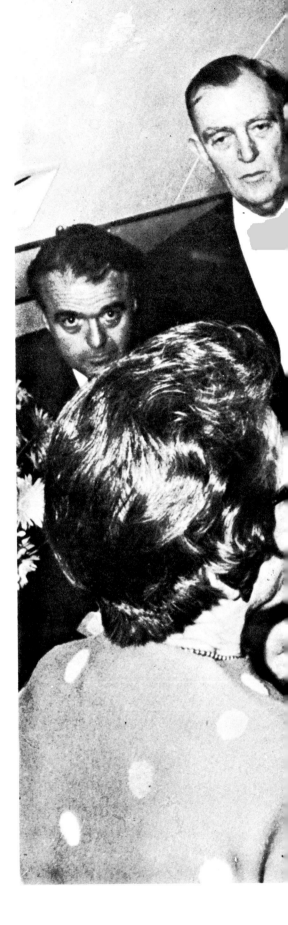

President Johnson gravely asks for nation's help
. . . "and God's" after he and Mrs. Johnson
return from Dallas on the plane which
also carried the body of the slain President.
It was Johnson's first address to a
stunned nation. At right, seven
members of President Kennedy's cabinet,
returned in mid-flight from a trip to
Japan upon hearing of the assassination.
Secretary of State Dean Rusk
(Center), talks with newsmen after
debarking. With him are (left to right),
Agriculture Sec'y. Orville Freeman;
Treasury Sec'y. C. Douglas Dillon; Rusk; Sec'y. of
Interior Stewart Udall; Commerce Sec'y. Luther
Hodges; Dr. Walter Heller, chairman of
Council on Economic Advisors, and
Labor Sec'y. W. Willard Wirtz.

Somber scene of activity as the President's body is gently placed into waiting Navy ambulance as a still shock-stricken wife, Mrs. John F. Kennedy appears at the plane's ramp entrance accompanied by the dead President's brother, Attorney General Robert Kennedy. The party had just arrived from Dallas where earlier in the day the President was shot.

Mrs. John F. Kennedy (above) her legs still smudged with blood enters ambulance in which rests her husband's body following air trip from Dallas and (right) the flag draped casket leaves Andrews Air Force Base for the White House.

Marching Marines precede the Navy ambulance carrying the body
of President Kennedy as it arrives at the
White House in the early hours of November 23rd (below).

The flag-draped casket of President Kennedy lies in state in the historic East Room of the White House . . . the same room, and on the very same Catafalque, on which another assassinated Chief Executive, President Lincoln, lay nearly 100 years ago.
An honor guard composed of all Military Services keeps a silent vigil.

Mourning and sadness throughout the world are emphasized by headlines, a sorrowful citizenry, special masses and the prayers of Pope Paul VI on the death of America's President.

Past Presidents of the United States
were among many world dignitaries who
paid their respects following
the assassination of John F. Kennedy. Harry S.
Truman arrives (above) and
Dwight D. Eisenhower walks up the White House
steps (center). The two former
Presidents are shown together (far right) with
Mrs. Eisenhower between them.

The Nation's Capitol
rises majestically in the
background as a
sad procession follows
the caisson-born
body of the late President
from the White House
to the Capitol's
Rotunda where it will lie
in state.

ROUTE
OF
CORTEGE

WASHINGTON, D.C.

ST. MATTHEWS CATHEDRAL

VIRGINIA

Union Station

Pennsylvania Ave.

WHITE
HOUSE

Arlington
Memorial
Bridge

Lincoln
Memorial

The Mall

KENNEDY
BURIAL PLOT

Independence Ave.

U.S. CAPITOL

Potomac River

Custis-Lee Mansion

ARLINGTON
NATIONAL
CEMETERY

PENTAGON

It is a crisp sunny morning in Washington as
the body of President Kennedy, born
on a caisson, arrives at the Capitol to lie in state.

President Kennedy's wife Jacqueline (left) shows her courage in spite of grief as she appears at the Rotunda where the body lies in state the day following the tragedy.
The family listens to eulogies in the Capitol rotunda, L-R: Robert Kennedy, Mrs. Stephen Smith, a sister, Peter Lawford, Mrs. Lawford, a sister and the President's widow. Children are Caroline Kennedy (front) and Sydney Lawford.

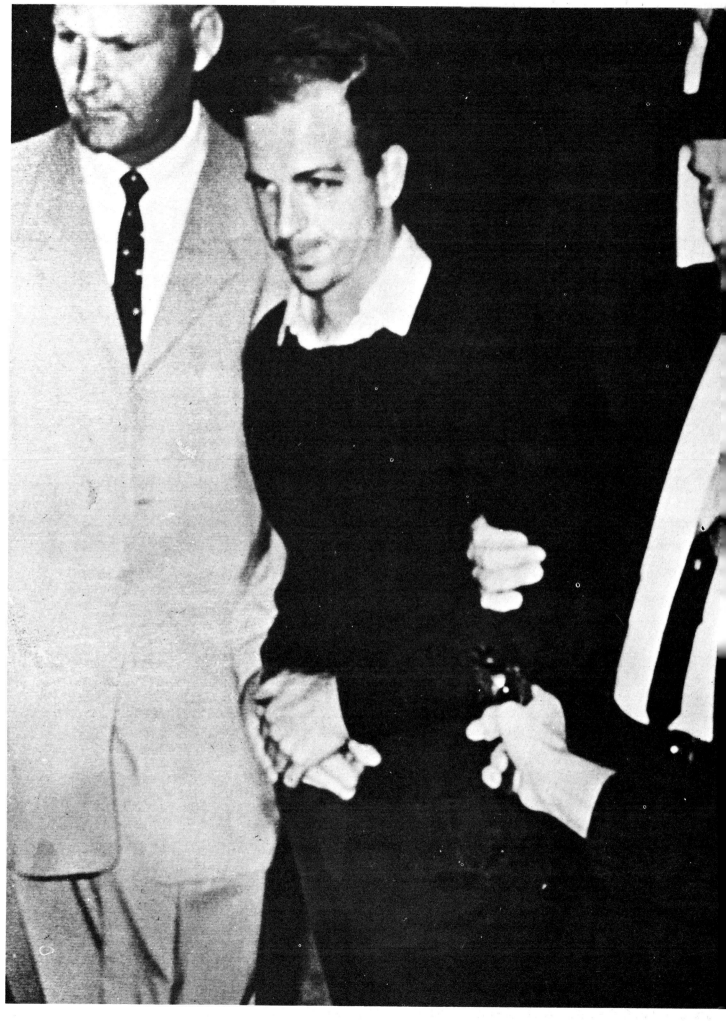

HISTORY IS MADE AS LEE HARVEY OSWALD, THE PRESIDENT'S SUSPECTED ASSASSIN, IS SHOT DOWN AS MILLIONS WATCHED THE DRAMA ON TELEVISION.
The bold, unbelievably rash shooting in the confines and security of the Dallas, Texas, police station left an already stunned nation speechless.

Rapid sequence of events finds Dallas plainclothe
men wrestling with a man (above) who shot Le
Harvey Oswald in the basement of the Dallas ci
jail. The man who did the shooting is Jack Rub
(left), owner of a nightclub in downtown Dalla
At right mortally wounded Lee Harvey Oswald
carried to an ambulance. He died a few hou
later, never regaining consciousness.

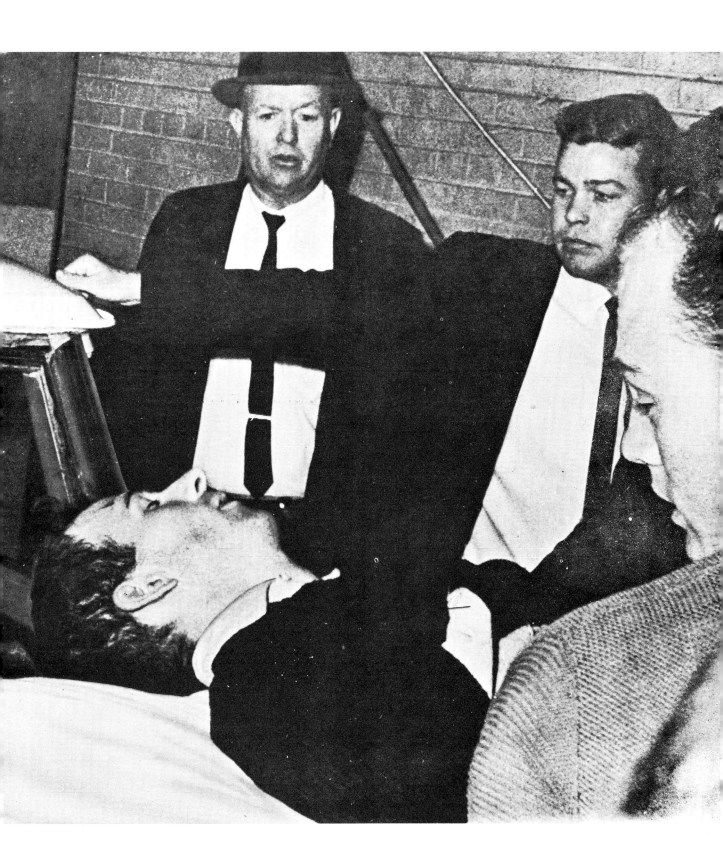

Mrs. Jacqueline Kennedy and her daughter, Caroline, wife and daughter of the late President, pay their last respects prior to removal of the casket for the funeral services and the march to Arlington National Cemetery.

The flag draped casket is carried from the Capitol as members of the family watch.

It was difficult to estimate the number of persons filing past the casket at left.

Many world leaders, no count was ever made, walk enmasse i
the funeral procession from the Capitol to St. Matthews Cathedra
At right are a few of these world leaders who came fro
all parts of the world to pay their respects
the late president Kennedy can be identified. From the left the
are: Heinrich Lubke, West German President; Charles c
Gaulle, President of France; Queen Frederik
of Greece; King Baudouin of Belgium; Emperor Haile Selass
of Ethiopia; and Diosdado Macapagal, President of the Philippine

The caisson bearing the body of the late President, drawn by six matched grey horses, led by a seventh mounted horseman and escorted by the honorar military pallbearers proceeds slowly toward St. Matthews Roman Catholic Church for funeral services.

Archbishop Richard Cardinal Cushing of Boston talks with the widow of the late President on the steps of St. Matthews (left). With her head unbowed, Mrs. John F. Kennedy wal between brothers-in-law, Robert on left and Edward as the procession moves from the Capitol for services.

chbishop Richard Cardinal Cushing (left)
nducts the funeral mass over flag-draped
sket of John F. Kennedy.

n his third birthday, John Kennedy Jr., hard-
aware of the sadly significant occasion,
lds a religious book as his sister Caroline
utches her mother's hand for reassurance.

llowing Mass, the body of the slain Presi-
ent is placed on caisson (left) as his son,
hn-John at right, manages his famous trib-
e, a salute as the family stand   in silence.

Francis Cardinal Spellman celebrates Requiem Mass for the late President in Vatican City before a symbolic coffin draped with an American Flag. The services, which coincided with those held in Washington, were conducted on Pope Paul's own personal Altar.

The cortege bearing the late President's body moves on Arlington National Cemetery. Lincoln Memorial, tribute to another President slain by assassin, is at top center.

A black veil covering Mrs. John F. Kennedy's face fails to hide her grief as the casket containing body of the slain President is lowered at graveside. Below, President deGaulle of France salutes, while West German Chancellor Ludwig Erhard (right) pays his homage.

Irish Cadets form an Honor Guard at Arlington National Cemetery as the casket is positioned over the burial spot.

Richard Cardinal Cushing blesses the casket of President Kennedy as military pallbearers hold back the flag.

Mrs. Kennedy puts her hand to her mouth to choke back her emotion as the flag is lifted.

ANOTHER FUNERAL ... ANOTHER SORROW

Services in Dallas Texas began about the time those for President John F. Kennedy were ending in Washington. Mrs. Marie Tippit, widow of policeman J. D. Tippit who was slain during the search for President Kennedy's assassin, is led from the Beckley Hills Baptist Church.

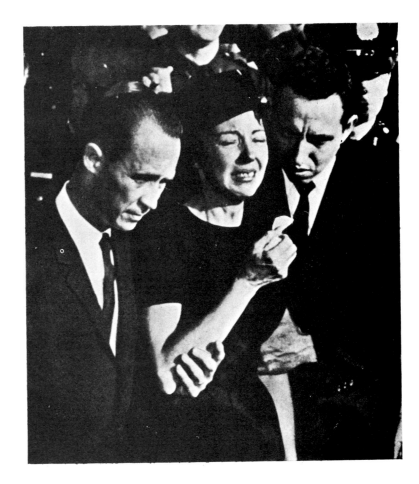

An Eternal Light
burns at the head of a dead
President's grave . . . lighted in
quiet memoriam
by Mrs. Jacqueline Kennedy.
It was her personal tribute to the
man who asked not what
his country could do for him . . .
but what he could do for
his country.
So ends Four Dark Days In History.

Mrs. Jacqueline Kennedy accepts the flag which covered the casket of her late husband.

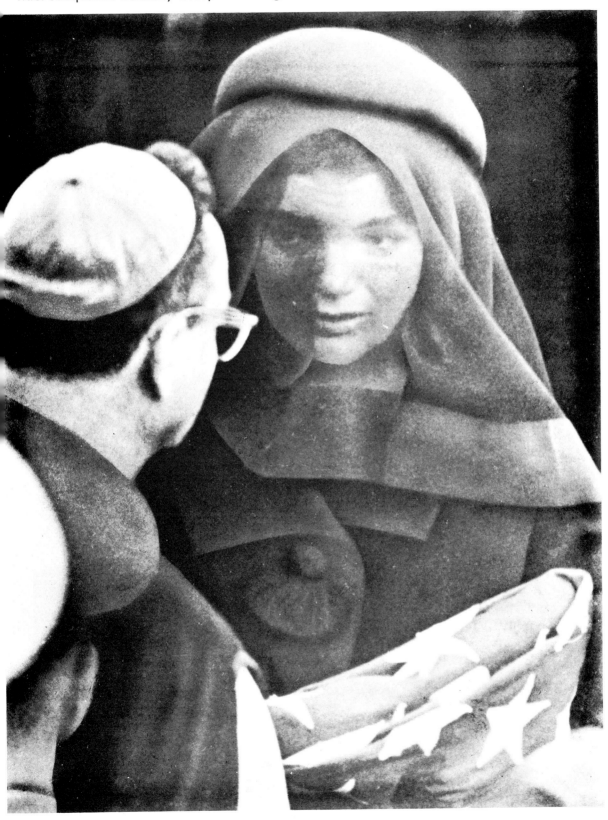

Congressional Record

United States of America

PROCEEDINGS AND DEBATES OF THE 88th CONGRESS, FIRST SESSION

Vol. 109   WASHINGTON, MONDAY, NOVEMBER 25, 1963   *No. 191*

House of Representatives

The House met at 12 o'clock noon.

DESIGNATION OF SPEAKER PRO TEMPORE

The SPEAKER pro tempore laid before the House the following communication from the Speaker:

THE SPEAKER'S ROOM,
November 25, 1963.
I hereby designate the Honorable JIM WRIGHT to act as Speaker pro tempore today.
JOHN W. McCORMACK,
Speaker of the House of Representatives.

PRAYER

The Chaplain, Rev. Bernard Braskamp, D.D., offered the following prayer:

Revelation 14: 13: *Blessed are the dead who die in the Lord from henceforth, yea saith the spirit that they may rest from their labors and their works do follow them.*

Most merciful and gracious God, we humbly acknowledge that in the life of each of us there are times of events and experiences when all our thoughts and feelings seem to impose silence.

As we assemble for prayer at this noon hour, we are not turning our eyes upon the ground whence no help can come but we are lifting them heavenward and unto Thee.

We thank Thee for the life and character and service of John F. Kennedy who walked and worked with us here in this Chamber and who now dwells with Thee in heavenly blessedness for thou hast opened unto him the gateway to the larger life and received him into Thy nearer presence.

Thou didst not loose him when Thou gavest him to us and so we have not lost him by his return to Thee and even though his sun went down while it was yet day we believe it has risen for him in eternal glory.

On this day, when his body is being carried to Arlington National Cemetery, we are not saying "Farewell" but only "Goodnight" for this is our faith that someday we shall dwell together in hallowed union and be forever with our blessed Lord in that fairer land whose language is music and where there is eternal joy.

We pray that Thou wilt give unto the members of his bereaved family and friends and to President Johnson and Speaker McCORMACK and to all the Members of Congress that strong faith which does not murmur or complain but which trusts and ties in courageously and confidently with the consolations of Thy grace and love and will enable them to carry on in faithfulness and fortitude.

Hear us through the merits and mediation of our blessed Lord. Amen.

THE JOURNAL

The Journal of the proceedings of Thursday, November 21, 1963, was read and approved.

MESSAGE FROM THE SENATE

A message from the Senate by Mr. McGown, one of its clerks, announced that the Senate had passed without amendment a bill of the House of the following title:

H.R. 8969. An act to provide, for the period ending June 30, 1964, temporary increases in the public debt limit set forth in section 21 of the Second Liberty Bond Act.

The message also announced that the Senate had passed bills of the following

21591

titles, in which the concurrence of the House is requested:

S. 298. An act to amend the Small Business Investment Act of 1958;

S. 1309. An act to amend the Small Business Act, and for other purposes; and

S. 2267. An act to amend Public Law 88–72 to increase the authorization for appropriations to the Atomic Energy Commission in accordance with section 261 of the Atomic Energy Act of 1954, as amended, and for other purposes.

The message also announced that the Senate agrees to the amendments of the House to a bill of the Senate of the following title:

S. 777. An act to amend the Arms Control and Disarmament Act in order to increase the authorization for appropriations and to modify the security procedures for contractor employees.

The message also announced that Mr. MONRONEY had been appointed a conferee on the bill (H.R. 8747) entitled "An act making appropriations for sundry independent executive bureaus, boards, commissions, corporations, agencies, and offices, for the fiscal year ending June 30, 1964, and for other purposes," in place of Mr. ROBERTSON, excused.

TRANSFER OF BUSINESS TO TOMORROW, NOVEMBER 26

Mr. MULTER. Mr. Speaker, I ask unanimous consent that the business in order for today shall be in order on tomorrow, and that special orders in order for today shall be transferred to tomorrow and shall precede those presently scheduled for tomorrow.

The SPEAKER pro tempore. Is there objection to the request of the gentleman from New York?

There was no objection.

PRINTING OF EULOGIES TO LATE PRESIDENT JOHN F. KENNEDY

Mr. MULTER. Mr. Speaker, I ask unanimous consent that the eulogies to our late President delivered in the rotunda on yesterday be printed at this point in the RECORD.

The SPEAKER pro tempore. Is there objection to the request of the gentleman from New York?

There was no objection.

BY SENATOR MANSFIELD

There was a sound of laughter; in a moment, it was no more. And so she took a ring from her finger and placed it in his hands.

There was a wit in a man neither young nor old, but a wit full of an old man's wisdom and of a child's wisdom, and then, in a moment it was no more. And so she took a ring from her finger and placed it in his hands.

There was a man marked with the scars of his love of country, a body active with the surge of a life far, far from spent and, in a moment, it was no more. And so she took a ring from her finger and placed it in his hands.

There was a father with a little boy, a little girl and a joy of each in the other. In a moment it was no more, and so she took a ring from her finger and placed it in his hands.

There was a husband who asked much and gave much, and out of the giving and the asking wove with a woman what could not be broken in life, and in a moment it was no more. And so she took a ring from her finger and placed it in his hands, and kissed him and closed the lid of a coffin.

A piece of each of us died at that moment. Yet, in death he gave of himself to us. He gave us of a good heart from which the laughter came. He gave us of a profound wit, from which a great leadership emerged. He gave us of a kindness and a strength fused into a human courage to seek peace without fear.

He gave us of his love that we, too, in turn, might give. He gave that we might give of ourselves, that we might give to one another until there would be no room, no room at all, for the bigotry, the hatred, prejudice and the arrogance which converged in that moment of horror to strike him down.

In leaving us—these gifts, John Fitzgerald Kennedy, President of the United States, leaves with us. Will we take them, Mr. President? Will we have, now, the sense and the responsibility and the courage to take them?

BY CHIEF JUSTICE WARREN

There are few events in our national life that unite Americans and so touch the heart of all of us as the passing of a President of the United States.

There is nothing that adds shock to our sadness as the assassination of our leader, chosen as he is to embody the ideals of our people, the faith we have in our institutions and our belief in the fatherhood of God and the brotherhood of man.

Such misfortunes have befallen the Nation on other occasions, but never more shockingly than 2 days ago.

We are saddened; we are stunned; we are perplexed.

John Fitzgerald Kennedy, a great and good President, the friend of all men of good will, a believer in the dignity and equality of all human beings, a fighter for justice, and apostle of peace, has been snatched from our midst by the bullet of an assassin.

What moved some misguided wretch to do this horrible deed may never be known to us, but we do know that such acts are commonly stimulated by forces of hatred and malevolence, such as today are eating their way into the bloodstream of American life.

What a price we pay for this fanaticism.

It has been said that the only thing we learn from history is that we do not learn. But surely we can learn if we have the will to do so. Surely there is a lesson to be learned from this tragic event.

If we really love this country, if we truly love justice and mercy, if we fervently want to make this Nation better for those who are to follow us, we can at least abjure the hatred that consumes people, the false accusations that divide us, and the bitterness that begets violence.

Is it too much to hope that the martyrdom of our beloved President might even soften the hearts of those who would themselves recoil from assassination, but who do not shrink from spreading the venom which kindles thoughts of it in others?

Our Nation is bereaved. The whole world is poorer because of his loss. But we can all be better Americans because John Fitzgerald Kennedy has passed our way, because he has been our chosen leader at a time in history when his character, his vision, and his quiet courage have enabled him to chart for us a safe course through the shoals of treacherous seas that encompass the world.

And now that he is relieved of the almost superhuman burdens we imposed on him, may he rest in peace.

BY SPEAKER McCORMACK

As we gather here today bowed in grief, the heartfelt sympathy of Members of the Congress and of our people are extended to Mrs. Jacqueline Kennedy and to Ambassador and Mrs. Joseph P. Kennedy and their loved ones. Their deep grief is also self-shared by countless millions of persons throughout the world, considered a personal tragedy, as if one had lost a loved member of his own immediate family.

Any citizen of our beloved country who looks back over its history cannot fail to see that we have been blessed with God's favor beyond most other peoples. At each great crisis in our history we have found a leader able to grasp the helm of state and guide the country through the troubles which beset it. In our earliest days, when our strength and wealth were so limited and our problems so great, Washington and Jefferson appeared to lead our people. Two generations later, when our country was torn in two by a fratricidal war, Abraham Lincoln appeared from the mass of the people as a leader able to reunite the Nation.

In more recent times, in the critical days of the depression and the great war forced upon us by Fascist aggression, Franklin Delano Roosevelt, later Harry S. Truman appeared on the scene to reorganize the country and lead its revived citizens to victory. Finally, only recently, when the cold war was building up the supreme crisis of a threatened nuclear war capable of destroying everything—and everybody—that our predecessors had so carefully built, and which a liberty-loving world wanted, once again a strong and courageous man appeared ready to lead us.

No country need despair so long as God, in His infinite goodness, continues to provide the Nation with leaders able to guide it through the successive crises which seem to be the inevitable fate of any great nation.

Surely no country ever faced more gigantic problems than ours in the last few years, and surely no country could have obtained a more able leader in a time of such crisis. President John Fitzgerald Kennedy possessed all the qualities of greatness. He had deep faith, complete confidence, human sympathy, and broad vision which recognized the true values of freedom, equality, and the brotherhood which have always been the marks of the American political dreams.

He had the bravery and a sense of personal duty which made him willing to face up to the great task of being President in these trying times. He had the warmth and the sense of humanity which made the burden of the task bearable for himself and for his associates, and which made all kinds of diverse peoples and races eager to be associated with him in his task. He had the tenacity and determination to carry each stage of his great work through to its successful conclusion.

Now that our great leader has been taken from us in a cruel death, we are bound to feel shattered and helpless in the face of our loss. This is but natural, but as the first bitter pangs of our incredulous grief begins to pass we must thank God that we were privileged, however briefly, to have had this great man for our President. For he has now taken his place among the great figures of world history.

While this is an occasion of deep sorrow it should be also one of dedication. We must have the determination to unite and carry on the spirit of John Fitzgerald Kennedy for a strengthened America and a future world of peace.

ADJOURNMENT AS A FURTHER MARK OF RESPECT FOR THE LATE PRESIDENT JOHN F. KENNEDY

Mr. MULTER. Mr. Speaker, I offer a resolution.

The Clerk read the resolution, as follows:

HOUSE RESOLUTION 571

IN THE HOUSE OF REPRESENTATIVES, U.S.,

Resolved, That the House of Representatives has learned with profound regret and sorrow of the tragic death of the late President of the United States, John Fitzgerald Kennedy, illustrious statesman and leader in the Nation and in the world.

Resolved, That as a token of honor and in recognition of his eminent and distinguished public services to the Nation and to the world the Speaker of the House shall appoint a committee of one hundred Members of the House to join a similar committee appointed on the part of the Senate to attend the funeral services of the late President.

Resolved, That the House tenders its deep sympathy to the members of the family of the late President in their sad bereavement.

Resolved, That the Sergeant at Arms of the House be authorized and directed to take such steps as may be necessary for carrying out the provisions of these resolutions and that the necessary expenses in connection therewith be paid out of the contingent fund of the House.

Resolved, That the Clerk communicate these resolutions to the Senate and transmit a copy thereof to the family of the late President.

The SPEAKER pro tempore. Without objection, the several resolving clauses are agreed to.

There was no objection.

The SPEAKER pro tempore. By direction of the Speaker, and by unanimous consent, the Chair appoints the following Members of the House to attend the funeral services:

Mr. McCORMACK
Mr. ALBERT
Mr. HALLECK
Mr. BOGGS
Mr. ARENDS
Mr. VINSON
Mr. CANNON
Mr. MARTIN of Massachusetts
Mr. PATMAN
Mr. SMITH of Virginia
Mr. COLMER
Mr. MAHON
Mr. COOLEY
Mr. GRANT
Mr. KEOGH
Mr. KIRWAN
Mr. POAGE
Mr. SHEPPARD
Mr. THOMAS
Mr. BROWN of Ohio
Mr. GATHINGS
Mr. JENSEN
Mr. McMILLAN
Mr. MILLS
Mr. KILBURN
Mrs. BOLTON of Ohio
Mr. BONNER
Mr. HARRIS
Mr. RIVERS of South Carolina
Mr. PHILBIN
Mr. KING
Mr. WHITTEN
Mr. ABERNETHY
Mr. AUCHINCLOSS
Mr. DAWSON
Mr. FEIGHAN
Mr. FISHER
Mr. HOEVEN
Mr. HOLIFIELD
Mr. HORAN
Mr. MADDEN
Mr. MORRISON
Mr. MURRAY
Mr. O'KONSKI
Mr. WINSTEAD
Mr. ANDREWS of Alabama
Mr. ROONEY of New York
Mr. BECKWORTH
Mr. CHENOWETH
Mr. WILSON of Indiana
Mr. FOGARTY
Mr. SIKES

Mr. CHELF
Mr. CORBETT
Mr. BYRNES of Wisconsin
Mr. FALLON
Mr. FULTON of Pennsylvania
Mr. MILLER of California
Mr. MORGAN
Mr. POWELL
Mr. PRICE
Mr. RAINS
Mr. TEAGUE of Texas
Mr. GARY
Mr. NORBLAD
Mr. THOMPSON of Texas
Mr. BENNETT of Michigan
Mr. BLATNIK
Mr. BURLESON
Mr. DONOHUE
Mr. EVINS
Mr. RIEHLMAN
Mr. TOLLEFSON
Mr. ABBITT
Mr. McCULLOCH
Mr. GREEN of Pennsylvania
Mr. ASPINALL
Mr. BATES
Mr. BOLLING
Mr. ELLIOTT
Mr. FORD
Mr. WILLIS
Mr. SAYLOR
Mr. ZABLOCKI
Mr. AYRES
Mr. CURTIS
Mr. SCHENCK
Mr. O'HARA of Illinois
Mr. BOLAND
Mr. BROYHILL of Virginia
Mr. FRELINGHUYSEN
Mr. O'NEILL
Mr. HOSMER
Mr. JOHANSEN
Mr. MACDONALD
Mr. THOMPSON of New Jersey
Mr. BURKE
Mr. CONTE
Mr. KEITH
Mr. MORSE

ADJOURNMENT

The Clerk will report the remainder of the resolution.

The Clerk read as follows:

Resolved, That as a further mark of respect to the memory of the late President the House do now adjourn.

The SPEAKER pro tempore. Without objection, the resolution is agreed to.

There was no objection.

A motion to reconsider was laid on the table.

The SPEAKER pro tempore. Pursuant to the foregoing resolution and as a further mark of respect to the deceased President, the House stands adjourned until 12 o'clock noon tomorrow.

Senate

The Senate met at 12 o'clock meridian, and was called to order by the President pro tempore.

AMENDMENT OF SENATE JOURNAL AND CONGRESSIONAL RECORD

Mr. METCALF. Mr. President, the sudden and tragic death of the President of the United States since the adjournment of the Senate on Friday last made it highly important and desirable that certain action should be taken by the Senate prior to 12 o'clock noon today—the hour to which the Senate on Friday adjourned.

That action, with which Senators are familiar, was taken at an unofficial meeting of Members of the Senate called by the majority leader and the minority leader for 10 o'clock a.m., today. In order that such proceedings may be given full legal effect, I submit the following unanimous-consent request; namely:

That the Senate Journal and the permanent edition of the CONGRESSIONAL RECORD, respectively, for Friday, November 22, 1963, with respect to the order and motion for adjournment until Monday, November 25, 1963, at 12 o'clock noon, be amended, at the appropriate places, therein, to provide that, instead of an adjournment until noon, the Senate adjourn until 10 o'clock a.m., on said day; and

That the informal meeting of the Members of the Senate, above indicated, be deemed to have been a duly authorized session of the Senate, and the action taken therein is hereby validated and approved as a part of its official proceedings of today.

The PRESIDENT pro tempore. Is there objection? The Chair hears none, and it is so ordered.

The proceedings of the informal meeting are as follows:

An informal meeting of Senators, called by the majority leader, the Senator from Montana [Mr. MANSFIELD], and the minority leader, the Senator from Illinois [Mr. DIRKSEN], was held at 10 o'clock a.m., in connection with arrangements for the funeral ceremonies for the late President of the United States, John F. Kennedy.

The meeting was called to order by the President pro tempore.

The Chaplain, Rev. Frederick Brown Harris, D.D., offered the following prayer:

God of the living and of the living dead: As in this hour we bow in the shadow of a people's grief, Thou dost hear the sobbing of a stricken nation. But we come with the comfort that Thou knowest what is in the darkness, and that the darkness and the light are both alike to Thee.

For the stewardship in the brief but epochal years of the young and gallant captain who has fallen at his post, we give thanks to Thee, the Master of all good workmen. In the profile of courage, of vision, and of faith which John F. Kennedy etched upon the darkened sky of these agitated times, in his exalted place of leadership, we behold the image of our America which alone will make sure the survival of our freedom.

And now that the valorous sword has fallen from his lifeless hands, he seems to be calling to us in the unfinished tasks which remain.

> Others will sing the song
> Finish what I began
> What matters I or they
> Mine or another's day
> So the right word be said
> And life the purer made.

In the Nation's poignant loss, may there come to those whose hands are at the helm of this dear land of our

21595

faith and love the vision which fortified Thy prophet of old as he bore witness:

In the year that King Uzziah died I saw the Lord high and lifted up.

So in this year of a tragic death, may there be granted to us a vision of the preeminent spiritual verities which abide and undergird and outlast the life and death of any mortal servant of great causes who toils for a while in these fields of time in the sense of the eternal, and then falls on sleep.

We pray in the name of the risen Christ who hath brought life and immortality to light. Amen.

DEATH OF JOHN FITZGERALD KENNEDY, 35TH PRESIDENT OF THE UNITED STATES

Mr. MANSFIELD. Mr. President, due to the sudden and tragic death of the President of the United States, a former colleague of ours in this body, it has been necessary to call this extraordinary meeting of the Members of the Senate before the hour formally appointed upon the adjournment of the Senate last Friday.

Mr. President, the Senate has assembled today to remark for the RECORD the death of John Fitzgerald Kennedy, President of the United States.

I shall be brief, for his life, too short, shut off too soon, speaks for him.

In these last hours, a profile in courage has emerged from the emulsion of his death. And the tears of those who knew him and those who did not know him will fix that profile forever in the experience of the Nation and the world.

John Fitzgerald Kennedy's courage was the human courage, the courage which all must have merely to live in this world, in the ever-present shadow of death. It was the special courage to defy the cold hand of death when it reaches out too eagerly, as twice it did—in the wounds of the war and in the grave illness of his Senate years. It was the quiet courage to accept death's finality when it would be denied no longer.

And his was an extraordinary courage. It was the courage to believe in, with all his heart, and to dedicate himself to, the attainment of the proposition that Americans—all Americans—are born with an equal right to life, liberty, and the pursuit of happiness.

His was a universal courage. It was the courage of one who had bled in war to seek, unashamed, a peace of decency among all nations. It was the courage to join, before all else, the family of man and, in the joining, to affirm, before all else, the integrity of human life in the face of the powers of violence to destroy and desecrate it.

This is the profile of the man who walked among us not long ago on the floor of the Senate. This is the profile of the man who emerged to reawaken the Nation to its finest meaning. This is the man who struck new sparks of hope in a world dark with unspeakable fears.

His death, Mr. President, has fused the many faces of courage into a single profile of courage set in the enduring frame of faith and reason. This is what

we have of him now. It is so little to have, and yet so much.

In a moment, I shall send to the desk a resolution of regret on the death of John Fitzgerald Kennedy. But that will not be the end. It will not be the end of our responsibility, of our debt to this decent man, this American who gave of himself until there was no more to give.

We will find, in his death, the strength to do what must be done to bridle the bigotry, the hatred, the arrogance, the iniquities, and the inequities which marched in the boots of a gathering tyranny to that moment of horror.

We will find, in his death, the strength to renew our faith in what is good in ourselves and in one another throughout this Nation.

We will find, in his death, the strength to follow the paths of reason on which he walked, until they lead us out of the morass of an all-consuming and cynical self-concern.

We will find, in his death, some of his love and reverence of life, some of his humility, some of his patience and forbearance, some of his wisdom, and some of his humor. And, so strengthened, we will join with the President in forging a new decency at home and a reasoned peace in the world.

God willing, these things we shall find, or God help us all.

Mr. President, I send to the desk a resolution which I submit on behalf of the 100 Members of the Senate.

The resolution (S. Res. 228) was read, as follows:

Resolved, That the Senate has learned with profound sorrow and deep regret of the tragic death of Hon. John Fitzgerald Kennedy, late the President of the United States, and a former Representative and former Senator from the State of Massachusetts.

Resolved, That in recognition of his illustrious statesmanship, his leadership in national and world affairs, and his distinguished public service to his State and the Nation, the Presiding Officer of the Senate appoint a committee, to consist of all the Members of the Senate, to attend the funeral of the late President at noon today.

Resolved, That the Senate hereby tenders its deep sympathy to the members of the family of the late President in their sad bereavement.

Resolved, That the Secretary communicate these resolutions to the House of Representatives, and transmit an enrolled copy thereof to the family of the late President.

The PRESIDENT pro tempore. The Chair recognizes the Senator from Illinois.

Mr. DIRKSEN. Mr. President, the memory of John Fitzgerald Kennedy lingers in this forum of the people. Here we knew his vigorous tread, his flashing smile, his ready wit, his keen mind, his zest for adventure. Here with quiet grief we mourn his departure. Here we shall remember him best as a colleague whose star of public service is indelibly inscribed on the roll of the U.S. Senate.

And here the eternal question confronts and confounds us. Why must it be? Why must the life of an amiable, friendly, aggressive young man, moved only by high motives, lighted on his way by high hopes, guided by broad plans, impelled by understanding and vision, be

brought to an untimely end with his labors unfinished? And why, in a free land, untouched by the heel of dictatorship and oppression, where the humblest citizen may freely utter his grievances, must that life be cut short by an evil instrument, moved by malice, frustration, and hate? This is the incredible thing which leaves us bewildered and perplexed.

One moment there is the ecstasy of living when one can hear the treble cries of scampering children over the White House lawn, the pleasure of receiving a Thanksgiving turkey which I presented to him but 3 days before the evil deed, the pleasure of conversation over many things, including his hopes for the future, the exciting fact of sunshine and green grass in late November, the endless stream of citizens coming to the President's House, the strident voice of the city rising from the hum of traffic, the animation of saluting crowds, and then the sudden strangling death rattle of dissolution. Who shall say, save that there is a divinity which shapes our ends and marks our days?

As the tumult and grief subside, as the Nation resumes and moves forward, and his own generation measures his works and achievements, what shall we say who knew him well—we in this forum, where he spent 8 years of his life—we who knew him best not as Mr. President but simply as Jack?

We saw him come to this body at age 35. We saw him grow. We saw him rise. We saw him elevated to become the Chief Magistrate of this Nation. And we saw him as the leader of both branches of this Republic assembled to deliberate over common problems.

In this moment when death has triumphed, when hearts are chastened, when the spirit reels in sheer bewilderment, what do we say now that the Book of Life has been closed?

Let me say what we have always said when he was alive, gay, happy, friendly, ambitious, and ready to listen.

He had vision that went beyond our own. His determination to effectuate a test ban treaty is a living example.

He was his own profile in courage. His unrelenting devotion to equality and civil rights attests that fact.

He was devoted to our system of constitutional government. His attitude toward the separation of church and state looms like a shining example.

He had the great virtue of spiritual grace. If at any moment he may have seemed frustrated over a proposition, it was so transitory. If he showed any sign of petulance, it was so fleeting. There were no souring acids in the spirit of John Kennedy.

If at any moment he may have seemed overeager, it was but the reflection of a zealous crusader and missioner who knew where he was going.

If at any moment, he seemed to depart from the covenant which he and his party made with the people, it was only because he believed that accelerated events and circumstances did not always heed the clock and the calendar.

If his course sometimes seemed at variance with his own party leaders or with the opposition, it was only because a deep conviction dictated his course.

On the tablets of memory, we who knew him well as a friend and colleague can well inscribe this sentiment:

"Senator John Fitzgerald Kennedy, who became the 35th President of the United States—young, vigorous, aggressive, and scholarly—one who estimated the need of his country and the world and sought to fulfill that need—one who was wedded to peace and vigorously sought this greatest of all goals of mankind—one who sensed how catastrophic nuclear conflict could be and sought a realistic course to avert it—one who sensed the danger that lurked in a continuing inequality in our land and sought a rational and durable solution—one to whom the phrase 'the national interest' was more than a string of words—one who could disagree without vindictiveness—one who believed that the expansion of the enjoyment of living by all people was an achievable goal—one who believed that each generation must contribute its best to the fulfillment of the American dream."

The te deums which will be sung this day may be wafted away by the evening breeze which caresses the last resting place of those who served the Republic, but here in this Chamber where he served and prepared for higher responsibility, the memory of John Fitzgerald Kennedy will long linger to nourish the faith of all who serve that same great land.

The PRESIDENT pro tempore. Is there objection to the present consideration of the resolution?

There being no objection, the resolution (S. Res. 228) was considered and unanimously agreed to.

The PRESIDENT pro tempore. The Chair appoints the entire membership of the Senate as a committee to proceed to the bier of our late President John F. Kennedy.

Mr. MANSFIELD. Mr. President, I ask Senators to join the leadership and proceed in a body to the bier on which our late departed colleague is now resting.

ADJOURNMENT

Mr. MANSFIELD. Mr. President, as previously ordered, the Senate will meet at 12 o'clock noon. I now move that this extraordinary meeting of Members of the Senate be now adjourned.

The motion was agreed to; and (at 10 o'clock and 19 minutes a.m.) the informal meeting of the Senate was adjourned.

The Senate proceeded in a body to the bier of the late President of the United States, John Fitzgerald Kennedy.

THE JOURNAL

Mr. METCALF. Mr. President, I ask unanimous consent that the Journal, as amended, be approved as if read.

The PRESIDENT pro tempore. Without objection, it is so ordered.

AUTHORIZATION FOR COMMITTEES TO FILE REPORTS DURING ADJOURNMENT OF THE SENATE

Mr. METCALF. Mr. President, I ask unanimous consent that committees of the Senate be permitted to file reports, with minority or individual views thereto, if appropriate, during the adjournment of the Senate.

The PRESIDENT pro tempore. Without objection, it is so ordered.

ADJOURNMENT

Mr. METCALF. Mr. President, as a further mark of respect to the memory of the late beloved President of the United States, I move that the Senate adjourn until 12 noon, tomorrow.

The motion was unanimously agreed to; and (at 12 o'clock and 3 minutes p.m.) the Senate adjourned until tomorrow, Tuesday, November 26, 1963, at 12 o'clock meridian.

"So when a great man dies,

For years beyond our ken,

The light he leaves behind him lies

Upon the paths of men."

HENRY WADSWORTH LONGFELLOW

PRESIDENTIAL PROTECTION

ON November 29, 1963, one week after Lyndon B. Johnson assumed duties as President of the United States he issued Executive Order No. 11130 creating the Warren Commission to investigate the assassination of President John Fitzgerald Kennedy, and later the killing of Lee Harvey Oswald, the man who allegedly shot the President.

The Commission was directed by President Johnson to evaluate all the facts and circumstances surrounding the assassination and the subsequent killing of the alleged assassin, Lee Harvey Oswald. Also to be investigated by the Warren Commission were a number of questions raised as a result of the assassination. A stunned and shocked America—and the nations of the world—demanded an explanation.

On December 9, the Federal Bureau of Investigation submitted to the Warren Commission a five-volume report which summarized the results of their investigation conducted immediately after the President was shot.

On December 18, the Secret Service submitted a report to the Warren Commission detailing the security precautions taken on the President's trip to Dallas and an account of the assassination as witnessed by Secret Service agents.

The Department of State then submitted a report on Lee Harvey Oswald's defection to Russia in 1959 and his return to the United States in 1962.

Next to submit a report on the assassination to the Warren Commission was the Dallas police department.

The Warren Commission then requested that the 10 major departments of the Federal Government, 14 independent government agencies or commissions and four Congressional committees all to submit information on the assassination and the background and activities of Lee Harvey Oswald and Jack Ruby.

All material was carefully analyzed and reviewed by the Warren Commission.

All witnesses testified to the Warren Commission in closed session except one. Although witnesses were permitted to give testimony in an open hearing if they desired, only this one exception requested to be heard publically. All witnesses were allowed to retain legal counsel if they so desired.

The Warren Commission members knew that some of the testimony presented before them would be inadmissible in a court of law. Since testimony could not always be taken in logical order, its partial publication might prove misleading.

In addition to hearing testimony, the Warren Commission took sworn depositions, statements and affidavits which they relied upon to round out their investigations.

The most difficult task facing the Commission was the uncovering of all the facts concerned with the assassination of President Kennedy. Furthermore, the Commission was to determine if the assassination was the product of a conspiracy, by either American or foreign persons.

Since Oswald was murdered before he could be tried in a court of law, the American people have been denied some measure of justice. In a trial, Oswald would be considered —under American standards of justice—innocent until proven guilty.

But the Warren Commission was empowered only to act as a fact-finding agency of the government, not as a judge and jury in the legal sense.

Finally, after 10 months of investigation, Chief Justice of the Supreme Court Earl Warren handed President Lyndon B. Johnson a copy of the Commission findings. The report was said to be "the truth as far as can be discovered."

In the best traditions of a Democracy, which depends upon an informed public to maintain the integrity of government, the findings of the Warren Commission were published in full. The American people and the world at large have long awaited these disclosures.

The following pages will present what is considered by the Editors, as the salient events leading up to, during and after the death of President John F. Kennedy as revealed in the Warren Commission Report.

MEMBERS OF COMMISSION

Biographical Information

The Honorable Earl Warren, Chief Justice of the United States, was born in Los Angeles, Calif., on March 19, 1891. He graduated from the University of California with B.L. and J.D. degrees, and was admitted to the California bar in 1914. Chief Justice Warren was attorney general of California from 1939 to 1943. From 1943 to 1953 he was Governor of California and in September 1953 was appointed by President Eisenhower to be the Chief Justice of the United States.

The Honorable Richard B. Russell was born in Winder, Ga., on November 2, 1897. He received his B.L. degree from the University of Georgia in 1918 and his LL.B. from Mercer University in 1957. Senator Russell commenced the practice of law in Winder, Ga., in 1918, became county attorney for Barrow County, Ga., and was a member of the Georgia House of Representatives from 1921 to 1931. He was Governor of Georgia from 1931 to 1933, was elected to the U.S. Senate in January 1933 to fill a vacancy, and has been Senator from Georgia continuously since that date.

The Honorable John Sherman Cooper was born in Somerset, Ky., on August 23, 1901. He attended Centre College, Kentucky, received his A.B. degree from Yale College in 1923, and attended Harvard Law School from 1923 to 1925. Senator Cooper has been a member of the House of Representatives of the Kentucky General Assembly, a county judge and circuit judge in Kentucky, and is now a member of the U.S. Senate, where he has served, though not continuously, for 12 years. He was a delegate to the Fifth, Sixth, and Seventh Sessions of the General Assembly of the United Nations, an advisor to the Secretary of State in 1950 at meetings of the North Atlantic Treaty Organization, and Ambassador to India and Nepal in 1955-56. He served in the 3d U.S. Army in World War II in Europe, and after the war headed the reorganization of the German judicial system in Bavaria.

The Honorable Hale Boggs was born in Long Beach, Miss., on February 15, 1914. He graduated from Tulane University with a B.A. degree in 1935 and received his LL.B. in 1937. He was admitted to the Louisiana bar in 1937 and practiced law in New Orleans. Representative Boggs was elected to the 77th Congress of the United States and in World War II was an officer of the U.S. Naval Reserve and of the Maritime Service. He has been a Member of Congress since 1946 when he was elected to represent the Second District, State of Louisiana, in the 80th Congress, and he is currently the majority whip for the Democratic Party in the House of Representatives.

The Honorable Gerald R. Ford was born in Omaha, Nebr., on July 14, 1913. He graduated from the University of Michigan with a B.A. degree in 1935 and from Yale University Law School with an LL.B. degree in 1941. Representative Ford was admitted to the Michigan bar in 1941. He was first elected to Congress in 1948 and has been reelected to each succeeding Congress. He served 47 months in the U.S. Navy during World War II. Representative Ford was elected in January 1963 the chairman of the House Republican Conference.

The Honorable Allen W. Dulles was born in Watertown, N.Y., on April 7, 1893. He received his B.A. degree from Princeton in 1914, his M.A. in 1916, his LL.B. from George Washington University in 1926, and LL.D. degrees. Mr. Dulles entered the diplomatic service of the United States in 1916 and resigned in 1926 to take up law practice in New York City. In 1953 Mr. Dulles was appointed Director of Central Intelligence and served in that capacity until 1961.

The Honorable John J. McCloy was born in Philadelphia, Pa., on March 31, 1895. He received an A.B. degree, cum laude, from Amherst College in 1916; LL.B. from Harvard, and LL.D. from Amherst College. He was admitted to the New York bar in 1921 and is now a member of the firm of Milbank, Tweed, Hadley & McCloy. He was Assistant Secretary of War from April 1941 to November 1945. Mr. McCloy was President of the World Bank from 1947 to 1949 and U.S. Military Governor and High Commissioner for Germany from 1949 to 1952. He has been coordinator of U.S. disarmament activities since 1961.

GENERAL COUNSEL

J. Lee Rankin was born in Hartington, Nebr., on July 8, 1907. He received his A.B. degree from the University of Nebraska in 1928 and his LL.B. in 1930 from the University of Nebraska Law School. He was admitted to the Nebraska bar in 1930 and practiced law in Lincoln, Nebr., until January 1953 when he was appointed by President Eisenhower to be the assistant attorney general in charge of the Office of Legal Counsel in the Department of Justice. In August 1956 President Eisenhower appointed Mr. Rankin to be the Solicitor General of the United States. Since January 1961 Mr. Rankin has been in private practice in New York City. He accepted the appointment as General Counsel for the President's Commission on the Assassination of President Kennedy on December 8, 1963.

SUMMARY AND CONCLUSIONS

The assassination of John Fitzgerald Kennedy on November 22, 1963, was a cruel and shocking act of violence directed against a man, a family, a nation, and against all mankind. A young and vigorous leader whose years of public and private life stretched before him was the victim of the fourth Presidential assassination in the history of a country dedicated to the concepts of reasoned argument and peaceful political change. * * * This report endeavors to appraise this tragedy by the light of reason and the standard of fairness. * * *

NARRATIVE OF EVENTS

At 11:40 A.M., C.S.T., on Friday, November 22, 1963, President John F. Kennedy, Mrs. Kennedy, and their party arrived at Love Field, Dallas, Tex. * * * After leaving the White House on Thursday morning, the President had flown initially to San Antonio where Vice President Lyndon B. Johnson joined the party. * * * Following a testimonial dinner in Houston for U. S. Representative Albert Thomas, the President flew to Fort Worth where he spent the night and spoke at a large breakfast gathering on Friday.

Planned for later that day were a motorcade through downtown Dallas, a luncheon speech at the Trade Mart, and a flight to Austin. * * * The Dallas motorcade, it was hoped, would evoke a demonstration of the President's personal popularity in a city which he had lost in the 1960 election. * * * Those responsible for planning, primarily governor John B. Connally, Jr., and Kenneth O'Donnell, a special assistant to the President, agreed that a motorcade through Dallas would be desirable. * * *

By midmorning of November 22, clearing skies in Dallas dispelled the threat of rain and the President greeted the crowds from his open limousine without the "bubbletop," which was at that time a plastic shield furnishing protection only against inclement weather. To the left of the President in the rear seat was Mrs. Kennedy. In the jump seats were Governor Connally, who was in front of the President, and Mrs. Connally at the Governor's left. Agent William R. Greer of the Secret Service was driving, and Agent Roy H. Kellerman was sitting to his right.

The motorcade left Love Field shortly after 11:50 A.M., stopping twice to greet well-wishers among the friendly crowds. * * * As the motorcade reached Main Street, a principal east-west artery in downtown Dallas, the welcome became tumultuous. At the extreme west end of Main Street the motorcade turned right on Houston Street and proceeded north for one block in order to make a left turn on Elm Street, the most direct and convenient approach to the Stemmons Freeway and the Trade Mart. As the President's car approached the intersection of Houston and Elm Streets, there loomed directly ahead on the intersection's northwest corner a seven-story, orange brick warehouse and office building, the Texas School Book Depository. Riding in the Vice President's car, Agent Rufus W. Youngblood of the Secret Service noticed that the clock atop the building indicated 12:30 P.M., the scheduled arrival time at the Trade Mart.

The President's car which had been going north made a sharp turn toward the southwest onto Elm Street. At a speed of about 11 miles per hour, it started down the gradual descent toward a railroad overpass under which the motorcade would proceed before reaching the Stemmons Freeway. The front of the Texas School Book Depository was now on the President's right, and he waved to the crowd. * * *

Seconds later shots resounded in rapid succession. The President's hands moved to his neck. He appeared to stiffen momentarily and lurch slightly forward in his seat. A bullet had entered the base of the back of his neck slightly to the right of the spine. It traveled downward and exited from the front of the neck. * * * Governor Connally * * * started to turn toward the left and suddenly felt a blow on his back. The Governor had been hit. * * * Another bullet then struck President Kennedy in the rear portion of his head, causing a massive and fatal wound. The President fell to the left into Mrs. Kennedy's lap.

Secret Service Agent Clinton J. Hill, riding on the left running board of the "followup" car, * * * jumped off the car and raced toward the President's limousine. In the front seat of the Vice-Presidential car, Agent Rufus W. Youngblood * * * vaulted into the rear seat and sat on the Vice President in order to protect him. At the same time Agent Kellerman in the front seat of the Presidential limousine turned to observe the President. Seeing that the President was struck, Kellerman instructed the driver, "Let's get out of here; we are hit." He radioed ahead to the lead car, "Get us to a hospital immediately."

Agent Greer immediately accelerated the Presidential car. As it gained speed, Agent Hill managed to pull himself onto the back of the car where Mrs. Kennedy had climbed. Hill pushed her back into the rear seat and shielded the stricken President and Mrs. Kennedy as the President's car proceeded at

high speed to Parkland Memorial Hospital, 4 miles away.

At Parkland, the President was immediately treated by a team of physicians who had been alerted for the President's arrival by the Dallas Police Department as the result of a radio message from the motorcade after the shooting. The doctors noted irregular breathing movements and a possible heartbeat, although they could not detect a pulsebeat. * * * In an effort to facilitate breathing, the physicians performed a tracheotomy. * * * Totally absorbed in the immediate task of trying to preserve the President's life, the attending doctors never turned the President over for an examination of his back. At 1 P.M., after all heart activity ceased and the Last Rites were administered by a priest, President Kennedy was pronounced dead. * * *

Vice President Johnson left Parkland Hospital under close guard and proceeded to the Presidential plane at Love Field. Mrs. Kennedy, accompanying her husband's body, boarded the plane shortly thereafter. At 2:38 P.M., in the central compartment of the plane, Lyndon B. Johnson was sworn in as the 36th President of the United States. * * * The plane left immediately for Washington, D.C., arriving at Andrews AFB, Md., at 5:58 P.M., E.S.T. The President's body was taken to the National Naval Medical Center, Bethesda, Md. * * * The autopsy report stated the cause of death as "Gunshot wound, head," and the bullets which struck the President were described as having been fired "from a point behind and somewhat above the level of the deceased."

At the scene of the shooting, there was evident confusion at the outset concerning the point of origin of the shots. * * * Within a few minutes, however, attention centered on the Texas School Book Depository Building. * * * The building was occupied by a private corporation, the Texas School Book Depository Co., which distributed school textbooks of several publishers and leased space to representatives of the publishers. * * * One eyewitness, Howard L. Brennan, had been watching the parade from a point on Elm Street directly opposite and facing the building. He promptly told a policeman that he had seen a slender man, about 5 feet 10 inches, in his early thirties, take deliberate aim from the sixth-floor corner window and fire a rifle in the direction of the President's car. Brennan thought he might be able to identify the man since he had noticed him in the window a few minutes before the motorcade made the turn onto Elm Street. At 12:34 P.M., the Dallas police radio mentioned the Depository Building as a possible source of the shots, and at 12:45 P.M., the police radio broadcast a description of the suspected assassin based primarily on Brennan's observations.

When the shots were fired, a Dallas motorcycle patrolman, Marrion L. Baker, was riding in the motorcade several cars behind the President. * * * Baker, having recently returned from a week of deer hunting, was certain the shot came from a high-powered rifle. * * * He raced his motorcycle to the building, dismounted, scanned the area to the west and pushed his way through the spectators toward the entrance. There he encountered Roy Truly, the building superintendent, who offered Baker his help. * * *

When they reached the second-floor landing * * * Baker thought he caught a glimpse of someone through the small glass window in the door separating the hall area near the stairs from the small vestibule leading into the lunchroom. Gun in hand, he rushed to the door and saw a man about 20 feet away walking toward the other end of the lunchroom. The man was emptyhanded. At Baker's command, the man turned and approached him. * * * Baker asked Truly whether he knew the man. * * * Truly replied that the man worked in the building, whereupon

Baker turned from the man and proceeded, with Truly, up the stairs. The man they encountered had started working in the Texas School Book Depository Building on October 16, 1963. His fellow workers described him as very quiet—a "loner." His name was Lee Harvey Oswald.

Within about one minute after his encounter with Baker and Truly, Oswald was seen passing through the second-floor offices. In his hand was a full "Coke" bottle which he had purchased from a vending machine in the lunchroom. He was walking toward the front of the building where a passenger elevator and a short flight of stairs provided access to the main entrance of the building on the first floor. Approximately 7 minutes later, at about 12:40 P.M., Oswald boarded a bus at a point on Elm Street seven short blocks east of the Depository Building. The bus was travelling west toward the very building from which Oswald had come. Its route lay through the Oak Cliff section in southwest Dallas, where it would pass seven blocks east of the rooming house in which Oswald was living, at 1026 North Beckley Avenue. On the bus was Mrs. Mary Bledsoe, one of Oswald's former landladies who immediately recognized him. Oswald stayed on the bus approximately 3 or 4 minutes, during which time it proceeded only two blocks because of the traffic jam created by the motorcade and the assassination. Oswald then left the bus.

A few minutes later he entered a vacant taxi four blocks away and asked the driver to take him to a point on North Beckley Avenue several blocks away from his rooming house. The trip required five or six minutes. At about 1 P.M., Oswald arrived at the rooming house. The housekeeper, Mrs. Earlene Roberts, was surprised to see Oswald at midday and remarked to him that he seemed to be in quite a hurry. He made no reply. A few minutes later Oswald emerged from his room zipping up his jacket and rushed out of the house.

Approximately 14 minutes later, and just 45 minutes after the assassination, another violent shooting occurred in Dallas. The victim was Patrolman J. D. Tippit of the Dallas police.

At approximately 1:15 P.M., Tippit was driving slowly in an easterly direction on East 10th Street in Oak Cliff. About 100 feet past the intersection of 10th Street and Patton Avenue, Tippit pulled up alongside a man walking in the same direction. The man met the general description of the suspect wanted in connection with the assassination. He walked over to Tippit's car, rested his arms on the

door on the right-hand side of the car, and apparently exchanged words with Tippit through the window. Tippit opened the door on the left side and started to walk around the front of his car. As he reached the front wheel on the driver's side, the man on the sidewalk drew a revolver and fired several shots, hitting Tippit four times and killing him instantly. * * *

As the gunman walked hurriedly back toward Patton Avenue and turned left, heading south * * * he passed alongside a taxicab. The driver, William W. Scoggins, had seen the slaying and was now crouched behind his cab on the street side. * * *

In a shoe store a few blocks farther west on Jefferson, the manager, Johnny Calvin Brewer, heard the siren of a police car moments after the radio in his store announced the shooting of the police officer in Oak Cliff. Brewer saw a man step quickly into the entranceway of the store and stand there with his back toward the street. When the police car made a U-turn and headed back * * * the man left and Brewer followed him. He saw the man enter the Texas Theatre, a motion picture house about 60 feet away, without buying a ticket. Brewer pointed this out to the cashier, Mrs. Julia Postal, who called the police. The time was shortly after 1:40 P.M. * * *

Within minutes the theater was surrounded. The house lights were then turned up. Patrolman M. N. McDonald and several other policemen approached the man. * * * The man drew a gun from his waist with one hand and struck the officer with the other. McDonald struck out with his right hand and grabbed the gun with his left hand. After a brief struggle McDonald and several other police officers disarmed and handcuffed the suspect and drove him to police headquarters, arriving at approximately 2 P.M.

Following the assassination, police cars had rushed to the Texas School Book Depository. * * * Shortly before 1 P.M., Capt. J. Will Fritz, Chief of the Homicide and Robbery Bureau of the Dallas Police Department, arrived to take charge of the investigation. Searching the sixth floor, Deputy Sheriff Luke Mooney noticed a pile of cartons in the southwest corner. He squeezed through the boxes and realized immediately that he had discovered the point from which the shots had been fired. On the floor were three empty cartridge cases.

A carton had apparently been placed on the floor at the side of the window so that a person sitting on the carton could look down Elm Street toward the overpass and scarcely be noticed from the outside. Between this carton and the half-open window were three additional cartons arranged at such an angle that a rifle resting on the top carton would be aimed directly at the motorcade as it moved away from the building. The high stack of boxes, which first attracted Mooney's attention, effectively screened a person at the window from the view of anyone else on the floor.

Mooney's discovery intensified the search for additional evidence on the sixth floor, and at 1:22 P.M., approximately 10 minutes after the cartridge cases were found, Deputy Sheriff Eugene Boone turned his flashlight in the direction of two rows of boxes in the northwest corner near the staircase. Stuffed between the two rows was a bolt-action rifle with a telescopic sight. * * *

As Fritz and Lt. J. C. Day were completing their examination of this rifle on the sixth floor, Roy Truly, the building superintendent, approached with information. * * * Earlier, while the police were questioning the employees, Truly had observed that Lee Harvey Oswald, one of the 15 men who worked in the warehouse, was missing. * * * Fritz left for police headquarters. He arrived at headquarters shortly after 2 P.M.

* * * Standing nearby were the police officers who had just arrived with the man arrested in the Texas Theatre. * * * The missing School Book Depository employee and the suspect who had been apprehended in the Texas Theatre were one and the same—Lee Harvey Oswald.

At 7:10 P.M. on November 22, 1963, Lee Harvey Oswald was formally advised that he had been charged with the murder of Patrolman J. D. Tippit. * * *

The formal charge against Oswald for the assassination of President Kennedy was lodged shortly after 1:30 A.M., on Saturday, November 23. By 10 P.M. of the day of the assassination, the FBI had traced the rifle found on the sixth floor of the Texas School Book Depository to a mailorder house in Chicago which had purchased it from a distributor in New York. Approximately 6 hours later the Chicago firm advised that this rifle had been ordered in March 1963 by an A. Hidel for shipment to Post Office Box 2915, in Dallas, Tex., a box rented by Oswald. * * *

On Sunday morning, November 24, arrangements were made for Oswald's transfer from the city jail to the Dallas County jail, about 1 mile away. * * * Earlier on Sunday, between 2:30 and 3 A.M., anonymous telephone calls threatening Oswald's life had been received by the Dallas office of the FBI and by the office of the County Sheriff. Nevertheless, on Sunday morning, television, radio, and newspaper representatives crowded into the basement to record the transfer. * * *

At approximately 11:20 A.M. Oswald emerged from the basement jail office flanked by detectives on either side and at his rear. He took just a few steps toward the car and was in the glaring light of the television cameras when a man suddenly darted out from an area on the right of the cameras where newsmen had been assembled. The man was carrying a Colt .38 revolver in his right hand and while millions watched on television, he moved quickly to within a few feet of Oswald and fired one shot into Oswald's abdomen. Oswald groaned with pain as he fell to the ground and quickly lost consciousness. Within 7 minutes Oswald was at Parkland Hospital where, without having regained consciousness, he was pronounced dead at 1:07 P.M.

The man who killed Oswald was Jack Ruby. He was instantly arrested and, minutes later, confined in a cell on the fifth floor of the Dallas police jail. Under interrogation, he denied that the killing of Oswald was in any way connected with a conspiracy involving the assassination of President Kennedy. He main-

tained that he had killed Oswald in a temporary fit of depression and rage over the President's death. Ruby was transferred the following day to the county jail without notice to the press or to police officers not directly involved in the transfer. Indicted for the murder of Oswald by the State of Texas on November 26, 1963, Ruby was found guilty on March 14, 1964, and sentenced to death. As of September 1964, his case was pending on appeal.

CONCLUSIONS

This Commission was created to ascertain the facts relating to the preceding summary of events and to consider the important questions which they raised. The Commission has addressed itself to this task and has reached certain conclusions based on all the available evidence. * * *

1. The shots which killed President Kennedy and wounded Governor Connally were fired from the sixth floor window at the southeast corner of the Texas School Book Depository. The determination is based upon the following:

   (A) Witnesses at the scene of the assassination saw a rifle being fired from the sixth floor window of the Depository Building. * * *

   (B) The nearly whole bullet found on Governor Connally's stretcher at Parkland Memorial Hospital and the two bullet fragments found in the front seat of the Presidential limousine were fired from the 6/5-millimeter Mannlicher-Carcano rifle found on the sixth floor of the Depository Building.

   (C) The three used cartridge cases found near the window on the sixth floor at the southeast corner of the building were fired from the same rifle. * * *

   (D) The windshield in the Presidential limousine was struck by a bullet fragment on the inside surface of the glass, but was not penetrated.

   (E) The nature of the bullet wounds suffered by President Kennedy and Governor Connally and the location of the car at the time of the shots establish that the bullets were fired from above and behind the Presidential limousine, striking the President and the Governor as follows:

   (1) President Kennedy was first struck by a bullet which entered at the back of his neck and exited through the lower front portion of his neck, causing a wound which would not necessarily have been lethal. The President was struck a second time by a bullet which entered the right-rear portion of his head, causing a massive and fatal wound.

   (2) Governor Connally was struck by a bullet which entered on the right side of his back and traveled downward through the right side of his chest, exiting below his right nipple. This bullet then passed through his right wrist and entered his left thigh where it caused a superficial wound.

2. The weight of the evidence indicates that there were three shots fired.

3. There is very persuasive evidence from the experts to indicate that the same bullet which pierced

the President's throat also caused Governor Connally's wounds. * * *

4. The shots which killed President Kennedy and wounded Governor Connally were fired by Lee Harvey Oswald. This conclusion is based upon the following:

(A) The Mannlicher-Carcona 6.5-millimeter Italian rifle from which the shots were fired was owned by and in the possession of Oswald.

(B) Oswald carried this rifle into the Depository Building on the morning of November 22, 1963.

(C) Oswald, at the time of the assassination, was present at the window from which the shots were fired.

(D) Shortly after the assassination, the Mannlicher-Carcona rifle belonging to Oswald was found partially hidden between some cartons on the sixth floor. * * *

(E) Based on testimony of the experts and their analysis of films of the assassination, the Commission has concluded that a rifleman of Lee Harvey Oswald's capabilities could have fired the shots from the rifle used in the assassination within the elapsed time of the shooting. * * *

5. Oswald killed Dallas Police Patrolman J. D. Tippit approximately 45 minutes after the assassination. This conclusion upholds the finding that Oswald fired the shots which killed President Kennedy and wounded Governor Connally. * * *

6. Within 80 minutes of the assassination and 35 minutes of the Tippit killing Oswald resisted arrest at the theatre by attempting to shoot another Dallas police officer.

7. The Commission has reached the following conclusions concerning Oswald's interrogation and detention by the Dallas police:

(A) Except for the force required to effect his arrest, Oswald was not subjected to any physical coercion by any law enforcement officials. * * *

(B) Newspaper, radio, and television reporters were allowed uninhibited access to the area through which Oswald had to pass when he was moved from his cell to the interrogation room and other sections of the building, thereby subjecting Oswald to harassment and creating chaotic conditions which were not conducive to orderly interrogation or the protection of the rights of the prisoner.

(C) The numerous statements, sometimes erroneous, made to the press by various local law enforcement officials, during this period of confusion and disorder in the police station, would have presented serious obstacles to the obtaining of a fair trial for Oswald. * * *

8. The Commission has reached the following conclusions concerning the killing of Oswald by Jack Ruby on November 24, 1963:

(A) Ruby entered the basement of the Dallas Police Department shortly after 11:17 A.M. and killed Lee Harvey Oswald at 11:21 A.M.

(B) Although the evidence on Ruby's means of entry is not conclusive, the weight of the evidence indicates that he walked down the ramp leading from Main Street. * * *

(C) There is no evidence to support the rumor that Ruby may have been assisted by any members of the Dallas Police Department in the killing of Oswald.

(D) The Dallas Police Department's decision to transfer Oswald to the county jail in full public view was unsound. * * *

9. The Commission has found no evidence that either Lee Harvey Oswald or Jack Ruby was part of any conspiracy, domestic or foreign, to assassinate President Kennedy. The reasons for this conclusion are:

(A) The Commission has found no evidence that anyone assisted Oswald in planning or carrying out the assassination. * * *

(B) The Commission has found no evidence that Oswald was involved with any person or group in a conspiracy to assassinate the President. * * *

(C) The Commission has found no evidence to show that Oswald was employed, persuaded, or encouraged by any foreign government to assassinate President Kennedy or that he was an agent of any foreign government. * * *

(D) The Commission has explored all attempts of Oswald to identify himself with various political groups, including the Communist party, U.S.A., The Fair Play For Cuba Committee, and the Socialist Workers Party, and has been unable to find any evidence that the contacts which he initiated were related to Oswald's subsequent assassination of the President.

(E) All of the evidence before the Commission established that there was nothing to support the speculation that Oswald was an agent, employee, or informant of the FBI, the CIA, or any other governmental agency. * * *

(F) No direct or indirect relationship between Lee Harvey Oswald and Jack Ruby has been discovered by the Commission. * * *

(G) The Commission has found no evidence that Jack Ruby acted with any other person in the killing of Lee Harvey Oswald. * * * Because of the difficulty of proving negatives to a certainty the possibility of others being involved with either Oswald or Ruby cannot be established categorically, but if there is any such evidence it has been beyond the reach of all the investigative agencies and resources of the United, States and has not come to the attention of this Commission.

10. In its entire investigation the Commission has found no evidence of conspiracy, subversion, or disloyalty to the U.S. government by any Federal, state, or local official.

11. On the basis of the evidence before the Commission it concludes that Oswald acted alone. * * *

The Commission could not make any definitive determination of Oswald's motives. It has endeavored to isolate factors which contributed to his character and which might have influenced his decision to assassinate President Kennedy. These factors were:

(A) His deep-rooted resentment of all authority. * * *

(B) His inability to enter into meaningful relationships with people. * * *

(C) His urge to try to find a place in history and despair at times over failures in his various undertakings;

(D) His capacity for violence as evidenced by his attempt to kill General Walker;

(E) His avowed commitment to Marxism and Communism. * * *

Each of these contributed to his capacity to risk all in cruel and irresponsible actions.

12. The Commission recognizes that the varied responsibilities of the President require that he make frequent trips to all parts of the United States and abroad. Consistent with their high responsibilities Presidents can never be protected from every potential threat. * * * Nevertheless, the Commission believes that recommendations for improvements in Presidential protection are compelled by the facts disclosed in this investigation. * * *

(1) The protective research section of the Secret Service, which is responsible for its preventive work, lacked sufficient trained personnel and the mechanical and technical assistance needed to fulfill its responsibility.

(2) Prior to the assassination the Secret Service's criteria dealt with direct threats against the President. Although the Secret Service treated the direct threats against the President adequately, it failed to recognize the necessity of identifying other potential sources of danger to his security. * * * In effect, the Secret Service largely relied upon other Federal or State Agencies to supply the information necessary for it to fulfill its preventive responsibilities. * * * The Commission has concluded that there was insufficient liaison and coordination of information between the Secret Service and other Federal Agencies necessarily concerned with Presidential protection. * * * A more carefully coordinated treatment of the Oswald case by the FBI might well have resulted in bringing Oswald's activities to the attention of the Secret Service. * * *

RECOMMENDATIONS

Prompted by the assassination of President Kennedy, the Secret Service has initiated a comprehensive and critical review of its total operations. * * * The Commission is encouraged by the efforts taken by the Secret Service * * * and suggests the following recommendations:

1. A committee of cabinet members including the Secretary of the Treasury and the Attorney General, or the National Security Councils, should be assigned the responsibility of reviewing and overseeing the protective activities of the Secret Service and the other Federal Agencies that assist in safeguarding the President. * * *

2. Suggestions have been advanced to the Commission for the transfer of all or parts of the Presidential protective responsibilities of the Secret Service to some other department or agency. * * *

3. Meanwhile, in order to improve daily supervision of the Secret Service within the Department of the Treasury, the Commission recommends that the Secretary of the Treasury appoint a special assistant with the responsibility of supervising the Secret Service. * * * One of the initial assignments of this special assistant should be the supervision of the current effort by the Secret Service to revise and modernize its basic operating procedures.

4. The Commission recommends that the Secret Service completely overhaul its facilities devoted to the advance detection of potential threats against the President. * * *

5. The Commission recommends that the Secret Service improve the protective measures followed in the planning, and conducting of Presidential motorcades. * * *

6. The Commission recommends that the Secret Service continue its recent efforts to improve and formalize its relationships with local police departments in areas to be visited by the President.

7. The Commission * * * recommends that the Secret Service be provided with the personnel and resources which the Service and The Department of the Treasury may be able to demonstrate are needed

8. Even with an increase in Secret Service personnel, the protection of the President will continue to require the resources and cooperation of many Federal Agencies. The Commission recommends that these agencies, specifically the FBI, continue the practice as it has developed, particularly since the assassination, of assisting the Secret Service upon request by providing personnel or other aid. * * *

9. The Commission recommends that the President's physician always accompany him during his travels and occupy a position near the President where he can be immediately available in case of any emergency.

10. The Commission recommends to Congress that it adopt legislation which would make the assassination of the President and Vice President a Federal crime. * * *

11. The Commission has examined the Department of State's handling of the Oswald matter and finds that it followed the law throughout. However, the Commission believes that the department in accordance with its own regulations should in all cases exercise great care in the return to this country of defectors who have evidenced disloyalty or hostility to this country or who have expressed a desire to renounce their American citizenship and that when such persons are so returned, procedures should be adopted for the better dissemination of information concerning them to the intelligence agencies of the government.

12. The Commission recommends that the representatives of the bar, law enforcement associations and the news media work together to establish ethical standards concerning the collection and presentation of information to the public so that there will be no interference with pending criminal investigations, court proceedings, or the right of individuals to a fair trial.

PRESIDENTIAL ASSASSINATIONS AND ATTEMPTS

In the course of the history of the United States four Presidents have been assassinated, within less than 100 years, beginning with Abraham Lincoln in 1865. Attempts were also made on the lives of two other Presidents, one President-elect, and one ex-President. Still other Presidents were the objects of plots that were never carried out. The actual attempts occurred as follows:

Andrew Jackson	Jan. 30, 1835.	
Abraham Lincoln	Apr. 14, 1865	Died Apr. 15, 1865.
James A. Garfield	July 2, 1881.	Died Sept. 19, 1881.
William McKinley	Sept. 6, 1901.	Died Sept. 14, 1901.
Theodore Roosevelt	Oct. 14, 1912.	Wounded; recovered.
Franklin D. Roosevelt	Feb. 15, 1933.	
Harry S. Truman	Nov. 1, 1950.	
John F. Kennedy	Nov. 22, 1963.	Died that day.
Gerald Ford	Sept. 5, 1975;	Sept. 22, 1975.

Attempts have thus been made on the lives of one of every five American Presidents. One of every nine Presidents has been killed. Since 1865, there have been attempts on the lives of one of every four Presidents and the successful assassination of one of every five. During the last three decades, three attacks were made.

It was only after William McKinley was shot that systematic and continuous protection of the President was instituted. Protection before McKinley was intermittent and spasmodic. The problem had existed from the days of the early Presidents, but no action was taken until three tragic events had occurred. In considering the effectiveness of present day protection arrangements, it is worthwhile to examine the development of Presidential protection over the years, to understand both the high degree of continuing danger and the anomalous reluctance to take the necessary precautions.

BEFORE THE CIVIL WAR

In the early days of the Republic, there was remarkably little concern about the safety of Presidents and few measures were taken to protect them. They were at times the objects of abuse and the recipients of threatening letters as more recent Presidents have been, but they did not take the threats seriously and moved about freely without protective escorts. On his inauguration day, Thomas Jefferson walked from his boarding house to the Capitol, unaccompanied by any guard, to take the oath of office. There was no police authority in Washing-ton itself until 1805 when the mayor appointed a high constable and 40 deputy constables.

John Quincy Adams received many threatening letters and on one occasion was threatened in person in the White House by a court-martialed Army sergeant. In spite of this incident, the President asked for no protection and continued to indulge his fondness for solitary walks and early morning swims in the Potomac.

Among pre-Civil War Presidents, Andrew Jackson aroused particularly strong feelings. He received many threatening letters which, with a fine contempt, he would endorse and send to the Washington Globe for publication. On one occasion in May 1833, Jackson was assaulted by a former Navy lieutenant, Robert B. Randolph, but refused to prosecute him. This is not regarded as an attempt at assassination, since Randolph apparently did not intend serious injury.

Less than 2 years later, on the morning of January 10, 1835, as Jackson emerged from the east portico of the Capitol, he was accosted by a would-be assassin, Richard Lawrence, an English-born house painter. Lawrence fired his two pistols at the President, but they both misfired. Lawrence was quickly overpowered and held for trial. A jury found him not guilty by reason of insanity. He was confined in jails and mental hospitals for the rest of his life.

The attack on Jackson did not inspire any action to provide protection for the Chief Executive. Jackson's immediate successor, Martin Van Buren, often walked to church alone and rode horseback alone in the woods not far from the White House. In August 1842, after an intoxicated painter had thrown rocks at President John Tyler, who was walking on the grounds to the south of the White House, Congress passed an act to establish an auxiliary watch for the protection of public and private property in Washington. The force was to consist of a captain and 15 men. This act was apparently aimed more at the protection of the White House, which had been defaced on occasion, than of the President.

LINCOLN

Even before he took the oath of office, Abraham Lincoln was thought to be the object of plots and conspiracies to kidnap or kill him. Extremist opponents apparently contemplated desperate measures to prevent his inauguration, and there is some evidence that they plotted

Abraham Lincoln, *William McKinley and James A. Garfield were all assassinated in office.*

to attack him while he was passing through Baltimore on his way to Washington.

For the inauguration, the Army took precautions unprecedented up to that time and perhaps more elaborate than any precautions taken since. Soldiers occupied strategic points throughout the city, along the procession route, and at the Capitol, while armed men in plain clothes mingled with the crowds. Lincoln himself, in a carriage with President Buchanan, was surrounded on all sides by such dense masses of soldiers that he was almost completely hidden from the view of the crowds. The precautions at the Capitol during the ceremony were almost as thorough and equally successful.

Lincoln lived in peril during all his years in office. The volume of threatening letters remained high throughout the war, but little attention was paid to them. The few letters that were investigated yielded no results. He was reluctant to surround himself with guards and often rejected protection or sought to slip away from it. This has been characteristic of almost all American Presidents. They have regarded protection as a necessary affliction at best and contrary to their normal instincts for either personal privacy or freedom to meet the people. In Lincoln these instincts were especially strong, and he suffered with impatience the efforts of his friends, the police, and the military to safeguard him.

The protection of the President during the war varied greatly, depending on Lincoln's susceptibility to warnings. Frequently, military units were assigned to guard the White House and to accompany the President on his travels. Lincoln's friend, Ward H. Lamon, on becoming marshal of the District of Columbia in 1861, took personal charge of protecting the President and provided guards for the purpose, but he became so exasperated at the President's lack of cooperation that he tendered his resignation. Lincoln did not accept it. Finally, late in the war, in November 1864, four Washington policemen were detailed to the White House to act as personal bodyguards to the President. Lincoln tolerated them reluctantly and insisted they remain as inconspicuous as possible.

In the closing days of the war, rumors of attempts on Lincoln's life persisted. The well-known actor, John Wilkes Booth, a fanatical Confederate sympathizer, plotted with others for months to kidnap the President. The fall of the Confederacy apparently hardened his determination to kill Lincoln. Booth's opportunity came on Good Friday, April 14, 1865, when he learned that the President would be attending a play at Ford's Theater that night. The President's bodyguard for the evening was Patrolman John F. Parker of the Washington Police, a man who proved himself unfit for protective duty. He was supposed to remain on guard in the corridor outside of the Presidential box during the entire performance of the play, but he soon wandered off to watch the play and then even went outside the theater to have a drink at a nearby saloon. Parker's dereliction of duty left the President totally unprotected. Shortly after 10 o'clock on that evening, Booth found his way up to the Presidential box and shot the President in the head. The President's wound was a mortal one; he died the next morning, April 15.

A detachment of troops captured Booth on April 26 at a farm near Bowling Green, Va.; he received a bullet wound and died a few hours later. At a trial in June, a military tribunal sentenced four of Booth's associates to death and four others to terms of imprisonment.

Lincoln's assassination revealed the total inadequacy of Presidential protection. A congressional committee conducted an extensive investigation of the assassination, but with traditional reluctance, called for no action to provide better protection for the President in the future. Nor did requests for protective measures come from the President or from Government departments. This lack of concern for the protection of the President may have derived also from the tendency of the time to regard Lincoln's assassination as part of a unique crisis that was not likely to happen to a future Chief Executive.

THE NEED FOR PROTECTION FURTHER DEMONSTRATED

For a short time after the war, soldiers assigned by the War Department continued to protect the White House and its grounds. Metropolitan Washington policemen assisted on special occasions to maintain order and prevent the congregation of crowds. The permanent Metropolitan Police guard was reduced to three and assigned entirely to protection at the White House. There was no special group of trained officers to protect the person of the President. Presidents after Lincoln continued to move about in Washington virtually unattended, as their predecessors had done before the Civil War, and, as before, such protection as they got at the White House came from the doormen, who were not especially trained for guard duty.

This lack of personal protection for the President came again tragically to the attention of the country with the shooting of President James A. Garfield in 1881. The President's assassin, Charles J. Guiteau, was a self-styled "lawyer, theologian, and politician" who had convinced himself that his unsolicited efforts to help elect Garfield in 1880 entitled him to appointment as a consul in Europe. Bitterly disappointed that the President ignored his repeated written requests for appointment to office and obsessed with a kind of megalomania, he resolved to kill Garfield.

At that time Guiteau was 38 years old and had an unusually checkered career behind him. He had been an itinerant and generally unsuccessful lecturer and evangelist, a lawyer, and a would-be politician. While it is true he resented Garfield's failure to appoint him consul in Paris as a reward for his wholly illusory contribution to the Garfield campaign, and he verbally attacked Garfield for his lack of support for the so-called Stalwart wing of the Republican Party, these may not have supplied the total motivation for his crime. At his trial he testified that the "Deity" had commanded him to remove the President. There is no evidence that he confided his assassination plans to anyone or that he had any close friends or confidants. He made his attack on the President under circumstances where escape after the shooting was inconceivable. There were some hereditary mental problems in his family and Guiteau apparently believed in divine inspiration.

Guiteau later testified that he had had three opportunities to attack the President prior to the actual shooting. On all of these occasions, within a brief period of 3 weeks, the President was unguarded. Guiteau finally realized his intent on the morning of July 2, 1881. As Garfield was walking to a train in the Baltimore and Potomac Railroad Station in Washington, Guiteau stepped up and shot him in the back. Garfield did not die from the effects of the wound until September 19, 1881. Although there was evidence of serious abnormality in Guiteau, he was found guilty of murder and sentenced to be hanged. The execution took place on June 30, 1882.

At least one newspaper, the New York Tribune, predicted that the assault on Garfield would lead to the President becoming "the slave of his office, the prisoner of forms and restrictions," in sharp and unwelcome contrast to the splendidly simple life he had been able to live before.

> The bullet of the assassin who lurked in the Washington railway station to take the life of President Garfield shattered the simple Republican manner of life which the custom of nearly a century has prescribed for the Chief Magistrate of the United States. Our Presidents have been the first citizens of the Republic—nothing more. With a measure of power in their hands far greater than is wielded by the ruler of any limited monarchy in Europe, they have never surrounded themselves with the forms and safeguards of courts. The White House has been a business office to everybody. Its occupant has always been more accessible than the heads of great commercial establishments. When the passions of the war were at fever heat, Mr. Lincoln used to have a small guard of cavalry when he rode out to his summer residence at the Soldier's Home; but at no other time in our history has it been thought needful for a President to have any special protection against violence when inside or outside the White House. Presidents have driven about Washington like other people and travelled over the country as unguarded and unconstrained as any private citizen.

The prediction of the Tribune did not come to pass. Although the Nation was shocked by this deed, its representatives took no steps to provide the President with personal protection. The President continued to move about Washington, sometimes completely alone, and to travel without special protection. There is a story that President Chester A. Arthur, Garfield's successor, once went to a ceremony at

Theodore Roosevelt

447

the Washington Navy Yard on a public conveyance that he hailed in front of the White House.

During Grover Cleveland's second administration (1893–97) the number of threatening letters addressed to the President increased markedly, and Mrs. Cleveland persuaded the President to increase the number of White House policemen to 27 from the 3 who had constituted the force since the Civil War. In 1894, the Secret Service began to provide protection, on an informal basis.

The Secret Service was organized as a division of the Department of the Treasury in 1865, to deal with counterfeiting. Its jurisdiction was extended to other fiscal crimes against the United States in later appropriations acts, but its early work in assisting in protecting the President was an unofficial, stopgap response to a need for a trained organization, with investigative capabilities, to perform this task. In 1894, while investigating a plot by a group of gamblers in Colorado to assassinate President Cleveland, the Secret Service assigned a small detail of operatives to the White House to help protect him. Secret Service men accompanied the President and his family to their vacation home in Massachusetts; special details protected the President in Washington, on trips, and at special functions. For a time, two agents rode in a buggy behind President Cleveland's carriage, but this practice attracted so much attention in the opposition newspapers that it was soon discontinued at the President's insistence. These initially informal and part-time arrangements eventually led to the organization of permanent systematic protection for the President and his family.

During the Spanish-American War the Secret Service stationed a detail at the White House to provide continuous protection for President McKinley. The special wartime protective measures were relaxed after the war, but Secret Service guards remained on duty at the White House at least part of the time.

Between 1894 and 1900, anarchists murdered the President of France, the Premier of Spain, the Empress of Austria, and the King of Italy. At the turn of the century the Secret Service thought that the strong police action taken against the anarchists in Europe was compelling them to flee and that many were coming to the United States. Concerned about the protection of the President, the Secret Service increased the number of guards and directed that a guard accompany him on all of his trips.

Unlike Lincoln and Garfield, President McKinley was being guarded when he was shot by Leon F. Czolgosz, an American-born 28-year-old factory worker and farmhand. On September 6, 1901, the President was holding a brief reception for the public in the Temple of Music at the Pan American Exposition in Buffalo. Long lines of people passed between two rows of policemen and soldiers to reach the President and shake his hand. In the immediate vicinity of the President were four Buffalo detectives, four soldiers, and three Secret Service agents. Two of the Secret Service men were facing the President at a distance of 3 feet. One of them stated later that it was normally his custom to stand at the side of the President on such occasions, but that he had been requested not to do so at this time in order to permit McKinley's secretary and the president of the exposition to stand on either side of McKinley. Czolgosz joined the line, concealed a pistol under a handkerchief, and when he stood in front of the President shot twice through the handkerchief. McKinley fell critically wounded.

Czolgosz, a self-styled anarchist, did not believe in rulers of any kind. There is evidence that the organized anarchists in the U.S.A. did not accept or trust him. He was not admitted as a member to any of the secret anarchist societies. No co-plotters were ever discovered, and there is no evidence that he had confided in anyone. A calm inquiry made by two eminent alienists about a year after Czolgosz was executed found that Czolgosz had for some time been suffering from delusions. One was that he was an anarchist; another was that it was his duty to assassinate the President.

The assassin said he had no grudge against the President personally but did not believe in the republican form of government or in rulers of any kind. In his written confession he included the words, " 'I don't believe one man should have so much service and another man should have none.' " As he was strapped to the chair to be electrocuted, he said: " 'I killed the President because he was the enemy of the good people—the good working people. I am not sorry for my crime.' "

McKinley lingered on for 8 days before he died of blood poisoning early on the morning of September 14. Czolgosz, who had been captured immediately, was swiftly tried, convicted, and condemned to death. Although it seemed to some contemporaries that Czolgosz was incompetent, the defense made no effort to plead insanity.

Franklin D. Roosevelt

Harry S. Truman

Czolgosz was executed 45 days after the President's death. Investigations by the Buffalo police and the Secret Service revealed no accomplices and no plot of any kind.

DEVELOPMENT OF PRESIDENTIAL PROTECTION

This third assassination of a President in a little more than a generation—it was only 36 years since Lincoln had been killed—shook the nation and aroused it to a greater awareness of the uniqueness of the Presidency and the grim hazards that surrounded an incumbent of that Office. The first congressional session after the assassination of McKinley gave more attention to legislation concerning attacks on the President than had any previous Congress but did not pass any measures for the protection of the President. Nevertheless, in 1902 the Secret Service, which was then the only Federal general investigative agency of any consequence, assumed full-time responsibility for the safety of the President. Protection of the

President now became one of its major permanent functions, and it assigned two men to its original full-time White House detail. Additional agents were provided when the President traveled or went on vacation.

Theodore Roosevelt, who was the first President to experience the extensive system of protection that has surrounded the President ever since, voiced an opinion of Presidential protection that was probably shared in part by most of his successors. In a letter to Senator Henry Cabot Lodge in 1906, from his summer home, he wrote:

> The Secret Service men are a very small but very necessary thorn in the flesh. Of course, they would not be the least use in preventing any assault upon my life. I do not believe there is any danger of such an assault, and if there were, as Lincoln said, "though it would be safer for a President to live in a cage, it would interfere with his business." But it is only the Secret Service men who render life endurable, as you would realize if you saw the procession of carriages that pass through the place, the procession of people on foot who try to get into the place, not to speak of the multitude of cranks and others who are stopped in the village.

Roosevelt, who had succeeded to the Presidency because of an assassin's bullet, himself became the object of an assassination attempt a few years after he left office and when he was no longer under Secret Service protection. During the Presidential campaign of 1912, just as he was about to make a political speech in Milwaukee on October 14, he was shot and wounded in the breast by John N. Schrank, a 36-year-old German-born ex-tavern keeper. A folded manuscript of his long speech and the metal case for his eyeglasses in the breast pocket of Roosevelt's coat were all that prevented the assassination.

Schrank had had a vision in 1901, induced possibly by McKinley's assassination, which took on meaning for him after Roosevelt, 11 years later, started to campaign for the Presidency. In this vision the ghost of McKinley appeared to him and told him not to let a murderer (i.e., Roosevelt, who according to the vision had murdered McKinley) become President. It was then that he determined upon the assassination. At the bidding of McKinley's ghost, he felt he had no choice but to kill Theodore Roosevelt. After his attempt on Roosevelt, Schrank was found to be insane and was committed to mental hospitals in Wisconsin for the rest of his life.

The establishment and extension of the Secret Service authority for protection was a prolonged process. Although the Secret Service undertook to provide full-time protection for the President beginning in 1902, it received neither funds for the purpose nor sanction from the Congress until 1906 when the Sundry Civil Expenses Act for 1907 included funds for protection of the President by the Secret Service. Following the election of William Howard Taft in 1908, the Secret Service began providing protection for the President-elect. This practice received statutory authorization in 1913, and in the same year, Congress authorized permanent protection of the President. It remained necessary to renew the authority annually in the Appropriations Acts until 1951.

As in the Civil and Spanish-American Wars, the coming of war in 1917 caused increased concern for the safety of the President. Congress enacted a law, since referred to as the threat statute, making it a crime to threaten the President by mail or in any other manner. In 1917 Congress also authorized protection for the President's immediate family by the Secret Service.

As the scope of the Presidency expanded during the 20th century, the Secret Service found the problems of protection becoming more numerous. In 1906, for the first time in history, a President traveled outside the United States while in office. When Theodore Roosevelt visited Panama in that year, he was accompanied and protected by Secret Service men. In 1918–19 Woodrow Wilson broadened the precedent of Presidential foreign travel when he traveled to Europe with a Secret Service escort of 10 men to attend the Versailles Peace Conference.

The attempt on the life of President-elect Franklin D. Roosevelt in 1933 further demonstrated the broad scope and complexity of the protection problems facing the Secret Service. Giuseppe Zangara was a bricklayer and stonemason with a professed hatred of capitalists and Presidents. He seemed to be obsessed with the desire to kill a President. After his arrest he confessed that he had first planned to go to Washington to kill President Herbert Hoover, but as the cold climate of the North was bad for his stomach trouble, he was loath to leave Miami, where he was staying. When he read in the paper that President-elect Roosevelt would be in Miami, he resolved to kill him.

On the night of February 15, 1933, at a political rally in Miami's Bayfront Park, the President-elect sat on the top of the rear seat of his automobile with a small microphone in his hand as he made a short informal talk. Fortunately for him, however, he slid down into the seat just before Zangara could get near enough to take aim. The assassin's arm may have been jogged just as he shot; the five rounds he directed at Roosevelt went awry. However, he mortally wounded Mayor Anton Cermak, of Chicago, and hit four other persons; the President-elect, by a miracle, escaped. Zangara, of course, never had any chance of escaping.

Zangara was electrocuted on March 20, 1933, only 33 days after his attempt on Roosevelt. No evidence of accomplices or conspiracy came to light, but there was some sensational newspaper speculation, wholly undocumented, that Zangara may have been hired by Chicago gangsters to kill Cermak.

The force provided since the Civil War by the Washington Metropolitan Police for the protection of the White House had grown to 54 men by 1922. In that year Congress enacted legislation creating the White House Police Force as a separate organization under the direct control of the President. This force was actually supervised by the President's military aide until 1930, when Congress placed supervision under the Chief of the Secret Service. Although Congress transferred control and supervision of the force to the Secretary of the Treasury in 1962, the Secretary delegated supervision to the Chief of the Secret Service.

The White House detail of the Secret Service grew in size slowly from the original 2 men assigned in 1902. In 1914 it still numbered only 5, but during World War I it was increased to 10 men. Additional men were added when the President traveled. After the war the size of the detail grew until it reached 16 agents and 2 supervisors by 1939. World War II created new and greater protection problems, especially those arising from the President's trips abroad to the Grand Strategy Conferences in such places as Casablanca, Quebec, Tehran, Cairo, and Yalta. To meet the increased demands, the White House detail was increased to 37 men early in the war.

The volume of mail received by the White House had always been large, but it reached huge proportions under Franklin D. Roosevelt. Presidents had always received threatening letters but never in such quantities. To deal with this growing problem, the Secret Service established in 1940 the Protective Research Section to analyze and make available to those charged with protecting the President, information from White House mail and other sources concerning people potentially capable of violence to the President. The Protective Research Section undoubtedly permitted the Secret Service to anticipate and forestall many incidents that might have been embarrassing or harmful to the President.

Although there was no advance warning of the attempt on Harry S. Truman's life on November 1, 1950, the protective measures taken by the Secret Service availed, and the assassins never succeeded in firing directly at the President. The assassins—Oscar Collazo and Griselio Torresola, Puerto Rican Nationalists living in New York—tried to force their way into Blair House, at the time the President's residence while the White House was being repaired. Blair House was guarded by White House policemen and Secret Service agents. In the ensuing gun battle, Torresola and one White House policeman were killed, and Collazo and two White House policemen were wounded. Had the assassins succeeded in entering the front door of Blair House, they would probably have been cut down immediately by another Secret Service agent inside who kept the doorway covered with a submachine gun from his vantage point at the foot of the main stairs. In all, some 27 shots were fired in less than 3 minutes.

Collazo was brought to trial in 1951 and sentenced to death, but President Truman commuted the sentence to life imprisonment on July 24, 1952. Although there was a great deal of evidence linking Collazo and Torresola to the Nationalist Party of Puerto Rico and its leader, Pedro Albizu Campos, the Government could not establish that the attack on the President was part of a larger Nationalist conspiracy.

The attack on President Truman led to the enactment in 1951 of legislation that permanently authorized the Secret Service to protect the President, his immediate family, the President-elect, and the Vice President, the last upon his request. Protection of the Vice President by the Secret Service had begun in January 1945 when Harry S. Truman occupied the office.

In 1962 Congress further enlarged the list of Government officers to be safeguarded, authorizing protection of the Vice President (or the officer next in order of succession to the Presidency) without requiring his request therefor; of the Vice President-elect; and of a former President, at his request, for a reasonable period after his departure from office. The Secret Service considered this "reasonable period" to be 6 months.

Theodore Roosevelt
TWENTY-SIXTH PRESIDENT   **1901-1909**

William Howard Taft
TWENTY-SEVENTH PRESIDENT   1909-1913

Woodrow Wilson
TWENTY-EIGHTH PRESIDENT   1913-1921

Warren G. Harding
TWENTY-NINTH PRESIDENT   1921-1923

Calvin Coolidge
THIRTIETH PRESIDENT   1923-1929

Herbert Hoover
THIRTY-FIRST PRESIDENT   1929-1933

Franklin D. Roosevelt
THIRTY-SECOND PRESIDENT   1933-1945

Harry S. Truman
THIRTY-THIRD PRESIDENT   **1945-1953**

Dwight D. Eisenhower
THIRTY-FOURTH PRESIDENT   1953-1961

John Fitzgerald Kennedy
THIRTY-FIFTH PRESIDENT   1961-1963

Lyndon B. Johnson
THIRTY-SIXTH PRESIDENT   1963-1969

Richard M. Nixon
THIRTY-SEVENTH PRESIDENT   **1969-1974**

Gerald R. Ford
THIRTY-EIGHTH PRESIDENT 1974

POWERS OF THE PRESIDENT

The Constitution states that "executive power shall be vested in a President" whose duty is to "take Care that the Laws be faithfully executed." From its brief outline of Presidential power, the Presidency has grown to be the unique institution it is today.

The President is Commander in Chief of the Armed Forces. He can make treaties by and with the advice and consent of the Senate, provided two-thirds of the Senators present concur. He can name Ambassadors and receive Envoys from other countries. He can appoint Supreme Court Justices and other U.S. officers whose appointments are not otherwise provided for, and which shall be established by law.

The President may call for the written opinion of the principal officer of any executive department concerning any aspect of his work. He may summon Congress to special session and adjourn both Houses in case of disagreement between them with respect to the time of adjournment—a privilege never yet used. He can veto bills, although Congress may override him. He can grant pardons and reprieves. He may make recommendations to Congress.

It has been the peculiar virtue of the highest post in the oldest republic on Earth that while some Presidents have done themselves little credit, none has dimmed the prestige of the office itself. Some, notably Washington, Lincoln, and the Roosevelts, enlarged the powers of the Presidency and were enlarged by their experiences in office. Others, who at first seemed too small for the Presidency, managed to fill it well. Only a few—notably, Grant, Harding, and Nixon—left tainted memories behind.

The Founding Fathers could not foresee the powers that would ultimately be given to the President, but they were wise enough both to allow for flexibility in the administration of the office and to establish limitations for it. Thus they left room for the occasional strong President, while ensuring that none could be other than an instrument of the people.

THE NINETEEN SEVENTIES

On August 9, 1974, Richard Nixon, the thirty-seventh President of the United States, resigned from office. The dramatic event concluded a two-year episode in American history which was replete with unprecedented events. The Vice President, in an unrelated matter, had been forced to resign from his post following an indictment on charges of criminal behavior. The Republican Party had been removed from the Presidential campaign in 1972 as members of the Committee to Re-Elect the President emerged in operations which ultimately led to the victor's demise. The war in Vietnam had been terminated, though hardly in the "peace with honor" fashion that the Chief Executive and the military had so desperately envisioned. And, within a matter of months, Gerald Ford, the thirty-eighth President of the United States, was sworn into office as the first president not to have been popularly elected to either the Vice Presidency or Presidency of the country.

The series of events known as Watergate are, in a sense, broader than the actual incidents themselves, vital to an understanding of American politics in the 1970's. One of the most fundamental questions raised by the events is the issue of an open, democratic government.

In a speech made in 1972, Nixon captured the essence of democracy, by maintaining that: "Fundamental to our way of life is the belief that when information which properly belongs to the public is systematically withheld from those in power, the people soon become ignorant of their own affairs, distrustful of those who manage them, and—eventually—incapable of determining their own destinies." The claim made by the President in support of an open government was viewed as both positive and vital to

Vietnamese farmer and his mutilated son during an impromptu press conference in Vietnam in 1970. After the news of the My Lai massacre had broken, many Vietnamese peasants came forward with similar stories about American atrocities in Vietnam.

democracy. It was a major factor in producing his overwhelming victory on November 7th. Yet, at the same time the speech was being delivered, the Committee to Re-Elect the President was engaging in multiple, illegal operations —all of which were kept secret. The record of Nixon's Administration clearly portrayed the extensive use of secret activities including domestic surveillance and international, subversive missions as well as other activities which violated the domain of information clearly and properly belonging to the public. Hence, the credibility gap first coined as a term describing President Johnson became the trademark of the Nixon Administration. Of the most critical challenges to Amerca in the 1970's, the issue of open government has come to the forefront.

Not until fairly recently has the constitutional basis for open government begun to emerge. There was no clear precedent in American history for banning secrecy and even participants in the Constitutional Convention held their meetings behind closed doors. The document produced and ratified in 1789 expressly provided for some secrecy within the operations of Congress and the first elected President refused on a number of occasions to submit information to the Legislature on the grounds that it should be withheld in the public interest.

There are, however, three fundamental doctrines which have developed out of interpretations of the Constitution which provide a means of promoting both a legal and political basis for open government. Given the experiences of the last year of the Nixon Administration, these doctrines are especially important in the 1970's—the separation of powers, the First Amendment and the concept of due process.

Separation of powers is generally perceived as a method of prohibiting one segment of government from interfering with the activities of another segment. It is closely related to the theory of checks and balances in that a certain amount of autonomy as well as coordination is necessary for reasonable

465

Aerial view *of the site of the My Lai massacre. The nation at first did not believe the stories about the slaughter of men, women, and children by U.S. soldiers in 1968. The controversy over the My Lai massacre went on during the first years of the decade of the 1970's.*

and effective conduct of a democratic government. Taken from another perspective, however, when autonomy through the separation of branches of government denies access to information or assistance in formulating decisions to another branch, it works against good government.

Taken to its extreme, the right to have information held by another branch of government in order to carry out rights and duties would result, in the case of Congress, in virtually unlimited access to any and all information possessed by the Executive branch. Because Congress is engaged in appropriation of funds, the enactment of laws and the overseeing of the work of the administration, its right of access to information would include almost the entire spectrum of data held by the executive. In practice, this obviously is not the case however.

The primary constitutional limitation imposed in this area is the doctrine of executive privilege. It has been promoted by the Executive branch historically and currently. There is little constitutional law on the subject, as evidenced in the disputes between the Nixon Administration and the Senate Select Committee during the Watergate hearings and the

A group of soldiers *stays behind white tape marking a cleared area in My Lai. The tape was to seal off the area of the massacre to allow a team of military investigators to search for evidence of the atrocities.*

subsequent impeachment hearings. The only courts which dealt directly with the issue were the District and Circuit Courts of Washington, D.C., which both ruled that the extravagant contention of the President and his attorneys that the information withheld was in the national interest was unsupportable. The exact scope of executive privilege, however, remains illusive. The Supreme Court refused to enter a judgment in the contest between the two branches of government exclusively on this matter and, consequently, it is likely to re-emerge time and again during this decade.

A second basis for arguing for the openness of government is found in the First Amendment. As the key element in the Bill of Rights, the amendment makes it clear that the government may not interfere with the right of individuals and groups to freedom of expression. Two additional interpretations of the amendment have recently been accepted on a wide basis and directly relate to the maintenance of open government.

The first deals with the right of reporters to have access to information. The Supreme Court has addressed itself to the problem in only one case, involving the power of grand juries to compel reporters to divulge sources of information. The issue was critical, with reporters maintaining that it was impossible to gather information accurately and freely without being able to pledge confidentiality. Opponents argued that information produced without a specific source was invalid and the Administration concurred.

In recognizing the fundamental importance of the First Amendment, however, the Supreme Court ruled that news gathering does qualify under the amendment's protections as a general principle. The specific case at hand, nonetheless, was rejected. Consequently, like the separation of powers issue, the application of the First Amendment has been broadened in the 1970's in some ways, and limited in others.

A second dimension of the First Amendment relates to the right of the American people to have access to information in order to make reasoned judgments on the conduct of government and the behavior of those who represent them. The right of the public to know is the obverse of the First Amendment right to engage in free speech, embracing the right to listen, read and observe. In order for the protection of freedom of speech and press to be meaningful, it must carry with it a means whereby considerable information is available. The Supreme Court first acknowledged the concept of the right to know in 1965 and reaffirmed its decision in another area in 1969. The essence of the latter decision was the statement that "It is now well established that the Constitution protects the right to receive information and ideas." In the 1970's, however, the Court has begun to express a certain amount of ambivalence on the subject. In its most recent decision, it declined to give any weight to the contention by a group of scholars that the government's refusal to allow a visa to a Belgian Marxist economist, who had been invited to lecture in the United States, violated their constitutional right to know. Consequently, the interpretations of the First Amendment, with all of their ramifications, remain illusive, despite the attempts to clarify the issue.

A third means of invoking constitutional doctrine to prohibit secrecy in government is derived from a recent expansion of the current concepts of due process of law. The ancient legal precept, first formulated in the Magna Charta and affirmed in American politics through the adoption of the Fourteenth Amendment, affirms that governmental decision-making must follow procedures which the community recognizes as being just and fair. Although due process has been confined primarily to the judicial system, where it has resulted in the rejection of the use of secret information in court procedures, the requirements of due process also apply to the executive branch of government. In the field of administrative law, for example, due process has witnessed its greatest expansion as a doctrine in the late 1960's and 1970's. Reliance upon evidence not disclosed to the parties involved is clearly prohibited and only in loyalty cases, where the government has appealed to national security, have the courts wavered at all on the matter. Additionally, and especially during the Watergate hearings, the right to compel disclosure of evidence in the possession of the government has steadily expanded.

The most difficult area to deal with in attempts to secure an open government continues to be the most important one —national security. The greatest amount of secrecy by the government is administered primarily through the classification system. There are, however, hundreds of examples of the use of the term "national interest" to suppress information which would clearly not jeopardize security. Beginning with the Eisenhower Administration and the U-2 incident and culminating with the Cambodian bombings for a year prior to the announcement that the American government was planning such attacks, the issue of the public's (or the Congress') right to information has been paramount.

Lieutenant William Calley *hesitating as he leaves the court-martial session at Fort Benning, Georgia, where he was on trial for his complicity in the My Lai killings.*

In a key decision, made precisely at the time that the Director of the F.B.I. was authorizing the use of wiretaps without warrants on the instructions of the Attorney General of the United States, the Supreme Court ruled on an essential aspect of secrecy in the name of national interest. In holding that wiretaps without a court order were not justified as a matter of national security, the Court rejected the basic contention that reasons of national security authorize the government to engage in operations which violate constitutional principles. The legal conclusion to be drawn, as well as the practical consideration of reducing credibility gaps between what the government says and what it in fact does, is that the national security exception to freedom of speech and executive privilege should be limited severely and on the basis of military necessity.

The efforts of the Senate Investigating Committee, headed by Frank Church, to explore the activities of the Central Intelligence Agency and establish some limits on its essentially free rein in decision-making both domestically and in foreign affairs represents a beginning in this direction. The Committee's interim reports, produced in late 1975, demonstrated that the secrecy covering the operations of the CIA had led to several assassination attempts, the invention of bizarre, James Bond-style weapons, the illegal use of drugs for experimentation on American citizens, the direct involvement in military coups overseas, the development of a domestic spying system called Operation Chaos, the violation of constitutional guarantees by opening and photographing 215,820 personal letters coming from and going to the Soviet Union between 1953 and 1973, and the ignoring of directives from the President's Office. Under the guise of national security, the CIA existed (and continues to exist despite the Congressional investigation) as an independent, autonomous organization which was quite capable of violating almost every major provision of the Constitution. Concurrently, as reported in the Rockefeller Commission study, the CIA maintained an agreement with the Justice Department that no CIA employee would be prosecuted for a criminal act—thus making a considerable number of American citizens exempt from the law.

Although the other commission reports, to be produced by a committee in the House of Representatives and the Church Committee in the Senate, have not yet been completed, there are strong indications that recommendations in five areas will be made, attempting to reduce the secrecy of the CIA and bring it back into the mainstream of governmental operations. This represents a major step in the direction of developing a more open government—a major challenge in the 1970's to the existence of a democratic political system in America.

The principal reforms which have been proposed by the Commission's investigation of the Central Intelligence Agency are:

(1) The CIA's 1947 Charter will be rewritten, or separate laws passed, explicitly prohibiting the Agency from gathering information on American citizens and requiring that the work of the organization be strictly limited to collecting and analyzing foreign intelligence.

(2) Conspiring to assassinate any foreign leader, whether on American territory or abroad will be dealt with as a criminal offense;

(3) Congressional responsibility for overseeing the Central Intelligence Agency will be concentrated in a single watchdog committee instead of dispersing the function among several committees, as is the current situation;

(4) The Central Intelligence Agency will be required to raise and make more precise its own standards of conduct, discipline and professionalism, to be more discriminating in selecting its agents, and to be more thorough in interpreting and analyzing the information which it receives; and

(5) The annual budget of the Central Intelligence Agency, as approved by the Congressional Committee, will be made public and reported in as much detail as national security allows.

Coupled with the concern over open government is popular dissatisfaction with the size of the Federal bureaucracy and the proliferation of programs which have mounted steadily since the New Deal. In a recent poll taken by CBS News, thirty-nine percent of the public expressed unhappiness with the direction of government and its apparent inability to provide services while maintaining economic stability. The dissatisfaction has substance, particularly when the records of the Great Society, the New Frontier and the Nixon Administration are taken into account alongside the inflationary cycle which has dominated the decade.

Although the total governmental spending for the past twenty years has remained fairly constant as a fraction of the Gross National Product and the Federal bureaucracy has increased only slightly in terms of the number of civilian employees, the size of federally funded social programs has grown astronomically.[1] The costs have mounted precipitously and the burden for payment has fallen primarily to the middle class, which contributes the major share of monies through the existing income tax structure. Simultaneously, the results of new programs have been questionable in many instances.

For example, although hundreds of millions of dollars have been appropriated for school enrichment programs annually since the turn of the decade, there is still no clear-cut evidence that they have produced improvement in either the quality of education or the educational achievement of students. Similarly, the massive expenditures made for the purpose of integrating public school systems have elicited no positive change—in fact, the number of desegregated schools in 1975 was lower than it had been in the 1960's Although only twelve percent of the population now falls beneath the so-called poverty line, compared with seventeen percent a decade ago, the number of people who hover just above poverty has remarkably increased.

Federal, state and local programs for direct aid payments to individuals have grown more than eight percent a year, while the nation's economy has witnessed only a 3.5 percent annual growth. The Social Security Administration is a testimony to the problems inherent in this discrepancy. Founded

[1]As of 1976, there are 14.6 million civilian employees of all levels of government and the total expenditure has reached $523.2 billion dollars or 37 percent of the GNP.

Pollution of the water *was another major concern as Americans began to realize that their environment was becoming poisoned in some areas of the country past the point where it would support life.*

during the depression, this almost universally applauded institution currently sends a monthly check to one in seven Americans. Despite the fact that the average amount received by an individual is two hundred dollars—a total which places millions of people just above the poverty level and in many cases below it—the shift in population trends and life expectancy has meant that the forty-five million dollar trust which supports the program will be insufficient by the end of the decade unless major reforms are instituted. Those reforms, according to the chief Administrator, James Cardwell, mean a higher tax rate for all citizens.

Similar problems plague the Agriculture Department's Food Stamp program which was conceived as a means of supplementing the anti-poverty program ten years ago. The program was initially directed at assisting some five hundred thousand people who fell dramatically below the poverty level and were therefore prone to malnutrition and starvation. With Congressional legislation and administrative fiat, the program has grown to a point where it serves twenty million people, including thousands of college students. To administer the program, the federal government has had to hire an additional seventeen hundred employees in Washington and create hundreds of state and county offices throughout the country, employing thousands of workers. Though eighty-five percent of the recipients still have an income of less than six thousand dollars for a family of four annually, an Agriculture Department survey of non-welfare households found that twenty-six percent of them were receiving more coupons than they qualified for under the provisions of the program.

The Medicare program, passed during the 1960's after thirty-five years of ardent opposition by the medical and insurance professions, is a classic example of a positive program which has had an unforeseen impact. There are currently twenty-four million eligible beneficiaries, raising the cost of the program to fifteen billion dollars, plus billions more in medical aid to the poor through such programs as Medi-Cal and Medic-Aid. Medicare has made the Federal government the major purchaser of health care, overtaxing both physicians and the public as time demands have increased by ten percent and revenue appropriated for the program has grown commensurately. Although the benefits

YOU ARE SWIMMING IN HOLLYWOOD SEWA

of the program cannot be denied, the average American has tended recently to focus on its abuses, which the media has covered extensively.

Program proliferation has not been confined to the provision of social services, however, and it is in the area of governmental regulation that a great deal of criticism has been directed. Although most of the public agrees that some form of federal regulation of the environment is necessary —an attitude which first emerged in the wake of the energy crisis of the mid-1970's—the approaches have been controversial. The creation of the Environmental Protection Agency in 1970 initiated a formal beginning to the national government's involvement in environmental issues and a great deal has been accomplished as the findings of investigative committees have been made available to Congress and the public. Regulations have resulted in a twenty-five percent reduction of hazardous sulfur dioxide concentrations nationwide, strip mining has been replaced with other methods of extracting natural resources, conservation programs have gotten underway, and fines have been imposed on industries which violate pollution standards. Nonetheless, the debate between environmentalists and proponents of free enterprise and the American ethic of progress continues to rage and the cost for environmental protection still is viewed by most Americans in terms of increases in the price of gasoline, electricity and heating.

The growth of the federal bureaucracy has been extended into the cities in a variety of forms other than directly administered national programs. In 1972, Nixon's Revenue Sharing Program was proposed and accepted by Congress. The program was a hallmark in a new concept of federalism and was heralded as a means of promoting decentralization. Pointing out that the original purpose for federalism had been to divide political power as well as economic resources between the central government and state and local units, the President argued persuasively that the new concept would enhance citizen participation, augment local spending for services which could not otherwise have been afforded by municipal governments, and encourage localities to take responsibility for their destiny. The plan was well received by Republicans and Democrats alike.

Following the decade of the 1960's which had been marked by large-scale demonstrations, wide-ranging and comprehensive programs, and a lack of community involvement, Revenue Sharing appeared to offer a substantial reaffirmation of basic American principles which seemed to many citizens to have been lost in the montage of national issues.

Across the nation, city officials began to draw up proposals for expenditures which would fall into the broadly defined categories established by Congress. Innovative ideas were translated into concrete programs and approvals were accompanied with large sums of money, administered by county governments. In the first two years of the existence of Revenue Sharing, the successes were numerous. New projects were started, existing services were augmented and public responses were almost uniformly favorable.

As with Medicare, however, unforeseen conditions emerged in the third year of the program's operation. The primary factor, which had not been adequately taken into account, was inflation. As demands for increases in salaries by city employees grew in response to the higher cost of living, and supplies and services necessary to the functions of city governments became more expensive each month, local officials began to rely more and more on Revenue Sharing funds to meet current financial requirements. Although using appropriated monies for salaries was illegal under the terms of the program, most cities found ways of accomplishing this. Although it was apparent by the early months of 1975 that federal funding was no longer being directed at the creation of innovative projects, demands for additional increments were continually sought and almost automatically approved. Citizen participation, which had increased substantially, proved to be an area of keen interest on the part of the Administration in Washington and despite violations of the intent of Revenue Sharing, Congress continued to respond. By the summer, it had become obvious that the majority of recipient governments were receiving annual allotments totaling a tenth of their actual budgets. Instead of adding ten percent on top of their budgets, cities had been forced to include the funds in their operating budgets, thereby defeating the original purposes of the program.

The most blatant case of the crisis which resulted from this kind of situation occurred in New York City in the Autumn. Although Revenue Sharing was by no means the singular cause of the financial collapse of the city, it was a major

The historic meeting *between the President of the United States and the Chairman of the Chinese Communist Party occurred in 1972. Here President Richard M. Nixon, right, talks with Chairman Mao, next to Nixon. At left is Premier Chou-En-Lai, with the translator between Chou and Mao.*

The rise in gasoline prices *pushed Americans into buying smaller cars in 1974. This idle Ford assembly line at the Baton Rouge plant points out the dramatic slump in automobile sales experienced by the major American automobile manufacturers in the early 1970's.*

contributor. In order to maintain high salaries for city employees, provide tuition-free universities, meet the impact of inflation and protect the credit rating of municipal bonds, Mayor Abraham Beam and his staff pursued a policy which had characterized the previous city administration—increasing dependence on the Federal government for the funding of all nonessential, and some essential, programs. By November, the city faced a financial crisis unprecedented in American history.

President Ford's immediate response was to insist that New York would have to work out its own problems without Federal assistance beyond what was already available. Most of the American public agreed with his stance, although Congressional committees in both Houses began to formulate plans for federally guaranteed loans.[2] By December, it had become apparent that the city would have to default on its commitments unless outside help was forthcoming. After a variety of proposals were rejected, the pressures built as Americans living throughout the country began to fear national ramifications if New York City declared bankuptcy, a decision was made to offer annual 2.3 billion dollar short-term loans to aid the city for a three-year period. Attached to the federally secured loans were several rigid conditions, designed to insure that the city would embark upon a dramatic program to rectify the existing financial crisis.[3] For the moment, the loans averted default and allowed the city to resume operations on a reasonably even keel.

[2] Mail to Congressmen in the initial days following the President's announcement ran at a hundred to one in favor of his stance; both House and Senate Committees produced measures which provided substantially greater amounts than were ultimately approved.

[3] Much of the burden of improving the financial status of the city has been relegated to the Mayor and to the Governor of New York state; cuts in city employees represent a major thrust of the revisions required.

The magnitude of the crisis was not confined to New York, however, even though the publicity given to it made it appear somewhat unique. Following the Federal government's decision to intervene, comprehensive investigations of cities throughout the country were launched. The early findings confirmed what many authorities had suspected—the thirty-five million people who had moved from central cities to the suburbs during the decade of the 1960's had carried with them a disproportionate amount of the revenue required to maintain metropolitan services, thereby drastically reducing the tax bases of major cities. At the time the loans were approved by Ford, ten large cities were on the brink of financial disaster and hundreds of smaller ones were almost completely dependent upon Revenue Sharing funds for their existence.[4]

Ironically, the new federalism had not resulted in a greater amount of independence on the part of local governments. Just the converse had happened. Yet, there are some important benefits to the program which should not be overlooked, even as the Congress currently is debating whether to extend Revenue Sharing beyond its June, 1976, termination date. The primary benefactors of the program have turned out to be the people who participated at the community level in developing uses for city appropriations. Community action groups have become essential to the operations of local government and have tended to make local democracy more operational than it has been in the past. The experiences derived from such participation have made local residents considerably more aware of their needs and the political means of satisfying them. This trend, regardless of the fate of Revenue Sharing itself, is likely to continue through the decade and beyond. Significantly, it is a remarkable demonstration of the resurgence of democracy at a time when it is most needed.

There are other areas which appear equally promising on the eve of America's Bicentennial, the most critical of which is that despite the epic of Watergate and public concerns over open and large government, the system has survived one of its most difficult tests. Although Nixon's popularity plummetted to an unprecedented twenty-seven percent im-

[4] These included Philadelphia, Wilmington, Newark, Jersey City, Hoboken.

Faced with more demand *than supply, the major American oil companies turned to advertising to sell their side of the energy crisis which hit American in 1974. Here are some of the advertise-* *ments from newspapers across the country illustrating the campaign the companies waged to convince the American public that they were being well served by the oil companies.*

mediately prior to his resignation, the attacks against the system as a whole which were leveled by protestors in the 1960's were not present in 1974. In fact, belief in the political institutions and procedures was enhanced through the televised Senate and House proceedings which precipitated the President's decision to step down from office. If Watergate was on the one hand an indication of the dangers of corruption at the highest reaches of government, its outcome was an applaudable testimony to the strength and viability of that government at the same time.

If Watergate has in many ways strengthened commitments to American institutions and political procedures, so also have a number of significant pieces of legislation which have been produced and implemented in the 1970's. Among the list of accomplishments, the extension of the franchise through the ratification of the Twenty-Sixth Amendment on June 30, 1971, stands out. By lowering the voting age to eighteen, the amendment added eleven million people to the electorate and completed a process of electoral expansion which had been initiated in the Nineteenth Century.

Coupled with this, restrictions which had been at the center of controversy in the previous decade have largely been removed. Voting rights have become more of a reality in the 1970's than ever before, especially through the implementation of registration drives, the abandonment of qualification tests for minority groups—including primarily Blacks and Mexican-Americans, and the availability of polling places at convenient locations. The violence which accompanied long marches in the South by voter registrants who worked conscientiously to enact legislative guarantees has largely been transformed into public acceptance of the existence of the right.

Considering that the total number of people who were Constitutionally qualified to vote in the first Presidential election represented less than four percent of the American population, the extension of the franchise is a remarkable tribute to the growth of equality and democracy. Although there remains a significant disparity between the number of qualified voters and those who actually cast their votes in any given election, the availability of the right to participate in the electorate has reached unprecedented proportions.[5]

The impact of the electorate in the 1976 elections will provide an interesting analysis of the political situation which has characterized the decade. To date, the milieu in which candidates in primary campaigns are operating is somewhat confusing. Immediately following the Watergate hearings, Congress passed a major campaign reform act, designed to reduce large-scale contributions by individuals and organizations, to place a ceiling on Congressional, Senatorial and Presidential expenditures, and to require full disclosure of contribution sources.[6] Initially a controversial measure, the reform act has finally reached the Supreme Court as the first primaries have gotten underway. The announcement of the Court's decision was made on the weekend of February 7-8, 1976 and reflected the contradictions which have been inherent in interpretations of the legislation from the beginning.

On all but one of the Constitutional issues raised by the 1974 bill, the opinions of the nine justices were divided. The central issue of balancing individual rights covered under the First Amendment to free political expression with the public's right to fair elections resulted in a situation in which both litigants in the case, taking diametrically opposed positions, claimed victory after the Court's decision was handed down. Although the Court upheld two major sections of the legislation—full financial disclosure of all campaign contributions and federal subsidies for Presidential candidates—its justification for nullifying other provisions ap-

[5]Unfortunately, the voter turnout among the under-21 segment of the electorate was low; in general elections, the pattern of the 1970's reflects a 60-70 percent turnout at the national level, with a 30 percent local vote and a 45-50 percent state election turnout.

[6]The original bill imposed the following limits: less than ten cents per voter or twenty million dollars in Presidential campaigns; twelve cents per voting age resident, or $150,000, whichever was greater, in Senatorial campaigns; and, $70,000 in House of Representatives campaigns.

Lieutenant William Calley *shown leaving the civil court in Columbus, Georgia, in 1974 following his release on a $1000 bond. Calley was serving a 20 year sentence for his conviction for his part in the My Lai massacres in Vietnam.*

The Indian Point No. 3 *nuclear generating plant in New York. The government stepped up production and installation of nuclear generating plants in the Seventies as a way to combat the expected shortage in fossil fuels for generating electricity. The construction of the nuclear plants created controversial opposition in many parts of the country.*

peared inconsistent, swinging back and forth from the First Amendment argument for freedom of expression to the collective argument for fair elections. In holding that to limit the amount of money that federal candidates can spend in an election is a restraint on their ability to communicate with the electorate was an infringement of individual protections under the amendment, the Court replaced this section by striking down both overall spending limits and the ceiling on what candidates can spend from their own personal resources. Although, from a Constitutional perspective, this decision follows a long tradition which is highly supportable, it nonetheless represents a failure on the part of the Court to extend First Amendment guarantees to all participants in the electoral process by discriminating against Presidential aspirants who elect to take the financial subsidy from the Treasury—a section of the law upheld by the Court. It does this by requiring that candidates who go through this process must suffer a penalty by being bound by the statutory limits of ten million dollars for primary campaigns and twenty million in the general election.

Presidential aspirants who reject the subsidy plan, on the other hand, along with candidates for Congressional and Senatorial positions, can raise and spend as much as they are able in the same way that they were allowed to act prior to the

passage of the Campaign Reform Act of 1974. The only segment of the population which is directly denied protection under the First Amendment by the Court's decision is that group of individuals who accept public funds as a basis for running for office.

Put another way, the effect of the decision is that money solicited from private sources provides candidates with greater freedom of expression than revenue taken from the United States Treasury. The freedom of the citizenry as a whole, or at least those individuals who make a decision to contribute to the Presidential campaign through an income tax contribution, is commensurately reduced.

In changing another section of the original bill, the Supreme Court maintained that a modification of the limitation of one thousand dollars for each individual contribution to a candidate's campaign could be augmented by supporting choices with advertising, mass mailings, billboards and headquarters so long as these things are not done with the

474

coordination or control of the candidate. The effect, in this instance, is to overturn the major justification for the 1974 legislation—the reduction of major influence by wealthy individuals and organizations on campaign politics.

The Court's single unanimous decision in the case is the finding that the joint appointment by the President and Congress of the Federal Elections Commission violates the separation of powers doctrine. It represents the most positive decision taken in regard to the entire Reform Act. The commission had been designed to enforce the provisions of the Congressional bill and as such was the only agency under direct Congressional control which was given law-enforcement powers—a prerogative which has always been assumed by the Administrative branch of government.[7] The Court, basing its decision on this point and on the ineffectiveness to date of the commission to regulate political activities, argued that the commission must be reconstituted within thirty days, and that responsibility for that action must be taken by Congress.

The ramifications of the Supreme Court's ruling remain uncertain as the primaries continue to capture the public's attention. Although it is doubtful that the full consequences will be explored prior to the conclusion of the elections in November, 1976, it does appear probable that the Congress will address itself in a serious and sober fashion to the entire issue of campaign reform in the 1977 sessions. In a positive sense, the Court's decision forces Congress to rethink the original legislation which had been passed hurriedly in response to the emotional impact of the Watergate revelations. The final outcome, to be determined at some date in the future, is likely to be preferable to both the original piece of legislation and the Supreme Court's recent alternative.

[7]Congressional control became possible because of the composition of the commission—four of the six appointees are members of Congress while the remaining two are appointed by the President. In addition, the House and Senate were given veto power over all of the commission's rulings.

Senator Frank Church, *right, and Senator John Stennis, during a heated debate over the senate's investigations into CIA activities.*

A week prior to the Court's decision, another event which was largely overlooked in the midst of the campaigns occurred. On February 11, 1976, the Selective Service System was officially terminated. After years of controversy, culminating in the creation and implementation of a volunteer army, peacetime conscription as a means of maintaining a standing army ended. It represented a highly democratic process which had been supported by a variety of ideologically disparate groups, ranging from the Young Americans for Freedom to the Students for a Democratic Society.

Just as Congress took an assertive role in the development of the volunteer army and in campaign reforms, it has begun to revitalize its powers in other areas as well. Despite the fact that Congress was the institution which the framers of the Constitution most feared would exert excessive authority, the record of the century makes it clear that the body has more frequently been dominated by the Executive branch than vice versa. Nonetheless, at the mid-point in the 1970's there are several indications that a restoration of a balance between the branches of government at the national level may be accomplished in the near future. The efforts of the Church Committee to investigate and regulate the Central Intelligence Agency are one example. Another is the fact that the Joint Committee on Atomic Energy has reached a point where it is more powerful than the Atomic Energy Commission. In areas concerning the national budget machinery and process, the Senate and the House have demonstrated a viable concern with improving the functioning of the General Accounting Office and raising its stature to the level of the Bureau of Management and Budget in the Administration. And, even though President Ford has vetoed an extraordinary number of bills during his nineteen months in office, Congress has been able to override his vote on several critical issues.

Of the tensions which have historically existed in the American political system, some appear to have been resolved successfully, while others remain both controversial and subject to conflicting interpretations. Although civil liberties have been expanded significantly over the course of the past two decades, the concept of individualism has been

Former Lieutentant *William Calley shown leaving the Fifth U.S. Circuit Court of Appeals in New Orleans, Louisiana, in 1975. The Army appealed the overturning of Calley's conviction in the My Lai massacre.*

the most part, the results as witnessed in the current decade indicate that the original concept of individual liberty and autonomy has had to be modified substantially. The inter-dependence of people in a highly technological age has become self-evident along with the fact that the ability of individuals to maintain a reasonable quality of life without some degree of societal and political assistance is generally impossible.

Recognition of this fact has been a positive achievement of the 1970's. Equality of opportunity remains a critical idea in American political philosophy, but the means whereby it can become meaningful and viable have changed considerably. While the previous decade emphasized the importance of equality, as such, in its massive civil rights movements and its accomplishment of equality under law for virtually all citizens in the United States, the current decade has given rise to a new interpretation of opportunity.

In view of the fact that it has become apparent that equality of opportunity is meaningless without opportunities being made available, the Federal government has taken the lead in promoting affirmative action programs, designed to transform the concept into reality. The reluctance of the Nixon Administration, particulary during its first term in office and under the guidance of Attorney General John Mitchell, to pursue actively affirmative action programs has given way to a more vigorous enforcement under the Ford cabinet. Although changes in the work force have not been dramatic, there are strong indications that the direction of the government is having an effect. In large measure, this is a strong testimony to the idea that attitudes can in fact be legislated and that compliance with required changes produces changes in behavior.

It is also a tribute to the endurance of the American political system that although major changes have been accomplished, the fundamental principles have in many instances been modified but not terminated. If there is one primary success of the 1970's it is the fact that the decade has withstood the impact of Watergate and emerged with a renewed sense of the interrelationships between democracy and a republican form of government. The democratic dimensions of the political system have been strengthened through the rise of interest in politics at the community level, through participation in the development of local programs, and through the development of a basic consensus reaffirming the underlying principles of American local, state and national government. The republican aspects of the system, particularly in the form of representative government, have been augmented through the passage of campaign reform acts, the resurrection of the Republican party after Watergate and the Democratic party after the Chicago Convention of 1968, and the amount of active participation in primary campaigns which characterizes the first months of the election year.

Taken together, the resurgence of interest in both democratic and republican ideas has produced a situation which, in many ways, is unparalleled in history. Despite the number of major problems which address the nation on its Bicentennial, there is an extremely widespread recognition that although the language of the original Constitution has been transformed to meet existing needs as they occurred, the basic intent of the document continues to be both relevant and viable. If faith in political leaders reached its low point with the Watergate revelations, confidence in the ability of the political system to operate effectively and justly has reached its high point in the aftermath.

altered. In major part, this is attributable to the fact that conditions in the United States have changed appreciably. The notion of a weak central government and a narrow interpretation of governmental powers subscribed to by the framers of the Constitution allowed for a broad definition of individualism. Thomas Jefferson, for example, argued that the purpose of government was to protect individuals from injuring one another, while providing them with maximum opportunities for conducting most of their other affairs on their own. Proponents of the free enterprise system have favored this interpretation, as noted especially in the decade of the Nineteen Twenties. On the other side, however, following a tradition established by James Madison, emphasis has been placed on the role of the government as a regulator of diverse and often conflicting interests. The relationship between the individual and the government has been determined primarily by the relationship between these two interpretations.

As the political demands placed on the government at all levels became increasingly complex, adjustments between public and private spheres of activity have been made. For

FOUR MORE YEARS

JANUARY 20, 1973

President Nixon *takes the oath of office from Chief Justice Warren E. Burger for the President's second term. Mrs. Nixon holds two family Bibles.*

TWO AQUEDUCT ARRESTS

EXTRA

LOS ANGELES EVENING HERALD
AN INDEPENDENT NEWSPAPER
The Evening Herald Grows Just Like Los Angeles
Reg. U. S. Patent Office. Copyright, 1927, by Evening Herald Publishing Company
VOL. LII THREE CENTS Hotels and Trains Five Cents THURSDAY, JUNE 30, 1927 Hotels and Trains Five Cents THREE CENTS NO. 207

LATEST NEWS

RUMOR BYRD MAY FLY TO VIENNA

BERLIN, June 30.—The Austrian Air Traffic Co. reported tonight that it had received a telegram from New York that Commander Richard E. Byrd of the America intends to fly to Vienna. If necessary he will stop at Paris to refuel, the report said.

TEN INJURED IN TRAIN WRECK

ROCHESTER, N. Y., June 30.—Ten persons were injured, four seriously, when a Rochester-bound passenger train of the New York Central railroad struck a work train, according to word reaching here today.

FINE PAIR FOR GIN POSSESSION

PORTERVILLE, Cal., June 30.—A. F. Ehmer and wife of San Francisco were arrested here today after police found 75 bottles of gin in their possession.

Walker Keeps Title by Knockout

BYRD LANDS IN PARIS

PAIR NABBED IN PROBE OF WATERLINE BLASTING

Major C. P. Watson of Big Pine and A. J. Betker of Bakersfield were arrested today on complaints issued by the district attorney of Contra Costa county charging them with illegal possession of TNT and nitro-glycerine, it was announced this afternoon at the Los Angeles bureau of power and light.

The arrests, it was stated are the result of the investigation into the recent dynamiting of the Los Angeles aqueduct.

Watson and Betker are charged, in three counts, with having had possession of the explosives after buying them in Martinez, northern California.

Watson, according to officials of the bureau of power and light, was an explosive expert in the army during the war.

Betker, officials stated, was one of the leaders in the Owens valley district against the city of Los Angeles.

Watson and Betker were taken after arrest to Martinez for arraignment on the charges.

Attorney William J. Clarke, special counsel for the bureau of power and light, stated that Watson located in Owens valley in 1924, when he is said to have purchased a ranch in that locality for $12,000. The city of Los Angeles, according to Clarke, offered Watson $24,000 for the property but he refused the offer.

Snow in Colorado Town as Midwest Gripped by Heat

By International News Service

BECKENRIDGE, Colo., June 30.—While the middle west was sweltering in a terrific heat wave, Breckenridge today was the scene of a midsummer snowfall, an inch of frozen crystals mantling the ground before noon.

Bells 4, Stars 5

MISSIONS—	Ab	R	H	Po	A	E
Swanson, cf.	4	1	3	0	0	0
Jones, 3b	2	0	0	0	1	0
Gillespie, 3b	1	0	0	0	2	0
Hooper, rf	3	0	0	1	0	0
Rose, lf	4	1	2	3	0	0
McDaniel, 1b	4	0	0	10	0	0
Parker, 2b	4	0	2	4	4	0
Rodda, ss	4	1	3	4	3	0
Whitney, c	2	0	0	3	2	1
Walters, c	2	0	0	0	0	0
Pillette, p	1	1	0	0	3	0
Weinert, p	0	0	0	0	2	0
Wade	0	0	0	0	0	0
Bryan	1	0	0	0	0	0
Totals	32	4	10	25	17	1

STARS—	Ab	R	H	Po	A	E
Lee, ss	3	1	0	2	3	0
Cook, c	0	0	0	1	2	0
Kerr, 2b	3	2	1	5	3	0
Twmbly, lf-rf	4	0	2	2	0	0
McNulty, cf	3	0	1	0	0	0
Frederick, rf	3	0	2	2	0	0
Sheehan, lf	1	0	0	1	0	0
Heath, 1b	4	1	2	11	0	0
Holley, 3b	2	0	0	1	2	0
Agnew, c	3	0	1	1	2	1
Gooch, ss	1	1	1	3	0	0
Fullerton, p	2	0	0	0	1	0
McCabe, p	0	0	0	0	0	0
Vitt	0	0	0	0	0	0
Totals	29	5	10	27	13	1

Missions . 010 002 100 — 4
Hollywood... 201 000 101 — 5

STARS DEFEAT MISSIONS IN THIRD

At San Francisco— R. H. E.
ANGELS ... 0 0 0 2 0
SEALS ... 0 5 2 1 0
Batteries—Wright and Hannah; May and Rego.

At Seattle— R. H. E.
OAKS ... 1 0 0 3 0
INDIANS ... 1 0 0 0 3
Batteries—Boehler and Read; Knight and Borreani.

At Portland— R. H. E.
SOLONS ... 1 0 1 0
BEAVERS ... 0 0 0 0
Batteries—Vincl and Koehler; Hughes and Yelle.

Hollywood defeated the Missions in the third game of their series today at Wrigley field. The score was 5 to 4.

FIRST INNING

BELLS—Swanson singled infield. Jones flied to Twombly. Swanson was out steal-

(CONTINUED ON PAGE TWENTY)

CHAMP K. O.'S MILLIGAN IN TENTH

LONDON, June 30.—Mickey Walker preserved his world's middleweight championship and the honor of American boxing tonight when he battered Tommy Milligan his Scotch challenger, into submission in the tenth round. It was a great fight while it lasted, but the so-called toy bulldog proved his right to the name by tearing Milligan apart in the infighting and, then shifting to the head, quickly cutting his man down.

FIRST TITLE BOUT

The fight was scheduled for 20 rounds and afforded England its first view of a world's championship contest in some years. The last was in Jimmy Wilde's day and previous to that the tight little isle had seen nothing of championship fisticuffing since the memorable Welsh-Ritchie lightweight fight in which the championship changed into British hands on a hairline decision.

There was no possibility of such a decision being rendered tonight, although the same referee, Eugene Corri, who rendered it, was the third man in the ring.

CAPACITY CROWD

A capacity crowd, including British blue bloods and American visitors, saw the fight and, in the early rounds, booed Walker for holding. He, however, proved to be merely feeling his man out and, after tiring him with body punishment, twice dropped him in the seventh round.

Walker came out for the eighth, primed for the "kill" and punished Milligan badly during the early moments. But the latter managed to hold Mickey even with his boxing.

However, three more knockdowns in the ninth had the Scot ready for the stretcher and he was thoroughly laid out in the tenth, his seconds tossing in the towel as Referee Corri was going through the motions of a count that obviously was unnecessary.

ROUND ONE

Walker and Milligan began operations with the national colors posted in their respective corners. They opened with a rush that set the crowd wild, both mixing vigorously at close quarters. They were almost violently aggressive, roughing each other in the clinches. The execution, however, was at a minimum, but Walker's old cut over

(CONTINUED ON FIRST SPORT PAGE)

10-Year-Old Girl, Struck by Truck, Seriously Injured

Tillie Verdugo, 10-year-old school girl of 1441 East Sixth street, was in the Receiving hospital late this afternoon in a critical condition as the result of being struck by a truck as she attempted to cross the street at Seventh street and Santa Fe avenue.

She is suffering from a fractured left leg, concussion of the brain and contusions on the body. The truck was driven by James Pelffio, 716 New High street.

GEHRIG AND RUTH GET HOMERS

AMERICAN LEAGUE

At New York— R. H. E.
Boston ... 0 0 6 0 0 0 0 0 0— 6 9 2
New York ... 3 2 1 3 1 3 0 0 x—13 19 3
Batteries—Harris, Welzer and Hoffman, Moore; Thomas, Moore and Collins.

At Washington— R. H. E.
Philadelphia . 2 0 2 0 0 0 1 0 0— 5 18 2
Washington . 1 0 2 0 1 0 0 1 1— 6 11 6
Batteries—Baker, Pate and Perkins; Lisenbee, Burke and Ruel.

At St. Louis— R. H. E.
Chicago ... 2 0 1 0 0 1 0 1 0— 5 9 0
St. Louis ... 0 0 0 0 0 0 1 0 0— 1 7 2
Batteries—Thomas and McCurdy; Stewart, Nevers and O'Neill.

At Cleveland— R. H. E.
Detroit ... 0 1 0 0 2 0 0 3 0— 6 11 2
Cleveland ... 1 0 0 0 0 2 0 0 2— 5 9 0
Batteries—Holloway and Bassler; Uhle, Buckeye and L. Sewell.

NATIONAL LEAGUE

At Boston (first game)— R. H. E.
New York ... 0 0 0 0 0 1 0 0 0— 1 6 1
Boston ... 0 3 0 1 1 0 1 0 x— 6 10 0
Batteries—Fitzsimmons, Boney and Devormer Cummings; Smith and Hogan.

At Boston (second game)— R. H. E.
New York ... 0 1 0 0 0 0 0 5 5—11 15 1
Boston ... 1 0 0 3 1 1 0 0 0— 6 15 5
Batteries—Benton, Songer and Taylor; McQuillan, Robertson, Edwards and Hogan

Brooklyn at Philadelphia, both games postponed; rain.

Only games scheduled.

NEW YORK, June 30.—Home runs by the Swatese twins, Gehrig and Ruth, bringing their individual totals to 25 for the season, featured the Yankees' 13-to-6 triumph over the Red Sox here today.

BOSTON	AB	R	H	O	A
Tobin, rf	3	1	2	0	0
Tarpert, rf	1	0	1	0	0
Rolings, 2b	1	0	0	0	1
Rogell, 3b	4	0	0	0	0
Carlyle, lf	5	1	2	0	0
Regan, 2b	3	1	0	5	2
Todt, 1b	5	1	2	8	0
Myer, ss	4	1	1	2	4
Shaner, cf	4	1	1	4	0
Hoffmn, c	3	0	0	5	1
B. Moore, c	1	0	0	0	0
Harriss, p	2	0	0	0	0
Welzer, p	2	0	0	0	3
Totals	38	6	9	24	11

NEW YORK	AB	R	H	O	A
Combs, cf	6	0	3	2	0
More't, 2b	6	3	2	0	6
Ruth, rf	4	2	2	1	0
Gehrig, 1b	5	2	3	13	0
Meusel, lf	4	2	3	1	0
Durr, lf	1	0	0	0	0
Lazzeri, ss	4	1	2	1	1
Dugan, 3b	4	0	1	0	1
Wera, 3b	0	0	0	0	0
Collins, c	3	2	2	9	0
Thomas, p	1	1	1	0	2
W. Mo're, p	4	0	0	0	2
Totals	42	13	19	27	12

Boston ... 0 0 6 0 0 0 0 0 0— 6
New York ... 3 2 1 3 1 3 0 0 x—13
Two-base hits—Meusel 2, Ruth, Collins.

(CONTINUED ON PAGE TWENTY)

FOG 'BURIES' FLIERS FOR 15 HOURS

ROOSEVELT FIELD, N. Y., June 30.—The weird record of flying across the Atlantic without sighting land or sea due to low and high freezing fogs that enveloped the gallant ship America, has been achieved by Commander Richard E. Byrd and his three daring companions, Grover Whalen, vice president of the America Transoceanic Co., related here today.

Commander Byrd late yesterday afternoon wirelessed that they had left sight of land and sea at 4 p. m when over the Newfoundland coast.

IN FOG 15 HOURS

Flying only by the readings of the delicate instruments, the four winged horsemen of America have been flying as if blindfolded through the freezing fog 10,000 feet above the Atlantic, for the past fifteen hours.

Meanwhile their radio instrument has been sending out its call signal out of the black night to tell the world a graphic story of the gallant fight made by the good ship America to wing her way through the dense enveloping arms of the dripping, cold fog and rain toward the Irish coast.

The America has been reported somewhere southwest of England, a few hundred miles from the French coast, at noon, eastern daylight time, today, according to careful plotting of experts at the Roosevelt field and based upon radio dispatches received.

The plane was expected in Paris between 4 and 5 o'clck (eastern daylight time).

Since 3 o'clock yesterday afternoon, before leaving Newfoundland, the four flying musketeers in their plane have been enveloped by a giant fog blanket, and advices from the European continent indicate that Byrd will have to battle adverse conditions to the very end.

CONTACT WITH ERIN

The air ministry at London, issued a weather forecast predicting rain over most of the British isles with fair intervals and unsettled conditions over the English channel and the southern part of the Irish sea.

Early today the America established wireless contact with Ireland. The monoplane communicated with the wireless station at Malin Head.

(CONTINUED ON PAGE SIXTEEN)

Here's Log of Byrd's Paris Hop

NEW YORK, June 30.—The story of Commander Richard E. Byrd and the flight of the America was told today in wireless messages direct from the monoplane and from ships at sea. Following is the log of the flight, eastern daylight saving time:

THURSDAY

1 a. m.—America's automatic signals still audible at Chatham, Mass., and believed to be 1500 miles away.

2:32 a. m.—America radios they have not sighted land or water since 4 p. m. yesterday, due to fog and low clouds.

3:00 a. m.—Steamship Belgenland, eastbound, reported hearing America's signal. Ship about 500 miles off Irish coast. America thought to be about 300 miles away.

4 a. m.—Liner Hamburg radioed here that America believed to be about 900 miles off Irish coast, E. D. T., according to "sextant estimate made by liner officials from call signals picked up from plane." Liner Hamburg was 275 miles southwest of Irish coast.

4:15 a. m.—Liner Paris radioed pick up America signal and believe plane about three-fourths of long water jump from Newfoundland.

7:00 a. m.—Byrd sent out following: "Our position at 7 a.m. was 49.33 north latitude, 18.10 west longitude. We are fine. Thank you. You have helped us a lot." This position given is 620 miles from tip of Ireland.

7:50 a. m.—Byrd sent following: "We have seen neither land nor water since 3 o'clock yesterday afternoon. Everything completely covered with fog for sixteen hours. But whatever happens I take my hat off to these three great fellows with me." This message was relayed here by liner Brothingham.

11 a. m.—Liner France reported picking up: "Three p. m. Greenwich latitude 50.06 north 7.57 west longitude bearing plane 235." No data on weather given.

11:05 a. m.—America wirelessed: "Grover Whalen: We hope to sight land at end of hour. Crew feeling fine after strenuous trip. (Signed) Byrd."

11:14—America reported to be slightly north and 200 miles west of Land's End, England, according to a radio from the steamship France intercepted by Lloyd's Land's End radio station.

12:00 Noon—America's signal "WTW" reported by French naval

(CONTINUED ON PAGE SIXTEEN)

U. S. FLIERS END HOP AFTER LONG BATTLE WITH FOG AND RAIN

LE BOURGET FLYING FIELD, PARIS, July 1.—Amid the acclaim of surging thousands of rioting Parisians, the silver and gold monoplane America, with Commander Richard E. Byrd and his three companions, landed here early this morning, completing the 3400-mile nonstop flight across the Atlantic ocean from New York city.

LE BOURGET FIELD, July 1.—Commander Byrd's monoplane America arrived in the vicinity of Le Bourget early this morning, but because of fog, darkness and a bad compass experienced difficulty in finding the airdrome. A radio at the field picked up a message from the America saying:

"We are flying around with a bad compass and cannot find airdrome or landing ground."

At this hour, 12:50 a. m. (7:50 p. m. Thursday, eastern daylight time), the America had not yet been sighted by the rain-drenched crowds at the field.

MESSAGE GARBLED

The message from the America was garbled and it could not be determined whether the operator was attempting to send a S O S. The signals came in strong, however, indicating that the plane was near the field but lost in the darkness.

At 1:10 a. m. a heavy downpour started and visibility was low. It was almost impossible to see anything in the air. Experts said it would be easy for Byrd to miss not only Le Bourget field but Paris as well, if he did not receive the radio bearings sent him. Byrd was then understood to be flying from the northward to the south.

OFF COURSE

The wireless stations at Viry, Chatillon and the field here began picking up signals from the America shortly after midnight. Chatillon is 10 minutes from Le Bourget.

The America evidently lost its way on the last leg of the dash for Paris.

Shortly after midnight here wireless signals indicated that Byrd had gone out of his way. The messages did not explain why but the message from Byrd in which he stated his compass "had gone bad" explained the mysterious disappearance of the transatlantic fliers after they left St. Brieuc near the coast of France.

At 12:20 a. m. today a loud speaker announcement from Le Bourget radio station said that Byrd in the monoplane America was believed to be nearing the landing field.

Since 10 o'clock last night the wireless posts at Havre, Cherbourg, Viry, Chatellon and Le Bourget had tried incessantly to pick up Byrd by sending his radio call, "WTW."

Byrd and his crew fought their way through rain and darkness across France after a heartbreaking flight through the freezing, clinging fogs over the Atlantic.

About 100 miles south of the well lighted route from Cherbourg to Paris, forced there by the heavy fog off southern England, Byrd felt his way through low, hanging rain clouds that pelted his plane constantly, dispatches indicated, at only about 80 miles an hour.

At 4:19 he passed over St. Brieuc, 80 miles east of Brest, the latter being 275 miles from Paris as the crow flies.

He passed over Ousaant Island.

(CONTINUED ON PAGE SIXTEEN)

Park Slaying Suspect Identified

Story Cols. 1-2

EXTRA

LOS ANGELES EVENING AND SUNDAY

Herald ▥ Examiner
EXPRESS

United Press International • Associated Press • Dow Jones
CLASSIFIED ADVERTISING Richmond 8-4111   All Other Calls Richmond 8-1212

VOL. C   NO. 314   FRIDAY, FEBRUARY 5, 1971   A   PRICE TEN CENTS

FRIDAY
LATEST
NEWS
SPORTS

ON THE MOON

Allies Score In Vietnam And Cambodia

U.S.-S. Vietnam Laotian border buildup strategy: Page A-4.

Khe Sanh — past and present meet; full page of pictures: Page A-6.

SAIGON (UPI) — The United States and South Vietnam massed nearly 50,000 men Thursday in giant twin drives to crush Communist sanctuaries and supply lines in Indochina. The Saigon government claimed its forces in Cambodia scored their biggest victory of the year and were poised to strike into Laos.

The combined allied operation in northwestern South Vietnam and Cambodia was believed to be the biggest of the Indochina War and drew warnings from Peking that mainland China would support the Communists "until final victory."

South Vietnamese troops reported their major victory of the year took place Thursday, in the Cambodian drive, which involves part of a 21,000-man Saigon force operating in Cambodia.

Military spokesmen said the South Vietnamese killed 69 Communists in a battle 18 miles east of the Cambodian provincial capital of Kompong Cham and 15 miles from the Vietnamese border.

It was the largest kill of Communists reported by Saigon either in Cambodia or South Vietnam since government troops claimed 74 dead last Dec. 29 in a battle in the same area.

Included in the big northern task force which was halted within sight of the Laotian frontier, were 9,000 Americans and 20,000 South Vietnamese who started the offensive six days ago. Casualties were

(Continued on Page A-2, Col. 3)

—Herald-Examiner Photo
MARY LOUISE HILL
Slain in Griffith Park

Suspect Is Sought In Slaying of Girl

An all points bulletin is out in the Southland today for a man wanted in connection with the strangulation slaying of a 13-year-old girl whose body was found in Griffith Park.

Drawn by the sound of clicking handcuffs, a hiker yesterday found the body in the mountainous 5000-acre area of Griffith Park, above the planetarium, about seven miles from downtown Los Angeles on the northeast edge of Hollywood.

Lying face up on a knoll, about 30 yards off a bridle path, the dead girl was fully clothed with her blouse pulled up around her neck.

Identified as Mary Louise Hill, 930 Venango Circle, the girl was a ninth grade student at Thomas Starr King Junior High School. Shortly after discovery of the body, her mother, Mrs. Cathryn Torri, gave birth

to twin baby girls at Fort MacArthur Hospital.

The hiker, not identified by police for his own protection, said he was walking along the trail near the famed Greek Theater when he noticed a man kneeling over a woman. He said he assumed the couple was in an embrace and turned to leave. Then he heard the sound of handcuffs being opened and removed.

He returned and saw a man, his back toward him, run about 50 yards to the bottom of a knoll where a silver grey car was parked. The hiker took the license number as the car drove away.

Police traced the car to Bertram Greenberg, 38, of 1006 S. Cajon Ave., West Covina, a 12-8 a.m. shift worker at a downtown

(Continued on Page A-2, Col. 1)

—UPI Telephoto

THIS IS HOW IT WILL BE DONE ON THE MOON

Using thumper geophone, Grumman test pilot depicting an astronaut sends charges into 'moon' in experiment at Bethpage, Long Island. Simulated terrain is Fra Mauro region, site of lunar landing.

—AP Wirephoto
APOLLO 14 COMMANDER ALAN SHEPARD JR.
Shown in outfit he wore during moon walk

—AP Wirephoto
LUNAR MODULE PILOT EDGAR MITCHELL
Suited up for 33½-hour stay in Fra Mauro highlands

FOG; MILD SANTA ANA WINDS DISAPPEAR

Winds shifted overnight to offshore as mild Santa Anas which breezed in from the mountains the past two days disappeared.

With the wind shift came fog and haze. Heaviest concentra-

tions of fog this morning were along the immediate coast but no major traffic or airport tieups were reported.

Temperatures dropped a bit with the Civic Center thermom-

eter climbing toward the mid-60s today and a high of 66 forecast for tomorrow following a predicted overnight low of 45 downtown and a hair above freezing in outlying suburbs.

Skies will remain hazy over the weekend and fair to hazy through Tuesday, according to the long range forecast. No rain is in sight for the Southland.

Antares is Safe After Touchdown On Fra Mauro

By DON BANE
Herald-Examiner Staff Writer

MANNED SPACECRAFT CENTER, Houston — Apollo 14 astronauts Alan B. Shepard and Edgar D. Mitchell set their lunar module Antares on the moon safely today.

They became the third pair of men to reach another celestial body, preceded only by the crews of Apollo 11 and Apollo 12.

Shepard reported the touchdown in the hilly Fra Mauro area of the moon 11 minutes after he and Mitchell fired the rocket engine on Antares to begin their descent. The two men will spend 33.5 hours on the surface.

Two exploratory walks, each lasting between four and five hours, are scheduled.

MANNED SPACECRAFT CENTER, Houston—Apollo 14 Astronauts Alan B. Shepard and Edgar D. Mitchell performed a complete checkout of the systems aboard Antares early this morning, and as suspense rose like a thermometer on a hot day here, the only thing that remained to do was fly down and land on the moon.

Some small doubt remained, until the systems checkouts began, whether the landing would indeed be made. Engineers had set limits on the level of Antares' suspicious battery which would determine a "go" or "no go" status for the landing.

But Shepard reported that both batteries were performing as they should, and the flight continued.

Finally, at 1:05 a.m. (PST), Shepard fired the rocket engine that would lower him and Mitchell to the moon, and the spacecraft dipped toward the ground.

Touchdown was scheduled 11 minutes later. As soon as the spacecraft landed, Shepard and Mitchell would again check all systems in case an emergency departure from the moon was necessary.

Shepard and Mitchell thus became the third pair of Americans to reach the surface of another celestial body.

During the long night of prelanding checks, one obstacle after another was overcome, until at last capsule communicator Fred Haise, veteran of Apollo 13, called up, "Kitty

Hawk and Antares, 697're go for separation."

Within two minutes, their crewmate Stuart Roosa was talking his way through the delicate maneuver, then advised, "Okay, Antares, you're free, out there."

Some small trouble was experienced with the steerable antenna aboard Antares. Shepard was unable to make it lock into position so it could pass information to and from Earth.

The spacecraft, however, has several backup antennas which maintain communications.

Like a couple of tourists at the zoo, Shepard in Antares and Roosa in Kitty Hawk grabbed their cameras and began taking pictures of each other.

Mitchell, meanwhile, had his hands full. At one point, when ground controllers asked him to reset an antenna, he said, "I'll leave you on for a few minutes. I'm damned busy right now."

Until last night, Mission Control was nearly deserted. Occasionally, members of the crew's family would visit, but for the most part all was quiet.

But last night the facility was jammed. Astronauts, high officials of the National Aeronautics and Space Administration and the families were on hand.

Present were George Low, acting NASA administrator; Apollo program director Rocco A. Patrone; Dr. Robert R. Gilruth, director of the Manned Spacecraft Center James A.

(Continued on Page A-2, Col. 6)

TODAY'S Top Features

Classified Advertising RI 8-4111
Other Departments RI 8-1212

SCIENCE AND TECHNOLOGY

"Yankee ingenuity" and "American know-how" are catchall phrases familiar to most inhabitants of the United States. The words represent a faith—sometimes a religious fervor—in progress, and an optimism that Americans can overcome any natural or man-made roadblock by means of "common sense" or trial and error.

While today this full-blown optimism may seem somewhat naive or worse—the kind of flag-waving best reserved for July 4—there is no doubt that faith in progress played a crucial role in this nation's history. More than 200 years ago, those first settlers to the continent found a wilderness: no roads, no cities, no schools, no hospitals, no seaports and little in the way of transportation. They could not go back so they made do with what they had, expanding it into what they really needed. This "making do" is the story of American science and technology.

1776-1800

MEDICINE

In 1799, George Washington died of a cold he caught while riding around his farm in the rain and snow. Life in the new United States seemed to be a constant battle against illness, for there was little known about how to cure even the mildest infections. Yellow fever, typhus and influenza were epidemics which quickly spread from one state to the other, and few of the nation's European-trained doctors could guess at a cure.

Medical advances from abroad arrived infrequently, and then were often resented. In 1721, for example, a smallpox epidemic raged in Boston. Cotton Mather, the clergyman and scholar, urged a local physician, Zabdiel Boylston, to undertake the nation's first inoculation against the disease, for

Mather had heard of successful experiments in Constantinople. Boylston agreed, and vaccinated his own sons, to satisfactory results. Nevertheless, the people of Boston were shocked at what they called an "impious" practice: mobs attacked Boylston's and Mather's homes, the two were vilified in the press and called upon to defend themselves. The controversy raged for months. Meanwhile Boylston vaccinated 200 people, using a virus taken from human smallpox victims. His fame spread to England, and in 1724 Boylston lectured on inoculation in London and was elected to the Royal Society, the leading scientific body of the day.

There were few hospitals in the new states, and the Revolutionary War showed how little doctors knew about medical practices. Soldiers with illnesses of all types were thrown in together where they were certain to catch the contagions of others. John Jones, called the "Father of American surgery," complained that there was little "pure air" in hospitals generally and military hospitals particularly. Benjamin Rush, one of the leading physicians of his day called hospitals "the Sinks of Human Life," asserting "they [the hospitals] robbed the United States of more citizens than the sword."

Medical education was limited at best, most doctors were trained by serving six-year apprenticeships, or by attending school in London or Paris. The first medical school was started in 1765 at the College of Pennsylvania (later the University of Pennsylvania) at the urging of Dr. John Morgan who was appalled at the low level of medical training available. Morgan urged reform of the profession, saying doctors should be barred from selling drugs, and medical students should have at least a minimal liberal education. Morgan was far ahead of his time, however, and his suggestions were ridiculed or ignored.

Morgan, however, was a great influence on the scientists of his time. He trained Benjamin Rush, one of the original signers of the Declaration, sometimes called the "father of experimental medicine," who diagnosed cholera and tooth infection, among other diseases. His cures, today, seem notably simplistic, relying on the purifying effect of heavy bleeding. For tuberculosis he recommended breathing fresh air, eating only vegetables and taking cold baths. Rush was one of the most popular medical teachers. He opened the nation's first free medical clinic in 1786 and advocated a host of liberal policies including humane treatment for the mentally ill. He published the first series of lectures on chemistry and won recognition in Europe for his description of treatment of yellow fever victims during the epidemic in Philadelphia of 1793.

Benjamin Franklin was probably the most influential scientist and because of him Philadelphia was the nation's center of medical and intellectual activity. Although nutrition and hygiene were not regarded as scientific endeavors at the time, Franklin wrote treatises on the advantage of body cleanliness, of sunshine and fresh vegetables, and of sun baths.

PHYSICS AND CHEMISTRY

Franklin's experiments lead in this area as well. After age 40, Franklin devoted himself to a study of heat. He discovered the scientific principles regarding air-conditioning and ventilation and the circulation of hot and cold air. He observed that air expanded with heat and condensed with cold, and suggested that people wear dark colors in the winter since they absorb more heat than do light colors.

Franklin was known as the world's leading expert in electrical science, not for his experiment with the kite, but for his theory as to the nature of electricity, including the nature of electrostatic conduction and the importance of insulation and grounding in electrical experiments. These theories were read aloud at the Royal Society in London and later published. But it is said Franklin's acclaim was greater abroad than in his home country.

Among the nation's first chemists was Dr. James Woodhouse who isolated the metal potassium and determined the superiority of anthracite over bituminous coal.

The nation's scientific community in those days was a small one. A person could function as a physician, a botanist and a chemist at the same time. Thus John Mitchell discovered a cure for yellow fever in 1730, which was used by Benjamin Rush, discovered some 25 new types of plants as a botanist, and later designed what was then the official map of French and English holdings in North America.

ASTRONOMY

Benjamin Rittenhouse was the leading astronomer. He began as a clockmaker at age 19, and in his 20's constructed telescopes. He became known as a land surveyor and settled the conflict of the boundary between Pennsylvania and Maryland, later to be known as the Mason-Dixon line. In 1770 he constructed a device which demonstrated the movement of the planets for the next 5,000 years, one of which exists today on display in the Franklin Institute. With instruments of his own device, he observed Venus traveling across the sun and computed the sun's parallax.

Astronomy was one of the leading sciences, important in establishing the longitude of the states. The Pennsylvania House of representatives allocated 100 pounds to the American Philosophical Society to create a tax-free land grant on which would be built an observatory on the State House lawn.

James Audubon, *whose drawings of American birds in the early years of the nineteenth century did much to popularize the science of naturalism. Audubon, and others like John Muir, worked in the area of nature study without having the academic background that the modern naturalist has. However, their love of nature and their careful cataloguing of flora and fauna helped establish the sciences of biology and botany in America.*

BOTANY

The nation's first botanist was John Bartram who was self-trained but nevertheless dedicated. He traveled through all the colonies gathering specimens and then sent them to Europe for classification. His gardens were often visited by Benjamin Franklin and George Washington. He discovered the tree *Franklinia alatamaha* growing wild, but apparently only two of the plants existed in nature. Whatever exists today of the *Franklinia* was apparently cultivated from the two plants originally found by Bartram.

TRAVEL

During the colonial period, roads were non-existent: the new settlers had to be content with the slim and rutted trails originally made by Indians. Colonial governments did their best to encourage road improvement, in some cases by passing laws requiring each citizen to work one day a year on road widening, removing trees either standing or lying in the way. Nevertheless, technology had not caught up with travel needs. New Amsterdam was one of the first colonies to fill in the rut holes of the roads, using loose stones which would be crushed by passing wheels. Oyster shells were dumped along the shore line to encourage drainage, gunpowder was used to remove boulders.

The first major advance in bridge building was the Leffingwell Bridge over the Shetucket River, some 120 feet in length and 28 feet above water. It was built according to the truss principle, with the full stress of the bridge resting on diagonal trusses. Previously, bridges were very rudimentary, consisting of logs thrown across the stream and then slats tied to the logs. At one time a bridge was built across the York River in Maine in 13 sections, each one supported by four pilings.

Sleighs were the common mode of transportation during winter months; during summer vehicles were designed to pass over mudholes and ruts in the roads. Basically, these consisted of two-wheeled carts with solid wood wheels more than five feet tall. Tires were wide and fit with iron by the blacksmith. The first public transportation was provided after 1700, with wagon service between New York and Philadelphia. By 1750 a Boston-New York stagecoach was running at irregular intervals.

Travel was slow. News of the battle of Lexington reached New York four days after the battle had begun, in eleven more days the citizens of South Carolina had the news.

Printing presses were imported from England until 1760. The first paper mill in the colonies began in 1690. Paper was made of rags and the process was messy and expensive, and then there were few trained typesetters.

The Revolution was a boon for American technology. The Continental Army needed uniforms, and the existing manufacturing processes were slow. Oliver Evans invented a machine to aid in wool processing, others revolutionized the spinning. Premiums were offered textile manufacturers if

Although the Industrial Age *was relatively late in crossing the Atlantic to America, once here industrial technology flourished. This towering Corliss steam engine, which was erected for the Centennial Exposition in 1876, generated 2,500 horsepower. Technological machinery grew rapidly during the latter quarter of the nineteenth century and by the twentieth century America was known throughout the world for her scientific and technological achievements.*

Luther Burbank, *center, planting one of the hundreds of hybrid plants he perfected during his long scientific career. Burbank, who died in 1926, is considered to be one of the greatest scientific geniuses America has produced.*

more material was produced. The momentum of the war was to be continued well into the 19th century.

The relatively small population and labor supply of the United States lent itself naturally to the machine age. Steam was harnassed and quickly put to work, both in transportation and in industry. Jethro Wood was one of the first to see that the simpler the manufacturing process, the quicker items could be produced. He is credited with the concept of "interchangeable parts," a principle which is the very foundation of the mass production system. Eli Whitney was the first to employ this concept when he manufactured firearms for the Federal government in 1798.

1800-1850

The nation became slightly more sophisticated as it neared the Civil War era. Some changes were highly visible. In 1820, for example, it took 78 days to take a message from Washington to Little Rock, Arkansas. Ten years later, that same message took 14 days. Some of the biggest changes obviously took place in road construction. In 1806, the Cumberland Road was authorized by a Congressional Act. It was one of the first macadam highways and was 20 feet wide. Those rutted, tree clogged roads were a thing of the past by 1855, replaced by plank roads which made travel twice as fast.

By 1845, the rudimentary wooden bridges as well were replaced by ones of iron, and there were covered bridges on highways. In fact, by 1850, bridge building had become a

science, with engineers involved in the analysis of stress.

Bridgebuilding attracted some of the great engineers of Europe. John August Roebling, born and educated in Germany, came to the United States to work on canals. He became a U.S. citizen in 1837 and spent most of his life designing wire rope suspension bridges which replaced the chain cable then widely used.

Roebling's feats appear truly heroic even today: he designed a double roadway bridge across the Niagara Falls in 1855, usable by railroad and vehicles, and engineers of the world held their breaths waiting for the bridge to collapse. When it did not, Roebling's achievement was copied by builders throughout the world. He completed a bridge over the Ohio River, and became most famous for the design of the Brooklyn Bridge which inspired Walt Whitman's poem of that name.

To the people of Roebling's day, the Brooklyn Bridge was an inspiration. Some said it was unbelievable, such a long, high, open span of bridge, navigable by any ship; it was an incredible engineering event. Yet it took 12 years for the New York city officials to approve the concept. Construction began in 1869, when Roebling was 60. At the bridge site, he contracted tetanus and died that same year, never to see the bridge completed.

Roebling's son, Washington Augustus, took over as chief engineer. Here too, events were ominous: Roebling, Jr. contracted caisson disease—the "bends," caused by faulty compression chambers used while constructing the deep underwater foundations—and he suffered from overexertion as well. He was confined to his home six blocks from the bridge where he supervised from his window in a wheel chair until the bridge's completion in 1883.

But one of the major engineering feats of this period was the Erie Canal, significant politically as well as scientifically. The ports of New York and New Orleans were in fierce competition for which one would dominate the nation's trade. With the Erie Canal, designed by Canvass White, the battle was over.

In the United States at this time there were no professionally trained engineers. Everything was done by trial and error. Canvass White, for example, had no schooling beyond age 17. White went to England in 1817 and explored the canal system, even looking at construction drawings. When he came back, he was the apparent expert in canal building. He designed the system of locks for the canal, and supervised construction, saving great expense by his discovery that New York state lime rock could be converted into concrete for the locks. So successful was his canal that he immediately set to work on the Delaware Canal and several others. The Canal Age had begun, but White was not to see it. He died at age 44, apparently having worked himself to death.

The Canal Age did not last long, at any rate. It was quickly superseded by the growth of railroads. At first the railroads were built up along the canal system. In 1850, New York state had the great share of the nation's 10,000 miles of railroad track.

One of the greater advances was that of the "T" rail by Robert L. Stevens, a ship builder who later became a rail promoter. Stevens went to England to order iron rails and discovered that travel would be more comfortable if the rails were placed on wooden ties over gravel. His "T" rail is still in use today. He also designed the rail spike, used to attach the rail to the tie.

Matthias W. Baldwin, a watchmaker, constructed the steam engine "Old Ironsides" for the Philadelphia & Germantown railroad. He introduced the steam-tight metal joint enabling trains to operate at twice the usual steam pressure. His company made 1,500 steam engines, most of which were still "fair weather" vehicles; passengers were warned on the schedule that the engine would be drawn by horses in case of bad weather.

The advent of the railroad throughout the country raised the question of energy consumption for the first time. The railroads, and the towns that grew up around them, were quickly eliminating all the forests whose wood was used for power. "Old Ironsides," for example, was wood burning, and wood was still cheaper than any other type of fuel. The "Tom Thumb" locomotive burned anthracite coal, regarded as being ahead of its time. The Baltimore and Ohio Railroad and the Reading Railroad were regarded as far-sighted when they built coal-burning engines as late as 1847. Wood-burners, however, existed until after the Civil War.

Water travel along the nation's internal rivers became common only after 1790, inaugurated by flatboat excursions from Pittsburgh to New Orleans. Commerce down the Mississippi grew quickly, however—mail was delivered by boat by 1800—and was aided by the advent of Henry M. Shreve's advances in steamboat technology, including the deck-mounted engine. Shreve demonstrated that riverboats could be used for commerce, and won a lawsuit against Robert Fulton and Robert R. Livingston to end the steamship monopoly they enjoyed and open the river to competition.

Industry was becoming increasingly mechanized. Begin-

An airplane *built by Samuel Langley perches precariously atop a houseboat in the Potomac River in 1903 (top picture) waiting to be launched. Langley had been experimenting with heavier than air craft for many years, and his attempt to launch an airplane from a floating base in 1903 was another of his many experiments with flight. This photograph was taken October 7, 1903, and moments after the picture was taken the airplane plunged into the Potomac. Langley tried to launch the aircraft again a month later, but met with the same results. Nine days after Langley's second attempt to take off from a floating base, the Wright Brothers made their historic first flight. Although Langley did not beat the Wright Brothers into space, his experiments with launching from a floating base did lead directly to the development of the modern aircraft carrier, bottom picture.*

The model plane, *Samuel Langley first used to prove that a heavier than air craft could fly, as it hangs in the Smithsonian Institution in Washington, D.C. The 90 second flight of this model plane proved the feasibility of winged flight, and sent several American scientists on the path to perfecting an airplane.*

Samuel Langley, *whose early experimentation with flight spurred the development of the airplane. For years Langley, who died in 1906, was secretary of the Smithsonian Institution.*

ning in 1825 farmers followed scientific principles in canning foods, and this new canning industry was an important factor in feeding soldiers during the Civil War. The power loom was introduced in 1813, and thus the mechanization of the clothing industry had begun. The first power news press was introduced in 1827, and the daily newspaper had become the "poor man's college."

American businessmen of the day felt certain that scientists were their partners and allies in building commerce and enterprise. This point was underscored in 1831 at the first chemical convention of New York City, attended by 500 delegates including representatives of industry. "Industrialists and scientists alike were disturbed over the markets," says one historian describing the purpose of the convention. The goal of the chemists was to find efficient methods of producing the nation's staples so as to compete with the foreign markets.

Scientists generally were enjoying a period of tremendous intellectual ferment, sharing information and becoming more concerned about the standards of their profession. The American Association for Advancement of Science began in 1842 as an organization of geologists and naturalists but expanded to include scientists trained in all areas. The American Medical Association was formed five years later. There was a lot to talk about, especially the newly-discovered cellular theory of functioning of living organisms. It was a time of "scientific awakening." James Smithson, a British chemist and mineralogist in 1846 bequeathed one half million dollars for the foundation of an "establishment for the increase and diffusion of knowledge among men," which is, of course, the Smithsonian Institution.

The Smithsonian made an immediate impact on the nation's scientific endeavors, publishing important research including the first studies of winds, storms and whirlwinds. Joseph Henry, the Smithsonian's first secretary, organized

the first volunteer team of meteorologists which led to the formation of the U.S. Weather Bureau in 1870. James Pollard Espy, a meteorologist, worked with Henry's weather corps after publication of his leading work on the "Philosophy of Storms" in 1841.

MEDICINE

While so much attention and money was being applied to the nation's industry and commerce, painfully little had changed with the nation's regard to sickness and health.

In 1800, for example, Benjamin Waterhouse introduced a new smallpox vaccination method from Europe, one which was much safer than that used by Zabdiel Boylston in 1725. Similar to Boylston, Waterhouse inoculated his own five year old son and others close to him. Seventy-five years had gone by but the people of Boston were still in an uproar regarding the vaccination process. A group of untrained persons got hold of some impure vaccine and a serious epidemic arose, for which Waterhouse was blamed. He complained to the local health board and demanded an investigation. The health board found Waterhouse harmless and concluded the vaccine—when properly administered—granted full immunity against the disease.

Ignorance of sanitary rules was apparently the attitude of the day. Oliver Wendell Holmes, a physician and poet, for example, shouted in the dark that unsanitary obstetricians had caused the spread of post-childbirth infection in women. His essays on the subject of cleanliness provoked a major controversy of the day.

S. Weir Mitchell was also well ahead of his time in advocating more human treatment of the insane, just as Benjamin Rush had urged some 50 years before. Mitchell urged

Albert Einstein, *left, and famed Dutch astronomer Willem Desitter look over formulae Desitter has worked out during a lecture at the Mount Wilson Observatory, in Los Angeles, California. Einstein came to this country to avoid persecution under the Nazi regime in Germany.*

so-called "alienists" who treated the mentally ill to conduct scientific research to rid the illness of its superstition. "I think asylum life is deadly to the insane," Mitchell wrote. "They are placed in asylums because of the widespread belief . . . to the effect that there is some mysterious therapeutic influence to be found behind your walls and locked doors. We hold the reverse opinion, and think . . . hospitals are never to be used save as the last resource."[1]

Mitchell was one of the first physicians to see the relationship between psychology and medicine, and pioneered the rest cure. He made important contributions in the structure and functioning of the brain.

The pre-Civil War era saw great advances in surgery, an outgrowth of the large number of medical schools which opened associated with major universities. Samuel D. Gross wrote the first treatment of pathological anatomy in the English language while a teacher at the Cincinnati Medical College. He was a founding father of the American Medical Association and wrote primary texts on surgery both for the army and for medical schools, on gastric and urinary disorders.

Advances in science continued to be made, however, even by those who lacked formal training. Samuel Guthrie, an unlicensed physician and chemist, is credited with discovering chloroform or "sweet whisky" in his New York laboratory in 1831. But the first use of anesthetic dates to 1846 when ether was administered prior to excision of a neck tumor. The attending surgeon that day was John Collins Warren, a professor at Harvard and the leading surgeon of his time.

Patent medicines were still very popular and were advertised in newspapers. In 1841, for example, the "oil" from rocks in Pennsylvania was said to cure a large number of ills.

Nevertheless, signs of civilization were appearing everywhere. New York City had one of the first horse-drawn streetcars in 1832. It went down 4th Avenue, held 30 passengers and cost 12½ cents. The first air-conditioner was placed in a Broadway theater in 1848. The nation's first gas company was established in Baltimore, Maryland in 1816 using coal gas for street lighting.

Technology was rapidly changing American life. John W. Draper, a physicist and astronomer, devised a way to stop action with a camera, and took the first pictures of a person with eyes open. He also took the first photo of the moon. Soap was pre-cut in uniform bars, rather than cut to order from a large chunk, by 1830, and the Sandwich, Massachusetts, glassworks were using standardized formulas by 1825, making glass cheap.

Each new advance called for increased amounts of energy. The nation used relatively little coal until about 1820; the coal that was used, however, was bituminous, a soft coal which burned with smoke as well as flame. From then on demand apparently doubled each year until at least the Civil War. This demand coincided with the growth of the Iron Age—the nation needed more tools than the local blacksmith could supply. In 1810, for example, 50,000 gross tons of pig iron were produced; by 1850, almost 600,000.

1850-1900

America was literally on the move. From 1850 to 1860, the railroad system tripled to 30,000 miles. In the year 1871, 7500 miles of track were laid, with roads extending to San

America's most famous *physicist Albert Einstein with the formulae describing one of his theories. This photograph, made in 1934, was taken while Einstein was addressing the American Association for the Advancement of Science. The formulae on the board is Einstein's proof of his theorem that matter and energy are the same thing in different forms, a theorem he first proposed in 1905.*

Francisco. This period saw the massive immigration of people from China for the purpose of building those roads, and American labor history is alive with the bitter social ramifications of that event.

There is no doubt that society changed as the railroads grew; there was demand for sleeping cars and eating cars, for comfort that was unnecessary during the shorter trips prior to 1850. Before the Civil War, railroad manufacturers responded to this need for comfort by equipping each seat with adjustable backs and legs. Trains were egalitarian, it is said, in that everyone regardless of wealth (except Negroes) was entitled to an easy journey.

But after the Civil War, that was no longer the case. The "palace" sleeping car *Pioneer* was introduced in 1867-68; the hotel car and dining car appeared on some lines that same year, combining sleeping and dining cars in one space. The drawing room car was a feature in the 1870's. For a short time these new extravagant railroad cars had difficulty fitting American tracks. They were too wide for the bridges and could not be used in normal traffic either. But in a few years time, the bridges and roads conformed to the designs of the George Pullmans and Webster Wagners who had luxury in mind, not only transportation.

Railroad was a romantic way to travel. The *Pioneeer* was said to offer service equal to the best American hotel. It had interiors paneled in black walnut, floors lined with the finest and thickest carpets, chandeliers were hung from the ceilings and French mirrors on the wall. The *Pioneer* made its first journey as a hearse, carrying the body of Abraham Lincoln to its resting place and in some way signifying the new post-war mechanized nation Lincoln had left behind. As one historian writes:

[1]S. Weir Mitchell, "Address before the 50th Annual Meeting of the American Medico-Psychological Association," in Brieger, Gert H., ed, *Medical America in the Nineteenth Century: Readings from the Literature* (Baltimore: The Johns Hopkins Press, 1972).

With Pullman's introduction of the palace-car *Pioneer*, the situation changed. For the rapidly increasing well-to-do, a special class was created in America, and in the course of time it came to be identified with the name 'Pullman.' Like Napoleon III, but with greater comfort, American industrialists were to have their private coaches that compressed into one car the luxury for which Napoleon III needed a whole train.[2]

This was indeed the day of the American industrialist. George Pullman had awakened in America a yearning for luxury and now it seemed anyone with some extra money was investing and reaping huge rewards. It was the age of the engineer, more than of the scientist. Yale and Harvard opened engineering schools in the 1870's. For those who were educated and knew how to use America's resources, this must have been an extraordinary time to live.

The country was alive with people looking for ways to make money. Benjamin Silliman, Jr., a chemist at Yale and son of Yale's first chemistry professor, in 1855 published his *Report on the Rock Oil, or Petroleum, from Venango County, Pennsylvania*, in which he outlined the uses of crude oil as a lubricant, for illumination and for paraffin. He saw the entire oil industry before him and talked of its great economic potential.

All Silliman needed was the land. George Bissell, a one time journalist apparently looking for a fortune, had already begun digging wells and trenches on his Oil Creek, Pennsylvania, property. He was losing money until he read Silliman's report. Bissell called Silliman and the two formed the Pennsylvania Rock Oil Company, the nation's first oil production concern. In 1858, Bissell conceived of digging artesian wells to look for oil and called in Edwin L. Drake, one of their stockholders to do the drilling. In 1859, in Titusville, the world's first oil well was completed, and oil struck at 69 feet. Bissell made a fortune, Silliman remained a chemistry professor until he died, and Drake's apparent poor business sense left him impoverished.

Oil was an idea whose time had come. In 1862 John D. Rockefeller at age 23 invested $4,000 in oil, and by 1870, he was in vertical control of much of the industry. Oil had become the country's second greatest export, surpassed only by cotton.[3] From 1862 to 1866, a Federal tax on oil netted the government $12 million (the tax was then repealed).

During those first oil-rich days, the nation was pumping more oil than it knew what to do with. By 1870, for example, the nation's homes and industry consumed only ⅓ of the total crude oil output, so the rest, naturally, was exported. Oil production kept on growing: between 1875 and 1880 the amount brought up from wells tripled and had tripled again by 1900, but the nation during that period could never use more than ⅔ of that which was produced. The turnover to oil was apparently slow, and the amount of fuel wood burned remained approximately constant during these first oil years.

The demand for coal grew enormously, however. Anthracite, or hard coal which burned without smoke, was preferred until the Civil War when industrialists caught on to the preferability of coke—once-fired bituminous coal—used in converting iron ore. From 1850 to 1870, coal production improved by 500 percent and all of it was used within the

[2] Siegfried Giedion, *Mechanization Takes Command: A Contribution to Anonymous History* (New York: W.W. Norton Co., 1948).

[3] Hans H. Landsberg and Sam H. Schurr, *Energy in the United States, Sources, Uses and Policy Issues* (New York: Random House, 1968).

Williams James, *known for his philosophical treatises, was one of the first American philosophers to base his theories of human behavior on scientific evidence, rather than on pure speculation.*

Thomas Hunt Morgan, *for years the director of the Kerchoff Laboratories of the Biological Sciences at the California Institute of Technology in Pasadena, California, received the Nobel Prize for Medicine in 1933. Morgan's research and experimentation was primarily in the field of anatomy.*

United States. Coal was used to refine steel and new improvements were made constantly in iron and steel production. The use of coke in Pittsburgh in 1860 made this the "steel city" of America.

The nation's entrepreneurs had the attitude that there was an endless supply of everything. Writes one historian:

> New machines were ever replacing the old. Capt. William Jones of Pittsburgh, one of the great steelmen of all time, became known as 'scrap pile Bill,' because he was always ready to throw out any piece of machinery as soon as a new and better one was introduced. He told a delegation of British producers that while they, the Britishers, tried to increase production by enlarging their machinery, in America production was increased by bringing in new machinery. [4]

The industrialists may have thought there was an endless supply, but the naturalists and botanists and people of the unpopulated countryside were concerned. The year's from 1850 to 1900 saw the growth of the nation's first organized ecology movement.

John Muir was a leader of the movement to create forest preserves, concentrating his actions in the Yosesmite Valley

[4] John W. Oliver, *History of American Technology* (New York: Ronald Press, 1956).

The application of scientific *theory has always been an integral part of research in America. This scene, showing a Ford auto body assembly system in Highland Park, Michigan, is typical of the kinds of manifold applications industry has taken from scientific investigation.*

area. Muir was a naturalist and an apparently vivid writer for his articles in the nation's monthly magazines aroused concern about the dwindling forests. Muir's 10 year effort on behalf of preservation culminated in 1890 with a bill establishing Yosemite National Park. The next year, Congress passed a law allowing the creation of similar preserves from the public domain. In 1896, Muir was named an advisor to the Forestry Commission.

Although the park system had been created, Muir found evidence that commercial interests were still encroaching. Once again, his articles drew public response and action to protect the preserves was taken. He prevailed upon President Theodore Roosevelt to increase greatly the lands in the public domain.

This period saw the increase in publication of works by "naturalists"—men who lived a simple life and felt that science was ruining society. The works of John Burroughs, who was a friend of both Muir and President Roosevelt, were influential statements of the anti-scientific philosophy of a certain segment of the public.

"Conservation" was the issue in 1900 that some think ecology had become by 1976. However, in 1900, President Theodore Roosevelt made conservation his own political issue, arguing that the public as a whole owned public lands and those lands must be protected from private interests. During his administration, he created 15 national monuments, including the Grand Canyon, added to the forest reserves, and generally raised the consciousness of those who had never before heard the country might run out of national resources.

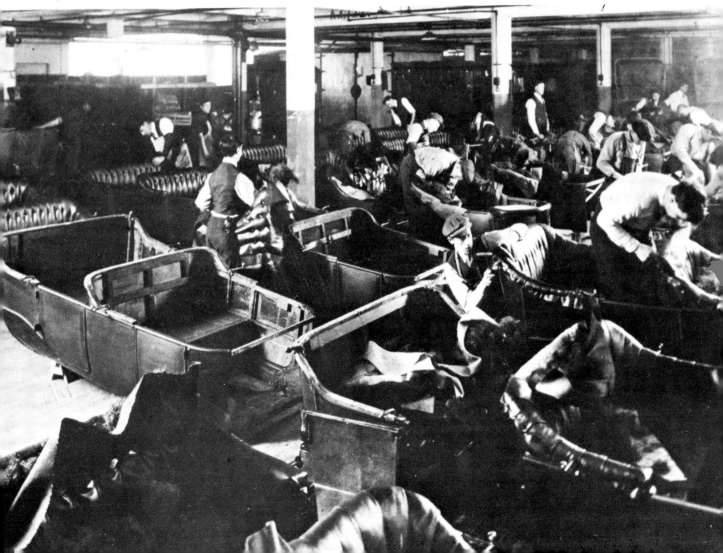

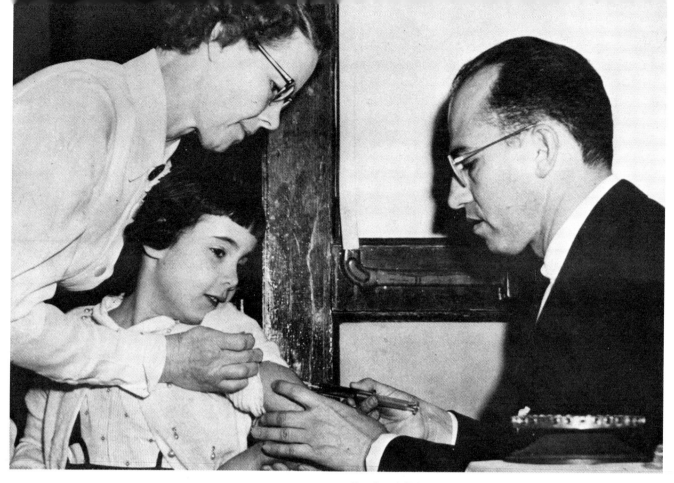

Dr. Jonas Salk, *who invented the world's first anti-polio vaccine, administers the vaccine to a little girl during part of a research program conducted in Pittsburgh, Pennsylvania, in 1956.*

Gifford Pinchot was named to head the forest reserves and he made the first systematic study of forestry in the country. He said that forests had to be used rather than preserved, but that such use must be scientific rather than raping the land of all the trees. He established the "constant annual yield" formula by which forests could be thinned but not killed.

THE MACHINE AGE

Though the Civil War resulted in many technological "firsts—among them proving the superiority of iron war vessels—the major impact of the war was in sealing the domination of the machine over American life. The South had a cheap slave labor supply and consequently had no need for labor-saving machinery. The North had to maximize its labor power and the machine was already a way of life in the North before the War.

More than merely an idealistic debate, however, the Civil War proved that mechanization was the only way to fight a war. The South, which had not yet fully accepted mass production of ammunition, guns or clothing, soon ran out of supplies. Thus, in the 1870's the nation as a whole moved into the machine age, with the South bringing up the rear.

This movement was especially seen in the great post-war activity in construction. Northern cities especially raised

Dr. Harlow Shapley, *internationally famous American astronomer, as he appeared in 1962. Shapley taught and did research at Harvard.*

With a chemical formula *on the board, and his hands on a model of the world, University of California professor of chemistry Harold C. Urey lectures a class in advanced chemistry. Urey, like hundreds of other theoretical scientists in America, combined a career of pure research and teaching.*

numerous major public building and private homes for the new millionaires. Architecture set the tone for the day, for, armed with iron and steel supports there was a major revolution taking place in building design.

Henry Hobson Richardson was a primary influence in what was to become the "modern" school of architecture. Richardson worked in Boston, designing Trinity Church and the Boston and Albany Railroad stations where the simplicity of his work became its hallmark. Richardson used quarry rock as a decorative material, believing in natural shapes and textures, and his shingled country houses impressed Stanford White and Charles McKim, leading architects in the 20th century. White and McKim designed the old Madison Square Garden (now torn down) in New York City and restored the Rotunda of the University of Virginia, originally designed by Thomas Jefferson. White is known best for the Washington Arch in Greenwich Village, but he preferred Madison Square Garden, and he had a home in its tower.

While White's style was clearly eclectic, his partner McKim was totally involved with classical architecture. McKim helped plan the development of Washington, D.C., and designed the area around the Capitol building including rough drawings of the Lincoln Memorial. McKim supervised the restoration of the White House in 1902-1903.

This neo-classical school represented by McKim would soon be at odds with the rise of the "modern" represented by the skyscrapers of Louis H. Sullivan. The Wainwright Building in St. Louis—the first true skyscraper—was designed by Sullivan in 1890, demonstrating his belief that "form follows function." His dedication to simplicity would be found in the Gage Building and the Auditorium Buildings in Chicago, the latter having near-perfect acoustics due to elevated rows of seats. Frank Lloyd Wright, among the most influential 20th century modern architects, was Sullivan's apprentice.

Sullivan's ideas, however, were not universally accepted. He was regarded by many as too radical, and he lost his financial backing.

Albert Einstein *on his 75th birthday, at his home in Princeton, New Jersey. Einstein's Theory of Relativity laid much of the theoretical groundwork for the development of atomic power. He died in 1955.*

George Washington Carver, *left, America's most famous Black scientist, and Henry Ford, when they met in Ford's Foods Laboratory in 1942. Carver's experiments led to hundreds of variations of new foods.*

The age of flight, *which began with the Wright Brothers in 1903, had by the Seventies progressed to the large luxury airliners shown here. The wing-span of this 747 is greater than the entire flight distance covered by the Wright Brothers in their first flight.*

The new American millionaires could afford the most accomplished architects for their homes. Richard Morris Hunt was among the most fashionable. He had designed the base of the Statue of Liberty and portions of the Metropolitan Museum of Art in New York City as well as the National Observatory in Washington, D.C. He designed in the same eclectic school as Stanford White and this was favored by the Vanderbilts, the Astors and the Belmonts for whom he designed mansions and estates. He was an influential member of the American Institute of Architects and among its founding members in 1857.

The exchange and expression of new ideas in architecture mirrored the reviving activity taking place throughout the nation's commercial and scientific communities which had been interrupted by Civil War. Leading American scientists and businessmen represented the United States at a series of international fairs which were significant for marking the nation's place among the world commercial giants. Europeans flocked to the nation's Centennial of 1876, and the Chicago World's Fair of 1893, to learn about American machinery and technology.

The industrialists discussed the latest innovative uses of energy—especially electricity. Arc lamps, powered by steam-driven generators, were first installed in John Wanamaker's department store in Philadelphia in 1878, and later in New York and Boston. The use of arc lamps to light merchandise in store-front windows created night-time window shopping as a fashionable pastime. Arc-lamps were introduced as street lighting replacing the gas lamps in 1879 in Cleveland, then in San Francisco and later in Wabash, Indiana, where the opening of the first light was a major social event.

Arc lamps were the accepted means of street lighting at least until 1900. They were used as lighting steam boats and were beacons in lighthouses. They were stage lights and search lights. In the meanwhile, of course, Thomas A. Edison and a host of fellow-inventors were busy working on the incandescent lamp which was completed in the 1880's but took some time to catch on. During this same period, Edison established the first central power station which was greatly more economical and eliminated the ugly churning individual power plants which were common basement fixtures of the time.

Edison's central generator was used for the opening of the Pearl Street Central Station in New York in 1882, and within four months the Edison Co. was lighting 5,000 lamps for 230 customers. It was clear that the electrical age had begun.

New York's transit system was already in full operation by 1900, but the subway itself was still an idea. The first experiment with subways lasted one year in 1870, when Alfred Ely Beach prevailed upon the city fathers to allow him to try out his pneumatic tube system. The subway's only car carried 22 people, was 9 feet wide and 312 feet long. For reasons that are not too clear, the subway ended after 400,000 people had ridden in it. Beach is given the credit as the "father" of the New York subway system, which now has 726 miles of track.

There was still a dependence upon horses in the years before 1900. In 1872, the city of New York suffered "the Great Epizoatic"—a viral epidemic which eventually killed one quarter of the nation's horses—and city transportation ground to a halt.

There were also new and improved roads, thanks primarily to Eli Whitney Blake's new stone crusher introduced in 1858. The roads were good, but apparently not good enough for automobile traffic. In 1879, George Seldon patented an internal combustion engine which, according to one theory, failed commercially because existing roads could not accommodate motorized vehicles.

In the American home, cleanliness was not yet next to Godliness. In the years before 1850, toilets and baths were provided when possible, though some large houses had more than one bathroom. In the years after 1850, as cities became more populated, the public grew more concerned about sanitation. Sewerage systems and water works were demanded, especially after the epidemics of 1884 and 1886, though the public was still involved in the question of bathing. *Everybody's Magazine,* for example, printed an article as late as 1904, "Is Bathing Good for Us?"

A series of inventions revolutionized the American communication system: the telephone, the typewriter and improved photography and printing. By 1900, President McKinley used the telephone frequently to talk to his party advisors. He had accepted it as a means of doing business. The first telephone line between Boston and Lowell, Massachusetts, was established in 1879; Bell Telephone, the first phone company, was organized in 1877, and that same year five Boston banks installed telephones with a single, common switching system.

Although the first transatlantic cable of 1858 was somewhat of a failure, the telegraph system itself became an indispensable link between cities. By 1870 there were long distance telegraph lines relaying through New York to cities throughout the country.

C. Latham Sholes constructed the first American typewriter, but sold the patent to the Remington Arms Co. in 1873 for $12,000 so they might improve upon his model. The first typewriters were principally used by writers, among them Mark Twain, and the clergy. Much later they became standard for business and the individual.

George Eastman made the first major renovation in cameras, inventing the Kodak, the first hand-held camera which needed no tripod. "Kodak" apparently was a word chosen at random.

MEDICINE

Despite all these technological advances, the fight against superstition in the area of public health was hard to win. For instance, in 1895, Francis Schlatter, a faith healer who dressed like Christ, set up a tent in Denver, Colorado and treated 2,000 to 3,000 persons daily.

The theory of the contagion of germs promoted in Europe by Lister was first being assimilated in the United States before 1880. In 1881, for example, President Garfield was shot at the Baltimore and Potomac Station in Washington. A host of doctors attended him, probing his wounds with instruments and with ungloved fingers. Stephen Smith, a leading doctor of the 19th century, writes about conditions at Bellevue Hospital in 1885, before antiseptic methods were generally accepted:

> The personal preparation of the surgeon and his assistants for the operation was limited to self-protection against soiling their clothes or person. No special thought was ever given to the condition of the hands and nails. The assistants came directly from other ward duties, their hands soiled by contact with the thousand impure matters which they must handle, and with slight or no washing.[5]

Despite the large number of medical schools of the time, the attitude towards broken bones still seems almost medieval; as Smith continues:

> Compound fractures were formerly regarded as proper cases for amputation, if the local injury exceeded a single fracture, with a simple penetration of the soft tissues. And even the simplest cases of compound fracture were reserved for treatment with many misgivings as to the result. The dictum of Munter that 'compound fractures commonly suppurate' [burst] was ever the guiding principle in the mind of the surgeon. If, therefore, the wound was extensive, or the bones comminuted, or a join involved, amputation was the rule.[6]

In the 1850's, through 70's, as Lister's ideas were heatedly

[5] Stephen Smith, "The Comparative Results of Operations in Bellevue Hospital," in Brieger, *op. cit.*, p. 204.

[6] *Ibid.*, p. 205.

[7] Samuel D. Gross, "The Factors of Disease and Death after Injuries, Parturition and Surgical Operations," in Brieger, *op. cit.*, pp. 190-196.

Dr. J. Robert Oppenheimer, *one of the leaders of the Manhattan Project. The Manhattan Project, conducted in secrecy during the Forties, led to the development of the atomic bomb.*

debated, hospital sponges were used from one patient to the next, merely washed off to remove the dirt and sand.

Lister won increasing numbers of converts in the United States after his appearance in Philadelphia in 1876 at the International Medical Congress, and yet those who believed in his methods continued to rationalize their radical position in medical journals. Doctors who tried the system sometimes gave it up saying it was too cumbersome keeping wounds clean, or that even after taking every precaution the undressed wound showed signs of infection.[7]

Nevertheless, increasing number of doctors were engaged in research against disease. William Henry Welch, for example, started the first pathology laboratory in the country in 1879 at Bellevue Hospital Medical College. He left to study bacteriology in Europe with Robert Koch and returned to become the first dean of Johns Hopkins Hospital Medical School. Welch discovered the bacillus which causes "gas gangrene" and was active in experimental medicine. Welch, along with Sir William Osler, gathered the best medical talent in the country to Johns Hopkins which quickly became the leading medical school in the United States.

William Stewart Halsted was one of those attracted to Johns Hopkins by Welch. He had been the leading surgeon in New York at Bellevue Hospital and performed the first successful blood transfusion in the country, giving blood to his own sister who was hemorrhaging after childbirth.

Halsted developed a philosophy of surgery which was a permanent influence on American medical education: he believed in the natural restorative powers of the body, and that the surgeon's and doctor's duty was to aid the body in recuperating. Therefore, sanitary conditions were a must, both in the operating room and in the hospital generally. He emphasized keeping the patient free of infection, that the blood flow can be controlled, and that body tissues must be treated with care. He demanded students wear rubber gloves while in an operating room.

Halsted also discovered the anesthetic qualities of cocaine

when injected into a nerve and became addicted to the drug while experimenting. It took him two years to kill the habit. Once cured, he joined Welch at Johns Hopkins and opened the first school of surgery in 1890.

Stephen Smith and James R. Wood, however, were examples of the leading surgeons of the day who accepted the practices of Lister and made contributions of their own. Wood, for example, was known for his deft neurosurgical techniques, and for his treatment of blood clots of the arteries. He was an expert in bone repair and regeneration. Wood helped found Bellevue Hospital in 1847 and helped it become the leading hospital of that generation.

Until the opening of the Mayo Clinic in 1889, the mid-west states of Minnesota, Iowa and the Dakotas had little in the way of adequate medical or surgical facilities. William and Charles Mayo were born in Minnesota where their father had a medical practice. After the sons went to medical school—at the University of Michigan and Chicago Medical College (now Northwestern University) respectively, the three had about the largest practice in the region.

The Mayo brothers started building a permanent hospital in 1883. It opened in 1889 and they were the only surgeons at the hospital until 1915. As they were fully aware of the medical and surgical developments occurring throughout Europe and the United States, the fame of the hospital grew. When various specialty surgeons came to the hospital, a group clinic practice was established, the first in the country. William Mayo then turned to his specialty, abdominal surgery, while Charles concentrated on thyroid and the nervous system. The Clinic has since become affiliated with the University of Minnesota and receives 150,000 patients a year from all over the world.

By the turn of the century, the nation's cities were still plagued by epidemic, especially typhus, small pox, and diptheria. Medical researchers were specializing in the area,

Experimentation in electronics *in the twentieth century resulted in the development of the motion picture camera, sound motion pictures, and the perfection of radio broadcasting. Pictured is the first radio station in America, KDKA, in Pittsburgh, Pennsylvania, which was established on November 2, 1920.*

but little headway was made until 1898 when Walter Reed, a 20-year veteran Army surgeon, and a group of postgraduate students at Johns Hopkins undertook a study of typhoid fever in Army camps. The commission's report was a significant contribution to the understanding of contagion in general.

In 1899, he and an associate published their research into yellow fever, and disproved the common notion that it was caused by a single type of bacillus. During the Spanish-American war, Reed, as the expert in the field, was sent to Cuba to investigate an outbreak of yellow fever among U.S. troops stationed there. His research confirmed the belief of fellow scientists that a certain mosquito was the carrier of the disease and the army began a program to eliminate the mosquito population. In the process of Reed's research on human subjects, several of his assistants, including Jesse Lazear, died of the disease.

Once the mosquito was isolated, yellow fever was controllable. By 1902 there were no cases of the disease in Cuba and Reed's work was praised as heroic. Reed then returned home only to die that same year of a sudden appendicitis.

Pure research in scientific laboratories—rather than research for the purpose of helping industry grow—was a new concept of education just beginning to catch on in the years before the 20th century. One can see during this period a growing schism in the ranks of the scientific community— one which will occupy them until the present day. The debate: does science exist to promote a "better way of life" or does it exist for itself, to help mankind find out about the universe, i.e., "practical" research versus "pure" research.

Schools like Johns Hopkins were apparently giving an ear to the pure research concept, and scientists like Ira Remsen, at the newly-formed Hopkins Chemical Laboratory, were among the major promoters of this new philosophy.

Remsen published books on chemical theory, including organic and inorganic matter, but also conducted research which led to the discovery of an artificial sweetener later known as saccharin. Remsen also started the engineering school at Johns Hopkins, and served as head of various chemical societies and the National Academy of Sciences. He worked as an industrial consultant and also did work on pure food laws for the government.

Dr. Edward Kendall, *shown at work in his laboratory where he worked on the development of cortisone. Dr. Kendall received the Nobel Prize for Medicine in 1950 for his pioneering work in developing cortisone and ACTH, a hormone which gives relief to arthritis sufferers.*

ASTRONOMY

In the field of astronomy, much as in medicine and in the sciences as a whole, researchers were forming professional organizations both within the United States and on an international basis. The first international conference of astronomers was held in Paris in 1896, largely at the instigation of Simon Newcomb, an American astronomer who three years later would become the first president of the newly formed American Astronomical Society.

These Associations not only evidence that there were more people studying in the particular field; but also reflect the growing sophistication of scientists regarding their world. No longer did astronomers, for example, believe that one man observing the heavens through a telescope could find out all there was to know about the movement of celestial bodies.

The work of Simon Newcomb especially reflects this philosphical turn. Newcomb, educated at Harvard's Lawrence Scientific School, became professor of mathematics at the U.S. Naval Observatory in Washington, D.C. While at the observatory he undertook the arduous task of correcting the existing tables regarding the positions and motions of the moon, the planets and the sun. Having finished that task, he standardized and constructed new tables of values and published the results in 1879, and then began the work of urging scientists in his own country to accept a single table. The international conference in Paris in 1897 was his reward, for the conference decided to adopt the worldwide use of astronomical constants, of which his work formed the major part.

Henry Draper carried on the interest in astronomy of his father, John W. Draper, both of whom studied radiant energy. Henry Draper introduced the first silver-on-mirror telescope in the United States and contributed many innovations in the photography of the stars. In 1872, he made the first record of the radiation of a star (called spectroscopy), and similarly studied the sun, planets and bright stars.

During the 1880's, he made the first spectrogram of a comet, and the first photograph of radiant gas (called a nebula). Draper graduated from the University of the City of New York, (now New York University), and became professor of natural science at Bellevue Hospital, later becoming professor of physiology and dean of the medical faculty. During the 1870's he was professor of analytic chemistry, and the year before he died succeeded his father to the chair of chemistry at the school.

The growing sophistication of U.S. astronomers regarding their endeavors can be seen in the work of Edward and William Pickering. Astronomers were no longer satisfied merely in describing stars and planets. They wanted to know about structure and motion. Thus, Edward Pickering, working at the Massachusetts Institute of Technology, and William, in inaugurating the Lowell Obsesrvatory in Flagstaff, Arizona, both were significant in their dedication to creating observatories with high-powered instruments for photo observations.

Edward Pickering (1846-1919) developed the first universally accepted scale by which to measure the brightness of the stars (stellar magnitude), and went on to measure the brightness of 80,000 of them. He collected a library of photographs of 300,000 observable stars which provided the first history of the universe. In the community of astronomers, however, he is best remembered, along with Annie Jump Cannon, for creating the Henry Draper Catalogue of the spectra (or emitted radiation) of 225,000 stars.

The impact of this work was monumental. Astronomers still use the Draper catalogue, which was regarded as a key to many problems in astronomy. He also began work on observing stars in the Southern Hemisphere.

William Pickering may well have felt overshadowed by the eminence of his older brother. However, he was a major

Dr. Norbert Wiener, *professor of cybernetics at the Massachusetts Institute of Technology.*

Science and politics *occasionally come together in American society. Here Nobel Prize winner Dr. Edward Kendall displays the molecular structure of cortisone while testifying before the Senate committee investigating the fixing of drug prices by the pharmaceutical industry in 1959.*

astronomer in his own right, best known for predicting the existence of the ninth planet, Pluto, which was actually discovered 10 years later in 1929. Earlier, he discovered the ninth satellite of Saturn (Phoebe) and Saturn's tenth satellite, actually confirmed in 1967.

Annie Jump Cannon was one of the few women in any field of the sciences to win acclaim during this period of American history. Although she worked under Edward Pickering in designing the monumental Henry Draper Catalogue, she did most of the actual work. She did not go unapplauded, however; historians have apparently given her her due in helping to change the very philosophy of science in the late 19th and early 20th centuries, in which specific evidence based on observation was called on to support theory.

She received numerous awards, and was the first women to receive an honorary doctorate from Oxford University in 1925.

The astronomical photographs of Edward Emerson Barnard, made at the Lick Observatory in Mt. Hamilton, California, were significant in their description of the Milky Way. Barnard came to astronomy by way of photography, and was one of the first to use a wide-angle lens which enabled him to get greater detail in his prints of the stars. Such detail helped in identifying nebulae. In 1892 he discovered Jupiter V, the fist new satellite of a planet to be discovered since Galileo discovered the first four. He apparently photographed everything: planets, comets, nebulae, and in 1916 he discovered Barnard's star, which had the greatest known angular motion relative to the earth.

1900 TO PRESENT

There is no question that the technology of the 20th century stands in the shadow of Henry Ford. With the acceptance

of the American automobile, and the mass production of cars on a grand scale, revolutionary changes were made in the life and society of the United States.

There are good sides to this as well as bad. As far as the worker is concerned—for every technological advance demands a working class capable of responding to its demands —the assembly line and the growth of American manufacturing has to be regarded as a discouraging event. The assembly line meant the increased demand for unskilled labor, for the repetition of tasks which were inartistic and relatively insignificant of themselves and in which the worker could feel little pride in craftsmanship.

> In the transition phase (of the assembly line) still predominant in industry, man acts as a lever of the machine. He must perform certain operations that are not yet carried out by mechanisms. True, the tempo of work is geared to the human organism; but in a deeper sense, the inexorable regularity with which the worker must follow the rhythm of the mechanical system is unnatural to man.[8]

Certainly there had been mass production during previous centuries; ammunition and guns were produced that way for the Civil War, and with the introduction of the cotton gin, the South, too, relied heavily on repetitive tasks from its slave population. No industrialist, however, exploited the assembly line as did Henry Ford.

For Ford, the American worker was just one more interchangeable part which must work at maximum efficiency for increased production of the automobile. His philosophy appeared to be only common sense to the vast number of American manufacturers and the assembly line itself became the basic characteristic of American labor throughout the 20th Century. "Scientific management" were the key words of the day, representing psychological techniques designed to have the workers produce more. "Scientific management" was only partially successful, however, and manufacturers were constantly looking for ways to replace still more humans by machines.

"We set out to build automobile frames without men," said one manufacturer in 1929. "It is highly probable that

[8] Giedion, *op. cit.,* p. 77.

watching our workers do the same thing over and over again, day in and day out, sent us on our quest for the 100% mechanization of frame manufacture."[9]

There is no question that the increased demand for unskilled labor to do repetitive tasks gave an additional push to the American labor movement. Ford and his plant, while heroic to the car-buying public, became a symbol of the class struggle during the 1930's. Charlie Chaplin's film *Modern Times* with his assembly line worker who goes mad and breaks his machine, is looked on as the social document of the day.

Despite these negative psychological and social ramifications, Henry Ford and the automobile represent a romantic interlude in American history. The United States began a love affair with the car in 1900 which has remained steadfast and unrequited, to this day.

The automobile was more than just a technological advance in the means of transportation: it was a sex symbol, a sign of status and wealth, it represented freedom and independence. American manufacturers and car owners themselves have for generations engaged in competition for who could design and own the most "beautiful" engine, or tail fin, or head light, or chassis. In contradtion to nations like Germany, for example, where the BMW and the Volkswagen remained virtually the same for 30 or 40 years, the American car buying public was fickle and needed a new model every year in a different color. Despite the waste of raw materials, and the ultimately draining demand for gasoline, the American automobile has remained a permanent fixture in the nation's psyche.

The American automobile has made possible the growth of cities such as Los Angeles in which the car is the single mode of transportation. Los Angeles, the car city, is many times larger than the subway-and-bus city of New York. The car makes these longer distances accessible.

It has enabled the nation to expand in a much more independent manner. Without the car, the United States might still be a nation of congestion alternating with emptiness, rather than the unplanned megalopolis which existed in the 1960's and 1970's.

Of course, this did not happen overnight:

> In 1910 there was 1 automobile for every 125 people aged eighteen or above. In 1920 there was 1 automobile for every eight adults, and the stock of automobiles had shot up in that decade from less than 500,000 to over 8 million. The pace remained rapid until the depression hit. By that time the number of adults per car had dropped to 3½. Between the aftermath of the depression and World War II it did not decline from that level. But in 1947 the ratio again began to drop, and by 1965 stood at about 1⅔ adults per car.[10]

The demand for gasoline rose concomitantly with the rise in automobile ownership. In 1920, gasoline represented 20 per cent of the total oil consumed; in 1930, it represented 40 percent. Technological advances were made in the refining of oil to get more gasoline from a barrel of crude oil. The petroleum industry also made decisions regarding the amount of oil which would go toward gasoline refinement: in 1930, two gallons of kerosene were produced from a barrel of crude compared with 24 gallons in 1900. Gasoline, however, yielded 18 gallons per barrel, compared with five during this same period. [11]

Of course, the nation's roads were still primarily of the

[9]*Ibid.*, p. 118.

[10]Landsburg, *op. cit.*, p. 41.

[11]*Ibid.*, p. 42.

crushed-stone variety, or of macadam, hardly sufficient for the rubber tires of automobiles. In fact, the new cars wore off the dust which held the macadam roads together. Until the 1920's, road construction relied on asphalt and tar, which was certainly an improvement over macadam, but not a solution to the problem.

That solution awaited the end of World War I, at which time the Army itself lent its support to a better roads campaign. A cross-country journey by 200 servicemen in 1919, over muddy and dusty roads, received tremendous publicity and resulted in passage of the Federal Highways Act.

The Act envisioned a system of highways leading to every city with more than 50,000 people. The building would be done exclusively in concrete, the most modern road-building material available. The latest advanced mechanical concrete mixers which operated automatically were introduced in the early 1920's, and new engineering techniques were said to stress the safety aspects of road construction, including the banking of curves.

The Pennsylvania Turnpike, authorized in 1937, represented the culmination of these road-building trends. It was a dual four-lane highway, 24 feet wide, and featuring a road divider, and was designed as an all-weather, high-speed road. It was called "The World's Greatest Highway," and was completed between Harrisburg and Pittsburgh in 1940. The complete road, which went from Philadelphia through the state farmland and mountains, featuring tunnels converted from railroad use, was open in 1951. The complete road, which went from Philadelphia to the Ohio border, was open in 1951. It traveled through cities, farmland, and mountains, used reconverted railroad tunnels and new bridges and pedestrian right of ways.

AIR TRANSPORTATION

Wilbur and Orville Wright's flying machine, patented in 1906, was immediately appropriated for defense purposes—first by France and Great Britain, and in 1908 by the United States War Department. After World War I, however, there was a surplus of planes and aircraft equipment and former servicemen who knew how to fly.

Planes were selling for less than automobiles, but the economy was not ready for the aviation industry, despite the efforts of entrepreneurs to open private air fields. Young men who wanted to continue flying were reduced to performing in the numerous flying stunt shows which were appearing throughout the country, or flying crop dusters around the farm states.

The first modern airliner appeared in 1936, the DC-3 carrying 21 passengers and cruising at 180 miles per hour. The DC planes were the first to prove that commercial air traffic could be lucrative. The four-engine "Stratoliner," seating 33 passengers and traveling at 250 miles per hour, was the next advance. The Civil Aeronautics Board, created in 1938, signified that the era of flight had begun.

Airplane technology increased rapidly during World War II, and it was only after the war's end that commercial airline traffic, including competition between airlines, would begin in earnest. The average American traveler regarded airplanes as a novelty throughout the 1950's. Air traffic only became a way of life, as common in its own way as the train had been during the 1880's, in the late 1960's.

MOTION PICTURES

The first motion pictures did not actually move at all; they

Developers of two anti-polio vaccines, *Dr. Albert Sabin, left, and Dr. Jonas Salk, as they appeared in 1954 while attending an international science congress on polio. Salk's vaccine was the first to be perfected, but Sabin developed an oral vaccine which, because it precludes the necessity of an injection, has found greater widespread usage throughout the world.*

were merely continuous action shots taken at extremely fast shutter speeds. Nevertheless, these pictures of horses in "motion," taken by Edward Muybridge in 1872, created tremendous excitement. His camera achieved shutter speeds up to $1/2000$th of a second, and made it appear that the horse was stationary and the scenery moving.

George Eastman and Thomas Edison joined in the development of the "Kinetograph," the first camera which could record a few seconds of action at a time. Before 1900 there was also a Phantoscope in 1894 by C. Francis Jenkins—a camera with a revolving lens—and the Vitascope—a motion picture projecting machine. By the be-beginning of the 20th century, audiences at vaudeville shows were presented with motion pictures.

Nevertheless, the motion picture industry was slow in formation. The Nickelodeon, "the world's first all-moving picture theater," opened in 1905 in Pittsburgh. The silent films were projected on a white sheet with phonograph background. Showings were continuous from nine in the morning until midnight. There were one or two reels of film, each 15 to 20 minutes. The public apparently adored the "movies" right away—as many as 5,000 people lined up to pay their nickels for a show.

George Melies is credited with producing the first "feature film"—*Cinderella*—which was followed quickly by other such full-length endeavors including Edwin S. Porters *The Great Train Robbery*.

Though the motion picture camera itself was stationary—it could not move forward for closeups or backward for broad landscape scenes without a completely new set up—major photographic advances were made within this limitation. D.W. Griffith's *The Birth of a Nation* and *Intolerance* were the first to use mob scenes and create the image of foreground and background.

The development of sound pictures—"talkies"—in the late 1920's awaited advancement of the radio and phono-

graph. While Thomas A. Edison and others had early experimented with the synchronization of sound on film, the first "phonofilm" device was introduced in 1926, the creation of Lee De Forest, an electrical engineer.

De Forest took his Ph.D. at Yale's Sheffield Scientific School and then worked for Western Electric in Chicago. On his own time, he received more than 300 patents, among them a device which made possible the use of headphones on wireless receivers. His invention of the audion, capable of amplifying radio signals and acting as a generator, was regarded as the greatest sound advance of the time. However, almost simultaneously, the audion was "invented" by Edwin H. Armstrong and Irving Langmir. A patent law suit developed and De Forest was victorious.

The phono film was just one of many electrical engineering developments by De Forest, who apparently never kept his mind on a project long enough to smooth out all the wrinkles. He sold the rights to the audion by World War I, then in 1919 developed his sound system. He made important contributions to the electric phonograph, the long-distance telephone, the television and radar. He called himself the "Father of Radio" and made the first broadcast, in 1910, of live music, featuring Enrico Caruso at the Metropolitan Opera.

Although Edwin Armstrong lost his battle for the audion, his sound advances were nevertheless significant. He is credited with perfecting the means by which radios pick up amplitude modulation (AM) frequencies, and for discovering the frequency modulation (FM) transmission which eliminated static. Armstrong thought FM was the greatest thing to happen to radio, but the radio industry apparently had other priorities. It took six years for FM receivers to be available, by which time Armstrong had started his own broadcasting station in New Jersey. In 1920 he perfected the system of circuits used for short-wave and "ham" radios.

While camera technicians and engineers had been experimenting with color film during the late 1890's, major advancement occurred during the 1920's. George Eastman's Kodachrome film was a typical development, relying in this case upon five coatings of color on a film. Dr. Leonard Troland, for example, developed a camera which took three pictures simultaneously with results on the order of those

achieved by Kodachrome. The first color films, among them the Walt Disney cartoons, used a method which borrowed from both of its predecessors, that of Herbert T. Kalmas of MIT who designed a dye-transfer method of printing.

The simultaneous advances in radio and sound film culminated with the creation of the television. Credit for this electronic marvel is given to Ernst F. Alexanderson who was born in Sweden but became a U.S. citizen in 1908. Alexanderson's experiments in radio frequency resulted in a more stable transoceanic radio system, refinements in sound amplification and the radio tuning system.

In 1927, Alexanderson designed a home television receiver while at General Electric which he demonstrated publicly the next year. By 1930, he had completed an entire television system in which the picture was projected on a

Professor Wallace Fenn, *left, and Dr. Albert Sabin, congratulating each other after both had won the Antonio Feltrinelli International Prize in 1964. Professor Fenn received the award for medicine, while Dr. Sabin received his award for applied surgery.*

theater screen. By the 1920's, however, the major communications companies of the nation were generally working on advances simultaneously. It is impossible to give Alexanderson full credit for television, for in fact, Vladimir Zworykin, working at RCA—where Alexanderson had once worked—introduced a crude television system in 1923. Zworykin is sometimes referred to as the "father of television," especially for his discovery of a high-efficiency scanning camera which allowed an all-electric television system to be created.

David Sarnoff and Allen B. DuMont—DuMont created the fine tuning dial—were the major promoters of television.

They headed RCA's efforts to make television a household necessity, but were in fact halted in their efforts by World War II.

CLOTHING

The post World War I period saw also an exciting advancement in the mass production and innovation of textiles, although for the people who crowded into sweat shops doing piece work it must have lost much of the glamor.

While the first man-made fibre, rayon, was developed in France, Germany and England, the U.S. followed quickly with nylon, a truly revolutionary fabric designed at the DuPont factory, by Dr. Wallace H. Carothers. Nylon was made public with much fanfare, advertised as a God-send to women who were desperate for silk stockings in the days before World War II. It demanded a new technology of its own, a melt spinning process, since the old hosiery knitting machines knotted with the fine yarn.

These new fibres—including orlon as a substitute for wool in the 1940's—were developed by chemists using technological advancements of the war years. World War I is sometimes referred to as a "chemist's war," World War II, a physicist's war. Chemists had been engaged in research to prevent meat spoilage, the properties of proteins, the maintenance of sanitary conditions, and the study of materials such as leather and paper. It was only during World War I that the nation's drug and chemistry industry was developed, since in prior years foreign competition had made the manufacture of chemicals unproductive.

With World War I finished, the chemists just continued their work. The cotton industry was mechanized, as was all of agriculture with a new emphasis on intensive farming.

Chemists discovered new ways of freezing foods and a greater attention was paid to nutrition. George Washington Carver was one of the heroes of the day, and one of the few Blacks to rise to a position of respect in the scientific community. Carver, an agricultural chemist, worked at Booker T. Washington's Tuskegee Institute in Alabama. He

plenish their soil, rather than continuing to plant only cotton which would rob the soil of nutrients. By such urgings, and with his discovery of hundreds of commercial uses of the peanut, Carver saved and expanded the Southern economy, for in 1914 a bollweevil epidemic had ruined the cotton crop.

Carver discovered the peanut could be used as milk and coffee substitutes, metal polish and shaving cream, in flour, linoleum and plastics.

ENGINEERING

Construction of the Panama Canal, creating a link between Atlantic and Pacific Oceans, presented both engineering and medical stumbling blocks. Ferdinand de Lesseps, a Frenchman, who had successfully built the Suez Canal, failed in his attempt to dig the canal in 1889, and the U.S. signed a treaty with Panama in 1903 allowing the U.S. to build the canal and operate it forever.

Building the canal was another story, however. The area was infested with yellow fever. The water levels of the Pacific and Atlantic differed significantly and required three sets of double locks to raise and lower the ships as they passed through.

In 1904, Col. William C. Gorgas of the U.S. Army was ordered to Panama to solve the yellow fever problem. He was

somewhat of an expert, having survived a bout with the disease in Texas in the 1880's and then serving with Walter Reed in Cuba where the infecting mosquito had been eliminated. By 1905, the canal zone was cleared of yellow fever and construction could begin. (Gorgas, however, remained the Army's yellow fever guinea pig, and he was sent to South and Central America as well as West Africa to control the disease.)

The actual construction of the canal was under the supervision of George W. Goethals, appointed to head the project by President Theodore Roosevelt in 1907. Goethals was somewhat of a tyrant, but he knew how to build canals, having just completed a similar project in Muscle Shoals along the Tennessee River and improvements along the Ohio and Cumberland Rivers.

The canal was completed in 1914, some 6 months ahead of schedule, but did not open until 1920. In all, the canal cost $380 million, including the Frenchman's aborted effort, sanitation control and the $10 million paid Panama for the original rights.

The Empire State Building, built in 1931, was the world's tallest building until 1970 when a mad rush for sky-high buildings made the 102-story building seem almost tiny. It was built in a spirit of competition, the first structure taller than the Eiffel Tower in Paris. It cost $40 million to build, contained 6,500 windows, and with its 220' television antenna stood one quarter of a mile tall. With its completion, the building and its observation tower took on romantic significance, was the subject of movies and novels and a tourist attraction in its own right.

The Empire State Building, along with Boulder Dam (now the Hoover Dam) and the Golden Gate Bridge, take on considerable significance against the social history of the day. During the 1930's when these projects were completed, the nation was in the midst of the depression, millions were out of work and soup lines were the witness to how desperate and needing man can be. But the great engineering projects were poetic feats: they demonstrated man's ability to exceed his limits, to span rivers, to create water in the desert and, of course, to find work in an economy where there seemed to be no possibility of growth.

The Golden Gate Bridge in San Francisco was one of the largest suspension bridges in the world, spanning 4,200 feet between towers. It was designed by Joseph Strauss in 1937, and cost $35 million.

Boulder Dam, 1938, was, up to that time, the most challenging water project in the world, involving the recharting of the turbulent Colorado River. It actually consisted of three dams, a canal, and reservoirs to provide water and power to both Nevada and California. It was designed by the U.S. Bureau of Reclamation at a cost of $385 million, and created one of the largest man-made lakes, Lake Mead.

THE SCIENCES

In the 20th century, scientific research has continually been international in nature, in that no one developed country has been significantly "ahead" of the others in making theoretical or practical advances.

This characteristic is an outgrowth of the trends of the late 19th century, when scientists were beginning to meet in international conventions to share information and their latest research. Although the spirit of competition has often been fierce—especially during World War II and the Cold War—it has been much more common to find scientists in one country only days or months away from reaching conclusions similar or identical to those announced as the most astounding breakthroughs in another country.

The international nature of scientific activity was confirmed in 1907 by the first announcement of the Nobel Prize in Stockholm. The prize was named after Alfred Nobel, the inventor of dynamite, and the cash awards are disbursed from money bequeathed from Nobel's estate. The Swedish Academy traditionally has named winners in three categories each year (a fourth category, economics, was added in the 1960's) which reflect the major international scientific achievements. With the exception of the years during the two World Wars, the prizes have been issued annually.

Nevertheless, there is a political nature to the awards themselves, and many scientists laboring in their laboratories, have made major scientific advances which never received note from the Nobel Committee.

PHYSICS

The work of research physicists during the period up to 1945 can now, in hindsight, be seen as leading directly and inevitably to the explosion of the first atomic bomb. Not that scientists who were studying radiation and the nature of energy could, in 1900, point to the production of the bomb as their goal, nor did they think then that they would be capable of destroying cities and countries by the laboratory work they had undertaken.

In fact, these physicists were still involved in "science for science sake" or pure research. They enjoyed the richest laboratories mankind has ever known, and they let themselves freely explore, for the love of learning, the nature of light, of energy and the composition of matter.

All of this "pure research," however, was done amid the background of the rise of Nazi and Fascist governments in Europe. The research laboratories of Germany, especially, were alive with scientists who were experimenting with nuclear fission (the splitting of the atom) and the structure of the atom itself. In the period 1900-1930, the laboratories in Europe saw tremendous research activity which only became the possession of the United States when hundreds of scientists emigrated from Hitler's Germany and Mussolini's Italy in the years prior to World War II. In fact, many of the Nobel Prize winners listed here as American were rewarded for work accomplished in their native countries.

1907—Albert A. Michelson (1852-1931) was born in Germany but came to the U.S. with his parents in 1854. His lifelong interest was the measurement of the speed of light and he designed instruments for this purpose. In the process of measuring light, however, Michelson and his colleague Edward W. Morley disproved the then-common theory that the space between the planets and stars was filled with ether. In disproving the so-called "ether wind" theory, Michelson and Morley provided support for certain aspects of Einstein's theory of relativity. Michelson was head of the physics department of the University of Chicago and made the first reliable measurement of the diameter of a star. He was the first American to win the Nobel Prize in Physics in 1907 for his optical measuring instruments and his work in meteorology and spectroscopy.

1921—Albert Einstein (1879-1955) was born in Germany and educated at the University of Zurich. Einstein's numerous contributions in physics are well known and are basically concerned with what happens to matter and light as they travel at ever increasing speeds. Einstein was among the first to think of matter and light as being affected by gravity, speed, and magnetic force, the so-called geometrization of physics.

From the standpoint of U.S. history, Einstein's discoveries had an immediate impact in the era before World War II. By the time he fled Nazi Germany for the United States, in 1933, Einstein had already won a Nobel Prize in 1921 for his work on photoelectricity. Some say he would have won that award in 1914 but for the anti-Semitic efforts of Philipp von Lenard, a German physicist and former Nobel winner himself. Lenard is said to have convinced the Nobel judges that Einstein's work was insignificant, and he was therefore passed over.

By 1933, as well, Einstein's general theory of relativity had already been formulated (1916) and this theory convinced him that the energy inside an atom was extremely powerful and dangerous. He became alarmed that Hitler might use the theories on the atom then being researched in his nation's laboratories for war purposes.

Einstein was not alone in his concern. Former German and Italian physicists now in the United States formed a lobbying organization and wrote President Franklin D. Roosevelt in 1939 imploring him to take counter measures. In the war-charged atmosphere of the day, this letter recieved much publicity, and Roosevelt was moved to act. He allocated funds for the newly-formed Manhattan Engineering District Project for physicists at the University of Chicago.

The government-sponsored research—at various university laboratories throughout the nation—resulted in the exploding of the first atomic bomb in Los Alamos, New Mexico, in 1945, and the subsequent beginning of the Atomic Age.

While much of the research of the Manhattan Project was based on atomic power, Edward Teller, another physicist with the Project had already begun working on the hydrogen bomb, which was immensely more powerful. Teller remained with the Manhattan Project after the war, becoming its assistant director in 1949. By 1951, the major theoretical problems of the hydrogen bomb had been solved.

Teller was a controversial member of the nation's community of physicists: he advocated continued nuclear testing, and was against any moratoriums or bans on the bomb in contrast to many members of the scientific community.

In his beliefs, Teller was most unlike J. Robert Oppenheimer, an American-born physicist who had been with the Manhattan Project since 1941 and, as one of its administrators, was known as the "father of the atomic bomb."

Despite his work on the atomic bomb project, Oppenheimer was in vocal opposition to the hydrogen bomb plan and voiced his opinion to President Harry S. Truman who nevertheless went on with it. Oppenheimer also advocated civilian and international control of atomic energy, espousing these and other "liberal" views.

Oppenheimer was highly regarded, receiving a presidential citation in 1946 and serving as a presidential advisor on atomic energy in the period up to 1952.

In the anti-communist hysteria which swept the nation in the 1950's, however, fanned by Sen. Joseph McCarthy of Wisconsin, Oppenheimer was to be discredited. He was accused of slowing down the hydrogen bomb project, of associating with communists, and disloyalty. He lost his security clearance.

Though he was cleared of all charges by the Atomic Energy Commission in 1954, he was nevertheless regarded as a security risk. He became head of the Institute for Advanced Studies in Princeton in 1947 and remained so until his retirement in 1966.

Gradually the smoke cleared and although officially he remained a security risk until his death, he was awarded the AEC's highest honor, the Enrico Fermi Award, in 1963 by President Lyndon B. Johnson.

The Nobel Prize in Physics was awarded to these U.S. scientists, in addition to Michelson and Einstein:

1923—Robert A. Millikan (1868-1953)—Millikan was honored by the Swedish Academy for his work with electrons and the photoelectric effect, specifically his determination that electrons had a constant charge. After receipt of the award, he was the first to isolate and name "cosmic rays"—radiation from outer space coming towards the earth. He worked with x-rays and ultraviolet radiation. Millikan received his Ph.D. from Columbia University, studied in Berlin and was an instructor and later professor at the University of Chicago. From 1922 to 1932 he represented the United States at the League of Nations committee for intellectual cooperation, and was director of the Norman Bridge Laboratory at the California Institute of Technology in Pasadena.

1927—Arthur Holly Compton (1892-1962)—shared with C.T.R. Wilson of Great Britain. The "Compton" effect, which he noted and explained, is an increase of wavelength of x-rays when they collide with electrons. The effect was a key contribution to the development of the quantum theory of energy. Compton took a Ph.D. at Princeton and served on the faculty of the University of Chicago until the end of World War II. He studied cosmic rays in the 1930's and in the 1940's studied the military application of atomic energy, culminating in his work for the Manhattan Engineering District, attempting to gather sufficient plutonium for one or more atomic bombs. The philosophical and moral aspects of his work in atomic energy are discussed in several books including *The Atomic Quest* (1956) and *The Human Meaning of Science* (1940).

1936—Victor F. Hess (1883-1964) (b. Austria)—Discovered cosmic radiation and received his award jointly with Carl D. Anderson (1905-   ). Anderson studied at California Institute of Technology working under Robert A. Millikan in the investigation of cosmic rays. His Nobel Prize was for discovery of the positron, a subatomic particle equal in mass to the electron but positively charged.

1937—Clinton J. Davisson (1881-1958) along with G. P. Thomson (1892-   ). Discovered that reflected electrons often act like waves. The discovery, reached almost simultaneously by both scientists, was regarded as significant proof of a then new theory that matter and radiation sometimes act in similar ways. Davisson had to borrow the money for his air fare to Stockholm, later commented that the award allowed him to live with greater sense of financial security.

1938—Enrico Fermi (1901-1954), (b. Italy)—Fermi's work on artificial radioactivity led almost directly to the explosion of the atomic bomb. Actually, his preliminary research bombarding uranium with neutrons was conducted in Rome. As the prevailing view of the day was that nuclear fission was impossible, Fermi could not see that he had nonetheless achieved it. He moved to the U. S. immediately after receiving his award in Stockholm. Fermi and other emigre scientists drafted the letter signed by Albert Einstein which expressed concern that Germany would get the bomb first. The small grant by FDR in 1942 sent Fermi to the University of Chicago. There the controlled chain reaction was achieved on Dec 2, 1942. He moved to the secret installation at Los ALmos, New Mexico and on July 16, 1945, the first atomic bomb was tested.

1939—Ernest O. Lawrence (1901-1958)—Lawrence invented the cyclotron or "atom smasher" in 1928, in which alternating fields of electrical currents are used to force atomic particles to extremely high speeds and energy levels. The promoter of the San Francisco Fair of 1938, he apparently wanted to exhibit the cyclotron but changed his mind when Lawrence mentioned loose neutrons could break out and sterilize the spectators. The first large scale cyclotron was completed in 1933 using an 80-ton magnet. In 1942 he demonstrated the conversion of stable elements into radioactive isotopes some of which were subsequently used as tracers in the treatment of cancer and other medical research. He became head of the University of California's Radiation Laboratory at Berekely in 1936. During World War II he was associated with Arthur H. Compton and Harold C. Urey in the production of plutonium for the first atomic bombs.

1943—Otto Stern (1888-1969) (b. Germany)—Stern worked with Albert Einstein in Prague and Zurich until 1914, then joined the University of Frankfurt. He came to the U. S. in 1933 and joined the staff of Carnegie Institute of Technology. His award was for research into atomic structure, including the magnetic properties of the atom and the discovery of the proton's magnetic moment, which added to the quantum theory.

1944—Isidor Isaac Rabi (1898-   ) (b. Austria)—Developed means by which the mechanical and magnetic properties of atomic nuclei could be observed. His discovery of the spectroscope became the basis for much of atomic research.

1945—Wolfgang Pauli (1900-1958) (b. Austria)—Discovered the exclusion principle in atomic theory.

1946—Percy Williams Bridgeman (1882-1961)—Faculty of Harvard University. Research into the effect of extremely high pressure on materials, including tests for thermal and electrical conductivity tensile strength and viscosity. He was able to generate pressure up to one million pounds per square inch. In 1949 he announced that visitors representing totalitarian nations were not welcome in his laboratory, and often wrote on the relationship between science and modern life, including *The Intelligent Individual and Society* (1938). He took his own life in 1961 while suffering from terminal cancer.

1952—Felix Bloch (1905-   ) (b. Switzerland) and Edward M. Purcell (1912-   )—Bloch and Purcell worked independently yet simultaneously discovered ways of measuring the magnetic moment of the atomic nuclei in a substance. Bloch worked with Enrico Fermi while in Europe, and upon coming to the United States in 1934, joined the faculty of Stanford University. During World War II he worked on the atomic bomb project at Los Alamos, New Mexico. In 1944-45 he joined a Harvard team investigating countermeasures to radar. Purcell worked on developing radar during World War II at Massachusetts Institute of Technology. Purcell and Bloch's efforts led to a new field of physics: magnetic resonance spectroscopy which not only measured magnetic moments but also chemical bonds and atomic binding in liquids and solids. After the war, Purcell pursued radio astronomy and developed a method to chart the distribution of hydrogen in the universe, revealing clouds of hydrogen within and between galaxies.

1955—Willis E. Lamb, Jr. (1913-   ) (b. Germany) and Polykarp Kusch (1911-   ) (American, b. Germany)—Both men worked on the structure of the atom, Lamb on hydrogen and helium atoms and Kusch on electromagnetic properties of the electron. Both explorations led to new discoveries in the field of particle interactions and radiation.

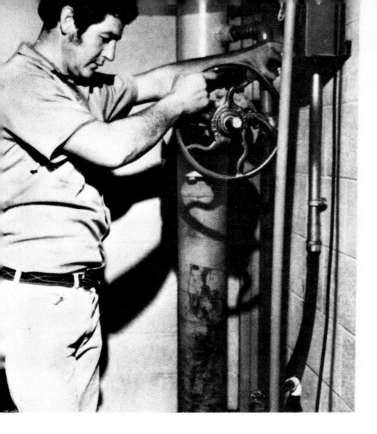

1956—John Bardeen (1908-   ) Walter H. Brattain (1902-   ); and William B. Shockley (1910-   ) (b. England)—While at Bell Laboratories, the three worked together on development of the transistor, which replaced the bulky vacuum tube and could both correct and amplify alternating currents. The invention revolutionized the electronics and communications industries.

1957—Tsung-Dao Lee (1926-   ) (b. China) and Chin Ning Yang (1922-   ) (b. China)—Lee and Yang took their undergraduate degrees in China before coming to the University of Chicago to study under Enrico Fermi. They earned their Nobel Prize at ages 31 and 35, among the youngest ever to receive the award. They disproved the principle of parity conservation in nuclear physics which pertained to the decay of particles, leading to the deeper study and investigation of atomic structure.

1959—Emilio G. Segre (1905-   ), (b. Italy) and Owen Chamberlain (1920-   )—Proved the existence of the anti-proton, a negatively charged particle with the same mass as the proton.

Segre conducted research with Enrico Fermi while at the University of Rome before coming to the U.S. in 1938. He became a citizen in 1944 and began work on the atomic bomb project in Los Alamos. After the war he again worked with Fermi and produced the first laboratory-made element, technetium, which probably does not exist in nature. He also aided in the discovery of the isotope plutonium-239 and the element astatine. These experiments in nuclear fission and radioactivity aided in the development of atomic weapons.

Chamberlain also worked on the Manhattan Project in Los Alamos on the atomic bomb, and studied under Enrico Fermi at the University of Chicago on the character of proton and neutrons, using the cyclotron. There was some question raised about the role of Oreste Piccioni in the discovery of the anti-proton. Piccioni, a professor of physics at the University of California in San Diego, claimed that the anti-proton was

his idea, and he asked Chamberlain and Segre to perform the experiments to prove its existence since he was not a citizen and couldn't get clearance. Piccioni sued in 1972 for $125,000, saying he waited until then because Segre and Chamberlain had promised him favors for keeping quiet. It was the first civil law suit arising from the Nobel Prize.

1960—Donald A. Glaser (1926-   )—Invented the bubble chamber, which quickly replaced the Wilson "cloud chamber" as a means of watching particle collisions. He received the award at age 34.

1961—Robert Hofstadter (1915-   ) shared with Rudolf L. Mossbauer of Germany—Research into the structure of the atom, including the size and shape of the proton and the neutron.

1963—Eugene P. Wigner (1902-   ) (b. Hungary) and Maria Goeppert-Mayer (1906-1972) (b. Poland) and J. Hans D. Jensen (1907-   )—German Theoretical work on the structure of the nucleus. Wigner had worked on the bomb with the Manhattan Project but after 1948 began work seeking international control of nuclear weapons. He has served twice on the Atomic Energy Commission, and received the AEC's Fermi Award. Maria Goeppert Mayer was one of the few women to be awarded the Nobel Prize. She arrived at her conclusions regarding the structure of the nucleus working independently at the University of Chicago and the Argonne National Laboratory. During World War II, she researched isotopes for the atomic bomb project while teaching at Sarah Lawrence College.

1964—Charles H. Townes (1915-   )—Townes' research into microwaves led to development of the atomic clock, the most accurate timing device known to man, and used to obtain present measurements of the earth's rotation. His method of microwave amplification was the "maser" which led to the laser beam, the same theory applied to light. He shared the prize with two Russian physicists who had independently arrived at the same theories.

1965—Richard P. Feynman (1918-   ); Julian S. Schwinger (1918); and Sin-itiro Tomonaga (Japanese)—Research into quantum electro-dynamics. The three men worked independently and arrived at similar mathematical explanations for the behavior of particles. Schwinger was a full professor at Harvard at age 29.

1967—Hans A. Bethe (1906-   ) (b. Germany)—Fled the Nazis in 1933 to Cornell University. Worked at Los Alamos in the theoretical research project and warned as early as 1947 about the dangers of radioactive fallout. In 1948 he refused to return to Los Alamos to the hydrogen bomb project headed by Edward Teller but the 1951 Korean War changed his mind. He wrote against nuclear warfare, excessive stockpiling of nuclear weapons and atmospheric testing. His Nobel Prize, however, was for research into the nuclear process of the stars, answering the question of how the stars could conserve their energy throughout a long life.

1968—Luis W. Alvarez (1911-   )—At MIT's Radiation Laboratory he designed with Lawrence Johnston a ground-controlled approach system that made possible all-weather aircraft landings. Worked on Los Alamos atomic-bomb project. His Nobel Prize was for heading a research team which investigated sub-atomic particles, significant in nuclear physics.

1969—Murray Gell-Mann (1929-   )—Research into elementary particles including the theoretical model called the "Eight Fold Way." He classified particles and their interactions.

1972—John Bardeen (1908-   ); Leon N. Cooper (1920-   ); and John R. Schrieffer (1929-   )—Explained superconductivity, that is, the characteristic of super-cold metals to lose their electrical resistance. Bardeen was one of three persons to win two prizes. Superconductivity is the perfect conductivity and the vanishing of magnetic induction.

MEDICINE

The 20th century opened with an explosion of its own regarding the field of medicine, that is, the issuance of a report in 1910 criticizing medical education in the United States and medical schools specifically. The report was written by Abraham Flexner, a graduate of Johns Hopkins University who criticized that school as well, although it was regarded as one of the best in the nation. Flexner did the report while on the staff of the Carnegie Foundation for the Advancement of Teaching. Modern medical education is said to date from the issuance of Flexner's report. Many schools were said to have been forced to close their doors after negative publicity.

During this period researchers investigated the way humans feel. Novocain was introduced in 1905. Walter Bradford Cannon, a physiologist, conducted extensive x-ray research into the movement of the stomach and the intestines. He concluded in 1912 that dryness of the throat or stomach contractions cause us to say we feel hungry. He did research on shock and perceived that emotions arise from the reaction of the sympathetic nervous system.

Alexis Carrel won the Nobel Prize in Medicine in 1912 for surgical techniques, including vascular suture and transplantation of blood vessels, but it is believed he passed off others' work as his own.

Contagious diseases continued as a major health factor in the overcrowded cities. In 1913 Bela Schick devised a skin test for diphtheria. In 1918, a flu epidemic spread through much of the country, killing hundreds of people daily. It is said 500,000 persons died of the flu.

"Typhoid Mary" was found working in a restaurant in 1906. In 1898 she had been discovered to be the carrier of a typhoid epidemic. When the authorities found her again she was working under an assumed name. After that, she was confined until her death in 1929.

Vitamins A & B were identified in 1912, and were said to be necessary for health.

American researchers also were concerned with the nature of blood and blood types. In 1930, Karl Landsteiner won the Nobel Prize for discovering A, B and O blood types, which led to refinement of the blood transfusion process. Landsteiner was born in Vienna and joined the Rockefeller Institute upon his emigration here in 1922. In 1940, he and Alexander S. Wiener discovered the Rh factor in blood. Landsteiner was also interested in viral diseases and especially studied polio.

The relationship between the liver and red blood cells was the subject of study by George R. Minot, William P. Murphy and George H. Whipple. All three jointly won the Nobel Prize in 1934. Their discoveries were significant in the treatment of pernicious anemia. Minot continued research on his own at Harvard and discovered Vitamin B_{12} as a standard treatment for anemia. It was Whipple's research on the effect of liver on dogs with anemia which initiated the project.

Continuing research has also yielded much new information on the relationship between genes and heredity. The foundation was laid by the work of Thomas Hunt Morgan who identified genes within chromosomes, support for his belief that there were individual mechanisms controlling heredity. His work earned him the Nobel Prize in 1933.

Herman Muller had worked closely with Morgan during the formation of the gene theory. Using Morgan's work as a base, he investigated the effects of X-rays on fruit flies and concluded that X-rays cause mutations. He earned a Nobel Prize for his work in 1946, and used his research to support his concerns regarding the effect of nuclear weapon radiation. During the 1930s, Muller taught genetics in Moscow, apparently returned to Western Europe and eventually came to the United States because of political disagreements with the Soviet system. He nevertheless favored the establishment of a sperm bank as a form of eugenics so the best qualities of men might be preserved.

The discoveries of ribonucleic acid (RNA) and deoxyribonucleic acid (DNA) were regarded in the scientific community as major breakthroughs in the hereditary process, since these substances carry the genetic code and translate it into protein. Arthur Kornberg and Severo Ochoa separately worked on various tasks in establishing the RNA-DNA link. They jointly shared the Nobel Prize in 1959.

It remained for Francis H. C. Crick and James D. Watson to describe the structure of these all-important RNA-DNA molecules and how they duplicate themselves. This sounds easy enough, but in truth, the double-helix structure the two evolved was crucial to the inner workings of heredity, and has been compared with the major scientific feats of all time, including Darwin's theory of evolution. In 1962, Crick and Watson shared the Nobel Prize with Maurice H. F. Wilkins, who also had done work in this field.

RNA and DNA were broken down further still into smaller

subunits in an attempt to discover just how the codes existed. Marshall W. Nirenberg announced in 1962 that he was able to convert ''brainless'' bacteria into tobacco virus proteins. The news was greeted as a sign that life could be created in a test tube. H. Gobind Khorana and Robert W. Holley, working independently in the United States, broke down the RNA molecule into its basic units. The three shared the Nobel Prize in 1968.

The application of these genetic advancements to bacteria resulted in the theory that natural selection affects the types of bacteria strains which survive. Specific research centered on the existence of ''phages''—viruses which disintegrate bacteria—and the manner in which the phages exchange genetic information. The research conducted by Max Delbruck, Alfred D. Hershey and Salvador E. Luria from the 1940's until the 1960's, was significant in the development of vaccines for polio, German measles, mumps and other viral infections. The three shared the Nobel Prize in 1969.

In 1974, Albert Claude and George Emil Palade shared the Nobel award with Christian Rene de Duve of Belgium for the creation of modern cell biology.

In addition to the breaking of the genetic code, 20th century researchers have been concerned with the elimination of disease, especially contagious disease, the nature of hormones, and metabolism, among other areas.

Edward A. Doisy, for example, discovered the chemical nature of the blood clotting factor, vitamin K, thereby initiating hemorrhage control, and won the Nobel Prize in 1943, in conjunction with the Danish biochemist Henrick Dam who had done similar work. Doisy also contributed significant research in the study of female sex hormones which has aided in the maintenance of endocrine balance.

During the years before World War II, research chemists, much like physicists, found their efforts leading toward the atomic age. In 1931, Harold C. Urey, for example, discovered heavy hydrogen, considered to be a rare isotope. He pursued the isotope research, questioning how the isotope might be separated, and developing the gas-diffusion process as a possible answer. This gas-diffusion process was used to separate uranium isotopes which led to the construction of the atomic bomb, though Urey was quite concerned with the ethical considerations of his discovery. He also developed a method for determining the age of geological formations, and posited a then new but now accepted theory of the origin of the solar system.

In the years since the war, however, significant chemical discoveries have been made in a wide range of areas including enzyme research and virus proteins. In 1954, the use of quantum mechanics by Linus Pauling gave rise to the theory that molecules are held together by valence bonds, for which Pauling won one of his three Nobel prizes (Physics and Peace were the others). Others have researched the electronic structure of the molecule, the nature of atomic weight, and the methods for dating fossils in an effort to determine the age of a planet.

SPACE

Just about the time man was preparing to date his planet, he was also making plans to leave it. For those old enough to remember the days before the Model T Ford—actually less than 50 years before!—the news, in 1957, that the Russians had a dog in a space satellite circling the earth, must have seemed like something out of science fiction.

In fact, it was the stuff of science fiction coming true. The space race became an All-American spectator sport, with lift-off and splash down live on television. And who were those astronauts but Superman come to life?! Every major newspaper and television station tried to arrange for exclusive interviews with the men who orbited the earth, then orbited the moon, and, finally, walked on the moon itself.

After the Russians launched Sputnik I in 1957, the U.S. space industry attempted to make up for lost time. The National Aeronautics and Space Administration set goals for America in space. President John F. Kennedy made it a matter of national pride that billions of dollars be allocated to get a man on the moon in 10 years.

In Stage I of the manned space flights, Alan Shepard in 1961 was the first man in the U.S. to leave earth in a space ship, although he had been somewhat upstaged by Yuri Gagarin's full orbit a month previous. John Glenn's first orbital mission occurred in 1962. In 1963, Gordon Cooper made a 22-orbit flight which lasted almost two days.

The Mercury Mission, however, demonstrated that the Russians were still ''ahead'' in space, for by the time of Cooper's mission in 1963, a Russian cosmonaut was preparing for an 81 orbit journey one month later.

Behind or not, the American public apparently loved hearing about men in space. There was a general fascination with weightlessness, with how it would feel to drink all your meals through a straw. ''Tang,'' an orange drink which was chosen for the astronauts in space, still uses that fact as an advertising claim in 1976.

Stage II, the ''Gemini'' program, was a series of flights experimenting with men in weightless conditions. Ground Control waited to see, would the men suffer from extreme depression, would they lose weight or get sick upon their return, how would they react to being in those incredibly involved space suits? The Gemini program included a 206 orbit flight lasting eight days. It helped prove a man—there were no women U.S. astronauts—could pilot a space ship and live in extremely cramped quarters with another human being and not get in a fight.

Communication with planet earth from space came in surprising loud and clear. At Christmas, 1968, the first Apollo mission circled the moon, and the American public heard three men who were speechless with bewilderment at seeing their home planet so far away. They expressed feelings of loneliness, of poetry at the earth's beauty, and how small it seemed. The first Apollo flight orbited the moon 10 times before making its way back to earth. They were gone five days, but in fact, they had entered another time zone.

Neil Armstrong was the first man to walk on the moon, and millions of people back on earth saw him do so live on color television on July 20, 1969. When he stepped onto the moon's surface, his voice—incredible to hear from so many millions of miles away—sounded like he was reading from a cue card: ''That's one small step for man, one giant leap for mankind.'' Yet in some ways the words do seem an accurate reflection of the space walk's significance. It might have felt something like that to watch from a television set at home in Spain as Columbus set foot in the New World.

The Apollo 13 was the only flight to have significant technological problems. The ship was crippled by an explosion on board, resulting in an extremely dangerous trip back to earth. The Apollo program ended in December, 1972

The greatest achievement *of American science so far is the landing of the astronauts on the moon in 1969. This photograph shows the Saturn 5 rocket thundering off its launch pad carrying the Apollo 11 space craft. Aboard the craft are Neil Armstrong, Michael Collins, and Edwin Aldrin on their historic flight to the moon.*

American physicists *have led the world in the development of nuclear energy for peaceful use. Theoretical research combined with American pragmatism has produced several nuclear generating plants across the country like the one pictured here at Rowe, Massachusetts.*

with a mission of 75 moon revolutions, and astronauts on the moon's surface.

The Skylab program was exactly that: an attempt to understand the nature of weightlessness and the environment of space. Three different missions radically extended the amount of time man would stay weightless, the final mission lasting almost three months.

At times the research opportunities of the manned space flights seemed hidden amid politically motivated statements of patriotism. President Richard M. Nixon, for example, once spoke to the members of one Apollo Mission via long distance "telephone" telling them their mission to the moon was the greatest event in the history of mankind.

By the end of the Skylab mission, the American public was disenchanted with space travel and the huge budget required to keep NASA's projects alive.

The grand finale was anti-climactic, at least in some opinions. The joint mission of the Apollo-Soyuz space flight in 1975, a demonstration of international cooperation between the U.S. and the Soviet Union, seemed a grand public relations event which never captured the excitement of space exploration.

During these same years, a series of unmanned probes were sent to the sun, to Venus and Mars, to Jupiter and Mercury. Each of these missions yielded information regarding the character of the planets. The 1974 pictures taken from Venus, for example, represent the first pictures of the planet nearest the sun.

Unmanned satellites have expanded the possibilities of international communication. Synchronized television reception via satellite is now a commonplace in many countries. Satellites have become important factors in weather prediction, information gathering by the military, and accumulated astronomical knowledge.

When the realization set in that space travel was possible, the more political question was raised: is space travel necessary? The reassessment of the space program at the end of the 1960's accompanied a period of retrenchment for the United States in a variety of areas.

This retrenchment was symbolized by an examination of the role of technology and "progress" in American history. It became clear that technological advances had been accomplished at a high social price: cities were polluted to the point that on some days in certain cities, little children could not play in school grounds for fear of smog exposure. The

automobile was a necessity, but had to be banned from New York City, among others, because there was no room for all the cars to park. And then again, these same cars, along with factories and homes, were using up a huge quantity of the world's petroleum. In the 1970's the Arab oil nations and the huge American oil companies had the American gasoline consumer literally over a barrel—an oil barrel in which they could name the price and the consumer must either pay or stay home.

Noise, air and water pollution were the catch words of the 1970's—all signs of technological "progress" gone mad. As bad, the tremendous excitement which had earlier greeted refinement of the computer as an information retrieval system with endless capabilities, had, in some cases, turned into fear that all that information might result in total loss of privacy.

The 1970's, then, were years when many in the United States were wondering just how far the nation had come in 200 years. In 1776, there was a job for everyone who could work; in 1976, the economists were predicting that 7 per cent unemployment may be a permanent figure in a no-growth economy.

The years of the 1970's were not years to be flying from planet to planet. There was trouble at home, just seeing if "Yankee ingenuity" and "American know how" were still alive.

BIBLIOGRAPHY

Brieger, Gert H., ed. *Medical America in the Nineteenth Century: Readings from the Literature.* Baltimore: The Johns Hopkins Press, 1972.

Burlingame, Rober. *Engines of Democracy.* New York: Scribners Sons, 1940.

Cox, Donald W. *Pioneers of Ecology.* Hammond, Inc., 1971.

Fortune, eds. *Great American Scientists.* Englewood Cliffs, N.J.: Prentice Hall, 1960, 1961.

Giedion, Siegfried. *Mechanization Takes Command: A Contribution to Anonymous History.* New York: W. W. Norton Co., 1948.

Jarrett, Henry, ed. *Perspectives on Conservation: Essays on America's Natural Resources.* Baltimore: Johns Hopkins Press, 1958.

Kranzberg, Melvin and William H. Davenport, eds. *Technology and Culture: An Anthology.* New York: Schocken Books, 1972.

Landsberg, Hans H. and Sam H. Schurr, *Energy in the United States, Sources, Uses and Policy Issues.* New York: Random House, 1968.

Oliver, John W. *History of American Technology.* New York: Ronald Press, 1956.

U. S. Dept. of Commerce, Bureau of the Census. *Historical Statistics of the United States; Colonial Times to 1957 and Abstract Supplement.* Washington, D.C.

U. S. Dept. of Commerce, Bureau of Census. *Statistical Abstract of the United States 1975.*

Van Doren, Charles, ed. *Webster's American Biographies.* Springfield, Mass, G. & C. Merriam Co., 1974.

Wallechinsky, David and Irving Wallace. *The People's Almanac.* Garden City, New York: Doubleday & Co., Inc., 1975.

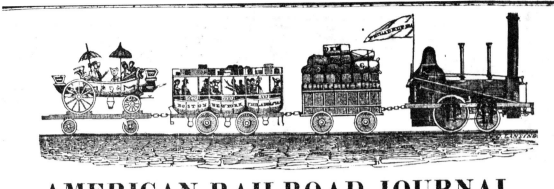

AMERICAN RAILROAD JOURNAL,
AND ADVOCATE OF INTERNAL IMPROVEMENTS.

PUBLISHED WEEKLY, AT No. 35 WALL STREET, NEW YORK, AT THREE DOLLARS PER ANNUM, PAYABLE IN ADVANCE.

By 1834, when this paper appeared, railroad building was already a top priority in developing the nation.

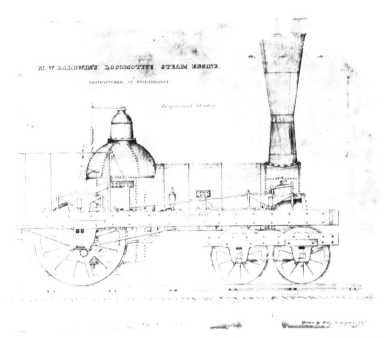

A sketch of a Baldwin locomotive of the period 1834–42

SCIENCE-TECHNOLOGY CALENDAR

1776
   First American war submarine, the *Turtle*, constructed by David Bushnell.

1777
   Jeremiah Wilkinson invented a process for cutting nails from cold iron.

1786
   First steamboat in America, built by John Fitch.

JULY 31, 1790
   U.S. Patent Office opened.

1792
   First important wooden truss bridge, type invented by Colonel Ewel Hale.

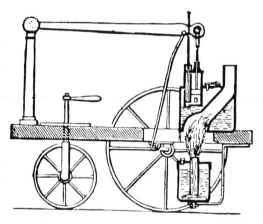

Cutaway view *of Murdock's model steam engine in 1784.*

OCTOBER 28, 1793
   Eli Whitney filed application for patent on cotton gin; patent was granted 2 years later on Mar. 14, 1794.

1797
   First American patent for clock taken out by Eli Terry for his newly devised method of employing wooden works in his clocks.

JUNE 26, 1797
   First U.S. patent for plow issued to Charles Newbold. After expending his entire fortune in developing practical plow of cast iron, Newbold was unable to sell it to farmers because of their fear of harmful effects of iron on soil.

1798
   Eli Whitney adapted suggestions of Le Blanc for manufacture of interchangeable parts for arsenal production of firearms supplied to U.S. government. The long series of misunderstandings which hampered success of cotton gin made Whitney turn to firearms manufacturing as a means of livelihood.

DECEMBER 14, 1798
   Patent awarded to David Wilkinson for machine that cut screw threads.

1809
   First screw-cutting machine in U.S. designed and produced by Abel Stowel in Massachusetts.

1812
   William Monroe began lead pencil manufacture with own formula for using ground lead.

1822
   First patent for making of false teeth awarded to C. M. Graham.

1825
   First technical innovation in making of glass since ancient times, mechanical pressing, by Deming Jarves at Sandwich, Mass.

JULY 23, 1829
   Patent issued to William A. Burt for 1st typewriter, called "typographer." It proved unworkable.

1831
   Mechanical reaper invented by Cyrus McCormick, who relied on principles of earlier inventions, especially cutter and reel principle of reaper made by Henry Ogle, an Englishman.
   Joseph Henry devised the electric bell.

1832
   John Ireland Howe invented machine to make pins.

1833
   1st steel plow produced in America by John Deere.

1834
   Cyrus McCormick patented early model of his famous reaper.

Fulton's drawing *of the paddle wheel mechanism for his steamboat,* Clermont.

Fanciful view *of early travel in America: a wind powered train about 1830.*

1835
   Samuel F. B. Morse invented the telegraph.

NOVEMBER 23, 1835
   Patent issued to Henry Burden for horseshoe-manufacturing machine.

DECEMBER 29, 1837
   Patent awarded to Hiram Pitts and John Avery Pitts for their invention of a combined portable thresher and fanning mill. "Chicago-Pitts" threshers were widely used throughout grain producing belt for more than a half century.

1838
   Chauncey Jerome first used standardized brass clock works,; manufacturing 600 clocks a day.

1846
First rotary printing press devised and produced by Richard M. Hoe, capable of turning out 8000 papers an hour.

SEPTEMBER 10, 1846
First sewing machine in U.S. patented by Elias Howe; father of the modern sewing machine.

1848
Power loom invented by Erastus B. Bigelow.

JUNE 27, 1848
First "air conditioning" patented by J. E. Coffee.

1849
Safety pin patented by Walter Hunt.

1850
First agricultural binder in U.S. invented by John E. Heath.

1851
First electric fire alarm system in America installed in Boston by Dr. William P. Channing and Moses Gerrish Farmer.

MAY 6, 1851
First patent for ice-making machine to John Gorrie.

AUGUST 12, 1851
Patent for a practical sewing machine granted to Isaac Merrit Singer, who very quickly organized the I. M. Singer & Company.

DECEMBER 16, 1851
Hiram Hayden received 1st patent for a process of shaping brass into bowls.

1852
First adequate safety device for hydraulic elevators developed by Elisha Graves Otis.
Alexander Bonner Latta invented first effective fire engine, a "steam" engine.

1853
Crystal Palace Exhibition of the Industry of All Nations held in New York city to demonstrate American inventions and industrial progress. Called a World's Fair, it was inspired by the London Exhibition of 1851.

1854
Paper collar invented by Walter Hunt.

The first oil gusher *in America,* Spindletop, *which spouted oil in January 10, 1901.*

1839
Samuel F. B. Morse, painter and inventor, brought from Paris first photographic equipment in U.S. Morse had learned the process from Daguerre, and he made the first daguerreotype portraits in America.

1842
John Bennet Lawes invented process for making superphosphate from rock phosphate and sulphuric acid, producing 1st commercial artificial fertilizer.
Samuel Colt, inventor of the famous Colt 45 revolver, began a series of experiments with explosive underwater mines and their electrical detonation.

MAY 24, 1844
First telegraph message, "What hath God wrought?" sent from U.S. Supreme Court room in Washington, D.C., to Baltimore, Md., by Samuel F. B. Morse, the inventor of the telegraph.

JUNE 15, 1844
Charles Goodyear patented the vulcanization process for rubber.

Artist's version *of the testing of the first successful incandescent lamp by Thomas Edison on October 21, 1879.*

Thomas Alva Edison *at his laboratory at Menlo Park, New Jersey.*

JULY 12, 1870
U.S. patent for discovery of process by which **celluloid** is produced awarded to John W. Hyatt, Jr., and Isaiah S. Hyatt.

1871
Andrew Smith Hallidie invented **underground continuous moving cable** and **mechanical gripper** for underside of streetcars, preparing the way for introduction of cable car in San Francisco and other cities in 1873.

1873
Cable street car, invented by Andrew S. Hallidie, 1st used in San Francisco, Calif.

OCTOBER 27, 1873
Joseph F. Glidden, received patent for improvement in **barbed wire**.

MARCH 7, 1876
First U.S. patent for the **telephone** awarded to Alexander Graham Bell.

1878
Patent for **phonograph** awarded to Thomas A. Edison.

MAY 8, 1879
First U.S. patent application for a gasoline-driven **automobile**, was filed by George B. Selden.

1880
First successful roll film for cameras patented by George Eastman.
Safety razor devised by Kampfe Bros.

JANUARY 27, 1880
Thomas A. Edison received patent for his **incandescent lamp**.

1882
New Yorker Henry W. Seely patented electric **flatiron**.
Electric fan developed by Schuyler Skaats Wheeler.

OCTOBER 7, 1856
Cyrus Chambers, Jr., awarded patent for **first practical folding machine** to fold book and newspaper sheets mechanically.

JUNE 23, 1857
Patent granted to William Kelly for inventing process by which pig iron is converted to **steel.**

SEPTEMBER 1, 1859
George M. Pullman's **first sleeping car** made its 1st run. It was a converted coach.

1860
First repeating rifle in U.S. produced by Oliver F. Winchester.

NOVEMBER 4, 1862
Patent issued to Richard Jordan Gatling for "revolving gun battery," the **1st machine gun**.

1863
Ebenezer Butterick invented **1st paper dress patterns** sold in U.S.

APRIL 14, 1863
Continuous roll printing press patented by William Bullock.

DECEMBER 1, 1863
Samuel D. Goodale secured patent for stereoscopic apparatus to show scenes in motion.

1867
Christopher Latham Sholes constructed **1st successful typewriter** and first used the word "typewriter."
"Now is the time for all good men to come to the aid of the party," slogan created by Charles Weller, a court reporter, to test efficiency of 1st practical typewriter.

JANUARY 16, 1868
William Davis, fish-market owner of Detroit, Michigan, granted patent for **refrigerator car**.

1869
Edison invention, the **electric voting machine**: 1st used in an election in 1892.

JUNE 8, 1869
First U.S. patent for suction-principle **vacuum cleaner** awarded to I. W. McGaffey.

Henry Ford *as he appeared in 1923.*

Machine which automatically *picks the lint from the cotton seed. Such machines have brought a revolution to American farming.*

Oil transportation *down the Mississippi in 1967. The boat pushes barges containing 41,000 tons of crude oil.*

1883

Lewis E. Waterman began experiments to produce **fountain pen**.

FEBRUARY 27, 1883

Patent issued to Oscar Hammerstein for **1st practical cigar-rolling machine**.

1885

Ottmar Mergenthaler invented **linotype machine.**

1886

Process for extracting **aluminum** from its ore invented by Charles Martin Hall.

1887

First successful electric trolley line built by Frank J. Sprague.

1888

Nikola Tesla developed the **induction motor.**

George Eastman of Rochester, N.Y., perfected **box camera** and **roll film.**

Astronaut Ed White *taking a stroll through space in 1965.*

The development and refinement *of the computer has brought about changes in virtually every aspect of American life.*

JULY 27, 1888
First electric automobile, designed by Philip W. Pratt. It was a tricycle driven by storage batteries.

1889
First movie film developed in America by Thomas A. Edison on a base devised by George Eastman.

Singer Manufacturing Company produced and marketed 1st electric sewing machine.

1890
First U.S. patent for a **pneumatic hammer** to Charles B. King.

Cyanide process of extracting **gold** from low-grade ore invented by 2 metallurgists (MacArthur and Forrest).

1891
Zipper patented by Whitcomb L. Judson.

First sun photography in America made possible by the invention of the spectro-heliograph by George E. Hale of the University of Chicago.

AUGUST 24, 1891
First patent in America for **motion picture camera** filed by Thomas Edison.

DECEMBER 29, 1891
First important radio patent awarded Thomas Edison for a "means of transmitting signals electrically . . . without the use of wires."

SEPTEMBER 1892
First gasoline automobile made in U.S. built by Charles and Frank Duryea.

SEPTEMBER 1892
An **electric automobile**, made by William Morrison, appeared on streets of Chicago.

1893
Leo H. Baekeland perfected the process by which Velox paper was produced.

DECEMBER 24, 1893
Henry Ford completed construction of his 1st gasoline engine that ran successfully.

1895
George Westinghouse made significant contribution to American industry by his construction of **huge power generators** at Niagara Falls. First generator capable of a widespread distribution of hydroelectric power.

JUNE 11, 1895
First U.S. patent for a **gasoline-driven automobile** by a U.S. inventor was issued to Charles E. Duryea.

JUNE 4, 1896
Henry Ford and his associates completed assembly of the **1st Ford automobile . .**

1899
The **Selden patent** brought about the most celebrated litigation in the history of the auto industry. Selden assigned exclusive license for his motor car to the Electric Vehicle Company. Suits initiated by this company led, in 1903, to the formation of the Association of Li-

Automatic welding *equipment today performs nearly 95 percent of all body welds on American cars.*

censed Automobile Manufacturers, which began to collect royalties from the industry for the Selden patent. The fledgling Ford Motor Company and a few other manufacturers not affiliated with the A.L.A.M. refused to pay the royalties, and suit was brought against the Ford company and one other in New York in 1903. The court upheld the validity of Selden's patent on Sept. 15, 1909. Ford appealed and the N.Y. Court of Appeals on Jan. 9, 1911, again ruled in favor of the Selden patent. But it was a pyrrhic victory for Selden and the Electric Vehicle Company: the patent was held to be restricted to the particular construction it described, and every important auto manufacturer used a motor significantly different from that of Selden's patent.

DECEMBER 17, 1903
First successful flight of a large sized heavier-than-air machine made at Kitty Hawk, N.C., by Orville and Wilbur Wright.

1908
Carl M. Wheaton announced **lethal gas** could be used as an effective weapon and offered the Army his formula, the result of 9 years of experimenting.

1909
First production of bakelite, which had been invented by Leo H. Baekeland.

1913

SUMMER, 1913
Henry Ford set up his **1st assembly line** for the production of Model T's.

JANUARY 13, 1914
Litigation over the **patents for balancing airplanes** settled by the U.S. Circuit Court of Appeals in favor of the Wright brothers against Glenn Curtiss.

JANUARY 25, 1915
First transcontinental telephone call made by Alexander Graham Bell, speaking from New York to Dr. Thomas A. Watson in San Francisco.

MAY 24, 1915
Invention of **"telescribe"** to record telephone conversations announced by Thomas A. Edison.

1916
Submachine gun invented by Brig. Gen. John Taliaferro Thompson. Gun was known as "Tommy gun."

1922
First successful use of **Technicolor** process made by Herbert T. Kalmus.

MARCH 13, 1923
Process for producing **sound motion pictures** by Dr. Lee de Forest: "Phonofilm."

NOVEMBER 6, 1923
Patent issued to Col. Jacob Schick for **1st electric shaver.**

NOVEMBER 30, 1924
Transmission of photographs from London to New York by **wireless telegraph** demonstrated by R.C.A.

JULY 30, 1928
First colored motion pictures in U.S. exhibited by George Eastman.

NOVEMBER, 1929
Patent issued to Sebastiano Lando for **coin-operated vending machine** which could not be defrauded.

1932
First polaroid glass devised by Edwin H. Land.

MAY 23, 1934
Dr. Wallace H. Carothers, a research chemist in the Du Pont laboratories, succeeded in spinning a synthetic fiber, it became famous as: **nylon.**

1938
Games Slayter and John H. Thomas perfected methods to manufacture **glass wool** or **fiberglass.**

APRIL 20, 1940
Electron microscope tested at R.C.A. Instrument magnified as much as 100,000 diameters. It had been developed by Dr. Ladislaus Marton and co-workers under the supervision of Dr. V. K. Zworykin.

MAY 15, 1940
Successful experimental **helicopter** manufactured by Vought-Sikorsky Corporation.

MAY 18, 1968
Sanford L. Cluett, inventor of Sanforizing, died at age 93.

SEPTEMBER 19, 1968
Chester F. Carlson, the inventor of xerography, died at age 62.

DECEMBER 12, 1971
David Sarnoff, broadcasting pioneer who helped found the electronics and communications industry, died at age 80.

HISTORICAL HEADLINES
ON
SCIENCE-TECHNOLOGY

EXTRA

Los Angeles Examiner

A Politically Independent Newspaper

Classified Advertising: Richmond 8-4111
All Other Calls: Richmond 8-1212

RACE RESULTS

10 CENTS   PCC   SEC. 1

SATURDAY, DEC. 7, 1957

U.S. 'MOON' BLOWS UP

Cause Mystery; Free World Shocked; Ike Demands Report

MERCILESS—AND DISHEARTENING—FLAMES CONSUME THE VANGUARD ON ITS LAUNCHING SITE AFTER IT BLEW UP YESTERDAY IN FLORIDA

—International News soundphoto.

Satellite Falls as Rocket Incinerates

GETTYSBURG, Pa., Dec. 6 — President Eisenhower, expressing disappointment, today demanded a full report from the Defense Department on the failure of the first U. S. attempt to launch a satellite.

White House News Secretary Hagerty reported Eisenhower expressed "disappointment" in his presence after learning that the Vanguard rocket had exploded at Cape Canaveral, Fla.

Hagerty said the Chief Executive immediately asked for a full report from the Pentagon.

STUNNING BLOW—

Failure to launch a U. S. satellite dealt a stunning new blow to American prestige in the Free World. In the United Nations there was an atmosphere of dismay.

Diplomats wondered with the failure coming in the final stage of buildup for the Allied Summit conference at Paris whether the incident did not make it urgent that President Eisenhower attend the Paris meet if physically able to do so.

According to Hagerty, the report is not expected for at least a few days. He

By DARRELL GARWOOD
International News Service
Atomic Science Editor

CAPE CANAVERAL, Fla., Dec. 6 — America's first attempt to launch an earth satellite ended in spectacular failure today when the Vanguard rocket blew up and burned on the firing site.

A terrific explosion, an awesome sheet of flame and a towering pillar of smoke marked the doom of the three-stage rocket two seconds after it was touched off at 11:45 a. m.

The six-inch sphere U. S. scientists had hoped to blast into orbit in outer space was retrieved when the third stage of the rocket in which it was housed was thrown safely clear.

The first and second stages of the missile were destroyed.

TOTAL LOSS—

Dr. John P. Hagen, director of the Vanguard project, said failure of the rocket was mechanical rather than a design problem. He said that "so far nobody knows for certain the cause of the accident."

Deputy Director Paul Walsh said "almost nothing can be salvaged from the wreckage."

Personnel at the Cape Canaveral Missile Center,

Turn to Page 2, Cols. 2-3

Turn to Page 2, Cols. 3-4

$41,100 Trash Costs Voted

Moving to keep the city's combustible rubbish pickup system from collapsing, the City Council yesterday made an emergency appropriation of $41,100 to meet Monday's payroll and to buy gasoline for the trucks.

The emergency fund was voted after the Council refused immediate approval of a request for $1,091,320 to keep the present rubbish equipment rolling and to buy and staff 40 additional trucks.

The Board of Public Works had requested $1,482,990. Councilmen said they were not satisfied with the explanation of the need made by Adm. Cushing Phillips, president of the Board of Public Works, and Warren Schneider, director of the Bureau of Sanitation.

PUT OVER—

The request was put over to Tuesday for more study.

Another emergency appropriation for $70,000 in payroll and gasoline was made three weeks ago.

Phillips warned the Council that even if it approves the $1,091,320 request the rubbish system may require another $120,000 for overtime and gasoline before March 1, unless the volume of rubbish declines.

The appropriations are in addition to the $3,150,670 in the annual budget for combustible rubbish pickup.

Turn to Page 4, Cols. 4-5

Where to Find It--

	Pages	Sec.		Pages	Sec.
Churches	6-7	1	Movies, Drama	12-13	1
Classified	6-15	2	Open Door	9	1
Comics	10	1	Radio	16	1
Crossword	7	2	Rudolph	8	1
Editorials	14	1	Southland Women	9	1
Financial	4-6	2	Sports	1-3	2
Fortune Finder	8	1	Television	15	1
Horoscope	9	1	Vital Statistics	6	2
Louella Parsons	13	1	Weather	5	2

Two Sections, Sec. 1 ◆ 54th Year, No. 361

2 Women Held in 'Trick-Treat' Killing

A woman who murdered for a kiss and the woman who assertedly induced her to kill were arrested yesterday in the Halloween "trick or treat" slaying of Peter Fabiano.

Mrs. Goldyne Pizer, 43, police said, confessed she shot Fabiano, 35, a man she did not know, as a "favor" to Mrs. Joan Rabel, 40.

DETAILS—

Police arranged for Mrs. Pizer to confront Mrs. Rabel in the office of Mrs. Rabel's attorney, Ralph Rosenstock. Once again Mrs. Pizer gave the details of the strange crime. Mrs. Rabel uttered not a word.

Fabiano was shot Halloween as he answered the ring of his doorbell at his home, 13236 Community street, Pacoima.

From the bedroom, Fabiano's wife, Betty, heard him say:

"It's a little late for this sort of thing, isn't it?"

Then she heard the sound of the shot.

Detectives deduced the

Turn to Page 5, Col. 3

Chest Appeal Issued

Courtlandt S. Gross, Community Chest campaign chairman, yesterday appealed to all volunteer workers to exert every effort to bring the current fund drive to a "successful conclusion" by December 12.

Here is his statement:

"More than ever this year are we dependent on the efforts of those of you who make up the volunteer residential workers organization.

"Appreciative as I am of what you have already done I must not fail to appeal to you not to let your interest and efforts lag at this critical moment of the campaign.

"If you will stay on your campaign job try your best to get contributions . . . increased contributions . . . together we can reach our goal as we must by the meeting at noon, December 12.

"Please remember there is no substitute for individual responsibility and individual effort in doing what I ask you to do. And further, remember that 167 health, welfare and children's services in the Community Chest are looking to you and depending on you . . . on you as an individual . . . for help."

EXTRA

The Weather
WARMER—Night and morning low clouds but mostly sunny today and tomorrow. No smog. High near 75.

LOS·ANGELES   EVENING

MIRROR · NEWS

Vol. XI—No. 197   ★ Largest Afternoon Home Delivery in the West   In Four Parts   THURSDAY, MAY 28, 1959   PART I   1★   MA 5-2311 — 145 S. Spring, Los Angeles 53 — TEN CENTS

—AP WIREPHOTO

THE FIRST SPACE APE—MONKEY ABLE
American-born rhesus in training at Pensacola, Fla.

Beatnik Bandit Pair Captured

An ex-actor's flair for dramatics resulted early today in the arrest of two men believed to be the beatnik bandits sought in a series of filling station and loan company stick-ups.

The pair approached Jack Boyle, 43, of 5827 Carlton Way, an attendant at a Rich-field service station at 5777 Hollywood Blvd., threatened him with a 2-ft. length of pipe and demanded the keys to an outside cash register.

Help Me, Mammy!

Boyle, a former actor, saw a police car passing, dropped to one knee and held out his arms in the traditional "Mammy!" gesture.

Officers Robert Kjorlien and Travis Hays wheeled in a tight turn into the filling station and grabbed one bandit. The second fled but was arrested in the same neighborhood 40 minutes later.

The bearded beatnik was identified as Thomas Harold Genter, 22, of 2850 Vineland Ave., North Hollywood, recently released on probation from San Quentin where he had done a year on a burglary conviction.

Also on Probation

His partner, Clarence W. Violette, 23, of 20258 Stag St., Canoga Park, told police he is out on probation on a forgery charge.

Both were booked at Hollywood station-on suspicion of robbery. Victims of other recent stick-ups will view the pair today.

Police believe the men to be the same duo who threatened Leon Kwapp, 57, of 937 Marview Ave., an attendant at a filling station at 7004 Laurel Canyon Blvd., North Hollywood, with pipes last night.

They forced Kwapp to lie on the floor and escaped with $30 from the till.

HARRY GENTER

—MIRROR NEWS Photos
CLARENCE VIOLETTE

EXPERTS REPORT!
ON KISSING—Youth Research Institute findings on teen-age romance, Page 1, Part II.

ON MID-1959—What last half of a busy year holds for U.S., ECONOSCOPE, Page 6, Part II.

TWO MONKEYS IN NOSE CONE RETURN ALIVE

Able, Baker Survive Trip; Hale, Hearty

CAPE CANAVERAL, May 28 (AP)—Two monkeys returned alive today from a 1,500-mile space ride in the nose cone of an Army missile.

CAPE CANAVERAL, Fla., May 28 (AP)—Two little monkeys rode a rocket 1,500 miles through space today and survived at least until the last minute of the trip back.

Their nose cone vehicle was recovered from the ocean but the task of opening it held up determination of their fate.

Scientists reported that signals from instruments attached to the animals showed only slight effects from the stress of blast-off and the weird ordeal of weightlessness in space.

Even that much represented a major step forward for the United States in the race with Russia to put a man into space.

If the monkeys survived the last minute, during which they were out of radio contact, and the actual impact, they would be the first animals known to have been into space and come back alive. That would amount to a massive break-through.

The last-minute loss of communication was not as usual. Contact becomes difficult as a space vehicle drops below the horizon.

The little passengers were hurled aloft at the tip of an Army Jupiter rocket at 2:35 a.m. (EST) (12:35 a.m. PDT). The nose cone was recovered from the water near Antigua Island at 4:08 a.m. by a Navy ship.

Altogether their 10,000-
Turn to Page 3, Column 1

Teener Idol Gets Ticket for Speeding

Ricky Nelson, 19-year-old screen, TV and recording star, was cited by police this morning on charges of driving too fast and not carrying an operator's license.

Officers Richard Baldwin and Danny Gardner stopped Ricky as he drove his foreign sports car east on Ventura Blvd., between Balboa Blvd. and Woodley Ave., Encino, at 2:15 a.m. today.

The citation was issued under the star's real name, Eric H. Nelson, 1822 Camino Palermo, Hollywood.

Ex-Husband Hosted by Liz, Eddie

ENGLEFIELD GREEN, Eng., May 28 (AP)—Elizabeth Taylor, honeymooning here with husband No. 4, played hostess last night to husband No. 2.

Actor Michael Wilding and his wife Susan were dinner guests at the tightly guarded 15-room mansion where Miss Taylor and Eddie Fisher are quietly spending the third week of their marriage.

While police patrolled the barbed wire barricades, Wilding played on the lawns with his two children by Miss Taylor — Michael Jr., 6, and Christopher, 4.

—AP WIREPHOTO
TRIP WAS NECESSARY, SO MONKEY BAKER LEARNED ALL ABOUT IT
Young space specimen peeks over microscope at peanuts he had for reward.

Argentina Battles Strikers

BUENOS AIRES, May 28 (AP) — Striking bank clerks clashed with police and thousands of railwaymen challenged troop's trying to force them to work as Argentina seethed today with industrial strife.

President Arturo Frondizi called out troops with tanks and machine guns to patrol the railway center of Junin.

He declared Junin, a junction city of 36,667 people, a military area after thousands of railwaymen refused to work in defiance of the government order last November mobilizing the nation's railwaymen in the armed forces.

Rain, Big Wind Lash Midwest

By the Associated Press

More severe thunderstorms, with tornadic winds in some areas, hit the middle part of the country last night.

Today's weather map indicated showers nearly everywhere except in the southern half of the country from the Rockies westward to the Pacific Coast.

The thunderstorm activity broke out from Western Texas to South Dakota. Tornadic winds, hail and rain swept areas in Northern, Western and Central Texas.

Heavy rains in Northeast Kansas and Northern Missouri caused flooding in some sections. A tornado alert was sounded as strong winds lashed Southeast Missouri.

A tornado struck near Gillette, Wyo., smashing farm buildings, a hangar and four airplanes.

A farmer was killed when struck by lightning during a severe thunderstorm in the Cadiz (O.) area.

Crew Saved in Ship Fire

PINAR DEL RIO, Cuba, May 28 (AP) — A Cuban navy launch rescued the captain and 28 crewmen of a Greek freighter on fire and grounded last night off the northwest coast of Cuba.

The ship's carpenter was the only fatality reported. He was killed in a boiler explosion which started the fire.

Ike to Tell Gromyko His Terms

WASHINGTON, May 28 (AP) — President Eisenhower is reported ready to tell Russia's Andrei A. Gromyko today he won't go to a summit conference unless East-West foreign ministers make substantial progress in easing tensions over Germany's future.

The President is expected to re-emphasize this attitude at an unusual White House meeting with the foreign ministers, who have been conferring in Geneva.

The four came here to attend yesterday's funeral for John Foster Dulles.

Word for Gromyko

Eisenhower has called Gromyko to meet with him in his office along with Secretary of State Herter, British Foreign Secretary Lloyd and French Foreign Minister Couve de Murville.

Eisenhower intends to avoid getting mixed up in the Geneva talks, but he means to tell Gromyko about the need for Soviet concessions on the German issue.

He arranged to meet alone with the foreign policy chief for a frank appraisal of prospects. The Geneva talks resume tomorrow with a secret meeting at Lloyd's villa.

Defies Threats

The President will make known his determination to avoid being blackmailed or threatened into an emergency meeting with Soviet Premier Khrushchev.

Eisenhower will spurn any summit-level talk unless the foreign ministers at least block out the framework of a new agreement reaffirming western rights to remain in Berlin.

CUBAN TAXES AIM AT HIGH SOCIETY

HAVANA, May 28 (AP) — Cuba's revolution is training its big guns on the rich with big cars and the high society that gets written up in the papers.

Now being drafted is a tax schedule which, among other things:

1—Puts the price of license plates for big new cars—mostly American—at $5,000.

2—Taxes newspapers $1 for each adjective they use in a society-page item.

3—Taxes the papers $100 every time the society page carries the name of a member of the nobility.

Capone Nemesis Succumbs at 68

MARION, Ind., May 28 (AP) — Don L. Kooken, 68, criminologist and last surviving member of the "T-Men Untouchables," died yesterday.

The self-styled untouchables were a group of Treasury agents who worked with Chicago police to break up the old Al Capone gang.

EXTRA
GLENN IN ORBIT!

SPORTS LATEST NEWS

LOS ANGELES EVENING AND SUNDAY
HERALD EXAMINER
EXPRESS
United Press International • Associated Press • Dow Jones
1111 S. Broadway, L.A. 54 • Phone RI. 8-4141 or RI. 8-1212

VOL. XCI — Four Sections Section A — 10 CENTS — TUESDAY, FEBRUARY 20, 1962 ★ — NO. 290

Horses 'Barefoot' In 'Anita Races

Floods Rage
Twisters Rip L.A. Area

Storm .... 1.71 inches
Season to date 17.42 inches
Last year ...... 3.99 inches
Normal to date .10.11 inches
(Nation's weather round-up, B-8; rain table, B-4.)

Water-logged Southern California today dug out from its third flood-loaded storm in two weeks, after a wild day yesterday which brought roaring twisters in Northridge and Santa Ana areas, 1.71 inches of rain in Los Angeles, and high winds elsewhere.

Gentler treatment was promised today, with only scattered showers and thunderstorms. Less than an inch of rain will fall, the Weather Bureau announced with wry humor.

ALL-NIGHT BATTLE

At Palmdale, more than 100 men won an all-night battle with swelling waters in four flood-control basins. With sandbags and reinforced dams, they capitalized on a brief respite from rain to secure Palmdale's business district from threatened flood.

PATIO COLLAPSES

"It sounded like a train going through the house," said Mrs. Harold Skaila of the twister which ripped through a six-block area of Northridge yesterday. She was painting her kitchen at 18606 Gledhill St. when the patio collapsed.

The twister tore roofs from houses, knocked over walnut and oak trees, blew down patio covers, fences and billboards and shattered glass windows.

TREES FALL

At Santa Ana, a long list of closed streets, slide-blocked roads and mud-filled areas was left behind the storm. At Rolling Hills, an eight-foot track opened under a $30,000 home under construction at Bowie Lane. The house is slowly tilting into the crack.

FAMILIES FLEE

In Santa Barbara County, floods drove families from homes in Montecito, Carpenteria and Goleta Valley. A state of emergency was declared.

At Huntington Beach, half the roof of a 100-man barracks housing Mexican

(Continued on Page 4, Col. 4)

JFK Plan for 1,600,000 Employes
Asks $1 Billion Pay Hike for Govt. Aides

By HELEN THOMAS

WASHINGTON, Feb. 20 (UPI)—President Kennedy today asked Congress for a $1 billion pay increase for 1,640,000 white-collar Government workers over the next three years to bring their salaries into line with private industry.

In a special message to the House and Senate, Kennedy proposed reform of the Federal pay system to provide for wage hikes ranging from 3.7 per cent for clerical to 35 per cent for top bracket employes.

The proposed 10 per cent boost in the Federal payroll would be spread over three annual stages, starting Jan. 1, 1963, with the first year accounting for about four and one-half per cent of the raise.

CITES NEEDS

Kennedy said that enactment of the reform plan was fundamental to the "maintenance of a standard of excellence in the Federal service." He said it was "essential if we are to achieve and maintain proficiency in the Federal government."

The President stressed the need for putting the pay of top-flight professional workers on a par with private enterprise, in order to attract and retain competent personnel.

The plan calls for the addition of two new top-level grades, grade 19 and grade 20, to the Federal pay scale.

At present the top classification is grade 18. The proposed legislation would apply

(Continued on Page 4, Col. 3)

U.S. Gives Congo $15 Million, Promises More

WASHINGTON, Feb. 20 (P)—The United States has given the Congo $15 million more in aid and promised another $18 million by the end of June.

The agency for International Development said yesterday that the $15 million grant—to be channeled through the United Nations—will be used for purchases of American goods, including industrial equipment, vehicles, drugs, food and technical assistance.

The latest gift brings the total of American aid to the struggling Congo economy to $82 million.

March 1 Target Date for New Steel Contract

PITTSBURGH, Feb. 20 (UPI)—The steel industry's has set an official target date of March 1 for a new contract agreement with the United Steelworkers.

R. Conrad Cooper of U.S. Steel Corp., chief negotiator for the "big 11" steel companies, and David J. McDonald, president of the USW, issued a joint statement following yesterday's session in which they said they are hopeful of a settlement before March 1.

Herald-Examiner Special Features

Run Sans Shoes in Blacksmith Pay Row

By GEORGE MAIN

Like the country boy on a warm summers day, the horses will go barefoot at Santa Anita this afternoon.

But, unlike the barefoot boy, who knew where he wandered, nobody knows what the horses will be doing today.

Having been shod with aluminum or steel shoes all their racing lives it is anyone's guess as to how they will react in their bare feet.

Handicapping today's card is like trying to guess how many beans are in the jar. Your guess is as good as the next bettors.

The debut of the barefoot horses came about when the horseshoers put in for a one buck raise from $17 to $18.

The owners and trainers balked at the raise and a stalemate resulted.

The owners are adamant in their refusal to pay and the horseshoers are just as firm about hiking the ante.

So, while mortal man stands well shod poor old dobbin will go to work in his bare feet.

What do shoes mean to a

(Continued on Page C-6)

Glenn Calls His Family From Atlas

ARLINGTON, Va., Feb. 20 (UPI) — Astronaut John H. Glenn phoned his wife direct from his space capsule today when the countdown preceding his scheduled orbital flight was halted at 22 minutes before blastoff.

The conversation between Glenn and his wife, Annie, lasted about five minutes.

TALKS TO CHILDREN

The Rev. Frank A. Erwin referred to Mrs. Glenn and the astronaut's family, David, 16, and Carolyn, 14, as well as friends and neighbors who were with them for the tense final countdown.

Glenn also talked with his son and daughter.

The two children of the astronaut planned to play hookey from school today to watch telecasts of the United States' first orbital flight,

---

—NASA Photo via Associated Press Wirephoto
AS ASTRONAUT GLENN ENTERED MERCURY CAPSULE FOR HISTORIC FLIGHT
Everything Was A-Okay Immediately From Blastoff, and Glenn Reported 'I Feel Fine—the View Is Tremendous!' as He Zoomed Into Orbit, the First American to Circle the Earth

Long Wait Over
Glenn's Big Day Traced

By FRED S. HOFFMAN

CAPE CANAVERAL, Fla., Feb. 20 (P)—With a confident wave, astronaut John H. Glenn jr. set out again today to conquer the biggest objective any Marine has ever tackled—the first American "beachhead" in orbit around the earth.

Glenn's green eyes, visible through the opening in his round, white space helmet, seemed to say "I'm going to make it this time" as he walked from his special training quarters at 5:02 a.m.

Just 245 days ago, Marine Lt. Col. Glenn started on this same journey, only to be thwarted by a heavy cloud cover just 20 minutes from launch time.

Then had come more delays because of weather and technical bugs. But now the waiting was over.

DAY CAME

The strong-jawed veteran of two wars had said salmly back on Jan. 27 that there would be another day—and that day had come.

His silver-coated space suit glinted in the glare of television lights as the 40-year-old Ohioan strode with a stiff-legged gait from the doorway

(Continued on Page 5, Col. 3)

Glenn's Mercury Craft Launched Into Orbit

Full page of Astronaut photos, A-22

CAPE CANAVERAL, Feb. 20 (UPI)—John Glenn went into orbit around the earth today—the first American to do so.

By ALVIN B. WEBB JR.

CAPE CANAVERAL, Feb. 20 (UPI)—The United States today launched Astronaut John H. Glenn Jr. on a planned space flight around the earth.

Glenn's Atlas rocket lifted from its launch pad at 9:48 a.m., after 10 frustrating delays which had kept the 40-year-old Marine lieutenant colonel grounded for the past two months.

It was the Free World's first attempt to put a man in orbit.

The mighty 93 foot Atlas Mercury space ship blasted from its launching pad at 9:45 a.m. (EST) and climbed steeply into a brilliant blue sky.

It began arching slowly to the northeast and continued its drive to put Glenn into orbit.

As it arched, a sprakling white vapor trail curled from its engines and contrail as it moved quickly towards space.

One minute after liftoff, Powers relayed from Glenn that all systems were go and that the flight was very smooth.

In a sequence action, the rocket's mighty 360,000 pound thrust engines belched into life and setn Glenn soaring into space with enough horsepower to drive 35,000 standard American autos.

Booster engines on the Atlas and an emergency escape tower—a safety protection for

(Continued on Page 5, Col. 1)

Glenn during the early touchy moments of blastoff—were jettisoned and sent tumbling into the Atlantic three minutes after launch.

Seconds later, the No. 1 tracking station at Bermuda picked up signals from Friendship 7.

Glenn reported his cabin pressuer was holding at 5.5 pounds.

He said that all systems were "go."

"I feel fine," Glenn said.

Fuel, oxygen and pressure

'Somebody Launched'

CAPE CANAVERAL, Fla., Feb. 20 (P)—Shortly before astronaut John H. Glenn Jr. entered his space capsule today, the public address system announced the birth of a baby to the wife of a technician working at the pad.

"Well," a worker remarked, "at least, somebody got launched today."

U.S. ROCKET HITS MOON

SPORTS LATEST NEWS

LOS ANGELES EVENING AND SUNDAY

Herald☆Examiner

United Press International • Associated Press • Dow Jones
CLASSIFIED ADVERTISING Richmond 8-4111
All Other Calls Richmond 8-1212 or Richmond 8-4141

VOL. XCII   Four Sections Section A   10 CENTS   THURSDAY, APRIL 26, 1962   ★   NO. 31

3 Slain in Chicago Gangland Killing

—Associated Press Wirephoto

TWO MEN AND WOMAN FOUND SHOT TO DEATH IN CAR IN GANG STYLE
Coroner Dr. Andrew J. Toman Examines Bodies (Arrow); Trio Slain With
Machine Gun or Repeating Rifle in Elmwood Park, Ill.

First Blast Brings Criticism

U.S. Pushes Aerial A-Tests

WASHINGTON, April 26 (UPI)—The United States pushed ahead today with atmospheric nuclear tests in the Pacific and sought to counteract criticism sparked by the first blast.

Will Seek Sanctions, Threat at Geneva

Russians Rant Over U.S. Nuclear Tests

By WELLINGTON LONG

GENEVA, April 26 (UPI)—The Soviet Union said today it would seek sanctions against the United States for resuming nuclear tests in the atmosphere.

The Soviet delegation to the 17-nation disarmament conference accused the United States of "challenging the whole world" with its explosion of a nuclear device in the Pacific yesterday.

U.S. Ambassador Arthur H. Dean told the conference the United States resumed nuclear tests in the air because it refuses to be duped or victimized again by the Soviet Union which broke the old voluntary moratorium.

FORCED TO TEST

Dean said the United States was forced to take the action because of Moscow's refusal of a cheat-proof test ban and its breaking of a pledge last fall not to test in the air.

Soviet Deputy Foreign Minister Valerian Zorin announced his government's in- **(Continued on Page 4, Col. 4)**

tentions to seek sanctions. But he did not spell out what form they envisaged.

He said the Americans were being hypocritical.

"The Soviet delegation cannot remain indifferent in the face of the shameful actions of the United States and with the conference will state its position with regard to sanctions," Zorin said.

Russia threatened to walk out of the Geneva disarmament talks, India protested and Japanese students had to be chased away by riot police when they marched on the U.S. embassy in Tokyo. Most of Western Europe stood by the United States.

The State Department announced that the "decision to test was taken reluctantly and with awareness of our responsibility as the most powerful defender of the free world and in the absence of an effective treaty to halt such tests."

"The United tSates has thrown away its mask," the Russian said. "The United States is unleashing a fresh arms race, and is bringing the world nearer to the abyss of nuclear war."

He said the Soviet Union **(Continued on Page 4, Col. 5)**

Hail of Bullets Rip Car

ELMWOOD PARK, Ill., April 26 (IP)—A volley of gunshots killed two men and a woman in gangland-style before dawn today as they motored along a quiet residential street in this Chicago suburb. The car crashed into a house.

Neighborhood residents said they heard a number of rapidly fired gunshots and police theorized the killer or killers used a machine gun or a repeating rifle.

The victims were identified tentatively by police as Phillip Scavo, 36, of Elmwood Park; Ronald Scavo of Chicago, and a woman at first thought to be a Marianne Martarono because of the name on an identification card ina wallet she carried. The owner of the wallet, however, said she lost it a month ago.

Phillip Scavo had $1118 in cash on his person, police said. Ronald Scavo carried $207.

The auto crashed into a home owned by Rudolf Kornfeind. Little damage was done to the house.

Mrs. Kornfeind told the Associated Press:

"I was awakened about 3:45 by a loud crash and a screech of brakes. My husband and I jumped out of bed and then we heard shots. My husband called police and I looked out the window.

"I saw a black car speeding away in a southerly direction. Then the police came."

Olsen said skid marks made by the victims' grey Thunderbird indicated the auto had been jammed into reverse gear, plowed across the Kornfeinds' lawn and smashed into the house.

The right front window of the sport car was shattered, apparently by the fusillade of shots. Police said the car was owned by Phillip Scavo.

CHURCH BURGLAR BAR

CAMDEN, N.J., April 26 (IP)—The Roman Catholic Diocese of Camden has ordered burglar alarms installed in every church.

Award Winning Car Values

You're in the running for an award-winning car value, when you check the special auto page in tomorrow's Herald-Examiner Classified. Choose from a complete selection of glamorous new and late-model cars at low down payments and easy terms. Don't miss the star line-up of best car buys in tomorrow's Herald-Examiner Classified.

**See Class. 370-382
Herald-Examiner Classified**

Sun Beams Over So. Cal.

(Nation's Weather on A-21)
Sunny skies beamed over Southern California today after a chilly night, and the Weather Bureau predicted a warming trend today would continue tomorrow.

Temperatures dropped to 50 in the downtown area last night, but climbed steadily to 68 today and probably will go higher tomorrow.

Fear Crackpot

Tighten Hearing Security

(Photo on A-3)

Hearings of the subcommittee of the House Committee on Un-American Activities, jarred yesterday by a bomb threat which emptied the Federal Building, resumed today in an atmosphere of even greater security precautions.

All persons going to the fifth floor, on which hearings are being held, will be searched before being allowed into the single express elevator, authorities said.

"This will prevent another crackpot call from interrupting the hearings," said U. S. Marshal George E. O'Brien.

PICKETS DWINDLE

Meanwhile, on the outside of the building, with the committee beginning work at 8 a.m., placard-carrying pickets again came late and dwindled even below the 100 which yesterday provided the sessions.

The "HUAC Recept Committee," as yesterday, is the only group providing pickets. The Fair Play For Cuba Committee and the Citizens Committee to Preserve American Freedom, which picketed Tuesday, failed to be represented.

While the committee announced at the beginning that the four-day sessions were closed and that no press reports would be given, Rep. Clyde Doyle, D-Calif., chairman, today gave a "status report."

"We're making headway," **(Continued on Page 8, Col. 3)**

U.S. Launches New Mystery Satellite

POINT ARGUELLO, Calif., April 26 (IP—The Air Force launched a mystery satellite from this West Coast missile base in the pre-dawn hours today.

Officials declined to give any details beyond the fact that the satellite employed a Blue Scout booster combination.

East Berlin Guns, Tanks Roll Out For May Day

BERLIN, April 26 (AP)—East German tanks and heavy guns rattled through the empty streets of East Berlin at dawn today, practicing for the annual May Day parade.

At one point they were only a few yards from the Communist wall.

East Berlin's May Day parade regularly includes heavy military equipment despite the Soviet-Western occupation agreement banning German military equipment from Berlin. The Western Powers usually protest the violation.

On the other side of the wall, West Berlin planned its own big May Day demonstration. Hundreds of thousands are expected to gather to hear speeches by West German President Heinrich Luebke and Mayor Willy Brandt. Gen. Lucius D. Clay, winding up his mission as President Kennedy's personal envoy, will appear.

AFL-CIO Asks Adoption of Race Ban Bar

WASHINGTON, April 26 (UPI)—The AFL-CIO was expected today to ask its 133 affiliated unions to adopt "plans for progress" programs to wipe out racial discrimination in labor's ranks.

The program, which already has AFL-CIO President George Meany's support, was scheduled to be considered by the federation's executive council at a two-day session here.

It was worked out by the AFL-CIO civil rights committee and President Kennedy's committee on equal employment opportunity under the leadership of Vice President Lyndon B. Johnson.

THE MASSIVE 'EAR' AT GOLDSTONE, CALIF., WHICH HEARD RANGER 4 HIT THE MOON
Ever Since Monday When the Atlas-Agena B Rocket Roared Up From Cape Canaveral, the 85-Foot Diameter
Goldstone Antenna Has Been Listening to Ranger's Progress; At 4:49.45 Sound Stopped, Proving 'Hit'

Spacecraft Tracked To Lunar Smashup By So. Cal. Station

By FRANK ELMQUIST
Herald-Examiner Staff Reporter

GOLDSTONE, Calif., April 26—At exactly 4:49.45 a.m., PST, today America landed on the moon.

That fact was confirmed here at this deep space tracking station.

Our lunar ambassador was a 730-pound gold and chrome plated spacecraft called Ranger 4. It was designed and put together for the National Aeronautics and Space Administration by the California Institute of Technology's Jet Propulsion Laboratory.

"It definitely hit the moon," said Clifford I. Cummings, lunar project director, as the jubilant scientists watching a closed circuit television screen saw the crosshairs of a simulated gunsight slowly approach the left side of the moon.

POSITION TRACED

The crosshairs indicated Ranger 4's position as it streaked through space. The 7-foot vehicle, itself, was too small to be detected visually.

Then the crosshairs of the gunsight touched the edge of the moon, and exclamations of delight were uttered by the two dozen persons following Ranger 4's progress here.

The faint radio beacon in Ranger was tracked with an 85-foot diameter dish-shaped antenna.

The spacecraft's speed, at impact, calculated at 5963 miles an hour, indicated the craft was destroyed at impact and its parts scattered along the moon's surface.

Ranger 4 cost America's taxpayers between $4 and $5 million, plus another $10,000 per pound to put it where it lies on the far side of the moon.

64-HOUR JOURNEY

The spacecraft made its 231,486-mile journey in 63 hours 59 minutes and 45 seconds. It was launched Monday by an Atlas-Agena B rocket from Cape Canaveral, Fla.

Ranger 4 had been designed to transmit television pictures of the moon's surface back to earth, and to send important information on moon quakes and meteoritic impacts from an instrumented capsule designed to make a relatively soft landing on the lunar surface.

In this, the spacecraft

failed. But it did hit the moon—an accomplishment for which there is no earthly comparison.

3 FLIGHTS SCHEDULED

In fact, Ranger 4's assignment was so difficult that NASA scheduled three flights, Ranger 3, 4 and 5 in the hope that one would be successful.

Ranger 3, the first effort, failed because of a malfunction in the Atlas booster. That was on Jan. 26 of this year. Ranger 3, injected into its lunar transfer path at excessive velocity, arrived in **(Continued on Page 6, Col. 1)**

Actress Mae Murray Dies

Story in Cols. 3-6

EXTRA

LOS ANGELES EVENING AND SUNDAY

HERALD — EXAMINER

CLASSIFIED ADVERTISING Richmond 8-4111   All Other Calls Richmond 8-1212 or Richmond 8-4141

LARGEST EVENING CIRCULATION IN AMERICA

8 STAR LATEST SPORTS
Complete N. Y. Stocks

VOL. XCIV Four Sections Section A   10 CENTS   TUESDAY, MARCH 23, 1965   8★   NO. 362

GEMINI: A SPACE FIRST
Twins Change Orbit; Safe

- *The Greenest Rookie's story: A-15.*
- *Those left behind: A-14.*
- *The voice of Molly Brown: A-14.*
- *Page of photos: A-26.*

By BOB CONSIDINE
Herald-Examiner Correspondent With Hearst Headline Service

CAPE KENNEDY, March 23—The U.S. space program took another step towards the moon today when astronauts Gus Grissom and John Young brilliantly demonstrated that spacecraft can be made to maneuver while in orbit.

The 38-year-old Air Force Maj. Grissom and 34-year-old Navy Lieut. Com. Young changed trajectories three times during their three laps "rollercoaster" trip around the world today.

Their Gemini space chariot splashed into the Atlantic at 2:20 p.m. EST (11.20 a.m. PST), an estimated 60 miles short of the exact point at which the space men had expected to land.

The astronauts' historic trip ended safely on an aircraft carrier's deck.

The only hitch in the near-perfect ride came at the finish, when Grissom missed his target—the aircraft carrier Intrepid—by 58 miles.

But this made little difference.

A Navy plane put three frogmen in the water to attach flotation gear to the spacecraft and a helicopter from the Intrepid lifted the astronauts out of the capsule later.

Grissom smiled broadly as he climbed from the helicopter on the Intrepid's deck and marched down a red carpet toward the admiral's cabin. Young followed close behind.

The astronauts had been blasted off Pad 19 here at Cape Kennedy at 9:24 a.m. (6:24 PST) by a thundering 430,000 horsepower Titan 2 rocket. Their momentous journey consumed 4 hours and 56 minutes.

In the course of their streak through space, Grissom and Young forced their space vehicle "Molly Brown" to do everything but nip-ups.

The most dramatic of the maneuvers performed by the astronauts was to shift the orbital path of their capsule as it raced along at 17,500 miles an hour above the earth.

This has never been done before.

Termed a "truly historic event" by the scientists and space officials associated with Project Gemini, the two astronauts slowed the speed of their vehicle by 33 miles an hour and lowered the high

(Cont. on Page 14, Col. 1-3)

Santa Anita Results

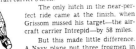

1 Rscl. Tass 7.20,3.40,2.60; FrncnsFlght 2.60,2.40; Grn.Hnv.4.60
SECOND—1 mile, claiming pace, all ages, purse $1500:

Scratched—Merrie Rita, Colonel Direct.
AT GOLDEN GATE
1 P inceBs 24.60,10.20,4.00; CaustnALt 11.40,4.60; GreekPni2.40

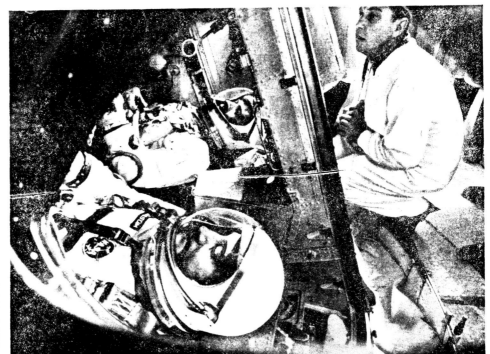

—United Press International Telephoto

MINUTES BEFORE THE BLASTOFF A TECHNICIAN (AT RIGHT) MAKES FINAL CHECK OF ASTRONAUTS
U.S. spacemen Virgil 'Gus' Grissom (bottom) and John Young off into the wild blue yonder aboard the Molly Brown

'Merry Widow' Mae Murray Dies

By JEAN BOSQUET
Herald-Examiner Staff Writer

MAE MURRAY
Before recent illness

Mae Murray, one of the brightest and most mercurial of Hollywood's glittering galaxy of stars 40 years ago, died today at 75 in the Motion Picture Country House and Hospital.

Death wrote the final paragraph in one of the most dramatic stories of stage and screen personalities after a prolonged illness caused by a stroke the dancer-actress suffered last August.

The closing out of the Murray career was like snuffing out the brightest tallow flame in a candelabra, hospital attendants said.

The effervescent little dancer who stubbornly refused to grow old was still trying to keep her age a secret at the end, and still considering herself a star.

"Once you become a star you are always a star," she recently said. "You don't have to keep making movies to remain a star."

Mae would never admit it, but records showed she was born Marie Adrienne Koenig in Portsmouth, Va., May 10, 1889, and began dancing in New York shows at 13.

She was to become a Ziegfeld star, a movie queen when they really were queens, and a bonafide — if unhappy — princess before the end of silent films.

She was to play out her butterfly role as "the girl with the bee-stung lips" on stage and off, on screen and off, until that ruthless stage manager, age, rendered Mae one

of the most pathetic relics of show business.

She was to rise to the pinnacle of Hollywood's gleaming heap of stardust as early as 1926 when she whirled through "The Merry Widow" with the great and tragic John Gilbert.

Only 10 years ago, the quicksilver of her stardom dimmed to all but Mae, she was fighting not only to retain her own glamor but to restore Hollywood's.

"Hollywood has drifted to Beverly Hills, leaving none of the magic and color that made it the goal of millions the world over," she declared.

"We must bring back the Hollywood of my starring days, we must line it with living trees and reglamorize the

(Cont. on Page 25, Col. 2-5)

TODAY'S Top Features

Sun Plays Peek-a-boo

(U.S. Weather, Tides, D-12)

It was a can't-make-up-its-mind kind of a day, but the weatherman keeps insisting that before the afternoon is over the sun will peep through and say "Howdy," like in the song.

The predicted high today was 64 degrees, the low tonight 53.

There were a few drizzles this morning in some of the coastal areas.

25 Below Zero

NEW YORK, March 23 (UPI) —Lowest temperature reported this morning in the United States was 25 below zero at Bemidji, Minn. Highest temperature yesterday was 85 at Imperial, Calif., and Islamorada, Fla.

TREASURE HUNT VERSUS PERMANENT COMMUNITIES

Americans inventiveness had its origins in the efforts of the first settlers to build homes and develop farms in the wilderness. These beginning efforts to provide the necessities of life were made with the aid of clothing, food, and tools brought from Europe. Thus the earliest colonial technology was based on the technology which had prevailed in Europe as a result of historical conditions there. But as the European food and European clothing were used up and worn out, the colonists' ability to survive depended upon their capability to grow or manufacture their own products and their skill in modifying European tools to solve the problems of the new environment.

England, more than any other European nation, had the people willing to settle in a new land. The movement from simple exploration and rapid exploitation to actual colonization in America was accentuated for the English when thousands of English Puritans, harassed by the Church of England and English royalty, first sought refuge in Holland, the home of the world's first democratic republic, and later on the Eastern coast of North America. Between 1630 and 1634 some 10,000 Puritans had come to New England with the intent of establishing permanent communities where they could put their ideals into practice. By the end of the American Revolution in 1790, the colonial population was three-fourths British descent and largely Protestant.

The English, of course, were not the only Europeans who explored and settled the New World. They play a predomi-

nant role in this story because it was the English who placed the stamp of their language, laws and customs on that major part of North America which eventually became the United States and Canada. Spain put a similar cultural stamp on Cuba, Puerto Rico, and most of South America but was more attentive to the search for gold and the conversion of souls to Catholicism than on establishing permanent settlements wherever their far flung treasure hunters touched. The French developed roots in Quebec but are more known for their fur trapping exploits, brilliant explorations of the great rivers of North America and establishment of trading posts than for colonization. The Peace of Paris of 1763, marking the close of the Seven Years' War in Europe and the "Old French and Indian War" in America finalized the end of France as a North American power. Portuguese explorers developed Brazil and Newfoundland but the small country of Portugal was too busy at the time with its vast trading empire elsewhere to challenge the Spanish acquisitions in South America. The Dutch had a short-lived empire in North America centered around their Hudson River trading posts at Fort Orange (Albany) and New Amsterdam (New York City) but the powerful Netherlands actually had no surplus population to emigrate to the New World as settlers. In 1664 the English Duke of York seized the Dutch outposts from Peter Stuyvesant without firing a shot, as if to underscore Dutch impotence, and renamed not only New Amsterdam but the whole province of New York after himself. Thus the management of the North American continent was to be English, not French or Spanish or Dutch.

This fact that England came to dominate North America is of crucial importance in understanding why the United States today is so much more prosperous than, for example, any

This drawing shows the young Thomas Alva Edison busy at work in his home laboratory. Edison, father of the phonograph, the movie camera, and hundreds of other electronic inventions, was one of America's greatest creative geniuses.

Robert Fulton *inventor of the steamboat. Fulton's creative genius was not always matched with a good business sense, and many of his later inventions proved to be commercial failures.*

An old print of Robert Fulton's fist steamboat, the Clermont *moving up the Hudson River in 1807. The* Clermont *was the beginning of steamboat transportation on American rivers, and Fulton's invention added greatly to the economic development of the new nation by making the transportation of goods cheap and safe.*

country in South America or of England itself in 1976. England was the home of the Industrial Revolution, and when the new English techniques of power generation, muscle saving machinery, and rapid transportation and communication were combined with the rich natural resources of underdeveloped and underpopulated North America, the stage for a new leap in human civilization was set. Had Spain or any other country than England achieved domination over North America, or had any combination of European powers simply duplicated in North America that crazy patchwork of European national borders which still impedes the free movement of materials and ideas in Europe, the United States, or any other political formation on the North American continent, would not have been able to develop as rapidly or as extensively.

TRANSFERRING THE OLD TECHNOLOGY

By 1776 almost the whole technology of Europe was transmitted to the colonists in North America. This transfer of information was accomplished by the skilled craftsmen of Europe who settled the towns and farms of the New World.

When the Jamestown, Virginia, settlement of the London Company faced starvation and disease in 1609 as a result of being ill-prepared for the task of surviving in the new world, Captain John Smith wrote back to his sponsors, "I entreat you send me 30 carpenters, husbandmen, gardeners, blacksmiths, masons and diggers-up of trees' roots rather than a thousand such as we have . . . In Virginia a plaine Souldier that can use a Pick-axe and spade is better than five Knights."

The London Company responded to Captain Smith's request by sending him six carpenters, some blacksmiths, one mason, and twelve laborers as well as tools for the craftsmen: axes, chisels, mattocks, knives and pike heads. Captain Christopher Newport also brought on his ship shot and powder, six mares and a horse, many chickens, goats, sheep, a hundred pigs and wheat.

In August 1611, Sir Thomas Gates arrived with 200 men, "nearly all artisans and mechanics." There were weavers, tanners, fishhook makers, blacksmiths, hemp and flax dressers, miners, bakers, brewers, and glass workers. By this time the London Company had given clear instructions to the settlers to abandon the search for gold and establish a self-sustaining colony.

The Virginia settlers soon learned that the newly discovered tobacco plant was an adequate substitute for gold which they had originally and unsuccessfully sought. John Rolfe, known as the first agricultural scientist in Virginia and the husband of the Indian "princess" Pocahontas, experimented with a number of varieties of tobacco plant to discover which plants would give the maximum yield. He also helped develop a system of cultivation where the top of the plant was cut off to produce a heavier middle leaf. Rolfe influenced the whole of American history by persuading the London Company to let him grow and cure tobacco. Tobacco production required considerable amounts of field labor and eventually led to the importation of slaves and the establishment of a plantation economy in Virginia.

As early as 1618 Virginia exported 50,000 pounds of tobacco to England. In 1621 the English Parliament considered prohibiting the importation of tobacco into England because of King James' opposition to smoking, but Parliament was persuaded that the enactment of this prohibition would ruin the Virginia colony.

The Pilgrims who came on the *Mayflower* to Plymouth in 1620 were well suited to develop a permanent colony. The "Saints," derisively called Puritans because they claimed to possess a purity of doctrine, had first migrated from Scrooby, England, to Holland, which at that time was the leading nation of the world in scientific and engineering developments. The Pilgrims had first settled in Amsterdam and then moved to Leyden but they were unable to conform to the customs of Holland. In 1617, Robert Cushman and John Carver were sent to England to negotiate a grant of settlement with the London businessmen who had territorial rights in America.

In their twelve years in Holland, the Pilgrims learned many skills from the industrious Dutch people, talents which they then brought to the new world. William Brewster, for example, had become a ribbon maker while in Leyden. William Bradford, whose journal is our main source of information about Plymouth Colony, called himself a fustian worker, which meant cloth worker. He learned this skill in Amsterdam. Others on the Mayflower had been previously employed in Holland as button makers, tailors, cobblers, metal workers, carpenters, printers, pike makers, pump makers, dyers and silk workers.

Also aboard the *Mayflower* were a supply of saws, hammers, chisels, nails, blacksmith tools, cooper's tools as well as some bar iron and some steel to be fabricated into tools as

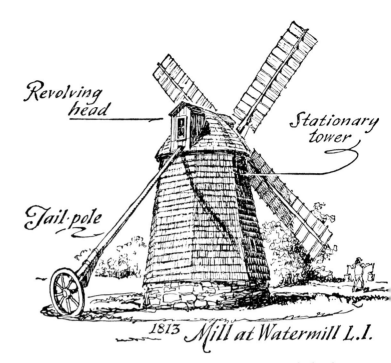

The Americans *retained many of Europe's proven methods of technology during the first years of the republic. Here is a sketch of an early windmill used on Long Island, New York. Although the Americans brought over European techniques, they modified them to fit into the pace of life in the new world.*

needed by the colonists.

Other New England settlements similarly attracted skilled craftsmen. The founders of Salem included two surveyors and six shipwrights, who arrived in 1629 and built by 1631 a 30-ton sloop, *Blessing of the Bay*.

The *Fortune* came to Cape Cod in November, 1621, carrying many artisans, including iron worker William Bassett of Middlesex, wool carder Robert Cushman of Kent, miller Stephen Deane, vintner William Hilton of Chester, nailer William Palmer of London, and armorer William Pitt of London.

When horses were brought to the new settlements, harness makers and saddlers were also induced to come. The new homes being built required glaziers, locksmiths, candle makers and carpenters. The new communities also advertised in Europe for shoe makers and blacksmiths while the newly developing fishing and maritime industries called for rope makers.

In 1624 the New Netherlands settlement promised free passage to America for craftsmen and tool workers. In 1654 Governor Rising of New Sweden asked his European sponsors to send pottery makers, brick makers, cabinet makers, shoe makers, tanners, lime burners and a hat maker to the Delaware settlement.

When William Penn advertised for European immigrants, he wanted "industrious husbandmen, carpenters, masons, weavers, shoe makers, and other mechanics, and industrious spirits that are oppressed about a livelihood . . ."

Twelve German families developed Germantown, Pennsylvania, in 1685 on the basis of their skills as mechanics and weavers. In 1714, Governor Spotswood of Virginia persuaded a small colony of Germans to develop a settlement for the purpose of mining iron ore. These settlers were provided with free houses for five years.

Settlements vigorously objected when felons and other "villains without crafts" were sent from the prisons of

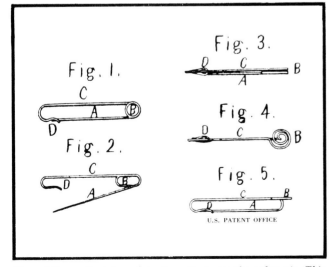

One of the earliest American *inventions was the safety pin. This ink sketch shows the operation of one of the first safety pins to receive a patent from the United States Patent Office.*

This reproduction *of a painting shows Samuel Morse, inventor of the telegraph, sending the first telegram from the chambers of the United States Supreme Court on May 24, 1884. Morse, seated in background, sent the message, "What Hath God Wrought?"*

Europe. It is estimated that Old Bailey prison alone supplied about 10,000 convicts for the American colonies between 1717 and 1775. Perhaps a total of about 50,000 convicts were sent to the colonies, the British government regularly vetoing any colonial laws forbidding importation of prisoners.

To conclude this brief account of how the technology of Europe was transmitted to the colonists in North America by skilled craftsmen, here is a portion of a letter to the Society for Propagating the Gospel describing the population of North Carolina in July, 1711, as consisting mainly of "carpenters, joiners, wheelwrights, coopers, tanners, shoe makers, tallow chandlers and what not." He also mentioned women workers, soap makers, starch makers and dyers. "He or she that can not do these things will have a bad time of it."

DEVELOPING THE AXE
AGRICULTURAL OPPORTUNITY

The first settlers at Jamestown and Plymouth used land in their immediate vicinity that was already cleared. Some of this cleared land had previously been used for planting by the local Indians, whose nature religion dictated a primitive form of crop rotation. They would leave fallow for many years a field that had produced a successful crop so the land would regain its strength. The European settlers were quick to cultivate this unoccupied land or ground that had been cleared by natural fire.

The earliest settlers learned from the Indians how to use this readily available land to plant corn, a native crop which yielded more per acre and grew faster than all their European seed. At the Plymouth Colony the Indians voluntarily taught the white foreigners how to plant and fertilize the corn seed with dead fish, but at Jamestown the Indians were forced to help. In 1609, for example, Captain John Smith captured two Indians and made them "teach us how to order and plant our fields." Under the supervision of these prisoners, the Jamestown colony initially planted 40 acres in corn and, within five years, had 200 acres devoted to corn cultivation.

As new settlers came, the instantly available fields could not supply sufficient crops and the forest had to be removed. At first the settlers used the Indian technique of bleeding the trees to death by "girdling" them. This technique of removing a complete circle of bark at the base of the tree required a

minimum amount of labor but the tree died slowly and still had to be removed. The main means for mastering the dense forest was the axe, which quickly became the traditional symbol of America's frontier. However, the European axe first available to the settlers was a heavy and awkward tool, not really suited for use in a thickly forested country, although it had served this purpose in England where the trees had been converted into ships so Britannia could rule the waves.

The American colonists observed that the native Indian axes and tomahawks, while often having a stone or flint cutting edge inferior to European steel, had handles that provided better grip than the traditional European axe because they were curved at the lower end and somewhat flared out. Taking this hint, American craftsmen redesigned the chopping axe handle and then produced a thinner, sharper and broader blade for the broad axe used in finishing the wood.

Benjamin H. Latrobe, the architect and civil engineer who designed the early Federal buildings for the U.S. government, described the improvements in the American chopping axe by noting that it acted upon the tree "more from its wedge-like form, its own weight and skillful swing, which gives it impetus, than from any great exertion of strength on the part of the woodsman . . . The American axe may well rank with maize and steam as one of three things which have conquered the western world."

BUILDING THE NEW HOMES

The trees cleared from the land in order to cultivate crops provided the material for building. The earliest settlers often lived temporarily aboard the ships which brought them but when the ships left, the colonists hastily erected primitive shelters which were often no more than holes in the sides of hills poorly covered with thatched roofs. The records show that the Pilgrims of Plymouth and the Puritans of the Massachusetts Bay Colony (the differences between "Pilgrims" and "Puritans" being that the Pilgrims of Plymouth were an extremist wing of the Puritan movement who not only

Samuel Morse *at the age of 59. Morse invented the telegraph in 1844. He also perfected the system of dots and dashes used in telegraphic communication which bears his name.*

The proliferation *of telegraph wires across the eastern seaboard within one decade of the invention of the telegraph led cartoonist Thomas Nast to create this humorous drawing of telegraph wires being strung in New York City in the 1880's. Note that the wires are being strung through a living room.*

Elias Howe, *developer of the automatic sewing machine, is shown in this ink sketch giving a demonstration of the machine's speed in 1845. Howe is racing five seamstresses while two garment factory owners look on.*

wanted to abandon the Church of England but preferred to destroy it, did not build these covered cellars but "English Wigwams" in which bent poles were covered with a thatched roof. These structures looked something like the frame-top of the later covered wagon.

Interestingly enough, the English colonists ignored all the architectural forms developed by the American Indian to provide adequate shelter from North American climate—the bark houses of the Penobscots, the long houses of the Iroquois, the tipis of the Crows, the mounds of the Mandans, the pueblos of the Zuni, the hogans of the Navajo, and the log dwellings of Puget Sound. The English colonists even ignored the sturdy log cabin, first introduced into America by Swedish settlers as early as 1638. There was only one kind of building suitable for a home: the wooden house of the type

they were used to in England. The boards for these buildings were first crudely prepared by European hand tools and later by wind or water-driven saws constructed by the colonists. The earliest of these wooden buildings, often having wooden chimneys insulated with clay, were very vulnerable to fire as the clay daubs would sometimes fall off. The Pilgrims reported in 1624 that out of 32 dwellings, seven were lost in one year due to fire.

The log cabin, a structure entirely unknown in England, was spread inland after 1718 by Scotch-Irish immigrants to the New World. (The North German immigrants who arrived in 1710 had also built log cabins as they had known them at home.) The advantage of the log cabin was that one man working by himself with an axe could quickly put together a cabin without saws, hammers, nails, pegs or plaster. The log cabin required no laborious sawing of boards and no long process of drying them. And with the help of a few neighbors, a log cabin could be put together with great speed. The log cabin also had the advantage of being perfectly tight and dry, unlike the leaky and illness-producing hovels originally built by all except the most well-to-do of the English.

One historian, Stewart H. Holbrook, noting that it was the rigid cultural habits of the British which prevented them from adopting the most suitable home devised for pioneering people, says that the introduction of the log cabin in 1638 was the most important single event between Columbus and the beginning of the American Revolution, a period of two hundred and eighty years.

During the period from 1700 to the start of the Revolution brick and stone began to replace wood in a number of settlements. The art of brick making had been brought over from Europe and most bricks were made on the building site. Some, however, were brought over as ballast on the ships which carried the colonists. In the Northern colonies, where field stones were easily and cheaply obtained, stone houses were built as early as 1639.

The mortar to build both stone and brick buildings required lime. When this could not be obtained from limestone, oyster

Although many men *were eventually awarded patents for various kinds of sewing machines, the machine perfected by Elias Howe, pictured here, was the best.*

shells collected in the shallows of the Atlantic were used to provide the lime. In the Southern colonies few stone buildings were erected due to the scarcity of stone.

DEVELOPING THE PLOW

The Pilgrims did not use a plow until twelve years after first landing at Plymouth. In 1637 there were only 37 plows in the Massachusetts Bay Colony.

The plow used by the Puritans was a bulky contraption of wood twelve feet long and drawn by eight or ten oxen with a man sitting on top to try to keep the tool from bouncing away from the ground. Despite the weight of the man on the ten foot beam, another man had to follow with a heavy iron hoe to dig up the places the plow had missed. By the time of the American Revolution strips of wrought iron were attached to the wooden moldboard, the part of the plow designed to overturn the sliced sod, which was often too heavy to be turned by the farmer.

Charles Newbold, of Burlington, New Jersey, took out the first patent on a plow in 1797. Newbold's plow was made of cast iron and could be guided by one man and two oxen. Thomas Jefferson, who had made the first scientific studies to determine the best shape for a plow's moldboard, took an interest in Newbold's invention, but the farmers that saw the plow swiftly and neatly turn the furrows mistakenly believed that the cast iron would poison the ground. So the American farmer, disbelieving or not even hearing of the work of Jefferson and Newbold, continued to drag a rough-hewn tree behind a small herd of oxen at plowing time.

In 1819, Jethro Wood of New York patented a cast iron plow of completely interchangeable parts. The various parts were made in separate pieces so any worn part could be quickly replaced, thus beginning an entirely new era in agricultural tools. But the continuing prejudice against cast iron for plowing forced Wood into financial difficulties. Toward the end of Wood's life, the American farmer began to abandon his soil-poisoning superstition and accepted Wood's invention, but dozens of patent infringers then forced Wood into court to defend his legal rights. In 1833 Congress came to the defense of Wood and, at the time of his death in 1834, thousands of iron plows were in use.

However, as the American farmer went further West and began to cultivate the virgin soil of Indiana, Illinois, Iowa, and Wisconsin, the roots of the long prairie grass and the heavy, sticky soil quickly dulled the soft iron plow which had been relatively efficient even in the stonier soil of New York, New Jersey, Pennsylvania, and Virginia. In 1833, blacksmith John Lane of Chicago attempted to solve the new problem by fastening strips of the finest saw steel available to a wooden plow. Lane did not patent his invention although it worked, and soon every country blacksmith who had heard of the improvement was fitting old hand saw blades to old wooden plows. Daniel Webster, trying to design a plow that would go deep enough to remove stumps, then produced a device too unwieldy for wide use.

It was left to John Deere, a giant young blacksmith of Grand Detour, Illinois, who probably had not even heard of the improved plow of John Lane, to design a light plow using the heavy steel of a circular mill saw which parted the sticky soil of the West as easily as the cast iron plow turned the sandy soil of the East. At first Deere imported saw steel from Germany, but in 1846 he had manufactured for him at Quincy, Illinois, the "first slab of cast plow steel" ever rolled in the United States. Deere thus started one of the most

Another sewing machine *which received a patent and became competition for the Howe machine was that one developed by Singer. This ink sketch shows Singer's original sewing machine.*

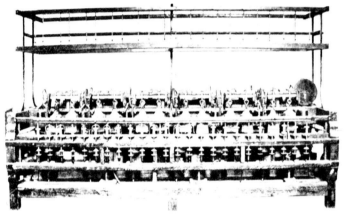

Samuel Slater, *an enterprising worker in the milling industry, traveled to England and worked for a while there in British mills. When he returned to America he brought with him in his memory the plans for the Arkwright spinning frame, which he then built and assembled in this country. The Arkwright spinning frame was only one of several intricate machines invented in England that Slater was able to "re-invent" from memory in this country.*

The first practical typewriter, *which was invented by three Americans—Christopher Sholes, Carlos Glidden, and Samuel Soule—in 1867.*

The invention of the cotton gin *by Eli Whitney radically changed the economy and culture of the South. Before its invention cotton was processed by hand, a slow and not particularly profitable system. After the invention of the gin, cotton became the staple commodity of Southern plantations and put the South in a position to rival the North in certain kinds of economic expansion.*

Railroad transportation *in America was greatly expanded through George Pullman's invention of the luxury railroad car. Pullman's development of overnight sleeping cars created a mass clientele for transcontinental travel.*

successful American companies manufacturing farm equipment, producing thirteen thousand steel plows in 1858 alone. Lane and Deere's contribution to plow manufacture made the cultivation of the great plains of the Mid-West possible and prepared the country to feed the future increase in population.

The development of the plow continued as other sections of American technology evolved. James Oliver, a young farmer from Indiana, bought a fourth interest in a South Bend foundry in 1855, and to everyone's surprise succeeded after twelve years in developing a cast iron casting that was soft and tough inside but hard and polished enough on the outside wearing faces for plowing the virgin prairie soil.

With the introduction of stronger and lighter plows, horses began to replace the slower moving oxen. In 1856, Obed Hussey of Baltimore built a steam-driven plow, and J.W. Fawkes of Lancaster, Pennsylvania, built in 1858 a steam contraption that pulled eight plows. But even though steam power by this time was producing a revolution in transportation technology, the steam engine proved too cumbersome and expensive for American farmers. Experiments with steam were abandoned with the introduction of the internal combustion engine, gasoline tractors in 1901 and disc gang plows on which the operator could ride.

DEVELOPING THE HARROW

Plowing, however, does not totally prepare soil for actual planting. The clods left by plowing must be broken up and the rough surface leveled. In colonial times, a branch of a tree with many small limbs was pulled over the soil to accomplish this pulverizing, a system not much advanced beyond the laborers of antiquity called "clodhoppers" who would break up the clods with a stick and their feet. A series of American improvements made by anonymous craftsmen resulted in the "A" harrow in which two pieces of timber fastened together in the angular shape of the first letter of the alphabet had metal teeth inserted in holes bored or burned in the wood.

In the 1860's a spring toothed harrow was developed which could be adjusted for depth and would not be clogged by roots or rocks. In 1847 G. Page devised and patented a single disc harrow. By the 1870's, multiple disc harrows, adjustable by section and with automatic scrapers, were in

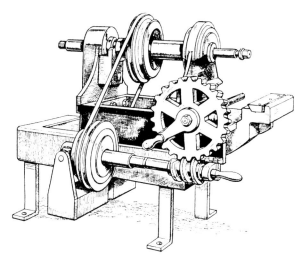

Eli Whitney *did not stop his inventing with the cotton gin. He went on to develop a system of mass producing muskets, and, with the invention of a machine used to milling interchangeable parts, pictured here, Whitney did much to establish factory production techniques in America.*

529

general use. No major improvement of the harrow has occurred in modern times but the preparation of the seed bed is now considered so important for efficient agriculture that four to six harrowing and rolling operations are common before planting.

The invention of improved locomotives *and more comfortable cars pushed the demand for railroad lines across the country. The joining of the nation by rail occurred at Promontory, Utah, on May 10, 1869. Union Pacific's locomotive No. 119, right, and Central Pacific's* Jupiter *were joined at the ceremony of the laying of the golden spike commemorating this historic event.*

MECHANIZED PLANTING

The early colonists planted their corn seeds Indian fashion, a few "to a hill" according to the old colonial jingle:

> One for the blackbird,
> One for the crow,
> One for the cutworm,
> And three to grow.

In the decade before the Civil War, hundreds of patents were issued for "corn droppers" attached to hoes, walking sticks, and horse drawn hoppers which could plant from six to eight acres per day. In the post-Civil War period an improved corn planter which counted the grains as they dropped and a corn "checker," operated by a trip wire so the seeds were dropped at regular intervals, permitted the planting of 12 to 15 acres per day. The time had passed when a farmer with a sack of grain around his neck would laboriously measure out a few corn grains to each hill.

Other grains and grass seeds were traditionally sown by hand. In 1701 a revolutionary grain drill was invented in England by Jethro Tull, who took parts of an organ, a wheel barrow and a cider mill to develop a seed box which would

Two of the greatest figures *in the history of American inventions, Henry Ford, left, and Thomas Edison, when they met at Ford's factory in Michigan. Their combined inventions and production techniques changed the course of civilization.*

Henry Ford, *right, admires his first automobile, built by him in 1892. Although Ford did not invent the automobile, his system of using mass production and interchangeable parts made possible the production of automobiles on a large scale, literally putting America on wheels.*

Edison's earliest efforts *were spent at perfecting the phonograph. This drawing shows a cross section of Edison's first phonograph and the method in which it operated.*

measure out the grain for planting and then cover the rows in one operation. In 1733, Tull published a book in which, according to one systematic historian, he devoted 12,662 words to describing the seed box alone before starting to discuss the rest of his grain drill. But Americans evidently did not pay attention to Tull's invention. In 1799, an American, Eliakim Spooner, re-invented the grain drill but so little attention was again paid to this device that Spooner's plans did not survive.

In 1840, J. Gibbons of Adrian, Michigan, patented a grain drill with a regulating device and, in 1842, two Pennsylvania farmers named Pennock patented a more successful grain drill, eventually selling several hundred of them. After the Civil War, when the Pennock patents had expired, grain drills were produced in quantity. Modern machines drill as many as 18 rows at a time, introduce fertilizer into the furrow, and cover the seed with loose soil. Few fundamental changes have occurred in grain seed drills since the mid-1870's. And until very recent times, the planting of vegetables, potatoes and many plants was done with the hands aided by the hoe and trowel.

THE MOST IMPORTANT AGRICULTURAL DEVELOPMENT

"As ye sow, so shall ye reap." The colonial harvesting of grain crops such as wheat, oats, rye, and barley was first done by hand with the scythe in the old world manner except that the steel blades were sharp as swords. However, the scythe limited the amount of land that could be profitably planted as

The Ford production line *in 1913. Henry Ford was the first person to begin mass producing automobiles. Here the bodies are being fitted to the chassis on Ford's first production line, set up near Highland Park, Michigan.*

The story of the invention *of the telephone is depicted in this drawing. Alexander Graham Bell, foreground, spilled some acid and called out to his assistant, "Mr. Watson, come here, I need you." The assistant, in the other room, heard Bell's words, and the invention of the telephone was made.*

one man could only cut about an acre per day, even with the improved blade. Shortly before the American Revolution, a new hand harvesting tool called a "cradle" was in use. The handle and the cutting blade of the cradle were similar to the old-fashioned scythe, but it also had a few wooden fingers attached to a frame shaped like, and parallel to, the blade which gathered the grain into neat bundles as it fell. This simple improvement made it possible for a strong man to cut three or four acres of grain per day and permitted the farmer to increase substantially his acreage of grain at a time when Washington's army needed to be fed.

The most important development in agricultural technology was the development, in the nineteenth century, of the harvesting machine called the reaper. The problem was that there was a natural bottleneck in the production of wheat. It all ripens at the same time in a given area and must be harvested within about a week—ten days in perfect weather, four in bad or the seed falls to the ground and all is lost. Under American conditions of cheap land it was not difficult for a farmer to raise more wheat than he could harvest for himself and one other family. Consequently, when there was a shortage in the American crop, as happened in 1838 when only 78 bushels were shipped from Chicago, grain had to be imported from Europe. But only ten years later, Chicago was shipping two million bushels of wheat because Cyrus McCormick had by then invented the reaper, and was selling hundreds of them to American farmers.

In 1816 a farmer in Virginia named Robert McCormick tried to build a reaper by duplicating the movements of a human harvester's arms but gave up this attempt in 1831.

Alexander Graham Bell, *inventor of the telephone.*

However, his son, Cyrus, who had worked alongside his father, built a moderately successful reaper in 1831 which he improved and patented by 1834. Unlike Bell's reaper, the McCormick machine was horse pullee as the actual cutter, a vibrating sickle-edged blade, was set at the side of the machine and right angled, along with a reel mechanism to bend the heads of the grain toward the knife.

One year before Cyrus McCormick obtained his patent, Obed Hussey, a Yankee sailor, had patented a reaper in which, following Bell, the cutting knife operated like a shear. This cutting knife, which consisted of vibrating notched fingers, eventually became the standard for all reapers and harvesters. However, Hussey stubbornly refused to improve his machine although it originally sold well and, as a result, was soon outstripped in sales by McCormick. In 1858 Hussey sold his interest in his reaping machine for $200,000 and turned to the invention of a steam plow as previously mentioned.

In 1841 McCormick had sold two machines for one hundred dollars each. In 1842 he sold seven at the same price. By 1844 he had sold another 79. By 1851 he was building 1,000 reapers a year. Six years later, in 1857, McCormick built 23,000 machines. His profit in that year alone was one and a quarter million dollars. By 1860, at the beginning of the Civil War, about 80,000 reapers in the mid-West helped produce a national wheat crop of two hundred million bushels. And four years later, at the end of the Civil War, the annual output of harvesting machines had grown to 70,000 units. This was an indication of how mechanized Northern agriculture had become as European de-

Model of the first telephone, *invented by Bell in 1875.*

THIS MODEL OF BELL'S FIRST
TELEPHONE IS A DUPLICATE OF THE INSTRU-
MENT THROUGH WHICH SPEECH SOUNDS WERE

mand for American wheat increased, as shortages of farm labor were brought about first by the gold rush and later by the Civil War, and as the building of railroads made possible the expansion of the wheat-growing territory. The McCormick reaper was thus as important to the development of the North as was the development of the Whitney cotton gin to the Southern economy.

OTHER AGRICULTURAL OPPORTUNITIES

The expansion of agriculture in the growing American economy demanded that breeds of animals be improved, adequate strains of grass developed to feed the livestock, irrigation systems planned, fences built, and new ways devised to preserve and pack seed, sometimes from abroad, for shipment to the American farmers who would plant them. Scientific societies were formed to promote agriculture and experimental gardens established to test theories. The tremendous increase in the quantity of grain being grown and threshed inspired the development of the grain storage elevator, a patent which was granted to Joseph Dart in 1842.

THE DAIRY INDUSTRY

For many years people in the cities had received their milk supply from local dairies which fed their cattle on discarded mash from breweries. With the introduction of better feeding methods and a better distribution system, New York, for example, began to receive whole milk which actually contained cream from more distant dairies, and the customers at first complained of the unexpected yellow scum. By 1852 shipments were being made in milk cans very similar to those of today. During the 1850's iced railroad cars were developed for the transportation of milk. Factory production of butter was developed. Cheesemaking was transferred from the home to the factory. Jacob Russell of Baltimore began the commercial production of ice cream in 1851. Gail Borden, one of the founders of the Texas Republic, applied for a patent in 1851 on a method for adding sugar and heating it in a vacuum so it could be shipped long distances. After a delay of three years, when he proved that his vacuum process was unique, his patent was granted and Borden was ready by

1861 to supply Civil War soldiers with canned milk, another factor along with those already mentioned which made the American dairy industry by 1860 the most important one of its kind in the world.

THE "FOUNDING FATHERS" AS FARMERS

Many of the "Founding Fathers" of the United States played a significant and direct role in this development of agriculture. George Washington, for one, carefully tested seeds, kept careful notes about the planting times and crop yields on his farms, noted the best seasons for harvest and listed the mechanical improvements introduced on his properties. Noting the way that tobacco depleted the soil, he experimented with strengthening the land through the rotation of crops such as lucerne, alfalfa, clover, and wheat.

Washington is known to have experimented with imported wheat seed from England, Siberia, and Poland. He sowed wheat in dry soil to see what resulted. In 1769 he exported 6,000 bushels of wheat to the West Indies. Much of this wheat was ground in his own mills. He spent time with his blacksmith perfecting a plow, designed an automatic seeder, bred sheep for better wool yield, raised the weight of his cattle by proper feeding and sheltering, imported pigs and mules, studied new threshing machines, and experimented with increasing the yield of oats.

Thomas Jefferson stated that "those who labor in the earth are the chosen people of God. Cultivators of the earth are our most valuable citizens. They are the most vigorous, the most independent, the most virtuous; they are tied to their country, and wedded to its interest and liberty by the most lasting ties." His farms at Monticello became experimental gardens where new crops, new methods of cultivation and new machinery were tried out. For hillsides, he proposed contour plowing. In his famous *Notes on the State of Virginia*, Jefferson scientifically described the physical features of the region and classified the observed plants in the greatest of detail. He compiled thousands of meteorological observations on rainfall, wind velocity, temperature, barometric pressure, and seasons of frost and heavy dew. He was elected a member of the French Academy of Agriculture for his work in designing an efficient plow, observed agricultural development in France, England and Italy with a view to introducing the latest developments in America and brought seeds from abroad for the experimental use of American farmers.

INDUSTRIAL DEVELOPMENT IN PRE-REVOLUTIONARY AMERICA

Glassmaking was the first industry in America, beginning as early as 1608 in Virginia when eight Polish and German craftsmen began making samples of window glass, glass bottles, lamps, tableware, and glass beads which were highly valued by the Indians near Jamestown as a medium of exchange. In 1639, a glass works was set up in Salem, Massachusetts, but produced some green and brown colored glass which was not very transparent. In 1764, Henry William Stiegel set up a large glass plantation in Pennsylvania similar to a large plantation he already owned to produce iron. His English and German glass workers produced some very fine flint glass tableware in a number of brilliant colors which are now collector's items.

Homes were first lit by candles made from the fat of deer or bear and later from beef or mutton tallow. Before the end of the 17th century, candles were made from the bayberry of the myrtle bush, which burned more slowly, produced more light and did not have the often offensive odor of smelly animal fat. By the mid 1700's, American whalers began to bring back a sufficient amount of spermaceti to make quantities of candles. These candles had the virtue of giving off about

This historic take off *occurred in 1910, barely three years after the invention of the airplane. Photograph shows Eugene Ely taking off from the deck of the cruiser* Birmingham.

three times more light than an ordinary tallow candle. The factory manufacture of candles began on a large scale in the late 1700's. Candle making was thus one of the first family chores to be removed from the home. A further improvement in lighting took place when glass and metal chandeliers for candles as well as candle reflectors began to be produced by skilled craftsmen for sale.

One of the earliest industries to develop in New England was devoted to the production of iron. Joseph Jencks, a master mechanic, erected the first furnace at Saugus (Lynn), Massachusetts, to produce pots, pans, nails, hinges, horseshoes and needed tools and received in 1646 from the Massachusetts General Court the first patent reportedly ever issued in America protecting his enterprise from competition for a period of 14 years. Jenks built America's first fire engine, cast a die for the first coined money, modified the English scythe and unsuccessfully attempted to produce wire commercially.

By 1776, there were nearly 200 iron forges operating in the colonies, more than in all of England and Wales. In 1775 colonial production of iron totalled 30,000 tons. America's total production of iron was one-seventh of the world's output, only Russia and Sweden producing more. (However, by the turn of the century the solution of technical problems permitting the use of coal in pig iron production caused an astonishing growth in Britain's production and use of iron). At the time of the Revolution the American colonies of England were producing very little steel.

Probably a greater deterrent to the development of large scale manufacturing in the colonies than British opposition was the high price of labor resulting from the desire of most of the colonists to take advantage of the cheap land available. When the colonies responded to the Stamp Act of 1765 by resolutions declaring their intent to promote colonial manufacture and the Board of Trade in Great Britain consequently

Harvey Firestone, *invented a process for vulcanizing raw rubber into a new commercially applicable rubber compound.*

This picture shows *the men responsible for the completion of the first transcontinental telephone cable on January 25, 1915. Seated at the center of the table is Alexander Graham Bell, inventor of the telephone.*

ordered all colonial governors to report on manufacturing in the colonies since 1734, the response of New York Governor Henry Moore was both typical and revealing:

"... The price of labour is so great in this part of the world that it will always prove the greatest obstacle to any manufactures attempted to be set up here, and the genius of the people in a country where everyone can have land to work upon leads them so naturally into agriculture that it prevails over every other occupation. There can be no stronger instances of this than in the servants imported from Europe of different trades; as soon as the time stipulated in their indentures is expired, they immediately quit their masters and get a small tract of land, in settling which for the first three or four years they lead miserable lives, and in the most abject poverty, but all this is patiently borne and submitted to with the greatest cheerfulness, the satisfaction of being landholders smooths every difficulty and makes them prefer this manner of living to that comfortable subsistence which they could procure for themselves and their families by working at the trades in which they were brought up . . ."

Nevertheless a hat industry functioned in the colonies because of the availability and cheapness of beaver, causing Parliament to respond with the Hat Act of 1732 limiting colonial competition with British manufacturers. English shipbuilders likewise protested to Parliament against the fact that perhaps one-third of the tonnage in the carrying trade of the empire just before the American Revolution had been built in the colonies, where fine ship timber was readily available. However, in this instance Parliament did not respond because English timber was scarce and it was obvious that Britain's commercial and naval strength depended upon the shipbuilding of the colonies. In the Naval Stores Act of 1704, Parliament even encouraged the manufacture of tar, pitch, turpentine, hemp, and masts in the American colonies to free Great Britain from dependence on Baltic countries for these items.

BENJAMIN FRANKLIN, COLONIAL RENAISSANCE MAN

Benjamin Franklin was perhaps the most inventive man of Colonial America. In 1742, Franklin introduced his first major invention, "The Pennsylvania Stove," which utilized the heating effects of circulating hot and fresh air, a considerable improvement upon the open English fireplace then generally used throughout the colonies despite the fact that this European design allowed four-fifths of the heat to escape up the chimney. In writing about this invention, Franklin commented on the inconvenience of the early colonial house and observed that by using his fireplace, "People need not crowd so close around the Fire, but may sit near the Window, and have the Benefit of the Light for Reading, Writing, and Needlework, etc. They may sit with comfort in any Part of the Room, which is a very considerable Advantage in a large family." Offered a patent for this "Franklin Stove" (as the invention came to be called) by the Governer of Pennsylvania, Franklin declined because "as we enjoy great advantage from the inventions of others, we should be glad of copy missing!

Franklin also studied smokey chimneys, invented bifocal spectacles, developed a long-handled grasping device for taking library books down from high shelves (which later became common in groceries), suggested daylight saving, designed an improved street lamp for Philadephia, built a flexible catheter to relieve his brother's bladder obstruction, founded the American Philosophical Society, invented a strange musical instrument called the "armonica" for which Mozart and Beethoven composed music, established the first circulating library in the country, was appointed in 1753 as one of two Deputy Postmasters General (and later as Postmaster General for the United States), in 1754 developed a plan for union of the colonies which led the writer Balzac to credit Franklin as having invented the United States of America, was a member of the Commission which drafted the Declaration of Independence, and was an active participant at the Convention of 1787 which framed the Constitution of the United States.

Franklin's accomplishments are almost too staggering to mention: He was also an abolitionist, athlete, composer, diplomat, economist, fireman, landlord, linguist, Freemason, nudist, manufacturer, spelling reformer, jolly good fellow and the inventor of hand-held paddles to speed swimmers. He was one of the true giants of all human history.

During the Revolutionary War there were also important developments in clothing manufacture. Christopher Tulley devised a spinning machine that would spin twenty-four threads of cotton or wool at one time. Oliver Evans developed a machine to manufacture the hand cards used in processing woolen cloth which cut and bent the iron teeth required at the rate of 3,000 a minute. Eastern Pennsylvania was the location of a factory for linen printing set up by Nathaniel Norgrove. Improvements in tanning technology resulted in leather uniforms for numbers of soldiers in the Continental Army although most colonial soldiers were clothed in the same belted homespun cotton shirt then used by farm laborers and called a smock-frock.

As a matter of fact, most of the current portraits showing revolutionary officers and soldiers in good uniforms are nothing but propaganda. Washington, himself, was far more accurate in noting how difficult it was to equip the new army with adequate clothing, shoes and tents. Writing about the soldiers at Valley Forge in 1777, he said, "Men are confined to hospitals or in farmers' houses for want of shoes. We have this day no less than two thousand eight hundred and ninety eight men in camp unfit for duty, because they are barefoot and otherwise naked." From Valley Forge Washington also wrote, "There are now in this Army . . . 4000 men wanting blankets, near 200 of which have never had one, altho' some of them have been 12 months in service." However, the principal reason why Washington's army went shoeless, blanketless, and hungry was not for an absolute lack of supplies but because farmers and merchants were reluctant to exchange merchandise for possibly worthless paper money. For example, the merchants of Philadelphia in 1781 refused to furnish General Greene with 5,000 uniforms although they had the cloth because the General wanted to pay them with French bills of exchange.

THE PATENTS OF OLIVER EVANS

In its very first Article, the new U.S. Constitution of 1787 provided that Congress shall "promote the Progress of Science and useful Arts by securing for limited times to Authors and Inventors the exclusive right to their respective writings and discoveries." Congress responded in 1790 with its first patent law granting a 14 year patent to any citizen or foreigner after a federal committee had determined that the discovery was truly original. Samuel Hopkins of Vermont was granted the first patent under this new law for "a new method of making pot and pearl ashes." The second patent was awarded for a new process of making candles. The third such patent was for new and improved flour milling machinery invented by Oliver Evans, called the "Father of Mechanized Flour Milling" because of his application of power to all phases of grain processing. Before Evans, power had been applied only to the operation of the millstone.

Evans also pioneered in other applications of steam power. In 1802 he was the first to attempt steam navigation on the lower Mississippi River. The steam engine involved was used later to operate a steam-driven saw mill, eventually leading to the introduction of the circular saw following the close of the War of 1812. In 1803 Evans was operating his machine shop in Philadelphia with steam power. In 1804 he constructed, at a cost of $3,700, a reciprocating steam engine with which he could break and grind twelve tons of plaster of paris in 24 hours. He also "applied to saw stone in Market Street [Philadelphia] where the driving of twelve saws, sawing at the rate of a hundred feet of marble in twelve hours, made a great show . . ." Although Evans complained that people doubted his steam engine even after seeing how much manual labor it replaced, he was given an order by the Philadelphia Board of Health in 1804 for a steam engine to be used in cleaning docks. Since the machine had to be built sixteen miles up the river in a shed that itself was a mile and a half from water, Evans designed his machine with both wheels and water paddles so it could get to its final destination under its own power. It was the first wheeled vehicle to move under its own power in America. By 1811 Evans was building steam engines of 70 horsepower. By 1814 steam power was being used to operate printing presses in New York City.

THE PATENT OFFICE BURNS DOWN

Following the Patent Act of 1790, there was such a flood of applications ranging from new processes to make nails to new types of lightning rods that the federal committee fell far behind in the processing of petitions. A revision made to the patent law in 1793, therefore, simply required the inventor to swear in his application that the invention was original and did not infringe upon existing patents. This 1793 law also restricted patent issuance to U.S. citizens. In 1811, inventors Oliver Evans, Robert Fulton, Eli Whitney and others hired a lobbyist in Washington to get the 1793 law changed but nothing was done to solve the grievances of the inventors until 1835, when Senator John Ruggles of Maine undertook a study of the American patent system. Ruggles reported to the Senate that, ''For more than forty years, the Department of State has issued patents on every application, *without any examination into the merits or novelty of the invention.* Many patents granted are worthless and void and conflict upon one another, and a great many law suits arise from this condition. Frauds develop. People copy existing patents, make slight changes and are granted patents. Patents become of little value, and the object of the patent laws is in great measure defeated.''

Ruggles' recommendations resulted in Congress passing a new patent law in 1836 re-establishing the provision that there be a preliminary examination of the novelty and patentability of the invention. Patents were given serial numbers and Senator Ruggles himself obtained Patent Number One for an improvement in locomotives. The new law was so much more stringent than the old that the number of patents issued dropped from seven hundred a year to half that number. However, disaster soon struck. The old hotel building which the government had bought to house the Patent Office, General Post Office and Washington City's Post Office burned down on December 14, 1836, destroying 7000 models, 9000 drawings and 168 rolls of records.

In 1842 the law was again modified to limit patents to seven years but this was then modified in 1861 to the present term of seventeen years. Since about 1880 the Patent Office has become so cluttered with models that the requirement for working models, although maintained, is insisted upon only in the case of perpetual motion machines or other devices that seem to violate what is known of the laws of nature. Almost four million patents have now been issued in the United States but the complexity of technology is so great that since about 1920 the number of patents issued in relation to population has actually been decreasing.

THE FIRST SUCCESSFUL AMERICAN FACTORY

After the American Revolution of 1776, many attempts were made to promote the factory system in the U.S. but, despite the prizes advertised by the new government, all attempts failed. The machinery available in the U.S. was inadequate because the British government refused to allow any of its new inventions to leave England. Britain forbade not only the exportation of completed machinery but of plans and the emigration of workers having the technical knowledge to construct and operate the machines. However, it was impossible for Britain to maintain this embargo forever and the American states advertised their prizes for the encouragement of U.S. manufacture in English newspapers. One such advertisement by the Pennsylvania legislature was read by a young Englishman, Samuel Slater, who had just completed an apprenticeship for a partner of Richard Arkwright and knew how to use and repair all of England's textile machinery. He carefully left England without taking any sketches of the machinery and without even telling his immediate family, until the day of departure, that his destination was the United States.

Arriving in Philadelphia in 1789, Slater contacted a famous Quaker merchant, Moses Brown. The young Englishman was offered all the profits less machinery cost of an inoperative textile manufactory owned by Brown if Slater could make the mill operate. Upon seeing the plant, however, Slater said, ''These will not do. They are good for nothing in their present condition. Nor could they be made to answer.'' Thereupon, Slater drew from memory the designs of the English textile machines developed by Arkwright and, with the help of an exceptional blacksmith, Oziel Wilkinson, built the first American factory. The plant opened on December 21, 1790. Based on the English factory system it was primarily staffed by children four to ten years old who, with their new machines, could easily outproduce any adult textile craftsman working by hand in the old manner. Slater, although not actually inventing or even improving on prior inventions, thus brought the industrial revolution to the United States much as the skilled craftsmen among the pre-Revolutionary colonists had brought all previous European technology to the New World.

ELI WHITNEY: THE COTTON GIN CHANGES THE SOUTH

By 1790, the institution of slavery was dying out in North America. Slaves cost more to maintain than they were able to produce. Eli Whitney was to change this. Two kinds of cotton were growing in the South. Sea Island cotton or long-staple would grow only in the sandy soil along the coast. Although limited in quantity, long-staple cotton was profitable because its fibers could easily be separated from the slippery black seeds by a device which looked like an old-fashioned clothes wringer, called by Southerners an ''engine,'' slurred to ''gin.'' Short staple or upland cotton, had fibers of two different lengths, the shorter tightly stuck to green seeds. Although short staple cotton could be grown anywhere, it was not profitable to cultivate it because the seeds had to be laboriously separated from the fibers by hand. Ten hours of hand work were needed to separate one pound of fiber from three pounds of the small green seeds. Eli Whitney, a young teacher from the North who had distinguished himself during the Revolutionary War as a nail maker and the country's sole producer of ladies' hatpins, became aware of this problem while living on a Southern plantation. In less than two weeks, Whitney had designed a machine which duplicated the hand movements required to clean the cotton. A wire sieve replaced the hand that would hold the seed, while a revolving drum with hook shaped wire teeth replaced the hand that would tease out the short fibers. A quickly rotating brush to clean the lint off the hooks completed the simple invention.

Enough upland cotton could now be cultivated and cleaned to provide the new textile mills of New England and of Old England as well. Cotton fabric, from being a luxury item, was now the poor man's cloth. Large plantations were developed, slavery increased, and a one-crop economy which exhausted the soil and required Western expansion became prevalent in the South. The foundation for America's great Civil War was thus laid as the Northern states did not want the South to dominate Congress with the votes of new Western states.

In 1791, America supplied only 138,234 pounds of cotton of a total world production of 490 million pounds. By the time of America's 150th anniversary, the U.S. alone was producing over 7 billion pounds of cotton primarily because of the cotton gin. The cotton gin permitted one slave to seed a thousand pounds of cotton in the time it originally took a slave to seed five pounds by hand.

In 1798, based mainly on his prestige as the inventor of the cotton gin, Whitney was given a contract from the federal government to make 10,000 muskets. Although he was unable to fulfill this contract in the required two years, Whitney, using machine tools that were guided by jigs and templates, succeeded in producing muskets with completely interchangeable parts. These unique machine tools and patterns, permitting the production of parts to standards of precision previously unobtainable, made possible the entire system of mass production. This was a revolutionary innovation of the Industrial Revolution, ranking along with the invention of the steam engine itself. Whitney's "American System of Manufacture" was eventually to transform the face of the North as much as his cotton gin transformed the face of the South.

FROM THE REVOLUTION TO THE CIVIL WAR

The development of the patent system, the cotton gin, the factory system, the mass production of interchangeable parts, the textile industry of New England, the design of mechanized farm equipment concluding with McCormick's reaper, set the stage for America's growth in the years between the American Revolutionn of 1776 and the Civil War of 1861. There were enormous changes in transportation, typified by the development of the steamboat and railroads, the canals and the clipper ships. The development of new printing presses, the telegraph, and the Atlantic Cable concept show the development of communication in this period. The vulcanization of rubber, the refining of sugar and oil, and new processes for producing iron and steel also took place. The sewing machine and automatic machinery for shoemaking revolutionized the clothing industry. The cities were developing and changing. It was a time of great expansion and growth.

Development of the first oil *well, Spindletop, in 1901, quickly led to numerous inventions in the drilling and refining of crude oil. This photograph is of an oil field in Texas in 1902.*

THE STORY OF THE STEAMBOAT

As early as 1784 James Rumsey of Virginia had built a small boat powered by a steam pump. By 1790, John Fitch, a watchmaker who manufactured guns for the Continental Army in the Revolutionary War, established regular steamboat passenger service on the Delaware River. He has been called the first successful builder of a steamboat in America. The *Perseverance*, the vessel he ran on the Delaware, lost money, however, because it was competing with the fastest coach lines in the U.S. and was so full of engine that there was insufficient room for paying passengers. John Stevens and his son, Robert, built a steamboat called the *Phoenix* in 1806, which was taken by sea from New York to Philadelphia, making it the first sea-going steamboat in the world.

However, August 17, 1807, the year that Robert Fulton took his steamboat, the *Clermont*, up the Hudson River from New York to Albany is usually considered as marking the beginning of steamboat navigation on American rivers. This is so even though some thirty steamboats had already been built, three of which were in practical use before the *Clermont*. Fulton's reputation had already been established before the *Clermont* for his work in canal design, the patenting in 1795 of a power shovel to be used in canal excavation and his work for the French in 1801 on the second submarine ever to be built after American David Bushnell's *Turtle*. Fulton built the 150 foot *Clermont* with a huge steam engine manufactured by Boulton and Watt in England. Bringing this engine into the United States was a considerable feat since the British government still maintained a strict embargo on machinery export. By 1815, the year of his death, Fulton had built 15 other steamers including the first steamship of war, the *Demologos*, used against the British in the War of 1812.

THE ERA OF CANALS

Since England and France had previously solved much of their internal transportation problems by the use of canals, America after its Revolution began to make the same effort. The first true canal was built in South Carolina between 1793 and 1800 at a cost of over one million dollars by a Swedish

engineer, Christian Senf. Senf singlehandedly engineered twenty-two miles of canal. The second canal built was the Middlesex Canal in Massachusetts connecting the Merrimac River to the Concord River and Boston Harbor. Finally the Erie Canal was built in New York at a cost of over seven million dollars although the original estimate was only five million. But the Erie Canal was well worth the cost. New York soon surprised New Orleans and Philadelphia in both population and wealth because the canal cut travel time and the expense of transporting freight inland from the port.

THE ERA OF RAILROADS

Most roads in the American colonies were simply trails so Americans then preferred to travel by water when they could. When Washington died at Mount Vernon, Virginia, on December 14, 1799, it took ten days for the news of this important event to reach Boston by stagecoach. Two days was the usual stagecoach time between New York and Philadelphia, although the road was the best in the country, a masterpiece of wood over mud. It was because transportation was so difficult that each community had to be more or less self-supporting. The fact that the United States became transformed within one hundred years from wilderness into a populous and prosperous country is largely due to the invention of the locomotive engine and its modification to North American conditions.

The key to a railroad is the rail system itself. The first railway in America began operation in 1828 to bring granite blocks for the Bunker Hill Monument three miles from the Quincy quarry to Boston. The actual hauling was done by horses. Steam locomotives had been proposed for America by Oliver Evans and John Stevens in the early 1800's, but it was not until 1830 that the Baltimore and Ohio Railroad was put into partial operation with the intention of using steam locomotives. Actually, the line was really opened with horse drawn cars and was briefly traveled in 1830 by Peter Cooper's *Tom Thumb*, the first American locomotive. As the *Tom Thumb* was much too light to pull a heavy load, weighing only one ton, the patriarch of American locomotives is considered to be the *Best Friend*, built at the West Point Foundry in 1830 for the South Carolina Railroad Company. Even the *Best Friend*, weighing four and a half tons, was considered too light for heavy hauling. A minimum weight of ten tons was considered necessary for the locomotive to include an adequate steam engine. The *Best Friend* pulled forty passengers in four cars at a speed of 21 miles per hour and had the distinction of being the first American locomotive to explode. This explosion led to the introduction of the "barrier car." The "barrier car" was a car loaded with bales of cotton and interposed between the locomotive and the passenger cars to protect the passengers in the event of the locomotive exploding.

Other famous names in the development of the American railroads include Matthew Baldwin, the jeweler who built the eight ton *Old Ironsides* which could haul 30 tons on a level road; John B. Jervis, who had the first eight-wheeled locomotive developed because the track would not sink under the distributed weight of the heavy engine; John Harrison, who developed the equalizing-lever which lessened the shock of the wheels going over bumps or hollows in the track; Mr. G. F. Swift, founder of the Swift meat-packing enterprise, who invented (in 1875) the refrigerator car to transport dressed meat; George Westinghouse, who developed the air brake, an important safety feature which braked all cars simultaneously; George Mortimer Pullman, who developed

luxurious sleeping and dining railroad cars for passenger use; and last but not least, mention must be made even without name of the many railroading men who invented elements of the vital signalling and automatic stop mechanisms of the modern systems. By 1850 there were almost 10,000 miles of railroads in operation. By 1860 this had tripled and half of the nation's internal commerce was being transported by rail.

THE ERA OF THE CLIPPER SHIP

Until the 1840's all large American ships were built large in the front and tapering toward a narrow stern. John W. Griffiths, marine architect of New York, wrote that this design was erroneously based on the idea that "because most of the various species of fish are largest near the head, and have their greatest transverse section forward of the center of their length, it must necessarily follow that the ship must be so constructed . . . The author can discover no analogy between the ship and fish in their evolutions through the trackless deep . . . The ship must contend with the buffetings of two elements, while the fish knows but one, and that one always tranquil." Based on this insight, Griffiths and another young American ship designer, Donald McKay, worked out the hull shapes which would present the least resistance to movement through water. The sharply pointed sterns and bows that developed, a radical departure from all ship building design before, along with longer hulls and vast expanse of sail, were the characteristic features of the American Clipper Ship that set new standards in speed for the entire world. The first clipper, the *Rainbow*, sailed to China in 92 days and literally flew home in 88 days. The second clipper built, the famous *Sea Witch*, was known as the fastest ship on the seas when it returned from Canton, China, to New York across the Pacific and around the Horn in 81 days.

Donald McKay's brother, Lauchlan, a carpenter, in 1839 wrote the first American treatise on shipbuilding, *The Practical Shipbuilder*, describing the then novel American method of building complete ship models to show lines of flotation. Lauchlan McKay eventually became one of the most famous American shipmasters of his time, breaking all kinds of speed records and having numerous adventures repairing ships at sea.

SAMUEL MORSE AND THE TELEGRAPH

The idea of using electricity to transmit information is as old as the first investigations into electricity. Franklin himself was involved in such experiments. Joseph Henry, a mathematics teacher in Albany, not only designed an electric transformer and the first electric motor (1831) but by 1831 also had sent a signal through a mile-long wire to activate an electric bell. By 1837 Samuel Morse, a portrait painter, developed a plan and a code for transmitting letters and words using an acid and zinc battery, a simple device for making and breaking the circuit, and an electromagnetic needle to receive the signal. Joseph Henry, who was by now doing other work in heat, light, and sound, generously aided Morse with advice to extend the range of Morse's device to thousands of miles by the use of relays and then helped Morse obtain a government grant of $30,000 in 1843. Morse constructed a forty mile overhead wire system from Washington and Baltimore under the terms of the government grant and, operating the Washington terminal, was able to receive news instantaneously from the Whig convention then being held in Baltimore. By 1848 many small communities were able to

This model of a modern oil refinery *points out the dramatic improvements brought about by inventors in the oil industry. The synthesis of oil into hundreds of products was the work of many anonymous inventors.*

receive news of the Mexican-American War from private telegraph lines established by Morse and his Magnetic Telegraph Company. In 1856, Hiram Sibley organized the Western Union Company and eventually gathered the best features of all the patents that by then had developed with Morse's patent as the basic core. The developing railroads began to recognize the usefulness of the telegraph system, giving a great impetus to both transportation and communication while many police and fire departments began adapting telegraphy to their needs.

THE DEVELOPMENT OF THE PRINTING PRESS

Christopher Sauer, a German publisher of Germantown, Pennsylvania, is usually given credit for constructing the first American printing press in 1760 and for casting the first type in 1772. By 1800 the manufacture of printing presses in North America had become an established business and foreign importation virtually ceased. In 1813 George Clymer invented his lever-operated Columbian press, prominently decorated with a cast-iron eagle that gave the machine its name. Otis Tufts and Peter Smith contributed to the operation of this press by a toggle joint which made the operation easier. In 1827 Samuel Rust built the Washington flat bed press which, with subsequent improvements, became such a standard for printing machines that American-made presses began to be exported to Europe. By 1827 Daniel Treadwell built a power operated press capable of 500 impressions per hour when it did not break down.

Until 1836, all types were cast by hand. In that year, however, an American, David Bruce, Jr., of New York, patented the first typecasting machine in which a pump forced molten type metal into a type mould to make a single letter at a time. In 1817 New York publishers Harper and Brothers had thirty-seven hand presses and one power press operated by a mule. The press was located on the third floor of a building, and every morning and evening the mule was hoisted to the third floor by a hoist.

Robert Hoe and his son, Richard, two of the most famous names in printing machinery history, began their careers in 1828 with a new kind of cylinder press still using type set in a flat-bed. By 1847 the Hoes had developed a revolving press in which the type was set into a cylinder. The revolving press could print 8,000 sheets of paper on one side in an hour and, with additional cylinders, could turn out 20,000 impressions an hour. A machine of this type weighed 60,000 pounds and was as large as a two-story house. It was not until after the Civil War that a self-feeding press which could print on both sides of the sheet at once was developed by William Bullock for the *Philadelphia Ledger*.

THE ATLANTIC CABLE

One of the most stupendous feats of science and technology prior to the Civil War was the laying of the Atlantic Cable to link up the telegraph systems of Europe and the United States. In 1842 Morse laid an experimental cable across New York harbor in which the wires were insulated from the water with tar. A more successful insulation was later developed from gutta percha, a latex similar to rubber obtained from Malaya. Mathew Maury made an important contribution to undersea cable technology with his 1852 topographic map of the Atlantic floor, showing the submarine mountain ranges and deeps and a plateau between Ireland and Newfoundland which could be the site of a telegraphic cable. Englishman William Thomson, later famous as Lord Kelvin, also solved a problem crucial to the Atlantic Cable when he showed how telegraphy could take place over long lines without relays. The organization of the whole project was undertaken by Cyrus W. Field, a retired paper merchant. After a few abortive efforts, an Atlantic cable was finally laid by August, 1858, but after a few days of transmission, the insulation on the cable failed. By 1866, another effort succeeded and the 15,000 miles of telegraph in Britain, the 80,000 miles of telegraph on the European continent, and the 48,000 miles of telegraph in the United States were finally linked.

THE LONDON EXHIBITION OF 1851

The large numbers of prizes and awards given to American inventors and their products at the London Exhibition of 1851 demonstrate the extent of American technological achievements by the middle of the nineteenth century. Less than three percent of the twenty thousand exhibits were American but twenty percent of the awards went to Americans. The McCormick reaper was demonstrated several times and the London Times said, "The reaping machine from the United States is the most valuable contribution from abroad . . . It is worth the whole cost of the Exposition." Because of the emphasis of the exhibition on peace, no prizes were given for firearms but the Colt Revolver invented by Samuel Colt, a repeating hand gun in which a revolving cylinder held multiple charges, won an honorable mention as did Palmer's target rifle and Robbins and Lawrence's military rifle. The Colt Revolver was described as one of the most important inventions in the entire history of firearms.

The sewing machine of Blodgett and Lerow of Boston, based on Elias Howe's shuttle principle, received a medal. Howe had received his patent in 1846 after another American inventor, Walter Hunt (the inventor of the safety pin) had abandoned his own work on a sewing maching and not taken out a patent for fear that seamstresses would be thrown out of work. Howe, probably without knowing of Hunt's work, developed the same kind of two needle machine in which a needle below the cloth "locked" a loop of thread formed by a needle above moving up and down through the cloth. The American shoe industry grew out of adaptations of the sewing machine and Civil War uniforms were made on Howe's machine. Headed by Isaac Singer, a combination of manufacturers paid Howe royalties after a bitter patent fight, and Howe became an extremely wealthy man. The prize medal of the London Exhibition gave the sewing machine enough publicity that the Singer Company was soon selling more machines in Europe than in the United States.

Charles Goodyear won an important medal at the London Exhibition for his India Rubber products exhibited including rubber boots, shoes, life boats, fabrics, knapsacks and cartridge belts. Prior to Goodyear's discovery that rubber could be "cured" with heat, anything made out of rubber would melt and become sticky in hot weather. After years of experimentation with many substances on a random basis, Goodyear accidentally discovered his vulcanization process when a piece of rubber was carelessly brought into contact with a hot stove. But Goodyear, after making a considerable fortune and seeing his discovery give rise to a whole industry, spent so much on promotion that he died in 1860 owing $200,000 despite his success at the London Exhibition.

The locks and safes developed by the American firm of Day and Newell were the only ones in the Great Exhibition which could not be picked. The Bond astronomical clock, produced by instrument makers William C. Bond and his son, George, director of the Observatory at Harvard, also won a prize and was so remarkable in eliminating the variance on accuracy of eye and ear by a recording system that one observer called it, "the most wonderful achievement of science since the days of Newton." Cotton and woolen goods were compared favorably with European products and won prizes. Whitney Hayden's cotton-drawing frame, Lowell's self-acting lathe and power loom, and Woodbury's wood-planing machine were praised. Products of the American iron and steel industry won awards, in part because an American, William Kelley, had independently discovered at the beginning of the 1850's the steel making process patented some years later by Englishman Henry Bessemer. In this important process, molten iron is converted into steel simply by burning out its carbon content with a blast of air. The discoveries of Kelley and Bessemer, while originally ridiculed, were the later basis of the steel age in which this strong, but malleable, metal was used for thousands of purposes.

As a result of the London Exhibition, and similar American triumphs at a subsequent Grand Exhibition in Paris in 1855, American patents were sold to European manufacturers, and distributors for American goods were set up throughout Europe. Charles Reade, an English author, in 1860 summed up the growth of American technology prior to the Civil War by writing, "American genius is at this moment ahead of all nations in mechanical inventions."

One of the major technological breakthroughs occasioned by the problems brought about by the Civil War was the discovery of Lamont Dupont for the North that sodium nitrate could be used instead of saltpeter in the manufacture of gunpowder. Another innovation was the use of the aerial balloon for reconnaissance by the North. While the French had used military balloons as early as 1794, it was Professor Thaddeus Lowe of New Hampshire, a protege of Joseph Henry, who designed and manufactured a number of balloons for specific military use. By using a barge as a base of operation, Lowe actually designed the first aircraft carrier in history. The South, in turn, benefitted from the invention by General Gabriel Rains of a land mine in 1862.

In 1862, Confederate Captain R. Williams invented a breech-loading machine gun which fired 40 times a minute at an effective range of 2,000 yards. When six of these guns were used in the Battle of Blue Springs, Tennessee, a Union soldier exclaimed, "We concluded that the enemy had some new fangled machine for throwing railroad spikes at us."

Both sides early realized the importance of railroads in transporting troops quickly over long distances. In 1862 some 2,000 Union troops were moved 400 miles in 40 hours by railroad from West Virginia to Washington to prevent Confederate General Lee from capturing the Capitol. Both sides, therefore, established special units trained to destroy trains, tracks and bridges. The North even had a special corps equipped with interchangeable parts of bridge spans and track to repair destroyed track and build new bridges. In 1863, the North began to use armored railroad cars equipped with small cannon to patrol the Baltimore and Ohio Railroad, the chief supply line for the Army of the Potomac.

The telegraph was used extensively by both sides during the Civil War. It was also the first war to be photographed adequately, using the wet-plate system developed by the Frenchman, Daguerre. By the Spring of 1864, the North was producing war materials and military supplies on a mass production basis and transporting troops efficiently by railroad through a central command efficiently linked with the battlefields by telegraph. Despite the early military victories of the South, the advanced machine technology of the North began to affect the outcome of the war. The North won in large part because its surplus of food, gunpowder, clothing, iron and steel, weapons and ammunition could not be matched by the primarily agricultural South.

THE OIL BOOM

It has already been noted that the early colonists first progressed from home-made animal fat candles to bayberry candles to illuminate their homes. The development was then to candles purchased from others, and then to whale oil as an illuminant. But as the price for whale oil increased, Americans began to look for a substitute. The first one found was an oil distilled from coal, called by its discoverer "kerosene." Abraham Gesner, a Canadian geologist, took out a patent on this distillate in 1854 but sales were not exceptionally high because of the smell of kerosene.

At this time petroleum had long been known to both Indian and white man, seeping up as it did in shallow pools. The Indians considered it a sacred substance and would burn it during special ceremonies. The white man would sell and buy it as "snake oil," a natural mineral oil that would cure anything. Many wells dug to obtain natural brine would be abandoned because of the bad-smelling mineral oil that would surface.

In 1857, A. C. Ferris realized that if he could find a way to remove the smell from the oil, he could sell it for lighting purposes. He employed a chemist, designed a special lamp and soon had to begin actually importing petroleum to meet the demand. He tried to dig some wells on land he purchased in Pennsylvania to obtain petroleum but was some miles away from an actual oil field. In May 1858 a Colonel E. L. Drake, in partnership with two New York attorneys, began to drill for oil in Pennsylvania using the same derricks used to drill salt wells. When Drake actually began to drill he faced the problem of a pool of water that gushed up by driving iron pipe through the water. But Drake did not actually strike oil until the next year when a seventy foot well began to yield eight barrels of oil a day. This quantity of oil was obtained when a pump—the first petroleum pump ever used—was attached to the pipe sunk in the ground. An oil rush immediately began in the area.

Two years later, the first flowing well was struck and steadily produced 300 barrels a day. (Oil was then selling for $40 a barrel). Not long after, the Phillips well on Oil Creek began to produce 3,000 barrels a day. A local paper wrote: "Less than ten years ago it is doubtful if a hundred thousand dollars were at any time in circulation in the country contiguous to Oil Creek. Now, it is not an uncommon thing in the same neighborhood for a million dollars to change hands in a single week . . .''

The drills, at first operated by foot power, soon were attached to steam engines and finally to electric motors. As the railroads were not anxious at first to extend their lines into oil country for fear the wells would suddenly dry up, oil was transported to the nearest railroad depots by rafts. Since Oil Creek itself was navigable only in a flood, once or twice a week the creek was artificially flooded by opening up old lumber dams. Hundreds of boats carrying as much as 40,000 barrels of oil would float into the Allegheny.

By 1876, California became an oil state, with an initial production of 12,000 barrels. (Previously, the Appalachian oil field being worked extended over the states of Pennsylvania, Ohio, New York, West Virginia, Kentucky, and Tennessee). By 1914 California was outproducing all other states with a production of almost 100 million barrels of oil. The Gulf Field of Texas and Lower Louisiana produced 530 barrels in 1899, nothing in 1900, and 18 million barrels in 1902.

THE CENTENNIAL CELEBRATION OF 1876

The 100th anniversary of the United States was celebrated with a great exhibition in Philadelphia. The Pennsylvania railroad constructed a line right to the fair grounds to transport the crowds. French sculptors then working on the Statue of Liberty were able to send only the torch-carrying hand, but that was mounted at the fair. People could survey the sights from the observation balcony below the torch. The Main Hall, the largest building in the world, contained thousands of exhibits from Great Britain, Spain, France, Germany and Russia but the dominant exhibits, of course, were the bewildering displays of American products from Gothic furniture to the new telephone of Alexander Graham Bell, invented that very year of 1876.

After the Main Building in size, came the Machinery Building, with its stories-high 1600 horsepower Corliss Steam Engine weighing 70 tons. The Machinery Building exhibits included the turret lathe invented by Robbins and Lawrence of Vermont in which a multiple tool holder permitted a succession of operations without unclamping the work. The universal milling machine, a device for machining flat surfaces, gear teeth and grooves which was first designed by Eli Whitney, also created a sensation. The Corliss bevel-gear cutting machine towered over the on-lookers as it operated. George Westinghouse (who was later to develop alternating electricity as a power source and invented the gas meter and

Inventions in the field *of chemistry by Americans is unmatched throughout the world. Here Wallace Carothers holds a sample of his modern invention, nylon.*

These modern harvesters *bear little resemblance to the first reaper, invented in 1834 by Cyrus McCormick, but they perform the same task. McCormick's invention before the Civil War, and subsequent refinements of it, have made America the world's largest producer of grains.*

automatic safety valves so gas could be used in the home and streets for cooking and lighting), exhibited his railroad air brake. Then 30 years old, Westinghouse had already equipped 38 percent of the 15,657 American locomotives and 14,055 railroad passenger cars with his airbrakes.

Opposite Machinery Hall, there was a large exhibition of photographic products. Photography had been invented in England and France in the early 1800's with the work of Humphry Davy, Thomas Wedgwood and Daguerre who created hand prints and photographs by exposing silver nitrate to light. Samuel Morse, the inventor of the telegraph, had met Daguerre in France in 1838. Upon returning to America, Morse set up one of the first portrait studios. However, the first photographic portrait was actually taken by American scientist John William Draper of New York University in 1839. The following year, Draper took the first picture of the moon. During the Civil War Matthew Brady made his famed front-line photographs using wet-plates and his assistants had then spread out over the country in the post-war period to photograph the explorations and growth. Alexander Gardner immortalized the spread of the Union Pacific Railroad while T. H. Sullivan snapped away in the Sierra Nevadas, on jungle expeditions in Panama, and at the Grand Canyon.

While the photographic exhibits at the Philadelphia Fair of 1876 were among the most popular, it was only the following year that 23 year-old George Eastman of Rochester, New York, began to experiment with dry photographic emulsions. By 1879 his first English patent was issued for "An improved process of preparing gelatin dry plates for use in photography and apparatus thereof." Eastman eventually succeeded in coating celluloid with a light sensitive solution to make the first rolled photographic film, finally designing a simple camera to use the roll film, his famous Kodak. These inventions made a new art form available to the masses. At the end

of his life when he headed one of the most famous American companies and had given away most of the 100 million dollars that he had earned, Eastman wrote to his friends, "My work is done. Why wait?" And then shot himself.

The third largest building at the Philadelphia Centennial celebration was the Agriculture Building, as if symbolizing how the U.S. was changing from a nation of farmers to a nation of mechanized industry. But agriculture was still the nation's biggest business despite the decreasing numbers of farmers. Under the influence of the mechanized equipment proudly displayed at the 1876 Fair, however, the family farm was being converted into the industrial farm. The plows, reapers and harvesters were getting bigger and more efficient in displacing labor. The most important technological change in agriculture, however, was the introduction of the steam engine as the power source for mechanized farm equipment.

Strangely enough, the seemingly minor invention of barbed wire in 1874 by Joseph Glidden of Illinois, also had a major impact on American agriculture and the whole future of the nation at this time. Many millions of cattle were roaming the vast treeless plains west of the Mississippi. Great profits were being made from these thousands of miles of free open range when the railroads hauled this beef eastward. However, the railroads were also bringing these profits to an end by selling off their huge grants of land as farms. (At the same time, the U.S. government, through the Homestead Act of 1862 was offering 160 acres of land free to anyone who would settle on the public domain lands of the Great Plains.) The railroads were even sending solicitors throughout Europe to get purchasers for their land, one agent persuaded one-third of the population of Iceland to buy railroad land and migrate. For ten years this great migration of peoples populated the edge of the Great Plains because no homesteader could cultivate crops while cattle freely roamed over plowed land. The introduction of barbed wire was to change all this. The homesteaders came in new waves on the railroad cars that had just carried beef eastward, holding legal deeds to land in their hands while the baggage cars were full of barbed wire to fence off their fields. The cattle rangers, used to free acess to to streams and grazing land, fought the homesteaders with great violence, but the long strands of barbed wire being strung all over the prairies proved too powerful for them.

THOMAS EDISON

One noted visitor to the Philadelphia Fair was 29 year-old Thomas Edison, already calling himself an "electrical engineer." From being a telegraph operator, Edison had advanced himself to co-owner of a laboratory which was in the business of making "inventions to order." He was producing stock tickers and other telegraphic mechanisms with his company, finally inventing devices on contract for Western Union. One system for multiple telegraphy developed by Edison in 1875 increased the value of Western Union by 15 million dollars. In 1877 Edison made a discovery for Western Union which eventually brought about the merger of Western Union and the American Bell Telephone Company into one international company.

By 1876, the year Edison visited the Philadelphia Fair, he was earning hundreds of thousands of dollars and could afford to indulge any whim. But what Edison wanted were not the usual toys of the rich man. "My one ambition is to be able to work without regard to expense. What I mean is that if I want to give up a whole month of my time and that of my whole establishment to finding out why one form of a carbon filament is slightly better than another, I want to do it without thinking of the cost. That galls me. I want none of the rich man's usual toys. I want no horses or yachts; I have no time for them. What I want is a perfect workshop."

In his workshop Edison made electricity an indispensable part of the modern world. He invented the filament light bulb in 1880 and a dynamo which would operate as lights were turned on and off. He devised a working phonograph as early as 1877. His second phonograph design of 1887 used wax cylinders for recording. In 1887 he thought of using Eastman's roll film in connection with his phonograph and, in 1891 patented a motion picture camera designed for perforated 35 millimeter film. In April, 1894, Edison opened the Kinetoscope Parlor on Broadway, New York, where a single viewer in a cabinet could watch motion pictures project at the rate of 46 frames a minute. Edison, however, believed that larger audiences would not be profitable and left the design of a better projection system to others. He also was content with a camera that weighed a ton, so lacking in portability that subjects to be photographed had to be taken to it.

In 1893 Edison applied for a patent on the famous "Edison Electric" automobile, developed an electric vote recorder for legislatures, invented waxed wrapping paper, the mimeograph, the carbon telephone transmitter, the central power station, poured concrete houses and much more. Edison invented a magnetic ore separator to process low grade ore, developed ore crushing machinery and spent several years operating his own iron mine. Edison's method of approaching a problem was first to read everything and then to try everything. With this approach he obtained 1093 patents in his lifetime.

Two more events that happened at the time of the Centennial Exposition at Philadelphia are worth noting here: the invention of the typewriter and the scientific work of J. Willard Gibbs.

MERGENTHALER'S LINOTYPE

In 1876, twenty two year old Ottmar Mergenthaler, a young machinist, had been in the United States for four years. He was working for a cousin who owned a machine shop in Washington, D.C. when a Virginian named Charles G. Moore brought a writing machine he had invented into the shop. Mergenthaler doubted the design and ten years later had changed Moore's original concept into the linotype, a machine which would cast type. An automatic method of typesetting, the linotype revolutionized newspaper and book production, making the modern daily newspaper possible along with the high speed printing press. But the linotype is a huge machine, noisy and complicated, and was hardly a personal writing machine. It remained for others to solve the problems involved in a true typewriter.

Besides some early European experiments at constructing a typewriter, it is known that an American, a Mr. Burt, received an American patent for a "typographer" prior to 1836. But all the records of Burt's invention were destroyed in the Patent Office fire. In 1843, another American, Charles Thurber, built a machine that operated too slowly but had a sliding carriage to hold the paper, and a way of moving the paper for the next line. Between 1847 and 1856 another American inventor, Alfred E. Beach, then editor of *Scientific American*, built several large typewriters out of wood on which he obtained hundreds of patents.

In 1867 Beach wrote an article in *Scientific American* about the advantages of an efficient typewriter, and the work being done by an American living in England, John Pratt. Three Americans in Milwaukee read this article and decided they could build a writing machine that would be a considerable improvement on Pratt's work. One was Christopher Latham Sholes, then editor of the Milwaukee *Sentinel*, the Collector of Customs, and the inventor of a method of printing newspaper subscribers' names on the margin of a paper so it could be delivered to them. Another was Carlos Glidden, and the third man was Samuel W. Soule, a machinist. In 1867 Sholes obtained a typewriter patent which he licensed, in 1873, to Philo Remington, son of the founder of the firearms company. Remington, however, could not sell the new machine in sufficient numbers and, thirteen years later, sold the typewriter design to independent interests. Remington sold out too early, however, for by 1890, fourteen years after the Centennial, the typewriter, and the telephone were standard equipment in most American offices.

FROM 1900 TO THE PRESENT

As the twentieth century opened, *Scientific American* magazine held a contest to review American progress. The prize-winning essay was written by Edward M. Byrn who characterized the last half of the nineteenth century as "an epoch unique in the world's history . . . when nine-tenths of all America's riches and physical comforts had come into existence . . . a gigantic wave of human ingenuity so fruitful in its wealth and so beneficial in its results" that it was impossible to comprehend.

Byrn noted that in 1850 there were no telephones, no

cables, no electric lights, photoengraving, or photolithographing. There were no cameras, no gas engines, no web-perfecting printing presses, no linotype machines, no passenger elevators, no asphalt pavements. Neither was there barbed-wire fencing, nor oil or gas wells, no ice machines, no phonographs, cash registers, typewriters, aluminum ware, Bessemer steel, sanitary plumbing, coal tars, or electric machines. All these had come into use by 1896 when Byrn was writing. What new has happened since then?

THE AUTOMOBILE

First of all there is the automobile. There is no one inventor responsible for the auto, either in Europe or America. Prior to 1890, automobiles were being manufactured in France, Austria, Germany and Italy. In 1892 Charles and Frank Duryea built and operated a one-cylinder gasoline-propelled car which they claimed to be the first successfully operated automobile in this country. Henry Ford built a gasoline "buggy" that same year but claims it did not run to his satisfaction until the following year. Alexander Winton built two big cars in 1897 and has the distinction of being the first man in the United States to build cars for sale. The first automobile show was held in 1900 in Madison Square Garden. By this time American industry had reached the point that there was an abundant supply of gasoline and there were adequate machine tools and trained workmen to produce interchangeable parts. In 1903 Henry Ford organized the Ford Motor Company, producing an inexpensive and serviceable car using mass production methods. By 1911 Vincent Bendix and Charles F. Kettering introduced a major innovation, the electric self-started. Car owners, truck operators and the government urged the building of good roads. Federal financing for roads became incorporated into a national defense act in 1916 when a German submarine appeared in Baltimore harbor.

THE AIRPLANE

The next revolution in transportation took place with the invention of the airplane. On May 6, 1896, Samuel Pierpont Langley, Secretary of the Smithsonian Institution, made two launchings of a steam-powered model plane with no one aboard. Subsequent attempts by Langley before his death in 1906 to launch a man-carrying plane failed but he left a heritage of engineering principles and instruments relating to wind resistance and air pressure which were to prove useful later. Nine days after Langley's last failure, Wilbur Wright successfully flew a heavier-than-air plane, which he and his brother Orville had designed. The historic date was December 17, 1903. The Wrights' patent application was filed March 23, 1903, and had sixteen claims, fully describing a system for controlling a flying machine.

When the First World War broke out in 1914, eleven years after the Wrights' first flight, the French Army had 1,500 planes and was able to requisition 500 additional civilian planes. The German Army at this time had 1,000 planes and a civilian reserve of 450. In sharp contrast, in 1917 the U.S. Army only had 55 planes, 51 obsolete ones and 4 obsolescent. The U.S. had built less than 200 planes since the Wrights' first flight, demonstrating how much more interested Europeans were in aviation than Americans. However, when the war came, the first Liberty engine for military aircraft was delivered in Washington on July 4, 1917, less than six weeks after its plans were completed. By November 1918, these engines were being produced at the rate of 150 per day. By the armistice, some 15,000 engines had been built, 5,000 of which were installed on planes built in the United States. The Lewis machine gun with its synchronized gears allowed the pilot to shoot through the

John Dessauer, *Chester Carlson, and Joseph Wilson shown here demonstrating their invention of a dry-copying machine. The invention of the dry-copying machine has revolutionized American business and industry economic practices.*

By 1967 the inventiveness *of American industry had not only developed thousands of new inventions, but had also perfected many inventions which had been made in an earlier age. Here a Bell Telephone Laboratory employee uses a "picturephone" to communicate with another Bell employee in another room.*

propeller. Bombing came late in the war with the development of adequate bomb sights.

RADIO

In 1896, Guglielmo Marconi, a twenty-two year old Italian, basing himself on the prior theoretical work of American physicist, Joseph Henry, and British physicist, James Clark Maxwell, and German Heinrich Hertz, and combining already existing apparatus, succeeded in constructing the first wireless telegraph. By 1897 Marconi got a British patent and extended the range of his device to ten miles. Sir Oliver Lodge worked out a way of tuning in on specific radio waves which he shared with Marconi in 1897. Englishman Joseph Fleming, who had previously worked with Edison, remembered some research done in the Edison laboratory which allowed him to produce the first radio vacuum tube, a "valve" which converted oscillating radio waves into spurts of electricity traveling in the same direction. Reception of the wireless telegraph was enormously improved. In 1906 American radio engineer Lee De Forest designed a new element into Fleming's simple "valve" which allowed the signal to be amplified. By connecting such tubes together, this "valve" could magnify a signal millions of times.

PRESENT AND FUTURE TECHNOLOGY

Since 1900 there have been two World Wars and a number of smaller military conflicts, each of which has intensified technological development from a more developed beginning base than did the Revolutionary or Civil War. It is also said that more than 90% of the scientists who have ever lived are alive today, adding to human knowledge at a rate previously unknown. These scientists are clustered in the universities, at government installations and in corporation laboratories where they often work in teams and with equipment unimaginable to scientists of 200 years ago. There has

been a tremendous revolution in the sources of power, in transportation, communication, materials, manufacturing processes and agricultural technology. Where are we now and where are we going?

In the area of power, humans are developing the nuclear generation of electricity and different kinds of portable power plants from gas turbines to improved steam and electrical engines. There is also exploration of solar energy, drawing power directly from the sun with solar cells. Scientists have already been able to duplicate in their laboratories the fusion process of welding together light atoms like hydrogen and lithium by which the stars themselves generate their vast power, but can not as yet do this in a controlled manner. If scientists succeed in this, there is limitless power available to humans and the anticipated consumption of all fossil fuels won't matter.

In the area of transportation, propeller planes have developed into jets. There are working models of "Ground Effect Machines" which support themselves by downward blasts of air and, floating only a few inches from the ground, do not require the developed roadways needed by automobiles. On the drawing boards are new systems for urban transportation including monorails with large capacity cars and monorails with smaller computer-operated cars that will take a passenger directly to the destination without transfer. More in the future, but not totally inconceivable according to some scientists, are personal body flying belts based on neutralization of gravity, portable rocket motors, and/or broadcast power. Conveyor belts for urban transportation are also in the design stage.

In the area of communication, color TV is quite common and the TV telephone is clearly on the horizon. Also developed and due to be marketed soon are several EVR (Electronic Video Recording) systems where a disc or tape will store a TV program and activate a video screen much as a phonograph record now operates a loudspeaker. Microfilming and the micro-fiche system are common in libraries and business and may easily be extended to the home, possibly to communicate subscription publications. Systems now in beginning-use to transmit business documents may also be developed to transmit periodicals to the subscriber. Since World War II the Xerox system of dry-

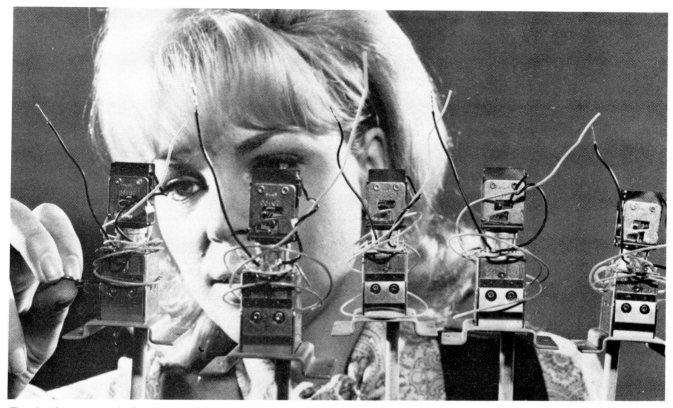

The development *in the late Sixties of the transistorized system and the micro- and mini-electric systems has changed the course of American inventions.*

process photocopying was developed by an independent inventor, Chester Carlson, and the Polaroid system of instant photography by Edwin Land, creating two new giant communication companies. Computer terminals in homes may become more than oddities, linking individuals with libraries and maybe subscription publications. Holography, the three dimensional photography invented by Professor Dennis Gabor, and other developments of laser light technology may also be developed as more than laboratory oddities. Long play records are a new development unveiled in 1948 by CBS Laboratories.

In the area of materials, plastics and silicones, synthetic diamonds and synthetic fabrics have changed the appearance of society already. Scientists are exploring the possibility that space mining or space manufacture under conditions of no gravity may result in new materials or products.

In the area of tools, manufacturing is just on the verge of being changed by tape controlled machine tools which may eliminate much skilled labor. Automation—the use of machines to run machines—has been much discussed in recent years. Improved electron microscopes and telescopes are scientific tools which have expanded the universe for humans. And in the late 1960's, Donald Wickes, while working at the Atomic Energy Commission's Sandia Laboratory in New Mexico, invented the Rolamite, a device made of a pair of rollers and a flexible band which may be as versatile as the gear or screw in a variety of applications.

In the area of agriculture, since the 1900's farming has been radically changed by the use of the tractor and huge harvesting combines. However, G.C. Hanna and Coby Lorenzen, researchers at the University of California campus at Davis, along with Stephen Sluka, patented in 1958 a successful tomato picker which may show a radically new direction for agricultural technology in that the seven ton machine works best with a tomato bred specially for machine

picking by plant breeder Hanna. Some scientists are also seriously exploring the possibility of farming the sea for food products such as plankton.

In terms of future exploration, although the American space program seems to be slowing down, scientists will be working for some time to come with the information already available from moon and planetary explorations of the last twenty years. A few scientists are concerned with undersea exploration, and still fewer seem concerned with penetrating the earth deeper than the 7,000 feet already attained in deep mines. On a planet 8,000 miles in diameter that is really scratching the surface! Some scientists are speculating that the development of robots may take place to solve the problems of outer space and inner earth exploration because both of these environments are hostile to humans born on the earth's surface.

In the area of medicine, the synthesis of the wonder drug, cortisone, by Upjohn Laboratories in the early 1950's and the manufacture of penicillin and other antibiotic drugs in the modern period are only the flashy tip of the iceberg of medical and pharmaceutical research now going on. X-Rays and the use of radioisoptopes, the development of the Salk vaccine for polio are also twentieth century developments that are notable. The use of suspended animation for space travel and to preserve people now dying of incurable disease until a cure is developed may be more feasible than it seems.

In the area of military technology, the twentieth century has seen the development of the tank, precision bombing with the Sperry bombsight, new explosives like TNT and plastic bombs, new automatic rifles, devices for night vision and atomic weapons. The Vietnam war also saw the use of weather modification, a new technology which can have tremendous consequences for human civilization.

These, in brief, have been the highlights of science and technology during the 200 year history of the United States. It is a story demonstrating an inner pattern of human inventiveness responding to problems by selectively combining the material and knowledge of the present.

Hughes Flies Huge Plane Over Los Angeles Harbor

View of Germany's Dismantled War Plants

Story on Page 1, Part I
GRACEFUL—Howard Hughes' $25,000,000 plywood flying boat soars above Los Angeles Harbor after Hughes, with 30 technicians and others aboard, skimmed water at 95 m.p.h. in "taxi test." Plane flew for nearly a mile.

'DESTROYER' DESTROYED — Huge Krupp works at Essen once spewed armaments for Hitler. Now girders and rubble strew floor as job of dismantling war plants goes on.

Story on Page 1, Part I
GROUNDED BY WINDS—The 30-foot fishing boat Jaye C, owned by G. E. Gillard of Redondo Beach, was driven by winds from brea kwater moorings to crack up on shore rocks.

MATERIAL FOR RECONSTRUCTION — Tiling taken from the roof of this section of former war plant in Berlin, now dismantled, will go into German reconstruction.

'THE EYE-DEA' — Lady with "philatelic eye" is Miss Sheila Rutter examining stamp at an exhibit in London.

Story on Page 1, Part I
NEW SON KISSES BRIDE—Mrs. Eddy Duchin, the former Mrs. Maria Teresa Winn of London, is kissed by husband's son, Peter Oelrichs Duchin, as band leader smiles approval.

AMERICAN ART: PAINTING AND SCULPTURE

The measure of any civilization must include its achievements in the arts . . .''

Colonial America with its Puritan and Quaker practicality was not a hospitable climate for the growth of a native art which resembled the art of Europe from where these dour, God-fearing people had come. Utility was the first test for any handicraft. Whatever art was produced in these early years must necessarily have had its specific function. The usefulness of an object was its principal value.

Nor did New England yet have its wealthy, ambitious merchants to patronize the arts; nor was there sufficient leisure time to invite the muse if one were an artist, nor time to contemplate man-made beauty. The trappings of wealth, the mark of one's material success were unimportant to these pious and frugal people. Art was not yet regarded on these shores as an emblem of the *nouveaux riches*. Nor was there yet any nobility obliged to commission portraits, or decorate new estates, or build monuments to commemorate their accomplishments.

Deeper yet was an aversion to finery; in the minds of these old world Protestants there was a connection between visual opulence and the Catholic or Anglican church against which their forebearers had rebelled. Colonial painters made commercial signs or simple ornaments for a coffin; sculptors carved gravestones or embellished wood with a rough-hewn design. Portraits did not flatter or idealize the sitter. And no artist yet dared to paint what he had never seen: events from the Bible, or from history.

But the urge to create is universal and the Puritan society of early colonial times had its special artisans, craftsmen, carpenters, metal joiners, stone cutters, smiths and furniture makers who might add to the simple, useful products of their trade some aesthetic ornament or refinement.

Later, as the small towns began to flourish, and distinctions of wealth and social station became more pronounced, the arts helped to create and define these differences. A man of wealth might commission some local painter to design and execute a coat of arms. Tombstones of the rich became a bit more ornate. Decorative patterns were incised into furniture, chased into metal, laid into brick work. But not possessing the skills of European masters upon whose work the local artisans based their traditional ornamentations, they simplified and modified, and thus began producing art with an emerging American flavor.

The origins of painting in America remain concealed behind the fog of history. The limner, or one who describes or portrays, particularly in paint, was an early tradition in colonial America. Usually self-taught and sometimes wandering from town to town, these first portrait painters most often rendered their subjects in a simple, flat pattern. Few possessed the skill or knowledge of perspective or the gift for creating the illusion of depth. The sitter was described in paint with an unembellished honesty, with an accurate likeness of face and bearing, and as accurately as the artist was capable.

Few of the works of these earliest limners can be unquestionably attributed to a specific artist. Certain names can be found in documents from the period—Nathaniel Mather mentions limner Joseph Allen, limner Lawrence Brown applied for permission to live in Boston in 1701, in 1679 Thomas Powell was paid in tobacco for decorating a church. But the paintings of these men no longer exist. And there are numerous paintings from the era which have no signatures. Unsigned portraits with strong stylistic similarities may either suggest authorship by the same artist, or by adept disciples of his ''school.''

Reproduction of a self portrait *of the famous American painter Gilbert Stuart, whose portrait of George Washington is one of the best known pictures of the first President. Stuart died in 1828.*

Three portraits of particular interest, painted perhaps by the same hand, reflect the stern rectitude of the New England era. *William Stroughton* of the Harvard Collection, *John Davenport* of the Yale University collection, and *Reverend Thomas Thatcher* whose portrait hangs in the Old North Church, Boston, all have faces of formidable character: glum, righteous, typically Puritanical.

In New Amsterdam (New York) the colonial establishment was painted with more sophistication. Volume and dimension were rendered more accurately by knowledgeable use of light and shadow, a legacy of the Dutch tradition. The portrait of Peter Stuyvesant in the New York Historical Society was painted perhaps by an artist with some formal training. The Duyckinck family of New Amsterdam produced a number of artist limners who practiced their trade for almost a hundred years, portraying notable citizens of the day. Unknown limners in the New York area recorded the faces of James Pierpont, Caleb Heathcote, a Mayor of New York, Robert Hunter, Governor of New York and New Jersey.

The portrait styles of these early native painters were imitative of European models, but usually somewhat unsophisticated in the refinements of technique. The art of New England derived from Tudor traditions and the art of the English court. New York painters were disciples of the Dutch school, usually more adept at modeling through the use of light and shadow. The New England painters were more able to penetrate into the character of their subjects, investing a portrait with the honest individuality of the sitter. The New York painters did not interpret their subjects, but rather presented them without artistic comment.

Limners who came to America from abroad usually brought with them a more accomplished Old World skill. Among these were the German-born Justus Englehardt Kuhn (d. 1717), the Swedish painter Gustavus Hesselius, who

arrived in America in 1711, and Scotsman John Smibert (1688-1751). Smibert was one of the most celebrated of painters in the colonies. He brought with him to America a modest reputation and formal training after leaving London where he felt the competition among painters was too difficult. After settling in Boston, Smibert presented the first art exhibition ever seen in America, displaying his own portraits of New England dignitaries along with his copies of old masters. He received numerous portrait commissions and was regarded by local connoiseurs of art as an artist of unprecedented excellence in the colonies.

Other limners of note from this period include the so-called Freake limner, painter of the double portrait of Mrs. Elizabeth Freake and baby Mary now hanging in the Worcester Art Museum. Joseph Blackburn, who painted in America from 1754 to 1763, and then possibly left America for England, was an accomplished technician and a number of his portraits are now owned by the New York Metropolitan Museum of Art. Robert Feke (c. 1705-c. 1750), Joseph Badger (1708-1765), and John Hesselius (1728-1778), son of Gustavus, were among the better known limners of the era in Boston, Philadelphia, and Maryland. Jeremiah Theus (c. 1719-1774) was the foremost limner of South Carolina.

The Dutch landowners or Patroons of New York, employed some six or seven limners on a regular basis and the portraits

Paul Revere *as painted by John Singleton Copley, circa 1756.*

Detail of Francis Guy's Winter Scene in Brooklyn *which he worked on from 1817 to 1820.*

of these unknown artists are the most accomplished of that region, which included the Hudson River valley. Although the pictures did not present a character study of their subjects, the strong colors and firm design place the work far above the quality of other limners of the period. A number of pictures from these so-called Patroon painters are owned by the Metropolitan Museum of Art in New York.

In 1738 two of America's most celebrated painters were born, both of whom possessed a talent and originality previously unseen in the colonies. Benjamin West (1738-1820) was born in Philadelphia, began painting at eight years old and by the age of fifteen had painted his first professional portrait commission. His earliest work was somewhat primitive, but demonstrated a familiarity with British and American engravings of high quality. By 1758, West was hailed in *American Magazine* as a ". . . sacred Genius!" He went to New York for the purpose of improving his skills and later traveled to Italy under the patronage of a prominent New Yorker. In Italy he studied the masters of the Renaissance painters, especially Raphael. On his way back to America, he stopped in London, intending only to stay briefly. So enthusiastic was his reception, however, that West decided to remain in England. He was appointed a charter member of the Royal Academy of Arts in 1768 and in 1772 King George III named West an official historical painter to the Crown.

Painting his scenes from the Bible, and from ancient and contemporary history, West presented his subjects in the flamboyant manner of neoclassicism. Dramatic and theatri-

cal poses characterized his compositions. His controversial painting *Death of General Wolfe* (National Gallery of Canada), violated all tradition by presenting the subjects in contemporary clothing rather than in Greco-Roman togas as the custom required. West became famous, wealthy, influential. He counted the most eminent Londoners among his friends.

As the first America-born painter to acquire an international reputation, West attracted a number of other American painters to his London studio where they studied under his tutelage. Among the more notable of West's students, were Gilbert Stuart, John Singleton Copley, Samuel F. B. Morse, Charles Willson Peale, Rembrandt Peale, Thomas Sully and John Trumbull. West was extremely generous to the painters who came to him seeking instruction, often giving them free lessons and studio accommodations. By the time West died in 1820 he had secured for himself not only a place in the history of American art, but a position as one of Europe's more influential eighteenth century painters.

John Singleton Copley (1738-1815) was a professional portrait painter in pre-Revolutionary Boston. He had painted many of the prominent Bostonians of his time including silversmith Paul Revere (Museum of Fine Arts, Boston), but was generally displeased with the status of painting in America.

In a letter to Benjamin West in London, Copley wrote, "Was it not for preserving the resemblace [sic] of particular persons, painting would not be known in this place."

He was exposed to the conventions of European painting

Asher B. Durand's Kindred Spirits *which he completed in 1849.*

Scene of a picnic, *painted about 1855 by Jeremiah Hardy.*

through his familiarity with Smibert's copies of the old masters, and through the tutorship of his stepfather, the engraver Peter Pelham, who had studied in England. Copley's early portraits were good but not extraordinary, yet he was later to evolve into the foremost American painter of his time. In 1766 he submitted his painting *Boy With The Squirrel* to the Society of Artists in London where the work was widely hailed as the best picture of its kind. West and Sir Joshua Reynolds, then president of the British Royal Academy of Arts, encouraged Copley to come to England where his skills as a painter might broaden through contact with European culture. Copley did not travel abroad, however, until 1774 and was never to return to America.

After a tour through Europe in which he studied the paintings of old masters, Copley settled in London with his family, fugitives from the American Revolution. In 1783 he became a full member of the Royal Academy. Copley's later painting, influenced by the direction of West and his colleagues, was concerned with historical events as subject matter. His former linear style which characterized his Boston portraits gave way to a bolder, more energetic brushwork freed of the previous restraints. Copley's famous picture *The Collapse of the Earl of Chatham in the House of Lords*, which hangs in The Tate Gallery, London, is illustrative of his later

style and his concern with history as drama.

In America, John Trumbull (1756-1843) became the first chronicler of contemporary history in a series of 12 narrative paintings depicting important events of the Revolution. His famous *Declaration of Independence* (Yale University Art Gallery), portrays forty-eight founders of the American Republic, thirty-six of whom Trumbull painted directly from life.

Trumbull, son of the colonial governor of Connecticut, was a graduate of Harvard and studied in London with Benjamin West. He was imprisoned for eight months by English authorities on suspicion of spying for the United States, and returned to America following his release. But he returned to London on two subsequent visits and stayed several years both times. He was commissioned in 1818 by the United States government to paint a series of scenes from the Revolutionary War for the rotunda of the Capitol in Washington.

Gilbert Stuart (1755-1828) probably painted the best known portraits of George Washington, including the nationally renowned but only partially completed picture of America's first president which was so widely reproduced and displayed in schoolrooms around the country. The original hangs in the Museum of Fine Arts, Boston. Another

Stuart portrait of Washington is the basis for the image used on America's one dollar bill, the most widely-circulated denomination of our paper currency.

Of all the numerous professional portrait painters of the day, Charles Willson Peale (1741-1827) was perhaps the most interesting. He was an exceptionally versatile man, achieving some success as an inventor, scientist, museum owner, saddle maker, soldier, naturalist and writer. He was born in Maryland, but fled Annapolis as an adult to escape his debtors. In Boston he saw the collection of paintings Smibert had assembled, and took some instruction from John Hesselius in return for a saddle. He also met John Copley whose influence on Peal's work would become increasingly apparent as the younger painter developed. Peale went to London in 1767 to study with Benjamin West and remained for two years and specialized in the painting of portraits and miniatures.

Returning to Annapolis in 1769 he settled into the profession of portrait painting but a scarcity of commissions in Maryland motivated his relocation to Philadelphia in 1776. During the Revolution he fought at the battles of Trenton and Princeton. His numerous portraits of Washington as a general are regarded as the most accurate pictures of him ever painted during this period. In the later years of his life, Peale devoted himself to the museum he created in which he intended to present an entire world in miniature. Eventually, the museum housed some 100,000 objects, including Peale's portrait gallery of Revolutionary heroes, and a huge collection of mounted animals and birds. Peale was one of the organizers

of the American Academy of Fine Arts in Philadephia, and among the founders of the Pennsylvania Academy of Fine Arts.

Ralph Earl (1751-1801) was one of the most distinguished American painters of his day, and a thoroughly disreputable drunkard, bigamist and wife-deserter. He painted portraits in the Copley manner, but his major accomplishment was the painting of what historians regard as probably the first historical pictures "ever attempted in America." Drawing sketches of the terrain at Lexington and Concord, Massachusetts, where the earliest battles of the Revolutionary War were fought, Earl then painted four large pictures of the events which were subsequently engraved and sold in large numbers.

Samuel F. B. Morse (1791-1872), a painter and sculptor of considerable gifts, would later become internationally celebrated for his invention of the telegraph. Morse had studied in London with Benjamin West and won early recognition for his sculpture *The Dying Hercules*, a preliminary study for a later painting, both of which are now owned by the Yale University Art Gallery. In 1825 he was commissioned to paint a full-length study of Lafayette (City Hall, New York). The work was acclaimed as one of his best and won for him a position of eminence among his artist colleagues in New York. In 1826 Morse founded the National Academy of Design, an organization run exclusively by artists, and antagonistic to the older, more conservative American Academy of Fine Arts. Giving up painting entirely about 1837, Morse devoted the remainder of his life to perfecting the telegraph.

One of the first American painters to specialize in the still life now appeared on the scene. Raphaelle Peale (1774-1825), son of Charles Willson Peale, began his career as a portrait painter, but is remembered principally for the balance, proportion and convincing texture of his still life paintings, among the more famous of which is *Still Life With Cake* (The Metropolitan Museum of Art, New York).

Rembrandt Peale (1778-1860), brother of Raphaelle, was also a student of Benjamin West, and a portrait painter of some note. His *The Court of Death* (Detroit Institute of Art), a huge historical picture, was described by Peale as "the first attempt in modern times to produce moral impressions on the ancient Greek plan without the aid of mythology, or conventional allegory." The painting toured for some thirteen months, was seen by an estimated 32,000 people and earned Peale more than $9,000.

In 1825 Peale was elected to the presidency of the American Academy of Fine Arts, succeeding John Trumbull. After a trip to Europe in 1828, Peale embarked upon an additional career of lecturing on famous portraits of George Washington.

John Vanderlyn (1775-1852) was among the finest draughtsman of his time and one of the first American painters to attempt a push beyond portraiture or historical painting into new areas of art. After studying in Paris, under the

The tranquil life *of the American northeast was captured on canvas by Fitz Hugh Lane in 1862 with his* Owl's Head.

patronage of Aaron Burr, Vanderlyn returned to New York and painted one of the most extraordinary landscape pictures of his time, a view of Niagara Falls (Senate House Museum, Kingston, New York). The Emperor Napoleon awarded Vanderlyn a Gold Medal for his painting *Marius Among the Ruins of Carthage* (M. H. De Young Memorial Museum, San Francisco). With Burr's killing of Alexander Hamilton in a duel, however, Vanderlyn's fortunes as a painter went into decline. He acquired a number of powerful enemies, including John Trumbull of the influential American Academy of Fine Arts. At last in 1837, apparently surmounting many of the problems which had compromised his career, Vanderlyn won a commission from the United States Congress to paint a panel for the Capitol rotunda. He worked in Paris painting *The Landing of Columbus* for almost eight years, and when the picture was finally installed, it was denounced by Vanderlyn's enemies as a modern French piece and certainly not painted by the artist to whom the commission was originally assigned.

The most unusual of Vanderlyn's painting is the circular panorama of *The Palace and Gardens of Versailles* (The Metropolitan Museum of Art, New York). The work was exhibited to the public with the intention of earning both fame and fortune for the painter. Vanderlyn's plan failed, like so many other projects of his, and he ended his days as a destitute beggar.

Vanderlyn's ambition to venture beyond the traditions of portraiture and historical painting was characteristic of a new trend in American painting which began developing about 1820. There was a new interest in landscape painting, prompted perhaps by a growing American romanticism and

the slow disappearance of the frontier, which even at this early date, was already apparent.

The Hudson River School of painters were exploring not only the region of their namesake, but venturing all up and down the Atlantic seaboard in quest of appropriate vistas for their brushes. Their landscapes bespoke a love of vast, pristine spaces, and they idealized in paint an already beautiful terrain. Thomas Cole (1801-1848) was one of the founders of the so-called Hudson River School, the first native American school or movement in painting, and was America's first major landscape painter. *The Oxbow* (The Metropolitan Museum of Art, New York) is typical of Cole's style.

Other important figures of the Hudson River School include John Neagle (1796-1865), Thomas Doughty (1793-1856), and Asher Brown Durand (1796-1886). All had in common their belief that man might find a higher moral purpose through his study of nature, and their pure landscapes would convey this power to the viewer.

American painting now also became increasingly concerned with the West, the unpopulated inland areas of the country, and the activities of common people in typical situations. American genre painting, as the concept was called, took commonplace scenes and average people as their subjects. The paintings were without moral and usually without message and most often depicted a well-observed, highly-detailed tableau of some ordinary activity. Nothing unpleasant is ever seen in genre painting. The new value conferred by President Andrew Jackson upon the common man is given pictorial form in the genre paintings of the 1830's, and thereafter. Anti-big money, sympathetic to labor, Jacksonian democracy was oriented toward people, and the genre painters expressed this new attitude. Pictures were no longer exclusively posed portraits, theatrically staged historical events, or half-imaginary landscapes; painting moved closer to the common experience.

Among the most important of genre painters was George Caleb Bingham (1808-1879). His genre paintings became widely known through their reproduction as engravings or lithographs. After studying painting in America he went to Düsseldorf, Germany, where he acquired a more refined knowledge of technique without losing his essentially American flavor. Among his most famous paintings is *Fur Traders Descending the Missouri* (Metropolitan Museum of Art, New York). Elected to the state legislature of Missouri in 1846, Bingham developed an interest in local politics as a subject for painting. His *The County Election* (The St. Louis Art Museum) depicts more than sixty people organized into a coherent composition.

Other celebrated genre painters include William Sidney Mount (1807-1868), Henry Inman (1801-1846), and Thomas Eakins (1844-1916), who would come to prominence after the Civil War. Numerous other American painters produced genre paintings during the course of their careers, but they cannot be classified exclusively within that category.

Sculpture in America before the Civil War had a variety of functions. Wealthy citizens and dignitaries of one kind or another often hired sculptors to fashion a portrait busts or three-dimensional likenesses of themselves, either for

George Catlin's Hidatsa Buffalo Hunt. *Catlin, an adventurer as well as an artist, often painted scenes of life among the plains Indians.*

America's most famous *painter of western life is Frederick Remington. His painting* Turn 'em Loose Bill *was sold in 1974 for a record price of $175,000.*

posterity, or for their own mantels. Tombstones gave way to stone figures for those who could afford it, and ornate figureheads were carved for Yankee clipper ships. Some sculptors learned their craft in America, more learned the art abroad in Italy.

Architectural sculpture, to decorate official government buildings, banks or other institutional buildings, and to grace the homes and gardens of the wealthy, was in great demand. A growing sense of history prompted innumerable sculpture commissions for heroic statues and busts of both the living and the dead, to commemorate their faces and achievements in marble or stone. The great Italian sculptor Antonio Canova, leading figure in the European revival of classicism in the early 19th century, was the principal influence upon American sculptors of the period.

Leading American sculptors of the early and middle 19th century include William Rush (1756-1833), Hiram Powers (1805-73), Horatio Greenough (1805-1852), and Thomas Crawford (1813-1857). Like the great Canova, their exemplar, they made sculpture in the classical style and affected the taste of a generation. The wooden statue of George Washington, by William Rush, may be seen in Philadelphia's Independence Hall. *Greek Slave,* by Hiram Powers, displayed a characteristic modesty peculiar to the era despite the figure's nudity. Greenough's *George Washington*, made for the nation's Capitol rotunda, shows the grim president seated upon an imperial throne, a toga draped across his bare upper torso while he holds his hand aloft like some ancient Caesar delivering an oration. Thomas Crawford's *Armed Freedom* stands atop the Capitol dome in Washington.

In the West now, beyond the Mississippi, George Catlin (1796-1872) wandered among the Indian nations drawing and painting documentary pictures of their people and customs. Albert Bierstadt (1830-1902) painted magnificent vistas of wilderness, typified in his *Merced River, Yosemite Valley* (Metropolitan Museum of Art, New York). John F. Kensett (1818-1872), a painter of the Hudson River School, left the civilized East to travel through Colorado and New Mexico to paint the rugged wonders of the West. Other painters by the dozens criss-crossed the territory leaving their record of the natural beauty and Indian life they encountered.

Meanwhile back East, illustrations of American life, including the West, were being printed in large numbers by the lithographic process of Currier and Ives. Reproduced from paintings or drawings, the Currier and Ives prints were immensely popular and collectively form a somewhat idealized pictorial chronicle of the era.

The so-called primitive, or unsophisticated painters, recorded what they saw without artifice or embellishment. Edward Hicks (1780-1849), among the most noted of 19th century American primitives, however, is an exception to the rule. His *Peaceable Kingdom*, of which some 25 versions exist, depicts an imaginary landscape in which "the lion lays down with the lamb" as prophesied in the Bible. The primitives derive from the earlier traditions of limners; most were self-taught and were not knowledgeable in the refinements of technique. Hicks, in fact, was a Quaker preacher and did not paint for a living.

Literally dozens of primitive painters of more than just passing interest created memorable works during the 19th century. Erastus Salisbury Field (1805-1900) is typical of the best of the primitives and his portrait of *Ellen Tuttle Bangs* (Metropolitan Museum of Art, New York) is characteristic of his style, in which his lack of formal training is obvious.

John James Audubon (1785-1851) spent only a few months of study in the Paris studio of Jacques Louis David, yet his paintings are an accurate, detailed and beautiful record of American bird life. Audubon devoted more than thirty years to producing a visual catalogue of every bird in America. He was also a write on the subject of birds, and his monumental *Ornithological Biography* is still considered a most authoritative volume.

With the nation reunited at the close of the Civil War, the Westward expansion began anew with homesteaders, prospectors and railroads spearheading the drive toward the Pacific. The Gilded Age descended on America; money, power and confidence put new spirit in the American swagger. The market for art was increasing, the day of the

Famed Civil War photographer *Matthew Brady. Brady and his assistants took the newly discovered process of photography and turned it into an art form with their photographs of scenes and personages of the Civil War.*

"Robber Barons" had dawned and the captains of commerce and industry would require art, and preferably old masters, to prove that they were civilized and cultured.

American artists now traveling abroad were exposed to the new, revolutionary experiments in paint with light and color which came to be known as Impressionism. The movement was met with extreme antagonism by the conservative French Academy and the public whose taste they dominated. Impressionism, however, with its concern for pure color, shimmering outdoor light and a speed and authority of execution, would soon come to influence a number of important American painters.

Earlier, however, Winslow Homer (1836-1910) painted scenes of sea and landscape in both somber, muted colors and a brilliant palette of high intensity, especially in his watercolors. As an illustrator for *Harper's Weekly*, Homer had sketched and painted Civil War scenes, the most famous of which is *Prisoners From the Front* (Metropolitan Museum of Art, New York). Homer brought American landscape painting out from its prevailing murky brown tonalities and into the sunlight, so to speak. His pure response to weather, light and place without pausing for intellectual reflection as he set these elements upon watercolor paper would later become a guiding principal of the Impressionist movement.

George Innes (1825-1894) began painting landscapes in the Hudson River School tradition but changed to a more classic style after studying French and Italian old masters on a trip to Europe. His *Peace and Plenty* (Metropolitan Museum of Art, New York) is bathed in the golden sunlight of the Venetian school which Innes adapted to depict the

Spectator *at the Chicago Art Institute studies the technique of the self portrait of American artist James McNeil Whistler.*

Madame X, *painted by John S. Sergent in 1884.*

York studio, Ryder was obsessed by painting and oblivious to everything else. Not completely knowledgeable in the effects of the materials he used—wax, candle grease, varnish, in addition to paint—his pictures have deteriorated badly over the decades. Some paintings he worked on for years, repeatedly glazing, applying successive layers of varnish, until the original shapes in the picture were reduced to ghostly silhouettes, undefined by line. Night scenes viewed in semi-darkness or in the light of a beclouded moon were his favorite subjects, and an unabashed romanticism inhabited these pictures. Among the better known of his pictures are *Flying Dutchman* (Smithsonian Institution, Washington, D.C.) and *Toilers of the Sea* (Addison Gallery of American Art, Phillips Academy, Andover, Massachusetts).

Mary Cassat (1845-1926), meanwhile, was living in France and absorbing ideas from the Impressionists, especially Manet and Degas. Born in Pittsburgh, the daughter of a wealthy banker, Mary Cassat went to Europe after study at the Pennsylvania Academy of Fine Art. She met and was befriended by the great Impressionist painter Edgar Degas and became deeply committed to the movement. Among her most famous paintings is *La Toilette* (Art Institute, Chicago) which depicts a mother tenderly bathing her child.

With Impressionism embattled against the forces of conservatism it gained an even more attractive image among

Mary Cassat, *expatriate of the nineteenth century.*

American landscape. Yet the greens and blues of the country side are not rendered in full brilliance, but rather muted and restrained, much like the Barbizon landscape painters of France from whom Innes took much inspiration.

Genre painting continued as an important aspect of the American art world but Thomas Eakins (1844-1916) selected everyday subjects and painted them with a realism and penetration far beyond the superficialities of the genre tradition. Eakins was not merely a superb realist with a skill for accurate reproduction; his paintings were an attempt to "Get the character of things," as he would so often tell his painting students at the Pennsylvania Academy of Fine Arts. One of his more celebrated paintings, *Max Schmitt in a Single Scull* (Metropolitan Museum of Art, New York) is typical of his mature, later period.

The great visionary painter and dark, nocturnal spirit of 19th century American painting was Albert Pinkham Ryder (1847-1917). Solitary, eccentric, living in a junk-filled New

Philadelphia artist *Franklin Watkins'* Solitaire.

young artists as the spirit of freedom in the arts. Childe Hassam (1859-1935) went to France in 1883 and became a quick convert to Impressionist theories of light and color. Returning to America, he brought the new movement with him, as would others. His *Union Square in Spring* (Smith College Museum of Art, Northampton, Massachusetts) displays all the love of color and shifting play of light which typified Impressionist painting.

Still there were American painters committed to older traditions and producing work of major significance. James McNeill Whistler (1834-1903) went to Paris in 1855 and settled in London in 1859. Whistler insisted that the artist not be dependent upon nature as observed, but rather should carefully select appropriate elements from any scene and rearrange them on canvas with an imposed harmony. Such a notion was considered revolutionary for its day. Whistler's notorious libel suit against critic John Ruskin ended in Whistler's favor with an award of one farthing in damages. Critic Ruskin in remarking on one of Whistler's pictures had accused the artist of ". . . flinging a pot of paint in the public's face." Although Whistler won the case, his wealthy London clientele deserted him. Aside from the apparent influence of the Spanish master Velázquez in Whistler's work, he was also influenced by Japanese prints. His most famous painting *Arrangement in Grey and Black No. 1: The*

Artist's Mother (The Louvre, Paris) became popularly known as *Whistler's mother*, and is a distant influence upon the non-objective painting which would explode upon the art world some years leter.

Like Whistler, John Singer Sargent (1856-1925) lived in London where he painted socialites, wealthy businessmen, and aristocrats and earned a reputation for dazzling technical proficiency. He is not, however, regarded as Whistler's equal as an artist owing to his lack of daring and refusal to experiment with new techniques or ideas. Yet on occasion his portraits reveal the hidden character of his affluent sitters in a subtlety which does not flatter. Among his more famous portraits are *MadameX—Madame Pierre Gautreau* and *The Wyndham Sisters*, (both Metropolitan Museum of Art, New York).

Out West in the last years of the 19th century Frederick Remington (1861-1909), sculptor and painter, was working out his own personal form of Impressionism beneath a burning sun as one critic remarked. No more accurate picture of the frontier in all its magnificent diversity exists that that record which Remington has bequeathed in his paintings and drawings. Attention to detail, superb skills as a draughtsman and colorist and a sensitivity for his subject inhabit his every picture. His sculpture was equally accomplished, freezing the swift movement of horses in bronze. A number of his works have been collected at the Remington Art Memorial, Ogdensburg, New York.

Now the 20th century dawned, the age of modernism and accelerated history. Old notions of art would shatter into fragments as new ideas and styles of painting never before dreamed of moved to center stage and grabbed the spotlight. Cubism, Futurism, Fauvism, Orphism, Synchronism, Symbolism, Dadaism, Surrealism, Precisionism, Constructivism, Expressionism, Supremacism, and a dozen other "isms" would evolve in the early years of the new century. And American artists would eventually emerge to lead the art world, instead of follow as they had for so long before.

American painters now found new areas to explore in the cityscape, un-romanticised and rendered realistically. The ordinary, everyday life of New York city would become the subject matter of a new movement of painters. Pure color and form itself would later become the "subject" of abstract painting. Later, yet, all reference to the visual reality of an external world would be eliminated entirely as non-objective painting moved into the vanguard. Revolutions, counter-revolutions, actions and reactions would characterize this most exciting of centuries in art since the Renaissance.

The realism of American painting in the early years of the 20th century came in revolt against the saccharine and mawkish sentimentality of academic painting, so popular during that period. Robert Henri (1865-1929), the great teacher,

N.C. Wyeth, *father of Andrew Wyeth, painted* Old Pew *as part of the illustrations he did for* Treasure Island *in 1911.*

painter and motivating force behind the new realism, encouraged his colleagues to take their subject matter from the vital, energetic life of the modern city. New York was a limitless feast, waiting to be devoured by their brushes. Satire and social commentary were characteristic elements in the pictures of this new group. Common people in everyday scenes were depicted in the unflattering realism of their major influences: Velasquez, Hals, Rembrandt, Goya and Daumier. Unlike the genre painters, the pictures of this new movement reflected their subjects without softening or changing whatever realities fell to their observation. Later, certain members of the group would splinter off into an even more realistic movement which would come to be known as "the ash can school," a term of derision, referring to the "ugly" subjects they chose to paint.

Originally, before moving to New York, the group had all been students at the Pennsylvania Academy of Fine Arts. Besides Henri, the group included painters George Luks (1867-1933), William Glackens (1870-1938), John Sloan (1871-1951), and Everett Shinn (1876-1953). Each of these artists would make important contributions to the history of American painting, especially in their rebellion against the rigid rules of the academics and the unrealistically "pretty" pictures they produced. Henri and Sloan later taught for years at New York's famous Art Students League, influencing thousands of disciples, many of whom became distinguished artists themselves.

In 1908 at the Macbeth Gallery in New York, three new artists joined the original realist group Henri, Luks, Glackens, Sloan and Shinn to form "The Eight," who showed their realistic paintings in protest against the National Academy of Arts and The Society of American Artists, which had rejected their work for exhibition. The three new group members were Maurice Prendergast (1859-1924), Arthur B. Davies (1862-1928) and Ernest Lawson (1873-1939). Surprisingly, the show of these "independents" was a financial if not a critical success. The term "ash can school" was first applied to these painters in a newspaper review of the show, but the public turned out in large numbers and some $4,000 worth of paintings were sold. When the New York exhibition concluded, it toured through eight other cities.

The same year Alfred Stieglitz (1864-1946) began regularly showing the work of the European avant garde at his famous "291" gallery on Fifth Avenue in New York. Exposed now to modernist ideas from abroad, American painters and sculptors in New York, along with a small but ever-growing group of collectors, fell under the influence of the radical ideas being imported. American artists were quick to absorb the revolutionary attitudes and transform them into art; a handful of daring collectors with adventurous tastes began buying the new work. In France, a number of American painters, several of whom were studying with modernist master Henri Matisse, formed the New Society of American Artists in Paris. Among them were Max Weber (1881-1961), and Alfred Maurer (1858-1932), influenced first by Matisse and his uninhibited use of color and simplified divisions of space and later by Picasso, Braque and other Cubists.

In the years before 1914, which marks the beginning of World War I, dozens of American artists came to Paris to study, to immerse themselves in the vitality of a militant revolt against tradition and to breathe the intoxicating air of freedom which seemed to pervade the "Capital of World Culture" as Paris was then regarded. Among the American painters then in Europe were Thomas Hart Benton (1889-1975), Charles Demuth (1883-1935), Arthur B. Davies

The End of the Trail, *completed by sculptor Earl Fraser in 1915.*

Famed American artist *Thomas Hart Benton, as he appeared in 1962.*

(1862-1928), Mardsen Hartley (1877-1943), Charles Sheeler (1883-1965), Joseph Stella (1880-1946) and Stanton Macdonald-Wright (1890-   ), all of whom would subsequently distinguish themselves as artists.

In 1913 Arthur B. Davies organized and presented the so-called Armory Show, officially introducing modern art to the American public. Held in the huge Sixty-Ninth Regiment headquarters building in New York city, the Armory Show displayed some 1,600 pieces of art, from the 19th century French painters Delacroix and Ingres to the contemporary Cubists. William Glackens, the American painter, selected a group of American artists to show their work along with the celebrated, and not-so-celebrated, Europeans. The entire exhibition was mounted under the auspices of the Association of American Painters and Sculptors, of which Davies was president. Marcel Duchamp's Cubist picture *Nude Descending a Staircase* inspired outrage and bewilderment among the generally conservative American public. Equally as upsetting to the streams of curious spectators who came to see the "explosion in a shingle factory" as one critic described Duchamp's picture, were the offerings of Picasso, Matisse, Braque, Kandinsky, Brancusi, Picabia, Léger, Roualt, Cézanne, Gaugin and Van Gogh—all giants of the modernist movement. The newspapers devoted an enormous amount of coverage to the event, most of it to ridicule and jeer at the work which was so troubling to American sensibilities and so contrary to the established traditions. But modern art had made its American debut and there'd be no turning back, once the mainstream of American art began moving in that direction. The show later traveled to Boston and Chicago and was generally received with the same derision, although hundreds of thousands came to gawk and no doubt derived a curious enjoyment from the spectacle.

With the outbreak of World War I in 1914, a number of Americans who had been living abroad returned home, bringing with them the new ideas they had acquired in Europe and infusing them into the body of American culture through their art. In New York, after the initial shock of the Armory Show, public and critics alike were now even more vigorously opposed to modernist art than before; what they had thought was a temporary joke had obviously come to stay, and had infected large numbers of American artists. A tiny handful of critics defended the new art, but they constituted a pathetic minority. Majority opinion held that the work was produced by "lunatics, charlatans and political subversives."

Implicit in the new art was the assertion of individuality, freedom from the unthinking conformities of mass culture, trust in the truth of the senses as against the artifice of learned responses, and a sense of adventure and inquiry. Such attitudes were to characterize in general the thinking and art of modernists for years to come. And eventually, the beliefs of these precedent-making artists would be enshrined as incontestable doctrine until the next wave of rebels arose to challenge them, preaching their own brand of dogma.

Cubism was a major trend in European painting through the war years, although other important styles or movements were developing simultaneously. Whatever new ideas appeared in European painting or sculpture, American artists adapted to their own uses. John Marin (1872-1953), the great watercolorist, used Cubist methods of reorganizing and fragmenting space on a flat, two-dimensional surface, using the New York city skyline and the American countryside for his subject matter. Charles Demuth, mentioned previously, took Cubist ideas and simplified them into a precision rendering of industrial scenes, cityscapes and abstractions, of which *I Saw The Figure Five in Gold* (Metropolitan Museum of Art, New York) is a typical example. Lyonel Feininger (1871-1956) was a musician, comic strip artist, toymaker and caricaturist who turned his strong sense of design and love of formalities both geometric and musical to painting. He produced a large body of work with a pronounced Cubist influence but a uniquely Feininger sensitivity and handling of large planes of volume and light. Exemplary of his style is *Bridge V* (Philadelphia Museum of Art), and *Gelmeroda VIII* (Whitney Museum of American Art, New York).

Joseph Stella, mentioned previously, combined the Italian Futurist concern with dynamic motion into the Cubist style of flat patterns to produce a body of work expressing the chaotic movement and frenzy of the modern city. *Battle of Lights, Coney Island* (Yale University Art Gallery) and *The Brooklyn Bridge* (Whitney Museum of American Art, New York), are illustrative of Stella's early and mature style, respectively.

Stanton Macdonald-Wright, cited before, was among the most important of early American abstract painters. Co-founder of the Synchronist movement, which reflects a strong Cubist influence, Macdonald-Wright attempted to create an optical sense of deeper space and fluid movement on the two-dimensional surface of the canvas through the scientific use of color and value. *Oriental: Synchrony in Blue-Green* (Whitney Museum of American Art, New York) is a good illustration of the Synchronist style.

With the end of World War I, there was a resurgence of activity in the arts in both Europe and America. Painters and sculptors moved more easily now from style to style, dropping old ideas, picking up new ones, and many defied easy classification. In Europe, Kandinsky had already painted the first non-objective (no recognizable subject matter) pictures a

Spring on the Missouri *by Thomas Hart Benton. Benton died in 1975.*

few years earlier. Malevitch followed with variations on that theme, but painted in strict hard-lined geometries, rather than the loose, freely brushed expressionism of Kandinsky. Picasso and Braque had introduced the collage—the use of pasted papers—and American artists were now utilizing the technique.

In America, a new regionalism in art was beginning to emerge which came perhaps in reaction against the foreign ideologies of modernism. Thomas Hart Benton, previously mentioned, Grant Wood (1891-1942) and John Steuart Curry (1897-1946) were among the most notable of this group of romantic yet realistic painters who idealized the American small town and country life in the Midwest. Grant Wood's famous *American Gothic* (Art Institute, Chicago) with its "typical" American farm couple, has an unmistakably satirical but gentle comment to offer. Benton's work is sometimes an idealized view of American life, or a cynical observation of it, as in his *Preparing the Bill,* owned by the estate of the artist. Curry's painting presents the American farmer as hero and protector, most fully realized in his *Tornado* (Hackley Art Gallery, Muskegon, Michigan). Thomas Hart Benton, the most outspoken regionalist, was ironically a teacher at the New York Art Students League, which would produce so many rebels against the regionalist attitude, including the great Abstract Expressionist Jackson Pollock (1912-1956).

Edward Hopper (1882-1967) was both a regionalist and a painter of urban America. Using simplified but still realistic forms and building solid compositions of architectural stability, Hopper also managed to invest each painting with a truth and emotion beyond the deceptively simple picture. A haunting loneliness pervades these scenes of New York City or New England countryside, painted with such deft handling of luminous sunlight and color. *Early Sunday Morning* (Whitney Museum of American Art, New York) and *Gas* (Museum of Modern Art, New York) are typical examples of his work.

Charles Burchfield (1893-1967) rendered the Midwest in a series of introspective watercolors which reflected a romantic influence tempered by a sharp and often satirical eye. His later works, many of which are based on recollections from his childhood, seem drenched in a sense of dramatic foreboding. Although theoretically a regionalist painter, Burchfield like Hopper transcends that easy definition since his work encompasses so much more than the term is able to describe. Representative paintings from his early and late period include *Church Bells Ringing—Rainy Winter Night* (Cleveland Museum of Art) painted 1917, and *April Mood*

Charles Demuth's I Saw the Figure Five in Gold, *based on some lines in a William Carlos Williams poem, was painted in 1928. Demuth committed suicide in 1937.*

(Whitney Museum of American Art, New York), painted 1955.

Georgia O'Keefe (1887-   ) first showed her art in 1916 at the "291" Gallery of Alfred Stieglitz, whom she later married. Flowers, Southwestern landscapes and the dried, bleached bones of the desert creatures near her New Mexico home have been the principal subject matter of Ms. O'Keefe's paintings. Inessential or superficial elements of the subject are taken out, or "abstracted" by Ms. O'Keefe until only a simple, powerful statement remains. Applying the same principle to her pictures of buildings, window casements and architectural elements, a new vision of these commonplace objects is achieved. Three paintings which illustrate the range of her concerns and her treatment of natural and geometric shapes are *Black Iris* and *Cow's Skull, Red, White and Blue* both (Metropolitan Museum of Art, New York), and *Lake George Window* (Museum of Modern Art, New York).

American sculpture from the turn of the century moved away from traditional restraints at a slower pace than painting. Monuments and sculptural ornaments commissioned for public buildings and institutions generally retained their typical Beaux-Arts European look, strictly academic, neoclassical, and competent but uninspiring. Much like their contemporaries The Eight, the realist painters previously mentioned, a small group of sculptors in New York took genre subjects and began transforming them into a new three-dimensional reality. Mahonri Young (1877-1957) first sculpted working-class figures and cast them in bronze. Subsequently, influenced perhaps by George Bellows, Young used the prizefighter as subject matter and *Boxer* (Whitney Museum of American Art, New York) demonstrates the drama and vitality of his style. Malvina Hoffman (1887-1967) studied sculpture first in America and later in Paris with the master Auguste Rodin. In 1911 at the Paris Salon she won a first prize in sculpture for a work much

influenced by her instructor. Returning to America, she settled in New York where she became celebrated for her technical virtuosity and energy. But her work belonged to an older era and none of the radical, daring ideas of the modernist movement intruded upon the purity of her style.

By contrast, Elie Nadleman (1882-1946), a transplanted Pole who had come to America by way of Munich and Paris, reflected his exposure to Cubism in the simplified forms and streamlined volumes of his figures. A more important influence on his work, however, would seem to be the ornamental curves of *Art Nouveau*, so popular in the early years of the 20th century. Nadleman's figures occupy space in a delicate, tentative way, elegant and stylized, but more refined than bold.

Another European immigrant who would profoundly influence the direction of American sculpture was Gaston Lachaise (1882-1935). The Parisian Lachaise came to America in 1906 with a solid academic background and several major group shows to his credit. After serving as assistant to the celebrated sculptors Henry Hudson Kitson (1863-1947) and Paul Manship (1885-1966), Lachaise began evolving his unique style of handling massive volumes in a rhythmic, lyrical weightlessness—which seems contradictory until one sees *Standing Woman* (Museum of Modern Art, New York), for example, demonstrating how these opposing elements are combined. His later works, just recently shown widely after years of censorship, are both more erotic and more expressionistically distorted than his earlier,

This portrait *of Harry Truman was painted by Thomas Hart Benton in 1972, and hangs in the lobby of the Truman Library in Independence, Missouri.*

Grant Wood's American Gothic, *completed in 1930.*

Artist Grant Wood *at work on an etching in 1942.*

more graceful figures.

William Zorach (1887-1966) began as a painter first, but in 1916 switched to sculpture which he produced by carving directly into his materials, an approach 20th century artists were giving up in favor of other methods. Abstracting and reducing his sculptural forms to simple shapes suggesting a distant Cubist influence, Zorach's earliest human and animal pieces were nevertheless representational images. Later in his career Zorach used a controlled expressionist distortion of form as so many of his colleagues did, including Lachaise.

John B. Flannagan (1895-1942) also carved directly into his materials, working principally in stone and producing a unique body of work which was both primitive and sophisticated simultaneously. Moving from the exaggerated shapes of expressionism into a more symbolic and quiet handling of stone, Flannagan's later work resembled both the work of romantic visionary painters of the past and the work of modernist Brancusi, a contemporary. *Chimpanzee* (Whitney Museum of American Art, New York) illustrates his affinity with Brancusi; *Jonah and the Whale* (The Minneapolis Institute of Arts) reveals the influence of earlier romantics.

Chaim Gross (1880-   ) also carved from stone and wood, allowing the shape and grain of his raw materials to suggest the final form, as illustrated in his *Mother and Child At Play*. Reuben Nakian (   ) produced simple abstractions in his early marble sculpture by pursuing its implicit grain and rendering the image as economically as possible. Jacob Epstein (1880-   ) found the sources of his earliest work in the Egyptian and Oriental art he had studied. Later, he would build with gobbets of clay quickly and impulsively applied, a series of potraits cast in bronze notable for their immediacy and strength.

Despite the exciting influx of modernist ideas from abroad, there were few American artists during this period of three decades whose sculpture was more than just competent. The artists mentioned above, of course, did not constitute the totality of American talent in the three-dimensional idiom. Alexander Archipenko (1887-1964) produced extraordinary Cubist *cum* Futurist pieces of geometric beauty and impact. Lorado Taft (1860-1936) acquired a reputation as a fine teacher and solid craftsman, although his public sculpture commissions were uninventive. Technical facility was not enough to commend an object as art, according to the new critics of the era. Sculpture in America for the first thirty years of the 20th century has been described by an eminent

circle as generally impoverished and lacking in experiment. American sculpture would miraculously blossom, however, in the next several decades and a brilliant array of new talent would emerge to transform completely the face of this ancient art.

With the Depression years a bleak, heavy mood descended on America, smothering temporarily the optimisms and enthusiasms which typified the 1920's. Bank failures, unemployment, poverty, hunger, Hoovervilles and all the attendant woes of the depression affected the work of a great number of American painters and sculptors. A strong social consciousness evolved in the American artist, and although many continued to pursue Surrealism, Expressionism and new modes of abstraction, the art of social protest arose as a grim reflection of the decade

Philip Evergood (1901-   ) abandoned an early concern with the painting of Biblical themes to take his subject matter from the everyday life of the 1930's which everywhere expressed the poignance and brutality of hard times. But Evergood's painting does not seduce with an easy sentimentality, but rather sees life in dramatic, almost Surrealistic images which bespeak all the chaos, heroism and corruption of the American scene. William Groper (1897-   ) painted the corrupt, windbag politician, bloated and well-fed while others starved. Ben Shahn (1898-1969) came to America from Russia as a child of eight, later studied lithography and developed his strong social conscience into an art of equal pictorial strength on returning from a trip to Europe as a young man. No longer content to paint merely an esthetic, sensual experience for the viewer, he turned to the representation of social injustice in powerful and compassionate terms. Pictures such as *The Passion of Sacco and Vanzetti* (Whitney Museum of Art, New York) and *Handball* (Museum of Modern Art, New York) illustrate Shahn's concern with social issues, and his superb gifts as an artist.

Also concerned with social problems but attacking them from a different angle was Jack Levine (1915-   ). He brought to the easel along with his considerable talents as a painter, a sharp sense of satire through which he penetrated into the heart of a character or situation. *The Feast of Pure Reason* (Museum of Modern Art, New York), in which politician, ward heeler and cop form an unholy trinity of corruption, demonstrates perfectly the measure of Levine's talent. Peter Blume (1906-   ) shared similar concerns with Shahn and Levine, but developed yet a third style with which to attack. Closely related to the Surrealist school of painting, but not strictly defined by that criterion, Peter Blume used real objects in unreal situations to produce an art of profound psychological resonance and social import. His masterpiece *The Eternal City* (Museum of Modern Art, New York) is much more than just an anti-Fascist protest piece. Its exacting realism, its Surrealistic juxtapositions and its references to past romanticism invade deeply into the psyche of the viewer.

George Grosz (1893-1959) came to America in 1932 from a troubled Germany about to fall under Nazi domination. Grosz had been a brilliant caricaturist and bitter commentator on the decadence of Berlin which preceded the rise of Hitler. Grosz became an American citizen in 1938, and taught for many years at New York's Art Students League. His American cityscapes, landscapes and nudes lacked the penetrating bite of his earlier satirical work, although several pictures gave form to his anticipation of the coming horrors of World War II. *A Piece of My World* (Newark Museum, Newark, N.J.), painted the year Grosz became an American citizen,

Grandma Moses *at work in her home in Eagle Bridge, New York.*

foreshadows the destruction and desolation soon to afflict the world.

Social injustice and rumors of war, however, were not reflected to any great extent in the work of Stuart Davis (1894-1964). More concerned with the formal aspects of painting (design, color, mass, line, etc.), Davis developed a pictorial style with its compositional roots in Cubism and its color disharmonies hearkening back to the Fauves or "wild beasts" of Paris. Davis, however, applied his color with an unbroken flatness, creating geometrical patterns of architectural stability, often enlivened by a rich, textural surface, and sometimes accented with fragments of words. Typical of his early style is *Lucky Strike* (Museum of Modern Art, New York), foreshadowing perhaps the advent of "Pop" art with its use of consumer products and advertising symbols as subject matter. *Owh! in San Pao* (Whitney Museum of American Art, New York), painted in 1951, illustrates his mature style.

Mark Tobey (1890-   ) was likewise concerned with the formal problems of painting. Influenced by his study of Chinese calligraphy, Tobey developed a style which he referred to as "white writing," which was a lyrical application of light brush work over a darker background. Using this mode first to define loosely a rough but recognizable image such as *Broadway* (Metropolitan Museum of Art, New York), Tobey later used the same technique in a non-objective style, of which *Edge of August* (Museum of Modern Art, New York) is a typical example.

Sculptors now also began experimenting on the borders of pure abstraction or the non-objective. Alexander Calder (1898-   ) first attracted wide attention with the exhibition

Barn Dance, *painted by Grandma Moses in 1950.*

Frank Lloyd Wright *standing in front of the Robie House he designed in Chicago.*

America's most famous *architect Frank Lloyd Wright, as he appeared in 1956.*

in 1932 of his wind-propelled mobiles, a semi-abstract sculptural object usually suspended from the ceiling and constantly in motion from the circulating air currents. In Calder's mobile *Lobster Trap and Fish Tail* (Museum of Modern Art, New York) the image is reduced to its bare essence. Later works would increase in size and evolve occasionally into a complete non-objectivity with close parallels to the Surrealist painting of Joan Miró. Isamu Noguchi (1904-   ) was born in America but spent his childhood in Japan. As an apprentice to Constantin Brancusi, he no doubt developed his affinity for highly finished, severely simple, semi-abstract shapes which characterized his early sculpture. His more mature work of polished stone is non-objective but suggestive of organic or biomorphic shapes, such as the typical *Capital* (Museum of Modern Art, New York).

Other important sculptors of the period just preceding World War II who were working in abstract styles include David Smith (1906-1965), Theodore Roszak (1907-   ), Ibram Lassaw (1913-   ), Seymour Lipton (1903-   ) and David Hare (1917-   ). All shared a common belief in sculpture as possessing far more potential than traditional restraints would allow. Many of these artists were already using metals and the welding torch in new ways to produce sculpture of a rich and spontaneous immediacy. Others would later adopt these techniques and give up the more conservative and older methods of carving, modeling and casting. On the eve of World War II, American sculpture was about to enter into three decades of its most inventive, productive and internationally influential period.

By the time America entered the war, the Federally-funded

WPA art project had been operating for some years and providing a meager living for many artists who would otherwise be unemployed. Many notable American artists were to emerge from the government's easel painting program or the mural projects which kept painters and sculptors busy creating art for post offices and public buildings all over America.

The booming war economy, however, soon provided a reason for ending the programs and American artists were on their own once more without government subsidy. From Europe now came a steady influx of artists in flight from the horrors of war and the oppressions of the dictatorial Nazis and Fascists. A sizeable community of foreign artists arose in New York, and many of these painters, sculptors, writers and musicians would remain to become American citizens. There was a strange reversal in these circumstances since now more European artists were coming to America than Americans going the other way.

Paintings of social protest geared now to the war effort flourished during the four years of American involvement, but there were other more powerful currents running wildly through the cultural underground which would eventually erupt in the explosion of vitality and originality known as Abstract Expressionism, or action painting or the New York school as it is variously called.

At the end of World War II America was the most powerful, richest and least injured of all the major nations embroiled in the conflict. Paris was no longer the capital of World Art. In America now a group of artists were probing deeper into their own psyches than the strict imagery of social protest pictures or even the strange juxtapositions of Surrealism might allow, although certain Surrealist principles lie at the base of the movement.

Basically, the Abstract Expressionists painted

American artist *Norman Rockwell.*

Reginald Marsh's Coney Island.

spontaneously, without conscious deliberation, letting their brushes explore and slash across the canvas, or letting their paint drip recklessly in an all-over pattern, or allowing accidental splashing and smudging of paint to stand as the basis of a composition. Behind such radical and apparent "anti-art" techniques was a profound aversion for the well-made, highly finished and intellectually calculated design. The senses and the impulses are more to be trusted, insisted these adventurous artists, than the cold deliberations of reason. Implicit perhaps in this radical thinking was a disenchantment with the so-called reason which bequeathed Hitler, Auschwitz, and Hiroshima to the world. Whatever the obvious or obscure origins of the movement, it exploded on the

Famed naturalist photographer Ansel Adams, as he appeared in 1974.

scene with a resounding concussion.

Like the Armory Show so many years before, the early exhibitions of Abstract Expressionist work were met with outrage and bewilderment. Two discerning and influential critics, however, were champions of the cause and helped pave the way for an easier and earlier acceptance of the work—if not among the general public, then at least among knowledgeable collectors and museum curators. Critics Harold Rosenberg and Clement Greenberg did much to explain and evaluate the work of this enigmatic and troubling group of artists.

Jackson Pollock (1912-1956) stands among the giants of the movement and is best known for his so-called "drip paintings." Despite what appears to be a formless, overall design, pictures like Pollack's *Number One, 1948* (Museum of Modern Art, New York) or *Autumn Rhythm* (Metropolitan Museum of Art, New York), have an underlying structure although they were painted spontaneously. To explain this paradox, critic Harold Rosenberg writes of the spontaneity of a master fencer, who responds to the thrust of a foil without thinking and yet deliberately. Pollock's paintings created a sense of deep space on a two dimensional surface without resort to the standard methods of spatial description. In his use of dripped paint as both line and shape, and using the act of painting itself as his subject matter, he broke from all past traditions including the heavy influence of Picasso and Miró in his earlier work. The act of painting itself as subject matter—this cryptic statement may best be understood if one follows the tracery of Pollock's restless dripping back and forth on canvas as one might read a map or a chart depicting the movement of his arm. Dead prematurely at forty-four in an automobile accident, Pollock's work is unique in Ameri-

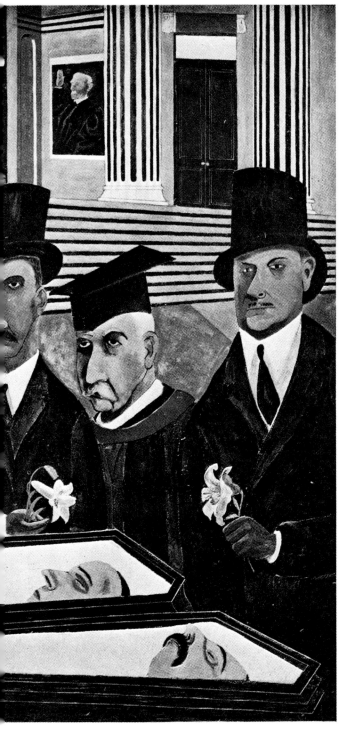

Ben Shahn's The Passion of Sacco and Vanzetti, *painted in the 1920's.*

can art and an enormous influence on painting around the world.

Willem de Kooning (1904-   ), another giant of Abstract Expressionism, also recreates the painting process on his huge canvasses, but a residue of pictorial origins remains buried in the thick impastos and non-objectivity of his later works, and is obvious in the earlier paintings. The most widely-publicized of de Kooning's paintings is *Woman I* (Museum of Modern Art, New York), one of a series of pictures on the same theme which the artist produced over a period of years. The figure sits in a flat, ambiguous space, defined by brutal and vigorous applications of a broad brush loaded with several colors at once. The process of painting a shape and painting it out, drawing with the brush and erasing is clearly visible on the tortured surface of the canvas, thereby again using the act of painting itself as part of the subject matter of the picture. Both earlier and later works of de Kooning move back and forth between recognizable subject matter and complete non-objectivity.

Franz Kline (1910-1962) simplified both the abstract and expressionist aspects of Abstract Expressionism into a series of black and white paintings of monumental scale and powerful impact. Using only a few broad strokes of black paint against a white background, Kline could suggest nuances of color, subtleties of space and terrific energies. Suggestions of Japanese calligraphy are apparent in Kline's paintings, but the artist is said to have developed his style after viewing

some oil sketches of his enlarged through a projector. Typical of the power Kline could evoke with minimum color and a compositional simplicity is *Painting Number 7* (The Solomon R. Guggenheim Museum, New York).

The influence of Hans Hoffman (1880-1966) can be seen in the three artists mentioned above, and vice versa, since the close associations of New York and constant exposure to the work and ideas of colleagues is bound to reflect and amplify itself in the art of painters who share common attitudes. Hoffman owned and operated his own painting school in New York and produced a number of brilliant young disciples who later went on to forge careers for themselves with uniquely personal styles only remotely similar to their master. In Hoffman's long career he was constantly experimenting with new ideas and techniques and his non-objective paintings were among the earliest in the Abstract Expressionist mode seen in America—even before the term had caught on. Typical of Hoffman's style is *Exuberance* (The Albright Gallery, Buffalo, New York) and *The Golden Wall* (Art Institute, Chicago).

Although Abstract Expressionism generally connoted an energetic, spontaneous approach to painting, there was another more thoughtful and less violent side to the movement. Among the practitioners of this contemplative but nonetheless powerful painting were Mark Rothko

(1903-1970), Barnett Newman (1905-1970), Bradley Walker Tomlin (1899-1953), Arshile Gorky (1905-1948) and Robert Motherwell (1915-   ).

Once the Abstract Expressionists established their dominance as the prevailing direction of American painting, the predictable disciples followed, among them such superbly gifted painters as Joan Mitchell (1926-   ), Larry River (1923-   ), Helen Frakenthaler (1928-   ), Jasper Johns(1930-   ) and Robert Rauschenberg (1924-   ). Some of these painters were enormously influential in their own right and we shall hear from them again as the inevitable reaction *against* Abstract Expressionism followed closely on the heels of its success.

The influence of Abstract Expressionism on international art was considerable. By the early 1950's the world was looking toward New York for the latest addendum to avant garde painting. America had assumed a leadership in the arts which previously had belonged to Paris. But there were other artistic tendencies at work in New York, and although the limelight was monopolized by the Abstract Expressionists, new artists would soon upstage them as the once-revolutionary painting first won wide acceptance and then declined into an academic parody of itself.

Sculpture during this period rediscovered some older influences and adapted them to a modern idiom. The sculpture of Pablo Picasso, with its use of found objects or "junk" items transformed into three-dimensional art, became a model from which younger American sculptors fashioned variations. Others used it as a point of departure to venture forward into new territory where sculpture previously had not explored. Richard Stankiewicz (1922-   ) welded rusted shards of machinery, iron and steel fragments from the american industrial scrap heap. The sculpture he created is rich and complex in shape, color and texture, formal qualities of art which had become increasingly important since the rise

of abstraction as a major direction in world art. *Instruction* (The Museum of Modern Art, New York) is a typical example of Stankiewicz's work. David Smith, previously mentioned, began grinding the surfaces of his sculpture into a rough, unfinished patina, almost like the vigorous brushwork of Abstract Expressionist painters. Louise Nevelson (1900-   ) won increasing acceptance for her colossal sculptures of wood scraps, discarded moulding, wooden architectural ornaments or furniture embellishments.

Robert Rauschenberg, previously mentioned, combined both found objects or "junk" items with the Abstract Expressionist brush-stroke to produce a series of what he called "combine paintings," of which *Bed* (Collection of Mr. and Mrs. Leo Castelli, New York) or *Lincoln* (Art Institute, Chicago) are early examples. Jasper Johns, also mentioned previously, used found objects in a series of paintings which first foreshadowed and eventually bridged the gap between abstract Expressionism and the new Pop art movement which became temporarily a major direction of both American and British artists.

Using symbols from popular culture—the advertising logo, the comic strip, the more gross and vulgar aspects of consumer taste and fashion—Pop artists launched an attack on the cherished values of Abstract Expressionism and a satirical broadside against the atrocities of mass production and the consequent debasement of taste and quality. Jasper Johns painted flat reproductions of the American flag, or huge maps of the United States in a loosely-brushed Abstract Expresionist manner. Roy Lichtenstein (1923-   ) took the cliches of comic strips, enlarged them to enormous scale, and presented what appeared to be single panels from some popular comic story. James Rosenquist (1933-   ), who had worked as a sign painter, created enormous canvases which showed a montage of common objects and symbols painted in a billboard realism, with exaggerated colors and somewhat stylized simplicity. His gigantic *F-111* (Collection Mr. Robert C. Scull, New York), 86 feet wide by ten feet high, is probably the largest painting of recent times. Claes Oldenburg (1929-   ), a painter and a sculptor, first showed roughly finished paintings and sculptures of advertising symbols and commonplace objects. Later, he made "soft sculpture" in polyvinyl and other plastics which included huge enlargements of hamburgers, popsicles, typewriters and toilets. Red Grooms (1937-   ) made huge, walk-in models of his favorite cities, New York and Chicago, fashioned from wood and moving objects, with accompanying music as part of the composition. Marisol Escobar (1930-   ) used blocks of raw wood upon which she drew and carved the bodies and faces of typical Americans in a cartoon-like rendering of reality. Robert Indiana (1928-   ) took the slogans and bromides of American culture and made paintings from them as if they were icons worthy of enshrinement. Love, Eat, Die, and other similar words were blown up and carefully lettered upon the canvas. The comment in each piece is partially satirical, partially accusatory.

Unquestionably the king of Pop, however, was Andy Warhol (1930-   ), who first attracted wide publicity with his multiple reproductions of the Campbell soup label and the Brillo box, which collectors acquired in large numbers. Again, the comment is satirical, derogatory, even vaguely disdainful of the affluent consumer who buys the Warhol picture of another picture. From advertising symbols Warhol moved to both stylized portraits of pop culture celebrities and portrait commissions of his patrons and collectors, using all

The dean of American *photographers, Edward Steichen, as he appeared in 1959.*

the instruments of the mass produced visual image, i.e., silk screen, lithography, photography, etc. A series of photographic silk screen paintings of automobile accidents, the electric chair and other horrors of civilization came next in Warhol's development and played a strange counterpoint against the previous frivolity of his subject matter.

Suddenly celebrated and made wealthy by some of the same public whose taste Warhol excoriated, he sought an even wider audience. He produced and directed a number of films for national release such as *Chelsea Girls* and *Trash*, to mention just a few. The films are erotic and satiric, spoofing the grandiose pretensions of the Hollywood "extravaganza" or the calculated obscurities of certain "art films." Other Warhol enterprises have included the formation of a rock music group called "The Velvet Undergrond," the publication of a national magazine entitled *Interview*, the authorship and several books including his *Autobiography*. All these cultural products issue from Warhol's New York headquarters which in his characteristic irony he calls "the Factory."

Pop sculpture expressed a variety of attitudes, including the three-dimensional genre studies of George Segal (1924-   ), whose life-sized figures in plaster were often cast directly from life, using a living person as an armature. Claes Oldenberg, previously mentioned, in his later sculpture created a series of giant-sized imaginary public monuments honoring various professions, trades and culture sym-

bols, building scale models of the objects in soft materials. A number of artists worked in the limbo between painting and sculpture, creating collages and constructions of three-dimensional objects on two-dimensional surfaces. Live performances, loudly-blasting radios and tape recorders, even art objects which destroyed themselves were added to the expanding panoply of Pop art possibilities. John Chamberlain (1927-   ) made sculpture of smashed and twisted automobile fenders which conveyed a spontaneous beauty close to the Abstract Expressionist aesthetic. Lee Bontecou (1930-   ) worked welded metal, wire and canvas on a two-dimensional ground made to hang on the wall. Tom Wesselman (1931-   ) first made paintings which resembled billboards, as did James Rosenquist, previously mentioned. Later, he produced life-sized rooms or environments using painted figures, actual objects, doors which opened, clocks which ticked off the time. By the time Pop art had been thoroughly exploited in the media, billboards began to look like paintings, automobile wreckage began to look like art, and art looked like everything.

While Pop art was asserting itself upon the American consciousness, as always there were other divergent ideas being pursued by painters and sculptors. Post-painterly abstraction, the name conferred by art historians upon the non-objective painting which evolved from Abstract Expres-

Originator of the mobile, *Alexander Calder, surrounded by one of his gigantic mobiles at the Perls Gallery in New York City.*

sionist concepts, soon emerged to challenge the dominance of pop art. There were major distinctions between the two styles, however. The Post-painterly abstractionists—of which there were numerous practitioners with nuances and subtleties of difference—no longer were concerned with thick impasto surfaces, broken color, the energetic brush-stroke, the bleeding of edges and the invasion of one color area into another. Instead, they minimized surface texture, staining their pigments directly into raw, unprepared canvas, so that fabric and picture became one. In these paintings of so-called colorfields one may trace the influence of Rothko, Pollock, Newman, Gorky, all Abstract Expressionists, but all also unique in their approach to the canvas. Among the notable painters of the era who used staining methods were Helen Frankenthaler, previously mentioned, Morris Louis (1912-1962), who was inflenced by Frankenthaler's work, Kenneth Noland (1924-   ), Jules Olitski (1922-   ), and Paul Jenkins (1923-   ).

Hard-edged painting, in which forms are precisely defined with a crisp division between each two areas, also belongs to the Post-painterly abstraction era, and has its roots in the paintings of Abstract Expressionist Barnett Newman, previously mentioned, and back to the precisionists, and even earlier to Mondrian and Malevitch, Europeans who pioneered in geometric abstraction. Among the major American artists working in this mode are Frank Stella (1936-   ) and Ellsworth Kelley (1923-   ). The later canvases of Stella are not shaped in the traditional square or rectangular format, but are irregular, curved, truncated, oblique, diamond-shaped, etc., to accommodate the chevrons, stripes or arcs of his paintings. Kelly painted in pure primaries—red, yellow and blue—or in stark black and white. In the work of both these artists there is no evidence of brushwork, and indeed the paint is often sprayed or rolled on with large brayers to eliminate the ''hand-made'' look of Abstract Expressionism. Joseph Albers (1888-   ) for years experimented with color combinations arranged as squares within squares, crisply delineated but concerned not so much with shape as with the optical effects of his arrangements.

Op-Art, or art concerned with perceptual paradox, illusion and the effects of complementary colors in dazzling juxtapositions, flourished briefly and was quickly picked up by interior decorators, commercial illustrators and fabric designers.

Sculpture, long divided into numerous branches and sub-branches, developed yet another aspect: movement. Kinetic sculpture, which moved on the power of gravity, electric motors or magnetic force became a brief but popular fad. Calder, mentioned previously, had set sculpture into an easy, flowing movement with his mobiles, driven by circulating air currents. But the new kinetic sculpture moved more quickly, and usually more frantically than the gentle circulation of Calder's pieces. The use of raw, unfinished steel also became popular for sculpture. Huge constructions fabricated with I-beams, or slabs of sheet steel, were being shown in galleries and museums. Steel became as commonplace in sculpture as was once marble and stone in classic times. Tony Smith (1912-   ) made giant geometrical pieces from corten steel, which turned under weathering into a rich, rusty surface which did not damage the material. Mark di Suvero (1933-   ) used structural steel beams in conjunction with railroad ties, scrap lumber, rope, rubber tires, other found materials, to create sculpture of surprising beauty and power. Typical of Tony Smith's work is *Cigarette* (Albright-Knox Art Gallery, Buffalo, New York). Mark di Suvero's *Pre-Columbian* (Storm King Art Center, Mountainville, New York) illustrates his typical eclectic use of materials.

Other sculptors in the mid 1960's turned to plastic materials which they transformed into an art of amazing diversity whose potential has only begun to be explored. Casing, vacu-forming, bending, using as clay, using as liquid, or in a dozen other methods, the artists working in platics probably have a range of possibilities in three-dimensional art previously undreamed of by the stone carvers of yesteryear. On the West coast artists such as Craig Kauffman (1932-   ) and Douglas Wheeler (1939-   ) made vacuum molded wall-hangings of colored plexiglas, illuminated by a shimmering neon light. Billy Al Bengston (1934-   ) combines plastic with paper, formica, steel, glass, ceramics or whatever else is available to make assemblages of symmetrical precision and psychedelic references. Duane Hanson (1925-   ) makes life-sized figures in plastic which are miraculously authentic reproductions of the human form.

The New Realism, or Sharp-Focus realism as it was also called, emerged in recent years as a reaction against the minimal abstractions of so many mainstream artists. Using subject matter from every area—cityscape, landscape, the commonplace and the banal, and even their own faces for portraiture—the New realists painted in a style of extreme photographic accuracy, although color was somewhat modified. Alfred Leslie (1927-   ), formerly an Abstract

Mark Rothko's Number 10, *painted in 1950.*

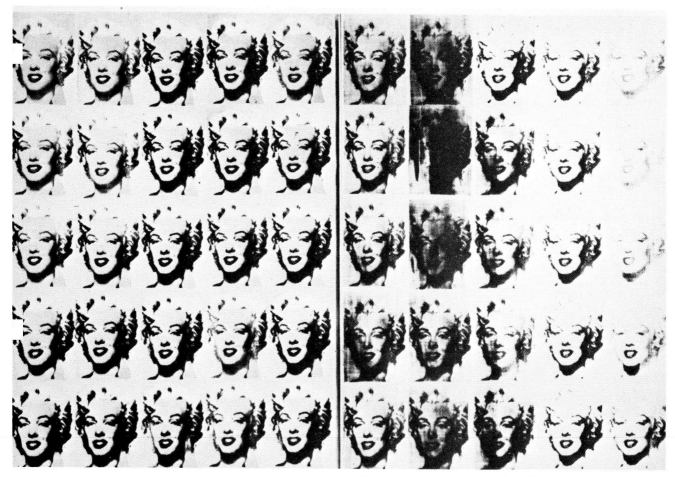

Marilyn Monroe Diptych, *executed by Andy Warhol in 1962.*

Expressionist, was among the major artists working this idiom. Philip Pearlstein (1924-   ) had been painting his brilliantly executed and realistic nudes long before the emergence of the movement, but won a wider audience for his work once the New realism was publicized nationally. Andrew Wyeth (1917-   ) had also been painting in a sharply realistic manner for years and was secure in his reputation long before realism was reclaimed by the avant garde of the late 1960's and early 1970's.

Other major American artists working in the New Realism included Joseph Raffael (1933-   ), who has since changed direction somewhat, Howard Kanovitz (1929-   ), Richard Estes (1939-   ), and Chuck Close (1941-   ). With the relaxation of censorship restrictions, art as well as literature has ventured into erotic subject matter with a new enthusiasm and the New realism has been a particularly appropriate idiom to express this new freedom. Often using photographs enlarged by projectors, the New realists returned to an older tradition which the very photographs they used were supposed to eliminate.

In New York, however, the Museum of Modern Art mounted a full scale show in 1968 called "The Art of the Real," which exhibited 33 completely abstract paintings. Only objects which claim to be nothing other than themselves are truly real, was the proposition implicit in the show of non-objective art. Merely to make a picture by copying from life (or from a photograph) has nothing at all to do with reality. And so a war of theoretics was waged while even newer ideas emerged to render both attitudes obsolete.

On the West coast now Robert Irwin (1928-   ) led a group of young artists who attempted to push beyond abstraction and into an area in which perceptual habits were tested

and challenged. Irwin himself had "painted" with light, with theater scrims and illuminated disks, to create perceptual illusions and comment on the nature of perceived reality. Conceptual art, in which the idea is more important than the executed piece, arose to stimulate and perplex the intellect. Artists who called themselves "sculptors" were scooping deep cavities from the ground and calling them "earthworks." Painters began "painting" with colored smoke. Such ephemeral materials, subject to constant change, and extremely difficult if not impossible to sell to collectors, were photographed instead, and the photographs and documentary records in the form of preliminary sketches or blueprints were sold while the actual art eroded, evaporated or otherwise extinguished itself.

Minimal painters and sculptors, using no recognizable pictorial elements or imagery, removing all emotional and symbolic content from the work and turning to mathematics and geometry for an organizational structure, moved to the forefront of American art to share attention temporarily with other main currents. An art based upon computer programming of images and moving pictures projected upon the read-out screen became popular, reflecting perhaps American fascination with the latest advances in technology. And again, the predictable cycle recurred in which certain artists reacted against an art they regarded as dehumanized, too scientific and unemotional.

The handmade object returned to art, this time in the form of crafts raised to the status of art. Macrame, or knotted ropes and strings, was used as a means to create significant sculpture, or as the artists called them, "wall-hangings." Adaptations were made of American Indian and Oriental handi-

The acrylic painting, Equivocation, *painted by Benjamin Cunningham in 1964.*

crafts, but without the previous utility of the objects built in to the new aesthetic transformation of tool into art. Some ironic closing of the artistic circle was suggested by this reaching backward to the origins of American art to find some novelty for the quickly-jaded public and the constantly questing artist.

The factionalism of American art since the end of World War II, despite the dominance of Abstract Expressionism for a decade or more, seems to suggest that the tradition of the avant garde, or at least an avant garde with only one direction, is ended. Too many fine artists are now working in too many different areas, and the mainstream has divided and sub-divided into dozens of fresh and swiftly running branches.

American art is now avidly sought by major museums all over the world. No collection of world art, and especially art of the 20th century, may consider itself comprehensive unless it contains a substantial selection of American masters. A museum in Australia just recently purchased Jackson Pollock's *Blue Poles* for a reported two million dollars! The painting, in Pollock's spontaneous drip style, which initially had been met with such derision, fetched more than any picture painted in modern times, including the much vaunted French Impressionists. Only the paintings of the old masters

have commanded higher prices. In a world which measures the value of everything in monetary terms, this incredible price confirms that American art has come of age—at least as a commodity.

But what of the intrinsic value of American art, if any? First, as a continuous record of our history, changing values and shifting attitudes, the visual arts provide a comprehensive record. Whatever biases naturally arise are counterbalanced by the antagonistic factions in any given period. The idealized vision of the genre painters, for example, opposed by the realism of The Eight. Second, and perhaps more important, American art embodies the very essence of the American spirit, as suggested by the last two hundred years of our history. A love of liberty, an unfaltering energy, a craving for new vistas and for the excitement of discovery—all those qualities which gave rise to our revolution and motivated our frontiersmen to move into uncharted territory—all those qualities are implicit in our art.

In an age when the individual and his freedom are threatened by a variety of enemies, including his own apathy and love of material comfort, art stands as an antidote and as a distant early warning system. Even more basic, however, is art as pleasure—pleasure for the mind and pleasure for the senses. Each year more American people are discovering this joy.

THE VOICE OF A NATION CAN
BE HEARD IN ITS LITERATURE . . .

Like any strong and lively youngster America sought to assert itself. The process continues today, moderated somewhat by a growing maturity, but ongoing nevertheless. As the nation evolved over two hundred years it forged its own identity, no longer imitating English examples, no longer looking to Europe for inspiration as once it did in earlier times.

A new America inscribed its own unique style upon the wild, uncharted vastness of a virgin continent. Later, of course, elements of that same style would proliferate around the world as Amerian culture was exported everywhere along with our wheat and consumer goods.

And so it was with American literature. Our first writers copied their cultural parents, echoing their ideas and literary manner. But slowly through the decades, separated by an ocean and no longer sharing a common national experience, American writers became more themselves and less the offspring of their English forebears. Then with a nation of their own and a growing body of history and tradition, American writers began defining the national character. By the middle of the twentieth century American writing had achieved an international eminence, enriching world literature with the story of these two hundred years and more of human enterprise.

The New World was a fearsome land, a wilderness populated by a primitive race which Columbus mistakenly named *Indian*. In a letter (1493) to his Spanish patrons Columbus reports on his "American" adventure, the discovery of San Salvador, Cuba, Hispaniola and other islands in the Caribbean. The character of New World writing thus had been set for the next two centuries; letters, chronicles and reports back to Europe would issue from the Spanish, Portuguese, French, and English who came to conquer, plunder and explore the new continent.

By 1607 and the establishment of the first permanent English settlement at Jamestown, a substantial body of writing already existed describing the geography and natural resources of America, and the peculiar customs of the "savages" who dwelt here.

The grand vitality of Elizabethan literature was fading by the time the Puritans arrived here with their strict and joyless ways and their difficult religion. The mood they imported, along with the Pilgrims, was sober, self-conscious, preoccupied with work, almost obsessed with theology. The theological journals of John Cotton (1585-1652), Thomas Shepard (1605-1649) and Thomas Hooker (1586-1647) are among the earliest works from the period and reflect the bleak, humorless life in the New England colonies in a style which matches the gloom of the era. By contrast, *The History of Plymouth Plantation*, begun in 1630 by Governor William Bradford (1588-1657), and *The History of New England*, by Governor John Winthrop (1588-1649), are both somewhat lighter in tone and offer a detailed and interesting daily account of the first hard years of these settlements.

Further South in Virginia the now-legendary Captain John Smith wrote the journal of his adventures in that colony. Later, in 1624, he would write a general history of Virginia, New England and the Summer Isles. His relationship with the Indian girl Pocahontas would in years to come be romanticized by new generations of American writers looking back upon these simpler times in search of national myths.

As the New England theocracy first flourished then declined, a host of clergymen wrote and published sermons. Increase Mather (1639-1723) and his son, Cotton (1663-1728), both wrote an enormous number of religious tracts, histories, biographies, and works on science. The infamous *Memorable Providences* (1689) by Cotton, describing the frenzies of witchcraft and the behavior of the possessed, was used as a guide to witch-hunting when that madness afflicted Salem in 1692. His *Magnalia Christi Americana* (1702), however, was a learned, well-researched church history of New England with much literary and historical value.

One of the great political thinkers of the early colonial period was unfortunately a writer whose heavy verbiage and obscure meanings flawed even the most popular of his books. Roger Williams (1603-1684), banished from the Massachusetts Bay colony for his dissent against the arbitrary

Samuel Langhorne Clemens, *who wrote under the* nom de plume *of Mark Twain, started out in life as a pilot on the Mississippi. He turned to journalism and from journalism moved to fiction. Among his works are* Tom Sawyer *and* The Adventures of Huckleberry Finn, *long cherished as classics of American literature.*

government, founded a settlement at Providence, Rhode Island. Here he put into practice the democratic principles so intolerable to the Puritan theocrats. As a Quaker, Williams insisted that a man's religion was his own concern and not a proper interest of government. These ideas were incorporated in his book *The Bloudy Tenent of Persecution for Cause of Conscience* (1644). The book discusses such enlightened concepts as the rights of man, a notion which was to characterize the American revolution.

The Calvinist faith of 18th century New England found its greatest expression in the writings of Jonathan Edwards (1703-1758). Despite his hellfire sermons and visions of an angry God, Edwards possessed a powerful intellect. His writing sought to demonstrate the absence of free will and prove the theory of predestination, thus encouraging the submission of man to the will of God. American philosophy is said to begin with Edwards, and his tragic sense still resonates in American writers two centuries later.

In Virginia, meanwhile, life seemed easier. A risque satire appeared in 1708, *The Sot-Weed Factor, or a Voyage into Maryland. . . By Eben. Cook, Gent.* The psuedonymous author was presumed to be a tobacco agent with a cynical view of southern institutions and Quaker business dealings which he satirized in mock-heroic style. In the *Westover Manuscripts,* first published in 1841, Colonel William Byrd (1674-1744), the founder of Richmond, expressed a wit and sophistication that embodied the concept of a southern aristocracy upon which later writers would build and embellish, and later southern gentlemen emulate.

At the American frontiers, in those days never too far from the center of these colonies, the culture of white man and Indian collided. William Hubbard's *Narrative of the Troubles With the Indians* (1677), and other first-person accounts in letters and diaries of the period, described the strange behavior of these so-called uncivilized peoples.

In Boston an authentic record of the times and customs was being kept by Samuel Sewall (1652-1730) in his *Diary.* Among the most revealing historical documents of the colonial era, Sewall's journal details the daily life of the royal colony, including the social, civic and political scene over a fifty year period from 1674 to 1729.

During the same period Philadelphia was developing a more liberal and relaxed society, hospitable and tolerant to new ideas. In this relatively free and easy environment so encouraging to the intellect, one of America's great Renaissance men lived, worked and flourished. Benjamin Franklin (1706-1790), a transplanted Bostonian, became in Philadelphia the embodiment of the Enlightenment which was then sweeping Europe and just beginning in America. Rational, liberal, humanitarian, scientific and practical, Franklin was related to the greatest of 18th century European thinkers, whose ideas gave fuel to the American and French revolutions.

As a colonial emissary to England and later as U. S. Ambassador to France, Franklin charmed the sophisticates of London and Paris with his penetrating satirical wit. His comic yet cosmopolitan turn of mind is best expressed in his *Autobiography* (1771-89) where the philosopher-scientist-statesman-inventor reflects upon the follies and triumphs of his long and eventful life. In the earlier *Poor Richard's Almanak* (1733-58), Franklin offered a compendium of proverbs, aphorisms, and practical advice, reflecting his commonsense philosophy. His pragmatic approach to the problems of daily life he also applied to the problems of politics. As a printer he was able to publish much of his own

writing, and as a bookseller he was able to disseminate it.

Among Franklin's earliest writings his *Dissertation on Liberty and Necessity, Pleasure and Pain* (1725) demonstrates his unwaivering intellectual honesty. The volume sets out to disprove the existence of a rational Deistic God, but instead persuaded Franklin of the logic of that concept. As a public-spirited citizen of increasing influence, Franklin published a series of pamphlets and essays on contemporary issues.

His interests and activities were constantly expanding. He formulated the positive-negative theory of electricity, invented the lightning rod, and became quite knowledgeable in science and economics. Franklin also published the first novel in America, a reprint of Richardson's *Pamela* (1744), and established America's first circulating library. Franklin's newspaper, the *Pennsylvania Gazette*, eventually became the largest in America during its hayday.

By the time Franklin entered politics he was rich and influential. As the English abuses of their American colonists increased and became more insufferable, Franklin became less a British subject and more a participant in events which would culminate in the revolution. He was appointed to the committee selected to draft the Declaration of Independence along with Thomas Jefferson, John Adams, Roger Sherman and Robert R. Livingston. Although Jefferson was assigned the responsibility of composing the first draft, Franklin's influence is also apparent in the document. In the last months before Franklin's death his continued belief in the rights of man prompted him to issue several strong essays advocating the abolition of slavery.

Thomas Jefferson, third President of the United States, was much less a prolific writer than Franklin, yet the beautiful language and lucid thought of *The Declaration of Independence* secures his place among the greatest of American writers and thinkers. Although he had written a number of papers on economics, state issues, and technical subjects, he published just one book, *Notes on the State of Virginia* (1784). Before publication of the *Declaration,* Jefferson's most widely-read work was *A Summary View of the Rights of British America* (1744), an anti-British pamphlet denouncing colonial oppressions.

Jefferson's ideology is among the cornerstones at the foundation of American government and society. A belief in liberty, faith in the integrity of the individual man, flexible laws, public education and decentralized government authority were essential to democracy in the Jeffersonian view.

Theater and the rise of American drama as a literary form would parallel the growth of American cities and was virtually unknown in 1776. Early in the 18th century English performers had played in the colonies, but the first American play, *The Contrast,* by Royall Tyler (1757-1826), was not performed by professional actors until 1787 in New York. The prohibition against theatrical performances was not changed in New England until Massachusetts led the way by repealing its law in 1793.

By the end of the colonial period and the establishment of a new nation, circulating libraries and literary groups at Harvard, Yale, Philadelphia, Boston, New York and elsewhere became a gathering place for college students to read and exchange ideas. In 1790 America passed a copyright law. A relative increase in leisure time, especially among women, expanded the potential audience for novels, poetry and drama. Newspapers began flourishing in towns along the Atlantic coast. And yet American writing still imitated British models. Typical American themes were presented in typically British literary style; political independence had been won, cultural dependence continued.

The 19th century dawned on America bringing with it the tempest of romanticism and its revolt against reason, already sweeping through Europe by 1800. The huge, unexplored American continent was a perfect stage for the development of romantic attitudes: an enchantment with the mysteries of nature, a love of the grand and heroic, a denial of tradition and the creation of a national myth.

In New York the Knickerbocker literary group had formed with novelists Washington Irving (1783-1859) and James Fenimore Cooper (1789-1851), its two most celebrated members. In 1807 the group published *Salmagundi*, a series of sketches satirizing life in Manhattan, a booming small town populated mainly by Dutch-English Americans, and soon to become an American publishing center.

As a young man Irving traveled through Europe, collecting materials for his famous sketches and acquiring a worldly refinement which would find expression in his later books. Among his most widely-read works are *Knickerbocker's History of New York* (1809) and *The Sketch Book* (1819-1820), an international best seller which contained the now classic "Rip Van Winkle" and "The Legend of Sleepy Hollow."

Notable among Irving's later works are *Tales of a Traveller* (1824), *The Alhambra: a series of tales and sketches of the Moors and Spaniards* (1832), and a history of Columbus and his voyages in four volumes starting in 1828. *Astoria*, published in 1836, was a vivid historical account of the fur-trading settlement founded in Oregon by John Jacob Astor, and which eventually made him a millionaire. Irving's *Life of George Washington* (five volumes, 1855-59), absorbed his last years and the final volume was published the year of his death.

Medallion *of James Fenimore Cooper, creator of the* Leather-Stocking Tales. *Cooper's work included both fiction and non-fiction but he is best known for his stories about life on the colonial frontier and the early struggles of the colonists with the indians.*

Irving is acknowledged as the first successful professional American writer and his substantial literary earnings allowed him to live in comfortable circumstances. As the first American man of letters to acquire international acclaim, he came to typify for a while the American sensibility, although his work belonged more to the Old World than the New. The melancholy mood and love of the mysterious past with references to a vague and glamourous classicism inhabited much of Irving's fiction and sketches, especially his *Bracebridge Hall* (1822), which would serve as a model for American short stories in the years to come.

James Fenimore Cooper, a prolific author of more than 30 novels, travel books, and essays, used American experience to create a literature which for the first time in the nation's brief history could truly be called characteristic of America. His *Leatherstocking Tales—The Pioneers* (1823), *The Prairie* (1827), *The Last of the Mohicans* (1826), *The Pathfinder* (1840) and *The Deerslayer* (1841)—described the wilderness experience at the American frontier and the daily contact between settlers and Indians. A central hero appears throughout these five novels, Natty Bumppo, the embodiment of American romanticism. Bumppo is an uneducated, "uncivilized," backwoodsman and scout, possessing the highest principles and a common sense philosophy which confers upon him an ideal nobility.

Cooper's literary treatment of the American Indian was almost reverential, and was widely criticized as unrealistic. He found the red man noble and possessing great moral character beneath what superficial observers saw as savagery.

The sea stories and historical novels which flowed from his energetic pen were charged with strong narratives and spirited action. Most notable among these were *The Spy* (1821), *The Pilot* (1823), *The Red Rover* (1828), *The Two Admirals* (1842), and *The Redskins* (1846). Cooper's novel on British high society, *The Precaution* (1820), was a failure, owing to his unfamiliarity with the subject and its imitative style.

Although many of the characters Cooper created were often wooden and his plots full of coincidence, many of the novels were masterpieces and were not only popular in America but also found an enthusiastic audience in Europe. The American adventure in a romantic wilderness stirred the European imagination and Cooper became widely known and respected abroad.

In his later years Cooper wrote, among other books, *Gleanings in Europe* (1837), a five-volume collection of travel letters; *The History of the Navy of the United States of America* (1839); and *The Crater* (1847), a Utopian allegory. His criticism of American democracy and its failure to perfect itself was expressed in Cooper's later works and brought him into the center of continuing controversy, inspired mainly by his political enemies.

At his death in 1851 Cooper had produced a body of literature typically American: it was written from firsthand experience, it dealt with the unique conditions of American life, it was based upon itself and not upon the traditions of Europe.

American poetry, meanwhile, had also come into its own. William Cullen Bryant (1794-1878) infused his poems with a quiet, reflective mood and a personal but restrained sensitivity, breaking the restrictive modes of the more formal British poets. Bryant's influence on successive generations of American poets is considerable and his acceptance of a moral obligation as a writer was a concept later poets would also embrace. Poetry, according to Bryant, conveys direct lessons of wisdom and can rouse the reader to passionate action.

Edgar Allan Poe, *whose stories of horror and suspense helped to create a new literary genre. Poe's poetry and short stories had a wide following, but his literary output was limited by his lifestyle. He died at the age of forty in 1849.*

Thus each poet has a responsibility to present only the most noble ideas.

As editor and part owner of the New York *Evening Post,* he was a leading spokesman for liberal causes of the day: free speech, free trade, and the abolition of slavery. He traveled frequently to Europe, participated in the cultural life of New York City and helped found the Republican Party. By 1825 Bryant was regarded as America's most distinguished poet.

In the more rural South, where life was somewhat slower than the brisk tempo of those booming cities along the Atlantic coast, a different aspect of the national literature was developing. John Pendleton Kennedy (1795-1870) wrote an exemplary novel of plantation life establishing a model for the genre which would influence writers for years to come. His *Swallow Barn* (1832) depicts the gentry of Virginia in their day-to-day activities, romanticized, of course, but creating the Southern plantation tradition and its legendary chivalry. John Esten Cooke (1830-1886) contributed additional works to the genre, notably *The Virginia Comedians* (1854) and *Henry St. John* (1859).

In the Southern cities of Baltimore, Charleston, and Richmond literary activity also flourished. Edgar Allan Poe (1809-1849) served as editor of the *Southern Literary Messenger,* a magazine based in Richmond, from which he was later fired for excessive drinking. The magazine *Southern Review,* published in Charleston, was an important forum for regional writing. The Southern tradition was most typified in Charleston's William Gilmore Simms (1806-1870) who wrote fiction, biography, history and poetry. His series of romantic historical novels, *The Yemassee* and *The Partisan* (both 1835), *Beauchampe* (1842), *Katherine Walton* (1851), the *Sword and the Distaff* (1853) and *Charlemont* (1856), was an accurate picture of the times, despite his idealized vision of the Southern aristocracy.

American literature now had a shape and a flavor. A great period of literary achievement was about commence which paralleled the increasing sense of national strength and American identity.

American romanticism now also evolved into something uniquely inself, although evidence of European influence necessarily remained. Ralph Waldo Emerson (1803-1882) seemed to reconcile the conflicting realities of American experience with the idealism of our national imagination. Self-reliance, a sense of morality and a belief in the agreement of moral and natural law were the keystones of Emerson's philosophy, which he described in his writing as a way of life, rather than a system of thought. As an essayist, Emerson was a master, and his *Nature* (1836), *The American Scholar* (1837) and *The Divinity School Address* (1838) are both fine examples of the form and important statements of his thinking. In 1841 he published a series, the first of the *Essays* based partially on his literary and scientific lectures. In 1844 the second series was published, further developing Emerson's ideas in a prose of persuasive rhetorical beauty, much like the inspired preaching he did as a young minister.

"Hitch your wagon to a star," said Emerson, expressing the spirit of American optimism and high aspiration. His transcendental philosophy proposed that "The highest revelation is that God is in every man." Such ideas were not only presented formally in his essays, but also as random musings in his *Journal,* which he had kept since his days as a student at Harvard. As a poet, Emerson is not as accomplished, although much of his verse is perceptive, truthful, and profoundly emotional. In the last years of his life he lived in Concord, Massachusetts, enjoying a well-deserved reputation as a sage of independent intellect and the embodiment of an American ideal: the infinite potential of the common man.

Another individualist and intellectual rebel in the Emersonian mode was Henry David Thoreau (1817-1862). Best known for his *Walden* (1854) and his earlier essay *The Duty of Civil Disobedience,* Thoreau's ideas have been more influential in the 20th century than they were in the time of their conception. Having spent a night in Concord jail for refusing on principle to pay his poll tax, Thoreau wrote the civil disobedience essay which many modern practitioners of passive resistance, including Ghandi of India, have used as a justification for their peaceful anti-government dissent.

A friend and disciple of Emerson, Thoreau was also a member of the New England Transcendentalist circle, a romantic movement in rebellion against the strict dogma of earlier Calvinist orthodoxies. A lonely, introspective communion with himself and nature is the continuing theme of his work, beginning with his *Journal,* started in 1837 and eventually published in fourteen volumes. Stressing the necessity to lead a solitary life, Thoreau's great subject was himself.

On July 4, 1845, Thoreau moved into a small cabin he had built himself on the shore of Walden Pond, about a mile from Concord. Here he spent two years in isolation, eliminating all nonessentials to simplify his life as completely as possible. Surrounded by nature he came to know the animals and plant life of the woods in which he lived. He wrote and read prodigiously in the ample leisure of his simple existence. The famed *Walden* and *A Week on the Concord and Merrimac Rivers* (1849) were later to emerge from that experience.

Thoreau's life-long quest for truth and his anti-materialism were ideas common to the Romantic—Transcendentalist thinkers of his era. But Thoreau expressed these ideas more persuasively and artfully than his colleagues.

"If one advances confidently in the direction of his dreams, and endeavors to live the life which he has imagined, he will meet with a success unexpected in common hours," wrote Thoreau, crystallizing American optimism and positivist faith.

Born two years after Thoreau, and outliving him by almost three decades, Herman Melville (1819-1891) saw America with a darker, more tragic sense. A profound cosmic doubt and perception of evil pervades the pages of his classic *Moby Dick* (1851), one of the great novels of American literature.

Melville was born in New York City, raised in a strict Calvinist family and early demonstrated the rebellious nature which would later inhabit the thoughts and motivate the deeds of his fictional heroes. At nineteen he went to sea as a cabin boy but eventually deserted his whaling ship in the Marquessas Islands. Captured by cannibals, Melville was held against his will but unharmed. He found himself enchanted by the jungle paradise and the idyllic existence of his captors, and would write about it some years afterward in his first novel *Typee* (1846), and in a sequel *Omoo* (1847). Australian whalers rescued Melville, and he subsequently served as a seaman aboard the man-of-war *United States,* drawing upon these adventures for such later works as *Redburn* (1849), *White-Jacket* (1850, and *Billy Budd,* not published until 1924.

In 1847 Melville married and settled down to several years of prolific output. In addition to the other works previously mentioned, *Mardi* (1849), *Pierre* (1852) and *The Confidence-Man* (1857) were published during this period. But the fame of Melville rests upon *Moby Dick,* a novel not well-received in its day, but some eighty years later rediscovered and appraised as a *classic* of major proportions. Resurrected from literary oblivion, Melville is venerated as a genius. His other novels, previously unread for years, were suddenly in demand and new editions were published.

Herman Melville, *author of* Moby Dick *and numerous other novels and short stories, was a friend and confidant of another American writer, Nathaniel Hawthorne. Melville's early life was spent aboard various whaling ships, and he used his personal experiences in the South Pacific in most of his books. Although he died in relative obscurity Melville today is regarded as one of America's greatest writers.*

Critics of the 1920's found qualities in *Moby Dick* which earlier appraisals of the novel failed to see as valuable. The book is rich and complex on several levels, mixing reality and symbol as its tormented hero obsessively seeks the white whale in defiance of God so it seems. The quest leads to a simultaneous victory and defeat, destroying the vengeful captain and the entire crew but one, the young survivor who narrates the story. Troubling questions on the nature of evil, and the destiny of man and his relationship to God are explored in the novel which resounds with a lyrical prose recalling the magnificent language of Shakespeare.

Melville himself, in a letter to his friend Nathaniel Hawthorne, said of *Moby Dick:* "I have written a wicked book, and feel as spotless as the lamb." Captain Ahab, half-mad in his pursuit of the dumb, innocent beast across vast oceans, is heroic yet sinful in his daring defiance of an inevitable fate. The modern American sensibility found in *Moby Dick* a metaphor for its own condition. And so Melville, who spent the last years of his life in obscurity as a customs clerk, was elevated to the pantheon of American writers decades after his unremarked death.

Nathaniel Hawthorne (1804-1864), a friend of Melville, was by contrast widely celebrated in his day for his novels, principally *The Scarlet Letter* (1850) and *The House of the Seven Gables* (1851). He is among the most gifted writers of the New England school and a gloomy Puritan sobriety is the dominant tone in much of his work. Notable also for his short stories, Hawthorne probed into the darker regions of his characters, much like Melville his contemporary. Edgar Allan Poe, himself a master of the short story form, was among the first critics to recognize Hawthorne's artistry.

Born into a Puritan household of meager means and humorless atmosphere, Hawthorne quickly developed the skeptical, insulated alienation from the world which characterized his life and gave its peculiar flavor to his work. In college, however, he met and befriended Franklin Pierce, who would later become President of the United States; Henry Wadsworth Longfellow, who would become a distinguished American poet; and Horatio Bridge who would help him acquire public recognition.

His talents as a writer were realized comparatively later in his life, and the first collection of his short stories, *Twice-Told Tales* (1837), was not published until his thirty-third year, and his first successful novel, *The Scarlet Letter,* when he was forty-six. In *The Scarlet Letter* Hawthorne explores the psychological effects of an adultery within a small Puritan community in which the adulterous woman must wear the constant public confession of her sin—the scarlet letter "A"—while her paramour, a Puritan minister, keeps the secret of his transgression. The novel is not a moral indictment of the sinners, but rather a tragedy of heroic dimensions in which the natural passion of love conflicts with the dogmatic religion of the society. The novel became an immense popular success, but Hawthorne was never again to achieve the same level of excellence. Yet his reputation was made, and his humanistic, ethical, yet detached view of life was further developed in subsequent writings.

Referring to himself as a "romancer" rather than a novelist in discussing his *The House of the Seven Gables,* Hawthorne points up an important distinction between the two forms. In essence, Hawthorne saw the romance as a less restrictive genre than the novel. In the novel, according to Hawthorne, the writer is obligated to record only the possible and probable of man's experience. In the romance a writer has more freedom. The Gothic labyrinth of colonial Salem and the accursed house of the seven gables in which the bizarre plot unfolds is certainly more romantic than realistic—and much less satisfying than his earlier novel.

In his later years, Hawthorne's most notable works are *The Blithedale Romance* (1852), *Tanglewood Tales* (1853), a collection of children's stories, and *The Marble Faun* (1860). Sin and salvation, Hawthorne's twin themes, recur again in his final novel, set in the American artists' colony in Rome. And again, Hawthorne observes it all with a critical detachment, neither moralizing nor condemning, but revealing the complexities of the human soul.

Edgar Allan Poe (1809-1849), the dark genius of American literature, seemed to embody in his tormented, drunken life and premature death the romantic myth of the brilliant but pre-doomed artist. Much of this myth was encouraged by Poe himself, although much of it was also justified. He was expelled from West Point for misconduct, fired from a variety of jobs for drinking and deliberately cultivated a shabby Bohemianism. But he was a writer of enormous talents and such eccentricities are secondary to his great achievements.

With Poe's first published poetry collection in his eighteenth year, *Tamerlane and Other Poems* (1827), it was already apparent that the young man possessed an extraordinary literary talent. The rhythmic, musical quality of his early verse would later evolve into the beautifully realized, almost melodic lyricism of poems like "The Raven" (1844), "Annabel Lee" (1845), and "The Bells" (1849). But before his poetry was properly appreciated in the United States, it was first "discovered" in France by Charles Baudelaire and Stéphane Mallarmé, both leading poets of the romanticist and symbolist avant garde.

Poe's magazine articles, his reviews, criticisms, and essays all demonstrated a first-rate intellect and a gift for innovation. He perfected the detective story, creating a character of enormous intelligence, wide-ranging knowledge and superior analytical powers who would serve as a model for the later Sherlock Holmes.

Always aware of his reading audience, Poe attempted to engage their emotions through the written word. Fear, thought Poe, was the most basic of emotions and so he wrote to create it in his readers. He produced a body of horror stories which he called "grotesque" and "arabesque," depending on his objective in each story. Among the more notable of these are "The Fall of the House of Usher" (1839), "The Black Cat" and "The Tell-Tale Heart" (1843), "The Cask of Amontillado" and "The Mask of the Red Death" (1846). Terror and suspense give power to these works, and their effects have been systematically worked out by the author.

The stories which Poe referred to as "ratiocinative" were exercises in the rational analysis of data and evidence to solve a riddle or crime. The best known stories in this style are "The Gold Bug" (1843) and "The Murders in the Rue Morgue" (1841).

As a literary critic and theoretician Poe's contribution to the culture of his time was considerable. His journey was inward to the frontiers of imagination and the psyche, rather than outward toward a growing trend in the direction of realism. He did not seek truth in his poetry; truth was a concern for science. What Poe sought was ". . .the rhythmic creation of beauty." And ultimately, unity became for him the essence of his art, even more than the beauty he pursued. A life of dissolution eventuated in Poe's tragic death in mid-career. He had lived totally within his art, as a magazine editor and writer, as a critic and as an example of his own ethic and conviction that art was a worthwhile profession.

Nathaniel Hawthorne, *whose puritan background was deeply influential in shaping his prose. Hawthorne's works, most notably* The Scarlet Letter, *are chiefly concerned with the idea of sin and salvation. He was the first major American writer to try to probe into the psychology of guilt and redemption.*

Meanwhile, another visionary was preaching the brotherhood of man in the coming democratic Utopia. Walt Whitman (1819-1892), the "good, gray poet" of America as he would later be called, was editing *The Brooklyn Daily Eagle* while writing the paeans of praise to his native land soon to be published collectively as *Leaves of Grass* (1855). "I am personal," said Whitman, speaking of his poetry, an attempt to record himself; his body and soul as a representative of humanity in general.

Americans were a noble race, insisted Whitman, and his poetry literally sang of their activities and aspirations from city to farm to wilderness. As a newspaper editor he wrote on civic affairs, public education, and prison reform, women's rights, abolition—in short, on all contemporary issues in which a civilized man of conscience would be interested. Some of the poems which were to appear in *Leaves of Grass* were first published in the *Eagle,* all embodying Whitman's notion of an America itself "essentially the greatest poem."

Leaves of Grass was continually reissued in expanded versions, new poems being added to each new edition. But initially it was not widely read although at least one great American writer recognized the genius of Whitman. "I greet you at the beginning of a great career," wrote Ralph Waldo Emerson, the sage of Concord, to the obscure newspaper editor who had published the slender volume of verse which would win him a place among the Olympians of American literature.

In the final edition of *Leaves of Grass* appeared such masterpieces of Whitman's poetry as "When Lilacs Last in the Dooryard Bloom'd" and "O Captain! My Captain!", elegies to the dead Lincoln in a doleful, funerary rhythm; and "Song of Myself," "Out of the Cradle Endlessly Rocking," and "Pioneers, O Pioneers" among others.

His creative work interrupted first and then transformed into new directions by the Civil War, Whitman worked in Washington, D.C., as a government clerk and war correspondent. Whatever free time he had was devoted to attending the wounded of both the U. S. and the Confederacy in the numerous hospitals nearby. There was no loss of his earlier optimism, but rather the developing of a more mature and sober objectivity to complement what was once almost an exclusively subjective idealism. *Specimen Days* (1882) is a prose account of his experiences as nurse.

Paralyzed partially in his later years, his poetry shows a similar decline in vitality, although generally it was nonetheless joyous in concept. His prose, particularly *Democratic Vistas* (1871), argued at length the ideas he had woven so economically and artfully into his poetry. American democracy once had offered man the potential for his fullest realization as an individual, wrote Whitman in effect, but at last the ideal and the reality no longer coincided. Yet the "experiment" could still succeed, said Whitman.

Whitman's life spanned the larger part of the 19th century, through America's childhood and adolescence, so to speak. By the time Whitman died in 1892, America was about to embark on an even greater adventure, the 20th century, in which frontiers not even known to exist previously were first discovered and then crossed. Whitman's final poems sang of an international community, a mystic religiosity rooted in a sense of the cosmic, and incontestable faith in man despite a developing cynicism in a nation growing materially rich.

Whitman's modern attitudes and exuberance ran contrary

Walt Whitman, *whose free form poetry helped shape the form and content of poetry for many generations. Whitman, particularly in* Leaves of Grass, *celebrated the abundance and magnitude of America and the spirit and vivacity of her people. Although he worked for many years as a journalist, Whitman is regarded today as one of America's premier poets.*

to the Puritan restraints and the provincialisms of several major American poets who shared a part of Whitman's century but not all of his philosophy and none of his genius. John Greenleaf Whittier (1807-1892), a New England Quaker, abolitionist and humanitarian, wrote sentimental verse of immense popularity. A lover of nature and simple things, his heroes were the common men and he wrote of their experience within the great drama which was American history. Among his most celebrated poems are "Barefoot Boy," "Snowbound," and "Maud Muller." He lead a long, active life as a writer, editor and bitter opponent of slavery, and won for himself a place among the most eminent writers of his day. And yet in the 20th century his importance has been reassessed in the light of changing literary values, and Whittier is generally regarded as minor.

Henry Wadsworth Longfellow (1807-1882) was even more popular in his day than Whittier. He was widely read and respected for his ability to express the simple aspirations of mankind in general and Americans in particular. In Longfellow's poetry the American past retreats into a mythological yesteryear in which present conflicts gave way to past harmonies. Thus such major works of his as *Evangeline* (1847), *The Song of Hiawatha* (1855) and *The Courtship of Miles Standish* (1858) are neither truth nor history, but pose rather as legend, and therefore are perhaps more attractive to an American audience moving each year further away from its origins.

James Russell Lowell (1819-91), poet, critic, Cambridge aristocrat, editor of *The Atlantic Monthly,* scholar, diplomat, self-described man of culture, intelligence, and conscience, was more versatile and cultivated than Whittier and Longfellow but less significant as a writer. Remembered today mainly for the humorous Yankee wit of *Bigelow Papers,* collected and published in 1867, Lowell in his own time was the consumate literary success. Perhaps Lowell's only peer as a brilliant wit and literary grandee was Oliver Wendell Holmes (1809-1894), a Boston physician with a Harvard degree and the best of social connections. His *The Autocrat of the Breakfast Table,* (1857) a collection of common sense essays, is most representative of his thinking.

Emily Dickinson (1830-1886), the secretive, reclusive poet of New England produced a body of imaginative, introspective writing. Despite the problems peculiar to women of that time and place, and her inability to find a publisher for her poems, she continued throughout her life to refine her art. The brilliant originality of her work, with its personal religion, intensity, apparent knowledge of love and death yet mysteriously ambiguous, was not properly appreciated until the 1920's, more than thirty years after her death.

The Civil War erupted with its calamitous effects upon the young nation, and arrested temporarily its growth. The nation divided "brother against brother" and the face of war exposed naked in the city and town and countryside, gave a new taste of reality and consequent maturity to a people who had not known such bloody strife. The early innocence was not irretrievably gone. The War Between the States would later be memorialized in countless poems and novels and dramas, retreating into memory into history and literature, but not quite into legend: it was too real and horrible. The Union prevailed, and President Abraham Lincoln himself added to the accumulating treasures of our national literature with his "Gettysburg Address" perfectly articulating the Northern attitude. The South had quite a different version of things.

Harriet Beecher Stowe's (1811-1896) *Uncle Tom's Cabin* (1852) created enormous anti-slavery sentiment in the North

Henry Wadsworth Longfellow *was a very widely read poet in his day. Using actual incidents from early American history, Longfellow formed a new American mythology in poetry in such works as* The Song of Hiawatha, Evangeline, *and* The Courtship of Miles Standish.

and was widely popular and controversial. At least 300,000 copies of the novel were sold in its first year of publication, an extraordinary best seller even by today's standards. Whittier's abolitionist poetry and his national prestige also added to the anti-slavery fever which was building to a crisis. The rights of man were at issue again, just as they had been on the eve of our revolution.

With the ending of the Civil War and the fusing again of two separate parts into a unified whole, a new era in American literary history began, designated by scholars as The Gilded Age. New frontiers were opening, skepticism and a scientific attitude were the new intellectual standards. Realism began encroaching upon the ivory towers of the "genteel tradition" of literature.

Into this post-war clamor stepped Mark Twain (1835-1910), a most original American genius and later a symbol of the nation's vitality and power. Samuel Langhorne Clemens was his real name, and he was the first major American writer born west of the Mississippi. Born in Florida, Missouri, and not Hannibal as the myth would have it, Mark Twain grew up along the Mississippi River which would provide him with so much material for his early work. He was a printer, a newspaper reporter, a river boat pilot, a traveler to New York, New Orleans, Nevada, California, even Hawaii, Europe, and Palestine, all as a young man. His first writings appeared in newspapers and were accounts of his adventures, satirical sketches or reports of local color from the areas he was visiting.

Twain's early humor was sharply observant but often delivered in the exaggerated, mock-serious wonderment of a country bumpkin. The open-mouthed, awe-struck innocent, however, could not conceal the shrewd, savvy intellect beneath. *The Celebrated Jumping Frog of Calaveras County and Other Sketches* (1867), a collection of stories on frontier life set in the boom towns and mining camps of the West, brought him a large and sympathetic audience almost immediately. Twain was closer to his post-Civil War audience perhaps than the New England writers who had dominated the national letters for so long. The country was moving West again, expanding across the Mississippi which Twain knew so well, and Twain possessed those qualities which typified the new Westerner. He was open to new experience; he was unimpressed by official authority and judged a man on his merits alone; he was wild and adventurous, unsophisticated perhaps, but tough to swindle, and illogically optimistic. Twain's optimism, however, would dissolve in later years, replaced by a bone-deep cynicism, and not because he was embittered by a series of personal calamities. His view was tempered by a knowledge of the men and institutions he wrote about, and a careful examination of his earlier work will reveal evidence of a consistancy in his attitude.

Taking his pen name from the old river boat term meaning two fathoms of water, Mark Twain sought direct contact with the subjects he would write about, although some of his later work would speculate on the past as a means of commenting on the present. *The Prince and the Pauper* (1882) and *A Connecticut Yankee in King Arthur's Court* (1889) were historical satires but applicable to the issues of the time in which they were written.

The Innocents Abroad (1869) and *Roughing It* (1872), the former an account of his trip to Europe, the latter an account of a trip to the American West, reinforced Twain's reputation as a satirist and knight-errant with hypocrisy as his sworn enemy. He had been married in 1870 and settled down in Hartford, Connecticut, to a long, productive period of work.

In 1873 Twain published *The Gilded Age,* a work of collaboration with Charles Dudley Warner in the same satirical tone of his earlier work. It was a popular success but not up to the standards Twain had previously set for himself. Perhaps the addition of Warner diluted Twain's power. *Tom Sawyer* was published in 1876 and described nostalgically the lazy, uncomplicated life of a small town boy along the Mississippi River in bygone days. Obviously drawn from Twain's own childhood, the book was written for a young audience, yet found appreciative readers of every age. Two subsequent works together with *Tom Sawyer* seem to form a related trilogy: *Life On The Mississippi* (1883) and *The Adventures of Huckleberry Finn* (1885). These latter two were not written for children, and although the subject matter is essentially the same as in *Tom Sawyer,* it is treated with a new depth and insight. And through it all ran the great river, the grand symbol of constant change and stability as well.

Ill health, domestic and financial problems plagued Twain's later years. He lost a substantial amount of money investing in a typesetting machine, and in publishing ventures. To repay his enormous debts, he undertook a world lecture tour, which exhausted him and taxed his health. Two of his daughters died and then his wife. Twain's later works with their total cynicism were written within this unhappy era, and how deeply was his work affected by personal circumstances is still debated by scholars and critics.

The international celebrity and consummate literary artist dipped his pen into acid and wrote the incisive essays which would be published posthumously as *The Mysterious Stranger* (1916), *What is Man? and Other Essays* (1917), and two volumes of his *Autobiography* (1924). First appreciated as a humorist and satirist, Twain's later reputation changed to assign him the distinction of being America's

Henry James *is the first major American expatriate writer. James lived most of his life in Europe, and his works generally deal with Americans living and traveling abroad. His major fiction—including such works as* The Ambassadors, The Wings of the Dove, The Awkward Age *and* Daisy Miller—*reveal an attention to detail as a means of defining character, which has been widely adopted by subsequent writers.*

most characteristic writer. The mood and truth of the Middle-West and West in Twain's time has been forever captured in his work.

While Twain enjoyed the limelight as America's premier writer, other authors of more modest gifts were making their important but less spectacular contributions to the nation's literature. William Dean Howells (1837-1920), produced a series of realistic novels the most significant of which was *The Rise of Silas Lapham* (1885), the story of a self-made millionaire. Bret Harte (1836-1902) advanced the art of the short story and added to America's frontier lore with the publication in 1870 of *The Luck of Roaring Camp and Other Sketches,* which also contained the famous "Outcasts of Poker Flat." In the South, Joel Chandler Harris (1848-1908) was writing his celebrated *Uncle Remus: His Songs and His Sayings* (1881). And a strange Utopia was envisioned by Edward Bellamy (1850-1898) in his *Looking Backward* (1888).

There was no shortage of authors to explore the American frontier and feed the voracious appetite of an expanding audience for such tales. Edward Eggleston (1837-1902) described the Indiana of simple farmers and agrarian homesteaders in his *Hoosier Schoolmaster* (1871) and *Circuit Rider* (1874). Way back in New England, the declining traditions of the region were chronicled by Sarah Orne Jewett (1849-1909) in *Deephaven* (1877) and *A Country Doctor* (1884).

While Whitman reigned as the poet of poets, other verse of secondary importance was being written by regionalist writers and writers still engaged to the old traditions. Among these were James Whitcomb Riley (1849-1916), and Eugene Field (1850-1895), author of "Little Boy Blue" and "Wyn-

ken, Blynken and Nod" but also a penetrating observer and critic of his times as revealed in his newspaper columns and random writings. Sidney Lanier (1842-1881) brought his Southern regionalist sensibility to poetry and his poem "The Song of the Chatahoochee" and *Science of English Verse* (1880) were among his more noteworthy achievements.

With American traditions now firmly established, a reaction against them was inevitable. Henry James (1843-1916), a novelist of great power and originality, turned his back on the American scene and sought a richer experience steeped in the traditions of Europe. London was his home for many years, and here James evolved into a superb artist of profound psychological insight, stylistic refinement, and complexity. Brother to the famed philosopher William, Henry James brought to his artistry a formidable intellect and a commitment to realism. The realism of James, however, is not mere fidelity to fact, but rather a realistic record of the *impressions* made upon the artist, or novelist.

With his first novel, *Roderick Hudson* (1876), James set a pattern for the totality of his work from which he would only occasionally vary. The story of Americans in Europe, the new culture colliding with the old, would preoccupy James, along with his psychological analysis and concern with the paradoxes confronted by the artist.

In a series of brilliant novels James explored and discussed his preoccupations in endless variations, the themes being restated time and again but continually refined under his deliberate artistry. *Daisy Miller* (1879), *Washington Square* (1881), *The Portrait of a Lady* (1881), *The Bostonians* (1886), *The Awkward Age* (1899), *The Wings of the Dove* (1902), *The Ambassadors* (1903) and *The Golden Bowl* (1904) were his major novels, observed and narrated for the most part by a detached witness to the events. His scrupulous attention to detail as a means of defining character and setting was a method to be widely adopted by subsequent novelists, and not restricted exclusively to American inheritors of the tradition.

His alienation from the land of his birth gave a peculiar displacement to the work of this celebrated expatriate who nevertheless tried to fathom the American character. So much of the work devoted to penetrating the psyche of Americans is set against a foreign backdrop. Yet James believed that the conflict and contrast inherent in such situations defined more clearly the two extremes.

Stephen Crane's (1871-1900) *Maggie: A Girl of the Streets* (1892) and the *Red Badge of Courage* (1895) with their realistic impressionistic technique and psychological insight won for this novelist an international reputation despite his premature death. Frank Norris (1870-1902), another realist, was noted principally for his unfinished trilogy of novels called *Epic of Wheat,* beginning with *The Octopus* (1901) and *The Pit,* published in 1903.

As the 19th century raced to its conclusion, with its accelerated sense of history, Henry James and Mark Twain were the two most widely acclaimed American writers of the day, and ironically they represented a polarity of attitudes. Realism for a while would take its place as the dominant literary mode. Again, American writers would find value in the work of their European colleagues and import a number of ideas from abroad.

Sigmund Freud and phychoanalysis would give novelists the tools to burrow ever deeper into their fictional characters, and into themselves as well. The work of French novelist Emile Zola and his naturalist techniques would also be absorbed by American writers. The modernist movement was well underway, sired by the Industrial Revolution, and the urban explosion. The final exhausted gasps of Feudalism were heard as the Mexican and Russian revolutions all but ended that archaic concept. And just before the century turned, America became a world power in her 1898 defeat of colonialist Spain in Cuba. American literature was about to enter an even more tempestuous period than the post-Civil War of the last century.

Jack London (1876-1916) expressed a new social consciousness and cynical view of American politics and economics. He was a Socialist by conviction and his philosophy colored much of his realistic writing. Like Twain before him, London held a variety of adventurous jobs including sailor, gold prospector in the Klondike, and newspaper man, all of which experience he drew upon for his novels and short stories. His radical political views had elements of the irreconcilable which reduced the impact of his art. *People of the Abyss* (1903), *Martin Eden* (1909) and *John Barleycorn* (1913) were all semi-autobiographical novels in the naturalist style, seeking to demonstrate that man is powerless in the face of natural laws. He was immensely popular, but less for the novels cited previously than for the more elemental drama written into *The Call of the Wild* (1903), *The Sea Wolf* (1904) and *White Fang* (1906).

Poetry at the turn of the century was in transition, moving away from the romanticism of Whitman on the one hand, and from European romanticism on the other. A new poetry was in the process of development, expressing a brooding disenchantment with America's unfulfilled promise. William Vaughn Moody (1869-1910) sought the re-establishment of old values as a panacea for the increasingly complex problems of a world outgrowing an earlier idealism. His dramatic verse

Jack London *was a writer who grew up in the rough and tumble atmosphere of the working class at the turn of the century. His socialism shaped his prose but most of his work has a quality of the irreconcilable which detracts from its value as social criticism. Like Twain before him, London was an adventurer as a youth and he used many of his personal adventures as the basis for his stories. Among his most famous works are* The Call of the Wild, White Fang *and* The Sea Wolf.

The Masque of Judgement (1900), *The Fire Bringer* (1904) and *The Death of Eve* (1912) all explore the concept of man's rebellion against God. Poet Edwin Arlington Robinson (1869-1935) pursued a different rebellion, looking for significance in the homely townspeople among whom he lived, and from whose lives he fashioned his art.

The so-called Genteel Tradition of American literature was still, in the first years of the 20th century, restraining the impulse of writers to break out of old attitudes. The Genteel Tradition, simply stated, held that no book or poem should be published unless it was "decent" and could "safely" be read by respectable young girls. By 1900, the "tradition" was tyrannical. Even Mark Twain had observed its repressive dictates by withholding his serious work from publication until after his death.

By 1910, however, the old literary taboos seemed to be crumbling of their own weight. New book publishers and magazines appeared on the scene, ready to feed the expanded audience for good writing and new ideas. Theodore Dreiser (1871-1945) had already been thwarted by the Genteel Tradition in 1910 when his publishers declined to distribute *Sister Carrie* after first printing it and then deciding the novel was obscene. The novel was first published in London before an American publisher felt bold enough to produce an edition in 1916.

Dreiser, formerly a newspaper reporter and magazine editor, saw the discrepancy between American ideals and the day-to-day actuality. He is regarded generally as a poor craftsman, but his meticulous accumulation of detail lends a density and sense of purpose to his novels which overwhelm his ineptitudes. Social groups and cosmic forces stand against Dreiser's heroes, and a man is powerless before them, or so his naturalistic novels contend. The most notable of these are *The Titan* (1914), *The Genius* (1915), and *An American Tragedy* (1925). Dreiser's travel books, essays and political commentary reveal a growing faith in socialism as a remedy for the afflictions of humanity and the dehumanizing society it was producing.

As Dreiser grappled with implacable social and cosmic forces, other writers of the same era were concerned with matters more mundane. O. Henry (1862-1910), was William Sydney Porter, famous for his surprise endings and *The Four Million* (1906), a collection of short stories in his characteritic style. Booth Tarkington (1869-1946) wrote a series of light novels on life in Indiana including the widely-read *Penrod* (1914) and *The Magnificent Ambersons* (1918). Willa Cather (1876-1947) eliminated much of the detail that fascinated Dreiser and wrote a lean, uncluttered prose describing Midwestern and Southwestern life. Her most celebrated novels include *O Pioneers* (1913), *The Song of the Lark* (1915) and *My Antonia* (1918).

In the years just preceding America's entry into World War I, a number of major American poets suddenly appeared on the scene. They were literary rebels, advocating a new freedom for verse, a concern with new ideas and a determination to restore poetry to its former importance. Collectively, the new poets formed a movement, and held a variety of attitudes in common: democracy and all its ramifications, including the unromantic growth of the city and industrialism, were appropriate poetic themes.

Robert Frost (1875-1963) was born in San Francisco but lived in New England from the age of ten, where he developed the characteristics which colored his poetry. He was simultaneously an adventurous, sophisticated writer and a Yankee conservative, a skeptic and yet a believer in man and nature. Unable to find a publisher in America for his verse, he

Robert Frost *as he appeared in 1952. He won four Pulitzer Prizes for his poetry. Frost's literary reputation grew steadily from the publication of his first book of poetry,* A Boy's Will, *in 1913. He used the poetic form to explore the American Yankee spirit, and such was his stature that he was asked to read his poetry at the inauguration of John Kennedy.*

Carl Sandburg, *the midwestern bard and literary descendent of Walt Whitman. Most of his poetry deals with the struggles and attitudes of the common man. In addition to his poetry, Sandburg also produced a six-volume biography of Abraham Lincoln. Among Sandburg's most notable poems are* ''Fog,'' ''Chicago'' *and* ''Smoke and Steel.''

went to England where in 1913 his first volume of poetry, *A Boy's Will*, was published. The following year he published *North of Boston*, and in 1915 both books were published in America, after receiving generous critical acclaim in England. He continued thereafter to produce a body of work of surpassing excellence, based principally on New England materials. Other noteworthy collections of Frost's poetry include *Mountain Interval* (1916), *New Hampshire* (1923), *West Running Brook* (1928) and *A Further Range* (1936). He won numerous awards, grants, fellowships, university residencies and the Pulitzer prize four times. He was invited to read from his own work at the inauguration ceremony of President John F. Kennedy.

Carl Sandburg (1878-1967), the Midwestern bard and literary descendent of Whitman, sang of the common man against the backdrop of city and factory, or alone within the vast rolling prairie of America. In a voice which rang with the cadences of the Illinois heartland in which he was born, Sandburg wrote in affirmation of the American experience, rural or urban. The sound of folk music and tales told around the campfire were heard in Sandburg's poetry, and indeed, on his lecture tours he often sang folk songs and played the guitar. Influenced first by imagist poets, Sandburg later added a naturalist flavor to his work in the accumulation of observed details. His poetry was first regarded as ''unpoetic.'' The poems were not rhythmic, not structured in accordance with the traditions of the day, and not concerned with the usual subjects of poetry. Later, of course, Sandburg would be acclaimed as one of the greatest poets America ever produced. His six volume biography of Abraham Lincoln (1926-1939), written in a lyrical prose much like poetry, won a Pulitzer prize for history in 1940. Sandburg's more notable poems include ''Fog'' (1916), ''Chicago'' (1914), ''Smoke and Steel'' (1920), ''Slabs of the Sunburned West'' (1922), ''Good Morning, America'' (1928), and ''The People, Yes'' (1936).

In contrast to Sandburg's immersion in Americana and the mythical ''common man,'' poet T. S. Eliot (1888-1965) was evolving in a totally different direction. He was born in St. Louis but later became a British citizen, and although he was alienated from the land of his birth, he became the most influential American poet and critic of the first fifty years of the 20th century.

Eliot liberated modern verse from the romanticism and moralism of the earlier era, and proposed a depersonalized voice in the poetry of modernism. Defining himself, Eliot said he was a ''classicist in literature, a royalist in politics and an Anglo-Catholic in religion.'' All these aspects of the man are apparent in his work. The voluntary exile from America was also partially detached from his own historical time as well, despite his modernist approach to writing; he looked backward upon the 17th century as a literary example. Among his more famous works are ''The Love Song of J. Alfred Prufrock'' (1915), ''The Waste Land'' (1929) and *The Cocktail Party* (1950), a play. He won the Nobel prize for literature in 1948.

Ezra Pound (1885-1972), another voluntary exile from the America of his birth, was almost as influential as Eliot on the younger American poets who followed after him. Certainly Pound influenced Eliot in the revolt against romanticism. Pound was a brilliant, erudite scholar with a wide-ranging knowledge of cultures both ancient and modern, including those of the Orient. He drew upon this material for his poetry, particularly the *Cantos*, a series of poems which Pound worked on throughout his life. The *Cantos* present allusions from obscure areas of world literature and are not at all

Ezra Pound, *who died in 1972, was another American writer who lived and worked for much of his life in Europe. Pound was a brilliant scholar and was influential in shaping the careers of many younger American writers in the 1920's. His longer works, particularly the* Cantos, *are filled with allusions to European and Eastern literature. During the Second World War Pound made numerous broadcasts for the Italian Fascists; following the war he was found insane and spent several years in a hospital for the mentally insane.*

concerned with the common man and American experience of Sandburg and Whitman. Living in Italy from 1924, Pound became a Fascist supporter and made anti-American propaganda broadcasts during World War II. He was later charged with treason, found insane and committed for a period of 12 years to a Washington, D.C., hospital for the mentally ill. On his release in 1958, he returned to Italy.

Amy Lowell (1874-1925), the Bostonian aristocrat from the same family as the distinguished James Russell Lowell, scandalized proper New Englanders with her cigar-smoking, Bohemian rebelliousness and untraditional poetry. An imagist poet of extraordinary talent, she also financed and published their periodical, *Some Imagist Poets.* The precepts of imagist poetry, set forth in that first issue of 1915, have become the credo of successive generations of modern poets the world over: use the language of common speech and always the exact word; new rhythms are required for new moods; poets must have absolute freedom in the choice of subject matter; poetry should present an image and not deal in vague generalities; poetry should be hard and clear, never blurred or indefinite; and poetry should have "concentration" of emotion as its essence. Among Ms. Lowell's more celebrated works are *Sword Blade and Poppy Seed* (1914), *Men, Women and Ghosts* (1916), *Pictures of the Floating World* (1919), all collections of her poetry; and *John Keats* (1925) and *Poetry and Poets: Essays* (1930).

Other important poets of the period included Stephen Vincent Benét (1898-1943), Vachel Lindsay (1879-1931), Edgar Lee Masters (1869-1950), and William Carlos Williams (1883-1963).

As poetry forged for itself a new, modern shape, so did the American novel, free now forever of the genteel tradition and

Sinclair Lewis, who died in 1951, was the first American to win the Nobel Prize for Literature. Lewis wrote about small town middle America, and his first well known novel was Main Street. *In 1922 he published* Babbitt, *a novel describing the life of a small town businessman which added a new word to the American lexicon. Among his other works are* Elmer Gantry, Arrowsmith, *and* Dodsworth.

probing into areas it had never been before. Even before World War I and the disenchantment that followed, literary frontiers were being crossed. In Chicago, where Sandburg and Dreiser had worked as newspaper men, other young writers were at work as journalists: Ring Lardner, Ben Hecht, and Ernest Hemingway. Sherwood Anderson (1876-1941) was a successful Chicago advertising copywriter. His first two novels, *Windy McPherson's Son* (1916) and *Marching* (1917) were undistinguished. But his third published work, *Winesburg, Ohio* (1919), a collection of short stories centered upon the life, inhabitants and values of a small Ohio town, achieved for him a national reputation. Hemingway and William Faulkner, novelists who would both later win the Nobel prize for literature, were influenced by Anderson's exploration into the soul of people unable to completely articulate their emotion and attitude.

Sinclair Lewis (1885-1951), America's first winner of the Nobel prize for literature, was a satirical novelist of immense influence and international celebrityhood. The several novels he published before World War I, however, were inconsequential and he remained relatively unknown until 1920. With the publication that year of *Main Street*, Lewis became instantly famous; he had captured in one brutally precise and satirical novel the phony boosterism, creeping conformity, growing hypocrisy, and commercialized culture of middle class America. In 1922 he published *Babbit*, contributing that descriptive word to our language which came to signify exactly the "type" Lewis was writing about. His other more memorable books include *Arrowsmith* (1925), *Elmer Gantry* (1927), *The Man Who Knew Coolidge* (1928), *Dodsworth* (1929), *It Can't Happen Here* (1935) and

Ernest Hemingway, *whose first novel* The Sun Also Rises *became the model of the so-called ''lost generation'' of Americans living in Europe following World War I, died in 1961. Hemingway won the Nobel Prize for Literature in 1954, specifically for the book* The Old Man and the Sea, *but by the time he had received the award his other works—among them* A Farewell to Arms, Death in the Afternoon, *and* For Whom the Bell Tolls—*had established him in the popular mind as one of America's leading writers.*

Kingsblood Royal (1947). The work of his later years declined in quality, but his influence on certain younger writers remained, especially his courage and honesty in challenging the sacred cows of American life. In his Nobel prize acceptance speech, which he later published under the title ''The American Fear of Literature,'' Lewis inveighed against the genteel tradition which for too long had repressed and intimidated American writers. The future of American literature, however, was assured, said Lewis, by such young writers as Hemingway, Thomas Wolfe, Thornton Wilder, John Dos Passos, Stephen Vincent Benét, Michael Gold and William Faulkner. Said Sinclair Lewis to the Swedish Academy which had voted him the coveted Noel prize, ''I have, for the future of American literature, every hope and every eager belief. We are coming out, I believe, of the stuffiness of safe, sane, and incredibly dull provincialism.'' He was correct, of course. But that process had already begun in the trenches of Verdun and Ypres some years earlier. A generation of Americans—a ''lost'' generation as author Gertrude Stein would later describe them—came face to face with the incredible horror of modern warfare in the muddy battlefields of Europe.

F. Scott Fitzgerald (1896-1940) joined the Army but missed the war, serving instead in the States. Yet Fitzgerald would come to embody, even more than Hemingway, that lost generation of post-War Americans who came to Europe seeking some elusive, nameless remedy for their disenchantment. The jazz age novelist was an immediate success with the publication in 1920 of his first novel, *This Side of Paradise*. In 1922 Fitzgerald published *The Beautiful and the Damned* and a collections of short stories, many of which had previously appeared individually in the *Saturday Evening*

Post. He went to Europe with his wife, Zelda, and overnight they moved into the charmed circle of Parisian expatriate life, over which presided the matriarchal Gertrude Stein. He met Hemingway now, and recommended the work of this extraordinary and yet unpublished young writer to his editor at Scribners. Fame and money and a taste for alcohol began eroding Fitzgerald's talent almost as soon as it had blossomed. The decline is most evident in certain short stories he wrote during this period. His quest for success and sensation among the wealthy, dissolute and amoral Americans in Europe gave him the materials for his novels, but also sealed him into his own destructive obsession. Before the fall, however, he wrote such widely praised novels as *The Great Gatsby* (1925), considered his masterpiece, and *Tender Is the Night* (1934). A third and unfinished novel *The Last Tycoon*, was published posthumously in 1941 and deals with Fitzgerald's experience in Hollywood as a screen writer in the last years of his life. He died in 1940 of a heart attack, his books out of print, his jazz age reputation all but swallowed up by the hungry year of depression which followed the crash of '29.

Ernest Hemingway (1898-1961), the restrained master of controlled artistry, the writer who saw the ''nothingness'' behind everything and showed it to a mass international audience, was also the victim of his own hand. But with Hemingway it was quick, decisive and there was no turning back; a shotgun did in an instant what took Fitzgerald years of dissipation to accomplish. He devoted a lifetime to exploring man's relationship to death and to a universe which seemed indifferent at best, hostile at worst. He left America as a young man, joining the war as an ambulance driver, turning his back on the culture which had produced him. Yet his earliest writing described his boyhood experience in the Michigan woods and his first confrontations with death, sex, love, and the loss of innocence that comes with the first knowledge of evil, human or cosmic. The stories are collected in a volume called *In Our Time* (1924), which established Hemingway as a master of the short story form. In 1925 *The Torrents of Spring* was published, a deliberate parody of the Sherwood Anderson style. *The Sun Also Rises* (1926) was his first novel and some critics believe it is his masterpiece. The disillusionment of post-War Americans living an aimless life of pleasure in Paris and Spain was described in the flat, understated prose which characterized Hemingway's life-long style. Jake Barnes, the novel's hero, postulates a credo which Hemingway exemplified in his life, and explored in his fiction: a man's senses determine what is good or evil, nothing else, and especially not institutional morality.

In 1929 *A Farewell To Arms* was published, further reinforcing Hemingway's reputation. *Green Hills of Africa* (1935), *Death in the Afternoon* (1932), a non-fiction work on bullfighting and *To Have and To Have Not* (1937) were published next and were not as critically well-received as his earlier work, although by now he was an international celebrity. With the publication of *For Whom The Bell Tolls* (1940) a new maturity and social consciousness was evident in Hemingway. The world was now standing at the edge and looking into the pit of World War II.

After the war Hemingway published two more major novels, one a failure—*Across the River and Into the Trees* (1950)—the other a masterpiece which included all of Hemingway's literary artistry and won for him the Nobel prize in 1954. The final novel of his career—although others were published posthumously—was *The Old Man and the Sea* (1952), a story of man in combat against nature and himself, with both principals ultimately victorious.

Although Hemingway dominated the thirties as America's most typical novelist, other major writers were also at work and making enormous contributions to the national literature. John Dos Passos (1896-1970), James T. Farrell (1904-   ), Thomas Wolfe (1900-1938), Edith Wharton (1862-1937), and Henry Miller (1891-   ) all wrote major works of fiction during the thirties, although censorship excluded from publication in America until 1960 Miller's two masterpieces, *Tropic of Cancer* and *Tropic of Capricorn*.

Theatre also flourished during this era, dominated since the 1920's by Eugene O'Neil (1885-1953), America's premier playwright and one of the most widely-performed dramatists in the English language outside of William Shakespeare. Combining naturalism, symbolism, the new Freudian insight into character, and the exaggerations of expressionism, O'Neill created a body of work unparalleled in our dramatic literature for its depth, revelation of emotion, and consummate artistry. In 1936 O'Neill won the Nobel prize for such plays as *The Emperor Jones* (1921), *The Hairy Ape* (1922), *Desire Under The Elms* (1924), *The Great God Brown* (1926), *Marco's Millions* (1927), *Strange Interlude* (1928), *Mourning Becomes Electra* (1931), *Ah, Wilderness* (1933), to cite only a partial list of his pre-Nobel prize production. Later, *The Iceman Cometh* (1946) and *A Moon For the Misbegotten* (1952) would re-establish O'Neill's reputation after a long decade of absence from the theatrical scene. Although much of O'Neill's drama was autobiographical, he withheld his *Long Day's Journey into Night* from production until after his death. The play reveals the anguish of O'Neill's family, with his father a failed actor, his brother an alcoholic, his mother a hopeless morphine addict and O'Neill himself, the young, aspiring writer, plagued with tuberculosis.

Other noted playwrights of the period included Elmer Rice (1892-1967), Maxwell Anderson (1888-1959), Clifford Odets (1906-1963), Robert Sherwood (1896-1955), John Van Druten (1901-1957), and Thornton Wilder (1897-1975).

World War II produced its new novelists, poets, dramatists, and young writers tempered and disillusioned by the experience of war, just as a previous generation of American writers had been catalyzed by World War I. New literary giants would emerge from America's new sense of itself as a victorious world power. And a new nihilism or denial of all value except the self and senses would also develop among certain writers, just as an earlier variation on this theme evolved after World War I. But post-war America could now look upon the possibility of the total destruction of the world: the atomic age had dawned, and a new freedom of expression came with it.

John Steinbeck (1902-1968) published novels both before and after the war, but he was concerned essentially with common, laboring people, farmers, men and women close to the soil, as were his literary predecessors, romantics like Whitman and Sandburg. The Salinas Valley of California, where Steinbeck was born, along with the Monterey sea coast and the dust bowl of Oklahoma provide the setting for much of his fiction. His theme was a simple affirmation of older values, the durability of man as an individual and the people as a group. In 1962 he won the Nobel prize for literature. Among his better known works are *To A God Unknown* (1933), *Tortilla Flat* (1935), *Of Mice and Men* and *The Red Pony* (1937), and *The Grapes of Wrath* (1939), which is generally regarded as his masterpiece. Following

William Faulkner, *who won the Nobel Prize for Literature in 1949, experimented with the interior monologue or stream of consciousness style in many of his works. The South is the setting for most of his novels, among them* As I Lay Dying, Light in August, *and* A Fable.

the war, his gradual disenchantment with the changing values of America was to find its most artistic expression in *The Winter of Our Discontent* (1961). Of his post-war novels *East of Eden* (1952) was the most widely read.

William Faulkner (1897-1962) explored the dark interior of man's psyche—murder, incest, rape in the gloomy, oppressive heat of Mississippi swamp country were the subjects and setting which preoccupied him. The South, with its mysterious resonances and dusty secrets harkening back to pre-Civil War days, gave a rich texture to Faulkner's courageous voyage inward among the tortured, sometimes perverted or idiotic minds of his characters. Experimenting with the technique of interior monologue or stream of consciousness, Faulkner attempts to record the process of thought with its strange, free-wheeling associations, its shifts back and forward in time. His more noteworthy books include *Soldier's Pay* (1926), *Mosquitoes* (1927), *Sartoris* and *The Sound and The Fury* (1929), *As I Lay Dying* (1930), *Sanctuary* (1931), *Light in August* (1932), *Absalom, Absalom!* (1936), *The Wild Palms* (1939), *The Hamlet* (1940), *Go Down Moses, and Other Stories* (1942), *Intruder in the Dust* (1948), *Requiem For a Nun* (1951), *A Fable* (1954), and *The Mansion* (1954). In 1949 he was awarded the Nobel prize for literature. Faulkner also wrote a number of motion picture scripts, including screen adaptations of Hemingway novels.

The novels of World War II were numerous, but only a relative handful had genuine artistic merit. Norman Mailer (1923-   ) wrote the blockbuster novel of the war, both a literary and a financial success of immense proportions. *The Naked and the Dead* (1948) followed an Army division

Eugene O'Neill, *considered by literary critics to be America's premier dramatist, died in 1953. His plays have been among the most widely performed in the English language outside of Shakespeare. O'Neill won the Nobel Prize for Literature in 1936. Among his more famous plays are* The Emperor Jones, Strange Interlude, The Iceman Cometh, *and* Long Day's Journey into Night.

James Jones, *author of* From Here to Eternity, *is shown at his desk working on another novel. Jones' novels are based closely on his experiences, particularly as a soldier in the Pacific during World War II. Among Jones' later works are* Some Came Running, The Thin Red Line, *and* The Pistol.

through an island invasion in the South Pacific, the subsequent campaign and the mopping up after their victory. Using the military unit as a metaphor for America, Mailer explores the minds of a variety of characters from the crypto-fascist general to his aristocratic but liberal aide, down through the ranks of officers and enlisted men until a panoramic picture of amazing diversity is assembled. Censorship problems arose before publication of the book, which seem somewhat Victorian in light of today's freedom of expression in publishing and motion pictures. Mailer's third novel, *The Deer Park* (1955) ran into censorship difficulties over explicit sexual scenes. Leaving the novel for a number of years, Mailer turned to journalism of a highly personal nature. *Advertisements For Myself* (1959), was a brilliant collection of short stories, fragments of novels-in-progress, autobiographical confessions, and incisive essays on literature and culture including his famous "The White Negro," a discussion of the philosophy of the "hipster," a latter-day underground rebel developing simultaneously with the "beatnik" of the late 1950's.

Mailer's two masterpieces of personal or subjective journalism are *Miami and the Seige of Chicago* and *The Armies of the Night*, both published in 1968. The former book dealt with the presidential conventions of 1968, including the riots of Chicago; the latter dealt with the march on the Pentagon in Washington in which thousands of anti-war protesters came to the nation's capital to express their disapproval of government intervention in Vietnam. In recent years Mailer has become an international celebrity and controversial figure, as a candidate for mayor of New York in 1968, as one of America's best and highest-paid writers and as a possible candidate for the Nobel prize.

James Jones' (1921-   ) most celebrated novel, *From Here to Eternity* (1951) ends with the beginning of World War II. Describing the pre-war American Army at Schoffield Barracks, Hawaii, Jones finds in the lonely figure of a company bugler a symbol for the common man and his essential integrity against the pressures of conformity represented by the Army. Other universal themes pervade the book, and the diversity of characters and situations accumulate into a broad picture of the American experience reduced to a military microcosm. For a number of years, Jones lived in Paris, and his subsequent novels were never as widely acclaimed as his first. Among the more notable of his later works are *Some Came Running* (1954) and *The Thin Red Line* (1962).

The "Beat" movement in American literature, was a modern-day romanticist attitude that would emerge in print from its underground obscurity in the years following the Korean War. But before the Beat phenomenon, a number of American novelists were working and evolving in separate directions which would open other frontiers of experience closed to the general reading public, which consumes only "popular" fiction.

Nelson Algren (1909-   ) in his *The Man with the Golden Arm* (1949) explored the world of the dope addict and professional small-time, big city hustler in a brutally realistic tragedy which won the first National Book Award.

Ralph Ellison (1914-   ) in his novel *Invisible Man* (1952), spoke to a wide and predominantly white audience about the black experience in America and particularly Harlem.

Saul Bellow (1915-   ), in a series of novels beginning with *Dangling Man* (1944), has evolved over more than thirty years into one of America's most widely-read and highly-acclaimed authors. His principle theme has been the confrontation between a sensitive, thoughtful man and an often mad society and sometimes even madder cosmos. His fictional characters have come from a variety of areas—the Jewish middle-class academic in *Herzog* (1965), *Mr. Sammler's Planet* (1973) and *Von Humbolt's Gift* (1975); a multi-millionaire WASP in *Henderson the Rain King* (1962); and a street-savvy Chicago hipster in *The Adventures of Augie March* (1953), to cite a few. Three-time winner of the National Book Award, Bellow was mentioned in 1975 as a possible candidate for the Nobel prize in literature.

American drama in the post-war years was a lively arena for new talents and new ideas, especially in the "off-Broadway" theaters with their non-commercial orientation. The Broadway stage, however, was divided between two giants, both playwrights representing different visions.

Arthur Miller (1915-   ) wrote realistic plays which were often staged in expressionist style. Man against himself and against an indifferent, amoral society in which material success seemed the only value was the theme which Miller most frequently explored. His more notable plays were *All My Sons* (1947), *Death of a Salesman* (1949), *The Crucible* (1953) and *A View from the Bridge* (1955).

Tennessee Williams (1914-   ) explored inward, probing into deepest areas of the human heart and mind in a succession of plays which sometimes seemed the dramatic counterpart of Faulkner's novels. Where Arthur Miller would suggest in his play some moral or ethical posture, Williams remained more clinical and detached. Among his celebrated works are *The Glass Menagerie* (1945), *A Streetcar Named Desire* (1947), *Summer and Smoke* (1949), *The Rose Tattoo* (1951), *Cat on a Hot Tin Roof* (1955) and *Sweet Bird of Youth* (1959).

Among some other playwrights of the era, Edward Albee (1928-   ), Paddy Chayefsky (1923-   ), Charles Gordone (1925-   ), Lorraine Hansberry (1930-1965), Lillian Hellman (1907-   ), William Inge (1913-1973), LeRoi Jones (Imamu Amini Baraka) (1934-   ) Clifford Odets (1906-1963), and Robert Sherwood (1895-1955), all made significant contributions to American literature.

A short five years after the end of World War II America was again at war, this time in Korea in what was euphemistically called a "conflict." The dream of peace had shattered as the nation moved from "hot war" to "cold war" and back again. Now a new literary movement was to arise, a "Renaissance" as some critics called it, a "know-nothing bohemianism" as others would say. But aside from their eccentric public behavior, a number of Beat writers made important additions to the nation's literature.

Dean of the Beat novelists was Jack Kerouac (1922-1969), a prolific writer whose work and lifestyle came to symbolize the philosophy of the movement. Like certain earlier romantics before them, the Beats trusted only their senses and the immediacy of experience. Drugs, sex, jazz were their "kicks," a personal morality outside the conventions of society allowed them to enjoy it all without a sense of guilt. America was a vast, lonely backdrop to the romantic adventures being played out in city and countryside, and a "beatific" or holy wisdom could be extracted from its open spaces, its junkies, winoes, whores, and criminals. Such was Kerouac's message, much like Walt Whitman before him: everything is holy. Kerouac's most widely-read novels include *On the Road* (1957), *The Subterraneans* (1958), *The Dharma Bums* (1958) and *Big Sur* (1962). There were many other novels, of varying literary and commercial success, plus several books of poetry. Kerouac seemed to speak for some of his generation of disaffected young people who had come of age after World War II and witnessed the growing discrepancy between the ideal and the actuality of American life.

John Clellon Holmes (1926-   ) published *Go* in 1952, a fictionalized account of the intellectual ferment and sexual adventures of leading figures in the Beat movement in New York city of the early 1950's. Kerouac, William Burroughs and Allen Ginsberg appear under thin disguises in the novel.

Allen Ginsberg (1926-   ) poet laureate of the Beat movement, and one of the most brilliant poets of recent times, broke new ground for American verse with his "Howl" (1956). Meant to be read aloud, with each line approximating the capacity of a human breath, "Howl" was praised, censored, denounced and eventually published around the world. Its startling, honest imagery; its bleak, pessimistic view of America and its final mystical, almost religious affirmation suggested the romanticism of Whitman, distorted through the lens of modern experience. Since "Howl" Ginsberg has continually grown and surpassed himself in the depth of emotion and technical achievement of his poetry.

Other notable figures of the Beat movement are poets Gregory Corso (1930-   ), and Lawrence Ferlinghetti (1919-   ), and novelist William Burroughs (1914-   ). There were numerous other writers of the period, some of whom claimed membership in the movement, others who claimed independence but were obviously partisans of the same cause.

Outside the Beat movement, with typical American vitality and variety, a plethora of writers were at work. Among the younger writers of literary merit who have come to national prominence in recent years are John Updike (1932-   ), Philip Roth (1933-   ), and Kurt Vonnegut (1922-   ), just to mention a few whose impact on American literature has been more than just incidental.

In America's 200th year, a quick look at the standard best-seller lists will indicate how far we've come as a nation from the Puritan restraints of colonial New England. Nothing is taboo, and anything with commercial value is published.

America's contribution to world literature during these past two hundred years has been monumental. No longer do American authors require the approval of their literary or cultural superiors in Europe before a novel or poem can be certified as art. American thinkers, critics, and essayists are now respected the world over and their writing is consulted avidly by Europeans and others just as we once looked to Europe for ideas. A unique and powerful body of writing has been bequeathed by America to the world, full of the spirit of revolt, courage, and intellectual honesty, despite its sometimes well-justified pessimism.

Within a year of its first publication in 1732, Benjamin Franklin's *Poor Richard's Almanac* had become the second most popular book in the colonies, surpassed only by the Bible. His maxims and sayings were read as eagerly as was his information on weather, tides, sunsets, and medical remedies.

AMERICAN MUSIC

Strange though it seems now, music was once the most continuing topic of controversy in this country. In fact, it might be said that the struggle to write and perform music freely was the microcosm for the struggle toward American freedom itself.

Though the thirst for freedom from European ties rose in crescendo as the 17th Century became the 18th, that thirst itself was always tied to a religious stoicism which looked upon enjoyment in general, and musical enjoyment in particular, as a bad influence. When, in 1720, no less a religious figure than Cotton Mather asserted that "heaven" was consistent with "regular singing," a cacophony of protests were heard.

The Europeans who had left the Elizabethan achievements and sophistication of Europe for America, were of a sparse, frontier temperament. Moreover, the means to perform and the audiences accustomed to advanced instrumental musical from Great Britain or France weren't available on the American landscape even for the Virginia-type aristocrats settling there. Thus American music in the early period was at best a mere combination of families singing in their homes, and groups of families singing in church, with a possibly pungent but very minor strain of American Indian influence.

Eventually, however, the rudimentary and unoriginal *Bay Psalm Books* gave way to original pieces by such musicians as John Tufts and Josiah Flagg (whose printer was none other than Paul Revere). And so the coming revolution would produce political freedom which in turn spawned freedom for music in the form of everything from conservatories to singing by children in grade schools. Thomas Jefferson performing Handel would not be uncommon. Francis Hopkinson, although no Handel, Beethoven, or Bach, would compose half a dozen pieces for the harpsichord dedicated to the first President of the United States, seeming to signal a new

musical era. Francis Scott Key's "Star-Spangled Banner," which he wrote anonymously in 1812 as "The Defence of Ft. McHenry," (though the melody itself was derived from an early English song), would be more than a political symbol. Though dissonant voices were not totally stilled, and though a tremendous influence of yet encapsulated and complex African music among the slaves on plantations was yet to be assimilated, for the first time the embryo of the true sound of America had passed the point of prematurity and was ready to be born.

One of the unique things which sprung from the music of America within the nineteenth century was a distinction completely taken for granted today: "popular" vs. "classical" music. The first truly popular American composer, Stephen Foster, was born on the fourth of July —exactly half a century after the Declaration of Independence. At the same time, it was no accident that this composer of such favorites as "My Old Kentucky Home," "Swanee River," and "Beautiful Dreamer," was an assiduous student of Beethoven and Mozart. For, though European-schooled critics would call Foster's music "household" and pejoratively "popular," within it was the seed of the ultimate American achievement: the fusion of classical and popular.

In the middle of the nineteenth century, though, nothing seemed further from reality than such a fusion. The United States was a sprawling, growing, technologically-oriented nation, the plains of Kansas and the gold mines of the West virtually cut off from the drawing rooms of the East. One outgrowth of this advancing technology was the proliferating manufacture of musical instruments in America, particularly pianos. Whereas at the turn of the century pianos were a relative rarity in the homes of Americans, by the beginning of the Civil War no less a cultural leader than Harriet Beecher

Stephen Foster, *the first popular musical composer in America. Although Europeans and American lovers of "serious" music belittled Foster's musical works, his popularity with the people have made him a favorite for many generations. Foster was one of the first composers to attempt to incorporate indigenous sounds into his compositions.*

A composite picture *showing some of the attractions of the Ziegfield Follies of 1921. Although the "extravaganzas" were short on content, they did give the audience grandiose and colorful stage settings and beautiful girls in beautiful costumes.*

Stowe advised that "the ideal American home" should contain this instrument, and thus they were selling at the rate of several thousand a day! One of those pianos was in the home of J.C.G. Graupner, who began the Boston Philharmonic Society.

Though many critics and musicians themselves consistently assert that technology is counter to creativity, the truth is that ultimately the advance of technology is a direct factor in the advance of music. The increased production and the increased quality of pianos would spur composers such as Charles E. Ives; a burgeoning economy would make more and better banjos, spurring "ragtime." The technological leaps of the nineteenth century may indeed have been a cornerstone of the high place in the world today of American music.

Certainly this is true of this century. The "moog synthesizers" of the 60's at once come to mind. Yet before that there was the dissemination of music to 30 or 40 million people at a time through TV and radio, to say nothing of a recording industry unparalleled in history, the finest works virtually every noted American composer and artist made available in each home for minimal cost!

Stephen Foster marks something else significant: the incorporation of black influence into the mainstream of American music, both in form and content. Though minstrel shows, which were growing in popularity, essentially derogated the Negro, Foster was at times able to elevate the patronizing to the poetic, the sentimental to the loving, as in "Nelly Was A Lady":

> *Toll de bell for Lubly Nell,*
> *My dark Virginny bride.*

Part of this evolution of music in the United States was the development of a real American classic of music. Though based upon strictly European models for a time, American

Another view *of the famed Ziegfield Girls from the 1920's. The shows were lavishly presented in an age when lavishness was thought to be essential to the American way of life.*

classical composing eventually began taking on a character of its own. The musical idiom of America seems at its best when tied to no tradition or, at the very least, an original assemblage of diverse traditions. So American Classical composing as a *genre* has never taken on a place of major importance in the history of the music of the world. Still, a number of American classical composers, and certain works in particular, rank with those of the great masters.

The first classical American musicians were Europeans whose goal was not truly to create a new American music, but to bring the old-world music to the new country. Thus, as the nineteenth century dawned, they established musical groups such as the Handel and Haydn Society. Americans such as William H. Fry (for his chamber music) and W. W. Gilchrest (for his symphonies) were lauded in their day, but became less important with the passage of years, until today their work is performed hardly at all. At that same time, for example, Walt Whitman and Henry David Thoreau were paying from their own pockets to see that their works were published, while other writers of the day, adhering more closely to classically accepted rules, were gaining wealth and notoriety from writing which several decades later would be of interest only to collectors.

The twentieth century told a different classical tale in America. Sessions composed concertos, symphonies and even an opera which, while still functioning within the generally accepted molds of established modes, filled those molds originally. Others, such as Hanson, were worthy of notice. But the true luminary of the period was Aaron Copland, born at about the same time as another man who fused classical and "pop" for America: George Gershwin.

Copland's "Billy the Kid" and "Appalachian Spring" are two of the most popular yet solid compositions in all of music. His "Third Symphony" and "Piano Fantasie," though somewhat lesser known, are greatly respected. For Copland's compositions are often unparalleled for conveying exact metaphorical meanings through non-verbal sounds—and sounds "of America." Many listeners, when first hearing "Appalachian Spring," exclaim that it can only be about spring, and only in our mountains!

In many quarters of America today, and for the decades since Copland and Gershwin wrote, there are composers attempting to forge experimental forms iconoclastically. That no further giants have yet appeared on the scene is not necessarily a failing of American musical genius. We are a country hardly two centuries old; how many centuries did it require to produce a handful of Beethovens and Bachs, Mozarts and Chopins, Tchaikovskys and Rachmaninoffs in a dozen countries?

But part of the reason why the United States is not best known for its classics is that so much of our musical energy has gone into other, more classically American forms.

The culmination of these currents and the unique and original highpoints of American music reached fruition after World War I in the forms of *jazz* and *musical comedy.*

As with any true, original art form, both are difficult to define. Musical comedy, however, usually has most of these elements: (1) Romanticism fused with humor, the first often expressed through a hero and heroine, the second through another couple or a third character; (2) A balance of song (and/or dance) with dialogue; (3) An initial overture, in which many of the songs are "previewed,"; (4) A "production number," often involving dance and designed to be impressive; (5) Two acts, the second of which ends with a reprise or "restatement song" from earlier. Yet this framework was stretched so greatly, for example, in George

Florenz Ziegfield, producer of the most famous musical extravaganzas in the history of American musical comedies. His stage productions, beginning in and running throughout the Twenties, were models of the elegant, sophisticated style of staging chorus line numbers.

song was but a "pop" tune because Bernstein perfectly accomplished what British critic T. S. Eliot called "the objective correlative"—the expression of complex and often theoretical ideas through one concrete, single scene, or action, or person, or even sound!

Each number, like a chapter of a great novel, both melodically and in words elucidates a principal character, while propelling a plot which builds in crescendo like the most expert of detective adventure thrillers.

"Something's Coming" sets forth the optimism of the hero, Tony, and simultaneously, emotionally sets up the audience for an important happening: his meeting the heroine, "Maria," at the dance "Tonight." Their backgrounds, their loyalties, are totally different, but not their hearts—and they fall irrevocably in love, sure that there must be a place for them "Somewhere."

The dance also brings the setting for a final confrontation between the Jets, who are Tony's friends, and the Sharks, led by Maria's brother, Bernardo. In a tragic accident, Bernardo dies at the hand of Tony.

The climax is a superb blending of sorrow and idealism: Tony is able to see Maria for a single instant before he is tragically shot, but from the shadows come forth both gangs, lifting his lifeless body from the cement, at last brought together "Somewhere," even if the lovers cannot be.

In this, we see why music itself has been called the purest art form, and why at moments of greatest happiness or sorrow there seems no adequate way to express one's feelings other than to sing or wail. At the same time, we have all

Gershwin's "Porgy and Bess" that many musical experts look upon "Porgy" as a fusion of the "musical" with opera. At the other extreme of the musical comedy continuum were the earlier "Ziegfield Follies," far less serious than "Porgy," far less unified, with the principal focus being a proliferation of production numbers.

Within these extremes are the hundreds upon hundreds of superb early American musical comedies. Some of the best examples are: Vincent Youmans' "No, No Nanette" in the mid-20's, Jerome Kern and Oscar Hammerstein II's "Showboat" in 1927, and several by George Gershwin at the turn·of the third decade of the twentieth century, including "Girl Crazy" and "Of Thee I Sing" (based upon the script by George S. Kaufman). The last signified the oncoming range and importance of musical comedy, winning a Pulitzer Prize.

The 30's and 40's thus saw such exemplary musicals as Rodgers and Hart's "I'd Rather Be Right" and their "Pal Joey" (written by famed novelist John O'Hara), and Rodgers and Hammerstein's "Carousel" and "South Pacific," the latter based on stories by James Michener. Possibly the all-time highpoint and model for the serious American musical occurred in 1957 with Leonard Bernstein's "West Side Story." Here, aided by fine Stephen Sondheim lyrics and Jerome Robbins choreography, Bernstein fused "musical-comedy" forms as no one had before.

The play is simultaneously topical and universal. Though dealing with a clash between Puerto Rican and Caucasian teenage gangs in New York City a generation ago, "West Side Story" has become increasingly topical and representative of the urban ethnic and racial crisis everywhere. In just one spirited and seemingly superficial song, "Gee, Officer Krupke!" every leading psychological and sociological theory toward the cause of violence is expressed—from inadequate parental love to adolescent crisis, man's inherently evil nature to larger environmental determinants. Yet to most of those millions who enjoyed "West Side Story," this

Al Jolson, *as he appeared as the "jazz singer" in 1927. Although Jolson went on to achieve an international reputation for his work in movies, he started out as a singer on Broadway.*

Dancer Martha Graham *as she appeared in 1932. Miss Graham and her dance troups did much to make modern dancing a popular art form in America and Europe.*

a prominent place alongside "Satchmo," were a number of mostly black musicians, such as pianist and composer Duke Ellington, bandleader Bill "Count" Basie and the blind artist of the keyboard, Art Tatum. Next, white musicians eagerly moved into the new world of jazz. In this already innovative field, the name of Stan Kenton stands out as supra-innovative. A pianist, leader and composer, Kenton was so iconoclastic that his critics argued he had gone beyond the limits of the supposedly "limitless" jazz structure! In the 40's, Dave Brubeck seemed to carry on the Kenton tradition of defying tradition, and later Brubeck's son—who often performed with his father—attempted to do the same.

An important offshoot of the jazz era was "the Big Band," playing mainstream music, which allowed people to dance, to participate. Yet the entire era seemed catalyzed, and to some extent created, by the one and only George Gershwin. Born in New York at the turn of the century, Gershwin's life was cut short by a cancer, short of his fortieth birthday. But in that brief span, he not only revolutionized the stage with "Of Thee I Sing" and "Porgy and Bess," he became the epitome of jazz itself forever through his "Rhapsody in Blue" and "An American in Paris." When Gershwin, whose brother Ira often wrote lyrics to George's more "pop" show songs, would travel by train, he felt he must keep pace with the lightning-like turning of the wheels in order to fuel his own music.

And so he did—and became, with Beethoven and Bernstein, a giant who irrevocably altered and heightened not only the inspiration which music gives us, but its very structure. Gershwin was not only a meteor which dazzled us with his flight, but a sun who will forever warm and give light. More of our lives than we suspect invisibly revolve about his sense of life. At his death, George Gershwin had plans, even farther-reaching, such as setting "The Gettysburg Address"

heard the truism, "Music speaks to us." And so, in the "musical comedy" of the twentieth century, the blending of the meanings of sound with the "sound" of meanings reached new heights in America and the world.

Not that musical comedies where the comedy was secondary dominated the scene. For every "West Side," there were several ebullient "Oklahomas," fantasy "Brigadoons," witty "My Fair Ladys," and nostalgic "Showboats." All these at their best, however, had two singular qualities in common: (1) a unique combination of diverse elements, some traditional, some modern, and, (2) the blending of those elements so beautifully that the "musical" seems a true dramatic play with the songs and the dances a natural, inevitable extension of the characters, the plot, the non-musical dialogue.

Thus, pianist arranger Norman Wallace of *International Who's Who of Musicians* has said:

"American musical comedy at its best is something which has never been produced elsewhere."

And so it is the same for jazz.

This uniquely American music can be traced to any number of influences. Yet, by its very nature—*improvisation*—jazz was new.

If it had a formal birthplace, however, jazz began in New Orleans, where relatively small groups (of various horns, drums, and, later, strings) mixed to produce original variations from either planned or spontaneous compositions. Nothing is outside the jazz periphery, be it war marches or the classic symphonies of European masters.

One of the earliest jazz performers, of course, was the famed singer and brass player Louis Armstrong. Soon taking

Agnes DeMille *in 1923. Miss DeMille worked as both a dancer and choreographer, staging dance numbers for musical reviews on Broadway as well as for the movies.*

to music. One cannot help but wonder how the landscape of the human soul would have been further changed had he lived to do it.

In the sixth decade of the twentieth century, a new phenomenon appeared on the American music scene: "rock."

Some say this musical form, which swept into virtually all strata of American culture for a time, was an inevitable outgrowth of what came before it; others say it was a defiance and desecration of American music, even music itself. Certainly, one can see the roots of some of the spirit and the rhythm of rock in the performances and material of Elvis Presley a decade before. It was true that much rock was either amateurish self-indulgent or an essential copy of "The Beatles" whose compositions first set the standards for rock, or British groups such as "The Who," whose rock opera "Tommy" validated this new musical form at its best.

Soon, then drawing upon its own unique roots, American rock carved its own niche in the history of music. Another highlight was "Woodstock"—a rock festival at Woodstock, New York, which lasted three days and drew nearly a half a million people from all over the United States. Though this

Isadora Duncan, shown here with some of her pupils in 1933, was another interpretative dancer who broke away from the classical form and structure of ballet to forge a new type of dance. She was instrumental in developing several dance groups in America.

festival was illumined by such British rock immortals as The Who and Joe Cocker, American performers such as Janis Joplin and Jimi Hendrix were the equal of any. Both these had mastered the mixture of rock with older forms, rhythm and blues, soul, and jazz.

Tragically, both also took their own lives within a few years after Woodstock, and this somehow seemed to catalyze a transformation of the violent emotions and bitter protests with which Joplin and Hendrix imbued their music to another level.

It was fitting, therefore, that the most famous performer at the Woodstock festival was an American woman, Joan Baez, who had never sung a note of rock in her nearly thirty years. Baez, long successful at embodying both current protest and basic human emotions within simple tunes, is representative of another important category of American music, a category found in every country since civilization began, a type of music which may at last tell more about a people than any other. Folk music.

Of all the countries in the world, America's folk music may be the most dynamic, because it is the most diverse. We are a huge country to begin with, bordered by Mexican and Central American influences on the south, French and other Canadian on the north, and, more important, a nation to which people from all other countries have emigrated, bringing the music of their own geographies with them—music which was then altered and nurtured by the new environment in an interaction with so many other different musical backgrounds.

Yet the crowning achievement of rock anywhere, and an achievement which transcended all cultural and musical lines, was the Broadway production of the American rock musical, "Hair." Heretical in ideas, presentation of nudity, and language, "Hair" made a permanent impact on American culture, as well as American music. Its unexcelled success was partly a result of a splendid eclecticism, mirroring the maturity of so much of American music. "Tribal" rhythms, "torchy" ballads existed side-by-side with farcical wit and pungent social comment; extemporaneousness was joined to classic artistry. Certainly some of the parts of "Hair" were not the equal of the creations of a Rodgers and Hammerstein, George Gershwin or Leonard Bernstein. But the "mix," like a kaleidoscope, worked perfectly because, finally, that mix was the theatrical and musical embodiment of an idea whose time had come.

Any new, lasting music produced in America inevitably finds its way into our folk songs. Virtually every American musical form can be traced back to folk, whether it was the rhythm-and-blues of the middle decades of the twentieth century (growing partly out of the ragtime and minstrelsy of almost a century before) or Elvis Presley's "country" music beginnings.

Irving Berlin, *dressed in an army uniform, in 1942. Berlin also wrote for the musical comedy stage, but with the outbreak of World War II he composed a number of songs intended to stir the country to patriotism.*

Cole Porter, *one of America's best known popular composers, as he appeared in 1940. Porter is known for the cleverness and sophistication of his lyrics. Many of his songs, written for Broadway productions, have become "standards" of American popular music.*

Lyricist Ira Gershwin, *left, and composer Jerome Kern shown at work in 1943 on the musical film* Cover Girl. *Kern wrote the Broadway musicals "Showboat," "Swing Time," and "The Cat and the Fiddle." Gershwin, who was the lyricist for his brother George for many years, wrote the lyrics for such musicals as "Porgy and Bess," "Lady in the Dark," and "Of These I Sing."*

Not incidentally, Mississippi, Presley's home, is the home of that body of American music called "country and western," long ignored by both American classical, semi-classical and pop authorities, as well as general audiences, despite a steady, growing influence upon all of them. In the 1960's and '70's, however, country and western artists broke through to national dominance, and "country" thus became a genuine and permanent part of American music.

In a sense, the foregoing is true of American music as a whole. Though as many as a dozen distinct facets of music have been innovated in the United States, as each developed, it transcendentally assimilated other facets and became a part of them as well, so that the music of the United States has, at its best, often grown into a united state.

Two composer-performers at their height at Bicentennial 1976, exemplify this: Paul Simon and Burt Bacharach.

The Missouri-born Bacharach, professionally educated in music at Mannes School in New York and Music Academy of the West in California, began as an arranger for such singers as Marlene Dietrich, but eventually achieved success for his own compositions. With lyricist Hal David, Bacharach produced the show "What's New, Pussycat" and, on his own, scores for such movies as "Butch Cassidy and the Sundance Kid" which included the famed tune "Raindrops Keep Fallin' On My Head."

Bacharach has produced a plethora of tunes which call up many major elements of music in America, from pop to jazz to soul to semi-classical. And it is noteworthy that many of these have been written singly. For, though much famous American music has emanated from theatrical shows, movies or TV, there is a solid body of work that came about singly, and was performed strictly for records or in nightclubs and concerts.

But possibly the epitome of this successful blending-transcending of forms, one which captured not only American but world-wide acclaim, are those of poet-composer Paul Simon.

Born in New Jersey in 1942, raised in New York, Simon achieved fame in teaming with singer Art Garfunkel. His first success of scope, however, was the score for the motion picture "The Graduate," from which his first hit, "The Sounds of Silence," emanated. However, the entire scope of music which Simon composed for this motion picture prophesied not only the quality but the range of his talents. The rhythmic "Mrs. Robinson" was also within that score,

Composer Jerome Kern. *Many of the songs he wrote for Broadway musicals have found their way into the common experience of American music.*

Composer Richard Rodgers *shown at the piano composing in 1943. Rodgers wrote the music for the show "Oklahoma," the first Broadway show to successfully integrate singing and dancing into a sound dramatic story. For many years "Oklahoma," which opened in 1943, was the longest running production on Broadway.*

George Gershwin, *who started in the music business as a composer of popular "Tin Pan Alley" songs, went on to write some of the most beautiful and enduring music in the history of American music. His "Rhapsody in Blue" is a masterful blending of classical and jazz traditions.*

Nat "King" Cole *as he appeared in 1948. Cole was one of the first Black singers to achieve national stardom as a recording artist. Cole also went on to star in a short-lived television program, and appeared in dramatic parts in movies.*

as well as the beautiful canticle "Scarborough Fair," plus a number of lesser-known tunes, ranging from Big Band parodies to rock-and-jazz creations.

Using new forms—such as the integration of actual radio broadcasts in "7 O'clock News/Silent Night"—yet always organically integrated with the message of the song, Simon went on to the inspiring "Bridge Over Troubled Water," reminiscent of a Negro spiritual, "Cecilia," drawing upon the "bop" of the forties with a touch of rock, and "The Fifty-Ninth Street Bridge Song" ("Feelin' Groovy"), a stream-of-consciousness paean to love of life.

His own? Simon titled the album issued just before Bicentennial 1976, "Still Crazy As Ever." If Simon, and those like him are "crazy," it is the insanity of genius. America in the middle decades of the twentieth century, while undoubtedly producing musical excellence, has been criticized for not producing great poets. However, is this because almost all of our great poets are putting their words to music? One only has to examine the lyrics of Simon's "Sounds of Silence," Joni Mitchell's "Chelsea Morning," Leonard Cohen's "Suzanne," to see surpassing poetry. Yet, the final value of

Frank Sinatra, *whose "crooning" reduced teenaged girls to shrieking fanatics, started out as a band singer with the Tommy Dorsey Orchestra. During the years of World War II Sinatra was the most popular singer in America.*

Lyricist Oscar Hammerstein, II *in 1953. Hammerstein, who during his career worked with composer Richard Rodgers, wrote the lyrics for such Broadway shows as "Oklahoma," "South Pacific," and "Carousel."*

Composer Irving Berlin *as he appeared in 1951. Berlin's musical productivity spanned several decades, and his music has become one of the most beloved in America.*

Paul Simon as a musician is that his melody is never subordinated to his message. The two are one.

It is impossible, of course, to list all of those American composers and performers not already cited who rival the Simons and Bacharachs, but the following cannot be omitted:

ROY ACUFF, country-and-western singer who spent decades with the "Grand Ole Opry."

MARIAN ANDERSON, the first Black to sing with New York's Metropolitan Opera.

HAROLD ARLEN, composer and pianist, who wrote such songs as "Stormy Weather" and "Blues In The Night."

JAMES BROWN, humanistic soul-rock singer and composer, who once rushed to Washington at the President's request to reason with rioters.

RAY CHARLES, unusual, influential blind jazz and pop singer-stylist.

NAT "KING" COLE, singer-pianist who was the leader of the "soft" style.

BING CROSBY, famed singer of such songs as "Going My Way" and "White Christmas."

NEIL DIAMOND, Brooklyn-born composer and performer who has run the gamut of creating music, from African rhythms to American evangelism, *Jonathan Livingston Seagull*, to intimate, autobiographical works such as "I Am, I Said!"

ARETHA FRANKLIN, the queen of "soul" singing.

FERDE GROFÈ, who studied at the famed Leipzig Conservatory in Germany, but returned to the United States to compose the indigenously American "Grand Canyon Suite" and many others.

WOODY GUTHRIE, probably the best-known American

Oscar Hammerstein, *left, and Richard Rodgers, center, along with producer Ralph Levy, watch rehearsals for their television special which was telecast in 1954. Rodgers and Hammerstein collaborated on a number of musicals which have become part of the popular tradition in American culture.*

Elvis Presley, *shown here the year he began his career in 1956. Presley created a sensation with his gyrating hips and new approach to music. Although Presley's music grew out of the black "rhythm and blues" sounds, his distinctive style and stage presence catapulted him to the number one position in music entertainment, a position he has continued to enjoy despite changing trends in popular music.*

folk singer, a fine guitarist and song writer as well. He composed "This Land Is My Land."

AL JOLSON, supposedly the first leading jazz singer, who was born in Russia but made the United States his adopted country. "Mammy," "California, Here I Come" and "Sonny Boy" are among the songs Jolson made world-famous with a singular jazz-pop style.

CAROLE KING, songwriter and singer whose "Tapestry" is the most popular record album in history.

ALAN LERNER, who with Frederick Loewe, accounted for "Brigadoon," "Paint Your Wagon," "My Fair Lady," and "Gigi."

ROD McKUEN, composer and singer, winner of the Grand Prix du Disc award. Some think McKuen's work is too popular and trite, others feel it to be surpassingly universal.

JOHNNY MATHIS, pop singer who, like Elvis Presley, mastered virtually all forms of music and whose popularity spans several decades.

ETHEL MERMAN, probably the greatest female musical

comedy singer.

GLENN MILLER, legendary bandleader of the 20's and 30's, who died in an untimely plane crash during World War II.

PAUL ROBESON, controversial black bass vocalist.

PETE SEEGER, noted folk singer and composer.

BEVERLY SILLS, leading opera soprano.

FRANK SINATRA, no doubt the most influential American pop singer, who gave a personalized, "honest" interpretation of lyrics which influenced all singers after him.

BARBRA STREISAND, singer who starred in "Funny Girl" and "Hello Dolly," giving a unique, ultra-emotional and personalized style to lyrics, much as Frank Sinatra did a generation before.

JIMMY WEBB, experimental composer-poet, who produced probably the most original, and possibly the longest song of quality ever written: "MacArthur Park."

LAWRENCE WELK, accordian player who later achieved great success as a bandleader on television.

Just as the music of these giants has influenced America, so American culture has had influence on American music. For some reason, for example, war has spawned many tunes and classical pieces, though not all of them good. Folk heroes and unusual feats have similarly inspired many muscial compositions, again not always lasting ones.

What does seem more significant is that virtually every American feels that in some form or another he is a "musician."

Possibly this is a result of our "all men are created equal," maybe it is simply a ramification of a deeply musical spirit in America. Whichever, there are few citizens in the United States who do not fancy themselves Frank Sinatras or Barbra Streisands, Beverly Sills or Enrico Carusos, when they step into the shower or play the lead in the local community productions. One of the oldest types of ads in American magazines asks for any songs the reader might have written, since there is always the chance . . . just as another long-time advertisement in American journals is for one to see if

Aaron Copland, *perhaps the most famous of America's "serious" musical composers. Copland's concert music is a skillful blending of the classical with American folk music.*

Martha Graham, *shown here performing "Appalachian Spring."*

The incomparable *Louis "Satchmo" Armstrong sitting with his horn in a Las Vegas, Nevada, dressing room following a performance in 1970. Armstrong rose from playing jazz in the New Orleans red light district to become America's best known jazz musician. In the early 1950's he traveled throughout the world as the unofficial ambassador of American good will.*

Frank Sinatra, *shown here performing in a special concert in 1974, has been the most enduring singer in the history of American popular culture. His career has spanned nearly four decades, and Sinatra has moved from singing to acting with the ease and grace of the born entertainer.*

he has artistic talent.

Obviously, talent is rare, yet, unlike other people, Americans feel they have at least a spark of that talent. Is this the germ of what has made us so open to new forms in music, and has led American music to be so rich and, at times, so exquisite?

At the very least, in the heart of each American, whether he chooses a Presley, a Copland, a Gershwin, or a Grand Ole Opry, it is "his own." He feels truly represented by the particular music which he chooses, more than by his political

Pearl Bailey, *shown here being sworn in as a senior advisor to the United States delegation to the United Nations, in 1975.*

representatives.

And for those that say that a Gershwin is no Bach, it can well be answered that a Gershwin, and a Copland before him and a Paul Simon after, are indeed the Bachs of the twentieth century.

American music, in its varied forms, has been enjoyed by more people and been integrated more into their lives than that of all the past "masters." Nevertheless, it has taken longer for those steeped in tradition to accept the greatness of American masters of music. One reason, of course, is that most venerate an accomplishment as much for what its age is as for what *it* is. No segment of our culture has ever been exempt from this.

An even more fulfilling reason is that the most lasting American music almost always seems to be that which broke away from tradition, even from American "tradition," in some crucial way.

Sometimes that breakaway is subtle and grows on us with time, as with Paul Simon's body of music. Sometimes the breakaway is brash and jolting, even abrasive, and takes years before much of it is even published, let alone accepted. Yet the majority of American musical geniuses have been recognized soon and young. Because we adore the new, at times too much, and so at times embrace the fad, the gimmick, and the novelty in music as in everything else. Many an instant success of today is the non-entity of tomorrow.

Yet this too is part of freedom and, if our political, social and business worlds have become more corrupt and rigid than we would like, the world of music has often become the outlet where we can be most free. Some compose, some perform, the vast, vast majority listen. And there will always be controversy about whether one form of music is superior to another, this composer or performer superior to that.

But music itself, contrary to its beginnings 200 years ago, is no longer an issue.

It is part of our lives; it has touched each and all of us.

It is a real, permanent, deep part of American character.

Tom Paine was a musician. Paul Revere was one.

But unlike paintings which can be reproduced and scientific formulas which can be explained on the printed page, music—especially America's diverse, driving, original music—must finally be listened to.

Listen to it.

It is the innermost sound of human emotion.

THE POPULAR ARTS

It is not an historical accident that for sixty years the movies have been one of America's most favorite and enduring popular forms of entertainment. The movies parallel the mainstream of American life, with its reliance on science and technology, because they, too, of all the popular arts, rely most heavily on science and technology for their very existence; and a history of the American film must begin with the inventors and inventions that made movies possible.

Like so many other modern contrivances the movies owe much of their existence to the genius of Thomas Edison. Late in the nineteenth century Edison became intrigued by Eadweard Muybridge's experimental still photographs of galloping horses. Although at the time (circa 1888) Edison was busily engaged with his work on developing what eventually became the phonograph, he began experimenting with a way of putting continuous still pictures in sequence which when projected would create the illusion of movement. While Edison concentrated most of his personal efforts at perfecting the phonograph, he left much of the experimentation of developing moving pictures to his assistant, William Dickson; Dickson's efforts at the Menlo Park, New Jersey, laboratories initially met with limited success. It took the invention of another American to make the moving picture theory a reality.

Early in 1889 George Eastman, working independently in Rochester, New York, invented and perfected continuous film. Before his invention photographic film had come in individual sheets, which made their use in motion picture cameras very haphazard. Eastman's new type of film, when coupled with Edison's primitive camera and projecting device, marked the practical beginning of the movies in America.

Realizing the economic benefits of his motion picture invention, Edison soon developed a machine for commercially showing pictures to the public which he named the Kinetoscope. For a penny the viewer looked through the Kinetoscope's peep hole and watched a one-minute film flash by. These early motion pictures were without stories and generally dealt with cultural curiosities—such as American Indians doing a war dance or a vaudeville magician doing a sleight of hand trick. Most of the films for the Kinetoscope were shot in an ersatz studio Edison had erected near his laboratories in 1893. Dubbed the "Black Maria" because of its tarpaper construction, Edison's one-room studio was the precursor of the Hollywood film studio. Despite their lack of any dramatic content, and their dreary repetition (the viewer saw the same one minute film over and over on the same machine) the Kinetoscope films were a commercial success, and by 1894 the term "peep show" had come into the American lexicon.

The "peep show" phenomenon grew and soon many major cities on the East coast had their store front "theaters" and arcades showing countless one-minute presentations to an enthusiastic public who could not get enough of the new form of entertainment.

The "peep shows'" popularity with the general public, however, was not matched in enthusiasm or acceptance by the more affluent members of society. At first most of the theater going public looked upon the "peep shows" as a vulgar form of show business, while the vaudeville audience continued to prefer the live acts on stage to their filmed counterparts on the Kinetoscope screen. All this changed, though, on April 23, 1896, when Edison produced his first Kinetoscope showing to a black tie audience as part of the vaudeville program at a large theater in New York City. From that day on the moving picture machine outgrew its "peep show" origins and soon became an important part of most vaudeville programs.

Although Edison recognized the money making potential of his camera for some inexplicable reason he failed to secure an international copyright on the machine. This oversight meant that, although the American copyright prevented others from capitalizing on Edison's invention in America, all an enterprising showman had to do was go to Europe, have a similar machine built there, and then bring it back to this country (along with films made in Europe) and set up his own theater. Many entrepreneurs took advantage of Edison's copyright oversight; other cameras and projectors were invented and marketed, and by 1899 there were a number of

D.W. Griffith, *the "father of the cinema" as he appeared in 1933. Griffith perfected many cinematic techniques which have become standard approaches in film making. His Birth of a Nation in 1915 was the screen's first epic. Griffith, along with Mary Pickford, Charlie Chaplin, and Douglas Fairbanks was responsibile for the creation of United Artists.*

"studios" established, mainly on the East coast, all of them competing with Edison's company for a share of the motion picture business.

Edison's strongest competitors were the American based Biograph Studio and the Pathé Studio in Paris. However, despite the fierce economic competition on the wide open market, the movies being produced were dismally alike in content.

The early film producers turned to the stage for their stories and actors, and the movies made during this period, whether scenes from popular plays and vaudeville acts or "originals" written specifically for the makeshift film "studios", were very stagey. The actors were unused to acting for the camera, and their gestures were much too broad for the intimateness of the celluloid image. On film those gestures which might have played well to the upper balconies of legitimate theaters were often comical instead of tragic; the movies borrowed their stories and techniques from the stage, and in most instances it was a poor choice of mimicry. The power of the cinema had not yet been discovered in dramatic terms. Movie makers during this period tended to think in quick one-shot scenes, with none of the dramatic intercutting common to modern films. However, one good example of the potential dramatic power of the new medium was evident in a short film made in 1896 called *The Kiss*, which showed May Irvine and John Rice re-creating for the screen their famous stage kissing scene. So strong was the effect of this scene on the audiences who saw it that ministers began speaking out against the movies, and the criticism raised against *The Kiss* was probably the first instance of local ministers trying to censor a movie.

In 1903 the art of movie making in America was born. Although there had been serious attempts at making more compelling stories in Europe before this date, it was not until seven years after the formation of the Edison movie making

Lillian Russell, *famed actress of the stage at the turn of the century, appeared in a short filmed version of one of her stage plays in 1899.*

company that any American broke away from the stagey one-reel melodramas which characterize this period. Edwin S. Porter, a director of limited dramatic background but one well versed in the intricacies of movie technology, made a film called *The Great Train Robbery* and started a tradition. For the first time in movie history a film was made which made use of a device unique to movies: cross cutting. Cross cutting is simply the technique of putting several different scenes, of varying lengths of time on the screen, together to form a whole. Cross cutting makes it possible for a movie

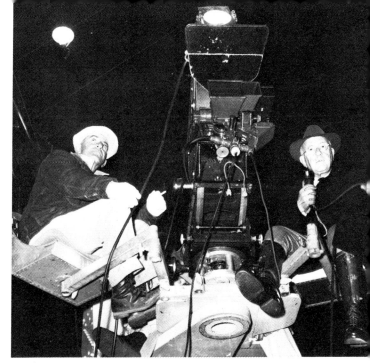

Movie technology *was slow in getting started, but once the film industry was established in Hollywood the technological development expanded in many directions, resulting in the creation of sound movies, color, and wide screen. Here director Cecil B. De-Mille, right, supervises a scene from atop a boom which also holds the 35mm camera.*

Clara Bow, *the "It Girl" of the 1920's. The Jazz Age ushered in new, more permissive cinema and Clara Bow was exemplary of the kind of femme fatale the movie going audience wanted to see during this decade.*

maker to show simultaneous action in different locations, and, hence, to heighten the dramatic tension in the audience. In *The Great Train Robbery* Porter told a relatively simple story of a hold-up, a chase, and a shootout at the end. However, by cross cutting the scenes *The Great Train Robbery* has the look of a movie, not the appearance and performance of a filmed stage play. Moving back and forth from the holdup scene, to the robbers escaping, to the posse being formed, and to the final shootout, Porter was able to tell the story without using many subtitles, and still make the plot clear to the audience. He ended the film by having one of the posse members fire his six-shooter directly at the camera, which, when projected, appeared as though he were aiming directly at the audience. The effect of this film was immediate and widespread. Audiences throughout the east coast clamored to see it, and Edison had to make several copies of the print to satisfy the demand. Artistically, *The Great Train Robbery* meant that the movies had a creative life of their own, that they did not have to rely on the stage for technique, and, in fact, had their own techniques and devices which needed only to be explored and developed.

The first developer of movies as an art form came along a short time after the making of *The Great Train Robbery*. D. W. Griffith was an out of work actor and playwright who had worked, as did many out of work stage actors in those days, for the fledgling film studios on the east coast. By 1907 Griffith himself was working at the Biograph Studio as a director. Here he made numerous one-reel (about 10-minute) films in the popular style of the day. Griffith soon realized that Porter's use of the cross cut was a great tool that only the movies had for telling stories. Griffith also noticed that many European directors were making use of the close-up shot, which revealed only a portion of the actor. As he worked on the quickie films Biograph turned out, Griffith began to experiment with camera position and editing and lighting. Between 1908 and 1912 Griffith turned out dozens of one

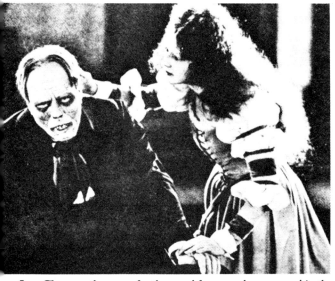

Lon Chaney, *the man of a thousand faces, as he appeared in the original version of* The Phantom of the Opera. *Chaney was a master of disguises and starred in several films during the silent era.*

Gloria Swanson *as she appeared in 1925. Miss Swanson was one of the best actresses to make the transition from the Broadway chorus line to starring roles in the movies.*

reelers, and with each film he learned something new about the art of movie making.

During this four-year period Griffith, who has come to be known as the Father of the Cinema, perfected the close-up, the wide angle shot, and the strictly cinematic technique of using objects in a film as actors. His story telling became almost completely visual; he relied very little on the use of title cards to move the plot along. Although these early films still suffered from a lack of high level dramatic content, they nevertheless told a relatively complicated story in an easy to follow manner. Griffith recognized that movies make their greatest effect on the emotions, not on the intellect. As Griffith formulated it, movies should make people feel; that the very mercurial nature of the enclosed cinematic mise en scene belies analysis at the time of viewing, and if the viewer is to have any reaction to the scene it must be the immediate, emotional one. Consequently, Griffith used new techniques which permitted him to convey to the audience the emotions of the scene in ways that had not yet been fully developed. He borrowed copiously from other directors, both European and American; but he developed and refined what he borrowed, so that although he often used approaches and techniques which were not original with him, his genius for filmmaking transformed the borrowed techniques into his own personal aesthetics as a film director.

In 1913 Griffith left Biograph and went to work for the Mutual Company. His reason for leaving Biograph was predicated mainly on his desire to make films longer than one or two reels. At Mutual he functioned more as an overseer of film production, directing individual scenes rather than the complete film. Again, however, Griffith was learning and waiting for an opportunity to direct a large film, both in length of running time and in content, and in 1914 Griffith was given the chance to direct his first epic. Some years earlier Griffith had read *The Clansman*, a novel about the Civil War, and he had harbored for some time the desire to

make a movie based on the book. When the chance came Griffith was ready, and in early 1915 he released the movie which he titled, *The Birth of a Nation*. Originally running almost three hours, *The Birth of a Nation* is Griffith's version of the Civil War and the Reconstruction Period following the war. Because the movie's length necessitated showings only in selected theaters around the country, and because an increased admission price was to be charged due to the cost of producing the film, it was not expected to reach the typical movie goer of the day. Nothing could have been further from the truth. The movie was an instant financial success; not only was *The Birth of a Nation* the first epic film, it was also the first film to generate widespread debate about the artistry of the motion picture. However, the film created another kind of reaction which Griffith had not expected.

Griffith was the son of a Confederate officer, and the South is viewed very sympathetically throughout the film. Southern aristocracy (which existed more grandiosely and humanely in Griffith's film than it did in reality) was held up as a model of gentility. The slaves were shown to be happy, foot shuffling creatures, docile and content with their lot in life—in fact, one scene shows the slaves cheering the Confederate soldiers as they ride off to battle. His general treatment throughout the film of the slaves is paternalistic: scene after scene shows them happy with their work in the cotton

Shirley Temple, *the first popular child actress. Shirley was loved by millions of movie fans around the world for her performances in dozens of movies in the Thirties.*

Scene from the Paul Muni *film* I am a Fugitive from a Chain Gang *made in 1932. The prison picture was just one of many film genre developed by Hollywood during the first few years of sound pictures.*

The gangster picture *was one of the staples of Hollywood film production during the Thirties. The Hays Office, which was the official Hollywood censorship board, had established a system of "compensating values" which meant that, among other things, crime was never to be successful on the screen. The gangster movies during the Thirties always ended badly for the bad guy. This scene from* Public Enemy *shows Jean Harlow, Edward Woods, center, and the number one screen bad guy of the period, James Cagney.*

Hollywood musicals *flourished with the advent of sound. In this scene from* Twenty Million Sweethearts *Dick Powell breaks into song while Ginger Rogers and Pat O'Brien look on admiringly. About ten years after he started out as a song and dance man, Powell made the transition to playing "tough guys" on the screen.*

fields, while the white plantation owner and his family enjoy the fruits of the slaves' labor. Despite this slightly distorted view of southern living and slave mentality, however, it was not those kinds of scenes which created controversy. The controversial scenes were those which occurred in the second half of the film (subtitled "Reconstruction") in which the Carpetbaggers and Scalawags were shown descending upon the war ravaged South, bringing with them corruption and barbarity. Again the Blacks, now freedmen, are shown in a distorted light: as thieves, drunkards, and corrupt politicians selling out to the Northern Carpetbaggers. As he builds the

dramatic tension in this part of the film, showing the once proud Southerners at the mercy of the former slaves and their Northern henchmen bent on completing the destruction of the South, he offers as the salvation of the South the one group which could rid the area of the arrogant freedmen and Northerners: the Ku Klux Klan. In fact, the Klan becomes the hero of the second half of *The Birth of a Nation.* So vociferous was the reaction to this portrayal of the Klan that riots occurred in Chicago and Philadelphia when the movie was shown there. Griffith was attacked as a racist; editorials denouncing the film's point of view appeared in several northern papers. No

The first great horror film *of the sound era was King Kong released in 1933. This still shows the giant ape atop a New York City skyscraper battling military airplanes.*

one questioned the artistry of the film, but its biased portrayal of the Blacks and its glorification of the Klan led to widespread denunciation. Griffith was stunned at this totally unexpected public reaction. While the controversy surrounding the film continued to rage, Griffith made plans for his next film, one that would be greater in scope than *The Birth of a Nation*, and one that he hoped would be an answer to his critics.

In 1916, the year following the release of *The Birth of a Nation*, Griffith came out with *Intolerance*. It is a massive film, with four main stories running through it: the life of Christ; the persecution of the Huguenots; the fall of Babylon; and a modern story involving an innocent man threatened with execution. As the title implies, the four stories are used to depict intolerance through the ages. *Intolerance* is Griffith's statement about hypocrisy; he treats the individuals as symbols of injustice rather than as individuals, and it marks a radical departure from the kinds of films he had made earlier. *Intolerance*, with its massive sets and complicated story line, was not a financial success—perhaps because the critics at whom it was aimed gave it generally mediocre reviews. Griffith was hurt financially by the film's lack of commercial success, and he never again tried to deal with such grandiose themes or use such extravagant sets. Three years after the release of *Intolerance* Griffith made what many consider his masterpiece. *Broken Blossoms* (1919) is a small picture in scope, but Griffith's artistry for story telling and his visual sense and form are manifest in every scene. A year later Griffith made another film, *Way Down East*, which was well received both critically and at the box office. However, after this film his career stagnated. Although he continued to make films for almost another fifteen years, his later movies were mostly re-hashing of earlier themes and earlier cinematic approaches. But the audiences changed; they were no longer enchanted by his delicate handling of

James Dunn *prepares to say goodnight to Shirley Temple in this scene from* Bright Eyes, *made in 1934.*

male/female relationships (during the Twenties his movies, which were sadly out of step with popular social mores, were not seriously considered by critics), nor was his handling of epic themes attractive to moviegoers already sated by other, more expensive and grandiose "spectaculars." Griffith continued living in Hollywood, but the movie industry which he had helped establish passed him by; his later years were spent in virtual isolation and relative poverty. He died on July 23, 1948, in Hollywood.

The rise of the American film industry created great changes not only in the movies themselves but also in the American social fibre. Movies quickly became one of the most popular forms of mass entertainment, and with the rise in the popularity of the motion picture came the motion picture star. At first the film actors were not identified on the screen; screen credits before 1910 listed the title, the studio or company which produced the film, and the director and technicians who had made the movie. However, the movie audience began showing their preferences to certain actors and actresses and a constant stream of letters poured into the studios in Hollywood asking for the names of actors and

The first great comedians *to emerge on the screen after the introduction of sound were the Marx Brothers. This is a scene from their famous "stateroom routine" in their movie* A Night at the Opera *made in 1935.*

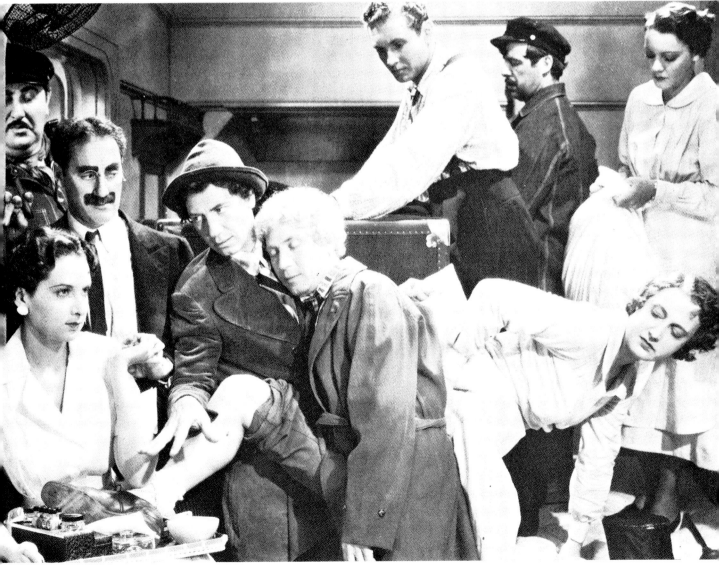

Olympic champion *Johnny Weissmuller became one of the most famous Tarzans in the history of that durable film series. He is shown here with Maureen O'Sullivan who played opposite him as Jane in several Tarzan films.*

actresses in particular films. In 1910 an actress sometimes listed as Little Mary, was finally revealed to be a child actress with the film name of Mary Pickford. Once the audience knew her name they flocked to her pictures, and the cult of the American Movie Star was born. Moviegoers throughout the country queued up whenever a Mary Pickford movie was being shown—they didn't care what the movie was, they wanted to see their favorite film actress. Carl Laemmle at Universal, noting the increased interest in Mary Pickford's movies once the audience knew her name, decided to capitalize on what most producers felt was a passing fancy, and fashioned his own over night screen star. He named her Florence Lawrence, and soon she was rivaling Pickford for boxoffice appeal. Miss Lawrence lacked the acting ability to long remain a threat to Pickford, but her manufactured biography and studio controlled life style marked the beginning of another facet of the burgeoning film industry: the star who was a product of public relations rather than talent.

Once Pickford had made the breakthrough and became well known, the floodgates were opened and dozens of formerly anonymous actors soon became household names. Rivaling Pickford in popularity was the screen comedian, Charlie Chaplin. Although another comedian, John Bunny, was perhaps the first comedic actor the movie audience knew by name, Chaplin's popularity grew so fast that by the outbreak of World War I his name and face were known around the world.

Chaplin had started as a vaudeville comedian in England, and came to America as part of a vaudeville company in 1912. While appearing with the Karno Comedy Company, Chaplin was seen by the legendary film director Mack Sennett, and in 1913 Sennett signed the "knockabout" comedian to a film contract. Chaplin went to work for Sennett in the early part of 1914, working first in a one-reel comedy *Making a Living*. It was in his second film for Sennett, *The Kid Auto Races at Venice*, however, that Chaplin began to develop the characteristic shuffle and gestures that have charmed millions of filmgoers. Chaplin's tramp costume came about almost by accident: he was sharing a dressing room with "Fatty" Arbuckle at the Sennett studios; while waiting to begin *The Kid Auto Races at Venice*, Chaplin put on a pair of Arbuckle's trousers, a coat from another comedian, a borrowed mustache from another—and within the period of a few hours Chaplin had created the character of the tramp which was his hallmark.

Chaplin's early career in Hollywood was shaped by Mack Sennett, whose Keystone Kops were one of the most popular of the silent comedies. Sennett had worked for the Biograph Studios as a director, but in 1912 he started his own studio, making nearly 140 one-reel comedies his first year. The Sennett brand of film comedy is described as slapstick; the pratfall, the pie in the face (the movie actress Mabel Normand is reportedly the first person to throw a custard pie in someone's face in a silent comedy) the madcap chase at the end—these were the characteristics of most Sennett films. He ran his studio like a repertoire company, and in the process developed many comedians—Charley Chase, Ben Turpin, Stan Laurel, Oliver Hardy—who went on to achieve movie greatness after they had left Sennett. However, none of his resident comedians had the talent and pathos of Chaplin, who soon outgrew the Sennett formula for film making and struck out on his own.

While Chaplin worked in other studios molding and shaping his character of the tramp in numerous films, D. W. Griffith was busy making his epic films, Mary Pickford was charming audiences in a series of love stories, and a transplanted British actor, Douglas Fairbanks, was starring in several movies which soon captured the hearts of women film goers. In 1919 the four of them—Griffith, Chaplin, Pickford, and Fairbanks—formed their own film production company, United Artists. The interest in movies had mushroomed to such an extent, that by 1919 the film industry was paying $32,000,000 annually in salaries in Los Angeles

The most highly awaited *film in the history of Hollywood was* Gone With the Wind, *released in 1939. The film starred Clark Gable, left, and Vivien Leigh, shown here on the first day of production.*

With the rise *of Hollywood stars came the fan magazines.* Silver Screen *was one of the first magazines devoted to stories about movie stars' private lives.*

alone—this from an industry which had not even existed ten years before! With the rise of the industry came the rise of the studios, and studio heads and individual producers soon began exerting an influence on actors and their personal lives which many well known screen personalities felt was stifling. When United Artists was formed it was with the idea that the so-called creative people (actors, actresses, directors) would have a greater hand in the film making process, and would have greater control over the film's content. As one Hollywood writer put it at the time, "The inmates are now running the asylum." Whatever shortcomings the directors of United Artists had as businessmen, Griffith, Chaplin, Pickford, and Fairbanks knew how to make a movie, and for the next few years each turned out some of their most memorable works.

By 1919 the one-reel length was a thing of the past, and most movies were being made in what has become the relatively standard length of one hundred minutes. In 1921 *The Four Horsemen of the Apocalypse* was released starring Rudolph Valentino. Almost overnight Valentino became a legend, and the myth of the Latin Lover was born. Valentino also starred in *The Shiek* and further rooted the idea of the dark, handsome leading man in the hearts of countless millions of women throughout the world.

Because of the adverse effects of World War I on European film production, Hollywood had a virtual monopoly on the world market, although the largest source of income was still the domestic audience. Competition between studios, however, forced many producers to emulate the latest hit of a rival studio, so that there was a great deal of repetition of

themes and characters in movies. The audiences did not mind; they never seemed to get enough of certain kinds of pictures, and by the end of World War I Hollywood had developed several "types" of movies which still exist. Cowboy movies were popular from the very beginning; indeed, the first narrative American film was a western. The first popular cowboy actor was William S. Hart. Hart began making movies shortly after the film industry was established in southern California and by 1914 was one of the best known figures in America. He was concerned in his movies with trying to capture the mood and feeling of the old west, and his westerns are very realistic. His "type" of western is filled with real locations, not Hollywood soundstage backdrops, genuine Indians, not actors dressed up like Indians, and he himself generally played the kind of western character who stood firm against the encroachment of civilization, who was tough but fair, and who struggled against the hostile environment of the land. Hart's films were particularly successful before World War I, but with the end of the war in 1918 a new kind of cowboy hero began to be seen.

The new Hollywood cowboy was much more of a romantic than those portrayed by Hart. Cowboy movies starring Tom Mix, Buck Jones, and Hoot Gibson soon replaced the realistic genre. These romantic cowboys made little effort to portray the American cowboy as a loner or social outcast, living in a hostile setting. Instead, the new cowboy was generally a trick rider and roper who regaled his audiences with feats of acrobatic horse riding, fancy shooting and trick roping, rather than portraying him as a hard working, sod busting builder of the western United States. The audiences loved the new Hollywood cowboys; Mix, Jones, and Gibson achieved a stardom greater than Hart had known before the war. Part of the reason for the audiences acceptance of this

The mouse that built an empire. Mickey Mouse shown here with another Disney cartoon character, Pluto.

romantic, distorted view of the cowboy undoubtedly lies in their satiation with the realistic, Hart-like western character. Another reason is that America was recovering from World War I; she had had enough of killing and brutality, and she preferred, even in her cowboy actors, to take a romantic view of things, to turn her back on reality and glory in the cinematic myths that Hollywood was creating about the western hero.

Another "type" of film which had developed was the melodrama. With the end of World War I and the coming of the Jazz Age, Hollywood entered freely into the national craze. Love stories were no longer simple boy/girl relationships; instead the Hollywood studios gave film audiences Theda Bara and dozens of other sultry, sexy and *loose* screen actresses. By 1922 the breakdown of Victorian restrictions meant that movies could use as their themes divorce, seduction, drug usage and other kinds of activities which would have shocked an audience ten years earlier. The private lives of Hollywood stars became everyday topics of conversation for millions of Americans, and the stars themselves began acting out their screen characters in private life. A fear of movie immorality was growing in certain parts of the country as films became more and more explicit in their portrayal of the new, liberated life styles of the Twenties. Then, in 1922 there was a series of real life disasters which changed Hollywood films for nearly fifty years.

Walt Disney, *famed producer of animated movies, is shown here going through some of the 400,000 drawings made for the film* Bambi, *which was released in 1942. Disney made the first full-length animated film,* Snow White and the Seven Dwarfs *in 1939.*

Orson Welles, *center, and Joseph Cotten, in a scene from* Citizen Kane, which was released in 1941. Citizen Kane *has been cited as one of the ten best movies ever made.*

In 1922 the very popular comedian Fatty Arbuckle was involved in a manslaughter case. Although he was never convicted of the crime, his career was over. A few months after the spectacular Arbuckle trial the famed Hollywood director William Desmond Taylor was killed. Mabel Normand, one of the most popular stars of the day, was one of the suspects in the killing. The matinee idol Wallace Reid was discovered to be addicted to heroin. These three stories shocked the country, and the groundswell to "clean up" the movies rolled across the country. Fearing that the Federal government might institute an agency to censor film content, the major studios got together and formed the Motion Picture Producers and Distributors of America. Although citing many reasons for the organization, the real purpose of the M.P.P.D.A. was to establish a censorship board within the industry, and thereby forestall the creation of a Federal censorship board. The M.P.P.D.A. installed the former Postmaster General Will Hays as head of the censorship board, and Hays quickly set about to bring movie content into line with what he considered to be acceptable moral standards.

Bascially what the Hays Office, as the censorship board came to be called, did was to establish a guideline for film content based on what Hays termed "compensating values." This rather ambiguous but rigidly enforced principle meant that no film would be permitted to be shown to a general audience which portrayed sin, crime, drugs, alcohol, divorce, and seduction as admirable or worthwhile activities. Nudity was not permitted. Couples had to be married in order to share the same bedroom, but not the same bed. If a man and woman were shown kissing on a couch, their feet had to remain on the floor at all times. In short, nothing was permitted which Hays felt would undermine the moral fibre of America.

The producers soon found, however, that their audiences were a bit more liberal in their social/sexual views than the Hays Office censors, and they quickly developed ways of giving the audience what it wanted while still meeting the Hays' edict of compensating values. For example, a movie could show a great deal of lascivious behavior, if in the final reel the immoral characters were either chastized and repentent or were shown to die a horrible death as a result of their immoral behavior. The great American director Cecil B. De Mille circumvented the Hays Office by making biblical spectacles which showed the heathen non-Christians engaged in immoral conduct. Since they were clearly the evil members of an ancient non-Christian morality, his pictures were given the censor's approval. In *The Ten Commandments* (1923) De Mille cleverly gave the audience several scenes of nudity and revelry, all of it skillfully camouflaged behind the veneer of telling the story of Moses and the tribes of Israel. Other producers followed suit, and, although the post-Hays Office films were never as explicit as films had been before the industry censorship board was established, movies continued to be made which contained nudity and barbarity; but now, instead of glorifying immorality, the movies showed it but condemned it.

Throughout most of the Twenties the film industry continued to enjoy an unprecedented financial success. Virtually every movie the studios turned out found an audience, and the greater the profits for certain kinds of films, the more versions of the "type" of film were made. Then, in 1922 a new kind of movie was made which started a completely new "type" of film.

Robert Flaherty, an explorer, self-taught mining engineer,

Katherine Hepburn, *left, and Humphrey Bogart, in a scene from their 1951 film* The African Queen.

and adventurer had spent sixteen months with the eskimos in the Yukon. During this time (from 1920 to 1921) he had filmed the day to day life of a group of Eskimos led by a man named Nanook. When he returned to civilization Flaherty assembled the footage of the primitive struggles of the Eskimos forced to survive in the frozen north and titled the film *Nanook of the North*. Flaherty was an engineer by training and temperament, but his film reflected the compassion and intelligence of the amateur anthropologist. *Nanook of the North* is a non-fiction film about the lives of a group of people struggling with the forces of nature. When the film was seen by the British historian John Grierson, he promptly labeled it a *documentary*, and thus added a new "type" of film to the growing number of movies being made.

The technique Flaherty used in *Nanook of the North* was not revolutionary, but the subject matter was. Flaherty basically set up his camera and had Nanook and his band of migrants go about their daily lives. What he captured on film was a document of Eskimo life; although the film purports to be an objective view of Eskimo life, Flaherty freely admitted that many of the scenes in the film were staged, not for theatrical effect, but because the actual occurrence did not happen while he was there with his cameras. For example, the famous seal killing scene had to be staged because Nanook and the other hunters had been unable to find and kill a seal for several months. Finally Flaherty shot a seal with a rifle, put the dead animal under the frozen ice, and then had Nanook and his family act as though they were struggling with the "harpooned" seal. As Flaherty explained it, "One often has to distort a thing to catch its true spirit." Flaherty justified his staging of certain scenes on the grounds that they were not necessarily distortions of actual events. He argued that as long as the filmmaker did not significantly change the actual event, the re-staging of the event still had the truth of the action being portrayed. Film audiences around the world agreed, and *Nanook of the North* was a commercial and critical success.

Although *Nanook of the North* brought a new kind of film genre to the studios, the industry preferred to continue making films in Hollywood because it was there—on the soundstages or in the nearby San Fernando Valley, where many outdoor scenes were shot—that the producers could have complete control over the shooting schedule and the film's content. However, the success of Griffith's two epic films had prodded a number of other filmmakers into considering making outdoor spectacles, and, not wanting to use the same locales as Griffith had used, they ventured further from Hollywood in search of settings. In 1923 James Cruze made the first epic western, *The Covered Wagon*; the success of this film prompted a young director named John Ford to make his first big western in 1924, *The Iron Horse*. With the various genres firmly established (the biblical spectacle, the melodrama, the comedy, the love story) Hollywood settled into a routine of filmmaking that matched other American industries in its production line approach to manufacturing entertainment.

The evolution of movies also affected the silent comedies. Although most of the same faces were still seen, the one-reelers of an earlier age had, by 1924, been replaced by longer running comedies with more plot. But they were, with the exception of Chaplin, mostly like slapstick one-reelers. Harold Lloyd starred in *The Freshman* in 1925, and, while the plot is centered on the exploits of Lloyd as a college man, most of the humor is derived from the break away props and hair raising hanging from the ledge type of situation. Buster

The singing cowboy *became a Hollywood fixture in the Thirties with the films of Gene Autry. Roy Rogers, however, became the most famous of the romantic singing cowboys. Here he is shown riding his horse Trigger.*

The Treasure of the Sierra Madre *starring Humphrey Bogart, center, Walter Huston, right, and Tim Holt, right. It has been estimated that another Bogart film,* Casablanca, *made in 1943, has been seen by more people, thanks to television re-runs, than any other movie ever made.*

Marilyn Monroe, *perhaps the most famous sex symbol ever created by Hollywood, as she appeared in 1952.*

Keaton, who was already an established vaudeville star before coming to Hollywood, made *The General* in 1926. Based on an actual occurrence during the Civil War, *The General* is a masterpiece of comedic story telling. Keaton is a railroad engineer who suddenly finds himself caught up in a madcap locomotive chase between two trains, one from the North, the other from the South. Keaton's inventiveness and use of props is nowhere better illustrated than in the scenes showing him desperately trying to bring the speeding locomotive under control, while at the same time rescuing the girl, and catching the evil doers. His deadpan acting underscores the frenzy of the action, and the final scene—where Buster gets the girl and rides off into the sunset—is a classic of the Keaton-styled underplaying of a scene.

The classic comedy of the silent era, however, was made in 1925 by Charlie Chaplin. *The Gold Rush* was written by, directed by, and starred Chaplin. Again he is the character of the Tramp, this time in the Yukon Territory during the gold rush days. Although the film is filled with many scenes involving trick photography and unusual sets and props—Charlie turning into a chicken, eating his boot for Thanksgiving dinner, and the cabin perched on the edge of a precipice, to name a few—the real humor of *The Gold Rush* grows out of Charlie's pathetic attempts to deal with the reality of man's greed. Time and again in the film Chaplin gives the audience an insanely funny scene, only to have the laughter catch in the throat as the Tramp is belittled or humiliated by the greedy and unsympathetic miners. *The Gold Rush* is a statement about the lengths men will go to attain wealth, and, in the final scene where Charlie gets the girl *and* the money, it is a statement about the ultimate goodness of men: the Tramp succeeds because of his consid-

eration for others.

During the late 1920's movie attendance began to decline. Competition from radio and the automobile made inroads into movie attendance, and the general rise in income meant that many people were now turning to other forms of entertainment. The drop in weekly movie attendance was so serious, in fact, that by 1926 the Warner Brothers' Studio was in desperate financial trouble. The moviegoing public was becoming increasingly satiated with the general run of pictures being turned out by Hollywood, and the Warner Brothers (Jack Warner in particular) knew that if the studio was to survive, they would have to come up with a new product to lure the audiences back into the movie theaters. They came up with sound, and its introduction ushered in a new era for the motion picture. Almost overnight the public forgot about the silent movie.

Sound in movies was nothing new. As early as 1889 Edison had experimented with synchronized sound on his Kinetoscope machine. The quality of the sound was poor, however, and Edison soon abandoned the project. Early efforts after the turn of the century to put sound and pictures together were based on using recording discs or records with the soundtrack on them. The problem with this approach was that the operator had to start the disc/record at precisely the same time the visual scene started; any delay would put the lip movement out of synchronization. Since it was virtually impossible to begin the sound at precisely the same time as the visual, audiences in 1909 (when this sound method was tried) were often forced to sit through an entire movie with

Marlon Brando *in a scene from his 1954 movie,* On the Waterfront. *Brando has been called America's greatest film actor by film historians.*

actors speaking, but hearing their words seconds after their lips had formed them. Another problem inherent in this approach was that the operator might inadvertently put the wrong disc on: such an occurrence happened with the one-reel version of *Carmen*, and the audience, instead of hearing arias from the opera, were treated to a banjo tune that belonged with another film.

The problem of having synchronized sound on film had been solved as early as 1923 by an engineering genius named Lee De Forest. His solution involved the use of photographing sound directly onto the film itself in varying widths of gray and black bands. The sound then would always be matched with the visual. Using De Forest's basic concept, the Bell Laboratories began experimenting with sound on film and by 1926 had developed a workable process. Jack Warner, looking for something that would attract audiences to his pictures, bought this process from Bell Laboratories, dubbed it *Vitaphone*, and set about making a series of fully synchronized shorts. When, by the end of 1926, it looked as though Warner Brothers' in particular and the whole industry in general might have to cut back drastically or go under, Warner Brothers' decided to make a full length picture using synchronized sound.

For the first film Warner selected a recent Broadway musical; to star in the film he approached several stars of the Broadway stage, but each rejected his offers, feeling that sound pictures, if they worked at all, would at best be a gimmick and would only hamper their stage careers. Finally his offer was accepted by a vaudeville singer, Al Jolson. Production on the film was done in relative secrecy. On the night of October 6, 1927, Warner Brothers' released the film, *The Jazz Singer*, as the first feature length talkie. Although the story is trite, the quality of the sound is poor, and barely one third of the dialogue is recorded, the audience response

was overwhelming. Almost overnight other studios began trying to acquire their own sound processes; the silent film era died a sudden death in America, and the race was on to produce the new phenomenon—the all talking picture.

William Fox secured the rights to a sound process and was soon making the first sound newsreel, The Fox Movietone News. Warner Brothers' followed the success of *The Jazz Singer* with the first completely all talking movie *The Lights of New York* in 1928. That same year Warner Brothers' also came out with another film, *The Terror*, in which not only did the characters speak and music was heard in the background, but also the credits for the film were spoken! So great was the public enthusiasm for sound pictures that movie attendance jumped from 60 million paid admissions in 1927 to more than 110 million paid admissions in 1919. By 1930 there were no commercially made silent films being produced in the United States.

The advent of sound brought more than economic changes to the American film industry. The influx of sound meant that sound departments had to be added to studios, and many actors and actresses who had flourished during the silent era found themselves out of work because they either could not deliver lines intelligently, or their voices were not appropriate (the leading man John Gilbert's career came to an end because his voice had a high pitched quality) or, as in the case of foreign actors, their accents were too pronounced. But devastating as the advent of sound was on certain individual actors, the microphone and recording equipment wreaked greater havoc on the industry in general. Because the early microphones were non-selective and picked up every bit of extraneous noise, movie making again moved into the soundstage, here the director could control the noise level. But even on the soundstage it was soon discovered that the whirring of the camera was picked up by the microphone; to overcome that problem the studios had to construct large soundproof rooms with glass on one side. The cameras were placed inside and photographed out, through the windows. The erection of these "hothouses" meant that actors' movement was severely restricted; scenes now had to be played within the limitations of the sound booth, and the fluidity of camera and actor movement, which had helped raise the silent movie to an art form, was now no longer possible. Early sound pictures were cinematically a giant step backwards as far as the art of movies was concerned. Films made during the late 1920's had the look of films made twenty years earlier: they were stagey, with little camera movement. Actors entered and exited as though in a stage play. Often, too, the quality of sound was erratic, because the volume might be set to register the actor nearest the microphone, while an actor standing further away might be barely audible. The problem of making sound pictures outdoors was somewhat alleviated by William Fox in a picture he made in 1929 called *In Old Arizona*. For this western about the Cisco Kid, the microphone was cleverly hidden in cacti, saddles, etc. to pick up the outdoor dialogue. Again, however, this was a stopgap solution, as the making of movies continued to be tyrannized by sound.

The coming of sound to Hollywood also meant that writers who knew how to write dialogue would have to be hired. Within a year of *The Jazz Singer* the Hollywood studios had hired a number of eastern writers and journalists whose job it was not to write movies so much as it was to write dialogue that sounded realistic and believable. Famous playwrights of the day were added to the studio personnel, but it was soon discovered that stage language and movie language were two different things; this problem was eased when Hollywood turned to journalists as script writers, and by 1931 every major studio had its own group of writers busily turning out scripts which were often little more than talking versions of silent movies.

It was during the early 1930's that the making of movies in Hollywood really moved into a factory production system. Virtually every facet of filmmaking—acting, directing, editing, sound, makeup, costume—was compartmentalized. To supply the public's almost insatiable hunger for sound pictures the studios worked year round, with many of the smaller studios turning out nearly a movie a week to meet the demand. In 1934 Joseph Breen took over as official industry censor, and the Breen Office, as the new Board was called, continued to function in much the same way as the Hays Office had, with the added responsibility of insuring that no double entendre or obscene language was heard on the screen.

The studio system, once it had overcome the problems of microphone placement (accomplished in part by the introduction of the "blimp" camera which permitted filming outside of the soundproof room) soon moved into an era of making movies in cycles. Whatever kind of movie was successful in one studio was certain to be copied by other studios. This copying of genre led to a series of films which were cyclical, and most of the movies from the 1930's fit into one of the major cycles.

One of the most popular and earliest type of films to be established after the introduction of sound was the gangster film. America was just coming out of the Twenties, and the lawlessness of that period was a perfect background for the kinds of action films the audiences enjoyed. *Little Caesar* starring Edward G. Robinson, was released in 1930; *The Public Enemy* with James Cagney was released a year later.

Elizabeth Taylor *as she looked for her role in* Cat on a Hot Tin Roof.

Sidney Poitier, *right, was the first Black American to win an Academy Award for best actor. Poitier won the Oscar for his performance in* Lilies of the Field, *shown here, in 1963.*

Tatum O'Neal, *shown here with her father Ryan, in a scene from* Paper Moon *for which the young actress received an Academy Award as best actress.*

The gangster picture was a radical departure from the melodramas of the silent era, with their racy dialogue, their screeching tires and machine gun blasts, and their introduction to the American public of a whole new kind of talk. For the first time in history the average American moviegoer began to go around talking about "taking people for a ride," and guns quickly became "gats" while women became known as "molls." Although the gangster films added a new dimension to the screen, their plots still had to conform to the standards of the Hays Office, and, if James Cagney was shown reaping the rewards for a life of crime for the first hour and a half, the audience knew that in the final ten minutes he was going to die a horrible and cowardly death.

Another type of genre popularized during the 1930's was the musical. Obviously before the introduction of sound such films could not exist, and one of the first things Hollywood producers did after sound became workable was to import musicals from the Broadway stage. The lack of sufficient stage musicals, however, soon forced filmmakers to begin making their own musicals, which they called "originals."

In 1930 Busby Berkeley was brought to Hollywood to help stage the musical numbers for the Eddie Cantor musical, *Whoopee.* Berkeley's imaginative camera positioning during the dance sequences was revolutionary. Placing the camera at obtuse angles, shooting the dancers reflected in mirrors, filming through waterfalls—all these techniques were used by Berkeley to give the dance sequences an abstract look. As dance routines they obviously could not have occurred on any stage, but on the screen their impact was immediate and strong. Audiences flocked to see Berkeley films, and soon, as had become the tradition in Hollywood, every studio had directors who imitated the Busby Berkeley approach.

The Depression which wracked America in the 1930's had a curious effect on Hollywood: it produced two new and different types of movie cycles. The first was the prison picture, perhaps best exemplified by the Paul Muni film *I Am a Fugitive from a Chain Gang* released in 1932. The prison

pictures generally showed the hero as a victim of the system; he was a good man who had either been given an unfair court decision, or had been the victim of a corrupting environment. In two other films that year, *Blonde Venus* and *Letty Lynton* the heroines, who were thinly disguised prostitutes, were shown to be the products of poverty who were forced into a life of shame to provide for their families. The prison pictures differed from the gangster pictures of the same era in that the gangster films tended to glorify crime (even if the hero died a horrible death at the end) while the prison picture tended to be more social criticism, arguing implicitly for changes in the social, legal, and economic scheme.

The second type of film cycle spawned by the depression was the romantic comedy. The comedic film had made a significant change from the early slapstick days of the Keys-

Controversy *surrounding the Academy Awards arose when George C. Scott refused to accept his Oscar as best actor for his performance in* Patton.

Barbra Streisand, *one of the biggest stars of the Seventies.*

tone Kops, and the advent of sound meant that comedians who could make people laugh with verbal humor could now make movies. The comedies of the mid-1930's, however, went one step further: they were often effective propaganda devices for selling the American way of life to a population caught in the throes of poverty. The comedies, and most of the musicals, showed people of the upper class involved in the meaningless dilemmas of boy meets girl, but all of it done with a flair of lavish costumes and dress. Ironically, many films during the height of the depression had scenes of enormous banquets, with endless tables filled with plentiful and exotic foods. The audiences flocked to see such films as *Footlight Parade* in 1933 and *100 Men and a Girl* which was released in 1937. The Ginger Rogers/Fred Astaire musicals of the 1930's proved to be one of the most popular and durable series of films Hollywood ever produced. In such films as *Top Hat*, released in 1935, Rogers and Astaire created a sophisticated world which existed only on the screen; their problems of falling in love and staying in love bore little resemblance to the day to day life of the average American, but their films offered a welcome respite to film goers who wanted to get away from the troubles, if only for a little while, outside the movie theater.

Although comedies continued to be a staple in the Hollywood production schedule, the introduction of sound brought many stage and radio comedians to the screen, and with them came a new kind of comedy. Among the earliest and most popular of these new film comedians were the Marx Brothers. The Marx Brothers had been headliners for years in the vaudeville circuit, but their brand of humor (particularly Groucho's) was as much verbal as visual. The popularity of sound films, however, soon lured them to Hollywood. Their first films were screen versions of their vaudeville shows, but in 1932 they made *Duck Soup*, which relied heavily on camera tricks for much of its humor, and the camera added a new dimension to the *bon mots* of Groucho. In 1935 *A Night at the Opera* was released, and the Marx Brothers were firmly established as one of the screen's biggest attractions.

Another vaudeville comedian, who had made the transition to radio, also began making films in the 1930's. W. C. Fields, a headliner for many years, incorporated many of his stage "bits" into his early movies. The golfing scene in *You're Telling Me*, released in 1934, was taken directly from his stage act, and the hilarious poker game, with Fields as the crooked player, was taken almost en toto from the stage and used in his film *Mississippi*, released in 1935.

If many of the films of the 1930's were attempts to take Americans' minds off the depression, there were a small but significant number of films made during that decade which attempted to show Americans that their country and its political and social system were basically workable. Frank Capra, a director of great imagination and insight, made *Mr. Deeds Goes to Town* in 1936, and *Mr. Smith Goes to Washington* in 1939; both films deal with the idealism of American democracy, and show how the American spirit of truth and fair play would, at least in the Thirties, triumph over duplicity and corruption. Another director who began making films in the Thirties in Hollywood was Alfred Hitchcock. Beginning with *The 39 Steps* in 1935 Hitchcock brought a new kind of film to the screen. His stories of intrigue and horror were touched with humor, and never before had the movie audience seen such a skillful blending of the macabre and the comedic. In such later films as *Secret Agent*, released in 1935, and *The Lady Vanishes*, made in 1938, Hitchcock showed the full integration of sight and sound to achieve dramatic and often frightening effects.

Ellen Burstyn, *who won the Academy Award as best actress for her performance in* Alice Doesn't Live Here, Anymore *in 1975.*

The animated film had been a part of the movie program in many theaters for several years. The first animated film by an American to have a commercial showing was *Gertie the Dinosaur* made by Winson McCoy in 1909, and although the animated movie, or *cartoons* as they came to be called in America, did not have the popularity of the live action films, by the 1930's there was one studio in Hollywood whose sole production was the manufacturing of cartoons. The Disney Studios, under the imaginative leadership of Walt Disney, had released its first sound film, *Steamboat Willie* in 1928. The popularity of this movie, which starred the inestimable Mickey Mouse, prompted Disney to make a series of musical animated shorts, which he called *Silly Symphonies*, and the success of these movies in turn led to the creation of animation departments at several studios. The Disney films of this period were perfectly suited to the 1930's audience's desire to see happiness and optimism portrayed on the screen. The great advantage that the Disney movies had over live action films was that they could manipulate the color and sound to create exactly the world they wanted; the suspension of disbelief was more easily accomplishesd by a depression wracked populace when they watched and heard the abstractions of the Disney cartoon. The animated American film, particularly those starring the list of cartoon characters developed by the Disney Studio, enthralled audiences throughout the 1930's; the enchantment and allure of the animated film reached a high water mark in 1938 when Disney released the first full length animated film, *Snow White and the Seven Dwarfs*. With this movie Disney ushered in a new type of American film, one that has become one of the staples of popular culture: the family movie.

The Thirties was also the era in which another filmmaker made his first real impact on the American screen. John Ford, who had started out in Hollywood in the early days, became a major figure in the world of film directors with the release of *The Informer* in 1935. Ford was a director whose social views found expression in his movies. He was a populist who sided with the common man against the institutions which attempted to take human dignity away from the poor and oppressed, and many of his movies can be viewed as stringent attacks upon those who would corrupt American institutions and ideals to gain money and power. Although *The Informer* won an Academy Award for its star, Victor McLaughlin, it was another film, *Stagecoach*, released in 1939, that brought Ford to the forefront of American direc-

Perhaps the movies' *most endurable star, John Wayne, as he* *appeared while filming* Rooster Cogburn.

tors. Ford's films are always attempts to portray people, little people, not so much as they are but as they should be, and *Stagecoach*, despite the exciting action sequences and the introduction of John Wayne as a serious film actor, is a movie showing the intimate interaction of people, rather than the excitement of fast paced events. It is a film about human values. Ford continued this psychological approach in another film, *The Grapes of Wrath*, released in 1940, and based on John Steinbeck's novel of the same name. As with his earlier films *The Grapes of Wrath* is a movie about people oppressed by corrupt institutions, but the essential goodness and humanity of the characters becomes a model for perseverance and human integrity that very few films of this era portrayed.

By the 1930's color films were no longer a novelty. Although its quality was not very good, color had been used in motion pictures as early as 1908. In 1918 Herbert Kalmus perfected a color process which he termed Technicolor, but the cost of the process was so high that very few producers were willing to make color movies. The chief use of color before the Thirties had been primarily as a gimmick to lure people into the theaters. A sequence in the original *Phantom of the Opera* left most audiences laughing rather than frightened. However, by the Thirties color was being used more often, particularly in the so-called "big" pictures. And no picture of the Thirties was any bigger than *Gone With the Wind*, released in 1939. Based on a best selling novel, *Gone With the Wind* was the most eagerly awaited movie in the history of Hollywood; it starred the most popular male actor in America at the time, Clark Gable; it literally had a cast of thousands; it was made in Technicolor; and it dealt with a love story told against the background of the Civil War. The pre-publicity attendant to the making of *Gone With the Wind* was like nothing that had ever come out of Hollywood before. The picture was given its premier showing in Atlanta, Georgia, and within weeks of its release had become the most popular movie since the invention of the movie camera.

It remained for another film, however, to raise the sound film several notches as an art form. In 1940 Orson Welles left his radio studio, where he had become famous as a radio actor, writer, and director, and came to Hollywood to make a movie. The movie he made, *Citizen Kane*, was revolutionary in content and approach. Because of his radio background Welles brought an understanding of the possibilities of sound to filmmaking which had not previously existed in Hollywood. His blending of sight and sound in *Citizen Kane* is nothing short of masterful, and the film is generally regarded as one of the ten best movies ever made. The film, however, shocked the Hollywood establishment, because it was a thinly disguised biography of William Randolph Hearst which treated him in an unflattering light. The film is sombre and at times even grotesque; it is uncompromising in its portrayal of power and the corruption that comes with too much influence. There are no last minute reconciliations for the romantic lovers, no lessening of the sharp edge of criticism of large corporate manipulations of personal lives. In short, it is a film that Hollywood was uncomfortable with. And, when the Hearst newspaper chain refused either to review the movie or allow advertisements announcing its showing, the Hollywood establishment more or less abandoned Welles to his fate. Apparently not one to be daunted by such a reaction, Welles made another film the following year, *The Magnificent Ambersons*, which was, in the opinion of many critics and film historians, superior to *Citizen Kane*. As the world approached war, the movie industry had matured and come into its own. It could, because of the popular-

ity of movies, afford to cast aside Welles as a renegade. Hollywood was respectable by 1941, and one had only to look at the grosses to see the respectability.

With the outbreak of World War II Hollywood re-tooled for the war effort just like any other major American industry. Although many of the standard kinds of movies continued to be made, to take Americans' minds off the war in Europe and in the Pacific, a new kind of film—the propaganda movie—soon began appearing in local theaters. Hollywood embraced the war effort with open arms, turning out literally hundreds of movies calculated to unite the American public behind the fighting forces. The propaganda films of the 1940's ran to two classes: those which belittled the Axis powers, and those which showed the American servicemen or American Allies as being invincible. The films relied very heavily on racial stereotypes (particularly in those films dealing with the war in the Pacific); they were relatively uncomplicated in plot structure (the bad guys were there and we were here and we had to go defeat them) and simplistic characterization (again the characters ran to stereotypes, this time American ones, with many movies peopled by characters named Tex, or Brooklyn, or Smitty, or any one of a dozen popular and easily recognizable American "types") and the themes were generally all the same—America and her Allies would win the war because her people were strong. Whatever the World War II propaganda movies lacked in dramatic content or cinematic style, they more than made up for in effectiveness in helping forge the country to the war effort. Popular actors of the day were used in numerous war stories, performing heroic feats that often bordered on the unbelievable; but the country wanted to believe them and it did, and Hollywood made a significant contribution to maintaining morale on the homefront. The movie industry also participated more directly in World War II by sending several of its most popular male stars off to fight. James Stewart, Clark Gable, and Tyrone Power, three of the most famous leading men of the day, all

The first television *receiver produced on a mass scale in America was this DuMont set made in 1938.*

served in the armed forces; and their presence in uniform assured America that the war was being fought not only by the common man, but also by the famous and wealthy. Several Hollywood directors, most notably John Huston, offered their services to the military for the duration of the war. These directors made documentaries of actual battles which were used as training films, and, in the case of Huston's *The Battle of San Pietro*, made in 1944, were also shown to the general public as an example of American heroism. The end of the war marked a return to normalcy for Hollywood, and the industry geared itself again to provide a wide range of entertainment for an entertainment starved populous.

In 1946 Hollywood's revenues reached $1,700,000,000. It was the biggest year of money making the industry had ever known, or ever would know. However, the prosperity in Hollywood was short lived. Television, that funny little black box with its small screen, had made its appearance in 1947 as a commercial threat to Hollywood. Then, the government, which had protected Hollywood ticket prices during the war, not only withdrew its support of tickets but ordered the studios to sell their theaters. The industry resisted divesting itself of theater chains, but the government countered by bringing anti-trust suits against several studios (the hardest hit was the 20th Century Fox Studios, which also owned a large chain of theaters on the west coast). Without its stranglehold on theaters, and with the inroads being made by television, Hollywood found that by 1949 the industry was in a tailspin, and drastic measures would have to be taken.

At first the movie industry ignored television, believing apparently that if movie people ignored the little box, it would go away. To insure that no established movie stars would be lured away to the new medium, Hollywood banned all film stars from appearing on television. An even more serious threat to the industry occurred in 1949 when workers within the industry demanded higher wages, and the taxes on land in southern California rose dramatically. These two calamaties caused several studios to cut back drastically their operations, and to sell off parts of their lots and lay off hundreds of their employees.

By 1952 it was apparent that Hollywood was losing the fight against television, and if movies were to have an audience at all they would have to provide a product that could not be found on the television screen. One of Hollywood's first efforts to lure the American public away from the television screen and back into the theaters was three-dimension movies. In 1952 *Bwana Devil*, a poorly made and hopelessly melodramatic movie, was released. It had been made in the stereoscopic processes involving two lenses which were then projected on the screen simultaneously. The audience had to wear plastic polaroid glasses to separate the two images, which then could be viewed in three-dimension. Although the 3-D effect was nothing new in still pictures, Americans turned out by the thousands to see the novelty in motion pictures. The success of *Bwana Devil* led to another movie the same year, *House of Wax*, a horror film starring Vincent Price, and *Fort Ti*, which was the fist 3-D western. The novelty of three-dimension soon wore off, however, because of two major reasons: one, the audience had to wear plastic glasses which were uncomfortable for those unaccustomed to wearing glasses, and, two, the quality of the films was rather poor—trite stories with barely adequate acting. The combination of these two drawbacks meant a quick end to this experiment in attracting greater crowds to movies.

The movie makers next turned to the wide screen in an attempt to gain a larger audience for the products. Cinerama,

Mr. Television, *Milton Berle, as he appeared on the Texaco Star Theatre. Berle was the first popular star of the infant medium, and his show, which began in 1948, literally brought television into the position to challenge the movies as America's most popular entertainment medium.*

a super-wide screen process involving three projectors, enjoyed some success in the early Fifties, but it too failed to attract the expected large audiences. *This Is Cinerama*, released in 1952, was not a story film, but rather a series of exciting outdoor scenes calculated either to frighten or sicken the audience. Although the novelty of being made seasick while watching a movie drew many customers at first, the lack of story soon made *This Is Cinerama* old hat to the movie audiences around the country. Cinerama was successful, though, in indicating that the wide screen might be the answer to luring more customers to the movies. In 1952 the 20th Century Fox Studios came out with a movie called *The Robe*, filmed in a wide screen process which the studio labeled CinemaScope. The success of this movie, and particularly the process in which it was filmed, convinced the heads of other studios that wide screen was the gimmick needed to get back the audience from television, and by the end of 1953 the widescreen movie was a common product of Hollywood.

The other major attraction that the movie industry tried to win back its audience was the use of color. Despite the success of color movies in the past (particularly *Gone With the Wind* and *The Wizard of Oz*, both released in 1939) color had not been a very popular commodity with the studios. For one thing the Technicolor process was both expensive and time consuming. The threat of television, however, forced Hollywood in the late 1950's to consider alternatives to the

Technicolor system. The competition to come up with a working alternative to Technicolor produced three viable processes—Eastman color, Deluxe, and Warnercolor. With these three added to the original, the competition drove the cost of color filming down, and by the 1960's the majority of films coming from Hollywood were in color.

The use of gimmicks (such as 3-D and Smellovision) and legitimate inventions (such as the wide screen and color) were not enough to save the movie industry from television, however, and in 1956 Hollywood began selling some of its older movies to the television networks. The race was over, and television had cut into the movie business to such an extent that never again would Hollywood have the kind of control over filmed entertainment that it had enjoyed for almost a half century.

Once the Hollywood establishment fully realized that it was not going to win the war with television, and that gimmickry and technology were not enough of an attraction to regain its audience, the studios settled back into the routine of making the types of movies that one could not see on television. Beginning in the early 1950's MGM Studios made *Singing in the Rain* in 1952, *The Bandwagon* in 1953, and *Seven Brides for Seven Brothers* in 1954—three of the best musicals ever made. They were big, clever, starred popular actors, in color, and had a sophistication and glamour that were far above television's ability to duplicate. Comedies such as *Some Like It Hot* in 1959 dealt with subject matter (men dressed as women) that was still taboo on television. The influx of foreign films into America, with their adult themes, also had their effect on the American film. Hollywood turned to more adult topics in the Sixties. An indication of the shift in types of subject matter from the Fifties to the Sixties is evident in the movies released in 1962. Gregory Peck received the Academy Award for Best Actor by appearing in *To Kill a Mockingbird*, a "safe" movie of that year, while 1962 also produced *The Days of Wine and Roses*, starring Jack Lemmon, in a story about alcoholism, and Burt Lancaster starred in *The Birdman of Alcatraz*, a film which dealt in part with the vagaries of prison life. In 1963 the first black actor to receive the Academy Award as Best Actor was in the person of Sidney Poitier who starred in *Lilies of the Field*. Two years later one of the most popular movies was *Cat Ballou*, starring Lee Marvin as a drunken, no-good, cowardly gunslinger.

In 1967 *Guess Who's Coming to Dinner*, starring Spencer Tracy and Katherine Hepburn, dealt with the subject of interracial marriage; in 1969 the movie *Charly* had as its subject the attempted rehabilitation of a mentally retarded man. The picture of the year Academy Award in 1969 was given to *Midnight Cowboy*, a film utterly frank and explicit in its portrayal of a male prostitute and his down and out friend. Jane Fonda received the Academy Award for Best Actress for her portrayal of a hardened call girl in the movie *Klute*. Not only was sex a big commodity in Hollywood by the 1970's; violence too had become standard fare in many American films. In 1973 the bloody and realistic *The Godfather* was such a success that it leapfrogged past *Gone With the Wind* as the highest grossing picture of all time.

The Godfather did not remain the number one grossing movie for long, though. In 1975 the movie *Jaws* created an international sensation, earning more than a billion dollars during its first year of release. Movies had partially found the solution to their battle with television: sex and violence.

While Hollywood and the film establishment was busily trying to compete with the television networks for an audience, film makers outside the mainstream of the industry were busy making films which pushed the sex and violence themes further than the studios were prepared to go. In 1970 an independent film maker came out with a sex film *Deep Throat* which helped to change the audience's tolerance for sex in the cinema. *Deep Throat* dealt explicitly, if a little simplemindedly, with the subject of sexual intercourse, and it was the first of the underground "sexploitation" films to gain a national audience. The response from churchmen was predictable, but people continued to see *Deep Throat*, perhaps as much out of curiosity to see how far movies would go in depicting sexual activity as out of any interest in the inherent qualities of the film. Whatever the reasons, the "sexploitation" film was, by the mid-1970's, a firmly entrenched popular film type. The movies, at least the "sexploitation" ones, had finally come up with a product that the television viewer wasn't likely to see on his home screen.

TELEVISION

Nearly thirty years before television had risen to serious competition for the movie industry, the first broadcast of a moving object via television was made. In 1923 C. Francis Jankins, an engineer who had been working on picture transmission for many years, broadcast a television picture from a radio station in suburban Washington back to his laboratory in Washington, D.C. Two years later scientists working for the Bell Laboratories telecast a live dancer atop a New York City building to a receiver located two floors below. The development of television was slow, primarily because of the technical problems involved. Work on perfecting a viable television transmission and receiving system was undertaken by a number of men in a number of electronically related companies, because the popularity of the movies had been a clear indication of the money making potential of the new medium if it could be perfected.

By 1928 short wave radio was being used to make transoceanic television broadcasts. On September 11, 1928, the first commercial television broadcast was made, a play titled *The Queen's Messenger*, which had to use two television cameras, one for the face of the actor reciting the lines, and another filming the background. In August of the same year New York Governor Alfred E. Smith's acceptance speech for the Democratic nomination for President was televised. By 1929 the major technological problems had either been worked out or were close to being solved for commercial television broadcasting. However, the stock market crash, coupled with the rise in popularity of the relatively less complicated medium of radio, meant that it would be well into the Thirties before the time and money necessary to perfect television transmission and reception would be spent.

In July, 1930, the National Broadcasting Company set up the first experimental television station in New York. The call letters for the first TV station were W2XBS, and the following year the Columbia Broadcasting System established the second experimental station, W2XAB, also in New York City. Although several experimental broadcasts were made using some of the famous radio personalities of the day, the images were very shadowy. The reason for the shadowy images lay in the number of lines per screen being transmitted; these early television transmitters sent out pictures at the rate of 60 lines per screen, as compared to the 525 lines per screen of the modern television received. It was not until 1935 when the breakthrough in technology made it possible to broadcast 245 lines per screen that TV really became a viable commercial medium.

Tap dancer Bill Robinson, *who was one of the guest performers on Milton Berle's first television program. The Berle show, later named the Texaco Star Theatre, at first was little more than a televised vaudeville show, with the guests performing their stage routines.*

In 1937 the development of an electronic "gun" made possible the transmission of a television image on a large-sized screen. In 1938 the NBC station W2XBS telecast *Susan and God*, starring Gertrude Lawrence, from a radio station in New York City. It was in the same year that the Du Pont Company began manufacturing television receivers on a large scale; the World's Fair of 1939 saw an expanded use of television transmission, and for the opening ceremonies of that Fair President Franklin Roosevelt's remarks were telecast, the first time a head of state had appeared on television.

While war clouds gathered again in Europe, the American television industry, such as it was in 1939, continued to make a number of "firsts." In that year was the first transmission of a variety program, starring Fred Waring and his Pennsylvanians; the first college baseball game; the first professional baseball game, between Brooklyn and Cincinnati; and the first professional boxing match, between Lou Nova and Max Baer. Macy's Thanksgiving Day Parade was first telecast that year, and a closed circuit telecast of a meeting of Rotary International in New York was made. By 1939 the first television personality was already being made—Dennis James had been serving as the master of ceremonies for many of Du Mont television programs. Telecasting from a small studio on Madison Avenue, James soon became a well known figure to the estimated two hundred owners of television receivers in the New York City area.

Television continued to make technological breakthroughs and to improve the quality of both its transmission and the programs being transmitted, but the war in Europe erupted

and soon America's technological and scientific interests were turned to the war effort. Again, as had happened with World War I, the development of television as a viable commercial medium would have to wait for the conclusion of a world war.

The Japanese attack on Pearl Harbor in 1941 was the subject of a 90 minute news broadcast by CBS, but so great was the impact of radio in reporting the news of the attack that television's efforts were lost. Another reason for television's second place to radio at this time was the practical problem—there were simply thousands of more radios than television receivers in America, and millions of Americans had been conditioned by almost a generation of radio to turn to it first for news of the day. With the attack on Pearl Harbor and America's entry in World War II, television programming came almost to a standstill. Only one network, the Du Mont, continued to make commercial telecasts throughout the war. Operating from station WABD in New York City, the network telecast entertainment programs starring singer Dick Haymes, comedian Henry Morgan, and Fred Waring and the Pennsylvanians. In 1943, however, television history was made indirectly when NBC sold its blue network. That network then became the American Broadcasting Company, while the old red network officially became the National Broadcasting Company. By 1943 there were television stations in several cities, among them Milwaukee, Philadelphia, and Schenectady, New York. In late 1943 the first musical comedy written especially for television, *The Boys from Boise*, was telecast on WABD in New York City.

The news of the surrender of Germany was telecast to the 7000 or so homes which had television receivers in 1945; opening sessions of the United Nations were also telecast that same year; but more important than the kinds of shows being telecast were the new technological advances in TV transmission. By the end of the war NBC had decided to link up a national television network and in 1946 the first step in that national network was taken when NBC began transmitting a signal which was relayed by an airplane flying in the stratosphere. By 1948, "stratovision" had improved to the extent that the Republican National Convention that year was telecast over a 525 mile area. The end of the war also meant the end of the freeze on television set manufacturing, and the boom to own a TV was on. Television programming itself did much to sell receivers during this period; it was estimated that the announced decision to telecast the Joe Louis-Jersey Joe Walcott championship fight was responsible for selling nearly 100,000 TV receivers. By 1948 television was on the edge of a monumental explosion in both technology and programming, and it was only a matter of time before the two came together to produce an industry.

The first smash hit program of commercial television occurred on September 14, 1948, when a seasoned vaudeville comedian named Milton Berle stepped in front of the cameras and announced the opening of the *Texaco Star Theatre*. The show used no writers at first; Berle and his guest stars simply did their vaudeville or nightclub routines. Appearing with Berle on that first show were Pearl Bailey, the ventriloquist Senor Wences, vaudeville comedians Smith and Dale, and the dancer Bill Robinson. Although the show was brash and harsh, and relied for much of its humor on slapstick routines (similar to the silent movie days), outrageous costumes and breakaway sets, the *Texaco Star Theatre* was an overnight sensation.

Within a matter of weeks Tuesday nights belonged to Berle and his televised zaniness. Across the country activity stopped as millions watched on little sets, or visited friends or neighbors who had receivers, or stood in front of appliance stores which had set up receivers in the windows so the public could see their favorite TV show. Berle's popularity was unmatched, and he soon became known in the fledgling industry as Mr. Television. An indication of Berle's popularity can be seen in his salary. In the initial year of the program he received $750 a week. By the second year, 1949, Berle was receiving $6000 a week. He remained as host on television for eight years, and, although the sponsorship of the program changed, Berle's brand of humor remained constant for eight years.

In 1949 another program that would rival Berle for humor and inventiveness appeared. Originally called the *Admiral Broadway Review*, it starred the many talented Sid Caesar. The name was changed to *Your Show of Shows* but the format remained essentially the same. While *The Texaco Star Theatre* was primarily a vaudeville type show, *Your Show of Shows* was a musical revue, running 90 minutes each week. Assisted by such clever comedians as Carl Reiner, Imogene Coca, and Howard Morris, Sid Caesar weekly went through comedy sketches, pantomimes, and lampoons of current movies. Less frenetic than Berle's type of humor, Caesar and his troupe appealed as much to the intellect as the funny-

bone, and Saturday night became Sid Caesar's domain. The success of *Your Show of Shows* was mitigated though by television's insatiable need for new and fresh material. When it went off the air in 1954 it was not because the public was tired of it, but rather because the strain of putting on a 90 minute weekly television show was too taxing. Even for such brilliant comedic writers as Neil Simon and Mel Brooks the press of weekly writing new material was too great, and the program finally went off. It would not be the last time a television program had to go off the air because the demands of the medium were too exhausting.

Ed Sullivan first began his *Toast of the Town* variety show in 1948. Sullivan, a Broadway gossip columnist originally, used a format which would not exhaust talent—he had different acts on each week. The program, during its more than twenty years on television, remained basically a televised vaudeville show, but its popularity was so great that the Sunday night viewing for millions of Americans meant the *Ed Sullivan Show*. Sullivan was the first to bring the television audience such performers as Martin and Lewis, Elvis Presley, and the Beatles; he balanced his programming of popular performers by presenting opera stars (often singing complete arias amid sumptuous sets) and serious figures from the worlds of politics, sports, and the legitimate stage.

In late 1948 the first popular cultural phenomenon spawned by television occurred when old Hopalong Cassidy movies began being shown on television. The films, 100 in all, starred William Boyd as the redoubtable Hopalong, and,

Rivaling Berle *as television's most popular comic is Jackie Gleason, here dressed up in the role of one of his many characters, with Art Carney on the right. Gleason's appeal to the audience was unmatched by any other entertainer during the latter part of the Fifties.*

although the movies were at best "B" pictures hardly ever seen in the movie houses except during Saturday morning kiddie matinees, their showing created an unprecedented rise in the number of viewers and led directly to the national cult of Hopalong Cassidy, which resulted in a number of ancillary products and promotions. Hopalong Cassidy was the first western hero of television, and William Boyd became a multi-millionaire.

Situation comedies, long a staple of radio, came to television in 1949 when *The Goldbergs*, starring Gertrude Berg, came on the screen. Other popular radio situations soon followed: *I Remember Mama* and *Life with Luigi*. 1949 also saw the first television of the popular radio program *The Life of Riley*, which originally starred Jackie Gleason. The early television comedies ran heavily to ethnic humor (*The Goldbergs* were Jewish, *Mama* was about a Swedish family, *Life with Luigi* was about Italians, and *Amos 'n' Andy* involved Blacks), and with the growing social consciousness of the American public, these programs had a short life span.

Serious drama on television also began in 1948 with such programs as *Studio One* and *Television Playhouse*. Both programs presented both original and well-known plays, and many important playwrights, actors, and directors had their first exposure with these two shows. In 1949 the first television daytime serial was broadcast; *One Man's Family*, long a favorite radio soap opera, originally starred Eva Marie Saint.

Programs designed especially for children began in 1947 with *Howdy Doody*. Also in the late 1940's the first nationally popular program to win the approval of the National Education Association, *Kukla, Fran, and Ollie*, went on the air. Walter Winchell brought his brand of staccato-fire journalism to television in 1950, and all three networks were busily competing to bring the daily news to the home viewer.

The 1950's have been referred to as the Golden Age of Television more for the proliferation of the television receivers and technological breakthroughs than for the fare being offered on the screen. In 1950 the Neilsen Rating System first became a fact of television life; also in that year radio made its final surge to recapture an audience lost to the TV set. It was a losing battle though, as the movies were finding out, because television by the 1950's was increasingly becoming a way of life for millions of Americans and nothing in popular culture was going to stop it, or even slow it down. In 1946 there had been only an estimated 10,000 sets in America; by 1951 there was an estimated 12,000,000. In September, 1951, the coaxial cable was completed, which made national television broadcasting a reality, and within a few months of the cable's completion TV antennas began to appear in the west and southwest in almost the same number as they had existed in the east for three years.

1951 also marked the appearance of a performer who was to become a show business legend. Jackie Gleason, although he had appeared as Riley in the *Life of Riley* program, began his own show in the fall of 1951 and his success was unrivaled even by Berle. The closest rival Gleason had for numbers of viewers came not from another comedian but, ironically, from a news program. Senator Estes Kefauver of Tennessee, who was chairman of a Senate committee investigating organized crime in America, permitted television cameras to film the committee's proceedings. Shown during the daytime hours of the Senate's meeting, the broadcast drew a surprisingly large audience. For the first time in history Americans by the millions were able to see firsthand how their government conducted its business. The Kefauver

Senate Hearings brought to the American public the names and faces of dozens of underworld figures (notably Frank Costello) and Kefauver tried to capitalize on his popularity as a television performer to garner the Democratic nomination of President in 1952.

News reporting in the early days of television had been little more than a reporter (John Cameron Swayze and Douglas Edwards were two of the first) reading the news. However, in 1951 Edward R. Murrow began his *See It Now* television documentary series. *See It Now* was an attempt to bring contemporary history into the living room; the program had the immediacy of the newsreel with the familiarity of the radio program. One of the highlights of the *See It Now* series occurred in 1954 when Murrow attacked Senator Joseph McCarthy of Wisconsin for his tactics of character assassination from the Senate floor. McCarthy asked for and was granted equal time in confronting Murrow, but so vicious was his attack on the newscaster that the appearance of the senator on *See It Now* marked the beginning of the end of his political career.

About a year later the Army-McCarthy hearings were held, and again the television cameras brought the proceedings into the living rooms of millions of Americans across the country. The audience sat enthralled for days as the investigations into communist influence in the armed forces proceeded and the legal wrangling between McCarthy and Army defense counsel Joseph Welch flared. Again McCarthy's insidious maneuverings were brought home to the American public and by the end of the hearing he was a broken man. Joseph Welch emerged from the television "debates" as a national hero.

It was on Christmas Eve, 1951 that the first opera written expressly for television was first performed. *Amahl and the Night Visitors*, composed by Gian Carlo Menotti, soon became a mainstay of the holiday season programming. Three years later the first "spectacular" was shown on television. The concept of NBC vice-president Pat Weaver, the "spectacular" was meant as a one of a kind special program. The first such program was *Satins and Spurs* starring Betty Hutton. However the show was poorly conceived and poorly performed and the first spectacular nearly became the last, so negative was the viewer response to *Satin and Spurs*. Strangely enough, perhaps the greatest spectacular ever shown on television was in the following year. On March 7, 1955, Mary Martin starred in the musical, *Peter Pan*. In two performances the perennial children's fantasy play had the largest audience ever to see a non-sporting event on television. *Peter Pan* proved that the American television public would watch a quality show superbly acted. With the success of *Peter Pan*, other performers were encouraged to star in spectaculars, and there followed such memorable programs as *An Evening with Fred Astaire* in 1958 and specials with Victor Borge and Maurice Chevalier in the same year. The movie industry, which had been fighting the incursions of television by several means mentioned previously, finally capitulated and in 1956 *The Wizard of Oz* was shown on television for the first time. Television programming had come a long way in ten years.

Late night programming on television had been mainly old movies and test patterns for years, but in 1950 a program called *Broadway Open House* was shown in New York City. Hosted by Jerry Lester and a bosomy actress named Dagmar, the program was a success. Four years later the program took on a national audience when Steve Allen became the host and the program's name was changed to *The Tonight Show*. Allen established the format of the talk show by inviting

Ed Sullivan, *right, and Bishop Fulton J. Sheen, two popular television personalities during the golden age of television in the Fifties.*

guests who, for the most part, sat around and talked. The show was lowkeyed, funny, occassionally informative, and a favorite with late night television viewers. In 1957 Jack Paar took over the show as host and his and the show's popularity continued to grow. Paar was an emotional performer who often cried at sad stories his guests told. He feuded with columnist Walter Winchell on the air, and once, offended that the NBC censors had excised an off-color joke from his opening monologue, he walked off the program in full view of the television audience. Paar's popularity was based partly on his controversial character, and when he had done on television what he had wanted to do, he retired in the early 1960's.

Another capitulation to television made by the movie industry occurred in 1954 when Walt Disney decided to put on an hour program each week on Sunday nights. The addition of the Disney name to television was perhaps the final straw for the movie industry on the west coast, and soon after *The Wonderful World of Disney* was a regular feature of Sunday television, several movie studios began getting into the business of making movies for television.

The Fifties were the Golden Age of Television in one respect at least. It was during this decade that many fine television dramas, written especially for television, were first performed live. In 1954 Reginald Rose's *Twelve Angry Men* was first shown; Rod Serling became known when his play *Patterns* was telecast in 1955, and in 1956 his *Requiem for a Heavyweight* starring Jack Palance was shown to the home audience. However, in 1957 a technological breakthrough

occurred which eventually precluded the frenzy of the live dramatic performance. TV record tape was perfected, which meant that television shows could now be made somewhat like movies are made; a scene could be stopped, actors, sets, etc., re-arranged, and the scene could go on. It also meant that two performances of the same program would not have to be given to accommodate the time differences across the country. Unlike the old kinescope (which was a process which transferred TV onto film) the TV tape was instantaneous, relatively inexpensive, and much easier to work with than film. Its invention and perfection in 1957 marked the beginning of a new era in television programming.

Of all the shows, both "spectaculars" and weekly programs, perhaps none has had the endurance of *I Love Lucy*. Starting out as a situation comedy the show soon became an American institution. Starring Lucille Ball, *I Love Lucy* is still being seen, more than twenty-five years after its inception in 1951. During the Fifties other show business names made the transition from radio to television, and Bing Crosby, Bob Hope, George Burns and Gracie Allen all had popular shows which were little more than filmed versions of their radio programs. The television series came into its own in the Fifties also, with such programs as *The Untouchables, Dragnet* and the World War II documentary *Victory at Sea* being among the most popular shows of the day. The cowboy, long a staple in the movie industry, moved into the great indoors of television following Hopalong Cassidy's earlier success, in such television series as *Wagon Train, Tales of the Texas Rangers,* and one of the most durable series in television history, *Gunsmoke,* which started out as a half hour program in 1955. Further evidence of movies losing the war of audiences to television occurred in 1957 when the legendary film director Alfred Hitchcock began his show, *Alfred Hitchcock Presents*. The first television dealing with doctors was *Medic*, starring Richard Boone, which came on the air in 1954.

Serious "cultural" programming came to television in 1952 when the Ford Foundation subsidized *Omnibus*, which was a Sunday afternoon show dealing with the legitimate stage and classical works of literature. Dr. Frank Baxter was host for a series of scientific programs under the auspices of the Bell Telephone Company. Baxter's programs were well received by the general public, and were a clear indication that educational television didn't have to be boring to be educational.

The first presidential nominating convention to be widely televised was the 1952 Convention of Republicans, in which Dwight Eisenhower reveived the nomination. A curious sidelight to this convention is the appearance of Richard Nixon on television defending himself against charges of accepting personal gifts meant for campaign purposes. Nixon appeared on evening television in what has been called the "Checkers speech" and was able to convince the American public of his honesty. It was an awesome display of television's ability to influence voters. Four years later the Republican Convention also gave America the news team of Chet Huntley and David Brinkley. The two were paired to serve as anchor men for the televised proceedings, but so popular were they with the viewing public that NBC made them joint anchormen on the Evening News, and thus launched television into serious journalistic competition among the three networks. News coverage during the Fifties included such firsts as a Presidential inauguration (Eisenhower's on January 20, 1953) the visit to America of Russian Premier Nikita Khrushchev in 1957, and the regular appearance of such news generating programs as *Face the Nation*, and *Meet the Press*.

Sports coverage also came of age during the Fifties, with weekly telecasts of prize fighting—Rocky Marciano, Ray Robinson, and Joe Walcott all fought for championships on TV. Although the sport of professional boxing was hurt by overexposure on TV, professional baseball and basketball, and college football benefitted from being on the small screen.

By 1956 an estimated two out of three homes in America had TV receivers, and a whole generation was growing up not knowing what the world was like without television. The influence of television was felt to be a positive one; movies had long since given up the struggle and television was the single most popular form of mass entertainment in America. Television had everything going for it, and then a series of events occurred which almost brought everything crashing down.

Quiz shows had long been a part of radio, and when television came in it was simply a matter of the quiz shows moving over onto television. In 1955 the first of the big television quiz shows went on the air called *The $64,000 Question*, the show was an immediate success, and soon after two other quiz shows came on—*The Big Surprise* (which offered a $100,000 first prize) and *Twenty-One*. America quickly became enamored with watching ex-jockeys, housewives, precocious children, and many other "experts" competing for the huge sums in prizes. Certain contestants who were quite knowledgeable about certain subjects were soon discovered to be quite dull, while other contestants gave more life to the shows. The livelier contestants seemed to be favored on the programs, and within weeks millions of

Americans were watching to see if their favorite contestant could go all the way to the big prize. The programs continued to draw massive audiences for three years; then, a former contestant on a quiz show called *Dotto* admitted that he had been given some answers, and the lid was blown off the quiz show fraud. Subsequent investigations revealed that many of the contestants on the give away shows had been either directly told the answers, or had been sufficiently coached to be able to figure the answers out from the wording of the question. The scandals which followed wrecked the credibility of television and indictments of quiz show producers followed lengthy investigations in the duplicity of the television industry. Although the popularity of the medium was too strong not to be able to weather the quiz show scandals, it was a dark period for television, and as the Fifties came to a close it was an ironic ending for the industry's so-called Golden Age.

Some of the most famous stars of the decade no longer had their own shows—Milton Berle, Sid Caesar, Red Buttons, Wally Cox were among the biggest of the era who went into the Sixties without a regular program on TV. The increased cost of television production meant that TV producers were no longer as willing to take chances on untried types of programs, and the pattern of duplicating popular programs became typical of television programming. As the industry moved into the Sixties the audience was faced with seeing "types" of shows—the western, the lawyer, the medical, the detective—in much the same way that theater audiences had had to choose between differing examples of the same genre of film a generation earlier. Television had also become a very big business in America by the end of the Fifties, and FCC investigations in unfair business operations on the part of the three major networks revealed examples of coercion and electronic blackmail to gain access to certain markets. By the beginning of the Sixties no one questioned the ubiquitousness of the TV antennas across the country; the only serious question facing television was, what would the industry do with the medium?

The influence of television in the daily life of the country is evident in the political career of John F. Kennedy. Spending large sums of money to buy exposure on TV, Kennedy was able to garner the Democratic nomination in 1960. His good looks and quick wit were an asset to campaigning in the new electronic age. Television played an important part in Kennedy's winning the election of 1960, too, because he was able to "win" the televised debates against his Republican opponent, Richard Nixon, and the people remembered what they had seen on TV when they went to vote. 1960 was the first election in which television played an important role in bringing the candidates to the people, and it was a lesson that was not lost on politicians.

One of the first serious attacks on the content of television programming occurred in 1961 when the then FCC Chairman Newton Minnow referred to TV as "a vast wasteland." Once Minnow's remarks were made public, the floodgates of criticism were opened and condemnation of television as being puerile and senseless flowed across the country. Parent-teacher groups attacked the medium for its lack of educational content in children's shows, while others railed against TV for the amount of violence depicted in many of the prime time programs. The attacks were met with silence at first, and then with a kind of backhanded sociology. Surveys taken by the television industry indicated that the vast majority of Americans felt that the programs on television were worthwhile and entertaining, and, although some concessions were made in programming, the industry silenced its critics by pointing to the increased numbers of Americans who turned to TV for relaxation and enjoyment.

The assassination of John F. Kennedy in 1963 proved to the country that television was a necessary and integral part of its daily life. Millions watched the news of the assassination from Dallas, for TV was now as fast in transmitting news events as radio was; and millions more were stunned to disbelief when they saw Lee Harvey Oswald being shot to death on TV by Jack Ruby. Television had brought the whole ghastly ordeal of the Presidential assassination into the living room, and the critics were silenced for a while.

The new mobility of television transmission in the Sixties meant that there was literally nowhere the TV camera and microphone couldn't go in searching for news. Dallas was just the beginning. The Chicago riots surrounding the 1968 Democratic Convention illustrated dramatically television's ability to go to the source of a news story and give people not only the facts but also the feel of the event. The space program was covered in minute detail by the television camera, and again the industry was able to show the country the effectiveness of bringing live, topical stories into the living room instantaneously and entertainingly. The remarkable TV transmission from the moon's surface on July 20, 1969, capped television coverage of the American space program.

Back on the earth, a newer phenomenon was occurring in television—color. Color TV transmission had started as early as the late Fifties, and in the early Sixties more and more ''specials'' were being shown in color. By 1965 NBC

began to advertise itself as the ''full color'' network, and the age of color had come to stay on the small screen. Programming itself saw relatively few changes from the Fifties. What had worked for the industry then continued to work for it in the Sixties, and, although many of the faces changed, the programming remained virtually the same. What did change was the impact that television began having on the life of the of the country. Television performers were no longer considered failed movie aspirants, but began generating a following of their own. Ancillary products involving popular stars or programs was becoming a satellite industry to television. Television history was made in 1965 when Bill Cosby became the first black American to be starred in a regular series.

Sports coverage was greatly expanded in the Sixties, with the TV cameras in attendance at both the 1964 and 1968 summer and winter Olympic Games. Television's first political cause celebre occurred in 1965 when the popular *Smothers Brothers Show* was taken off the air for political remarks made about the conduct of the Vietnam war. Popular shows such as *Bonanza* and *That Was the Week That Was* had huge audiences. Specials such as the *Miss America Beauty Pageant* became an annual affair on the TV screen.

As television moved into the Seventies it could look back on its coverage of sporting events, political campaigns, and even the Vietnam war with some measure of pride. In less than one generation television had become a basic fact in American life, with the ability to mold and shape opinion, educate and entertain. Despite its cultural limitations, television has served America well, and nowhere in human history has there ever been a more powerful tool for shaping the lives of Americans.

Jack Paar, *left, and Senator John F. Kennedy during Kennedy's appearance on Paar's late night talk show in 1960. Paar took over the late night time from Steve Allen, and made the talk show one of the most popular kinds of television program.*

Man's "greatest adventure" *reached a climax on July 20, 1969, when Neil Armstrong became the first man on the moon as seen by millions of TV viewers.*

From Radio *to Television's small image, as shown in this view of Edward R. Murrow in 1949. Color TV was introduced first in 1951, but discontinued until 1953. Some of the leading television innovators are seen on this page as viewed on the small screen.*

The Howdy Doody Show (1947–60), originally **The Puppet Playhouse.** The puppet Howdy Doody, Buffalo Bob, and Clarabell the Clown starred in the first popular children's TV show.

The Texaco Star Theatre, featuring Milton Berle (1948–53). So popular that he became known as Mr. Television, Berle had prominent guests on his variety show, but he was the main attraction.

Your Show of Shows (1949–54). The team of Sid Caesar and Imogene Coca, with Howard Morris and Carl Reiner, brought memorable comedy and Broadway-quality revues into the home every week.

I Love Lucy (1951–57). Starring Lucille Ball and Desi Arnaz, seen here with Ethel Mertz and William Frawley (left), this comedy is among the leaders of the daytime reruns that have proliferated on every channel.

Gunsmoke (1955–75). Shown are James Arness and Dennis Weaver, two of the stars of what became the longest running Western on television. Gunsmoke was a forerunner among adult Westerns.

As the World Turns (1956–). Although not the oldest soap opera on television, this daytime serial attracted 10 million viewers. Some of its stars have been with the show since its inception.

Perry Mason (1957–66). Perry (Raymond Burr) and his secretary, Della Street (Barbara Hale), confer in a scene from this series, based on Erle Stanley Gardner's stories of a criminal lawyer who never lost a case.

Dr. Kildare (1961–66). Typical of several medical series, this popular show starred Richard Chamberlain as Dr. Kildare and Raymond Massey as Dr. Gillespie. Some "Dr. Kildare" movies had preceded it.

The Tonight Show (1954–57), host Steve Allen; **The Jack Paar Show** (1957–62); **The Tonight Show Starring Johnny Carson** (photo) (1962–).

Super Bowl Joint Telecast (1967); **Super Bowl** (1968–). The climax of the professional football season attracted 56 million viewers in 1975, the largest audience up to then for a single sporting event.

OSCAR

Hollywood's prize baby came from humble beginnings. The Academy Awards started — almost as an afterthought — from a much bigger seed-idea born in the brain of M-G-M's powerful bossman, Louis B. Mayer.

One Sunday afternoon at his Santa Monica beach home, L.B. told two guests, Conrad Nagel and Fred Niblo, that there should be an organized group, composed of Hollywood's elite, which might serve several purposes, one of which would be to help arbitrate labor disputes then running rampant through the movie studios. Due to Mayer's general enthusiasm — and persistence — the idea flowered with little delay.

On May 4, 1927, a group of 36 industry leaders (including Mayer, Nagel, Niblo, Mary Pickford, Douglas Fairbanks, Joseph Schenck, Frank Lloyd, and Cedric Gibbons) got together to discuss the idea further and — one week later — on May 11, 1927, they held a banquet in the ballroom of the Biltmore Hotel. Besides breaking bread, they told 300 black-tie guests their idea. Mayer footed the bill for the banquet, but let Douglas Fairbanks do the talking.

"Our purpose is positive, not negative," Fairbanks told them. "We are formed to do, not undo." Among the organization's secondary aims: "to encourage the arts and sciences of the profession by awards of merit for distinctive achievement." At the end of the banquet, nearly everyone in the room signed a check for $100 and became a pioneer Academy member. Thus, the Academy of Motion Picture Arts and Sciences was officially born, founded as a non-profit organization, chartered under California law.

When the labor unions came into focus in Hollywood, the original Mayer aim of Academy arbitration quickly died away. But that other aim — "awards of merit" — took hold and never let go.

The late Cedric Gibbons, a long-time executive art director at M-G-M, was chosen to design some kind of award to be given those honored. While listening to a long discussion of certificates, scrolls, medals and plaques, he quietly jotted down the sketch of a man in a dynamic, militant pose, holding a crusader's sword and standing on a reel of film. That original sketch became the model for the Academy Award that still exists today. Energetic writers persisted in circulating the story that Gibbons drew the first Oscar sketch on a tablecloth.

"It was done on paper" he said in 1947. "I made the sketch during a meeting of board members. We were sitting around a table, all right, but it was a big polished table in the board room and there was no tablecloth."

Sculptor George Stanley executed the statue for a $500 fee. Standing 13½ inches tall and weighing 6¾ pounds, it was cast by Alex Smith, composed of 92.5% tin and 7.5% copper. Bronze-filled and gold-plated, at a cost of $100. During the war, when metal was hard to get, the Oscar was made of a plaster cast and gold leaf. Those statues were later replaced by the Academy when metal was again available. Current Oscars have a Britannia metal base, highly polished, then plated with 10 karat gold and again highly polished and covered with a final 24-karat gold plate. Actual dollar cost of an Oscar today is $60. Statuettes today weigh in at 11 pounds. The Southern California Trophy Company, in association with Dodge, Inc., makes the Oscars each year.

In the early years, a winner could hock his Oscar, melt it down, or shoot craps for it if he wanted. Since the award was copyrighted on September 2, 1941, however, members are forbidden by Academy rules to sell or "otherwise dispose of it nor permit it to be sold or disposed of by operation of law without first offering to sell it back to the Academy for $10."

Today the annual Academy Award presentations are the organization's most colorful function, but the AMPA&S is a busy establishment with many other projects. Over the years, the Academy has assembled a large library, gathered an extensive collection of research material, and issued bulletins of industry news. The organization publishes a quarterly directory of actors and actresses for help in casting offices, engages in public enterprises and has special screenings of movies in its own theatre.

From the first organizational banquet in 1927 and the second banquet when awards were first handed out, on to the present day, the Academy Award story is filled with change, struggles, clashes, and controversy. It is often criticized, but it remains as democratic an operation as any in existence. Any time personal opinion is expressed—and the yearly awards express the opinions of several hundred individuals—there is bound to be disagreement and verbal fire. The Academy expects this, and goes on its own merry way —studying methods, making adjustments and altering rules in an effort to be fair.

The Academy Award wasn't the first award given to movies and their makers (*Photoplay Magazine* started a yearly popularity poll in 1920; the National Board of Review started annual awards the same year; *Film Daily* awards, along with countless others, have popped up every year since) but it remains the most powerful of them all. Part of the Oscar power comes from the fact it is voted by members within the industry, honoring its own. Another stems from the fact—as the following pages show—that Oscar is a jumble of paradoxes: it has been known to flush life into a sagging career and blot out a promising one; it can be won by a dash of sentiment or crumble the career of a potent personality. The little statue is ruled, and voted, by human beings who are sometimes vulnerable to sentiment, sometimes blinded by color and razamataz. These people are conscientious and try to rule with their heads, but they are human and sometimes rule with their emotions. Every year the Oscar is required to take the pulse of these hundreds of people active in all branches of the motion picture industry. Their human emotions make the Oscar something of a saint, something of a rascal, but they give him life as surely as Dr. Frankenstein gave life to his monster.

BEST ACTRESS, 1938
BETTE DAVIS
in "Jezebel"

BEST ACTOR, 1942

JAMES CAGNEY

in "Yankee Doodle Dandy"

BEST ACTOR, 1944

BING CROSBY
in "Going My Way"

BEST ACTRESS, 1948

JANE WYMAN
in "Johnny Belinda"

BEST ACTOR, 1956

YUL BRYNNER

in "The King and I"

Great Stars of the Silver Screen

Left to right, *top row: Charlie Chaplin, Stan Laurel and Oliver Hardy, Rudolph Valentino, Lillian Gish, Clara Bow, Harpo, Chico, and Groucho Marx. Second row: Mary Pickford (in circle), Buster Keaton, Douglas Fairbanks, Sr. (in circle), Nelson Eddy and Jeanette MacDonald, Greta Garbo (in circle). Third row: William S. Hart (with revolver), Gloria Swanson, Jean Harlow (in circle), Ginger Rogers and* *Fred Astaire, W. C. Fields and Mae West. Fourth row: Joan Crawford, Rita Hayworth, Spencer Tracy (in circle), Marlene Dietrich, Bette Davis (in circle), Cary Grant, Clark Gable. Fifth row: Judy Garland, Edward G. Robinson, James Cagney, Marilyn Monroe, Shirley Temple, Gene Kelly, Humphrey Bogart. Sixth row: John Wayne, Gary Cooper, Elizabeth Taylor, Marlon Brando, Katharine Hepburn.*

William Hahn's 1868 painting "It's My Turn."

Grandstand thrills *and hoopla fill the Sells Brothers poster (above) of the 1890's. But nothing could match the Ringling Brothers, Barnum and Bailey show, at its height during the 1930's. It absorbed 11 older shows and featured three rings, five stages, and a hippodrome track—all under a Big Top that seated 10,000 "children of all ages." Among the most popular features of the great tent circuses was the sideshow (right), which alternately amused and appalled ticketholders with brief stints by a galaxy of human oddities, some truly talented, others sadly deformed. In recent years sideshows have become less popular, and most circuses have been forced by economics to perform only in indoor arenas.*

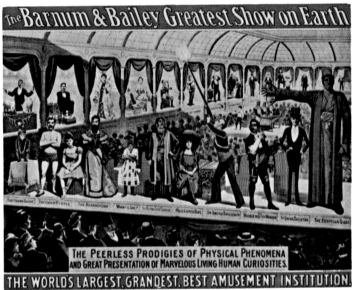

The **Barnum & Bailey** Greatest Show on Earth

THE PEERLESS PRODIGIES OF PHYSICAL PHENOMENA AND GREAT PRESENTATION OF MARVELOUS LIVING HUMAN CURIOSITIES.

THE WORLD'S LARGEST, GRANDEST, BEST AMUSEMENT INSTITUTION.

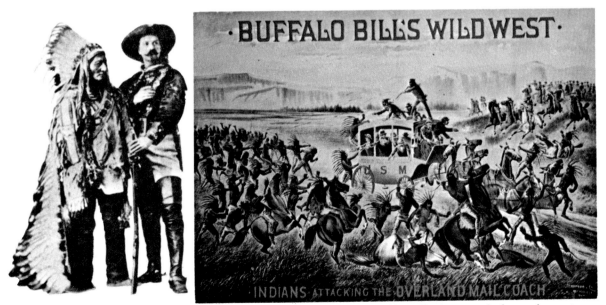

BUFFALO BILL'S WILD WEST

INDIANS ATTACKING THE OVERLAND MAIL COACH

Former foes *(above left) Sitting Bull and Buffalo Bill were united by show business. During the 1880's the former leader of the Sioux* *performed in the Wild West Show's most popular feature—the reenactment of an Indian attack on a stagecoach, pictured in the poster above.*

HISTORICAL HEADLINES
ON
POPULAR ARTS

SECOND EXTRA SECOND

our Newspaper
no private axes to grind, elfish personal interests to e and no financial strings ng to any other source of er or influence.

Los Angeles Record

CITY EDITION 2 CENTS

-first Year — Entered as second-class matter, April 1, 1895, at the postoffice at Los Angeles, California, under the Act of March 3, 1879. — LOS ANGELES, MONDAY, AUGUST 23, 1926 — Published Daily Except Sunday at Record Building, 612 Wall Street — Number 9837

VALENTINO DEAD

LLYWOOD MOURNS .M 'SHEIK'S' DEATH

By JIMMY STARR

OLPH VALENTINO, the een's greatest lover, died orning, and Hollywood is aving waited all night long the latest report of the screen sheik's condition.

norning, as the news came wire, Hollywood bowed its e more for one of its famous

years ago "Rudy" started onal wave of the Argentine hen he appeared in "The orsemen" for Metro, but he to real popularity when he as the leading man with yres in "The Sheik."

e was his performance in ture that he automatically a star in his own right when was released.

famous role as the sheik he whole world imitating.

* * *

Y youth in the country ied Rudy's Argentine peon which he had worn in Four Horsemen." Then in of "The Sheik" he made complexions and sleek hair ore popular.

was born in the Italian vil-Castellaneta, on May 6, 1895 s ago). He was christened Alfonso Raffaelo Pierre Guglielmi di Valentina guolla.

first appeared and received edit seven years ago under tion of James Young. His that time was Rudolpho de o.

in "Roads to Romance." Young directed with Earle for Vitagraph, that Valen-enlisted to do an Apache So clever were his terpsi-steps that he was given ys' work at $15 a day.

* * *

$45 was Valentino's Holly-d fortune. Later on he ap-with Universal as a villain m starring Carmel Myers. o won a small role with Kimball Young in "Eyes of

part grew until he was final-ed for the leading male role Four Horsemen," which Rex was directing for Metro

Mathis, scenarist, is credited ving first "discovered" the reen sheik. However, James who directed Rudy for Vita-as the first to go on record g said Valentino would be a ar some day.

ino received not more than week while making "The orsemen." His estimated the time of his death was $8000 and $10,00 per week.

appearing in the Ingram fea-dy was engaged to appear Alice Lake in "The Un-Sea." This part attracted ntion, as did "The Four n" role, of Nazimova, who him immediately for the part nd Duval in her version of

* * *

CHA RAMBOVA, who r became Mrs. Rudolph no the second, was art di-for Nazimova. It is be-hat Valentino's association mbova while making the a film resulted in their e, which took place two ater.

"Camille" Valentino was under Ingram's direction Conquering Power," once pearing with Alice Terry ex Ingram) who won na-me as his leading woman.

June Mathis departed from rio staff of Metro studios ed the Famous Players orporation, she immediately thought of Valentino and saw that he was engaged for "The Sheik."

After this Rudy played opposite Dorothy Dalton in "Moran of the Lady Letty" and opposite Gloria Swanson in "Beyond the Rocks."

Then came Fred Niblo's version of "Blood and Sand," which placed Valentino, after a series of mediocre films, back into the limelight once more.

Studio trouble resulted over the small salary he was receiving, and Valentino started suit to break his contract with the Lasky organization.

* * *

AFTER many weeks of discussion, a new company, the Rudolph Valentino Productions was organized by J. B. Williams. Valetino completed "The Young Rajah" for Lasky and then went directly to New York, fighting his case and also making public appearances and fulfilling a dancing engagement in Chicago's largest ballroom.

Upon his return to Hollywood, with most of his accumulated fortune wasted upon lawyers in New York, Rudolph was heartsick and discouraged. His new company, which wanted to produce "Cobra," brought only trouble to Rudy's mind. His affairs at home were in turmoil and Rambova is blamed for part of the friction at the studio, which arose between Valentino and his company.

Valentino's small fortune was now practically gone and he was in dire need of funds, once more as he had been four years before.

After considerable trouble, both with his company and his wife, Rudolph decided to disband his organization and signed with Joseph M. Schenck, head of United Artists corporation, who had offered him a long term contract at a huge figure and a percentage interest in his pictures.

* * *

THE friendship between Valentino and Schenck began when the latter aranged $5000 bail after Valentino had been arrested for bigamy and was lodged in the county jail.

It was this move of Schenck's, who had never met the screen idol, personally, which gave Valentino implicit faith in the producer.

Valentino's first picture under the Schenck management was "The Eagle," directed by Clarence Brown and marked a decided departure from any of his other productions.

It was hailed for bringing back a new Rudolph. Then came the sequel to "The Sheik," entitled "Son of the Sheik," for the opening of which Rudolph went to New York when an operation became necessary.

New York meant much to Rudolph, who had once been an apprentice landscape gardener in Central park. This was long before Rudolph had talked himself into a short vaudeville engagement with Bonnie Glass, and it was this act which drew the attention of Joan Sawyer, one of Broadway's famous dancers, who asked Rudolph to form a dancing partnership with her, which after weeks of severe training, resulted into one of the most famous of dancing teams.

* * *

RUDOLPH claimed at that time that he did not want to be a dancer and with a little money he worked his way to San Francisco where he danced for several months, then later coming to Hollywood with only a hope that he could really crash the studio gate.

Rudolph's dream after he became a star was to play "Romeo and Juliet" opposite Norma Talmadge, who was outside his door at the hospital when he passed away. Mrs. Schenck had promised Rudolph a chance to

[CONTINUED ON NEXT PAGE]

LAST ROLE PLAYED

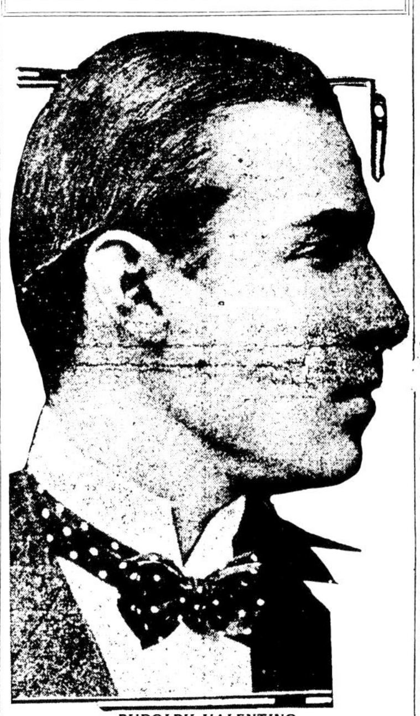

RUDOLPH VALENTINO

* * *

Here's 'Official' Life of 'Sheik'

Here's the official biography of Rudolph Valentino as kept in the files of United Artists' Corporation:

RUDOLPH Alfonzo Raffaelo Pierre Filibert Guglielmi di Valentina d'Antonguolla was born in the little village of Castellaneta, Italy, May 6, 1895. His mother was the daughter of a learned Parisian doctor, Pierre Filibert Barbin. His father, Giovanni Guglielmi, was in his youth a captain of Italian cavalry and later a veterinary doctor.

When Valentino was 11, his father died. He was sent to Dante Alighieri college, where he finished the course at 13. Then he went to a military college where he is said to have been more interested in romantic novels than in studies. It is recorded he was once sent home because he broke out of a room in which he was confined for discipline in order to see the king, a visitor to the school.

* * *

VALENTINO next enrolled in the Royal Academy of Agriculture to learn to be a scientific farmer; he was graduated with highest honors in his class. Several months of life in Paris and Monte Carlo followed. When the prodigal returned to his home it was decided by his family that if he were going to continue the reckless life he had pursued in France, it were better he be shipped to America.

* * *

SO RUDOLPH VALENTINO arrived in New York December 23, 1913. Although most of his money was spent in cafes, he did learn one thing that was to prove invaluable to him,—how to dance. His money gone, he had to seek a job and his first position was as superintendent of the Long Island estate of Cornelius Bliss, Jr.

His next position was as an apprentice landscape gardner in Central Park, New York. At the Civil Service bureau, he was told he was ineligible for a regular position there.

Quite penniless and literally homeless, this phase of the future star's dramatic career was best summarized by the statement that he took any little odd jobs he could get,—shining brass on cars, sweeping out, what not.

Finally the head waiter at Maxim's employed him as a dancer, and so his professional career began. As dancing partner to Bonnie Glass and later with Joan Sawyer, he attained same reputation.

But the Italian scientific farmer cherished hopes of forsaking the dancing profession, which was never close to his heart, to become a farmer in California. Toward this end he joined a musical comedy troupe headed for the coast, which organization pleased Fate by stranding in San Francisco.

* * *

VALENTINO was advised by a friend he had known in the east, Norman Kerry, to try motion pictures, and on the bounty of Kerry he traveled to Los Angeles, where he did not get a job in the movies.

For a long time, Valentino could not even secure the most menial form of studio employment. One day

[CONTINUED ON NEXT PAGE]

Last Conscious Word Uttered at 3 O'clock

BULLETIN

By United Press.

NEW YORK, Aug. 23.—Rudolph Valentino, who came to this country as an emigrant and rose to the heights of fame as an actor, died at the Polyclinic hospital here today.

Humbly born, the son of a farmer in Italy, he died with four skilled physicians at his bedside and with the country waiting each word from his sick room almost as it waits for a word from the sick room of a president.

Death came at 12:10 P. M.

Dr. Harold Meeker, one of the attending physicians who was with the actor throughout the night and morning, said he believed the last conscious words were spoken at 3:30 a. m.

At that time, Valentino, still thinking he was to recover from an operation for appendicitis and gastric ulcers, spoke of the days he would spend in recuperation and asked the doctor about trout fishing.

"Do you have plenty of rods and hooks?" the actor asked Dr. Meeker.

At 4 a. m. Valentino became irrational and talked mostly in Italian.

Two hours later he was semi-conscious and lapsed into a coma at 8. From then on he occasionally opened his eyes when his name was called. He died without pain. The cause of death, in medical parlance was "septic pneumonia and septic endocarditis."

Scientists considered a blood transfusion and Edward Day, engineer at the hospital, volunteered a pint of his blood. It was decided, however, that the actor was too weakened to stand the extra strain on his heart.

The corps of physicians then ordered an X-ray. It was found that the pleurisy, which brought about a relapse Saturday when Valentino seemed on the road to recovery, had been followed by septoendocarditis (poisoning of the wall of the heart).

The last official bulletin was issued shortly before noon, when it was admitted that the actor was "rapidly failing."

His temperature had mounted to 105. His pulse was hammering at the rate of 140 strokes to the minute. His respiration was 30 to the minute.

In a few moments the actor was dead.

The operation was performed a week ago Sunday. Valentino had been in New York in connection with the release of one of his pictures, "The Son of the Sheik." He had attended several parties and was in a gay mood most of the week preceding his illness.

After he had been stricken by acute appendicitis he was taken to the hospital.

The ulcerous condition was said to be more of a menace to his health than the appendicitis.

At first it was believed the operation had been completely successful. On Tuesday it was known that peritonitis had developed, but physicians said it was localized.

The hospital, meanwhile, was besieged by personal and telephone calls from thousands of those whose hours had been made happier by Valentino's screen appearance.

Once there was a report of his death, and extra girls were assigned to telephone duty at the Polyclinic.

"Mr. Valentino is alive and his condition is the same," intoned the operators to the callers and a gasp of relief followed.

Father Congodo administered the last rites of the Catholic church to the dying man shortly after 10 a. m. today. Just before Valentino died, Father Bennon, of the Church of St. Malachi, known as the Actors' church, in Forty-ninth street, arrived in the sickroom.

Joseph M. Schenck announced Valentino's death. He came downstairs at 12:15 and read the brief bulletin signed by Drs. Paul E. Durham, G. Randolph Manning and Howard D. Meeker.

The relapse came Saturday. Valentino still showed a remarkable constitution and physicians took hope from his courage. However, the disease traveled slowly but certainly toward the heart and death could not be denied.

After news of his death came today, the telephone girls were immediately beseiged once more.

By Thursday of last week Valentino was in better spirits and hopes were high that his recovery would be complete. He even consented to an interview, through George Ullman his personal manager.

Valentino had lost consciousness shortly before the end.

* * *

Pola Faints at News of Death

Unconscious and hysterical by turns, crying out her grief over the death of Rudolph Valentino, Pola Negri, reported fiancee of the dead film star, was under the care of two physicians in her Ambassador hotel bungalow today.

The Polish film star's grief was touching.

Informed of Valentino's death by newspapermen, Miss Negri fainted.

Frantically her maid, crying out for aid, summoned the hotel house physician. A few moments later the star's private doctor arrived. Restoratives returning her to consciousness, Miss Negri wept bitterly. The star was completely unnerved. A few moments later and her grief turned to hysteria.

In her dialect of mixed English and Polish, Miss Negri screamed again and again the name of Valentino.

Again physicians quieted her.

As news reached the studio where she had been working night and day on her new picture, "Hotel Imperial," in an effort to finish her work in order that she might rush to her lover's bedside, officials dispatched messengers, hoping to be able to reach the actress before she had heard the story from other sources.

They were too late.

Mr. and Mrs. Charles Eyton, close personal friends of the star, were the only ones admitted to her hotel bungalow.

Mrs. Eyton remained with Miss Negri, seeking to comfort her.

The star's hysterical condition prevented her from issuing any statement. It could not be learned if she plans to go to New York, should the funerel be held there.

All work on Miss Negri's picture was abandoned.

At her bungalow home none could say whether the star will rush to New York or not.

At the Famous Players studio flags were lowered to half-mast immediately upon receipt of the news.

Work on all stages was abandoned, the film players assembling in groups. It was the same at other studios in Hollywood and Culver City. There too the flags were lowered.

As the news spread through the great stages on the Famous Player-Lasky "lot" and at United Artists, directors shouted their commands of "cut," and cameras stopped clicking.

Film players rushed to executive offices and grouped about asking for further news after the first bare announcement of the star's death.

Women film stars wept. Many of the male players made no effort to hide their tears. The genuine affection with which Valentino was held by his film world was clearly evident.

Only Los Angeles Newspaper With All Leading News Services— Associated Press, International News, United Press, Dow-Jones

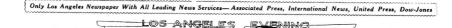

LOS ANGELES EVENING HERALD AND Express
AN INDEPENDENT NEWSPAPER

Registered United States Patent Office
The Evening Herald and Express Grows Just Like Los Angeles

HERALD-EXPRESS PHONE Richmond 4141

LATEST NEWS

WEATHER FORECAST

Los Angeles and Vicinity—Fair tonigh Tuesday, with low clouds or fog night and ing. Little change in temperature. Gentle w

VOL. LXVI | Hotels and Trains Five Cents | THREE CENTS | MONDAY, AUGUST 10, 1936 | THREE CENTS | Two Sections Section A | NO. 1

MARY ASTOR'S DIARY

STAR'S WRITTEN WORDS TELL OF KAUFMAN AFFAI

300,000 Jam Hollywood for Legion Parad

'Fell Like a Ton of Bricks' for Writer, Actress Relates

In lavender ink, Mary Astor wrote in a diary love secrets and bared details of a romantic interlude she experienced with George S. Kaufman, Puliitzer prize winning playwright. Today, Joseph Anderson, attorney for her former husband, Dr. Franklyn Thorpe, in the court battle over the custody of their daughter, Marylyn, released excerpts from the "lavender diary." They follow:

Tuesday, Jan. 14, 1934.

Well, here is another New Year and I'm doing my usual wondering about what's going to happen to me.

To go back to that May entry, I flew east with the Gallaghers, stayed about two weeks and had a heavenly time—and I did meet a man, professional, somewhat older and rather well-to-do only his first initial is G—George Kaufman—and I fell like a ton of bricks—as only I can fall—it was just one of those things—I met him the Friday after I arrived, at the Algonquin.

A friend had told me to look him up and I had phoned him Monday—he was out of town but he phoned me Friday a. m. and made a luncheon engagement for Saturday with me—the same day I had lunch with Natalie Lewy, and in he came—he seemed very nice, talked to us a few minutes, made some remark about the fact that it was lucky we had met so he would know me on the morrow and wouldn't have to wear a red carnation or something. That evening I had dinner with a young man, I've forgotten his name—at "Twenty-One" and there he was again.

Saturday he called for me at the Ambassador and we went to the Casino for lunch and had a very gay time. He was such fun—we drove back down town and sneaked in at the Music Box where his show, "Of Thee I Sing," was playing, stayed a minute and then went next door (Shubert theater) where "Gay Divorcee" was showing and it was very cool and pleasant and Fred Astaire was dancing so beautifully to such a beautiful number, "Night and Day," and the theater was half empty, so we stayed, and he was looking at me more than at the stage, and I liked it.

HAD A DRINK SOMEPLACE AND THEN WENT TO LITTLE FLAT

Sunday night we had dinner and saw "International House" at the Paramount and laughed a lot and liked each other even more. Monday I had a preview engagement with Bennett Cerf for dinner but George called me up and said he knew about a tea party that might be fun and would I go—I would and did but the tea party wasn't fun and we left in about 15 minutes—it was very hot so we got a cab and drove around the park a few times and the park was—well, the park—and he held my hand and said he'd like to kiss me, but didn't—Tuesday night we had dinner at "Twenty-one" and on the way to see "Run, Little Chillun," he did kiss me—and I don't think either of us remember much about what the show was about—afterwards we had a drink some place and then went to a little flat in Seventy-third street where we could be alone and it was all very thrilling and beautiful

I didn't see very much of anybody else the rest of the time—we saw every show in town, had grand fun together and went frequently to Seventy-third street. I remember one morning about 4 we had a sandwich at Reubens and it was just getting daylight so we drove through the park in an open cab and the street lights went out and the birds started singing and it was cool and dewy and pretty heavenly. The evening I left we had dinner at "Twenty-one"—and a bottle of lovely wine—he had a car and drove me to the airport,—kissed me goodby—

Monday, January 15.

That was six months ago and it's still good—we write to each other often; about every two weeks—flowers and telegrams for Xmas and New Year's; once when Franklyn was away he called me long distance and we talked for half an hour—his last letter finished with "Think of me, my darling, because I certainly think of you. If it's lasted this long on both sides it must be something pretty good—too good to let drop."

STRANGE LOVE AFFAIR; LETTER DAMPENS ARDOR

September 17.

Tomorrow afternoon at 4:00 I leave Grand Central for N. Y., arriving there at 10:55 a. m. Wednesday. Staying at the Essex House and am very excited. Got a lot of new clothes (can't be bothered to shop when I'm there—it takes too much time). It will be six months since I've seen George—what a strange love affair! I can't say it's very satisfactory. He is rehearsing "Merrily" and I will be there for the opening which is second best—how I would love to have been in it. Oh dear, everything in my life seems to go off half-cocked—maybe I expect too much. George's letter, always friendly, always unexciting, dampens my ardor a bit.

At any rate it will be nice to be beau-ed around to theaters

(CONTINUED ON PAGE FIVE)

JAM COURT FOR ASTOR HEARING

The Mary Astor-Dr. Franklyn Thorpe court fight over custody of their 4-year-old daughter Marylyn was reopened today after a week's interim during which strenuous efforts were made to reach a settlement out of court.

Long before the session started the courtroom of Superior Judge Goodwin J. Knight was jammed with curious fans eager to listen to the cross-examination of Miss Astor by Joseph Anderson, counsel for Dr. Thorpe.

Anderson said he would base his cross-examination on more information obtained from the diary kept by the star in which she is said to have mentioned a dozen or more well known screen figures.

KAUFMAN LEAVES, REPORT

It was reported today that George S. Kaufman, playwright, had left the city rather than answer the subpoena served on him at Catalina nearly 10 days ago, following the introduction of his name into the record of the case as a close friend of Miss Astor.

Will H. Hays, "czar" of the motion picture industry, is said to have been exerting the influence of his official position at the behest of leading film executives in an attempt to arrange a settlement out of court.

Judge Knight was quoted prior to the opening of court today as saying that he will permit the introduction of "pertinent" portions of Miss Astor's diary into evidence as bearing relevantly on her fit-

(CONTINUED ON PAGE FIVE)

Herald-Express Special Features

Fair Weather for Southland; High Humidity Expected

With Southern California still under the influence of a tropical air mass stirred up by last week's Mexican hurricane, fair weather was predicted today, but the humidity was expected to continue high.

Temperature here yesterday was 83 degrees, and it was 67 this morning. Hotter was Yuma with 102, and Imperial with 100. Scattered showers fell in various parts of the state, 02 in Los Angeles, .03 on Mt. Wilson and 30 of an inch at Santa Barbara.

Other thunderstorms fell in Arizona and New Mexico.

—Vote American—

Gen. Cortina New Governor of Lower California District

By Associated Press

MEXICO CITY, Aug. 10.—President Lazaro Cardenas today appointed Gen. Rafael Navarro Cortina governor of the northern district of Lower California, succeeding Gen. Gabriel Gavira, resigned.

General Cortina formerly was commander of the military garrison in Mexico City.

—Vote American—

Liquor Shares in Spurt That Rallies N. Y. Stock Mart

By International News Service

NEW YORK, Aug. 10.—An upward spurt in liquor shares rallied stocks today after an advance into new high ground had been temporarily halted.

Southern Pacific and Union Pacific reached new highs for the year.

United States Steel and Bethlehem converted small losses into modest gains.

In coppers, Kennecott advanced a point to a new top at 47. Anaconda also hit a new high.

NETHERLANDS GIRL WINS SWIM TITLE

BERLIN, Aug. 10.—America trailed in both the men's and women's swimming meets today in the unofficial score based on a count of 10-5-4-3-2-1. Score in the men's events was: Japan 12, Hungary 10, Germany 2, United States 1. In the women's events the score stood: Holland 15, Argentina 5, Germany 4, United States 1. America dominated the track and field competition, which ended yesterday, with a final score of 203, followed by Finland 80¼, Germany 69¾, Japan 51 13-22 and Great Britain 43 1-11.

BERLIN, Aug. 10.—Rita Mastenbroek of Holland won the Olympic Women's 100-meter free style swimming championship today as Janet Campbell of Argentina captured runner-up honors.

The German girl, Miss Arendt, led Miss Mastenbroek by almost a length at halfway mark, and then the Dutch star and Miss Campbell cought her 20 meters from home and fought it out between them, with Miss Mastenbroek hitting the finish line inches in front. Miss Arendt was third.

YANKS LOSE POLO

Meanwhile the United States water polo team was eliminated from further competition by losing its second start of the Olympic competition to Belgium, 4 to 3. The Yankee team, composed

(CONTINUED ON PAGE THIRTEEN)

Olympic Games Results

By Associated Press

BERLIN, Aug. 10.—Today's Olympic swimming summaries:

WOMEN'S 100-METER FREE STYLE FINAL—Mastenbroek, Holland, first, 1:05.9 (new Olympic record); Campbell, Argentina, second, 1:06.4; Arendt, Germany, third, 1:06.6; Denouden, Holland, fourth, 1:07.6; Wagner, Holland, fifth, 1:08.1; Olive McKean, United States, sixth, 1:08.4; Katherine Rawls, United States, seventh, 1:08.7.

800-METER RELAY (first two in each heat and the two fastest thirds qualify for tomorrow's final).

FIRST HEAT—Won by France (Paris, Nakache, Cavalero, Einer), 9:21.7; second, Canada, 9:40; third, Brazil, 9:42.5; fourth, Philippines, 9:45.8; fifth, Bermuda; sixth, Greece.

SECOND HEAT—Won by United States (Charles Nutter, Ralph Gilman, Paul Wolf, Jack Medica), 9:10.4; second, Hungary, 9:20.8; third, Great Britain, 9:30.8; fourth, Denmark, 9:39.6; fifth, Austria, 9:58.4. (Poland finished fifth, but disqualified for beating gun.)

THIRD HEAT—Won by Japan (Yusa, Sugiura, Taguchi, Arai), 8:56.1, (betters former Olympic record, 8:58.4, made by

(CONTINUED ON PAGE FIFTEEN)

Here's Line of March In Veterans' Parade

Here is the line of march and the list of organizations participating in the mammoth American Legion parade, beginning at 2 p. m. today in Hollywood as contained in orders issued by Brig.-Gen. Henry H. Arnold, grand marshal:

LINE OF MARCH

The line of march is as follows: from Hollywood boulevard and Vine street, west along Hollywood boulevard to La Brea avenue; south on La Brea avenue to Sunset boulevard; east on Sunset boulevard into disbandment area, east of Vine street.

REVIEWING STAND

The parade will be reviewed by Governor Frank F. Merriam. The reviewing stand is located on the south side of Sunset boulevard at Wilcox avenue.

ORDER OF MARCH

Motorcycle police escort, Chief James E. Davis, commanding.

Grand marshal, Brig. Gen. Henry H. Arnold, U. S. Army, and staff.

Sheriff's mounted posse escort, Sheriff Eugene Biscailuz, commanding.

Distinguished guests.

(a)—HEADQUARTERS DIVISION—Lieut. Col. John C. French, U. S. A., retired, commanding.

(1)—Sixty-third U. S. Coast artillery regiment (AA), Lieut. Col. R. Duncan Brown, U. S. A., commanding.

(2)—160th Infantry, California National Guard, Col. Harcourt Hervey, U. S., N. G., commanding.

(3)—Naval Militia, Lieut. Commander L. F. Brown, U. S. N. R., commanding.

(b)—DIVISION NO. 1: Willard Stewart, marshal.

(1)—San Gabriel post drum and bugle corps—national champions.

(2)—Massed colors, department sergeant of arms, William K. Krietz, commanding.

(3)—Hollywood post mounted patrol escort, Walter Long, commanding.

(4)—Department Commander Dan Emmett and staff.

(5)—Mounted auxiliary troop escort, Margaret Kaedig, commanding.

(6)—Department auxiliary president, Ethel Marsh, and staff.

(7)—Grand Chef de Gare, 40 et 8, Tom S. Estabrook, and staff.

(8)—Le Chapeau, 8 et 40, Bessie Cooper and staff.

(9)—Districts 3 and 4.

(c)—DIVISION NO. 2—William B. Nash, marshal.
Districts 12, 8 and 5.

(d)—DIVISION NO. 3—Bob Ryan, marshal.

(1)—Districts 6 and 11.

(2)—Los Angeles Police post band—state champions.

(3)—Districts 17, 2 and 19.

(e)—DIVISION NO. 4—Ivan Deputy, marshal.
Boy Scouts units.

(f)—DIVISION NO. 5—Warren Dunnell, marshal.
Districts 20, 1, 21, 22 and 18.

(g)—DIVISION NO. 6—E. M. Streeter, marshal.
Districts 15, 7, 16, 9 and 14.

(h)—DIVISION NO. 7—Walter Harrison, marshal.

(1)—Districts 10, 13 and 23.

(2)—Massed combat division flags.

(3)—District 24.

Pope Sends Protest to Spain Over Priest Murders by Reds

By United Press

VATICAN CITY, Aug. 10.—The Holy See protested energetically to the Madrid government today against the slaying of priests, the ejection of nuns from hospitals, the burning of churches and "the profanation of bodies" during the Spanish civil war. The Vatican's note asked the Madrid government to intervene and terminat "excesses," or at least to deplore publicly the "sacrileges."

By United Press

HENDAYE, French-Spanish Frontier, Aug. 10.—Two hundred picked loyalist miners hurled dynamite from a catapult today into the army barracks at Oviedo, which Spanish rebels have been holding for three weeks against fierce attack.

Walls of the barracks were reported crumbling and on fire.

The miners from the Asturias district resumed the attack at dawn in co-operation with loyal troops.

Two hundred of the miners, picked as expert dynamite men, were detailed to man a catapult which the Loyalists built. During

(CONTINUED ON PAGE FOUR)

50,000 VE IN COLORF TEN-MIL PAGEAN

Hollywood was the mec 300,000 Southern Califo today as they trekked t motion picture capital to the parade of 50,000 Worl veterans who will part in the huge American California convention n pageant.

At the same time the conve first business session swun action in the huge conventic in Warner Bros.' Sunset bou studio, at which nominatio department officers will be including the post of comm vice commander at large, ch and sergeant-at-arms.

TEN-MILE PARADE

Meanwhile more than a sc resolutions dealing with d tions against Communism, n defense, veterans' welfare child welfare were in the ha the various committees of th vention.

The parade will start at 2

The big parade of forme vice men, representaative women's auxiliaries and ch will be more than 10 miles and will form in side streets vicinity of Hollywood boul and Vine street.

More than forty floats, which will be from the host c zation, Hollywood Post o American Legion, depicting canism, rehabilitation, comm welfare, junior activities, reli the poppy float, will be in th of march.

PLANES TO CIRCLE CRO

Airplane squadrons from army and navy will circle ov line of march, and in the will be the entire 160th In regiment, Los Angeles' own tional Guard outfit, while Sixty-third Coast artillery re

(CONTINUED ON PAGE SIX

She Married Her Boss for the Advantages He Offered Her

Hardened and grasping, se ing money and position, stood silent while her e ployer divorced his wife marry her. But she refu to give him the family a domesticity he craved.

NOW SHE REGRETS I

Read why in this girl's let today in the Beatrice Fair column on Page A-8 of t newspaper.

Death of a U-Boat—Dramatic Story in Pictures See Page 1, Part 2

LESLIE HOWARD LOST; NAZIS DOWN AIRLINER

Only Los Angeles Newspaper With All Leading News Services—Associated Press, International News, United Press, Dow-Jones

LOS ANGELES EVENING HERALD AND EXPRESS

NIGHT FINAL

HERALD-EXPRESS PHONE Richmond 4141

HERALD-EXPRESS BUILDING 1243 Trenton Street

Registered United States Patent Office
The Evening Herald and Express Grows Just Like Los Angeles

HERALD-EXPRESS PHONE Richmond 4141

VOL. LXXIII Two Sections Section A WEDNESDAY, JUNE 2, 1943 H★ NO. 58

—International News Sound Photo

Damage inflicted on a marauding Nazi U-boat in a mid-Atlantic sea battle is shown in this photo. Arrows indicate points where terrific depth charges and hot gun fire from the deck of the Coast Guard Cutter Spencer crippled the sub and finally sent it plunging to the bottom. See Page 1, Part 2 for full page of pictures on sub's death fight with United States warship.

COAL STRIKE TO FDR

U. S. SHIP SINKS NAZI U-BOAT IN DRAMATIC FIGHT

By WATSON FENIMORE
International News Service Staff Correspondent

WASHINGTON, June 2.—The Navy today described a ramatic sea engagement between an American Coast uard cutter and a German U-boat in mid-Atlantic in which he undersea craft was destroyed by withering, point-blank unfire. More than 40 men aboard the raider were captured.

The victory was credited to the oast Guard cutter Spencer and s veteran crew. The incident ccurred "several weeks ago" hile the cutter was helping uard an important United Naons convoy.

Sound Operator Harold V. Anerson, 24, of Kewanee, Ill., deected the U-boat lurking just beeath the surface in the path of huge convoy.

'BOMBED' TO SURFACE

Wheeling into action, the Spener blasted the raider to the surace with depth charges and then aked the U-boat from stem to ern with cannon and machine un fire. Coast Guard Photographer Jack January of St. Louis, Io., described the opening action s follows:

Suddenly, Nazi heads began to ppear at the conning tower of he sub and the first man out warmed toward the U-boat's hree deck guns. By that time our machine guns and cannon vere on the beam, and they nocked off Germans like so nany clay pigeons."

The Spencer, a heavily-armed, 27-foot craft, was in charge of omdr. Harold S. Berdine, 41, of taten Island, N. Y. It also

(Continued on Page 11, Column 5)

Today's Baseball

(For stories of today's baseball games, see Page A-17.)

COAST LEAGUE

At Gilmore Field— R. H. E.
Seattle .....0 0 0 0 1 0 1 0 2—4 9 2
Hollywood ...0 0 5 0 0 0 2 2 *—9 15 1
Batteries—Elliott, Molitor and Sueme; Smith and Brenzel.

At Sacramento (first game) R. H. E.
Los Angeles..0 1 0
Sacramento .1 0 0
Batteries—Lynn and Holm; Pintar and Peterson.

San Francisco at San Diego, twilight game.

AMERICAN LEAGUE

At Boston—1st game, 12 innings R. H. E.
St. Louis .. 0 0 0 3 1 0 0 0 0 0 0 3—7 14 0
Boston..... 3 0 0 0 0 1 0 0 0 0 0 0—4 7 1
Batteries—Hollingsworth, Caster and Hayes; Dobson, Ryba and Partee.
Winning pitcher—Caster. Losing pitcher—Dobson.

At Boston (second game)— R. H. E.
St. Louis.... 2 0 0
Boston..... 2 0 0
Batteries—Ostermueller, Galehouse and Ferrell; Terry and Peacock.
NCleveland at Washington, night game.

At New York— R. H. E.
Chicago..... 0 0 0 0 0 0 0 1 1—2 8 0
New York... 0 0 0 0 1 0 0 0 0—1 5 2
Batteries—Wade and Tresh; Borowy and Hemsley.

At Philadelphia— R. H. E.
Detroit ......0 0 0 4 0 1 0 2 0—7 14 0
Philadelphia 0 0 1 0 0 0 0 0 1—2 5 2
Batteries—Overmire and Parsons; L. Harris, Clyde, Kyczynski and Wagner.

NATIONAL LEAGUE

At Cincinnati— R. H. E.
New York...1 4 0 0 0 0 0 1 0—6 11 3
Cincinnati 1 2 4 4 0 1 0 1 *—13 18 2
Batteries—Feldman, Lohrman, Coombs, Adams, Sayles and Lombardi; Walters, Shoun and Lakeman.

At Chicago— R. H. E.
Philadelphia 1 0 1 2
Chicago 0 0 0 0
Batteries—Rowe and Livingston; Passeau and Hernandez.
Brooklyn at St. Louis, night game.
Boston at Pittsburgh, night game.

Warships Shell Italy Isle

By DANIEL DE LUCE
Associated Press Staff Correspondent

ALLIED HEADQUARTERS IN NORTH AFRICA, June 2.—British warships in their second bombardment of Pantelleria in less than 48 hours yesterday heavily shelled the harbor area, barracks and batteries of the Italian island, it was announced today.

United States Flying Fortresses joined the air offensive against the battered island 45 miles off the Tunisian coast while other American attacks were made on the islands of Sicily and Sardinia.

The warships blasted Pantelleria Sunday night and then returned yesterday afternoon, an Allied headquarters communique announced, to carry out a heavy shelling without loss although there was some retaliatory fire from the shore.

The communique's announcement of the bombardment said:

"The island of Pantelleria was successfully bombarded by naval surface forces on the night of May 30-31. There was no effective opposition and our ships sustained no casualties or damage.

"Another successful bombardment of the island took place during the late afternoon of June 1. Hits were obtained on the barracks and battery areas. There was some retaliation from the shore, but our ships sustained no casualties."

The Italian fleet dispersed along the Italian west and east coasts appeared powerless to intervene against the British navy and no enemy air attacks against the warships were reported.

'Navy Bill' Ingram Dies

(For details see Page A-17.)

By Associated Press

LOS GATOS, Cal., June 2.—Major William A. "Navy Bill" Ingram, United States Marine Corps, former football coach at Annapolis Naval Academy and the University of California, died at his home here last night.

Bomber Lost

Newsman Is Saved by Being 3 Minutes Late

By EUGENE BURNS
Associated Press Staff Correspondent

A RAT ISLAND BASE, Alaska, May 15.—(Delayed)—While carrying food and supplies to fellow American soldiers fighting on Attu Island, First Lieut. A. N. Brannon and the crew of nine aboard his Liberator bomber failed to return to this base last night.

Lieutenant Brannon of Jackson, Miss., began carrying supplies on May 11 to American soldiers above the cloud lines on Attu.

Incidentally, I was scheduled to go on this flight to Attu yesterday—the mission from which he has not returned. I missed it by three minutes.

War Bonds

'Invest 25 Pct. by End Of 1943'—Morgenthau

By Associated Press

NEWARK, N. J., June 2.—Secretary of the Treasury Morgenthau, launching a streamline organization for war bond sales, said today the average American family should be investing one-fourth of its income in the bonds by the end of 1943.

Kill 1500 Attu Japs, Capture 4

By JOSEPH A. BORS
International News Service Staff Correspondent

WASHINGTON, June 2.—The Navy revealed today that the American reconquest of Attu Island in the Aleutians cost the Japanese 1500 dead and four captured during the first 20 days of fighting.

At the same time, the Navy said that American ground troops continued their "mopping up operations" against isolated Japanese forces on the tiny North Pacific Island.

News that 1500 Japs have been slain was the first over-all estimate from Washington of Japanese losses during the bitter fighting on the island. The total is expected to be much higher when all Japanese remnants are mopped up.

The Tokio radio recently estimated its force on the island at between 2000 and 3000 troops, but no such figure was given out by official quarters in Washington.

MAY BE MORE

The estimated 1500 dead indicated that many other enemy troops may be buried in the snow-filled passes and mountain ridges, since all organized Japanese resistance on the island has ended.

The fact that only four Japanese were captured testified to the hard fighting during the three weeks that followed the American invasion on May 11.

Although Japanese propaganda broadcasts have estimated Ameri

(Continued on Page 11, Column 1)

Herald-Express Special Features

Senate Passes Tax Bill

By Associated Press

WASHINGTON, June 2.—The Senate passed legislation today putting the nation's income taxpayers on a pay-as-you-go basis and sent it to the White House, with the expectation that it soon will become a law.

Final passage was on a vote of 62 to 19.

Reportedly headed for presidential acquiescence, either by Mr. Roosevelt's signature or his failure to veto it, the bill represents four months of congressional labor to put 44,000,000 income taxpayers on a current basis for the first time, by cancelling 75 to 100 per cent of their back levies.

O. K.'D BY HOUSE

The measure, approved by the House yesterday by a 256 to 114 vote, will be in the President's hands soon after its signature by presiding officers of the two houses.

There would be these practical results to the average taxpayer:

He will find himself for the first time in his life paying the federal taxes on his income as he earns it, either through a 20 per cent payroll levy which would go into effect July 1, or through quarterly installments made on the basis of his estimated net receipts for the year.

12½ PER CENT ADDED

He will find, in most instances, 12½ per cent added to the amount he expected to pay out this year in income taxes, plus an identical 12½ per cent the following year, but those extra bills won't be due until March 15 of 1944 and 1945.

He will find from 75 to 100 per cent of what he now owes in income taxes abated, but to him that will remain largely a bookkeeping operation until his income declines or until the second certainty—death—steps in. (He will never get any money back, just pay less at some future and uncertain date.)

He will have to pay his June 15 installment on last year's income just as if Congress had never considered changing the system that has existed since 1913.

(For how senators voted on tax bill, see Page A-10.)

Cut Women's Rayon Stockings Quota

WASHINGTON, June 2.—Manufacturers of rayon hosiery and other civilian products formerly made of silk and nylon were cut approximately one-sixth below their present quotas today by the War Production Board.

Summons Ickes, WLB To Meet

By International News Service

WASHINGTON, June 2.—President Roosevelt late today summoned the War Labor Board and Secretary of the Interior Harold Ickes to the White House for a conference in an effort to end the two-day-old strike in the nation's coal fields.

The conference was scheduled immediately with W. L. B. Chairman William H. Davis and six members of his board certain to attend.

Members of the board at the emergency meeting with Davis are Frank Graham, Wayne Morse and George H. Taylor, representing th epublic; Ruben Robertson, representing th eemployers; Van A. Bitner, representing the C.I.O., and Robert Watt, representing he A. F. L.t

White House Secretary Stephen T. Eearly said that the President had called Ickes and the W. L. B. to th esession and that coa "is the onl ysubject which would be discussed."

NELSON IN WARNING

Earlier, Donald M. Nelson, chairman of the War Production Board, warned that the coal strike would start shutting down vital war factories "i na day or two."

Early made the announcement of the White House conference after the W. L. B. referred the case to the White House for such action as the President "deems appropriate."

The W. L. B. also ordered John L. Lewis, president of the United Mine Workers' Union, and coal operators to halt their conferences to effect a truce in the two-day-old strike. While this action

(Continued on Page 6, Column 4)

Weather

Temperature in L. A. Down 10 Degrees

It cooled off 10 degrees yesterday.

The Weather Bureau disclosed today that yesterday's maximum temperature, recorded on the ground floor of its observatory, was 68 degrees, as compared with 78 the day before. Maximum readings on the roof of the station were 67 yesterday and 76 Monday.

Yesterday morning's minimum was 59, as compared with 59 on Monday.

Dim-out is effective from 8 p. m. tonight until 5:42 a. m. tomorrow.

Nazis Bag Howard Plane

(For story of Leslie Howard's work in filmland, see Page A-6. Pictures on Page A-3.)

By Associated Press

LONDON, June 2.—The British Overseas Airways Corp. announced tonight that one of its airliners, apparently attacked by enemy aircraft, was missing with 13 passengers and a crew of four between Lisbon and England. Unofficial reports said Leslie Howard, noted London and Hollywood actor, was one of the passengers.

Names of the passengers and details of the reported attack were not issued immediately.

The announcement said:

"The British Overseas Airways Corp. regrets to announce that a civil aircraft on passage between Lisbon and the United Kingdom is overdue and must be presumed lost.

"The last message received from the aircraft stated that it was being attacked by an enemy aircraft.

"The aircraft carried 13 passengers and a crew of four.

"Next of kin have been informed."

NEWSMAN ABOARD

Later the British Press Association quoted reliable sources as confirming that the actor was one of the passengers on the plane.

The plane left Lisbon yesterday morning and was due in England last evening.

Kenneth Stonehouse, former chief of bureau at Washington for Reuters News Agency, who was en route to London to take a new assignment, was said to be aboard the aircraft with Mrs. Stonehouse.

The report from Lisbon said the plane with its Dutch crew was shot down in the stormy Bay of Biscay about half way between Lisbon and England and hat concern was felt over weather reports which indicated it would have been difficult for the passengers to take to their rubber boats.

A Berlin broadcast, reporting from Lisbon that the plane was missing, said "it was feared it met with an accident."

Earlier the German communique reported that Nazi reconnaissance planes had shot down three Allied bombers and "one transport" over the Atlantic.

The Lisbon account said Alfred Chaenwall, a film director, and

(Continued on Page 6, Column 5)

EXTRA

Times Telephone Numbers
- **MAdison 5-2345** for all calls except those concerning classified advertising.
- **MAdison 9-4411** for all classified advertising calls.

Los Angeles Times

EQUAL RIGHTS

LIBERTY UNDER THE LAW   TRUE INDUSTRIAL FREEDOM

9 A.M. FINAL

VOL. LXXVI   IN FOUR PARTS   9   MONDAY MORNING, JANUARY 14, 1957   80 PAGES   DAILY 10c

HUMPHREY BOGART, 56. DEAD OF CANCER

L.A. Escapes With Minor Flood Loss

Illustrated on Page 3, Part I

The thirsty soil of Southern California apparently blotted up most of Saturday night's rain as fast as it fell and flood control officials were overjoyed when they had no floods to control.

The weatherman said there was a possibility of a few light showers near the mountains today and increasing cloudiness tomorrow.

Los Angeles had 2.05 inches of precipitation at the time showers ceased yesterday morning. This brought the

Rainfall figures on Page 2, Part I.

season's rainfall to 3.30 inches; last year, 2.84 inches. Mt. Wilson reported 2.97 inches, Burbank the same figure, Palos Verdes 1.45, Topanga Canyon 3.25, San Bernardino 1.50 and Santa Barbara 2.70.

Damage was most feared in the Malibu and Zuma Beach areas where the recent fires burned off the vegetation, but although nearly three inches of rain fell in the Topanga Canyon area and about half that much near Zuma Beach no bad slides were reported.

Constant Check Kept

Howard Earl, County Civil Defense Director, said the burned-over area in the Malibu and Zuma Beach districts is constantly being checked by civil defense and disaster crews and personnel and heavy equipment are on constant alert basis to handle any emergency which may arise from additional rain.

The ground appears to have been well saturated by the water and more rain might create a serious condition, Earl warned. He said four helicopters are taking off as frequently as possible with 300-pound loads of rye seed

Turn to Page 4, Column 4

FEATURES INDEX

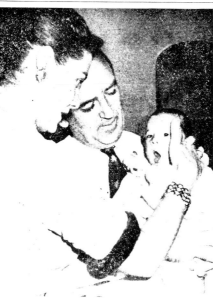

M'CARTHY A PARENT—Five-week-old Tierney Elizabeth McCarthy isn't too impressed with being center of attraction as she yawns while parents, Sen. and Mrs. Joseph McCarthy, admire her. She was adopted in New York, taken to Washington. *Story on Page 7, Part I.*

Parker Compares Novel With McDonald Story

Striking Similarities Don't Prove Anything, Chief Says; Variations in Account Studied

Police Chief William H. Parker took advantage of a gloomy Sunday to finish reading "The Fuzzy Pink Nightgown," a kidnap novel found in the Encino home of Marie McDonald, and among the fictionalized incidents he thought similar to the actress' own spectacular account was this:

The pair of hoods who in . . . as well as differences in the book abduct a movie actress send out to a delicatessen for turkey sandwiches.

The Police Chief previously indicated things have come to "the lie detector stage," but whether the actress, back in seclusion since failing Saturday to identify a private detective who fit her description of the younger of her kidnapers, will willingly submit to the polygraph remains to be seen.

She has hinted she would not be averse to such a test, but Atty. Jerry Giesler takes

Parker said he will confer with detectives today to decide the next move in the continuing inquiry into The Body's disappearance and subsequent reappearance a week ago last Friday.

Lie-Detector Test

"We're at the point now," Parker said, "of trying to compile a specific list of variations between Miss McDonald's version when she was questioned in the hospital at Indio and the version she gave before police movie cameras during her re-enactment.

Turn to Page 4, Column 2

Burglar Alarm Traps Man in H'wood Church

A 29-year-old transient was trapped in the pastor's office of the Hollywood Presbyterian Church last night when he set off a burglar alarm by breaking a pane of glass in a door, Hollywood Division police reported.

Sgt. C. A. Nicholl answered the burglar alarm with several radio car crews. Sgt. Nicholl said Rodman Archer was found hiding behind a desk in the office of Dr. Raymond Lindquist.

Before Archer was booked at Hollywood Station Jail on suspicion of burglary, he assertedly told police he entered the church when it still was open yesterday and remained after it was locked up for the night.

THE WEATHER

U.S. Weather Bureau forecast: Variable cloudiness today with the chance of a few light showers, mostly near the mountains. Increasing cloudiness tomorrow. Temperatures about the same. High today about 64.

Youth Corps Bus Crash Injures 26

By a Times Correspondent

IDYLLWILD, Jan. 13 — Twenty-six persons, most of them teen-agers, were injured today when a private bus returning them to Los Angeles from a James Cadet Corps retreat crashed into a tree on Circle Drive here.

The California Highway Patrol said eight injured were taken to Hemet Community Hospital, 18 were treated at the scene by a private physician, and two other passengers escaped unhurt.

Reaches for Board

The CHP officers said the bus was driven by Salvation Army Maj. Bramwell Glaeser, 44, of 3334 W 119th St., Inglewood. Patrolmen quoted Glaeser as saying the crash occurred when a clipboard with his list of passengers fell to the floor of the bus and he bent to retrieve it. Glaeser received chest injuries.

Injured Named

Hemet Community Hospital officials said they also treated the following victims: Mrs. Victoria Nottle, 56, and her son, William, 15, of 8132 Virginia Ave., South Gate; Donald McDougald, 19, of 1904 Compton Ave., Redondo Beach; James Watt, 12, of 1603 W 85th St.; Sandra Patton, 17, of 740 Glasgow Ave., Inglewood; Judy O'Dell, 16, of 13301 Tiller Ave., Orange, and Joseph Millington, 14, of 717 S Essey Ave., Compton.

Doctor Assists

Summoned by the Highway Patrol, Dr. H. G. Cleary of Hemet administered first aid at the crash scene to the other 18 injured.

Young McDougald was said to have sustained the most extensive injuries, severe lacerations of the face and scalp when his head struck the windshield.

300 Flee Fire in Alaska in Subzero Cold

FAIRBANKS, Alaska, Jan. 13 — A fire in this city's largest apartment building killed one person, injured 14 others and forced more than 300 men, women and children to flee into 15-below-zero weather today.

Trapped by smoke that swirled through the nine-story Northward Building, some tenants leaped into nets to safety.

DIES OF CANCER—Veteran Screen Actor Humphrey Bogart died early today, victim of cancer. He was 56.

IKE BEGINS TOUR OF DROUGHT AREAS

Eisenhower Flies Into Texas on First Leg of Southern Great Plains Inspection

Illustrated on Page 12, Part I

SAN ANGELO, Tex., Jan. 13 — President Eisenhower flew into Texas tonight on the first leg of a 4500-mile tour of the drought-hit Southern Great Plains.

The President, flanked by Secretary of Interior Seaton and Secretary of Agriculture Benson, was greeted by Texas Gov. Shivers at the Goodfellow Air Force Base. A crowd estimated at 7000 to 10,000 cheered the President's arrival.

The President halted briefly after emerging from his plane, the Columbine III, while the air base band played "Hail to the Chief." Then, smiling and waving, he walked down the landing ramp and posed with Seaton and Benson for photographers. Benson was slow in getting into line for the picture.

Rapid Inspection

"Ezra, Ezra," called the President, "come here and get your picture taken."

The President was driven immediately to the Officers' Club, where he retired for the night.

Early tomorrow he will begin a series of ground and aerial inspection tours which will take him to Oklahoma, New Mexico and Arizona.

After leaving San Angelo,

the President will fly to West Woodward, Okla., near the Panhandle, for another inspection, and then proceed to Clovis, N.M., and Tucson, Ariz.

From Arizona, President Eisenhower will go to Pueblo, Colo., and Garden City, Kan., ending his tour at Wichita, Kan.

Before flying back to the capital, the President will confer at Wichita with farmers, ranchers and officials from 15 Midwest and Southwest States.

Maintained Optimism Until End

Humphrey Bogart, 56, one of Hollywood's most famous names, died at 2:10 a.m. today of cancer.

The veteran character actor, an Academy Award winner in 1951, lapsed into a coma yesterday from which he never revived, his physician, Dr. Maynard B. Bandsmag, said.

Operated on last March for cancer of the esophagus, Bogart still was optimistic about his illness as late as Saturday night, Dr. Bandsmag said death was due to a general spread of the original cancer.

Steadily Weaker

Bogart had grown steadily weaker in recent months and for the final few weeks had been in some pain. However, a nerve tissue operation had relieved the pain somewhat.

The actor's wife, Actress Lauren Bacall, was at Bogart's side when he died. She asked that no photographers visit the house this morning and said she wanted their two children, Stephen, 8, and Leslie, 4, to leave for school as usual.

Pungent Retorts

In recent weeks, Bogart from time to time had been besieged with requests to confirm or deny reports that his malignancy was making deadly inroads upon his system.

With the typical jocularity that had come to be associated with him in facing the press or the public under trying conditions, he

Turn to Page 2, Column 4

LAST-MINUTE NEWS

EX-SEN. C. WAYLAND BROOKS DIES

CHICAGO, Jan. 14 (Monday) (AP) — Former Illinois Sen. C. Wayland Brooks died as the result of a heart attack early today in Passavant Hospital. He was 59. He entered the hospital Jan. 8. Brooks served as Senator from 1940 until 1948, when he was defeated by Sen. Paul Douglas (D) Ill. He was elected to serve the unfinished term of the late Sen. James Hamilton Lewis (D) Ill. He was a leader in the Illinois Republican Party since 1932.

Ship Rides Out Storm

HONOLULU, Jan. 13 (AP) — The freighter SS Charles F. Dant of Portland, Or., docked here tonight after riding out a severe Pacific storm that turned its cargo of gold-copper concentrates into a slosh mess below-decks.

EXTRA

The Weather
WARMER—Sunny and warmer today with high near 68. No eye irritation. Chance of rain this week end.

LOS ANGELES EVENING
MIRROR NEWS

LATE NEWS
RACING

Vol. XI—No. 88 | Largest Afternoon Home Delivery in the West | In Four Parts | WEDNESDAY, JANUARY 21, 1959 | PART I | 1★ | MA 5-2311—145 S. Spring, Los Angeles 53—TEN CENTS

CECIL B. DE MILLE DIES: HEART FAILS

High Wages Hurt Movies ---Goldwyn

Samuel Goldwyn sounded a sharp and ominous warning to his fellow producers and studio chieftains as he accepted a Screen Producers Guild Milestone Award at its annual awards dinner last night at the Beverly Hilton.

"Conditions in the film industry today are worse than I have ever known them in the 47 years I have been connected with motion pictures," he declared in blasting what he called excessive salary demands of stars, writers and directors.

Goldwyn made it clear that he was talking about conditions under which pictures are made today rather than a decline in theater attendance.

Audience Remains

"For although box-office receipts have dropped off about 20% from their high in 1947, there is still a great audience for good pictures," Goldwyn declared.

Decrying the high salary demands of stars at $500,000, $750,000 and $1 million for pictures plus a share of the gross or of the profits, Goldwyn flatly blamed the studio management and producers.

"I can't really blame art-

Turn to Page 12, Column 2

Break Due in Tie-up of Markets

BY DON HARRIS
Staff Labor Writer

A major break in the 21-day-old grocery industry dispute appeared imminent today.

And the indications were that a settlement may come quickly — if joint negotiations are resumed today as expected.

Joseph T. DeSilva, chief spokesman for the Retail Clerks Union, gave the tip-off last night at a press conference when he unveiled the latest revised union contract proposal.

It called for a 66.8-cent hourly wage package, including fringe benefits, spread over a five-year contract, plus a cost-of-living escalator clause.

Basis for Negotiations

Robert K. Fox, Food Employers Council president, although assailing the proposal as "still exorbitant," immediately conceded that it furnished a "basis for resumption of negotiations."

And State Conciliator Merle Wissler, who has been working around the clock with both sides since joint talks broke off Jan. 9, said he hoped that joint negotiations could be reopened today.

Officially, the employers are still sticking to their offer of a 50-cent hourly

Turn to Page 12, Column 1

Atlas Death Due Today

CAMBRIDGE, Mass., Jan. 21 (AP) — Atlas, the American satellite which broadcast President Eisenhower's Christmas message of peace to the world, was expected to plunge to its fiery death today.

The plunge was expected to take place in the vicinity of the Hawaiian Islands.

Atlas, the 4½-ton rocket, was America's biggest artificial moon. It completed just under 500 trips around the earth since it was launched from Cape Canaveral, Fla., Dec. 18.

CAL. LAWMAKERS SLAP WORK LOSS

WASHINGTON, Jan. 21 (AP) The California congressional delegation has united behind a move to assure the State a fair share of defense contracts.

Rep. John F. Shelley (D) sounded a warning yesterday that the state of Washington is moving in on naval facilities in the San Francisco Bay region, and getting military supply operations from California.

Rep. Donald Jackson (R) said the Douglas Aircraft Co. had been reduced from third to 37th in the number of military aircraft contracts, with a resultant increase in unemployment in the Los Angeles area.

The delegation heard the reports at its organization meeting, in which Rep. Harry R. Sheppard (D) was elected chairman, succeeding Rep. Gordon McDonough (R).

Rep. J. Arthur Younger (R) was elected vice-chairman and Rep. Jeffery Cohelan (D), secretary.

The delegation authorized the appointment of a committee to investigate reports that California aircraft industries are losing defense contracts to other states and to Canada.

Engines Fail on Mikoyan Airliner

ARGENTIA, N.F., Jan. 21 (AP) — Anastas Mikoyan spent an unexpected night at the U.S. naval air base in Newfoundland after the Scandinavian airliner carrying the Soviet deputy premier homeward was forced down with two engines out.

Mikoyan — apparently unshaken by the mishap which set nerves jangling in more than one world capital—was to board another plane today to resume his flight to Copenhagen.

He ended his 16-day visit to the United States yesterday and started home with a party of five, including his son Sergo.

Sabotage Discounted

A Scandinavian airline spokesman in New York expressed doubt that sabotage lay behind the mishap last night while the four-engine DC7 was high over the Atlantic. There were 35 passengers and 14 crew members aboard.

The spokesman said the plane had been under close guard after it arrived at Idlewild yesterday and that New York police had inspected it thoroughly before its departure.

The airline ordered a plane from Copenhagen to Newfoundland to pick up the stranded passengers.

The pilot, Capt. Carl Schulzberg, reported that he found a defective supercharger on No. 4 engine while 108 miles from Gander, N.F., his scheduled stopping point.

"While we were trying to adjust this mechanical condition, a fire broke out in engine No. 1 which lasted five or six seconds," he said.

Argentia was the nearest alternate airport.

CECIL B. DE MILLE

Storm Kills 12; More Snow Due

KANSAS CITY, Jan. 21 (AP) A giant storm lashed the nation with snow, freezing rain, bitter cold and even thundershowers in the South as it crept across the midcontinent today.

The storm area stretched from Northern New Mexico to Cape Cod on the coast of New England and from the southern Great Lakes into the Mississippi Valley.

As it moved northeastward today, it dealt its harshest blows to the Midwest — Kansas, Missouri, Iowa, Nebraska and Illinois. Southern Michigan appeared next in line.

12 Die in Storm Traffic

Twelve deaths have been attributed to the storm. All of the victims were killed in traffic accidents on ice or snow-covered roads.

Three were killed in New Mexico. Montana, Pennsylvania and Iowa each reported two deaths, and Oklahoma, Kansas and Illinois had one each.

In a special summary this morning, the Weather Bureau said the storm took the form of snow, cold and high winds, that kicked up blizzard conditions in Nebraska, Iowa and the flatlands of central Kansas.

Freezing Rain Falls

Immediately ahead of the snow, there was a narrow band of freezing rain. And in the south, thundershowers accompanied spring-like temperatures.

There was even a tornado last night in Mississippi. The funnel touched the ground near Vicksburg, but apparently did no damage.

The heaviest snowfall this morning was in Eastern Kansas and Northern Missouri. Kansas City lay in the center of the area.

More Snow Expected

Parts of New Mexico, Colorado, Wyoming, Oklahoma, Nebraska and Iowa still were getting snow. The northern three-quarters of Illinois had 6 or more inches on the ground — with more expected.

And Southern Michigan, still digging out of a heavy snow yesterday, braced itself for more of the same, perhaps as much as 6 inches.

The Weather Bureau forecast continued heavy snow today from Northeastern Kansas through Iowa and into the Great Lakes region.

Generally, snow depths ranged from five to eight inches, with a high of 12 inches at Douglas, Wyo. Temperatures in the southern part of the snow area were in the teens, but reached five to 10 below zero from the upper Mississippi Valley westward through the northern plains.

MIRROR NEWS INDEX

Hollywood's Greatest Career Ends at 77

Cecil B. De Mille, 77, greatest of Hollywood's producer-directors, died today of a sudden heart attack at his home.

The film industry was stunned by the death of the autocratic, legendary executive, whose early extravaganzas gave meaning to the "colossal, stupendous" descriptive terms now common to movies.

De Mille was noted for his films on religious themes, which reportedly have grossed a total of more than $750 million over the world since 1925.

He suffered a near-fatal heart attack while filming "The Ten Commandments" in Egypt several years ago, but insisted on finishing the film.

Famous as Starmaker, Showman

Known as a starmaker, De Mille had skyrocketed some of the greatest names in Hollywood into marquee lights.

De Mille had directed more than 70 films, and exhibitors' reports said only two lost money. No other director approached his record.

Funeral arrangements are pending.

De Mille was born Aug. 12, 1881, the son of a playwright.

From Colonial Family

He came of an old colonial family. His first American ancestor came to this country in 1658. The De Mille family later settled in North Carolina in 1820.

His home was at 2010 De Mille Dr., near Griffith Park.

Some of his famous screen credits were for "The King of Kings," a story of the life of Jesus; two versions of "The Ten Commandments," the story of Moses; "The Sign of the Cross," "Samson and Delilah," "Union Pacific," and scores of other "colossals."

5 Billion View Works

Paramount Pictures, with which he was long affiliated, said his productions had been seen by more than 5 billion people, twice the earth's population.

Evangelist Billy Graham called De Mille "a prophet in celluloid who has had the privilege of bringing the Word of God to more people throughout the world than any other man."

De Mille was one of the pioneers of the film industry, and expanded the sweeping concepts of D. W. Griffith in the use of vast crowds of extras to give authenticity to his works.

The great director had been in failing health for a year.

He was in a hospital last fall for an intestinal ailment.

He had been ill for a week before his death, but the heart attack today was unexpected.

Daughter at Bedside

His daughter, Cecilia, and her husband, Joseph Harper, were with him when he died.

De Mille's brother William, also a famed director, died in 1955.

De Mille's father, William Sr., had studied for the ministry, but later formed a theater partnership with David Belasco. The De Mille boys grew up in the theater atmosphere.

Started on N.Y. Stage

De Mille started his career as an actor. He had a successful career on the New York stage, playing in "The Warrens of Virginia," "The Prince Chap" and other hits before he came to Hollywood with the early migration of stage stars to filmland.

His real career began, however, when he took up the megaphone and puttees that marked the early day Hollywood director.

De Mille married Constance Adams, daughter of a New Jersey judge, while touring with E. H. Sothern in 1902. They had four children, two sons and two daughters.

GOLD HOAX

Texan Admits Big Lie

DALLAS, Tex., Jan. 21 (AP) D. E. Jones' 86 bars of gold were just plain bull — not bullion — the U.S. Secret Service said today.

Jones, 38-year-old father of eight children, told Secret Service officers yesterday, "There wasn't any gold." He had just flunked a lie detector test.

Forrest V. Sorrels, agent in charge of the Dallas office of Secret Service, said Jones made the admission.

Told of Rich Cache

Earlier, the Corsicana, Tex., filling station attendant said he found the multi-million-dollar cache in East Texas while picking berries.

But the idea of the tale started last summer, he said, "while the boys were sitting around the filling station talking about buried gold."

A farmer thought gold was buried on his farm.

Jones' curiosity was aroused so he went to a banker to find out what to do if he found the gold.

The banker sent him to a lawyer. With 7 cents in his pocket, Jones went to an attorney and signed a contract.

People started bothering Jones for a cut in his "discovery," he said, so Jones moved to Corsicana and the filling station job.

Last week Jones started telling the story again. The Secret Service stepped in and yesterday Jones pointed to a gold-filled tooth.

"More gold here than I found," he said.

RAIN HERE SEEN IN DISTANT STORM

There's a chance of rain this week end, says the weatherman.

His five-day forecast calls for possible showers over the entire Southland from a weather front moving southeast from a position 1,500 miles off the Oregon coast.

Northerly winds up to 40 m.p.h. swept mountain and foothill areas during the night, but will subside today.

The forecast is for sunny, smog-free skies with a high of 68.

200 YEARS OF AMERICAN SPORTS

During the Colonial Period sports, as they have come to be played in more modern times, hardly existed. The colonists were generally of a class which had not engaged in game playing in Europe—such activities were usually the province of the aristocracy—and most of their time was taken up with creating a new life for themselves which did not include sports of any kind. The lack of recreation was much more prevalent in the New England colonies than in the South. The southern colonies, because of the greater reliance upon slave labor, devoted a great deal of time to such activities as horse racing, boat racing, cricket (an English game brought over intact by the more aristocratic Southern settlers) and cock fighting. Most of the games played in the South were of such a nature that gambling soon became a large part of the sports scene in the warmer climates of the colonies.

Journals existing from as early as 1820 indicate that crowds for horse races, regattas, and foot races often exceeded 20,000 spectators, and as the towns slowly grew into cities, the number of people who became more interested in watching sporting events, rather than participating in them, also grew. Most of the contests were patterned on their European counterparts, and included such new world touches as racoon fighting in pits, bear baiting (although common in Europe the colonists added to the spectacle by putting several bears in the same pit at the same time) and contests of strength between men and alligators.

Perhaps the first recognizable game played in North America was Lacrosse. Originally an Indian game (the Indians referred to it as *baggataway*), Lacrosse in the early years of the republic was a rough and wide-open game generally played on a massive field with numerous players on each side. Although the colonists refined Lacrosse by adding rules and a definite playing time, it remained a bloody and

Jim Thorpe, perhaps America's greatest athlete, was named to the All-American team three times, and was selected by football writers as the greatest football player for the first half of the twentieth century.

dangerous game for several years. The first recorded game of Lacrosse played by the colonists under their rules occurred in 1611, and the brutality of the contest so angered the colonial governor that he threatened to put the players in jail for mayhem.

Meanwhile in New England the Puritanical life precluded much sporting activity, and a number of laws were already in existence in 1628 which made the playing of most games, wagering, and engaging in sport on the Sabboth a crime. The Dutch settlers in New York, however, labored under no such social views, and participated in a number of games, the most popular of which was a game they called *Bowling Green*. Played outdoors on a well manicured lawn, the object was to roll a heavy ball across a green alley and try to knock over a series of wooden blocks at the other end. It was a mild game played by men, women, and children. The Dutch, however, had another game which was played exclusively by men. Called *gander pulling*, the game was played by first stringing a rope across a fast running current and then tying a goose, head down, to the rope. Men then rowed vigorously down the current and as they passed under the goose they attempted to pull its head off. The winner was the one who managed to yank off the goose's head without falling into the current.

Most of the sporting contests in the early colonial period were local and generally unorganized affairs. By 1665, however, horse racing had become so popular throughout the colonies that an attempt was made to standardize the courses and lengths. In that same year the first organized and publicized horse race was held on Long Island.

One hundred years before the development of baseball the English game of Cricket was played in the colonies. Because of its mother-country origin, the game had a wide following, and in 1751 a Cricket match was played between teams representing New York and London—a contest which historians say was the first international contest played by an American team.

Another game imported from England was Gouging, in which two combatants fought under rules which permitted kicking, biting, kneeing, and, of course, gouging. The object of this violent game was to gouge out the opponent's eye. Gouging soon spread from the southern colonies (where it was more popular than in New England) and moved into the Ohio Valley and onto the frontier. By 1805, however, because of its barbarity, gouging was outlawed.

Sporting events involving animals were particularly common in the South during the first one hundred years of America. Bear baiting (in which a bear was tethered to the ground and a pack of dogs upon it), cock fighting, and fox hunting all flourished. As the colonies grew and prospered and became, in effect, more civilized, the games played reflected a trend away from the sports which pitted one man against another, and turned increasingly toward those games which pitted animals against animals.

Horse racing, long a popular sport, was upgraded significantly in 1788 when the great British thoroughbred *Messenger* was brought to America. Although *Messenger* was a thoroughbred who ran on a flat track, the Americans soon discovered that his progeny made excellent trotting horses, and with the proliferation of his line a new sport was developed in America—the trotting and pacing race. Horse racing—both thoroughbred and trotters—continued to be the single most popular sport in America, generating great rivalries in each section of the country. The sectional rivalry reached its peak in 1823 when a match race between the northern champion *Eclipse* and the southern champion *Sir Henry* was held at the Union Race Course in Long Island. A crowd of more than 100,000 people watched as *Eclipse* won the best two out of three heats and garnered the winning purse of $20,000 for his owner. The match race between *Eclipse* and *Sir Henry* was the first sporting event which caught the interest and imagination of the entire nation, and was the precursor of what was to come in American sports.

Despite the interest in horse racing Americans continued to devote some of their leisure time to the pursuit of boxing—both as spectators and participants. The first heavy weight champion of America was a Virginia slave named Thomas Molineaux. Molineaux traveled to England in 1810 where he met the British champion, Tom Cribb. Cribb won the fight, in a dubious decision over the Black man, and Molineaux soon fell into a life of debauchery and ended his fighting career penniless and alone.

Another international ring battle generated a great deal of public interest on both sides of the Atlantic when, in 1860, the American champion Johnny Heenan fought English bareknuckle champ Thomas Sayers in London. A whole shipload of supporters accompanied Heenan to London for the fight, while the British aristocracy and sporting crowd turned out in great numbers to watch the contest. The fight lasted two hours and twenty minutes, and was declared a draw. Both men were awarded championship belts—Heenan for America, Sayers for Britain—and both retired from the ring shortly after this historic fight. Although prize fighting flourished in most sections of America, it was many years before there was another fight which generated the kind of support and enthusiasm which the Heenan-Sayers fight had.

The history of baseball starts with the British game of *rounders*. Played on an open field, *rounders* originally started out as a game between only three players; but, as the size of the towns grew and the open space became more limited, additional players and bases were added to each side, until by the 1830's the game was re-christened "town ball" and was played extensively throughout the country. The game continued to be played by men, women, and particularly children until, in 1846, two amateur teams of

Lacrosse *was perhaps the first organized game played in the New World. The Indians played Lacrosse in North America long before the Europeans came. Above is a picture of the game as it is played today.*

By 1665 *horse racing was such a popular sport in the Colonies that an attempt was made to standardize the lengths and types of courses. One of the first race courses in the new Colonies was located in Long Island.*

The great English *thoroughbred* Messenger *was brought to this country in 1788 and began a new type of racing in America—the trotter. Above is the famed American trotting horse,* Dan Patch.

men, both from New York City, played a game under rules adopted the previous year. The rules called for nine men to a side, a diamond shaped playing area, and three outs to a side. It was the first game of baseball, as Americans know it, to be played.

Alexander Cartwright was the American responsible for these new rules and regulations governing the playing of baseball. Although not all sections of the country adopted these rules at first (particularly in New England, where the

Abner Doubleday, *above, who served as a Union general in the Civil War, is credited with being the originator of modern day baseball. He is said to have originated the game in 1839 at Coopers- town, N.Y.*

runner was still thrown at to be out), Cartwright, through his travels around the country, did a great deal to standardize the game. By 1859, the game's popularity had spread to the college level, when in that year Amherst played Williams as part of a two day sporting weekend. By the advent of the Civil War the game had become generally standardized, and organized semi-professional teams existed in most of the eastern cities.

SPORTS FLOURISH ACROSS THE LAND

Although sports had become an integral part of the Ameri- can nation, America, by the end of the Civil War, still regarded her games provincially, with certain rules for the same game used in different sections of the country. However, within a decade of the end of the Civil War, a sports boom hit America changing her attitudes towards the playing of games, and altering forever the simplicity of sports in an earlier age. In one fifteen year period, from 1876 to 1891, there were no fewer than seven national or intercol- legiate organizations founded to govern and regulate the playing of certain sports. It was during this period that three major organizations—The U.S. Lawn Tennis Association, the National Baseball League, and the U.S. Golf Association—were formed.

It was also during this period that the sport of bicycle racing first got its start. Called originally *velocipedes,* these early bicycles were wooden framed iron wheeled contrap- tions which were heavy and cumbersome; yet, such was the interest in the new invention, that within a short time of their appearance on the scene, velocipede schools soon opened around the country.

Shooting, an activity engaged in by Americans from the very beginning of the colonial period, was organized and regulated in 1871 into the National Rifle Association. In 1874 competitive shooting had grown to such an extent that the American shooting team met a shooting team from Ire- land in a $9000 winning-team-take-all match. The Ameri- cans barely won, and two years later the same team traveled to England where it defeated the British shooting experts.

The effect of the Civil War on American sports was mixed. Horse racing, long the most popular sport south of the Mason-Dixon line, nearly ceased to exist during the war. In the North, however, horse racing found new interest, and several tracks were built following the close of hostilities. Tracks sprang up in several eastern cities, and two tracks were even added to the growing number in the west. Perhaps

the most historic track to be built in American history was constructed shortly after the end of the Civil War, when a group of industrialists and thoroughbred enthusiasts erected, in Louisville, Kentucky, a track they named Churchill Downs (named after the grandfather of Winston Churchill). The popularity of the track grew and in 1875 the first Ken- tucky Derby was run, won by the colt *Aristides.*

Rowing, which had begun earlier as a participant sport and evolved into a popular spectator sport on the east coast, had, by the end of the Civil War, grown to major proportions

Originally called velocipedes, *the proliferation of bicycles throughout America after the Civil War led to the rise of profes- sional bicycle racing in the twentieth century. Above is the start of a six-day bicycle race in Madison Square Garden in 1938.*

Hunting, *which began as a way of life in America, soon developed into a sport. Above is a typical scene during duck season in the mid West.*

The Kentucky Derby, *the premier thoroughbred race in America, is run each year at Churchill Downs. The famed race course was built in 1874, and is named after the grandfather of Winston Churchill.*

Walter Camp, *known as the father of American football, as he appeared as a member of the 1879 Yale football team. Camp helped to standardize football regulations, and developed new types of football strategy. In 1889 Camp selected the first All-American football team.*

By 1888 *golf had become such a popular sport in America that the first golf course was laid out in Yonkers, New York. Bobby Jones, above, after his playing days constructed golf courses around the country.*

among colleges and universities. A number of private rowing clubs had also been established; in 1870 a series of collegiate rowing competitions were held among eastern colleges such as Harvard, Yale, and Amherst. Rowing provided America with her first college hero—the oarsman—who soon won the hearts and imaginations of women and children. In 1875 a regatta involving thirteen colleges was held on Lake Saratoga, but it was such an unwieldy affair that many colleges withdrew from competition and formed their own rowing unions.

Another singularly historical event occurred during this same period when on November 6, 1869, in New Brunswick, New Jersey, teams from Rutgers and Princeton met to play the first game of intercollegiate football. Each team comprised twenty-five players, and the game more closely resembled soccer than modern day football. The Rutgers team won the first game six to four; a week later the Princeton footballers won, but the third game was never played. The following year Rutgers defeated Columbia College, and then the playing of intercollegiate football was suspended until 1872 when Yale and Columbia met in what was to be the actual beginning of collegiate football in America. Although football, like baseball, evolved from British games, it was not until 1891 that rules, techniques, and playing areas were codified and the game took on its uniquely American look. Walter Camp, often called the father of American football, was responsible for organizing, and codifying the rules so that by the turn of the century football was a reasonably standard game throughout the country. Among his achievements Camp introduced the concept of tackling below the waist, and awarding a team a first down if it completed a prescribed number of yards; Camp also picked the first All-American teams in 1889.

Football in the late nineteenth century was played with a blunt-nose ball; the players wore little protective equipment—generally a pair of moleskin pants and a padded vest; helmets were unheard of, and players purposely let their hair grow to act as a buffer to head injuries. The collegiate game started on the east coast, spread quickly through the midwest, and by 1892 had established itself on the west coast when Stanford played California University in the first game among large colleges west of the Mississippi. So popular had the game become that the annual Thanksgiving Day game between Yale and Princeton was one of the sporting events of the year on the east coast.

The great John L. Sullivan, *one of the great bareknuckle champions of all time, as he appeared during the height of his career. From 1882 to 1892 Sullivan completely dominated the professional boxing world.*

Fifteen years after the conclusion of the Civil War the game of tennis had established itself on the east coast, and the first important tennis tournament in American history was held at Staten Island. In 1881 the first tournament sanctioned by the U.S. Lawn Tennis Association was held, and that initial winner, Richard Sears, went on to win another seven consecutive years. By the 1890's the game had outgrown its elite east coast aura and was prospering among the wealthy leisured class in most parts of the country.

Although golf had been imported from England several years before, the first golf course in America was laid out in 1888 near Yonkers, New York. Five years later the game had grown such in popularity that a club was built in Chicago, and in 1895 the first amateur championship was held in Newport, Rhode Island.

Golf and tennis continued to be the domain of the rich until well into the twentieth century, but the common folk also had their sports, and their sports heroes; standing at the top of the popularity pyramid during the 1890's were the bareknuckle fighters, and premier among them was a fighter who was perhaps the greatest ring champion this country ever had—John L. Sullivan. Fighting under differing rules and with varied equipment, Sullivan dominated the professional boxing world for ten years, from 1882 to 1892. He met and defeated all comers, from many nations, during his reign, but perhaps his greatest victory occurred in 1889 in Richburg, Mississippi, when he met the self-proclaimed world champion, Jake Kilrain. Their championship fight, the last bare-knuckle fight in sporting annals, went seventy-five rounds, lasted two hours and sixteen minutes. Sullivan emerged the winner, proving for all that he was indeed the champion of the world.

Although Sullivan was the world champion, he failed to defend his title for three years. During that three year span a San Francisco bank clerk, James J. Corbett, was busy perfecting his style. While Sullivan was a puncher and mauler, Corbett exhibited the kinds of finesse and grace and speed common to the modern-day fighter. He fought a series of bouts throughout the country, and in 1892 challenged the indolent champion Sullivan to a championship fight. They met in New Orleans on September 7, in the first championship fight using padded gloves and following Marquis of Queensbury rules. Corbett's style of feinting and jabbing completely befuddled the out of shape Sullivan, and in the twenty-first round Sullivan went down for the count. A new champion was crowned, and with him professional prize fighting entered a new era.

If prize fighting was the violent sport most closely followed by the general public, then it was to baseball that they turned their interests for finesse. In 1876 the National League of Professional Base Ball Clubs was formed with eight teams, and thus professional baseball in America was off and running. The game of baseball during this period looked like the modern game in most respects, but as it grew and developed the strategy so common in the modern game slowly worked its way in. So, too, did the baseball heroes, becoming household words in America. The first name to come out of professional baseball is Cy Young, the only man to win over 500 games in his career. During his twenty-one year

Gentleman Jim Corbett, *above, defeated John L. Sullivan for the heavyweight championship of the world in 1892. Corbett's style of jabbing and moving ushered in a new style in professional boxing.*

diamond career Young won 511 games, a mark which is likely to stand for all time. Baseball for many enthusiasts is a game of statistics, and soon local sports journalists were busy keeping track of baseball statistics, giving the game a uniqueness—for only in baseball can the modern fan have some idea of the relative greatness of the athletes from one generation to the next.

In January, 1892 a physical education instructor at the Y.M.C.A. Training College in Springfield, Massachusetts, conducted a new game he had invented the previous winter. The man was Dr. James Naismith, and the game was basketball, the only original team sport to come from America. As conceived by Naismith, basketball was to be a game of finesse and skill, rather than of brute force. The original "baskets" for the game were literally two wooden peach baskets, suspended eight feet from the gymnasium floor. An attendant, seated atop a ladder near each basket, retrieved the ball (originally a soccer ball) after each successful shot, and threw it to the players. During the course of the first games it occurred to someone to cut out the bottom of the peach basket, and suddenly a new and different game was born. The game of basketball quickly caught on, particularly in the colder eastern cities, and by the turn of the century basketball was being played in Y.M.C.A. and college gymnasiums and outdoor courts around the country.

Despite the influx of new games involving balls, bats, and hoops, the basic games which called for speed and strength also continued to develop in America during the 1890's, and before. Intercollegiate competition in track and field was held annually in the 1880's, and in 1871 the first cinder track was built in America. So proficient were American runners and hurdlers, in fact, that in the 1896 Olympic Games held in Athens many European athletes accused the Americans of being professionals. Although nothing could have been further from the truth (the American athletes at the first modern Games were all college athletes who had paid their own way to Athens), the Americans did make off with nine first place medals from the total of twelve events.

Americans by this time were inveterate sports buffs and team followers, but during the 1890's there were a number of athletes whose prowess lay outside team or organized sports competition who also caught the public's imagination. One of the most notable of these athletes was the bicycle racer "Mile a Minute" Murphy. On June 30, 1899, Murphy rode his bicycle over a marked mile course behind a Long Island Railroad car. When the officials checked their stop watches they were amazed: Murphy had completed the mile in less than one minute. The news of Murphy's prodigious feat quickly spread through the country, and the handsome young Irishman went on to a successful career as a vaudeville performer. Another athlete of remarkable talents was the woman sharpshooter, Annie Oakley. Annie's feats with a rifle were so legion that she traveled throughout the world, taking on men sharpshooters in thousands of demonstrations of accuracy.

20TH CENTURY SPORTS

With the turn of the century America entered into a new era of sporting activity. Golf and tennis continued to be played mostly by the wealthy classes; boxing, because of its still frontier-like brutality, was banned in a number of states; baseball was still in its fledgling stages, and football continued to be a game of brawn played by college boys.

Barney Oldfield, *America's first racing car hero, stands next to his famed "999" which he drove to a world record speed of 90 miles an hour. Oldfield, driving "999," did much to establish the sport of auto racing in America.*

Amos Alonzo Stagg, *left, and Knute Rockne, as they watch the national track championships in 1930. Stagg and Rockne in their coaching careers produced several national championship teams.*

However, a new sport came to America shortly after the turn of the century that was destined to gain great popularity and capture the imaginations of countless millions.

Auto racing came on with a rush in America and by 1904 the Vanderbilt Cup Races were held annually on Long Island. By 1909 crowds of several thousands lined the race course to see their favorites roar by, and in 1911, in Indianapolis, Indiana, a track was completed expressly for the racing of automobiles, which was destined to become the single greatest sporting event in America. The Indianapolis 500 ranks with any other single sporting contest for drama, excitement, and violence, and many of the features of the modern automobile had their premier testing on the racetrack at Indianapolis.

In spite of the inherent dangers in auto racing, it was another sport's fatalities which nearly drove it from the American sporting scene. College football in 1905 accounted for five deaths as a direct result of injuries sustained on the playing field. So adverse were the public outcries against this game that no less a personage than Theodore Roosevelt helped establish a new set of rules for football in 1906 which were designed to open up the game and remove its more violent aspects. The game did not become less exciting, only less brutal. Another feature which was added to college football was the appearance of the full-time professional coach. Amos Alonzo Stagg, who had played football at Yale, was hired as the football coach at the University of Chicago in 1892, and he remained there for another forty years. Stagg's contributions to the growth of football were mostly in the area of strategy: he was the first one to develop the forward pass, the backfield shift, and the quick kick. It remained for another football coaching pioneer, Glenn "Pop" Warner, however, to give football a more modern look. Warner coached at several colleges, and during his active coaching days invented and developed the single and double wings and the crouching start position for backfieldmen. As football spread throughout the colleges, so also did football rivalries, and in 1903 the Michigan and Minnesota teams played for the "Little Brown Jug," thereby starting a number of rivalries which have gone on for more than seventy years.

Although the forward pass was permitted as early as 1906, it was not until 1913 that its effectiveness as an offensive weapon became apparent. In that year the Notre Dame team went east to play the West Point eleven. The quarterback for Notre Dame completed 13 of 17 passes that day, and his team went on to defeat the heavily favored Army team 35 to 13. The end who caught many of the passes that day was an unknown Notre Dame football player named Knute Rockne.

Prize fighting, although banned in many states, had a resurgence of interest shortly after the turn of the century. A number of tough and able fighters in the heavyweight division—Jim Jeffries, Jack Sharkey, Bob Fitzsimmons—kept alive the interest in the sport. But perhaps the most interesting fighter of this pre-World War I era was Jack Johnson, the Black man who won the title from Tommy Burns in Sydney, Australia in 1908. Johnson returned to this country and agreed to fight the ex-champion Jim Jeffries. Jeffries had been a popular hero, but he was sadly out of shape. Johnson soon became the target of the racism inherent in the American sports of the day. The two fought in Reno, Nevada in 1910, and the superior Johnson won in the fifteenth round on a knockout. Winning the championship and then defeating Jeffries did not ease the troubles Johnson had with the white sports fans; in fact, from 1910 on his trouble in America increased, and he finally had to flee the country to avoid prosecution under a federal law which forbade taking women across a state line for immoral purposes. Johnson stayed away from America but continued to fight in other countries. Finally he fought for the championship against an American fighter, Jess Willard, in Havana, Cuba in 1915. Johnson lost the match and his championship, but there are many who believe that he was more the victim of racism than of Willard's gloves.

The year the century turned was also the year of the formation of the American League in baseball. Organized by an ex-sportswriter, the American League was hard pressed at first to gain an equal footing with the older and better established National League. For two years the two leagues fought and squabbled over players and rules, but during those two years the ex-sportswriter, Bancroft Johnson, used his time to organize his league into one which was of equal calibre to the National League. He enticed Connie Mack to move his team from Milwaukee to Philadelphia. Johnson had a genius for promotion, and he soon rivaled the senior league in attendance. By 1903 the two rival leagues had agreed upon standard rules and ironed out other, player-related differences, and the first World Series was played. Baseball, now expanded to two eight team leagues, continued to grow in popularity, and in 1910 President Taft threw out the first ball of the season, therein cementing for several generations the idea that baseball was the national pastime.

The first great, almost mythical, hero to emerge from baseball after the amalgamation of the leagues into professional competition was Ty Cobb. Cobb was a perfectionist and tireless student of the game of baseball. Baseball was his

Connie Mack, *center, and two of his most famous players, Mickey Cochrane, left, and Lefty Grove, on the eve of the 1931 World Series. Mack's moving his team from Milwaukee to Philadelphia did much to strengthen professional baseball near the turn of the century.*

The first great player *to emerge from the amalgamation of the two professional leagues was Ty Cobb, shown sliding into third base. Cobb's aggressive play, although it often earned him the enmity of fellow players, earned him a place in the Hall of Fame for his numerous records.*

passion, and his dedication to the game was so intense that within a few years his aggressive play had so antagonized opposing players, umpires, and team mates alike that he had few friends within organized baseball. However, his records speak for themselves. He held the stolen base record for nearly fifty years; he batted over four hundred three times in his career; he singlehandedly won hundreds of games, and he was the baseball batting champion twelve times. Cobb's temperamental opposite was another legendary player, Honus Wagner, sometimes called the "Flying Dutchman." Wagner was a consummate ballplayer, handling virtually all positions with uncanny ability, although he preferred playing shortstop. His records are equally impressive: not until he was forty did he ever hit below .300 for a season; eight times he was National League batting champion; seventeen consecutive years he batted over .300. Another legendary baseball bit of lore was achieved during this pre-World War I era when the Chicago Cubs trio of Joe Tinker, Johnny Evers, and Frank Chance captured America's imagination with their remarkable double play combinations. All three were hotly competitive players (Evers and Tinker did not speak to one another off the field for years); this triumvirate went on to establish baseball as a game of quickness and finesse.

The turn of the century also marked the beginning of a new era in tennis. In 1900 a young Harvard student, Dwight Davis, offered a winning cup to the team which could beat him and his fellow Harvard players. English tennis enthusiasts responded to the challenge and sent a team of three players over for the contest which was destined to become perhaps the most prestigious in all of sports. Davis Cup competition between countries continued until the outbreak of World War I.

Two years before the outbreak of the "war to end all wars" the fifth modern Olympics were held in Stockholm, Sweden. It was during this Olympiad that an athlete established for himself the reputation for being perhaps the greatest individual athlete America ever produced.

Jim Thorpe was an American Indian of incredible abilities. During the 1912 Games he won *both* the pentathalon and decathalon (his score in the pentathalon was twice as great as his nearest competitor). So impressive were his performances that the king of Sweden proclaimed him as the world's greatest athlete. Personal tragedy awaited Thorpe after his stunning successes in Stockholm, however. It was discovered he had played semi-professional baseball the year before the Olympics, and his gold medals and Olympic trophies were taken away from him, and the records he established were erased from the record books.

The same year that Thorpe was winning gold medals at the Olympics he was also named to the All-American Football Team by Walter Camp. Playing for the Carlisle Indian School, Thorpe led his team to victories over nearly every major college team of the day. In his last year as a college player he scored twenty-five touchdowns, a remarkable record. He could run, block, and kick with the best of his day, and he was voted the Greatest Football Player for the first half of the 20th century.

When Thorpe finished his college days he signed to play professional with the New York Giants. John McGraw, the manager of the Giants, used Thorpe only sparingly, claiming that the huge but well coordinated Indian could not hit the curve ball. Thorpe ended his big league baseball career with the Boston Braves, and despite his lifetime batting average of .327, he did not excel in America's favorite pastime. Thorpe went on to play professional football for a number of years with the Canton, Ohio, Bulldogs. His personal life, touched with the death of a son and long and stultifying bouts with alcohol, detracted greatly from his athletic talents and prowess, and Thorpe gradually sank into old age and obscurity.

When his collegiate *playing days were over Thorpe turned to professional sports. He played baseball for a while with the New York Giants and Boston Braves, but gained his greatest professional success as a football player.*

THE GOLDEN AGE OF SPORTS

With the release of tensions following the end of the First World War America embarked on a binge of athletic frenzy that has never been equalled in her history. Records were established in numerous sports that have stood for over fifty years; athletes' names, which became famous during the 1920's and 30's have since become part of American mythology—Jesse Owens, Red Grange, Jack Dempsey, Babe Ruth, *Man O' War*—still mean American excellence in athletic competition.

The Golden Age of American Sports actually began in 1919 when Jack Dempsey defeated Jess Willard for the heavyweight championship of the world, and *Man O' War* began his career as one of the greatest thoroughbreds of all time. *Man O' War*, also called "Big Red" by his attentive and loving followers, was so impressive a specimen of horseflesh that he was the odds on favorite the very first time he raced. During the 1919-1920 racing seasons *Man O' War* won twenty out of twenty-one races (his lone loss was more the result of a dubious starting by an official and a poor ride by his jockey); during one eleven race stretch, he set world records in eight of the races; and he won one race (the Lawrence Realization Stakes) by a hundred lengths.

Swimming, long thought to be nothing more than a pleasant activity on the weekends at the beach or in a public pool, came of age in 1921 when a phenomenal swimmer named Johnny Weissmuller, then only a sixteen year old schoolboy, won the 50 and 220 yard freestyle events. Weissmuller went on to Olympic competition where, in 1924, he met another legendary swimmer, Duke Kahanamoku, and defeated him in the 100 meters race, having to establish a world's record to beat the aging Hawaiian.

Swimming of another sort also sprang full blown onto the American scene during the 1920's when Gertrude Ederle became the first woman to swim the English Channel. In 1926 she swam the cold waters of the Channel in the record time of fourteen hours and thirty-one minutes.

It was early in the decade of the Twenties that a man emerged who was destined to go down in American sports history as one of the most inspirational and ablest coaches in collegiate football. Knute Rockne, the immigrant boy from Norway who had helped his Notre Dame defeat Army by using the forward pass a decade earlier, became the head football coach at his alma mater in 1919. From then until his death in 1931 Rockne's teams were perennially one of the college football's powerhouses, and Rockne himself established the game of football as a conditioner to the game of life. In 1924 the famed Four Horsemen rode out of Notre Dame campus under Rockne's coaching to amass a string of victories that captured the country's imagination, and firmly settled the stubby little coach in the heart of his countrymen. During this time, when intercollegiate football began hitting the big time as a spectator sport and intersectional rivalries flourished, Rockne produced five teams which finished the season undefeated, an accomplishment never again matched by a coach at a large university.

If Rockne was the coaching great name of this period, then the name of the player who enthralled the fans must belong to the inestimable Red Grange. Called the "Galloping Ghost" by his faithful followers who numbered in the thousands, Grange played for the University of Illinois. So great were his abilities that he was three times named to the All-American teams. In one game against Michigan, in 1924, Grange scored five touchdowns and led his team to a 39-14 victory over the then unbeaten Michigan team. Following his career at Illinois Grange went on to play professional football for the Chicago Bears, where he compiled an equally impressive record as a runner. It was mainly through Grange's feats and popularity that professional football was pulled up from its small times origins and placed in the limelight of spectator sports.

No single athlete dominated the Golden Age of Sports, but Jack Dempsey came close. Called the "Manassa Mauler" by his legions of followers, Dempsey defeated Willard in Toledo, Ohio, in 1919, inflicting on the giant champion the worst beating he had ever received. Dempsey first defended his crown against the French champion Georges Carpentier in an historic match. It was the first million dollar gate for a prizefight, and the first championship fight to be broadcast over the radio. In 1923 Dempsey fought Luis Firpo in what many sports historians consider the most brutal and dirtiest championship fight of all time. Dempsey knocked Firpo down seven times in the first round, and once Firpo got up

Man O' War, *one of America's greatest thoroughbreds, as he appeared during the post parade for a race in 1920.* Man O' War *won one of his victories (in the Lawrence Realization Stakes) by more than 100 lengths.*

Gertrude Ederle, *30 years after her famous swim of the English Channel. In 1926 Miss Ederle swam the English Channel in the record time of fourteen hours and thirty-one minutes.*

from the canvas and proceeded to knock Dempsey out of the ring. The match was a grudge fight. In the second round Dempsey knocked him down at will, and then stood over him and pummeled the fallen challenger as he tried to get up. Dempsey next fought Gene Tunney for the championship. Tunney, although a large man, was more graceful and agile than the champion, and when they met in 1926 in Philadelphia, Tunny's strategy of hitting and moving completely befuddled Dempsey, and the challenger went on to win the championship.

Nearly a year later the two met again in what has become known as the "long count" championship. For six rounds the second title fight proceeded identically as the first, with Tunney weaving, hitting, jabbing, and generally staying out of reach of Dempsey's lethal right hand. In the seventh round Dempsey caught Tunney in the corner and bludgeoned him to the canvas. The referee, Dave Berry, motioned Dempsey to the far neutral corner (a regulation both fighters had agreed to prior to the fight). Dempsey, instead, remained standing over the fallen Tunney. When, after several seconds, Dempsey moved to the neutral corner, Barry started his count. The interim had given Tunney several precious seconds to clear his head. He arose at the nine count and went on to successfully defend his title. Probably no victory in American ring history created as much controversy as the famous "long count" of the second Tunney-Dempsey fight held in Chicago on September 22, 1927.

If Dempsey had a rival for most famous athlete in this period it was the most awesome baseball player of all time, Herman "Babe" Ruth. Ruth came to the major leagues in 1914, and from then until 1919 he played for the Boston Red Sox, playing in the outfield and as a starting pitcher. Ruth

The famous Four Horsemen *of Notre Dame—Don Miller, left, Elmer Layden, Jim Crowley, and Harry Stuhldreher—as they appeared following the victory over Army in 1924.*

Harold "Red" Grange *as he looked as a college player for the University of Illinois in 1923. Named three times to the All-American Team, Grange went on to play professional football for the Chicago Bears.*

Jack Dempsey, *known as the Manassa Mauler, as he trained for his "comeback" fight in 1927. Dempsey gained the heavyweight championship in 1919 by defeating Jess Willard.*

Jack Dempsey *is down on one knee in the eighth round of his re-match with Gene Tunney. The re-match held in Chicago in 1927 was the scene of the famous "long-count," one of the most controversial decisions in American ring history.*

The legendary Babe Ruth *shown as he hit one over the fence in 1934. In 1927 he hit 60 home runs, a record that stood for nearly fifty years. Ruth began his baseball career as a pitcher, but his prodigious feats at the plate are what earned him a place in the Hall of Fame.*

moved to the New York Yankees in 1920 and the following year he led them to the World Series, the first time the Yankees had ever played in the annual championship. During succeeding years Ruth went on to establish seasonal records for hitting and for number of home runs. In 1927 he hit a record number 60 home runs, a record that lasted nearly fifty years. In 1925 another famous name was added to the Yankee lineup. Lou Gehrig took over the first base position on June 1 of that year and for the next fourteen years he was never out of the starting lineup, compiling an amazing 2,130 consecutive game playing record.

If Grange and Ruth and Gehrig dominated the team sports during the Golden Age, and Dempsey glowed brightest in the violent sports, it fell upon a tall and at times ascetic young man to achieve mastery of the finesse game. Bill Tilden dominated tennis during the Twenties. Ten straight years he was ranked as the top male player in the world and won six consecutive national championships at Forest Hills. He was the first American to win the British Championship at Wimbledon, and he was a member of the Davis Cup team that won seven straight championships. In all he won more than seventy major championships during his astonishing career, but he did not know when to get out of big time competition, and "big Bill," as his fans called him, ended his days playing exhibition matches and in personal tragedy.

While Bill Tilden was dominating men's tennis during the decade, a slight but strong young girl came out of California to show the eastern and international tennis crowd how tennis was played on the west coast. Helen Wills won her first national women's championship at the age of seventeen. During the next fifteen years she won seven American titles at Forest Hills and eight at the more prestigious British championships at Wimbledon.

Golf, the other finesse sport, was dominated by an equally romantic character from the South, Bobby Jones. Beginning big time competition at fourteen, Jones went on to win every international golfing championship of his day. From 1923 to 1930 Bobby Jones won thirteen major championships, a feat not likely to be soon equalled. In 1930 he won the Grand Slam of golf by winning the Master's, the British Open, the British Amateur, and the American Amateur. In all he won more major tournaments than any other golfer, and retired in glory at the height of his career.

Although sports participation and spectator enthusiasm did not drop off immediately with the end of the Golden Age,

Baseball greats *Babe Ruth and Lou Gehrig, in the Yankees' uniforms, as they appeared in 1930. The A's are Al Simmons, left, and Jimmy Foxx. Ruth and Gehrig formed the one-two punch that established the Yankee dynasty in the Twenties.*

"Big Bill" Tilden *as he appeared in a tennis tournament in 1933. Tilden dominated men's tennis during the Golden Age of American Sports, being ranked ten consecutive years as the number one male tennis player in the world.*

Helen Wills *during a doubles match in 1926. Miss Wills won her first national championship at the age of seventeen, and during her career won seven Forest Hills titles and eight Wimbledon championships.*

Babe Didrikson *shown winning the long jump at the AAU outdoor track meet in 1911. The following year Babe made an international reputation for herself by winning two gold medals at the Olympic Games in Los Angeles.*

it was not until the 1932 Olympics in Los Angeles that another individual athlete came along who could rival the athletic stars of the Twenties for ability and charisma. Babe Didrikson, a shy farm girl from Texas, went on to win more titles in more varied sports than any other athlete in American history. In the 1932 Olympics she won the 80 meter hurdles race, the javelin throw, and placed second in the high jump. Turning professional after these Olympics, she toured the country as a basketball player in season, then switched to baseball, in season, and traveled the country. She also continued to give exhibition matches in billiards. Tiring of the traveling involved with these makeshift teams, Babe sat out professional competition for several years so she could regain her amateur standing in golf. That completed, she went on to win sixteen straight golf tournaments, capping her string of accomplishments by winning the British Women's Amateur golf title. In her later years she worked hard to develop the Ladies Professional Golf Association. She died of cancer in 1956, having been voted the greatest woman athlete in the first fifty years of the 20th century.

The Olympics, this time the 1936 Games in Berlin, provided America with another great, near legendary athlete. Jesse Owens, a Black sprinter from Ohio State University, had already established himself as the premier speed runner and hurdler in America by setting five world records and tying a sixth during an incredible *one day* burst of athletic prowess at the Big Ten track and field championships in 1935. The following year the indefatigible Owens led his Olympic team to Berlin.

The Berlin Games were shaped, for the first time in athletic history, by political considerations. Hosted by the Nazi dictatorship of Adolph Hitler, whose psychopathic ideas of race superiority pitted the Black American athletes against many of the so-called Nordic athletes from Germany, the Games were meant to be a verification of the Nazis' racial superiority theory. Single-handedly Jesse Owens destroyed the myth of Nordic superiority. He won four gold medals: in the 100 and 200 meter dashes, in the long jump, and he was the lead runner on the gold medal winning four-man 400 meter relay team. Never before had running competition at the Olympic level been so dominated by any one athlete.

Four years later the mythical fifteen feet ceiling, which had frustrated pole vaulters for years, came crashing down when the American Cornelius Warmerdam cleared the bar at 15 feet, 1⅛ inches to establish a new world record. It was twenty-two years before pole vaulters cleared sixteen feet.

The Winter Olympics were held in Lake Placid, New York in 1932, and it was really the beginning of serious winter sports competition on the international level for America. So quickly did the Americans take to the winter games that by 1941 a transplanted Norwegian, Torger Tokle, set the world's record for the ski jump.

Red Grange established professional football in this country, but it took the efforts of three other men to cement it firmly in the public's attention. Professional football in the decade prior to the Second World War was a fully organized yet lightly considered game. The college brand of football ranked first in the spectators' hearts, but Bronko Nagurski, Don Hutson, and Sammy Baugh, each of whom had had illustrious college careers, brought the professionals into contention with college football for the fans' interest.

Baugh, playing for the Washington Redskins; Hutson, laboring for the Green Bay Packers, and Nagurski, for the Chicago Bears, helped establish new and varied records (some of which still remain), but more importantly for professional football, they each brought a degree of talent, finesse, and raw courage to the game and gave it the impetus it needed to catch on in a big way. By the advent of World War II professional football was a thriving business, and, thanks to the earlier efforts of Baugh, Nagurski, and Hutson, college players could now consider extending their playing days in the professional ranks.

It was mainly to college football, however, that the nation turned to during World War II, and the college game came up with players whose achievements matched the needs of a country oppressed by a foreign war. The famous West Point teams of the war years produced Doc Blanchard and Glen Davis. Referred to as "Mr. Inside" and "Mr. Outside" respectively, Blanchard and Davis, for the first time in American history, gave the country heroes whose exploits on the athletic fields were a direct precursor of the country's exploits on the battlefields. During the war years perhaps the greatest football rivalry to develop was between the Fighting Irish of Notre Dame and the Cadets of the Military Academy. Although they faced each other in 1944, '45 and '46, it was the last game that is remembered most fondly. Both teams were very evenly matched, with Army having three All-Americans to Notre Dame's two—one of them the phenomenal Johnny Lujack. So evenly were the two teams matched that the game ended in a 0-0 tie, bringing to an end the period of football domination by the West Point Cadets.

As much as Americans had grown to love the organized mayhem of the football field, there was still a substantial number of fans who followed boxing. Prize fighting had fallen on lean years after the golden days of Dempsey and Tunney. For nearly ten years the heavyweight division labored under the efforts of large but generally inept fighters; and the dearth of competent fighters meant that the sport itself was growing flabby. But a young Black fighter from Detroit with an impressive knockout record began to make his move up through the professional ranks. Joe Louis, nicknamed the "Brown Bomber," finally got his chance at the championship by fighting and defeating the current champ, Jim Braddock. Louis went on to score impressive victories over every contending heavyweight. Perhaps his most rewarding victory came over the German Max Schmeling. Schmeling had beaten Louis earlier (before the Detroit slugger had become champion), and since that first battle Schmeling had gone on to become an ardent follower of Hitler and an espouser of the Fascist rascist ideology. When they met the second time it took Louis only two minutes and four seconds to dispose of the German boxer, proving, as Jesse Owens had done three years earlier at the Berlin Olympics, the fallacy of the master race theory.

668

Following her track career Babe Didrikson, above, turned to playing softball and basketball exhibitions around the country. Later Babe turned exclusively to golf, winning at one point sixteen straight tournaments.

Jesse Owens shown at the start of one of the heats in the 200 meter dash during the 1936 Olympic Games. Owens' performance at the Berlin Games established him as one of the legendary track figures in American history.

Jesse Owens on the victors' stand seconds after receiving the gold medal for the long jump. In addition to this gold medal, Owens also won gold medals in the 100 and 200 meter dashes, and was the lead runner on the first place American 400 meter relay team.

Army greats *Glenn Davis, left, and Felix "Doc" Blanchard, as they appeared in 46., Blanchard and Davis, known as "Mr. Inside" and "Mr. Outside," were consensus All-Americans at West Point.*

Bronislaw "Bronko" Nagurski *was a three-time All-American football player from the University of Minnesota. Nagurski went on to play nine seasons with the Chicago Bears, helping to bring professional football into the sports limelight.*

Joe Louis, *center, lands a solid punch to the body of Max Schmeling during their re-match in 1938. Schmeling had beaten Louis in an earlier fight, but in the re-match Louis stopped the German in the first round.*

Baseball stars *Ted Williams, left, and Joe DiMaggio in the American League locker room following the 1941 All-Star Game. Both Williams and DiMaggio are enshrined in the Baseball Hall of Fame.*

While the football and baseball teams continued to dominate the attention of the team sports fans, and while Louis reigned supreme as heavyweight champ, another sport was silently making its way into the American sports conscious. Basketball, Dr. Naismith's American invention, gradually came out of the Y.M.C.A. gyms, found its way into high schools, and then colleges, and caught on with the general public in such a way that by the end of the 1950's New York City's Madison Square Garden was regularly sold out for college basketball games, and there was not a major city in the country that did not have a large auditorium capable of holding fans clamoring to see the roundball game.

By 1938 the National Invitational Tournament pitted the very best twelve college teams in the country against one another in a double elimination tourney. The game of basketball suffered a major setback in the late Forties and early Fifties, however, when it was discovered that a number of college players had accepted bribes to shave points (so that the professional gamblers could win on the point spread for each game). Basketball waited for the public to forget its dark days, and also, it waited for the agile big man who would come on in the 60's to dominate the game.

Baseball, meanwhile, saw the demise of the legendary Babe Ruth, and the rise of the superstar who dominated the game during the Forties, Joe DiMaggio. Son of an Italian fisherman in San Francisco, DiMaggio established the record for the highest number of consecutive games with a hit; known as the "Yankee Clipper," DiMaggio's quiet strength and unemotional demeanor earned him a close spot in the hearts of baseball fans for over a decade.

In 1951 the Baseball Hall of Fame was enlarged to accommodate the name plaques and memorabilia of the famed players from the past.

Horse racing, long the sport of the rich in America, had, with the proliferation of tracks throughout the country and the introduction of pari-mutuel betting, by the 1930's also became the sport of the masses. In 1938 one of the great match races of the sport in America was held which pitted the gitty little California *Seabiscuit* against the Triple Crown winner, *War Admiral*. The son of *Man O' War*, *War Admiral* was the 1937 horse of the Year, while *Seabiscuit* had already finished his track career. Nevertheless the little California horse broke out in front and led the whole race, winning by four lengths.

The Grand Slam of tennis was won again during the Thirties when a young Californian, Don Budge, burst on the world tennis scene and walked away with the American, British, French, and Australian Championships. Although by this time Bill Tilden had long been retired, the inevitable comparison between him and Budge was a recurring item in the sports pages. Later, in 1937, Budge went on to prove his domination of the game when he led the American team to a four-to-one victory over the British for the Davis Cup, bringing that honored trophy back to American shores for the first time since Tilden's days.

In the mid-'40's America saw the rise of another great tennis player destined to make his mark on the world sports scene. Jack Kramer, the young man with the golden hair, worked his way up through the ranks of big time amateur tennis by winning a string of junior matches. When he made the move to national competition, his winning ways continued, and by the end of 1945 Kramer was the established star of the tennis world. Playing with his unflappable partner, Ted Schroeder, Kramer amassed a number of doubles victories in USLTA competition, and in 1946 and 1947 the two

Seabiscuit *leads War Admiral around the first turn during the "dream race" at Pimlico race track in 1938. Seabiscuit led the whole race and went on to defeat the son of* Man O' War *by four lengths.*

Ben Hogan *shown blasting his way from a trap during the National Open Golf Tournament in 1950. Following a near fatal automobile accident Hogan went on to win both the U.S. and British Opens in 1953.*

led their team to victories over the Australians to once again bring the Davis Cup home to America. Mainly because of their play the Davis Cup remained in America during most of the Forties, and it was only in 1950, three years after Kramer had turned professional, that America relinquished her hold on the famed tennis trophy.

With the retirement of Bobby Jones, golf, while it had not exactly fallen on lean years, did not have the kind of player whose exploits could move the gallery. Then, also like Jones coming up from the South, Sam Snead appeared on the golfing scene. Playing in his famed Panama hat, Snead went on to score an incredible string of national tournament victories that quickly moved him to the forefront of American golfers. During his long career Snead won more tournaments than any other professional golfer, among them: three Professional Golfers Championships, three Master's Tournaments, the British Open, and three Canadian Opens. Despite his winning ways, Snead was never able to win the U.S. Open; his most heart breaking performance in that tournament occurred in 1939 when he lost the championship on the last hole.

Challenging Snead during the late Thirties and early Forties was the little scrapper from Texas, Ben Hogan. Hogan admitted that he was not, like golfers who had preceded him in national ranking, a natural golfer. But what Hogan lacked in natural talent he more than made up for in determination and courage. Often playing in pain from injuries sustained in a near fatal auto accident, Hogan, in the early Forties, went on to win fifty-six tournaments in his abbreviated but illustrious career. Although Hogan was at times a mercurial player, his courage and determination played an important part in prolonging his career, when, after the accident, and written off by the golfing crowd as never being able to seriously compete again, Hogan came roaring back to win the U.S. Open for the third time in 1951. Hampered by recurring pain, Hogan struggled along the professional circuit, and, finally in 1953 he capped his courageous career by winning both the U.S. and British Opens.

Professional boxing had gone into a decline with the retirement of Joe Louis in 1949. Louis' vacant crown was given to a journeyman fighter named Ezzard Charles, who had won a series of victories in the elimination fights to find a successor to Louis. Louis, in trouble with the government over back taxes, decided on a comeback. On September 27, 1950, he fought Charles for the championship, but, unfortunately for the Brown Bomber, he was sadly out of shape, and Charles went on to retain his championship by a decision.

Charles was challenged by an aging boxer named Joseph Walcott. Called "Jersey Joe" by the fans, Walcott was a sentimental favorite with the crowds, but he was never much

Ted Williams, *as he looked taking batting practice in 1946, when he established the modern single season batting average with a .406 mark in 1941.*

Maureen "Little Mo" Connolly *shown warming up for the 1952 Forest Hills tournament. Miss Connolly won the tournament the year before at the age of sixteen. In 1952 she added the Wimbledon championship to her records.*

Florence Chadwick, *famed long distance swimmer of the fifties, is shown swimming the treacherous Hellespont. Miss Chadwick successfully swam the English Channel in 1950, and in the process broke Gertrude Ederle's record for the same feat by more than an hour.*

of a champion, although he did defeat Charles in defending the heavyweight title.

Baseball had, at the end of the Second World War, taken on a new life and several heroes emerged during the Forties and Fifties who matched and occassionally surpassed the records of an earlier age. Joe DiMaggio continued to reign supreme with the Yankees, but in Boston a young Californian named Ted Williams went on to set the modern single batting average record by hitting .406 in 1941. And in St. Louis Stan ''The Man'' Musial was carving out a place for himself in the baseball Hall of Fame.

Women's tennis in the Forties was completely dominated by a young phenom from California, Maureen Connolly. Maureen (known to her fans as ''Little Mo'') won the National Women's Singles Championship at Forest Hills in 1951 at the age of sixteen. In 1952 Maureen went on to add the British Championship at Wimbledon to her string of victories. Not until the early Seventies would a woman tennis player come along who would capture the hearts and cheers of the crowd as Maureen Connolly had done in the Fifties.

In 1950 an unknown typist, Florence Chadwick, stunned the sports world by swimming the English Channel in under an hour faster than the record established by the legendary Gertrude Ederle. Florence broke the 24 year old record by swimming from France to England. In 1951 the indomitable Chadwick repeated the feat, this time swimming from England to France.

1948 marked the beginning of one of the greatest careers in the history of American thoroughbred racing. *Citation* won nineteen of twenty races in 1948, capping this incredible string of victories by winning the Triple Crown. So awesome were *Citation's* abilities that in one race, the Pimlico Special, no owner could be found to enter a horse against him, and the great horse raced around the track alone. *Citation's* jockey was the all-time great, Eddie Arcaro, and the two of them rode onto victory after victory during the early Fifties. When *Citation* was finally retired he had won more than $1,000,000, the first horse in history to do so.

From 1947 through 1956 professional basketball was the sole domain of a genial giant from De Paul University, George Mikan. Playing for the Minneapolis Lakers, Mikan almost singlehandedly took professional basketball from a minor league sport and gave it the excitement and crowd appeal necessary to move into the big time. So prodigious were his abilities that he was once selected as the greatest basketball player in history.

The 1948 Olympic Games in London again proved to be the background for another American stellar performance. Bob Mathias, the youngest American to ever wear the Olympic uniform to date, won the modern decathalon. Mathias repeated his remarkable performance four years later in Helsinki, Finland, walking off again with the gold medal in the decathalon.

Tennis found an new champion and a new delight for the gallery in the late Forties when Pancho Gonzales emerged from the pack to win the championship at Forest Hills in 1948. Gonzales, always a volatile character on the court and off, went on to dominate tennis well into the Fifties, and, after his move into professional tennis, the inestimable Gonzales continued his winning ways.

In 1947 an event occurred in baseball which had as much sociological significance as it did athletic importance. The first Black player to play in the major leagues, Jackie Robinson, was signed by Branch Rickey to play for the Brooklyn Dodgers. Perhaps never before in the history of American sport has any athlete had the kind of psychological pressure

Citation, *winner of the Triple Crown in 1948, is shown after winning the Chesapeake Stakes at Harve de Grace Race Track. Citation was the first horse in history to win more than $1,000,000.*

on him that Robinson faced his first few years in the majors. A superior athlete and ardent student of baseball, Robinson went on to silence his racist critics by generally outplaying his white counterparts. Despite some resistance from Southern players, Robinson established himself as a big leaguer, and the color line in baseball was broken forever.

In 1950 the University of Oklahoma, under the tutelage of Bud Wilkinson, won the national collegiate football championship. The ''Sooners'' went on to set a collegiate winning record as yet unmatched in football history.

In 1952 an ex-GI, Rocky Marciano, knocked out Jersey Joe Walcott and won the heavyweight championship of the world. Marciano, a punishing boxer who did not mind taking two punches to land one, was undefeated in forty-nine straight fights at the time he won the championship. Although the heavyweight division during the Fifties was somewhat bereft of sound contenders, Marciano defended his crown several times, managing always to emerge the winner.

The cultural and political malaise of the Fifties was somewhat reflected in the world of sports. Although national championships in various amateur and professional sports continued to be held, no single athlete during the early Fifties emerged to capture the imaginations of the fans. Instead, what began to occur was the gradual shift from the ''sports-for-sports'' ethic which had permeated athletic competition since the colonial days, to the high-powered moneyed game. Television was undoubtedly partly responsible for this. But as America moved into the international arena politically, her sports also took on the look and feel of international struggles. The 1952 Olympics in Helsinki, for example, was the first great showdown between the American and Russian

Eddie Arcaro, *one of America's all time great jockeys, displays a big grin and gives himself a congratulatory handshake shortly after having ridden* Hill Prince *to victory in the 1950 Preakness.*

Rocky Marciano, *left, lashes out at Jersey Joe Walcott during their Heavyweight championship fight in 1952. Marciano stopped Walcott in the thirteenth round to win the heavyweight crown.*

Bob Seagren *clears the bar at 17 feet during indoor meet at Madison Square Garden in 1973. The introduction of the fibre-glass pole pushed the height of the bar over 17 feet in 1963.*

track and field teams, and was a portent of things to come in international competition. Baseball, long considered the national pastime, began to slip in attendance, and several teams—most notably the Brooklyn Dodgers and New York Giants—moved to new cities. The move by the Dodgers, lamented in New York City, brought big league baseball to the west coast and opened up the country for genuine national champions. Professional football continued to belabor with an essentially eastern league, but it too moved westward during the Fifties with the result that new and larger audiences were made west of the Mississippi. Professional and collegiate basketball (the latter finally having lived down the point shaving scandals of the early Fifties)also moved into the arenas of big time, moneyed competition. Boxing was in a state of relative calm, while the thoroughbreds continued to produce champions, but none of them of the caliber of an earlier age. Tennis during the Fifties became almost the sole property of the Australians, although Gonzales and Kramer continued to shine as professional stars. Television and the added mobility provided by the automobile competed with sports for America's attention. But, as had happened so often in the past, the cultural challenge presented by sports was met, not on the diamonds or courts, but on the running track.

In 1954 the mythical four minute mile barrier was broken by an Englishman, Roger Bannister, and the world was off on a binge of record breaking performances. Within a year of Bannister's record breaking run four men had broken his record; the seven foot high jump, long thought to be an impossibility, was set, and the new fibre-glass poles permitted pole vaulters to clear the equally mythical height of seventeen feet. In 1963, the American John Pennel cleared seventeen feet, the first man ever to vault that height. The 1964 Olympics produced Bob Hayes, called at the time the world's fastest human, who set the record for the 100 meter dash at 9.1 seconds.

Moving into the 1964 Olympics, a contingent of American teenagers literally rewrote the record book in swimming. Don Schollander, an eighteen year old freestyler, won four gold medals at the Tokyo Games. Schollander's record for the 400 meter freestyle was 52 seconds faster than the mark established by Johnny Weissmuller. Sharon Stouder, a fifteen year old girl, came away from the Tokyo Olympiad with three gold medals in swimming.

The setting of new records, after years of relative mediocrity, found its way into the professional baseball record book. In 1961 Roger Maris broke Babe Ruth's home run record. However, because of the added number of games in the modern season, the baseball commissioner decreed that Ruth's record still stood as the 154 game record. The following year Los Angeles Dodger Maury Wills also broke a long standing baseball record when he stole 104 bases, thereby breaking Ty Cobb's forty-seven year old record. However, again the longer seasonal play brought the new record into dispute, and Wills' record is in the record book with a footnote explaining the differences between the old and new records. From 1949 through 1960 the New York Yankees won an unprecedented ten pennants, establishing a record for team championships. The Yankee manager, the irascible Casey Stengel, guided the Yankess during this dynasty, making him one of the most winning managers in baseball history.

Professional football also moved into the record books in a number of varied ways. Because of the explosive growth of the game, new teams were added and finally, in 1960, a new league (the American Football League) was formed. At first the new league posed no real competition for the older and established National Football League. The NFL, which traced its origins back to 1925 and the days of Red Grange and the Chicago Bears, continued to fill its stadiums each Sunday, giving fans the kind of controlled violence the nation of television watchers was quickly coming to expect from professional athletics. Starting in 1957 Jim Brown, playing for the Cleveland Browns, began to set new rushing records in the NFL. Not since the days of Grange had professional football fans seen such a dynamic runner. Brown's performances were so formidable that he was considered to be the greatest running back in the history of professional football. In 1964 his yardage gained passed the 10,000 mark—the first runner in football history to gain such yardage.

The advent of the AFL also brought a new dimension to professional sports in America. Owners from both leagues began to compete financially for the services of college stars. When Joe Namath, an All-American from the University of Alabama, signed a professional contract with the New York Jets of the AFL for a reported $405,000, it was believed to be the highest salary ever paid for an untried professional athlete in the history of American sports.

Muhammad Ali, *left, blasts Joe Frazier during first round of their 1975 championship fight in Manila. Ali won the Heavyweight title from Sonny Liston in 1964.*

Arnold Palmer *established his superiority in golf in the early Sixties by winning the U.S. Open in 1960 and the British Open in 1961 and 1962. Palmer, who is followed around the links by ''Arnie's Army,'' has won four Master's Tournaments.*

In boxing, Rocky Marciano remained the undefeated heavyweight champion for four years. When he retired in 1956 undefeated he left the division vacant. A series of elimination matches were held that year and Floyd Patterson, the youngest man to ever win the heavyweight championship, came out on top. Despite a rather mediocre career in the ring, Patterson did establish a record: he was the first ex-heavyweight champion to ever regain his title.

In 1962 Patterson lost his title to a huge but lethargic fighter named Sonny Liston. Liston knocked out Patterson in the first round of their title fight. A year later, in Las Vegas, Nevada, the two met for a rematch. The result was precisely the same: Patterson did not last through the first round. The stage was now set for the entrance of perhaps the most flamboyant fighter America has ever known. Liston was the champion, but he defended his title rarely. No one was thought capable of stopping the huge fighter, and the only serious contender was a twenty-two year old former Olympic light-heavyweight champion.

The championship fight was scheduled for Miami Beach, Florida, on February 25, 1964. The champion and challenger traded punches for three rounds, and then in the fourth Liston connected, but the challenger remained on his feet. In the sixth round the challenger turned the tables on Liston and gave him a terrible beating, so bad, in fact, that the champion couldn't answer the bell for the seventh round. A new champion was born that night who was destined to make sport history in America. The new champ was Cassius Clay, later to change his name to Muhamad Ali.

Golf also grew up into a mass sport in the Sixties. Television brought the once gentlemanly game into every living room, and by the early Sixties the names of professional golfers were as well known as those of any other athlete. Arnold Palmer emerged as the most popular, and the best, golfer of the early Sixties. Followed around by huge galleries (dubbed ''Arnie's Army'' by sportswriters) Palmer established his superiority of professional golf by winning the U.S. Open in 1960, the British Open in 1961 and 1962, and capped his remarkable performances with four Master's titles in 1958, 1960, 1962 and 1964. Palmer became a millionaire almost overnight in this era of big purses, and he, along with another golfer, brought the game into the forefront of American spectator sports.

In 1962 the golfer destined to rival and then exceed Palmer's incredible string of victories came onto the professional circuit. Jack Nicklaus, considered by many to be perhaps the greatest golfer of all time, won the U.S. Open in 1962 at the age of twenty-two. Palmer and Nicklaus blazed a trail across the American golf scene that may not ever be seen

Jack Nicklaus *watches ball after he chipped toward green in 1975 Ryder Cup play. Nicklaus challenged Palmer for golf's number one position during the mid and late sixties.*

Secretariat, *with Ron Turcotte in the saddle, crosses the finish line alone to win the 1973 Kentucky Derby. Secretariat won the Triple Crown in 1973.*

again. No only did they manage to win every major tournament between them, they also were responsible for creating in the American mind the idea that golf was a game that could be enjoyed by everyone, and thus they heralded in the new age of sports participation in this country.

In horse racing the Sixties brought America one of the great thoroughbreds of all time. *Kelso*, with a lifetime earnings of nearly $2,000,000, was five times nominated as the Horse of the Year, a record never equalled by any other thoroughbred. Not until the rise of *Secretariat* nearly a decade later did a horse so capture the hearts of the racing public.

In the 1960's professional basketball burst forth on the sports scene. Aided by lucrative television contracts, and blessed with a new generation of large and graceful players, the National Basketball League produced some of the most exciting and memorable moments for sports fans during this decade. Although the professional basketball dynasty of the Boston Celtics began in the late 1950's, by the Sixties such names as Bob Cousy and Bill Sharman were household words. With the coming of Bill Russell into the NBA the era of the big man came into the game. Russell, followed a few years later by another giant and graceful player, Wilt Chamberlain, showed America that basketball was not a game of tall ungainly freaks, and with their inspired play a whole generation of American children had found new sports heroes.

Auto racing also flourished during the 1950's, 60's and into the 70's. The Indianapolis 500 remained as the premier racing event in the world, each year attracting more than 300,000 spectators. The Indianapolis race, if the largest racing event in the world, has also been the scene of some of the most ghastly crashes. During the 1964 running of the race one of the most spectacular crashes in the 500 history occurred, involving nearly every car in the starting field. The famed driver Eddie Sachs was killed. Although the race has been won by a number of renowned drivers over the years, of the modern drivers the name of A.J. Foyt stands supreme. Foyt has competed in more races than any other living driver, and has won virtually every major championship in America. The often contentious Foyt also has won races at nearly every kind of automobile racing.

Despite the mass popularity of the Indianapolis 500, another kind of auto racing began making inroads into speedcar events in the early Sixties. Stock car racing, a unique brand of auto racing growing out of America's seventy-year infatuation with the automobile, began as a small time activity in the South. By the late Sixties stock car drivers were among the best paid athletes in the country, and the names of Richard Petty, Cale Yarborough, and Bobby Allison were known outside of the southern states, and the Daytona 500 had come to rival the Memorial Day race in Indianapolis for spectator appeal and drama.

In 1963 the Davis Cup was returned to America. Tennis in the Sixties grew into a big time game. Spurred on by the rise in popularity in tennis participation, and with the advent of a number of professional leagues, tennis players in the Seventies once again became the darlings of the sporting world. Althea Gibson, a Black woman, won two championships each at Forest Hills and Wimbledon. But the single most electric player to emerge during the Sixties was the phenomenal woman from California Billy Jean King. Billy Jean swept down the international tennis establishment and went away with every major championship. Always outspoken, Billy Jean often criticized the officials, both those at the court

Wilt Chamberlain, *wearing a face mask to protect his nose, drives in toward the basket against Connie Dierking. Chamberlain and Bill Russell helped establish professional basketball in the early sixties as one of America's most popular spectator sports.*

A. J. Foyt, *shown here in a Lotus-Ford racer during a practice run for the 1965 Indianapolis 500. Foyt has competed in virtually every kind of auto racing and is one of the most winning drivers in auto racing history.*

Stock car racing, *which started in the South, is one of the most popular forms of auto racing in America. Above is the start of the 1971 Daytona 500, the premier event in this uniquely American type of racing.*

and those running the tournaments. Although outspoken, she usually manged to win, and her combination of winning tournaments while at the same time speaking out against the stodgy management of big time tennis gradually broke down the barriers of institutionalized tennis and made the way clear for younger players to move into the big time. Following King as the premier lady tennis player of the Seventies was Chris Evertt, a young player from Florida, who catapulted to fame when she won the British Open. Her male counterpart, Jimmy Connors, also an outspoken critic of the existing tennis establishment, dominated tennis during the Seventies in much the same way that Tilden had dominated the game nearly a half century earlier.

Sports in the latter half of the Seventies have grown into big business. Virtually all of the popular team sports, and many of the individual sports (including golf and tennis) are propped up by lucrative television contracts. College football has become a big business, with the various bowl games accounting for millions of television viewers, while the professional football championship (dubbed the Super Bowl in 1966) draws the largest single day television audience in the world.

Olympic competition has also come to the television generation, and such Olympic stars as Mark Spitz and his record breaking seven gold medals at the 1972 Olympics in Munich have been added to the list of American sports heroes.

The 1976 Super Bowl, won for a second time by the Pittsburgh Steelers, was viewed by more than 75,000,000 viewers. And the 1976 World Series was one of the most exciting and well played Series in modern memory, proving perhaps once again that, although the games themselves may have changed over the past 200 years, the excellence of American games remains undiminished.

No one growing up in America has escaped the lure of sports, for they have been an integral part of the American scene for more than two hundred years. Their development from informal and nearly formless games and diversions to highly regulated and sophisticated amateur and professional sports mirrors closely the growth of the country. The essence of American sports and the essence of American life has been excellence through competition. If the battles of England were won on the playing fields of Eton, then the battles of America to establish and maintain a way of life were won on every sandlot diamond, vacant lot gridiron, and big city makeshift court. The particular sport is not important; if someone throws a ball, or jumps over a barrier or runs or lifts or soars or glides or swims or matches his strength with another—Americans want to do it. And if the individual discovers that he can't do it, then he'll pay in either time or money to watch someone else do it.

American history is filled with the names of courageous generals, astute politicians, and outrageous characters, but no names conjure the same respect or awe as those of our sports heroes. Ruth and Gehrig, John L. Sullivan and James J. Corbett, ''Bill Bill'' Tilden, the ''Brown Bomber,'' Ty Cobb, Willie ''the Shoe'' Shoemaker, Gertrude Ederle, Jesse Owens, *Man O' War*, Connie Mack, Barney Oldfield, Jim Thorpe, Babe Didrikson Zaharias, Blanchard and Davis, Cy Young, Red Grange, *Secretariat*, Muhammad Ali—these and a thousand others are all etched deeply onto the American conscious. Some have been elevated almost to deity, while others have occasionally become our national scapegoats. But whether winner or loser, man or animal, they are our heroes, and our lives have been enriched and broadened by their athletic disasters and accomplishments.

Billie Jean King *returns a backhand against Chrissy Evertt during one of their matches in 1975. Mrs. King won a number of amateur championships (including Forest Hills and Wimbledon) before turning professional. As a professional she has been instrumental in popularizing tennis as a spectator sport.*

Mark Spitz *competes in the butterfly stroke as part of the 400 meter medley during the 1972 Olympic Games in Munich. Spitz won a record seven gold medals during the Munich Games.*

Hank Aaron *holds the historical ball that he knocked out of the park to break Babe Ruth's home run record in 1974. Aaron's record blast came in a game against the Los Angeles Dodgers.*

AMERICAN SPORTS CALENDAR

1779

A popular diversion of lower and middle classes around Charlottsville, Va., was **sprint races,** quarter-mile races between two horses of very great speed. This was also called "quarter-racing."

NOVEMBER 3, 1780

3 days of **racing** on Hempstead Plains, Long Island, included: Gentleman's Purse, Ladies' Subscription, and race run by women riders. Gentlemen fond of fox hunting met daily at dawn at Loosely's King's Head Tavern.

1784

Nightly deer hunting expeditions in Carolinas became misdemeanor because of accidental slaughter of many domestic cows and horses.

MAY, 1788

Famous gray stallion, **Messinger,** believed to be original sire of fine breed of trotting horses, 1st in America, arrived from England.

1790

Horse racing fans began to take interest in blood and breed of horses. The offspring of *Medley,* an earlier champion, *Belair, Gimcrack,* and *Calypso* won repeatedly at races.

1793

Lexington, Ky.: Town trustees ordered an end to **horse racing** in the streets. It was frightening the pedestrians.

1796

Billiards frequently played in South according to contemporary reports. Francis Baily noted dozen tables in Norfolk alone.

1798

Breeding of horses in U.S. began in earnest in 1798. This year, *Diomed,* great English champion who had won Epsom Derby in 1780, was brought to U.S. *Diomed* sired many famous American horses, including *Eclipse* and *Lexington.*

1798

Sporting Magazine of England reported a **hawk** that had been shot in Yorkshire had attached to its leg a brass band inscribed, "Belonging to the Governor of New Halifax, America, A.D., 1762."

1800

Gouging, popular frontier sport, reached peak of popularity in Ohio Valley. Ultimate goal was gouging out of an opponent's eye with the thumbnail. Thumbnails were grown long for this purpose. This style of fighting was imported from England into South and spread westward.

Ball game, which later became **baseball,** played by boys using cricket balls but not cricket bats.

1802

New York State passed law forbidding **public races.** Only races in state were held by private Jockey Clubs.

Expectation won sweepstakes at Richmond, doing 2 miles in 3:47. After race, he was sold for $4000.

1803

Race horse *Peacemaking* set **30 year record** running 2 miles in 3 min. 54 sec.

1806

First picture of **football game** on American soil showed Yale students kicking ball under stern eye of Puritan Yale president Timothy Dwight. Football had been kicked around at Yale for 45 years by this time.

JUNE 5, 1806

First horse to trot a mile in under 3 min. was *Yankee,* covering distance in 2.59.

1808

Famous race horse named *Diomed* died.

DECEMBER 10, 1810

First unofficial **heavyweight champion** of U.S., Tom Molineaux, freed slave from Virginia beaten in 40th round by Tom Cribb, English champion, in fight at Copthall Common, England.

1811

Competitive rowing races came into prominence. Race between *Knickerbocker* and *Invincible* of Long Island from Harsimus, N.J., to Battery attracted thousands. Race was won by *Knickerbocker.*

1813

Craps ist introduced to U.S. by Bernard Xavier Philippe de Marigny de Mandeville, rich playboy of New Orleans, La. It was an adaptation of "hazards," a French dice game, which Marigny had played in English coffeehouses. American name derived from Johnny Crapaud, soubriquet for Louisiana Creoles. Crapaud later syncopated to Craps. Marigny lost most of his wealth playing the game.

1816

New mile record in horse racing set by *Timoleon.* Time was 1:47.

In **1st "pugilistic encounter"** in America, Jacob Hyer beat Tom Beasley in grudge fight and called himself America's 1st champion, being so recorded. Bare knuckles, London Prize Ring Rules.

Football, *today a popular spectator sport, was banned at Yale in 1822 for being too brutal.*

Photo finish *of a horse race is common sight today, but in 1800 public horse racing was banned in New York.*

1817

Paw-paw was a game of chance with sea shells used as dice.

1818

First recorded trotting contest occurred when *Boston Blue* did the mile in less than 3 minutes, winning his supporters $1000.

First mention of **bowling at pins** made in *Rip Van Winkle,* Washington Irving's story of Dutch settlers in New York. Bowling at pins, as well as lawn bowls, probably popular for some years by this time.

1820

First football games appeared in American colleges. It was form of hazing used especially at Yale and Harvard. Sophomores and freshmen were supposed to kick ball around, but sophomores generally kicked freshmen instead. These "games" were banned during 1830's because of large number of injuries.

1821

New York State relaxed laws against **public horse racing,** permitting tracks to open in Queens County. This led to building of Union Course on Long Island.

1822

Football at Yale College prohibited.

MAY, 1823

First great horse racing event in America was between *American Eclipse* from North and challenger *Sir Henry* from South for purse of $20,000. *American Eclipse* won 2 out of 3 heats, doing 4-mile stretch in 7:49 and 8:24.

1824

Estimated crowd of 50,000 witnessed **boat race** in New York harbor for a purse of $1000.

1825

Organization of **New York Trotting Club,** which constructed racing course on Long Island, 1st especially devoted to trotting.

First U.S. gymnasium was established at Northampton, Mass., by Charles Beck.

1826

Charles Follen, Harvard College instructor, introduces **physical education** into college education. He taught the Friedrich Jahn system.

1827
2nd handbook for American sportsmen, *American Shooter's Manual* published in Philadelphia.

JULY 23, 1827
First swimming school in America opened in Boston, Massachusetts.

1828
America's 1st archery club formed.

AUGUST, 1829
American Turf Register and Sporting Magazine, 1st American publication of its kind, founded by John Stuart Skinner in Baltimore, Md. Magazine devoted to improvement of thoroughbred horses, racing, hunting, shooting, fishing and the habits of American game.

1830
Sam Patch became national hero during this decade by a series of daring, well advertised leaps from bridges and banks of waterfalls. His 1st great triumph was a 90-ft. jump into the Passaic River from the bridge at Patterson, N.J. He began touring country after this success, and was well paid for his efforts. His next spectacular achievement was a drop into Niagara Falls from the highest point on Goat Island, a drop of more than half the height of the falls. His last and fatal leap was into the Genesee Falls from the Genesse River, "a distance of 125 feet."

Walking feat, which Joshua Newsam of Philadelphia covered 1000 miles in 18 days.

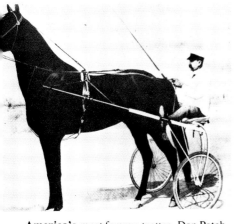

America's *most famous trotter,* Dan Patch.

FEBRUARY 11, 1830
Continued interest in cock fighting indicated by a great main held in Harrisburg, Pa., in which $100 was put up for each fight.

SEPTEMBER 18, 1830
Race between horse and "Tom Thumb," 1st locomotive built in America, won by horse. Locomotive pulled 40 passengers over 9-mile course from Riley's Tavern to Baltimore, but sprang leak in boiler and failed to finish.

DECEMBER 10, 1831
A popular weekly racing sheet, *Spirit of the Times,* founded by William Trotter Porter. Its stated purpose was to raise reputation of racing and other sports.

1832
First sports editor in U.S., William Trotter Porter, was given that position and title after he sold his newspaper *The Spirit of the Times* to *The Traveller.*

1833
Rudimentary form of baseball played in Philadelphia by Olympic Ball Club. Home plate was situated between 2 bases. Like cricket, a ball hit behind the batter was considered a "hit," and runners struck by the ball were "out."

1834
First "hurdle race" run in America took place at the Washington, D.C., Jockey Club. 6 fences were distributed over the mile stretch, the winner being awarded a plate valued at £100.

First printed rules for "baseball" appeared in Robin Carver's *The Book of Sports.* Rules for game called "Rounders" copied verbatim from English book. Little resemblance to modern baseball.

1835
Nearly 30 thousand spectators saw famous 10-mile foot race at Union Course, Long Island. An offer made in New York of $1000 to any man who could run 10 miles in less than an hour drew 9 contestants. Henry Stannard of Killingsworth won, covering the 1st mile in 5:36, last mile in 5:54, and the entire course in 59.44.

1839
Col. Abner Doubleday laid out 1st baseball diamond at Cooperstown, N.Y.

1840
1st international cricket match in which a U.S. team participated took place in Toronto, where an underrated New York club beat the Toronto club by the slim margin of 1 point.

MAY 20, 1842
The intersectional horse races took place at Union Course. Long Island, between *Fashion* (entry from North) and *Boston* (entry from South) for a purse of $20,000. *Fashion* broke all records by doing the 4 miles in 7:32.

1843
Rowing introduced to Harvard when William Weeks, a student, bought and outfitted a shell. Yale set up boat and crew in 1844.

1844
International track meet took place at Hoboken, N.J., in which John Gildersleeve of New York outran Britishers in a 10-mile race for a purse of $1000; his time, 57:01½.

1845
Cartwright dedvised 1st formal rules for playing baseball. Most significant differences from rules applied at present were: game was terminated when 1 team made 21 aces (runs); the ball had to be pitched underhand; only 1 base was allowed when the ball bounced off the playing field; a ball caught on the 1st bounce was out.

JUNE 19, 1846
First recorded baseball game in history played at Elysian Field, Hoboken, N.J., between the New York Nine and the Knickerbockers. The New York Nine won, 23-1, but Davis , their pitcher, was fined 6 cents for swearing at the umpire. Alexander Joy Cartwright, founder of Knickerbockers, wrote rules for the game, which are still followed in large part today.

1848
Baseball rules altered to provide that a runner was out at 1st base if ball was held by a fielder on the bag before the runner could reach it.

1849
The American Fistiana published. It was a history of American boxing which listed the main events of the 40 years previous and gave an account of the $10,000 purse match between Sullivan and Hyer.

FEBRUARY 7, 1849
Tom Hyer, unofficial American heavyweight champion, met Yankee Sullivan, an Englishman who was touring the country taking on all comers, and knocked him out. This was Hyer's last fight as no one else challenged him.

JUNE 3, 1851
First baseball uniforms worn by New York Knickerbockers. Outfits consisted of straw hats, white shirts, and blue full-length trousers.

AUGUST 22, 1851
Schooner-yacht America unexpectedly won over 15 British vessels in 60-mile yacht race around the Isle of Wight. The trophy won became known as "The America's Cup."

AUGUST 3, 1852
Yale and Harvard held 1st intercollegiate rowing race on 2-mile course at Lake Winnepesaukee, N.J. Harvard won by 4 lengths.

1853
Intercity baseball rivalry between an All-New York team and an All-Brooklyn 9. New York won 2 out of 3 matches.

First newspaper story on baseball appeared in New York *Mercury* written by Sen. William Cauldwell.

OCTOBER 12, 1853
John C. Morrissey, who claimed the heavyweight boxing championship was challenged by Yankee Sullivan. Sullivan led for 36 rounds, but during a rest period, climbed out of the ring to take on a few Morrissey supporters who had been heckling him. He failed to get back into the ring on time and the referee awarded the decision and the title to Morrissey.

1854
Trotting horse, Flora Temple, broke all records by running the mile at Kalamazoo, Mich., in 2:19½—1st time a horse had run below 2:20. News flashed throughout nation by telegraph made her a national legend.

Baseball rules stipulated exact weight and size of the baseball for 1st time. Ball had to weigh between 5½ and 6 oz. and have a diameter of between 2¾ and 3½ in.

Baseball, *long considered America's favorite pastime, was first played with "modern rules" in 1846.*

1857

First baseball association formed. 25 amateur baseball clubs became National Association of Baseball Players.

New **baseball rule** fixed the length of a game at 9 innings and provided that an interrupted game would be legal after 5 innings.

OCTOBER 6, 1857

American Chess Association organized at 1st American Chess Congress, New York City.

Paul C. Morphy, 20-year-old chess wizard from New Orleans, La., won American chess championship. Morphy is recognized as **1st American international chess master.**

1858

National Association of Baseball Players organized to include 16 New York City clubs. Association adopted, with a few changes, rules which had been created by New York Knickerbocker Baseball Club, including standardized measurements for ball and bat, distance between bases, etc. Many of these rules still in force today.

APRIL 12, 1858

First billiard championship of U.S. held at Fireman's Hall, Detroit, Mich. Michael J. Phelan defeated John Seereiter in match lasting 9½ hours.

JULY 20, 1858

First admission charge to a baseball game (50¢) levied for the contest between Brooklyn and the New York All Stars at Fashion Race Course in Long Island. New York defeated Brooklyn by a score of 22-18.

APRIL 12, 1859

Michael Phelan of New York City became **1st national billiard champion** by defeating John Seerciter of Detroit, Mich., in 2,000-point match for $15,000 stake. Game was 4-ball carom on 6-pocket table.

JULY 26, 1859

Harvard won **1st intercollegiate regatta** over Yale and Brown at Lake Quinsigamond, Worcester, Mass. Race, in 6-oared shells, was 3 miles.

OCTOBER 3, 1859

International cricket match took place in Hoboken between an All-England 11 and an All-U.S. 22 from Philadelphia and New York. The English team was victorious by a score of 64 runs and an inning, after a match that lasted 3 days.

1860

Game of **croquet** introduced from England and enjoyed a large following.

"7th-Inning Stretch" became common at baseball games. It refers to the custom of spectators standing up in their seats and stretching just before the home team comes to bat in the 7th inning. The custom serves 2 functions, 1 practical and 1 superstitious. The spectator not only relieves his cramped muscles but he brings good luck to his team as well because of the traditional luck of the number "7" in dice.

1860

First organized baseball game in San Francisco played.

Yale met Harvard in **1st inter-collegiate billiards match.**

1861

First baseball trophy offered by newspaper, *New York Clipper.*

1862

First enclosed baseball field opened at Union Grounds, Brooklyn, N.Y.

1863

New baseball regulation provided that both balls and strikes were to be called.

Roller skating introduced to America by James L. Plimpton. He invented the 4-wheel skate, which worked on rubber pads.

First attempt to "steal a base" made by Eddie Cuthbert of Philadelphia when Keystones played against Brooklyn Atlantics.

MAY 5, 1863

Joe Coburn knocked out Mike McCoole in a 63-round **American boxing championship** bout held at Charleston, Md.

1864

John Morrissey, ex-prize fighter, built **race track** at Saratoga, N.Y., and organized 1st race meets there. He named 1st stakes race The Travers after local family; it is still run today, the oldest race of its kind in U.S.

First American croquet club founded. It was the Park Place Croquet Club of Brooklyn, New York.

1865

John Wesley Hyatt received patent for a **composition billiard ball,** and was awarded $10,000 prize by a billiard ball manufacturer who up to this time had to use expensive ivory.

1866

Brooklyn's team, the Atlantics, played the Athletics of Philadelphia for the unofficial **baseball championship** of U.S. Brooklyn defeated the Athletics 27 to 10.

First deliberate **bunt** in baseball laid down by Dickey Pearce of Brooklyn Atlantics.

James Gordon Bennett's 107 ft. schooner, the *Henrietta,* won **1st trans-oceanic yacht race.** The *Henrietta* engaged 2 other schooners in a race from Sandy Hook, N.J., to the Isle of Wight. Her time was 13 days, 21 hours, 45 minutes.

JUNE 17, 1866

New York City Athletic Club founded.

1867

Ruthless won the **1st annual Belmont Stakes.** Jockey was F. Morris; time was 3:05 for winnings valued at $1850. Race held at Jerome Park, N.Y.

1867

Record for long-distance walking set by **Edward P. Weston,** who did the distance from Portland, Me., to Chicago in 26 days, and won for his efforts $10,000.

1868

First baseball uniforms introduced by Cincinnati Red Stockings. Featuring knickerbockers, they were ridiculed at first.

Vogue for **ice skating** led to the meeting of an American skating congress in Pittsburgh, whose purpose was to formulate regulations for the sport.

NOVEMBER 11, 1868

First amateur track and field meet (indoors) held by the New York Athletic Club. The New York A.C., which had been orga-

nized Sept. 8th, later held outdoor meets, established rules for the conduct of meets, built the 1st cinder track.

1869

"Battery" 1st employed in baseball parlance to describe the combination of pitcher and catcher. Term derived from telegraphy where combination of transmitter and receiver formed a battery.

Fenian won the 3rd annual **Belmont Stakes.** Jockey was C. Miller; time was 3:04¼ for winnings valued at $3350.

Poughkeepsie (N.Y.) Ice Yacht Club formed, 1st such society in U.S. It was followed by New Hamburgh and Hudson River Ice Yacht Clubs.

MARCH 15, 1869

First professional baseball team was Cincinnati Red Stockings who announced regular payments to players and began a successful 8-month tour of East and Middle West.

JUNE 15, 1869

American boxing champion Mike McCoole, won on a foul in 9th round from Tom Allen of England in what was probably **1st international bare knuckles boxing match** at St. Louis, Mo.

NOVEMBER 6, 1869

First intercollegiate football game played at New Brunswick, N.J. Rutgers beat Princeton 6-4 in a game more like soccer than football as it is played today. There were 25 men on each team and no running with ball was allowed.

1870

Roller skating spread throughout America as it did throughout world. By 1863, 4 rollers had been added to "parlor skates" and a young skater, William H. Fuller, developed art of figure skating, which he displayed on a tour around the world.

One of the most **popular spectator sports** was walking. Gilmore's Gardens in New York City would usually sell out when famous heel-and-toers raced there.

2 popular sports were cricket and baseball.

Famous international boat race took place in New York between British yacht *Cambria* and host of entries from New York Yacht Club. Race was won by an American boat, the *Magic.*

Pimlico race track built in Baltimore, Md., by a group of racing enthusiasts who were encouraged by the success of the course at Saratoga Springs, N.Y., in 1864.

Kingfisher won the 4th annual **Belmont Stakes.** Jockey was W. Dick; time was 2:59½ for winnings valued at $3750.

Belmont Stakes, *one third of the famed Triple Crown, was first run in 1867.*

MAY 10, 1870

Jem Mace of England, who claimed **world heavyweight boxing championship** upon retirement of Tom King, also of England, fought Tom Allen, another claimant, in a 10-round bout near Kennersville, La. Mace was declared winner.

Columbia, Princeton and Rutgers were playing their earliest **football matches.** The game which was played was technically soccer.

Yale and Harvard met in a **crew race** on a circular course at Worcester, Mass. Yale came in 1st, but was disqualified for having run into Harvard.

AUGUST 16, 1870

Fred Goldsmith demonstrated that the **curve ball** was not an optical illusion before a crowd at Capitoline Grounds, Brooklyn. Goldsmith set up 3 poles in a straight line and hurled a ball that went to the right of the 1st pole, to the left of the 2nd, and to the right of the 3rd.

1871

Interest in rifle shooting led to formation of **National Rifle Association.**

First professional baseball association organized, National Association of Professional Baseball Players, which replaced the amateur National Association.

New **baseball rule** permitted the batter to call for a high or low pitched ball as he desired. This rule was rescinded in 1887.

Harry Bassett won the 5th annual **Belmont Stakes.** Jockey was W. Miller; time was 2:56 for winnings valued at $5450.

1872

New baseball rule permitted the pitcher to snap his delivery of the ball. However, the pitcher was still restricted to an underhand, below-the-waist motion. Present day regulations for size of ball also set this year: not less than 5 nor more than 5¼ oz., and not less than 9 nor more than 9¼ in. in diameter.

Joe Daniels won the 6th annual **Belmont Stakes.** Jockey was J. Rowe; time was 2:58¼ for winnings valued at $4500.

1873

Famous decision by **President White of Cornell:** "I will not permit 30 men to travel 400 miles to agitate a bag of wind," when refusing Cornell football players permission to meet Michigan at Cleveland.

Bookmakers 1st appeared at U.S. race tracks. 1st few were English but Americans soon learned the skill, and the days of informal wagering between owners or between spectators were over.

The **Fair Grounds race course** was opened in New Orleans, La., to operate on a system of prolonged meetings patterned after John Morrissey's races begun in Saratoga Springs in 1864.

The No. 1 national idols during the 1870's were **riflemen.** More than 100,000 people attended one national rifle shooting tournament held at Creedmoor, Long Island, N.Y. in 1873. No. 2 were **oarsmen.** As many as 60,000 men, women, and children lined the banks of the Harlem River in New York City to watch and wager on the sculling contests.

Survivor won the 1st annual **Preakness Stakes,** at Pimlico, Md., paying 11-1. Jockey was G. Barbee; time was 2:43 on a slow track for winnings valued at $1800. Preakness Stakes is one of the 3 classic races in American racing. It is associated with the Kentucky Derby and the Belmont Stakes in importance,

and a horse which has won all three has earned the Triple Crown of American racing.

Springbok won the 7th annual **Belmont Stakes.** Jockey was J. Rowe; time was 3:01¾ for winnings valued at $5200.

SEPTEMBER 23, 1873

Tom Allen of England, who claimed **world's heavyweight boxing championship** after retirement of Jem Mace, fought Mike McCoole near St. Louis, Mo. Allen won and was declared world champion.

OCTOBER 19, 1873

Yale, Princeton, Columbia, and Rutgers met at 5th Avenue Hotel, New York City, to draft 1st code of rules for **football.** Rules chosen were more like soccer than modern football and were abandoned in a few years in favor of the "Boston Game" played at Harvard.

1874

Rugby football introduced on American campus in a match between Harvard and McGill University of Canada. Canadian rules for the game greatly interested the sports-minded of America and were instrumental in development that led to modern football.

Culpepper won the 2nd annual **Preakness Stakes,** paying 8-1. Jockey was M. Donohue; time was 2:56½ on a muddy track for winnings valued at $1900.

Saxon won the 8th annual **Belmont Stakes.** Jockey was G. Barbee; time was 2:39½ for winnings valued at $4200. Distance was 1½ miles.

Mary Ewing Outerbridge brought **lawn tennis** to America from Bermuda. She set up her net on grounds of Staten Island Cricket and Baseball Club, where she and a friend played 1st game in U.S.

Formation of the **Coaching Club** reflected popularity of 4-in-hand coach driving as a fad of the American upper classes.

First appearance of **football uniform** at match between Harvard and Tufts.

Baseball glove introduced by Charles G. Waite, 1st baseman for a Boston team. Glove was unpadded.

Tom Ochiltree won the 3rd annual **Preakness Stakes,** Jockey was L. Hughes; time was 2:34½ on a slow track for winnings valued at $1900.

Calvin won the 9th annual **Belmont Stakes.** Jockey was R. Swim; time was 2:42½ for winnings valued at $4450.

MAY 17, 1875

First Kentucky Derby held at Churchill Downs, Ky., the winner being *Aristides,* ridden by Jockey Lewis for a purse of $2850.

First Kentucky Derby *run at Churchill Downs was in 1875.*

1876

Polo brought to America by James Gordon Bennett, famous publisher of New York *Herald.* Sport was launched at Dickel's Riding Academy, New York City.

Catcher's mask used in baseball invented by F.W. Thayer, of Harvard University.

Professional baseball entrenched in America with the formation of the National League. League was composed of the following teams: the Athletics of Philadelphia; Hartford; Boston; Chicago; Cincinnati; Louisville; St. Louis; and the Mutuals of New York. 1st president of the League was Morgan G. Bulkley. 1st pennant winner was Chicago with a season record of 52 wins and 14 losses.

First American amateur to run **100 yds. in 10 secs.** was Horace H. Lee of Pennsylvania.

Algerine won the 10th annual **Belmont Stakes.** Jockey was W. Donohue; time was 2:40½ for winnings valued at $3700.

Intercollegiate Association of Amateur Athletes of America founded at Saratoga, N.Y., by delegates from 14 U.S. colleges participating in crew and track events held on July 20-21. Organization was earliest significant intercollegiate sports association in U.S. Amherst, Bowdoin, Brown, CCNY, Columbia, Cornell, Dartmouth, Harvard, Princeton, Trinity, Union, Wesleyan, Williams, and Yale were original members.

Shirley won the 4th annual **Preakness Stakes,** paying 2-1. Jockey was G. Barbee; time was 2:44¾ on a good track for winnings valued at $1950.

APRIL 2, 1876

In **1st official National League baseball game** Boston beat Philadelphia, 6-5, with Jim O'Rourke getting the 1st hit.

MAY 15, 1876

Vagrant won 2nd **Kentucky Derby** at Churchill Downs, Ky. in 2:38¼ for a purse of $2950. Jockey was Swim; owner was W. Astor.

Rules for college *football were first standardized in 1876.*

MAY 23, 1876

Joe Borden pitched **1st no-hitter** in the history of the National League. The Boston pitcher lost his effectivness soon after and ended the season as the club's grounds-keeper.

SEPTEMBER 7, 1876

Joe Goss of England defeated Tom Allen in 27 rounds at Covington, Ky. The victory earned Goss the **world's heavyweight boxing championship.**

NOVEMBER 23, 1876

At invitation of Princeton, delegates from Yale, Harvard, Rutgers, Columbia, and Princeton met at Massasoit House, Spring-field, Mass., to discuss **rules for football.** Princeton had recently adopted Harvard's rules which in turn were chiefly based on the rules of the British Rugby Union, and these were adopted by all colleges represented at the meeting. Intercollegiate Football Association, 1st such organization in U.S., grew out of the meeting.

1877

New baseball rule exempted hitter from time at bat if he was walked. This rule affected the scoring of a batter's average rather than actual play. Another new rule stipulated that a substitute player could replace a starting player only before the 4th inning. **National League baseball pennant winner** was Boston with a record of 31 wins, 17 losses.

Cloverbrook won the 5th annual **Preakness Stakes.** Jockey was C. Holloway; time was 2:45½ on a slow track for winnings valued at $1600.

Cloverbrook won the 11th annual **Belmont Stakes.** Jockey was C. Holloway; time was 2:46 for winnings valued at $5200.

MAY 22, 1877

Baden Baden was the winner of the **3rd Kentucky Derby,** held at Churchill Downs, Louisville, Ky. He won $3300 running the 1½ miles in 2:38 on a fast track, under jockey Walker.

1878

Interest in archery led to formation of **National Archery Association.**

Duke of Magenta won the 6th annual **Preakness Stakes,** paying 2-5. Jockey was C. Holloway; time was 2:41¾ on a good track for winnings valued at $2100.

Duke of Magenta won the 12th annual **Belmont Stakes.** Jockey was L. Hughes; time was 2:43½ on a mnuddy track for winnings valued at $3850.

National League baseball pennant winner was Boston with a season record of 41 wins and 19 defeats.

MAY 21, 1878

Day Star won the **4th Kentucky Derby** at Churchill Downs, Louisville, Ky. He won $4050 on a good track in 2:37¼, under jockey Carter.

OCTOBER 10, 1878

Earliest American **jockey record** was Jimmie McLaughlin's riding of winners in all 3 races in Nashville, Tenn. One of the races was run in 2 heats, of which McLaughlin won both.

1879

Interest in **fox hunting** revived among wealthy of New York and New England.

New baseball rule allowed a batter to reach 1st base after receiving 9 balls. The requirements for a "walk" to 1st base were reduced to 8 balls in 1880, 7 in 1881, 6 in 1884, raised to 7 again in 1885, reduced to 5 in 1887, and 4 in 1889. This last requirement for a base on balls has persisted until the present time.

Spendthrift won the 13th annual **Belmont Stakes,** paying 2-5. Jockey was L. Hughes; time was 2:47 on a good track for winnings valued at $2800.

Grenada won the 8th annual **Preakness Stakes,** paying 1-6. Jockey was L. Hughes; time was 2:40½ on a fast track for winnings valued at $2550.

MAY 20, 1879

Lord Murphy won the **5th annual Kentucky Derby** held at Churchill Downs, Louisville, Ky. His time was 2:37 on a fast track under jockey Schauer, and earned $3550.

JUNE 24, 1879

First Childs Cup won by University of Pennsylvania in 9:23. The cup was presented this year by George W. Childs of Philadelphia, Pa. Columbia, Pennsylvania, and Princeton are the only schools eligible to win the cup. Cornell and Navy occasionally participate by invitation, but if they win, may not claim the prize. The Childs Cup is the oldest trophy in sprint racing; was limited to 4-oared crews until 1887; 8-oared crews since 1889.

FALL, 1879

Providence won the **National League baseball pennant** with a season record of 55 victories, 23 defeats.

1880

Increasing interest of **women participating in sports** during this decade. Besides tennis, archery and croquet, they went in for riding, cycling, swimming, boat racing, fencing, and skating.

New baseball rule stipulated that a batter was out if he was hit by a batted ball.

Grenada won the 14th annual **Belmont Stakes,** paying 2-5. Jockey was L. Hughes; time was 2:47 on a good track for winnings valued at $2800.

Grenada won the 8th annual **Preakness Stakes,** paying 1-4. Jockey was L. Hughes; time was 2:40½ on a good track for winnings valued at $2000.

MARCH 18, 1880

Fonso was the winner of the **6th annual Kentucky Derby.** He ran the 1½ miles in 2:37½ under jockey G. Lewis, winning $3800.

JUNE 21, 1880

Paddy Ryan, an American, defeated Joe Goss in the 87th round of a fight for the world's heavyweight boxing championship held near Colliers Station, W. Va.

Autumn: Chicago won the **National League baseball pennant** with a season record of 67 victories, 17 defeats.

1881

New baseball rule increased the distance of the pitcher from home plate from 45 ft. to 50 ft.

United States Lawn Tennis Association born at meeting of the leaders of the Eastern clubs where tennis was played. A pattern of play was set and adopted all over the world. National championship was held at Newport, R.I., Aug. 31. Richard D. Sears won the 1st

men's singles crown.

Saunterer won the 15th annual **Belmont Stakes,** paying 5-2. Jockey was T. Costello; time was 2:47 on a heavy track for winnings valued at $3000.

Saunterer won the 9th annual **Preakness Stakes,** paying 3-2. Jockey was W. Costello; time was 2:40½ on a good track for winnings valued at $1950.

MAY 17, 1881

Hindoo won the **7th annual Kentucky Derby.** He earned $4410 in this race running a fast track in 2:40 under jockey J. McLaughlin. *Hindoo* was one of the 1st great American race horses, going on to win 18 out of 20 races this year.

FALL, 1881

Chicago won the **National League baseball pennant** with a season record of 56 victories, 28 defeats.

OCTOBER 15, 1881

American Angler, owned and edited by William C. Harris, published in Philadelphia, Pa. It was the **1st American fishing journal.**

1882

Rival baseball organization formed as **American Association** which flourished for some years, introducing some innovations into league rules later adopted by National League. It formed working agreement with National League in 1886.

Phil Casey, one of Ireland's great handball players, immigrated to Brooklyn, N.Y. Casey built a **handball court** and opened a school, introducing a new sport into the U.S. with the help of some fellow immigrants from the British Isles.

National Croquet Association formed, to revise and standardize rules of game.

Boxing achieved nationwide popularity through efforts of world bare-knuckle champion, John L. Sullivan, who toured the U.S. putting on boxing exhibitions, with gloves under the Marquis of Queensberry rules, and offering $500 to any man who could last 4 rounds with him. Bare-knuckle fighting had been frowned upon by respectable people until this time.

Prize fighting *under Marquis of Queensbury Rules was first introduced in America in 1882.*

U.S. Intercollegiate Lacrosse Association founded. Members were Harvard, Princeton, and Columbia; Yale and NYU admitted the following year.

Vanguard won the 10th annual **Preakness Stakes,** paying 1-7. Jockey was W. Costello; time was 2:44½ on a good track for winnings valued at $1250.

Forester won the 16th annual **Belmont Stakes,** paying 1-5. Jockey was J. McLaughlin; time was 2:43 on a fast track for winnings valued at $2600.

U.S. lawn tennis men's singles champion, Richard D. Sears.

FEBRUARY 7, 1882

John L. Sullivan won the American heavyweight championship when he defeated Paddy Ryan in 9 rounds at Mississippi City. This contest was fought with bare knuckles.

MAY 16, 1882

The 8th annual **Kentucky Derby** was won by *Apollo.* He won $4500 running on a good track in 2:40½ under jockey Hurd.

JUNE 24, 1882

Only major league baseball **umpire** ever expelled for dishonesty, Richard Higham, was expelled from National League.

Fall: Chicago won the **National League baseball pennant** for the 3rd time in a row with a season record of 55 victories, 29 defeats.

SEPTEMBER 25, 1882

First major league baseball doubleheader (2 games for the price of 1) held between Providence and Worcester.

1883

George Kinney won the 17th annual **Belmont Stakes,** paying 1-12. Jockey was J. McLaughlin; time: 2:42½ on a fast track for winnings valued at $3070.

Jacobus won the 11th annual **Preakness Stakes.** Jockey was G. Barbee; time: 2:42½ on a good track for winnings valued at $1635.

G.M. Hendrie of Springfield, Mass., won the **1st recorded bicycle race.** It was called a race for the championship although only 2 riders participated. Hendrie later became famous as an automobile and motorcycle builder.

U.S. lawn tennis men's singles champion, Richard D. Sears.

MAY 1, 1883

First National League baseball game played; Philadelphia beating Providence, 4-3.

MAY 23, 1883

The 9th annual **Kentucky Derby** was won by *Leonatus,* ridden by jockey W. Donohue. The track was heavy, time: 2:43, winnings $3760.

JUNE 2, 1883

First baseball game played under electric lights in Fort Wayne, Ind. Fort Wayne beat Quincy, 19-11, in 7 innings.

JUNE 16, 1883

First Ladies' Day baseball game staged by the New York Giants. On Ladies' Day, both escorted and unescorted ladies were admitted to the park free of charge.

FALL, 1883

Boston won the **National League baseball pennant** with a season record of 63 victories, 35 defeats.

OCTOBER 22, 1883

First annual New York Horse Show opened at Gilmore's Gardens, New York City, organized by National Horse Show Association of America.

1884

New baseball regulation removed all restrictions on the manners in which pitchers could hurl the ball. Pitcher was compelled, by another rule to take only 1 step before delivering his pitch.

First baseball championship of America won by Providence of the National League at the Polo Grounds, N.Y. The Providence team swept a 3-game series from the Metropolitans of New York who won the American Association title.

First Negro to play baseball in a major league was Moses Fleetwood Walker of Toledo in the American Association.

Greyhound racing introduced at Philadelphia, Pa.

Panique won the 18th annual **Belmont Stakes,** paying 11-10. Jockey was J. McLaughlin; time: 2:42 on a good track for winnings valued at $3150.

Knight of Ellerslie won the 12th annual **Preakness Stakes,** paying 3-5. Jockey was S.H. Fisher; time was 2:39½ on a fast track for winnings valued at $1905.

U.S. lawn tennis men's singles champion, Richard D. Sears.

MAY 16, 1884

10th annual Kentucky Derby won by *Buchanan,* time: 2:40¼ on a good track, the winnings $3990. The jockey was Isaac Murphy, one of the great American jockeys. Murphy, a Negro, won 4 American Derbies and 3 Kentucky Derbies in addition to many other important races during the 1880's, often riding inferior horses.

FALL, 1884

Providence won the **National League baseball pennant** with a season record of 84 victories, 28 defeats.

Tyrant won the 19th annual **Belmont Stakes,** paying 10-9. Jockey was P. Duffy; time: 2:43 on a good track for winnings valued at $2710.

Tecumseh won the 13th annual **Preakness Stakes,** paying 2-5. Jockey was J. McLaughlin; time: 2:49 on a heavy track for winnings valued at $2160.

U.S. lawn tennis men's singles champion, Richard D. Sears.

MAY 14, 1885

Winner of the 11th annual **Kentucky Derby** was *Joe Cotton* in 2:37¼ on a good track under jockey Henderson; earnings $4630.

FALL, 1885

Chicago won the **National League baseball pennant** with a season record of 87 victories, 25 defeats. The **baseball championship series** ended in a tie between Chicago, the National League winners, and St. Louis of the American Association. In the 7-game series both teams won 3 games each and 1 game ended in a draw.

DECEMBER 20, 1885

William B. Curtis **weight-lifting strongman,** reported to have hoisted 3,239 lbs.

1886

First international polo match took place between an English 4 and an American at Newport, R.I. The visiting team easily swept the match 10 to 4 and 14-2.

Inspector won the 20th annual **Belmont Stakes,** jockey was J. McLaughlin; time: 2:41 on a fast track for winnings valued at $2720.

The Bard won the 14th annual **Preakness Stakes,** paying 13-5. Jockey was S.H. Fisher; time: 2:45 on a good track for winnings valued at $2050.

U.S. lawn tennis men's singles champion, Richard D. Sears.

JANUARY 1, 1886

First Tournament of Roses in Pasadena, Calif., staged by the Valley Hunt Club which had been founded by Charles Frederick Holder. Holder suggested that the members decorate their carriages with the natural flowers of California on New Year's Day and that after a parade of these carriages, a program of athletic events be devised to round out the day.

MAY 14, 1886

Ben Ali, the favorite, won the 12th annual **Kentucky Derby.** Time: 2:36½ on a fast track for winnings valued at $4890. Jockey was P. Duffy.

AUTUMN, 1886

Chicago won the **National League baseball pennant** with a season record of 90 victories, 34 defeats. St. Louis of the American Association won the **baseball championship** of America, defeating the Chicago team, winners of the National League title, 4 out of 6 games.

1887

First real golf club in the U.S. was the Foxburg Golf Club, founded in Foxburg, Pa., as a result of John Mickle Fox's trip to Scotland where he learned the game. There were clubs calling themselves "golf clubs" in Savannah and Charleston as far back as 1795 and '96, but there is no record of their members ever playing golf.

Hanover won the 21st annual **Belmont Stakes,** paying 1-20. Jockey was J. McLaughlin; time: 2:43½ on a heavy track for winnings valued at $2900.

First golf club *for membership play was completed in 1887.*

1887

Dunbine won the 15th annual **Preakness Stakes,** paying 4-1. Jockey was W. Donoghue; time: 2:39½ on a fast track for winnings valued at $1675.

U.S. lawn tennis men's champion, Richard D. Sears; **1st U.S. women's champion,** Ellen F. Hansell.

MARCH 2, 1887

American Trotting Association organized at Detroit, Mich.

MAY 11, 1887

Montrose won the 13th annual **Kentucky Derby**, paying 10-1. Jockey was I. Lewis, time: 2:39¼ on a fast track for winnings valued at $4200.

MAY 26, 1887

First day of **legal betting** at tracks in New York state.

FALL, 1887

Detroit won the **National League baseball pennant** with a season record of 79 victories, 45 defeats.

1888

Track records as they stood this year:
100 yd. dash—10 sec. flat
220 yd. dash—22 sec.
¼ mi.   —47¾ sec.
½ mi.   —1:55²/₅
1 mi.   —4:21²/₅
10 mi.   —52:58³/₅

The 100 yard dash *record was first set at 10.0 seconds in 1888. Modern record is nearly one second faster.*

New York won the **baseball championship**, defeating the St. Louis team 6 games to 4.

Major league record for most consecutive games won by a pitcher in a season set by Tim Keefe of New York. He won 19 straight games.

Refund won the 16th annual **Preakness Stakes**, paying 4-1. Jockey was F. Littlefield; time was 2:49 on a heavy track for winnings valued at $1185.

Sir Dixon won the 22nd annual **Belmont Stakes**, paying 2-5. Jockey was J. McLaughlin; time was 2:40¼ on a fast track for winnings valued at $3440.

U.S. lawn tennis men's singles champion, Henry W. Slocum Jr.; **women's singles champion**, Bertha L. Townsend.

JANUARY 21, 1888

Formation of **Amateur Athletic Union of the U.S.** A.A.U.'s aim: to preserve "sport for sport's sake." Its high ideal and success in attaining it is respected all over the world.

MAY 14, 1888

Macbeth II, an 8-1 shot, ridden by jockey Covington, won the 14th annual **Kentucky Derby**. Time: 2:34½ on a fast track for $4780.

AUTUMN, 1888

New York won the **National League baseball pennant** with a season record of 84 victories, 47 defeats.

1889

"Texas Leaguer" became baseball parlance for a weak hit just over the heads of the infield but short of the outfield players. Term was 1st used to describe the short hits of Arthur Sunday, a player from the Texas League,

The first *All-American Football Team, picked by Walter Camp, was in 1889. Pictured above is famed football coach Amos Alonzo Stagg.*

who was able to maintain a batting record of .398 with the help of these "Texas Leaguers."

First all-American football team selected by Walter Camp, who picked 11 players as best in their positions. His selections appeared annually in *Collier's Weekly* until Camp's death in 1925, when Grantland Rice took over.

Erie won the 23rd annual **Belmont Stakes**, paying 7-5. Jockey was W. Hayward; time was 2:47 on a good track for winnings valued at $4960.

Buddhist won the 17th annual **Preakness Stakes**, paying 1-30. Jockey was H. Anderson; time: 2:17½ on a fast track for winnings valued at $1130. This year the distance was 1¼ miles. There were no races between 1889 and 1894.

U.S. Lawn tennis men's singles champion, Henry W. Slocum Jr.; **women's singles champion**, Bertha L. Townsend.

MAY 9, 1889

Spokane, ridden by Kiley, won the 15th annual **Kentucky Derby**. *Spokane*'s time was 2:34½, the record for this race was a 1½-mi. run (the length of the race was shortened to 1¼ mi. in 1896). The track was fast and the winner earned $4970.

JUNE 5, 1889

Career of boxer **James J. Corbett,** a young bank clerk, began with his defeat of Joe Choyinski in 27 bloody rounds. Corbett finished the battle with a left hook, a blow he is said to have invented.

JULY 8, 1889

Last bare-knuckle championship fight, between John L. Sullivan and Jake Kilrain at Richburg, Miss. Sullivan defeated Kilrain after 75 grueling rounds, and claimed the world's championship since Kilrain had fought a draw with the champion of England, Jem Smith. After this bout boxing with gloves and under Marquis of Queensberry rules was introduced.

AUTUMN, 1889

New York won the **National League baseball pennant** with a season record of 83 victories, 43 defeats. Team then won the **baseball championship** for the 2nd consecutive year, defeating Brooklyn of the American Association.

NOVEMBER 14, 1889

Journalist **Nellie Bly** (Elizabeth Cochrane) started on her famous journey around the world for the New York *World,* which took her 72 days, 6 hrs., and 11 mins., at that time a

record. She completed her trip Jan. 25, 1890, thus beating the record set in Jules Verne's famous fictional story, *Around the World in Eighty Days*.

1890

"Baltimore Chop": Term originated with the Baltimore Orioles, who were adept at securing this tricky hit.

Burlington won the 24th annual **Belmont Stakes**, paying 6-1. Jockey was S. Barnes; time: 2:07¾ on a fast track for winnings valued at $8560. Distance was 1¼ miles.

U.S. lawn tennis men's singles champion, Oliver S. Campbell; **women's singles champion**, Ellen C. Roosevelt.

MAY 14, 1890

Issac Murphy rode his 2nd **Kentucky Derby** winner when he brought Corrigan's *Riley* in 1st in the 16th running of classic race. Time: 2:45 on a heavy track; winnings were $5460.

AUTUMN, 1890

Brooklyn won the **National League baseball pennant** with a season record of 86 victories, 43 defeats. **Baseball Championship of America** ended in a tie between the Brooklyn and Louisville teams. Of the 7 games played both teams won 3 games each and 1 game was played to a draw.

NOVEMBER 29, 1890

First **Army-Navy football game** was played at West Point, N.Y. The score, Navy 24, Army 0. This was the 1st game in what became an annual game between the 2 service academies (missing 1909, '17, '18, '28, '29). Usually held in Philadelphia's Municipal Stadium, it now draws over 100,000 privileged spectators and is viewed by millions on a nation-wide television broadcast.

1891

Basketball invented by Dr. James A. Naismith, physical education instructor at YMCA Training College (now Springfield College) in Springfield, Mass., as an indoor substitute for baseball and football.

Dr. James Naismith, *above, invented the game of basketball in 1891.*

New baseball rule permitted the insertion of a substitute player at any time during a game, removing restriction imposed in 1877 which allowed a substitute to enter the game only before the 4th inning.

Foxford won the 25th annual **Belmont Stakes**, paying 8-1. Jockey was E. Garrison; time: 2:08¾ on a fast track for winnings valued at $5070.

U.S. lawn tennis men's singles champion, Oliver S. Campbell; **women's singles champion**, Mabel E. Cahill.

Bob Fitzsimmons became **1st American boxer to hold 3 international titles;** he held middleweight, light heavyweight, and heavyweight crowns.

MAY 13, 1891

Isaac Murphy rode his 3rd **Kentucky Derby** winner (2nd straight) when he brought the favorite *Kingman* in 1st. Slow time of 2:52½ on a good track. Winnings were $4680.

FALL, 1891

Boston won the **National League baseball pennant** with a season record of 87 victories, 51 defeats.

OCTOBER 18, 1891

First International 6-day bicycle race in the U.S. run in the old Madison Square Garden in New York City. Riders used high wheelers and worked alone, pumping until exhausted, then resting, then starting again to total 142 hours. 1st winner was "Plugger Bill" Martin. Record under one-man rules was established in 1898 by Charlie Miller at Madison Square Garden; he rode 2,093.4 miles. Most of his competitors ended in hospitals, ill from exhaustion.

NOVEMBER 21, 1891

Yale won the **Intercollegiate football championship,** defeating Harvard 10 to 0 at Hampden Park, Springfield, Mass.

NOVEMBER 28, 1891

Army defeated Navy at Annapolis, Md., by a score of 32 to 16 at their 2d annual contest.

1892

Expression **"Garrison finish"** born when jockey Ed "Snapper" Garrison came from the rear of the field and won the Suburban Handicap at Sheepshead Bay by 3 in.

Patron won the 26th annual **Belmont Stakes,** paying 6-5. Jockey was W. Hayward; time was 2:17 on a muddy track for winnings valued at $6610.

U.S. lawn tennis men's singles champion, Oliver S. Campbell; **women's singles champion,** Mabel E. Cahill.

MARCH 18, 1892

Jockeys prohibited from using anything but a whip and a spur on a horse during a race. Ruling prompted by the discovery that jockey Cook used an electric spur while riding *Gyda* at Guttenburg, N.J. Cook was ruled off the track.

MAY 11, 1892

18th annual **Kentucky Derby** won by the favorite, G.J. Long's *Azra*, ridden by jockey Clayton. Time, 2:41½ on a heavy track; value, $4230.

AUTUMN, 1892

Boston won the **National League baseball pennant** with a season record of 102 victories, 48 defeats.

SEPTEMBER 7, 1892

First heavyweight boxing champion under the Marquis of Queensberry rules requiring gloves and 3-minute rounds was **James J. Corbett** when he knocked out the great John L. Sullivan in the 21st round at New Orleans, La. Sullivan was world bare knuckle champion and there are claims that he was 1st champ under Marquis of Queensberry rules because of previous fight with gloves.

NOVEMBER 26, 1892

Navy defeated Army at West Point in their annual football game: score of 12 to 4.

DECEMBER 31, 1892

Great American race horse was *Hindoo*, who by the end of 1892, after 3 years of racing, had won 31 of 36 starts and never finished out of the money.

1893

Ice hockey introduced to the U.S. at Yale and Johns Hopkins University.

Rise of **bicycling** as a popular diversion in America.

First national fly casting tournament held at the Chicago World's Fair (Columbian Exposition) by the newly formed Chicago Fly Casting Club. Accuracy, Accuracy Fly, Delicacy Fly, Long-distance Bait, and Long-distance Fly events were held at distances of 75, 80, and 85 ft.

New baseball rule established the distance between the pitcher and home plate at 60 ft. 6 in.

Comanche won the 27th annual **Belmont Stakes,** paying 20-1. Jockey was W. Simms; time: 1:53¼ on a fast track for winnings valued at $5310. Distance was 1⅛ mi.

U.S. lawn tennis men's singles champion, Robert D. Wrenn; **women's singles champion,** Aline M. Terry.

MAY 10, 1893

19th annual **Kentucky Derby** won by favorite *Lookout* in 2:39¼ on a fast track under jockey Kunze, winning $4090.

AUTUMN, 1893

Boston won the **National League baseball pennant** with a season record of 86 victories, 44 defeats.

NOVEMBER 30, 1893

Princeton defeated Yale by a score of 6 to 0 at New York to win the **Intercollegiate Football Association championship.**

DECEMBER 2, 1893

At Annapolis, Md., **Navy** beat Army, 6-4, in their 4th annual football classic.

1894

Highest batting average ever compiled in one season by a major league baseball player was Hugh Duffy's .438. He was a member of the Boston Nationals.

New baseball rule replaced the pitching box with a slab 12 x 4 in. Other rules stipulated that a foul bunt was to be considered a strike and player who sacrificed was not to be charged with a time at bat for scoring purposes.

Henry of Navarre won the 28th annual **Belmont Stakes,** paying 1-10. Jockey was W. Simms; time: 1:56½ on a fast track for winnings valued at $6680.

Assignee won the 18th annual **Preakness Stakes,** paying 4-1. Jockey was F. Taral; time: 1:49¼ on a fast track for winnings valued at $1830. Distance was 1¹/₁₆ mi.

Jockey Club incorporated. Club's purpose was to "encourage the development of the Thoroughbred horse" and "establish racing on such a footing that it may command the interest as well as the confidence and favorable opinion of the public."

U.S. lawn tennis men's singles champion, Robert D. Wrenn; **women's singles champion,** Helen R. Helwig.

MAY 15, 1894

20th annual **Kentucky Derby** won by the favorite, *Chant*, ridden by jockey Goodale.

Time: 2:41 on a fast track for winnings valued at $4020.

JUNE 16, 1894

Squeeze play 1st employed in baseball by George Case and Dutch Carter, players on the Yale team, in a game against Princeton.

AUTUMN, 1894

Baltimore won the **National league baseball pennant** with a season record of 89 victories, 39 defeats.

DECEMBER 22, 1894

United States Golf Association formed U.S.G.A. held its **1st amateur championship** in 1895 at Newport, R.I. C.B. Macdonald won over the 32 entrants. **1st open championship,** held the next day, was won by Horace Rawlins.

1895

New baseball regulation established the infield "pop fly" rule. Other rules classified foul tips as strikes, restricted the length of a bat to 42 inches, and increased the size of the pitcher's slab from 12 x 4 in. (1894) to 24 x 6 in.

Belmar won the 29th annual **Belmont Stakes,** paying 6-1. Jockey was F. Taral; time: 2:11½ on a heavy track for winnings valued at $2700. Distance: 1¼ mi.

Belmar won the 19th annual **Preakness Stakes,** paying 3-1. Jockey was F. Taral; time: 1:50½ on a fast track for winnings valued at $1350.

U.S. lawn tennis men's singles champion, Fred H. Hovey; **women's singles champion,** Juliette P. Atkinson.

MAY 6, 1895

21st annual **Kentucky Derby** won by the favorite *Halma*, ridden by J. Perkins. Time: 2:37½ on a fast track for winnings valued at $2970.

AUGUST 31, 1895

First "professional" football game played in Latrobe, Pa., when Latrobe's team of profit-sharing players met the Jeannette, Pa., team. Latrobe hired a substitute quarterback, John Brallier, for $10 expenses, making him the game's **1st professional player.**

AUTUMN, 1895

Baltimore won the **National League baseball pennant** with a season record of 87 victories, 43 defeats.

SEPTEMBER 9, 1895

American Bowling Congress formed in Beethoven Hall, N.Y. The A.B.C. became the ruling body of bowling, standardized rules and equipment and planned national tournaments. Modern tenpin game became standard.

1896

U.S.G.A. amateur championship won by H.G. Whigham at Shinnecock Hills, N.Y. He defeated J.G. Thorp 8 and 7. **Open championship** won by James Foulis with a score of 152.

Hastings won the 30th **Belmont Stakes,** paying 8-5. Jockey was H. Griffin; time: 2:24½ on a fast track for winnings valued at $3025. Distance: 1⅜ mi.

Margrave won the 20th annual **Preakness Stakes,** paying 4-5. Jockey was H. Griffin; time: 1:51 on a fast track for winnings valued at $1350.

U.S. lawn tennis men's singles cham-

pion, Robert D. Wrenn; **women's singles champion,** Elisabeth H. Moore.

APRIL 6, 1896

First modern Olympic Games in Athens, Greece, dominated by a small group of Americans who arrived just as the roll of athletes for the 1st events was being called. The U.S. team won 9 of the 12 events.

MAY 12, 1896

The **Kentucky Derby** was shortened to 1¼ miles and the favorite, M.F. Dwyer's Ben Brush , made the new distance in 2:07¾ on a good track to win the 22nd Derby and $4850. Jocky was W. Simms.

FALL, 1896

Baltimore won the **National League baseball pennant** with a season record of 90 victories, 39 defeats.

NOVEMBER, 1896

1st U.S. hockey league, the Amateur Hockey League, organized in New York City.

Modern ice hockey, *pictured above, got its start in America with the organization of the first hockey league in New York City in 1896.*

1897

U.S.G.A. amateur championship won by H.G. Whigham at Chicago, G.C., Wheaton, Ill. He defeated W.R. Betts, 8 and 6. **Open championship** won by Joe Lloyd with a score of 162.

Scottish Chieftain won the 31st annual **Belmont Stakes,** paying 9-5. Jockey was J. Scherrer; time: 2:32¼ on a fast track for winnings valued at $3550.

Paul Kauvar won the 21 annual **Preakness Stakes,** paying 6-1. Jockey was Thorpe; time: 1:51¼ on a sloppy track for winnings valued at $1420.

U.S. lawn tennis men's singles champion, Robert D. Wrenn; **women's singles champion,** Juliette P. Atkinson.

MARCH 17, 1897

"Gentleman Jim" **Corbett** defeated by "Bob" Fitzsimmons on St. Patrick's Day in a 14-round contest. Corbett added the term, **"Solar plexus,"** to the prizefighting vocabulary. It was 1st boxing match photographed by a moving picture camera.

MAY, 4, 1897

23rd **Kentucky Derby** won by J.C. Cahn's *Typhoon II,* ridden by F. Garner. Time: 2:12½ on a heavy track for winnings valued at $4850.

FALL, 1897

Boston won the **National League baseball pennant** with a season record of 93 victories, 39 defeats.

684

1898

U. S. lawn tennis men's singles champion, Malcolm D. Whitman; **women's singles champion,** Juliette P. Atkinson.

U.S.G.A. amateur championship won by Findlay S. Douglas at Morris County G.C., Morrisson, N.J. He defeated W. B. Smith, 5 and 3. **Open championship** was won by Fred Herd at Myopia Hunt Club, Hamilton, Mass., with a score of 328.

Bowling Brook won the 32nd annual **Belmont Stakes,** paying 7-2. Jockey was F. Littlefield; time: 2:32 on a heavy track for winnings valued at $7810.

Sly Fox won the 22nd annual **Preakness Stakes,** paying 8-5. Jockey was W. Simms; time: 1:49¾ on a good track for winnings valued at $1500.

MAY 4, 1898

24th **Kentucky Derby** won by J. E. Madden's *Plaudit.* Time: 2:09 on a good track for winnings valued at $4850.

AUTUMN, 1898

Boston won the **National League baseball pennant** with a season record of 102 victories, 47 defeats.

1899

New baseball rule required a pitcher to complete a throw to 1st base if he had motioned in that direction to pick a runner off.

U.S. lawn tennis men's singles champion, Malcolm D. Whitman; **women's singles champion,** Marion Jones.

U.S.G.A. amateur championship won by H. M. Harriman at Onwentsia Club, Lake Forest, Ill. He defeated Findlay S. Douglas, 3 and 2. **Open championship** was won by Willie Smith at Baltimore, G.C. with a score of 315.

Half Time won the 23rd annual **Preakness Stakes,** paying 1-1. Jockey was R. Clawson; time: 1:47 on a fast track for winnings valued at $1580.

Jean Bereaud won the 33rd annual **Belmont stakes,** paying 5-21. Jockey was R. Clawson; time: 2:23 on a fast track for winnings valued at $9445.

MAY 4, 1899

The 25th **Kentucky Derby.** Winner was the favorite *Manuel,* ridden by jockey F. Taral. Time: 2:12 on a fast track for winnings valued at $4850.

JUNE 9, 1899

James J. Jeffries became **world heavyweight boxing champion** after knocking out Bob Fitzsimmons in 11th round at Coney Island, N.Y.

AUTUMN, 1899

Brooklyn won the **National League baseball pennant** with a season record of 88 victories, 42 defeats.

DECEMBER 2, 1899

Army defeated Navy, 17-5, in the annual **Army-Navy football game** held at Franklin Field, Philadelphia, Pa.

1900

New **baseball rule** introduced the 5-sided home plate.

Increase in the popularity of tennis was the putting up of the **Davis Cup** by Dwight F. Davis for competition in tennis between U.S. and England. This year the U.S. team won the cup.

U.S. lawn tennis men's singles cham-

pion, Malcolm D. Whitman; **women's singles champion,** Myrtle McAteer.

U.S.G.A. amateur championship won by Walter J. Travis at Garden City G.C., N.Y. He defeated Findlay S. Douglas, 2 up. **Open championship** was won by Harry Vardon of England at Chicago G.C. with a score of 313.

Ildrim won the 34th annual **Belmont Stakes,** paying 7-2. Jockey was N. Turner; time: 2:21½ on a fast track for winnings valued at $14,790.

Hindus won the 24th annual **Preakness Stakes,** paying 15-1. Jockey was H. Spencer; time was 1:48²⁄₅ on a fast track for winnings valued at $1900.

JANUARY 29, 1900

American League formed in Chicago.

MARCH 18, 1900

Maud S., one week less than 26 years old, died. Race track queen longer than any other horse of her generation. Her record for mile was 2:08.75, made at Cleveland, Oct. 20, 1891. Owned by Robert Bonner, who had bought her from William H. Vanderbilt for $40,000.

APRIL 15, 1900

First well-organized **automobile race** in U.S. held at Springfield, L.I. Won by A. L. Riker with an electric car; he covered 50 mi. in 2 hr., 3 min.

Although *they were a far cry from the supercharged racer pictured above, the first organized auto race was held on Long Island in 1900.*

MAY 3, 1900

26th annual **Kentucky Derby** won by the favorite, C. H. Smith's *Lieutenant Gibson,* ridden by jockey J. Boland. Time was 2:06¼ on a fast track, value: $4850.

AUTUMN, 1900

Brooklyn won the **National League baseball pennant** with a season record of 82 victories, 54 defeats.

1901

U.S. lawn tennis men's singles champion, William A. Larned; **women's single champion,** Elisabeth H. Moore.

U.S.G.A. amateur championship won by Walter J. Travis at Atlantic City, N.J. He defeated W.E. Egan, 5 and 4. **Open championship** won by Willie Anderson at Myopia Hunt Club, Hamilton, Mass., with a score of 331.

Commando won the 35th annual **Belmont Stakes,** paying 7-10. Jockey was H. Spencer; time was 2:21 on a fast track for winnings valued at $11,595.

The Parader won the 25th annual **Preakness Stakes,** paying 9-20. Jockey was Landry; time: 1:47¹⁄₅ on a heavy track for winnings valued at $1605. Distance was 1 mi. and 70 yds.

APRIL 29, 1901

27th annual **Kentucky Derby** won by F.B. Van Meter's *His Eminence* ridden by jockey J. Winkfield. Time: 2:07¾ on a fast track for winnings valued at $4850.

AUGUST 21, 1901

"Iron Man" Joe McGinnity expelled from the National League for stepping on umpire Tom Connolly's toes, spitting in his face, and punching him.

AUTUMN, 1901

Pittsburgh won the **National League baseball pennant** with a season record of 90 victories, 49 defeats.

Chicago won the **1st American League baseball pennant** with a season record of 83 victories, 53 defeats.

NOVEMBER 30, 1901

Army defeated Navy in their annual football contest by a score of 11 to 5. The game was held at Philadelphia, Pa.

1902

U.S. lawn tennis men's singles champion, William A. Larned; **women's single champion,** Marion Jones.

U.S.G.A. amateur championship won by L. N. James at Glen View G.C., Golf, Ill. He defeated E. M. Byers, 4 and 2. **Open championship** won by Lawrence Auchterlonie at Garden City G.C., N.Y., with a score of 307.

Old England won the 26th annual **Preakness Stakes,** paying 9-5. Jockey was L. Jackson; time: 1:45⁴/₅ on a sloppy track for winnings valued at $2240.

Masterman won the 36th annual **Belmont Stakes,** paying 13-5. Jockey was J. Bullman; time: 2:22½ on a fast track for winnings valued at $13,220.

First postseason bowl football game was held at the Tournament of Roses. Michigan defeated Stanford, 49-0.

MAY 3, 1902

28th annual **Kentucky Derby** won by T.C. McDowell's *Allan-a-Dale,* ridden by jockey J. Winfield. Time: 2:08¾ on a fast track for winnings valued at $4850.

AUGUST 8, 1902

Davis Challenge Cup won by the American team defeating the British 3 matches to 2 at the Crescent Athletic Club grounds, in Brooklyn, N.Y.

AUGUST 19, 1902

National Lawn Tennis Championship was won by W.A. Larned, who defeated R.F. Doherty in the final round, at the Casino, Newport, R.I.

AUTUMN, 1902

Pittsburgh won the **National League baseball pennant** with a season record of 103 victories, 36 defeats.

Philadelphia won the **American League baseball pennant** with a season record of 83 victories, 53 defeats.

NOVEMBER 29, 1902

Army defeated Navy, 22-8, in their annual football classic at Franklin Field, Pa.

1903

U.S. lawn tennis men's singles champion, Hugh L. Doherty of England; **women's singles champion,** Elisabeth H. Moore.

U.S.G.A. amateur championship won by

Walter J. Travis at Nassau G.C., Glen Cove, N.Y. He defeated E. M. Byers, 5 and 4. **Open championship** won by Will Anderson at Baltusrol G.C., Short Hills, N.J., with a score of 307.

Flocarline won the 27th annual **Preakness Stakes,** paying 8-1. Jockey was W. Gannon; time: 1:44⁴/₅ on a fast track for winnings valued at $1875.

Africander won the 37th annual **Belmont Stakes,** paying 3-5. Jockey was J. Bullman; time: 2:23¹/₅ on a fast track for winnings valued at $12,285.

APRIL 27, 1903

Opening of **Jamaica Race Track** in Long Island, N.Y.

MAY 2, 1903

29th annual **Kentucky Derby** won by C. R. Ellison's *Judge Himes,* who paid off at 12-1. Time: 2:09 on a fast track for winnings valued at $4850. Jockey was H. Booker.

OCTOBER, 1903

Boston, of the American League, won the 1st annual **World Series** for baseball's world championship, by beating Pittsburgh, of the National League, 5-3.

NOVEMBER 28, 1903

Army defeated the Navy in their annual contest by a score of 40 to 5 at Franklin Field, Philadelphia.

1904

Recognition for **jiu-jitsu** started by Pres. Roosevelt, who had a Japanese instructor call regularly at the White House.

New baseball rule limited the height of the pitching mound to 15 in. above the plate.

U.S.G.A. amateur championship won by H. Chandler Egan at Baltusrol G.C., Short Hills, N.J. He defeated Fred Herreshoff, 8 and 6. **Open championship** won by Will Anderson at Glen View, G.C., Golf, Ill., with a score of 303.

U.S. lawn tennis men's singles champion, Holcombe Ward; **women's singles champion,** May G. Sutton.

Delhi won the 38th annual **Belmont Stakes,** paying 3-2. Jockey was G. Odom; time: 2:06³/₅ on a fast track for winnings valued at $11,575. Distance was 1½ mil.

Bryn Mawr won the 28th annual **Preakness Stakes,** paying 3-2. Jockey was E. Hildebrand; time: 1:44¹/₅ on a fast track for winnings valued at $2355.

The New York Giants, National League champions, **called off the World Series.**

APRIL-MAY, 1904

Frank J. Marshall, of Brooklyn won the **international masters' chess tournament,** held at Cambridge Springs, Pa., and at St. Louis, Mo., without the loss of a single game. Among the contestants were Lasker, the world's champion and Pillsbury, U.S. champion, as well as champions of France, England, Russia, and Austria.

MAY 2, 1904

30th annual **Kentucky Derby** won by *Elwood,* who paid 10-1. Time: 2:08½ on a fast track for winnings valued at $4850. Jockey was F. Prior.

MAY 5, 1904

First "perfect" major league game pitched when Cy Young of Boston Americans did not allow a single Philadelphia player to reach 1st base.

Cy Young, *above, pitched the first "perfect" major league game in 1904.*

MAY 14, 1904

First Olympic Games held in America opened as part of the St. Louis Exposition in St. Louis, Mo. U.S. won 21 events in this, the 3rd Olympiad.

OCTOBER 8, 1904

Automobile racing began in America with 1st **Vanderbilt Cup race** sponsored by William K. Vanderbilt. Cup won by A. L. Campbell in foreign-built Mercedes before 25,000-30,000 spectators. He beat 17 other starters after 10 laps around 28.4-mi. course.

NOVEMBER 26, 1904

Army beat the Navy by a score of 11 to 0 in the annual football contest at Franklin Field, Philadelphia.

1905

New world heavyweight boxing champion, Marvin Hart, knocked out Jack Root in 12 rounds.

Drastic rules revisions made this season by the Rules Committee of Football as a result of Pres. Roosevelt's threat to abolish football after he had seen a newspaper picture of a badly mangled football player.

U.S.G.A. amateur championship won by H. Chandler Egan at Chicago G.C., Wheaton, Ill. He defeated D.E. Sawyer, 6 and 5. **Open championship** won by Willie Anderson at Myopia Hunt Club, Hamilton, Mass., with a score of 314.

U.S. lawn tennis men's singles champion, Beals C. Wright; **women's singles champion,** Elisabeth H. Moore.

Cairngorm won the 29th annual **Preakness Stakes,** paying 9-5. Jockey was W. Davis; time: 1:45⁴/₅ on a fast track for winnings valued at $2200.

Tanya won the 39th annual **Belmont Stakes,** paying 11-5. Jockey was E. Hildebrand; time: 2:08 on a fast track for winnings valued at $17,240. Distance: 1¼ miles.

MAY 10, 1905
Three horses ran in the **Kentucky Derby.** Winner was the favorite, S. S. Brown's *Agile,* ridden by jockey J. Martin. He ran the 1¼ miles in 2:10¾ on a muddy track, earning $4850.

OCTOBER 9-14, 1905
New York, NL, defeated Philadelphia, AL, 4-1 in the 2nd annual **World Series.**

DECEMBER 2, 1905
Army and **Navy** tied in their classic football contest, 6-6, at Princeton, N.J.

1906
U.S. lawn tennis men's singles champion, William J. Clothier; **women's singles champion,** Helen Homans.
U.S.G.A. amateur championship won by E. M. Byers at Englewood, N.J., G.C. He defeated G.S. Lyon, 2 up. **Open Championship** won by Alex Smith at Onwentsia Club, Lake Forest, Ill., with a score of 295.
Burgomaster won the 40th annual **Belmont Stakes,** paying 2-5. Jockey was L. Lyne; time: 2:20 on a fast track for winnings valued at $22,700. Distance: 1⅜ mi.
Whimsical won the 30th annual **Preakness Stakes,** paying 9-5. Jockey was W. Miller; time: 1:45 on a fast track for winnings valued at $2355.

FEBRUARY 23, 1906
Tommy Burns defeated Marvin Hart in 20 rounds at Los Angeles, Calif. and claimed the **heavyweight title.** James J. Jeffries refereed the fight.

APRIL, 1906
U.S. won **Olympic Games** at Athens with 75 points against England's 41 and Sweden's 28.

MAY 2, 1906
32nd annual **Kentucky Derby** won by the favorite *Sir Huon,* ridden by R. Troxler. Time: 2:08⅘ on a fast track for winnings totaling $4850.

OCTOBER 9-14, 1906
Chicago, AL, defeated Chicago, NL, 4-2 in the 3rd annual **World Series.**

NOVEMBER 28, 1906
Philadelphia Jack O'Brien became the **heavyweight champion** when he fought a 20-round draw with Tommy Burns in Los Angeles, Calif.

DECEMBER 1, 1906
Navy beat the Army by 10 to 0 in their annual football contest at Franklin Field, Philadelphia.

DECEMBER 29, 1906
First annual convention of the **Intercollegiate Athletic Association** held. Formed as an educational organization to establish sound requirements for intercollegiate athletics.

1907
U.S.G.A. amateur championship won by Jerome D. Travers at Euclid Club, Cleveland. He defeated Archibald Graham, 6 and 5.

Open championship won by Alex Ross at Philadelphia Cricket Club, Chestnut Hill, Pa., with a score of 302.
U.S. lawn tennis men's singles champion, William A. Larned; **women's singles champion,** Evelyn Sears.
Don Enrique won the 31st annual **Preakness Stakes,** paying 15-1. Jockey was G. Mountain; time: 1:45⅖ on a slow track for winnings valued at $2260.
Peter Pan won the 41st annual **Belmont Stakes,** paying 7-10. Jockey was G. Mountain; winnings were valued at $22,765.

MAY 6, 1907
33rd annual **Kentucky Derby** won by J. Hal Woodford's *Pink Star,* paying 15-1. Time: 2:12⅗ on a heavy track for winnings valued at $4850. Jockey was A. Minder.

OCTOBER 8-12, 1907
Chicago, NL, defeated Detroit, AL, 4-0 in the 4th annual World Series. 1st game ended in tie score.

NOVEMBER 30, 1907
Navy defeated Army 6 to 0 in their annual football classic at Franklin Field, Philadelphia.

DECEMBER 2, 1907
Tommy Burns knocked out Gunner Moir in 10 rounds at London, England. Burns was the sole legitimate claimant to the **heavyweight championship** of the world.

1908
Irving Brokaw popularized figure skating.
New baseball rule prohibited pitchers from soiling new baseballs.
U.S.G.A. amateur championship won by Jerome D. Travers at Garden City, N.Y., G.C. He defeated Max Behr, 8 and 7. **Open championship** won by Fred McLeod at Myopia Hunt Club, Hamilton, Mass., with a score of 322.
U.S. lawn tennis men's singles champion, William A. Larned; **women's singles champion,** Mrs. Maud Bargar-Wallach.
Colin won the 42nd annual **Belmont Stakes,** paying 1-2. Jockey was J. Notter; winnings were valued at $22,765.
Royal Tourist won the 32nd annual **Preakness Stakes,** paying 1-2. Jockey was E. Dugan; time: 1:46⅖ on a fast track for winnings valued at $2455. Distance was 1¹/₁₆ miles.

FEBRUARY 12, 1908
Around-the-world automobile race from New York City to Paris by way of Alaska and Siberia sponsored by the *New York Times* and *Le Matin* began at 11 a.m. 6 cars, French, German, Italian, and American, participated. First, the huge German "Protos" driven by Lt. Koepens and the American "Thomas Flyer" with George Schuster at the wheel. German team was penalized for shipping their car to Seattle by rail, so the Americans were declared the winner on July 30.

MAY 5, 1908
24-1 long shot, *Stone Street,* won the 34th annual **Kentucky Derby** in 2:15⅕ on a heavy track, to win $4850.

AUGUST 29, 1908
American Olympic team distinguished itself in the track and field events by winning 15 firsts out of a possible 28, in London.

SEPTEMBER 23, 1908
Greatest dispute in baseball in decisive game at Polo Grounds, N.Y., of Chicago-New York pennant race. The last of 9th, score tied at 1-1, 2 out, New York was at bat with 2 men on. Bridwell hit safely to center field, scoring runner. Chicago players claimed that when **Fred Merkle,** man on 1st, saw the winning run score, he started to walk toward the clubhouse without touching 2nd base, invalidating play. Johnny Evers, Chicago 2nd baseman, tried to get the ball, to tag Merkle out. But fans streamed onto the field, and bedlam reigned. Pres. Pulliam of National League decided to call the game a tie. Fans invented the terms "boner" and "bonehead" to apply to Merkle's play.

OCTOBER 10-14, 1908
Chicago, NL, defeated Detroit, AL, 4-1 in the 5th annual **World Series.**

NOVEMBER 28, 1908
Army won over Navy 6 to 4 in their annual football contest at Franklin Field, Philadelphia.

DECEMBER 26, 1908
"Jack" Johnson, Negro stevedore from Galveston, Tex., fought and defeated the **world heavyweight champion,** "Tommy" Burns of Canada, at Sydney, Australia.

1909
U.S.G.A. amateur championship won by R. A. Gardner at Chicago, Ill., G.C. He defeated H. Chandler Egan, 4 and 3. **Open championship** won by George Sargent at Philadelphia, Pa., Cricket Club with a score of 290.
U.S. lawn tennis men's singles champion, William A. Larned; **women's singles champion,** Hazel V. Hotchkiss.
Effendi won the 33rd annual **Preakness Stakes,** paying 20-1. Jockey was W. Doyle; time: 1:39⅘ on a fast track for winnings valued at $3225. Distance was 1 mile.
Joe Madden won the 43rd annual **Belmont Stakes,** paying 11-5. Jockey was E. Dugan; time: 2:21⅗ on a slow track for winnings valued at $24,550.

MAY 5, 1909
Winner of the 35th annual **Kentucky Derby** was the favorite, J. B. Respess's *Wintergreen,* ridden by V. Powers. Time for 1¼ mi. was 2:08⅕ on a slow track for winnings valued at $4850.

OCTOBER 8-16, 1909
Pittsburgh, NL, defeated Detroit, AL, 4-3 in 6th annual **World Series.**

The first *Around-the-World auto race, similar to concourse racing of the Thirties, pictured above, was held in 1908.*

1910

Hugh Chalmers offered a **Chalmers car** as 1st prize for the leading batter in the Major Leagues. The winner, Ty Cobb.

Caught: a **Chinook salmon** weighing 83 lbs, out of the Umpqua R. in Oregon. This was the largest fresh water fish ever snared by rod and reel.

U.S.G.A. amateur championship won by W. C. Fownes, Jr., at the Country Club, Brookline, Mass. He defeated W. K. Wood 4 and 3. **Open championship** won by Alex Smith at Philadelphia, Pa., Cricket Club with a score of 298.

U.S. lawn tennis men's singles champion, William A. Larned; **women's singles champion,** Hazel V. Hotchkiss.

Layminster won the 34th annual **Preakness Stakes,** paying 8-1. Jockey was R. Estep; time: 1:40³/₅ on a fast track for winnings valued at $3300. Distance was 1 mile.

Sweep won the 44th annual **Belmont Stakes,** paying 1-10. Jockey was J. Butwell; time: 2:22 on a fast track for winnings valued at $9700.

MAY 10, 1910

The winner of the 36th annual **Kentucky Derby** was the favorite *Donau* ridden by jockey F. Herbert. His time was 2:06²/₅ on a fast track, and his winnings totaled $4850.

JULY 4, 1910

Heavyweight Champion **Jack Johnson** defeated Jim Jeffries in 15 rounds at Reno, Nev.

1911

U.S.G.A. amateur championship won by Harold H. Hilton at Apawamis Club, Rye, N.Y. He defeated Fred Herreshoff, 1 up in 37 holes **Open championship** won by John J. McDermott at Chicago G.C. with a score of 307.

U.S. lawn tennis men's singles champion, William A. Larned; **women's singles champion,** Hazel V. Hotchkiss.

Watervale won the 35th annual **Preakness Stakes,** paying 13-10. Jockey was E. Dugan; time: 1:51 on a fast track for winnings valued at $2700. Distance was 1⅛ mile.

Record for **most baseball games pitched by one pitcher** set when Cy Young finished his career after pitching 906 games in his 21 years in the major leagues (516 in the national, 390 in the American). Young also secured record for the **most games won by a single pitcher** in the major leagues—511 of the 906 games he pitched.

MAY 13, 1911

Winner of the 37th annual **Kentucky Derby** was R. F. Carman's *Meridian*, who cut 1²/₅ sec. from the previous year's time, running the 1¼ mi. in 2:05 on a fast track, under jockey G. Archibald, to win $4850.

SEPTEMBER 4, 1911

Frank A. Gotch successfully defended his **World's wrestling championship** against George Hackenschmidt of Russia at Chicago, Ill. Gotch achieved the 2 necessary pin falls in 19:50.4 sec.

OCTOBER 14-26, 1911

Philadelphia, AL, defeated New York, NL, 4-2 in 8th annual **World Series.**

NOVEMBER 25, 1911

Navy defeated Army, 3-0, in their annual classic at Franklin Field, Philadelphia.

1912

James Thorpe won both the decathlon and the pentathlon at the Olympics held in Stockholm, Sweden, and was proclaimed the "world's greatest athlete." Thorpe's medals and honors were taken from him when it was learned that he had played semiprofessional baseball as part of a summer job while in college.

Jim Thorpe, who won pentathalon and decathalon in 1912 Olympics, went on to play professional football.

U.S.G.A. amateur championship won by Jerome D. Travers at Chicago, Ill., G.C. He defeated Charles Evans, Jr., 7 and 6. **Open championship** won by John J. McDermott at Buffalo, N.Y., C.C. with a score of 294.

U.S. lawn tennis men's singles champion, Maurice E. McLoughlin; **women's singles champion,** Mary K. Browne.

Colonel Holloway won the 36th annual **Preakness Stakes,** paying 23-10. Jockey was C. Turner; time: 1:56²/₅ on a slow track for winnings valued at $1450.

MAY 11, 1912

Winner of the 38th annual **Kentucky Derby** was favorite, *Worth*, ridden by C. H. Shilling. The time: 2:09²/₅ on a muddy track; the value to the winning owner was $4850.

OCTOBER 8-16, 1912

Boston, AL, defeated New York, NL, 4-3 in 9th annual **World Series.** 2nd game ended in a tie.

NOVEMBER 30, 1912

Navy defeated Army, 6-0, in their annual football classic Franklin Field, Philadelphia.

1913

Major league record for the **most consecutive shutout innings pitched in 1 season** set by Washington's pitcher Walter Johnson, when he pitched 56 consecutive innings, allowing no runs.

U.S. lawn tennis men's singles champion, Maurice E. McLoughlin; **women's singles champion,** Mary K. Browne.

U.S.G.A. amateur championship won by Jerome D. Travers at Garden City, N.Y., G.C. He defeated J. G. Anderson, 5 and 4. **Open championship** won by Francis Ouimet at The Country Club, Brookline, Mass., with a score of 304. Francis Ouimet, only 20, beat a field which included 2 great English golfers, who

had been conceded the match. Ouimet and golf made the headlines.

Buskin won the 37th annual **Preakness Stakes,** paying 7-5. Jockey was J. Butwell; time: 1:53²/₅ on a fast track for winnings valued at $1670.

Prince Eugene won the 45th annual **Belmont Stakes,** paying 3-1. Jockey was R. Troxler; time: 2:18 on a fast track for winnings valued at $2825.

MAY 10, 1913

91-1 long shot, T. P. Hayes's *Donerail*, won the 39th annual **Kentucky Derby.** These were the longest odds ever paid on a winner of this race, a $2.00 mutual ticket on *Donerail* paying $184.90 to win. His time was the fastest yet, 2:04⁴/₅ on a fast track; his prize money amounted to $5475. Jockey was R. Goose.

JULY 25, 26, 28, 1913

The United States Tennis team won the **Davis Cup** in the challenge round against the British Isles, at Wimbledon, England, 3 matches to 2.

OCTOBER 7-11, 1913

Philadelphia, AL, defeated New York, NL, 4-1 in 10th annual **World Series.**

NOVEMBER 1, 1913

First Army-Notre Dame football game. Notre Dame defeated Army by constant use of forward pass.

NOVEMBER 29, 1913

Army defeated Navy, 22-9, in their annual football classic.

1914

The **Yale Bowl,** seating almost 80,000, opened, reflecting the increasing popular interest in football.

U.S.G.A. amateur championship won by Francis Ouimet at Ekwanok C.C., Manchester, Vt. He defeated Jerome D. Travers, 6 and 5. **Open championship** won by Walter Hagen at Midlothian C.C., Blue Island, Ill., with a score of 290.

U.S. lawn tennis men's singles champion, R. Norris Williams II; **women's singles champion,** Mary K. Browne.

U.S. lost the **Davis Cup** matches to Australia at matches held at the West Side Tennis Club, Forest Hills, N.Y.

Holiday won the 38th annual **Preakness Stakes,** paying 21-5. Jockey was A. Schuttinger; time: 1:53⁴/₅ on a fast track for winnings valued at $1335.

Luke McLuke won the 46th annual **Belmont Stakes,** paying 9-5. Jockey was M. Buxton; time: 2:20 on a fast track for winnings valued at $3025.

MAY 9, 1914

Winner of the 40th annual **Kentucky Derby,** H.C. Applegate's *Old Rosebudn*, ran the 1¼ mi. in the fastest time yet, 2:03³/₅ on a fast track under jockey J. McCabe, winning $9125.

OCTOBER 9-13, 1914

Boston, NL, defeated Philadelphia, AL, 4-0 in 11th annual **World Series.**

NOVEMBER 28, 1914

Army defeated Navy 20-0 in their annual football classic at Franklin Field, Philadelphia.

1915

Modern major-league record for the **most**

bases stolen in 1 season is 96, set by Ty Cobb.

National tennis championship site now **Forest Hills,** New York.

The Finn won the 47th annual **Belmont Stakes,** paying 7-5. Jockey was G. Byrne; Time: 2:18²/₅ on a fast track for winnings valued at $1825.

Rhine Maiden won the 39th annual **Preakness Stakes,** paying 6-1. Jockey was D. Hoffman; time: 1:58 on a muddy track for winnings valued at $1275.

U.S.G.A. amateur championship won by Robert A. Gardner at C.C. of Detroit, Grosse Point Farms, Mich. He defeated J. G. Anderson 5 and 4. **Open Championship** won by Jerome D. Travers at Baltusrol G.C., Short Hills, N.J., with a score of 297.

U.S. lawn tennis men's singles champion, William M. Johnston; **women's singles champion,** Molla Bjurstedt.

In Cambridge, Mass., Norman Taber of the U.S. **ran the mile in 4:12.6,** nearly 2 seconds under the old record.

APRIL 5, 1915

Jess Willard of Kansas took the **heavyweight championship** from Jack Johnson in a 23-round bout at Havana, Cuba.

MAY 8, 1915

Only filly to win the **Kentucky Derby** was *Regret,* which took the 41st running of the Churchill Downs classic in 2:05²/₅ on a fast track to win $11,450. Jockey was J. Nutter.

OCTOBER 8-13

Boston, AL, defeated Philadelphia, NL, 4-1 in the 12th annual **World Series.**

OCTOBER 9, 1915

Driving a Stutz at 102.6 mph, Gil Anderson won the Astor cup and set a **new auto speed** record at Sheepshead Bay, N.Y.

NOVEMBER 27, 1915

Army defeated Navy 14-0 in their annual football classic, held this year at the Polo Grounds, New York City.

1916

Major league record for the **most shutouts** pitched in 1 season set by Grover Cleveland Alexander of Philadelphia Phillies, who pitched 16 shutout games.

Friar Rock won the 48th annual **Belmont Stakes** paying 5-2. Jockey was E. Haynes; time: 2:22 on a muddy track for winnings valued at $4100.

Damrosch won the 40th annual **Preakness Stakes,** paying 13-2. Jockey was L. McAfee; time: 1:54⁴/₅ on a fast track for winnings valued at $1380.

U.S. lawn tennis men's singles champion, R. Norris Williams II; **women's singles champion,** Molla Bjurstedt.

U.S.G.A. amateur championship won by Charles Evans Jr. at Merion Cricket Club, Haverford, Pa. He defeated Robert A. Gardner, 4 and 3.

JANUARY 1, 1916

First permanent annual Rose Bowl football game held between Washington State College and Brown University, Washington State winning 14-0.

APRIL 10, 1916

First professional golf tournament held at the Siwanoy course in Bronxville, N.Y.,

by the Professional Golfers' Association of America.

MAY 13, 1916

Winner of the 42nd annual **Kentucky Derby** was *George Smith,* ridden by J. Loftus. Time, a new record, was 2:04 on a fast track; winnings, $9750.

SEPTEMBER 30, 1916

Longest winning streak in modern baseball history was stopped at 26 games, when the N.Y. Giants were beaten by the Boston Braves, 8-3, in the 2nd game of a doubleheader.

OCTOBER 7-12, 1916

Boston, AL, defeated Brooklyn, NL, 4-1 in the 13th annual **World Series.**

OCTOBER 24, 1916

Battling Levinsky outpointed Jack Dillon in a 12-round fight in Boston and proclaimed himself the **light-heavyweight champion.**

NOVEMBER 25, 1916

Army defeated Navy in their annual football classic, 15-7, at the Polo Grounds, New York City.

1917

U.S. lawn tennis men's singles champion, Lindley Murray; **women's singles champion,** Molla Bjurstedt.

Hourless won the 49th annual **Belmont Stakes.** The jockey was J. Butwell. The winning 3-year-old carried 126 pounds and earned $5800.

Kalitan won the 41st annual **Preakness Stakes,** paying 10-1. Jockey was E. Haynes; time: 1:54³/₅ on a fast track for winnings valued at $4800.

JANUARY 1, 1917

2nd annual **Rose Bowl** game, Oregon defeated Pennsylvania by a score of 14 to 0.

MAY 2, 1917

The **1st double no-hit 9-inning baseball game** in the major leagues was played in Chicago. Jim Vaughn of the Cubs and Fred Toney of Cincinnati both pitched the full game without allowing a hit. The Reds scored in the 10th to win 1-0.

MAY 12, 1917

First imported horse to win the **Kentucky Derby** was *Omar Khayyam,* who won the 43rd running of the Churchill Downs classic in 2:04³/₅ on a fast track to win $16,600.

JUNE 23, 1917

Ernie Shore joined the select company of **perfect-game pitchers** (no hits, no runs, no man reached 1st base), as he led Boston to a 4-0 victory over Washington.

AUGUST 19, 1917

First baseball game played in New York's **Polo Grounds** resulted in the arrest of managers John McGraw of the Giants and Christy Mathewson of the Cincinnati Reds for violating New York Blue Law prohibiting Sunday ball playing.

OCTOBER 6-15, 1917

Chicago, AL, defeated New York, NL, 4-2 in 14th **World Series.**

1918

42nd annual **Preakness Stakes** was run in

2 sections this year. *War Cloud,* ridden by jockey J. Loftus, won the 1st on a sloppy track, paying 17-10. Time: 1:53³/₅ for winnings valued at $12,250. *Jack Hare, Jr.,* ridden by C. Peak, won the 2nd on a good track, paying 9-10. Time: 1:53²/₅ for winnings valued at $11,250.

Johren won the 50th annual **Belmont Stakes,** paying 11-5. Jockey was F. Robinson; time: 2:20²/₅ on a fast track for winnings valued at $8950.

U.S. lawn tennis men's singles champion, R. Lindley Murray; **women's singles champion,** Molla Bjurstedt.

JANUARY 1, 1918

Mare Island Marines defeated Camp Lewis by a score of 19 to 7 in the 3rd annual **Rose Bowl** football game.

MAY 11, 1918

Exterminator, known as "Old Bones," won the 44th annual **Kentucky Derby.** He ran the muddy track in 2:10⁴/₅ and won $14,700. His jockey was W. Knapp.

SEPTEMBER 1, 1918

Baseball season cut short by order of the Sec. of War, Baker. World Series started early, Sept. 5th, Boston Red Sox winning first game, 1-0, on pitching of Babe Ruth.

SEPTEMBER 5-11, 1918

Boston, AL, defeated Chicago, NL, 4-2 in the 15th annual **World Series.**

DECEMBER 16, 1918

Jack Dempsey knocked out Carl Morris in 14 seconds at New Orleans.

Jack Dempsey *knocked out Carl Morris in 14 seconds at New Orleans in 1918.*

1919

U.S. lawn tennis men's singles champion, William M. Johnston; **women's singles champion,** Mrs. Hazel Hotchkiss Wrightman.

U.S.G.A. amateur championship won by S. D. Herron at Oakmont, Pa., C.C. He defeated Robert T. (Bobby) Jones, Jr., 5 and 4. **Open championship** won by Walter Hagen at Brae Burn C.C., West Newton, Mass., with a score of 301.

Sir Barton won the 51st annual **Belmont Stakes,** paying 7-20. Jockey was J. Loftus; time: 2:17²/₅ on a fast track for winnings valued at $11,950.

Sir Barton won the 43rd annual **Preakness Stakes,** paying 7-5. Jockey was J. Loftus; time: 1:53 on a fast track for winnings valued at $24,500.

1919

JANUARY 1, 1919

Great Lakes Naval Training Station defeated Mare Island Marines by a score of 17 to 0 in the 4th annual **Rose Bowl** football game.

MAY 10, 1919

First horse to win the **Kentucky Derby** and then go on to win the Preakness and the Belmont Stakes, gaining the mythical "Triple Crown," was *Sir Barton,* who won the 45th Kentucky Derby in 2:09⁴/₅ on a muddy track to win his owner, J. K. L. Ross, $20,825.

JULY 4, 1919

Jack Dempsey became **Heavyweight Champion of the World** when he scored a technical knockout over Jess Willard after 3 rounds of a scheduled 12-round match at Toledo, Ohio. Willard, who held the title since he defeated Jack Johnson in 1915, was 37 years old, weighed 243 lbs., and was 6 ft. 6½ in. tall. Dempsey was 24 years old, weighed 187 lbs., and was 6 ft 1 in. tall.

OCTOBER 1-9, 1919

Cincinnati, NL, defeated Chicago, AL, 5-3 in the 16th annual **World Series.**

NOVEMBER 29, 1919

Navy defeated Army, 6-0, in the annual **Army-Navy** game held at the Polo Grounds, New York City.

1920

Boxing fully legalized in New York state when "Walker Law" passed.

U.S.G.A. amateur championship won by Charles Evans, Jr., at Engineers C.C., Roslyn, N.Y. He defeated Francis Ouimet, 7 and 6. **Open championship** won by Ted Ray of England at Inverness Club, Toledo, Ohio, with a score of 295.

U.S. lawn tennis men's singles champion, William T. Tilden II; **women's singles champion,** Mrs. Molla Bjurstedt Mallory.

Man o' War won the 52nd annual **Belmont Stakes,** paying 1-20. Jockey was C. Kummer; time: 2:14¹/₅ on a fast track for winnings valued at $7950.

Man o' War won 44th annual **Preakness Stakes,** paying 4-5. Jockey was C. Kummer; time: 1:51³/₅ on a fast track for winnings valued at $23,000.

Davis Challenge Cup won by U.S. at Aukland, New Zealand with U.S. defeating Australia 5-0.

JANUARY 1, 1920

Harvard edged out Oregon by a score of 7 to 6 in the 5th annual **Rose Bowl** football game.

APRIL-SEPTEMBER, 1920

U.S. won 1st place in the **Olympic Games** held in Belgium, scoring 212 points, 1st 9 times, 2nd 12, 3rd 9, 4th 10, 5th 9, and 6th 5. The 2nd place team was Finland with 105 points.

MAY 8, 1920

Paul Jones, a 16-1 long shot, won the 46th annual **Kentucky Derby** in 2:09 on a slow track, winning $30,375. Jockey was T. Rice.

SEPTEMBER 28, 1920

Chicago grand jury indicted 8 members of **Chicago White Sox** for "throwing" World Series between White Sox and Cincinnati Reds in 1919.

OCTOBER 5-12, 1920

Cleveland, AL, defeated Brooklyn, NL, 5-2 in the 17th annual **World Series.**

NOVEMBER 8, 1920

Judge K. M. Landis, of Chicago, appointed Baseball Commissioner by a joint decision of both major leagues.

Keenesaw "Judge" Landis *was appointed Commissioner of Baseball in 1920.*

NOVEMBER 20, 1920

Navy defeated Army, 7-0, in their annual contest at the Polo Grounds, New York City.

1921

U.S. tennis team successfully defended the **Davis Cup** by defeating the Japanese team 5-0. The U.S. singles players were William T. Tilden and William M. Johnson; Richard Norris Williams 2nd and Watson M. Washburn made up the doubles team.

Grey Lag won the 53rd annual **Belmont Stakes,** paying 2-1. Jockey was E. Sande; time: 2:16⁴/₅ on a fast track for winnings valued at $8650.

Broomspun won the 45th annual **Preakness Stakes,** paying 1-1. Jockey was F. Coltiletti; time: 1:54¹/₅ on a slow track for winnings valued at $43,000.

U.S. lawn tennis men's singles champion, William T. Tilden II; **women's singles champion,** Mrs. Molla Bjurstedt Mallory.

U.S.G.A. amateur championship won by Jesse P. Guilford at St. Louis, Mo., C.C. He defeated Robert A. Gardner, 7 and 6. **Open championship** won by James M. Barnes at Columbia Club, Chevy Chase, Md., with a score of 289.

JANUARY 1, 1921

California defeated Ohio State by a score of 28 to 0 in the 6th annual **Rose Bowl** football game.

MAY 7, 1921

The winner of the 47th annual **Kentucky Derby** was *Behave Yourself,* who ran the 1¼ mi. in 2:04¹/₅ on a fast track to win $38,450. C. Thompson was the jockey.

JULY 2, 1921

Jack Dempsey-Georges Carpentier championship heavyweight fight, **1st prize fight with a million dollar gate,** held at Jersey City, N.J. Dempsey won by knock-out in 4th round.

AUGUST 3, 1921

Judge K.M. Landis, Commissioner of Baseball, ruled that the **Chicago White Sox** players charged with throwing games during the World's Series and regular season, though acquitted, would not be permitted to play again.

OCTOBER 5-13, 1921

New York, NL, defeated New York, AL, 5-3 in the 18th annual **World Series.**

NOVEMBER 26, 1921

Navy defeated Army, 7-0 in the annual **Army-Navy football game** held at the Polo Grounds, New York City.

1922

U.S. won the **Davis Cup** for the 3rd consecutive year defeating Australia in the challenge round 4 to 1, the U. S. doubles team (W. T. Tilden 2nd and V. Richards) losing the only match. W. M. Johnston and W. T. Tilden 2nd played the singles matches for the U.S.

Pillory won the 54th annual **Belmont Stakes,** paying 6-1. Jockey was C. H. Miller; Time: 2:18⁴/₅ on a fast track for winnings valued at $39,200.

Pillory won the 46th annual **Preakness Stakes,** paying 11-1. Jockey was L. Morris; time: 1:51³/₅ on a fast track for winnings valued at $51,000.

U.S. lawn tennis men's singles champion, William T. Tilden II; **women's singles champion,** Mrs. Molla Bjurstedt Mallory.

U.S.G.A. amateur championship won by Jess W. Sweetser at The Country Club, Brookline, Mass. He defeated Charles Evans, Jr., 3 and 2. **Open championship** won by Gene Sarazen at Skokie C.C., Glencoe, Ill., with a score of 288.

JANUARY 1, 1922

Washington and Jefferson College and California University played to a scoreless tie in the 7th annual **Rose Bowl** football game.

MAY 13, 1922

The winner of the 48th **Kentucky Derby** was *Morvich,* the favorite, who ran the 1¼ mi. in 2:04³/₅ on a fast track, winning $46,775. A. Johnson was the jockey.

AUGUST 28, 1922

Oldest American international team golf match, Walker Cup match between U.S. and Great Britain, established with opening play at National Golf Links of America, Southampton, N.Y. U.S. team won on 2nd day, 8 to 4.

Walker Cup *golf competition between England and America started in 1922.*

OCTOBER 4-8, 1922

New York, NL, defeated New York, AL, 4-0 in the 19th annual **World Series. First radio broadcast** of a baseball game direct from the field was Graham McNamee's announcing of this Series.

NOVEMBER 25, 1922

Army defeated Navy, 17-14, in the annual **Army-Navy Football game** at Philadelphia, Pa.

1923

U.S. won the **Davis Cup** for the 4th year in succession by defeating the Australian team in the challenge round 4 matches to 1, W. M. Johnson (U.S.) losing the first singles match to J. O. Anderson (Austr.) W. T. Tilden 2nd and R. N. Williams were the other 2 members of the U.S. team.

U.S. lawn tennis men's singles champion, William T. Tilden II; **women's singles champion,** Helen N. Wills.

U.S.G.A. amateur championship won by Max R. Marston at Flossmoor, Ill., C.C. He defeated Jess W. Sweetser, 1 up. **Open championship** won by Robert T. (Bobby) Jones, Jr. at Inwood, N.Y., C.C., with a score of 296.

Vigil won the 47th annual **Preakness Stakes,** paying 9-2. Jockey was B. Marinelli; time: 1:53³/₅ on a fast track for winnings valued at $52,000.

Zev won the 55th annual **Belmont Stakes,** paying 4-5. Jockey was E. Sande; time: 2:19 on a good track for winnings valued at $38,000.

JANUARY 1, 1923

Southern California defeated Pennsylvania State by a score of 14 to 3 in the 8th annual **Rose Bowl** football game.

APRIL 18, 1923

Yankee Stadium in New York City opened. It became the home park of the New York Yankees of the American League.

MAY 19, 1923

Earle Sande won his 1st **Kentucky Derby** when he rode *Zev* to victory in the 49th Churchill Downs classic, winning $53,600. Time, 2:05²/₅ on a fast track.

SEPTEMBER 14, 1923

Dempsey-Firpo fight held at the Polo Grounds, New York City. Dempsey knocked out the challenger in the 2nd round and retained his heavyweight championship. In the 3 min. 57 sec. of fighting time there was a total of 11 knockdowns, the most famous of which occurred in the 1st round when Firpo knocked the champion out of the ring.

OCTOBER 10-15, 1923

New York, AL, defeated New York, NL, 4-2 in the 20th annual **World Series.**

NOVEMBER 24, 1923

Navy and **Army** tied, 0-0, in their annual football classic at the Polo Grounds, New York City.

1924

National football champion, Notre Dame, played 9 games and won them all under the guidance of coach Knute Rockne, who had been a member of the 1913 Notre Dame team which upset Army.

U.S.G.A. amateur championship won by Robert T. (Bobby) Jones, Jr., at Merion Cricket Club, Haverford, Pa. He defeated George

Knute Rockne coached Notre Dame to the national collegiate football championship in 1924.

Von Elm, 9 and 6. **Open championship** won by Cyril Walker at Oakland Hills C.C., Birmingham, Michigan., with a score of 297.

U.S. lawn tennis men's singles champion, William T. Tilden II; **women's singles champion,** Helen N. Wills.

U.S. Tennis Team successfully defended the **Davis Cup** for the 4th year in succession by defeating the Australian team in the challenge round 5 matches to 0. William T. Tilden 2nd, Vincent Richards, and William M. Johnston made up U.S. team.

Nellie Morse won the 48th **Preakness Stakes,** paying 12-1. Jockey was J. Merimee; time: 1:57¹/₅ on a heavy track for winnings valued at $54,000.

Mad Play won the 56th annual **Belmont Stakes,** paying 2-1. Jockey was E. Sande; time was 2:18⁴/₅ on a good track for winnings valued at $42,880.

JANUARY 1, 1924

Washington and Navy played to a 14-14 tie in the 9th annual **Rose Bowl** football game.

MAY 17, 1924

50th annual **Kentucky Derby** won by *Black Gold.* Time: 2:05¹/₅ on a fast track; the value, $52,775; jockey was J. D. Mooney.

JULY 13, 1924

For 8th consecutive time, U.S. team took 1st place in **Olympic Games,** held at Paris, with 255 points.

OCTOBER 4-10, 1924

Washington, AL, defeated New York, NL, 4-3 in the 21st annual **World Series.**

NOVEMBER 29, 1924

Army defeated Navy, 12-0, at Baltimore Stadium.

DECEMBER 31, 1924

Exterminator ended his 8th and final year of racing with a record of 50 wins in 100 starts and $252,996.00 in total earnings.

1925

U.S.G.A. amateur championship won by Robert T. (Bobby) Jones, Jr., at Oakmont, Pa., C.C. He defeated Watts Gunn, 8 and 7. **Open championship** won by Willie Macfarlane at Worcester, Mass., C.C.`with a score of 291.

U.S. lawn tennis men's singles champion, William T. Tilden II; **women's singles champion,** Helen N. Wills.

Coventry won the 49th annual **Preakness Stakes,** paying 22-1. Jockey was C. Kummer; time: 1:59 on a fast track for winnings valued at $52,700. Distance: 1³/₁₆ mile.

American Flag won the 57th annual **Belmont Stakes,** paying 9-20. Jockey was A. Johnson; time was 2:16⁴/₅ on a fast track for winnings valued at $38,500.

National football champion was Dartmouth, coached by Jesse B. Hawley. They were undefeated and untied in 8 games.

JANUARY 1, 1925

Notre Dame defeated Stanford by a score of 27 to 10 in the 10th annual **Rose Bowl** football game.

MAY 16, 1925

Earle Sande drove home his 2nd **Kentucky Derby** winner, *Flying Ebony* in the 51st annual Churchill Downs classic at Louisville, Ky. Sande rode *Flying Ebony* in 2:07³/₅ on a muddy track to win $52,950.

SEPTEMBER 12, 1925

The U.S. won the **Davis Cup** for the 6th year in succession by defeating the French team 5 matches to none in the challenge round at Philadelphia. W. T. Tilden 2nd and W. M. Johnston won the singles matches for the U.S. and R. N. Williams and Vincent Richards were the victors in the doubles match.

OCTOBER 7-15, 1925

Pittsburgh, NL, defeated Washington, AL, 4-3 in the 22nd annual **World Series.**

NOVEMBER 28, 1925

Army defeated Navy, 10-3, in their annual contest, at the Polo Grounds, New York City.

1926

First woman to swim the English Channel was **Gertrude Ederle** of New York. 19 years old, she accomplished the feat in 14 hr. 31 min.

National football champion was Stanford, coached by Glenn (Pop) Warner. They were undefeated and untied in 10 games.

Display won the 50th annual **Preakness Stakes,** paying 19-1. Jockey was J. Maiben; time: 1:59⁴/₅ on a fast track for winnings valued at $53,625.

Crusader won the 58th annual **Belmont Stakes,** paying 7-10. Jockey was A. Johnson; time: 2:32¹/₅ on a sloppy track for winnings valued at $48,550. Distance: 1½ mi.

U.S. lawn tennis men's singles champion, René Lacoste of France: **women's singles champion,** Mrs. Molla Bjurstedt Mallory.

U.S.G.A. amateur championship won by George Von Elm at Baltusrol G.C., Short Hills, N.J. He defeated Robert T. (Bobby) Jones, Jr., 2 and 1. **Open championship** won by Robert T. (Bobby) Jones, Jr., at Scioto C.C., Columbus, Ohio, by a score of 293.

JANUARY 1, 1926

Alabama edged out Washington by a score of 20 to 19 in the 11th annual **Rose Bowl** football game.

MAY 15, 1926

The 52nd annual **Kentucky Derby,** won by *Bubbling Over* in 2:03⁴/₅ on a fast track. First prize money amounted to $50,075. Jockey: A. Johnson.

SEPTEMBER 11, 1926

The United States Tennis team won the **Davis Cup** for the 7th year in succession defeating the French team in the challenge round 4 matches to 1, at the Germantown Cricket Club, Philadelphia, Pa. W.T. Tilden 2nd lost the only match for the U.S., losing to J.R. Lacoste, 4-6, 6-4, 8-6, 8-6. W.M. Johnston, R.N. Williams, and V. Richards were the other members of the U.S. team.

SEPTEMBER 23, 1926

Gene Tunney became the **Heavyweight Champion** of the world by defeating defending champion Jack Dempsey by a decision in a 10-round fight held at the Sesquicentennial Stadium, Philadelphia.

NOVEMBER 27, 1926

Army and Navy played to a 21-21 tie in the annual **Army-Navy football game** held at Soldiers Field, Chicago, Ill.

OCTOBER 2-10, 1926

St. Louis, NL, defeated New York, AL, 4-3 in the 23rd annual **World Series.**

1927

Two major league records set when **Walter Johnson,** the Washington Sentors' pitcher, ended the last season of his 20-year career, having pitched 113 shutouts and struck out 3497 opposing batters.

First **Golden Gloves** amateur boxing matches held, sponsored by New York *Daily News*.

This year's **national football champion** was Illinois. Their record: 7 wins, no losses, 1 tie.

Bostonian won the 51st annual **Preakness Stakes,** paying 3-1. Jockey was A. Abel; time: 2:01³/₅ on a good track for winnings valued at $53,100.

Chance Shot won the 59th annual **Belmont Stakes,** paying 2-7. Jockey was E. Sande; time: 2:32²/₅ on a fast track for winnings valued at $60,910.

U.S. Lawn tennis men's singles champion, René Lacoste of France; **women's singles champion,** Helen N. Wills.

U.S.G.A. amateur championship won by Robert T. (Bobby) Jones, Jr., at Minikahda Club, Minneapolis, Minn. He defeated Charles Evans, Jr., 8 and 1. **Open championship** won by Tommy Armour at Oakmont, Pa., C.C. with a score of 301.

JANUARY 1, 1927

Alabama and Stanford battled to a 7-7 tie in the 12th annual **Rose Bowl** football game.

MAY 14, 1927

The winner of the 53rd annual **Kentucky Derby** was *Whiskery* ridden by jockey L. McTee. The time: 2:06 on a slow track; the value was $51,000.

SEPTEMBER 10, 1927

France took the **Davis Cup** from the United States 3 matches to 2 at Philadelphia, the U.S. team winning 1 singles match and the doubles match.

SEPTEMBER 27, 1927

Home run record set when Babe Ruth hit his 60th home run of the season off Tom Zachary, Washington pitcher, in Yankee Stadium.

OCTOBER 5-8, 1927

New York, AL, defeated Pittsburgh, NL, 4-0,

in the 24th annual **World Series.**

OCTOBER 7, 1927

Tommy Loughran won the **Light Heavyweight title** by defeating Mike McTigue by a decision in a 15-round contest held at New York City.

NOVEMBER 26, 1927

Army defeated Navy, 14-9 in the annual **Army-Navy football game** held at the Polo Grounds, New York City.

1928

This year's **national football champion** was the University of Southern California, coached by Howard Jones. Their record: 9 wins, no losses, 1 tie.

Vito won the 60th annual **Belmont Stakes,** paying 10-1. Jockey was C. Kummer; time: 2:33¹/₅ on a fast track for winnings valued at $63,430.

Victorian won the 52nd annual **Preakness Stakes,** paying 9-1. Jockey was R. Workman; time: 2:00¹/₅ on a fast track for winnings valued at $60,000.

U.S. lawn tennis men's singles champion, Henri Cochet of France; **women's singles champion,** Helen N. Wills.

U.S.G.A. amateur championship won by Robert T. (Bobby) Jones, Jr., at Brae Burn C.C., West Newton, Mass. He defeated T. Philip Perkins, 10 and 9. **Open championship** won by Johnny Farrell at Olympia Fields, Matteson, Ill., with a score of 294.

JANUARY 1, 1928

Stanford edged out Pittsburgh by a score of 7 to 6 in the 13th annual **Rose Bowl** football game.

MAY 19, 1928

The winner of the 54th annual **Kentucky Derby** was the favorite *Reigh Count,* ridden by jockey C. Lang. Time: 2:10²/₅ on a heavy track; the value, $55,375.

JULY 29-AUGUST 12, 1928

The United States emerged with top honors in the 9th **Olympic Games** held at Amsterdam, Holland, scoring a total of 131 points, with 24 1sts, 21 2nds, and 17 3rds. Americans also established 17 new Olympic records, 7 of which are world records.

OCTOBER 4-9, 1928

New York, AL, defeated St. Louis, NL, 4-0 in the 25th annual **World Series.**

1929

Year's **national football champion:** Notre Dame, still coached by Knute Rockne. Record: 9 wins, no losses, no ties.

Blue Larkspur won the 61st annual **Belmont Stakes,** paying 13-10. Jockey was M. Garner; time: 2:32⁴/₅ on a sloppy track for winnings valued at $59,650.

Dr. Freeland won the 53rd annual **Preakness Stakes,** paying 19-5. Jockey was L. Schaefer; time: 2:01³/₅ for winnings valued at $52,325.

U.S. lawn tennis men's singles champion, William T. Tilden II; **women's singles champion,** Helen N. Wills.

U.S.G.A. amateur championship won by Harrison R. Johnston at Pebble Beach Course, Del Monte, Calif. He defeated Dr. O.F. Willing, 4 and 3. **Open championship** won by Robert T. (Bobby) Jones, Jr., at Winged Foot G.C., Mamaroneck, N.Y., with a score of 294.

JANUARY 1, 1929

Georgia Tech edged out California by a score of 8 to 7 in the 14th annual **Rose Bowl** football game.

MAY 18, 1929

The winner of the 55th **Kentucky Derby** was *Clyde Van Dusen,* ridden by jockey L. McAfee. The time: 2:10⁴/₅ on a muddy track; the prize, $53,950.

OCTOBER 8-14, 1929

Philadelphia, AL, defeated Chicago, NL, 4-1 in the 26th annual **World Series.**

1930

Irish Sweepstakes, a lottery on behalf of several Irish hospitals, inaugurated.

National football champions was once again Notre Dame, coached by Knute Rockne. Their record: 10 wins, no losses, and no ties.

First A.A.U. James E. Sullivan Memorial Trophy for outstanding amateur athlete of the year won by golfer, Robert (Bobby) Jones. Award for amateur athlete who does most to advance cause of good sportsmanship.

Gallant Fox won the 54th annual **Preakness Stakes,** paying 1-1. Jockey was E. Sande; time: 2:00³/₅ on a fast track for winnings valued at $51,925.

Gallant Fox won the 62nd annual **Belmont Stakes,** paying 8-5. Jockey was E. Sande; time: 2:31³/₅ on a good track for winnings valued at $66,040.

U.S. lawn tennis men's singles champion John H. Doeg; **women's singles champion,** Betty Nuthall of England.

JANUARY 1, 1930

Southern California defeated Pittsburgh by a score of 47 to 14 in the 15th annual **Rose Bowl** football game.

MAY 17, 1930

Earle Sande rode his 3rd **Kentucky Derby** winner, the great *Gallant Fox*, who went on to win the Triple Crown. The time was 2:07³/₅ on a good track; the prize, $50,725.

JUNE 12, 1930

Max Schmeling of Germany became **Heavyweight Champion of the World** when he was awarded the victory over Jack Sharkey, who fouled him in the 4th round at New York City.

Bobby Jones, *right, holds British Amateur Championship Cup he won*

SEPTEMBER 27, 1930

Robert Tyre "Bobby" Jones became 1st golfer to win the 4 most important golf matches by taking U.S. Amateur Tournament at Philadelphia, Pa.

OCTOBER 1-8, 1930

Philadelphia, AL, defeated St. Louis, NL, 4-2 in the 27th annual **World Series.**

DECEMBER 13, 1930

Army defeated Navy, 6-0 in the annual **Army-Navy** football game held at Yankee Stadium

1931

National football champion was Southern California, coached by Howard Jones. Their record: 9 wins, 1 loss, no ties.

Twenty Grand won the 63rd annual **Belmont Stakes,** paying 4-5. Jockey was C. Kurtsinger; time: 2:29³/₅ on a fast track for winnings valued at $58,770.

Mate won the 55th annual **Preakness Stakes,** paying 41-10. Jockey was G. Ellis; time: 1:59 on a fast track for winnings valued at $48,225.

U.S. lawn tennis men's singles champion, H. Ellsworth Vines Jr.; **women's singles champion,** Mrs. Helen Wills Moody.

U.S.G.A. amateur championship won by Francis Quimet at Beverly C.C., Chicago, Ill. He defeated Jack Westland, 6 and 5. **Open championship** won by Billy Burke at Inverness Club, Toledo, Ohio, with a score of 292.

Ty Cobb, *longtime All-Star baseball player, participated in the 1934 All-Star Game in St. Louis.*

JANUARY 1, 1931

Alabama defeated Washington State by a score of 24 to 0 in the 16th annual **Rose Bowl** football game.

MAY 13, 1931

In the famous **"false start race,"** at Jamaica, N.Y., the entire field of horses went completely around the track before they were recalled. 1st and 2nd in the false start were *Rideaway* and *Clock Tower;* in the official race *Clock Tower* came in 1st, *Rideaway* 2nd.

MAY 16, 1931

Twenty Grand set a new **Kentucky Derby** record, ridden by jockey C. Kurtsinger, ran the 1¼ mi, in 2:01⁴/₅ on a fast track, winning $48,725.00.

OCTOBER 1-10, 1931

St. Louis, NL, defeated Philadelphia, AL, 4-3 in the 28th annual **World Series.**

DECEMBER 12, 1931

Army defeated Navy, 17-7 in the annual **Army-Navy football game** held at Yankee Stadium.

1932

Olympic Games were held in U.S., the winter events at Lake Placid, N.Y., and the summer events at Los Angeles. U.S. won 11 of the 23 events.

This year's national **football champion** was Michigan, coached by Harry Kipke. Their record: 8 wins, no losses, no ties.

U.S.G.A. amateur championship won by C. Ross Somerville at Baltimore, Md., C.C. He defeated Johnny Goodman, 2 and 1. **Open championship** won by Gene Sarazen at Fresh Meadow C.C., Flushing, N.Y., with a score of 286.

U.S. lawn tennis men's singles champion, H. Ellsworth Vines, Jr.; **women's singles champion,** Helen Hull Jacobs.

Faireno won the 64th annual **Belmont Stakes,** paying 5-1. Jockey was T. Malley; time: 2:32⁴/₅ on a fast track for winnings valued at $55,120.

Burgoo King won the 56th annual **Preakness Stakes,** paying 16-5. Jockey was E. James; time: 1:59⁴/₅ on a fast track for winnings of $50,375.

JANUARY 1, 1932

Southern California defeated Tulane by a score of 21 to 12 in the 17th annual **Rose Bowl** football game.

FEBRUARY 4, 1932

Winter Olympic Games, 1st held in U.S., opened at Lake Placid, N.Y., with ceremony led by Gov. Franklin D. Roosevelt.

MAY 7, 1932

The winner of the 58th annual **Kentucky Derby** was *Burgoo King,* ridden by E. James. Time: 2:05¹/₅ on a fast track; the prize, $52,350.

JUNE 21, 1932

World Heavyweight Boxing Championship won by Jack Sharkey, who took 15-round decision over Max Schmeling at New York.

SEPTEMBER 28-OCTOBER 2, 1932

New York, AL, defeated Chicago, NL, 4-0 in the 29th annual **World Series.**

OCTOBER 13, 1932

Kid Chocolate knocked out Lew Feldman in round 12 of featherweight boxing championship match held at New York City.

DECEMBER 3, 1932

Army defeated Navy, 20-0, in their annual contest at Franklin Field, Philadelphia.

1933

First **totalizator** used at an American race track installed at Arlington Park, Chicago, Ill. This completely electrical device prints and issues betting tickets at the rate of 50 per min.;

sorts, adds, and transmits totals to indicator boards, flashing new information every 90 sec.

This year's national **football champion** was, for the 2nd straight year, Michigan, coached by Harry Kipke. Their record this year: 7 wins, no losses, 1 tie.

U.S.G.A. amateur championship won by George T. Dunlap, Jr., at Kenwood C.C., Cincinnati, Ohio. He defeated Max R. Marston, 6 and 5. **Open championship** won by Johnny Goodman at North Shore C.C., Glen View, Ill., with a score of 287.

U.S. lawn tennis men's singles champion, Frederick J. Perry of England; **women's singles champion,** Helen Hull Jacobs.

Hurryoff won the 65th annual **Belmont Stakes,** paying 15-1. Jockey was M. Garner; time: 2:32³/₅ on a fast track for winnings valued at $49,490.

Head Play won the 57th annual **Preakness Stakes,** paying 9-5. Jockey was C. Kurtsinger; time: 2:02 on a slow track for winnings valued at $26,850.

JANUARY 1, 1933

Southern California defeated Pittsburgh by a score of 35 to 0 in the 18th annual **Rose Bowl** football game.

MAY 6, 1933

Broker's Tip, ridden by D. Meade, won the 59th annual racing classic at Churchill Downs, in 2:06⁴/₅ on a fast track, winning $48,925.

JUNE 21, 1933

World Heavyweight Championship won by Italian giant, Primo Carnera, who knocked out Jack Sharkey at Long Island City Bowl.

JULY 6, 1933

American League defeated the National by a score of 4 to 2 in the **1st All-Star Baseball Game.** Contest was held at Comiskey Park in Chicago.

OCTOBER 3-7, 1933

New York, NL, defeated Washington, AL, 4-1 in the 30th annual **World Series.**

NOVEMBER 25, 1933

Army defeated Navy, 12-7 in the annual **Army-Navy football game** played at Franklin Field, Philadelphia, Pa.

DECEMBER 17, 1933

Chicago Bears defeated the New York Giants, 23 to 21, for the **1st National Professional League Championship.** Played at Chicago, Ill.

1934

This year's **National Football Champion** was Minnesota, coached by Bernie Bierman. Their record: 8 wins, no losses, no ties.

U.S. lawn tennis men's singles champion, Frederick J. Perry of England; **women's singles champion,** Helen Hull Jacobs.

U.S.G.A. amateur championship won by W. Lawson Little, Jr. at The Country Club, Brookline, Mass. He defeated David Goldman, 8 and 7. **Open championship** won by Olin Dutra at Merion Cricket Club, Haverford, Pa., with a score of 293.

Peace Chance won the 66th annual **Belmont Stakes,** paying 3-1. Jockey was W. D. Wright; time: 2:29¹/₅ on a fast track for winnings valued at $43,410.

High Quest won the 58th annual **Preakness Stakes,** paying 9-20. Jockey was R. Jones; time: 1:58¹/₅ on a fast track for winnings valued at $25,175.

JANUARY 1, 1934

Columbia defeated Stanford by a score of 7 to 0 in the 19th annual **Rose Bowl** football game.

MAY 5, 1934

Cavalcade won the 60th annual **Kentucky Derby.** The time was 2:04 on a fast track; the prize $28,175. The jockey was M. Garner.

MAY 12, 1934

U.S. golfers defeated golfers of Great Britain in the International **Walker Cup Match** held at St. Andrews, Scotland. The score was 9 matches for the U.S. to 2 for Great Britain, and 1 match halved.

JUNE 14, 1934

Max Baer scored a technical knockout over Primo Carnera, **World's Heavyweight Champion,** in the 11th round of a fight held in New York city. Max Baer, the new champion, received $40,000 for his efforts while the deposed champion, Carnera, received $122,000. Carnera, at 6 ft. 6½ in. and 260 lbs., was one of the biggest men ever to hold the Heavyweight Championship.

JULY 10, 1934

American League defeated the National by a score of 9 to 7 in the 2nd annual **All-Star Game.** Contest was held in the Polo Grounds in New York city.

OCTOBER 3-9, 1934

St. Louis, NL, defeated Detroit, AL, 4-3 in the 31st annual **World Series.**

DECEMBER 1, 1934

Navy defeated Army, 3-0, in the annual **Army-Navy football game** held at Franklin Field, Philadelphia, Pa.

1935

National College Football Champion was Southern Methodist. Their record: 12 wins, no losses, no ties.

U.S. lawn tennis men's singles champion, Wilmer L. Allison; **women's singles champion,** Helen Hull Jacobs.

Great Britain defeated the U.S. 5 to 0 in the challenge round of the **Davis Cup** International Matches.

U.S.G.A. amateur championship won by W. Lawson Little, Jr., at C.C. Cleveland, Ohio. He defeated Walter Emery, 4 and 2. **Open championship** won by Sam Parks, Jr., at Oakmont, Pa., C.C. with a score of 299.

Omaha won the 67th annual **Belmont Stakes,** paying 7-10. Jockey was W. Saunders; time: 2:30⅗ on a sloppy track for winnings valued at $35,480.

Omaha won the 59th annual **Preakness Stakes,** paying 9-10. Jockey was W. Saunders; time: 1:58⅖ on a fast track for winnings valued at $25,325.

JANUARY 1, 1935

Alabama defeated Stanford by a score of 29 to 13 in the 20th annual **Rose Bowl** football game.

MAY 4, 1935

61st annual **Kentucky Derby,** won by *Omaha* ridden by W. Saunders. He ran the 1¼ mi. in 2:05 on a good track and won $39,525 for his owners. He went on to win the Preakness and the Belmont Stakes and to gain the Triple Crown.

MAY 24, 1935

Reds and Phillies play **1st major league night game** at Crosley Field, Cincinnati, Ohio. Cincinnati 2; Philadelphia 1.

JUNE 13, 1935

World's Heavyweight Championship won by James J. Braddock over Max Baer on points in 15 rounds.

JULY 8, 1935

American League defeated the National by a score of 4 to 1 in the 3rd annual **All-Star Game.**

OCTOBER 2-7, 1935

Detroit, AL, defeated Chicago, NL, 4-2 in the 32nd annual **World Series.**

NOVEMBER 30, 1935

Army defeated **Navy,** 28-6, in their annual contest at Franklin Field, Philadelphia.

1936

National Football Champion was Minnesota, coached by Bernie Bierman. Their record: 7 wins, 1 loss, no ties.

Baseball's Hall of Fame established in Cooperstown, N.Y., by group of baseball leaders. Shrine and museum planned to honor "Immortals" of the game.

Baseball *Hall of Fame was established in 1936. Dizzy Dean, above, is one of many baseball greats enshrined at Cooperstown.*

Granville won the 68th annual **Belmont Stakes,** paying 16-5. Jockey was J. Stout; time: 2:30 on a fast track for winnings valued at $29,800.

Bold Venture won the 60th annual **Preakness Stakes,** paying 9-5. Jockey was G. Woolf; time: 1:59 on a fast track for winnings valued at $27,325.

U.S. lawn tennis men's singles champion, Frederick J. Perry of England; **women's singles champion,** Alice Marble.

U.S.G.A. amateur championship won by John W. Fischer at Garden City, N.Y., G.C. He defeated Jack McLean, 1 up. **Open championship** won by Tony Manero at Baltusrol G.C., Short Hills, N.J., by a score of 282.

JANUARY 1, 1936

Stanford defeated Southern Methodist by a score of 7 to 0 in the 21st annual **Rose Bowl** football game.

MAY 2, 1936

Bold Venture won the 62nd annual **Kentucky Derby,** running the 1¼ mi. in 2:03⅗ on a fast track and winning $37,725 for his owner. Jockey was A. Hanford.

JULY 7, 1936

National League defeated the American by a score of 4 to 1 in the 4th annual **All-Star Game.** Contest was held in Boston.

SEPTEMBER 30-OCTOBER 6, 1936

New York, AL, defeated New York, NL, 4-2 in the 33rd annual **World Series.**

NOVEMBER 28, 1936

Navy defeated Army, 7-0, in the annual **Army-Navy football game** held at Municipal Stadium, Philadelphia, Pa.

1937

National football champion was Pittsburgh, coached by John Sutherland. Their record: 9 wins, no losses, no ties.

War Admiral won the 61st annual **Preakness Stakes,** paying 7-20. Jockey was C. Kurtsinger; time: 1:58⅖ on a good track for winnings valued at $45,600.

War Admiral won the 69th annual **Belmont Stakes,** paying 9-10. Jockey was C. Kurtsinger; time: 2:28⅖ on a fast track for winnings valued at $38,020.

U.S. defeated Britain 4 to 1 in the challenge round of the **Davis Cup** International Matches.

U.S. lawn tennis men's singles champion, J. Donald Budge; **women's singles champion,** Anita Lizana of Chile.

U.S.G.A. amateur championship won by Johnny Goodman at Alderwood G.C., Portland, Ore. He defeated Ray Billows, 2 up. **Open championship** won by Ralph Guldahl at Oakland Hills C.C., Birmingham, Mich., with a score of 281.

JANUARY 1, 1937

Pittsburgh defeated Washington by a score of 21 to 0 in the 22nd annual **Rose Bowl** football game.

MAY 8, 1937

War Admiral, son of Man o' War, won the 63rd annual **Kentucky Derby.** His time was 2:03⅕ on a fast track and he won $52,050 under jockey C. Kurtsinger. *War Admiral* went on to win the Triple Crown.

War Admiral *shown winning the 1937 Kentucky Derby.*

JUNE 22, 1937

World Heavyweight Boxing Championship won by Joe Louis, who knocked out James J. Braddock in 8th round at Chicago, on June 22. Louis was 2nd Negro to hold title.

JULY 7, 1937

American League defeated the National by a score of 8 to 3 in the 5th annual **All-Star Game.** Contest was held in Washington.

OCTOBER 6-10, 1937

New York, AL, defeated New York, NL, 4-1 in the 34th annual **World Series.**

NOVEMBER 27, 1937

Army defeated Navy, 6-0, in the annual **Army-Navy football game** held at Municipal Stadium, Philadelphia, Pa.

1938

This year's **national college football champion** was Texas Christian, coached by Leo Meyer. Their record: 10 wins, no losses, no ties.

U.S.G.A. amateur championship won by Willie Turnesa at Oakmont, Pa., C.C. He defeated B. Patrick Abbott, 8 and 7. **Open championship** won by Ralph Guldahl at Cherry Hills Club, Englewood, Colo., with a score of 284.

U.S. lawn tennis men's singles champion, J. Donald Budge; women's singles champion, Alice Marble.

U.S. defeated Australia 3 to 2 in the challenge round of the **David Cup** International Matches.

Pasteurized won the 70th annual **Belmont Stakes,** paying 8-1. Jockey was J. Stout; time: 2:29²/₅ on a fast track for winnings valued at $34,530.

Dauber won the 62nd annual **Preakness Stakes,** paying 3-2. Jockey was M. Peters; time: 1:59⁴/₅ on a sloppy track for winnings valued at $51,875.

JANUARY 1, 1938

California defeated Alabama 13 to 0 in the Rose Bowl.

MAY 7, 1938

An 86-10 long shot, **Lawrin** won the 64th annual **Kentucky Derby.** He ran the 1¼ mi. in 2:04⁴/₅ on a fast track and won $47,050. He was ridden by Eddie Arcaro.

JULY 6, 1938

National League defeated the American by a score of 4 to 1 in the 6th annual **All-Star Game.** Contest was held in Cincinnati.

OCTOBER 5-9, 1938

New York, AL, defeated Chicago, NL, 4-0 in the 35th annual **World Series.**

NOVEMBER 26, 1938

Army defeated Navy, 14-7, in their annual contest at Municipal Stadium, Philadelphia.

DECEMBER 11, 1938

New York Giants defeated Green Bay Packers 23-17 at New York city for the **National Professional Football Championship.**

1939

National Football Champion was Texas A. and M., coached by Homer Norton. Their record: 10 wins, no losses, no ties.

Johnstown won the 71st annual **Belmont Stakes,** paying 1-8. Jockey was J. Stout;

694

---

time: 2:29³/₅ on a fast track for winnings valued at $37,020.

Challedon won the 63rd annual **Preakness Stakes,** paying 6-1. Jockey was G. Seabo; time: 1:59⁴/₅ on a muddy track for winnings valued at $53,710.

Australia defeated the U.S. 3 to 2 in the challenge round of the **Davis Cup** International Matches.

U.S. lawn tennis men's singles champion, Robert L. Riggs; women's singles champion, Alice Marble.

U.S.G.A. amatuer championship won by Marvin Ward at North Shore C.C., Glen View, Ill. He defeated Ray Billows, 7 and 5. **Open championship** won by Byron Nelson at Philadelphia, Pa., C.C., with a score of 284.

JANUARY 1, 1939

Southern California defeated Duke, 7 to 3, in the **Rose Bowl.**

MAY 6, 1939

Winner of the 65th annual **Kentucky Derby** was the favorite *Johnstown* ridden by J. Stout. *Johnstown* ran the 1¼ mi. in 2:03²/₅ on a fast track, winning $46,350.

JULY 11, 1939

Baseball's 7th annual **All-Star Game** won by the American League, 3-1, at the Yankee Stadium in New York city. Joe DiMaggio hit a home run for the winners.

OCTOBER 4-8, 1939

New York, AL, defeated Cincinnati, NL, 4-0 in the 36th annual **World Series.**

DECEMBER 2, 1939

Navy defeated Army, 10-0, in the annual **Army-Navy football game** held at Municipal Stadium, Philadelphia, Pa.

1940

National football champion was Minnesota, coached by Bernie Bierman. Their record: 8 wins, no losses, no ties.

First man to pole vault 15 feet was **Cornelius Warmerdam.**

U.S. lawn tennis men's singles champion, W. Donald McNeill; women's singles champion, Alice Marble.

U.S.G.A. amateur championship won by Richard D. Chapman at Winged Foot G.C., Mamaroneck, N.Y. He defeated W. B. McCullough, 11 and 9. **Open championship** won by W. Lawson Little, Jr. at Canterbury G.C., Cleveland, Ohio, with a score of 287.

Bimelech won the 72nd annual **Belmont Stakes,** paying 13-10. Jockey was F.A. Smith; time: 2:29³/₅ on a fast track for winnings valued at $35,030.

Bimelech won the 64th annual **Preakness Stakes,** paying 9-10. Jockey was F.A. Smith; time: 1:58³/₅ on a fast track for winnings valued at $53,230.

JANUARY 1, 1940

Southern California defeated Tennessee, 14 to 0, in the **Rose Bowl.**

MAY 4, 1940

A 35-1 long shot, *Gallahadion*, won the 66th annual **Kentucky Derby.** Under jockey C. Bierman he ran the 1¼ mi. in 2:05 on a fast track and won $60,150.

JULY 9, 1940

The American League defeated the National League, 1-0, to win the 8th annual **All-Star Baseball Game.**

OCTOBER 2-8, 1940

Cincinnati, NL, defeated Detroit, AL, 4-3 in the 37th annual **World Series.**

NOVEMBER 30, 1940

Navy defeated Army, 14-0, in the annual **Army-Navy football game** held at Municipal Stadium, Philadelphia, Pa.

1941

This year's **National College Football Champion** was, for the 2nd straight time, 4 titles in all, Minnesota, coached by Bernie Bierman. Their record: 8 wins, no losses, no ties.

U.S. lawn tennis men's singles champion, Robert L. Riggs; women's singles champion, Mrs. Sarah Palfrey Cooke.

U.S.G.A. amateur championship won by Marvin Ward at Omaha, Neb., G.C. He defeated B. Patrick Abbott, 4 and 3. **Open championship** won by Craig Wood at Colonial Club, Fort Worth, Tex., with a score of 284.

Whirlaway won the 73rd annual **Belmont Stakes,** paying 1-4. Jockey was E. Arcaro; time: 2:31 on a fast track for winnings valued at $39,770.

Whirlaway won the 65th annual **Preakness Stakes,** paying 11-10. Jockey was E. Arcaro; time: 1:58⁴/₅ on a fast track for winnings valued at $49,365.

JANUARY 1, 1941

Stanford defeated Nebraska, 21 to 13, in the **Rose Bowl.**

MAY 3, 1941

The present record time for the **Kentucky Derby** 2:01²/₅, was made by *Whirlaway* with Eddie Arcaro up, in the 67th running of the Churchill Downs classic. The winner's prize was $61,275. *Whirlaway* went on to win the Preakness and the Belmont Stakes to take American racing's Triple Crown.

JUNE 2, 1941

Baseball's "Iron Man," **Lou Gehrig,** died in N.Y.C. Longtime first baseman for the Yankees, he had played in a record 2130 consecutive games.

JULY 8, 1941

The American League won the 9th annual **All-Star baseball game** at Detroit, beating the National League 7-5.

JULY 17, 1941

Cleveland pitchers Al Smith and Jim Bagby, Jr., halted the hitting streak of Yankee center fielder Joe DiMaggio. He had **hit safely in 56 consecutive games** from May 15 through July 16, a major-league record.

OCTOBER 1-6, 1941

New York, AL, defeated Brooklyn, NL, 4-1 in the 38th annual **World Series.**

NOVEMBER 29, 1941

Navy defeated Army, 14-6, in their annual classic in Municipal Stadium, Philadelphia.

1942

National College Football Champion: Ohio State, coached by Paul Brown. Their record: 9 wins, 1 loss, no ties.

U.S. lawn tennis men's singles champion, Frederick R. Schroeder, Jr.; women's singles champion, Pauline M. Betz.

Alsab won the 66th annual **Preakness Stakes,** paying 1-2. Jockey was B. James;

Joe Louis *shown knocking out Billy Conn to retain Heavyweight Championship in 1941.*

time: 1:57 on a fast track for winnings valued at $58,175.

Shut Out won the 74th annual **Belmont Stakes,** paying 7-2. Jockey was E. Arcaro; time: 2:29¹/₅ on a fast track for winnings valued at $44,520.

JANUARY 1, 1942

Oregon State defeated Duke 20-16 in the **Rose Bowl** game, played for the 1st time at Durham, N.C.

JANUARY 9, 1942

Joe Louis knocked out Buddy Baer in the 1st round.

MAY 2, 1942

The winner of the 68th annual **Kentucky Derby** was the favorite *Shut Out,* ridden by W.D. Wright. He ran the 1¼ mi. in 2:04²/₅ on a good track to win $64,225.

JULY 6, 1942

The American League scored 3 runs in the 1st inning on home runs by Rudy York and Lou Boudreau to beat the National League, 3-1, in the 10th annual **All-Star game.**

SEPTEMBER 30-OCTOBER 5, 1942

St. Louis, NL, defeated New York, AL, 4-1 in the 39th annual **World Series.**

1943

Outstanding basketball teams of the year were the University of Illinois, which won its 2nd straight Big Ten championship, and the University of Wyoming, Rocky Mountain conference champs who went on to win the N.C.A.A. tournament.

Stan Musial of the Cardinals and Spurgeon Chandler of the Yankees were named **most valuable baseball players,** respectively, of the National and American leagues.

N.Y. Giants' relief pitcher Ace Adams set a new 20th-century baseball record of 70 games pitched.

National College Football Champion was Notre Dame, coached by Frank Leahy. Their record: 9 wins, 1 loss, no ties.

The Heisman Memorial Trophy was awarded to Angelo Bertelli, Notre Dame quarterback named by sportswriters as the **outstanding collegiate football player of the year.**

U.S. lawn tennis men's singles champion, Lt. (j.g.) Joseph R. Hunt; **women's singles champion,** Pauline M. Betz.

Count Fleet won the 67th annual **Preakness Stakes,** paying 1-7. Jockey was J. Longden; time: 1:57²/₅ on a good track for win-

nings valued at $43,190.

Count Fleet won the 75th annual **Belmont Stakes,** paying 1-15. Jockey was J. Longden; time: 2:28¹/₅ on a fast track for winnings valued at $35,340.

JANUARY 1, 1943

Georgia defeated U.C.L.A., 9 to 0, in the **Rose Bowl.**

APRIL 8, 1943

Detroit won the last of 4 straight games in the Stanley Cup finals, defeating Boston 2-0 to become National League **hockey champions.**

MAY 1, 1943

Winner of the 69th annual **Kentucky Derby** was the favorite *Count Fleet,* J. Longden up. His time was 2:04 on a fast track; prize, $60,725. He went on to win the Triple Crown.

JULY 13, 1943

Baseball's 11th annual **All-Star Game** won by the American League, 5-3, at Philadelphia.

OCTOBER 5-11, 1943

New York, AL, defeated St. Louis, NL, 4-1, in the 40th annual **World Series.**

NOVEMBER 27, 1943

Navy defeated Army, 13-0, at Michie Stadium, West Point.

1944

This year's **National College Football Champion** was Army, coached by Earl Blaik.

The Heisman Memorial Trophy was awarded to Leslie Horvath, Ohio State quarterback named by sportswriters as the **outstanding collegiate football player of the year.**

Green Bay Packers defeated the New York Giants 14 to 7 for the **National Professional Football Championship.**

P.G.A. Championship, held at Spokane, Wash., Byron Nelson lost, 1 down, to the relatively unknown Indiana pro Robert Hamilton.

U.S. lawn tennis men's singles champion, Sgt. Frank A. Parker; **women's singles champion,** Pauline M. Betz.

Pensive won the 68th annual **Preakness Stakes,** paying 33-20. Jockey was C. McCreary; time: 1:59¹/₅ on a fast track for winnings valued at $60,075.

Bounding Home won the 76th annual **Belmont Stakes,** paying 16-1. Jockey was G.L. Smith; time: 2:32¹/₅ on a fast track for winnings valued at $55,000.

JANUARY 1 1944

Southern California defeated Washington, 29 to 0, in the **Rose Bowl.**

MARCH 3, 1944

Bob Montgomery outpointed Beau Jack in 15 rounds at Madison Square Garden to win the **lightweight championship.**

MAY 6, 1944

Winner of the 70th annual **Kentucky Derby** was the favorite *Pensive,* ridden by C. McCreary. The time, 2:04¹/₅ on a good track; the prize, $64,675.

JULY 11, 1944

The National League won the 12th annual **All-Star baseball game** at Pittsburgh, 7-1.

OCTOBER 4-9, 1944

St. Louis, NL, defeated St. Louis, AL, 4-2 in the 41st **World Series.**

NOVEMBER 25, 1944

Kenesaw Mountain Landis, commissioner of organized baseball for nearly 24 years, died.

DECEMBER 2, 1944

Army defeated Navy, 23-7.

1945

This year's **national football champion** was again Army, coached by Earl Blaik. Their record: 9 wins, no losses, no ties.

U.S. lawn tennis men's singles champion Sgt. Frank A. Parker; **women's singles champion,** Mrs. Sarah Palfrey Cooke.

Boxer of the year was Rocky Graziano, who in 5 fights scored 5 knockouts, including 2 over welterweight champ Fred Cochrane.

Pavot won the 77th annual **Belmont Stakes,** paying 2-1. Jockey: E. Arcaro.

Polynesian won the 69th annual **Preakness Stakes,** paying 12-1. Jockey was W.D. Wright.

JANUARY 1, 1945

Southern California defeated Tennessee 25 to 0 in the **Rose Bowl.**

JANUARY 26, 1945

The **N.Y. Yankees baseball club was sold** by the heirs of the late Jacob Ruppert and Edward G. Barrow to a syndicate headed by Lawrence McPhail and including Daniel Topping and Del Webb. Estimated price was $2.8 million.

APRIL 24, 1945

Sen. **Albert B. "Happy" Chandler** named high commissioner of baseball to fill post caused by death of Judge Landis.

JUNE 9, 1945

Eddie Arcaro rode his 3rd **Kentucky Derby** winner, *Hoop Jr.*

AUGUST 10, 1945

Controlling interest in the **Brooklyn Dodgers** baseball club was acquired by Branch Rickey, Walter O'Malley, and John L. Smith.

OCTOBER 3-10, 1945

Detroit, AL, defeated Chicago, NL, 4-3 in the 42nd **World Series.**

DECEMBER 2, 1945

Army defeated Navy, 32-13.

1946

This year's **National Football Champion** was Notre Dame, coached by Frank Leahy. Their record: 8 wins, no losses, 1 tie.

U.S. lawn tennis men's singles champion, John A. Kramer; **women's singles champion,** Pauline M. Betz.

U.S.G.A. amateur championship won by Ted Bishop at Baltusrol G.C., Short Hills, N.J. He defeated Smiley Quick, 1 up. **Open championship** won by Lloyd Mangrum at Canterbury G.C., Cleveland, Ohio, with a score of 284.

Assault won the 70th annual **Preakness Stakes,** paying 7-5. Jockey was W. Mehrtens; time: 2:31²/₅ on a fast track for winnings valued at $96,620.

Assault won the 78th annual **Belmont Stakes,** paying 7-5. Jockey was W. Mehrtens;

time: 2:30⁴/₅ on a fast track for winnings valued at $75,400.

U.S. defeated Australia 5 to 0 in the challenge round of the **Davis Cup** International Matches.

JANUARY 1, 1946
Alabama defeated Southern California by a score of 34 to 14 in the **Rose Bowl.**

MAY 4, 1946
Assault won the 72nd annual **Kentucky Derby.** He ran the 1¼ mi. in 2:06³/₅ on a slow track, winning $96,400. The jockey was W. Mehrtens.

JULY 9, 1946
American League shut out the National League, 12-0, in the 13th annual **All-Star game** held in Boston after a lapse of one year. Ted Williams hit 2 home runs for the winners and Charlie Keller hit one.

OCTOBER 1-3, 1946
National League pennant race ended in league's **1st tie:** Brooklyn and St. Louis had same reason record of 96 wins, 58 losses. St. Louis won play-off on Oct. 3 by taking 2 games straight, 4-2 and 8-2.

OCTOBER 6-15, 1946
St. Louis, NL, defeated Boston, AL, 4-3 in the 43rd annual **World Series.**

NOVEMBER 30, 1946
Army defeated Navy, 21-18, to win the annual **Army-Navy football game** at Municipal Stadium, Philadelphia, Pa.

1947
First Negro baseball player in National League when Jackie Robinson signed with Brooklyn Dodgers.

National College Football Champion was Notre Dame, coached by Frank Leahy. They were undefeated and untied in 9 games.

U.S. lawn tennis men's singles champion, John A. Kramer; **women's singles champion,** A. Louise Brough.

U.S. defeated Australia 4 to 1 in the challenge round of the **Davis Cup** International Matches.

U.S.G.A. amateur championship won by Robert H. Riegel at Pebble Beach Course, Del Monte, Calif. He defeated Johnny Dawson, 2 and 1. **Open Championship** won by Lew Worsham at St. Louis, Mo., C.C., with a score of 282.

Faultless won the 71st annual **Preakness Stakes,** paying 21-5. Jockey was D. Dodson; time: 1:59 on a fast track for winnings valued at $98,005.

Phalanx won the 79th annual **Belmont Stakes,** paying 23-10. Jockey: R. Donoso; time: 2:29²/₅ on a fast track for winnings valued at 78,900.

JANUARY 1, 1947
Illinois defeated U.C.L.A. by a score of 45 to 14 in the **Rose Bowl.**

MAY 3, 1947
Winner of the 73rd **Kentucky Derby** was *Jet Pilot* ridden by Eric Guerin. He ran the 1¼ mi. in 2:06⁴/₅ on a slow track, winning $92,160 for his owners.

JULY 8, 1947
The 14th annual **All-Star game** won by the American League, 2-1, at Chicago on July 8. Johnny Mize hit a homer to account for the

loser's only run.

SEPTEMBER 30-OCTOBER 6, 1947
New York, AL, defeated Brookly, NL, 4-3 in the 44th annual **World Series.**

NOVEMBER 29, 1947
Army defeated Navy, 21-0, in their annual contest at Municipal Stadium, Philadelphia.

1948
The **National Football Champion** was Michigan. The coach, Bernie Oosterbaan. The record: 9 wins, no losses, no ties.

U.S. lawn tennis men's singles champion, Richard A. Gonzales; **women's singles champion,** Mrs. Margaret Osborne du Pont.

U.S.G.A. amateur championship won by Willie Turnesa at Memphis, Tenn., C.C. He defeated Ray Billows, 2 and 1. **Open championship** won by Ben Hogan at Riviera C.C., Los Angeles, Calif., with a score of 276.

Ben Hogan *won the U.S. Open Golf Championship in 1948.*

Citation won the 80th **Belmont Stakes,** paying 1-5. Jockey: E. Arcaro; time: 2:28¹/₅ on a fast track for winnings valued at $77,700.

Citation won the 72nd annual **Preakness Stakes,** paying 1-10. Jockey: E. Arcaro; time was 2:02³/₅ on a heavy track for winnings valued at $91,870.

U.S. defeated Australia 5 to 0 in the challenge round of the **Davis Cup** International Matches.

JANUARY 1, 1948
Michigan defeated Southern California by a score of 49 to 0 in the **Rose Bowl.**

MAY 1, 1948
Eddie Arcaro rode his 4th **Kentucky Derby** winner, *Citation*, in the 74th running of the Churchill Downs, classic. *Citation's* time was 2:05²/₅, winning $83,400.

JULY 13, 1948
The American League defeated the National League, 5-2, to win the 15th annual **All-Star baseball game** at St. Louis, Mo.

JULY 29-AUGUST 14, 1948
U.S. won the unofficial championship of the 14th **Olympic games** held at London, England, with a team score of 547.5. Sweden was 2nd with a score of 308.5.

OCTOBER 6-11, 1948
Cleveland, AL, defeated Boston, NL, 4-2 in the 45th annual **World Series.**

NOVEMBER 27, 1948
Army and Navy tied, 21-21, in the annual **Army-Navy football game.**

1949
The **national football champion** was Notre Dame.

U.S. lawn tennis men's singles champion, Richard A. Gonzales; **women's singles champion,** Mrs. Margaret Osborne du pont.

U.S.G.A. amateur championship won by Charles R. Coe at Oak Hill C.C., Rochester, N.Y. He defeated Rufus King, 11 and 10. **Open championship** won by Cary Middlecoff at Medinah, Ill., C.C., with a score of 286.

Capot won the 73rd annual **Preakness Stakes,** paying 5-2. Jockey: T. Atkinson; time: 1:56 on a fast track for winnings valued at $79,985.

Capot won the 81st annual **Belmont Stakes,** paying 11-2. Jockey: T. Atkinson; time: 2:30¹/₅ on a fast track for winnings valued at $60,900.

U.S. defeated Australia 4 to 1 in the **Davis Cup** International Matches.

JANUARY 1, 1949
Northwestern defeated California by a score of 20 to 14 in the **Rose Bowl.**

MAY 7, 1949
A 16-1 long shot, *Ponder*, won the 76th annual **Kentucky Derby** running the 1¼ mi. in 2:04¹/₅ on a fast track and winning $91,600. Jockey up was S. Brooks.

JUNE 22, 1949
New **World's Heavyweight Champion,** Ezzard Charles, out-pointed "Jersey Joe" Walcott in 15 rounds.

JULY 12, 1949
The 16th annual **All-Star game** at Ebbets Field in Brooklyn, N.Y. was won by the American League, 11-7. Ralph Kiner and Stan Musial hit home runs for the losers.

Stan Musial, *longtime St. Louis Cardinals player, was member of the National League All-Stars in 1949.*

OCTOBER 5-9, 1949
New York, AL, defeated Brooklyn, NL, 4-1 in the 46th annual **World Series.**

NOVEMBER 26, 1949
Army defeated Navy, 38-0, to win the annual **Army-Navy football game.**

1950
National College Football Champion was Oklahoma, coached by Charles Wilkinson. Their record: 10 wins, no losses, no ties.

Man o' War named the greatest horse of the 1st half of the 20th Century by an Associated Press poll.

U.S. lawn tennis men's singles champion, Arthur Larsen; **women's singles champion,** Mrs. Margaret Osborne du Pont.

Australia defeated the U.S. in the challenge round of the **Davis Cup** International Matches 4-1.

U.S.G.A. amateur championship won by Sam Urzetta at Minneapolis, Minn., G.C. He defeated Frank R. Stranahan, 1 up. **Open championship** won by Ben Hogan at Merion G.C. Ardmore, Pa., with a score of 287.

Middleground won the 82nd annual **Belmont Stakes,** paying 27-10. Jockey: W. Boland; time: 2:28³/₅ on a fast track for winnings valued at $66,350.

Hill Prince won the 74th annual **Preakness Stakes,** paying 7-10. Jockey: E. Arcaro; time: 1:59¹/₅ on a slow track for winnings valued at $56,115.

JANUARY 1, 1950

Ohio State defeated California by a score of 17 to 14 in the **Rose Bowl.**

MAY 6, 1950

The 77th annual **Kentucky Derby** was won by *Middleground*, who just missed tying *Whirlaway's* Derby record of ¹/₅ sec. With jockey W. Boland up he won $92,650, running the fast track in 2:01³/₅ .

JULY 11, 1950

The National League finally won an **All-Star game,** beating the American League, 4-3, at Chicago, after losing 4 straight mid-season classics. Ralph Kiner and Red Schoendienst hit homers for the winners.

OCTOBER 4-7, 1950

New York, AL, defeated Philadelphia, NL, 4-0 in the 47th annual **World Series.**

DECEMBER 1, 1950

Navy defeated Army, 14-2, in their annual contest at Municipal Stadium, Philadelphia.

1951

National College Football Champion was Tennessee, coached by Col. Robert Neyland. The "Volunteers' " record: 10 wins, no losses, no ties.

U.S. lawn tennis men's singles champion, Frank Sedgman of Australia; **women's singles champion,** Maureen Connolly.

Australia defeated U.S. 3-2 in the challenge round of the **Davis Cup** International Matches.

U.S.G.A. amateur championship won by Billy Maxwell at Saucon Valley C.C., Bethlehem, Pa. He defeated Joseph F. Gagliardi, 4 and 3. **Open championship** won by Ben Hogan at Oakland Hills, C.C., Birmingham, Mich., with a score of 287.

Counterpoint won the 83rd annual **Belmont Stakes,** paying 5-10. Jockey was D. Gorman; time: 2:29 on a fast track for winnings valued at $82,000.

Bold won the 75th annual **Preakness Stakes,** paying 4-1. Jockey: E. Arcaro; time: 1:56²/₅ on a fast track for winnings valued at $83,110.

JANUARY 1, 1951

Michigan defeated California by a score of 14 to 6 in the **Rose Bowl.**

FEBRUARY 3, 1951

$144,323 won by *Great Circle* in the **Santa**

Willie Shoemaker *won the Santa Anita Maturity aboard* Great Circle *in 1951.*

Anita Maturity. The jockey was Willie Shoemaker.

MAY 5, 1951

Jockey Conn McCreary rode his 2nd **Kentucky Derby** winner *Count Turf.* Time: 2:02³/₅ ; prize, $98,050.

JULY 10, 1951

The **All-Star game,** won by the National League, 8-3, at Detroit. Six home runs were hit; Stan Musial, Bob Elliot, and Gil Hodges connecting for the National League and Vic Wertz and George Kell hitting for the losers.

JULY 14, 1951

First horse to win $1 million was *Citation,* by winning the Hollywood Gold Cup, Inglewood, Calif.

JULY 18, 1951

World Heavyweight Championship won by "Jersey Joe" Walcott when he K.O.'d Ezzard Charles in 7th round at Pittsburgh. At 37 Walcott was oldest man to gain title.

OCTOBER 4-10, 1951

New York, AL, defeated New York, NL, 4-2 in the 48th annual **World Series.**

DECEMBER 1, 1951

Navy defeated Army, 42-7, in their annual contest at Municipal Stadium, Philadelphia.

1952

National College Football Champion was Michigan State, coached by Clarence "Biggie" Munn. Their record: 9 wins, no losses, no ties.

U.S. lawn tennis men's singles champion, Frank Sedgman of Australia; **women's singles champion,** Maureen Connolly.

Australia defeated the U.S. 4 to 1 in the challenge round of the **Davis Cup** International Matches.

U.S.G.A. amateur championship won by Jack Westland at Seattle, Wash., G.C. He defeated Al Mengert, 3 and 2. **Open championship** won by Julius Boros at Northwood Club, Dallas, Tex., with a score of 281.

One Count won the 84th annual **Belmont Stakes,** paying 13-1. Jockey: E. Arcaro; time: 2:30¹/₅ on a fast track for winnings valued at $82,400.

JANUARY 1, 1952

Illinois defeated Stanford by a score of 40 to 7 in the **Rose Bowl.**

MAY 3, 1952

Jockey Eddie Arcaro rode his 5th **Ken-**

tucky Derby winner, *Hill Gail,* running a fast track in 2:01³/₅ . The prize was $96,300.

JULY 8, 1952

Baseball's 19th annual **All-Star Game** at Shibe Park, Philadelphia won by the National League team, 3-2. Jackie Robinson and Hank Sauer hit home runs for the winners.

SEPTEMBER 23, 1952

World **Heavyweight Championship** won by Rocky Marciano, who knocked out "Jersey Joe" Walcott in 13th round at Philadelphia. It was Marciano's 43rd straight win as professional boxer, no bouts lost.

OCTOBER 1-7, 1952

New York, AL, defeated Brooklyn, NL, 4-3 in the 49th annual **World Series.**

NOVEMBER 29, 1952

Navy defeated Army, 7-0, in their annual contest at Municipal Stadium, Philadelphia.

1953

U.S. lawn tennis men's singles champion, Tony Trabert; **women's singles champion,** Maureen Connolly.

U.S.G.A. amateur championship won by Gene Littler at Oklahoma City, Okla., G. and C.C. He defeated Dale Morey, 1 up. **Open championship** won by Ben Hogan for 4th time at Oakmont C.C., Pittsburgh, Pa., with a score of 283.

This year's **national college football champion** was Michigan State with a perfect season; team was coached by Clarence (Biggie) Munn who was named "coach of the year."

Native Dancer won the 77th annual **Preakness Stakes,** paying 1-5. Jockey: E. Guerin; time: 1:57⁴/₅ on a fast track for winnings valued at $65,200.

Native Dancer *won the Preakness in 1953.*

Native Dancer won the 85th annual **Belmont Stakes,** paying 9-20. Jockey: E. Guerin; time: 2:28³/₅ on a fast track for winnings valued at $82,500.

Australia defeated the U.S. 3 to 2 in the challenge round of the **Davis Cup** International Matches.

JANUARY 1, 1953

Southern California defeated Wisconsin by a score of 7 to 0 in the **Rose Bowl.**

MARCH 18, 1953

The shifting of the **Boston Braves'** baseball franchise to Milwaukee, Wisc., approved by the National League. This year Milwaukee became the most baseball-happy town in the U.S. leading both leagues in attendance, 1,826,397, National League record.

MAY 2, 1953

A 25-1 long shot, *Dark Star*, won the **Kentucky Derby;** time: 2:02; his prize, $90,050. Jockey: H. Moreno.

JULY 14, 1953

The National League won the 20th annual **All-Star game** at Cincinnati, Ohio, beating the American League, 5-1.

SEPTEMBER 16, 1953

The shift of the **St. Louis Browns'** baseball franchise to Baltimore, Md., approved by the American League, the Browns to begin the following season as the **Baltimore Orioles.**

SEPTEMBER 20-OCTOBER 5, 1953

New York, AL, defeated Brooklyn, NL, 4-2 in the 50th annual **World Series.** This was the 1st time a team has won 5 consecutive World Series.

NOVEMBER 28, 1953

Navy defeated Army, 7-0, at Philadelphia.

1954

U.S. lawn tennis men's singles champion, E. Victor Seixas, Jr.; **women's singles champion,** Doris Hart.

U.S.G.A. amateur championship won by Arnold Palmer at Detroit C.C., Grosse Point Farms, Mich. He defeated Bob Sweeny, 1 up. **Open championship** won by Ed Furgol at Baltusrol G.C., N.J., with a score of 284.

High Gun won the 86th annual **Belmont Stakes.** Jockey: E. Guerin; Time: 2:30⁴/₅ for winnings valued at $89,000.

Hasty Road won the 78th annual **Preakness Stakes.** Jockey: J. Adams; Time: 1:57²/₅ for winnings valued at $91,600.

JANUARY 1, 1954

Michigan State defeated U.C.L.A. by a score of 28 to 20 in the **Rose Bowl.**

MAY, 1954

The winner of the 80th **Kentucky Derby** was *Determine* ridden by R. York. His time: 2:03; the prize, $102,050.

JULY 13, 1954

The 21st annual **All-Star baseball game** was won by the American League 11-9.

SEPTEMBER 29-OCTOBER 2, 1954

New York, NL, defeated Cleveland, AL, 4-0 in the 51st annual **World Series.**

NOVEMBER 8, 1954

The American League approved the transfer of the **Philadelphia Athletics** baseball franchise to Kansas City, Mo.

NOVEMBER 27, 1954

Navy defeated Army, 27-20.

DECEMBER 26, 1954

The Cleveland Browns defeated the Detroit Lions, 56-10, to win the **National Professional Football Championship.**

1955

This year's National College Football Champion was Oklahoma, coached by Charles Wilkinson.

The Cleveland Browns defeated the Los Angeles Rams, 34-14 at Los Angeles, to win the **National Professional Football** Championship.

U.S.G.A. Amateur Golf Championship won by Harvie Ward at the Country Club of Virginia, Richmond, Va. He defeated William Hyndman, 9 and 8. **Open Championship** was won by Jack Fleck at Olympic C.C., San Francisco, Calif. He defeated Ben Hogan, 69 to 72 in a playoff match.

Nashua won the **Belmont Stakes.** Jockey: E. Arcaro; time: 2:29. Winnings were valued at $83,700.

Nashua won **Preakness Stakes.** Jockey: E. Arcaro; record time was 1:54³/₅ .

U.S. lawn **Men's Tennis Singles Champion,** Tony Trabert; **Women's Singles Championship** won by Doris Hart.

JANUARY 1,1955

Ohio State defeated Southern California 20-7, in the **Rose Bowl** football game.

MAY 7, 1955

The **Kentucky Derby** won by *Swaps*. Time: 2:01⁴/₅ . Jockey: Willie Shoemaker up, he won $108,400.

JULY 12, 1955

The National League won the 22nd **All-Star baseball game,** beating the American League, 6-5, in a 12-inning contest held at Milwaukee, Wisc.

SEPTEMBER 28-OCTOBER 4, 1955

Brooklyn, NL, defeated N.Y. Yankees, AL, 4-3 in the 52nd annual **World Series.**

NOVEMBER 26, 1955

Army defeated Navy, 14-6 in the annual **Army-Navy game** at Philadelphia, Pa.

1956

National College Football Champion was Oklahoma, coached by Bud Wilkinson.

U.S.G.A. Amateur Golf Championship won by Harvie Ward, Jr., for the 2nd year in a row. **Open Championship** was won by Cary Middlecoff at Rochester, N.Y.

Fabius won the **Preakness Stakes.** Time: 1:58²/₅ . Jockey was Willie Hartack.

U.S. lawn **Men's Tennis Singles Champion,** Ken Rosewall; **Women's Singles Championship** won by Shirley Fry.

MAY 5, 1956

Needles won the **Kentucky Derby.** Time: 2:03²/₅ . Jockey: D. Erb, he won $123,450.

JUNE 16, 1956

Needles won the **Belmont Stakes.** Time: 2:29⁴/₅ . Jockey: D. Erb.

JULY 10, 1956

The National League won the 23rd **All-Star baseball game,** beating the American League 7-3 at Washington, D.C.

OCTOBER 3-10, 1956

New York, AL, defeated Brookly, NL, 4-3 in the 53rd annual **World Series.** On Oct. 8, Don Larsen, New York Yankee right-hander, pitched the **first no-hit, no-run game in World Series history** to beat Brooklyn 2-0.

NOVEMBER 30, 1956

Floyd Patterson knocked out Archie Moore in the 5th round of their **heavyweight championship fight** in Chicago. Patterson, 21, was the youngest man ever to win the championship.

DECEMBER 1, 1956

The 57th annual **Army-Navy game** at Philadelphia, Pa., was tied 7-7.

DECEMBER 30, 1956

The New York Giants defeated the Chicago Cardinals 47-7 at New York to win the **National Professional Football** Championship.

1957

National College Football Champion was Alabama Polytechnic Institute.

The Detroit Lions defeated the Cleveland Browns 59-14 to win the **National Professional Football** Championship.

U.S.G.A. Amateur Golf Championship won by Air Force Lt. Hillman Robbins of Memphis, Tenn. **Open Championship** was won by Dick Mayer of La Jolla, Calif., who defeated defending champion Cary Middlecoff in an 18-hole playoff.

U.S. lawn **Men's Tennis Singles Champion,** Malcolm Anderson; **Women's Singles Championship** won by Althea Gibson.

The Milwaukee Braves set a **baseball attendance record** for the National League of 2,215,404 fans attending games during the year.

JANUARY 1, 1957

At the annual **Rose Bowl** football game, Iowa beat Oregon State 35-19.

FEBRUARY 23, 1957

The Yale Univ. freestyle relay **swimming team set a new record** of 3:18 ³/₁₀ in the 400-yard freestyle event at New Haven, Conn.

APRIL 27, 1957

Bob Gutowski, an Occidental College senior, set a new **pole-vault record** of 15 feet 8¼ inches at Palo Alto, Calif.

MAY 4, 1957

The **Kentucky Derby** won by *Iron Liege*. Time: 2:02¹/₅ ; jockey Bill Hartack rode for $107,950.

MAY 18, 1957

Bold Ruler won the 81st annual **Preakness Stakes** at Pimlico. Jockey: Willie Shoemaker; time: 1:56¹/₅ .

JUNE 15, 1957

Gallant Man won the **Belmont Stakes.** Jockey: Willie Shoemaker; time: 2:26³/₅ .

JULY 9, 1957

The **All-Star baseball game** was won by the American League. Score: AL 6, NL 5.

JULY 19, 1957

Don Bowden was **first American to run mile in less than 4 minutes.** His time was 3 min., 58.7 seconds at Stockton, Calif.

OCTOBER 2-10, 1957

Milwaukee, NL, defeated New York, AL, 4-3 in the **World Series.**

NOVEMBER 30, 1957

Navy defeated Army 14-0.

1958

U.S.G.A. Amateur Golf Championship won by Charlie Coe when he defeated Tom Aaron 5 and 4. **Open Championship** was won by Tommy Bolt in Tulsa, Okla.

JANUARY 1, 1958
Ohio State defeated Oregon State 10-7 in the **Rose Bowl.**

MARCH 25, 1958
Sugar Ray Robinson won the **middleweight boxing championship** by outpointing Carmen Basilio in 15 rounds at Chicago.

MAY 3, 1958
The **Kentucky Derby** won by *Tim Tam.* Time: 2:05. Jockey: Ismael Valenzuela up, he won $160,500.

MAY 17, 1958
Tim Tam won the **Preakness Stakes.** Jockey: Ismael Valenzuela; winnings were $97,900.

JUNE 7, 1958
Cavan won the **Belmont Stakes** for $73,440. Jockey: Pete Anderson.

JUNE 28, 1958
Nancy Ramey of Seattle swam the women's 100-meter butterfly in a **world record** time of 1:9⅗ during a meet in Los Angeles.

JULY 8, 1958
The American League won the **All-Star baseball game,** beating the National League 4-3.

AUGUST 6, 1958
During a meet in Budapest, Hungary, Glenn Davis of Columbus, O., set a new **world record in the 400-meter hurdles** in 49.2 seconds.

SEPTEMBER 6, 1958
Mark Antony, a 4-year-old colt, set a **world record for the mile and 70 yards** when it won the Manchester Handicap at Rockingham Park, N.H., in 1:39.2.

SEPTEMBER 7, 1958
U.S. lawn **Men's Tennis Singles Championship** won by Ashley Cooper; **Women's Singles Champion** was Althea Gibson for the second year in a row.

OCTOBER 1-9, 1958
New York, AL, defeated Milwaukee, NL, 4-3 in the 55th annual **World Series.**

OCTOBER 9, 1958
Yogi Berra, New York Yankee catcher, finished participating in his 10th World Series; he tied records for World Series participation set by **Babe Ruth** and **Joe DiMaggio.**

DECEMBER 28, 1958
The Baltimore Colts defeated the New York Giants 23-17 at New York to win the **National Professional Football** Championship.

1959

FEBRUARY 1, 1959
Zachariah Davis was designated for the **Baseball Hall of Fame.**

MAY 25, 1959
A Louisiana ban on bouts between **Negro and white boxers** was declared unconstitu-tional by the United States Supreme Court.

JUNE 26, 1959
Ingemar Johansson of Sweden won the **world's professional heavyweight boxing title** by knocking out Floyd Patterson in a bout in New York City.

JULY 13, 1959
Cliff Lumsden won the Atlantic City (N.J.) professional **swim marathon.** Finishing in 10 hr. 54 min. 5 sec., he won $5,000.

JULY 20, 1959
Tennis national clay court championships were won by Bernard Bartzen, men's singles; Sally Moore, women's singles; Bernard Bartzen and Grand Golden, men's doubles; Sandra Reynolds and Renée Schuurman, women's doubles.

AUGUST 16, 1959
The **American Soap Box Derby** was won by Barney Townsend, an Indiana 13-year-old.

AUGUST 23, 1959
U.S. tennis amateur championship winners included: Neale Fraser, men's singles; Maria Bueno, women's singles; Neale Fraser and Roy Emerson, men's doubles.

AUGUST 28-31, 1959
Australia retained the **Davis Cup** as its team (Neale A. Fraser, Roy Emerson, Rod Laver) defeated the U.S. challengers (Alex Olmedo, Barry MacKay, and Earl Buchholtz, Jr.) at Forest Hills, N.Y.

SEPTEMBER 7, 1959
Pan American Games concluded with the U.S. first and Argentina second.

OCTOBER 8, 1959
National League Los Angeles **Dodgers won the World Series** by defeating the American League's Chicago White Sox, 13-6 in the 6th game.

OCTOBER 10, 1959
The PGA announced that Art Wall, golf pro of Pocono Manor, was the **leading golf prize winner** for 1959. Wall had won $53,142 on the PGA tournament circuit.

OCTOBER 29, 1959
The **Cy Young award** was given to Chicago White Sox' Early Wynn as the best major league pitcher of 1959.

NOVEMBER 4, 1959
The Baseball Writers' Association named **Ernie Banks,** shortstop for the Chicago Cubs, the most valuable National League player of 1959.

NOVEMBER 5, 1959
The **American Football League** announced that eight professional teams will begin play in 1960. The newly formed American League will rival the National Football League.

NOVEMBER 12, 1959
The Baseball Writers' Association named Nellie Fox, 2nd baseman for the Chicago White Sox, the **most valuable American League player** of 1959.

NOVEMBER 17, 1959
Willie McCovey, first baseman of the San Francisco Giants, was named **rookie of the year** in the National League, 1959.

NOVEMBER 18, 1959
Bob Allison, center fielder for the Washington Senators, was named **rookie of the year** in the American League, 1959.

NOVEMBER 21, 1959
Progressing, ridden by Hedley Woodhouse, won the **Pimlico Futurity** in Baltimore for $71,635.

DECEMBER 1, 1959
The **Heisman Trophy** for outstanding 1959 college football player was awarded to Billy Cannon, halfback for Louisiana State Univ.

DECEMBER 2, 1959
Joe Brown retained the **world lightweight title** by scoring a TKO over Dave Charnley.

DECEMBER 4, 1959
Gene Fullmer successfully defended his **world middleweight championship** by a 15-round decision over Ellsworth "Spider" Webb.

DECEMBER 6, 1959
The New York Giants won the **Eastern Championship of the National Football League** by defeating the Cleveland Browns 48-7.

DECEMBER 8, 1959
Boxing Writers Association selected **Ingemar Johansson** "fighter of the year."

DECEMBER 12, 1959
The Sebring (Fla.) Grand Prix, auto racing classic, was won by Bruce McLaren of New Zealand. Driving a Cooper-Climax, he drove 218.4 miles in 2 hr. 12 min. 36.6 sec.

Sebring *Grand Prix was won in record time by New Zealander Bruce McLaren in 1959.*

DECEMBER 18, 1959
The **Bert Bell award** for the outstanding National Football League player of 1959 was given to John Unitas, quarterback for the Baltimore Colts.

DECEMBER 27, 1959
The **Baltimore Colts** retained the National Football League Championship by defeating the New York Giants 31-16.

1960

JANUARY 1, 1960
Rose Bowl game: Washington defeated Wisconsin, 44-8.

JANUARY 2, 1960
Brooklyn's 16-year-old chess wonder, Bobby Fischer, successfully defended the **U.S. chess championship** in a tournament in New York City.

Sugar Ray Robinson, *right, shown here against Gene Fullmer, won the Middleweight crown in 1960.*

JANUARY 12, 1960

Dolph Schayes, of the Syracuse professional basketball team, reached a **15,013 point total** for his career. Schayes, famed for his rebounding ability, was the first player in NBA history to score more than 15,000 points.

JANUARY 22, 1960

The National Basketball Association all-star game was won by the Eastern Division in a 125-115 victory over the West.

JANUARY 22, 1960

Paul Pender defeated Sugar Ray Robinson in a 15-round split decision to gain world recognition as **middleweight boxing champion.**

JANUARY 30, 1960

The $166,490 **Santa Anita Maturity** was won by *First Landing* for $80,490. Eddie Arcaro was the jockey.

JANUARY 30, 1960

U.S. figure skating championships were won in Seattle by: Carol Heiss, women's singles; David Jenkins, men's singles; Margie Ackles and Charles Phillips, Jr., dance pairs.

FEBRUARY 7, 1960

Arnold Palmer, 30-year-old professional golfer, won the $100,000 **Palm Springs Desert Classic** for $12,000. In the same tournament, Joe Campbell won a special $50,000 prize for shooting a hole in one.

FEBRUARY 14, 1960

The **Daytona International** 500-mile stock car race was won for $19,600 by Robert Johnson, driving a 1959 Chevrolet. The $88,245 race was run at Daytona Beach, Fla.

FEBRUARY 18-28, 1960

Unofficial team championship of the 1960 Winter Olympics was won by the U.S.S.R. at Squaw Valley, Calif. Sweden was 2nd and the U.S. 3rd.

FEBRUARY 23, 1960

Demolition of Ebbets Field, one-time home park of the Brooklyn Dodgers (now the Los Angeles Dodgers), was begun.

MAY 30, 1960

The **500-mile race at the Indianapolis Speedway** was won by Jim Rathmann of Miami. Completing the course in 3 hr. 36 min. 11.36 sec., with an average speed of 138.757 mph, Rathmann won $110,000.

JUNE 18, 1960

The U.S. Open golf championship was won by Arnold Palmer. The tournament was played in Denver, Col.

JUNE 20, 1960

A knockout of **world heavyweight boxing champion,** Ingemar Johansson, Floyd Patterson became the first fighter in boxing history to lose and then regain the heavyweight championship.

JULY 13, 1960

The **Powder Puff Derby** (women's transcontinental air race) was won by Mrs. Aileen Saunders. She flew 2,709 miles in 18 hr. 27 min.

AUGUST 28, 1960

The U.S. tennis men's **doubles championship** was won by Roy Emerson and Neale A. Fraser of Australia. The **women's championship** was won by Darlene R. Hard of Calif. and Maria Esther Bueno of Brazil.

OCTOBER 5-13, 1960

The **World Series** was won by the Pittsburgh Pirates, defeating the New York Yankees 4 games to 3.

OCTOBER 8, 1960

The P.G.A. designated Arnold Palmer the **professional golfer of the year.**

OCTOBER 18, 1960

Manager of the New York Yankee baseball team, **Casey Stengel, was fired.**

1961
JANUARY 1, 1961

Washington defeated Minnesota 17-7 in the annual **Rose Bowl.**

JANUARY 2, 1961

Bobby Fischer, 17-year-old **chess champion,** defeated Pal Benko, Hungarian Grand Master.

FEBRUARY 25, 1961

Northrup R. Knox defended the **U.S. amateur tennis championship** by defeating Jimmy Bostwick.

FEBRUARY 25, 1961

The $145,000 **Santa Anita Handicap** was won by *Prove It* for $100,000. Willie Shoemaker was up.

MARCH 13, 1961

Floyd Patterson retained the **heavyweight championship of the world** when he knocked out Ingemar Johansson in the 6th round.

MARCH 25, 1961

The **world championship endurance auto race** in Sebring, Fla., was won by Phil Hill of Santa Monica, Calif., and Olivier Gendebien of Belgium, who shared the $1,500 prize.

MAY 6, 1961

The **Kentucky Derby** was won by *Carry Back*. Johnny Sellers was up.

1961
MAY 30, 1961

The **Indianapolis Speedway Memorial Day 500-mile race** was won by A.J. Foyt, Jr.

JUNE 5, 1961

The **Belmont Stakes** was won by *Sherluck*. Braulio Baeza was the jockey.

JUNE 9, 1961

Four ex-college basketball players and 17 current players were accused of bribery in connection with a college basketball "point shaving" plot. Gamblers Aaron Wagman and Joseph Hacken were accused as co-conspirators.

JUNE 10, 1961

Archie Moore retained the **world light-heavyweight championship** by defeating Giulio Rinaldi in a 15-round decision.

JUNE 16-17, 1961

The **National Collegiate Athletic track and field championships** in Philadelphia were won by Southern California.

JUNE 17, 1961

Gene Littler won the **U.S. Open** golf championship.

JULY 11, 1961

The National League defeated the American League, 5-4, in the first game of the annual **All-Star baseball series.** The second game of the two-game series ended in a tie, 1-1, as the game was called because of rain at the end of the ninth inning.

JULY 29, 1961

Ridan, with Bill Hartack up, won the **Arlington Futurity.**

JULY 30, 1961

Jerry Barber defeated Don January to win the **P.G.A. national golf championship.**

NOVEMBER 15, 1961

Roger Maris of the New York Yankees was designated **the most valuable player** of the year in the American League. Frank Robinson received the award for the National League on Nov. 22.

Roger Maris *broke Babe Ruth's single season home run record in 1961.*

DECEMBER 4, 1961
Floyd Patterson world heavyweight champion, knocked out Tom McNeeley in the 4th round of a bout in Toronto, Canada.

DECEMBER 31, 1961
The pro-championship of the National Football League was won by the Green Bay Packers of the West defeating the New York Giants of the East.

1962
Maury Wills of the Dodgers was named most valuable player in the National League.

JANUARY 1, 1962
The Rose Bowl, Minnesota defeated U.C.L.A. 21-3; Alabama won 10-3 over Arkansas in the Sugar Bowl; Texas beat Missisippi 12-7 in the Cotton Bowl; Penn State downed Georgia Tech 30-15 in the Orange Bowl.

FEBRUARY 2, 1962
Marine corporal John Uelses became the 1st man to pole-vault 16 ft., at the Milrose games in Madison Square Garden. Using a springy fiberglass pole, he cleared 16 ft. ¼ in. The following night at Boston he raised the mark to 16 ft. ¾ in.

FEBRUARY 10, 1962
Jim Beatty, the 1st American to run an indoor mile in less than 4 minutes, was clocked at 3:58.9 in Los Angeles, a new indoor mile record.

MARCH 2, 1962
Wilt Chamberlain, star of the Philadelphia Warriors, dropped in 36 goals and 28 foul shots against the N.Y. Knicks, to become the 1st basketball player to score 100 points in a game.

MARCH 24, 1962
TV fight fans watched welterweight contender Emile Griffith hammer champion Benny (Kid) Paret senseless in Madison Square Garden. Paret died 10 days later without regaining consciousness.

MARCH 24, 1962
In the final of the NCAA basketball tournament at Louisville, Cincinnati for the 2nd year beat Ohio State, 71-59. Nevertheless, Ohio State was voted best collegiate team by the news service polls; Ohio State star Jerry Lucas was named outstanding college player of the year.

APRIL 3, 1962
Eddie Arcaro retired.

APRIL 9, 1962
In a 3-way playoff of the Masters tournament at Augusta, Ga., Arnold Palmer scored a 68 to win by 3 strokes over Gary Player. Dow Finsterwald finished 3rd.

1962
APRIL 22, 1962
The National Hockey League's Stanley Cup was won by the Toronto Maple Leafs, as they defeated the Chicago Black Hawks 4 games to 2.

MAY 5, 1962
Decidedly won the Kentucky Derby with Hartack up. Time: 2:00²/₅; the purse was $119,650.

MAY 19, 1962
Greek Money won the Preakness Stakes with Rotz up. The time: 1:56⅕; the purse was $135,800.

MAY 30, 1962
Roger Ward, driving a Leader Card, set a new race record of 140.292 mph, to win the Memorial Day classic at the Indianapolis Speedway.

JUNE 4, 1962
Sports announcer Clem McCarthy, 79, died.

JUNE 9, 1962
Jaipur won the Belmont Stakes with Shoemaker up. The time: 2:28⁴/₅; the purse: $109,550.

JUNE 17, 1962
Jack Nicklaus capped his smashing 1st year as a pro by winning the U.S. Open championship at Oakmont, Pa. He and Arnold Palmer had finished regulation play in a tie at 283; Nicklaus won the playoff 71 to 74.

Jack Nicklaus *won the U.S. Open Championship in 1962.*

JULY 21-22, 1962
In the annual meeting between track and field teams of the U.S. and Russia, the American men's team won by a score of 128-107, at Palo Alto, Calif. The U.S.S.R.'s strong women's team bested the U.S. ladies, 66-41.

JULY 22, 1962
Gary Player of South Africa became the 1st non-resident of the U.S. to win the P.G.A. championship, carding a 278 to defeat Bob Goalby by 1 stroke at Newton Square, Pa.

SEPTEMBER 8, 1962
The richest purse in thoroughbred racing history, $357,250, was offered in the Arlington-Washington Futurity, a race for 2-year-olds. The winner's share, $142,250, went to Candy Spots.

SEPTEMBER 15-25, 1962
The U.S. successfully defended the America's Cup, yachting's most important international trophy, for the 18th time. The challenging Australian 12-meter sloop Gretel was defeated in 4 races out of 5 by Weatherly, the U.S. defender.

SEPTEMBER 25, 1962
After 2 minutes 6 seconds of the 1st round in their heavyweight boxing title match Sonny Liston knocked out Floyd Patterson to gain the crown. Fans paid $100 for ringside seats.

OCTOBER 16, 1962
The New York Yankees won the 7th game of the World Series 1-0 against the San Francisco Giants, to become world champions for the 20th time.

NOVEMBER 15, 1962
Archie Moore was stopped in the 4th round by Cassius Clay. It was Clay's 16th victory, and his 13th knockout.

DECEMBER 23, 1962
The Dallas Texans defeated the Houston Oilers 20-17, to win the AFL championship. The game went to 2 extra quarters, and was decided by a field goal by Tommy Brooker.

DECEMBER 30, 1962
The NFL championship was won by the Green Bay Packers, who defeated the N.Y. Giants 16-7 in the playoff at New York.

1963
JANUARY 1, 1963
In the Rose Bowl U.S.C. defeated Wisconsin 42-37; Mississippi won 17-13 over Arkansas in the Sugar Bowl; Louisiana State beat Texas 13-0 in the Cotton Bowl; and Alabama defeated Oklahoma 17-0 in the Orange Bowl.

JANUARY 5, 1963
Rogers Hornsby of major-league baseball, died in Winters, Tex.

MARCH 21, 1963
Davey Moore died.

MARCH 23, 1963
In the finals of the NCAA basketball tournament at Louisville, Loyola of Chicago defeated the University of Cincinnati, 60-58.

APRIL 7, 1963
At the Augusta Masters golf tournament, Jack Nicklaus edged Tony Lema by 1 stroke, to win with a score of 286.

APRIL 18, 1963
The Toronto Maple Leafs won the National Hockey League's Stanley Cup, defeating the Detroit Redwings 4 games to 1.

APRIL 24, 1963
Boston Celtics' guard Bob Cousy, 34, retired from competition after leading his team to their 5th straight NBA championship. The Celtics downed Los Angeles 4 games to 2 in the title playoffs.

MAY 4, 1963
Chateaugay won the Kentucky Derby, with Baeza up. Chateaugay also took the Belmont Stakes, but missed racing's "triple crown" by finishing 2nd to Candy Spots in the Preakness.

MAY 18, 1963
Candy Spots, with Shoemaker up, won the Preakness Stakes and a purse of $127,500.

MAY 30, 1963
At Indianapolis Speedway, Parnelli Jones drove an Agajanian-Willard Battery Special an average speed of 143.137 mph to take top prize of $148,513.

JUNE 8, 1963
The Belmont Stakes was won by Chateaugay, Baeza up.

JUNE 23, 1963

In a playoff match at Brookline, Mass., Julius Boros won the **U.S. Open** golf title, defeating Arnold Palmer and Jacky Cupit.

JULY 7, 1963

U.S. tennis amateur Chuck McKinley downed Fred Stolle of Australia 9-7, 6-1, 6-4 in the finals, to win the **Wimbledon singles title.**

JULY 9, 1963

The **All-Star game** was won 5-3 by the National League team.

JULY 22, 1963

Sonny Liston knocked out Floyd Patterson in 2 minutes 10 seconds of the 1st round.

AUGUST 5, 1963

Craig Breedlove set an unofficial **world auto speed record** of 407.45 mph on the Bonneville Salt Flats, Utah, driving a 3-ton, 3-wheeled, jet-powered auto. The U.S. Auto Club established a new class for its records: "Jet-Powered Vehicles."

AUGUST 24, 1963

Don Schollander of Santa Clara became the 1st man to break the 2-minute mark for the 200-meter freestyle swim. At Osaka, Japan, he won the event with the time of 1:58.4.

AUGUST 24, 1963

John Pennel became the **1st man to pole-vault 17 ft.,** a feat which won him the James E. Sullivan Memorial Award as the outstanding amateur athlete of the year.

SEPTEMBER 29, 1963

Stan Musial played his last game today for the St. Louis Cardinals, retiring at 42 to take an executive position with the club.

OCTOBER 2-6, 1963

The Los Angeles Dodgers won the **World Series** in 4 straight games from the New York Yankees. Dodger pitching held the Yanks to 4 runs in the Series. In the opener, Koufax set a Series record by striking out 15 men; he came back in the 4th game to win 2-1 over Whitey Ford. His Series performance capped a brilliant season for Koufax: he had fanned 306 men, hurled a no-hitter, and won 25 of his 30 games. He was named the National League's most valuable player, and won the Cy Young award as the outstanding pitcher in the majors.

NOVEMBER 8, 1963

Six of 8 trotters in the 6th race at **Roosevelt Raceway,** N.Y., were involved in a pile-up. Fans who had laid bets on the daily double were outraged when the race was declared offical, rioted all over the track and started a $20,000 fire. In the melee, 20 persons were injured.

DECEMBER 26-29, 1963

In Adelaide, Australia, the U.S. tennis team won the **Davis Cup** defeating an Australian team 3-2.

1964
FEBRUARY 25, 1964

Sonny Liston could not answer the bell for the 7th round because of an injury to his left arm, and surrendered his title to **Cassius Clay** on a TKO.

MARCH 21, 1964

At Aintree, England, the **Grand National Steeplechase** was won by *Team Spirit*, the 1st American horse to win the event in 26 years.

MARCH 21, 1964

In the final game of the **NCAA basketball tournament** at Kansas City, U.C.L.A. defeated Duke University 98-83.

APRIL 25, 1964

In the **Stanley Cup** playoffs, the Toronto Maple Leafs won the cup, defeating the Detroit Red Wings 4 games to 3.

MAY 2, 1964

Northern Dancer, Bill Hartack up, won the 90th **Kentucky Derby.**

MAY 16, 1964

The **Preakness Stakes** was won by *Northern Dancer*, Hartack up.

MAY 30, 1964

A.J. Foyt of Texas, driving a Sheraton-Thompson Special, won the annual Memorial Day race at **Indianapolis Speedway.** He averaged 147.350 mph on the 500-mile course, a new record.

MAY 31, 1964

The **longest game in baseball history,** the Giants defeated the Mets 8-6 after 7 hours and 23 minutes of the 2nd game of a double-header.

JUNE 6, 1964

The **Belmont Stakes** winner was *Quadrangle,* whose share of the purse was $110,850.

JUNE 20, 1964

Golfer Ken Venturi scored in the **National Open,** winning by 2 strokes over Tommy Jacobs at the Congressional Club in Washington, D.C. Venturi was voted pro golfer of the year.

JUNE 21, 1964

Jim Bunning of the Phillies pitched a **perfect game** against the Mets.

Cassius Clay *(later Muhammad Ali) won the Heavyweight championship in 1964.*

SEPTEMBER 15-21, 1964

Defending the America's Cup, yachting's oldest trophy, the U.S. boat *Constellation* easily outdistanced a British challenger in 4 races off Newport, R.I. The *Constellation* was the product of a U.S. syndicate of yachtsmen; its nominal skipper, Eric Ridder, took over on the final legs from helmsman Robert Bavier. In a total of 97.2 miles and about 17 hours of sailing, the *Constellation* racked up a victory margin of 48 minutes and 11 seconds. At times she was practically out of sight of her rival.

SEPTEMBER 25-28, 1964

For the first time in the history of **Davis Cup** tennis competition, the challenge round was played on clay courts. Roy Emerson and Fred Stolle led a strong Australian team that took the trophy from the U.S.

OCTOBER 7-15, 1964

Pitcher Bob Gibson of the St. Louis Cardinals struck out 31 batters in 3 games, a Series record, as his team took the **World Series** 4 games to 3 from the N.Y. Yankees.

OCTOBER 10-24, 1964

At the 18th **Olympic Games** in Tokyo, strong swimming and track and field teams won the U.S. 36 gold medals for 1st place. The Russians took 30 1st-place medals, the Japanese 16.

OCTOBER 31, 1964

At Aqueduct race track in New York, the 7-year-old gelding **Kelso** won the Jockey Club Gold Cup. His time, 3:19.2, broke his own American record for 2 miles. For the 5th time in a row, *Kelso* was voted Horse of the Year.

DECEMBER 27, 1964

In Baltimore, fullback Jimmy Brown led the Cleveland Browns in a massive ground offensive that swamped the Baltimore Colts 27-0, and brought the Browns the **National Football League championship.**

1965

JANUARY 1, 1965

Michigan beat Oregon State 34-7 in the **Rose Bowl;** Louisiana State won 13-10 over Syracuse in the Sugar Bowl; Texas beat Alabama 21-17 in the Orange Bowl; and Arkansas defeated Nebraska 10-7 in the Cotton Bowl.

FEBRUARY 13, 1965

16-year-old Peggy Fleming of Pasadena won the U.S. ladies **senior figure-skating** title at Lake Placid; Gary Visconti of Detroit took the men's title.

FEBRUARY 15-16, 1965

A Scottish terrier, Ch. Carmichael's Fanfare, was chosen best in show at the **Westminster Kennel Club** show in New York.

MARCH 17, 1965

Amos Alonzo Stagg, a coach for more than 60 years, died at 102 in Stockton, Calif.

MARCH 21, 1965

The Boston Celtics won their 7th consecutive pro **basketball championship,** defeating Los Angeles 4 games to 1. Their big center

Peggy Fleming *won the U.S. Ladies Figure Skating Championship at the age of 16 in 1965.*

Bill Russell won the Sam Davis Award as the most valuable pro player of the year. The Celtics gave him a new 3-year contract that called for an annual salary of about $100,000.

APRIL 3-4, 1965
At the **International Kennel Club** Show in Chicago, best-in-show honors were awarded to a Doberman pinscher, Ch. Ru-Mar's Tsuchima C.D.

APRIL 11, 1965
Jack Nicklaus won the **Masters Golf Tournament** at Augusta, Ga., with a score of 271.

MAY 1, 1965
At Montreal, the Montreal Canadians won the **Stanley Cup,** defeating the Chicago Black Hawks 4 games to 3. Bobby Hull, Hawks' left wing, was named most valuable player in the National Hockey League.
Lucky Debonair, ridden by Shoemaker, won the **Kentucky Derby** purse of $112,000.

MAY 2, 1965
Arnold Palmer won golf's **Tournament of Champions** at Las Vegas.

MAY 15, 1965
Tom Rolfe, Turcotte up, won the **Preakness Stakes** and a purse of $128,100.

MAY 25, 1965
Cassius Clay and Sonny Liston fought a 1-minute skirmish. Clay retained the **N.B.A. heavyweight crown.**

MAY 31, 1965
At **Indianapolis Speedway,** Jim Clark of Scotland won a record $166,621 and hit the all-time high average speed of 150.680 mph in the Memorial Day classic. He drove a Ford-powered Lotus.

JUNE 5, 1965
The **Belmont Stakes** purse of $125,000 was won by *Hail to All,* ridden by Sellers.

JUNE 21, 1965
U.S. Open golf championship was won by Gary Player of South Africa. He became the 3rd man to win golf's 4 top pro titles; only Gene Sarazen and Ben Hogan had taken the U.S. and British Opens, the Masters, and the P.G.A. during their careers.

AUGUST 15, 1965
Dave Marr won the **P.G.A. championship** with a record score of 280, at Ligonier, Pa. He was named P.G.A. player of the year.

AUGUST 30, 1965
N.Y. Mets manager **Casey Stengel** announced his retirement, after 55 years in baseball.

SEPTEMBER 9, 1965
Sandy Koufax of the L.A. Dodgers pitched a **perfect game** (no man got to 1st base) against the Chicago Cubs.

Sandy Koufax *of L.A. Dodgers pitched "perfect" game in 1965.*

OCTOBER 14, 1965
The L.A. Dodgers won their 4th game of the **World Series,** defeating the Minnesota Twins 2-0.

NOVEMBER 16, 1965
William D. Eckert, retired U.S.A.F. lieutenant general, was elected **baseball commissioner.** He succeeded Ford Frick, who retired after having held the post since 1952.

NOVEMBER 22, 1965
Cassius Clay stopped ex-champ Floyd Patterson in the 12th round of what had been billed as a fight for the **heavyweight championship.**

DECEMBER 26, 1965
The Buffalo Bills defeated the San Diego Chargers 23-0 to win the **American Football League championship,** their 2nd straight, at San Diego. The Green Bay Packers took the Western Conference title in the National Football League with a 13-10 win over the Baltimore Colts

1966

January 1, 1966
Michigan State, unbeaten in regular season play, bowed to UCLA, 14-12, in the **Rose Bowl.**

MARCH 5, 1966
At Albuquerque, Bob Seagren set a new indoor record of 17 ft. ½ in. for the **pole vault.**

MARCH 11, 1966
James (Sunny Jim) Fitzsimmons, died in Miami at 91. Sunny Jim was active in racing for 78 years, first as a jockey and then as the sport's most famous trainer. At his retirement in 1963, he had saddled nearly 2300 winners and had earned his stables more than $13 million.

MARCH 12, 1966
Bobby Hull of the Chicago Black Hawks scored his 51st goal, in a game with the New York Rangers at Chicago. Hull thus became the first player to score more than 50 in a season.

MARCH 12, 1966
Jockey **Johnny Longden,** 59, retired after 40 years of racing and after riding his 6032nd 1st-place horse—the most ever for a jockey—in the San Juan Capistrano Handicap at Santa Anita. Longden had also ridden 4914 2nds and 4272 3rds in a total of 32,397 races. His mounts earned $24,665,800.

MARCH 27, 1966
Ken Miles and Lloyd Ruby won the **Sebring 12-hr. endurance race** in a Ford Roadster XL with an average speed of 98.631 mph.

MARCH 29, 1966
Cassius Clay won a 15-round decision over George Chuvalo, Canadian title-holder.

APRIL 11, 1966
At Augusta, golfer Jack Nicklaus won the **Masters** tournament for the 3rd time and became the first man to do it 2 years running.

APRIL 25, 1966
Emile Griffith won the **middleweight boxing title** from Dick Tiger of Nigeria in a 15-round decision.

APRIL 28, 1966
The Boston Celtics won the **National Basketball Association** playoffs, beating the Los Angeles Lakers, 4 games to 3, and allowing coach Red Auerbach to retire with his 8th successive championship. Auerbach was replaced by Bill Russell, Celtic center, the first Negro to coach a major U.S. sports team.

MAY 5, 1966
At Detroit, the Montreal Canadiens beat the Red Wings 3-2, winning the finals of the **Stanley Cup playoffs,** 4 games to 2, and the team's 2nd consecutive National Hockey League championship.

MAY 7, 1966
Kauai King, a son of the great *Native Dancer,* led all the way to win the **Kentucky Derby** and $120,500 prize money.

MAY 21, 1966
Kauai King, ridden by D. Brumfield, won the **Preakness** at Pimlico. The purse: $129,000.

MAY 21, 1966
World **heavyweight boxing champion** Cassius Clay defeated England's Henry Cooper in 6 rounds in London.

MAY 30, 1966
At the **Indianapolis Speedway,** Graham Hill won the classic 500.

JUNE 4, 1966

Amberoid, ridden by W. Boland, won the $117,700 purse of the **Belmont Stakes.**

JUNE 8, 1966

The **National and American football leagues** announced that they would merge for the 1970 season.

JUNE 20, 1966

Billy Casper, PGA Golfer of the Year, won his 2nd **U.S. Open** in a playoff with Arnold Palmer.

JUNE 25, 1966

Buckpasser set a new world record of 1:32³/₅ for the mile in winning the Arlington Classic.

JULY 2-3, 1966

The world **decathlon** record of 8089 points, held by C.K. Yang, was bested twice at Salina, Kans., by Russ Hodge (8130) and Bill Toomey (8234).

JULY 9, 1966

Jack Nicklaus won the British Open.

JULY 12, 1966

Baseball's **all-star game** was won by the National League 2-1 in 10 innings.

JULY 16-17, 1966

All other countries lost out in a **5-nation swimming meet** in Moscow that saw the long-awaited match of the U.S. and Soviet teams of both sexes. The U.S. won 11 of the 17 events, the Soviets the remaining 6.

JULY 17, 1966

Jim Ryun, 19-year-old college freshman, ran **the mile** in 3:51.3, trimming 2.3 sec. from the world record.

Jim Ryun *set world record for the mile run in 1966.*

JULY 18-21, 1966

In the U.S. Amateur Athletic Union's **national outdoor swimming championships** at Lincoln, Neb., Don Schollander won 5 gold medals and set world records in the 200- and 400-meter freestyle events. In all, 5 world records were broken at the meet, and 15 American records fell and 3 were tied.

JULY 23, 1966

John Pennel set an outdoor record of 17 ft. 6¼ in. in the **pole vault.**

JULY 24, 1966

Golfer **Tony Lema** was killed in the crash of a private plane near Munster, Ind.

JULY 24, 1966

Al Geiberger, with an even par score of 280, won the **PGA championship** at Akron, Ohio.

AUGUST 6, 1966

In London, Brian London failed to land a single solid punch against **heavyweight champion Cassius Clay** and was knocked out in the 3rd round.

SEPTEMBER 10, 1966

Cassius Clay defeated the German champion Karl Mildenberger in 12 rounds.

OCTOBER 9, 1966

In Baltimore the Orioles shut out the Dodgers for the 3rd straight game—and 33 consecutive innings—to sweep the **World Series** in 4 games, 5-2, 6-0, 1-0, 1-0.

OCTOBER 22, 1966

In Mexico City the crowd began fighting after referee Billy Conn stopped the **lightweight title bout** between Carlos Ortiz and challenger Sugar Ramos in the 5th round because of a cut over Ramos' eye. An official overruled the referee and gave the title to Ramos when Ortiz refused to continue the fight. The next day the World Boxing Association declared the title vacant and it was agreed that the two fighters would meet again in 1967.

NOVEMBER 14, 1967

In the Houston Astrodome, Cassius Clay defeated Cleveland Williams by a TKO in the 3rd round.

NOVEMBER 19, 1966

In the **collegiate football game of the year,** the undefeated teams of Michigan State and Notre Dame battled to a 10-10 tie at East Lansing.

DECEMBER 16, 1966

Boxer José Torres lost the **light heavyweight title** to Dick Tiger of Nigeria.

1967

FEBRUARY 2, 1967

Formation was announced of a 2nd pro basketball league, the **American Basketball Association,** with former NBA star George Mikan as commissioner.

MARCH 4, 1967

At the **women's world figure-skating championships** in Vienna, Peggy Fleming of the U.S. fell during her freestyle event but went on to win the world title.

MARCH 12, 1967

The Chicago Black Hawks clinched the **National Hockey League** championship, the team's first title in its 41 years of existence, but then lost the Stanley Cup semifinals to Toronto, 4 games to 2. Toronto won the finals May 2, defeating Montreal, 4 games to 2.

MARCH 25, 1967

UCLA beat Dayton, 79-64, to win the **NCAA basketball championship.**

APRIL 9, 1967

Gay Brewer won the **Masters golf championship.**

APRIL 24, 1967

The Philadelphia 76ers, led by center Wilt Chamberlain, defeated the San Francisco Warriors, 4 games to 2, to win the **National Basketball Association championship.**

MAY 6, 1967

Proud Clarion, a 30-1 shot, won the **Kentucky Derby.**

MAY 14, 1967

Mickey Mantle hit his 500th home run, the 6th man in baseball to reach that lifetime mark.

MAY 20, 1967

Damascus won the **Preakness Stakes.**

MAY 31, 1967

A. J. Foyt drove his Coyote-Ford an average of 151.205 mph to win the **Indianapolis 500.**

JUNE 3, 1967

Damascus won the **Belmont Stakes.** The 3-year-old colt was the first to win 3 divisional titles: Horse of the Year, best 3-year-old, and best handicap racer. He won 12 of 16 races and earned $817,941, the most ever in a year.

JUNE 18, 1967

Jack Nicklaus won golfing's **U.S. Open championship** with a score of 275, 1 stroke better than the record set by Ben Hogan in 1948. Nicklaus, named the PGA Golfer of the Year, won more than $200,000 in prize money this year.

JUNE 20, 1967

Heavyweight boxer **Muhammad Ali** (Cassius Clay) was given a 5-year sentence and fined $10,000 for refusing to be drafted. Ring authorities had earlier stripped him of his world title, rejecting, as did the jury, his claim to exemption as a minister of the pacifist sect the Nation of Islam.

JUNE 23, 1967

Jim Ryun cut 0.2 sec. from his own **world record for the mile** with a run of 3:51.1 in the AAU Championships at Bakersfield, Calif. At the same meet, Paul Wilson cleared 17 ft. 7¾ in., adding ¾ in. to the **world record for the outdoor pole vault** just set June 10 by Bob Seagren.

JULY 8, 1967

At Wimbledon, England, **Mrs. Billie Jean King** of the U.S. swept the women's singles, the doubles (with Rosemary Casals), and the mixed doubles (with Owen Davidson).

JULY 11, 1967

At Anaheim, the National League won baseball's **all-star game,** 2-1.

JULY 14, 1967

Eddie Mathews of the Houston Astros became the 7th man in baseball to hit **500 home runs.**

JULY 21, 1967

Jimmy Foxx, member of the Baseball Hall of Fame and one of the great hitters of all time, died at 59.

JULY 23-AUGUST 6, 1967

A U.S. team of 401 athletes overwhelmed all opponents at the 5th **Pan-American Games** in Winnipeg. The U.S. squad won 120 of 171 gold medals, 63 silver medals, and 42 bronze; its wrestlers won all 23 of their bouts and its swim team broke 13 world records.

JULY 24, 1967

Golfer Don January won the **PGA championship** in Denver, in a playoff with Don Massengale.

AUGUST 20, 1967

In the Women's National AAU Outdoor Championships at Philadelphia, swimmer **Debbie Meyer,** 15, cut an incredible 22.9 sec. from the world record to win the 1500-meter freestyle event in 17:50.2. **Catie Ball** set a new world record of 2:39.5 for the 200-meter breaststroke. On Aug. 19 she had set a new record of 1:14.6 for the 100-meter breaststroke, and she set 2 more world records on Sept. 30. Miss Meyer this year also set new world freestyle record times of 4:29 for 400 meters, 9:22.9 for 800 meters, and 9:44.1 for 880 yd.

AUGUST 21-29, 1967

In the U.S. doubles championships at Brookline, Mass., **Mrs. Billie Jean King and Rosemary Casals** won the women's title. Mrs. King, with Owen Davidson, also won the mixed doubles.

SEPTEMBER 10, 1967

At Forest Hills, N.Y., **Mrs. Billie Jean King** won the U.S. women's singles tennis championship, completing her sweep of both the U.S. and British singles, doubles, and mixed doubles championships. John Newcombe of Australia won the men's singles.

SEPTEMBER 12-18, 1967

The U.S. yacht *Intrepid* bested Australia's *Dame Pattie* in 4 straight races to win for the U.S. the **America's Cup.**

SEPTEMBER 24, 1967

Jim Bakken of the St. Louis Cardinals broke all **pro football kicking records** with 7 field goals in 1 game.

SEPTEMBER 30, 1967

In London, U.S. swimmer **Catie Ball** set 2 new world records, winning the 110-yd. breaststroke in 1:17 and the 220-yd. breaststroke in 2:46.9.

NOVEMBER 18, 1967

In the **collegiate football game of the year,** Southern California and its star runner O.J. Simpson defeated UCLA and its great quarterback Gary Beban, 21-20. Beban won the Heisman Trophy as the best player of the year; Simpson, a junior, led major-college players in rushing, with 1415 yd.

DECEMBER 31, 1967

At Green Bay, Packers' quarterback Bart Starr sneaked the ball from the 1-yd. line for a

touchdown that beat the Dallas Cowboys, 21-17, for the **National Football League championship.** The Oakland Raiders routed the Houston Oilers, 40-7, to win the **American Football League title.**

JANUARY 1, 1968

In the **Rose Bowl,** Southern California defeated Indiana 14-3.

JANUARY 14, 1968

In the **Super Bowl,** the Green Bay Packers of the National Football League defeated the Oakland Raiders of the American Football League 33-14.

FEBRUARY 1, 1968

Lawson Little, famed golfer, died at age 57.

FEBRUARY 6-18, 1968

In the **Winter Olympic Games,** held in Grenoble, France, the U.S. won only 1 gold medal, taken by figure skater Peggy Fleming.

FEBRUARY 13, 1968

In the **Westminster Kennel Club Show** a Lakeland terrier, Ch. Sting-ray of Derrybah, won the best-of-show.

MARCH 22, 1968

The UCLA basketball team defeated the University of Houston in the **NCAA** semifinals, and went on the next day to win the championship.

APRIL 14, 1968

Bob Goalby won the **Masters golf tournament** when leader Roberto DeVincenzo was disqualified for having signed an incorrect scorecard.

APRIL 19, 1968

Tommy Bridges died at age 61.

MAY 2, 1968

The Boston Celtics won the **National Basketball Association Championship** by defeating the Los Angeles Lakers, 4 games to 2.

MAY 4, 1968

Dancer's Image won the **Kentucky Derby,** but was disqualified 3 days later on the grounds that he had been given a pain-killing drug. *Forward Pass* was then declared the winner.

MAY 11, 1968

The **Stanley Cup** was won by the Montreal Canadians.

MAY 18, 1968

Forward Pass won the annual **Preakness Stakes**.

MAY 27, 1968

George Halas retired as coach of the Chicago Bears.

MAY 30, 1968

Bobby Unser, driving an Eagle-Offenhauser, won the **Indianapolis 500.**

JUNE 2, 1968

Stage Door Johnny won the annual **Belmont Stakes.**

JUNE 14, 1968

Lee Trevino won the **U.S. Open golf championship,** beating Jack Nicklaus by 4 strokes.

JUNE 15, 1968

Sam Crawford, member of baseball's Hall of Fame, died at age 88.

JULY 6, 1968

Billie Jean King won the women's singles championship at Wimbledon.

JULY 9, 1968

In **baseball's all-star game,** played at the Astrodome, the National League beat the American League, 1-0.

JULY 21, 1968

Julius Boros won the PGA golf championship by 1 stroke, beating Arnold Palmer and Bob Charles.

AUGUST 20, 1968

Earl Sande, highly successful jockey, died at age 69. He won the Kentucky Derby 3 times and took almost $3 million in purses.

AUGUST 24, 1968

Dr. Fager **set a world record** for the mile, running it in 1:32^1/$_5$ at Arlington.

SEPTEMBER 9, 1968

Arthur Ashe won the **U.S. Open tennis** championship for men's singles by beating Tom Okker of the Netherlands.

SEPTEMBER 14, 1968

New Zealand bred **Cardigan Bay,** the first harness racer to earn more than $1 million, was retired at age 12.

OCTOBER 10, 1968

The Detroit Tigers won the **World Series** beating St. Louis, 4-1, in the 7th game.

OCTOBER 12-27, 1968

In the **Olympic Games** at Mexico City, the U.S. took 45 gold medals, the U.S.S.R. took 29, and Hungary finished 3rd with 10. Many records were broken, and spectacular performances were turned in by U.S. athletes Bob Beamon, who broke the world broad-jump record by 21 in. with a jump of 29 ft. 2½ in., and Dick Fosbury, who won the high jump at 7 ft. 4½ in., going over the bar backward.

OCTOBER 18, 1968

U.S. track stars Tommie Smith and John Carlos were suspended from Olympic competition for giving a **black-power salute** during the ceremony in which they were awarded victory medals.

DECEMBER 6, 1968

Baseball Commissioner William D. Eckert was relieved of his post at a meeting of team owners.

DECEMBER 15, 1968

Former world heavyweight champion (1915-1919) **Jess Willard** died at age 86.

DECEMBER 28, 1968

The U.S. tennis team, led by Arthur Ashe and Clark Graebner, won the **Davis Cup** from the Australians by a score of 4-1.

1969

JANUARY 1, 1969

In the **Rose Bowl,** Ohio State defeated Southern California by a score of 27-16.

JANUARY 12, 1969

The New York Jets scored 16-7 upset over

the Baltimore Colts, giving the American Football League its 1st major triumph over the National League and its 1st **Super Bowl** victory.

FEBRUARY 7, 1969

At Hialeah, Diana Crump became the **1st woman jockey** to race at a U.S. parimutuel track. Her mount finished 10th in a field of 12.

FEBRUARY 22, 1969

Barbara Jo Rubin became the **1st winning woman jockey** at a U.S. thoroughbred track, with a victory at Charles Town in West Virginia.

FEBRUARY 25, 1969

A 3-year pact was signed ending a **baseball players' boycott of spring training** in a pension dispute. Club owners agreed to increase their pension contributions and to reduce eligibility for a pension to 4 years.

MARCH 2, 1969

Tim Wood of Detroit won the **men's world figure-skating championship** at Colorado Springs. Gabriele Seyfert of East Germany won the women's title.

MARCH 2, 1969

During a **drag race at Covington, Ga.,** a car going 180 mph smashed into spectators, killing 11 and injuring many.

MARCH 2, 1969

UCLA won the **NCAA basketball tournament** for the 3rd straight year, beating Purdue 97-92.

APRIL 13, 1969

George Archer won the **Masters golf championship** at Augusta, Ga.

MAY 3, 1969

Majestic Prince, Bill Hartack up, won the **Kentucky Derby.** The winner's prize: $113,200.

MAY 5, 1969

The Boston Celtics took the **National Basketball Association championship,** beating the Lakers 108-106, in the 7th game.

MAY 10, 1969

Plans were completed for the 1970 **merger of the 2 pro football leagues** into a new National Football League with 2 conferences of 13 teams each. The old NFL was renamed the National Conference and 3 of its teams (Baltimore, Cleveland, and Pittsburgh) were shifted to the American Conference (the old AFL).

MAY 17, 1969

Majestic Prince, Bill Hartack up, won the **Preakness Stakes.**

MAY 30, 1969

In the **Indianapolis 500,** Mario Andretti won driving a turbo-powered Ford-Brawner Hawk designed by Andy Granatelli, and set a track record of 156.867 mph.

JUNE 6, 1969

Joe Namath, quarterback of the New York Jets, announced that he would retire from football rather than give up his interest in a restaurant that Commissioner Pete Rozelle said had become a hangout for gamblers. On July 18, Namath reversed his decision.

JUNE 7, 1969

In the **Belmont Stakes,** *Arts and Letters* easily took Horse of the Year honors.

JUNE 8, 1969

In ceremonies at Yankee Stadium, star outfielder **Mickey Mantle** formally retired after 18 years with the Yankees.

June 15, 1969

Orville Moody won the **U.S. Open golf championship** at Houston by a single stroke over Deane Beman, Al Geiberger, and Bob Rosburg. The PGA named Moody Golfer of the Year.

JUNE 21, 1969

John Pennel added 1½ in. to the **world pole vault record,** clearing the bar at 17 ft. 10½ in. in a night meet at Sacramento.

Vince Lombardi *led his Green Bay Packers to Super Bowl Championship over Oakland Raiders in 1968.*

JUNE 23, 1969

Joe Frazier defeated leading heavyweight contender Jerry Quarry with a KO in the 7th round. Frazier was the recognized champ in 7 states; Jimmy Ellis, recognized by the World Boxing Association as champion, did not defend his title this year. Muhammad Ali (Cassius Clay) remained absent from the ring as he fought his draft case in the courts.

JULY 23, 1969

In Washington, D.C., the National League won baseball's **all-star game** beating the American League 9-3.

AUGUST 13, 1969

Bowie Kuhn, temporary **commissioner of baseball** since Feb., was formally appointed to that post with a 7-year contract.

AUGUST 30, 1969

At Oakmont, Pa., Steve Melnyk won the **USGA men's amateur golf championship** with a record 5-stroke margin.

AUGUST 31, 1969

Former world heavyweight boxing champion **Rocky Marciano** was killed in a plane crash near Newton, Iowa. He had retired undefeated in 1956.

AUGUST 31, 1969

In a time trial at Indianapolis, **Nevele Pride** trotted a 1-mile track in 1:54⁴/₅, breaking the record of 1:55¼ set by *Greyhound* in 1938.

The 4-year-old stallion, named Harness Horse of the Year for the 3rd straight time, was syndicated for $3 million in Oct. and retired to stud. His career earnings were $871,738.

SEPTEMBER 9, 1969

Australian Rod Laver, who had already won the Australian, French, and Wimbledon singles titles, completed the **grand slam of tennis** by winning the U.S. men's singles championship at Forest Hills. It was only the 3rd such sweep in history: Laver had done it in 1962, Don Budge in 1938.

SEPTEMBER 19-21, 1969

The U.S. retained the **Davis Cup,** defeating the Romanian tennis team, 5 matches to 0, at Cleveland Heights. Arthur Ashe and Stan Smith played the U.S. singles, Smith and Bob Lutz the doubles.

SEPTEMBER 22, 1969

San Francisco Giants outfielder **Willie Mays hit his 600th home run,** becoming the only player other than Babe Ruth to reach that mark.

OCTOBER 5, 1969

Walter Hagen, one of the all-time golfing greats, died.

OCTOBER 6, 1969

The New York Mets won the **National League playoffs,** having defeated the Atlanta Braves in 3 straight games, 9-5, 11-6, 7-4. In Minnesota the Baltimore Orioles routed the Minnesota Twins in 3 consecutive games also, 4-3, 1-0, and 11-2, to win the **American League playoffs.**

OCTOBER 7, 1969

14 blacks were dropped from the University of Wyoming football team after they defied the coach's ban against protests and wore black armbands in support of a stand by the Black Students' Alliance. The BSA wanted the university to sever sports ties to Brigham Young University, a school run by Mormons, who have barred Negroes from their church's ministry.

OCTOBER 16, 1969

The New York Mets won the **World Series,** taking 4 of 5 games from the favored Baltimore Orioles: 1-4, 2-1, 5-0, 2-1, 5-3.

OCTOBER 18, 1969

Chester Marcol of Hillsdale (Michigan) College kicked a **62-yd. field goal,** the longest on record for either amateur or pro football.

NOVEMBER 22, 1969

Ohio State lost, 24-12, to Michigan. The game tied the 2 clubs for the **Big 10 football championship** and qualified Michigan for the Rose Bowl.

DECEMBER 6, 1969

A protest by the governor of Pennsylvania (where Penn State was undefeated in 30 games in 3 years) failed to deter Pres. Nixon from presenting a plaque to Texas as the **best football team in the nation** after it defeated Arkansas, 15-14.

DECEMBER 10-11, 1969

Bill Toomey set a new world record of 8417 points for the decathlon. He won the Sullivan Award as the best amateur athlete of the year.

JANUARY 1, 1970
The University of Southern California at the **Rose Bowl** game, upset Michigan 10-3.

JANUARY 11, 1970
In professional football's **Super Bowl** game, played in Tulane Stadium, New Orleans, the Kansas City Chiefs defeated the Minnesota Vikings 23-7.

FEBRUARY 7, 1970
At Tulsa, Okla., the U.S. **men's figure-skating championship** was won by Tim Wood of Colorado Springs, Colo.

FEBRUARY 15, 1970
Billy Kidd of Stowe, Vt., won the men's combined title in the **Alpine World Ski Championships** at Val Gardena, Italy. Kidd's was the 1st U.S. world title in Alpine combination.

FEBRUARY 16, 1970
Joe Frazier became recognized as the heavyweight champion of the world by winning over Jimmy Ellis in a 5th-round knockout in New York City.

MARCH 7, 1970
At Ljubljana, Yugoslavia, Tim Wood won the **men's world figure-skating championship.**

MARCH 21, 1970
UCLA won the **NCAA basketball tournament** defeating Jacksonville University, 80-69.

APRIL 13, 1970
Billy Casper won the **Masters golf championship** at Augusta, Ga.

MAY 2, 1970
The **Kentucky Derby** was won by *Dust Commander,* ridden by Mike Manganello. The purse was $170,300.

MAY 8, 1970
The **New York Knickerbockers** won the NBA title beating the Los Angeles Lakers 113-99 in the 7th and deciding game of the playoffs.

MAY 10, 1970
The Boston Bruins won the National Hockey League's **Stanley Cup** defeating the St. Louis Blues 4-3 to complete a 4-game

Drag racing, pictured above, became a popular sport by 1960's. Drag racing accident in 1969 at Covington, Ga. killed 11 spectators.

sweep. The Bruins' Bobby Orr was named the league's most valuable player.

MAY 16, 1970
Personality, with Eddie Belmonte up, won the **Preakness Stakes** at Baltimore.

MAY 30, 1970
The **Indianapolis 500** was won by Al Unser, driving a Colt-Ford.

JUNE 6, 1970
The **Belmont Stakes,** the 3rd of the triple-crown horse races, was won by *High Echelon,* with John Rotz up, earning $115,000.

JUNE 18-20, 1970
At the NCAA outdoor championships at Des Moines, Iowa, Ralph Mann of Brigham Young University broke the **world record 440-yd. hurdles** with 48.8 seconds.

JUNE 21, 1970
The **U.S. Open golf championship,** held at Chaska, Minn., was won by Tony Jacklin, of Great Britain, by 7 strokes over Dave Hill. He was the first Englishman in 50 years to win it.

JULY 14, 1970
In Cincinnati the National League won baseball's **all-star game** for the 8th consecutive year, defeating the American League in the 12th inning 5-4.

AUGUST 16, 1970
Dave Stockton won the **PGA championship** by 2 strokes.

AUGUST 23, 1970
At the AAU national outdoor swimming meet, at Los Angeles, Gary Hall of Indiana University broke 3 world records.

AUGUST 29-31, 1970
Arthur Ashe and Cliff Richie, the U.S. retained the **Davis Cup** by defeating West Germany, 5-0, in Cleveland.

SEPTEMBER 3, 1970
Vince Lombardi died in Washington, D.C., at age 57. In 9 seasons he led the professional Green Bay Packers to 6 Division titles and 5

National Football League championships.

SEPTEMBER 7, 1970
At the Del Mar horse racing track **Willie Shoemaker** rode his 6033rd winner, breaking Johnny Longden's record. In his career, Shoemaker had earned more than $4 million.

SEPTEMBER 13, 1970
Veteran Australian tennis player Ken Rosewall won the **U.S. men's singles championship** at Forest Hills, N.Y.

SEPTEMBER 28, 1970
Off Newport, R.I., the **America's Cup** was won by the U.S. yacht *Intrepid* which took 4 of 7 heats from the Australian contender *Gretel II.*

OCTOBER 2, 1970
14 members of the **Wichita State University football team** were killed when their chartered plane crashed in the Rocky Mts.

OCTOBER 5, 1970
In the **National League playoffs,** the Cincinnati Reds beat the Pittsburgh Pirates in 3 straight games: 3-0, 3-1, 3-2. The Baltimore Orioles routed the Minnesota Twins in 3 straight games, 10-6, 11-3, 6-1, to win the **American League playoffs.**

OCTOBER 15, 1970
The Baltimore Orioles won the **World Series,** taking 4 of 5 games from the Cincinnati Reds: 4-3, 6-5, 9-3, 5-9, 9-3. Brooks Robinson, the Baltimore 3rd baseman, was named the outstanding player of the series.

OCTOBER 23, 1970
A **land speed record** of 622.407 mph was set by Gary Gabelich of Long Beach, Calif., driving a rocket-powered car.

OCTOBER 26, 1970
Muhammad Ali (Cassius Clay) fought his first regulation bout in 3½ years in Atlanta, Ga. The fight with Jerry Quarry was stopped after 3 rounds because of cuts over Quarry's left eye, and Ali was declared the winner.

NOVEMBER 8, 1970
Tom Dempsey of the New Orleans Saints pro football team kicked a **record 63-yard field goal** to give the Saints a 2-point victory over the Detroit Lions.

NOVEMBER 14, 1970
In Kenova, W. Va., 43 members and coaches of the **Marshall University football team** were killed when their chartered plane crashed.

NOVEMBER 18, 1970
Heavyweight title defended by Joe Frazier in Detroit, Mich. Frazier won with a 2nd-round knockout of Bob Foster of Washington, D.C., the light-heavyweight champion.

NOVEMBER 24, 1970
Jim Plunkett, Stanford University quarterback, was named winner of the Heisman trophy as the nation's outstanding collegiate player.

DECEMBER 7, 1970
Muhammad Ali (Cassius Clay) fought his 2nd big return bout, knocking out Oscar Bonavena of Argentina in the 15th round.

JANUARY 1, 1971
In the **Rose Bowl,** Ohio State was upset by Stanford University, 27-17.

JANUARY 5, 1971
World heavyweight boxing champion (1962-1964) **Sonny Liston** was found dead at age 38.

JANUARY 17, 1971
With 5 seconds left to play, Jim O'Brien kicked a field goal to break a tie and give the Baltimore Colts a 16-13 **Super Bowl** victory in Miami over the Dallas Cowboys.

FEBRUARY 28, 1971
The **PGA championship** tournament at Palm Beach Gardens, Fla., was won by golfer Jack Nicklaus by 3 strokes over Billy Casper.

MARCH 8, 1971
The **heavyweight championship of the world** resulted in a unanimous decision in favor of Frazier in the 15-round bout.

MARCH 25, 1971
UCLA won the **NCAA basketball championship,** beating Villanova.

APRIL 7, 1971
New York city began operation of the country's 1st legal **off-track betting system (OTB).**

Bobby Jones, one of America's legendary golfers, died on December 18, 1971.

APRIL 10-14, 1971
A U.S. **table-tennis team** visited **Communist China** and played several exhibition matches in Peking.

APRIL 11, 1971
The **Masters golf championship** was won by Charles Coody by 2 strokes over Jack Nicklaus and John Miller.

APRIL 30, 1971
The **Milwaukee Bucks won the National Basketball Assn. title,** defeating the Baltimore Bullets.

MAY 1, 1971
Canonero II, Gustavo Avila up, won the **Kentucky Derby,** worth $145,500.

MAY 15, 1971
The **Preakness Stakes** was won by *Canonero II,* Gustavo Avila up. The winner's purse was worth $137,400.

MAY 29, 1971
Al Unser won the **Indianapolis 500** in a P.J. Colt chassis with a Ford rear-mounted engine.

JUNE 5, 1971
In the **Belmont Stakes,** *Pass Catcher* was the winner.

JUNE 21, 1971
Lee Trevino won the **U.S. Open golf championship** in Ardmore, Pa. On July 10 he won the British Open championship, to become the 4th U.S. player to win both titles in the

same year.

JUNE 28, 1971
Muhammad Ali won a 4-year legal battle for vindication when the Supreme Court reversed his 1967 draft-evasion conviction.

JULY 25, 1971
Golf's richest tournament, the **Westchester Classic** played in Harrison, N.Y., was won by Arnold Palmer who received a top purse of $50,000.

JULY 26, 1971
Muhammad Ali fought Jimmy Ellis in Houston and stopped him in 12 rounds.

AUGUST 8, 1971
The **U.S. professional tennis championship** was won by Australian Ken Rosewall, one of the top contenders on the international pro circuit.

AUGUST 26, 1971
Wellington Mara, owner of the **New York Giants football team** said he would move to New Jersey when a new 75,000-seat stadium was completed in 1975.

SEPTEMBER 9, 1971
Gordie Howe, of the National Hockey League, announced his retirement at age 43 to take a position in the front office of the Detroit Red Wings.

SEPTEMBER 15, 1971
Winners of the singles titles at the **U.S. Open tennis championship** at Forest Hills, N.Y., were Stan Smith and Mrs. Billie Jean King.

SEPTEMBER 21, 1971
It was announced that the **Washington Senators** would move to Texas for the 1972 season of the American League in baseball.

OCTOBER 3, 1971
Mrs. Billie Jean King became the 1st female athlete in history to earn more than $100,000 in a single year.

OCTOBER 17, 1971
Pittsburgh Pirates defeated Baltimore Orioles in baseball's **World Series.** The Pirates won 2-1 in the deciding 7th game.

OCTOBER 26, 1971
In Buenos Aires, Bobby Fischer defeated the Soviet Union's Tigran Petrosian and became the 1st American to clear elimination matches for the **world chess championship.** He was scheduled to meet world champion Boris Spassky of the Soviet Union in 1972.

OCTOBER 30, 1971
Ed Marinaro of Cornell set a new **collegiate rushing record** with a 3-year career total of 4132 yards.

NOVEMBER 19, 1971
Sports broadcaster **Bill Stern** died at age 64.

DECEMBER 18, 1971
Bobby Jones, one of the world's great sports figures, died at age 69. He was the only golfer to win the golfing grand slam in 1 year—the British Amateur, the U.S. Open, the British Open, and the U.S. Amateur—a feat he accomplished in 1930.

Billy Kidd *in the special slalom event of the World Championships at Stowe, Vermont, in 1970.*

JANUARY 1, 1972
Results of the college bowl games: In the Orange Bowl, Nebraska beat Alabama 38-6; Stanford edged past Michigan 13-12 in the Rose Bowl; and the Sugar Bowl victory went to the Oklahoma Sooners 40-22 over the Auburn Tigers.

JANUARY 16, 1972
The Dallas Cowboys defeated the Miami Dolphins in the Superbowl, 24-3.

JANUARY 19, 1972
Sandy Koufax, Yogi Berra, and E. Wynn were elected to baseball's Hall of Fame.

JANUARY 30, 1972
James Hussey, Hatteral Inlet, N.C., set a world record in saltwater fishing with his 31 lb. 12 oz. Bluefish.

FEBRUARY 6, 1972
Grier Jones won the Hawaiian Open.

FEBRUARY 16, 1972
Wilt Chamberlain of the Los Angeles Lakers set an NBA record with a total of 30,000 points scored.

Surfer near Galveston, *Texas rides the waves created by hurricane Fern in June 1971.*

MARCH 22, 1972
Kareem Abdul-Jabbar, Milwaukee's center, elected most valuable player in NBA.

MARCH 24-26, 1972
Betsy Cullen took the $85,000 first prize in the Sears Classic.

MARCH 25, 1972
Defeating Florida State University 81-76, UCLA won its sixth straight NCAA basketball championship.

APRIL 1-13, 1972
First players strike in the 102 years of organized baseball.

APRIL 9, 1972
Jack Nicklaus won his fourth Masters tournament.

MAY 7, 1972
The L.A. Lakers won their first NBA championship 114-100 over the New York Knicks.

MAY 11, 1972
The Boston Bruins won the Stanley Cup over the New York Rangers.

MAY 27, 1972
Indianapolis 500 won by Mark Donahue.

JUNE 4, 1972
Doug Sanders won the Kemper Open tournament in Charlotte, N.C.

JUNE 15-18, 1972
U.S. Open, Pebble Beach, Calif. won by Jack Nicklaus.

JULY 8, 1972
Billie Jean King receives first place in the All-England Open, Wimbledon.

JULY 15, 1972
Lee Trevino won the British Open golf tournament.

AUGUST 10-13, 1972
Jack Nicklaus took the first place prize of $250,000 in the Westchester Classic.

AUGUST 28, 1972
In the Munich Olympics, Mark Spitz earned the first two of his seven gold medals: 200-Meter Butterfly and U.S. team 400-Meter Freestyle.

AUGUST 29, 1972
Setting a world record in the 200-Meter freestyle, Mark Spitz won his third Olympic gold medal.

AUGUST 31, 1972
Victory in the 100-Meter Butterfly and U.S. team freestyle relay brought Mark Spitz his fourth and fifth gold medals.

SEPTEMBER 3, 1972
Mark Spitz won his sixth gold medal in the 100-Meter freestyle.

SEPTEMBER 4, 1972
With the U.S. team taking first place in the 400-Meter medley freestyle, Mark Spitz received his seventh gold medal.

SEPTEMBER 9, 1972
Billie Jean King won the U.S. Open Tournament at Forest Hills, New York.

Mark Spitz *shown winning his fourth gold medal (this one for the 100 meter butterfly) at the 1972 Olympic Games in Munich.*

American diver Micki King *showing her form in the women's diving competition at the 1972 Olympic Games.*

709

OCTOBER 15, 1972
The U.S. team won its fifth consecutive Davis Cup.

OCTOBER 22, 1972
In the 69th World Series, the Oakland A's beat the Cincinnati Reds

OCTOBER 24, 1972
Jackie Robinson, the first black to play major league baseball, died at the age of 53.

NOVEMBER 21, 1972
In a nontitle fight, Muhammad Ali knocked out light heavyweight Bob Foster.

DECEMBER 16, 1972
Defeating the Baltimore Colts 16-0, the Miami Dolphins became the first NFL team to finish the season undefeated and untied.

DECEMBER 31, 1972
In the Sugar Bowl, the Oklahoma Sooners beat Penn State 14-0.

JANUARY 1, 1973
In the Rose Bowl, it was Southern California 42, Ohio State 17. Nebraska beat Notre Dame 40-6 in the Orange Bowl.

Bob Seagren *clears the bar at 17 feet, six inches to win the pole vault in the first professional track meet in America, held in Pocatello, Idaho, in 1973.*

Some of the 1500 entries *for the 77th running of the Boston Marathon in 1973.*

JANUARY 14, 1973
Super Bowl victory went to the Miami Dolphins 14-7 over Washington Redskins.

JANUARY 22, 1973
George Foreman knocked out Joe Frazier in the second round of their fight held in Kingston, Jamaica.

FEBRUARY 4, 1973
John Schlee won the $40,000 Hawaiian Open.

FEBRUARY 18, 1973
The Daytona 500 prize of $33,500 was captured by Richard Petty.

MARCH 26, 1973
UCLA won its seventh NCAA championship in their game against Memphis State, 87-66.

MARCH 29, 1973
Boston Celtics center, Dave Cowens, was chosen most valuable player in the NBA.

MARCH 31, 1973
Muhammad Ali lost his fight with Ken Norton. Ali's jaw broken in the first round.

APRIL 9, 1973
Tommy Aaron won the Masters tournament.

APRIL 27, 1973
Steve Busby pitched a no-hitter in the Kansas City-Detroit game.

MAY 10, 1973
NBA title taken by the New York Knicks 102-93 over the Los Angeles Lakers.

MAY 15, 1973
Nolan Ryan pitched a no-hit game for the California Angels against Kansas City 3-0.

MAY 19, 1973
The $13,000 prize in the World series of Poker, played in Las Vegas, went to walter Clyde Pearson of Nashville, Tenn.

JUNE 9, 1973
Secretariat became the first Triple Crown winner since Citation in 1948.

JUNE 17, 1973
Shooting a course record of 63, Johnny Miller won the U. S. Open prize of $35,000.

JULY 15, 1973
Nolan Ryan of the California Angels pitched

Bobby Riggs *rushes the net against Billie Jean King during their historic "Battle of the Sexes" held at the Astrodome in Houston, Texas in September, 1973.*

Joe Namath, *quarterback for the New York Jets, lets go with a long bomb in a game against Cincinnati in 1973.*

his second no-hitter of the season in a game against Detroit, 6-0.

JULY 24, 1973
The National League beat the American League 7-1 in the 44th All-Star game.

JULY 27, 1973
At Chicago's Soldier Field, the Miami Dolphins beat the college football All-Stars 14-3.

AUGUST 8-11, 1973
Steve Rajeff, San Francisco, won the American Casting Assoc. combined championships title——"Grand all around champion."

AUGUST 20-25, 1973
Hiram Bradley, Vest, Ky. and Barbara

Frederick, Camdenton, Mo., were chosen "champion of champions" in the 74th Grand American Trapshooting Tournament.

SEPTEMBER 6, 1973
Men's freestyle record for 400-Meters set by Rick DeMont.

SEPTEMBER 15, 1973
Secretariat set a new world record for 1⅛ miles.

SEPTEMBER 20, 1973
After 22 years in baseball, Willie Mays retired.
Billie Jean King beat Bobby Riggs in the "Tennis Match of the Century" played at the Houston Astrodome.

SEPTEMBER 29, 1973
Henry Aaron, outfielder for the Atlanta Braves, finished the season with 713 home-runs, one short of Babe Ruth's record.

OCTOBER 7, 1973
Cale Yarborough, driving a Chevrolet, took first place in the $17,725 National 500 held in Charlotte, N.C.

OCTOBER 10, 1973
National League won by Mets in series against Cincinnati.

OCTOBER 11, 1973
The Oakland A's won the American League playoff against Baltimore Orioles.

OCTOBER 21, 1973
The National League's most valuable player was Pete Rose, Cincinnati outfielder.

DECEMBER 4, 1973
The Heisman Trophy was presented to John Cappelletti, Pennsylvania State University tailback.

DECEMBER 6, 1973
Sandy Hawley broke the record set by Willie Shoemaker in 1953 for most races won by a jockey in one year.

JANUARY 1, 1974
The annual college bowl games saw Ohio State's Buckeyes beat the University of Southern California 42-21 in the Rose Bowl. In the Orange Bowl, it was Penn State 16, Louisiana State 9.

JANUARY 13, 1974
In Super Bowl, the Miami Dolphins beat the Minnesota Vikings, 24-7.

FEBRUARY 17, 1974
Richard Petty won the Daytona 500.

MARCH 16-24, 1974
Purdue won the National Basketball Invitation Tournament with a score of 87-81 against Utah.

MARCH 26, 1974
George Foreman retained his heavyweight title against Ken Norton.

Jimmy Connors *shown in competition during the 1974 U.S. Open Tennis Tournament at Forest Hills, New York. Connors won the men's singles championship.*

APRIL 8, 1974

Henry Aaron hit his 715th home run, breaking Babe Ruth's record.

APRIL 14, 1974

Gary Player won the Masters tournament in Augusta, Georgia.

APRIL 25, 1974

Mario Andretti, driving an Alpha Romeo at 136.607 mph, won the Manza.

MAY 4, 1974

Cannonade won the Kentucky Derby prize of $274,000.

MAY 12, 1974

Boston Celtics, beating the Milwaukee Bucks 102-87, for their 12th NBA championship.

MAY 19, 1974

Philadelphia Flyers won Stanley Cup against Boston Bruins.

MAY 26, 1974

Johnny Rutherford, driving at 158.589 mph, won the Indianapolis 500. His prize was $245,032.

JUNE 8, 1974

Little Current won the Belmont Stakes.

JUNE 16, 1974

The U.S. Open victory went to Hale Irwin.

JULY 13, 1974

Gary Player won the British Open.

JULY 23, 1974

In the 45th All-Star Game, the National League beat the American League 7-2.

AUGUST 11, 1974

Lee Trevino won the 56th PGA national championship.

AUGUST 25, 1974

A new record in 1,500-Meters freestyle swimming was set by Tim Shaw.

SEPTEMBER 9, 1974

Jimmy Connors and Billie Jean King won the U.S. Open at Forest Hills, New York.

SEPTEMBER 17, 1974

America's Cup won by the U.S. entry—The Courageous, in race against the Southern Cross of Australia.

SEPTEMBER 28, 1974

Nolan Ryan, California Angels, pitched the third no-hitter of his career in game against the Minnesota Twins.

OCTOBER 5-9, 1974

American League pennant won by Oakland A's over Baltimore Orioles; the National League pennant won by Los Angeles Dodgers over Pittsburgh Pirates.

OCTOBER 17, 1974

Oakland A's won the World Series against the Los Angeles Dodgers. They are the first team in 21 years to win the title 3 years in a row.

OCTOBER 30, 1974

Knocking out George Foreman in a fight televised from Zaire, Muhammad Ali regained the heavyweight title of the world.

NOVEMBER 2, 1974

Henry Aaron traded by Atlanta Braves to Milwaukee Brewers.

NOVEMBER 12, 1974

Los Angeles Dodgers' Steve Garvey was chosen the National League's most valuable player.

NOVEMBER 21, 1974

Jeff Burroughs named most valuable player in the American League.

DECEMBER 5, 1974

The Birmingham Americans won the first World Football League championship over the Florida Blazers, 22-21.

DECEMBER 17, 1974

Muhammad Ali named fighter of the year by the Boxing Writers Association.

DECEMBER 26, 1974

Legislation allowing girls to play Little League baseball was signed into law by President Ford.

DECEMBER 31, 1974

In the Sugar Bowl, Nebraska beat Florida 13-10.

JANUARY 1, 1975

In the Rose Bowl, the University of Southern California beat Ohio State 18-17. Orange Bowl victory went to Notre Dame 13-11, over University of Alabama.

JANUARY 12, 1975

In Super Bowl it was the Pittsburgh Steelers 16, Minnesota Vikings 6.

FEBRUARY 9, 1975

With a four-under-par 68, Johnny Miller won the Bob Hope Desert Classic.

FEBRUARY 16, 1975

Jimmy Connors became the first player in recent history to win the National Indoor Tennis tournament three times straight.

MARCH 31, 1975

NCAA championship taken by the UCLA, 92-85 over University of Kentucky.

APRIL 5, 1975

Chris Evert won her third Virginia Slims tennis championship in four years.

APRIL 13, 1975

Jack Nicklaus won his fifth Masters Tournament.

Tom Sneva *miraculously escaped serious injury when he was involved in this flaming crash during the running of the 1975 Indianapolis 500.*

Billie Jean King *goes up for an overhead smash during a match in the latest addition to professional American sports, world team tennis. Match was played in 1975.*

Bobby Unser *comes into the pits following his winning of the 1975 Indianapolis 500 motor race.*

MAY 12, 1975
The Houston Aeros, defeating the Quebec Nordiques, won the World Hockey championship Avco Cup for the second year.

MAY 25, 1975
Bobby Unser won the Indianapolis 500.

MAY 27, 1975
Stanley Cup championship went to the Philadelphia Flyers over Buffalo Sabres.

JUNE 3, 1975
New York Cosmos of the North American Soccer League completed a 3 year, $7 million contract with the Brazilian soccer star, Pele.

JUNE 20, 1975
Marty Liquori set a meet record for the 5,000 meter run in the AAU championships.

JULY 5, 1975
Wimbledon won by Arthur Ashe over Jimmy Connors. Ashe first black man to take the title.

JULY 20, 1975
Sandra Palmer won the U.S. Women's Open golf championship.

AUGUST 10, 1975
Jack Nicklaus won his fourth PGA championship.

AUGUST 13, 1975
Tom Watsen won the $16,500 British Open.

AUGUST 23, 1975
Ed Halicki, San Francisco Giants, pitched a no-hit game against the New York Mets, 6-0.

SEPTEMBER 1, 1975
Pitching his 200th strikeout for the 8th straight season, Tom Seaver of the New York Mets set a new major league record.

SEPTEMBER 6, 1975
Forest Hills, won by Chris Evertt.

Richard Petty *crosses the finish line to win the Tuborg 400 race for stock cars at the Riverside Raceway in 1975.*

Halfback Wendell Tyler *holds ball aloft in triumph as he crosses the goal line during UCLA's stunning upset victory over Ohio State in 1976 Rose Bowl game.*

SEPTEMBER 28, 1975
New major league record was set by four Oakland A's pitchers in a shut-out game against the California Angels, 5-0. It was the first no-hitter by more than 2 pitchers.

OCTOBER 1, 1975
Muhammad Ali retained his heavyweight title in a 14 round fight with Joe Frazier.

OCTOBER 22, 1975
The Cincinnati Reds won their first World Series in 35 years in a 4-3 upset of the Boston Red Sox.

NOVEMBER 12, 1975
Cy Young award for pitching given to Tom Seaver for the third time.

NOVEMBER 18, 1975
Joe Morgan voted most valuable player in the National League.

NOVEMBER 26, 1975
The American League's most valuable player award went to Fred Lynn.

DECEMBER 10, 1975
Bill Veeck bought the Chicago White Sox from John Allyn for $9.75 million.

DECEMBER 17, 1975
Arthur Ashe named No. 1 male tennis player by the U.S. Tennis Association.

JANUARY 1, 1976
Ohio State upset by U.C.L.A. in Rose Bowl, 23-10.

JANUARY 18, 1976
The Pittsburgh Steelers beat the Dallas Cowboys 21-17 in Super Bowl.

Chris Evert *returns shot during the World Tennis Tournament in Tokyo in November, 1975. Evert won the women's singles title in the $100,000 tournament.*

713

HISTORICAL HEADLINES
ON
AMERICAN SPORTS

SLAV FORTS SINK 4 WARSHIPS

ONE CENT
CITY AND COUNTY

LOS ANGELES
EVENING HERALD
AN INDEPENDENT NEWSPAPER
Reg. U. S. Pat. Off. The Evening Herald Grows Just Like Los Angeles.

BOX SCORE EDITION

VOL. XLII. ONE CENT In Los Angeles City and County Elsewhere Two Cents Hotels and Trains Five Cents MONDAY, OCTOBER 15, 1917 ONE CENT In Los Angeles City and County Elsewhere Two Cents Hotels and Trains Five Cents NO. 298

WHITE SOX WORLD CHAMPIONS

Troops Called to Quell Teuton Riots

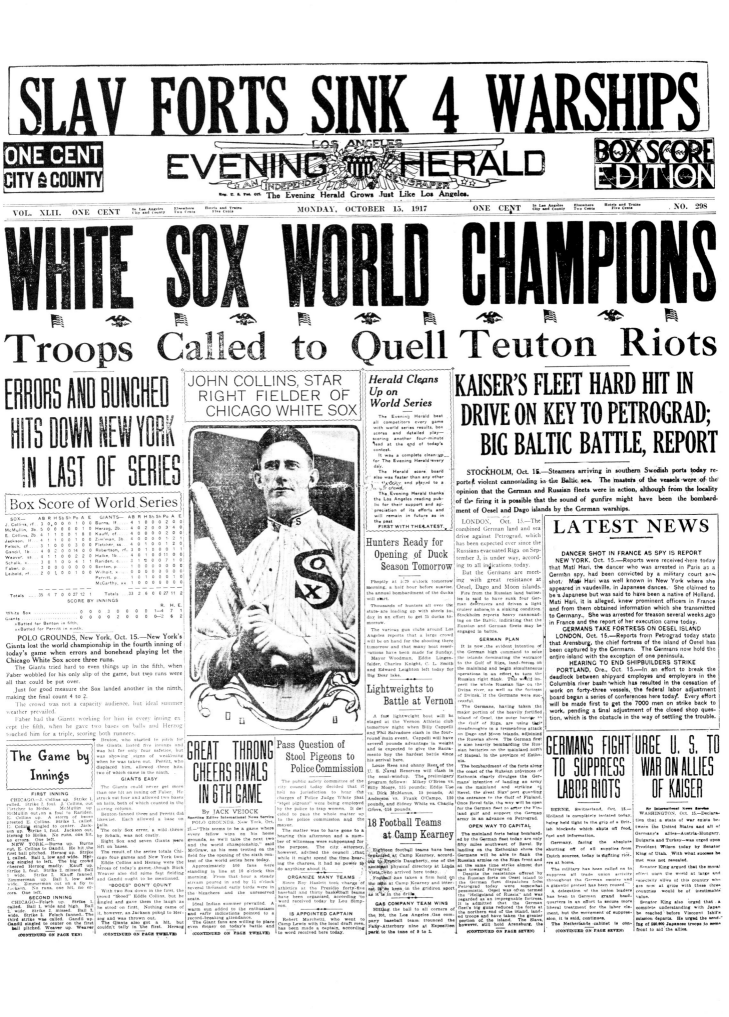

ERRORS AND BUNCHED HITS DOWN NEW YORK IN LAST OF SERIES

Box Score of World Series

SOX—	AB	R	H	Sb	Sh	Po	A	E
J. Collins, rf	3	0	0	0	0	1	0	0
McMullin, 3b	5	0	0	0	0	0	1	0
E. Collins, 2b	4	1	1	0	0	1	8	0
Jackson, lf	4	1	1	0	0	1	0	0
Felsch, cf	3	1	0	0	0	3	0	0
Gandil, 1b	4	0	2	0	0	14	0	0
Weaver, ss	4	1	1	0	0	2	2	0
Schalk, c	3	0	1	0	0	4	1	1
Faber, p	3	0	0	0	0	0	0	0
Leibold, rf	2	0	1	0	0	1	0	0
Totals	35	4	7	0	0	27	12	1

GIANTS—	AB	R	H	Sb	Sh	Po	A	E
Burns, lf	4	1	0	0	0	2	0	0
Herzog, 2b	4	0	2	0	0	3	4	0
Kauff, cf	4	0	0	0	0	2	0	0
Zim'man, 3b	4	0	0	0	0	1	2	1
Fletcher, ss	4	0	1	0	0	1	2	0
Robertson, rf	3	0	1	0	0	0	1	1
Halke, 1b	4	0	1	0	0	11	0	0
Rariden, c	3	1	0	0	0	7	1	0
Benton, p	1	0	0	0	0	0	0	0
Wilhoit, x	0	0	0	0	0	0	0	0
Perritt, p	1	0	1	0	0	0	1	0
McCarthy, xx	1	0	0	0	0	0	0	0
Totals	33	2	6	0	0	27	11	2

SCORE BY INNINGS

										R.	H.	E.
White Sox	0	0	0	3	0	0	0	0	1	4	7	1
Giants	0	0	0	0	2	0	0	0	0	2	6	2

xBatted for Benton in fifth.
xxBatted for Perritt in ninth.

POLO GROUNDS, New York, Oct. 15.—New York's Giants lost the world championship in the fourth inning of today's game when errors and bonehead playing let the Chicago White Sox score three runs.

The Giants tried hard to even things up in the fifth, when Faber wobbled for his only slip of the game, but two runs were all that could be put over.

Just for good measure the Sox landed another in the ninth, making the final count 4 to 2.

The crowd was not a capacity audience, but ideal summer weather prevailed.

Faber had the Giants working for him in every inning except the fifth, when he gave two bases on balls and Herzog touched him for a triple, scoring both runners.

Benton, who started to pitch for the Giants, lasted five innings and was hit for only four safeties, but was showing signs of weakening when he was taken out. Perritt, who displaced him, allowed three hits, two of which came in the ninth.

GIANTS EASY

The Giants could never get more than one hit an inning off Faber. He struck out four and allowed two bases on balls, both of which counted in the scoring column.

Benton fanned three and Perritt did likewise. Each allowed a base on balls.

The only Sox error, a wild throw by Schalk, was not costly.

Eight Sox and seven Giants were left on bases.

The result of the series totals Chicago four games and New York two.

Eddie Collins and Herzog were the heroes of today's game, though Buck Weaver also did some fast fielding and Gandil ought to be mentioned.

"BOOES" DON'T COUNT

With two Sox down in the first, the crowd "booed" Eddie Collins, but he singled and gave them the laugh as he stood on first. Nothing came of it, however, as Jackson poked to Herzog and was thrown out.

The Giants also got a hit, but couldn't tally in the first. Herzog

(CONTINUED ON PAGE TWELVE)

The Game by Innings

FIRST INNING

CHICAGO.—J. Collins up. Strike 1, called. Strike 2, foul. J. Collins, out Fletcher to Holke. McMullin up McMullin out on a foul to Rariden. E. Collins up. A storm of booes greeted E. Collins. Strike 1, called. E. Collins singled to center. Jackson up. Strike 1, foul. Jackson out, Herzog to Holke. No runs, one hit, no errors. One left.

NEW YORK.—Burns up. Burns out, E. Collins to Gandil. He hit the first ball pitched. Herzog up. Strike 1, called. Ball 1, low and wide. Herzog singled to left. The big crowd cheered Herzog madly. Kauff up. Strike 1, foul. Strike 2, missed. Ball 1 wide. Strike 3. Kauff fanned. Zimmerman up. Ball 1, low and wide. Zimmerman out on a fly to Jackson. No runs, one hit, no errors. One left.

SECOND INNING

CHICAGO—Felsch up. Strike 1, called. Ball 1, wide and high. Ball 2, wide. Strike 2, missed. Ball 3, wide. Strike 3. Felsch fanned. The third strike was called. Gandil up. Gandil singled to center on the first ball pitched. Weaver up. Weaver

(CONTINUED ON PAGE TEN)

JOHN COLLINS, STAR RIGHT FIELDER OF CHICAGO WHITE SOX

GREAT THRONG CHEERS RIVALS IN 6TH GAME

By JACK VEIOCK
Sporting Editor International News Service

POLO GROUNDS, New York, Oct. 15.—"This seems to be a game where every fellow wins on his home grounds, so we'll take the next two and the world championship," said McGraw, as his men trotted on the field for the opening of the sixth contest of the world series here today.

Approximately 500 fans were standing in line at 10 o'clock this morning. From that hour a steady stream poured in and by 11 o'clock several thousand early birds were in the bleachers and the unreserved seats.

Ideal Indian summer prevailed. A warm sun added to the enthusiasm and early indications pointed to a record-breaking attendance.

The Giant fans are willing to place even money on today's battle and

(CONTINUED ON PAGE TWELVE)

Pass Question of Stool Pigeons to Police Commission

The public safety committee of the city council today decided that it had no jurisdiction to hear the charges of Police Judge White that "stool pigeons" were being employed by the police to trap women. It decided to pass the whole matter up to the police commission and the mayor.

The matter was to have gone to a hearing this afternoon and a number of witnesses were subpoenaed for the purpose. The city attorney, however, advised the council that while it might spend the time hearing the charges, it had no power to do anything about it.

ORGANIZE MANY TEAMS

Since Roy Haslett took charge of athletics at the Presidio forty-five baseball and thirty basketball teams have been organized, according to word received today by Lou Simpson.

IS APPOINTED CAPTAIN

Robert Marchetti, who went to Camp Lewis with the local draft men, has been made a captain, according to word received here today.

Herald Cleans Up on World Series

The Evening Herald beat all competitors every game with world series results, box scores and detailed play—scoring another four-minute lead at the end of today's contest.

It was a complete clean-up for The Evening Herald every day.

The Herald score board also was faster than any other [illegible] and played to a bigger crowd.

The Evening Herald thanks the Los Angeles reading public for their support and appreciation of its efforts and will remain in future as in the past

FIRST WITH THE LATEST.

Hunters Ready for Opening of Duck Season Tomorrow

Phoptly at 5:29 o'clock tomorrow morning, a half hour before sunrise, the annual bombardment of the ducks will start.

Thousands of hunters all over the state are loading up with sheels today in an effort to get 25 ducks tomorrow.

The various gun clubs around Los Angeles reports that a large crowd will be on hand for the shooting there tomorrow and that many boat reservations have been made for Sunday.

Mayor Woodman, Eddie Lingenfelder, Charles Knight, C. L. Smith and Edward Leighton left today for Big Bear lake.

Lightweights to Battle at Vernon

A fast lightweight bout will be staged at the Vernon Athletic club tomorrow night when Billy Cappelli and Phil Salvadore clash in the four-round main event. Cappelli will have several pounds advantage in weight and is expected to give the Sacramento boy the hardest battle since his arrival here.

Louie Rees and ohnny Rees of the U. S. Naval Reserves will clash in the semi-windup. The preliminary program follows: Mikey O'Brien vs. Billy Moore, 135 pounds; Eddie Use vs. Dick McManus, 15 pounds, Al Anderson vs. Frank O'Campo, 130 pounds, and Sidney White vs. Charlie Grove, 116 pounds.

18 Football Teams at Camp Kearney

Eighteen football teams have been organized at Camp Kearney, according to Francis Daugherty, one of the assistant physical directors at Linda Vista, who arrived here today.

Football has taken a firm hold on the men at Camp Kearney and interest is as keen in the gridiron sport as it is in the drills.

GAS COMPANY TEAM WINS

Hitting the ball to all corners of the lot, the Los Angeles Gas company baseball team trounced the Fahy-Atterbury nine at Exposition park to the tune of 9 to 2.

KAISER'S FLEET HARD HIT IN DRIVE ON KEY TO PETROGRAD; BIG BALTIC BATTLE, REPORT

STOCKHOLM, Oct. 15.—Steamers arriving in southern Swedish ports today reported violent cannonading in the Baltic sea. The masters of the vessels were of the opinion that the German and Russian fleets were in action, although from the locality of the firing it is possible that the sound of gunfire might have been the bombardment of Oesel and Dago islands by the German warships.

LONDON, Oct. 15.—The combined German land and sea drive against Petrograd, which has been expected ever since the Russians evacuated Riga on September 3, is under way, according to all indications today.

But the Germans are meeting with great resistance at Oesel, Dago and Moon islands.

Fire from the Russian land batteries is said to have sunk four German destroyers and driven a light cruiser ashore, in a sinking condition. Stockholm reports heavy cannonading on the Baltic, indicating that the Russian and German fleets may be engaged in battle.

GERMAN PLAN

It is now the evident intention of the German high command to seize the islands dominating the entrance to the Gulf of Riga, land forces on the mainland and begin simultaneous operations in an effort to turn the Russian right flank. This would imperil the whole Russian line on the Dvina river, as well as the fortress of Dvinsk, if the Germans were successful.

The Germans, having taken the major portion of the heavily fortified island of Oesel, the outer barrier to the Gulf of Riga, are using their dreadnoughts in a tremendous attack on Dago and Moon islands, adjoining the Russian shore. The German fleet is also heavily bombarding the Russian batteries on the mainland north of Hapsal, in the province of Esthonia.

The bombardment of the forts along the coast of the Russian provinces of Esthonia clearly divulges the Germans' intention of landing an army on the mainland and striking at Revel, the great Slav port guarding the entrance to the Gulf of Finland. Once Revel falls, the way will be open for the German fleet to enter the Finland gulf and support the German army in an advance on Petrograd.

OPEN WAY TO CAPITAL

The mainland forts being bombarded by the German fleet today are only fifty miles southwest of Revel. By landing on the Esthonian shore the Germans will be able to flank the Russian armies on the Riga front and at the same time strike almost due east toward Petrograd.

Despite the resistance offered by the Russian forts on Oesel island to the German fleet dispatches from Petrograd today were somewhat pessimistic. Oesel was often termed the "Heligoland of Russia" and was regarded as an impregnable fortress. It is admitted that the German fleet's big guns reduced the forts at the northern end of the island, landed troops and have taken the greater portion of the island. The Slavs, however, still hold Arensburg, the

(CONTINUED ON PAGE SEVEN)

LATEST NEWS

DANCER SHOT IN FRANCE AS SPY IS REPORT

NEW YORK, Oct. 15.—Reports were received here today that Mati Hari, the dancer who was arrested in Paris as a German spy, had been convicted by a military court and shot. Mati Hari was well known in New York where she appeared in vaudeville, in Japanese dances. She claimed to be a Japanese but was said to have been a native of Holland. Mati Hari, it is alleged, knew prominent officers in France and from them obtained information which she transmitted to Germany. She was arrested for treason several weeks ago in France and the report of her execution came today.

GERMANS TAKE FORTRESS ON OESEL ISLAND

LONDON, Oct. 15.—Reports from Petrograd today state that Arensburg, the chief fortress of the island of Oesel has been captured by the Germans. The Germans now hold the entire island with the exception of one peninsula.

HEARING TO END SHIPBUILDERS STRIKE

PORTLAND, Ore., Oct. 15.—In an effort to break the deadlock between shipyard employes and employers in the Columbia river basin which has resulted in the cessation of work on forty-three vessels, the federal labor adjustment board began a series of conferences here today. Every effort will be made first to get the 7000 men on strike back to work, pending a final adjustment of the closed shop question, which is the obstacle in the way of settling the trouble.

GERMANS FIGHT TO SUPPRESS LABOR RIOTS

BERNE, Switzerland, Oct. 15.—Holland is completely isolated today, being held tight in the grip of a British blockade which shuts off food, fuel and information.

Germany, facing the absolute shutting off of all supplies from Dutch sources, today is fighting rioters at home.

The military has been called on to suppress all trade union activity throughout the German empire and a gigantic protest has been roused.

A delegation of the union leaders has been to German grand headquarters in an effort to secure more liberal treatment for the labor element, but the movement of suppression, it is said, continues.

The Netherlands cabinet is con-

(CONTINUED ON PAGE SEVEN)

URGE U. S. TO WAR ON ALLIES OF KAISER

By International News Service

WASHINGTON, Oct. 15.—Declaration that a state of war exists between the United States and all of Germany's allies—Austria-Hungary, Bulgaria and Turkey—was urged upon President Wilson today by Senator King of Utah. With what success he met was not revealed.

Senator King argued that the moral effect upon the world at large and especially allies of this country who are now at grips with these three countries would be of inestimable value.

Senator King also urged that a complete understanding with Japan be reached before Viscount Ishii's mission departs. He urged the sending of 500,000 Japanese troops to some front to aid the allies.

SPORTS TWO CENTS

LOS ANGELES EVENING HERALD

AN INDEPENDENT NEWSPAPER

The Evening Herald Grows Just Like Los Angeles

EXTRA

VOL. XLIV. TWO CENTS FRIDAY, JULY 4, 1919 TWO CENTS NO. 210

DEMPSEY WINNER

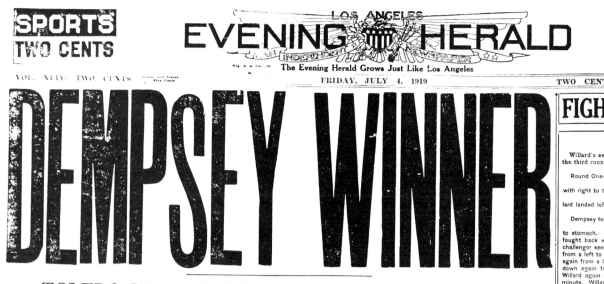

TOLEDO, July 4.—Jack Dempsey won the world heavyweight title by defeating Champion Jess Willard in the big pugilistic battle here today before a record crowd. Dempsey will defend his title.

FANE NORTON WIRES BOTH MEN LOOK FIT AS THEY ENTER RING

By FANE NORTON

Evening Herald Sporting Editor, who went to Toledo to cover the big fight

RINGSIDE, TOLEDO, July 4.—The blistering sun was shooting like an individual searchlight, straight down on every spectator and principal as the challenger and challenged entered the ring, and the record boxing battle of history got under way.

Both men looked fit, but it was plain that even the short distance of 12 rounds under the blistering heat would tax any athlete, no matter how well trained, to the utmost of his endurance.

Dopesters figured that this condition was in Dempsey's favor, but Willard appeared smiling and confident.

The crowd was a little slow in gathering, but it came in record proportions, though not so large as expected, with its coats off, fans in its hands and its straw hats tilted against the slant of the sun.

Right near me sat two well known Los Angeles men—Frank Chance, who piloted the Angel ball team to victory, and William A. Curley, who once was managing editor of The Evening Herald. I also saw Joe Reuhl, former manager of the Alexandria hotel, who when he was an Angeleno was one of the greatest fight fans of them all. Evidently he still feels that way, even if he does live in Kansas City.

DODGE THE HEAT

In spite of the extreme heat the crowd was good natured and there was a great deal of raillery as the preliminaries were gone through.

Never before in the history of boxing had such a problem confronted those delegated to handle the people at a big sporting event. There are a number of automobile roads leading to within less than a mile of the arena, but these roads merge into one big circular boulevard that runs completely around the park in which the arena is situated.

WALK TO ARENA

Toledo street car facilities were taxed to the utmost and thousands of fans started from the city early to walk the four miles to the arena. Traffic congestion completely upset the plans of autoists and many machines were abandoned some distance from the arena while their occupants continued to the scene of battle on foot.

Some of the biggest boats on the

(CONTINUED ON PAGE TWO)

OCEAN FLYER REACHES AMERICA

By International News Service

NEW YORK, July 4.—The big British dirigible R-34 had crossed the Atlantic in about 60 hours and soared above St. Johns, capital of Newfoundland, this afternoon.

At her present rate of speed she will not arrive at Mineloa, L. I., until tomorrow.

In her history-making flight across the Atlantic the R-34 encountered far less trouble with the elements than is usually experienced by an ocean liner.

1000 FEET IN AIR

Only once was she was driven out of her course.

That was late last night when arriving 300 miles off the Newfoundland coast she ran into a great fog bank and rainstorm. She was flying at an altitude of about 1000 feet at that time.

Instead of swinging southwest toward St. Johns, as he originally planned, Maj. Scott laid the airship's course straight westward, riding along the northern edge of the storm clouds and seeking clear weather. Shortly after 3 o'clock this morning, New York time, he found it, according to a wireless message to the British air ministry.

The dirigible's nose swung about and pointed southward as a clear sky

(CONTINUED ON PAGE SIX)

THE CHAMPION

JACK DEMPSEY

TIGERS LOSE TO BEES IN OPENER

Eddie Herr's Salt Lake crew won a 2 to 1 victory over Bill Essick's Vernon Tigers this morning at Washington park.

Leverenz, on the mound for the Bees, held the Tiger squad to five bingles. "Wheezer" Dell was nicked for nine bingles. Neither side made an error.

With two down in the second inning, the Bees scored the first run, after Johnson singled to center, took second on a passed ball and scored on Mulligan's single to center.

THE FOURTH

L. A. WOMAN DIES

Mrs. Laura A. Hall, formerly of Los Angeles, died at a Bakersfield hospital as a result of an operation. She was born in Seward, Neb., in 1872 and lived in Los Angeles for 20 years.

BOX SCORE

MORNING GAME

BEES—	AB	R	H	2B	3B	Hr	Sb	Sh	Po	A	E
Maggert, cf.	4	0	0	0	0	0	0	0	6	1	0
Krug, 2b	4	0	0	0	0	0	0	0	0	4	0
Mulvey, lf	4	0	0	0	0	0	0	0	1	1	0
Rumler, rf	4	1	3	1	0	0	0	0	3	0	0
Sheely, 1b	3	0	2	0	0	0	1	1	19	0	0
Johnson, ss	4	1	1	0	0	0	0	0	3	3	0
Mulligan, 3b	4	0	2	0	0	0	1	0	0	0	0
Byler, c	3	0	0	0	0	0	0	0	4	1	0
Leverenz, p	3	0	1	0	0	0	0	0	0	1	0
Totals	33	2	9	1	0	0	2	1	27	11	0

TIGERS	AB	R	H	2b	3b	Hr	Sb	Sh	Po	A	E
J. Mitchell, ss	4	0	1	0	0	0	0	0	4	5	0
Chadbourne, cf	4	0	0	0	0	0	0	0	1	0	0
Meusel, 3b	3	0	0	0	0	0	0	0	1	1	0
Borton, 1b	3	0	0	0	0	0	0	0	9	2	0
Edington, rf	3	0	0	0	0	0	0	0	2	1	0
High, lf	3	1	1	0	0	0	0	0	2	0	0
Fisher, 2b	3	0	2	1	0	0	0	0	2	1	0
Brooks, c	3	0	1	0	0	0	0	0	6	1	0
Dell, p	3	0	0	0	0	0	0	0	0	2	0
Totals	29	1	5	1	0	0	0	0	27	13	0

SCORE BY INNINGS

Bees	0	1	0	0	0	0	1	0	0	—2
Tigers	0	1	0	0	0	0	0	0	0	—1

THE FOURTH

Shimmie Contest Closed by Police

By United Press

STOCKTON, July 4.—The crowds seemed to like it fine, judging from the attendance, but Police Chief Simpson has branded the shimmie "obscene and immoral" and closed the "shimmie contest" at a local theater.

SPECTATORS STRIP IN ...IELING ...

By FRANK G. MENKE

Staff Correspondent International News Service

ARENA, BAYVIEW PARK, TOLEDO, Ohio, July 4.—Sun rays—broiling, staggering, blinding in their intensity—shimmered down this afternoon on the biggest crowd that ever saw a pugilistic clash.

And under the pitiless beating of the sun which warmed typewriters and telegraph instruments almost to a point where they were untouchable, Jess Willard and Jack Dempsey fought their battle with the heavyweight championship of the world at stake.

THOUSANDS COME

Thousands of persons who came here early so as to witness every fistic move made in this vast stadium, quitted the stands shortly after their arrival and sought refuge under them—and the remainder until time for the big fight to begin.

Willingly they sacrificed seeing a few preliminary bouts rather than risk prostration. And, as a result, huge sections of the stands were peopled but sparsely until the big fighters entered the ring.

SPECTATORS STRIP

Those who had the courage to remain in the sun-baked stadium, which itself radiated the heat like a dozen furnaces, divested themselves early of coat and collar and many went to the extreme of doffing down to their B. V. D's long before fight time.

And all the while aeroplanes, ready to carry away the mail and photos, hovered overhead like vultures waiting for prey—that the scorching sun seemed to have promised them.

Two hours before fight time it was apparent that the promoter's dreams of a million crowd would be rudely dispelled. There was only a sprinkling of reserved seat holders in sight. The really surprising fact, however, was the bleachers were less than one-third filled.

SPECULATORS STUNG

Outside the park unhappy ticket speculators who had been kidded into believing that the Willard-Dempsey skit would be put on before a packed house, offered pasteboards at far below the costs.

Seats of the $60 variety were hawked—and without purchasers—for $40 and all the other varieties were offered at from 20 to more than 60 per cent below cost. One saddened "spec" had six $30 seats—total cost $180.

"Anybody can have 'em for $60," he pleaded.

But no one was interested.

Jack Dempsey may not emerge a victor in this afternoon's clash, but

(CONTINUED ON PAGE TWO)

PRELIMINARY BOUTS BRING KNOCKOUTS FOR TWO

By International News Service

RINGSIDE, TOLEDO, Ohio, July 4.—The arena was a third filled when the first preliminary to the championship battle started at 11:02, one hour after the scheduled time.

The early preliminaries were a tip-off as to how the heat was affecting the fighters.

The first affair was a six-rounder between Tommy O'Boyle, a Toledo bantam, and Solly Epstein of Indianapolis.

The boys started off at a fast clip and maintained it through the first round and part of the second.

Then they began to slow down in their work and through the last three merely dragged their way through the three minutes of fighting.

FIRST KNOCKOUT

At the finish—the fight was a draw—both boys were near collapse.

Whirlwind Wendt and Wop English, another bantam, met in a scheduled six rounder. They mixed it for about a minute and, although no real blow was struck during a flurry, Wendt seemed to collapse. He placed his hand on his head and as he did so English hit him—and Wendt was a knockout victim. It was some time before be could be revived.

The third preliminary had a finish somewhat similar. It brought together Johnny Lewis of Toledo and Tommy Long of Detroit.

LIGHTWEIGHTS BATTLE

They were lightweights. They fought along rather briskly in the early part of the first round, but near the end Long begun to show the effects of the heat. He came out for the second rather groggy and went down with the first real punch that Lewis struck. Long got up at the count of seven and weathered out the round, but in the third he appeared lifeless in his actions and one solid wallop on the chin finished him.

The fourth preliminary brought together Johnny Rose of Milwaukee and Battling Bellaire of Brooklyn, who fought a six-rounder at the middleweight limit.

SPEEDY START

Both men started off at a rather speedy clip, but slowed down in the third round and from then on swung blows that lacked steam. They alternated the rest of the way by staggering around the ring and holding each other in forward clinches. Rose was given the decision.

Shortly before 2 p. m. the arena appeared just about half full. That meant a crowd of 30,000 or 40,000—depending upon the exact seating capacity of the big stadium. No official announcement of just how many persons it can accommodate had been made other than "around 80,-

(CONTINUED ON PAGE TWO)

FIGHT BY ROUND

Willard's seconds tossed a towel into the ring at e... the third round.

Round One—Willard led left for the jaw. Dempsey ... with right to the stomach. Willard stood confidently ... lard landed left and right to the head.

Dempsey took a left on the nose. He countered wi... to stomach. Dempsey hooked left to the head. Wi... fought back with both hands as Dempsey went in ... challenger seemed to gain confidence. Willard ... from a left to the jaw, took count of seven and ... again from a left to the jaw, took count of ... down again from a smash on the jaw. Dempsey sc... Willard again with right and left. He was up again ... minute. Willard went down the fourth time. He went d... the fifth time from a volley of rights and lefts. Demp... was smashing him to all parts of the ring. Dempsey ...

him through the ropes with left and right. Willard we... the floor in a neutral corner. The round ended with Wi... on his haunches in a neutral corner. He was being cou... out when the bell rang.

Round Two—Dempsey ran to Willard's corner, sm... ing rights and lefts to the jaw. The champion fought b... but was unable to stand the terrific bombardment. De... sey deliberately measured Willard and then crossed r... to the point of the chin, but Willard did not fall. Demp... missed a smashing left hook. Willard's left eye was c... ing and he bled from the cheek.

The semi-final was cut to eight rounds, bringing the m... bout 12 minutes nearer. It ended at 3:30 with Tremaine ... winner. The verdict of Billy Rooks of Detroit was gree... with jeers and the crowd began to shout, "Bring on ... fighters." Immediately the semi-final ended a new canv... was stretched over the ring. A group of marines then g... a bayonet drill which provoked cheers from the cro...

... Dempsey entered the ring at 3:56.

Willard entered the ring at 3:58.

The cheers for Willard were but ... whisp... oari... with those ...

As soon as he jumped through the ro... Jess ... across the ring and shook hands with Demp... The c... pion towered above the challenger.

YANKS WIN INTER-ALLIED SHOT PUT

PERSHING STADIUM, Paris, July 4.—Americans w... all three places in the finals of the shot put today and sec... and third places in the 800-meter run. Over 50,000 sp... tators packed the stadium. Frenchmen captured all th... places in the marathon. Results in the other events w... 800-meter run, won by Mason, New Zealand; Earl Eby, C... cago, second; T. M. Spink, Chicago, third. Time, 1:55 2... Shot put, won by Reg Caughey, Ukiah, Cal.; H. Liversed... Oakland, Cal., second; Wallace Maxfield, Bloomfield, N. ... third. Distance, 13.776 meters.

GEN. PERSHING SENDS JULY 4 MESSAGE

WASHINGTON, July 4.—The following message fr... Gen. Pershing was received this afternoon by the commit... in charge of the celebration here today: "Each annivers... of this great day brings us added reason to rejoice, but ... day we celebrate the greatest victory for freedom won, w... our allies, by the clean hands of our courageous soldie... backed by the united will of the American people."

GEN. HOFFMAN REINSTATED BY HUNS

COPENHAGEN, July 4.—Gen. Hoffman, who was d... missed from his command on the old eastern battlefront ... the German government, has been reinstated, according ... information reaching the Central News from Berlin today.

500 CHILDREN MANAGE FOURTH CELEBRATION

GRASS VALLEY, Cal., July 4.—The Independence d... celebration here is in charge of 500 children under 10 ye... of age. Neil Whiting, 9, is chairman of the day. Malco... Crass, 6, is grand marshal of the parade, in which the ch... dren will take the leading part. The grownups held th... returned veterans' parade last evening. Veda Bradley, ... recited the Declaration of Independence and Jack Curno... 8, was orator of the day. A chorus of 500 children's voi... was a feature of the celebration.

COLORADO SPRINGS RESIDENCE DISTRICT FLOOD

COLORADO SPRINGS, Colo., July 4.—Several blocks ... the wealthy residence district in the north end of this c... were buried under four feet of water as a result of a clou... burst last night. Two automobiles were washed into t... stream. Police and firemen worked steadily in an effort ... clear the cellars and streets of water. The storm was ge... eral in the Pike's Peak region. The Denver and Colora... bridge over Sand Creek was washed away.

HUNS NOT TO ANSWER SHIP SINKING NOTE

BERLIN, July 4.—The German government does not ... tend to answer the note from the entente protesting again... the sinking of German ships at Scapa Flow. It was point... out today that no answer was required. The governme... is inclined to believe the allies will not press the issue.

THERE IT GOES—A familiar cry when the Babe was at bat. In 1927 the Babe smacked 60 home runs, a record that has stood 21 years and might well stand 20 more.

SPORTS-LOVING NATION MOURNS DEATH OF HOMER KING BABE RUTH

Dread Malady Takes Life of Beloved Baseball Player

NEW YORK, Aug. 16 (U.P)—Babe Ruth, 53, baseball's beloved home-run king, died in his sleep at 8:01 tonight, ending a career that had been devoted to baseball for more than a quarter of a century.

The famed Sultan of Swat, for 22 years a major leaguer, the man who hit 714 home runs in his lusty lifetime and who hit a record 60 in the 1927 season alone, died quietly after a two-year fight against cancer of the throat.

The Babe fought to the end, and in his last weeks only his stout heart kept him alive. His booming voice was all but gone, and his strength was sapped.

Ruth's family and close friends were by his side when he died. They had been on the alert for nearly a week, ever since Ruth was placed on the critical list last Wednesday after a pulmonary congestion set in.

Concern over Ruth's condition, expressed during the last few days in messages from all parts of the country and from distant points throughout the world, also was felt in the White House.

President Truman had telephoned the hospital last week from the capital to find out how the Babe was getting along. Tonight, advised of Ruth's death, the Chief Executive arranged to send a message of condolence to Ruth's widow.

In Albany, Gov. Thomas E. Dewey and his Vice-Presidential running mate, Gov. Earl Warren, expressed regret at the death of Babe Ruth.

"A spectacular baseball player whose equal may never be reached, Babe Ruth was above all a great American . . . In his passing I have lost a good friend," Dewey said.

Warren said, "Few men in American history have been a greater inspiration to the youth of our land . . . Throughout his life he played the game fair and hard and never gave up to the very end."

At his suite in the Waldorf-Astoria, former President Herbert Hoover described Ruth as "one of the great sportsmen of the United States."

Hoover Halls

Mr. Hoover then recalled a public gathering in Los Angeles when he was approached by a small boy who asked for his autograph.

"Would you mind giving me three?" the boy asked.

Mr. Hoover complied but asked the boy why he wanted three.

"Because it takes two of yours to trade for one of Babe Ruth's," he replied.

The One and Only

Two employees at the hospital where Ruth had lingered out his last illness were affected visibly when word of the Bambino's death spread throughout the institution.

Said 50-year-old William Stevenson:

"Gee, it's tough. I seen him when he opened up in the Yankee Stadium in 1923. I have not seen

Turn to Page 2, Column 5

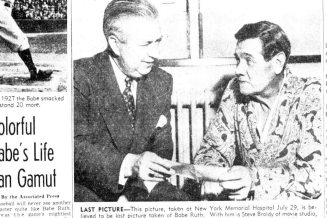

LAST PICTURE—This picture, taken at New York Memorial Hospital July 29, is believed to be last picture taken of Babe Ruth. With him is Steve Broidy of movie studio, who is presenting him with check for Ruth Foundation for underprivileged children.
(AP photo)

SPORTSCRIPTS

By PAUL ZIMMERMAN TIMES SPORTS EDITOR

LONDON, Aug. 16—Avery Brundage, Hollywood hotel owner and parttime Southern California resident as he likes to point out, isn't a man to duck a controversial issue as was shown in the winter Games in Switzerland when he got himself right in the middle of the ice hockey team controversy.

For that reason, it is remarkable that the London Olympic Games failed to project Brundage, member of the International Olympic Federation and president of the American Olympic Committee, into anything more exciting than the usual discussion of "broken time" and the true meaning of amateurism.

Broken time involves the question of whether Olympic athletes should be paid by Olympic associations for money lost by being taken away from their normal professional or labor pursuits while competing in the world championships.

NEVER CHANGE

Brundage goes back to the dictionary and points out that amateurism means competition for the love of the game only and he adds that he feels professional sports belong on the entertainment pages of the newspapers since they are staged purely and simply for the enjoyment of the public and not the pleasure of the competitor.

Anyway, he insists you never can change the amateur rule because it is elemental.

The fact that Brundage was not in the middle here may be taken as a compliment to the athlete competing. There was no real untoward incident and the American team, especially, conducted itself as a group of ambassadors should.

WELL-BEHAVED

There were no champagne parties; no cases of athletes getting out of line; nothing of an exciting nature to report although the usual sensational element of the press tried to make incidents such as the absurd inference that one of our champions was a little tipsy at the reception staged by King George VI.

Brundage says this is by far the best-behaved American team we have taken to the Games. It may be for that reason that he was quick to push the protest of Coach Dean Cromwell when the American 400-meter team was disqualified — a disqualification that was overridden as soon as the motion pictures were seen.

Even if the pictures had shown that Barney Ewell and Lorenzo Wright had completed their baton pass outside the restraining zone, it is probable that Brundage, a member of the reviewing jury, would have argued for our team.

IMPORTANT THING

"I have always contended," said Brundage before he went in to view the films, "that the important thing in athletic competition is consideration of the competitor. Technicalities that prevent the best athletes from gaining a championship, so long as the violations are not of a serious nature and do not aid in that victory, do not merit consideration."

It is quite likely that Brundage would have projected himself into a controversy here, had the pictures failed to substantiate the American contention that the 400-meter relays were honestly run and victory well earned.

POINT OF VIEW

A long-time athletic competitor himself, Brundage is an official who certainly can see the contestant's point of view. The fact that he is a self-made man of considerable wealth while continuing amateur competition in his early years undoubtedly is one of the strong reasons why he is so set in his ways on the subject of absolute amateurism.

Although he has said that he is ready to resign as head of the American Olympic Committee, most of those who know Brundage well do not believe that it will be possible for him to turn his back completely on amateur athletics.

P.S.: Regardless of your personal feelings concerning the man, you have to admit that he has given freely of his time and money to further the cause of amateurism.

Colorful Babe's Life Ran Gamut

By the Associated Press

Baseball will never see another character quite like Babe Ruth. He was the game's mightiest slugger and most glamorous figure. He was the highest paid performer and greatest gate attraction. He was also its heaviest-fined "bad boy" and, as time marched on, its "forgotten man."

A street urchin from the dock district of Baltimore, the Bambino captured the fancy of the American public.

His tremendous slugging revolutionized baseball in the turbulent twenties, yet records still are on the books that he made as a young southpaw pitcher. For glamour, color, thrills and achievement Ruth's career was unparalleled. During the "Golden Era" of sport after the first World War, Ruth shared with Jack Dempsey, Bobby Jones and Big Bill Tilden.

Got $80,000 Salary

In 1930 and 1931 he drew a salary of $80,000 per season, $5000 more than the President of the United States. And the $2,000,000 Yankee Stadium, largest and most modern baseball plant in the land, is still known as "The House that Ruth Built."

His early life is shrouded in mystery. Little is known of his parents and the date of his birth is uncertain. Old records say he was born at Baltimore, Feb. 7, 1894, but baseball records and his 1934 passport give Feb. 6, 1895, as the date.

Both his poverty-stricken parents were still living when 6-year-old George was taken off the streets and placed in St. Mary's Industrial School of Baltimore. School didn't interest the lad and he was soon back with his parents. But not for long, because they had neither the time nor means of preventing him from running wild with street gangs. So Father Matthias at St. Mary's took the young rebel back to school again to teach him the trade of shirtmaker.

Coached by Cleric

It wasn't long before Ruth found a real friend in Brother Gilbert, the school's baseball coach. He discovered that young George had more natural baseball ability than any lad in school. When Ruth became 18, Brother Gilbert recommended him to Jack Dunn, owner and manager of the Baltimore Orioles.

Dunn took out guardian papers and agreed to give Ruth $600 for the 1914 season. Ruth always claimed that his biggest thrill came when he went back to St. Mary's and told his schoolmates that he had signed a contract with the Orioles and was a real professional baseball player.

Ruth was a natural from the start. In his first season he won 22 games and lost nine for Baltimore and Providence. Before the season ended he was sold to the Boston Red Sox along with Pitcher Ernie Shore for $30,000. The Red Sox farmed him out to Providence but recalled him before the end of the season and he won two games and lost one.

First Homer

The next season Ruth, who had picked up the nickname of Babe while with Baltimore, hit his first major league homer against the New York Yankees May 6, 1915. Before he called it a day in 1935 Ruth hit 714 home runs, a mark that seems to stand.

Many say that if he had remained on the mound he would have gone down as one of the great left-handers. In 1915, his first full season with the Red Sox, he won 18 games and lost 8. The next season he copped 23 and lost 12 and achieved an earned run average of 1.75.

It wasn't until 1920 that he re-

Turn to Page 2, Column 5

Ruth Had One Name for All

The Babe always had trouble remembering names of teammates and rival players. So he called everybody "Kid." In '29, when Mickey Cochrane was at his peak as star catcher of the Athletics, he passed Babe on the street and said, "Hello, Babe." The Babe nodded and said, "Hello, kid," and strode on. Mickey ran after him, grabbed his arm and spun him around. "Listen, you," growled Mickey, "my name is Mickey Cochrane—and don't call me 'kid'." But the very next day the Babe saw Mickey again and said, "Hello, kid." And Mickey just shrugged his shoulders and let it go at that.

'YOUTH' VS. 'AGE'

'YOUTH' VS. 'AGE'

"Youth" vs. "age," a question that has cropped up countless times in athletic history, will get still another airing when the Los Angeles Rams face the Washington Redskins for Los Angeles Times Charities, Inc., in the Los Angeles Coliseum on the night of Sept. 2.

The "age" will be supplied by Washington's Sammy Baugh, who, like Old Man River, keeps right on rolling along. Sammy's only 34 years old—young for a U.S. Senator but practically Social Security age for a professional football player.

His foe, representing "youth" and the Rams, will be Glenn Davis, 23-year-old Army lieutenant, who left frustrated tacklers sprawled on gridirons all over the East and Midwest during his four years as a West Point performer.

Baugh, who won't tell where he keeps his private fountain of youth, holds virtually every passing record in the National League. And this year railbirds say he's better than ever before.

Davis, a Southern California product, has never had a chance to show his wares here since his high school days. Until now, that is.

Although they're two entirely different types of players, they both have one thing in common—greatness. Who is greater? Come out and see for yourselves.

Tickets for the game may be obtained at any of the following locations:

Southern California Music Co., 737 S Hill St.; Desmond's, 616 S Broadway and 5500 Wilshire Blvd.; Denels Music Shop, 6634 Hollywood Blvd.; Los Angeles Rams, 273 S Beverly Drive, Beverly Hills; Los Angeles Times Information Desk, 202 W 1st St.; all Mutual ticket agencies.

All tickets $3.60 and $2.50, including tax.

THE BABE—The famous grin, the lovable face, the big homely nose—the one and only, the great Babe Ruth. Today the whole sports world mourned his passing.

LIFELONG HERO PASSES

Ruth Most Colorful of All Sports Greats

BY AL WOLF

Th' Babe is dead.

Th' Babe was our hero.

So it's not going to be a pleasant task writing this piece.

Babe Ruth was our hero when we were playing ball with the other neighborhood kids on weed-strewn vacant lots, with paving slabs for bases and a "nickel brick" for a ball. He was our hero long before we ever saw a professional game and he was still our hero when he died, long removed from the game.

No other sports figure ever challenged him closely for our affection and adoration. No one probably ever will.

Babe Ruth was much more than a great athlete—and he was a sensational fielder and a superb pitcher as well as the mightiest slugger of all time. He was more than the greatest personality in America's greatest game. Babe Ruth was the ultimate personification of an era in which sports "grew up" —from the Police Gazette to the front pages, from barns and bleachers to massive stadiums, from boozy, suspendered masculinity to socialite festoonings, from shoestring operations to big business.

The impetus that brought about this change in sports' status came in the postwar plenitude of the 20s.

And interest did not recede again with the stunning crash that ended that decade. There was a slight pause, until money again became something other than a museum piece, then a new forward surge that made fans of everybody, poured millions through the turnstiles and put athletes into the upper brackets, both socially and financially.

Color did it.

Sports in the "Roaring Twenties" were blessed with a tremendous concentration of athletic artists whose muscular talents were embellished by that tangible something that

Turn to Page 2, Column 3

RUTH CALLED SHOT IN '32 WORLD SERIES

Of all Babe Ruth's homers, the most incredible was the one he blasted in the third game of the '32 World Series between the Yankees and Cubs in Chicago. Wrathful over the dugout taunts of the NL'ers, Babe warned Pitcher Charley Root he was going to hammer the first good pitch into the center field stands. Every fan in the crowd of 49,986 saw Babe dramatically wag his bat in the direction of the stands—and then belt the ball precisely into them!

Flags to Fly at Half-Mast Tonight

President Clarence Rowland said last night that all flags in Pacific Coast League baseball parks will be at half mast tonight, honoring the memory of Babe Ruth. There will be one minute of silent tribute to the Babe before tonight's games.

"He was just the greatest of all baseball players," said Rowland. "He was America's sports hero— a hero to young and old. There will never be another like him."

TODAY IN SPORTS

BASEBALL—Oakland vs. Los Angeles. Wrigley Field. 8:15.
HORSE RACING—Del Mar. first post 2.
MIDGET AUTO RACING—Culver City Speedway, time trials 7, first race 8:15.
WRESTLING—South Gate Arena. 8:30.
GIRLS' SOFTBALL—Monrovia vs. Bambies. Montebello Park. 8:30.
PRO BOXING—Olympia Auditorium. 8:30 p.m.

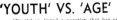

TOGETHER AGAIN—The Babe (right) shown in his heyday with Yankee teammate, Lou Gehrig. Lou died in 1941. Babe was seventh member of 1927 Yankee team to die.
(AP photo)

BABE RUTH'S CAREER

Game's greatest home run hitter.
Born, Feb. 6, 1895, at Baltimore, Md.
Height, 6ft 2in. Weight, 215. Threw and batted lefthanded.

Vice-president and assistant manager, Boston, N.L., April, 1935; released, June, 1935; coach, Brooklyn, June 18, 1938 until end of season.
Outstanding performances—Elected to Hall of Fame 1936; named most valuable player, American League, 1923; cracked an All-Star major league record, hitting 60 and 1921, of American League batters, 1924; first in hitting home runs, 1918 (11) tied with Walker of A's 1919–20–21–23–24 (tied with Gehrig) 1926–27–28–29, scored most runs, season—177 (1921); batted in 2209 runs, holds major league record for most long hits, season—119 (1921); made most extra bases on long hits, season—253 (1921); most total bases season—457 most extra bases on long hits, season—846 (1921); most home runs, lifetime—714; most home runs, lifetime—60 (1927); most home runs in succession—first game, May 21, 1930 and May 20, 1930; most home runs with bases filled, season—4 (1919); most bases on balls, lifetime—1336.

(statistical table continues)

Year	Club	League	Pos	G	AB	R	H	HR	SB	BA	PO	A	E	FA
1914	Baltimore													
1914	Providence	(I.L.)	P-OF	46	121	27	28	1	4	.231	30	87	6	.951
1914	Boston	(A.L.)	P	5	10	1	2	0	0	.200	3	14	0	1.000
1915	Boston	(A.L.)	P-OF	42	92	16	29	4	0	.315	9	63	5	.935
1916	Boston	(A.L.)	P	67	136	18	37	3	0	.272	14	83	4	.960
1917	Boston	(A.L.)	P	52	123	14	40	2	0	.325	14	101	2	.983
1918	Boston	(A.L.)	P-1B-OF	95	317	50	95	11	6	.300	220	58	14	.952
1919	Boston	(A.L.)	P-OF	130	432	103	139	29	7	.322	222	34	19	.931
1920	New York	(A.L.)	OF	142	458	158	172	54	14	.376	259	21	19	.936
1921	New York	(A.L.)	OF	152	540	177	204	59	17	.378	348	17	13	.966
1922	New York	(A.L.)	OF	110	406	94	128	35	2	.315	226	14	9	.964
1923	New York	(A.L.)	OF	152	522	151	205	41	17	.393	378	19	11	.973
1924	New York	(A.L.)	OF	153	529	143	200	46	9	.378	340	18	14	.962
1925	New York	(A.L.)	OF	98	359	61	104	25	2	.290	207	15	6	.974
1926	New York	(A.L.)	OF	152	495	139	184	47	11	.372	308	11	7	.978
1927	New York	(A.L.)	OF	151	540	158	192	60	7	.356	328	14	13	.963
1928	New York	(A.L.)	OF	154	536	163	173	54	4	.323	304	9	8	.975
1929	New York	(A.L.)	OF	135	499	121	172	46	5	.345	240	5	4	.984
1930	New York	(A.L.)	OF	145	518	150	186	49	10	.359	266	10	10	.965
1931	New York	(A.L.)	OF	145	534	149	199	46	5	.373	237	5	7	.972
1932	New York	(A.L.)	OF	133	457	120	156	41	2	.341	209	10	9	.961
1933	New York	(A.L.)	OF	137	459	97	138	34	4	.301	215	9	7	.970
1934	New York	(A.L.)	OF	125	365	78	105	22	1	.288	197	5	6	.971
1935	Boston	(N.L.)	OF	28	72	13	13	6	0	.181	39	1	2	.952
Major league totals				2503	8399	2174	2873	714	123	.341	4673	358	175	.968

WORLD SERIES RECORD

Year	Club	League	Pos	G	AB	R	H	HR	BA	PO	A	E	FA
1915	Boston	(A.L.)	P	1	1	0	0	0	.000				
1916	Boston	(A.L.)	P	1	5	0	1	0	.200				
1918	Boston	(A.L.)	P-OF	3	5	0	1	0	.200				
1921	New York	(A.L.)	OF	6	16	3	5	1	.313				
1922	New York	(A.L.)	OF	5	17	1	2	0	.118				
1923	New York	(A.L.)	OF	6	19	8	7	3	.368				
1926	New York	(A.L.)	OF	7	20	6	6	4	.300				
1927	New York	(A.L.)	OF	4	15	4	6	2	.400				
1928	New York	(A.L.)	OF	4	16	9	10	3	.625				
1932	New York	(A.L.)	OF	4	15	6	5	2	.333				
World Series Totals				41	129	37	42	15	.325	73	12	3	.977

ALL-STAR GAME RECORD

	AB	R	H	2B	3B	HR	RBI	BA	PO	A	E	FA
1933 Americans	4	2	2	0	0	1	2	.500	2	0	0	1.000
1934 Americans	2	0	0	0	0	0	0	.000	2	0	0	1.000
All-Star game totals	6	2	2	0	0	1	2	.333	4	0	0	1.000

PITCHING RECORD

Year	Club	League	G	W	L	ER	BB	SO	ERA
1914	Baltimore-Prov.	(I.L.)	35	22	9				
1914	Boston	(A.L.)	4	2	1				3.91
1915	Boston	(A.L.)	32	18	8				2.44
1916	Boston	(A.L.)	44	23	12				1.75
1917	Boston	(A.L.)	41	24	13				2.02
1918	Boston	(A.L.)	20	13	7				2.22
1919	Boston	(A.L.)	17	9	5				2.97
1920	New York	(A.L.)	1	1	0				
1921	New York	(A.L.)	2	2	0				
1930	New York	(A.L.)	1	1	0				
1933	New York	(A.L.)	1	1	0				
Major League Totals			163	1220	92	46	477	979	

WORLD'S SERIES PITCHING RECORD

Year	Club	League	G	W	L	ER	BB	SO	ERA
World's Series Totals			3	3	0	8	10	10	0.87

AGAINST THEIR WILL: 200 Years of Black-American History

In 1776 there were half a million slaves in this country. Every one of them had been brought to North America by force, sold into slavery for a price, and kept in bondage against his will.

The essence of Negro American history flows not from the American Revolution, but from the first slave shipment from Africa, a shipment which began as early as the first colony in Jamestown.

The first mention of slavery appeared in the diaries of the planter John Rolfe in 1619, in Jamestown, one year before the landing of the Mayflower. Portuguese traders had been selling African slaves since early 1400 and to them, the discovery of North America was merely one more market for their human merchandise.

The African kingdoms of Ashanti and Dahomey grew wealthy by capturing members of rival tribes, and selling them to the traders in exchange for rum and gunpowder. Initial attempts to use native American Indians as slaves proved a dismal failure. As the demand for slaves grew, English traders joined the market, eventually dominating it, along with the French and Dutch. Prices for slaves varied with the kingdom of origin: Angolan slaves were regarded as "worthless," those from Ashanti were "good workers but too rebellious," those from Senegal, "too prone to theft," the Eboes of Nigeria were "timid and despondent," the Pawpaws of Dahomey were the best grade "most docile and best disposed."

Recent research has estimated two million slaves were brought over from Africa between 1680 and 1786. During the Portuguese monopoly, the annual import rate was 5,000 slaves. After free trade began in 1750, the number rose dramatically: 160,950 slaves brought to the colonies between 1750 and 1759. Slaves were provided to the Spanish colonies as well. For the slaves the journey was traumatic and often ended in death; there are estimates that 13 percent of those leaving Africa never made land.

Once here, slaves were subjected to control by "slave codes" enforcing servitude and separating black from white in social matters. In 1664, Maryland passed a law which set the model for other colonies, making slavery hereditary.

THE SLAVE MARKET

Slave trading was big business in the colonies up to the War for Independence. New England ships were used to bring slaves from Africa via the West Indies to North America. A lucrative trade triangle was established, New Englanders trading their fish and produce for West Indian sugar and rum and buying slaves with rum.

The Mississippi River was likewise alive with the slave market. Savannah, St. Louis, the District of Columbia, Alexandria, Richmond, and New Orleans were among the major trading cities. William Wells Brown, a slave and later an abolitionist writer, was forced to supervise the slave market:

I was ordered to have the old men's whiskers shaved off, and the gray hairs plucked out where they were not too numerous, in which case we had a preparation of blacking to color it, and with a blacking brush we would put it on. This was a new business to me, and was performed in a room where the passengers could not see us. These slaves were also taught how old they were by Mr. Walker, and after going through the blacking process they looked ten or fifteen years younger.

We landed at Rodney, and the slaves were driven to the pen in the back part of the village. Several were sold at this place,

TO BE SOLD,
A Negro Man that underſtands Cooking and Houſe-work ; alſo a young Ne-ro Girl ; both have had the Small-Pox.
Enquire of the Printers.
Maſs.Gaz. Aug 29 1769.

An advertisement *for a slave sale which appeared in a colonial newspaper. Such advertisements were common in newspapers throughout the colonies.*

during our stay of four or five days.

Before the slaves were exhibited for sale, they were dressed and driven out into the yard. Some were set to dancing, some to jumping, some to singing, and some to playing cards. This was done to make them appear cheerful and happy.

My business was to see that they were placed in those situations before the arrival of the purchasers, and I have often set them to dancing when their cheeks were wet with tears. As slaves were in good demand at that time, they were all soon disposed of, and we again set out for St. Louis.

In the years before the Revolution, slaves were bought both North and South. In this new land, with farming and industry expanding, there was much for slave labor to do. They worked in iron works, factories, on wharves, in mills, in shops and as apprentice craftsmen. But it was on the large Southern plantations, where cotton and tobacco were commercial crops, that slaves made the biggest impact. Where the southern farmer planted only his food or small trade, he was no more disposed to use slaves than was the small Northern farmer.

The Boston Massacre *in 1770 resulted in the deaths of several colonists, among them Crispus Attucks, a runaway slave. Attucks received a public funeral.*

America's first heavyweight *professional boxing champion was a freed slave, Tom Molineux. Molineux fought the British champion, Tom Cribb, two times, but failed to gain a victorious decision in either fight.*

Reproduction of a cartoon *from the Revolutionary War showing a Hessian mercenary receiving directions from a slave.*

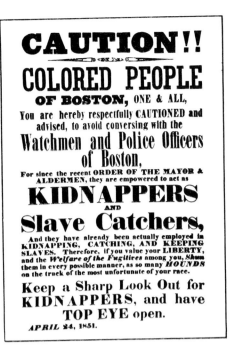

Public bulletin *which appeared in Boston in 1851 warning runaway slaves in that city to be on the alert for bounty hunters who would capture them and return them to their owners in the South.*

The interior of a slave-holding cell *in St. Louis, Missouri circa 1850. Such cells were used to hold slaves until they were brought to the auctioning block for sale to plantation owners.*

Life on the plantation was "a little nation by itself," Frederick Douglass, a fugitive slave and the major black leader of the post-Revolutionary Period, has written. The plantation had "its own language, its own rules, regulations and customs." He described the living quarters and conditions:

> *The sleeping apartments . . . have little regard to comfort or decency. Old and young, male and female, married and single, drop down upon the common clay floor, each covering up with his or her blanket—the only protection they have from cold or exposure. The night, however, is shortened at both ends. The slaves work often as long as they can see, and are late in cooking and mending for the coming day; and, at the first gray streak of morning, they are summoned to the field by the driver's horn.*
>
> *More slaves are whipped for oversleeping than for any other fault. Neither age nor sex finds any favor. The overseer stands at the quarter door, armed with stick and cowskin, ready to whip any who may be a few minutes late. When the horn is blown, there is a rush for the door and the hindermost one is sure to get a blow from the overseer.*

While the vast majority of slaves worked the fields, under the watchful eye of the overseer, some of them—the so-called "better class"—worked in the plantation house as butler, maid, or cook.

On the eve of the American Revolution the colonies had grown used to slavery. George Washington and Thomas Jefferson both owned slaves; the Quakers argued for an end to the slave trade but were owners themselves. The New England colonies were quick to protest the Sugar Act of 1764, raising a tax on foreign molasses, as hurting their triangle trade routes to Africa.

When the colonies declared their independence from England, it was white America alone that was speaking, and when the Declaration spoke in august Lockean terms that "all men are created equal" and entitled to "life, liberty and pursuit of happiness" it was to white men they were referring.

The slaves, however, were listening. They heard the rhetoric of independence and they believed it as well. Beginning in the early 1760's, slaves in New England began bringing "suits of service" asking the courts for their freedom and for compensation for their past labors. Jenny Slew of Ipswitch, Massachusetts, won her freedom and four pounds in 1765. Four other slaves futilely petitioned the slave-owning Massachusetts Governor Thomas Hutchinson for their freedom, seeking to leave for the coast of Africa.

Though New Englanders were not eager to award slaves their freedom, they were willing to use acts of heroism by slaves as propaganda for the Revolution. Crispus Attucks, for example, was one of five persons killed by British troops in 1770 during the Boston Massacre. The five were buried in a spectacular public funeral and honored as heroes in a solemn parade.

During the war itself, the hope of freedom motivated large numbers of slaves to enlist for the causes of both colonist and king. Negroes participated in the early battles of Lexington, Concord, and Bunker Hill, only to be barred from serving in the newly formed Continental Army on the grounds such service would encourage runaways.

The British Lord Dunmore, governor of Virginia, immediately invited the enlistment of all Negroes, promising them freedom in exchange for service. When huge numbers of Negroes flocked to the British cause, George Washington, commander of the Continental Army, was sorely embarrassed and extremely worried that all the slaves would flee, and he immediately reversed his policy. In all, 5,000 Negroes served with the colonists seeing battle throughout the war. The British, however, used them as spies or guides or in the war camps themselves, but rarely as soldiers. When the war ended, these former slaves shipped off with the British for Canada, the West Indies and Nova Scotia. There were said to have been 4,000 from Savannah, 6,000 from Charleston and 4,000 leaving with the British from New York.

Much as Washington expected, however, large numbers of slaves fled the plantations of the south for freedom and

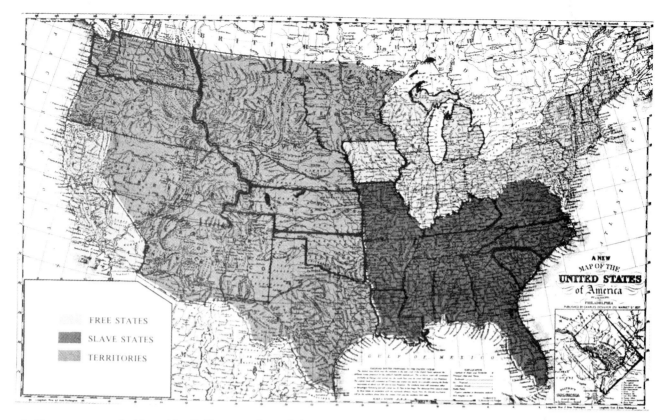

probably never served either side. Jefferson estimated that some 30,000 slaves fled Virginia in 1778; Georgia is said to have lost at least 10,000.

"You are another man's property and I have not money sufficient to buy all of you and set you free."

—Gen. Andrew Jackson

The Founding Fathers arrived at Philadelphia for the Constitutional Convention of 1787 with an opportunity to wipe the slate clean regarding slavery. For years, many of them had blamed the British for the existence of slavery and the slave trade. Jefferson himself had written a position paper asserting that the abolition of slavery was a great desire of the

As anti-slavery feeling *began to grow in the North, woodcuts such as this one became a common feature in newspapers and bulletins.*

Map showing the division *of the states and territories between free and slave in the 1856 election. The newly organized Republican Party campaigned on an anti-slavery platform in this election.*

colonists but that the British had stymied all their efforts in this direction. When it came time to act, however, the framers of the Constitution continued in the British tradition.

The key to the continued existence of slavery after the Revolution lies in the character of the Founding Fathers themselves, for they were generally rich men who measured wealth in terms of material goods and land. To a man they believed slaves were property. Whether or not they believed in slavery as an institution—and many of the Northern delegates wanted it eliminated—they were not about to deprive another man of property fully paid for without compensation for the loss. Though these Northern delegates might return home and successfully end slavery in their states, they apparently could not or would not impose such new laws on the nation as a whole.

Given this supreme respect for private property, the Constitutional Convention debated the political power issues regarding slavery but left the moral considerations for another day. There was adequate reason to believe that if the question of continued slavery was pressed too forcefully, the Union might never be formed at all.

The issue of slavery was like a chip on the South's shoulder, causing it to fear Federal intervention by the new central government in areas apparently remote for the question of the Negro. Delegate James Madison, writing of the Convention in the 10th Federalist Paper, said voting blocs formed early, centering not around "difference of size, but by other circumstances; the most material of which resulted partly from climate, but principally from the effects of them having or not having slaves."

The Southern delegates were prepared to do verbal battle to preserve slavery—or bolt, despite the fact that only one-fifth of all southern landowners had slaves. The delegations from Georgia and South Carolina, large plantation states, made the threat explicit during the debate on how slaves should be counted. Representation of the states in the new Congress was a key issue at the Convention. The North, afraid the South would outvote it on key issues, argued that since slaves were property, they should not count at all. The South, of course, wanted the slaves to count equally with free men, thereby enlarging their populations and adding to representative power.

The result was the ''three-fifths compromise,'' which was incorporated into Article I, Section 2 of the Constitution:

> *Representatives and direct Taxes shall be apportioned among the several States which may be included within this Union, according to their respective Numbers, which shall be determined by adding to the whole Number of free Persons, including those bound to Service for a Term of Years, and excluding Indians not taxed, three fifths of all persons.*

Similar property questions underlay the debate on the resumption of the slave trade, which had been halted during the War. Although some Northern states wanted to end the trade immediately, they were outvoted; the delegate from South Carolina rising to say his states could never accept a constitution prohibiting slavery in any form. The delegate from Virginia, owning 200 slaves himself, condemned the slave trade and wanted it eliminated; but he was accused of wanting to bolster the price and value of slaves already within his state lines.

Thus, the Pennsylvania Abolition Society, which had provided delegate Benjamin Franklin with a motion to outlaw the slave trade altogether, dropped its intention rather than upset the South further.

Given the heat of the debate and the threat of Southern withdrawal, it is no surprise the delegates passed a motion continuing the slave trade for the present but outlawing it as of 1807. They similarly decided that any runaway be returned to his master, whether he was found in a slave state or free state.

THE PUSH WESTWARD

In the first 100 years of the new Republic, white America delegated the Negro to second and third class status. Those slave who bought their freedom, and there were few enough of them, would find themselves cast with the ''mark of Cain,'' either resented or despised, even where the most ''liberal'' abolitionists congregated.

Though the slave's choices were minimal, there were still choices to be made: he could accept his bondage and adapt; he could escape, or riot. Many historians have noted the apparent relative absence of slave revolts and questioned

The famous ''Underground Railway'' *which was organized by Northerners, runaway slaves, and sympathetic Southerners to clandestinely transport freedom-seeking slaves out of the South to the sanctuary of the North.*

Abràham Lincoln, *who signed the Emancipation Proclamation which freed the slaves in the United States.*

hty seventh.

Abraham Lincoln
the President:
William H. Seward,
Secretary of State.

The signatures of Abraham Lincoln, _and his Secretary of State Seward, affixed to the Emancipation Proclamation._

Popular view _of the respect the freed slaves had for Lincoln in 1862. Although Lincoln had signed the Proclamation earlier, the freeing of the slaves did not become an enforceable law until Congress passed the Thirteenth Amendment._

how that could be. Certainly there were slave rebellions, with men like Nat Turner and Denmark Vesey capable of rounding up dozens of their fellows, escaping from plantations and walking many miles, often killing many whites along the way.

Even the most spectacular of these, however, were poorly organized, quickly quashed and the insurgents put to death. Intermittent rioting by slaves in the Northern cities, in the pre-Revolution days, resulted in the calling of the state militia in some circumstances. And from time to time, rumors that slaves were to be set free would rush through the South, resulting in further uprisings.

But compared with the Black slave rebellions in Haiti and in Latin America, the slave of the South was noticeably quiet. Was it true, as the Southern slaveowner argued, that Blacks were happy under the slave system and felt protected by it? Modern historians researching the period, and the testimony of runaway slaves themselves, suggest that this was hardly the case. Stanley Elkins, in his master work _Slavery,_ compared the attitudes of slaves toward their masters in the South, with those of inmates of German concentration camps during World War II. In both cases, Elkins writes, there was little chance of escape, little chance for life to improve. Thus, the reaction of both slave and inmate was to identify fully with his master.

"In the concentration camp, the result was an almost complete submissiveness on the part of the inmates; in American slavery, the slave became a Sambo, an irresonsible, docile child who accepted the value system and culture of his masters.

Frederick Douglass argued that slaves stayed docile because of the divisive tactics of plantation owners, who calculatedly played off house slaves against laborers and gave out petty rewards of extra holidays or extra food to keep the slaves quiet.

Nevertheless, freedom and rebellion were never far from the slave's mind, Douglass writes. In songs and stories, they identified with the Israelites who were in bondage in Egypt, prayed for a Moses, and included words of escape in even their happiest activities. Others have suggested that rebelliousness and doing poor work were calculated acts by slaves, as substitutes for uprisings.

There was little realistic hope for freedom in the newly-settled area of the West. In 1787, the Northwest Ordinance prohibited slavery or involuntary servitude in that Territory, but provided that runaway slaves would be returned. In 1857, the _Dred Scott_ case clarified the matter: Scott, a slave, was taken by his master to Chicago, a free state, and then to Wisconsin territory and then back to Missouri. Scott sued for his freedom on the grounds he had lived in a free state. The majority of the U.S. Supreme Court found slaves were property and masters could take their slaves anywhere in the territories and retain title. Scott was a rare slave because he suspected he had rights. Most slaves were illiterate and barred by law from getting an education, regardless of how rudimentary.

This photograph, _taken in 1862 by a Union soldier, shows how little life had changed for the freed slaves, who became endentured servants on plantations where they formerly had been slaves._

George Washington Carver, *eminent American scientist, and founder of the first institution of higher learning for black Americans, as he appeared in 1939.*

The rise of the Ku Klux Klan *following the Civil War was an ominous obstacle in the newly-freed slaves' move to equality. This photograph, taken at a 1924 Klan rally outside Los Angeles, shows a swearing in ceremony for new members.*

Though slavery was prohibited in all the Northern states soon after the Revolution, Negroes who hoped to escape discrimination were bound to be disappointed. "Between the . . . classes there are lines of demarcation drawn wide, distinct and not to be violated with impunity," wrote Samuel Jones of Pittsburgh in 1826. Along the frontier, new white settlers hungered for signs of civilization and enjoyed looking down on Negroes.

Nevertheless, the yearning for freedom was strong, and slaves did run from the South. In fact, for 200 years, Negroes have been leaving the South for the North; the wave of migration has never ceased. Though forbidden by law to leave the plantation, and knowing they risked capture and certain return throughout their precarious journey, thousands of slaves made their escape. Once in the North, some of them would journey back but this time as part of the Underground Railroad, which began in 1804 to bring other slaves to freedom. The Railroad's truly active period began in the 1830's, when it was a well-oiled network of people—Southern, Northern, free Black and white—who were willing to hide out Negro slaves.

The Black populations of cities west and north ballooned with runaways, and the North was soon the scene of racial violence. In Philadelphia in 1819, three white women stoned a Negro woman to death. When a leading abolitionist sought to resettle a group of freed slaves in Ohio, the German settlers there voiced opposition and forced them to move on. In 1830, a mob drove eight Negroes out of Portsmouth, Ohio; New York City and two others in New York State saw rioting in 1834 and 1839. "They are not slaves indeed, but they are pariahs, debarred from every fellowship save their own despised race," wrote one Northern observer.

Still the migration could not be stopped; between 1830 and 1860, for example, Michigan's Negro population jumped from 2,500 to 6,700. Once in the cities, however, the free Negroes enjoyed the right to organize for their rights and soon started abolitionist societies.

Frederick Douglass, for example, who had been taught to read by his former owner, spoke at a continuing series of abolitionist conventions and started his own newspaper, *North Star*. In their attempts to end slavery, free Negroes were aided by white abolitionist societies which had formed after the Revolution but had their peak activity during the 1830's. This group of abolitionists, however, parted company with the free Negro when it became apparent the white answer to slavery was to ship the Negro back to Africa. The American Colonization Society, founded in 1817, actually started a colony of 1,420 American Negroes in Liberia. Colonization, the society argued, was the "solution" to the race problem, since it was doubted the two peoples could ever live together in harmony.

Colonization, however, appealed to the Southern plantation owner as well as the Northern "do gooder." To the plantation owner, a colony of freed slaves was as good a place as any to deposit "troublemakers." By 1832, more than a dozen legislatures had given official approval to the Society, many of them in the slave states.

Most Negroes however, had no desire to go to Africa and repudiated the colonization aims. As one free Negro wrote to an abolitionist newspaper:

"I would ask some of our pretended white friends and the members of the American Colonization Society, why they are so interested in our behalf as to want us to go to Africa? . . . Will some of those guardian angels of the people of color tell me how it is that we, who were born of the same city or state with themselves, can live any longer in Africa than they? I

consider it a most absurd assertion that any man of common sense could make . . . we consider the United States our home, and not Africa as they wish to make us believe; and if we do emigrate, it will be to a place of our own choice.

Three thousand free Negroes took to the streets of Philadelphia in 1817, protesting colonization, and their leaders denounced the white abolitionists of the Society as "arrant hypocrites" who were the "Negro's worst enemies." Yet the division in the abolitionist community played right into the hands of the slave society. Even as the free Negroes were organizing, conditions in the slave South were worsening.

In 1790, the cotton gin was invented by Eli Whitney, a remarkable invention in terms of cotton production which consequently created an unceasing demand for slave labor and new land to cultivate. Cotton was quickly becoming the number one cash crop in the nation, a major export item. Although the slave trade with Africa was to have ceased in 1807, by law passed at the Constitutional Convention, the black market import of thousands of slaves continued at least until 1858. The newly-annexed territory of Texas was port of entry for the new cotton states of Florida and Louisiana. An internal slave trade among the states was thriving as well, with young black women sold for high prices and plantation owners boasting of their "slave production."

In the years leading to the Civil War in 1861, the sectional differences between North and South, apparent even at the beginnings of the new nation, became most vivid. While the South expanded agriculturally, becoming more dependent on slavery, the North was increasingly industrialized, and in need of free labor.

Historians today suggest that the North seized upon the issue of slavery as a focus for long-simmering sectional rivalries. After all, the North was actually no more convinced of the inherent equality of the Negro in 1860 than it was in 1776. Thus, slavery is seen as a moral justification for a war stemming out of rivalries between industrialism and agrarianism, the city and the farm, the needs of the west for new

"Amos and Andy" *one of the most popular radio shows in America during the Forties, was a white man's version of life among the blacks. Amos and Andy were in fact played by white men, Freeman Gosden and Charles Correll, and their characterizations soon became stereotypes of black behavior for millions of white Americans.*

Field workers *picking cotton in 1942. Despite nearly one hundred years of freedom, the blacks in the South continued to work in much the same manner as their grandparents had done as slaves.*

roads and the north for new shipping ports, between the cotton and grain states for new markets.

These antagonisms between North and South were whipped into flame by the abolitionists, actually a thorn in the sides of both sections. The abolitionists atempted to convince the North that the South was a land of planters ''living in great white-pillared mansions, drinking intemperately and consorting with female slaves.'' These plantation owners formed a ''slaveocracy'' in conspiracy to develop and protect cotton markets at the expense of northern grain.

When abolitionists dropped their endorsement of colonizing they inspired dread in the hearts of Southerners as well, who envisioned their slaves walking out on them and the cotton kingdom crumbling. Southerners soon envisioned all Northerners as abolitionists.

One of the first black leaders *to gain a national reputation was the evangelist ''Father Divine''. Although generally dismissed as a religious charlatan by most whites, Father Divine's evangelistic crusades did raise money which helped provide work and food for Blacks during the Depression.*

Those Southern whites who were against slavery moved North in great numbers depriving the South of any real debate on the issue. With its strong commitment to slavery and the need for new slave states in the Union, the South stopped apologizing for slavery and started defending it. Rumors of secession started to spread.

Hatred of the abolitionists was already at a fever pitch at the time of John Brown's raid on Harper's Ferry, Virginia, in 1859. Brown was an active abolitionist who had taken part in anti-slavery action in Kansas and participated in the Underground Railroad. In 1859, seeking a more dramatic action to free slaves, he and 50 others seized the Federal arsenal at Harper's Ferry, in hopes of securing ammunition. Federal and state authorities were on immediate alert. Many of Brown's men were killed and Brown was taken captive. ''The effect of this raid on the South was electrifying,'' wrote John Hope Franklin. ''It made slaveholders think that the abolitionists would stop at nothing to wipe out slavery . . . The whole South was put on a semi-war footing, with troops drilling regularly as far south as Georgia . . .''

Brown's raid and subsequent hanging, along with the election of Abraham Lincoln in 1860, are regarded by some as the key acts leading to the Civil War. By the time of Lincoln's election, seven states had already seceded. Lincoln had a clear record against slavery, saying it was hostile to the poor man. In his election race for Senate in 1858, Lincoln had issued his famous ''House Divided'' speech on slavery.

A house divided against itself cannot stand. I believe this nation cannot endure, permanently half slave and half free.

I do not expect the Union to be dissolved—I do not expect it to fall—but I do expect it will cease to be divided.

It will become all one thing, or all the other. Either the opponents of slavery will arrest the further spread of it, and place it where the public mind shall rest in the belief that it is the course of ultimate extinction, or its advocates will push it forward, till it shall become alike lawful in all the states, old as well as new—North as well as South.

Even for his own Civil War period, Lincoln was no radical regarding the rights of Negroes. At best he was an enlightened Republican politician: hating slavery, concerned about property rights, and wondering how in the world the Negro will ever fit into white America. He was certainly not an extreme abolitionist like Charles Sumner, who advocated the truly liberal ''equal rights for all.'' Even as Lincoln was ruminating over the Emancipation Proclamation, he still wanted to compensate the slaveholders for turning their property free. And up to the last, he hoped Negroes might go back to Africa and sincerely hoped a colony might be formed in Liberia.

But he was also realistic. He saw the war drag on; he knew the North could use the military power of the Southern slaves once freed, and he realized there was no chance now for a colony in Liberia. With the nation torn in two and chaos reigning, compensation was impossible.

Still, if he were going to emancipate the slaves, he wanted to do so legally, within the framework of the Constitution. He had no support at all for emancipation within the Congress. His own advisors told him not to do it. Nevertheless, feeling in his heart that slavery must end, Lincoln seized upon the Northern military victory at Antietam, and under his powers as Commander-in-Chief, issued the Emancipation Proclamation as a necessary war measure to quell the Southern rebellion. As of January 1, 1863, the slaves would be free.

The document, long awaited by Negroes and abolitionist whites, was received with tremendous excitement and celebration. The day of the speech, large crowds gathered in a

Members of the 101st Airborne Division *with fixed bayonets were called in to prevent racial confrontations when the Little Rock, Arkansas high school was ordered to desegrate in 1957.*

The face of the white student *in the background characterizes the feelings of many Little Rock, Arkansas citizens when the federal government ordered the desegregation of the city's largest high school. The desegregation of the school was the beginning of the modern civil rights for blacks movement in America.*

vigil, awaiting word that it had finally been delivered.

"The general reaction in the North was unfavorable," writes John Hope Franklin. "Many whites felt that the war was no longer to save the Union but to free the Negro, and some soldiers resigned rather than participate in such a struggle . . . The real reaction was seen at the November elections. Although the Republicans maintained a majority in Congress, the Democrats won in many Northern communities and gained substantially in both House and Senate."

If the newly-freed Negroes were elated at the Emancipation and the war's final victory for their cause, that excitement was short-lived. Reconstruction—rebuilding the war-ravaged South—proved to be a bitter process in which the Negro was to be the scapegoat.

There were 4.9 million Negroes in the United States in 1870, 3.8 million of them in what had been the Confederacy. The freed men were in dire need of jobs, of land, and of laws to ensure their rights, and the chief question was how far the victorious North would go in meeting these needs.

For 100 years historians have debated how the situation might have been different if Lincoln had lived. But with Lincoln's assassination in 1865, the black Americans lost a political ally, someone who had deeply considered their plight, and with him a chance for meaningful governmental assistance.

President Andrew Johnson, though pledging to take up where Lincoln had left off, obviously was more concerned with healing the nation than with securing the rights of newly-freed slaves. He vetoed a Civil Rights bill, declaring Negroes were not yet ready for the privileges and equality of citizenship. He vetoed continued aid to the slaves—refusing to make the Freedmen's Bureau refugee organizing permanent—on the grounds it would do more for Blacks than had ever been done for Whites. He gave no leadership to the abolitionist program of turning over confiscated plantation land to the Negroes and without such leadership the plan never crystallized.

Initially there was Congressional action despite Johnson. The veto of the Civil Rights bill was overridden. The 14th and 15th Amendments, defining citizenship and prohibiting disenfranchisement on the grounds of race, became law. And while Northern troops remained in the South, a modicum of peace was restored.

With the help of Northern industrialists and Republican politicians who came South, blacks were initially successful in forming state political organizations. Before 1900, 17

This one room school house *near Madison, Maryland, was typical of the kind of schooling facilities blacks had open to them prior to the Supreme Court decision to desegregate public schools.*

Negroes served in both Houses of Congress and two served in the Senate. Strides were made in education as well: the Freedmen's Bureaus opened schools and colleges, among them Fisk University in Tennessee and Howard University in Washington.

These successes were minimal, however, compared with the disastrous economic impact of emancipation and the end of the war. When the Northern whites left the South without securing the Negroes an economic base, the Negro was left to poverty, and in most cases dependence upon his former master. Reconstruction was a dismal failure from the Black perspective. By 1871, the law disenfranchising most of the Confederate population had been repealed and general amnesty proclaimed. Thus, the Southern whites were soon back in power. Even before the troops had left, however, the old leadership was beginning to mobilize against what it saw as "Negro domination." The Ku Klux Klan and other white "fraternal" organizations were taking extralegal action against "uppity" Negroes, with lynchings and mob violence occurring sporadically.

Once the Southern Democrats were back in power, the real torture for Blacks began. Throughout the South, Black Codes were enacted, restricting the rights of freedmen to travel, to rent houses in "white districts," and to hold meetings. Negroes would have to post bond in order to work, and have work permits signed by their bosses.

Thus began the "Strange Career of Jim Crow," so labeled by historian C. Vann Woodward, the system of racial apartheid which lasted until the late 1950's and which became more onerous and more confining as the years went on. It was becoming difficult to say which was worse: the degradation of the plantation slave system, or the ostracism and humiliation of the post Civil War South. The antebellum South, Woodward says, at its worst at least recognized the interdependence of the races to make the plantation work.

Despite passage of the 15th Amendment, the Southern Democrats soon effectively disenfranchised the Negro population through a series of voting tests which most Negroes certainly could not pass: a literacy test, a poll tax demanding payment for the exercise of the franchise, and the requirement that proof be offered that one's ancestors had the right to vote. Separate voting booths for Blacks and Whites were required for those who could pass scrutiny, and then Negroes were rarely told the correct time and place of elections.

Such segregation laws were eventually approved by the U.S. Supreme Court in cases such as *Plessy V. Ferguson* which said "separate but equal" facilities were constitutional. As life in the "Deep South" took its depressing turn, Negroes again fled for the cities of the North and West.

And once again violence flared. New York City had a race riot in 1900, Springfield, Illinois, had one in 1908. "White supremacy" was once again supported by "scientific evidence" and anti-Negro "conventions" once again were well attended. Vaudeville shows featured whites dressed in black face.

BOOKER T. WASHINGTON
(1858-1915)

How was the Negro population to react to such racial hostility? With the memories of slavery still fresh and the excitement of freedom still shining, five million black persons waited for leadership.

Into the power vacuum stepped Booker T. Washington, certainly one of the most powerful Negro leaders in American history. Washington, born a slave, had become leader of the newly-formed Afro-American League, headed a huge political and economic empire based in Tuskegee, Alabama. He based his power on millions of dollars of foundation grants to Negro schools. Washington counseled exactly what white America wanted to hear: that the Negro should wait for full equality; that he should show by perseverance and hard work, through learning a job and doing it well, that he deserves full rights and responsibilities of citizenship. As a reward for his message of accommodation, Washington was sought out by presidents—he lunched with Theodore Roosevelt in the White House—governors, political leaders throughout the country.

Washington was the man to see about political appointments and the receipt of grants from white captains of industry. Tuskegee Institute became a true intellectual and scientific mecca for outstanding Blacks and was soon accepted by Southern whites as well. Washington's power was formidable and most of the black population idolized him.

However, a growing rank of black activists realized that in a sense, Washington had sold their rights down the river. Washington counseled them to accept the loss of voting

Smoke fills the bus *carrying "Freedom Riders" testing the segregation of bus stations in the South in 1961. The "Freedom Riders" were one of the first organized groups to begin demonstrating for equality for Blacks in the Sixties.*

Whites surround a bus *near Anniston, Alabama, to prevent it from leaving the local bus station carrying "Freedom Riders." Moments after this picture was taken the white demonstrators set fire to the bus, but there were no injuries to the Freedom Riders inside.*

rights and equal accommodations on street cars, something these activists said cost the Negroes their self respect even more than their freedom.

W. E. B. DuBOIS
(1868-1963)

W. E. B. DuBois had never known slavery, and consequently could never understand Washington's acceptance of second-class status. DuBois, the first Black to receive a Ph.D. from Harvard University, was a brilliant intellectual and the philsophical son of Frederick Douglass in his demand that the Negro be accepted equally as a member of society.

In 1905, DuBois started the Niagara Movement which eventually became the National Association for the Advancement of Colored Peoples (NAACP), at the time regarded as a "radical" organization.

We refuse to allow the impression to remain that the Negro-American assents to inferiority, is submissive under oppression and apologetic before insults. Through helplessness we may submit, but the voice of protest of 10 million Americans must never cease to assail the ears of their fellows, so long as America is unjust.

–Principles of the Niagara Movement

The NAACP sought greater police protection for Southern Negroes, crusaded against lynching and lawlessness and generally refused to conform to the ideas of complacency against racism sponsored by Washington. These positions kept the organization poor for decades, and deprived DuBois of the support of white philanthropists. The NAACP had to wait until the 1920's for massive Negro support.

Under the prevailing ideology of Booker T. Washington, living conditions for the Negro population became increasingly poverty-ridden. Once the Negro had "accepted" white supremacy, he had condemned himself to almost 80 years of silence and despair. Certainly people like W. E. B. DuBois' NAACP continued to organize for Negro rights, but waited until World War I ended for a great surge in membership.

The First World War aggravated the yearnings of the Negro for equality, but resulted only in increased frustration. More than 360,000 Negroes entered military service, many seeing action overseas. Just as in the American Revolution,

the Negro population believed the rhetoric of a war being fought to "make the world safe for democracy" and expected that American society would awaken to hypocrisy at home. Such was not the case, however. Twenty-five race riots resulted in the first six months of 1919. "The greatest period of interracial strife the nation had ever witnessed," wrote John Hope Franklin in 1944. Mobs ruled the cities for days, burning and shooting and during the first year following the war more than 70 Negroes were lynched, several of them veterans still in uniform.

The disappointment of the Negro soldier had turned to anger. Wrote DuBois in 1919:

We return from the slavery of uniform which the world's madness demanded us to don to the freedom of civil garb. We stand again to look America squarely in the face and call a spade a spade. We sing: This country of ours, despite all its better souls have done and dreamed, is yet a shameful land.

*It **lynches, it disenfranchises** its own citizens. . . . It encourages **ignorance**. . . . It steals from us . . . It insults us . . .*

*We **return**. We **return from fighting**. We **return fighting**.*

Make way for Democracy! We saved it in France, and by the Great Jehovah, we will save it in the U.S.A., or know the reason why.

The post-war era up until the 1940's saw a massive exodus of Blacks from the South to the Northern urban areas, for the South was enacting a new series of "Jim Crow" laws which showed Blacks they were not wanted. These laws included separate taxi cabs for Blacks and whites, separate water fountains and rest rooms. Atlanta in 1932 prohibited amateur baseball clubs of different races from playing within two blocks of each other.

In 1933 Texas barred "Caucasians" and "Africans" from boxing and wrestling together, and Arkansas in 1937 required segregation at all race tracks and gaming establishments. This post-war period saw the greatest rise in Ku Klux Klan membership.

In 1944, Swedish sociologist Gunnar Myrdal in his landmark book on American race relations wrote, "Segregation is now so complete that the white Southerner practically never sees a Negro except as his servant and in other stan-

A rally *of the National Association for the Advancement of Colored People held in Jackson, Mississippi, in June 1961. The demonstrators were in Jackson to test that city's segregation laws.*

dardized and formalized cast situations.''

Powerless in the South, millions of Negroes moved to the North only to find their living conditions increasingly dreadful. The years between 1920 and 1940saw the rise of the new urban ghetto, in cramped quarters, with exorbitantly high rents. The number of Negroes living outside the South grew in the 1940's from 2.4 million to 4.6 million. The mass exodus after World War I was spurred by the new urban Negro newspapers which encouraged southern Negroes to come North. ''To die from the bite of frost is far more glorious than at the hands of the mob,'' wrote one newspaper in 1917. Most cities, however, were either unwilling or unable to adequately house the huge numbers of migrants.

In 15 years before 1930, Detroit's Negro population jumped from 6,000 to 100,000; New York's grew from 150,000 to 327,000 between 1920-1930.

In 1931, President Herbert Hoover's Committee on Negro Housing urged a desperately needed program of urban renewal, and was virtually ignored. The Committee found throughout the nation the Negroes were living in houses unfit for human habitation.

''Only a small percentage of the houses in the congested Negro districts are provided with baths, either tub or shower . . . In an investigation made by the Board of Public Welfare near Garrison Square (Kansas City, Mo.) only two bathtubs were found in 827 Negro houses.''

Medgar Evers, *Field Secretary for the National Association for the Advancement of Colored People, who was assassinated in 1963. The assassination of Evers touched off demonstrations in several cities.*

Not surprisingly, the cities had high crime rates, poor health conditions and juvenile delinquency. Social workers were called on to help, but of course to no avail.

The New York Urban League reported two years later on its national survey on the ''Effects of Urbanization'':

In Chicago, Negro girls and young women have constituted nearly one-third of females confined in the jails. The Dept. of Correction of New York reported for 1930 that of 59,000 males arraigned in the four courts, 16,391, or about 28 percent, were Negroes—five times as great as the population should warrant. One would think that Negroes are especially fond of going to jail. According to studies made by the National Urban League, unemployment runs all the way from four to six times that of the city as a whole. In juvenile delinquency, crime, disease and the other ills that so vitally affect family life, the story is generally the same. Harlem is referred to in a report of the New York Vice Committee as a place where whites go on a moral vacation.

This 1933 survey found Chicago Negroes paying $20 for a room for which whites had previously paid $4 or $5. In New York, Negroes paid $110 a month for a room whites had paid $55 for. Negroes were found to change apartments once every 15 months while whites moved once in five years.

MARCUS GARVEY
(1887-1940)

In the despair following the First World War, the imagination of the black ghetto was struck by the crusade of a Jamaican printer named Marcus Garvey who founded the Universal Negro Improvement Association. Closely linked philosophically with the beliefs of Booker T. Washington,

The use of police dogs *against civil rights demonstrators was widespread. Here a dog lunges at a demonstrator who offers no resistence to the vicious charge.*

Malcom X, *who became one of the leading spokesmen for the Black Muslim sect. In 1964 Malcolm X left the Black Muslims and formed his own organization, the Muslim Mosque. He was shot and killed while addressing a Black audience in Harlem in 1964.*

Garvey counseled Blacks to start their own businesses, to accept their separate status and feel glorified in the black race. His crusade was initially a financial success—Garvey raised more than $1 million within the Negro community at a time when the NAACP had a $50,000 budget. Garvey was not, however, business oriented. His steamship lines, slated to voyage between New York, the West Indies, and Africa, failed and Garvey served two years in jail for fraud. He had plans to take over the African colonies owned by Germany before World War I but was ignored by the League of Nations. His attempt to colonize Liberia ultimately failed. However, in terms of unifying the black urban populations, and instilling racial pride in those desperately needing it, Garvey was doubtless a success.

During the Great Depression of the 1930's, life changed little for the Negro, except for the fact that he was now no longer alone in his poverty. Millions of Americans were unemployed, on soup lines, in despair. The social policies of President Franklin Delano Roosevelt may not have been aimed directly at the Negro, but he benefited from any social legislation that was enacted: the soup lines fed him along with whites; the WPA gave him a job too. Roosevelt captured the Negro vote, the first major shift away from the Republican Party since the Civil War.

Roosevelt recognized the black population and consulted with its leadership—a major boost for his image—but was slow to enact legislation specifically on its behalf. As a result, Negro leadership organized as never before. A. Philip Randolph, founder and head of the powerful Brotherhood of Sleeping Car Porters and Maids (one of the first successful attempts to unionize Negroes), now organized the militant March on Washington. He demanded that Negro contractors get a bigger share of the lucrative war industry, and threatened to bring 100,000 Negroes to Washington if Roosevelt did not sign the law creating a Fair Employment Practice Committee to supervise these defense contracts. Under such pressure, Roosevelt relented, signing the FEPC into law.

World War II was marked, as were wars preceding it, by the service of Negro soldiers who saw battle as enlisted men and draftees in the major theaters of action. However, these soldiers were increasingly aggravated at segregation in the armed forces and the racial abuse they often suffered. The war proved to be an eye opener for many Blacks: they went to France and reported how well the French treated their own Negro soldiers and came back in despair. Negro leaders implored Roosevelt to end the color line, and expressed shock that the government could maintain such racially biased policies and still call upon black men to fight for there country. Roosevelt did little in response.

A black soldier wrote to the NAACP: ''A new Negro will return from the war—a bitter Negro if he is disappointed again. He will have been taught to kill, to suffer, to die for something he believes in, and he will live by these rules to gain his personal rights.''

In the administration of Harry Truman, the Negro took the

Black frustration *at the slow movement of de-segregation finally erupted in Detroit, Michigan, in 1965. More than 600 Michigan National Guardsmen were called in to assist 600 Detroit policemen in quelling the Detroit riot.*

Black demonstrators *surround a police car during the rioting which broke out in the Los Angeles section called Watts in the summer of 1965. California National Guardsmen were moved in to help put down the rioting and looting.*

A National Guard officer *stands at the ready during the 1967 racial strife which broke out in Detroit. By the time of the second Detroit riot the chant, "Burn, Baby, Burn" had become the characteristic refrain of many Black demonstrators.*

first small steps toward gaining political equality. A combination of factors conspired to push Truman to action: the new militance of the Negro organizations, the promise of A. Philip Randolph that the Negro would not fight again (a new war was already beginning in Korea), and the ideological warfare between the U.S. and the Soviet Union.

There was no question that poverty and deprivation, had made the Communist Party seem attractive to thousands of Blacks. And Truman knew that Federal activity to alleviate their plight would also improve the image of the United States around the world.

Regardless of his political reasoning, Truman doubtless was one of the first U.S. Presidents to make the cause of the Negro an important goal in his political platform. His administration is noteworthy for the following Civil Rights actions:

- Integration of the armed services.
- Integration of Federal employment.

- Appointment of a Civil Rights committee which called for "elimination of segregation, based on race, color creed or national origins."
- Enactment of a Fair Employment Practice law.
- Advocacy of an end to segregation in interstate transportation.
- Advocacy of anti-poll tax and anti-lynching laws.
- Advocacy of a fair election law.

Many of Truman's recommendations remained exactly that, in fact only the military service integration was fully successful. Yet his leadership as President helped in some perhaps small ways to prepare the way for the major Civil Rights legislation of the 1960's.

Truman's policies seem like activism indeed compared with the silence on racial issues of Dwight D. Eisenhower

A Black demonstrator *gives a National Guardsman a thumbs down sign during the rioting which occurred in Newark, New Jersey in the summer of 1967.*

The Black movement *moved into the larger arena of anti-war demonstrating in 1968. Here a Black leader uses a bull horn to arouse a crowd during a mass rally in front of the San Francisco City Hall.*

who followed Truman to the White House. "I don't believe you can change the hearts of men with laws or decisions," Eisenhower said.

While the Presidency and the Congress sleep-walked through the last eight years of the 1950's, the cause of Civil Rights was taken up in truly grand manner by the U.S. Supreme Court. The Court, under Chief Justice Earl Warren (appointed by Eisenhower who was surprised at the results) sought to undo in a decade almost 200 years of disservice and degradation suffered by black Americans. Beginning in 1954 with the landmark *Brown v. Board of Education*, the Warren court asserted that "separate but equal" facilities were not constitutional. "In the field of public education the doctrine of 'separate but equal' has no place. Separate educational facilities are inherently unequal," Chief Justice Warren wrote.

The *Brown* case sent shock waves through the South and unleashed a new series of violent actions against Negroes by segregationists who quickly formed White Citizens' Councils to defend their views. Lynchings, mob violence, and bombings were once again a fact of Southern life. Once again "scientific" explanations, offered by men with scholarly credentials, were used to support the views of those who feared their world would end if children of different races sat side by side in school.

This time, however, the Negro was not silent. Negroes did not accept white Southern attempts to bar children from schools by violence. They responded in record numbers by organizing for political strength.

MARTIN LUTHER KING, JR.
(1929-1968)

The Rev. Dr. Martin Luther King, Jr. became Baptist minister in Montgomery, Alabama, in1954, the year of the *Brown* decision. In the atmosphere of violence which surrounded his church, King preached non-violence, but also non-acceptance. King's non-violent activities began simply with a bus boycott in Montgomery, thousands of Negroes protesting segregation. The boycott led to the founding of the Southern Christian Leadership Conference and the Student Non-Violent Coordinating Committee which for the next decade dramatically focussed the attention of white America on the suffering of black people in the South. King was inspired by the non-violence of the Indian leader Mahatma Ghandi.

Dr. Martin Luther King *on the night of his final public appearance. King was in Memphis, Tennessee, to address a rally of city sanitation workers when he was assassinated by James Earl Ray. The assassination occurred the day after this picture was taken.*

By 1968 the civil rights *campaigns had embraced the larger issue of poverty in America. Here the Reverend Ralph Abernathy leads a mule drawn wagon at the head of a Poor People's Campaign near Edwards, Mississippi.*

His method of protest was to challenge onerous laws in a non-violent manner, fully expecting violence in return. He staged sit-ins at segregated lunch counters and similar public facilities, calling huge crowds of Negroes together in violation of public meeting and riot ordinances. He spent many days in jail as a result of his activities.

His speeches were like sermons, full of biblical images and identification of the Negro with the slaves in Egypt. And he could move audiences—white and black—to see the validity of his own dream of freedom for his people. In 1960, when King was sent to jail without bail after a staged boycott, President John F. Kennedy personally intervened and had him freed.

In April, 1963, a series of demonstrations resulted in the jailing of 3,300 Negroes and that same year King made good A. Philip Randolph's threat of the 1940's and brought 200,000 people of both races to a March on Washington. He went North to protest housing discrimination and South for a series of voter registration drives. And for all his efforts, he received the Nobel Peace Prize of 1964.

The summer of 1964 saw several thousand Northern college students journeying to the South to sign up Blacks who had just been made eligible to vote by the Civil Rights Act of 1964. Three of them were kidnapped and murdered by white vigilantes, part of the continuing series of violent acts against Civil Rights workers by White Citizens Councils and the Klan.

Nevertheless, by the time King was assassinated in April, 1968, during a labor protest march, a major split in the Civil Rights movement had already occurred. King's non-violent tactics seemed cast in the mold of Booker T. Washington compared to the Du Bois-like anger of a growing number of Blacks, who thought the world was not changing fast enough.

Huey Newton, Eldridge Cleaver, the Black Muslim sect and its leader Malcolm X now repudiated the aid of white Northern ''liberals'' and counseled the ''brotherhood'' of

The Reverend Ralph Abernathy, *who succeeded Dr. Martin Luther King as head of the Southern Christian Leadership Conference after King's assassination in 1968.*

Blacks throughout the world. A black "revolution"—a violent one if need be—was necessary, they said, to open the eyes of America to the needs of its minority people.

No I'm not an American. I'm one of the 22 million black people who are the victims of Americanism. One of the 22 million black people who are the victims of democracy, nothing but disguised hypocrisy. So I'm not standing here speaking to you as an American, or a patriot, or a flag-saluter, or a flag-waver—no, not I. I'm speaking as a victim of this American system. And I see America through the eye of the victim. I don't see any American dream; I see an American nightmare.
—*Malcolm X*

Once again the black community was split, and there was talk once again of going back to Africa. Basketball star Lew Alcindor became Kareem Abdul Jabar as increasing numbers of Blacks changed their names and joined the Black Muslim movements in honor of their African heritage. "Black is beautiful" and "Black Power" were slogans of the day.

And for those white American still asleep to the frustrations of the black populations, the urban ghettos exploded in violence. Watts, Detroit, and Newark, were just a few of the cities burned during the "long hot summers" of the 1960's.

The Reverend Jesse Jackson *who rose to prominence as head of the Operation Breadbasket program of the SCLC. Later, Jackson, shown here in 1972, formed his own organization, People United to Save Humanity.*

Blacks ironically set fire to property in their own community as if to demonstrate how little they actually had.

In the end, it probably took the combined action of King and his critics to get legislation which finally created statutes guaranteeing Negro rights.

The bombing of a Baptist church in Birmingham by white vigilantes, killing four young Negro girls, led eventually to the Civil Rights Act of 1964. Originally proposed by Kennedy, a host of bills were forced through Congress by President Lyndon Johnson after Kennedy's assassination. The 1964 Act prohibited different voting standards for Blacks and whites, barred discrimination in public accommodations and public facilities and barred Federal aid to any program which practiced racial discrimination.

Today is a triumph for freedom as huge as any victory that's ever been won on any battlefield.

Yet to seize the meaning of this day we must recall darker times.

Three and a half centuries ago the first Negroes arrived at Jamestown. They did not arrive in brave ships in search of a home for freedom. They did not mingle fear and joy in expectation that in this new world anything would be possible to a man strong enough to reach for it.

They came in darkness and they came in chains. And today we strike away the last major shackle of those fierce and ancient bonds.

Today the Negro story and the American story fuse and blend. And let us remember that it was not always so. The stories of our nation and of the American Negro are like two great rivers. Welling up from that tiny Jamestown spring, they flow through the centuries along divided channels.

When pioneers subdued a continent to the need of man they did not tame it for the Negro. When the Liberty Bell rang out in Philadelphia it did not toll for the Negro. When Andrew Jackson threw open the doors of democracy they did not open for the Negro. It was only at Appomattox a century ago that an American victory was also a Negro victory. And the two rivers, one shining with promise, the other dark-stained with oppression, began to move toward one another.

Yet for almost a century the promise of that day was not fulfilled.

Today is a towering and certain mark that in this generation that promise will be kept. In our time the two currents will finally mingle and rush as one great stream across the uncertain and the marvelous years of the America that is yet to come.
—*Pres. Lyndon B. Johnson's speech on signing the Voting Rights Act, August 6, 1965*

Similarly, violence by Southern law enforcement officials against hundreds of non-violent protesters—in the full view of the nation's television cameras—finally resulted in the Voting Rights Act of 1965, prohibiting literacy tests and all other devices as qualification for election in the Southern states.

And thanks to the encouragement of the black "separatists" black parents demanded and received greater control of their schools in the Northern ghettos—focussing attention on racial injustices in an area used to pointing its finger at the South. Universities were forced through sit-ins and campus violence to include "black studies courses" featuring the legacy of Africa and "black culture"—areas of study previously missing from curricula. In the private and public sector "affimative action" programs were ordered to get Blacks into jobs previously barred to them.

Out of this period came a new black pride, a sense of contribution made by Blacks in the past and in the future. At the time of his death, Martin Luther King, Jr. had become a

forceful opponent of the war in Vietnam, asserting too many Blacks were being sent to fight a white man's war.

The economic condition of the Blacks in America changed slowly. While unemployment and drug addiction continued to be more prevalent in black areas than in white, there were also signs of progress. Many major baseball, basketball and football superstars were black, commanding contracts equal to or surpassing their white contemporaries. In politics, Blacks maintained constituencies based largely on the issues rather than on color. Mayor Tom Bradley of Los Angeles, for example, was elected with a sizeable vote from the white suburban middle class of the nation's second largest city. In the 1972 presidential campaign, Gov. George Wallace tried hard not to mention that he first came to public attention as a segregationist—physically blocking the door of the University of Alabama so in 1963 the first Blacks could not enter.

Yet the first half of the 1970's seemed in many respects to mirror the Eisenhower years of the 1950's. President Gerald R. Ford seemed to share Eisenhower's view that legislation cannot change men's hearts, and he therefore did nothing to stem the racial violence in Boston between whites and blacks over busing of school children to achieve racial integration. His predecessor, Richard M. Nixon, apparently shared the opinion of his Vice President, Spiro Agnew, when Agnew suggested, "If you've seen one ghetto you've seen them all."

Nixon made severe financial cutbacks in the Federal "War on Poverty" programs begun by Lyndon B. Johnson and had few ties with the black community. The U.S. Supreme Court—packed with conservative members appointed by Nixon—seemed determined to undercut all the progress of the Warren years. Also during the 1970's, whites increasingly fled the urban centers for the suburbs, leaving poor Blacks to the ghettos. Because the ghettos were relatively free of rioting, some commentators assumed that life had improved, though the rate of incidental violence continued to rise.

The nation's racial problems still were far from solved. Life in the ghettos still sounded much like it did in 1930—overcrowded with frustrated people who lack hope. If there were more middle class Blacks, more educated Blacks, and more laws to protect their rights, there was also rampant unemployment affecting Blacks in greater numbers than whites and an unwillingness of the Federal government to take leadership. In the year of the Bicentennial, the nation still faced the question of when—or whether—the Negro would become an equal participant in the mainstream of American life.

Roy Wilkins, *longtime head of the National Association for the Advancement of Colored People.*

Angela Davis, *who rose to national attention when she was denied a full time teaching position in a university because of her political views. Davis, an admitted member of the communist party, turned her firing from the academic position into a movement for racial equality. Later she was indicted on a murder-conspiracy charge in California. Here she is shown at a press conference following the all-white jury's innocent verdict in the murder-conspiracy charge.*

Los Angeles Times

Brown Casts Aside Usual Yardsticks

Unorthodox Approach Makes It Difficult to Measure Record

BY TOM GOFF

SACRAMENTO—Jerry Brown, who wants to be President after 15 months as governor of California, shows himself more clearly each day to be a very bright and very ambitious young politician with a formula calculated to take him to the top.

He makes it difficult, to be sure, for those who would measure his record against the traditional yardsticks.

He marches to a different beat. He does not fit yesterday's mold—or maybe even today's. He surrounds himself with a transcendental mystique that seduces the unwary and titillates even the most calloused.

But when the bottom line is reached, the name of the game is politics and the master player, he hopes, is Jerry Brown.

The scale against which Brown, himself, would measure the success of his Administration is as alien to most people associated with government as the new math introduced into the schools a few years ago was to the typical middle-aged parent.

Government traditionalists of all political persuasions expect Brown to do things, to propose things, to offer positive solutions to the problems of the time.

They want to measure him as they did his predecessor, Ronald Reagan,

An Analysis

against the success of a welfare reform or the failure of a tax-limitation plan.

Brown refuses to oblige them. He considers "six-point programs," legislative "laundry lists" and "blue ribbon commissions" out of date.

Such things promise more than they can produce, Brown says, and, in any event, he is not convinced that a governor—or a President—can change the course of government—except in extraordinary circumstances—more than slightly in the direction he wants to see it move.

So Brown, to date and with only a few exceptions, has resisted these traditional leadership approaches. He prefers to talk, to philosophize, to ask questions.

Questions rather than answers have become a Brown trademark. They are the major weapon in his arsenal. And he insists his constant and repetitious probing is vital, particularly if it exposes an inconsistency or casts light on an exaggerated government promise.

At least a couple of examples stand out. One represents a win for Brown; the other a loss.

Brown determined early in his administration that the state office of Criminal Justice Planning, with a staff of well over 200 civil servants might be a waste of money.

His questioning of the program convinced him he was right. He succeeded in just about quartering the staff with no loss of effectiveness insofar as its funneling of federal funds to local government was concerned.

Brown also cast a wary eye on the California Commission for Economic Development, a program under the

Please Turn to Page 3, Col. 2

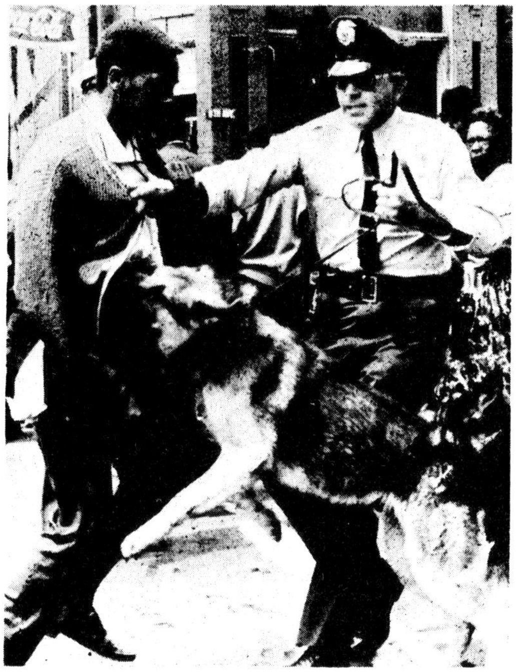

Civil rights protests, inspired by Martin Luther King, took place in many cities, North and South, in 1963, and often led to violence. In the photograph above, police dogs are being used against black demonstrators in Birmingham, Alabama.

L.A. Warned It Faces Serious Fiscal Future

Mayor's Panel Calls for Action Now to Deal With Situation

BY JOHN F. LAWRENCE

The city of Los Angeles faces a serious financial situation that will be nearly impossible to deal with unless solutions are found promptly, a study committee appointed by the mayor concluded in a report released Thursday.

"Los Angeles is not on the verge of a New York-type fiscal catastrophe, but mounting problems of the inner city and the growing disparity between expenditures and revenues clearly demonstrate severe financial problems ahead," the study group stated.

"It is a matter of semantics to debate whether we are in a crisis or there is one immediately ahead," it added. "The plain truth is that the forthcoming years will bring a fiscal crunch much tighter than any in the past decade or two . . ."

The study was conducted by the Ad Hoc Committee on City Finances, set up by Mayor Bradley last fall in the wake of the New York City crisis. Its members are leading Los Angeles business and professional figures.

The committee's conclusions generally reinforce warnings which have been coming from the mayor and other local leaders for some time. Similarly, the committee's prescription for dealing with the budget squeeze pulls together a number of proposals made in the past.

Some of those proposals have received a cool reception before and probably will be so received again. The most controversial of the committee's recommendations, for example, were directed at improving productivity of city workers and eliminating the city Charter requirement that workers receive a prevailing wage—a wage in keeping with gen-

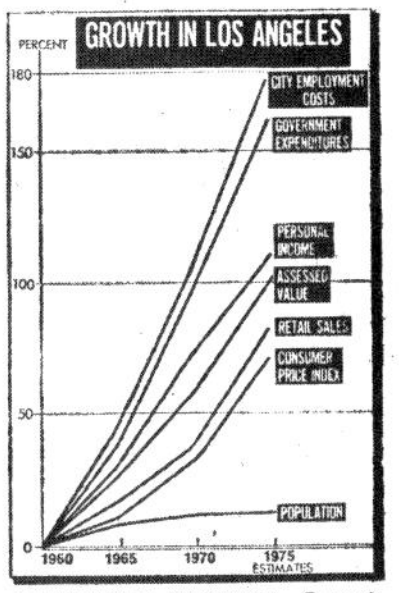

MOUNTING PROBLEM—Growth in cost of L.A. city government as contrasted to increase in population, business in city.

eral industry and government standards in the community.

Ricardo F. Icaza, secretary-treasurer of Retail Clerks Union Local 770 and the lone labor representative on the committee, did not endorse these two recommendations.

Asked about the prevailing wage proposal at a press conference Thursday, Mayor Bradley argued that with the onset of more formal collective bargaining between the city and its employes the prevailing wage requirement becomes a floor from which negotiations move upward. He argued that either collective bargaining or a prevailing wage system should be used, not both. Prevailing wages obviously would continue to be a central consideration in the bargaining.

The mayor conceded, however, that only one member of the City Council supports putting a Charter amendment to make this change on the ballot.

Steps to improve productivity, the mayor observed, require "joint nego-

Please Turn to Page 27, Col. 1

Winds Up to 80 M.P.H. Hit Area; Air Crash Kills 6

BY MICHAEL SEILER

Snow, hail, rain and winds gusting up to 80 m.p.h. struck the Southland Thursday, dropping the visibility to near zero in some desert areas and churning up turbulence that apparently caused a plane crash that killed six persons.

The twin-engine commuter plane plunged into the San Jacinto Mountains 16 miles south of Palm Desert, killing the commuter line's pilot, copilot and four passengers.

Federal Aviation Administration investigators said the plane was battered by high winds just before it crashed into 3,200-foot hills less than a quarter of a mile from California 74.

The aircraft, bound from San Diego to Palm Springs, was operated by Sun Aire Line, headquartered at Borrego Springs in San Diego County.

Killed were the pilot, Larry Bossler, the copilot, Dennis Card, and four passengers: Paul McNalley, 5, and James Cottingham, 16, of San Diego, and John R. Janney and Michael Mohr, about 22, of Palm Springs.

Wind-driven snow began to pile up in the mountains, with Big Bear reporting winds of 40 m.p.h. In the desert, gusts up to 80 m.p.h. hit the Goldstone Tracking Station near Barstow.

Observers said wind-driven rain in Barstow appeared to be almost horizontal at times. The California Highway Patrol reported overturned campers on Interstate 40 and Interstate 15 with near zero visibility near Baker.

More than 6,000 minor power outages were reported in the Los Angeles area.

The unstable weather was caused by a cold front moving down the coast and a deep low pressure system over Nevada. They were expected to move out of the area today, leaving Los Angeles under clearer but still windy skies.

Please Turn to Page 31, Col. 1

ing that a particular justice continues to sit and vote on the merits.

"I have never known of a lawyer to withdraw for that purpose," said Michael Rodak, clerk of the court. "Occasionally there's a last-minute switch because the lawyer has become ill or had a falling-out with the client. But this idea of withdrawing so that a justice won't have to is a new one on me."

The recommendation that the firm step aside came from University of Chicago law professor Philip B. Kurland, who was retained as the Pasadena board's counsel last year after a nationwide search for a constitutional law scholar to direct the high court appeal. Kurland works as a part-time consultant for the Chicago firm and brought it into the case.

In a special meeting last month, the Pasadena board accepted Kurland's recommendation and dismissed both him and the Rothschild firm as lawyers of record. At Kurland's urging, the board replaced him with former University of Chicago law dean Phil C. Neal, another expert on the Constitution.

Dies in Glendale

Fiery Political Orator Was Damned, Revered

BY TED THACKREY JR.

Gerald L.K. Smith, the fiery orator denounced by many as a hate-mongering bigot—and revered by others as a Christian patriot—died Thursday in Glendale.

A spokesman for Glendale Community Hospital said Smith, 78, was admitted there on Monday for treatment of pneumonia. He said Smith died due to complications at 5:30 p.m. Thursday.

Interment will be at Eureka Springs, Ark., where a crypt has been prepared.

Smith, who once called Franklin D. Roosevelt a "cat's-paw of the Jew bankers," while boosting Louisiana Gov. Huey (Kingfish) Long's presidential candidacy, had been the storm center of controversy for more than half a century.

Gerald Lyman Kenneth Smith was the descendant of four generations of circuit-riding "hellfire and brimstone" preachers, born in Pardeeville, Wis., and reared on a diet of Bible fundamentalism and hard work.

Facts concerning his education are few and tend to fluctuate; he described himself at times as a graduate of Valparaiso University and Butler College, both in Indiana.

Regardless, it was a seemingly inborn talent for pulpit oratory, first developed in his apprenticeships at

Please Turn to Page 18, Col. 1

onstrations amid police fears that the student unrest could lead to a repetition of the May, 1968, uprising that nearly caused a government overthrow. But violence so far has been limited.

The demonstrations climaxed weeks of student restiveness that had already developed into a strike now paralyzing the French university system. Virtually all the country's 75 universities are affected to some degree.

The Paris clash apparently started when police refused to let demonstrators leave the prescribed march route along the Left Bank of the Seine. Student marshals waded into the fight to try to control their own people.

The two-mile march moved on at a swift pace toward the Education Ministry, with loudspeaker vans blaring, "Keep the bosses off the campus," and students chanting, "No to university factories."

The major left-wing student union which organized the protest claims the government reforms will give industry an undue voice in running university affairs.

Miss Hearst Also Victim of Malnutrition, Doctor Says

BY JERRY BELCHER

REDWOOD CITY —Patricia Hearst, recuperating well from a collapsed right lung, also is suffering from malnutrition, according to the staff doctor who has been treating her at Sequoia Hospital here.

In addition, Dr. Donald Rowles reported that chest X rays made Thursday morning showed a dollar-sized, air-filled "bleb" or blister at the top of her right lung.

He said it was a rupture of the bleb which caused the collapse of the lung Tuesday evening requiring insertion of a chest tube into the right plural cavity to reexpand the lung.

Rowles, a chest surgeon, said if the bleb should rupture again, another tube would have to be inserted or Miss Hearst might have to undergo surgery.

However, according to Rowles, the 22-year-old newspaper heiress was in improving" and ate a hearty breakfast Thursday morning.

Rowles said he still could not say definitely what brought on the pneumothorax condition, although he conceded that Miss Hearst's emotional state may have played some part in it.

He mentioned her malnutrition only in passing and gave no indication that it was of a serious nature.

The prisoner-patient, under heavy guard on the second floor of the hospital, was visited for more than two hours Thursday by her parents, Randolph and Catherine Hearst, and her younger sister, Victoria.

After the visit, Hearst said the doctor told him his daughter was suffering from "mild malnutrition."

"She seems to be better," he said. "Her color is better than yesterday."

Hearst said he did not attribute his daughter's weight loss—she is now

300 PROTEST SHORTENED ACAPULCO STAY

Melee on Italian Cruise Ship Reported

ACAPULCO (AP)—Crewmen on an Italian liner rolled out high pressure fire hoses and threatened to use them to quell a near riot by 300 angry passengers protesting a shortened Acapulco stay on the ship's round-the-world cruise, consular sources reported Thursday.

Port sources said a few fistfights had broken out between the crew of the Galileo Galilei and the passengers, but no one had been injured in the melee a week ago.

The ship, said to be carrying about 1,500 passengers and 350 crew members, last was reported steaming for the Caribbean, but its precise location was not known. It is due in Genoa, Italy, on April 25.

One passenger said he and his wife had been "manhandled over the side" during the Acapulco fracas, that alarms had sounded, putting the crew on full-scale alert, and that the fire hoses actually had been turned on.

The ship's owners, the firm of Lloyd Triestino, said that fire passengers had been ordered off the ship and that they had left with the "help of Mexican police" during what they called a "grave incident."

The owners confirmed that the crew had been ordered to be ready to use the fire hoses, but insisted they had not been turned on.

The Acapulco consular sources and the ship's owners said the incident had occurred April 7 shortly after the 27,700-ton Galileo Galilei, named for the astronomer, anchored in Acapulco Bay after sailing from Tahiti.

Lloyd Triestino said that en route to Acapulco the Galileo had answered a distress call from a freighter to pick up an injured seaman, which cost 13½ hours sailing time.

The ship was scheduled to stay in Acapulco 20 hours but because of a 13½-hour delay, it had to cut its stay in Acapulco short, and this sparked the protest, the company said.

The Acapulco consular sources said the five passengers ordered off the ship, three Britons and two West Germans identified by the captain as ringleaders of the protest, had been flown back home.

"I don't know if they plan to sue the owners of the ship or what. But they certainly were angry as anything," said West German Consul Walter Kayser, who dealt with the two West Germans.

He identified the evicted passengers as Hans Joachim Tinti, a 28-year-old officer in the West German air force; Ingrid Bents, a 29-year-old woman friend; Mr. and Mrs. Raphael

FEATURE INDEX

THE WEATHER

National Weather Service forecast: Variable cloudiness but mostly sunny today and Saturday. Some gusty winds both days, especially below the canyons. Highs today in the low 60s and Saturday in the mid 60s. High Thursday 58; low, 53.

Complete weather information and

THE MILITARY: A SOLID ROOT

Any comparison between the rag-tail citizen army that amassed itself around General George Washington at Valley Forge, and the institution that is commonly known as the Department of Defense would be impossible. The courage and pride of those early fighting men are no less equaled with the men of today's military, who have inherited all of the majestic fighting qualities of their forefathers, those early fighters for freedom who were forged in the steel of Lexington, Concord, and the deadly snows of Valley Forge.

The torch that was passed hand to hand through Fort Sumter, Gettysburg, and Appomattox was grasped by the trembling fingers of the men at Belleau Wood, St. Mihiel, and the Meuse-Argonne and carried onward by other Americans, who screamed their battle cry at Normandy, Anzio, Leyte, Tarawa, Korea, and Vietnam. Americans who have faultlessly given their all without question, without rancour, and who have stood shoulder to shoulder, second to none with the greatest fighting spirit and courage known in the history of mankind.

THE UNITED STATES ARMY . . .
THE HUMBLE BEGINNINGS

Although there are various dates that are proposed for the day that the Continental army was established, June 14, 1776, is the accepted modern date. This would have had a most debilitating effect on the men of the "Old North Regiment" of the colonial militia in Massachusetts in 1636, but their heritage remains the same.

At the outbreak of the Revolutionary War Americans were to prove early that they were not to be expected to do the conventional thing in battle. Learning from the Indians that

Marines *of the 28th Regiment of the Fifth Division raise the American flag on Mt. Suribachi following the capture of Iwo Jima in 1945. The battle for Iwo Jima was one of the bloodiest in U.S. Marine history.*

blue was harder to see in the woods and red a better target, they acted accordingly. It didn't matter to George Washington that it was Christmas and normally armies took the day off; he abraded tradition by crossing the Delaware River and surprising his enemy. The general alluded to his men as, "A mixed multitude . . . under very little discipline order of government." Added to this observation was a British citizen in Boton who wrote, "despicable wretches compose the banditti of this country . . . a most rude, depraved, degenerate race, and it is a mortification to us that they speak English." That rabble of despicables rose to the occasion unlike anything a European army could have possibly visualized.

In 1776, gunners at Fort Moultrie, Charleston Harbor mutilated the British Navy, who were trying to land troops on an adjacent island, where British Admiral Sir Peter Parker suffered the ultimate indignity of having to withdraw upon having his pants set afire, as the colonials looked on with glee and laughter.

At Trenton, following Christmas day, Washington, one hour before dawn, split his forces and, attacking the main street from opposite sides, routed the Hessians, making them surrender after an hour and a half of fighting. Washington captured 918, killed 30, with two frozen to death. The non-disciplined group, who amassed for a parade later in the day, was observed by a Marylander who noted, ". . . that's the finest group of men I'd ever seen out of step."

If the citizen soldier of 1776 lacked military discipline and professional army acumen, he more than made up for it by his ability to see the thing through and learn from it.

The early muskets that the army used were almost as detrimental to the user as to the intended victim . . . "If the wind was blowing, it was almost impossible to place any powder in the pan, and if the uneven mixture of sulpher, carbon and saltpeter was damp there was little reason to put it into the rifle at all."

Observe the firing instructions and commands of a musket rifle from the British Manual, that was followed by the continentals. . . .

The Lame Deer Creek *episode as portrayed by Frederic Remington. During the push to settle the west the Cavalry played an important role in maintaining order in regions long under the control of Indian tribes.*

Reproduction *of a painting showing Colonel Theodore Roosevelt at the head of his charging Rough Rider Regiment during the Spanish-American War. The Charge up San Juan Hill in 1898 electrified the country and made Roosevelt a national figure.*

1. Half-cock your firelocks!   (1 motion)
2. Handle your cartridges!   (1 motion)
3. Prime!   (1 motion)
4. Shut your pans!   (2 motions)
5. Charge with cartridges!   (2 motions)
6. Draw your rammers!   (2 motions)
7. Ram your cartridge! .   (1 motion)
8. Return your rammers!   (1 motion)
9. Shoulder your firelock!   (2 motions)
10. Poise your firelocks!   (2 motions)
11. Cock your firelocks!   (2 motions)
12. Present!   (1 motion)
13. Fire!   (1 motion)

It isn't too hard to realize that in the first few battles of the war the continentals were severely handicapped by adhering to the ritualistic manual, and often with serious results. One soldier, forgetful of the proximity of his uncorked powderhorn, started a conflagration that burned for several hours and caused him considerable discomfort for several weeks. Another having snapped his rifle on a ''delayed'' charge was, upon recocking and firing, promptly kicked to death. John McMurtry, not realizing that there was a load in his rifle, sent a bullet through a double partition of inch boards, a single board of berth, the chest of a man named Penn, and left a mark against a brick chimney.

Nothing came easy for the First Continental Army. Yet it continued to win against the motherland. In 1781 it won at Yorktown with the aid of 6,000 French allies, and forced Cornwallis to abandon his position. As Cornwallis' troops

Some *of the Rough Riders who participated in the Spanish-American War in 1898.*

Photograph *of some members of the U.S. Army Signal Corps laying telephone lines in support of American forces during the Spanish-American War.*

left Yorktown they encased their flags and marched away to the tune of a Turkish song, "The World Turned Upsidedown."

It was the beginning of the end for Britain, and the beginning of a tradition that was to follow each succeeding generation that would go into battle for the stars and stripes.

The army came of age in 1782 and a medal was given to wounded troops by General George Washington, that in 1932 became the famed Purple Heart.

After minor skirmishes, the British were finally thrown out of their last two strongholds, Savannah and Charleston.

The Nation's first military academy was established, March 16, 1802, which was to form the nucleus for a whole generation of army officers and set up standards that would be copies and imitated throughout the world. Here, the lessons that were learned from the British war became the matrix for the small band of men, ten cadets and seven officers, who were the vanguard of thousands of the most successful officers in history, and several presidents as well.

The Army's mettle was reinforced in the war of 1812. It was a war that had its roots in a British blockade of American shipping and the army suffered a beating at the hands of the combined British and Indian forces in Canada. The British fought their way past Bladensburg, Maryland, sweeping into the capitol city of Washington, and promptly set fire to the nation's capitol. Several bullet holes remain in the capitol today that are mute testimony to the British anger of the times.

The Navy took on the powerful British fleet in the Azores and Florida and in the Chesapeake Bay, and won the Battle of New Orleans.

The army's contribution was spectacular in view of the fact that its mission was accomplished with understrength regiments and an undertrained part-time militia.

Historian Henry Adams said, "The American rifle has no equal in the world when used in American hands."

In 1836 the young army faced another crisis when Texas, which had recently joined the union, was invaded by the Mexican government. General Zachary Taylor engaged the enemy and fought them across the Rio Grande river, winning the battle of Monterrey, and in November occupied Saltillo. It was a young and inexperienced army which fought the Mexicans, but it made up for its greenness with spirit, resolve and acts of bravery. Dressed in their handsome dragoon uniforms of light blue and gray the soldiers fought the battles

of Cerro Gordo and Molino del Rey, in good style.

With the able assistance of two young officers, Col. Robert E. Lee and Lt. Ulysses S. Grant, U. S. forces occupied Mexico City, forcing Santa Anna from his presidency.

In return for their hard earned victory, the peace treaty confirmed the Texas boundry and transferred to the United States all territory that is now California, Nevada, Utah, most of Arizona and New Mexico, and parts of Colorado and Wyoming for $15,000,000.

It was the first time in American Army history that it was required to administer a system of military government in a foreign country.

The Civil War need not be chronicled here, except to comment on the fact that when brother opposed brother the result was twofold. It was the costliest war in the country's history, and perhaps the most violent. Secondly, the army probably gained more gut experience in this conflict, that was ultimately to harden it into one of the finest fighting military units in the history of man.

However, just prior to the Civil War, the Union army had reduced itself to approximately 16,000 troops, most of whom were serving in the west and southwest trying to protect white settlers from hostile roaming tribes of Indians. It was an uneasy peace. The government was sworn to protect all of the citizens in this territory and that included those native to it as well as the new settlers. It wasn't going to be an easy job and there were injustices on both sides.

The Indian campaigns are distasteful to both army historians and contemporary Indians. The wounds are as yet unhealed and solutions still unresolved. Suffice to say, the thin military forces were scattered in 68 permanent posts and 70 temporary forts, ostensibly to map frontier territories. Four of these army survey routes were ultimately used for the guidelines to the railroads inching west.

In May of 1856 Lawrence, Kansas was sacked by a pro-slavery mob, and two days later, the fanatic John Brown, who was a rabid abolitionist, was hard pressed by the army after he and his three sons escaped after shooting and hacking to death five southern sympathizers at Pottawatomie Creek. Three years later, with about eighteen followers, Brown tried to spark a slave rebellion in West Virginia by seizing Harpers arsenal. He was captured by troops commanded by Colonel R. E. Lee. Brown and six henchmen were tried and convicted for treason and hanged.

On February 9, 1861, Jefferson Davis became president of the confederacy, and in a few months an already hardening army of the Union was making contingency plans to fight Davis, armed with new breechloading rifles. Briefly, after the firing of the initial guns at Fort Sumter, the two blood brother giants went to grips on the battlefield.

Into the serene and almost indescribable beauty of the Shenandoah Valley 20,000 yipping and screaming confederates, under the command of an eccentric graduate of V. M. I., march with utter abandon. His name is "Stonewall" Jackson, and he confused, baffled, and destroyed four Union armies of some 60,000 men and threatened Washington before he was subdued.

Early in the conflict, Robert E. Lee showed his superior generalship by driving the Union from Richmond and invading the north, almost winning the war in the first few months.

It was five years of bloody fighting, with neither side giving nor asking quarter, ending at the courthouse at Appomattox, a defeated Lee having his sword handed back to him by an admiring Grant. It was to cost this country 1,000,125 casualties, but it was to forge deep within the bowels of the new emerging army a fortitude and resolution that was to stand it in good stead within a few short years, and present to the world at large the strength and power of the new nation that was only now emerging out of the wilderness and gazing with eager eyes to the outer borders of her far boundaries, and starting to reach her hand out to other peoples in other lands, without realizing what a giant she had become.

With the turn of the century, the army strode into it with the newest weapons available, one of which was the Gatling gun, invented by an American, and promising the horrible prospect of multitudinous deaths by just a squeeze of a trigger.

The Germans were quick to realize the potential of the new gun and went to work developing a better model and producing it in wholesale lots. The building of the Panama Canal, which would never have been completed without the help of men like Walter Reed, who with the assistance of older volunteers helped wipe out the dread disease, Yellow Fever. The Germans were unimpressed and with the assassination of the heir to the Hapsburg throne, soon all Europe was thrust into the conflagration. Treaty linked with treaty, honored by treaty upon treaty, and like a tumbling house of cards, "the show was on."

A view *of U.S. Soldiers involved in trench warfare during World War I. Before the Americans arrival in 1916 the war had bogged down in a stalemate of trenches which extended nearly the length of the war zone.*

It was a war in which America didn't want to get involved, but it was a war that was inevitable in the fate line of the country. German sympathies were strong in this country and British sympathies were equally as emotional among Americans.

The war ground itself into a long trenchline that stretched from the small town of Nieuport on the Belgium coast to the base of the Swiss alps. Four hundred miles of stench from dried blood, and rotting flesh. Armies had been trained to maneuver, and parry, and thrust at one another, but here was something that was difficult for the commanders of that day to understand: a war lock and stale front that changed little in four years.

Those years allowed defenses to become so sophisticated and elaborate that some of them had their own pianos and fashionable furniture fifty feet underground. Not that it was that way all over; for the most part it was a four foot trench and "standing up to your knees in mud." This is what faced the American army when it got the call to arms on April 6, 1917.

As usual and to the good fortune of the civilized world, the Americans came up with a brilliant man. His name was General John J. (Blackjack) Pershing, his nickname derived from his having commanded an all Negro troop which was employed fighting the Indian wars in the southwest. When the war was opened Pershing was running Pancho Villa into the depths of Mexico. He quickly saddled another kind of horse and brought with him a small detachment of troops to Europe. It was a pitifully small group of soldiers, but it was representative of a whole angry nation, and the vanguard of almost another million men to follow. What seeds they planted in Europe in two years of fighting were to burn itself in the memory of a whole generation of people twenty-five years later, when their sons were to be called back to Europe to finish off the job that the first group of Americans started in 1917.

Pershing had to fight political battles as well as military ones. The French, always looking for extra cannon fodder, wanted to sift the Americans into their lines and take their place beside the French Poilu. The English were of the same determination, but Pershing, under terrible pressure, denied his allies that luxury, and stated that he would have his army fight as an American unit and that to prove their point they would take the hardest part of the line to fight their war in. A

Here an *American soldier prepares to throw a handgrenade during a battle fought near Aneauville, France in 1918. The American soldiers, called "Doughboys" in the First World War, entered the European conflict in 1916.*

lot of sidelong glances and smirks greeted Pershing as he made his statement, but he was determined to have a complete American army and didn't want his men fighting under foreign generals who would not have understood their independent temperament.

He got his wish, faster than he anticipated. The Germans made a breakthrough of the lines opposite St. Mihiel. The First Division was thrust into the line in April 1918, and stopped the Germans cold. So cold that the brilliant German General Erich von Lundendorff stated bitterly, "Most unorthodox tactics. These Americans are reckless. They don't fight like the others!" He was forced to break off his attack and retire back to his old position with the Americans in hot pursuit.

General Pershing's doughboys changed the tactics from deadlock and stalemate to maneuver and pliability. They had broken the rack in the new game of billiards. The First Division captured Cantigny, and the Second took the Bois de Belleau; this latter division was blessed with two regiments of United States Marines, who complimented their army brothers like a melodious chord on a church organ.

Battling alongside the French, stumbling over the language barrier and barbed wire, the Americans helped push back the Germans through the thick Compiegne Forest. The Soissons counterattack changed the war for the Germans. With the aid of primitive tank and air support the United States' First and 26th Divisions eliminated the German salient below Verdun. Verdun, where a million German and French dedicated soldiers fought and died under three feet of mud and bloody remnants of decayed flesh. There had been no battle like it before and none after, perhaps the most hideous rendering of human flesh in the history of mankind, and the American army went into that stinking valley, between the bare muddy hills honeycombed with barbwire and shell holes, and threw the Germans back. It was more than a victory; it was the forging of a tremendous military army and completed the final victory, in the final offense of the great war.

There were plenty of heroes. Sgt. Alvin York stands out as the foremost, certainly the most noted. But in the trenches on both sides of the conflict stood other men. General Douglas

General John "Blackjack" Pershing *leads a victory parade down the Champs Elysees following the end of World War I. The parade of American soldiers through the heart of Paris occurred on July 14, 1919.*

MacArthur led the famous Rainbow division and the fighting 69th regiment, while a young Captain named Harry S. Truman led the rowdy wine drinking Battery D 129th Field Artillery into the Vosges Mountains fighting.

In the intervening years between 1918 and 1941 the army, like the rest of the nation, went through a series of belt tightening regimens. There was a national depression. Jobs were scarce, much of the populace was on relief, and there were no appropriations for defense or for added expenditures for the armed services.

A small voice crying in the wilderness was that of General Douglas MacArthur, who warned the nation that complacency in the Pacific would lead to an attack by the Japanese. It wasn't until 1940 that the government heard him and started to put some muscle into the army. It was too little too late, and as a result Pearl Harbor and World War II was an inescapable conclusion. While the Army was effective in the Pacific, with masterful campaigns in New Guinea, the Phillippines, and at Okinawa, the full force of the men in khaki was felt in the European conflict.

In November 1942, a green army led by General George Patton, a feisty general who had almost mystical insight into the procedures of modern war, made amphibian landings in North Africa and smashed the pro-Nazi French at Casablanca, Fidala, Oran, and Algiers. They then joined the British forces in Tunisia and, at the Kasserine Pass, the two armies joined up and captured Bizerte causing the fall of Tunis, assuring the collapse of military speculation in Africa by Nazi Germany.

On June 6, 1944, the allied armies led by the Americans landed on French soil to begin the final thrust of the war in Europe. Germany had already been weakened by the fall of Italy and Rome by American armies and General Mark Clark. After a costly and bloody battle on the beaches of Normandy the army broke through the hedgerows and started streaking toward Paris.

Lt. Gen. Omar Bradley's First Army allowed the Third Army to spring forward with its armored divisions from Saint-Lo toward central France. The men in their tanks relieved Orleans on August 16, and after a 250 mile drive against stiff opposition cracked the enemy resistance and marched victoriously into the capitol city of Paris.

Patton, never satisfied with the progress of his successful daily advances, finally ran out of petrol just as he had the bulk of the Germans in his grasp. He was furious and stated: "My

A group *of American soldiers celebrating the news of the Armistice near St. Mihiel, France in 1918. The Armistice ending the first World War was signed on November 11, 1918.*

men can eat their belts, but my tanks gotta have gas."

By mid October the logistics problem was partially eased and the Allies forged a solid front from the Swiss border to the North Sea, a tragic reminder of the front lines of the First World War, and was portentive of what might occur if the Allies did not move forward hastily. With this in mind the First Army thrust toward the Rhine river and eight divisions under Lt. Gen. Courtney Hodge were ravaged securing the Huretgen Forest.

When the Belgiums received a large force of supply ships the Germans forged a campaign to take Antwerp. Both sides raced for the city of Bastogne, with the result that the 101st Airborne Division was surrounded. The Bulge was flattened by some of the most bloody and meritorious fighting of the

Benito Mussolini, *right, and Adolf Hitler, second from right, as they paid homage at the Shrine of Martyred Fascists in 1938. Also pictured are Count Ciano, left, and von Ribbentrop, diplomatic officers for the two major Axis powers in the Second World War.*

Second World War, with the American army arising victorious, snapping at the rag-tail remnants of the fleeing Germans.

In the Colmar pocket the Americans not only cleared the Germans out of France, but the army was given its most decorated hero of the war, a Texas sharecropper's son, Audie Murphy.

The army raced across Germany in a series of uninterrupted victories and on May 7, 1945, at a school house in Reims, France, Eisenhower sent out this message to his troops and to the world . . . "The mission of this allied force was fulfilled at 0241 local time." The war in Europe was over!

In the Pacific, the army, executing a series of island hopping, under the able direction of General MacArthur, worked itself into a position to re-land on the islands of the Philippines and retake the islands in time to hand that country its independence as a new nation. The army, with the help of Chiang Kai-shek working hand in hand with General Joe Stillwell, fought across Burma via the Ledo road and created a passage from India to China. The war terminated before the combined forces of Chiang and the army could thrust its way up the coast to defeat the quick fleeing Japanese.

The army lay poised, ready to strike at the heart of the Japanese homeland, and some of the troops were already boarding ships for the final invasion of the war when it was suddenly and surprisingly ended with the conclusive voice of the atomic bomb at Nagasaki and Hiroshima.

It was a costly victory, causing 1,078,162 total casualties, of which the United States army incurred 884,135. But it was not without its rewards as well, for out of the forge of the furnaces of bloody Europe the United States army graduated with honors and rose with strength and a new found spirit and muscle that gained the respect and fear of all the world.

The final two phases of army history are neither glorious nor satisfying as far as the army is concerned. With the outbreak of the Korean conflict, and as the hordes of North

The Army Air Corps *barracks at Hickam Field on fire after the Japanese attack on Pearl Harbor on December 7, 1941.*

Korean soldiers swept down from the north scattering the inept South Korean army in its wake, the only body of men who could possibly stop them were the weak and untried civilian United States army soldiers who were stationed in Japan as an occupation force and ill equipped for frontline fighting.

Regardless of their lack of training for combat, these men went into battle against a superior force and stopped the enemy under the able direction of General Douglas MacArthur, who was shortly afterward designated as Commander of all the United Nations armies in Korea. Despite its 6,000 casualties, the now toughened army not only held its position, but under a masterful stroke by MacArthur landed at Inchon and cut the enemy off from his supplies and thoroughly routed him, making him retreat back to his own borders and beyond. MacArthur had won the war in Korea.

But, unforeseen by the chief of staff, a brand new war erupted when approximately 200,000 Chinese attacked below their border, driving the United Nations forces into a 75 mile retreat which stiffened and held below the 38th parallel.

American GI's performed the major role, winning such battles as "Pork Chop Hill," about which Military Historian S. L. A. Marshall stated, "The Americans won, not simply by the superior weight of their artillery, but because of the infantry, man for man, in hand to hand combat."

It was to be a bitter struggle for the army who fought a war and finished a fight that it couldn't win, couldn't lose, and couldn't quit. It was the first no-win mission in army history, and it was to be followed by another bitter struggle, much the same as Korea, four years later in Vietnam.

Beginning in 1951 the United States army was inched into Vietnam through the soon to be designated Military Assistance Command. In 1961 President Kennedy brought total support for the army of the Republic of Vietnam to 16,000 personnel. In 1964, after an attack on American navy ships, President Johnson ordered air attacks against North Vietnam. Hanoi rejected the many peace offers and continued its struggle in spite of terriffic losses in men and equipment. It was an uneasy war, that once again tied the army's hands behind its back and made it fight against all of the principles that can earn it victory.

Lieutenant General George Patton, *left, commander of the Seventh Army, General "Hap" Arnold, center, U.S. Army Air Forces chief, and Lieutenant General Mark Clark, Allied Fifth Army commander, as they await the arrival of President Roosevelt to Sicily following the Teherean Conference.*

Photograph *of the Normandy beachhead following the Allied invasion on June 6, 1944. The armada formed for the invasion of Europe was the largest collection of men and materiél ever assembled in the history of warfare.*

A Japanese photograph *of American prisoners of war during the infamous Bataan Death March following the fall of Bataan in April, 1942.*

View of *American soldiers going ashore on Omaha Beach, France, during the D-Day assault in 1944.*

Photograph *of American paratroopers jumping behind German lines in southern France in 1944.*

General Douglas MacArthur *keeping his promise to the Filipinos of "I Shall Return", wades ashore at Leyte Island in October, 1944.*

Bunched together in conclaves, and limited to patrols and boundry lines which was as self defeating as any enemy could be, the army frustrated itself against a seldom seen enemy and against a building resentment at home. It was not only an unpopular war from the army's point of view, but it was manifestly unpopular in the civilian ranks as well.

ITEM: January 3, 1976

LONDON (A. P.)—"The Soviet Navy has become the most potent in firepower of any fleet that ever existed, but the American sailor is better than the Soviet navy man."

Capt. John Moore, Editor
"Jane's Fighting Ships"

It was not the first time in history that the United States Navy had been relegated to the position of underdog. In its infancy the new fleet, commissioned on October 13, 1775, was struggling with its two "swift sailing vessels" against the sea might of the British empire. And what tipped the balance of the scales? The answer lies in the fact that these thirteen colonies sat on the edge of a large body of water, and when England made the mistake of tightening her control over newly won Canada from the French with her sea power, she erred when she underrated the small band of pirateers that sprang up in the rivers and inlets of the colonies and cut her supply line to the mother country. It was an error that would lead to her defeat less than a decade later.

It was to be a pirateers war that the Americans would wage, with her French allies, against England, and when viewed from the American side it was revealed that the infant navy never was able to muster more than a twenty-seven ship navy in all that long war, but its courage and spirit were never questioned, and when that war was finally terminated it was the seed for what was to ultimately become the greatest sea power the world had ever known.

It was not without its first heroes, brave men who had two things in common: courage and aggressiveness. They believed in carrying the fight to the enemy, and for nearly two hundred years their names have been a hallmark and an inspiration to the men who have followed in their footsteps. Johnathan Haraden, Lambert Wilkes, Gustavus Conyngham, Joshua Barney and John Barry, all early navy heroes who have had their names honored by having destroyers named after them, and finally one name that is probably the symbol of the United States throughout the world: John Paul Jones. Brave, proud, hot tempered and with a zealous fever of patriotism, when asked by the British to surrender his "Bon Homme Richard" Jones politely told them, "I have not yet begun to fight."

The Navy had a rebirth after the revolution when out of necessity there arose a need to protect American shipping from the African pirates and our former allies, the French, who had begun to harass all shipping in the Mediterranean. The Congress, spurred on by President Adams, instituted a program of ship building and encouragement of the formation of a full fledged navy which was to operate under the aegis of the Secretary of War.

In 1799 the frigate U.S.S. Constellation, under Captain Truxtun, defeated the French *Insurgent* and a year later the *Vengeance*. During this undeclared war the young Navy came of age, and it showed the world that the former colonists could not only build better ships, but fight with them with more skill and imagination than their European counterparts. This was to stand the Navy in good stead when England declared war in 1812.

Munich crowds *intermingled with freed prisoners watch American tanks and troops passing down Dachauerstrase on their way to occupying the city of Munich.*

An Allied correspondent *examines the remains of what was once a barber shop in Hiroshima. Tiled tub at right is all that remains to identify the former Japanese shop. The dropping of the atomic bombs on Hiroshima and Nagasaki brought a quick end to the war in the Pacific and precluded the landing on the Japanese mainland, which military experts said would have cost a million American casualities.*

Soldiers *of the 24th Infantry Division round up Chinese communist prisoners of war during mountain fighting in Korea in 1951.*

Water spouts *in a series of geysers as shells from a Japanese warship land near a U.S. Navy Escort Carrier during the Battle of the Philippine Sea in 1944.*

While one U.S. Navy ship *(background) zig zags through shells from a Japanese destroyer, the crew of an Escort Carrier (foreground) rushes to launch its planes during the Battle of the Philipine Sea.*

U.S. Navy gunners *watch as a Japanese dive bomber burns off the surface in the Pacific. U.S. Navy planes had shot the Japanese bomber moments before this photo was taken.*

President Madison saw no hope of a successful sea action against the powerful and immense British fleet, and it was his intention that we should dismantle what ships we had and place their guns ashore to defend the coast. Loud protestations were heard from "Preble's Boys," such as William Bainbridge and Charles Stewart, to give the Navy a chance. Madison relented, saying that one cruise for each American vessel would be allowed before she was to be dismantled and scrapped.

Endeavoring to break the British blockade Issac Hull, in the frigate *Constitution*, sailed from Boston without orders to seek the British. Finding the British frigate *Guerriere* he defeated her soundly and thrilled Americans while shocked and unbelieving Britishers received the news with incredulity. The U. S. ships *Essex* and *Wasp* also defeated British ships, making the country aware of what the Navy could do and inspiring the forces on the ground to fight with further determination. Stephen Decatur, in his frigate *United States*, captured the *Macedonian;* the *Constitution* scored again by sinking the *Java*.

Despite all of these small Navy victories the British were able to effectively hold their blockade and finally sail up the Potomac and burn Washington, D. C They failed in their attempt to burn Baltimore, and inspired Francis Scott Key to write the "Star Spangled Banner" after watching an all-night British attack fail against Fort McHenry. Only on Lake Erie were the British to fail miserably, and Commodore Perry's gaining control of the inland seas swept the British and her domination of the northwest out of the continent for good, establishing once and for all the complete independence of the American states in the new world.

Between 1812 and the Civil War the Navy led the world in advanced ship design, and developed a tradition of aggressiveness and effectiveness in sea warfare. Steam propulsion and rifled cannon made their appearance during the War of 1812.

The opening of Japan to the western world was one of the most significant acts of naval enterprise of the nineteenth century. Commander Matthew Perry prepared himself and his force carefully for this delicate operation, and with careful patience and skill opened the Japanese mainland to the rest of the world.

It was not until the Civil War that the Navy really came into its own with a promise of spearheading the world in naval enterprise on new ideas for warships and manifestly professional ability to blockade and maintain the country's eastern shore from all outside intervention and interruption of

her Union's desires. It was apparent that the Navy would have few engagements on the high seas, but that blockading and support of troops would be of paramount importance. It was necessary to blockade the agricultural South and cut off its trade of cotton for war goods. To discourage southern privateers, the Union Navy made forages and landings against the southern coast. Several forts along the Carolina and Florida coasts were highly successful, but what was more important was the fact that it proved naval guns were more effective than those that were land based and immobile. It was a lesson that was to stand in good stead in a war seventy years in the future.

Probably the most singular naval advancement that came out of the Civil War was the introduction of the iron clads. The Confederacy had raised a ship, the *Merrimac,* from its half sunken situation in Chesapeake Bay near Norfolk at Hampton Roads. They decided to create an iron clad out of the ship. Iron clads were not a new idea. When the Union realized what the Confederates were up to in Hampton Roads, they quickly hired an engineering genius named John Ericsson to "set to and deliver us an iron clad before the rebs get one." It was a desperate race and it was obvious that the first navy to procure an iron clad would rule the sea. It is an ironic fact of history that both ships were completed about the same time, and when the *Merrimac* ventured forth on her maiden voyage she promptly sunk the Union ships *Cumberland* and *Congress,* and was damaging the *Minnesota* when she retired for the evening. The next day as she ventured forth to wipe out the rest of the Union Navy she was confronted by the *Monitor,* who had made her way down the coast from New York, and engaged the southern ship in battle. It came out a tie and neither side claimed victory, but the *Merrimac* was never again to come out of her secure position in the harbor and was for all purposes rendered useless by the *Monitor's* constant vigilance.

One of President Lincoln's last acts was to order twenty more *Monitors* to be built and it was the start of the first all iron clad ships to sail the high seas. After the battle of the iron clads most of the remainder of the naval battles fought were on rivers and along the coast. It was during the approach to Mobile, and the end of confederate naval opposition, that the famous "Damn the torpedos, full speed ahead" was given by Admiral Farragut from the rigging of his flag ship *Hartford*. The torpedos were really mines that had been planted in the river.

After the Spanish American War the United States emerged as a world naval power, and when the First World War erupted the Navy was more than ready to take its part and sweep the German Navy from the high seas. The emergence of the U-Boat was a significant revelation that came out of the world war and was to play an important factor in the war that would shortly follow.

The Depression that followed the world war forced the Navy into thin and hard times. The country, more interested in the great national depression, funded monies to internal national interests and the Navy went on a starvation diet, tightening its belt and hoping for more prosperous times.

Always mindful of world affairs, ever glowering with its eagle eyes, the Navy was more than aware of the threatening build-up of Japanese strength in the Pacific, and its pleas to a deaf-eared congress fell like rose petals on the floor. It was not until the war in Europe erupted in 1939 that the country realized it had better pad its naval effectiveness. Ironically, most of that padding went down into the depths with the attack on Pearl Harbor. For the first time in United States history the Navy would be called upon to not only defend the

The U.S. Coast Guard *ship the* Unimak, typical of the ships the Coast Guard uses to patrol the coastlines of America.

Admiral William F. "Bull" Halsey, *Commander of the Third Fleet in the Pacific during World War II is shown talking with his staff following a war conference on Leyte in late 1944.*

country but also to wage a major war on both land and sea with a highly sophisticated enemy.

The Japanese had the third largest fighting navy in the world at the inception of the international conflict. It wouldn't be too many years before the United States Navy would not only grind down that effective number, but actually reduce the Japanese navy to an ineffectual fighting machine, unable to either supply itself with materials or protect any of its troops garrisoned on remote Pacific islands. However, it would not be without a herculean struggle. The Japanese were able to follow up their navy victory by subduing the Philippines and moving down the chain of Pacific islands through the Marshalls and down to New Britain, placing themselves in a position to attack Australia, whose troops and main defenses were mostly in Britain and Africa.

It was a dark hour that faced the nation and the response was clear from the Navy. The first counterblow the Navy could muster would be against the Japanese inland bases of Wotje, Kawajalein and Jaluit, by the *Yorktown* and *Enterprise* air groups. It jolted the Japanese and kept them off balance long enough for the Navy to recover her Pearl Harbor losses, resupply her fighting fleet and go out looking for trouble.

The first major battle between the Japanese and United States carrier task forces took place in the Coral Sea, after which the battle is named. The object of the *Lexington* and the *Yorktown* was to prevent the Japanese from landing at Port Moresby in Western New Guinea, in May of 1942. The Japanese struck first sinking an American fleet tanker, the *Neosho,* and her escorting destroyer, the *Sims,* thinking that this was a carrier task force. Once deluded, the *Lexington's* planes found the carrier *Shoho* and sunk her. Unfortunately, on the next day the *Lexington* was destroyed and the *Yorktown* damaged. A heavy price to pay, and while certainly not a victory for the American forces, it was the first initial thrust made against the Japanese, and served notice that the American Navy was well trained, ready and eager to fight. Firm resolve followed that sea battle and a new respect for the enemy ramrodded navy spines and girded them for future sea engagements.

On June 4, 1942, a main Japanese carrier force hit Midway Island, two hundred sixteen planes in all, and did only moderate damage to the land bases there. As the Japanese planes returned to their mother ships to re-arm they were hit by torpedo planes from the *Hornet* and the *Enterprise,* who came in without fighter escort; as a result three Japanese carriers were sunk with all of their planes aboard. The fourth

U.S. Marines *under bombardment from Japanese artillery, dig in on the beaches following the landing on Iwo Jima.*

carrier, *Hiryu,* was sunk at dawn the next day. It was a disastrous defeat for the Japanese and one from which they would never recover. The rest of the fleet turned westward to Japan. The Japanese's brilliant Admiral Yamamoto had given up on his attempt to take Midway and his planned attack on Hawaii, and it was obvious to all professional Navy men that Japan had lost the fine cutting edge of her ceremonial Samurai sword. After American victories at Guadalcanal, the Marshalls, and the Gilberts, the U. S. Navy was able to roam the Pacific at will. Mass production at home of fighting ships was beginning to tell and with an intelligent and ambitious submarine efficiency against the Japanese it was soon apparent that what had once been the most formidable fighting navy in the Pacific was nothing more than a barnacled hull of its former self.

The famous "Turkey Shoot" as the Navy supported the Marine landings in the Marianas was to bag 402 Japanese airplanes. Saipan was captured, the Philippines fell, Iwo Jima became a memorial and the Japanese were soundly and decisively thrashed, reducing them to a nonexistent sea power. What few carriers they had left were inefficient because the pilots who manned the planes were inexperienced and unable to operate equitably in the air with the experienced Navy pilots that were shooting them down at will. Other facets of Navy warfare occurred in the Mediterranean, but Hitler's navy was so ineffective against a more professional and better equipped British one, that other than aiding and keeping the shipping lanes clear, the navy's task was relatively light. It is generally acknowledged that the victory in the Pacific was accented most vigorously by the action of the Navy and her land arm, the Marine Corps. It was the first time that a major power had eliminated another major power in war so thoroughly through sea power.

The Navy was to play a part in both the Korean and Vietnam wars. Not so decisively as in the Second World War, but effectively and importantly. It was at the famous

Bodies of dead Marines *who never made it ashore float in the water following the amphibious landing on Tarawa. The landing on Tarawa was part of the U.S. Marines hopscotching across Pacific islands during World War II.*

Inchon landings that the Navy softened the area with bombardments and helped land the Marines, which resulted in a brilliant stroke that broke the backs of the North Koreans and spelled defeat for their army which was fighting in the south of the country at the time, cutting off their supplies and making their ensuing retreat a military rout. In Vietnam, the Navy was a floating base protecting our soldiers and Marines who were struggling with the no-win war on land. They effectively blockaded and mined northern harbors, and were a prohibiting factor and obstacle controlling the seas, enabling the fighting men and civilians to perform their duties ashore, duties that without the stout work of the Navy would not have been able to have been performed at all.

Often confused with the Navy is the United States Coast Guard. The relationship between the two services stops at the uniform. The history of the Coast Guard goes back more than a century and a half. Although the nation dates from the Declaration of Independence, July 4, 1776, but the constitutional government we know today did not start until 1789, the year George Washington was inaugurated. The next year, August 4, 1790, Washington signed a bill authorizing the construction of "ten boats" for guarding the coast against smugglers. It was the beginning of the Coast Guard. The father of the Coast Guard was Alexander Hamilton, the first secretary of the Treasury, and it was in his interest that the service was formed, to provide a fleet to insure the tonnage dues and import duties from vessels entering United States waters. By the time the revolution was over smuggling had become a habit and way of life along the coastal waters of the Atlantic, and the young nation was in danger of imminent bankruptcy due to losses incurred by the brigands. It was to this end that the Coast Guard took the responsibilities and this country was insured that she have taxation with representation, and to make the people aware of the new customs laws and fight public apathy toward the smugglers and their utter disdain toward governmental laws under its young constitution. By 1799 the young fleet had a two-masted ship, the *Massachusetts,* plus the 51 ton *Scammel,* two 50 tons ships, the *Active* and *Pickering,* and the 40 ton *Diligence.* The 35 ton *Argus, Vigilent, Virginia,* and *South Carolina* had only four guns and the *General Greene,* a 35 ton sloop, had but three. Hamilton told congress in a worried tone about the extravagance of the fleet: ''The first cost of one of these boats, completely equipped, may be computed at one thousand dollars.''

The Coast Guard participated in the War of 1812 with her cutters bringing in the British warships, *Patriot, Wade,* and *Shamrock,* the latter carrying $20,000 in gold and silver. The cutter *Vigilent* took the British privateer *Dart* in a running battle between Newport and Block Island.

Although the British navy was too powerful a force to defeat, the small Coast Guard ships and cutters performed what was tantamount to a sea gorilla war, by sniping and foraging from small inlets and bays doing credit to the service and adding to the historical tradition throughout the conflict. A sea skirmish that epitomizes Coast Guard fighting spirit is recorded by British Captain John Crerie . . . ''On the night of June 12, 1813, three barges from the *Narcissus* attempted to take the American cutter *Surveyer* by surprise action in the York River. Though we outnumbered them 50 to 13 the cutter crew wounded seven and killed three of our company before she was captured. The determined way in which her deck was disputed, inch by inch, in hand to hand fighting, was a marvelous example of spirit and determination.'' Captain Crerie was so impressed that he returned to Captain William Travis of the cutter ''The sword you had so nobly used.''

The Coast Guard suffered through the growing pains of the Civil War and a brief respite into 1917 where she actually suffered more losses in proportional strength than any other of the services.

It was not until the Second World War that she truly came into her own. Shifted from the Department of Treasury to

Marines *wade ashore on Okinawa with no resistence from the Japanese garrison on the island. Okinawa was under the control of the Marines in 1945.*

A U.S. Marine *cocks his arm to throw a handgrenade at a Japanese bunker during fighting on Tarawa. Smoke from the ensuing battle fills their emplacement.*

serve under the Navy, its manpower hit the peak. Not only were her duties to serve and defend the coastal areas of both coasts, the diminutive service's personnel grew to a peak of 171,168. There were only ten thousand more men ashore than at sea, where they served spectacularly. As in World War I, most of their tasks were relegated to chasing submarines, a rather deadly assignment, with small cutters and escorts. No mighty war ships these, but venomous and expertly manned.

Perhaps the most spectacular enterprise the Coast Guard was to participate in was the landings on the invasion beaches in the south and central Pacific; a battle hardened marine observed on the Tinian landings: ''I'd rather go in with the Coast Guard than anybody; at least I know they'll get me on the sand!'' And get them on the sand they did, through Guadalcanal, Attu, North Africa, Salerno, Eniwetok, Normandy, Southern France, Luzon, Guam, Saipan, Iwo Jima, and Okinawa.

The Coast Guard had the dubious distinction of being the first of her sister services to get hit by a Kamakazi Zero at Okinawa. The L. S. T. *884,* her mangled hull penetrated by the Zero's flaming engine, which erupted inside the ships tank deck and set Marines aflame as they sat burning in their amtracks, waited only a moment before performing a fake landing on the southern side of that island. Her guns fired inspite of a 38 degree list and explosions that rendered her and her company immobile and reduced to a burned out husk. Her guns were never quiet as she was gutted with fire and began to sink.

The Coast Guard remains the nation's guardian and first thin line of defense against all intruders. Today she is under the direction of the Transportation Department, where she keeps a weather eye out at sea for military and civilian distress situations. In the chilly north she has the constantly busy duty of tracking down icebergs that present a menace to navigation, and with her small but elite air wing she is a composite picture in miniature of all the military services combined.

While it must be respectfully admitted that the Marine Corps had its birth under the broad timbers of ''Tuns Tavern'' in Philadelphia, the actual historical recruiting history of the Marine Corps goes back to a day when Major Samuel Nicholas, newly appointed commandant of the infant corps, was busily recruiting men for his new army. They were recruited out of various taverns in Philadelphia. Forty men were enlisted in the service and it was not until June the

following year that Robert Mullan, a tavern keeper, was appointed as a recruiter. Mullan was a captain of a marine detachment on the frigate *Delaware,* and as a good man fond of a drink now and then, made his rendezvous and headquarters at "Tuns Tavern," where a successful recruitment of healthy young men was carried out. Two of the earliest men recruited by Mullan were Issac Walker and "Orange Negro." Both men were Blacks and it is assumed that since both men were paid the same wages as all the others recruited that their duties were the same. Thus the Marine Corps was born, amid the heavy aromatic fumes of rum and tobacco smoke, and the gruff lusty gravel voices of freedom loving men.

The Marines immediately established themselves as a service apart from any other in the defense of their country. The early officers were required to have maritime service and were trained in land tactics as well. While it is true that their main duties were to be the fighting unit and boarding parties of the frigates on which they were stationed, it is equally true that they were as eager as their army counterparts to get their feet on dry land and "Trade a ball or two" with their enemy. They indeed did trade a ball or two in the Revolutionary War, and though a small unit they served with the naval forces in the Bahamas and with the lake fleets of the Continental Navy, which was successful in defeating British war ships in that area. After that war the Marine Corps like the Navy simply went out of existence.

The Marine Corps as it exists today was formed by the act of July 11, 1787, at the beginning of the naval war with France. Marines formed part of the landing force that operated against a nest of pirates in Cuba and in 1836 and 1837 helped the army fight the Creek and Seminole Indians in Georgia and Florida. During the Mexican war a detachment of marines marched with General Scott to Mexico City participating in the final battle against the Mexicans, defeating them at the Castle of Chapultepec, and marched on the National Palace and The Halls of Montezuma.

A group of Marines, *after landing on the beach at Bougainville, struggle to push a landing craft back into deep water after it was beached when the tide went out. Note the landing craft in the background being pounded by the heavy surf.*

During the Civil War the Marines served ashore and afloat, participating in the battle of New Orleans and against coastal defenses on the Atlantic seaboard. They took part in a number of land engagements including the fight at Bull Run. One noteworthy incident was the participation of Marines in the capture of abolitionist John Brown and the suppression of an uprising and riot at Harper's Ferry.

In scattered actions during the brief peace between the Civil War and the war with Spain the Marines found time to make their first Korean expedition when they stormed Fort Chojijin and Kangwha Island with infantry and artillery. This was an ominous portent for a war that was to be fought seventy years later.

It was not, however, until the First World War that the Marines blossomed into a complete fighting outfit, second to none. When Pershing was asked by the French army to step into the lines and try to stop a successful breakthrough by the German army, he was quick to send in the 2nd Division which was housing the Fourth Brigade of Marines, including the 5th and 6th Regiments. The Germans were pouring through the French lines and the Poilus were beating a hasty retreat from the area. When they saw the Marines moving past them and into the fiery gap, the French shouted a warning, "Retreat, Retreat, the huns are coming. . . ." and got as an answer. . . . "Retreat hell . . . we just got here!!" Pouring into the gap the Marines distinguished themselves at the battle of Belleau Woods, Soisson, Blanc Mont Ridge, St. Mihiel, and the Argonne. It was in the Battle for Belleau Woods that the Marines stopped the Germans flat, and after a terrible struggle, hand to hand, with bayonets and trench knives earned the creditable nickname "Devil Dogs", or as the Germans called them, "Teufel-Hunden."

Little known Marine air units were conspicious in that on October 14, 1918 Lt. Ralph Talbert and his sergeant Robert

Guy Robertson were both given the Congressional Medal of Honor for valorous duty in action against the enemy while flying their two seated bomber.

Although their valor and bravery was accented in the First World War, it was not until the war in the Pacific, during the great conflict against the Japanese, that the Marines emerged as a total and complete fighting branch of the War Department. The Marines were the first United States land fighting unit to go on the offensive against the enemy in that war. That operation was in the Solomons, by the 1st and 2nd Marine Divisions on Guadalcanal. Fighting in intolerable jungle conditions, cut off from their food supply by a hostile enemy navy, they fought several battles against Japanese land forces, and won these battles supplied themselves with the only food available on the island. Later, when the United States Navy was able to relieve their plight, they wiped the enemy off of the island quickly and efficiently and were to form the fighting nucleus for the most terrifying fighting machine in the world.

Fighting up the island chain the Marines took Tarawa, a small porkchop shaped atoll in the Gilbert Islands. It took them three days of the bloodiest fighting in the history of warfare to overwhelm their persistent enemy. They were to incur 3,166 casualties in those three days, but they were to take five thousand Japanese soldiers to their graves as a result of the terrible campaign.

Bloodied at Tarawa and Guadalcanal, there were more carnage makers ahead for the Marines. The Marianas were to prove a particularly hard nut to crack and Saipan was a difficult campaign for the Marines because of the treacherous terrain that they had to fight over. It was a natural for the defenders, who could hide in caves and in mountain ravines and take their toll with artillery and heavy machine gun and mortar fire. But the 2nd and 4th Divisions were equal to the task, and after a tiresome six weeks of continuous battle the Marines were finally victorious as they walked to the southern end of tiny Tinian Island. Little did they know that with the capture of Tinian in a few short months, on August 6, 1945, an Air Force B-29 would take off with a special payload in her belly, the atomic bomb.

Iwo Jima provided the Marines with another glorious but bloody chapter in their long history, and later, with the 10th Army, the Marines helped take Okinawa, the last Japanese

U.S. Marines *advancing through the mountains of Korea as part of the United Nations' Forces involved in fighting the Communist Chinese in 1951.*

bastion outside of her homeland. Marines were boarding the ships to begin that invasion of Japan when the war came to its abrupt and surprising end.

Later in Korea and in Vietnam the Marines were again to distinguish themselves valiantly and heroically in historic battles at the brilliant Inchon landings that demolished the North Koreans, and later the fight to the sea at the Choshin Reservoir, where they avoided a "Dunkirk" by their incredible fighting abilities. In Vietnam, the handbound war that limited them to conclaves and border restrictions, the Marines distinguished themselves with honor and dedication to the country that allowed the Corps to follow its country's dictates, and is ever ready and willing to take the battle to her enemies.

If flying heavier than air crafts started with the illustrious Wright brothers then it was perfected by a brash group of young eagles over the skies of Northern France, as they tore themselves to shreds in the air war of 1914-18. Clumsy canvas boxes of flaming coffins were their chariots, and the initiating of a heritage that is still being perfected today in what has evolved into the United States Air Force. The beginnings of the Air Force were properly seeded under the aegis of the French and British, and initially called the "Lafayette Escadrille." Young Americans, mostly college men from Yale, Princeton, Harvard, and Georgetown, eager to fight, although their country was at peace, went overseas to join the French in their fight against "The Hun." They went as ambulance drivers, soldiers, and finally entered the fledgling, but rapidly learning French Air Force. When the United States finally entered the conflict, the young fliers transferred into the infant United States Army Air Force. Having no planes of their own, since their country hadn't had the foresight to get into "war planes" until it was too late, they were forced to use French Spads and English S. E. 5a's. The acknowledged head of the first American squadron was a man named Raul Lufbery. He was not a native American but was born in France of an American father. After his mother died he was raised in the United States. He became an ace in the French Air Force and transferred into the new American service after she entered the war. He not only became the spiritual and inspirational leader but also their first ace. He died jumping out of his flaming plane. One of the pilots reporting on his death was Captain Eddie Rickenbacker, who was America's foremost ace in the war and was responsible for taking 26 German air planes out of the sky before the conflict was over.

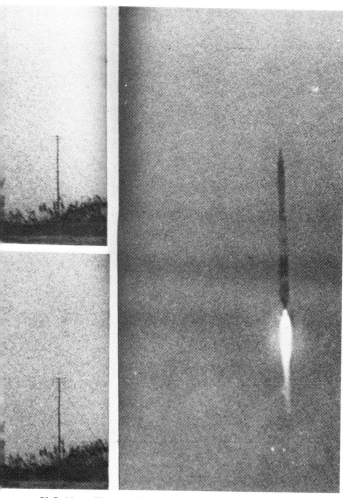

U.S. Navy Vanguard *missle being launched from Cape Kennedy.*

Meanwhile, in the Pacific, the Navy fliers were holding most of the responsibility in their hands with planes based on air craft carriers. However, when islands became available, the Army Air Corps was able to get its new and vaunted B-29s into the air over the skies of Tokyo and Yokohama. Ultimately the Air Corps earned the final responsibility of delivering the atomic bomb over two Japanese cities, Nagasaki and Hiroshima. The devastation was virtually total. Other bombs were saddled up and waiting. It was the final stroke of the war and it was to be delivered by the youngest service defending its country. The onus of responsibility has continued with the Air Corps, which on July 26, 1947, was retermed the Air Force by the Unification Act and established as a separate military service.

Today, the United States Air Force stands as America's first line of defense, and probably its last as well. There are no moments of the day when highly efficient bombers are not manned and ready and in the air.

SELECTED BIBLIOGRAPHY

Maurice Matloff, General Editor, *American Military History.* Office of the Chief of Military History, U.S. Army, Washington, D.C.

Col. Marcus Skarstedt and Col. Thanxton Hanson, *Vanguard of Freedom.* The Association of the United States Army.

The Blue Jackets Manual. 18th Edition. United States Naval Institute, Annapolis, Maryland.

Charles R. Smith, *Marines in the Revolution.* History and Museums Division, Headquarters, U.S. Marine Corps. Wash. D.C.

Guidebook for Marines. Leatherneck Association, Inc., Washington, D.C.

Henry I. Shaw, *Tarawa.* Ballantine Books #8; Ballantine Books, Inc., New York, New York.

Eddie V. Rickenbacker, *Fighting the Flying Circus.* Avon Books, New York, New York.

Arch Whitehouse, *Heros and Legends of World War I.* Doubleday and Company, Icc.

Richard Johnston, *Follow Me!.* Random House, New York, New York.

Our Early Navy, Parts 1 and 2. All Hands Magazine, U.S. Navy Publication.

Coast Guard History. Public Information Division, Washington, D.C.

Historically Famous Lighthouses. Public Information Division, Washington, D.C.

Pictures permitted by courtesy: United States Army; United States Navy; United States Marine Corps; Public Relations Bureau, 1100 Wilshire Blvd., Los Angeles, California.

Additional information taken from: *The 1972 World Almanac.* Newspaper Enterprise Association, New York, New York.

Gene Gurney, *The Flying Aces of World War I.* Windward Books, Random House, New York, New York.

William Addleman Ganoe, *The History of the United States Army.* D. Appleton-Century Company, London, England.

If the young American Flying Corps was steeled in the furnaces of France then they were mellowed and tempered by the uneasy peace that followed. General Billy Mitchell proved to his contemporaries that air power would be a factor when he sunk an old navy ship with a squadron of airplanes. He was to suffer a court martial and suspension of duty for his brashness. The department of the army gently gestured the air wing aside and continued to count on the cavalry to forge the new fronts of the future wars that would be fought. Adolph Hitler changed that idea when in 1939 his blitzkrieg and control of the air forced Poland to her knees, and when American generals saw the results of the Battle of Britain and how "so much was owed by so many to so few." Pearl Habor caught both the Navy and the Air Corps off guard and it would take two more years of uphill fighting to balance things in the Pacific. Meanwhile, concentrating on heavy bombers, and combining their talents with the British, America proved that saturation bombing of a highly industrialized nation could almost single handedly bring an enemy to its knees.

Learning from the stagnation of the First World War the Air Corps set its task to systematically demolish Nazi Germany. For the first time in history whole cities and their populations were destroyed and leveled to the ground. Many times whole flights of planes and bombers did not return from their missions. There was a wholesale slaughter in the air on both sides, but ultimately victory came to the Allies, and probably just in time, because the Germans had just developed a jet air craft and were about to go into mass production with it.

EXTRA!

ALL THE NEWS ALL THE TIME

Largest Home Delivered Circulation
Largest Advertising Volume

Los Angeles Times

EQUAL RIGHTS

LIBERTY UNDER THE LAW — TRUE INDUSTRIAL FREEDOM

IN THREE PARTS

PART I — GENERAL NEWS

Times Office: 202 West First Street
Los Angeles 53, Cal.
Times Telephone Number MAdison 2345

VOL. LXIII   CC**   TUESDAY MORNING, JUNE 6, 1944   DAILY, FIVE CENTS

INVASION!

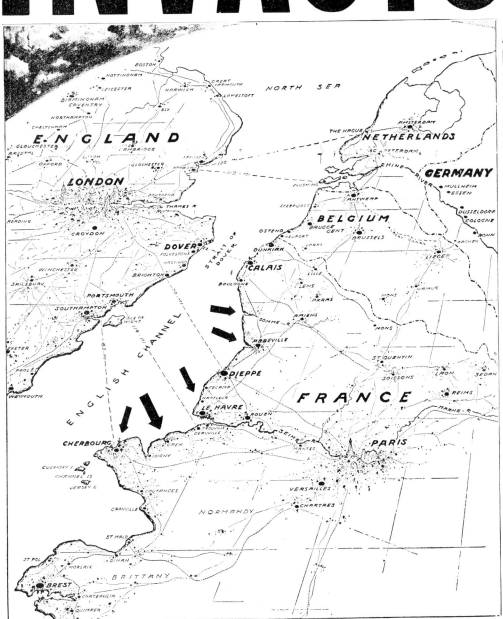

WHERE ALLIES ARE STRIKING—Arrows indicate the ports and coastal regions where Allied armies of invasion were reported swarming ashore in France early this morning.

Allied Landings Begun in France, Eisenhower Says

SUPREME HEADQUARTERS, ALLIED EXPEDITIONARY FORCE, June 6. (A.P.) Gen. Dwight D. Eisenhower's headquarters announced today that Allied troops began landing on the northern coast of France this morning strongly supported by naval and air forces.

Text of the communique:

Under the command of Gen. Eisenhower Allied forces, supported by strong air forces, began landing Allied armies this morning on the northern coast of France.

The Germans said the landings extended between Le Havre and Cherbourg along the south side of the bay of the Seine and along the Northern Normandy coast.

Parachute troops descended in Normandy, Berlin said.

Berlin first announced the landings in a series of flashes that began about 6:30 a.m. (12:30 a.m. E.W.T.)

The Allied communique was read over a trans-Atlantic hookup direct from Gen. Eisenhower's headquarters at 3:32 E.W.T. (12:32 a.m. P.W.T.) designated "Communique No. 1."

Montgomery Leads Assault

A second announcement by Shaef said that "it is announced that Gen. B. L. Montgomery is in command of the Army group carrying out the assault. This army group includes British, Canadian, and United States forces."

The Allied bulletin did not say exactly where the invasion was taking place, but Berlin earlier gave these details:

Allied naval forces, including heavy warships, are shelling Le Havre. "It is a terrific bombardment," Berlin said.

Allied parachute troops floating down along the Normandy coast were landing and being engaged by German shock troops.

Other Allied units were streaming ashore into Normandy from landing barges.

Eisenhower Order of Day

In a special order of the day issued to all soldiers, sailors and airmen under his command, Gen. Eisenhower said:

"We will accept nothing except full victory."

Eisenhower told his men they were "embarking on a great crusade toward which we have striven these many months," and warned them that they were facing a tough, well-prepared enemy.

Berlin said the "center of gravity" of the fierce fighting

Turn to Page A, Column 1

Invasion—and 'The Times'

This is D-Day. The greatest continuing news story in the history of man has begun—and will continue until Victory. Americans, and all the people of the earth, now eagerly await every new development, watch every Allied move and Nazi countermove.

The detailed story of invasion, complete with all the available maps and pictures, will be brought to Times readers with the speed, thoroughness and accuracy that have always made The Times the West's most dependable . . . and depended upon . . . newspaper!

VIOLENCE IN AMERICA—
A DECAYING LIMB

Hernando de Soto landing in Florida in search of gold in the fabled Seven Cities, with an entourage of 720 men and 237 horses, was to leave a trail of blood and violence across Georgia, the Carolinas, Tennessee, Alabama and into the Mississippi Valley near the edge of the Gulf of Mexico.

Scattered in his wake were a heap of mutilated native bodies, who for the most part didn't have the faintest idea why they were being slaughtered. Whole villages were slaughtered, women and children literally torn apart by the huge dogs that the Spaniards set upon them.

The Indians battled for their homes and reprisals were often taken to avenge the dead Spaniards. Some were killed by the sword and others were made porters and slaves in the continuing growing caravan of death. An ancient chronicler tells us "The land over which the governor (deSoto) traveled lay wasted and was without maize."

Eventually turning back to his starting point, de Soto's lust for gold had cooled radically and with it his will to live. He died on the banks of the Mississippi River in an ironic ending that mingled his blood with those whom he had sent on before him. The key note had been set and the symphony had begun. Others were to take on the chorus and join in on the "Valse of Violence."

The English carried on the bloody tradition in the mid 16th century laying the framework in Virginia with another kind of violence, religious bigotry.

The roots of this phase of violence in America had its early origins in Europe between the Catholics and the Protestants. The latter, fearful of their lives, hoped for a refuge in the new world. The violence was to occur and reoccur from time to time for the next four hundred years.

The small Protestant colony made its settlement in the calm waters of the River of May in northern Florida. They thought they had finally reached their land of peace and tranquillity. However, other men had other thoughts. In August, 1565, a fleet commanded by Pedro Menendez de Aviles, Adelantado of Florida, sailed into the River of May and had on his person an asiento, or what is called in modern terms, a contract, issued by the King of Spain, Philip II, which called for the liquidation of the Protestant foothold in what Philip described as "one of our dominions." De Aviles, who was an erratic and fanatic Catholic, eager to uphold his contract to the letter, was not without logical and rational justification for his upcoming actions, and even clarified his stand when he said, "I do this not unto the Frenchmen with whom my King and country are at peace, but unto heretics." With his success was to come the governorship of Florida, as added incentive. Attacking the "heretics" with vigor and acumen they slaughtered the colony to a man and celebrated their brilliant victory by tearing their dead and vanquished enemies' eyeballs out of their heads.

In 1620, when the Mayflower had hardly settled in her berth, two more English ships arrived loaded and ready with sixty men who intended to found a colony nearby. This immediately incurred the wrath of the Pilgrims who did everything they could to make it extremely difficult for the new arrivals, who hardly needed any new visitation upon them, for they had indolently neglected their crops and stolen from the Indians. This of course had a dampening effect upon the Indians who had gotten tired of the whippings and harassment from the Puritans. The Pilgrims punished the

Puritans by whippings and pillory, and when this proved futile they decided to placate the Indians by condemning one of the colonists to death. At first the culprit was a young man, but since he could contribute to the welfare of the community, they chose a feeble old man, innocent of any crime, for their example. Strange rationale but seemingly accurate.

This didn't assuage the local tribes at all and they became more restive and news of an impending attack girded Miles Standish, who was known as "Captain Shrimpe," to get rid of two menaces at once, the Colonists and the Indians.

Pretending friendship for the Indians he lured them into a meeting and smoked a peace pipe. All went according to schedule, and when the Indians were at peace within the meeting hut the soldiers fell upon the Indians and hacked them to death. Standish personally accounted for one savage whom he sliced to death with his knife. Then the Pilgrims fell upon any and all natives in the area, chasing them into the swamps.

Standish saved one Indian boy, an eighteen year old, whom he retained for a public hanging to set an example. After chasing them into the swamps Standish returned triumphantly with the Indian chief's head and nailed it to the wooden stockade fence of Plymouth, having it become "one of the sights of Plymouth."

It wasn't so easy to eliminate the Puritans of New England, for they too were a hearty breed as vigorous and sinewy as their Pilgrim counterparts. They were to prove this later at a small town in Massachusetts called Salem.

It was from the mischievousness of three young girls, Elizabeth Parris, her cousin Abigail Williams and the self confessor to the hoax, Anne Putnam, that the Salem witch trials and hangings eminated in 1692.

Wanting to have some innocent fun and to scare the rest of the villagers the girls feigned senselessness, and were diagnosed as "obsessed by a diabolic spirit." In too deep to acknowledge that the were pretending, the young girls kept up the sham until so many townspeople were killed and jailed that it threatened to deplete the town completely. Some two hundred people were jailed and any and all excuses for personal revenge precipitated an accusation and swift punishment.

The crusade needed a spiritual head and no better candidate than Cotton Mather stepped into the breech. Mather, who was a clergyman and writer, had tremendous influence in the community and stated, "We must set down every incidence of divine judgements, tempests, floods, earthquakes, as are unusual, strange apparitions, or whatever else shall happen that is prodigious, witchcrafts, diabolical possessions, remarkable judgements upon noted sinners, eminent deliverances and answers to prayers. . . Hangman, do your duty!!"

The trials and persecutions would probably have gone on indefinitely were it not for the fact that the accusers had made a fatal mistake. Someone accused the wife of one of the most bitterly antagonistic witchhunters, Reverend John Hale, of being a witch. The reverend minister suddenly had a change of heart and mind about the whole matter and denounced the trials as nothing but idle superstition, bringing the whole thing to a rather abrupt close.

The Revolution was not without its share of violence away from the battlefields. Simon Girty had witnessed his

General George Custer, *who led 225 members of the Seventh Cavalry to their deaths in a battle against Cheyenne and Sioux warriors at the battle of Little Big Horn.*

father being killed by an Indian in a drunken brawl. It didn't have either a salutary or bitter effect on his attitude because rather than fight against the Indians he sided with them and the British during the Revolutionary War. He and his Indian troop raided Fort Pitt and after the battle was seen proudly admiring the two scalps that he draped from his belt.

Fighting his way into Kentucky he came back from that forage with a series of scalps, "enough to adorn the doorway to my cabin." As an additional prize he captured a white woman that he turned over to the squaws for the pleasure of "having something to burn." He then took his band of men and moved down to New Orleans, where he and his men successfully raided a boating party, who were loaded down with supplies from Fort Pitt, and after the unexpected attack and quick victory killed forty-two of the seventy Americans and captured the rest for slaughter and torture.

Three months later he commanded the capture of Ruddled Station which he took by subterfuge when he assured the men at the post that the British would have charge of all men taken prisoners. As the gates to the small fort swung open he allowed his Indians to run wild and the ensuing massacre was quick and final. In a later incident he allowed his men to burn a prisoner a day for nine days and as they were about to burn the last prisoner Girty talked the Indians into allowing him to go free and carry the word back to other settlers as an example of what would happen to them in the future.

During the 1830's a mass migration of laborers and manual workers began to migrate from Ireland to this country. Poor and ill trained, most of them were of the Catholic faith and almost immediately aroused the indignation of the local natives who feared that a papal state was forming in this country. Most of the violence poured in the streets of the urban communities, and most of that in the large eastern cities. "Ulcerating slums along the five points in Manhattan caused a great deal of civil strife and it may have been the era of the greatest urban violence that America has ever experienced."

When Catholic leaders objected to Bible teaching in public schools, preferring their own Douay version, Protestants viewed this as a papal movement and immediately began a

movement, formed around the American Bible Society, that spread anti-Catholic literature around the country. It was to set up a period of almost forty years of violence between the natives and their victims, the Irish Catholics.

In 1843 violence erupted in Boston. The citizens of Charleston across the bay from Boston were the initiators. The Ursuline Sisters had set up a small convent where they taught school, not only to a small number of Catholic children, but also to daughters of well-to-do Protestants. The violence stemmed from a minor incident of a girl, Rebecca Reed, who was supposedly writing a book entitled, *Six Months In a Convent*. Rumors started by brickyard workers suggested that the Catholics were involving the girls in moral impurity and offered that Rebecca had escaped "imprisonment by the nuns." Native Protestants now appeared on the street with their banners and posters. It was all the native crowd needed; they tore into the nunnery shouting that it must be destroyed. Windows were smashed and doors were battered down, Bibles and other class books were piled up in the dining center and set afire. Added to the flames as kindling were the statues and other religious arti-

Jesse James *and his killer Bob Ford. James was one of the first western badmen to gain a national reputation for his illegal exploits. With his brother Frank, James led a group of bank and train robbers on a reign of holdups throughout the western states. He was shot in the back and killed by Ford.*

PAT GARRET
KILLED BILLY THE KID.

William Bonney, *known as "Billy the Kid" and Pat Garret, the sheriff who finally killed the infamous western outlaw. Bonney was an easterner who went west and found the lawlessness of the region perfectly suited to his psychopathic personality. He reportedly killed more than 22 men during his lifetime, and was eventually shot and killed by Garret who had tracked the youthful desperado for many months.*

A reproduction *of a woodcut showing the outlaw Jesse James being shot in the back by Bob Ford at St. Joseph, Missouri on April 3, 1882. James had gone into partial retirement from bank robbing and was living in St. Joseph under the name of Mr. Howard at the time Ford discovered his identity and killed him for the reward money.*

America's greatest era *of lawlessness and violence was ushered in with the passage of legislation which made the manufacturing of alcohol for other than medicinal purposes illegal. Photograph shows two truckloads of illegal liquor which had been seized after a raid near Falmouth, Massachusetts in April, 1931. The Coast Guardsmen are guarding the illegal alcohol.*

This scene, *from a newspaper ink sketch of the time, is typical of the violence which exploded from time to time in the labor disputes before the turn of the 20th century. Here nearly 900 New York City police escort a horse drawn railway car down the street in an effort to break the strike started by the Street Railway Employees union in 1886.*

cles and within moments the entire building was in flames. The nuns were able to get more of the students out the back door and to safety before the building was completely demolished.

Shortly thereafter, in St. Louis, one of the worst riots in the city's history occurred when a band of native Protestants, goaded on by the rumor that an Irish Catholic had stabbed a member of the American Native Party in the back, raided Catholic homes, plundering and killing until ten men were killed and thirty seriously wounded. One of the leading papers in the city reported, "Men have been butchered like cattle, property destroyed and anarchy rules supreme."

In Philadelphia on May 3, 1844, the Native Americans demonstrated against the Irish Catholics, marching through

the Irish neighborhood threatening and cursing its frightened inhabitants. Someone fired a gun, and in a moment a general gun battle was in progress with "Irish women by their men's sides directing them as to where to fire and whom to strike. Even small boys took a hand in the affray." A row of houses where the Irish had taken refuge at Ninth and Poplar streets was set on fire. Another crowd burned St. Michaels church, the pastor's house, and a nearby convent. The fire spread from there to two more rows of houses and these burned to the ground because the Protestants wouldn't allow the fire department to have access to the flaming inferno.

In New York City, in 1854, a street preacher named West led an assault against a man in the street, "because he looked to be Irish." This was the beginning of the Know-Nothing mobs and demonstrators against the Catholics and other minorities, who were to become so powerful on the national scale as to receive this admonishment from a minor politician in Illinois, whose name was Abraham Lincoln . . . "How can anyone who abhors the oppression of Negroes be in favor of degrading classes of white people? As a nation we began by declaring that 'all men are created equal.'"

In 1619 a ship, newly arrived from Africa, carried with it the seeds of some of the most serious social and racial problems that would face the country in the next three hundred and fifty years. In Jamestown, John Rolfe recorded a minor event in his diary. . . . "About the last of August came in a Dutch man-of-war that sold fifty niggers." With that single act and many that were to follow violence had a new ally in this country. Bigotry, bias, hate and vitriolic venom all wrapped up neatly in the form of an enslaved group of humans from Africa, who had no choice in their bondage, and no direction over their destiny.

Criminal action against the slave started early in the history of human bondage in this country. In America no matter how intelligent, ambitious, loyal or cooperative a black man might be, he was still regarded as a lesser entity not on any peerage level with his white masters. The law gave him no protection.

In South Carolina in 1740, the killing of a slave was punishable by a fine of 700 pounds. In the event of an accidental death this was reduced to 350 pounds. In Georgia,

Labor violence *grew during the Thirties as factory conditions and long hours forced American workers to the streets to vent their frustrations at the lack of tolerable conditions. Here truckdrivers in Minneapolis, Minnesota, battle with police in May, 1934. Police and National Guard units were often used on the side of factory to quell workers' demonstrations.*

the murdering of a slave was not punishable at all if death occurred accidentally, "in a sudden heat of passion when giving a slave moderate correction." The only restraint placed upon the white slave owner in his relations with a Negro was that of the protection of property. If a white man killed another man's slave he could be sued for damages.

In 1838, Micajah Ricks of North Carolina advertised to find a run away slave ". . . the woman is tall and black. A few days before she left I branded her with a hot iron on the left side of her face. I tried to mark her with the letter "M", and she kept a cloth over her face and a fly bonnet over her head so as to cover the burn."

An account from the court record in Balwin County, Georgia, reveals an interesting chronicle of fourteen years of "Slave owner justice."

Richard T. Frankensteen, *United Auto Workers Organizational Director, is attacked near the entrance of the Ford River Rouge plant by strike breakers hired by the auto industry. The attack on Frankensteen was one of the first acts of violence in the bloody auto industry dispute which raged throughout much of the Thirties.*

These two effigies, *one labeled "General Motors Stool Pigeon" and the other "George Boysen", the leader of the Flint Alliance which was trying to prevent auto workers from organizing, are hanging from the Fisher Body Company's Plant Number Two. The striking auto workers had occupied the building in 1937 as part of the general strike against the auto manufacturing industry.*

1812 Major convicted of rape and hanged

1815 Tom convicted of murdering a fellow slave sentenced to branding on each cheek with the letter "M" and to thirty-nine lashes on his bare back for three successive days.

1816 John, a slave of William McGeehee, convicted of theft of a hundred dollar bill was sentenced to whipping in a similar fashion.

1818 Aleck, found guilty of assault. Received fifty lashes on three days in succession.

1819 Rodney, sentenced to death by hanging for arson.

1822 John convicted of burglary but recommended to mercy. Sentenced to be branded with a "T" on the right cheek and to receive three times thirty-nine lashes. The same John on the same day was sentenced to death for assaulting a white man.

1825 John Ponders George convicted of burglary. Jury recommended mercy but the death sentence was passed anyway.

1826 Elleck, convicted of assault received the death sentence.

Finally, there is an excerpt from a testimony of a slave woman on the type of treatment that she received from the hands of her master. ''He ties me to that stake and every half hour for four hours they lay ten lashes on my back. For the first couple of hours the pain am awful. I'se never forget it.''

Walter Grimes, a particularly intelligent slave, speaking in 1825 stated, ''If it were not for the stripes on my back which were made while I was a slave, I would, in my will, leave my skin a legacy to the government, desiring that it be taken off and made into parchment and then bind the constitution of glorious, happy, free America. Let the skill of an American slave bind the chapter of American Liberty!'' It could come as no great shock to anyone then, when the Black man, under this punishing vassalage, suddenly turned to his own particular type of revenge and violence.

David Walker, a free Black who lived in Boston, gave a series of speeches and printed a phamphlet which he called, ''Walker's Appeal in Four Articles,'' which he published in 1829: ''Never make an attempt to gain our freedom or natural rights until the way is clear. When that hour arrives, make your move and be not afraid. Let twelve good Black men get armed for battle and they will put to flight fifty whites.''

Between the years 1750 and 1850 there were more than 250 revolts or attempted revolts against the slave masters. Often this was slave against master, but many times whole staffs of Blacks rose up and committed kinds of rebellions, such as arson, poisoning food, and murder.

In Virginia, in 1831, a young Black man, angered and having had enough of the brutal treatment that was heir to a slave/master relationship, decided to revolt. He was thirty-one years old and had been taught to read. Most of that reading

J. Edgar Hoover, *as he appeared in 1969. Hoover single-handedly built the Federal Bureau of Investigation into one of the most effective crime fighting organizations in the world. He personally took credit for the capture of many infamous bank robbers in the Twenties and Thirties, and used the publicity resulting from these arrests to insulate the FBI's mystique in the minds of millions of Americans.*

was out of the Bible and somehow Turner began to interpret the writings as being pointed directly at him, with the direct result that he believed himself to be the Black deliverer sent from God to free his brothers. Foreman of a small plantation, he convinced eight of his fellow slaves to follow him and without any formal plan of operation attacked his master's family with a hatchet and broad axe. The seven minute carnage left five whites dead, including a small baby which had its head cleaved like a green cantaloupe. Armed with a few guns, the gang, now joined by fifty or more other escaped slaves, moved from the plantation killing all whites that they came across. The slaughter continued for three days, as men and women were killed and children were hacked to death.

Mary Barkeley Blackford, who was the wife of a planter, recorded this account in her diary. . . ''A few minutes after the Negroes were seen riding up to the house they were inside and had commenced their work of slaughter. The mother of the master who had always enjoyed the affection of her Negroes was the first to be killed. Her own servant had nothing to do with the insurrection.''

The insurrection terminated as it had begun, in bloodshed. Marching towards the county seat the rebels came upon the plantation of a wealthy planter named Parker. Feeling their taste of victory, the slaves intended recruiting Parker's vassals. Turner, with an innate instinct, was against the move but was overruled by his subordinates, who sent to Parker's house and found a plentiful supply of cider and other liquors. Their spending a few leisure hours of drinking and creating general mayhem allowed Parker to muster eighteen volunteers who attacked and dispersed his men with birdshot and

Labor violence *during the Thirties was not always between police and strikers. Here one of twenty men injured during a fight between members of the rival American Federation of Labor and Congress of Industrial Organizations is helped to his feet. The clash between rival unions occurred frequently in 1939.*

fowling pieces. Turner, who had been absent during the battle, returned with other men, but he too was routed by the plantation owners and Turner escaped into the swamps. He eluded a posse for several months but was finally captured. He was hanged with eighteen others of his group in return for the fifty or so whites who had died during his brief uprising.

This was to bring to an end the southern contention that Negroes were docile in their slavery and loved their masters. The misconception that slaves labored happily under their bondage was to perpetuate itself adamantly into the twentieth century, with vestiges of that erroneous idea still believed in certain contemporary circles. The myth of harmonious Black consent in their vassalage has had a tenaciously lingering death.

If the Black slavery idea had a hard death, then another group of vigilantes were to parallel that idea with one of their own, an idea as stubborn and persistent as any visited upon man's violence and hatred responses.

The Ku Klux Klan started among college students who had been Confederate officers. They remembered offenses during the great internal struggle that laid waste to the land, that offered freedom from slavery as the base roots of the Civil War.

Andersonville Prison in Georgia was a prime example of man's inhumanity to man when it was revealed that conditions inside the prison were so bad that over 12,000 men died from starvation, beatings, and disease. It was reported that

Jack ''Legs'' Diamond, *racketeer in New York City, is shown in the company of one of his attorneys leaving a Federal Courthouse following his indictment for conspiracy to violate the Prohibition law.*

the stench from its rotting interiors could be ''smelled for over a mile.''

Another Civil War figure that came to the attention of post war dissenters, who was a paradox even among southern admirers, was William Clark Quantrill. Quantrill wandered around Utah and finally ended up in Kansas where he carried out his most vicious crimes against any and all authority. He was wanted for horse stealing and killing several pro-slavery farmers. He was also a slave stealer, and joined the Cherokee Indians as a renegade and helped attack and kill regular army troops at Wilson's Creek.

Fighting ostensibly under the Confederate banner he burned and looted the town of Olathe, Kansas, then raided the town of Lawrence, Kansas, where he and his gang murdered more than 150 defenseless men and boys, leaving the town in flames. It was from this seedy and questionable background that the Klan had its demeritorious beginnings.

The first grand wizard was an ex-Confederate cavalry man, General Nathan Bedford Forest, who was guilty of being part of the massacre of soldiers and their dependents at Fort Pillow. There Forest ordered 229 of the 262 Negro defenders of the fort killed, burning most of them at the stake. Burning was to become a favorite past time for the Ku Klux Klan as its tentacles spread their way across the country.

By 1886 the Klan was able to boast a membership of over 500,000 and its terrorist actions could number well in the millions. ''If a black man was believed to be guilty of having seduced a white woman, he was castrated, tarred and feathered, then lynched. Likewise, if a white woman was believed to have encouraged the sexual advances of a black man, she was murdered, usually only after she had been shaven bald and made to parade through the streets nude, the words 'nigger lover' painted (or carved by pen knife) upon her chest and back.''

Alphonso ''Scarface'' Capone, *leader of the underworld in the Chicago area for many years. Capone's rise in the underworld was unrivaled for its violence and power. Although he was arrested on several occassions, once he had climbed to the top of the power ladder, police officials had no luck in bringing convictions. He was finally convicted of income tax evasion and sentenced to a Federal prison.*

George Nelson

Two views *of the gangster George "Babyface" Nelson at the height of his crime spree in 1933. Nelson and others such as Clyde Barrows, Machine Gun Kelly, and Ma Barker became legendary characters through the romanticizing of the illegal activities by the press.*

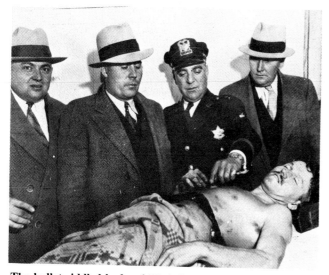

The bullet riddled body *of "Babyface" Nelson in an undertaker's salon near Chicago in 1934. Nelson's body was found by authorities shortly after he and Federal agents had exchanged gunshots near Niles Center, Illinois on November 23, 1934.*

The Klan burned down black schools as fast as the government could build them. If a Black was found to have a prosperous farm they would burn it to the ground or murder the inhabitants by burning or lynching. They broke into jails, took the prisoners and smashed their skulls. The wave of terror became so wide spread that finally the founder of the Klan, Forest himself, could take no more and dissolved the Klan in 1869.

Dissolution was ineffective because the Klan had had its taste of violence and revenge against the Blacks and other minorities and was to continue its trubulent maurauding for another hundred years.

Approximately five thousand Blacks were lynched by white mobs between 1865 and 1955 and this figure does not include legal lynchings or actions taken by self-empowered kangeroo courts. In race riots alone over five hundred Blacks were killed between 1865 and 1940.

In the middle 1800's violence wasn't the bedmate of

Blacks, Irish and Catholics only, for there was another form of racial violence just as insidious and perhaps with even less justification. The opening stanza of a popular song of the gold rush period, which reflected only minutely the feelings of Californians toward the Chinese of the mid-1850's, had these lyrics, "John Chinaman, John Chinaman, but five short years ago, I welcomed you from Canton, John, but I wish I hadn't though."

The Chinese that first set foot on these shores, according to the *Sacramento Bee* in 1866, stated that his name was Chum Ming, a Cantonese. He was to become highly successful in the gold mines during the early months of the gold rush. This was to inspire others of his country to join in the quest for the yellow element.

They came from China via Peru and would soon grow to several thousand. Whereas the Californians called the Mexicans and Indians various derogatory names, they had a few equally appalling cognomens for the Chinese as well. If the Mexicans and Indians were "Greasers" and "Diggers" then the Chinese were "Chinks," "Celestials," "Heathens," "Coolies," "Slant Eyes" and "Moonfaces."

The Chinese, being a placid people by nature, were patient and cool toward their tormentors, and unlike the Mexicans, Indians, and black slaves and freedmen, did not retaliate. Instead, unable to vent their hate in a reciprocal way, miners used old internal Chinese clan troubles to antagonize so that every now and then the Chinese would take up arms against one another with the sad result that many were killed in the process.

The Chinese were discriminated against because it was said that they were dirty and brought filthy habits over with them, namely the smoking of opium. It was feared that young American girls would corrupt themselves through the Chinese influence.

John Dillinger, *a few months before he was killed by FBI agents. The pistol in his left hand is the wooden model he reportedly used in his escape from the Crown Point, Indiana jail. This photograph was taken at his father's home near Moore, Indiana three months before his death.*

The body of Benjamin ''Bugsy'' Siegel in his Beverly Hills, California, home, where he was killed on June 20, 1947. Siegel was one of the best known underworld figures to move to the West Coast in the Forties where he reportedly tried to establish a syndicate in the large west coast cities.

There were a percentage of prostitutes, both white and Chinese, and it is also recorded that the Chinese ladies of the evening had little time off from their job and little need for customers. Mark Twain noted in his ''Roughing It'' that ''a disorderly Chinese is rare, and a lazy one does not exist.'' With all of this evidence of an orderly minority, there still existed a number of horrendous actions against the peaceful people. ''Not having a Chinaman's Chance'' was not just an innocent phrase.

Judge Roy Bean, self appointed ''law of the west,'' looked through three or four law books and noted, ''damned if I can find where it's against the law to kill a Chinaman!'' This was in a trial against a man who had taken the life of a Chinese who had been accused, (rightly or wrongly) of petty thievery. Chinese were hanged, shot, taken advantage of and generally looked down upon by society. The murder of Orientals became so commonplace in Los Angeles that newspapers seldom printed the story.

If the Chinese were having it difficult in the old west they were in good company with the original inhabitants of the area, the American Indians. ''There is more law in a Colt Six Gun that in all the law books'' ran a popular expression in the old west. Another anecdote saw ''three legged Willie,'' who was a pioneer judge in Texas, trying to explain the law to another Texan of equal persuasions, watched the man pull a bowie knife from a sheath and lay it on the judge's desk . . . ''Here's the law of Texas, Judge.'' Willie calmly pulled out his six shooter and placed it next to the bowie knife and responded, ''Yes, and by God here is the constitution of Texas.'' If gun culture was the child of western justice, then the western and plains Indians were its innocent victims.

Estimates of Indians massacred in the United States since 1789 vary from 4,000 to 10,000. Thousands more were killed by alcohol, smallpox, measles, chickenpox and other diseases that were unheard of before the coming of the white man.

In the middle of the 1800's it became the Indians' turn to taste the bitter fruit of violence. Centered in the conflict were the Cheyenne, Arapaho, Sioux, Crow and other members of the Great Plains tribes. Worthy of note was Chief Black Kettle, a Cheyenne warrior who had the dubious distinction

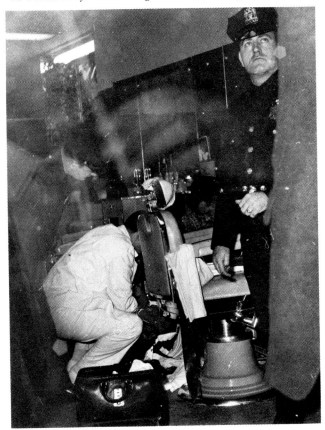

A medical examiner checks the body of Albert Anastasia in a barber shop where he was shot and killed on October 25, 1957. Anastasia was an overlord in the New York City underworld at the time he was killed by two masked gunmen while having his hair cut.

of having been the victim of violence on two occasions. First at Sand Creek, Colorado, and later at the Washita River in Oklahoma.

In 1864 his band had been given permission from the commander at Fort Lyons to camp at nearby Sand Creek for the winter. It was understood that as long as they flew the Stars and Stripes over their tepees they would not be bothered.

Earlier that summer a group of volunteers under the command of a Methodist minister, Colonel J. M. Chivington, arrived at Fort Lyons, ''in search of Indians.'' It was well known in Denver that the minister's orders to his troops suggested that all Indians that they encountered were to be killed, whether ''friendly or not.''

Black Kettle had been so secure in his camp, under the flag, that he had long since ceased to post sentries around his camp. It was upon this quiet early morning scene that James Beckwourth, a black mountain man and the discoverer of Beckwourth Pass in California, noted that ''orders by the Colonel stated that we 'take no prisoners,' 'to kill all,' 'little and big,' and that the only good Indian was a dead Indian.''

A lieutenant, James D. Conner, of the New Mexico Volunteers related this narrative of the attack to a Congressional investigating committee several months later. ''At about daybreak on the morning of the 29th of November we came in sight of the camp of the friendly Indians aforementioned, and were ordered by Colonel Chivington to attack the same, which was accordingly done. The village of Indians consisted of from one hundred to one hundred fifty lodges, and as far as I am able to judge, of from five hundred to six hundred souls, the majority of which were women and children; in going over the battleground the next day I did not see a body of man, woman or child but was scalped, and in many instances their bodies were mutilated in the most horrible manner. Men and women and childrens private parts cut out, etc. I heard one man say that he had cut out a womans private parts and had them for exhibition on a stick. According to the best of my knowledge and belief these atrocities that were committed were with the knowledge of J.M. Chivington and I do not know of his taking any measure to prevent them.''

The Colorado Volunteers returned to Denver with their scalp trophies and three terrified Indian children who were later put on exhibition at a local opera house.

The Congressional Committee concluded after hearing all of the testimony that, ''It is difficult to believe that beings in the form of men, and disgracing the uniform of the United States soldiers and officers could commit or countenance the commission of such acts of cruelty and barbarity.''

Meanwhile Black Kettle and other Cheyenne and Arapaho survivors, kept under close supervision, were moved to the mouth of the Arkansas River on October 14, agreeing to give up all claim to the eastern Colorado land and live south on the lands belonging to the Kiowas. The ensuing results were predictable and inevitable. In the early hours of November 27, 1868, almost four years to the day, Black Kettle was to suffer the ultimate humiliation and final act of his life, as he was to be betrayed for the last time.

Probably engendered by a general order from General Ord who was in command of the Department of California of the Military Division of the Pacific, which proclaimed a general extermination policy toward the Indians, and in an official letter which stated in part, ''I encouraged the troops to capture and root out the Apache by every means and to hunt them down as they would wild animals. This they have done with unrelenting vigor.''

With this authority prevailing at the time it wasn't terribly difficult for the final assault on Black Kettle and the vestiges of his band of men. In the early hours of that fateful November dawn General George Armstrong Custer and four detachments of his famed Seventh Cavalry attacked Black Kettle's camp in the Washita River. So quick and efficient were his troops that in a few short minutes they were in control of the village. However, the Cheyenne warriors were not to go down to defeat so lightly, they fought back bravely and desperately. Hand to hand combat ensued between the soldiers and Indians and a general butchery of Indians occurred. There would probably have been a total slaughter of the band had it not been for a great number of Arapahos, Kiowas, and Comanches camped in the vicinity and already responding to the sounds of battle when Custer and his men retreated. As it was the carnage was almost complete.

Custer claimed to have destroyed fifty-one lodges and captured nine hundred horses and a number of skins, food, and arms. His report claimed that his troops killed one hundred and three Indians, and numbered among the victims were Black Kettle and his wife. Custer's own casualties amounted to about thirty-five killed or wounded.

In the late nineties the nation looked forward to a century of progress and prosperity. It was on the edge of a modern industrial revolution. Mass production was in its infancy, sweat shops and the exploitation of the myriads of immigrants who were used for cheap labor, and the first stirring of unionizing was beginning to take roots in the minds of the workers and ambitiously angry men.

From 1900 to 1919 the country was in a transition. New faces were on the scene: vast numbers of immigrants who were trying to shake off the shackles of the old world and eager to start life with a freshness unseen before in the new

Roger Touhy *slowly dying after being ambushed as he returned home on December 16, 1959. Touhy had been released from prison 23 days earlier where he had served a 25 year sentence in Stateville penitentiary for a kidnaping crime he maintained he did not comit. Touhy died from the shotgun wounds.*

Mobster Joseph Valachi *shown on his arrival at a Senate hearing room to testify into the government's investigation into organized crime in America. Valachi was a member of a crime syndicate which operated on the east coast for many years.*

one. In this transition violence against the Negro was again pronounced because he had moved in from the rural districts and into the urban areas to look for advancement in the rapidly erupting industrial movement. The only thing the exodus from the south and rural area brought the Black was further misery and ghettoization. Disenfranchised and disillusioned, they remained a target for hate and retaliation until after the First World War.

Suddenly, a new type of violence began to rear its ugly head, the labor riots. The labor disputes properly belong to the latter part of the 19th century where they slipped into the present century as a residual effect of the seeds that were planted in incidents such as the Haymarket riots on May 4, 1886.

It began innocently enough at the McCormick works in Chicago on May 3, and would have gone unnoticed except that several policemen panicked and shot into the crowd killing several workers. A meeting was called for the next day at a square on Randolph Street, called Haymarket. As the large crowd gathered the policemen began to get uneasy. They were still uneasy over the previous day's shooting and were expecting retaliation from the workers. The crowed, in full force at the appointed time, was addressed by their leaders. Among them were avowed Anarchists and the grumblings were getting heated when the police began to disperse them.

From somewhere, some anonymous hand threw a bomb at the policemen. Seven of them fell to the ground dead. Many more of their number were wounded. In retaliation, seven Anarchists were arrested and charged with murder because they were accomplices in the killing, and because they had repeatedly and publicly advocated such acts against the servants of the government. They were convicted and sentenced to death. Four were hanged, one committed suicide and two had their sentences commuted to life imprisonment.

In 1900 a strike by the United Mine Workers resulted in a clash that caused one strikebreaker to be killed. Strikers were killed in Old Forge, a colliery, in 1902, and another was slain at Duryea. As these strikes went on in the anthracite fields other men were slain by troops and policemen, until finally a Congressional committee investigating the private armies that had been hired by the mine owners found that workers had been forcibly kept in stockades and compelled to work by armed guards. "There was an armed guard at each end of the car and passangers were not allowed to leave the train, and when they got into camp they were forced to work there by the deputies of the car companies, being authorized by the sheriff to appoint whatever deputies they chose."

In 1912 at a copper strike in Michigan, the operatives of the Waddell Private Detective Agency spread rumors that their men had been fired on from a particular home. Deputies surrounded the home and fired into it with the result that one man was killed and a baby, though wounded, did survive. The victims were totally innnocent.

In 1911, at the Illinois Central Shopman's strike several men were killed and a number of railroad cars were burned. Five Negroes working for the railroad were killed and several wounded. This was the result of strikebreakers, and not at the hands of the strikers.

Violence and the Roaring Twenties went hand in hand, and it was not until the coming of the New Deal in 1933 that a series of laws were passed regulating labor relations and disputes with the result that a further easing of labor violence ensued.

All was not so peaceful in Chicago on Memorial Day, Sunday, May 30, 1937. It wasn't enough that the country was laboring in the terrible throes of the great Depression, and that it had not learned the lessons of the Pullman Strike, a short forty-two years before, where the arrival of Federal troops and police were to put down the roving gangs of strikers with guns, billies, and bayonets. When the carnage was finally over, it was revealed that it had taken fourteen thousand troops, and five thousand Federal marshalls to bring the strike to an end, resulting in the lives of thirteen strikers killed and fifty three seriously wounded. Several hundred strikers had been arrested.

Memorial Day. A day for remembering the nation's dead. It was a holiday and a lot of the workers were out of work at the Republic Street Mill, which made the holiday even more incongruous. Three steel companies had merged, Little Steel, Youngstown Sheet and Tube, and Republic. It had necessitated a lay-off of seventy-five workers from Republic and had engendered a great deal of anger from the Depression-plagued workers. The right of peaceful picketing had been refused to the strikers by police who had broken up the picketers as they attempted to rally around the mill. The

This photograph *shows Sam Giancana as he entered a Federal court building in Chicago in 1974. Giancana, who had been a Chicago crime syndicate leader for several years, had been linked to alleged CIA plots to kill Cuban prime minister Fidel Castro. Giancana was killed in his Oak Park, Illinois home in 1975.*

Police officials *unearth the bodies of two high school students near Bennet, Nebraska. The two students had been shot to death, and at the time the bodies were discovered the police had no clues as to the killer, who turned out to be Charlie Starkweather. The bodies were found on January 29, 1958.*

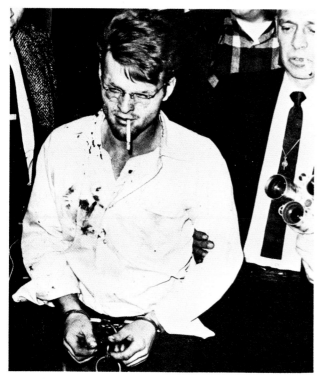

Charlie Starkweather *being led to waiting police care following his capture. Starkweather led police in seven mid-western states on a chase which finally ended near Lincoln, Nebraska. He was executed for murder.*

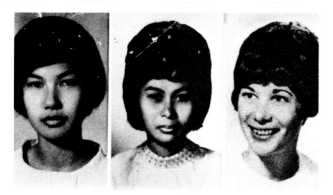

Three of the eight nurses *slain in a dormitory on July 14, 1966. The eight were systematically murderd by Richard Speck.*

Richard Speck, *left, as he leaves the courthouse following his conviction for murdering eight Chicago student nurses. Speck received the death sentence in 1967.*

pickets kept coming back for three days, and as always the police kept dispersing the strikers and they were not allowed to voice their dissent.

Sam's Place was a cafe where the strikers would rally and formulate their plans and discuss the clubbings and arrests by their fellow workers. On the 30th, women and children, because of the Sunday holiday, were at Sam's Place, dressed up in their Sunday best. The rally took on the color and tone of a holiday celebration. Leo Krzycki, a union organizer and principal speaker, addressed the crowd. He reported that the mayor had affirmed the workers' right to picket and protest. He joked with the crowd and they were all in an extremely good mood.

Some of the women sang and finally a vote was taken that the meeting should proceed across the fields and picketing should begin against the Republic Steel Mill. The audience strolled out in a gay and fun spirited manner that hardly could be misconstrued as a march. It was hardly evident that this gay group of people, singing and laughing among one another, were actually marching to their deaths.

At the head of the column was a small petite lady, hardly ninety pounds and not five feet tall, whose name was Mrs. Lupe Marshall; she was a social worker from the Hull House community center. Someone heard her call to a worker who had picked up a stone, "Drop that, we don't want none of that stuff." There were no guns among the marchers and no clubs or placards. Only a mass of laughing and singing humanity. A platoon of fifty policemen had been seen walking out of the mill that morning and it was their objective to make the striking workers appear to be part of a Red plot to take over the mill. The two groups met and the only protection that the marchers had between them and the armed and angry policemen were two American flags.

Without any warning, seemingly out of nowhere, several shots were fired into the crowd. Women screamed and some of the strikers managed to throw a few stones. Then within minutes the area was like a battlefield, and suddenly bodies of men and women, dying and dead were lying at the feet of the policemen. Lupe Marshall, appalled at the death and carnage occuring around her, pleaded with a policeman. Another policeman cursed her as she turned, bent down and helped a bloodsoaked victim. As she was in this bent position a policeman came up behind her and split her skull with a billie club. She fell to the ground and miraculously recovered her conciousness within moments and continued to attend her fallen comrade.

The police packed the bodies into a paddy wagon, one on top of another, until the interior of the vehicle was a mass of mangled human beings. Lupe Marshall was busy trying to help people inside the wagon in spite of her head which was now blood clotted and "an ugly sight."

The victims couldn't stand up in the wagon and were falling all over each other. The floor of the wagon soon became soaked in blood and the dying groans of praying men were heard almost in muted echoes. A man died in Lupe Marshall's lap as she was trying to give him a cigarette.

What happened at the hospital was almost worse than the rest. The hospital was overwhelmed with the dead and wounded and the police tried to keep the nurses aids and volunteers from helping. Lupe Marshall tried to help a wounded boy but the police drove her away.

When the final count was in, seventeen men were dead and ten more seriously wounded. The number of major wounds was about one hundred and fifty and the number of lesser wounds and gas victims will never be known.

The reason stated by policemen for their firing into the

crowd was that the marchers were communists, (many were booked as communists) and that "they came along smoking cigarettes like they were doped. I suppose they were smoking marijuana, they seem to be chanting a long monotonous chant which seemed to go. . . 'C. I. O., C. I. O.'' At the Senate investigating committee Senator LaFollette answered, "Is that what smoking marijuana does to one?''

Labor strikes and the attendant violence seemed to be a daily occurrence in the Depression days of the thirties, and almost no major company or concern escaped its ferocity. However, while labor strife was the topic of many newspaper headlines, there were other forms of diabolical criminality that were pervasively evident during the period.

One of the more celebrated cases was the Lindbergh baby kidnapping, and subsequent murder. The infant son of Charles and Anne Morrow Lindbergh was taken from his nursery in the second floor of the Lindbergh home in New Jersey. A ranson of fifty thousand dollars was paid for the return of the baby, and after several months of waiting the infant was found dead, a few hundred yards from where he was abducted, in the woods of the Lindbergh estate.

George Bruno Hauptman was apprehended a year later while exchanging some of the gold standard ransom notes at a gasoline station. The subsequent trial was to find him guilty and he was sentenced to die by electrocution, professing his innocence to the last as the sentence was carried out. With it many laws were enacted regarding kidnapping, one of which was that the crime was to be a Federal offense carrying the death sentence with it.

Other shadowy figures were moving on the periphery of social acceptance. These were the mafia inspired remnants of the bootleg era. Bonnie and Clyde were rampaging throughout the mid-west, and others, inspired by a new murder

James Earl Ray, *convicted assassin of Dr. Martin Luther King, during an interview conducted in prison in 1973. Ray was given a 99 year sentence for the assassination, and is serving his time in the Tennessee State Prison.*

machine, the Thompson sub-machine gun, were using it to the best of their pervertability. Bank robberies were showing up with such frequency that it was a running serial in the local papers as they reported the exploits of Francis Keating, Machine Gun Kelly, Pretty Boy Floyd, Ma Barker, Ray Terrill, Baby Face Nelson, and head and shoulders above the dung heap, John Dillinger.

Their exploits were viewed by a radio listening public as dark heroes reflecting the adversity and indifference of the times. No one knows how long it would have gone on if another larger slaughter hadn't been just off stage in the wings, awaiting its entrance: World War II.

With the public's attention turned toward Europe the country was given a slight breathing spell, but the persistent head of violence was merely taking a breather for better things to come.

Upon America's entrance into the war a sudden splurge of patriotism and brotherhood prevailed for a time. Most of the country's youth was under the Gordian Knot of the military, and to be outside of that paternal organization during the war years was to be ostracized from society and looked upon as either a shirker, incompetent, slacker, 4F, or, "zoot suiter."

On Thursday evening, June 3, 1943, a group of youngsters of Mexican descent had held a meeting in a police sub-station in Los Angeles. Usually these meetings were held in a school house, but since it was closed the police volunteered their premises. The subject of the meeting was gang violence between two opposing neighborhood groups. The meeting ended peacefully and the police took the boys home and dropped them off at the corner nearest their home.

At another corner of the city, eleven sailors had strayed slightly from their usual haunts in downtown Los Angeles, either by mistake or design. Whatever the reason, they happened upon a gang of young "Pachucos" and a fight began between the two elements.

As a fight it wasn't much; most of the sailors suffered cuts and bruises with no one really seriously injured. Police were dispatched to the area and no arrests were made. However, rumors quickly spread among the military that the sailors had been set upon by a roving gang of civilians wearing zoot suits, and suddenly violence had a cause and a symbol, draped pants and young civilians. Both were to be major targets for the frustrated military men of the area.

Two hundred sailors gathered downtown for the expressed purpose of "getting them." They hired twenty taxi-cabs and cruised downtown looking for Pachucos. A Mexican boy was spotted and the sailors gathered around him and beat him into insensibility. Moving on past a line of police officers who looked the other way, the sailors found four other boys. Two were seventeen years old, one was nineteen and the other one was twenty-three. They were beaten into unconsciousness and left on the street for the ambulance to pick up. Satisfied that they had done a good night's work, the sailors retired.

The headlines in the next day's papers screamed, "SAILOR TASK FORCE HITS L. A. ZOOTERS! ZOOT SUIT GANGSTERS FLEE FROM MIDDIES!" Promptly rumors spread that a sailor's wife had been raped and that a Marine had been killed by a zoot suiter.

Taken over literally by the servicemen, and bloated with angry civilians, the mob set out to do its work. They mauled every boy they found wearing a zoot suit, dragged anyone of Mexican descent out of theaters and beat him mercilessly. Streetcars were boarded and anyone of dark complexion was taken off and beaten. Negroes, Philipinos, and Italians were suspect.

Police procedure was simple and thoroughly uncomplicated. Wherever they saw a group of military men they knew trouble was not far behind. Following at a leisurely pace they would watch the men do their damage and when the action was over they would make an appearance.

Sailors went into one central city bar and, angry at not finding any zoot suiter on the premises, decided to take the bar apart, which they did. Carefully following the sailors the police arrested eleven boys who were beaten up on Carmolita Street; six more were arrested several blocks ahead.

With the seeming inability of the local police to contain or control the carnage, the military finally stepped in and put down the riots with their own military police. Los Angeles had been declared off limits and all servicemen in the area were confined to their bases and forbidden to go on leave.

That ended the rioting on the west coast. It was never officially stated as to how many young civilians were beaten and injured in the riots, and to speculate would be haphazard at best. However, a side reflection on the incident is recorded in the Los Angeles *Times:* ''at the outset zoot suiters were limited to no specific race; they were Anglo-saxon, Latin, and Negro. The fact that later on their numbers seemed to be predominately Latin was in itself no indictment of that race at all. No responsible person at any time condemned Latin-Americans as such.''

We had emerged out of the area of wholesale violence, on the battlefield with the ending of the war, and out of the streets, with the Detroit race riots in 1942-43 where, when the damage was finally assessed and the tally recorded, nine white people were dead, and twenty-five Negroes dead, and we were moving into the area of violence committed by individuals.

On September 6, 1949, Howard Unruh, a quiet Bible student, walked out of his mother's apartment and methodically began to shoot people down in the street with his souvenir Luger. One after another he shot and killed thirteen people and wounded many others. He fled to his mother's apartment and was finally taken very calmly without resistance by police who asked him . . . ''how many have you killed?'' Unruh smiled and calmly answered, ''I don't know yet. I haven't counted them, but it looks like a pretty good score.'' Later police psychiatrists declared him insane and he is presently in the New Jersey State Mental Hospital in Trenton.

On November 17, 1950, another New Jersey man, Ernie Ingenito, of Vineland, got angry at his wife because she had refused to allow him to see his children. He invaded his in-laws' house where the children were staying and, armed with an army carbine, he shot and wounded his wife and killed his father-in-law. Angry at his mother-in-law and considering her the main cause of his marital troubles, he followed her to the home of her parents and killed her and four more of his in-laws, wounding three others before his work of carnage had been complete. He was sentenced to life in prison.

In late January, 1958, Charley Starkweather and his girlfriend, an immature fourteen year old, went on a killing rampage that covered several states. They began by killing three members of the girl's family and ultimately went on to take eight more lives. Starkweather admitted to all of the killings, although later he told police that his girlfriend also helped. Charley Starkweather went to the electric chair on June 25, 1959.

Violence in the sixties and seventies has taken another form. Away from any formula, violence seems capable of erupting in any and all directions. Violence which heretofore seemed to have a basis of logical reasoning behind it, no

Elmer Wayne Henley *shown entering Bexar County courthouse for trial for his part in the Houston homosexual torture-killings. Henley was found guilty in six of the 27 murders which occurred in the Houston area.*

Authorities *shown removing a body from a shallow grave near Jefferson County, Texas in 1973. This was one of 27 victims of a bizarre homosexual torture-death ring which operated in the Houston area.*

772

Sirhan Sirhan, *convicted assassin of Senator Robert Kennedy.* *Sirhan was given a life sentence.*

matter how unrational that basis may have been, has moved into an area of enigmatic irrationality.

Viewed in its proper perspective, the Charles Manson killings seemed to have erupted out of no casual basis at all, rather out of a response or plea to society that is more a scream for recognition than an entreaty.

The mass rioting and demonstration of college students during the recent Vietnam conflict arose out of an earnest endeavor to right a moral and ethical wrong rather than out of a base of anger and long standing racial or social indignation.

Cases of mindless attempts at assassination or attempted assassinations of presidents and high state officials reflect frustration, and attempted murderers use these methods to get an idea across as a protest more than for individual hatred or revenge.

The direction of violence in the mid-seventies apparently is moving along a disjointed path that has encompassed kidnapping, letter bombing, and sabotage. Violence has moved out of the local arena and into the center ring of the bigtop tent, with the result that no violence is isolated in a small area of limited interests, but rather into the national picture where its insidious action is felt by us all.

SELECTED BIBLIOGRAPHY

Bernard de Voto, *The Course of Empire*. Houghton Mifflin Company.

J. W. Schulte Nordholdt, *The People that Walk in Darkness*. Burke Publishing Company, Ltd.

Irving J. Sloan, *Our Violent Past*. Random House.

Thomas Rose (ed.), *Violence in America*. Random House.

W. Eugene Hollon, *Frontier Violence*. Oxford University Press.

Ovid Demaris, *America the Violent*. Cowles Book Company.

David Wallechinsky and Irving Wallace, *The Peoples Almanac*. Doubleday Company, Inc.

Herbert Aptheker, *Nat Turner's Slave Rebellion*. Grove Press, Inc.

Dean Lipton, *The Truth about Simon Girty*. Adventure Classics.

HISTORICAL HEADLINES
ON
ASSASSINATIONS

THE TWICE-A-WEEK DETROIT FREE PRESS.

VOL. 78. NO. 48. (NEW SERIES VOL. 15. NO. 31.) THE DETROIT FREE PRESS: TUESDAY, JUNE 16, 1903. PRICE: THREE CENTS.

FAMOUS BAD MEN OF THE FRONTIER

Western Knights of the Revolver who Were Sure Shots and Became Officers of the Law.

BEN DANIELS A TERROR TO EVILDOERS IN THE SOUTH-WEST.

TEXAS STREET, DODGE CITY, WHEN IT WAS KNOWN AS "HELL WITH THE LID OFF."

PAT SHUGRUE, ONE OF THE NERVIEST MARSHALS WHO MADE A SPECIALTY OF CORRALING "BAD MEN"

WILD BILL HICKOCK.

TEXAS JACK, ONE OF THE GENTLEST OF MEN, BUT LIGHTNING WITH THE GUN

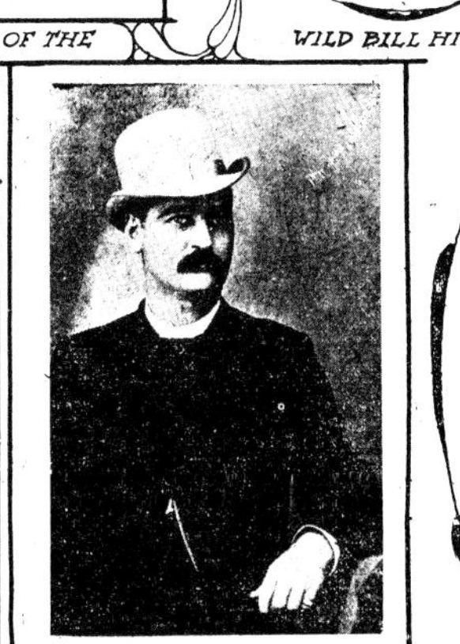

BAT MASTERSON, PROBABLY THE BEST KNOWN OF ALL LIVING GUN FIGHTERS FROM A PHOTOGRAPH TAKEN IN THE STIRRING DAYS OF DODGE CITY.

LUKE SHORT, A CELEBRATED GUN FIGHTER OF DODGE CITY DAYS.

THE recent killing of Outlaw James McKinney in a Chinese joss house at Bakersfield, Cal., has served to recall some of the plucky deeds of famous frontier marshals who never hesitated to enter any place or to confront any odds when striving to make an arrest. McKinney, who shot Charles Blakey, known as the cowboy pianist, at Kingman, Ariz., was a desperado of the worst type. He was known to be a sure shot and quick with the gun. Consequently, after his brutal and unprovoked murder of Blakey, when McKinney turned up at Bakersfield, the town marshal knew that he was facing death as soon as he got within range of McKinney's gun. But McKinney's fire from the joss house was returned with such good effect that the outlaw was killed, though not until he had slain Deputy W. E. Tibbets and mortally wounded City Marshal T. J. Packard, of the opposing party.

Deeds like this were not uncommon in the west a few years ago. In fact, when a man accepted the marshal's star or service badge he knew pretty well that he was taking long chances in a game with death, particularly if he happened to be in a community that was favored with the presence of many men of the "bad" type. Towns like Dodge City and Hayes City, Ks.; Tombstone, Ariz., and Leadville, Col., were the bright particular gathering places of the knights of the revolver, and the history of the "bad men" and of the takers of "bad men" is so mingled that one is at a loss to know today where to find the line that marks the desperado from the upholder of the law. In fact, it was a common custom in the west to select as sheriff a man who had a record as a killer. Many a "bad man" has accepted the badge of marshal or sheriff and has made a notable record in office. Seemingly there was a certain pride in assuming the badge of authority and going among the lawless element as a representative of law and order, though perhaps this same lawless element would have recognized the marshal as a bright and leading light only a short time before.

Dodge City and Hayes City, Ks., though now the most peaceful towns in the world, have had a number of marshals with double records. Dodge City in particular, which was the center of the buffalo hunters, horse stealers, cowboys, soldiers and adventurers of all sorts a generation ago, points with pride to its gun fighters whose records are those of lawbreakers as well as law enforcers.

Wild Bill's Bravery.

As good an example of the "bad man" turned marshal as one can point out is "Wild Bill" Hickock, whose fame will endure as long as that of his cousin, "Buffalo Bill." "Wild Bill" was known as a fighter in the various cities from Dodge to Denver and from Tombstone to Deadwood. He began his fighting career in the civil war, one of the most famous of his exploits being the spiking of the guns of Fort Pillow. The federal fleet did not dare ascend the Missouri under the guns of the fort. "Wild Bill" was dropped into the river, having around his neck a string of light files with which to spike the cannon. He strangled the sentry, climbed inside the fort and forced the files into the priming holes of the cannon. When he was spiking the last gun he was discovered. He escaped over the wall, swam away, notified the fleet, and the federals came up the river past the helpless fort.

When "Wild Bill" was living on the Big Blue, near Manhattan, Kansas, eight pro-slavery men visited his cabin with the intention of killing him. He was at the spring when they came, but he shot two of them dead, got into the house and shot four more before his pistol was empty. The two remaining men sprang upon him, but he killed them both with his knife. Such feats made "Wild Bill" famous throughout the entire west, and there was a rivalry among the lively cities of the frontier to secure him as a marshal. He was one of the most picturesque figures of the old days. His hair was long, black and curling. His mustache gave a fierce look to his face and his keen eyes made him a man who would be picked out as extraordinary in any crowd. He had the shoulders of a Hercules and the waist of a woman, and his physical strength was phenomenal.

His chief characteristic, however, was the quickness with which he could draw his revolvers. He never took aim, but the weapons were discharged as soon as they were drawn from their resting places. This fact doubtless saved him from death a hundred times. He always depended on the fraction of a section advantage which his own quickness gave him over his opponent.

Other Exploits.

In Hays City, two soldiers undertook to kill "Wild Bill" and they crept on him from behind. One of them knocked him down with the butt of a revolver. As he lay on the ground, half stunned, "Will Bill" instinctively drew his terrible revolvers and both soldiers were killed before they could complete their work.

At another time a noted gambler sought to kill "Wild Bill." Hickock not only shot the gambler dead, but killed one of the man's friends who was running to assist him. Then he paid the funeral expenses of both men. A refractory alderman of Hays City, whose vote was needed, swore that not even "Wild Bill" could take him to the council chamber. "Wild Bill" walked up to the man, threw him on his shoulders, and carried the alderman into the council chamber like a sack of flour. As a marshal "Wild Bill" made a wonderful record and usually his mere appearance was enough to make a lawbreaker submit to arrest. This hero of a hundred battles, like nearly all other men who have depended on the revolver, met an ignominious death in a saloon at Deadwood, being shot in the back by an Irishman with whom he had had an altercation.

Bat Masterson, who is known today in sporting circles from coast to coast, was one of the coolest fighters in the days when the revolver was the last resort in argument. Today Masterson is an inoffensive, blue-eyed, plump-handed chap who can write a rattling good newspaper article, who is soft of speech and whose long divorce from any scene of violence has even led some people into the error of thinking that his record as a frontiersman terror was imaginary. But any well-informed western man knows that Bat Masterson has fought his way out of many death traps and has triumphed over many close shooting enemies merely through his cool head and steady hand. Masterson, in 1877, though a mere boy at the time, was sheriff of Ford county, Kansas, and his brother Ed, a handsome youth, was marshal of Dodge City. While Ed was attempting to disarm some cowboys before they entered a dance hall, he was shot through the lungs. Bat killed two of the cowboys and chased the others ignominiously out of town. This gave Bat a widespread reputation as a revolver fighter, although he had gained local prominence some time before by his skill as a buffalo hunter and an Indian fighter. Bat was concerned in nearly all the exciting incidents that made Dodge City one of the liveliest spots on the map. Usually he was enforcing law and order, however, and later on in Leadville he did not less heroic work.

"Hell With the Lid Off."

In the palmy days of the gun fighter, Texas street, Dodge City, was known as "hell with the lid off." A railroad bisected the street, giving it the appearance of a double avenue. On both sides of the railroad were saloons and dance halls with a slight minority of general stores. The motley collection of men who visited Dodge City at all hours of the day and night, buffalo hunters, scouts, soldiers, Indians, gamblers and the riffraff that invariably scents out such a headquarters for crime, thronged Texas street and the other avenues of commerce.

Naturally, the maintenance of order at Dodge City was no light matter, and the election of a marshal meant a great deal more than the appointment of a police captain in any city today. Probably the best marshal Dodge City ever had was Patrick Shugrue. This little horseshoer never found it necessary to kill a man, although he arrested many notorious "gun" fighters, some of them being taken under circumstances which were decidedly humiliating to themselves.

It was Shugrue's rule to seek out his man and calmly say, "You may consider yourself under arrest." Apparently, these words had a hypnotic effect, for it was seldom that there was any attempt at resistence. On one occasion, it is related that a "bad man" sent word to Shugrue to come and take him. Shugrue obligingly went to the "bad man's" place of business and as he opened the door a revolver was discharged almost in his face. With lightning quickness, Shugrue knocked the muzzle of the weapon upwards, but the powder burned his face and hand. The marshal quickly had the would-be assassin on the floor, the "bad man," naturally thinking his days were numbered. But instead of discharging his revolver, which was held at the coward's head, Shugrue simply said, "I ought to kill you, but you may consider yourself under arrest."

Shugrue began his career shoeing horses for the United States government at Fort Dodge. Soon he opened a blacksmith shop of his own, and in 1878 was elected constable. He arrested a few horse thieves, who were numerous on the border at that time, and then announced his candidacy for the marshalship. The city administration was against him, and it was rumored that on election day a great number of deputies inimical to Shugrue would see that the little blacksmith's friends would not get a chance to put their man in office. But Shugrue telegraphed Bat Masterson and Wyatt Earp and on election morning they were on hand with the simple announcement that Pat Shugrue was to get a fair show. The appearance of these two noted "gun" fighters on the scene changed the plan of the city administration, and the anti-Shugrue deputies did not materialize. The blacksmith carried every precinct and began the operations which gained him fame as the gentlest captor of the very worst "bad men" in the United States. It is said that Shugrue never lost a prisoner, which is the more remarkable from the fact that he never found it necessary to shoot one. His sole object was to do his duty in accordance with the law, and the wildest inhabitant of Dodge City never forgot this fact, and consequently never failed to respect the peace officer as a brave man among brave men.

Ben Daniels, who came into the public eye a short time ago on account of the controversy over his appointment as United States marshal of Arizona, was a prominent figure at Dodge City in its wildest days. Daniels was every inch a gun fighter, and he had made a big reputation as a killer, when the people, following a happy custom, decided that it would be better to have such a man as a peace officer than a peace destroyer. Daniels's career at Dodge City gained him such fame as a gun player that when the new and noisy gold camp of Cripple Creek began to loom up, Sheriff Bowers, of El Paso Co., Col., sent for this Kansas revolver expert. Bob Taylor was brought up from Indian Territory at the same time, and "Kid" Wallace and Grant and Lem Crumley were also imported, and all were made deputy sheriffs at the time of the great Cripple Creek strike in 1893. Grant Crumley, only a short time ago, shot and killed Sam Strong, the millionaire owner of the Strong mine, about which much of the tragedy of the great strike was acted. Daniels showed his nerve during the strike in a way that recalled the Dodge City days. The strikers, headed by veterans of the labor wars of the Coeur d' Alenes, under command of the mysterious "General" Johnson and Jack Smith, were entrenched behind earthworks on Bull Hill. They had cannon and their position was considered impregnable, but Daniels, one morning, organized a company of mounted deputies and started out with the avowed purpose of capturing and hanging "General" Johnson. Just at this time the National Guard, under command of Davis H. Waite, of "bloody bridles" fame, flung itself between Daniels and the strikers, and prevented a conflict which would have been nothing short of a battle on a large scale.

When the Spanish-American war broke out, Daniels enlisted in Roosevelt's Rough Riders and went through the campaign in a manner that gained him the personal commendation of President Roosevelt.

Luke Short, another member of the Dodge City circle, made his name famous in the days of Masterson, Daniels, et al, by the prominent part he took in the festivities along Texas street. Every "gun" fighter has his peculiarities of style, like every other individual who depends on his skill and quickness in living up to his reputation. Short, unlike Dave Mather of Dodge City, was an open and fearless fighter. Mather, who was undersized, shuffled along the street with his hat pulled down over his eyes and had a trick of throwing up his hands and whining and protesting when some fellow "bad man" "got the drop" on him. Invariably Mather's opponent would neglect to fire and his pistol arm would drop at his side. Instantly Mather's own gun would leap forth and the coroner of Dodge City would have another case to attend to. Luke Short never adopted this style. He participated in some of the hottest fights in the history of Kansas, both in Hayes City and Dodge City, but no man could ever say that Short took a mean advantage. His prowess as a "gun" fighter gained him appointment as sheriff and marshal, and like other "bad men" who rose to these official positions, he made a good officer, taking pride in his ability to bring the worst outlaw to justice.

Gentle Texas Jack.

Probably the gentlest of all the border characters of the stirring days of Dodge City was J. B. Omohundro, better known as "Texas Jack." Omohundro was a protege of "Buffalo Bill." He dressed much after the style of Cody and was much in demand among Buffalo hunters as a guide. He was one of the most skilled Indian fighters that ever blazed a trail through the wilderness, and he was one of the first white men to penetrate Yellowstone park, entering that great place of natural wonders soon after Jim Bridger made his famous trip into the Yellowstone. "Texas Jack" never provoked a quarrel, but when in one he was known as anything but a quitter. He was called upon, in his day, to bring many men to justice, but, like Pat Shurgee, he seldom found it necessary to make a "gun" play. "Texas Jack" was taken up by the Papyrus Club, of Boston, on a trip east in the early days, and was made much of at the "Hub." His picturesque frontier regalia as he walked down the main streets of Boston attracted no little attentio and the frontiersman liked the not riety so much that he remained f some time in Boston, becoming a cal celebrity. Unlike most of t knights of the pistol, "Texas Jac did not die "with his boots on." P monary troubles carried off this ge tle character, and his grave ne Leadville, Colorado, is often visited t day by men who knew and admir him in times when really gentle m were few.

The Worst "Bad Men."

Probably the worst "bad men" w ever gave trouble to the marshals the southwest were "King" Fisher a the Thompson Brothers, Ben and B Fisher was a bully through a through, fierce and assertive. Wh he entered a barroom his eyes circl round to see who he could browbe On one occasion Fisher so thorough bullied Bill Longley, a "bad man" no small reputation, that Long never again cocked his hat over o eye and put on his "bad man" swa ger. Fisher not only made him sh the white feather, but took from h his revolver and shoved it across t bar to pay for the drinks for crowd.

Fisher had a sense of humor, wh was evidenced when he put up a si board at the forks of a public ro The sign post read: "This is 'Ki Fisher's road. Better take the othe Needless to say, most people took t other road, even though it was fart around."

Ben Thompson was another hum ist, and he and his brother Bill play many wild pranks with their rev vers, to the terror of the populace a to the undoing of many marshals. was Ben Thompson who broke up cattlemen's banquet at Austin shooting every plate off the table a breaking the neck off every bot while not a cattleman dared shoot return. The wholesome fear Thompson can be realized when it known that the desperado rode int county court room on his musta with a six-shooter in either hand, a pleasantly informed judge and j that he would like to see any coy in the crowd with nerve enough take him. Nobody moved and Thon son rode from the room as debon as you please, despite the fact t there were several unserved warra out for him on charges of murder.

Thompson met a dramatic death. was persuaded to visit the Pal theater at San Antonio, Tex. As entered his seat in the front row the balcony, a volley of rifle sh rang out. Thirty men in the parq fired by signal and the desperado riddled with bullets. "King" Fish who was with Thompson, was ki outright, and Thompson tumbled fr the balcony into the pit, morta wounded. Before the desperado d however, he drew a gun and ki two men, one of them being the who had prevailed upon him to c to the theater. Thompson's brot Bill quickly heard the news, ral his followers and swept down on theater. A barricade of well arm men under cover kept them back w repeating rifles. The cowpunch poured into town to avenge the de of "King" Fisher. The militia called out and for six weeks San tonio was under martial law. At the cowboys retired, leaving deaths of Thompson and "King" F er unavenged.

The Pessimist in June.

He can't enjoy these lovely, fragr
days,
For misery holds him all along
ways;
"Just think," he says, "the fact
sadly clear,
We won't have June again for
long year."

Bound to Do as He Pleases

Rebecca—"Father is going to ma for the third time."

Rachel—"He must be sentimenta

Rebecca—"Oh, no; he's just ob nate."

With a Bunch of Violets.

Fair springs the violet—and yet
Within my breast it wakes regret;
For pain's surcease—pledge fond
true—
I gathered these, and dreamed of

Full Page of Lindbergh Pictures—Page 7

CALIFORNIA FORECAST

Los Angeles and Vicinity—Fair Thursday and Friday; moderate temperature.
San Francisco and Vicinity—Fair and mild Thursday and Friday.

MEAN TEMPERATURES

LOS ANGELES	58	New York	45
San Francisco	54	Chicago	35
San Diego	55	Detroit	33
Seattle	38	Boston	46
Portland	43	Washington	46
Omaha	40	Atlanta	70

CHARACTER QUALITY AMERICA FIRST! ENTERPRISE ACCURACY

Los Angeles Examiner EXTRA

AN AMERICAN PAPER FOR THE AMERICAN PEOPLE — THE GREAT NEWSPAPER OF THE GREAT SOUTHWEST

Reg. U. S. Pat. Off.

VOL. XXIX—NO. 83 For Complete Weather Reports, See Page 9, Part II. S LOS ANGELES, THURSDAY, MARCH 3, 1932 Two Sections—Part One PRICE FIVE CENTS

BABY LINDY EXPECTED BACK TODAY!

Father Confident; 'By Noon,' He Says

Today

Blue Eyes, Golden Hair
Britain Enjoys Her Tariff
Taxing Public Pleasures
Is Uncle Sam Spending? Yes

By Arthur Brisbane
(Copyright, 1932, King Features Synd., Inc.)

his is the description of the lbergh child:

Twenty months old, blue eyes, golden hair, fair complexion, chubby boy, resembling his er. He is about normal size child his age, has just begun ddle, and is learning to talk."

ery word of that description strike deep into the heart of child's mother.

hoever they are that stole the bergh child, they must know their only hope of safety, or hereafter, lies in return- the child promptly to its er's arms.

e kidnapers can have the y that they demand. They rely absolutely on any prom- that Colonel Lindbergh may in connection with paying money, and the return of the

til this problem is solved, and ittle boy is safe again with ather and mother, it is un- y to talk of "most severe hment" for the crime of kid- g, or of anything but this s safety.

en Great Britain had "free " and this country was liv- nside of tariff walls, tariff d wicked to the British.

v they have tried protection, t seems to agree with them. will repay tomorrow one ed and fifty millions of the hundred million dollars bor- from this country last Au- to bolster the falling pound. ntly confident that the is all right, Britain has the ban on exchange pur- and gives her stock ex- full swing again.

oretically, it seems barbar- r the world's different na- to live inside a tariff wall, shutting out his neighbor. ractically, if you have money end, it is a good thing to it with members of your family, first; your own na- econd.

new cry in England: "Buy ," is yielding results. ord Beaverbrook can carry gh his plan of free trade in- the Empire, all of its units g with each other without tions, as our forty-eight trade with each other, no houses between, there will ew British boom.

York state acts unwisely in at this time, moving pic- and other amusements of ople. Such a tax has never aid and should not be laid, in times of extreme pros- if at all.

difficult enough, under ex- circumstances, to keep the in a cheerful mood, discour- active dissatisfaction, with- ying an odious tax on the harmless amusement.

a sad comment on New state's government that it tax or suppress the tens of nds of speakeasies that ex- New York City alone, taking dreds of millions from the s pocketbook, and must get ome by taxing an industry in greatest difficulties.

e Government could get for a reasonable share of the c sum that its public offi- directly and indirectly, get ootleggers and other crimi- would not need to tax the s pleasures.

rnor Roosevelt and Lieu- Governor Lehman, if they ough this tax, will find that ave made a political mis-

e tax is enforced, each thea- uld put at its entrance a tin to which the public would ired to drop the amount of , the box appropriately in- with the names of the poli- responsible.

e may be hoarding, but Un- n is NOT. In fact he is "teeny-weeny" bit beyond ans.

e last eight months, he one billion, three hundred rty-four million and some ndreds of thousands of dol- d spent three billions, one d and fifteen millions and odd thousands. In other he spent exactly one bil- even hundred and eighty- llion, seventeen thousand ndred and ninety-six dol- ore than he took in.

interests YOU, because you taxed to make up the dif- . Uncle Sam has no choice. at the rate of almost two d and twenty million dol- month, more than seven dollars a day, beyond your means optimism.

e days of Grover Cleveland, al expense of the United Government per year was an one-third the present for eight months.

IS EXPENSIVE. Shov- ut your money to other es is also expensive.

prohibition is expensive, g the country, according fessor Seligman, of fifteen d million dollars a year in-

ct, everything seems to be ve except cotton, oil, coal, **sugar, labor.**

JAPAN ORDERS 'CEASE FIRING' AT SHANGHAI

Warfare Stopping Now That 'Lives of Nationals Safe,' Say Military, Naval Leaders

Woosung Forts, Last of City's Defenses to Hold Out Fall; Nanziang, Kating Also Seized

BULLETIN!

SHANGHAI, March 3 (Thursday). — (A.P.) — Japanese military and naval authorities decided to cease military operations at Shanghai immediately, an official statement issued this afternoon said.

The statement said:

"Now that Japanese military and naval authorities have accomplished their object, the protection of Japanese lives and property, and secured the safety of the International Settlement, they have decided that their military operations be stopped forthwith."

Admiral Kenkichi Nomura, Japanese naval commander, ordered Japanese naval forces to cease hositilities shortly before 3 o'clock this afternoon (11 p. m. Wednesday, Pacific time).

SHANGHAI, March 3 (Thursday).—(AP)—Japanese military headquarters announced the occupation of Kating, smore than 15 mile northwest of Shanghai, shortly after 3:30 this afternoon (11:30 p. m., Los Angeles time).

SHANGHAI, March 3 (Thursday).—(AP)—Dispatches from Nanking which reached here shortly after the Japanese announced that hostilities would end today said Chinese National Government leaders there issued a statement declaring "all energies should be turned toward resisting Japanese aggression."

The statement caused some confusion here.

(Copyright, 1932, by Associated Press)

SHANGHAI, March 3 (Thursday).—A huge Japanese landing party finally wrested the forts of Woosung from the Chi-

(Continued on Page 6, Column 1)

LORD CURZON ART GOING ON BLOCK

LENOX, Mass., March 2.—(AP)—The Lord George Nathaniel Curzon of Kedleston art collection will be brought to this country from England for disposal on the block, Cortland Field Bishop of Lenox announced today.

The collection is worth approximately a million pounds.

Bishop recently announced his American art galleries in New York had taken over the famous Sir William Bennett collection for sale at auction.

Senate Dooms 'Lame Duck' by Vote of 73 to 3

Norris Constitutional Amendment Now Goes to States for Ratification

WASHINGTON, March 2.—(Universal Service.)—A fight begun almost single-handed fourteen years ago by Senator George W. Norris (Republican) of Nebraska, to force Congress to approve a Constitutional amendment abolishing lame duck sessions, came to a successful conclusion today.

This was accomplished when the Senate, by a vote of 73 to 3, adopted the conference report on the Norris resolution submitting the lame duck amendment to the states for ratification as the Twentieth Amendment to the Constitution.

Voting against the Norris proposal were Senator Porter H. Dale of Vermont, Jesse H. Metcalf of Rhode Island and Charles W. Waterman of Colorado, all Republicans. Senator Hiram Bingham (Republican) of Connecticut, was paired against the resolution.

States to Act

The House, under Speaker Garner's leadership, adopted the conference report last Monday.

As no action by the President is required, the proposed amendment will be submitted by Secretary of State Stimson to the states at once for ratification.

Under the amendment, Congress will convene annually on January 3, instead of thirteen months after the November elections, as at present, and the President and Vice President will be inaugurated on January 20, instead of March 4.

Bruening Favors German Participation

BERLIN, March 2.—(AP)—Chancellor Henrich Bruening today earnestly advocated German participation in the 1932 Olympiad at Los Angeles in a letter to Theodore Lewald, president of the Reichs athletic commission.

Middle West Sleet Hampers Air Travel

CHICAGO, March 2.—(AP)—Sleet storms in eastern Iowa, northern Missouri, and southern Illinois today had disrupted airplane travel and broken many of the communication lines.

Decision on Mooney Pardon Due Soon

SACRAMENTO, March 2.—Decision on Tom Mooney's pardon application will be announced within two weeks, Governor Rolph declared here today.

Where Did Money Go?

BY ARTHUR "BUGS" BAER

While the Senate is investigating Wall Street we would also like to learn some form-fitting answers to a few loose questions.

Who yanked the rip cord on that 1929 balloon?

Why did the boys keep yelling prosperity even after their voices sounded like an opera singer going down for the third time and no boat in sight?

If the Stock Exchange is a private club, why was everybody as welcome as thirty-five pounds of air in flat tires?

Why did they build Wall Street in back of a graveyard? And why didn't any of us pushovers take the hint?

(Copyright, 1932, Distributed by Universal Service, Inc.)

(If Transylpopoff wants to have a war with Hertzogingam they'll have to travel on their stomachs, because big bankers refuse to supply plush cars. ***See Page 14, Part 2.)***

Latest Photo of Missing Boy

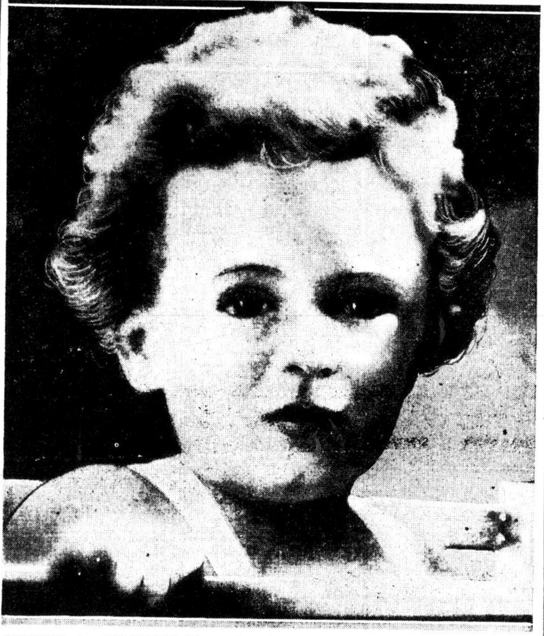

CHARLES A. LINDBERGH JR., curly-headed, blue-eyed son of famous flyer. THIS PICTURE, made only two weeks ago, is his most recent.—I. N. R. telephoto.

ANTI-DRYS BACK BEER TAX BILL

WASHINGTON, March 2.—(Universal Service.)—A beer bill designed to raise $500,000,000 in revenue for the Federal Government was approved by the Republican and Democratic anti-prohibition blocs in the House today.

ALBANY, N. Y., March 2.—(AP)—Party lines failed to hold all of the Republican majority in the New York Assembly today, enough of them joining with a solid Democratic group to pass two anti-prohibition resolutions.

Twenty-four Republicans lined up with 56 Democrats to memorialize Congress to repeal the Eighteenth Amendment and restore liquor control to the states.

A Democratic resolution asking Congress to permit 4 per cent beer also was passed by the Assembly.

COLLAPSE OF DAM TRAPS FAMILIES

GALLUP, N. M., March 2.—(AP)—Collapse of the McGaffey dam, south of here, today forced three families to take refuge on high ground as their homes were flooded.

Warned by the roar of water as the dam, built to form a recreational lake, gave way, the families of Manuel Diaz, Glenn Morri and N. V. Davis were able to escape. Diaz, his wife and one daughter climbed on tables and cupboards and remained there until the water receded enough to allow them to get out.

Kidnapers, Here's Diet Grieving Mother Sends

HOPEWELL, N. J., March 2.—(AP)—To the kidnaper of the Lindbergh baby:

Here is a heart-broken appeal direct from the mother of the child you stole.

The baby has been sick and its recovery may depend on the treatment it gets from you. You must be especially careful about the diet.

Mrs. Lindbergh issued to the press today the strict diet she has been following since the baby fell ill. She did this in the hope you might read this story and that there was some spark of humanity even in the heart of a baby thief.

Here is the diet, accompanied by the fervent prayer of a grieving mother:

One quart of milk during the day.

Three tablespoons of cooked cereal morning and night.

Two tablespoons of cooked vegetables once a day.

One yolk of egg daily.

One baked potato or rice once a day.

Two tablespoons of stewed fruit daily.

Half a cup of orange juice on waking.

Half a cup of prune juice after the afternoon nap.

And fourteen drops of a medicine called Viosterol during the day.

That's all, kidnaper. That's what the baby's mother wants you to give the boy.

CHILD WEARING SLEEPING SUIT

HOPEWELL, N. J., March 2. — (Universal Service.)—This is what the Lindbergh baby looked like and what he wore when kidnaped from his parents' home here:

Age—1 year, 8 month, 8 days, (born June 22, 1930.

Height—2 feet 9 inches.

Weight—30 pounds.

Eyes—Blue

Hair—Fair, curly.

Complexion—Fair.

Clothing—One-piece sleeping suit of fine white balbriggan, size 2, with long sleeves and stitched feet.

It was fitted with six pearl buttons between crotch and neck and three across the hips at the back.

The baby walked a little and could speak a few simple nursery words.

'YOUR SON SAFE,' SAYS POSTCARD

NEWARK, N. J., March 2.—(AP)—A post card was mailed to Colonel Charles A. Lindbergh from here today, reading:

"Baby safe. Instructions later. Act accordingly."

The clerk at the Plane street and Central avenue postal station, where the mail box is located, informed police he had sold only two cards of the type of the one addressed to Lindbergh during the morning. One was to a woman and the other to a man.

The description pictured the man as about 40, 5 feet 3 inches tall, and weighing 140 to 150 pounds.

The vicinity of the substation was a scene of wild confusion as a great crowd gathered, but was held in check by a detail of 200 police and firemen.

Colonel Ready to Pay $50,000 Demanded in Ransom Note; Orders Wooded Estate Cleared for Mystery Caller

State Troopers Keep All Road to Home Open; Believed Awaiting Imminent Return of Boy

BULLETIN!

HOPEWELL, N. J., March 3 (Thursday).—(A.P.)—Col. Charles A. Lindbergh was heard to remark to a group of state troopers early today he is "very confident" his kidnaped baby would be returned by noon today.

After the Colonel left the barrier in the road to return to his home the state troopers said to a reporter:

"Get back where we can't see you, boys, 'way back. We're expecting someone to come through here in the morning and we don't want cars parked along the road, because they might get frightened."

The reference to the parked cars was directed to the automobile in which the reporter had driven up to the private road from Hopewell. Four state police were on guard at the gate. Colonel Lindbergh before he left the gate to return to his house was also heard to remark something about "waiting for somebody before noon."

By Seymour Berkson
Universal Service

HOPEWELL, N. J., March 2. — The world's most famous baby, Charles A. Lindbergh Jr., will be back in the eager arms of his father and mother tomorrow by dawn—unless there is some unexpected hitch in negotiations with the child's kidnapers.

This was disclosed tonight after Colonel Lindbergh himself prepared to pay $50,000, and at 6 p. m. informed police authorities stationed at his estate that he expected to have his 20-months-old son back safe and sound "within twelve hours."

Asks All to Leave

That the flying colonel, despairing of finding the child's kidnapers without endangering his son's life, was following ransom instructions left by the abductors was indicated late tonight when he personally ordered his estate cleared not only of newspapermen and curious spectators, but of state troopers as well.

Colonel Lindbergh himself came down the narrow, winding road leading from his wooded estate and implored everybody to leave. For the first time since tragedy descended on his household last night he even ventured a smile as he told a group of newspapermen:

"I appreciate all you have done for me but I must ask you to leave the grounds here clear. It is imperative. Please do not ask me why."

He refused to confirm or deny that he had arranged to pay the $50,000 ransom demanded in the note left in his son's crib last night and he refused to state whether or not he had been in direct communication.

Returns to House

When the questions began to come faster than he could answer them, he merely said, "Please do not embarrass me now," and returned to his house.

His action in clearing the estate was interpreted as meaning one of two things:

Either he was arranging for the surrender of the infant at some lonely spot in the woods surrounding his own estate or he was preparing to drive to some distant rendezvous and felt compelled to take precautions that he would not be followed and the negotiations spoiled.

That an important development — regarded as the virtually certain return of the child—was ex-

WILL suppression
* * *
OF crime news
* * *
SUPPRESS crime?
* * *
INSTEAD it may
* * *
INCREASE crime
* * *
AS suppression
* * *
OF divorce news
* * *
ENCOURAGED divorce
* * *
IN old England,
* * *
WARNS G. K. Chesterton
* * *
IN a forceful
* * *
MARCH of Events
* * *
ARTICLE on Page 12

CRIME
America's Danger and Disgrace
END IT!

KIDNAPED, MUTILATED, MURDERED —The skeleton of Brooke Hart, twenty-two-year-old aristocratic youth of San Jose, California, viewed by Deputy Coroner Walter Flierl after its discovery by horrified hunters in the mud flats of lower San Francisco Bay. It was the finding of this body, after long suspense, during which tremendous indignation was inflamed that set the spark which aroused the San Jose mob to batter down the doors of the jail and "string up" John M. Holmes and Thomas H. Thurmond, confessed kidnapers of the boy. This case became a national issue when the late Governor Rolph declared he would pardon any of the lynchers that might be apprehended. He said: "That was a fine lesson to the whole nation. There will be less kidnaping now . . . if anyone is arrested for the good job, I'll pardon them all." But the wave of kidnapings did not stop

FURY OF THE MOB—The first moment of the rush on the jail as the vengeance-thirsty lynch-mob fight through a tear-gassed barrage and begin the demolition of the door of the Santa Clara County Jail to get at the two kidnapers, whom they soon hanged on trees in a park opposite the jail. Note the debris scattered by the first blows of the iron pipe battering-ram. The mob soon numbered hundreds. Note sheriff's office in background.

WITHOUT PROCESS OF LAW—Here hangs the body of Thomas H. Thurmond, one of the kidnapers and murderers of young Brooke Hart, lynched by the mob impatient of American justice. Note the faces in the foreground, turning toward the camera. This eloquent picture was taken in the dark, for in the dark such deeds are done John M. Holmes, Thurmond's partner in the crime, was swinging from a nearby tree in the park at the time.

OUR CIVILIZATION! What Must We Americans Do to Prevent Honor and Decency from Perishing in Our Land

CHARACTER · QUALITY · AMERICA FIRST! · ENTERPRISE · ACCURACY

Los Angeles Examiner

AN AMERICAN PAPER FOR THE AMERICAN PEOPLE · THE GREAT NEWSPAPER OF THE GREAT SOUTHWEST

Reg. U.S. Pat. Off.

Complete SPORTS & MARKETS

VOL. XXIX—NO. 109 | LOS ANGELES, TUESDAY, MARCH 29, 1932 | Two Sections—Part One | P | PRICE FIVE CENTS

PASTOR FLIES TO LINDY WITH NEWS OF CHILD!

Today

Generous French Loans Out Shooting News Red and White Men Go Saved by Snow

By Arthur Brisbane

MIAMI BEACH, Fla., March 28.—The Paris newspaper under the heading *Politique et Finance* prints a list of loans made by France to foreign countries since the war ended. They total THIRTEEN BILLION TWO HUNDRED AND SEVENTY-SEVEN MILLION FRANCS. Not including a loan to Czecho-Slovakia, of six hundred million francs, made last January 20th, a three hundred million-franc loan to Finland or a loan made to Polish railroads of four hundred million francs.

The French editor's heading, "Politics and Finance," is well chosen. France has lent Rumania two billions and ninety million francs. Rumania, lying in the shadow of the Russian bear, is important.

France has lent two thousand million francs to Poland, plus four hundred millions lent to Polish railways. Poland, or Russia, and adjoining property, including the famous corridor taken from Germany, is important to France.

France has lent to neighbors, near and far. Seven hundred and seventy million francs to Turkey; twenty-three million francs to poor old China. This list of generous French loans to the various foreign governments helps you to understand why France feels unable to repay money borrowed from us SINCE THE WAR.

You know that this country has forgiven all sums lent to France during the war. We wiped that out, and requested only repayment of debts that France has incurred since the war ended.

President Hoover made a public statement to that effect and was surprised that it was never published in any newspaper in France except a couple of unimportant Pahis papers published in he English language.

Having taken from Germany so much valuable property, Alsace and Lorraine, cash, colonies, etc., France naturally fels a little anxious about her military position, with Germany and Russia on the east growing so powerful.

It is natural that France should prefer building up military allies in Europe to repaying money borrowed from us, but why should Uncle Sam be called "Uncle Shylock" by those that took his money and don't intend to pay? That seems an unnecessary touch.

The news continues as usual in our "highly civilized" country. In the Southeast two policemen are killed, troops ordered out to prevent lynching. Three thousand miles away off in the Northwest you read: "Two bandits rob thirty passengers aboard train." It was an interesting robbery. One of the bandits is believed to be a womap. Among men lined up and robbed were two detectives that had pistols in their suitcases. There is much authority in the pistol that points first.

Georgia reports the killing of two prohibition agents, with the shooter found guilty. In another corner of the United States, Basil Banghart, colled "a member of Detroit's Purple Gang," shoots his way out of the county jail, wonds the jailer, commandeers a taxicab and escapes.

We certainly live in a shooting age and the shooters themselves are immune.

The Chicago Herald and Examiner says Frank Nitti, called "Capone's chief lieutenant," just came back from fifteen months in Leavenworth prison, learns that he is "marked for death." There is no joking about such a mark, and it makes the marked one nervous.

Yesterday Leslie V. Shaw, Secretary of the Treasury under Theodore Roosevelt, died, aged 84. At about the same time Chief Bacon Rind, once ruler of the Osage Indians, passed on to the happy hunting grounds, aged 72. A cancer killed him.

Chief Bacon Rind was six and one-half feet high, and important from the white American point of view, because he was chief and adviser of the richest lot of Indians on earth. Oil made them rich. How could large-hearted white men, carefully picking out the worst lands to give to the Indians, imagine that oil worth hundreds of millions was hidden under those barren lands?

Did the white man's statesmen and the Osago chief travel together on the mysterious journey that we all take when life ends? Did one go to one heaven, the other to another heaven? Is one an Indian and the other a white man in the future life? Or are both totally unlike Indians and white men?

That which our heroic "devil dog" marines and all the power of our Government couln not do, appears to have been done by a creature so small you could not see it with the naked eye.

Sandino, leader of Nicaragua's insurgent band, is laid up with a violent attack of malaria, under a doctor's care, unable to ride or shoot. And he is not the first victim of the tiny germs that Anopheles mosquitos implant in your blood.

Some historians believe that malaria, distributed by mosquitos from the marshes around Rome wiped out Roman power of resist-

(Continued on Page 2, Columns 3-4)

Garner Planning House Appeal for Balanced Budget

Nation's Credit Must Be Unimpaired, Says Speaker

PREJUDICE HIT

Worst Kind of Levies Better Than None, Texan Adds

WASHINGTON, March 28.—(Universal Service.—Speaker John N. Garner, from the floor of the House, will deliver a vigorous appeal for a tax bill that will balance the budget and keep unimpaired the credit of the nation, it was indicated tonight.

He disclosed today he was considering making such an appeal when the ways and means committee reports a substitute plan for raising revenue to replace the general manufacturers' sales tax, which the House, under lash of insurgents, knocked out last week.

The committee expects to make its report tomorrow, although it may be delayed until Wednesday.

Opposes Prejudices

From the start of the bitter fight over the tax bill, Speaker Garner has insisted that the paramount necessity is to pass a bill that will balance the budget and thereby maintain the credit of the Government at home and abroad.

He issued two statements during the bitter row over the sales tax, emphasizing this condition.

While he ignored a sales tax spread over industries generally, and not singling out a few to be victims, as the most practical way to balance the budget, the Speaker said that in the present emergency the method of raising the taxes was inconsequential, compared with the prime object of balancing the budget.

Prejudices against various types of taxation should be laid aside for the ultimate goal, he said.

Not Duty to Dictate

Speaker Garner has maintained from the start of the fight over the tax bill that it was not his duty to try to dictate to the House what method should be taken to raise the taxes.

But with the insurgent bloc that fought and killed the sales tax threatening to pass a bill that will not balance the budget, he believes it to be his duty to use every means at his command to fight for a balanced budget, he said.

When Chairman Joseph Byrns (Democrat), Tennessee, of the powerful appropriations committee, in the fight against the sales tax, said it was not necessary to balance the budget, his statement was applauded by insurgents on both sides of the aisle.

They justified their votes against the sales tax on the judgment of Chairman Byrns.

With sentiment increasing for a bill that will balance the budget, Garner today was of the opinion he had better use his high office in an open appeal to his colleagues.

Garner said:

"In my opinion, the Federal

(Continued on Page 2, Columns 3-4)

Blizzards, Gales Hit New England in Easter's Wake

Holiday Motorists Marooned by Drifts; Hampshire Snow 7 to 12 Inches Deep

NEW YORK, March 28.—(AP)—Blizzards buffeted New England **today, gales swept the Eastern Seaboard,** snow drifts marooned Easter holiday motorists as Easter Monday became a belated winter day.

Snow from seven to twelve inches deep, the heaviest of the winter, blanketed New Hampshire. Railroads sent out snow flangers for the second time this winter, and snow plows were used.

North of Lowell, Mass., a storm felled twenty-five telephone poles, cutting the city off from communication to points north. It blew down trees and ripped an advertising sign twenty feet long off a building in Lowell.

Birds Frozen

Game wardens at North Adams, Mass., reported flocks of early robins, bluebirds and song sparrows died in the freezing winds.

A northeaster howled on the Maine Coast, and mountainous waves lashed against the rocks.

At Bellefonte, Iowa, the electrocution of Quincey Wallandz, wife murderer, was delayed more than two and a half hours when witnesses were delayed by storm and there was trouble with electrical apparatus.

Viceroy Says Force in India for Peace

DELHI, March 28.—Lord Willingdon, Viceroy of India, told the Chamber of Princes today that Britain is determined to maintain peace in India, and that use of force was solely to prevent chaos.

Commenting upon the work of the round table conference committee working here, Lord Willingdon expressed the hope a Federal system would be established soon.

Lydia Macy Sues N. Y. Mate in Reno

RENO, March 28.—Lydia B. Macy today filed suit for divorce against Valentine E. Macy Jr. of New York City, charging cruelty. The Macys, socially prominent in New York, were married in Pasadena November 7, 1925.

I. C. C. to Conduct 6-Hour Day Inquiry

WASHINGTON, March 28.—The Interstate Commerce Commission will begin hearings May 11 to determine what effect the proposed six-hour day would have on operation, service and expenses of all classes of railway employees.

'SLUSH FUND' FOR JURISTS' PAY RISE AIRED

Grand Jury Investigating Receivership Scandal May Sift New Sensational Report

Contributions of thousands of dollars by certain local politicians to the "slush fund" that was said to have financed in part the fight in the Legislature for higher salaries for Superior Court judges may be one of the sensational phases of the grand jury investigation of the receivership racket.

This was learned yesterday, when it was reported that at least $2000 was donated by a politician and his cohorts in an effort to ingratiate himself with members of the bench.

Foreman Charles S. Hutson of the grand jury, at a conference late yesterday, reiterated the determination of that body to go to the bottom of the American Mortgage Company scandal and related matters.

Judgment Reserved

"But we must reserve our judgment, as a grand jury, until we are completely in possession of all the facts," Hutson said.

In private conversations, however, another grand juryman said that if the judges who received gifts from receivers were shown to have reciprocated for these donations with favorable court decisions "with that intent," he was in favor of asking their removal from their high judicial positions.

Betrayal Harmful

Although the grand jury also was preparing to inquire into 350 other receiverships now active in Los Angeles County, members of the bench and bar pointed out this meant no reflection on those receivers who handled their trusts with honesty and capability.

It was pointed out that receiverships are necessary in litigation and are only harmful when this trust is betrayed.

Mark Hanna's Kin Gets Second Threat

WASHINGTON, March 28.—Reporting receipt of a second telephone threat that if she does not produce $2000 her daughter, Daisy, 6, will be kidnaped, Mrs. Betty Hanna Davidson, granddaughter of the late Mark Hanna, appealed to police today to make a thorough investigation.

Incendiaries Burn Convent in Madrid

MADRID, March 28.—The convent occupied by a branch of the Antequeria Trinitarian monks was burned to the ground by incendiaries here today. An attempt to burn another monastery was frustrated when civil guards fired on a Communist mob, wounding one.

I. C. C. Approves Rail Line Abandonment

WASHINGTON, March 28.—The Interstate Commerce Commission today authorized the Colorado & Southern Railroad to abandon seven and one-half miles of line in Boulder County, Colorado.

CHINESE REBEL FORCES MARCH ON CHANGCHUN

Japanese Troops in Manchuria May Be Obliged to Defend Instead of Attack

BY EDWARD S. HUNTER

HARBIN, March 28.—The Japanese force assigned to wipe out Chinese rebel armies in the Tokyo-dominated new state of Manchoukou may be forced to defend the new capital, Changchun, within a few days.

The steady approach of Chinese rebel forces moving north on Changchun from Tun Ua and southward from Nungan, 400 miles from Changchun, has created a new problem for Japanese troops.

Nungan was captured by the rebels today, forcing the flight of the Kirin loyal troops. Gen. Ma Chanshan, former Chinese patriot now aligned with the Japanese, was forced to dispatch a brigade to Chaotung to reinforce Japanese troops besieged at Fuyu.

The band approaching from the south is expected to arrive at Mingula tomorrow, according to Japanese military posts. In fighting over the week-end, the Japanese lost 15 killed and 24 wounded, and reported the Chinese losses at 180 killed and wounded.

Trocps Seize City

Gen. Ting Chao, leader of the allied rebel armies, is beset by Japanese and Kirin provincial troops now at Fangcheng, fifty miles from Ting's headquarters here. The Kirin troops yesterday captured Tungpin.

The Japanese are also faced with refusal of Soviet officials to cooperate with them. Russians still are purchasing Chinese grain here despite the Japanese-imports embargo. The Soviet section of the Chinese Eastern Railway has withdrawn most of its rolling stock to Manchuli, hampering Japanese campaigning along the railroad.

TOKYO, March 28.—Rumors of a Communistic uprising in Korea

(Continued on Page 3, Column 6)

L. A. Flyer Detained as Liquor Smuggler

SAN DIEGO, March 28.—Picked up accidentally by Federal border guards after his plane had been forced down by a clogged oil line near San Juan Capistrano, Maynard Dowell, 27, Los Angeles airplane pilot, was held today by Federal authorities on a charge of smuggling 175 gallons of alcohol into the United States.

2 L. A. Stanford Men Hurt in Auto Crash

KING CITY, March 28.—Two Stanford students, returning from an Easter holiday visit to their homes in Los Angeles, were injured today when their automobile skidded off the highway near here. They are J. R. Lewis and William M. French. Both were taken to Palo Alto Community Hospital.

Ex Mayor Gets 3 1-2 Years in Vice Case

DETROIT, March 28.—Dr. Rudolph G. Tenerowicz, resigned Mayor of Hamtramck, Mich., and three co-defendants, found guilty of vice conspiracy, were each sentenced to three and a half years in prison by Judge Homer Ferguson today.

Burmese Rebel Head Killed During Raid

CALCUTTA, March 28.—Po Hnya, notorious Burmese rebel leader, was killed today in a raid on Toungoo, Burma, said reports from Rangoon. Five of the rebel chieftain's followers were reported captured.

British Flyer Sets New London-Capetown Record

CAPETOWN, S. A., March 28.—J. A. Mollison, British aviator, set a new record for the flight from London to Capetown today when he landed here at 7:50 p. m.

The plane was partly wrecked when the undercarriage struck soft sand in landing on the beach, but the pilot was not hurt.

Mollison's unofficial time of four days nineteen hours and eleven minutes took almost a day from the record set by Peggy Salsman, British girl flyer, of five days eight hours and thirty-seven minutes.

Amy Johnson, British girl who set records in flights from London to Australia and Soviet Russia, arrived here today by steamer to head the celebration welcoming Mollison.

A Suitable Symbol for Insurgent Democrats

THE Democratic insurgents in Congress have given Mr. Hoover a very agreeable Easter memento.

They have presented him with a reelection to the Presidency in this year of grace nineteen hundred and thirty-two.

How delighted Mr. Hoover must have been this happy Easter to contemplate the bright-colored reelection egg which the insurgent Democrats and the insurgent Republicans had so generously and so certainly presented to him.

The jackass rabbit is the emblem of the insurgents.

Rabbits have always had something to do with Easter—not everybody knows exactly what or why.

But everybody knows now that the jackass rabbits have laid at Mr. Hoover's feet this delightful Easter present that he hardly expected to get.

THE jackass rabbit, as the emblem of the insurrectionary Democrats, is a fitting combination of the jackass, which is the appropriate emblem of the regular Democratic party, and the white rabbit, which is the accepted symbol of timidity—not to mention stupidity.

The jackass rabbit, therefore, emblem of the Democratic revolutionists, expresses admirably and perfectly the interesting and obvious fact that this new Bolshevist party possesses the brains of the ass and the heart of the white rabbit, and is therefore devoid of the wisdom to see its obligation to the Nation, and devoid of the courage to perform its obligation even if it could see it.

Mr. Hoover, of course, can be grateful to the jackass rabbit for the pleasant Easter surprise of reelection to the Presidency which they have given him, but the rest of the country has nothing to thank the jackass rabbit for.

The jackass rabbits have become a pest in Washington, a scourge, as they have been heretofore in some other parts of the country, and the only thing for the citizenship of the Nation to do is to adopt the usual measures in dealing with jackass rabbits, and have a jackass rabbit drive at the election this fall, and get as many as possible of these destructive animals in a corral and proceed to knock them politically on their silly heads.

NATURALLY, the result of this drive will be the reelection of Mr. Hoover, and that is not pleasant to contemplate, but anything is better than having the Government of our great country in the control of jackass rabbits.

General Grant once said that no matter in what a desperate plight the Republicans might be they need not despair, because the Democrats, true to their party emblem, would always do some jackass thing to give the Republicans the victory.

Until quite lately the regular Democrats in Congress, under the able leadership of Speaker Garner, were making such a commendable record as to seem wholly to belie this statement.

Then came the great plague of jackass rabbits, like the great plagues in the Bible, or like the seven years of famine, or the seven years' itch, or the great wind in Ireland—something always to be remembered and deplored—something that will go down in history as the ultimate of affliction, the acme of imbecility, something to prove that, after all, General Grant was emphatically and incontrovertibly RIGHT.

What the jackasses did not do to reestablish the Republican party and to reelect Mr. Hoover to the Presidency, the jackass rabbits did.

They ran out on Speaker Garner, and believe you me, brother, a jackass rabbit may not be able to see very far ahead; he may not be able to hear the people's voice, even with those long ears of his

(Continued on Page 2, Columns 6-7)

RECTOR TELLS CONTACT WITH KIDNAPERS

Clergyman in Plane Braves Storm to Rush Optimistic Report to Hopewell, N. J.

Holds Two-Hour Secret Parley With Colonel; Declares Stolen Boy Wll Be Returned

HOPEWELL, N. J., March 28.—(AP)—On a mission he considered important he flew nearly 300 miles through storms which had grounded most other planes, the dean of a Norfolk (Va.) church came here today to tell Col. Charles A. Lindbergh of a "contact" made with the kidnapers of the famous flyer's son.

After an hour behind closed doors with the Colonel, the clergyman, the Very Rev. H. Dobson-Peacock, started back home with the statement there probably would be another conference with Lindbergh within three or four days.

He declined to discus the information he had passed on to the father of the child, who was stolen twenty-seven days ago from his crib, but twice he spoke of the "optimism" he and two other prominent Norfolk residents, acting with him as intermediaries, have that the missing baby will be returned to his parents.

"The conference was the result of a contact made with the kidnapers," he said.

"Dis Colonel Lindbergh receive your information with optimism?" he was asked.

'Optimistic'

"I cannot speak for Colonel Lindbergh," he replied. "All I can say is we are optimistic."

He apparently referred to himself, John H. Curtis, Norfolk boat builder, and Rear Admiral Guy H. Burrage, retired, who have been associated since March 9 in efforts to obtain the return of the child.

Over the week-end Curtis made a mysterious airplane trip to meet the abductors. His associate, however, did not make it clear this afternoon whether the "contact" to which he referred had been made

Wives Do Have Some Rights!

You've probably read about the English judge who ruled that a woman's body is not the property of her husband—and caused a world-wide stir. Possibly you were one who agreed with him—or mayhap you thought him all wrong. But on this morning's March of Events page comes Mary Borden to give the English woman's view of this judicial decision which has upset our views. And whatever you think of the judge and his decision, you'll find her column filled with common sense which if followed would make more marriages happy.

And just think of the other fine writers who contribute today—Vincent Starrett, Adela Rogers St. Johns, Charles Hanson Towne, Bruno Lessing, Idwal Jones and a host of others. Why, unless you turn and read Page 11 now, you won't get the FULL VALUE from YOUR Examiner.

THE CRIMINAL GUN MOWS DOWN EVEN WOMEN

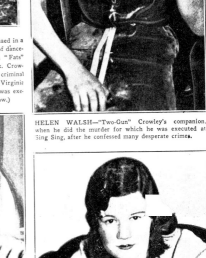

MURDERED FOR THE VICE-RING—Virginia Brannen, subpoenaed in a New York crusade against a syndicate operating vicious resorts under the guise of dance-halls, was murdered for $300 paid to Francis "Two-Gun" Crowley and Rudolph "Fats" Durniger in an automobile, and her body thrown on a lonely road in The Bronx. Crowley and Durniger were two of the toughest products of New York's juvenile criminal population. Durniger was later executed for the murder of poor, deluded young Virginia Brannen, a victim of poverty and organized crime in New York, and Crowley was executed for the murder of Policeman Hirsch, in Long Island. (See right, and below.)

HELEN WALSH—"Two-Gun" Crowley's companion, when he did the murder for which he was executed at Sing Sing, after he confessed many desperate crimes.

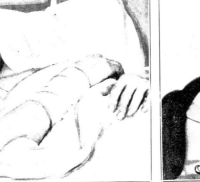

CROWLEY'S FORT—A detective leans through the shattered door of the West 90th st. apartment where Crowley was besieged in a sensational raid by New York police, and where he and his young girl companion, Helen Walsh (see photo at right, above), were wounded and captured. Note bullet-holes in the door and wall. More than three hundred metropolitan police engaged in the spectacular daylight battle, which raged for hours, and ended only when Crowley had spent his ammunition and was shot. (See right.)

AFTER BATTLE—Francis "Two-Gun" Crowley in the hospital under heavy guard after he was shot and taken. He was later tried and executed for murder of a policeman who held up his car while he was driving with Helen Walsh. Crowley, an undersized waif of the mid-Manhattan slums, had committed almost every known type of desperate crime before he was 20.

THE GIRL WHO TOLD—Young Billie Dunn, (above), jilted by "Two-Gun" Crowley, who preferred Helen Walsh (above), gave the information which led the police to the hiding place of Crowley, 20-year-old cop-killer, vice-ring executioner, robber, racketeer and "problem child" of the New York tenement belt, in trouble from childhood and electrocuted at 20 for one of numerous murders. Bitter hatred of policemen was the motivating impulse of his distorted, reckless young life. He "died game!"

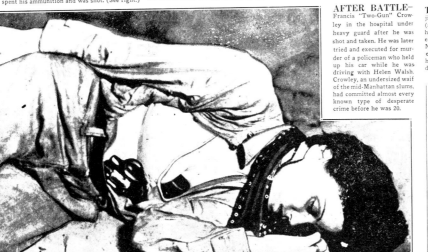

HER LAST MESSAGE—Portrait of pretty Helen Eaton (see left) before she began her last prison sentence, and, superimposed, a facsimile of the note she left in her cell as she made her armed farewell break for liberty.

FUGITIVE FROM THE "BIG HOUSE"—Attractive Helen Eaton, escaping prisoner from the Arkansas Women's Prison, repeated jail-breaker, was shot by a convict trusty a few miles from the prison. The picture reveals her body as it lay in the roadside showing the .45 with which she was about to defend her life and liberty. She had torn open her waist and was about to "draw" when the shotgun blast dropped her, lifeless. At 22, the beautiful young girl had killed two men, the second while on parole from the sentence for killing the first. She confessed and was "doing" ten years when she got away, leaving a note saying: "I'll never be taken alive!" (See right.)

OUR NATION'S SHAME! More of These Remarkable Pictures Will Appear in This Newspaper Next Sunday

Bare Lindbergh Baby Kidnaper's Code Note Telling of Abduction Plar

SPECIAL EXTRA EDITION

Only Los Angeles Newspaper With All Leading News Services— Associated Press, International News, United Press, Dow - Jones

NRA MEMBER U.S. WE DO OUR PART

LOS ANGELES EVENING HERALD Express
AN INDEPENDENT AND NEWSPAPER

Reg. U. S. Pat. Office. Copyright, 1934, by Evening Herald Publishing Company
The Evening Herald and Express Grows Just Like Los Angeles

SPORTS
COMPLETE N.Y. STOCKS-BONDS

WEATHER FORECAST
Los Angeles and Vicinity—Fair tonight and Sunday with cloudy night and morning; seasonable temperature and humidity; gentle to moderate wind.

VOL. LXIV THREE CENTS Hotels and Trains Five Cents SATURDAY, SEPTEMBER 22, 1934 Two Sections Section A THREE CENTS NO. 155

DILLINGER AIDE SLAIN AS 2 ESCAPE DEATH CELLS

LINEUPS FOR TODAY'S TROJAN GRID BATTLES

Here are the lineups for the U. S. C.-Oxy and U. S. C.-Whittier football games, starting at 1 o'clock this afternon in the Los Angeles Coliseum:

FIRST GAME

U. S. C.— No.	Player	Position	—OCCIDENTAL Player	No.
	Kidder	L. E.	Rowland	75
	[illegible]	L. T.	[illegible]	37
[illegible]	Beard	L. G.	Cleland	85
15	Hall	C.	Nunn	68
25	Sanders	R. G.	Howe	59
64	Rorison	R. T.	Gough	69
66	Ostling	R. E.	Beebe	70
24	Howard	Q.	Lewis	78
71	Belko	L. H.	McMillan	79
29	Wing	R. H.	Sheridan	76
42	Smith	F.	Cosby	74

SECOND GAME

U. S. C.— No.	Player	Position	—WHITTIER Player	No.
37	Bescos	L. E.	Christopher	16
35	Jorgenson	L. T.	Dahlitz	53
44	McGinley	L. G.	Rusk	27
34	Carpenter	C.	Hannon	19
32	Dittberner	R. G.	Soeberg	69
33	Harper	R. T.	Dietrick	31
21	Browning	R. E.	Stevenson	50
13	Warburton	Q.	Notthoff	24
47	Propst	L. H.	Hutchison	21
18	Clemons	R. H.	Arrambide	22
23	Wotkyns	F.	Nelson	16

SOUTHERN CALIFORNIA ROSTER

13 Warburton, q.	35 Jorgenson, lt.	55 Lady, rt.	74 Spraggins, rh.
12 Rogers, c.	36 R. Matthews, re.	56 Bardin, rg.	75 Powers, f.
15 Hall, c.	37 Bescos, le.	57 Coughlin, lt.	76 Brandt, rt.
16 Kovac, rg.	38 Fuhrer, re.	58 Lynch, f.	77 Kirkpatrick, lh.
18 Clemens, rh.	39 Beard, lg.	59 Kuhn, c.	78 Grider, g.
19 Reboin, lh.	40 Larabee, re.	60 Burchard, rh.	79 F. Tatsch, t.
20 Cameron, q.	41 Gill, le.	61 Thurlow, le.	80 E. Rogers, t.
21 Browning, re.	42 Smith, f.	62 G. Matthews, q	81 Elliott, e.
23 Wotkyns, f.	43 Clayton, re.	63 Kraintz, f.	82 Beatty, h.
24 Howard, q.	44 McGinley, lg.	64 Rorison, lt.	83 Schultz, f.
25 Sanders, rg.	45 H. Tatsch, lt.	65 Murray, rt.	84 Hardeman, g.
26 Kidder, le.	46 Sutherland, lh.	66 Ostling, re.	85 Talbot, e.
27 Davis, q.	47 Propst, lh.	67 Hull, rt.	86 Preininger, t.
28 Houlgate, c.	49 Bishop, e.	68 Hofer, lh.	87 Boone, t.
29 Wing, rh.	50 G. Davis, rg.	69 Munch, q.	88 Crawford, e.
31 Wilburg, rg.	51 Loughborough, rh.	70 De Hetre, c.	89 Cascales, g.
32 Dittburner, rg.	52 W. Dye, rg.	71 Belko, lh.	90 Kuntz, q.
33 Harper, rt.	53 McNeish, rt.	72 Busby, lt.	
34 Carpenter, c.	54 Webb, rh.	73 Rodeen, re.	

OCCIDENTAL ROSTER

50 Arpes, h.	59 Howe, g.	68 Nunn, c.	79 McMillan, f.
51 Packer, h.	60 Hunt, t.	69 Gough, t.	80 Bates, h.
52 Punaro, h.	61 Moore, t.	70 Beebe, e.	81 Heffern, g.
53 Nauman, e.	62 McBratney, e.	71 Villard, h.	82 Kingston, q.
54 Powell, e.	63 Voron, e.	72 Carter, h.	83 Hammack, c.
55 Winterburn, h.	64 Woods, t.	73 Tuttle, h.	84 Lyons, h.
56 Appy, c.	65 Knudson, e.	74 Cosby, f.	85 Cleland, g.
57 Gemmell, t.	66 Barrett, t.	75 Rowland, e.	86 Snyder, g.
58 Reed, g.	67 Demarest, e.	76 Sheridan, q.	

WHITTIER ROSTER

2 Bishop, q.	17 Tebbs, le.	26 Langdon, rh.	47 Dozier, rg.
3 Sheively, lh.	18 Rupard, le.	27 Rusk, g.	50 Stevenson, re.
5 Siegmund, lh.	19 Hannon, c.	30 Cogswell, lg.	53 Dahlitz, lt.
9 Sanders, re.	21 Hutchison, rh.	31 Dietrick, rt.	55 La Form, lt.
12 Peiper, lg.	22 Arrambide, rh.	33 Hunt, c.	59 N. Sowers, lt.
13 Kendle, rh.	23 Richardson, h.	35 Bettsinger, g.	65 Kirchner, rg.
15 Patterson, re.	24 Notthoff, q.	39 Kemp, re.	69 Soeberg, f.
16 Nelson, f.	25 Robinson, f.	44 Hoffman, rg.	73 E. Sowers, rt.

TROJANS OPEN GRID SEASON AGAINST OXY AND WHITTIER

By GEORGE T. DAVIS

Southern California's '34 football eam with its green, heavy line and ght, speedy backfield, was ready o swing into action today at the oliseum in a double-header against ccidental and Whittier.

The Trojans were scheduled to eet Oxy at 1:00 o'clock, with the Vhittier game slated for 3:15 clock. Coach Howard Jones was o start the second team, led by Bill Ioward at quarterback, against the engals, with the varsity, featuring Cotton" Warburton in the starting uarterback position, being held in eserve for the Poets.

A year ago the Trojans defeated Oxy and Whittier by scores of 39-0 and 51-0, respectively, and a crowd of 35,000 spectators was expected to flock to the Coliseum today to compare the present Trojan machine with that of 1933.

While the results of the games were not in doubt, the fight for positions on the Southern California varsity was expected to furnish plenty of activity for the fans. One of the greatest fights for recognition was anticipated between Bill Howard and Dave Davis, the latter a sophomore flash, for the right to understudy Warburton at quarterback.

Howard, because of his greater experience, was to get the call to-

(CONTINUED ON PAGE NINE)

PLOT TOLD IN LETTER TO CONVICT

By Associated Press

COLUMBUS, Ohio, Sept. 22.—Evidence that Bruno Hauptmann, arrested in the Lindbergh kidnaping case, had sent a code letter to an Ohio penitentiary convict late in 1931 or early in 1932, revealing he intended to kidnap the famous aviator's child, was disclosed here today by Preston E. Thomas, veteran warden of the old prison.

The warden disclosed that the prisoner, George Paul, alias Paullin, made a trip to New Jersey with him shortly after the kidnaping, in the hope he could return the child to its parents. But, said the warden, "New Jersey officers took no interest in it and we returned to Columbus."

VIEWS PICTURE

Shown a picture of Hauptmann today, the convict said instantly:

"That's the man."

The Lindbergh baby was kidnaped March 1, 1932, and the code letter was received by Paul late in 1931 or early in 1932.

The code in the letter consists of taking the second word in each sentence and making a separate sentence out of the second words.

The letter follows:

"'I **WILL** write you a few lines today to let you know that all is well. Old **KID**, how I wish you were here with us. A **NAP** is taken by Mildred every afternoon since she came from the hospital. Mr. **LINDY** went to Red Bank last week and while skating caught a severe cold and has pneumonia. Old **BABY** wish you could have been with us last week as we surely had a grand time. I **HOPE** everything is going well with you. As **FOR** me things are not going so good. Oh, **ME**, oh my.'

(Signed) BRUNO.

KEY REVEALED

Thus the key to the code brought out the startling statement:

"Will kidnap Lindy baby. Hope for me."

(Editor's Note—The letter was written entirely in the same style, the second words in each sentence in the above, being merely capitalized in print to emphasize the secret code message.)

"On account of the peculiar wording and disconnected sentences the letter was particularly noted by Miss A. A. Thomas, mail censor," the warden said. "Soon after the kidnaping of the Lindbergh baby, I received several notes from Prisoner Paul asking for an interview. His request was not granted at the time. Then came a note to me at night that he must see me at once and that

(CONTINUED ON PAGE EIGHT)

DIG UP NEW ABDUCTION EVIDENCE

By Associated Press

NEW YORK, Sept. 22.—Henry Uhlig, 28, friend of Isadore Fisch, the man Bruno Hauptmann said entrusted the Lindbergh ransom money to him, was taken to the police station today for questionng.

By Associated Press

WASHINGTON, Sept. 22.—An intensive study of Henry Uhlig and Isadore Fisch, two friends of Bruno Hauptmann, has been undertaken by the justice department. Hauptmann told police that Fisch gave him the $13,750 of the Lindbergh ransom money that was found hidden in his garage. Fisch and Uhlig later sailed for Europe and Fisch died in Germany. Both are naturalized aliens.

NEW YORK, Sept. 22.—Police revealed today that department of justice agents were seeking a friend of Bruno R. Hauptmann who supposedly visited the Hauptmann garage after the Lindbergh case suspect was arrested. The ransom money was found in the garage by federal agents.

The unidentified man who visited the garage, police said, lives in Mount Vernon, at a place not far from the Hauptmann home. The Mount Vernon house has been watched and the telephone wires tapped.

The man is an American about 40 years old.

Meanwhile, police digging in the cellar of the Hauptmann house emerged with a suitcase, two bundles and a small package which they carried away in an automobile.

Reports that Hauptmann had con-

(CONTINUED ON PAGE FOUR)

Surprise Shower Falls in Westwood; Fair Is Forecast

Heavy fog dripped on Los Angeles streets today, while outright showers amounting to .02 inch fell in Westwood and at points along the beach. It was a surprise gift of moisture from the weather which had been extra hot and excessively dry for days. But the weather man said the hot spell did not cause the extremely damp fog and mist today.

The temperature was moderate, 64 being recorded at the weather bureau.

Fogs, ranging from heavy on the coast to light in the interior, and mist prevailed in the early morning hours, but cleared lightly as the day advanced. The forecast was for fair tonight and tomorrow.

The temperature yesterday reached a high of 73 degrees and dropped to a low of 62 degrees at dawn.

DILLINGER AIDES TRY ESCAPE, SHOT

Charles Makley, Dillinger gangster who was killed today in an effort to escape from an Ohio prison death cell, and Harry Pierpont, a "trigger man" who was critically wounded in the attempted break, are pictured shackled to John Dillinger in a dramatic court scene after their capture in Arizona. Makley and Pierpont today tried the Dillinger "dummy gun" trick, using "weapons" carved of soap. Arrows show the handcuffs that linked the mobsters to Dillinger. Now death is replacing steel in binding the gangsters together.

BARE DEAD MAN MYSTERY IN LINDY CASE

Copyright, 1934, by Associated Press

LEIPZIG, Germany, Sept. 22.—Leipzig police headquarters informed the Associated Press today that the body of Isidor Fisch probably would be disinterred for post mortem examination if the New York police should request it.

Copyright 1934 by International News Service throughout the world. Reproduction in whole or in part strictly forbidden.

LEIPZIG, Sept. 22.—Buried in his grave for six months, Isadore Fisch stepped back into the world limelight in connection with the Lindbergh case today when investigation revealed that, although he went to America as a poor immigrant in 1925, he was able by 1932 to support members of his family in lavish style with money from the United States.

At the same time, his family disclosed to International News Service that Fisch was well acquainted with Bruno Richard Hauptmann, held as receiver of the Lindbergh ransom, who has told police he received it from Fisch and cached it in his Bronx garage.

Before he died here early this

Watch for Herald-Express Football Extra

King Football rules again!

Up and down the coast and over the whole country, the gridiron sport comes into its own today. At the Coliseum the Trojans play Oxy and Whittier in a double-header; at U. C. L. A., Pomona and San Diego play the Bruins.

Stanford meets San Jose, Loyola of New Orleans plays Rice, Texas faces Texas Tech and other outstanding teams swing into action.

For the complete scores and colorful details of leading contests, be sure to get your Evening Herald and Express FOOTBALL EXTRA.

With the final gun at the Coliseum, it will be on the street. Watch for it. As usual, you will find it

FIRST WITH THE LATEST AND THE BEST.

Stars and Portland Play Sixth Game This Afternoon

Hollywood and Portland meet in the sixth game of the current series at Wrigley field this afternoon, with Wally Hebert due to pitch for the Stars and Hal Turpin for the visitors. The probable batting order:

PORTLAND—	HOLLYWOOD—
Bongiovanni, cf	Levey, ss
Wilburn, ss	Haney, 3b
Burns, 1b	Durst, lf
Claybaugh, lf	Jolley, rf
Moore, 3b	Bell, cf
Blackerby, rf	Jacobs, 1b
P. Coscarart, 2b	Bassler, c
Cox, c	R. Doerr, 2b
Turpin, p	Hebert, p

U. S. YACHT WINS 4TH RACE OF CUP SERIES

By Associated Press

ABOARD U. S. C. G. CUTTER ARGO, OFF NEWPORT, Sept. 22.—In as thrilling a race as ever was sailed for the America's cup the defending Rainbow today defeated the British challenger Endeavour in the fourth race of the current series to even the count at two victories each.

She won by a minute 16 seconds.

SEE-SAW TALENT

No more see-saw contest ever was waged than that of the two racing yachts today as first one and then the other led.

The American boat was first away, crossing the starting line 20 seconds ahead of the invader, but Endeavour made up that margin and in a thrilling bow-to-bow dash rounded the first 10-mile buoy 27 seconds ahead.

Rainbow began to go to town from there, quickly closed the gap, took the lead and rounded the second turning mark at 20 miles with a lead of 59 seconds.

She lost some of her advantage in the early stages of the last 10 miles, but came faster at the finish

(CONTINUED ON PAGE ELEVEN)

FOIL MAKLEY, PIERPONT FAKE GUN BREAK

COLUMBUS, Ohio, Sept. 22.—Charles Makley, former John Dillinger gangster, was shot to death today by Ohio penitentiary guards who frustrated an attempt by Makley and Harry Pierpont to win their freedom from the death cell at the prison.

Pierpont was wounded critically and may die.

The two attempted to duplicate the stunt of their former chieftain in bluffing their way out of the penitentiary with fake weapons.

Where Dillinger successfully made his way out of Crown Point, Ind., jail last spring by covering a guard with a pistol fashioned of wood, Pierpont and Makley were unsuccessful in attempting to bluff Ohio prison guards with weapons made from soap.

The weapons, those who saw them said, were "perfect imitations" of a .32-caliber revolver and an automatic pitsol.

The attempted break took place while Warden Preston E. Thomas was talking with newspapermen in his office, telling them of a tip that had been given a convict prior to the Lindbergh kidnaping that the crime was to be attempted. The tip came in a letter

Herald-Express Special Features

CHARACTER QUALITY · AMERICA FIRST! · ENTERPRISE ACCURACY

RED LINE

Los Angeles Examiner
AN AMERICAN PAPER FOR THE AMERICAN PEOPLE · THE GREAT NEWSPAPER OF THE GREAT SOUTHWEST

RED LINE

LOUIS READY FOR BATTLE
See Sports Section

VOL. XXXIII—NO. 37   P   LOS ANGELES, FRIDAY, JANUARY 17, 1936   Two Sections—Part I—FIVE CENTS

HOFFMAN REPRIEVES BRUNO

EATH PENALTY POSTPONED
Escapes Electric Chair in New Move

30 MORE DAYS OF LIFE GIVEN TO MURDERER

Prisoner and Wife Elated Over Stay; Governor Withholds Reasons for Granting Mercy

TRENTON, N. J., Jan. 16.—(AP)—Bruno Richard Hauptmann, convicted Lindbergh baby killer, was saved temporarily from the electric chair late today with a 30-day reprieve from Governor Harold G. Hoffman.

It came only 29 hours before the hour of execution.

"I am granting a reprieve," the Governor said, "for divers reasons which I do not care to disclose at this time."

The reprieve, though only for thirty days, actually assures Hauptmann of at least eight more weeks of life, and perhaps three months, due to the fact it will be necessary to resentence him.

Governor Hoffman acted soon after the United States Supreme Court, in a one-sentence decision by Chief Justice Hughes, denied Hauptmann's appeal for a writ of habeas corpus and a stay of execution.

ONLY ONE REPRIEVE

There will be only one reprieve, "unless the evidence should warrant" another, the Governor said. If Hauptmann is to be finally saved, it must be through the presentation of sufficient new evidence to warrnt Justice Thomas W. Trenchard, who presided at the Flemington trial, granting a request for a new trial, or for a new plea for clemency to the State Pardons Court.

The Governor announced his decision in his office shortly after talking with Mrs. Anna Hauptmann, who presumably had called upon him to plead for her husband's life.

There was no formal statement by the Governor, who spoke extemporaneously. He said:

"The Attorney General and I have been in conference on this matter, and I have decided to announce a reprieve of thirty days.

"We have agreed that this will not be challenged."

WILL SIGN

A delay in preparation of the reprieve order caused the Governor to leave his office before signing it. It will be signed early tomorrow, it was said.

Hauptmann received word of his new lease on life from two of his attorneys—C. Lloyd Fisher and Frederick A. Pope.

Pope quoted the condemned man as saying "Thank you," as his face lighted up, and he asserted he was "sure something would happen" to prevent execution.

The "grapevine" carried the news quickly throughout the big prison.

PRISON IN UPROAR

The inmates lifted their voices in shouts:

"Hauptmann! Hauptmann!"

"Reprieve! Reprieve! Reprieve!"

They beat upon the cell doors, and the noise spread swiftly from cell block to cell block.

Finally it diminished and faded out.

The Governor made the an-

(Continued on Next Page, Col. 8)

HATCHET ATTACK RELATED
Boy, Girl Say Father Wounded Them

MARY SUAREZ, who told court she sustained broken arm trying to shield her brother.

SHE IDENTIFIES the hatchet with which her father assertedly threatened to "dipe out family."

'Wipe Out Family' Threat Told

"Light glaring in my eyes awakened me. There stood my father with a hatchet in his hand. Then he struck me on the head with it."

Saying that his father, Jesus Suarez, 54, Spaniard, frequently had threatened to "wipe out the whole family," Joseph Suarez and his sister, who sustained a broken arm in trying to shield her brother, yesterday were the chief witnesses against their parent.

"We were always scared," the girl said before Municipal Judge William R. McKay, under questioning by Deputy District Attorney Terrys Gambord. "Father was always threatening us. Then, the night of December 23, he grabbed the hatchet and started after us. He hit Joe on the head. My arm was broken when I tried to grab father's arm."

Judge McKay held the father for trial in Superior Court on charges of attempted murder.

JOSEPH SUAREZ shows judge where he was struck on side of head by weapon he testified his father wielded.

PROSECUTOR'S JUROR QUIZ GIVES CLEW

District Attorney Perjury Case to Reach Into Past, Latest Indication by Shoemaker

Entry into the perjury trial of District Attorney Buron Fitts of spectacular financial, moral and political cases in the last five years became a certainty late yesterday as the lines of battle grew clearer in the slow and painstaking selection of jurory.

With the law of averages promising a jury composed largely of women, Special Prosecutor Clyde C. Shoemaker gave a clew in his questioning that the prosecution will reach into the past to bring into sharp relief the notorious "Hollywood love mart" and the collapse of the California Reserve Corporation, whose former president, George Gregory, is Fitts' brother-in-law.

DEFENSE WEAPONS

In the other camp, Chief Defense Attorney Jerry Giesler has already raised as one of his chief weapons the claim that the 1934 grand jury, which indicted Fitts, was "hand-picked" and "politically motivated."

Despite several changes, eight women of the housewife type, and four men, ratio of the day before, remained in the box late yesterday, prospective judges of whether Fitts gave false testimony concerning an orange grove transaction during investigation by the grand jury of his dismissal of morals charges against John P. Mills, local real estate man, in the "love mart" case.

The panel was tentatively accepted by the defense and shortly before noon the prosecution began interrogation.

2 MEN EXCUSED

Seven to five feminine in first panel, the majority of women was increased by the lottery of the venire selection, Court Clerk James Shaw drawing the names of two women to replace two men who were excused, and then drawing the name of a man to replace a woman.

Thus the law of averages, observers held, should serve to retain the feminine predominance in future drawings occasioned by the excusing of talesmen or peremptory challenges.

There were clear hints that the defense would be satisfied with such a jury.

WARNING BY JUDGE

Presiding Judge Pat R. Parker warned the courtroom full of veniremen that the jury would be locked up at night, when testimony starts, and called upon them to present legitimate excuses promptly when called if they wished to be relieved of duty.

uestioning by both sides during the second day of jury selection gave rich promise of sensational testimony to come.

Prominent among early witnesses, it was indicated, will be Lucien Wheeler, one of numerous private detectives whose testimony is expected to give flavor to the case.

DEED IN CASE

Wheeler was Mills' private investigator during the morals case prosecution, and to him, it is said, is charged purchase

BRUNO RICHARD HAUPTMANN, who has been granted thirty-day reprieve from electrocution.

PRISONER, WHO was convicted of Lindbergh baby kidnap-murder, won respite from "Jersey justice."

—International News Photo

WATERGATE

On November 7, 1972, Richard Nixon was re-elected to the Office of the Presidency by the largest popular vote ever recorded in American history. Over forty-seven million people cast their support at the polls and the Committee to Re-Elect the President revelled in the accomplishment of what its members considered an unprecedented mandate. The campaign itself had been a marked deviation from previous Republican strategies, with the Committee isolating the President from established Party structures and activities as much as possible. Of the seventy million dollars in campaign contributions raised by the Committee, very few were appropriated to Congressional campaigns or to the Party apparatus. Even the slogan was indicative of the separation between the two organizations—"Re-Elect the President." In the end, the President was the direct beneficiary of the strategy, while Republican candidates for other offices were defeated in an almost equally dramatic fashion.

It was not until the inauguration of Nixon for his second term that a number of factors in the campaign were made public, however, and the course of the events to follow was largely predicated on those covert, and often illegal, actions which left their indelible impact on the nation under the name of Watergate. In major part, the incidents which produced the Watergate break-in and the subsequent events which led to the resignation of both the Vice President and the President of the United States had their origin in the White House and the Attorney General's Office several months before the Committee to Re-Elect the President was formed. In two primary areas, the legacy which the Committee assumed in the early months of 1972 had been molded by the end of 1971.

On June 13, 1969, John Mitchell had announced that, as Attorney General, he believed that the President had the authority to engage in wiretapping without a court order. Despite the prevailing interpretation of the Fourth Amendment which disallowed

Nixon faced a televised news conference with Associated Press Managing Editors where the President of the United States felt obliged to say, **"I'm not a crook."** For the second time in his life he seemed to be a man backed up against the wall, pulling out the lining of his pockets and emptying the contents before the world.

such an action, Mitchell appointed F.B.I. Director J. Edgar Hoover as head of a commission to formulate plans for internal intelligence gathering in the summer of 1970. Three weeks later, the commission presented a forty-three page document to the President and the Attorney General, recommending two kinds of activities— mail coverage, and breaking and entering. Although the document carried a warning that such activities were "clearly illegal," the report was well-received by the White House as a means of dealing effectively with the Chief Executive's growing concern over domestic subversion, particularly among the ranks of the anti-war demonstrators. The first actual manifestation of the use of questionable forms of surveillance occurred in the summer of 1971, when Nixon ordered the initiation of activities designed to "stop security leaks and to investigate other sensitive security matters." Following the publication of the first installment of the *Pentagon Papers* in the Sunday edition of the New York *Times*, the President operationalized the order by organizing a special, secret investigation unit to be supervised by John Ehrlichman and staffed by Krogh, Liddy and Young. In direct response to Ellsberg's indictment on charges of possessing documents related to the national defense in regard to the release of the papers, the first actions of the unit were directed at the burglary of Ellsberg's psychiatrist's office in Beverly Hills, California, on the night of September 4.

Over the course of the next few months, as the Committee to Re-Elect the President took form, participants engaged in a series of discussions about campaign tactics and fund-raising. Compounded by the President's concern with internal subversion, the decision of the committee to opt for a victory of unprecedented margin began to dominate conversations. Initial plans reflected the zeal of the investigative unit members, who became closely aligned with the Committee, and one of the earliest requests was for permission to engage in a variety of activities aimed at undermining the Democratic contestants' campaigns. Hired as counsel for the Committee, Liddy announced privately that a detailed plan had been devised which would cost approximately a million dollars and would emphasize "mugging squads, kidnapping teams, prostitutes to compromise the opposition, and electronic surveillance." The request was denied by Mitchell, who was acting as chief con-

WHITE HOUSE ORGANIZATION CHART

1971-72, WITH SUBSEQUENT PERSONNEL CHANGES NOTED

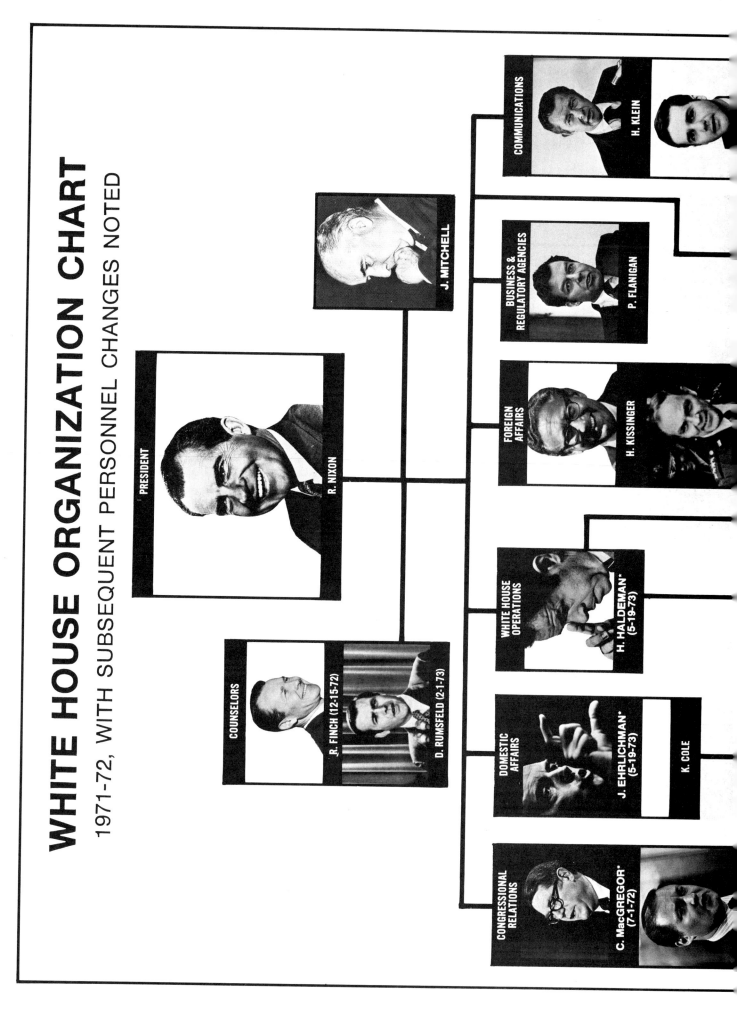

PRESIDENT
R. NIXON

J. MITCHELL

COUNSELORS
R. FINCH (12-15-72)
D. RUMSFELD (2-1-73)

COMMUNICATIONS
H. KLEIN

BUSINESS & REGULATORY AGENCIES
P. FLANIGAN

FOREIGN AFFAIRS
H. KISSINGER

WHITE HOUSE OPERATIONS
H. HALDEMAN* (5-19-73)

DOMESTIC AFFAIRS
J. EHRLICHMAN* (5-19-73)
K. COLE

CONGRESSIONAL RELATIONS
C. MacGREGOR* (7-1-72)

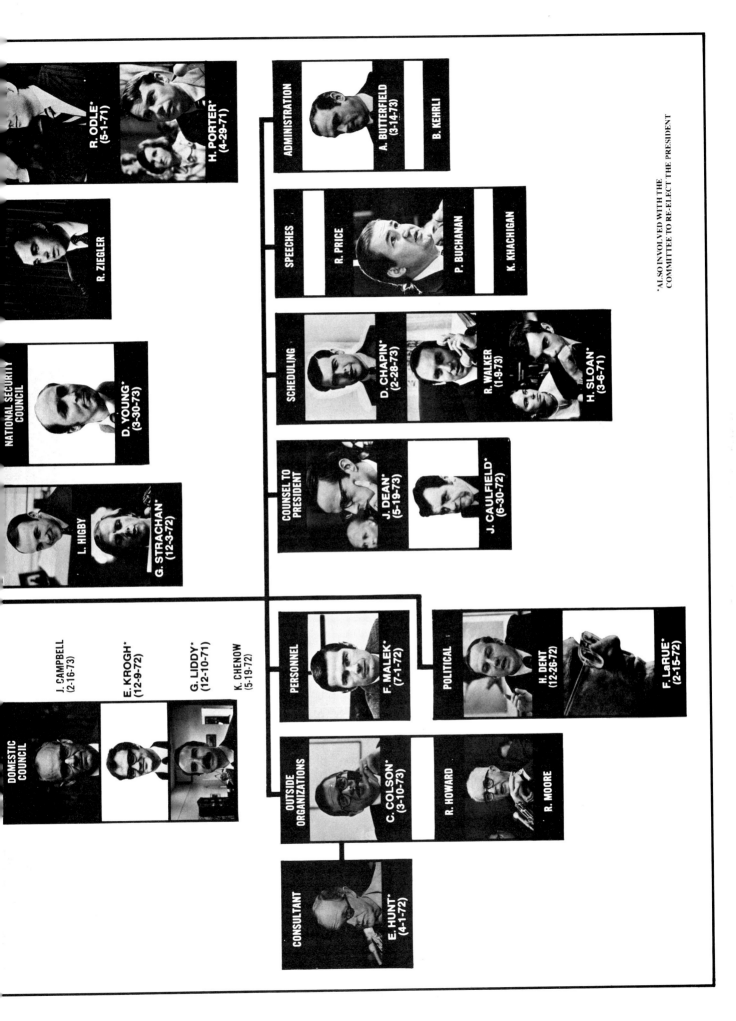

R. ODLE*
(5-1-71)

H. PORTER*
(4-29-71)

R. ZIEGLER

NATIONAL SECURITY
COUNCIL

D. YOUNG*
(3-30-73)

L. HIGBY

G. STRACHAN*
(12-3-72)

ADMINISTRATION

A. BUTTERFIELD
(3-14-73)

B. KEHRLI

SPEECHES

R. PRICE

P. BUCHANAN

K. KHACHIGAN

SCHEDULING

D. CHAPIN*
(2-28-73)

R. WALKER
(1-9-73)

H. SLOAN*
(3-6-71)

COUNSEL TO
PRESIDENT

J. DEAN*
(5-19-73)

J. CAULFIELD*
(6-30-72)

DOMESTIC
COUNCIL

J. CAMPBELL
(2-16-73)

E. KROGH*
(12-9-72)

G. LIDDY*
(12-10-71)

K. CHENOW
(5-19-72)

PERSONNEL

F. MALEK*
(7-1-72)

POLITICAL

H. DENT
(12-26-72)

F. LaRUE*
(2-15-72)

OUTSIDE
ORGANIZATIONS

C. COLSON*
(3-10-73)

R. HOWARD

R. MOORE

CONSULTANT

E. HUNT*
(4-1-72)

*ALSO INVOLVED WITH THE
COMMITTEE TO RE-ELECT THE PRESIDENT

John Mitchell, Attorney General of the United States, announced that he believed that the President had the power to engage in wiretapping without a court order despite the prevailing interpretation of the Supreme Court that the Fourth Amendment disallowed such action. After frequent use of wiretap devices, the Court again reaffirmed its earlier decision. The use of wiretaps in the Watergate break-in became the central focus of the ensuing investigations.

sultant to the Committee, but the idea remained dominant in later discussions. Progressively, the Committee envisioned the widespread use of intelligence-gathering and sabotage as means of securing a dramatic re-election of the President; the assistance of governmental agencies was incresingly solicited in the effort, under the auspices of the White House.

On February 4, a new strategy was introduced. Reducing the funding requested, Liddy informed the Attorney General that half a million dollars would cover the expenses of a plan to break into the Watergate Hotel in Washington, D.C., for the purpose of placing wiretaps on the telephones of the Democratic National Committee Offices and securing photographs of important materials related to the campaign. Again, the plan was denied, but this time only after the Attorney General had officially resigned from his position and taken control of the leadership of the Committee.

On April 7, just over a month after Mitchell changed roles, the break-in plan was approved, with authorization for James McCord, the special coordinator of the Committee, to take action within thirty days. Over the course of a month, $85,000 was spent on the purchase of tape recorders, transmitters, antennas, and walkie-talkies to be used in the break-in scheme. Then, in accordance with the second phase of the plan, McCord and a team of associates rented room 419 at the Howard Johnson Motor Lodge, directly across the street from the Watergate complex, and began to finalize plans for the first actual attempts on the weekend of May 26 and 27. On Friday evening, the first effort at breaking and entering failed. On Saturday night, a second attempt was again aborted. Finally, on Sunday, the team successfully entered the Democratic Headquarters, photographed documents and implanted wiretaps on the telephones. The next day, McCord began monitoring conversations while Liddy secretary transcribed them for use by the Committee to Re-Elect the President.

Not completely satisfied with the material amassed from this effort, another attempt was sanctioned and scheduled for June 17. At 2:30 a.m., McCord's team was discovered and arrested on charges of second degree burglary. The police confiscated cameras, electronic surveillance equipment and an attache case containing numerically sequenced hundred dollar bills. Within the next thirty-

six hours, events transpired at a phenomenal pace. The incident was reported by the press, with Mitchell responding almost immediately that the Committee was in no way responsible—a statement which was soon to be refuted. At 10:30 on Monday morning, John Dean, acting as special counsel to the President, ordered the removal of all potentially incriminating evidence from White House offices. A few hours later, the Supreme Court handed down a decision, rejecting Mitchell's 1969 interpretation of Executive privilege in the use of wire-tapping, maintaining that no domestic person or group could be subjected to electronic surveillance under any circumstances without a specific warrant issued by a court of law. A day later, the Justice Department announced that it would begin a full investigation of the Watergate break-in and, on Wednesday, the Democratic National Committee filed a million dollar civil suit against the Committee to Re-Elect the President. By the first week of July, Liddy had been formally fired from his post on the Committee and John Mitchell had resigned as chairman.

Two weeks before the Republican National Convention began in Miami, Florida, the press carried a story in which the staff of the Committee publicly admitted that campaign contributions had been used in the Watergate affair. The public, however, responded in a way which had been conditioned by past experiences and which reflected the fact that very little was as yet known about the activities of the Committee—polls revealed that the majority of the American people believed that the break-in was merely part of campaign tactics which were commonly used by both political parties and that Watergate was not an extraordinary event. Republican delegates echoed this opinion, renominating Nixon on the first ballot on July 22.

Ensuing charges, indictments, and convictions did little to alter the initial impression of the public. Following an eight count indictment against the five men arrested in the break-in, including Liddy and Hunt, by a Federal Grand Jury in the Capitol, the Washington *Post* charged that "the break-in is a result of a massive campaign of sabotage directed by the White House, financed by a secret fund and controlled by John Mitchell." Nonetheless, on November 7, Nixon was overwhelmingly returned to office by one of the greatest margins in history.

Between the time of the election and the day of the inauguration, two critical events occurred. The first was the confirmation by the White House that a special investigative unit, known as the plumbers, did indeed exist. The second and equally important announcement was that the Committee to Re-Elect the President was unable to account to the national committee on campaign finance for the expenditure of a million dollars worth of campaign contributions. These two events triggered a series of actions which forced the creation of a Senate Select Committee, designed to explore fully the break-in and other related activities of the Committee. Under the leadership of Sam Ervin, the committee was approved by a vote of seventy to zero; the seven-member group was destined to become engaged in one of the most dramatic and historic processes in American history.

Simultaneously, as debates raged over an announcement that secret tapes existed in the Oval Office which contained transcribed conversations of meetings between the President and members of the Committee, investigations of the Vice President's background were being actively pursued on the grounds that there was reason to believe that Agnew had been involved in income tax evasion and campaign contribution fraud in the state of Maryland a few years earlier. In spite of the growing evidence of misconduct at the highest levels of government, both Nixon and Agnew retained a substantial amount of popular support. In a poll taken in February, 1973, sixty-eight percent of the American public indicated that they believed Nixon was doing an admirable job and, despite the controversiality of the Vice President's rhetoric and style, more than half of the public continued to support him.

Within the ensuing nine months, the exposure of monumental events and activities on the part of both individuals would have a profound effect on public opinion, however. On Wednesday, October 10, Agnew surrendered the Vice Presidency of the United States. He had been charged with enriching himself at the public expense in the period from 1969 to 1972 in return for awarding contracts to Maryland firms. Although he had entered a plea of no contest, Judge Hoffman argued that the plea was "the full equivalent to a plea of guilty." Refraining from imposing a prison sentence, the judge levied a ten thousand dollar fine and placed Agnew on probation for three years.

During the summer prior to Agnew's Federal Grand Jury hearing and ultimate resignation from the Vice Presidency, the issue of executive privilege was reaching its climax in the battle between the White House and the Senate Select Committee. On July 18, two months after Archibald Cox was named as Special Prosecutor and Elliot Richardson was sworn in as the Attorney General of the United States, Cox formally requested the transmittal of the tapes to the Irvin Committee. On July 23, Nixon denied the request, claiming executive privilege and arguing that much of the material recorded was highly sensitive from a national security perspective. Two responses were forthcoming—Democratic Representative Robert Drinan, from Massachusetts, introduced an impeachment resolution to the House, charging the President with high crimes and misdemeanors, and a suit was filed in court, attempting to force the President to turn over the tapes to the Special Prosecutor.

Despite Nixon's contention that the President was answerable "to the nation, but not to the Courts," Judge Sirica, the presiding officer of the Washington District Court, ordered him to provide him with the tapes to enable him to make a reasonable judgment as to their use by both the Grand Jury and the Senate Select Committee. On the day of Agnew's resignation, the President yielded to the Court order—in part at least, indicating that, under the pressure of a series of events which were rapidly occurring, he could no longer politically afford to defy Sirica's orders.

Faced with clamorous public indignation at his decision to withhold the tapes from the Jury, the development of a strong movement towards impeachment in the House of Representatives, the possibility of a citation for contempt of Court, and an indirect warning from Judge Sirica that the Watergate Grand Jury would continue, the President reversed himself and instructed his White House Counsel, Charles Wright, to advise the Court that the tapes would be handed over. Wright's announcement was made at a dramatic hearing before Judge Sirica and astonished the entire country.

Spiro T. Agnew surrendered the Office of Vice President of the United States on Wednesday, October 10, in an unprecedented action. Agnew was charged with enriching himself at the public expense in the period between 1969 and 1972 in return for awarding contracts to Maryland firms while he was serving as Governor of the State. Although he had entered a plea of no contest, the presiding judge in the case argued that the plea was "the full equivalent to a plea of guilty."

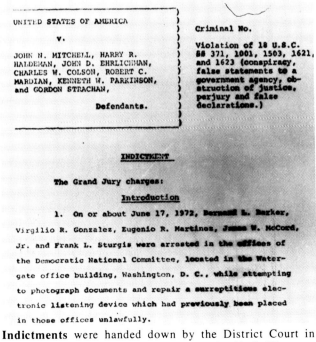

Indictments were handed down by the District Court in Washington, D.C. against the individuals involved in the Watergate break-in and cover-up. The majority of individuals indicted were employed by the Committee to Re-Elect the President and most had had previous positions in the government prior to the Watergate events.

Every poll of public opinion and every day's flood of mail and telegrams into Washington showed a high degree of anti-Nixon sentiment among the American people.

Was this another diversionary tactic by Mr. Nixon or was the White House especially upset that Cox had made good on his promise to follow any trail "wherever that trail may lead" in his investigation? The White House seemed especially upset about Cox's determination to pursue dozens of criminal allegations extending far beyond the Watergate break-in, such as:

1. The "townhouse project" which raised up to $4 million in campaign funds for Nixon-favored Congressional and *Gubernatorial candidates in the 1970 election. The question of how the money was raised and what became of it is potentially one of the most explosive scandals yet to come.*
2. Witnesses had accused secret service agents and White House advance men of interfering with the civil rights of anti-Nixon demonstrators performing peaceful protests during the 1972 rallies in Illinois and Tennessee.
3. Possible abuses involving claims of danger to national security and the misuse of government agencies, including the Internal Revenue Service.
4. Five companies, Goodyear Tire & Rubber Company, Gulf Oil Company, Minnesota Mining & Manufacturing Company, Braniff Airways Inc., and American Airlines are only a few of the illegal corporate contributors to Nixon's 1972 campaign, which have been made public, so far. Cox's investigators were looking into possible violations by several dozen other firms and labor unions.
5. The White House "plumbers" activities involving "national security."
6. The authorized campaign to tap the telephones of certain administration aides and outside newsmen.
7. An alleged $100,000 cash donation to Mr. Nixon from billionaire, Howard Hughes, handled through Mr. Nixon's close friend, C. B. (BeBe) Rebozo, in 1969 and '70. Rebozo, reportedly had told investigators he kept the money in a safe deposit box and returned it to Hughes early this year, and in

Some of about 300 protestors supporting Nixon's impeachment marched outside Los Angeles' Century Plaza Hotel as the president addressed about 1,000 members of business organizations inside. Police said the demonstration was peaceful. Nixon entered the hotel through an underground garage and did not see the marchers.

fact, did not even tell Nixon of the gifts existence. Both the Cox staff and the Senate Watergate Committee seem very curious as why Rebozo would allow $100,000 to languish for three years in a safe deposit box at his bank.

8. The merger of International Telephone and Telegraph Corporation with the Hartford Fire Insurance Company.

9. Cox said he had been denied the files on a milk industry contribution to President Nixon's re-election campaign and had been told to "keep the hell out of" the burglary of the office of Daniel Ellsberg's psychiatrist.

When he asked former Attorney General Elliot L. Richardson for the file on the milk industry case, he said, Richardson agreed and said he would call the White House to report he was letting Cox have the files.

The next day, Cox said, Richardson informed him that the President's attorneys had said Cox was not to see the milk file.

"When the milk industry gave $1.5 to $2 million in contributions, and then milk price supports are raised, it kind of makes you wonder," Cox said.

The order to stop his investigation of the break-in at the office of Ellsberg's psychiatrist came from the President.

"The President said, 'Keep the hell out of that.'" Cox said. "Even though the same men were involved."

When the office of the special prosecutor was set up, these were the duties officially outlined for the special prosecutor:

"Full authority for investigating and prosecuting offenses against the United States arising out of the unauthorized entry into Democratic National Committee Headquarters at the Watergate, all offenses arising out of the 1972 Presidential election for which the special prosecutor deems it necessary and appropriate to assume responsibility, allegations involving the President, members of the White House staff or Presidential appointees, and any other matters which he consents to have assigned to him."

Needless to say, at the time President Nixon abruptly fired Archibald Cox, the special prosecutor had set in motion a wide ranging investigation into possible wrongdoings out of the 1972 Presidential election.

From the news conference held October 23, 1973, in Washington by fomer attorney General Elliot. L. Richardson:

"There can be no greater privilege and there is not greater satisfaction than the opportunity to serve one's country. I shall always be grateful to President Nixon for giving me that opportunity in several demanding positions.

"Although I strongly believe in the general purposes and priorities of his Administration, I have been compelled to conclude that I could better serve my country by resigning my public office than by continuing in it. This is true for two reasons: first, because to continue would have forced me to refuse to carry out a direct order of the President; second, because I did not agree with the decisions which brought about the necessity for the issuance of that order.

"In order to make clear how this dilemma came about, I wish to set forth as plainly as I can the facts of the unfolding drama which came to a climax last Saturday evening [October 20]. To begin, I shall go back to Monday of last week [October 15]. Two courts—the District Court and the Court of Appeals of the District of Columbia—had ruled that the privilege protecting presidential communications must give way to the criminal process, but only to the extent that a compelling necessity had been shown.

"The President had a right of further review in the Supreme Court of the United States. He had a right, in other words, to try to persuade the Supreme Court that the long-term public interest in maintaining the confidentiality of presidential communications is more important than the public interest and the prosecution of a particular criminal case, especially where other evidence is available.

''Had he insisted on exercising that right, however, the issue would have been subject to continuing litigation and controversy for a prolonged additional period—and this at a time of acute international crisis.

''Against this background, the President decided on Monday afternoon to make a new effort to resolve the impasse. He would ask Senator John Stennis [Democrat, of Mississippi], a man of impeccable reputation for truthfulness and integrity, to listen to the tapes and verify the completeness and accuracy of a record of all pertinent portions. This record would then be available to the grand jury and for any other purpose for which it was needed. Believing, however, that only the issue of his own involvement justified any breach of the principle of confidentiality and wishing to avoid continuing litigation, he made it a condition of the offer to provide a verified record of the subpoenaed tapes that access to any other tapes or records would be barred.

''I regarded the proposal to rely on Senator Stennis for a verified record—for the sake of brevity, I will call it the Stennis proposal—as reasonable, but I did not think it should be tied to the foreclosure of the right of the Special Prosecutor [Archibald Cox] to invoke judicial process in future situations. Accordingly, I outlined the Stennis proposal to Mr. Cox later on Monday afternoon and proposed that the question of the other tapes and documents be deferred. Mr. Cox and I discussed the Stennis proposal again on Tuesday morning. On Wednesday afternoon, responding to Mr. Cox's suggestion that he could deal more completely with the proposal if he had it on paper, I sent him the document captioned ''A Proposal'' which he released at his Saturday press conference. On the afternoon of the next day he sent me his comments on the proposal, including the requirement that he have assured access to other tapes and documents.

Senator Sam Ervin, *the Chairman of the Senate Select Committee, and Senator Howard Baker, the Vice Chairman, experience a light moment during the investigation of the Watergate break-in and subsequent cover-up actions. The Committee engaged in months of investigations which ultimately resulted in the* Rodino Committee in the House of Representatives—a committee which was responsible for pursuing the impeachment of the President.

Archibald Cox *faces newsmen in his Washington office as he reads his prepared statement criticizing President Nixon's refusal to surrender tape recordings, documents and memoranda relating to Watergate. Cox was fired for opposing the President.*

''The President's lawyers regarded Mr. Cox's comments as amounting to a rejection of the Stennis proposal, and there followed the breakoff of negotiations reflected in the correspondence with Charles Alan Wright [White House legal consultant], released by Mr. Cox.

''My position at that time was that Senator Stennis' verified record of the tapes should nevertheless be presented to the District Court for the court's determination of its adequacy to satisfy the subpoenas, still leaving other questions to be dealt with as they arose. That was still my view when, at 8 p.m. Friday evening, the President issued his statement directing Mr. Cox to make no further attempts by judicial process to obtain tapes, notes or memoranda of presidential conversations. A half hour before this statement was issued, I received a letter from the President instructing me to give Mr. Cox this order. I did not act on the instruction but instead, shortly after noon on Saturday, sent the President a letter restating my position. . . .

''The President, however, decided to hold fast to the position he had announced the night before. When, therefore, Mr. Cox rejected that position and and gave his objections to the Stennis proposal as well as his reasons for insisting on assured access to other tapes and memoranda, the issue of presidential authority versus the independence and public accountability of the Special Prosecutor was squarely joined.

''The President, at that point, thought he had no choice but to direct the Attorney General to discharge Mr. Cox. And I, given my role in guaranteeing the independence of the Special Prosecutor as well as my belief in the public interests embodied in that role, felt equally clear that I could not discharge him. And so I resigned.

''At stake, in the final analysis, is the very integrity of the governmental processes I came to the Department of Justice to help restore. My own single most important commitment to this objective was my commitment to the independence of the Special Prosecutor. I could not be faithful to this commitment and also acquiesce in the curtailment of his authority. To say this, however, is not to charge the President with a failure to respect the claims of the investigative process. Given the importance he attached to the principle of presidential confidentiality, he believed that his willingness to allow Senator Stennis to verify the subpoenaed tapes fully met these claims.

''The rest is for the American people to judge. On the fairness with which you do so may well rest the future well-being and security of our beloved country. . . .''

These are three of the men indicted by a federal grand jury on charges they tried to block the Watergate investigation. From left are former Assistant Attorney General Robert C. Mardian, former presidential aide Gordon G. Strachan and Kenneth W. Parkinson, an attorney for Nixon's re-election finance committee.

President Nixon continued to deny any association with the activities which occurred in the Watergate incidents and for a period of time public opinion supported him. As the Senate Select Committee hearings revealed evidence suggesting possible knowledge on his part, however, public opinion began to change and his support diminished substantially.

A suit which was filed October 20, 1973, by consumer advocate, Ralph Nader, Senator Frank E. Moss (D-Utah) and representatives Bella S. Abzug (D-New York), and Jerome R. Waldie (D-California), sought to force acting Attorney General, Robert H. Bork, to reinstate Cox and re-establish the office of the special prosecutor, which was officially abolished by President Nixon.

Federal Judge Gerhard Gesell, on November 14, 1973, ruled that acting Attorney General Robert Bork, was not legally able to fire Archibald Cox primarily because of the Justice Department's regu-

These four men were indicted by a federal grand jury in Washington on charges they tried to clock the Watergate investigation. From left are former Presidential aides H. R. Haldeman and John D. Ehrlichman, former White House special counsel Charles W. Colson and former Attorney General John N. Mitchell.

lations setting up the special prosecutor's office. In his eleven page opinion Judge Gesell said that "This turn-about was simply a ruse to permit the discharge of Mr. Cox" and that it violated the Justice Department's regulation under which the special prosecutor task force was established, "the special prosecutor will not be removed . . . except for extraordinary improprieties on his part." Judge Gesell further stated in rebuttal to Bork's claim that the regulation did not legally bind the attorney general "it is settled beyond dispute that under such circumstances an agency regulation has the force in effect of law . . . and is binding upon the body that issues it . . . even more directly on point, the Supreme Court has twice held that an executive department may not discharge one of its officers in a manner inconsistent with its own regulations." The judge further stated that it made no difference, that three days after Cox's firing, Bork revoked the regulation. He ruled that Bork's revocation was illegal, "an agency's power to revoke its regulations is not unlimited," because a "virtually identical regulation" was issued three weeks later, the judge concluded that the original action was "arbitrary and unreasonable, and must be held to have been without force or affect."

Although Cox refused to seek re-instatement, Gesell said, the establishment of the special prosecutor's office and the appointment of Jaworski were "not necessarily . . . illegal" and probably were needed "to carry on the important work in which Mr. Cox had been engaged . . . but that fact does not cure past illegalities," acting Attorney General Bork said, because of Cox's return to Harvard made the whole case moot. Judge Gesell stated because the firing of Cox "precipitated a widespread concern, if not lack of confidence, in the administration of justice" and made clear a "pressing need to declare a rule of law that will give guidance for future conduct" of the Watergate prosecution. Further stating, Judge Gesell wrote, if the case were declared to be moot "the challenged conduct of the Attorney General could be repeated with regard to the new Watergate special prosecutor if he presses too hard."

Judge Gesell's ruling on the Cox firing was unequivocal and was directed against acting Attorney General Robert Bork, who carried out Mr. Nixon's order to fire Mr. Cox after Attorney General Elliot Richardson and Deputy Attorney General William Ruckelshaus resigned rather than to do so.

The immediate job of investigating the charges against Nixon and the possible grounds for impeachment fell to the House Judiciary Committee, chaired by dapper Rep. Peter W. Rodino Jr. (D–N.J.). After the Senate's Ervin Committee started its inquiries and hearings in the spring of 1973, the Rodino Committee began to study the background of the impeachment process and the potential grounds for impeachment. When John Dean testified before the Senate Committee in June 1973, and the anti-Nixon

Preparing for the final debate, *Rep. Delbert Latta (R–Ohio) stacks up all the books of evidence released by the Judiciary Committee during its seven months of inquiry into grounds for impeachment.*

tide began mounting, O'Neill told Rodino to move into action, to be prepared for what seemed the inevitable course of events. Rodino set up a special staff to study the question of impeachment. In December 1973, Rodino named John Doar as special counsel to the Judiciary Committee. In January of 1974, the committee's investigation finally started to move ahead in high gear.

During the first half of the year the committee pressed its investigation, subpoenaed many witnesses, and heard testimony behind closed doors. A large part of this testimony was "leaked" to the press by various Congressmen; details are recorded in our monthly *Calendars* and elsewhere in the pages of *The Breaking of a President 1974.* There were headlines and more headlines, charges and counter-charges. In July the Rodino Committee made public a large part of its evidence in a series of massive volumes, and announced that it had wound up its investigation and was ready to debate the question of whether or not to impeach Nixon. A dramatic televised debate followed, in which all the 38 members of the committee had their say; and a further drama went on behind the scenes. Proposed articles of impeachment were introduced, debated, wrangled over, amended. In less than a week, a set of workable drafts of articles was finally hammered out.

On the warm Saturday night of July 27th, the four tumultuos days of debate, climaxing the seven-month inquiry, came to an end, and while the nation watched its television screens in fascination, the fateful roll-call began. The faces of the 38 members of the committee were strained and solemn. One by one their names were called, and one by one they cast the most momentous vote cast by any Congressmen (or women) in a century.

Predictions and speculations were fulfilled: all six Republican Congressmen joined all 21 Democrats to recommend that Richard Nixon be impeached by the House, and to seek his removal from office through a Senate trial.

Mr. Railsback: *Aye*. Mr. Fish: *Aye*. Mr. Hogan: *Aye*. Mr. Butler: *Aye*. Mr. Cohen: *Aye*. Mr. Froehlich: *Aye*.

By the historic roll-call vote, the first article of impeachment was adopted, 27 to 11, by the debate-weary committee at 7:07 p.m. The bi-partisan nature of the vote made it highly probable that the full House would also vote to impeach the embattled President. The first article in its final form, the full text of which appears in these pages, alleged that Nixon had committed multiple

acts designed to obstruct justice, in his attempts to conceal the origin and background of the Watergate break-in and "other unlawful covert activities."

The degree of bi-partisanship in the Judiciary Committee vote was larger than had been expected, and constituted an effective rebuttal to the White House claims that the impeachment proceedings were a partisan "witch hunt" and that the Rodino Committee was a "kangaroo court." The six Republicans voting for impeachment represented the Midwest, the South, and New England. The wide range of GOP support indicated that still more of the wavering Republicans would align themselves against the President when it came to a decisive vote by the full House. Other Southern Congressmen were expected to be influenced by the highly articulate roles played in the committee debate by the leading Southern Democrats: Walter Flowers of Alabama, James Mann of South Carolina, and Ray Thornton of Arkansas.

The climactic backstage maneuvers that led to the historic vote were now revealed. Chairman Rodino himself had long since been convinced that the committee's vast accumulation of evidence, as presented by Special Counsel John Doar and Minority Counsel Albert Jenner through the eleven weeks of closed hearings, and spelled out in 36 notebooks of "statements of information," thoroughly warranted the impeachment of Richard Nixon. As the climactic committee vote approached, Rodino's principal aim was to secure maximum support in his committee, for any articles of impeachment that would be recommended to the House. There was no hope, he knew, of winning the support of some ten Republicans who were firmly committed to standing by Nixon; but he was confident that the articles could be drafted in such a way as to win the votes of the other Republicans, who had indicated they were seriously disturbed by Nixon's Watergate actions. Yet Rodino also faced the problem of not making the charges against the President so limited and narrow, that the liberal Democrats would insist on making the language tougher, or adding more articles which might be dubious. He was worried, too, about some of the Southern Democrats, whose home districts were heavily in favor of the entrenched President.

Rodino and the Democratic leaders, in the final weeks moved guardedly to enlist the help of the Southern Democrats on the committee. Flowers, Mann and Thornton had indicated they were offended by Nixon's flaunting of the Constitution and his flagrant abuse of the FBI, IRS and CIA. The key to gaining maximum support for the proposed articles was, as one House leader explained to newsmen, to "put together the Southern Democrats and the Republicans."

Tense conference: *Reps. William Cohen (R–Maine), lower left, Tom Railsback (R–Ill.), upper left, and Harold Froehlich (R–Wis.), confer during a recess in the debate.*

Ladies of the Committee: *Reps. Barbara Jordan (D–Tex.), left, and Elizabeth Holtzman (D–N.Y.), right, were the two women members of the 38-member House Judiciary Committee which debated President Nixon's impeachment.*

The key man was Alabama's Walter Flowers, who was so conscientious that he had developed an ulcer over the impeachment question. Flowers was well aware that his home state was partial to Nixon; he seemed the most likely Democrat to vote against impeachment, despite his expressed misgivings over Nixon's conduct in the Watergate scandal. As the showdown approached, Rodino and others urged Flowers, and also Mann of South Carolina, to meet with some of their moderate Republican colleagues and try to find areas of agreement. Soon, private meetings were being held between the three Southerners, Flowers, Mann and Thornton, and four as yet uncommitted Republicans: Cohen, Butler, Fish and Railsback. This group remained on the fence between those who were pushing all-out for impeachment, and those who clung loyally to the President.

Another strategic backstage role was played by Democrat Jack Brooks of Texas. A strong Nixon opponent, Brooks prepared and distributed to the 38 committee members a lengthy, generalized series of proposed impeachment articles which he knew were too broad and too strong for most of the members who had not yet made up their minds. But the Brooks strategy worked: the distribution of his not-too-carefully-drawn articles had the intended effect of causing a number of other members to start working on drafts of articles of their own. "It got the members thinking," one staffer explained. "They began to wake up to the fact that they shouldn't leave it to Doar and his staff, that they should draw up their own articles." Thus the process was.

In a few days there were two groups working on the drafts of articles. One was a partial Democratic caucus, influenced by Jack Brooks but not controlled by him. The other was the coalition of Southern Democrats and impeachment-minded Republicans. The two groups practically overlapped, with the Southerners shuttling between them.

Unexpectedly, the coalition group moved more quickly toward agreement than did the all-Democratic committeemen. By Tuesday night, according to one of the coalition members, "We had a consensus in two major areas: the abuse of power and the obstruction of justice." By this time, it was apparent to vote-counters that at least four of the Republicans—Cohen, Railsback, Butler and Fish—would vote to recommend impeachment.

The views of the Southern Democrats and Northern Republicans in the seven-member coalition had a great deal in common. Walter Flowers expressed his feeling succinctly to a *Time* reporter: "I had a yearning, an innate desire to find the President innocent. But I put the blinders on, like the old mule used to wear going

Rep. Paul S. Sarbanes *((D–Md.) emphasizes a point during debate on final draft of the articles of impeachment. Sarbanes introduced the original draft of the first article voted by the committee.*

Spectators listen intently *to the committee's debate, while television camera grinds, bringing to the nation the first congressional hearing to be televised in history.*

Rep. Walter Flowers *(D–Ala.) played a key role in bringing members of differing viewpoints together for draft of the articles. He is shown (left) huddling with Chairman Rodino, just before the final vote on Article One.*

Rep. William Hungate *(D–Mo.) reads a newspaper as he awaits start of the panel's debate at evening session.*

Rep. Lawrence Hogan *(R–Md.) presents his arguments on the impeachment articles. Listening is Rep. M. Caldwell Butler (R–Va.). Hogan's public statement on the eve of the final debate, that he would vote to impeach Nixon, swayed several committee members who were undecided.*

down the road with the wagon behind him. I couldn't see anything except the road.'' Flowers said he was particularly disturbed by the March 21, 1973, White House tape: ''. . . The matter-of-fact way in which the payment of hush-money was discussed. It shocked my conscience, I'll tell you . . . And you take the whole sordid mess and compare it with the public pronouncements of the President, and it just doesn't fit. . . . I felt that if we didn't impeach, we'd just ingrain and stamp in our highest office a standard of conduct that's just unacceptable.''

Flowers wielded an important influence on the Republicans in the group. He told the undecided ones at a private meeting: ''This is something we can't just walk away from. It's happened, and now we've got to deal with it.'' His persuasive and candid eloquence swayed Caldwell Butler of Virginia, who later told newsmen: ''I knew at that second that he was right.''

Unexpectedly and abruptly, a fifth Republican, conservative Lawrence Hogan of Maryland, on July 23rd publicly announced his break with Nixon. Hogan, who had kept his intentions quiet, called a press conference in which he bitterly denounced the President. Hogan solemnly told the assembled reporters:

''The evidence convinces me that my President has lied repeatedly, deceiving public officials and the American people. Instead of cooperating with prosecutors and investigators, as he said publicly, he concealed and covered up evidence, and coached witnesses so that their testimony would show things that were really not true. He praised and rewarded those who he knew had committed perjury. He actively participated in an extended and extensive conspiracy to obstruct justice.''

Hogan explained that he had originally begun listening to the evidence with a ''firm presumption'' that Nixon was innocent. ''But after reading the transcripts,'' he said, ''it was sobering: the number of untruths, the deception and the immoral attitudes. At that point, I began tilting against the President, and my conviction grew steadily.''

Suddenly, one evening while driving home, he realized that he had actually made up his mind to vote to recommend impeachment. ''There was just too much evidence. By any standard of proof demanded, we had to bind him over for trial and removal by the Senate.''

By Wednesday of that final week, the two groups drafting impeachment articles had come closer together. The coalition group had already decided upon two general articles: obstruction of justice and abuse of power; and now the Democratic group was nearing agreement on the same two articles. The Democrats were still considering a third article charging Nixon with contempt of Congress. Rep. Mann was largely responsible for drafting the Democratic articles, which were later introduced by Harold Donohue of Massachusetts when the final nationally televised debate began on Wednesday night, July 24th. Chairman Rodino set the tone of the historic debate, the first ever to be televised, when he said in his opening remarks:

''Throughout all of the painstaking proceedings of this committee, I as the chairman have been guided by a simple principle, the principle that the law must deal fairly with every man. For me, this is the oldest principle of democracy. It is this simple but great principle which enables man to live justly and in decency in a free society . . . Make no mistake about it. This is a turning point whatever we decide. Our judgment is not concerned with an individual but with a system of constitutional government. . . . Whatever we now decide, we must have the integrity and the decency, the will and the courage to decide rightly. Let us leave the Constitution as unimpaired for our children as our predecessors left it to us.''

In their opening statements, the members one after another expressed their anguish and concern over the decision they faced. The Republicans suffered most. Said Cohen: ''I have been faced with the terrible responsibility of assessing the conduct of a President that I voted for, believed to be the best man to lead this country, who has made significant and lasting contributions toward securing peace in this country, throughout the world, but a President who in the

793

Chief Counsel John Doar *bites on a pencil as he listens to committee members offer their arguments for and against impeachment.*

Rep. Charles Wiggins *(R–Calif.) looks thoughtful as he reads the press statement by Rep. Lawrence Hogan just before the debate got under way.*

A show of hands: *Members of the committee raise their hands to signify they want to speak out on an amendment to one of the proposed articles of impeachment. In foreground is Rep. Elizabeth Holtzman (D–N.Y.)*

THE ARTICLES OF IMPEACHMENT

Following are the three Articles of Impeachment as drawn up and passed by the bipartisan House Judiciary Committee after dramatic debate on July 27, July 29, and July 30, 1974:

ARTICLE 1

In his conduct of the office of President of the United States, Richard M. Nixon, in violation of his constitutional oath faithfully to execute the office of President of the United States and, to the best of his ability, preserve, protect, and defend the Constitution of the United States, and in violation of his constitutional duty to take care that the laws be faithfully executed, has prevented, obstructed, and impeded the administration of justice, in that:

On June 17, 1972, and prior thereto, agents of the Committee for the Reelection of the President committed unlawful entry of the headquarters of the Democratic National Committee in Washington, District of Columbia, for the purpose of securing political intelligence. Subsequent thereto, Richard M. Nixon, using the powers of his high office, engaged personally and through his subordinates and agents in a course of conduct or plan designed to delay, impede and obstruct investigations of such unlawful entry; to cover up, conceal and protect those responsible and to conceal the existence and scope of other unlawful covert activities.

The means used to implement this course of conduct or plan have included one or more of the following:

—Making or causing to be made false or misleading statements to lawfully authorized investigative officers and employes of the United States;

—Withholding relevant and material evidence or information from lawfully authorized investigative officers and employes of the United States;

—Approving, condoning, acquiescing in, and counseling witnesses with respect to the giving of false or misleading statements to lawfully authorized investigative officers and employes of the United States and false or misleading testimony in duly instituted judicial and congressional proceedings;

—Interfering or endeavoring to interfere with the conduct of investigations by the Department of Justice of the United States, the Federal Bureau of Investigation, the office of Watergate special prosecution force and congressional committees;

—Approving, condoning, and acquiescing in the surreptitious payment of substantial sums of money for the purpose of obtaining the silence or influencing the testimony of witnesses, potential witnesses or individuals who participated in such unlawful entry and other illegal activities;

—Endeavoring to misuse the Central Intelligence Agency, an agency of the United States;

—Disseminating information received from officers of the Department of Justice of the United States to subjects of investigations conducted by lawfully authorized investigative officers and employes of the United States for the purpose of aiding and assisting such subjects in their attempts to avoid criminal liability;

—Making false or misleading public statements for the purpose of deceiving the people of the United States into believing that a thorough and complete investigation has been conducted with respect to allegations of misconduct on the part of personnel of the executive branch of the United States and personnel of the Committee for the Reelection of the President, and that there was no involvement of such personnel in such misconduct; or

—Endeavoring to cause prospective defendants, and individuals duly tried and convicted, to expect favored treatment and consideration in return for their silence or false testimony, or rewarding individuals for their silence or false testimony.

In all of this, Richard M. Nixon has acted in a manner contrary to his trust as President and subversive of constitutional government, to the great prejudice of the cause of law and justice and to the manifest injury of the people of the United States.

Wherefore Richard M. Nixon, by such conduct, warrants impeachment and trial, and removal from office.

ARTICLE 2

Using the powers of the office of President of the United States, Richard M. Nixon, in violation of his constitutional oath faithfully to execute the office of President of the United States and, to the best of his ability, preserve, protect, and defend the Constitution of the United States, and in disregard of his constitutional duty to take care that the law be faithfully executed, has repeatedly engaged in

---

process by act or acquiescence allowed the rule of law and the Constitution to slip under the boots of indifference and arrogance and abuse."

"How distasteful this proceeding is for me," protested Butler of Virginia, who said he had worked with Nixon in every one of the President's national elections, "and I would not be here today if it were not for our joint effort in 1972." Railsback of Illinois sought escape. "I wish the President could do something to absolve himself," he said. Charles Sandman of New Jersey abandoned his fighting manner to explain: "For the first time in my life, I have to judge a Republican, a man who holds the most powerful office in the world . . . This is the most important thing I shall ever do in my whole life, and I know it."

New York Democrat Charles Rangel said: "Some say this is a sad day in America's history. However, I think it could perhaps be one of our brightest days. It could be really a test of the strength of our Constitution, because what I think it means to most Americans is that when this or any other President violates his sacred oath of office, the people are not left helpless."

Most members revealed their position on impeachment, and there were few surprises. Wisconsin's Democrat Robert Kastenmeier contended that "President Nixon's conduct in office is a case history of the abuse of presidential power." New York Democrat Elizabeth Holtzman: "A seamless web of misconduct so serious that

it leaves me shaken." Brooks of Texas claimed that the committee evidence traced "governmental corruption unequaled in the history of the United States." Asked Republican Cohen: "How in the world did we ever get from the Federalist Papers to the edited transcripts?"

In the view of many members of the majority, failure to impeach would do far greater harm to the nation's welfare than would a Senate trial. Surprising his colleagues with the vehemence of his stand, Republican Butler declared: "If we fail to impeach, we will have condoned and left unpunished a course of conduct totally inconsistent with the reasonable expectations of the American people . . . and we will have said to the American people, 'These deeds are inconsequential and unimportant.' "

Democrat Thornton claimed that such a failure "would effectively repeal the right of this body to act as a check on the abuses that we see." After reeling off a list of specific improper Nixon acts, Railsback warned of another result. Speaking of the nation's young people, he claimed: "You are going to see the most frustrated people, the most turned-off people, the most disillusioned people, and it is going to make the period of LBJ in 1968, 1967, look tame."

"To become Congressmen and Congresswomen," noted Missouri Democrat William Hungate, "we all took the same oath of uphold the Constitution which Richard M. Nixon took. If we are to

conduct violating the constitutional rights of citizens, impairing the due and proper administration of justice and the conduct of lawful inquiries, or contravening the laws governing agencies of the executive branch and the purposes of these agencies. This conduct has included one or more of the following:

1. He has, acting personally and through his subordinates and agents, endeavored to obtain from the Internal Revenue Service, in violation of the constitutional rights of citizens, confidential information contained in income tax returns for purposes not authorized by law, and to cause, in violation of the constitutional rights of citizens, income tax audits or other income tax investigations to be initiated or conducted in a discriminatory manner.

2. He misused the Federal Bureau of Investigation, the Secret Service and other executive personnel, in violation or disregard of the constitutional rights of citizens, by directing, or authorizing such agencies or personnel to conduct or continue electronic surveillance or other investigations for purposes unrelated to national security, the enforcement of laws, or any other lawful function of his office; he did direct, authorize, or permit the use of information obtained thereby for purposes unrelated to national security, the enforcement of laws, or any other lawful function of his office; and he did direct the concealment of certain records made by the Federal Bureau of Investigation of electronic surveillance.

3. He has, acting personally and through his subordinates and agents, in violation or disregard of the constitutional rights of citizens, authorized and permitted to be maintained a secret investigative unit within the office of the President, financed in part with money derived from campaign contributions to him, which unlawfully utilized the resources of the Central Intelligence Agency, engaged in covert and unlawful activities, and attempted to prejudice the constitutional right of an accused to a fair trial.

4. He has failed to take care that the laws were faithfully executed by failing to act when he knew or had reason to know that his close subordinates endeavored to impede and frustrate lawful inquiries by duly constituted executive, judicial, and legislative entities concerning the unlawful entry into the headquarters of the Democratic National Committee, and the coverup thereof, and concerning other unlawful activities including those relating to the confirmation of Richard Kleindienst as attorney general of the United States, the electronic surveillance of private citizens, the break-in into the office of Dr. Lewis Fielding, and the campaign financing practices of the Committee to Reelect the President.

5. In disregard of the rule of law, he knowingly misused the executive power by interfering with agencies of the executive branch, including the Federal Bureau of Investigation, the Criminal Division, and the Office of Watergate Special Prosecution Force, of the Department of Justice, and the Central Intelligence Agency, in violation of his duty to take care that the laws be faithfully executed.

In all of this, Richard M. Nixon has acted in a manner contrary to his trust as President and subversive of constitutional government, to the great prejudice of the cause of law and justice and to the manifest injury of the people of the United States.

Wherefore Richard M. Nixon, by such conduct, warrants impeachment and trial, and removal from office.

ARTICLE 3

In his conduct of the office of the President of the United States, Richard M. Nixon, contrary to his oath faithfully to execute the office of President of the United States and, to the best of his ability, preserve, protect, and defend the Constitution of the United States, and in violation of his constitutional duty to take care that the laws be faithfully executed, has failed without lawful cause or excuse to produce papers and things as directed by duly authorized subpoenas issued by the Committee on the Judiciary of the House of Representatives on April 11, 1974, May 15, 1974, and June 24, 1974, and willfully disobeyed such subpoenas. The subpoenaed papers and things were deemed necessary by the committee in order to resolve by direct evidence fundamental, factual questions relating to presidential direction, knowledge or approval of actions demonstrated by other evidence to be substantial grounds for impeachment of the President. In refusing to produce these papers and things Richard M. Nixon, substituting his judgment as to what materials were necessary for the inquiry, interposed the powers of the Presidency against the lawful subpoenas of the House of Representatives, thereby assuming to himself functions and judgments necessary to the exercise of the sole power of impeachment vested by the Constitution in the House of Representatives.

In all of this, Richard M. Nixon has acted in a manner contrary to his trust as President and subversive of constitutional government, to the great prejudice of the cause of law and justice, and to the manifest injury of the people of the United States.

Wherefore, Richard M. Nixon, by such conduct, warrants impeachment and trial, and removal from office.

---

be faithful to our oaths, we must find him faithless in his." Iowa Democrat Edward Mezvinsky expressed a similar thought, arguing that Nixon should be brought "to account for the gross abuse of office," and that "we must all ask ourselves, if we do not, who will?"

The President's defenders were led by Sandman, California's Charles Wiggins and Indiana's David Dennis. Sandman called the impeachment of President Andrew Johnson in 1868 "one of the darkest moments in the government of this great nation," and added: "I do not propose to be any part of a second blotch on the history of this great nation."

"This case must be decided according to the law, and on no other basis," noted Wiggins. Posing sharp legalistic questions, Wiggins insisted that perhaps only half of one volume among the committee's ooks of evidence would be admissible in a Senate trial of the President. "Simple theories, of course, are inadequate. That is not evidence. A supposition, however persuasive, is not evidence. A bare possibility that something might have happened is not evidence."

Mississippi Republican Trent Lott argued with vigor that "for every bit of evidence implicating the President, there is evidence to the contrary." The case against Nixon, contended Iowa Republican Wiley Mayne, consists of "a series of inferences piled upon other inferences."

Rep. Wayne Owens (D–Utah), at left, confers with Rep. Lawrence Hogan (R–Md.) as the debate continues on drafts of the proposed impeachment articles.

Escorted from hearing: *An unidentified young woman is escorted out of the committee's hearing room by a security officer. She and a young man were ordered ejected by Chairman Rodino after they made a noisy outburst.*

In rebuttal, many of the committee Democrats in their turn rattled off specific presidential acts and conversations, particularly from the President's tapes, that they considered solid evidence. The general reply was offered by Republican Cohen: "Conspiracies are not born in the sunlight of direct observations," he said. "They are hatched in dark recesses, amid whispers and code words and verbal signals, and many times the footprints of guilt must be traced with a searchlight of probability, of common experience." Moreover, circumstantial evidence is admissible in trials, Cohen noted, and it is often persuasive. He cited as an example that someone who had gone to sleep at night when the ground was bare and awoke to find snow on the ground could reasonably conclude that snow had fallen while he slept.

Father Robert Drinan, a Massachusetts Democrat, argued that it was wrong not to cite Nixon for the secret bombing of Cambodia just because it would not "fly" or "play in Peoria." He asked:

"How can we impeach the President for concealing a burglary but not for concealing a massive bombing?" New York Republican Henry Smith, considered against impeachment, indicated that the Cambodia bombing was the one Nixon offense that he might consider impeachable. The opening statements publicly confirmed Republican defections from the President that had become apparent in the closed-door sessions on the eve of the debate. Demonstrating a willingness to impeach on at least one article were Illinois' Robert McClory, Railsback, Fish, Butler and Cohen. Froehlich hinted that he might go along with an article on the obstruction of justice in the Watergate cover-up.

Hogan followed his previous attack on Nixon with another assault. Referring to the occasion when Nixon and his aides discussed E. Howard Hunt's demands for money in the March 21, 1973, White House conversation, Hogan protested: "The President didn't, in righteous indignation, rise up and say, 'Get out of here! You are in the office of the President of the United States. How can

Rep. Elizabeth Holtzman (*D–N.Y.*) *glances through a book of the White House tape transcripts as she listens to debate on the impeachment articles.*

Rep. Robert Drinan (*D–Mass.*), *a Catholic priest, looks solemn as he listens to arguments for and against the first impeachment article, charging Nixon with obstructing justice.*

Bright television lights *took their toll on the eyes of the weary committee members during the lengthy sessions of debate. Shown rubbing their eyes are Rep. George Danielson (D–Calif.), at top; Rep. Charles Rangel (D–N.Y.), bottom left, and Rep. M. Caldwell Butler (R–Va.), bottom right.*

you talk about blackmail and bribery and keeping witnesses silent?' . . . And then throw them out of his office and pick up the phone and call the Department of Justice and tell them there is obstruction of justice going on. But my President didn't do that. He sat there, and he worked and worked to try to cover this thing up to it wouldn't come to light.''

The impeachment forces went to work on new drafts as soon as the round of general debate was concluded on Thursday night. Chairman Rodino joined the group of Democrats assembled in Counsel Zeifman's office, among them Flowers and Mann, who now held the virtual proxy votes of moderate Republicans. Their aim was to find the right language that would placate the more liberal Democrats, hold the Southerners as well as the Republicans, and yet be technically sound enough to withstand the anticipated assault from the Nixon loyalists.

The drafting was resumed Friday morning, delaying the start of that day's public session. Finally, with little substantive change but a tightening of wording, the articles were introduced as an amendment to the Donohue articles by Maryland Democrat Paul Sarbanes.

In the general debate, the first division stemmed from an attempt by Republican McClory to delay proceedings for ten days if the President would promptly agree to give the House Judiciary Committee the same tapes he had been ordered by the Supreme Court to yield to Judge Sirica for use in the impending Watergate cover-up trial. Actually, McClory conceded that he had little expectation of a favorable response from Nixon. McClory's tactic was aimed at strengthening a contempt of Congress article against the President he planned to introduce. The motion was defeated 27 to 11 in the first test of the committee's voting lineup.

The committee fell into a second argument over just how specific or general the articles of impeachment ought to be. The Nixon loyalists, joined by more moderate Republicans, insisted that the proposed articles were much too vaguely phrased. Democratic defenders of the articles contended that the supporting facts should

Chairman Rodino, *looking weary, scratches his cheek as another session of debate begins on the second impeachment article.*

The impeachment vote: *Clerk keeps tally as the committee members vote, 27 to 11, to adopt Article One, recommending the impeachment of President Nixon for obstructing justice.*

Rep. Harry Smith III *(R–N.Y.) studies the Constitution of the United States as the committee debate goes on.*

be included in the committee's final report and not jammed into the brief impeachment articles.

Sandman moved to strike the first paragraph of the Sarbanes articles and threatened to make the same move against eight other paragraphs. When a vote was finally taken late Friday night, Sandman's move was defeated by the same 27 to 11 margin.

By the next day, Sandman dropped the fight over specificity. "The argument was exhausted yesterday," he conceded to the committee, then withdrew his other eight motions to strike portions of the article under consideration. But now the Democrats turned the tables, introducing motions to strike paragraphs as a means of debating the facts behind each charge.

Wiggins and Dennis of the Nixon loyalists were pitted against Democrats George Danielson, Wayne Owens and Hungate. Every time a vote was taken on Flowers' motions to eliminate paragraphs, the proposals lost decisively; most of the time Flowers merely responded "Present," not voting on his own motion.

Finally all of the amendments were dispensed with and Chairman Rodino asked for the vote on the articles presented by Sarbanes, as amended slightly, even though all knew what the general outcome would be. The only questionable vote was that of Froehlich, who cast a low-voiced "Aye."

Several of the Congressmen bowed their heads as the vote was taken. Thornton closed his eyes as if in prayer. Democrats Mann and Republican Wiggins appeared close to tears. Almost all the "Ayes" were delivered in low tones. The first "No"—from Edward Hutchinson—sounded more positive.

After the Sarbanes substitute article passed, the final vote on the article as amended was anti-climactic, even though it marked the

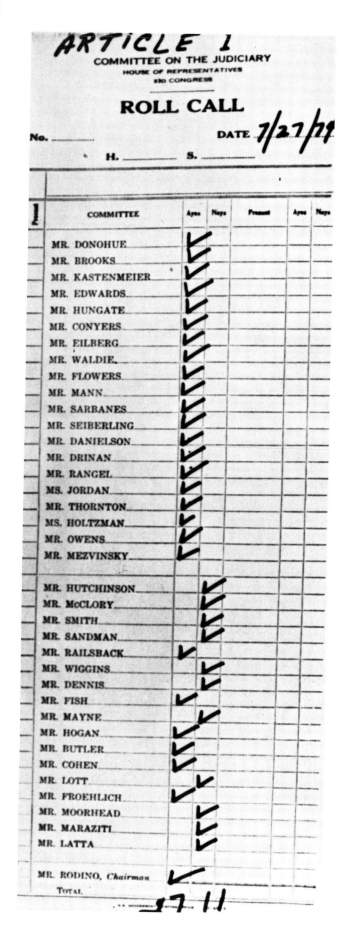

Roll call tally sheet *kept by clerk shows how each member voted on the first of the three articles of impeachment. Final tally was 27 to 11 in favor of the article.*

THE DAMNING TAPES

"Don't go any further into this case—period!"

The damning evidence that finally convinced Nixon's staunchest supporters, including his own lawyer, that he had been deeply involved in the Watergate cover-up, was contained in three transcripts which he released to the public on August 5th, along with his statement that portions of the tapes of these . . . conversations are at variance with some of my previous statements." He could say that again! The revelatory transcripts, which sealed Nixon's doom when he had to release them on order of the Supreme Court, were of conversations between Nixon and H.R. Haldeman, then White House chief of staff, on June 23, 1972, only six days after the Watergate break-in. Here are the most incriminating passages:

First meeting (10:04-11:39 a.m.)

HALDEMAN: Now, on the investigation, you know the Democratic break-in thing, we're back in the problem area because the FBI is not under control, because [Acting FBI Director L. Patrick] Gray doesn't exactly know how to control it and they have—their investigation is now leading into some productive areas—because they've been able to trace the money—not through the money itself—but through the bank sources—the banker. And, and it goes in some directions we don't want it to go... [Nixon Campaign Chairman John N.] Mitchell came up with yesterday, and [then White House Counsel] John Dean analyzed very carefully last night and concludes, concurs now with Mitchell's recommendation that the only way to solve this, and we're set up beautifully to do it, ah, in that ... That the way to handle this now is for us to have [Deputy CIA Director Vernon] Walters call Pat Gray and just say "Stay to hell out of this—this is ah, business here, we don't want you to go any further on it." That's not an unusual development, and ah, that would take care of it.

PRESIDENT: What about Pat Gray—you mean Pat Gray doesn't want to?

H: Pat does want to. He doesn't know how to, and he doesn't have, he doesn't have any basis for doing it. Given this, he will then have the basis. He'll call [then Deputy Associate FBI Director Mark Felt in, and the two of them—and Mark Felt wants to cooperate because he's ambitious—

P: Yeah.

H: He'll call him in and say, "We've got the signal from across the river [the CIA] to put the hold on this." And that will fit rather well because the FBI agents who are working the case, at this point, feel that's what it is.

P: This is CIA? They've traced the money? Who'd they trace it to?

H: Well, they've traced it to a name, but they haven't gotten to the guy yet.

P: Would it be somebody here?

H: [Republicans' Midwestern Finance Chairman] Ken Dahlberg.

P: Who the hell is Ken Dahlberg?

H: He gave $25,000 in Minnesota and, ah, the check went directly to this guy [Watergate Burglar Bernard] Barker.

P: It isn't from the committee, though, from [Nixon Campaign Finance Director Maurice H.] Stans?

H: Yeah. It is. It's directly traceable and there's some more through some Texas people that went to the Mexican bank, which can also be traced to the Mexican bank—they'll get their names today.

P: Well, I mean, there's no way—I'm just thinking if they don't cooperate, what do they say? That they were approached by the Cubans [the Watergate burglars]. That's what Dahlberg has to say, the Texans too, that they—

H: Well, if they will. But then we're relying on more and more people all the time. That's the problem, and they'll stop if we could take this other route.

P: All right.

H: And you seem to think the thing to do is get them to stop?

P: Right, fine.

H: They say the only way to do that is from White House instructions. And it's got to be to [CIA Director Richard] Helms and to—ah, what's his name ...? Walters.

Pensive Trio: *Chairman Rodino, at right, Rep. Jack Brooks (D-Tex.), left, and Jerome Zeifman, general counsel, all have pensive looks on their faces prior to start of the committee's debate on Article Three.*

official passage of the first impeachment article against Nixon. "Article One of that resolution of impeachment will be reported to the House," Chairman Rodino announced before recessing the committee.

The debate resumed on Monday, but the conclusion was a foregone one; the impeachment tide could not be resisted. Another Republican vote was picked up — McClory of Illinois — who had opposed Article One.

The second article recommending impeachment was passed Monday night, July 29th, by a vote of 28 to 10.

The article accused the President of numerous acts that allegedly violated his oath of office and the Constitution, including asserted violations of citizens' constitutional rights and the misuse of the FBI, the CIA, the IRS, the Justice Department and the office of the Watergate special prosecution force.

As expected, the committee's 21 Democrats voted solidly for Article Two, as they had done for Article One.

Republicans in addition to McClory voting for Article Two were the same ones who voted for Article One. They were Reps. Tom Railsback (Ill.), Hamilton Fish Jr. (N.Y.), Lawrence J. Hogan (Md.), M. Caldwell Butler (Va.), William Cohen (Me.) and Harold V. Froehlich (Wis.).

White House lawyers *arrive to deliver to the U.S. District Court in Washington the first batch of 20 of the 64 incriminating tapes which the Supreme Court ordered Nixon to turn over to Judge Sirica for the Watergate cover-up trial. Surrender of the tapes coincided with windup of the Rodino committee hearings after the three impeachment articles were voted. White House lawyer James St. Clair is second from left.*

McClory called Article Two "the crux of our responsibilities here" and said that while it might be "less dramatic and less sensational" than the Watergate cover-up article, it bore directly on the President's responsibility to protect the Constitution and to take care to see that the laws were faithfully executed.

He said: "There is a clear violation of the President's responsibility when he permits multiple acts of wrongdoing by large numbers of those who surround him in possession of great responsibility and influence in the White House."

Although Nixon's supporters on the committee defended him during the debate, there was little of the rancor or bitterness that marked debate on the first article. Nor were the proceedings as solemn as those involving Article One, when the committee members were deliberating the first vote to impeach a President since 1868.

On Tuesday night, July 30th, the Judiciary Committee ended its historic debate after deciding to recommend that Nixon should be tried in the Senate for defying committee subpoenas, but should not be tried for income tax evasion nor for the secret bombing of Cambodia.

By a 21-17 vote, predominantly along party lines, the committee recommended that the House impeach Nixon for refusing to comply with four subpoenas it had issued for evidence in its impeachment inquiry.

The committee rejected, by a 26-12 vote, a proposed article by Rep. Edward Mezvinsky (D–Iowa) that accused the President of income tax evasion and unlawfully receiving the benefit of government expenditures at his homes in San Clemente and Key Biscayne.

It earlier rejected, also by a 26-12 vote, a proposed article that accused the President of constitutional violations in the secret bombing of Cambodia during the Vietnam war.

It now remained for the 435-member House, where support for Nixon had seriously eroded during that climactic week, to decide whether or not to impeach the embattled President on any or all of the three articles recommended by the Rodino Committee. The House Rules Committee moved swiftly to set a meeting for the following week to set rules of procedure for debate in the House, where only a simple majority voting for impeachment would be necessary to put Nixon on trial in the Senate. Conviction in a Senate trial would require a two-thirds majority, or 67 senators.

The House debate was expected to begin by August 12th and to be completed by August 23rd. Since impeachment by the House was virtually certain in the eyes of congressional leaders, the Senate started drawing up plans to begin a trial in the first part of October.

But Nixon's own actions obviated all this, and the record is now history. After being confronted by Gen. Haig, Presidential Attorneys Fred Buzhardt and James D. St. Clair, who had learned of further incriminating tapes and threatened to resign if they were not made public, Nixon on August 5th grudgingly released three tapes, made only six days after the Watergate break-in, which showed that Nixon himself instructed Bob Haldeman to block the investigation. St. Clair said he had first learned of this evidence while listening to the tapes turned over to Judge Sirica, and he and Haig agreed that the President must make them public. Nixon finally released the damning transcripts, together with a statement acknowledging that they were "at variance with some of my previous statements." He could say that again!

Immediately after the black revelations of August 5th, Nixon's support in Congress dwindled rapidly. Republicans Charles Wiggins of California and John Rhodes of Arizona joined the growing list of those who said they would vote for impeachment. All ten of the House Judiciary Committee members who had opposed impeachment now annonced that they had reversed their positions.

On August 7th, Senators Barry Goldwater and Hugh Scott and House Republican leader Rhodes conferred with Nixon at the White House. Goldwater told newsmen that the President had made "no decision" on whether to resign.

The next evening, August 8th, Nixon quit, effective the following day.

P: Walters.

H: And the proposal would be that [then Domestic Adviser John] Ehrlichman and I call them in, and say, ah—

P: All right, fine. How do you call him in—I mean you just—well, we protected Helms from one hell of a lot of things.

H: That's what Ehrlichman says.

P: Of course, this Hunt, that will uncover a lot of things. You open that scab, there's a hell of a lot of things, and we just feel that it would be very detrimental to have this thing go any further. This involves these Cubans, Hunt and a lot of hanky-panky that we have nothing to do with ourselves. Well, what the hell, did Mitchell know about this?

H: I think so. I don't think he knew the details, but I think he knew.

P: He didn't know how it was going to be handled, though—with Dahlberg and the Texans and so forth? Well, who was the asshole that did? Is it Liddy? Is that the fellow? He must be a little nuts.

H: He is.

P: I mean he just isn't well screwed on, is he? Is that the problem?

H: No, but he was under pressure, apparently, to get more information, and as he got more pressure, he pushed the people harder to move harder—

P: Pressure from Mitchell?

H: Apparently.

P: All right, fine, I understand it all. We won't second-guess Mitchell and the rest. Thank God it wasn't [Presidential Counsel Charles W.] Colson.

H: The FBI interviewed Colson yesterday. They determined that would be a good thing to do. To have him take an interrogation, which he did, and that—the FBI guys working the case concluded that there were one or two possibilities—one, that this is a White House—they don't think that there is anything at the election committee—they think it was either a White House operation and they had some obscure reasons for it—non-political, or it was a—Cuban and the CIA. And after their interrogation of Colson yesterday, they concluded it was not the White House, but are now convinced it is a CIA thing, so the CIA turnoff would—

P: Well, not sure of their analysis, I'm not going to get that involved. I'm (unintelligible).

H: No, sir, we don't want you to.

P: You call them in.

H: Good deal.

P: Play it tough. That's the way they play it, and that's the way we are going to play it.

H: O.K....

P: When you get in ... say, Look, the problem is that this will open the whole, the whole Bay of Pigs thing, and the President just feels that, ah, without going into the details—don't, don't lie to them to the extent to say no involvement, but just say this is a comedy of errors, without getting into it, the President believes that it is going to open the whole Bay of Pigs thing up again. And, ah, because these people are plugging for (unintelligible) and that they should call the FBI in and (unintelligible) don't go any further into this case—period!... Well, can you get it done?

H: I think so.

Second meeting (1:04-1:13 p.m.)

P: O.K. ... just say (unintelligible) very bad to have this fellow Hunt, ah, he knows too damned much, if he was involved—you happen to know that? If it gets out that this is all involved, the Cuba thing, it would be a fiasco. It would make the CIA look bad, it's going to make Hunt look bad, and it is likely to blow the whole Bay of Pigs thing, which we think would be very unfortunate—both for [the] CIA, and for the country, at this time, and for American foreign policy. Just tell him [presumably FBI Director Gray] to lay off. Don't you?

H: Yep. That's the basis to do it on. Just leave it at that.

Third meeting (2:20-2:45 p.m.)

H: Well, it was kind of interest[ing]. Walters made the point and I didn't mention Hunt, I just said that the thing was leading into directions that were going to create potential problems because they were exploring leads that led back into areas that would be harmful to the CIA and harmful to the Government ... Gray called and said, yesterday, and said that he thought—

P: Who did? Gray?

H: Gray called Helms and said I think we've run right into the middle of a CIA covert operation.

P: Gray said that?

H: Yeah ... So at that point he [Helms or Walters] kind of got the picture. He said, he said we'll be very happy to be helpful (unintelligible) handle anything you want. I would like to know the reason for being helpful, and I made it clear to him he wasn't going to get explicit (unintelligible) generality, and he said fine. And Walters (unintelligible). Walters is going to make a call to Gray. That's the way we put it and that's the way it was left.

Rep. Jack Brooks *(D–Tex.), who played an important role in spurring the members to draw up their arguments in concrete article form, puffs on his cigar as he listens to debate on Article Two of the three adopted.*

Rep. Robert McClory *(R–Ill.), speaks passionately in support of Article Three, which he drafted and introduced, as the historic session neared its conclusion.*

"AMERICA NEEDS A FULL-TIME PRESIDENT . . ."

Following is the complete text of President Nixon's resignation address to the nation from the Oval Office on Thursday night, August 8, 1974:

Good Evening. This will be the 37th time I will have spoken to you from this office where so many decisions have been made that shaped the history of this nation.

Each time I have done so to discuss with you some matters which I believed affected the national interest. In all the decisions I have made in my public life I have always tried to do what was best for the nation.

Throughout the long and difficult period of Watergate, I have felt it was my duty to persevere, to make every possible effort to complete the term of office to which you elected me.

In the past few days, however, it has become evident to me that I no longer have a strong enough political base in the Congress to justify continuing that effort.

As long as there was such a base, I felt strongly that it was necessary to see the constitutional process through to its conclusion; to do otherwise would be unfaithful to the spirit of that deliberately difficult process, and a dangerously destabilizing precedent for the future.

But with the disappearance of that base I now believe that the constitutional purpose has been served and there is no longer a need for the process to be prolonged.

I would have preferred to carry through to the finish no matter the personal agony that would have been involved. And my family unanimously urged me to do so.

But the interest of the nation must always come before any personal consideration.

From the discussions I have had with congressional and other leaders, I have concluded that because of the Watergate matter I might not have the support of the Congress that I would consider necessary to back the very difficult decisions and carry out the duties of this office in the way the interests of the nation will require.

I have never been a quitter. To leave office before my term is completed is abhorrent to every instinct in my body.

As President I must put the interests of America first. America needs a full-time President and a full-time Congress, particularly at this time with problems we face at home and abroad.

To continue to fight through the months ahead for my personal vindication would almost totally absorb the time and attention of both the President and the Congress in a period when our entire focus should be on the great issues of peace abroad and prosperity without inflation at home.

Therefore, I shall resign the Presidency effective at noon tomorrow.

Vice President Ford will be sworn in as President at that hour in this office.

As I recall the high hopes for America with which we began this second term I feel a great sadness that I will not be here in this office working in your behalf to achieve those hopes in the next two and a half years.

But in turning over direction of the government to Vice President Ford, I know, as I told the nation when I nominated him for that office 10 months ago, that the leadership of America will be in good hands.

In passing this office to the Vice President, I also do so with the profound sense of the weight of responsibility that will fall on his shoulders tomorrow and, therefore, understanding the patience, the cooperation he would need from all.

As he assumes that responsibility, he will deserve the help and the support of all of us. As we look to the future, the first essential is to begin healing the wounds of this nation; to put the bitterness and the divisions of the recent past behind us and to rediscover those shared ideals that lie at the heart of our strength and unity as a great and as a free people.

By taking this action, I hope that I will have hastened the start of that process of healing which is so desperately needed in America.

I regret deeply any injuries that may have been done in the course of the events that led to this decision. I would say only that if some of my judgments were wrong, and some were wrong, they were made in what I believed at the time to be the best interest of the nation.

To those who have stood with me during these past difficult

months, to my family, my friends, to many others who joined in supporting my cause because they believed it was right, I will be eternally grateful for your support.

And to those who have not felt able to give me your support, let me say I leave with no bitterness toward those who have opposed me, because all of us, in the final analysis, have been concerned with the good of the country however our judgments might differ.

So, let us all now join together in affirming that common commitment and in helping our new President succeed for the benefit of all Americans.

I shall leave this office with regret at not completing my term, but with gratitude for the privilege of serving as your President for the past 5½ years. These years have been a momentous time in the history of our nation and the world. They have been a time of achievement in which we can all be proud, achievements that represent the shared efforts of the Administration, the Congress and the people.

But the challenges ahead are equally great, and they too will require the support and the efforts of the Congress and the people working in cooperation with the new administration.

We have ended America's longest war, but in the work of securing a lasting peace in the world, the goals ahead are even more far-reaching and more difficult.

We must complete a structure of peace so that it will be said of this generation, our generation, of Americans, by the people of all nations, not only that we ended one war, but that we prevented future wars.

We have unlocked the doors that for a quarter of a century stood between the United States and the People's Republic of China.

We must now insure that the one quarter of the world's people who live in the People's Republic of China will be and remain not our enemies but our friends.

In the Middle East, one hundred million people in the Arab

". . . I regret deeply any injuries that may have been done in the course of the events that led to this decision. I would say only that if some of my judgments were wrong, and some were wrong, that they were made in what I believed at the time to be the best interest of the nation."

countries, many of whom have considered us their enemy for nearly 20 years, now look on us as their friends. We must continue to build on that friendship so that peace can settle at last over the Middle East and so that the cradle of civilization will not become its grave.

Together with the Soviet Union we have made the crucial breakthroughs that have begun the process of limiting nuclear arms. But we must set as our goal not just limiting, but reducing and finally destroying these terrible weapons so that they cannot destroy our civilization and so that the threat of nuclear war will no longer hang over the world and the people.

We have opened the new relation with the Soviet Union. We must continue to develop and expand that new relationship so that the two strongest nations of the world will live together in cooperation rather than confrontation.

Around the world, in Asia, and Africa, in Latin America, in the Middle East, there are millions of people who live in terrible poverty, even starvation. We must keep as our goal turning away from production for war and expanding production for peace so that people everywhere on this earth can at least look forward in their children's time, if not in our own time, to having the necessities for a decent life.

Here in America, we are fortunate that most of our people have not only the blessings of liberty, but also the means to live full and good and, by the world's standards, even abundant lives. We must press on, however, to a goal of not only more and better jobs, but of full opportunity for every American, and of what we are striving so hard right now to achieve, prosperity without inflation.

For more than a quarter of a century in public life I have shared in the turbulent history of this era. I have fought for what I believed in. I have tried to the best of my ability to discharge those duties and meet those responsibilities that were entrusted to me.

Sometimes I have succeeded and sometimes I have failed, but always I have taken heart from what Theodore Roosevelt once said about the man in the arena: "whose face is marred by dust and sweat and blood, who strives valiantly, who errs and comes short again and again because there is not effort without error and shortcoming, but who does actually strive to do the deeds, who knows the great enthusiasms, the great devotions, who spends himself in a worthy cause, who at the best knows in the end the triumph of high achievements and who at the worst, if he fails, at least fails while daring greatly."

I pledge to you tonight that as long as I have a breath of life in my body, I shall continue in that spirit. I shall continue to work for the great causes to which I have been dedicated throughout my years as a congressman, a senator, a Vice President and President; the cause of peace not just for America but among all nations, prosperity, justice and opportunity for all of our people.

There is one cause above all to which I have been devoted and to which I shall always be devoted for as long as I live.

When I first took the oath of office as President five and one-half years ago, I made this sacred commitment: "to consecrate my office, my energies and all the wisdom I can summon to the cause of peace among nations."

I have done my very best in all the days since to be true to that pledge. As a result of these efforts, I am confident that the world is a safer place today, not only for the people of America, but for the people of all nations, and that all of our children have a better chance than before of living in peace rather than dying in war.

This, more than anything, is what I hoped to achieve when I sought the Presidency. This, more than anything, is what I hope will be my legacy to you, to our country, as I leave the Presidency.

To have served in this office is to have felt a very personal sense of kinship with each and every American. In leaving it, I do so with this prayer: may God's grace be with you in all the days ahead.

INDEX

A

G

L

P

S

T

U

V

W

Y

ARTICLES OF THE CONSTITUTION

AMENDMENTS TO THE CONSTITUTION

Z

SUPREME COURT DECISIONS